THE GOOD HOUSEKEEPING
STEP-BY-STEP
COOK BOOK

THE GOOD HOUSEKEEPING
STEP-BY-STEP
COOK BOOK

Colour Library Books

Editor-In-Chief	Gill Edden
Managing Editor	Amy Carroll
Managing Art Director	Stuart Jackman
Project Editor	Yvonne McFarlane
Art Editor	Debbie Mackinnon
Associate Art Editor	Sandra Schneider
Editors	Christine Davis
	Vicky Hayward
	Norma MacMillan
	Maria Mosby
Designers	Derek Coombes
	Isobelle Pover
Assistant Designers	Julia Harris
	Nick Harris
	Gary Marsh
Contributing Editor	Helena Radecka

CLB 3089

This 1993 edition produced exclusively for
Colour Library Books Ltd, Godalming, Surrey

ISBN-0-86283-964-5

Printed in Italy

Introduction

*For our newest cookery book we chose to adopt a fresh approach which,
we hope, reflects all the requirements of our readers.
Putting ourselves in your place, we thought that most meals, formal or
informal, posed two questions to the creative cook: 'What shall I cook?'
and 'How do I prepare it?'. The mouthwatering colour photographs at the
beginning of the book will quickly supply the answer to the first question.
By turning to the page referred to under the colour photograph of your
chosen dish, you will find the perfect solution to the second question.
Here we give step-by-step instructions, often accompanied by
step-by-step illustrations, which will enable you to produce
any of the recipes with complete confidence.*

*As well as supplying recipes for any occasion we have included lots of
information and ideas which will make this book of great practical value
in the kitchen. Freezing, preserving, baking and entertaining are just a few
of the subjects covered. Advice on selecting foods from basic fruits and
vegetables to exotic spices and cheeses is given in a way that is easily
accessible. A guide to kitchen equipment includes such developments as
food processors, mixers and blenders as well as
the more familiar kitchen tools.*

Comprehensive, practical and fun to use, The Good Housekeeping
Step-by-Step Cook Book *will prove indispensable to everyone who wants to
enjoy cooking what they eat and eating what they cook.*

Contents

BEFORE YOU COOK

The recipes in this book will help you make the most of your cooking. Precise measurement of ingredients and step-by-step instructions mean you can prepare a dish perfectly, the first time and every time. Background information is given with each chapter and many cooking techniques are illustrated in detail.

Before you begin to prepare a recipe for the first time, read it carefully and check that you have allowed enough preparation time. Before starting to cook, assemble utensils and measure all the ingredients needed for the recipe to be sure you have everything. Avoid substituting key ingredients unless the recipe suggests an alternative. Be cautious, too, about doubling or halving recipes: although some can be adjusted successfully, many cannot. Seasonings and spices can safely be varied according to personal taste, but it is always a good idea to follow the recipe directions exactly the first time you use it.

Do as much advance preparation of ingredients as possible before you start mixing and cooking. Decide whether you are going to work with metric measures, in grams and litres, or with imperial measures, in pounds, ounces and pints, and don't try to combine the two. Measure all ingredients accurately, using the correct scales, measuring spoons or measuring jugs (opposite). Prepare utensils in advance too, where appropriate. If, for instance, a greased and floured cake tin is called for, have it ready before you need it. Always preheat the oven to the required temperature before starting to cook, referring to the manufacturer's instructions for timing. For best results, cook at the temperature specified in the recipe and start checking to see whether the food is cooked towards the end of the time suggested in the recipe. Position oven shelves so that the food will be in the centre of the oven.

HOW TO USE THIS BOOK

First look at the colour index to find a dish you would like to prepare. The captions will tell you briefly about the dish, the number of servings, how long you should allow for preparation and the page on which the recipe appears.

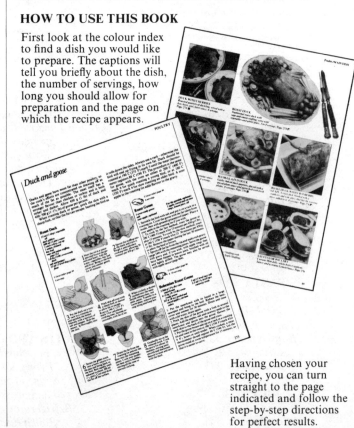

Having chosen your recipe, you can turn straight to the page indicated and follow the step-by-step directions for perfect results.

Measuring ingredients

USING THE CORRECT MEASURING EQUIPMENT
Accurate measurements are essential if you want the same good results each time you make a recipe.

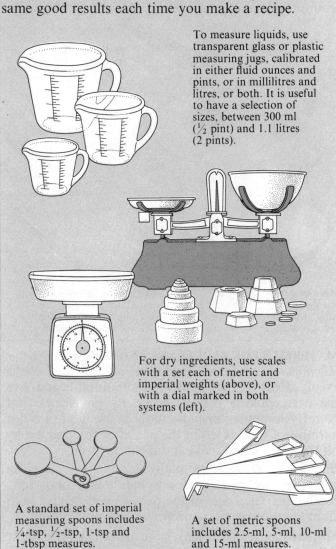

To measure liquids, use transparent glass or plastic measuring jugs, calibrated in either fluid ounces and pints, or in millilitres and litres, or both. It is useful to have a selection of sizes, between 300 ml (½ pint) and 1.1 litres (2 pints).

For dry ingredients, use scales with a set each of metric and imperial weights (above), or with a dial marked in both systems (left).

A standard set of imperial measuring spoons includes ¼-tsp, ½-tsp, 1-tsp and 1-tbsp measures.

A set of metric spoons includes 2.5-ml, 5-ml, 10-ml and 15-ml measures.

MEASURING FATS
To measure accurate amounts of fats such as butter, margarine and lard, weigh out the required amount as for dry ingredients. If the fats are melted, measure as for liquids in a standard measuring spoon. For approximate amounts, divide the block as shown.

Dividing up a block of fat: Most fats are packed in blocks weighing 250 g (8.8 oz). Where approximate amounts are needed, as for frying, a complete block can be divided into 50-g (2-oz) portions, using the guidelines on the wrapper.

MEASURING DRY INGREDIENTS
When measuring foods which require preparation, pay special attention to the wording used in the recipe. For example, *450 g (1 lb) peas, shelled,* is a different measurement from *450 g (1 lb) shelled peas.*

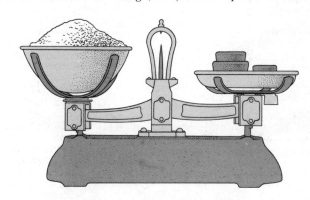

Use scales for all except the smallest amounts. With a lever balance, the levers should be exactly level; with a spring balance be sure the pointer is exactly on the mark you require.

To measure dry ingredients with a spoon, first scoop the ingredient lightly from the storage container.

Then level the surface with the edge of a straight-bladed knife.

MEASURING LIQUIDS
Always read the line on a measuring jug at eye level when checking the volume of liquid.

Place the measuring jug on a level surface and slowly pour the liquid into the measuring jug until it reaches the required mark.

If using a measuring spoon, pour the liquid just to the top. Don't hold the spoon over the mixture to which you will be adding liquid, in case you pour out too much.

Choosing pots and pans

SAUCEPANS AND CASSEROLES

Good pans should conduct the heat evenly. The diameter of the pan should be similar to that of the hot plate or burner in use. The inside of the pan should be smooth, with the corners rounded.

Saucepans: Lids should fit closely. Handles should be strong, firmly fixed and a comfortable length. Both handles and knobs are best in a heat-resisting material. Short handles on either side are best for large, heavy saucepans.

Double saucepan: This consists of two saucepans, one of which fits inside the other and has a lid; ideal for sauces.

Casserole: A flameproof casserole can be used on the hob and in the oven.

HOW TO MEASURE PANS

Choose the correct size of pan to hold comfortably the amount of food being cooked. If a size is expressed in liquid capacity, fill it just full to the top to measure.

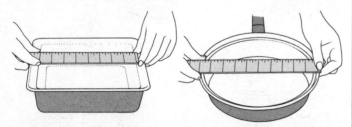

For baking tins, measure the top inside for length, width or diameter; measure inside for depth.

Sizes for frying pans are expressed as the top outside diameter, excluding the size of the handle.

FRYING PANS AND GRIDDLES

Look for a frying pan with a heavy, flat base and a comfortable handle; a close-fitting lid is useful.

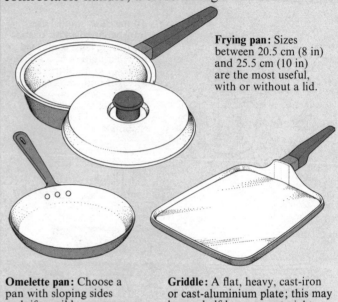

Frying pan: Sizes between 20.5 cm (8 in) and 25.5 cm (10 in) are the most useful, with or without a lid.

Omelette pan: Choose a pan with sloping sides and, if possible, a non-stick coating.

Griddle: A flat, heavy, cast-iron or cast-aluminium plate; this may have a half-hoop or a straight handle, or two short handles.

MATERIALS FOR SAUCEPANS AND FRYING PANS

Aluminium is a good conductor of heat and cooks evenly. Heavy-gauge pans are more durable and give the best cooking results, especially on electric hot plates. Aluminium may discolour in use but this is not harmful; if food is left in the pan after cooking it may pit the surface and make it difficult to clean.

Stainless steel is exceptionally durable, easy to clean and does not react to foods but it is a poor heat conductor. The bases of the pans should be clad with aluminium or copper to improve heat distribution.

Vitramel-coated pans may be made of cast iron, light steel or aluminium; the vitramel (vitreous enamel) coating is fused to the metal to give a hard, glass-like surface that is resistant to scratching and pitting. Cast-iron pans with this finish are heavy to use, but give excellent heat conduction. A vitramel interior surface may lead to food sticking and burning; a vitramel exterior and a non-stick or alternative finish inside is preferable. Vitramel cannot be cleaned with abrasives.

Copper is good looking and an excellent conductor of heat, but should be heavy gauge and lined with another metal as foods may create a chemical reaction on direct contact with copper. Constant cleaning is necessary.

Ceramic glass is safe at extremes of temperature and can be transferred directly from freezer to oven; lids may be of ordinary ovenglass and should not be subjected to sudden temperature changes. It is a poor heat conductor, so take care that food does not burn.

Choosing baking equipment

CAKE AND LOAF TINS

A selection of basic shapes and sizes will serve for most cakes and breads, but a few unusually shaped tins will help make your baking more attractive.

Cake tins: Round or square, with a shallow tin for sandwich cakes.

Loaf tin: This is used for bread, teabreads and certain types of cake.

Ring tin: This is used for savarins and certain decorative cakes.

Spring-release tin: The side section can be removed without disturbing the base. These often come with alternative bases.

Swiss roll tin: Shallow rectangular tray, usually no more than 2.5 cm (1 in) deep.

Brioche tin: Used for brioche loaves and decorative desserts.

Patty tins: These are used for small cakes and tarts.

GREASING AND FLOURING TINS

It is best to grease and flour tins to prevent sticking, except for those with a non-stick finish. If lining is also required, see page 383. Cup cakes can be baked in paper cake cases placed inside patty tins.

The easiest way to grease tins is with a pastry brush, using oil or melted butter. Or you can use solid fat in a piece of greaseproof paper.

OTHER BAKING EQUIPMENT

While not essential, the equipment illustrated below will always be useful.

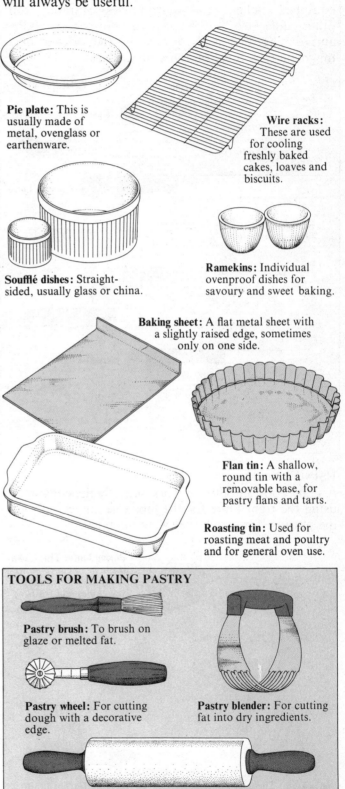

Pie plate: This is usually made of metal, ovenglass or earthenware.

Wire racks: These are used for cooling freshly baked cakes, loaves and biscuits.

Soufflé dishes: Straight-sided, usually glass or china.

Ramekins: Individual ovenproof dishes for savoury and sweet baking.

Baking sheet: A flat metal sheet with a slightly raised edge, sometimes only on one side.

Flan tin: A shallow, round tin with a removable base, for pastry flans and tarts.

Roasting tin: Used for roasting meat and poultry and for general oven use.

TOOLS FOR MAKING PASTRY

Pastry brush: To brush on glaze or melted fat.

Pastry wheel: For cutting dough with a decorative edge.

Pastry blender: For cutting fat into dry ingredients.

Rolling pin: This should be as long as possible, to give the most even rolling.

Cutting tools

BASIC CUTTING TOOLS

A basic collection of cutting tools is vital in any well-equipped kitchen. Store sharp knives separately from other cutlery, so that the edges do not become dulled and damaged; a slotted rack in the drawer or a magnetic rack hung on the wall are ideal.

Paring knife

Chef's knife

Bread knife

Carving knife

Two-pronged fork

Steel

Boning knife

Serrated knife

Kitchen scissors

USING A KNIFE

A good cook's ability to work skilfully depends upon using the right knife for the job. Use knives only for the purpose for which they were intended.

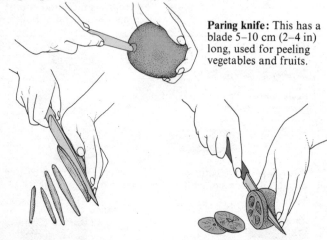

Paring knife: This has a blade 5–10 cm (2–4 in) long, used for peeling vegetables and fruits.

Chef's knife: This has a longer, broader, tapered blade to be used for general cutting, slicing and chopping.

Serrated knife: This knife is useful for many small slicing jobs, especially tomatoes or citrus fruits.

CHOPPING WITH A CHEF'S KNIFE

The length of the blade and the weight of a chef's knife are designed to make chopping easier. Where the blade joins the handle, there is room for knuckle clearance.

CHOPPING HERBS

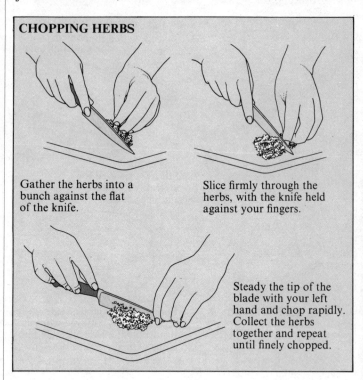

Gather the herbs into a bunch against the flat of the knife.

Slice firmly through the herbs, with the knife held against your fingers.

Steady the tip of the blade with your left hand and chop rapidly. Collect the herbs together and repeat until finely chopped.

SHARPENING KNIVES

Carbon steel knives give the best cutting edge and are the easiest to sharpen, but unless you take special care of them they easily stain and become rusty. Stainless steel knives are much easier to care for but are difficult to sharpen to a really good edge. Hollow-ground stainless steel retains its sharpness well, but cannot be re-sharpened at home. For sharpening, a steel or carborundum used correctly give the best results but, for the less adept, a manual or electric sharpening machine will give quite a good edge.

Using a steel: Hold the steel upright; place the blade edge, near the handle, at an angle of 20° to the tip of the steel.

Draw the blade down towards you and across the steel until the knife tip almost reaches the handle of the steel. Repeat on both sides five or six times.

Mixing tools

These are some of the basic tools available for mixing, stirring and beating.

Wire balloon whisk: For whisking egg whites, stirring sauces, whipping cream.

Rotary whisk: For whipping cream, beating eggs and other light mixtures.

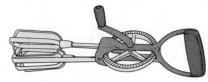

Electric mixer: This may be either hand-held, or (right) a stand-mounted, heavy-duty machine for whisking and beating, with attachments for mincing, slicing, kneading, grinding, puréeing, shredding etc.

Food processor: This chops, minces, grinds, shreds and slices, and mixes pastry and doughs.

Blender: This blends, purées, mixes, grinds and chops a wide range of foods and liquids.

SPOONS AND SPATULAS

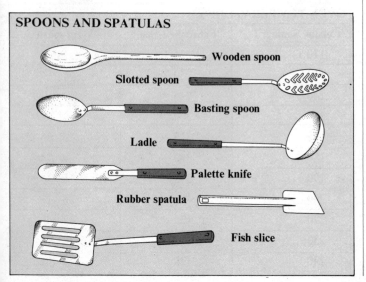

Wooden spoon

Slotted spoon

Basting spoon

Ladle

Palette knife

Rubber spatula

Fish slice

Other useful equipment

KITCHEN AIDS

In addition to the basic measuring, cutting and mixing tools, there is a variety of other equipment that makes a cook's life easier.

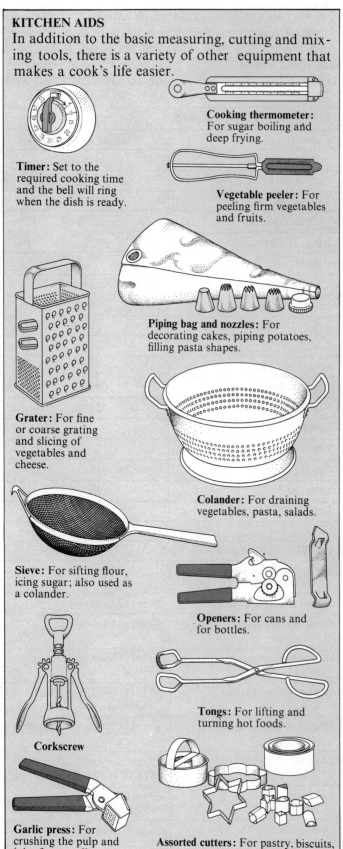

Timer: Set to the required cooking time and the bell will ring when the dish is ready.

Cooking thermometer: For sugar boiling and deep frying.

Vegetable peeler: For peeling firm vegetables and fruits.

Piping bag and nozzles: For decorating cakes, piping potatoes, filling pasta shapes.

Grater: For fine or coarse grating and slicing of vegetables and cheese.

Colander: For draining vegetables, pasta, salads.

Sieve: For sifting flour, icing sugar; also used as a colander.

Openers: For cans and for bottles.

Tongs: For lifting and turning hot foods.

Corkscrew

Garlic press: For crushing the pulp and juice from garlic.

Assorted cutters: For pastry, biscuits, doughnuts and confectionery.

Reference charts

The recipes in this book are given with both metric and imperial measures, but if you want to convert your own recipes, the first chart will help you. Below that are some useful ways of measuring small amounts. A deep frying guide will ensure the food is crisp and golden every time you fry in deep fat, using a thermometer to gauge the temperature accurately. Finally, if you buy a new cooker with an unfamiliar temperature setting dial, the last chart will help you relate it to the settings you are accustomed to using.

EQUIVALENT MEASURES

Capacity	Working approximation
¼ pint (142 ml)	150 ml
½ pint (284 ml)	300 ml
1 pint (568 ml)	600 ml
½ litre (0.88 pints)	18 fl oz
1 litre (1.76 pints)	1¾ pints
Weight	
1 oz (28.35 g)	25 g
2 oz (56.7 g)	50 g
4 oz (113.4 g)	100 g
8 oz (226.8 g)	225 g
~~12 oz (340.2 g)~~	350 g
1 lb (453.6 g)	450 g
1 kilogram (2.2 lb)	2¼ lb
Length	
1 in (2.54 cm)	2.5 cm
6 in (15.2 cm)	15 cm
12 in (30.4 cm)	30.5 cm
1 metre (39.37 in)	3 ft 3 in

USEFUL EQUIVALENTS FOR SMALL AMOUNTS

Flour, cornflour, cocoa, custard powder 25 g (1 oz)	45 ml (3 level tbsp)
Sugar, rice 25 g (1 oz)	30 ml (2 level tbsp)
Fresh breadcrumbs 25 g (1 oz)	90 ml (6 level tbsp)
Dried breadcrumbs 25 g (1 oz)	60 ml (4 level tbsp)
Golden syrup or treacle 40 g (1½ oz)	15 ml (1 level tbsp): use a warmed spoon
Double or whipping cream 150 ml (¼ pint)	300 ml (½ pint) whipped cream
1 lemon	45 ml (3 tbsp)* juice and 15 ml (1 tbsp)* grated rind
1 orange	60 ml (4 tbsp)* juice and 30 ml (2 tbsp)* grated rind
Long grain rice 25 g (1 oz)	65 g (2½ oz) cooked rice
Approximate amounts	

DEEP FRYING GUIDE

Food	Temperature	Time
Chipped potatoes *(see page 293)* 0.5 cm (¼ in) thick	190°C (375°F)	7 minutes plus 3 minutes
Potato croquettes 8 cm (3½ in) long (egg and breadcrumb coating)	190°C (375°F)	3–4 minutes
Scotch egg 8 × 8 cm (3½ × 3½ in) (egg and breadcrumb coating)	160°C (325°F)	10 minutes
Chicken Kiev *(see page 265)* 10 × 6 cm (4 × 2½ in) (egg and breadcrumb coating)	160°C (325°F)	15 minutes
Fish fillets 1 cm (½ in) thick (batter or egg and breadcrumb coating)	177–188°C (350–370°F)	5–10 minutes
Doughnuts	175–180°C (350–360°F)	5–10 minutes
Whitebait, floured	177–188°C (350–370°F)	2–3 minutes

OVEN TEMPERATURES

°Celsius Scale	°Fahrenheit Scale	Gas mark
110°C	225°F	¼
130	250	½
140	275	1
150	300	2
170	325	3
180	350	4
190	375	5
200	400	6
220	425	7
230	450	8
240	475	9

COLOUR INDEX

Colour index contents

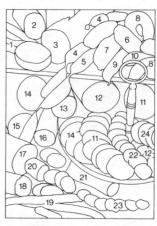

Appetisers

(Left to right): EGG AND ROE ROUNDS □ SMOKED SALMON SQUARES □ CURRIED TUNA PUFFS ◩ WATERCRESS AND CREAM CHEESE CANAPES □ TUNA AND DILL ROUNDS □ BLUE CHEESE AND ASPIC CANAPES ◩ ANCHOVY AND CHEESE CANAPES □ ASPARAGUS CANAPES □ Pages 115–116

PATE DE CAMPAGNE
Minced pork and chicken cooked with mushrooms, sherry, pistachio nuts and seasonings. 8 servings. Page 122 ■

DEEP-FRIED WALNUTS (left) *Makes 450 g (1 lb).* □ **CURRIED ALMONDS** *Makes 275 g (10 oz).* □ **CHEESE TWISTS** *Makes 96.* ◩ All page 114

RILLETTES DE PORC
Pork cooked with garlic and herbs, then pounded and shredded and served cold with toasted French bread. 6 servings. Page 124 ■

GUACAMOLE
Avocado mixed with tomato, onion, garlic, lemon juice and chilli powder and served with crisps. Makes 400 ml (¾ pint). Page 124 □

SPINACH PATE
Chilled loaf of spinach, spring onions, carrots, cream and eggs, flavoured with basil and cayenne. 10 servings. Page 122 ■

CHICKEN LIVER PATE
Cooked chicken livers puréed with butter, garlic, cream, tomato paste and sherry or brandy. 10 servings. Page 122 ◩

RADISH SPREAD (left) *400 ml (¾ pint).* Page 294 □ **CHEESE SPREADS** (front, rear and right) *10 servings each. Page 124* ■

18

PEPPER AND HERB CREAM CHEESE
Home-made cheese flavoured with herbs and coated with crushed black peppercorns.
12 servings. Page 123 ■

SPRING ONION DIP (left) □ **BLUE CHEESE DIP** (centre) Both page 124 □
YOGURT AND CREAM CHEESE DIP
Page 125 □

BAGNA CAUDA
Hot, creamy garlic and anchovy dip, served with crisp fresh vegetables and breadsticks.
12 servings. Page 125 ◪

FRESH VEGETABLES WITH CHILLI-TOMATO DIP *Chilled crisp vegetables served with a spicy dip. Makes 600 ml (1 pint). Page 125* □

DUCK PATE IN ASPIC
Boneless duck and pork layered with smooth chicken liver mixture, baked, chilled and coated with aspic. 10 servings. Page 123 ■

PEPPERY MAYONNAISE DIP
Onion, chives, chilli sauce and curry powder in mayonnaise, served with vegetables.
Makes 225 ml (8 fl oz). Page 124 □

TUNA DIP
Canned tuna, blended with mayonnaise, anchovies, lemon juice and paprika. Makes 400 ml (¾ pint). Page 125 □

STEAK BITES
Marinated rump steak, grilled and cut into cubes, with a spicy mustard sauce. Makes 48.
Page 119 ◪

SWEDISH MEATBALLS
Sherry-flavoured meatballs served with a creamy consommé sauce. Makes 40.
Page 119 ◪

Appetisers

TINY PATE-STUFFED TOMATOES
Small tomatoes filled with a mixture of pâté, soured cream and creamed horseradish. Makes 450 g (1 lb). Page 126 □

SAUSAGE-STUFFED MUSHROOMS
Mushrooms stuffed with chopped sausages, Mozzarella cheese and breadcrumbs, then baked. Makes about 30. Page 117 □

MARINATED ARTICHOKE HEARTS AND MUSHROOMS *Artichoke hearts, mushrooms and peppers, marinated in a garlic dressing. 6 servings. Page 319* ◩

CHINESE CHICKEN WINGS
Chicken wing pieces cooked with spring onions, soy sauce, sherry and ginger; serve hot or cold. Makes about 36. Page 121 □

CAPONATA
Chilled cooked aubergines, courgettes, mushrooms, tomatoes and celery in a tangy dressing. 6 servings. Page 300 ■

CELERY HEARTS VINAIGRETTE
Celery cooked in stock, then marinated in a green pepper and pimento mixture; serve chilled. 6 servings. Page 321 ■

SPICY CARROTS ◩ **COCKTAIL ONIONS** ◩ **HERBED MUSHROOMS** ■
All page 126

SPANAKOPITAS
Phyllo pastry triangles stuffed with spinach and cheese, baked until golden and served hot. Makes 60. Page 121 ◩

TOSTADAS
Hot Mexican tortilla wedges topped with spicy beef, cheese, lettuce, tomato sauce and olives. Makes 36. Page 118 ◩

HORS D'OEUVRE VARIES
Selection of cold meats, fish and cheese on a lettuce-lined platter: Mortadella, sardines, ham, salami and provolone. In bowls (left to right):
MARINATED TUNA AND RED CABBAGE ☐ MARINATED CAULIFLOWER ☐ MARINATED AUBERGINE ◪
MARINATED GREEN BEANS ◪ All page 126

APPETISER AVOCADOS
Avocado slices with a hot, spicy sauce, garnished with crumbled bacon. 6 servings.
Page 303 ☐

LEMON FRUIT SALAD
Orange and lemon slices marinated in French dressing with tarragon, served in a lettuce-lined bowl. 4 servings. Page 322 ☐

STEAMED ASPARAGUS
Tender asparagus served hot with hollandaise sauce or melted butter, or cold with French dressing. Page 278 ☐

21

Appetisers

PISSALADIERE
French-style pizza topped with sliced onions, anchovies, stuffed olives and cheese. Makes 36 canapés. Page 117 ■

HOT CANAPES: *Individual Broccoli Quiches* ◪ *Hot Mushroom Turnovers* ◪ *Cheesy Prawn Canapés* ☐ *Münster and Onion Triangles* ☐ *Pages 116–118*

SAUSAGE ROLLS
Sausagemeat rolled in shortcrust pastry and baked until golden; serve hot. Makes 24. Page 121 ◪

GRAVAD LAX
Scandinavian-style fresh salmon, rubbed with sugar, seasoning and brandy, then pressed with fresh dill weed for 24–36 hours; cut into thin slices and serve with lemon wedges. 12–14 servings. Page 119 ■

RUMAKI
Marinated chicken liver and water chestnuts, wrapped in bacon and grilled. Makes 18. Page 121 ◪

ESCARGOTS A LA BOURGUIGNONNE
6 servings. ☐ **SCALLOPS IN PERNOD**
6 servings. ☐ *Both page 120*

GRILLED GRAPEFRUIT
Grapefruit halves sprinkled with brown sugar and sherry and grilled until golden. 4 servings. Page 307 □

GINGERED MELON WEDGES
Honeydew melon wedges sprinkled with icing sugar and ground ginger; serve chilled. 4–6 servings. Page 310 □

TORTELLINI IN CREAM SAUCE
Home-made pasta dumplings stuffed with chicken and ham, served with a cream and Parmesan sauce. 4–6 servings. Page 335 ■

SCRAMBLED EGGS ARCHIDUCHESSE
Scrambled eggs with ham, mushrooms and asparagus tips, served on fried bread. 4 servings. Page 144 □

STUFFED EGGS
Hard-boiled eggs, halved and then stuffed with a mixture of the yolks, mayonnaise and various flavourings. 4 servings. Page 141 □

EGGS EN GELEE
Stuffed hard-boiled eggs garnished with pimento and olives and set in jellied consommé. 4 servings. Page 141 ■

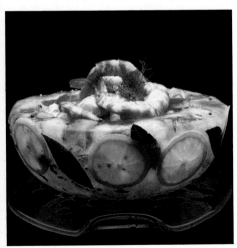

MARINATED PRAWNS
Prawns marinated in a spicy dressing with dill weed, served in a decorative crystalline ice bowl. 6 servings. Page 120 □

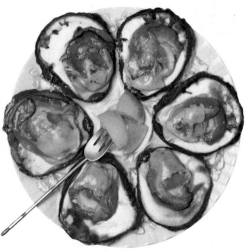

OYSTERS 'AU NATUREL'
Fresh raw oysters served in their shells on cracked ice, with lemon and brown bread and butter. Page 161 □

PRAWN COCKTAIL
Shelled prawns in tomato mayonnaise dressing, on shredded lettuce. 4 servings. Page 164 □

23

Appetisers

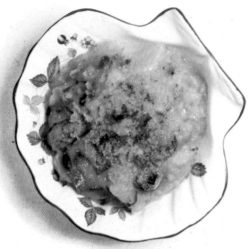

COQUILLES ST JACQUES
Scallops in white wine, mixed with creamy mushroom sauce, topped with breadcrumbs and grilled. 4 servings. Page 163 ◪

SCALLOPS AND BACON
Seasoned scallops wrapped in bacon rashers and grilled. 4 servings. Page 163 ☐

BAKED OYSTERS WITH SPINACH
Oysters on the half shell, baked with herbed spinach topping, bacon, and grated cheese if you wish. 6 servings. Page 161 ☐

FRIED WHITEBAIT
Whole whitebait, tossed in flour, deep fried until golden and served with lemon, brown bread and butter. 4 servings. Page 175 ☐

FISH MOUSSE
A poached white fish, mayonnaise and cream mixture set with gelatine and decorated. 4 servings. Page 183 ■

FRIED OYSTERS
Shelled oysters coated with salt biscuit crumbs and shallow fried until golden. 6 servings. Page 161 ☐

MOULES A LA MARINIERE
Mussels cooked in white wine with shallots, thyme, bay leaf and parsley. 4 servings. Page 160 ◪

BLINIS
Tiny, light pancakes topped with soured cream and lumpfish roe and served hot. Makes 40. Page 118 ■

INDIVIDUAL ASPARAGUS SOUFFLES
Fresh asparagus in rich sauce lightened with egg whites and baked in ramekins. 8 servings. Page 149 ◪

FRENCH ONION SOUP
Sautéed onions cooked in brown stock, poured into bowls, topped with toast slices and cheese, then grilled. 4–6 servings. Page 130 ▨

CHICKEN AND RICE SOUP
Chicken stock and rice thickened with egg yolks, flavoured with lemon juice and garnished with lemon slices. 4–6 servings. Page 130 ▢

LOBSTER BISQUE
A lobster soup enriched with cream, lobster butter, lemon juice and white wine. 4–6 servings. Page 132 ▨

CREAM OF MUSHROOM SOUP
A puréed mushroom soup, flavoured with onion and garlic and finished with mushroom slices. 4–6 servings. Page 131 ▨

GAZPACHO
Cucumber, tomatoes, green pepper, onions and garlic puréed with oil and vinegar and served chilled. 4–6 servings. Page 129 ▨

CHILLED CUCUMBER SOUP
A refreshing vegetable soup, finished with cream and garnished with cucumber slices. 6 servings. Page 129 ▨

CREAM OF GREEN PEA SOUP
A smooth pea soup with onion and béchamel sauce, enriched with cream and garnished with mint. 4–6 servings. Page 130 ▨

JELLIED CONSOMME
A beef consommé, chilled until lightly jellied and served with grapes and chopped onion. 4–6 servings. Page 129 ▩

CREME VICHYSSOISE
Leeks, potatoes and onion cooked in stock and puréed, with cream added before the soup is chilled. 4–6 servings. Page 130 ▨

25

Main course dishes

PRAWN SOUP
Shellfish soup flavoured with onion, lemon juice and herbs and thickened with egg yolks and cream. 4–6 servings. Page 132 □

FISH CHOWDER
A hearty and nourishing soup of cubed haddock, sliced potatoes and onion, and bacon rashers cooked in a tomato-flavoured fish stock with cloves and a bay leaf. 4–6 servings. Page 132 ◪

BOUILLABAISSE
A rich soup of mixed fish and shellfish, flavoured with tomatoes, onions, garlic, celery and herbs. 4–6 servings. Page 137 ◪

PRAWN CHOWDER
Whole prawns, sliced onion and diced potatoes in a thin soup with cheese added for extra flavour. 4–6 servings. Page 132 □

CURRIED COD CHOWDER
A mildly curried white fish and vegetable chowder, garnished with chopped parsley and chives. 4–6 servings. Page 132 ◪

CHICKEN SOUP WITH DUMPLINGS
A substantial chicken soup with vegetables and tiny suet dumplings. 4–6 servings. Page 136 ◪

GOULASH SOUP
A traditional Hungarian beef and tomato soup, mildly spiced with paprika and served with soured cream. 4–6 servings. Page 135 ■

GERMAN LENTIL SOUP
Lentil soup flavoured with ham, carrot, celery, onion and herbs. 4–6 servings. Page 134 ■

HARICOT BEAN AND BACON SOUP
A winter soup based on dried haricot beans and flavoured with bacon, tomatoes and celery. 4–6 servings. Page 137 ■

SPLIT PEA SOUP
A traditional English soup combining the flavours of split peas and ham by cooking the vegetable with a ham bone and adding chunks of the cooked meat to the finished soup. 4–6 servings. Page 135 ■

BEEF AND BEETROOT SOUP
A main dish soup made with chunks of beef, beetroot and shredded cabbage, served with soured cream. 4 servings. Page 134 ■

CREAMY CHEDDAR CHEESE SOUP
Chicken stock and milk form the basis of this cheese soup served with toasted pumpernickel cubes. 4–6 servings. Page 136 □

MULLIGATAWNY SOUP
A curried soup with chicken chunks, bacon, carrot, celery and apple, served with a spoonful of rice. 4–6 servings. Page 136 ◪

OLD FASHIONED BEEF AND VEGETABLE SOUP *A hearty soup with chunks of mixed vegetables and stewing beef. 4–6 servings. Page 134* ◪

MINESTRONE
The classic Italian mixed vegetable and pasta soup, served with a large bowl of grated Parmesan cheese. 4–6 servings. Page 135 ◪

Main course dishes

SOFT- AND HARD-BOILED EGGS
Boiled eggs, either soft with a barely set yolk and creamy white, or hard with a solid yolk and firm white. **Page 140** □

CREOLE EGGS
Hard-boiled eggs simmered in a herby tomato and green pepper sauce, spooned over hot boiled rice. 4 servings. **Page 142** □

STUFFED EGGS A LA MORNAY, WITH BROCCOLI *Hot stuffed eggs and broccoli spears with mornay sauce, lightly grilled. 4 servings.* **Page 142** □

SCRAMBLED EGGS
Beaten eggs and milk, cooked gently in butter and served immediately on hot buttered toast. **Page 144** □

SHRIMP SCRAMBLE
Scrambled eggs with shrimps, served on toasted muffins or roll halves. 2 servings. **Page 144** □

PLAIN OMELETTE
A classic plain omelette of beaten eggs cooked in butter until just set and golden. 1 serving. **Page 145** □

FRIED EGGS
Whole eggs, fried in a little melted dripping or bacon fat until the whites are firm and the yolks just set. **Page 143** □

BAKED EGGS
A simple dish of whole eggs seasoned with salt, pepper and paprika and baked in a ramekin. **Page 143** □

EGGS BAKED IN CREAM
A rich recipe for baked eggs with a little cream added to them before they are baked. 4 servings. **Page 143** □

CLASSIC CHEESE SOUFFLE
A thick cheese sauce lightened with beaten egg whites and baked until puffy and golden brown. 4 servings. Page 148 ◪

CHICKEN SOUFFLE
A substantial soufflé that contains cooked chicken pieces and chopped mushrooms. 4 servings. Page 149 ◪

SPINACH SOUFFLE
A soufflé with finely chopped, cooked spinach, chopped onion and grated Parmesan cheese. 6 servings. Page 149 ◪

CHEESE AND BACON SOUFFLE
Chopped fried bacon and grated Cheddar cheese are used as the flavourings in this delicious savoury soufflé. 2 servings. Page 149 ◪

SALMON PUFF
A fish soufflé made with canned salmon and seasoned with mustard and Worcestershire sauce. 4 servings. Page 149 ◪

SOUFFLE OMELETTE
A puffy omelette, made by beating the egg whites separately before folding them into the yolks. 1 serving. Page 146 ☐

POACHED EGGS
A whole shelled egg cooked in simmering water until just set, served on hot buttered toast. Page 142 ☐

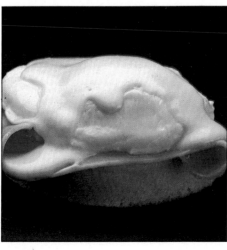

EGGS BENEDICT
Slices of ham and lightly poached eggs served on toasted muffin halves with hollandaise sauce. 4 servings. Page 142 ☐

SPINACH PANCAKES (front)
4 servings. Page 147 ☐
CURRIED SHRIMP PANCAKES
4 servings. Page 147 ☐

Main course dishes

SWISS FONDUE
Melted Swiss cheeses, kirsch and seasonings, cooked and served in a fondue pot, with bread chunks for dipping. 4 servings. Page 155 □

CHEDDAR AND CIDER FONDUE
A variation on the classic fondue, made with Cheddar cheese, cider and brandy. 4 servings. Page 155 □

CHEESE PUDDING
A baked savoury pudding of cheese, eggs and milk poured over a base of bread cubes. 4 servings. Page 155 □

RACLETTE
Thinly sliced Raclette cheese baked until just melted and served alone or with vegetables. 4 servings. Page 154 □

ITALIAN CHEESE TOAST
Toasted French bread, topped with Italian cheese, grilled and then coated with anchovy and caper sauce. 4 servings. Page 154 □

WELSH RAREBIT
A traditional dish of creamy melted cheese and brown ale, served on toast. 4 servings. Page 154 □

CHEESE ON TOAST
Grated cheese blended with milk, mustard and Worcestershire sauce, spread on toast and grilled until golden. 4 servings. Page 154 □

SWISS CHEESE AND TOMATO BAKE
Croûtons and tomato slices baked in a pie dish with grated Gruyère cheese, beaten eggs and milk. 4 servings. Page 154 ◩

QUICHE LORRAINE
*A savoury shortcrust flan, filled with an egg
custard flavoured with bacon and cheese.
4 servings. Page 156* ◪

ITALIAN CHEESE AND HAM PIE
*A deep, double-crust pie with a moist cheese, ham and egg filling; may be
served either hot or cold. 4–6 servings. Page 157* ◪

CHEESE AND ONION QUICHE
*A shortcrust flan case filled with sautéed
onion rings, grated Gruyère cheese, beaten
egg and cream. 4 servings. Page 157* ◪

CHEESE, SAUSAGE AND SPINACH PIE
*Mozzarella and curd cheeses with spinach,
sausages and eggs, baked in a shortcrust
pastry case. 4–6 servings. Page 156* ◪

FRIED CHEESE PATTIES
*Cheese and onion patties, coated with egg and
breadcrumbs, fried and served with tomato
sauce. 6 servings. Page 157* ■

CHEESE BREAD RING
*A home-made yeast bread ring, filled with
grated Edam cheese and decorated with
almonds. Makes 1 ring. Page 446* ◪

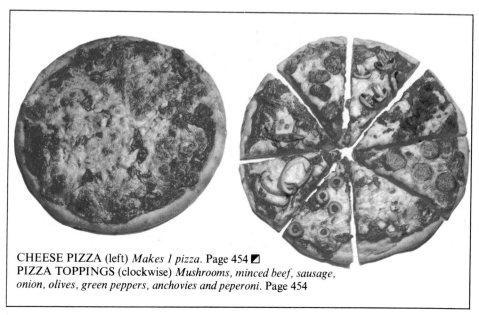

CHEESE PIZZA (left) *Makes 1 pizza. Page 454* ◪
PIZZA TOPPINGS (clockwise) *Mushrooms, minced beef, sausage,
onion, olives, green peppers, anchovies and peperoni. Page 454*

Main course dishes

SPAGHETTI CON FORMAGGIO
*Spaghetti cooked until it is just tender,
then tossed in a creamy sauce made with four
Italian cheeses. 4 servings. Page 331* □

BAKED MACARONI CHEESE
*Macaroni in a cheese sauce, covered with
breadcrumbs and baked until crisp and
golden. 4 servings. Page 332* □

ONE-PAN MACARONI CHEESE
*A fast, easy variation of macaroni cheese
with onion, green pepper and olives in the
thick cheese sauce. 4 servings. Page 332* □

SPAGHETTI ALLA CARBONARA
*Spaghetti tossed with crispy bacon pieces,
eggs, cream and grated Parmesan
cheese. 4–6 servings. Page 331* □

SPAGHETTI WITH HAM AND PEAS
*Peas and strips of cooked ham in a mild
cheese sauce, tossed with spaghetti. 4 servings.
Page 331* □

RAVIOLI and JUMBO RAVIOLI
*Home-made pasta cases with a cheese, meat
or spinach filling, served with tomato sauce
and Parmesan cheese. 4 servings. Page 333* ■

SPAGHETTI AND MEATBALLS
*A substantial dish of spaghetti and well-seasoned beef meatballs, fried
until brown and then cooked in tomato sauce. Serve with grated
Parmesan cheese. 6 servings. Page 331* ◪

**CAVATELLI WITH ITALIAN MEAT
SAUCE** *Delicious home-made pasta shapes
served with a beef and tomato sauce flavoured
with oregano. 4 servings. Page 332* ■

STUFFED PASTA IN MEAT SAUCE
*Cooked cannelloni stuffed with cheeses,
layered with a spicy sausage and beef sauce
and Parmesan. 4 servings. Page 334* ■

MANICOTTI
*Home-made pasta filled with Ricotta,
Mozzarella and Parmesan cheeses, then
baked in a veal sauce. 4 servings. Page 334* ◪

CANNELLONI
*Home-made pasta rolled round a spinach,
meat and cheese filling and topped with
Parmesan sauce. 4 servings. Page 335* ■

LASAGNE
*A baked dish of cooked lasagne sheets
layered with minced beef, Ricotta and
Mozzarella cheeses. 4 servings. Page 336* ◪

VEAL LASAGNE
*A variation on lasagne, made with veal in
a white sauce and finished with grated
Parmesan cheese. 4–6 servings. Page 336* ◪

AUBERGINE LASAGNE
*Layers of cooked lasagne sheets, fried
aubergine slices, Mozzarella cheese and
tomato sauce. 4 servings. Page 336* ◪

CHEESE-STUFFED PASTA
*Large pasta shells with a cheese and parsley
stuffing, baked in tomato sauce. 4 servings.
Page 334* ◪

PUERTO RICAN BEANS AND RICE
*Tender rose cocoa beans flavoured with salt
pork, onion and green peppers, served with
boiled rice. 6 servings. Page 280* ■

AUBERGINE PARMIGIANA
*Crisply fried aubergine slices layered with a
tomato sauce, Mozzarella and grated
Parmesan cheese. 6 servings. Page 299* ◪

Main course dishes

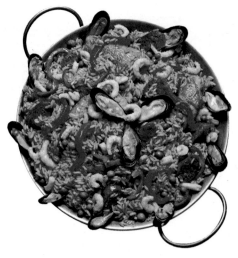

PAELLA
Mixed shellfish, chicken and sausages with peppers, tomatoes and garlic, cooked with saffron rice. 6–8 servings. **Page 165** ◩

STEAMED CLAMS
Clams, steamed until the shells have opened, served with melted butter and the cooking broth. 6 servings. **Page 162** ◻

DRESSED CRAB
The white and dark meats from a cold cooked crab, seasoned and flavoured separately, then served in the shell. 3–4 servings. **Page 166** ◩

CRAB TOASTS
A rich mixture of crab meat, butter, milk, sherry and breadcrumbs, served hot on buttered toast. 4 servings. **Page 167** ◻

SCALLOPS BONNE FEMME
Sautéed scallops and mushrooms in a creamy wine sauce, sprinkled with cheese and parsley and served with toast. 4 servings. **Page 163** ◻

PRAWN CURRY
Prawns in a curried sauce made with onion, apple, chicken stock, chutney, tomato paste, lemon juice. 3–4 servings. **Page 165** ◩

GRILLED PRAWNS WITH GARLIC BUTTER *Dublin Bay prawns grilled in garlic butter, with oregano and lemon juice. 4 servings.* **Page 164** ◻

STIR-FRIED PRAWNS
A Chinese dish of prawns, stir-fried with ginger, paprika, almonds, spring onions, Chinese cabbage, mange tout and mushrooms, then flavoured with a mixture of soy sauce and sherry. 4 servings. **Page 165** ◻

GRILLED LOBSTER WITH SHRIMP SAUCE *Grilled lobster halves with shrimp sauce spooned over the top and a garnish of parsley sprigs. 2 servings. Page 169* ◪

LOBSTER THERMIDOR
Cooked lobster meat folded into a wine and cheese sauce, returned to the lobster shells, sprinkled with grated cheese and grilled until golden. 2 servings. Page 169 ◪

GRILLED CRAWFISH TAILS
Grilled crawfish tails served with melted butter or with a mustard and herb butter. 2 servings. Page 169 ☐

CRAB GRATINE
A cheesy crab meat mixture baked in the crab shell and garnished with fried banana slices. 4 servings. Page 167 ◪

CRAB CAKES
Crab meat flavoured with mayonnaise, parsley and seasonings, fried until crisp. Serve with tartare sauce. 4 servings. Page 167 ☐

CRAB IMPERIAL
A well-seasoned mixture of crab meat, green pepper, milk and lemon juice, thickened and baked until golden. 4 servings. Page 167 ◪

GRILLED HERRINGS
Whole herrings with the heads and fins removed, grilled and served with mustard sauce. 4 servings. Page 174 ☐

BAKED STUFFED RED SNAPPER
A whole red snapper stuffed with a savoury veal and bacon forcemeat, covered and baked until tender. 3–4 servings. Page 176 ◪

35

Main course dishes

POACHED SALMON
Whole salmon, poached in court bouillon and then chilled. Before serving, it is skinned and garnished with lemon slices, parsley sprigs and cubes of aspic made from the stock. **Page 176** ■

GRILLED SESAME TROUT
Marinated trout coated with melted butter and toasted sesame seeds, grilled and served with the juices. 6 servings. **Page 174** ■

QUENELLES WITH CREAM SAUCE
Minced fish and white sauce, moulded into ovals and poached, then served with a rich, creamy sauce. 4–6 servings. **Page 182** ◪

TROUT AND ALMONDS (top) *4 servings.* Page 175 □   SOLE MEUNIERE
4 servings. Page 175 □

GRILLED FISH WITH COURGETTES
White fish fillets topped with a spicy barbecue sauce and grilled with mushroom caps and cheesy courgettes. 4 servings. **Page 177** □

SOLE AU GRATIN
Rolled sole fillets poached in milk, coated in a cheese sauce then grilled until golden. 4 servings. **Page 178** □

MEDITERRANEAN COD WITH VEGETABLES *Cod fried in breadcrumbs and dill, served with Mediterranean vegetables. 4 servings.* **Page 178** □

SOLE STUFFED WITH PRAWNS
Sole fillets with a prawn and mushroom stuffing, simmered in white wine and served with a creamy sauce. 6 servings. Page 180 ☐

TARRAGON FISH
White fish fillets grilled with tarragon, oil and lemon juice, served with lemon wedges and parsley. 4 servings. Page 177 ☐

STUFFED PLAICE MOULDS
Plaice fillets, baked in ramekins with a seafood stuffing to make individual filled fish cups. 4 servings. Page 179 ◪

STUFFED MACKEREL FILLETS
Mackerel fillets with apple stuffing, baked and finished with gherkins and an apple juice glaze. 4 servings. Page 180 ☐

POACHED WHITE FISH WITH HOLLANDAISE SAUCE *Filleted fish simmered in court bouillon, with hollandaise sauce. 4 servings.* Page 179 ◪

BAKED FILLETS WITH LEMON SAUCE *Fish fillets in a sauce made with lemon juice and chicken stock, garnished with sliced olives. 4 servings.* Page 179 ☐

CREAMED FINNAN HADDIE
Smoked haddock and hard-boiled eggs folded into a cream sauce, garnished with egg yolk and parsley. 4 servings. Page 180 ☐

FRIED FISH ALLA MARGHERITA
Sole or plaice fillets, lightly fried, then simmered in a thick tomato sauce. 4 servings. Page 178 ☐

DEEP FRIED FISH FILLETS
Fish fillets coated in batter and deep fried until the coating is crisp and golden. 4 servings. Page 177 ☐

Main course dishes

MARINATED HALIBUT STEAKS
Halibut marinated in oil, vinegar, herbs and seasoning then grilled until just tender. 4 servings. Page 182 ■

SALMON STEAKS WITH CUCUMBER SALAD *Chilled, poached salmon steaks served with a sliced cucumber and onion salad. 6 servings. Page 181* ▨

HALIBUT STEAK WITH AUBERGINE SAUCE *Grilled halibut with a rich sauce of aubergine, tomatoes, onion, green pepper and white wine. 4 servings. Page 181* □

COD STEAK WITH MUSHROOMS AND SPINACH *A large cod steak, lightly fried in butter and served with spinach and mushrooms. 4 servings. Page 182* □

SALMON MOUSSE
A shaped mousse made with canned salmon and béchamel sauce, decorated with thinly sliced radishes. 6–8 servings. Page 184 ■

FISH CAKES
Small cakes of cooked fish and potato, fried until crisp and golden and served with hollandaise sauce. 4 servings. Page 183 □

COUNTRY FISH PIE
White fish and salmon, with mushrooms and hard-boiled eggs in a parsley sauce, with a flaky pastry crust. 6 servings. Page 183 ▨

TUNA AND SPAGHETTI BAKE
Spaghetti with tuna, cheese and mushrooms in béchamel sauce, baked until golden and bubbling. 4 servings. Page 184 ▨

TUNA LOAF WITH CUCUMBER SAUCE *Flaked tuna, breadcrumbs, egg, celery and onion, baked and served with cucumber sauce. 4–6 servings. Page 184* ▨

ROAST STUFFED TURKEY AND RICH GRAVY *A whole turkey stuffed at both ends and roasted until tender, served with a rich gravy made from turkey giblet stock. 18–20 servings.* Page 249 ■

TURKEY MOLE
Turkey and avocado with a sauce flavoured with sesame seeds and chocolate. 4 servings. Page 267 ◪

ROLLED AND GLAZED TURKEY ROAST *Boned and rolled turkey meat basted during cooking with a sweet glaze. 12 servings.* Page 250 ■

SAUCY TURKEY WINGS
Turkey wings browned in oil, then baked in celery sauce until tender. 4 servings. Page 258 ◪

BONED AND STUFFED TURKEY
A whole boned turkey roasted with an apricot and ginger stuffing. 25–30 servings. Page 251 ■

TURKEY AND SAUSAGE KEBABS
Chunks of turkey meat marinated in soy sauce and sherry, threaded on to skewers with pieces of sausage, spring onion and pineapple, then grilled until tender. 6 servings. Page 263 ◪

Main course dishes

TURKEY IN CIDER
*Braised turkey in a mushroom, cream and
cider sauce, served here with toast flowers.
4–6 servings. Page 260* ■

TURKEY ROQUEFORT SALAD
*Cold turkey in a Roquefort cheese and soured
cream dressing, served on peach halves.
4 servings. Page 269* □

CHICKEN SALAD
*A light salad of chicken, celery and green
pepper with a mayonnaise dressing, served on
lettuce. 4–6 servings. Page 269* □

TURKEY-TAMALE CASSEROLE
*Mexican chilli-braised turkey with red kidney
beans, celery and tomatoes, topped with
cornmeal batter. 6 servings. Page 260* ◪

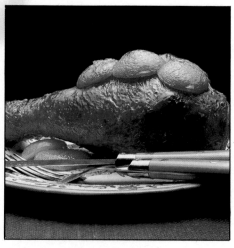

APRICOT-GLAZED TURKEY
DRUMSTICKS *Braised turkey drumsticks
brushed with an apricot jam glaze and
garnished with apricots. 4 servings. Page 260* ◪

CHICKEN GALANTINE
*A whole boned chicken, stuffed, roasted and
chilled, then coated with cream sauce and
garnished. 6–8 servings. Page 250* ■

TURKEY CORDON BLEU
Turkey breast slices stuffed with Gruyère cheese and ham, braised in wine and served with a cream sauce. 6 servings. Page 259 ◪

FRENCH ROAST CAPON
A capon roasted with herbs and stock, to give the bird a delicious flavour and keep the flesh moist. 8 servings. Page 251 ◾

BRAISED CHICKEN WITH SOURED CREAM SAUCE *Chicken braised with carrots and celery, served with a soured cream sauce and hot, fluffy rice. 4 servings. Page 255* ◪

CHICKEN IN PORT
Boneless chicken breasts braised in port and served with mushrooms, onions and a rich cream sauce. 4–6 servings. Page 258 ◪

CHICKEN PAPRIKA WITH SPAETZLES
Chicken cooked in a casserole in a paprika-flavoured sauce, with tiny German dumplings. 4 servings. Page 254 ◪

DEEP SOUTH CHICKEN CURRY
Chicken joints in a mildly curried sauce, served with hot rice tossed with almonds and raisins. 4–6 servings. Page 255 ◪

CHICKEN SEVILLE
Braised chicken in a herb and tomato sauce, with green pepper, ham and olives. 6 servings. Page 256 ◪

NUT-STUFFED CHICKEN BREASTS
Boneless chicken breasts filled with a peanut stuffing, baked and served with a light gravy. 6 servings. Page 252 ◪

FRENCH FRIED CHICKEN
Chicken joints fried crisp in batter, then finished in the oven. 4 servings. Page 264 ☐

41

Main course dishes

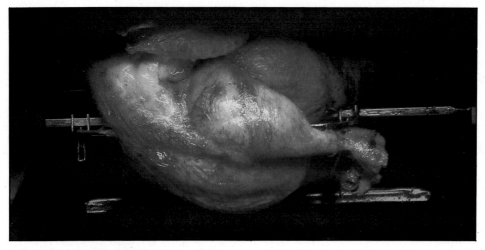

ROTISSERIED CHICKEN
A whole chicken, grilled on a spit and basted during cooking with the melted chicken fat. A 1.6-kg (3½-lb) chicken gives 4 servings. Page 261 ◪

FESTIVE CHICKEN WITH
ASPARAGUS *Chicken breasts and asparagus spears braised with white wine and blue cheese. 6 servings.* Page 260 ◪

CHICKEN CHORIZO
A garlic-flavoured, braised chicken dish with diced ham, Spanish sausages and a sweet-sour sauce. 6 servings. Page 256 ◪

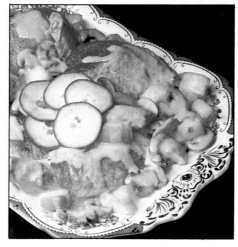

CHICKEN WITH CUCUMBER
Braised chicken quarters and cucumber in a soured cream, sherry and mushroom sauce. 4 servings. Page 255 ◪

SOURED CREAM CHICKEN
ENCHILADAS *Fried tortillas with chicken, chilli and mushrooms, baked with soured cream and cheese. 6 servings.* Page 270 ◪

SAVOURY CHICKEN
Chicken quarters steeped in a garlic marinade and grilled indoors or over a barbecue until tender. 4 servings. Page 261 ■

POLLO CACCIATORE
An Italian dish of chicken joints with small onions, tomatoes, green pepper and herbs, in red wine. 4 servings. Page 255 ◪

PARTY CHICKEN AND PRAWNS
Chicken breasts and prawns cooked in a rich tomato sauce flavoured with onion, garlic, herbs and port. 6 servings. Page 257 ☐

CHICKEN EN COCOTTE WITH APPLES AND CREAM *Chicken braised in cider with apples, onion and celery. 4 servings. Page 257* ◲

BARBECUED ROAST CHICKEN *An oven-roasted chicken, basted with a barbecue sauce during cooking. 4 servings. Page 251* ◲

CHICKEN IN A POT *A whole chicken, braised with onions, carrot, bacon and Jerusalem artichokes. 6 servings. Page 258* ■

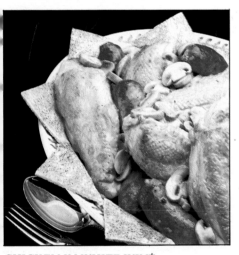

CHICKEN IN WHITE WINE *Chicken breasts braised with pork sausages and mushrooms in a white wine sauce. 4 servings. Page 259* ◲

CHICKEN WITH LEMON SAUCE *Tender chicken pieces braised in a sharp lemon juice, olive oil, onion and garlic sauce. 4 servings. Page 256* ■

ROAST CHICKEN *Simple roast chicken served with traditional accompaniments. 4 servings. Page 251* ◲

CHICKEN AVGOLEMONO *Boneless chicken breasts and sliced courgettes in an egg yolk and lemon sauce, served with pilaf. 4 servings. Page 259* ◲

CHICKEN SALAD VARIATIONS *4–6 servings each. Page 269* □

Main course dishes

FRIED CHICKEN WITH PARSLEY SAUCE *Chicken joints, shallow fried in oil until the skin is crisp and served with a stock-based parsley sauce. 4 servings. Page 263* ☐

BAKED CHICKEN *Chicken pieces, dipped in egg and breadcrumbs, basted with butter and baked until tender and golden. 6 servings. Page 252* ◪

BOILED CHICKEN WITH PARSLEY SAUCE *A whole chicken boiled with onion, cloves and a bouquet garni and accompanied by parsley sauce. 6 servings. Page 267* ■

COQ AU VIN *Chicken joints flamed in brandy, then braised in red wine and stock with bacon, mushrooms and onions. 4 servings. Page 257* ◪

CHICKEN IMPERIAL *Chicken breasts, fried in butter and braised in cream and sherry, with mushrooms and chopped onion. 4 servings. Page 258* ☐

CHEESE AND ANCHOVY GRILLED CHICKEN BREASTS *Chicken breasts rubbed with anchovy and onion and grilled with Mozzarella cheese. 6 servings. Page 263* ◪

CHICKEN BREASTS WITH ARTICHOKE HEARTS *Braised chicken breasts, finished with soured cream and artichoke hearts. 6 servings. Page 259* ◪

ARROZ CON POLLO *A Spanish dish of rice and chicken joints with tomatoes, pimentos, stuffed olives, sausages and peas. 4 servings. Page 254* ◪

CHICKEN KIEV *Chicken breasts filled with garlic and parsley butter, coated with breadcrumbs and deep fried. 4 servings. Page 265* ■

STIR-FRIED CHICKEN AND MUSHROOMS *Thinly-sliced chicken flavoured with ginger and sherry and stir-fried with vegetables. 4 servings.* Page 266 □

CHINESE CHICKEN WITH VEGETABLES *Chicken, celery, green pepper, bean sprouts and water chestnuts, stir-fried with almonds. 3–4 servings.* Page 266 □

CHICKEN SZECHUAN STYLE *Marinated chicken pieces and spring onions, stir-fried in an orange sauce and garnished with carrot. 4 servings.* Page 266 □

BUTTERY GARLIC CHICKEN *Chicken joints in a marinade of butter with garlic, honey, spices and herbs, grilled and served with tomatoes. 4 servings.* Page 262 ◪

SAUCY CHICKEN WITH AVOCADO *A rich dish of chicken braised in dry sherry, topped with avocado slices folded into a creamy sauce. 4 servings.* Page 256 ◪

SIMMERED CHICKEN WITH PASTA *Lasagne, layered with chicken and mushroom sauce. 4–6 servings.* Page 268 ◪

CHICKEN FRICASSEE *Boiled chicken and vegetables in an egg yolk, cream and lemon sauce, with grilled bacon rolls and parsley. 4 servings.* Page 267 ◪

CHICKEN MARYLAND *Crisply coated fried chicken, traditionally served with fried bananas and corn fritters. 4 servings.* Page 264 □

CHICKEN VOL-AU-VENTS *Vol-au-vent cases filled with chopped chicken and vegetables in a sherry-flavoured sauce. 4 servings.* Page 269 ◪

Main course dishes

TANDOORI CHICKEN
Chicken marinated in yogurt, spices and lemon juice and either grilled or barbecued over a charcoal fire. 8 servings. Page 261 ■

CHICKEN POT PIE
A mixture of chicken pieces and vegetables in a cream and stock sauce, topped with shortcrust pastry. 4–6 servings. Page 268 ■

CRUNCHY DRUMSTICKS
Chicken drumsticks marinated in orange juice, then rolled in oats and butter and fried until crisp. 4 servings. Page 264 ■

CHICKEN CROQUETTES
4 servings. Page 270 □

CHICKEN WITH CHILLI MARINADE
Chicken quarters, marinated in a mild chilli relish with horseradish and garlic, and then grilled. 4 servings. Page 262 ■

LEMON CHICKEN ON SPINACH LEAVES *Sautéed chicken breasts in a lemon sauce, arranged on a base of shredded raw spinach. 6 servings. Page 264* □

CREAMY CHICKEN HASH
Diced cooked chicken and potatoes, reheated in a creamy sauce. 4 servings. Page 269 □

CHICKEN ROULADES
Chicken breasts, stuffed with ham, cheese and rosemary, then coated in egg and breadcrumbs and fried. 4 servings. Page 265 □

CHICKEN BAKED IN WINE
Chicken halves, marinated in white wine and oil with chopped spring onions and parsley and baked. 4 servings. Page 252 ■

CHICKEN LIVER SAUTE
Chicken livers, sautéed with onion and served in a sherry sauce with crisp toast triangles. 4 servings. Page 270 ▢

LEMON GLAZED POUSSINS
Rôtisseried poussins, brushed with a sweet glaze of lemon and apple juice. 4 servings. Page 272 ◩

CHICKEN LIVERS ALOHA
A Hawaiian-style dish of sautéed chicken livers with pineapple chunks. 4 servings. Page 270 ▢

POUSSINS WITH APRICOT STUFFING
Roast poussins, glazed with golden syrup and sherry and served with apricot and walnut stuffing. 4 servings. Page 272 ◼

GRILLED POUSSIN HALVES
A halved poussin, grilled and served with parsley-flavoured rice and grilled pineapple rings. 2 servings. Page 272 ▢

POUSSINS WITH RED SULTANA SAUCE
Whole poussins, filled with a wheatgerm and celery stuffing, roasted in butter, then served with a redcurrant and sultana sauce. 4 servings. Page 271 ◩

SPRING CHICKEN CASSEROLE
Spring chicken joints, casseroled with tomatoes, carrots and dumplings. 3–4 servings. Page 271 ◩

Main course dishes

POUSSINS MARSALA
Poussin halves braised in Marsala, topped with a whipped cream, paprika, garlic and cheese sauce. 6 servings. Page 271▨

HONEYED SPRING CHICKEN
Marinated spring chicken quarters, fried, glazed with honey and served on shredded lettuce. 2–3 servings. Page 272 ■

PEKING DUCK WITH THIN PANCAKES
A Chinese dish of crisp-skinned, roast duck. The duck is carved into small pieces which are served with hoisin sauce and spring onions, rolled up inside the pancakes. 4 servings. Page 275 ■

BOHEMIAN ROAST GOOSE
Rich roast goose, served sliced, with a sauerkraut and apple stuffing flavoured with caraway seeds. 8–10 servings. Page 273 ■

ROAST GOOSE
A whole roast goose with characteristically crisp skin, garnished here with grilled apple rings. 6 servings. Page 273 ■

SHANGHAI DUCK
Braised duck in the Chinese style, with whole leeks, sliced leeks and carrots in a soy and ginger sauce. 4 servings. Page 274 ■

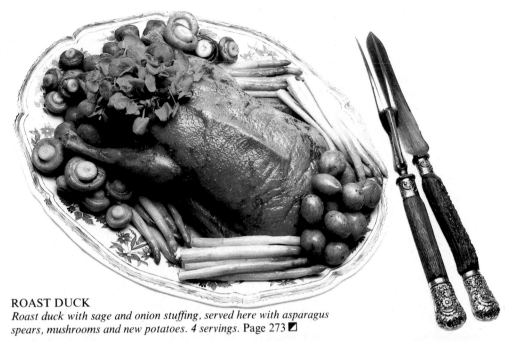

DUCK WITH CHERRIES
Moist roast duck quarters with a port- and orange-flavoured brown sauce and cherry garnish. 4 servings. **Page 274** ■

ROAST DUCK
Roast duck with sage and onion stuffing, served here with asparagus spears, mushrooms and new potatoes. 4 servings. **Page 273** ◪

DUCK A L'ORANGE
A classic French dish of roast duck in an orange, wine and brandy sauce, garnished with orange slices. 4 servings. **Page 274** ■

PLUM-GLAZED DUCK
Garlic-flavoured duck quarters, glazed with a spicy plum sauce. 4 servings. **Page 276** ■

ROAST DUCK WITH CRANBERRY GLAZE *A roast duck brushed with a cranberry and wine glaze that has the roasting juices added to it. 4 servings.* **Page 276** ◪

CHESTNUT STUFFING (left) *for a 4.5-kg (10-lb) turkey.* **Page 253** ☐
SAUSAGE AND APPLE STUFFING (right) *for a 4.5-kg (10-lb) turkey.* **Page 253** ☐ **RICE STUFFING** *for a 1.8-kg (4-lb) duck.*
Page 253 ☐

From left, **CURRANT-MINT JELLY**
Makes 225 ml (8 fl oz). ☐ **LEMON SAUCE**
Makes 300 ml (½ pint). ☐ **CRANBERRY**
SAUCE *Makes 400 ml (¾ pint).* All page 276 ☐

Main course dishes

ROAST RIB OF BEEF WITH YORKSHIRE PUDDING
Tender roast beef, on the bone, served with individual Yorkshire puddings, thin gravy and horseradish cream. 6 servings. Page 191 ■

BOEUF EN DAUBE
Top rump of beef braised with onions, carrots, salt pork, white wine, herbs and black olives. 6 servings. Page 195 ■

BOILED BEEF WITH WINTER VEGETABLES *Boneless brisket simmered with swede, cabbage, carrots and potatoes. 6–8 servings. Page 205* ■

CREAMED BEEF AND NOODLES
Braised chuck or blade steak with soured cream and dill sauce, served over noodles. 6 servings. Page 200 ◪

STEAK SAUTERNES
Pan-fried fillet steaks with a white wine, mushroom and ham sauce, served on toast circles. 4 servings. Page 198 ☐

CALIFORNIAN BEEF STEW
Steak cubes, with onions, mushrooms, peas and olives, stewed in red wine and stock. 6 servings. Page 203 ■

CAESAR STYLE BRAISED STEAK
Fillet or rump steaks, braised in Worcestershire and anchovy sauce, served on garlic bread. 4 servings. Page 201 ◪

LONDON GRILL
Seasoned entrecôte or rump steak, grilled with halved tomatoes and mushrooms basted with French dressing. 4 servings. Page 196 ☐

MEAT LOAF (rear) *6–8 servings.* ◪
PINEAPPLE MEAT LOAF *6–8 servings.* ◪
Both page 206

FILLET STEAK WITH MUSTARD-CAPER SAUCE *Pan-fried steaks with a creamy, vermouth-flavoured sauce. 6 servings.* Page 195 ☐

BEEF POT ROAST WITH SWEET AND SOUR CABBAGE *Braised boneless top rib of beef. 6–8 servings.* Page 194 ■

MACARONI BAKE
Minced beef, macaroni, tomato sauce and cottage, Parmesan and Mozzarella cheeses, baked together. 4–6 servings. Page 209 ◪

VEGETABLE-TOPPED ROAST BEEF
Boned and rolled sirloin, topped with grated carrots and celery leaves, served with red wine gravy. 6–8 servings. Page 191 ◪

CELERY-STUFFED BEEF STEAK
Flank steak 'sandwich' with fresh celery filling, braised and served with ginger-flavoured sauce. 6 servings. Page 201 ■

CARBONNADE OF BEEF
Chuck or blade steak simmered in beer with onions, garlic and herbs. 6–8 servings. Page 199 ■

Main course dishes

HAMBURGERS
Seasoned minced beef patties, fried or grilled and served in a bun with a choice of toppings. 4 servings. **Page 205** □

SIMPLE BEEF POT ROAST
Topside or brisket of beef braised in beef stock and water until tender. 6 servings. **Page 193** ■

STEAK DIANE
Fried entrecôte steaks, flamed with brandy and served with a sherry, shallot and chive sauce. 4 servings. **Page 196** □

INDIVIDUAL BEEF WELLINGTONS
Fillet steaks with mushrooms and onion, wrapped in flaky pastry and baked until golden brown. 8 servings. **Page 192** ■

INDIVIDUAL LEMON BARBECUED MEAT LOAVES (rear) *6 servings.* □
CHILLED MEAT LOAF *6–8 servings.* ■
Both **page 207**

CHILLI CON CARNE
Chilli-flavoured stew of minced beef, red kidney beans, tomatoes, green pepper and onion. 6 servings. **Page 209** ◪

MEXICAN BEEF POT ROAST
Chuck or blade steak cooked with chillies, green peppers, sweetcorn, onions and tomato paste. 6–8 servings. **Page 194** ■

PRESSURE-COOKED BEEF STEW
Marinated beef chunks, cooked quickly in a pressure cooker with salt pork, red wine and vegetables. 6 servings. **Page 203** ■

ENTRECOTE MIRABEAU
Grilled entrecôte steaks topped with a lattice of anchovies and served with anchovy butter. 4 servings. **Page 196** □

MINUTE STEAKS WITH FRESH TOMATO SAUCE *Fried minute steaks with tomato, spring onion and basil sauce. 6–8 servings. Page 198* □

ORIENTAL ANISEED BEEF *Chuck or blade steak braised with spring onions, soy sauce, sherry, ginger and aniseed. 6 servings. Page 200* ◪

DILLED MEATBALLS (top) □ **MUSH-ROOM AND CHEESE MEATBALLS** (left) *Both 6 servings.* □ **BURGUNDIED MEATBALLS** *4 servings.* □ All page 208

STEAK MEDICI *Fried sirloin steaks with sliced mushroom and port sauce. 4 servings. Page 197* □

TERIYAKI BEEF KEBABS *Marinated cubes of rump steak grilled on skewers with chunks of fresh pineapple. 6 servings. Page 198* ■

BEEF POT ROAST WITH PEPPERS *Chuck steak braised with dry sherry and soy sauce, served with cooked peppers. 6–8 servings. Page 194* ■

BOEUF BOURGUIGNON *Steak cubes stewed with bacon, shallots, mushrooms, garlic, brandy and red wine. 6 servings. Page 202* ■

QUEUES DE BOEUFS AUX OLIVES NOIRES *Oxtail cooked with brandy, white wine, herbs and black olives, served with rice. 6–8 servings. Page 204* ■

STEAK AND KIDNEY PIE *Chunks of steak and kidney cooked in stock and wine or beer, then topped with pastry and baked. 6 servings. Page 203* ■

Main course dishes

BEEF AND CHESTNUT CASSEROLE
A hearty casserole of chuck or blade steak, tomatoes, pimentos, red wine, garlic sausage and chestnuts. 6 servings. Page 204 ■

SAUERBRATEN
Beef silverside, marinated for several days then braised and served with soured cream sauce. 6–8 servings. Page 193 ■

CHUNKY BEEF WITH CELERY
Beef top rib pieces cooked with celery, red kidney beans, stock and sherry. 4 servings. Page 199 ■

DEVILLED PORTERHOUSE STEAK
Steak coated with spicy mustard butter and breadcrumbs and grilled until golden. 6 servings. Page 197 □

WHOLE STUFFED CABBAGE
Cabbage leaves filled with a spicy minced beef and rice mixture, simmered gently in a tomato sauce. 6 servings. Page 209 ■

MARINATED BEEF CASSEROLE
Chuck or blade steak marinated with garlic, then cooked with button onions, mushrooms and bacon. 6 servings. Page 199 ■

BEEF STEW
Chunks of stewing steak simmered in stock with onions, garlic, potatoes, carrots and peas. 6 servings. Page 202 ■

BEEF WITH SOURED CREAM AND MUSHROOMS *Slow-simmered chuck or blade steak served with noodles and a soured cream sauce. 6 servings. Page 201* ◪

COUNTRY POT ROAST
Topside or silverside cooked in tomato juice with carrots, onions, celery, garlic and herbs. 6–8 servings. Page 192 ■

FRUITED BEEF POT ROAST
Silverside or boned brisket braised in cider with dried apricots and prunes. 6–8 servings.
Page 195 ■

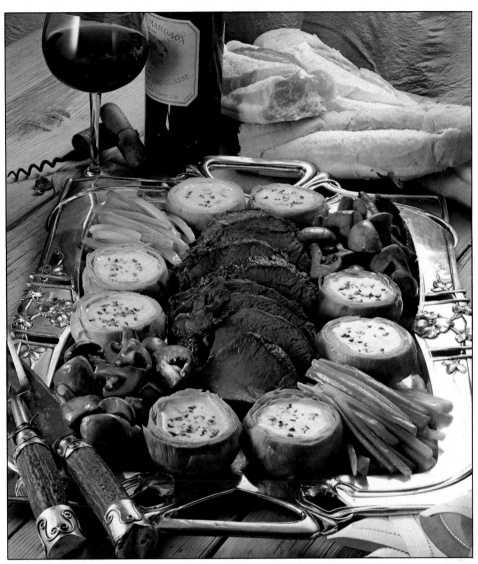

OXTAIL RAGOUT
Browned oxtail cooked in canned tomato soup with carrots, onions and broad beans.
6–8 servings. Page 204 ■

CHATEAUBRIAND
Grilled châteaubriand or fillet steak cut into thick slices and served on a platter, surrounded by cooked globe artichokes filled with béarnaise sauce, and mushrooms, carrots and celery. 4 servings. Page 195 □

BEEF POT ROAST WITH BROAD BEANS *Topside beef with onion, garlic, Worcestershire sauce, parsnips and broad beans. 6–8 servings.* Page 193 ■

SWISS STEAK WITH PEPPER-TOMATO SAUCE *Chuck steak cooked in tomato sauce with onions, garlic and green peppers. 6 servings.* Page 200 ■

CARPET BAG STEAK
Luxurious dish of rump or fillet steak stuffed with oysters and mushrooms and grilled. 4 servings. Page 197 □

Main course dishes

ROAST LOIN OF PORK
Succulent roast loin of pork, on the bone, served with gravy made from the pan juices. 6–8 servings. Page 212 ■

BREADED PORK FILLET
Pork fillet slices coated with rosemary-flavoured egg and breadcrumbs and fried. 4–6 servings. Page 213 ◪

PRUNE-STUFFED PORK
Roast loin of pork stuffed with prunes, served with cream and redcurrant jelly sauce. 6–8 servings. Page 212 ■

BARBECUED SPARERIBS
Pre-cooked American pork spareribs, brushed with tomato and chilli sauce and barbecued. 4 servings. Page 216 ◪

PORK CHOPS WITH PRUNE AND APPLE STUFFING *Baked pork chops topped with prune, apple, rice and almond stuffing. 4 servings.* Page 215 ■

COUNTRY SPARERIBS
Pork sparerib chops baked in apple juice with potatoes, carrots, onions and cabbage. 4 servings. Page 216 ◪

PORK BAPS WITH BARBECUE SAUCE
Fried pork steaks in baps or rolls, with a simple tomato barbecue sauce. 6 servings. Page 214 □

PORK SPARERIBS WITH SAUERKRAUT *American pork spareribs, browned then simmered in lager with sauerkraut. 6 servings.* Page 216 ◪

PORK HOCKS WITH HARICOT BEANS
Pork hocks or spring joints, simmered with haricot beans, button onions and carrots.
6 servings. Page 217 ■

BURRITOS
Mexican tortillas filled with a spicy pork and beef mixture, red kidney beans and Cheddar cheese. 6 servings. Page 217 ■

STIR-FRIED PORK AND VEGETABLES
(rear) *6 servings.* Page 213 □ PORK
CHOPS ORIENTALE *6 servings.* Page 214 ■

ORANGE PORK CHOPS
Browned pork chops simmered with paprika and served with a spicy orange sauce.
6 servings. Page 215 □

ROAST PORK WITH PIQUANT SAUCE
Roast blade of pork, on the bone, basted with sweet-sour tomato sauce. 6–8 servings.
Page 213 ■

PORK RAGOUT
Cubed pork shoulder meat stewed with green peppers and red wine, with rice and stuffing balls. 4 servings. Page 217 ◩

MARINATED PORK AND ONION
KEBABS *Marinated, boneless, cubed pork sparerib, grilled or barbecued with onions.*
4 servings. Page 213 ■

BRAISED PORK CHOPS
Pork chops braised in the frying pan, served with pan gravy; with flavouring variations.
4 servings. Page 214 □

GRILLED PORK CHOPS WITH
PINEAPPLE *Chump chops marinated in a pineapple and soy sauce mixture, then grilled with pineapple rings. 6 servings. Page 215* ■

Main course dishes

WHOLE BOILED HAM
Boiled whole ham, brushed with honey to glaze and finished in the oven.
Serve hot with vegetables and parsley sauce, or cold with an assortment
of bread and rolls. 30–36 servings. Page 221 ■

BRAISED BACON
Boneless gammon or collar bacon simmered
in stock with onion, carrots, turnip, celery
and herbs. 8 servings. Page 220 ■

BARBECUED BACON AND PEACHES
Boil-in-the-bag bacon covered with chilli-
flavoured sauce and baked with fresh peach
halves. 4 servings. Page 220 ◪

BACON CHOPS WITH BROWN
LENTILS *Braised bacon chops served on a*
mixture of brown lentils, onion, celery and
mushrooms. 4 servings. Page 222 ■

58

PINEAPPLE-GLAZED BAKED HAM
Par-boiled ham, covered with a pineapple and brown sugar glaze and then baked in the oven. 12–15 servings. Page 220 ■

GAMMON RASHERS WITH FRUIT SAUCE *Gammon rashers braised in orange juice with prunes and dried apricots. 6 servings. Page 222* □

CHOUCROUTE GARNI
Bacon and pork simmered in wine and stock with onions, potatoes, frankfurters and sauerkraut. 6–8 servings. Page 222 ◪

GAMMON STEAK HAWAII
Gammon steak and bananas cooked in a brown sugar, butter and vinegar sauce. 6 servings. Page 221 □

LEMONY GAMMON STEAKS
Grilled gammon steaks basted with a lemon, mustard and sugar glaze, and topped with lemon slices. 6–8 servings. Page 222 □

GLAZED HAM LOAF
Minced ham, carrot and onion loaf, baked with a pineapple glaze and garnished with pineapple slices. 4 servings. Page 223 ◪

ROAST GAMMON
Roast gammon, glazed with marmalade and mustard, then garnished with orange slices and cloves. 10 servings. Page 220 ■

CHEESE-TOPPED GAMMON RASHERS *Grilled gammon rashers topped with apple rings and Cheddar cheese. 4 servings. Page 222* □

IDEAS FOR LEFTOVER HAM (from top): HAM CASSEROLE □ HAM CHEF SALAD □ HAM, NUT AND FRUIT SALAD □ GLAZED KEBABS □ Page 223

Main course dishes

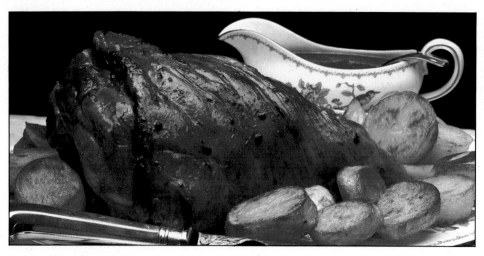

ROAST LEG OF LAMB
Leg of lamb, spread with a juniper berry and mustard mixture and roasted with sliced potatoes. Serve with sauce made from the pan juices, flavoured with gin and redcurrant jelly. 6–8 servings. **Page 226** ■

LAMB CURRY
Cubes of lamb simmered in spicy curry sauce, served with rice and a selection of side dishes. 6 servings. **Page 231** ■

LAMB CUTLETS WITH FRUIT SAUCE
Lamb cutlets dipped in egg and breadcrumbs, then grilled and served with gooseberry and apple sauce. 4–6 servings. **Page 229** □

MARINATED LEG OF LAMB
Leg of lamb marinated in an orange juice, wine, garlic and chilli mixture, then roasted. 6 servings. **Page 227** ■

BRAISED NECK OF LAMB
Middle neck of lamb braised in a spicy prune sauce. 4 servings. **Page 230** ■

LANCASHIRE HOT-POT
Layers of middle neck lamb chops, kidneys, onions and potato slices, baked in a casserole. 4 servings. **Page 230** ■

BARBECUED BREAST OF LAMB
Breast of lamb pieces baked with a honey, orange and chilli sauce and orange slices. 4 servings. **Page 229** ■

PERSIAN LAMB WITH ALMONDS
Minced lamb, cooked with almonds, lime juice and mint, served on spinach leaves with tomatoes. 4 servings. **Page 231** □

ROAST RACK OF LAMB WITH APRICOT GLAZE *Best end of neck of lamb, seasoned and roasted with an apricot jam glaze. 4 servings. Page 227* ◪

LAMB RIBLETS WITH PINEAPPLE *Lamb riblets in a spicy honey sauce, topped with pineapple chunks and baked in the oven. 6 servings. Page 229* ◪

ROQUEFORT LAMB CHOPS (rear) *8 servings. Page 228* □ **GINGERED LAMB CHOPS** *6 servings. Page 228* □

ROTISSERIED LEG OF LAMB *Boned and rolled leg of lamb, marinated in a spicy wine mixture and spit roasted. 6–8 servings. Page 227* ■

MIDDLE EAST LAMB STEW (rear) *6–8 servings. Page 230* ■ **LAMB STEW ROSE** *6 servings. Page 231* ■

LAMB CHOPS A L'ORANGE *Chump chops brushed with an orange marmalade, sherry and garlic mixture and grilled. 4 servings. Page 228* □

BARBECUED LAMB KEBABS *Lamb cubes, aubergine and peppers marinated in a spicy tomato mixture, then barbecued on skewers. 4 servings. Page 228* ■

MARINATED BONED LEG OF LAMB *Boned leg of lamb, marinated in wine flavoured with garlic and oregano, then roasted until tender. 6–8 servings. Page 226* ■

LAMB PATTIES *Lemon- and herb-flavoured minced lamb patties wrapped in bacon rashers and grilled. 6 servings. Page 231* □

Main course dishes

LEMON TARRAGON VEAL ROAST
Boneless shoulder of veal seasoned with lemon rind and tarragon, then roasted. 6–8 servings. Page 234 ■

SPICED LEG OF VEAL
Leg of veal, pot roasted with apple juice, onions and spices, and garnished with poached apple wedges and celery leaves. 6–8 servings. Page 235 ■

SALTIMBOCCA
Sautéed veal escalopes finished in sherry sauce with ham and Gruyère cheese. 4 servings. Page 236 □

VEAL MILANESE
Stewed veal with white wine, tomatoes, carrot, celery, garlic and basil, garnished with lemon rind. 6 servings. Page 237 ◪

VEAL ESCALOPES WITH LEMON
Sautéed veal escalopes in a white wine and lemon sauce, garnished with lemon slices. 4 servings. Page 236 □

VEAL PAPRIKA
Stewed veal with paprika, onion and soured cream, served on a bed of noodles. 6 servings. Page 237 ◪

ROAST LOIN OF VEAL MARSALA
Loin of veal, seasoned with herbs and roasted, served with a mushroom and Marsala sauce. 6–8 servings. Page 234 ■

VEAL PARMIGIANA
Breadcrumbed escalopes, sautéed then topped with tomato sauce and Mozzarella and Parmesan cheeses. 6 servings. Page 236 □

WIENER SCHNITZEL
Breadcrumbed escalopes, sautéed in butter and garnished with lemon, parsley, anchovies and capers. 6 servings. Page 236 □

VEAL A LA HOLSTEIN
Wiener schnitzel topped with a fried egg. 6 servings. Page 236 □

TOMATO-PAPRIKA VEAL
Pot roasted leg of veal in a tomato and paprika sauce enriched with soured cream. 6–8 servings. Page 235 ■

COUNTRY VEAL POT ROAST
Boned fillet end of leg, cooked in canned cream of mushroom soup with carrots, onion and herbs. 6–8 servings. Page 234 ■

BLANQUETTE DE VEAU
Simmered chunks of veal with mushrooms and onions in a vermouth and cream sauce, garnished with dill. 6 servings. Page 237 ◪

VEAL AND PEPPERS
Escalopes sautéed in butter and served with peppers and onions which have been cooked in a spicy vinegar mixture. 8 servings. Page 235 □

Main course dishes

ROAST PHEASANT
A brace of pheasants, barded with bacon, spread with butter and roasted.
Serve surrounded with fried breadcrumbs, garnished with watercress and
accompanied by gravy made from the pan juices. 4 servings. **Page 241** □

RAISED GAME PIE
Pheasant or pigeon meat with sausagemeat,
ham and chuck steak, baked in a hot water
crust pastry case. 6 servings. **Page 243** ■

ROAST LOIN OF VENISON
Loin of venison marinated in red wine with
flavourings, then roasted and served with
gravy. 8 servings. **Page 241** ■

BRAISED PARTRIDGE WITH
CABBAGE *Partridges braised in chicken*
stock with cabbage, bacon, carrots, onions
and herbs. 4 servings. **Page 242** ◪

CASSEROLE OF RABBIT WITH
JUNIPER BERRIES *Rabbit joints cooked in*
red wine with bacon rolls, garnished with
toast triangles. 6 servings. **Page 242** ■

HARE TERRINE
A minced hare and sausagemeat mixture,
layered with fillets of hare meat. 6 servings.
Page 243 ■

JUGGED HARE
A rich dish of braised hare, bacon and vegetables; the gravy is thickened with the hare's blood. 6 servings. Page 242 ■

BOILED OX TONGUE
Salted ox tongue boiled with vegetables and flavourings, then skinned, boned and pressed. 8–10 servings. Page 239 ■

SWEETBREADS MEUNIERE
Breaded veal sweetbreads, grilled and served with a buttery lemon sauce. 3–4 servings. Page 239 ◪

POACHER'S PIE
Rabbit joints, bacon, potatoes and leeks with stock and herbs, covered with shortcrust pastry. 4 servings. Page 243 ◪

FRIED LIVER AND BACON
Calf's or lamb's liver, fried in bacon fat and served with bacon rashers and lemon wedges. 4 servings. Page 238 ☐

KIDNEYS MADEIRA
Lamb's kidneys sprinkled with Madeira, coated with a well-seasoned sauce and grilled. 4 servings. Page 239 ☐

ROAST BARON OF HARE
Baron of hare stuffed with a spicy veal and bacon forcemeat and roasted. 4 servings. Page 241 ◪

LIVER JARDINIERE
Ox liver slices braised with onions, green peppers and tomatoes and topped with crumbled bacon. 4 servings. Page 238 ☐

SAUTEED VEAL KIDNEYS
Veal kidneys, mushrooms and spring onions braised in stock and Madeira and served with toast triangles. 4 servings. Page 239 ☐

Main course dishes

SALADE NICOISE
Hard-boiled egg, with French beans, tuna, tomato wedges, potato, anchovies and olives on lettuce. 4 servings. Page 324 ◪

CHEF'S SALAD
Dressed lettuce with tomato and egg wedges and strips of cheese, cold cooked chicken and ham. 6 servings. Page 324 ☐

CRAB LOUIS (rear) *4 servings.* Page 325 ☐
PINEAPPLE AND CHEESE SALAD
4 servings. Page 325 ☐

CHUNKY EGG SALAD
Large chunks of egg tossed in a mayonnaise dressing with celery and green pepper, on a bed of lettuce. 4 servings. Page 325 ☐

BUFFET SALAD
Layers of cheese, ham, tomato and lettuce in a substantial moulded salad, served with a mustard mayonnaise. 6 servings. Page 325 ◪

RICE SALAD
Chopped onion, green pepper and ham mixed into a tomato and thyme-flavoured rice salad. 6 servings. Page 325 ◪

HERRING SALAD
Smoked fish, apple and plain and pickled vegetables in cream, chilled well to allow the flavours to blend. 4 servings. Page 324 ■

PRAWN SALAD (left) *6 servings.* Page 325 ☐
TUNA SALAD (centre) *6 servings.* Page 325 ☐
SALMON SALAD *6 servings.* Page 325 ☐

Side dishes

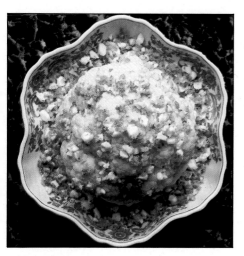

CAULIFLOWER POLONAISE
A whole boiled cauliflower, topped with buttery fried breadcrumbs, parsley and chopped egg. 6 servings. Page 284 □

BAKED CREAMED SPINACH
Chopped cooked spinach mixed with a cream sauce and beaten egg whites, baked until lightly set. 4–6 servings. Page 295 □

RATATOUILLE
Aubergines, peppers, courgettes and tomatoes stewed with onion, garlic and herbs. 4–6 servings. Page 298 ◪

STIR-FRIED COURGETTES (front)
4 servings. Page 286 □ **FRENCH BEANS WITH COURGETTES AND BACON**
6 servings. Page 299 □

COURGETTES IN SOURED CREAM
Sliced courgettes, fried with garlic and served in a soured cream sauce. 4 servings. Page 286 □

RUNNER BEANS WITH CHEESY TOPPING (front) *4 servings. Page 281.* □
RUNNER BEANS WITH SAGE BUTTER *4 servings. Page 281* □

ONIONS IN CREAM SAUCE (left)
4 servings. Page 291 □ **GLAZED ONIONS** *4 servings. Page 290* □

CRISPY FRIED ONIONS (left)
4 servings. Page 291 □ **FRIED ONIONS** *4 servings. Page 291* □

JACKET BAKED ONIONS
Whole baked onions, with centres chopped and mixed with cheese and parsley, then replaced. 4 servings. Page 290 ◪

Side dishes

BOSTON BAKED BEANS
A traditional American dish of baked haricot beans flavoured with salt pork, onions, black treacle and spices. 4 servings. Page 279 ■

SOUTHERN STYLE BLACK-EYE BEANS (rear) *4–6 servings. Page 280* ■
SPICY BEANS AND SWEETCORN
6 servings. Page 280 ■

FRENCH BEANS WITH THYME
French beans cooked with onion, bacon and thyme until they are just tender. 4 servings. Page 280 ☐

BRAISED FENNEL
Halved fennel bulbs braised in chicken stock, which is then thickened with beurre manié to make a sauce. 4 servings. Page 287 ☐

SPICED CARROTS (rear) *4–6 servings. Page 284* ☐   **GLAZED CARROTS**
4 servings. Page 284 ☐

TURNIP PUREE
Turnips simmered in chicken stock until tender, then mashed with butter, cream and seasonings. 4 servings. Page 297 ☐

CREAMED PARSNIPS
Sliced parsnips in an orange-flavoured sauce made with the cooking liquid, sprinkled with chopped parsley. 4 servings. Page 291 ☐

SWEET AND SOUR BEETROOTS
Sliced cooked beetroots in a piquant onion, sugar and vinegar sauce, served hot or cold. 6 servings. Page 281 ■

BROAD BEANS WITH SOURED CREAM (left) *4 servings.*
BROAD BEANS WITH WATER CHESTNUTS *4 servings. Both page 279* ☐

SAUTEED AUBERGINE SLICES (front)
4 servings. **Page 278** □ AUBERGINE
WITH CARAWAY SEEDS *4 servings.*
Page 278 □

SUMMER VEGETABLE BOWL
*French beans, sweetcorn, courgettes and celery,
with green pepper and onions, topped with
bacon and tomatoes. 6 servings.* **Page 298** □

SAUTEED MUSHROOMS (front)
4 servings. **Page 289** □ MUSHROOMS IN
SOURED CREAM *6 servings.* **Page 289** □

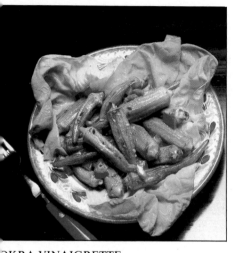

OKRA VINAIGRETTE
*An unusual salad of okra and red pepper in an
olive oil dressing flavoured with garlic and
thyme. 6 servings.* **Page 290** ■

STIR-FRIED CABBAGE AND
COURGETTES *Shredded white cabbage and
sliced courgettes fried in garlic-flavoured oil
until tender and crisp. 4 servings.* **Page 299** □

BRAISED MIXED VEGETABLES
*French beans, carrots and mushrooms, lightly
braised with thyme and butter. 4–6 servings.*
Page 298 □

CHICORY AU GRATIN
*A rich dish of whole blanched chicory heads
baked in Gruyère cheese, butter and single
cream. 6 servings.* **Page 285** □

CABBAGE BRAISED IN CIDER
*Quartered green cabbage braised with onion
and cooking apples in a cider and chicken
stock sauce. 4 servings.* **Page 283** ◪

MARINATED CABBAGE (left) *6 servings.* ◪
FRIED CABBAGE (rear) *6 servings.* □
SWEET AND SOUR RED CABBAGE
CASSEROLE *4 servings.* ■ All page 283

69

Side dishes

SWEETCORN WITH FLAVOURED BUTTERS *Sweetcorn cobs served with chilli butter* (left), *dill butter* (front) *and chive butter.* Page 296 □

STIR-FRIED ASPARAGUS
Asparagus pieces, lightly stir-fried until tender but still crisp. 6 servings. Page 278 □

LEEKS AU GRATIN
Cooked leeks in cheese sauce, with a breadcrumb and cheese topping, grilled until lightly browned. 4 servings. Page 288 □

HERB SAUTEED GREEN PEPPERS (front) *4 servings.* Page 292 □
MARINATED PEPPERS *6 servings.* Page 292 □

STUFFED GREEN PEPPERS (left) *4 servings.* Page 300 □ **PEPPER AND TOMATO SAUTE** *4–6 servings.* Page 299 □

STIR-FRIED MIXED VEGETABLES
Carrot, broccoli, onion and whole button mushrooms, stir-fried in oil with seasonings. 6 servings. Page 299 □

BUTTERY CUCUMBER RINGS
Seeded cucumber rings sautéed gently in butter until tender and lightly browned, and served hot. 4 servings. Page 286 □

PEAS AMANDINE
Fresh peas, slivered almonds, fried chopped onion and bacon tossed together in double cream. 4 servings. Page 292 □

SIMMERED CARROTS AND CELERY
Sliced carrots and celery cooked until just tender in a little seasoned water and oil. 4–6 servings. Page 298 □

BAKED POTATOES
Potatoes brushed with oil or butter, baked until soft and topped here with cheese. 4 servings. Page 293 ◩

ROAST POTATOES (left) *4 servings*. Page 293 ☐
CREAMED POTATOES (centre) *4 servings*. Page 293☐
CHIP POTATOES *4 servings*. Page 293☐

SAUTE POTATOES (front) *4 servings.*
Page 293 ☐ **POTATO HASH** *6 servings.*
Page 294 ☐

POTATOES ANNA (front) *4 servings*.
Page 294 ◩ **POTATOES AU GRATIN**
6 servings. Page 294 ◩

RIBBON VEGETABLES
Grated courgettes, carrots and parsnips, simmered with water and butter until just tender. 4 servings. Page 298 ☐

SAUTEED CELERY
Thin slices of celery, sautéed with thyme, bay leaves, salt and pepper. 4 servings. Page 285 ☐

**JERUSALEM ARTICHOKES IN
LEMON CREAM** *Jerusalem artichokes, sautéed in butter and lemon juice, then tossed in cream and nutmeg. 4 servings. Page 287* ☐

**BRUSSELS SPROUTS WITH
BUTTERED CRUMBS** (front) *4 servings*.
Page 282 ☐ **BRUSSELS SPROUTS
WITH BACON** *4–6 servings*. Page 282 ☐

Side dishes

FRIED GREEN TOMATOES (front)
4–6 servings. Page 296 ☐   HERBY BAKED
TOMATOES (left) *4 servings.* SCALLOPED
TOMATOES *6 servings.* Both page 297 ☐

STUFFED TOMATOES
Whole tomatoes baked with a stuffing made
with tomato pulp, ham, onion, breadcrumbs,
parsley and cheese. 4 servings. Page 296 ☐

BUTTER-BASTED SWEDES
Chunks of swede baked with melted butter
and sprinkled with buttered wholemeal
breadcrumbs. 4 servings. Page 295 ◪

STIR-FRIED BROCCOLI (front) *4–6*
servings. Page 282 ☐   BAKED BROCCOLI
WITH GRUYERE *6 servings.* Page 282 ☐

MARROW FRITTERS (front) *4 servings.*
Page 289☐   SPICED MARROW
4 servings. Page 289 ☐

FRIED APPLE WEDGES (left)
4 servings. Page 301☐   BAKED
BANANAS *4 servings.* Page 303☐

CRANBERRY AND APPLE RELISH
Whole cranberries and thickly sliced apples simmered with cider
vinegar, demerara sugar, orange rind and mixed spice until pulpy, to
make a sharp fruit relish. Makes 700 g (1½ lb). Page 305 ◪

SPICED NECTARINE SLICES
Cold nectarine slices in a spiced syrup, to
serve as a relish with ham or poultry.
16 servings. Page 311 ◪

BOILED RICE (left) *3–4 servings.*
Page 338 □ **BUTTERY BAKED RICE**
4 servings. Page 338 □

PILAF WITH BACON AND PEAS
Rice cooked in chicken stock until tender but still moist, with peas, finely chopped sautéed onion and crisply fried bacon pieces mixed through it. 6 servings. Page 339 □

SPANISH RICE
Rice baked in tomato sauce with onion and green pepper, then topped with cheese and bacon. 6 servings. Page 340 ◪

**CASSEROLED RICE WITH
MUSHROOMS** *Long grain rice, mushrooms, celery and onion baked with beef stock and thyme. 4 servings.* Page 340 □

BOILED RICE WITH PEPPERS
White, long grain rice boiled with sautéed, chopped peppers and spring onions. 3–4 servings. Page 338 □

RICE RING
Hot cooked rice tossed with butter and parsley, then moulded into a ring shape. 4 servings. Page 341 □

BOILED WILD RICE
Dark, nutty, wild rice simmered in water until tender and served here with a knob of butter. 3–4 servings. Page 338 □

BAKED RICE AND NOODLES
A mixture of mildly curried rice and noodles, baked in chicken stock with sautéed onion and mushrooms: 6 servings. Page 340 ◪

Side dishes

HERBED ORANGE RICE
Orange and thyme flavoured rice with pieces of celery and a little grated onion.
6 servings. Page 341 □

CURRIED RICE
Cooked rice and golden fried onions in a rich, creamy, curry sauce. 3–4 servings.
Page 339 □

CHINESE FRIED RICE
Lightly scrambled eggs mixed with fried rice, soy sauce and bacon, sprinkled with chopped spring onions. 3–4 servings. Page 341 □

RISOTTO ALLA MILANESE
Italian rice, cooked in white wine with stock and saffron, with butter and Parmesan stirred in before serving. 4 servings. Page 339 □

HOME-MADE NOODLES
Long noodles cut from home-made pasta dough, cooked in chicken stock until tender but still firm. 6 servings. Page 330 ■

NOODLE RING
Hot cooked noodles, tossed with butter, spooned into a ring tin and baked in a bain marie. 6 servings. Page 330 □

HOME-MADE SPINACH NOODLES
Ribbon noodles made from a fresh spinach pasta dough, served tossed in butter and black pepper. 8 servings. Page 330 ■

TAGLIATELLE ALFREDO
A rich dish of noodles coated in butter, Parmesan cheese and creamy milk.
4 servings. Page 330 □

CAESAR SALAD
Lettuce, anchovies and garlic croûtons, tossed with French dressing, raw egg and Parmesan cheese. 4 servings. **Page 318** □

SPINACH SALAD WITH LEMON AND MUSTARD DRESSING *Shredded spinach and lettuce, chicory and sliced mushrooms in a tangy dressing. 4–6 servings.* **Page 318** □

CUCUMBERS IN SOURED CREAM
Thinly sliced, peeled cucumber tossed in a soured cream and lemon juice dressing and served chilled. 6 servings. **Page 319** □

CALIFORNIA SALAD
Avocado slices and shredded lettuce, tossed in a herb dressing and garnished with walnuts. 4–6 servings. **Page 318** □

TOMATOES VINAIGRETTE
A salad of sliced tomatoes with French dressing and chives, garnished here with chopped parsley. 4 servings. **Page 319** □

MIXED VEGETABLE SALAD
Diced potatoes, peas and carrots in a mayonnaise dressing, topped with thinly sliced cucumber. 4 servings. **Page 320** ◨

MIXED GREEN SALAD BOWL
A light, tossed salad of Cos and Webb lettuces, peas, cucumber, spring onions and celery. 4–6 servings. **Page 318** □

DANISH CUCUMBER SALAD
Wafer-thin cucumber slices in sweetened vinegar, flavoured with fresh dill weed. 4 servings. **Page 319** ◨

HOT POTATO SALAD
Diced potato, chopped bacon and sautéed onion heated through in a seasoned cider vinegar dressing. 4 servings. **Page 320** ◨

Side dishes

COLESLAW
Finely shredded cabbage, grated carrot and onion, sliced celery and green pepper, coated in mayonnaise. Serve in a salad bowl or in a natural bowl made with the outer leaves of the cabbage. 4 servings. Page 319 □

PERFECTION SALAD
A moulded salad of cabbage, celery and pimentos in a cider vinegar and lemon juice jelly. 4–6 servings. Page 323 ■

CURRIED PASTA RING
Cooked pasta shells, ham, celery and apple, mixed with curried mayonnaise and moulded in a ring tin. 4–6 servings. Page 323 ◪

BRAISED LEEKS VINAIGRETTE
Leeks braised in chicken stock until tender, then chilled in a wine vinegar marinade with pimentos. 6 servings. Page 321 ■

GERMAN SAUERKRAUT SALAD
Canned sauerkraut and grated dessert apples in a dressing of olive oil, sugar and pepper. 4–6 servings. Page 321 □

MIXED BEAN SALAD
Cooked dried beans, tossed with coriander-flavoured French dressing and finished with sliced onion. 6 servings. Page 321 ■

TURKISH BEAN SALAD
A Middle Eastern salad of haricot beans, tomatoes and black olives in a mint dressing. 4–6 servings. Page 321 ■

TOMATO JELLY RING
A well-flavoured tomato purée set with gelatine to make a jelly ring, served with yogurt dressing. 4 servings. Page 323 ■

WALDORF SALAD
A classic salad combining crisp apples and celery with walnuts and raisins in a lemon mayonnaise. 4–6 servings. **Page 322** □

ZESTY TANGERINE SALAD
Tangerine segments, sliced celery and pimento tossed in French dressing and served over lettuce leaves. 4 servings. **Page 315** □

SALAD DRESSINGS AND SAUCES
Some well-known and some unique dressings and sauces, flavoured with varying ingredients. **Page 326** □

GREEK SALAD
Crisp salad greens, tomato wedges, black olives, crumbled feta cheese, capers and anchovy fillets tossed in an olive oil and red wine vinegar dressing. 6 servings. **Page 320** □

Baking

WHITE BREAD
An everyday loaf with a golden crust and fine-textured crumb, made with a plain white yeast dough. Makes one 900-g (2-lb) loaf. Page 434 ■

QUICK WHEATMEAL BREAD
An easy loaf made with wheatmeal flour. Makes one 700-g (1½-lb) loaf. Page 434 ◩

LIGHT RYE BREAD
A white rye dough flavoured with caraway and shaped into round loaves. Makes two 450-g (1-lb) loaves. Page 435 ■

WHOLEMEAL BREAD
Wholemeal flour gives a nutty flavour to this crusty brown bread. Makes two 900-g (2-lb) loaves. Page 436 ■

MARBLE LOAF
Two doughs rolled up to give a marbled effect. Makes two 1.1-kg (2½-lb) loaves. Page 435 ■

RYE AND WHOLEMEAL PLAIT
Dark rye dough and honey-sweetened wholemeal dough combined in an egg-glazed plait. Makes one 900-g (2-lb) loaf. Page 437 ■

PLAITED HERB BREAD
Makes one 700-g (1½-lb) loaf. Page 437 ■

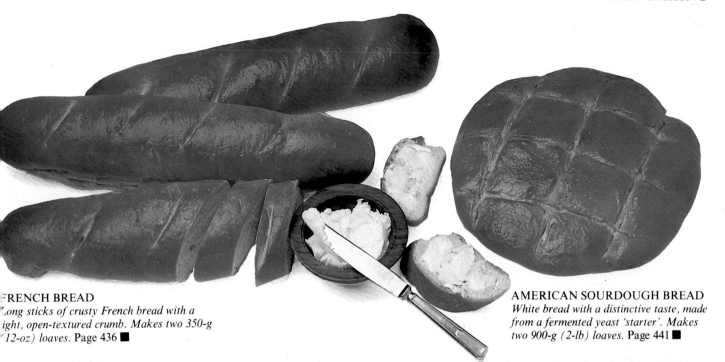

FRENCH BREAD
Long sticks of crusty French bread with a light, open-textured crumb. Makes two 350-g (12-oz) loaves. **Page 436** ■

AMERICAN SOURDOUGH BREAD
White bread with a distinctive taste, made from a fermented yeast 'starter'. Makes two 900-g (2-lb) loaves. **Page 441** ■

OATMEAL BREAD (above and right)
A moist bread of rolled oats and golden syrup, baked in cake tins or casseroles. Makes two 450-g (1-lb) loaves. **Page 438** ■

CHEESE CASSEROLE BREAD (left)
A savoury white bread made with milk and flavoured with grated Cheddar cheese. Makes one 900-g (2-lb) loaf. **Page 438** ■

SESAME SEED BREAD (centre)
Sweetened white bread dough, glazed with milk and sprinkled with sesame seeds. Makes two 450-g (1-lb) loaves. **Page 438** ◪

POTATO BREAD (right)
A white bread with mashed potato and beaten eggs mixed into the yeast dough. Makes two 1-kg (2¼-lb) loaves. **Page 438** ■

Baking

ROLL SHAPES
Pages 439–440 ■

VIENNA ROLLS

TWISTS

DINNER ROLLS

FAN ROLLS

CRESCENTS

WINDMILLS

POPPIES

KNOTS

BATCH ROLLS

FLOURY BAPS
Light, open-textured baps finished with a dusting of flour. Makes 36 rolls. Page 441 ■

PARKERHOUSE ROLLS
Rounds of yeast dough coated in melted butter and folded in half before proving and baking. Makes 36 rolls. Page 441 ◪

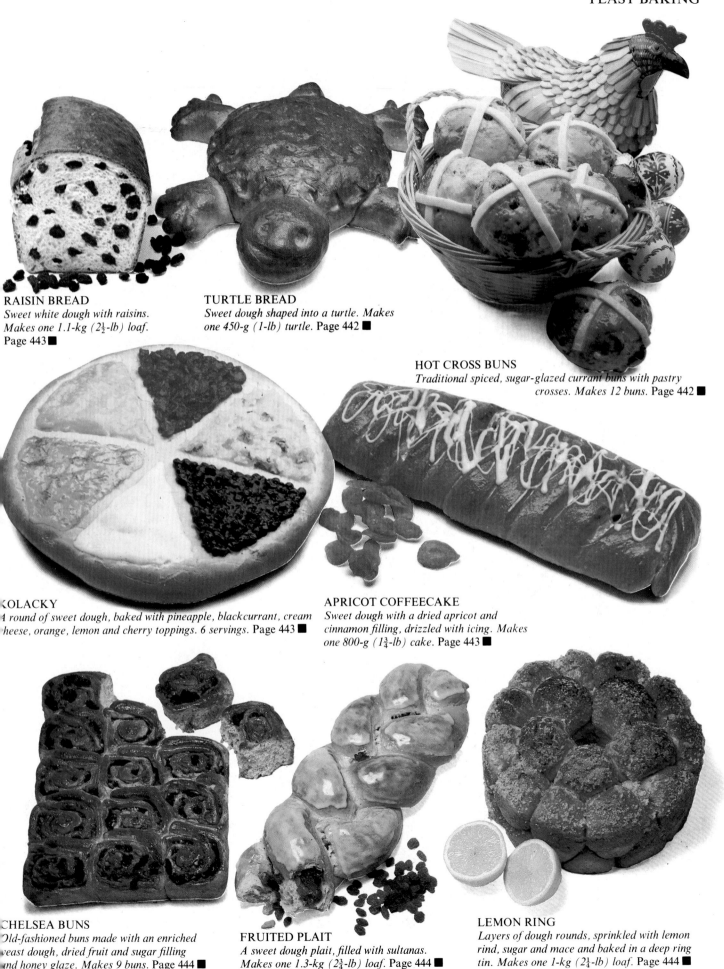

RAISIN BREAD
Sweet white dough with raisins.
Makes one 1.1-kg (2½-lb) loaf.
Page 443 ∎

TURTLE BREAD
Sweet dough shaped into a turtle. Makes
one 450-g (1-lb) turtle. Page 442 ∎

HOT CROSS BUNS
Traditional spiced, sugar-glazed currant buns with pastry
crosses. Makes 12 buns. Page 442 ∎

KOLACKY
A round of sweet dough, baked with pineapple, blackcurrant, cream
cheese, orange, lemon and cherry toppings. 6 servings. Page 443 ∎

APRICOT COFFEECAKE
Sweet dough with a dried apricot and
cinnamon filling, drizzled with icing. Makes
one 800-g (1¾-lb) cake. Page 443 ∎

CHELSEA BUNS
Old-fashioned buns made with an enriched
yeast dough, dried fruit and sugar filling
and honey glaze. Makes 9 buns. Page 444 ∎

FRUITED PLAIT
A sweet dough plait, filled with sultanas.
Makes one 1.3-kg (2¾-lb) loaf. Page 444 ∎

LEMON RING
Layers of dough rounds, sprinkled with lemon
rind, sugar and mace and baked in a deep ring
tin. Makes one 1-kg (2¼-lb) loaf. Page 444 ∎

Baking

APRICOT BUTTERFLY ROLLS *Makes 20.* Page 445 ■

BRIOCHES *Makes 12 small or 1 large brioche.* Page 447 ■

CROISSANTS *Makes 12.* Page 448 ■

PARTY DOUGHNUTS (left) *Makes 10–12.* Page 449 ■ **JAM DOUGHNUTS** *Makes 10–12.* Page 449 ■

RUM BABAS *Soaked in honey-rum syrup and topped with cream. Makes 16 babas or 1 savarin.* Page 450 ■

DANISH PASTRIES *Selection of pastries* (from left) IMPERIAL STAR, FOLDOVER, CUSHION *and* COCKSCOMB. *Makes 16 pastries.* Page 451 ■

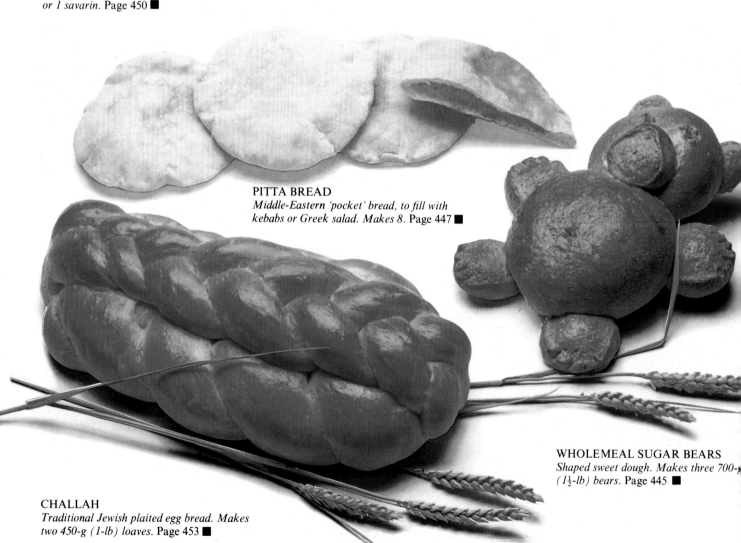

PITTA BREAD *Middle-Eastern 'pocket' bread, to fill with kebabs or Greek salad. Makes 8.* Page 447 ■

WHOLEMEAL SUGAR BEARS *Shaped sweet dough. Makes three 700-g (1½-lb) bears.* Page 445 ■

CHALLAH *Traditional Jewish plaited egg bread. Makes two 450-g (1-lb) loaves.* Page 453 ■

CARDAMOM CHRISTMAS WREATH

A spicy sweet bread flavoured with cardamom and decorated with dough holly berries and leaves. Makes one 1.4-kg (3-lb) wreath. Page 453 ■

STOLLEN

Rich, sweet bread filled with fruit and nuts. Makes three 550-g (1¼-lb) loaves. Page 452 ■

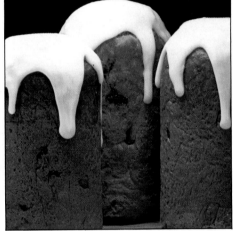

MUFFINS

Coated in corn meal and traditionally cooked on a griddle, for serving split, toasted and buttered. Makes 18. Page 446 ■

KULICH

A rich, fruited, Russian Easter bread baked in a coffee tin. Makes three 450-g (1-lb) loaves. Page 452 ■

POPPY SEED POTICAS

Rolled around a poppy seed and walnut filling, potica dough is baked in a coil. Makes two 550-g (1¼-lb) loaves. Page 448 ■

ENRICHED WHITE ROLLS

Moist, soft rolls, enriched with milk and eggs, which can be varied in many ways. Makes twelve 50-g (2-oz) rolls. Page 439 ■

RAISIN AND CARAWAY SODA BREAD

A coarse-textured bread to be served in thick slices, spread with butter. Makes one 1.3-kg (2¾-lb) loaf. Page 429 ◪

COURGETTE BREAD

An unusual bread, moistened with grated courgettes and crunchy with walnuts. Makes two 700-g (1½-lb) loaves. Page 429 ◪

Baking

LEMON TEABREAD
A sweet bread brushed with a lemon juice and sugar glaze after baking. Makes one 900-g (2-lb) loaf. **Page 428** ◪

CHOCOLATE, DATE AND NUT LOAF
A chocolate-flavoured bread, with sliced dates and chopped walnuts. Makes one 900-g (2-lb) loaf. **Page 429** ◪

NUT BREAD
An easy-to-make bread filled with chopped walnuts. Makes one 900-g (2-lb) loaf. **Page 428** ◪

CORN BREAD
Baked in a square tin, corn bread is cut into squares and served warm. Makes one 450-g (1-lb) loaf. **Page 428** ☐

CORN STICKS
Corn bread batter can also be baked in a ring tin, as muffins, or as corn sticks, shown here. Makes 14–18 sticks. **Page 428** ☐

WAFFLES
A milky batter baked in a waffle iron, with serving ideas for breakfast or tea. Makes 6. **Page 427** ☐

SCOTCH PANCAKES
A thick pouring batter cooked on a griddle or heavy frying pan to give soft, moist pancakes or 'drop scones'. Serve with butter and jam. Makes 10 large 10-cm (4-in) or 15 small 5-cm (2-in) pancakes. **Page 426** ☐

POTATO PANCAKES
Grated potato and onion, mixed with egg and flour and fried until golden brown. Makes 16. **Page 426** ◪

PEACH-FILLED TEABREAD
Makes one 700-g 1½-lb) loaf. **Page 430** ◩

CHERRY TEABREAD
Makes one 1.3-kg (2¾-lb) loaf.
Page 430 ◩

NUT-LAYERED TEABREAD
Makes one 900-g (2-lb) loaf.
Page 430 ◩

POPOVERS
Egg batter quickly baked in ramekins or soufflé dishes; serve hot with butter. Makes 8.
Page 427 ◩

QUICK MUFFINS (left) *Makes 12.* Page 424 □ **SCONES** *Makes 10–12.* Page 423 □

MUFFIN VARIATIONS
(clockwise from top) blackcurrant, orange, bran, plain and wholemeal muffins. Page 424 □

QUICK RING DOUGHNUTS *and* **DOUGHNUT 'HOLES'** *Deep-fried dough rings and centres, sprinkled with sugar. Makes 20 of each.* Page 425 □

BEIGNETS
Deep-fried choux paste balls, served hot with a dessert sauce. Makes 30. Page 425 ◩

BOSTON BROWN BREAD
Traditional American bread, flavoured with black treacle and raisins. Makes two 450-g (1-lb) loaves. Page 429 ◩

INDIAN PURIS (left) *Makes 8 puris.* Page 431 ◩ **ONION CRACKERS** *Makes 16.* Page 431 ◩

Baking

DEEP DISH PEACH PIE
Sliced fresh peaches sprinkled with sugar and cinnamon in a deep shortcrust pastry case with twist decorations. 6 servings. Page 348 ◪

CREAM-TOPPED CHOCOLATE PIE
Chilled, rich chocolate filling in a shortcrust or crumb crust case, topped with whipped cream. 8 servings. Page 350 ■

BLACKBERRY PIE
A double-crust pie made with fresh blackberries and spices. 6 servings. Page 346 ◪

CHERRY PIE
Sweetened fresh cherries in shortcrust pastry. 6 servings. Page 346 ◪

APPLE PIE
Apples flavoured with spices and lemon, in shortcrust pastry. 6 servings. Page 346 ◪

PUMPKIN PIE
Spicy, sweet pumpkin filling (fresh or canned) in a shortcrust pastry case, served hot with whipped cream. 6 servings. Page 349 ◪

PECAN PIE
Pecans or walnuts with a dark, sweet custard in an open pie made with shortcrust pastry. 6–8 servings. Page 356 ◪

PRUNE, APRICOT AND NUT FLAN
A shortcrust pastry case filled with a dried fruit mixture and topped with toasted nuts; serve cold. 8 servings. Page 347 ■

LEMON CHIFFON PIE
light, lemon filling set with gelatine in an open shortcrust case, decorated with whipped cream and lemon rind. 8 servings. Page 352 ■

DEEP DISH PLUM PIE
Fresh plums, sweetened and lightly flavoured with almond essence, baked in a deep-dish pastry case and topped with a lattice of pastry strips. Serve hot or cold. 6 servings. Page 348 ◿

FRUIT CREAM TARTS
Pâte sucrée tart cases filled with rich custard, topped with fresh fruit and glazed. Makes 12. Page 357 ■

OLD ENGLISH EGGNOG PIE
Chilled, rum-flavoured custard in a sweet flan case, sprinkled with nutmeg and grated chocolate. 6 servings. Page 353 ■

STRAWBERRY EGGNOG PIE (left)
6 servings. Page 353 ■   COFFEE EGG-NOG PIE *6 servings. Page 353* ■

BLUEBERRY PIE
Spicy, fresh blueberry filling in a double-crust shortcrust pie, with an unusual square opening in the centre. 6 servings. Page 346 ◿

CHOCOLATE CREAM PIE
Unbaked chocolate crumb crust filled with a light chocolate mixture, decorated with whipped cream. 8 servings. Page 353 ■

WALNUT TARTS
A rich walnut filling made with golden syrup and treacle, in pâte sucrée cases; serve cold with whipped cream. Makes 12. Page 357 ◿

Baking

FRENCH APPLE FLAN
Apple purée in a sweet pastry case, topped with dessert apple slices and glazed with apricot jam. 8 servings. Page 348 ■

STREUSEL-TOPPED PEAR PIE
Sliced pears sprinkled with a sweet, spicy crumble mixture containing grated Cheddar cheese. 8 servings. Page 347 ◪

PEACH PIE
A shortcrust pastry case filled with sliced fresh peaches and topped with pastry twists. 6 servings. Page 347 ◪

ORANGE CHIFFON PIE
Fluffy orange jelly in a crumb or shortcrust case, chilled and decorated with cream and fresh orange segments. 8 servings. Page 352 ■

CUSTARD TART
Simple egg custard, sprinkled with ground nutmeg, baked in a shortcrust pastry case. 6 servings. Page 349 ◪

PEANUT PIE
Rich filling of eggs, peanut butter, salted peanuts, golden syrup and treacle, decorated with cream. 8 servings. Page 356 ◪

CHERRY AND KIRSCH FLAN
Almond pastry case with a kirsch-flavoured cream filling, topped with fresh cherries. 8 servings. Page 355 ■

SPICED PUMPKIN CHIFFON PIE
Chilled, light pumpkin filling in a coconut and biscuit crumb crust. 8–10 servings. Page 354 ■

FUDGY NUT PIE
Nutty chocolate fudge mixture baked in a shortcrust pastry case; serve with ice cream. 8 servings. Page 356 ◪

OFFEE LIQUEUR FLAN
*ia Maria- and coffee-flavoured filling,
hilled in an unbaked chocolate crumb crust.
servings.* **Page 354** ■

RASPBERRY RIBBON FLAN
*Raspberry jelly layered with a light cream
cheese mixture in an open shortcrust flan.
8 servings.* **Page 354** ■

**CHOCOLATE AND RUM-LAYERED
FLAN** *Chocolate and rum-flavoured
custards layered in a ginger crumb crust and
chilled. 8 servings.* **Page 355** ■

LEMON MERINGUE PIE
*shortcrust pastry case filled with a
lightly tart lemon mixture and topped with
oft meringue. 6 servings.* **Page 351** □

PEACH MERINGUE TARTS
*Sliced ripe peaches baked in pâte sucrée
cases, topped with meringue and baked again.
Makes 12.* **Page 357** ◪

CHRISTMAS RUM FLAN
*Crystallised fruit and rum cream in an
unbaked crumb crust, decorated with whipped
cream and fruit. 8 servings.* **Page 355** ■

MINCE TARTS
*Home-made mincemeat, diced apples,
chopped walnuts and brandy baked in
shortcrust cases. Makes 12.* **Page 357** ■

CREAM-TOPPED VANILLA PIE
*Chilled vanilla custard in a crumb crust or
shortcrust case, covered with whipped cream.
8 servings.* **Page 350** ■

CREAMY BANANA PIE
*A pastry flan case filled with chilled vanilla
custard and sliced bananas, topped with
lemon rind. 8 servings.* **Page 350** ■

Baking

DEVIL'S FOOD CAKE
Chocolate and soured cream cake filled and iced with rich chocolate frosting. Makes one 20.5-cm (8-in) cake. Page 384 ◨

SILVER-WHITE SANDWICH CAKE
A light, white cake sandwiched and iced with chocolate butter cream. Makes one 20.5-cm (8-in) cake. Page 385 ◨

TREACLE SPICE CAKE
Spicy, moist, black treacle cake, served topped with whipped cream. Makes one 23-cm (9-in) square cake. Page 387 ◨

MADEIRA CAKE
Sweet, buttery cake; may be topped with citron peel. Makes one 18-cm (7-in) round cake or a 900-g (2-lb) loaf cake. Page 386 ◨

WHISKED SPONGE CAKE
Feather-light sponge layers sandwiched with whipped cream and dusted with icing sugar. Makes one 18-cm (7-in) cake. Page 389 ◨

MARBLE CAKE
Orange and chocolate mixtures swirled and baked together. Makes one 23-cm (9-in) cake. Page 386 ◨

SACHERTORTE
Hazel nut and chocolate cake sandwiched with jam and coated with icing. Makes one 23-cm (9-in) cake. Page 394 ◨

CHERRY CAKE
Moist loaf cake with glacé cherries. Makes one 21.5 × 11 cm (8½ × 4½ in) cake. Page 388 ■

WALNUT SPONGE RING CAKE
Light sponge cake with finely chopped walnuts, baked in a ring tin. Makes one 20.5-cm (8-in) cake. Page 389 ◨

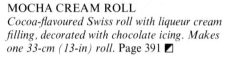

RICH DARK FRUIT RING
Currants, sultanas, glacé cherries, almonds and peel in a spicy ring cake. Makes one 25.5-cm (10-in) cake. Page 393 ■

SWISS ROLL
Delicate, plain sponge rolled around a jam filling and dredged with sugar. Makes one 33-cm (13-in) roll. Page 391 ◪

MOCHA CREAM ROLL
Cocoa-flavoured Swiss roll with liqueur cream filling, decorated with chocolate icing. Makes one 33-cm (13-in) roll. Page 391 ◪

PETITS FOURS
Small, decorative sponge cakes, sandwiched with jam and almond paste. Makes 30. Page 392 ■

ANGEL FOOD CAKE
A light ring cake, made with egg whites, sugar, flour and flavourings. Makes one 20.5-cm (8-in) cake. Page 390 ◪

LIGHT SPICE CAKE
Cinnamon, allspice, cloves and nutmeg cake, filled and coated with whipped cream. Makes one 20.5-cm (8-in) cake. Page 387 ◪

HAZEL NUT GATEAU
A rich hazel nut cake sandwiched with sweetened whipped cream and decorated with finely chopped hazel nuts and piped cream. Makes one 23-cm (9-in) cake. Page 395 ■

MOIST APPLE CAKE
Cake made with apples, walnuts and raisins, decorated with icing sugar. Makes one 20.5-cm (8-in) square cake. Page 388 ■

Baking

VICTORIA SANDWICH CAKE
A creamed sandwich cake, filled and iced with butter cream. Makes one 20.5-cm (8-in) cake. **Page 384** ◪

PINEAPPLE UPSIDE-DOWN CAKE
Pineapple chunks and maraschino cherries baked in a Victoria sandwich mixture. Makes one 33 × 23 cm (13 × 9 in) cake. **Page 384** ◪

COFFEE SPONGE CAKE
Coffee-flavoured sponge mixture with chopped walnuts added. Makes one 20.5-cm (8-in) ring cake. **Page 392** ◪

BRAZIL NUT AND FRUIT LOAF
Loaf cake rich with Brazil nuts, dates and maraschino cherries. Makes one 25.5 × 15 cm (10 × 6 in) cake. **Page 393** ■

CHOCOLATE FEATHER SPONGE CAKE *Light cocoa-flavoured sponge baked in a ring tin and dusted with icing sugar. Makes one 20.5-cm (8-in) cake.* **Page 389** ◪

BLACK FOREST CHERRY TORTE
Chocolate sponge, layered with whipped cream and cherries, richly decorated. Makes one 23-cm (9-in) cake. **Page 395** ■

BANANA CAKE
Banana-flavoured sandwich cake, filled and coated with whipped cream. Makes one 20.5-cm (8-in) cake. **Page 388** ◪

DELUXE COCONUT CAKE
A cake layered with coconut custard, then frosted and sprinkled with coconut. Makes one 20.5-cm (8-in) cake. **Page 386** ◪

CHOCOLATE AND WALNUT LAYER CAKE *Three-layer cake with chocolate walnut filling and smooth chocolate icing. Makes one 18-cm (7-in) cake.* **Page 387** ◪

CHRISTMAS CAKE
Rich, dark fruit cake, soaked in brandy then covered with almond paste and royal icing. Makes one 20.5-cm (8-in) cake. Page 393 ■

ORANGE AND LEMON GENOESE SPONGE RING *Lemon-flavoured cake iced with lemon and orange crème au beurre. Makes one 20.5-cm (8-in) cake.* Page 390 ■

THREE-TIER ROSE SPONGE CAKE
Whisked sponge layers, split and filled with lemon butter cream, iced with delicate pink icing and decorated with piped white butter cream. Makes one three-tier cake with 30.5-cm (12-in) base. Page 396 ■

CHOCOLATE CUP CAKES *and* **CHOCOLATE CAKE**
The same cocoa-flavoured mixture can be used to make 24 individual cup cakes or a 20.5-cm (8-in) sandwich cake. Both are iced with coffee cream cheese frosting or chocolate glacé icing. Page 385 ◪

EGGNOG GATEAU
Sponge with nutmeg and rum flavouring, layered and iced with chocolate butter cream. Makes one 20.5-cm (8-in) cake. Page 394 ■

Desserts

SUMMER SPONGE GATEAU
A light sponge ring, split then filled and topped with ripe strawberries and whipped cream. 12 servings. Page 369 ◪

STRAWBERRY SOUFFLE
Fresh strawberries, egg whites and cream set with gelatine to make a cold, light dessert. 4–6 servings. Page 361 ■

POTS DE CREME
Rich mousse, flavoured chocolate or mocha, topped with sweetened whipped cream. 6 servings. Page 362 ■

APPLE STRUDEL
Delicate strudel or filo pastry rolled around a spicy apple, raisin and walnut filling. 8 servings. Page 370 ◪

FLOATING ISLANDS
Chilled vanilla custard topped with soft, poached meringues and golden sugar syrup. 4 servings. Page 365 ◪

CREAM PUFF RING
Choux pastry ring filled with confectioners' custard, topped with chocolate satin icing and strawberries. 6–8 servings. Page 367 ◪

CREPES SUZETTE
Classic French crêpes, heated in an orange and curaçao sauce and flamed with brandy. 6 servings. Page 368 ◪

PANCAKES WITH SOURED CREAM AND ORANGE SAUCE *Served hot, decorated with chopped orange. 6 servings.* Page 368 ◪

EVERLASTING SYLLABUB
A frothy cold dessert of whipped cream with lemon rind and juice, sugar, brandy and sherry. 4 servings. Page 369 ■

HOT CHOCOLATE SOUFFLE
Thick chocolate sauce, enriched with egg yolks, lightened with stiffly whisked egg whites and baked. 6–8 servings. **Page 363** □

INDIVIDUAL CHOCOLATE SOUFFLES
Chocolate soufflé mixture baked in individual soufflé dishes or ramekins and served with whipped cream. 6 servings. **Page 363** ◩

CREAM PUFFS
Baked choux puffs filled with confectioners' custard or whipped cream and dusted with icing sugar. Makes 8–10. **Page 366** ◩

SWAN ECLAIRS
Choux paste piped into swan shapes and filled with a rich, creamy custard. Makes 12. **Page 367** ■

APRICOT CREAM FLAN
Chilled almond custard in a walnut pastry crust, topped with apricot halves. 8 servings. **Page 360** ■

CHOCOLATE CUPS WITH STRAWBERRY CREAM
Plain chocolate shells filled with strawberries and sweetened whipped cream. 8 servings. **Page 370** ◩

BAVAROIS
A moulded mixture of custard, whisked egg whites and whipped cream, decorated with fresh fruit. 6–8 servings. **Page 360** ■

WALNUT CHIFFON PIE
Walnut, biscuit crumb and egg white pie, topped with sweetened whipped vanilla-flavoured cream. 8 servings. **Page 365** ■

BANANA SOUFFLE
A rich yet light, hot soufflé flavoured with bananas, nutmeg and vanilla; serve with whipped cream. 4 servings. **Page 364** ◩

Desserts

CHOCOLATE AND CHERRY SOUFFLE
A cold soufflé of plain chocolate, canned black cherries, kirsch and whipped cream. 4 servings. Page 361 ■

JAM SPONGE PUDDING (left) *4 servings.* Page 374 ◪ EGG CUSTARD SAUCE (centre) *Makes 300 ml (½ pint).* Page 359 □ CASTLE PUDDINGS (rear) *4 servings.* Page 374 ◪ APPLE AND GINGER ROLY-POLY (right) *4–6 servings.* Page 374 ◪

GALATOBOUREKO (front and rear) *Makes 20 pieces.* Page 371 ■ BAKLAVA (centre) *Makes 20 pieces.* Page 371 ◪

CHRISTMAS PUDDING
Traditional steamed fruit pudding. Garnish with holly, flame with brandy and serve with brandy butter. Makes 2 puddings. Page 375 ■

CREME CARAMEL
Individual baked vanilla custards with caramel syrup, served chilled. 6 servings. Page 359 ■

CHOCOLATE AND CINNAMON TORTE *Baked biscuit rounds sandwiched with cocoa cream, topped with grated chocolate. 10–12 servings.* Page 373 ■

CREME BRULEE WITH FRESH FRUIT
Baked cream and egg yolks with a burnt sugar topping, served chilled, with fresh fruit. 4–6 servings. Page 359 ■

STRAWBERRY MERINGUES
Individual meringue nests, filled with vanilla ice cream and topped with strawberries. 6 servings. Page 365 ■

LIME SOUFFLE MILANAISE
A creamy cold soufflé flavoured with the juice and rind from fresh limes. 4–6 servings. Page 362 ■

ZABAGLIONE
Light, frothy egg yolks, sugar and Marsala, whisked in a basin over heat and served warm. 4 servings. Page 360 □

CHOCOLATE MERINGUE FLAN
Meringue basket filled with chilled rich chocolate and whipped cream mixture. 8 servings. Page 365 ■

ORANGE LIQUEUR SOUFFLE
A hot soufflé flavoured with orange rind and curaçao, served with whipped cream. 6 servings. Page 364 ◪

STRAWBERRY SHORTCAKE
A rich, round shortcake, split in half and filled and topped with strawberries and cream. 8 servings. Page 369 ◪

SHERRY TRIFLE
Sponge cake and macaroons soaked in sherry, topped with custard and whipped cream. 4–6 servings. Page 372 ■

CHOCOLATE ECLAIRS
Choux paste fingers filled with confectioners' custard and topped with chocolate satin icing. Makes 12. Page 366 ◪

Desserts

CRANBERRY SOUFFLE
A cold soufflé made with fresh or frozen cranberries and decorated with sugared berries. 6–8 servings. Page 362 ■

APPLE TURNOVERS (rear) *Makes 8.* Page 372 ◪ **CREAMED RICE** *4 servings.* Page 341 ▢

STRAWBERRY BLINTZES
Pancakes filled with sweetened cottage and cream cheeses, served hot, topped with fresh strawberries. 6 servings. Page 368 ◪

SOUFFLE OMELETTE WITH STRAWBERRIES *Fluffy sweet omelette filled with fresh strawberries, sprinkled with icing sugar. 1 serving.* Page 146 ▢

UNBAKED CHEESECAKE
Custard and cottage cheese filling in a biscuit crumb crust, topped with fruit. 6–8 servings. Page 159 ■

BAKED RICH CHEESECAKE
A rich pastry case with an orange-flavoured cream cheese filling, topped with a layer of soured cream. 8 servings. Page 158 ■

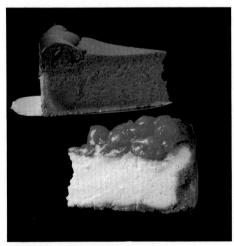

CHOCOLATE CHEESECAKE (top)
8 servings. Page 158 ■ **CHERRY CHEESECAKE** *8 servings.* Page 158 ■

LUXURY CHEESE FLAN
Cream cheese filling in a spiced biscuit crumb crust, topped here with canned peach slices. 6–8 servings. Page 159 ■

CREAM CHEESE AND RHUBARB PIE
A pastry case layered with rhubarb and cream cheese mixtures and soured cream, decorated with almonds. 6 servings. Page 159 ■

RED CHERRY SOUP
Made with fresh cherries and red wine; garnished with cream and mint. 4–6 servings. Page 133 ◼

COLD RASPBERRY SOUP
Puréed raspberries, spiced with cinnamon, flavoured with port and chilled. 6 servings. Page 133 ◼

STRAWBERRY SOUP
A refreshing summer soup of strawberries and white wine with a lemony tartness. 4–6 servings. Page 133 ☐

STRAWBERRY AND RHUBARB SOUP
Strawberries and rhubarb cooked in fresh orange juice, then sweetened and blended to a smooth purée. Serve chilled, garnished with sliced strawberries. 4–6 servings. Page 133 ◼

BLACKCURRANT SOUP
Fresh blackcurrants; cooked and sieved, then thickened and flavoured with white wine and lemon juice. 6 servings. Page 133 ◼

Desserts

CINNAMON APRICOTS IN CREAM
*Fresh apricot halves spiced with cinnamon
and baked with double cream. 4 servings.*
Page 302 □

STRAWBERRIES ROMANOFF
*Fresh strawberries soaked in port; served
topped with Chantilly cream, and feuilles
royales if you wish. 6 servings.* Page 305 ◪

SUMMER PUDDING (left) *4 servings.*
Page 304 ■ **GOOSEBERRY FOOL**
4 servings. Page 305 ◪

BRANDIED CHERRY SAUCE (left)
Makes 400 ml (¾ pint). Page 305 □
BILBERRY SAUCE *Makes 600 ml
(1 pint). Served with ice cream.* Page 304 □

STEWED PLUMS (top) *4 servings.*
Page 314 □ **PLUMS IN PORT** (right)
6 servings. Page 314 ◪ **CREAMY PLUM
SAUCE** *Makes 400 ml (¾ pint).* Page 314 □

ORANGES A LA TURQUE (left)
4–6 servings. Page 312 ■ **ORANGE
PRALINE MOUSSE** *12 servings.* Page 312 ■

MIXED BERRY COMPOTE
*Strawberries, raspberries and blackcurrants
or blueberries, topped with ice cream and
grated orange rind. 4–6 servings.* Page 304 ◪

GRAPEFRUIT AMBROSIA
*Grapefruit segments mixed with fresh or
desiccated coconut and clear honey.
4 servings.* Page 307 □

POACHED PEACHES (top) *6 servings.*
Page 312 □ **BUTTERY BAKED
PEACHES** *6 servings.* Page 312 □

PEARS IN WHITE WINE (top) *6 servings.*
Page 313 ◪ PEARS IN CHOCOLATE
SAUCE *4 servings.* Page 313 ◪

MINTED GRAPES
*Seedless white grapes marinated in honey,
lime juice and mint and served chilled.
4 servings.* Page 306 □

BAKED APPLES (rear) *4 servings.*
Page 301 □ STEWED APPLES *4 servings.*
Page 301 □

GINGERED KIWI FRUIT
*Sliced kiwi fruit and orange segments in
sugar syrup with crystallised ginger.
4 servings.* Page 307 ◪

FLAMBEED BANANAS IN ORANGE
SAUCE (left) *6 servings.* Page 303 □
NECTARINES BRULEES *4 servings.*
Page 311 ◪

MARINATED WATERMELON (top)
4–6 servings. Page 310 ◪ CANTELOUP
WATER ICE *Makes 1.2 litres (2 pints).*
Page 310 ■

STEWED RHUBARB (top) *4 servings.*
Page 315 □ RHUBARB CRUMBLE
4 servings. Page 315 □

FRESH FRUIT SALAD WITH
CARDAMOM SAUCE *Melons, peaches,
plums and pears with a cream cheese and
spice dressing. 4 servings.* Page 322 □

MEDITERRANEAN FRUIT BOWL
*Pineapple, melons, oranges, nectarines or
apricots, plums, grapes and lime, chilled in
aniseed syrup. 4–6 servings.* Page 322 ◪

101

Desserts

VANILLA ICE CREAM
Egg custard with cream and vanilla, frozen in an ice cream churn. Makes 2.7 litres (5 pints) or 12 servings. Page 376 ■

HOME-MADE ICE CREAM VARIATIONS (left to right): *Spiced Banana* ■ *Strawberry* ■ *Chocolate* ■ *Pistachio* ■ *Peach* ■ All page 377

PEPPERMINT ROCK ICE CREAM
Ice cream flavoured with crushed peppermint rock. Makes 2.7 litres (5 pints) or 12 servings. Page 377 ■

NESSELRODE ICE CREAM MOULD
Vanilla ice cream, candied fruit, sultanas and nuts, layered with sponge fingers and frozen. 6 servings. Page 379 ■

STRAWBERRY MILK ICE *Makes 1.8 litres (3¼ pints) or 6 servings.* Page 378 ■
REFRIGERATOR COOKIES *Makes 45.* Page 411 ◿

PINEAPPLE SHERBET
Fresh pineapple purée, frozen with sugar syrup and whisked egg whites. Makes 1.1 litres (2 pints) or 10 servings. Page 380 ■

BAKED ALASKA
Vanilla ice cream and frozen raspberries, layered with sponge fingers, covered with meringue and baked. 4–6 servings. Page 378 ◿

ICED ORANGE MOUSSE (left) ■
ICED CANTELOUP MOUSSE ■ *Both make 1.8 litres (3¼ pints) or 12 servings.* Both page 380

STRAWBERRY-ORANGE ICE *Makes 1.1 litres (2 pints) or 10 servings. Page 381* ■ **CANDIED ORANGE PEEL** *Makes 225 g (8 oz). Page 311* ■

RAINBOW ICE CREAM GATEAU *Layered ice creams and black cherries in a gingernut biscuit crust, topped with walnuts. 6 servings. Page 379* ■

MINTED SHERBET RING *Pineapple sherbet ring flavoured with crème de menthe, filled with strawberries and coconut. 4–6 servings. Page 380* ■

LEMON WATER ICE *Lemon shells filled with fresh lemon ice and decorated with mint sprigs. Makes 900 ml (1½ pints) or 6 servings. Page 381* ■

WATERMELON ICE *Watermelon blended with icing sugar and lemon juice and frozen. Makes 1.1 litres (2 pints) or 10 servings. Page 381* ■

PRALINE BOMBE *Moulded strawberry and vanilla ice creams with almond praline centre, decorated with vanilla-flavoured whipped cream and strawberries and served with a rich chocolate sauce. 6 servings. Page 379* ■

Snacks

BOSTON BROWNIES
Makes 12. Page 404 ◪

CINNAMON BISCUITS
Makes 36. Page 413 ■

**DOUBLE CHOCOLATE
DROPS** *Makes 36.*
Page 406 ◪

**CHRISTMAS
WREATHS**
Makes 24. Page 409 □

**CHOCOLATE PEANUT
DROPS** *Makes 36.* Page 407 □

OAT COOKIES
Makes 36. Page 407 □

WALNUT CLUSTERS
Makes 36. Page 407 □

ORANGE AND RAISIN COOKIES
Makes 25. Page 407 □

SHORTBREAD
Makes 12. Page 40.

**ALMOND AND COCONUT
BARS** *Makes 12.* Page 404 ◪

**COCONUT MERINGUE
COOKIES** *Makes 24.*
Page 408 ◪

**DANISH ALMOND
COOKIES** *Makes 35.*
Page 409 ◪

**MARBLED FUDGE
BARS** *Makes 36.* Page 405 ◪

CHOCOLATE COOKIES
Makes 20. Page 406 □

GINGERBREAD MEN
Makes 18. Page 413 ◪

BRANDY SNAPS
Makes 20. Page 407 □

SHELL COOKIES
Makes 12. Page 409 □

GINGER AND CINNAMON COOKIES
Makes 30. Page 406 □

NUT ROCKS
Makes 24–26. Page 408 ◨

CITRUS PINWHEELS
Makes 48. Page 411 ◨

NEAPOLITAN COOKIES
Makes 64. Page 411 ■

HAZEL NUT DROPS
Makes 24. Page 408 ◨

LINZER COOKIES
Makes 30. Page 405 ◨

LUSCIOUS APRICOT SQUARES
Makes 16. Page 404 ◨

WALNUT BARS
Makes 20. Page 404 ■

PEANUT BUTTER COOKIES
Makes 25–30. Page 408 ◨

TOASTED OAT AND RAISIN COOKIES *Makes 48.* Page 406 □

CARDAMOM COOKIES
Makes 30.
Page 409 □

ALMOND BUTTER BISCUITS *Makes 32.*
Page 412 ◨

SPICE BISCUITS
Makes 36. Page 413 ◨

PRUNE RIBBON COOKIES
Makes 27. Page 405 ◨

SHREWSBURY BISCUITS
Makes 20–24. Page 412 ◨

Snacks

VIENNA COOKIES (centre) *Makes 36.*
RINGLETS (rear) *Makes 32.* RASPBERRY
THUMBPRINTS *Makes 36. All page 410* ◪

CHOCOLATE DIPPED BUTTER
COOKIES *Soured cream and almond dough
pressed into tree shapes, dipped in chocolate
glaze. Makes 27. Page 410* ◪

SANDWICH BISCUITS
*Rich rolled biscuits sandwiched with tinted
butter cream. Makes 36. Page 412* ◪

TOFFEE APPLES
*Dessert apples dipped in buttery demerara
sugar syrup, then left to cool and set.
Makes 6–8. Page 302* ◪

LOLLIPOPS
*Boiled sweets or jelly tots set in a corn syrup
mixture, in paper cup moulds. Makes 12.*
Page 417 ◼

POPCORN BALLS
*Popped corn and glacé cherries coated with
syrup and shaped into balls. Makes 12.*
Page 418 ◪

WALNUT AND CHOCOLATE
FUDGE *Makes 700 g (1½ lb).*
Page 415 ◪

PEANUT BRITTLE
Makes 900 g (2 lb).
Page 418 ◪

NUTTY BUTTERSCOTCH
FUDGE *Makes 700 g (1½ lb).*
Page 415 ◪

VANILLA KISSES
Makes 350 g (12 oz).
Page 415 ◪

TOFFEE
Makes 350 g (12 oz). Page 416 ◪

MARZIPAN FRUITS
Makes 1.4 kg (3 lb). Page 419 ■

WALNUT CRUNCH
Makes 700 g (1½ lb). Page 418 ◪

WHITE CLOUDS
Makes 700 g (1½ lb).
Page 417 ◪

PECAN PENUCHE
Makes 900 g (2 lb).
Page 415 ◪

FONDANT BONBONS
Makes 1.1 kg (2½ lb).
Page 418 ■

FONDANT CREAMS *Makes
1.1 kg (2½ lb).*
Page 417 ◪

PEPPERMINT PATTIES
Makes 1.1 kg (2½ lb).
Page 419 ◪

ORANGE AND ALMOND CARAMELS
Makes 700 g (1½ lb).
Page 416 ◪

NOUGAT
Makes 550 g (1¼ lb).
Page 416 ◪

**CHOCOLATE-DIPPED FRUIT AND
NUTS** *Makes 60 fruits and 12 nut clusters.*
Page 420 ◪

**MELTAWAY
CHOCOLATE MINTS**
Makes 450 g (1 lb).
Page 420 ◪

CHOCOLATE RUM TRUFFLES
Makes 450 g (1 lb). Page 420 ■

Sandwiches

OPEN STEAK SANDWICHES
Fried minute steaks on toast, served with gravy and garnished with watercress. 4 servings. Page 457 □

OMELETTE SANDWICHES
Ham, green pepper and onion omelette served between toast slices. 4 servings. Page 456 □

BACON BURGERS
Crisply fried back bacon in toasted hamburger buns. 6 servings. Page 456 □

CURRIED BEEF IN PITTA BREAD
Minced beef curried with onion, apple and raisins, served in pitta bread with yogurt. 6 servings. Page 457 ■

CROQUE MONSIEUR
Ham and Gruyère cheese sandwiches with mustard, brushed with butter and toasted in the oven. 8 servings. Page 455 □

SLOPPY JOES
Minced beef cooked with onion, green pepper, baked beans and sausages and ketchup, served in crusty rolls. 6 servings. Page 456 □

BARBECUED PORK ROLLS
Pork shoulder meat simmered in a spicy sauce, served in crusty rolls with lettuce and tomato. 6 servings. Page 455 ■

MOZZARELLA LOAF
Mozzarella cheese and olives in a crusty, sesame seed loaf, baked until the cheese has melted. 6 servings. Page 455 □

FRIED SALT BEEF AND SAUERKRAUT SANDWICHES *Chilli mayonnaise, Gruyère cheese, sauerkraut and salt beef in rye bread. 4 servings. Page 456* □

ITALIAN HERO SANDWICHES
Hot Italian sausages with onions and red or green peppers in long crusty rolls. 4 servings. Page 457 ☐

CHICKEN TACOS
Fried Mexican tortillas with chicken filling, topped with lettuce, tomatoes, cheese and Tabasco sauce. 6 servings. Page 456 ◩

POOR BOY
Ham, Gruyère cheese, cucumber and tomato with egg and mayonnaise dressing in French bread. 6 servings. Page 457 ☐

CLUB SANDWICHES
Layers of toast with a crisp bacon, turkey, salad and mayonnaise filling. 2 servings. Page 457 ☐

WATERCRESS AND WALNUT
SANDWICHES (front) *4 servings.* ☐
CURRIED PRAWN (left) ☐ CRUNCHY
TUNA SANDWICHES ☐ All page 458

PATE PINWHEELS (right) *Makes 30.* ☐
RIBBON SANDWICHES *Makes 50.* ☐
Both page 459

DANISH OPEN SANDWICHES
(Top row, left to right) *Egg, black lumpfish roe and red pepper* ☐
Prawns with mayonnaise ☐ *Danish blue cheese, black grapes and walnuts* ☐ *Marinated herring with onion and tomato on lettuce* ☐

(Bottom row, left to right) *Rare roast beef with fried chopped onion* ☐
Smoked salmon on lettuce ☐ *Salami and cucumber twists* ☐
Cold roast pork with orange twists and crumbled bacon ☐ All page 458

Preserves

RASPBERRY JAM
Raspberries simmered in their own juice with sugar, to make a softly set jam. Makes 3 kg (6½ lb). Page 467 ◨

STRAWBERRY JAM
A thick, whole-fruit jam made with fresh, firm strawberries and sugar with lemon juice added to help it set. Makes about 2.3 kg (5 lb). Page 467 ◨

FOUR FRUIT JELLY (front). Page 468 ■
BLACKCURRANT JELLY. Page 468 ■

CHERRY JAM (top) *Makes about 2.3 kg (5 lb).* Page 467 ◨ **DRIED APRICOT JAM** *Makes about 2.3 kg (5 lb).* Page 467 ■

PLUM JAM
Chunky jam made with ripe plums and flavoured with the kernels from the stones. Makes about 4.5 kg (10 lb). Page 467 ◨

GOOSEBERRY JAM (front and rear) *Makes about 4.5 kg (10 lb).* Page 467 ◨ **BLACKBERRY AND APPLE JAM** *Makes about 4.5 kg (10 lb).* Page 467 ◨

THREE FRUIT MARMALADE (left) *Makes about 4.5 kg (10 lb).*
Page 469 ■   LIME MARMALADE (centre) *Makes about 2.3 kg
(5 lb).* Page 469 ■   SEVILLE ORANGE MARMALADE *Makes
about 4.5 kg (10 lb).* Page 468 ■

PICKLED ONIONS
*Small onions steeped in spiced vinegar for
at least 3 months. Makes 2.7 kg (6 lb).*
Page 470 ■

GREEN TOMATO CHUTNEY
*Unripe tomatoes simmered in vinegar with
apples, onions, sultanas, sugar and spices.
Makes about 1.4 kg (3 lb).* Page 469 ■

DOWER HOUSE CHUTNEY
*A thick preserve of plums, tomatoes, apples,
onions, dried fruit, sugar and spices. Makes
2.3 kg (5 lb).* Page 469 ■

SPICED ORANGE RINGS
*Sweet orange slices simmered until soft, then
steeped in spicy vinegar syrup. Makes 2.3 kg
(5 lb).* Page 470 ■

PICCALILLI
*Mixed summer vegetables, soaked in brine
then preserved in vinegar and mustard.
Makes 3.2 kg (7 lb).* Page 470 ■

SPICY MINCEMEAT
*Apples, dried fruit and candied peel, suet, sugar, spices and brandy
in the traditional Christmas preserve. Makes about 2.3 kg (5 lb).*
Page 470 ■

Drinks

LEMON DRINK
*Fresh lemon rind and juice, sugar and water;
serve chilled, diluted with soda. Makes
3.7 litres (6½ pints).* **Page 471** □

MULLED WINE
*Red wine heated with cinnamon, cloves and
orange and lemon slices. Makes 900 ml
(1½ pints).* **Page 471** □

**HOT CIDER CUP WITH BAKED
APPLES** *Cloves, allspice and nutmeg in a
hot cider and fruit juice cup. Makes 4 litres
(7 pints).* **Page 472** □

DAIQUIRIS (left) □ **BLENDED
WHISKY SOURS** □ *Both make
1.1 litres (2 pints).* **Page 472**

CITRUS PUNCH (left) *Makes 3.7 litres
(6½ pints).* **Page 471** □ **PINEAPPLE
CRUSH** *Makes 1.7 litres (3 pints).*
Page 471 □

GLOGG
*Warm punch with red wine and vodka or gin,
flamed. Makes 2.2 litres (4 pints).* **Page 471** ■

COCKTAILS (from left): BRANDY ALEXANDER □ VIRGINIA MINT JULEP □ MARGARITA □ OLD
FASHIONED □ TOM COLLINS □ MANHATTAN □ STINGER □ MARTINI □ BLOODY MARY □ PARTY
BLOODY MARY □ All pages 472–473

RECIPES

APPETISERS

Appetisers and cocktail savouries should stimulate the taste buds without blunting the appetite. The simplest cocktail snacks require no cooking at all, but more substantial finger food is a good idea if guests are likely to have more than one or two alcoholic drinks. Choose the appetiser for a main meal with the rest of the menu in mind and serve it in small portions so that your guests will be able to enjoy the rest of the meal.

Cocktail snacks

Colour index
page 18

96 twists

Cheese Twists

150 g (5 oz) plain flour
50 g (2 oz) corn meal
5 ml (1 level tsp) salt
150 g (5 oz) Cheddar
  cheese, grated

50 g (2 oz) blended
  white vegetable fat
25–35 ml (5–7 tsp) water
grated Parmesan cheese

1. Put the flour, corn meal and salt in a bowl and mix well. Cut or rub in the cheese and fat until the mixture resembles coarse breadcrumbs. Stir in 25 ml (5 tsp) water and shape the dough into a ball, adding a little more water if necessary.
2. Halve the dough. Place one half between two sheets of waxed paper and roll it out to a rectangle about 30.5 × 25.5 cm (12 × 10 in). Cut the rectangle in half lengthways, then crossways into 1-cm (½-in) strips.
3. Remove each strip from the paper and turn the ends in opposite directions to make twists. Lay the twists on a baking sheet, pressing the ends down to prevent them curling.
4. Bake at 220°C (425°F) mark 7 for 6–8 minutes until golden. Remove from the oven and sprinkle with grated Parmesan. Remove twists to a wire rack to cool; repeat with the remaining dough.

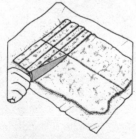

Cutting the strips: Use a sharp knife to divide the rolled dough into narrow, even-sized strips.

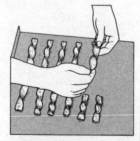

Twisting the strips: Hold each strip; turn the ends in opposite directions to form a twist.

Colour index
page 18

Makes 450 g
(1 lb)

Deep-fried Walnuts

1.5 litres (2½ pints) water
450 g (1 lb) shelled
  walnuts
100 g (4 oz) sugar

oil or fat for deep frying
pinch salt

1. Put the water in a large saucepan and bring to the boil. Add the walnuts, bring back to the boil and cook for 1 minute; drain immediately.
2. Rinse the walnuts under hot running water and drain again. Toss them with the sugar.
3. Heat the oil to 180°C (350°F). Add a few of the walnuts and fry for 5 minutes until golden.
4. Remove the nuts from the oil and drain in a coarse sieve over a bowl, sprinkling with salt and tossing lightly to prevent them sticking together. Transfer to waxed paper; cool. Repeat with remaining nuts. Store in a tightly covered container.

Colour index
page 18

Makes 275 g
(10 oz)

Curried Almonds

20 g (¾ oz) butter or
  margarine
275 g (10 oz) almonds,
  blanched

15 ml (1 level tbsp)
  curry powder
10 ml (2 level tsp) salt

1. Melt the butter in a roasting tin; add the almonds and toss until they are evenly coated.
2. Toast in the oven at 150°C (300°F) mark 2 for 30 minutes, stirring occasionally. Add the curry powder and salt and toss well. When cold, store in a tightly covered container.

CHILLI CASHEWS: Prepare the nuts as above, but replace the almonds with *salted cashews* and the curry powder with *chilli powder*.

HOT PEPPERY WALNUTS: Prepare the nuts as above, but replace the almonds with *225 g (8 oz) halved walnuts* or pecans and curry powder with *10 ml (2 tsp) soy sauce* and a *dash of Tabasco sauce*; use only *5 ml (1 level tsp) salt*. Makes 225 g (8 oz)

Cold canapés

Colour index
page 18
40 canapés

Curried Tuna Puffs

choux paste made with 65 g
(2½ oz) flour,
page 366
210-g (7½-oz) can tuna
100 ml (4 fl oz)
mayonnaise, page 462
25 g (1 oz) celery, trimmed
and finely chopped
2 hard-boiled eggs, shelled
and chopped
15 ml (1 level tbsp) curry
powder
1.25 ml (¼ level tsp) salt

For the garnish:
25 g (1 oz) parsley,
chopped

1 Grease a large baking sheet, then carefully spoon the choux paste into a piping bag fitted with a 1-cm (½-in) plain round nozzle.

2 Pipe the pastry on to the baking sheet to make 20 mounds, spaced well apart. Bake at 190°C (375°F) mark 5 for 20–25 minutes until browned.

3 Transfer the puffs to a wire rack and leave until completely cool.

4 Meanwhile, mix the tuna in its own oil with a fork until finely flaked.

5 Stir in the mayonnaise, celery, hard-boiled eggs, curry powder and salt until evenly blended. Cover and chill.

6 Cut each puff in half to make two shells and re-move any uncooked paste from the centres.

7 Spoon about 10 ml (2 tsp) filling into each shell. Garnish with chopped parsley.

Colour index
page 18
24 canapés

Egg and Roe Rounds

2 250-g (8.8-oz) packets
sliced pumpernickel
3 hard-boiled eggs, shelled
6 stoned black olives

mayonnaise, page 462
30 ml (2 level tbsp) red
lumpfish roe

1. Cut two rounds from each slice of pumpernickel, with a 5-cm (2-in) plain round cutter.
2. Slice the eggs and cut each olive into four.
3. Spread a little mayonnaise on the centre of each round and place a slice of egg on top. Finish with a little lumpfish roe and a slice of olive.

Colour index
page 18
24 canapés

Tuna and Dill Rounds

2 250-g (8.8-oz) packets
sliced pumpernickel
mayonnaise, page 462
1 small cucumber, sliced
210-g (7½-oz) can tuna,
drained
60 ml (4 tbsp) soured cream

5 ml (1 level tsp) dried
dill weed
5 ml (1 tsp) lemon juice
pinch pepper
7.5 ml (1½ tsp) finely
chopped canned pimento

1. Cut two rounds from each slice of pumpernickel with a 5-cm (2-in) plain round cutter. Spread each one with a little mayonnaise and top with a cucumber slice. Chop any leftover cucumber.
2. Mix the chopped cucumber, 45 ml (3 tbsp) mayonnaise, the tuna, soured cream, dill, lemon juice and pepper. Spoon a little of the mixture on to each round and top with chopped pimento.

Colour index
page 18
20 canapés

Watercress and Cream Cheese Canapés

5 thin slices white bread or
toast
75 g (3 oz) cream cheese

1 bunch watercress, washed
and trimmed

1. Trim the crusts from the bread and spread the slices with cheese. Cut each slice into four triangles.
2. Top each triangle with a sprig of watercress.

Colour index
page 18
20 canapés

Smoked Salmon Squares

5 thin slices white bread,
toasted
75 g (3 oz) cream cheese,
softened
75 g (3 oz) smoked salmon,
sliced

For the garnish:
pared rind of 2 large
lemons, cut into
thin strips

1. Trim the crusts from the toast and spread the slices with cheese; cut each slice into four squares.
2. Cut the salmon slices to fit and arrange on top of the cheese. Garnish with strips of lemon rind.

Colour index
page 18
24 canapés

Anchovy and Cheese Canapés

2 250-g (8.8-oz) packets
sliced pumpernickel
150 g (5 oz) Cheddar
cheese spread
10 ml (2 level tsp) creamed
horseradish

50-g (2-oz) can anchovy
fillets, drained and
cut into strips
6 pimento-stuffed olives,
sliced

1. Cut two rounds from each slice of pumpernickel with a 5-cm (2-in) plain round cutter.
2. Mix the cheese spread and horseradish and spread some on each round of pumpernickel. Top with strips of anchovy fillet and olive slices.

Cold canapés

Blue Cheese and Aspic Canapés

Colour index
page 18

20 canapés

15 g (½ oz) powdered
  gelatine
447-ml (15¾-fl oz) can
  tomato juice
75 ml (5 tbsp) soured
  cream
30 ml (2 tbsp) crumbled
  blue cheese
5 thin slices white bread or
  toast

For the garnish:
capers

1 Dissolve the gelatine in a little of the tomato juice in a small basin over a pan of hot water, then stir in the rest of the tomato juice.

2 Pour the tomato juice mixture into a Swiss roll tin and chill thoroughly for about 30 minutes or until set.

3 Meanwhile, mix the soured cream with the blue cheese. Trim the crusts from the bread.

4 Spread the soured cream and blue cheese mixture on the bread and cut each slice into four triangles.

5 Cut the tomato aspic into small cubes and place a few on each triangle. Garnish the canapés with the capers.

Asparagus Canapés

Colour index
page 18

20 canapés

5 thin slices white bread or
  toast
mayonnaise, page 462
425-g (15-oz) can white
  asparagus spears,
  drained

1 whole canned pimento,
  drained and cut into
  thin strips
2 gherkins, sliced

1. Trim the crusts from the bread slices and spread the slices lightly with mayonnaise; cut each slice into four small squares.
2. Halve the asparagus spears and place a few pieces of asparagus on each square of bread, trimming them if necessary. Garnish each canapé with pimento strips and a gherkin slice.

Hot canapés

Individual Broccoli Quiches

Colour index
page 22

36 canapés

shortcrust pastry made with
  175 g (6 oz) flour,
  page 343
25 g (1 oz) butter or
  margarine, melted
150 g (5 oz) frozen
  broccoli, thawed and
  chopped

50 g (2 oz) Gruyère cheese
  grated
50 ml (2 fl oz) single cream
50 ml (2 fl oz) milk
2 eggs
2.5 ml (½ level tsp) salt

1 Grease and lightly flour thirty-six 3.5-cm (1¾-in) deep patty tins.

2 Roll out the pastry on a lightly floured surface to about 0.3-cm (⅛-in) thickness.

3 Cut out thirty-six rounds with a 5-cm (2-in) fluted cutter, re-rolling the pastry scraps to make the full number of rounds.

4 Line the patty tins with the pastry rounds and brush them lightly with melted fat; chill for 30 minutes. Drain the broccoli thoroughly on kitchen paper towel.

5 Spoon about 5 ml (1 tsp) broccoli into each pastry case and sprinkle a little grated cheese over the top. Whisk together the cream, milk, eggs and salt.

6 Spoon about 15 ml (1 tbsp) egg mixture into each case. Bake at 200°C (400°F) mark 6 for 25 minutes or until a knife inserted into the centre comes out clean.

INDIVIDUAL SPINACH QUICHES: Prepare as above, but replace the broccoli with **150 g (5 oz) frozen chopped spinach**, thawed and drained; replace the Gruyère cheese with **50 g (2 oz) mature Cheddar cheese** and sprinkle with **grated Parmesan** before baking.

Pissaladière

Colour index
page 22

6 canapés

275 g (10 oz) strong white
  flour
5 ml (1 level tsp) salt
225 ml (8 fl oz) water
15 g (½ oz) fresh yeast
45 ml (3 tbsp) vegetable oil
4 onions, skinned and sliced
50-g (2-oz) can anchovy
  fillets, drained and
  chopped

2.5 ml (½ level tsp) dried
  oregano
226-g (8-oz) jar pimento-
  stuffed olives, drained
  and sliced
100 g (4 oz) Gruyère
  cheese, grated

1. Sift 100 g (4 oz) flour and the salt into a large bowl.
Heat the water until tepid and blend in the yeast
until smooth. Gradually beat the yeast liquid into
the flour with a wooden spoon until the flour is just
moistened, then beat hard for a further 2 minutes.
Beat in another 50 g (2 oz) flour to make a thick
batter; continue beating for a further 2 minutes,
then stir in another 100 g (4 oz) flour to make a soft,
slightly sticky dough.
2. Turn the dough on to a lightly floured surface and
knead for about 8 minutes, until it is smooth, elastic
and no longer sticky, adding more flour if necessary.
Shape the dough into a ball. Place it in a large
greased bowl, cover with oiled polythene and leave
to rise until it has doubled in size.
3. Meanwhile, heat the oil in a large frying pan and
fry the sliced onions gently for about 10 minutes,
stirring frequently, until soft but not coloured.
Remove from the heat and stir in the chopped
anchovy fillets and oregano.
4. Turn the dough on to a floured surface and knead
lightly for 2–3 minutes, then invert the bowl over the
dough and leave to rest for 15 minutes.
5. Place the dough on a greased baking sheet and roll
it out to a 36.5 × 30.5 cm (13½ × 12 in) rectangle.
Spread the onion mixture over the dough, arrange
the olives on top; sprinkle with cheese.
6. Bake at 220°C (425°F) mark 7 for 20–25 minutes
until the crust is golden and the edges are crisp. To
serve cut into small pieces with a sharp knife.

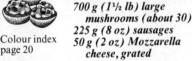

Sausage-stuffed Mushrooms

Colour index
page 20

About
30 canapés

700 g (1½ lb) large
  mushrooms (about 30)
225 g (8 oz) sausages
50 g (2 oz) Mozzarella
  cheese, grated

60 ml (4 level tbsp) fresh
  white breadcrumbs

1. Remove the stems from the mushrooms. Reserve
the caps and chop the stems.
2. Fry the sausages until brown. Remove them from
the pan, allow them to cool slightly and chop them
finely. Return the pieces to the pan and brown them
all over. Drain the sausage pieces and spoon off all
but 30 ml (2 tbsp) fat from the pan.
3. Reheat the remaining fat, add the mushroom
stems and cook, stirring, for 10 minutes until tender.
4. Remove from the heat; stir in the sausage pieces,
cheese and breadcrumbs. Spoon the mixture into the
mushroom caps.
5. Place the mushrooms in a roasting tin and bake at
230°C (450°F) mark 8 for 15 minutes until tender.

Münster and Onion Triangles

Colour index
page 22

24 canapés

275 g (10 oz) Münster
  cheese
½ onion, skinned

250-g (8.8-oz) packet
  sliced pumpernickel

1. With a sharp knife, slice the cheese thinly. Cut the
onion crossways into thin slices and separate each
slice carefully into rings.
2. Place two slices of cheese on top of each slice of
pumpernickel, trimming them to fit, and top with
the onion rings.
3. Grill the slices under high heat for 3–5 minutes
until the cheese is bubbly and the onion slightly
browned. Cut each slice into four triangles and serve
immediately, while hot.

CHEDDAR AND TOMATO TRIANGLES:
Prepare the Münster and onion triangles as above,
but replace the Münster cheese with *mature Cheddar
cheese* and top each triangle with a *thinly sliced
tomato* before grilling.

Cheesy Prawn Canapés

Colour index
page 22

20 canapés

10 slices white or
  wholemeal bread
25 g (1 oz) butter or
  margarine
2.5 ml (½ level tsp) dried
  thyme
100 g (4 oz) shelled
  prawns, chopped
50 g (2 oz) Gruyère cheese,
  grated

75 ml (5 tbsp) mayonnaise,
  page 462
25 g (1 oz) fresh white or
  wholemeal breadcrumbs
1.25 ml (¼ level tsp) salt

For the garnish:
paprika

1. Cut two rounds from each slice of bread with a 5-
cm (2-in) fluted round cutter; use the trimmings to
make breadcrumbs.
2. Melt the butter or margarine in a small saucepan
and stir in the dried thyme. Brush the herb butter
over the bread rounds and place them on a baking
sheet. Bake at 200°C (400°F) mark 6 for 10 minutes
until golden.
3. Meanwhile, put the chopped prawns in a bowl
with the Gruyère cheese, mayonnaise, breadcrumbs
and salt and mix well. With your fingers, lightly
shape the mixture into 20 small balls about the size
of a walnut.
4. Lightly press a prawn ball on to each baked bread
round and grill under high heat for about 10
minutes, until golden and bubbling. Garnish with
the paprika.

Cutting out rounds: Use a
5-cm (2-in) fluted round
cutter to stamp out the
bread rounds.

Adding the topping: Press
the prawn balls lightly on
to toasted rounds, then
grill until hot and golden.

Hot canapés

Colour index
page 24

40 canapés

Blinis

*175 g (6 oz) plain flour,
    sifted*
150 ml (¼ pint) milk
15 g (½ oz) fresh yeast
2 size 6 eggs, separated

*150 ml (¼ pint) soured
    cream*
pinch salt
25 g (1 oz) lumpfish roe

1. Put half the flour in a bowl. Heat the milk until just tepid, then blend in the yeast. Tip the yeast liquid on to the flour and mix to a soft dough. Put it in a greased bowl, cover with oiled polythene and leave to rise in a warm place for 2 hours.
2. Add the remaining flour, egg yolks, 15 ml (1 tbsp) soured cream and salt to the dough and mix well to make a thickish batter.
3. Whisk the egg whites until stiff peaks form and fold them into the batter. Cover again with oiled polythene and leave to prove in a warm place for about 30 minutes.
4. Lightly grease a griddle or heavy frying pan with oil, heat it and spoon 5 ml (1 tsp) batter at a time on to the hot griddle to make tiny pancakes. Cook until the tops are set and the undersides just golden; turn and cook the other sides. Spread the cooked pancakes in a single layer on a heated serving plate and keep them hot.
5. Spoon the remaining soured cream into a piping bag fitted with a 1-cm (½-in) star nozzle. Pipe a little on to each pancake and top each one with a little lumpfish roe.

BLINIS WITH COD'S ROE: As an alternative topping, omit the soured cream and spread each blini with a little *smoked cod's roe*.

Colour index
page 20

36 canapés

Tostadas

*6 Mexican tortillas,
    page 431*
vegetable oil
*350 g (12 oz) lean minced
    beef*
*1 small onion, skinned and
    chopped*
*20 ml (4 level tsp) chilli
    powder*
2.5 ml (½ level tsp) salt

*2.5 ml (½ level tsp) dried
    oregano*
*225 ml (8 fl oz) tomato
    sauce, page 337*
*100 g (4 oz) Cheddar
    cheese, grated*
*few leaves Webb lettuce,
    shredded*
*100 g (4 oz) stoned black
    olives, sliced*

1. Cut each tortilla into six wedges. Heat about 0.5 cm (¼ in) oil in a frying pan and fry a few tortilla wedges for 30 seconds. Turn them and cook for a further 30 seconds, or until golden and crisp. Remove from the pan with a slotted spoon and drain on kitchen paper towel. Spread them in a single layer on a large serving dish and keep hot while you fry the remaining tortilla wedges in the same way.
2. Put the beef and onion in a saucepan and cook, stirring occasionally, for about 10 minutes, until the meat is browned and the onion soft. Spoon off any excess fat. Stir in the chilli powder, salt, oregano and half the tomato sauce. Cook the mixture, stirring, for a further 2 minutes.
3. Spoon a little meat mixture on to each tortilla wedge. Top each one with a little cheese, lettuce, tomato sauce and some olive slices and serve the tostadas immediately.

Party appetisers

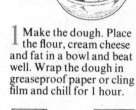

Colour index
page 22

20–25 canapés

Hot Mushroom Turnovers

20 g (¾ oz) butter
*100 g (4 oz) mushrooms,
    finely chopped*
*1 small onion, skinned and
    finely chopped*
2.5 ml (½ level tsp) salt
pinch dried thyme
*15 ml (1 level tbsp) plain
    flour*
30 ml (2 tbsp) soured cream
1 egg, beaten

For the dough:
75 g (3 oz) plain flour
*120 g (4½ oz) cream
    cheese, softened*
*50 g (2 oz) butter or
    margarine, softened*

1 Make the dough. Place the flour, cream cheese and fat in a bowl and beat well. Wrap the dough in greaseproof paper or cling film and chill for 1 hour.

2 Melt the butter in a frying pan and fry the mushrooms and onion until tender. Add the salt and dried thyme.

3 Blend in the flour and soured cream, remove the pan from the heat and allow to cool slightly.

4 Roll out dough and, using a 6-cm (2¾-in) plain round cutter, cut out rounds. Re-roll remaining dough and cut more rounds.

5 Place 5 ml (1 tsp) of the mushroom mixture on one half of each round.

6 Brush the edges with egg and fold the dough over the filling. Seal the edges with a fork. Prick the tops and place the turnovers on a baking sheet.

7 Brush the turnovers with egg, cover and chill until time to serve. Bake at 230°C (450°F) mark 8 for 12 minutes or until golden and serve hot.

Steak Bites

Colour index
page 19

48 steak bites

100 ml (4 fl oz) red wine
1 clove garlic, skinned and
    crushed
900 g (2 lb) rump steak, cut
    2.5 cm (1 in) thick
25 g (1 oz) butter or
    margarine
7.5 ml (1½ level tsp) dry
    mustard

5 ml (1 tsp)
    Worcestershire sauce
1.25 ml (¼ level tsp) salt
few dashes Tabasco sauce

For the garnish:
parsley sprigs

1. Mix the red wine and the garlic in a shallow dish and add the steak. Cover and leave to marinate for about 1½ hours, turning the steak once, then drain the steak and reserve the marinade.
2. Place the steak on a greased rack in the grill pan, and grill under high heat for about 5 minutes on each side for rare steak, 7 minutes if you prefer the steak medium-done.
3. Meanwhile, melt the butter or margarine in a small saucepan and stir in the dry mustard, Worcestershire sauce, salt, Tabasco sauce and 30 ml (2 tbsp) of the reserved steak marinade. Simmer gently until the mixture is heated through.
4. When the steak is done, cut it into 2.5-cm (1-in) cubes and place them in a chafing dish or heated serving dish, with the cooking juices. Pour the seasoned butter mixture over the steak and garnish with parsley sprigs. Serve the steak bites with cock-tail sticks.

Swedish Meatballs

Colour index
page 19

40 meatballs

450 g (1 lb) lean minced
    beef
175 g (6 oz) dried
    breadcrumbs
100 ml (4 fl oz) dry sherry
2.5 ml (½ level tsp) ground
    mace
2.5 ml (½ level tsp) salt
pinch pepper
300 ml (½ pint) double or
    whipping cream

40 g (1½ oz) plain flour
30 ml (2 tbsp) vegetable
    oil
25 g (1 oz) butter or
    margarine
298-g (10½-oz) can
    condensed consommé
bay leaf

1. Mix the beef with the breadcrumbs, sherry, mace, salt, pepper and 175 ml (6 fl oz) cream. With floured hands, shape the mixture into about 40 small meat-balls. Spread 25 g (1 oz) flour on a sheet of greaseproof paper and roll the balls in the flour until coated; reserve any leftover flour.
2. Heat the oil in a large frying pan and fry half the meatballs until well browned all over. Drain well on kitchen paper towel and keep hot while you cook the remaining meatballs. Wipe the frying pan clean with kitchen paper towel.
3. Melt the butter or margarine in the same pan, blend in the remaining flour and cook for 1–2 minutes, stirring all the time. Gradually stir in the undiluted consommé and remaining cream. Bring to the boil, stirring constantly, then add the meatballs and bay leaf. Reduce the heat, cover and simmer for 15 minutes or until the meatballs are tender. Discard the bay leaf. Spoon the meatballs and sauce into a heated serving dish or a chafing dish and serve with cocktail sticks.

Gravad Lax

Colour index
page 22

12–14 first
course servings

30 ml (2 level tbsp) salt
20 ml (4 level tsp) sugar
5 ml (1 tsp) black
    peppercorns, crushed
700 g (1½ lb) middle-cut
    fresh salmon, scaled,
    with skin on and bones
    removed
15 ml (1 tbsp) brandy
bunch fresh dill weed

For the garnish:
fresh dill weed
lemon wedges

1 Mix together the salt, sugar and pepper and rub the mixture over the fish; sprinkle with brandy.

2 Put one third of dill in shallow dish. Place one piece of salmon, skin side down, on top.

3 Put another third of the dill on top. Add the remaining salmon, skin side up, and top with the remaining dill.

4 Cover the salmon and dill with cling film and put a heavy plate over it. Weight the plate down with heavy cans and chill the salmon thoroughly for 24–36 hours.

5 Scrape the dill and seasonings off salmon and place it, skin side down, on a serving board.

6 To serve, garnish with dill and lemon. Cut the salmon in thin slanting slices, away from the skin.

GRAVAD LAX WITH MUSTARD SAUCE:
Prepare as above and serve with a sauce made from 100 ml (4 fl oz) made mustard, 100 ml (4 fl oz) vegetable oil, 75 ml (5 level tbsp) sugar, 60 ml (4 tbsp) white vinegar, 5 ml (1 tsp) soured cream and a pinch of salt blended together; chill. Stir in 60 ml (4 tbsp) chopped fresh dill weed just before serving.

Party appetisers

Marinated Prawns

Colour index
page 23

6 first course
servings

*700 g (1½ lb) fresh or
frozen uncooked jumbo
prawns, in the shell
½ stick celery, washed and
trimmed
bay leaf
6 black peppercorns
20 ml (4 level tsp) salt
100 ml (4 fl oz) vegetable
oil*

*65 ml (2½ fl oz) lemon
juice
50 ml (2 fl oz) vinegar
22.5 ml (1½ tbsp) mixed
pickling spice, tied in a
muslin bag
5 ml (1 level tsp) sugar
2 sprigs fresh dill weed*

1. Shell the prawns, leaving the tails on. Put them in a large saucepan of boiling water with the celery, bay leaf, peppercorns and 10 ml (2 level tsp) salt. Simmer for 3 minutes; drain well.
2. Toss the prawns and flavourings with the remaining ingredients, reserving one sprig of dill. Chill.
3. To serve, drain the prawns well and discard the flavourings. Garnish with fresh dill.

PARTY MARINATED PRAWNS: Prepare as above, but double the quantities and serve them with cocktail sticks, spooned into a crystalline ice bowl (below).

MAKING A CRYSTALLINE ICE BOWL

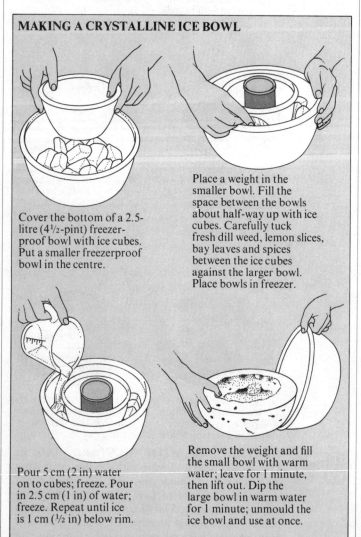

Cover the bottom of a 2.5-litre (4½-pint) freezer-proof bowl with ice cubes. Put a smaller freezerproof bowl in the centre.

Place a weight in the smaller bowl. Fill the space between the bowls about half-way up with ice cubes. Carefully tuck fresh dill weed, lemon slices, bay leaves and spices between the ice cubes against the larger bowl. Place bowls in freezer.

Pour 5 cm (2 in) water on to cubes; freeze. Pour in 2.5 cm (1 in) of water; freeze. Repeat until ice is 1 cm (½ in) below rim.

Remove the weight and fill the small bowl with warm water; leave for 1 minute, then lift out. Dip the large bowl in warm water for 1 minute; unmould the ice bowl and use at once.

Escargots à la Bourguignonne

Colour index
page 22

6 first course
servings

*2 cans escargots (30 snails)
with shells*

For the garlic butter:
*175 g (6 oz) butter,
softened
2 shallots, skinned and
finely chopped*

*2 cloves garlic, skinned and
crushed
10 ml (2 tsp) chopped
parsley
pinch mixed spice
salt and pepper*

1. To make the garlic butter, mix together the butter, shallots, garlic, parsley and mixed spice. Add salt and pepper to taste.
2. Drain the snails and push one into each shell. Press as much of the garlic butter as possible into each shell.
3. Place the shells in special snail dishes or in a shallow ovenproof dish and put in the oven at 220°C (425°F) mark 7 for 10 minutes. Serve hot.

PRAWNS A LA BOURGUIGNONNE: Using the garlic butter ingredients as above, melt the butter in a large frying pan, add the shallots and garlic and cook until the shallots are soft but not coloured. Stir in *450 g (1 lb) shelled prawns*, the parsley, mixed spice, salt and pepper. Cover and cook gently for 10 minutes. Serve in individual heated dishes, with thinly sliced *brown bread* and *butter*.

MOULES A LA BOURGUIGNONNE: Clean thoroughly about *4 dozen mussels* (page 160), place them in a large saucepan and cook in garlic butter as for prawns à la bourguignonne. The mussels are cooked when the shells open. Serve the mussels in their shells in heated soup plates with the butter spooned over.

Scallops in Pernod

Colour index
page 22

6 first course
servings

*12 large fresh scallops or
700 g (1½ lb) fresh or
frozen scallop meat
22.5 (1½ level tbsp) flour
40 g (1½ oz) butter
1 onion, skinned and finely
chopped*

*175 ml (6 fl oz) Pernod
7.5 ml (1½ tsp) lemon juice
salt and pepper*

For the garnish:
chopped parsley

1. To prepare fresh scallops, rest the hinge of a shell on a flat surface and insert a small knife into one of the openings on either side of the shell, just above the hinge. Prise it open slightly and, keeping the knife close against the flat shell, sever the muscle attaching the meat to the shell. Remove the meat and discard the black sac and remaining muscle. Repeat with the remaining scallops and scrub six of the shells to use as dishes. To prepare frozen scallop meat, thaw it in the refrigerator, then rinse in cold water, drain and dry on kitchen paper towel.
2. Toss the prepared scallop meat in the flour.
3. Melt the butter in a large frying pan, add the onion and fry gently for 2 minutes. Add the scallops and cook for a further 5 minutes.
4. Stir in the Pernod and lemon juice and season to taste. Simmer gently until the liquid is heated through, then spoon into the scallop shells or individual heated serving dishes. Garnish with parsley and serve hot.

Spanakopitas

Colour index page 20

60 pastries

30 ml (2 tbsp) olive oil
1 small onion, chopped
227-g (8-oz) packet
frozen chopped spinach,
thawed and squeezed
dry
75 ml (5 level tbsp) grated
Parmesan cheese

pinch pepper
1 egg, beaten
175 g (6 oz) bought
phyllo or strudel pastry
(6 sheets)
100 g (4 oz) butter,
melted

1 Heat the oil in a saucepan, add the onion and fry gently until tender. Remove the pan from the heat and stir in spinach, cheese, pepper and egg.

2 Cut each phyllo sheet widthways into ten 5-cm (2-in) strips. Place the strips on waxed paper and cover with a slightly damp tea towel.

3 Brush one strip of the phyllo with melted butter and place 5 ml (1 tsp) of the spinach mixture at end of strip.

4 Fold one corner of the strip diagonally over the filling, so that it forms a triangle.

5 Continue folding the pastry at right angles until you reach the end of the strip, forming a neat, triangular package. Repeat with remaining strips and filling.

6 Place the packages, seam side down, in a large tin, and brush with melted butter. Bake at 220°C (425°F) mark 7 for 15 minutes until golden. Serve hot.

TIROPITAS: Crumble *100 g (4 oz) feta cheese* and stir in *100 g (4 oz) ricotta* or cottage cheese, *30 ml (2 tbsp) chopped parsley, 1 egg,* beaten, and *1.25 ml (¼ level tsp) pepper.* Prepare phyllo pastry as above; fill with the cheese; bake as above.

Sausage Rolls

Colour index page 22

24 rolls

shortcrust pastry made with
400 g (14 oz) flour,
page 343

450 g (1 lb) sausagemeat
flour
milk to glaze

1. Roll out the pastry thinly, on a lightly floured surface, to form a rectangle. Cut it lengthways into two strips and trim the edges.
2. Halve the sausagemeat. Dust both pieces with flour; shape into two rolls the length of the pastry.
3. Lay a roll of sausagemeat down the centre of one pastry strip. Brush the long edges of the pastry with milk, fold one side over the sausagemeat and press the edges firmly together to seal. Repeat to make a second roll.
4. Brush the rolls with milk; cut them each into 4–5 cm (1½–2 in) slices. Place on a baking sheet.
5. Bake at 200°C (400°F) mark 6 for 15 minutes, then reduce the temperature to 180°C (350°F) mark 4 and cook for a further 15 minutes or until the pastry is golden. Serve hot.

Chinese Chicken Wings

Colour index page 20

About 36 portions

1.4 kg (3 lb) chicken wings
30 ml (2 tbsp) vegetable oil
3 spring onions, cut into
7.5-cm (3-in) pieces
100 ml (4 fl oz) soy sauce
100 ml (4 fl oz) medium or
dry sherry
60 ml (4 tbsp) tomato
ketchup

30 ml (2 level tbsp) sugar
1.25 ml (¼ level tbsp)
ground ginger
3 star anise, optional

To serve, optional:
1 large head crisp lettuce,
shredded

1. Cut off the chicken wing tips at the joint and discard; cut each wing in half at the joint.
2. Heat the oil in a large saucepan, add the chicken wings and two thirds of the spring onions. Fry them for 7 minutes, stirring all the time. Reduce the heat and add the remaining ingredients. Stir well; cover and cook for 25 minutes, stirring occasionally.
3. Remove the lid and cook for a further 10 minutes, stirring frequently, until almost all the liquid is absorbed and the chicken wings are tender.
4. Serve hot or cold on a bed of shredded lettuce. Garnish with the reserved spring onion pieces.

Rumaki

Colour index page 22

18 rumaki

225 g (8 oz) chicken livers
about 9 rashers streaky
bacon, rinded and halved
227-g (8-oz) can water
chestnuts, drained
100 ml (4 fl oz) soy sauce

2.5 ml (½ level tsp) curry
powder
1.25 ml (¼ level tsp)
ground ginger

1. Rinse the chicken livers, dry them with kitchen paper towel and cut them into chunks. Wrap each piece of bacon around a chunk of liver and a water chestnut; fasten with wooden cocktail sticks.
2. Stir together the soy sauce, curry powder and ginger, add the livers and toss carefully. Cover and chill for at least 1 hour, turning occasionally.
3. Just before serving, drain the rumaki and place them in a single layer on a rack in the grill pan. Grill under high heat, turning frequently, for about 10 minutes or until the liver is cooked. Serve hot.

Pâtés

Pâté de Campagne

Colour index page 18

8 first course servings

30 ml (2 tbsp) vegetable oil
100 g (4 oz) mushrooms, chopped
50 g (2 oz) onion, skinned and chopped
1 clove garlic, skinned and finely chopped
50 ml (2 fl oz) medium sherry
2.5 ml (½ level tsp) dried thyme
pinch ground nutmeg
7.5 ml (1½ level tsp) salt
2.5 ml (½ level tsp) pepper

225 g (8 oz) lean pork, minced
225 g (8 oz) boneless chicken, minced
100 g (4 oz) pork fat, minced
50 g (2 oz) shelled pistachios, chopped
30 ml (2 tbsp) chopped parsley
1 egg, beaten
225 g (8 oz) streaky bacon, rinded

1 Heat the oil in a large saucepan and gently fry the mushrooms, onion and garlic until tender, stirring from time to time.

2 Add the sherry, thyme, nutmeg, salt and pepper; bring to the boil. Cover and simmer for 5 minutes, stirring occasionally. Remove the saucepan from the heat.

3 Stir in the minced pork, chicken and pork fat, the chopped pistachios and parsley and the beaten egg. Beat together until the meats are well mixed.

4 Reserve a few bacon rashers. Line a 450-g (1-lb) loaf tin with the remaining rashers, letting the ends hang over the sides.

5 Pack the meat into the tin firmly. Fold over the bacon ends and top with reserved bacon. Bake at 180°C (350°F) mark 4 for 1¼ hours. Cool the pâté, then cover and chill.

6 Loosen the pâté from the sides of the tin with a palette knife dipped in hot water. Turn it out on to a flat serving plate. To serve, cut the pâté neatly into thick slices.

Chicken Liver Pâté

Colour index page 18

10 first course servings

700 g (1½ lb) chicken livers
75 g (3 oz) butter
1 onion, skinned and finely chopped
1 large clove garlic, skinned and crushed
15 ml (1 tbsp) double cream

30 ml (2 level tbsp) tomato paste
45 ml (3 tbsp) sherry or brandy
sprig of parsley

1. Rinse the chicken livers in cold water and dry them thoroughly with kitchen paper towel. Melt the butter in a frying pan and fry the livers, stirring occasionally, for about 10 minutes until they change colour.
2. Reduce the heat and add the chopped onion and the garlic. Cover and cook for about 5 minutes, then remove them from the heat and leave to cool slightly. Stir in the double cream, tomato paste and the sherry or brandy.
3. Purée the mixture in a blender or press it through a sieve, then turn into a small bowl and chill until required. Garnish with parsley.

Spinach Pâté

Colour index page 18

10 first course servings

700 g (1½ lb) frozen chopped spinach, thawed
50 g (2 oz) butter or margarine
1 bunch spring onions, trimmed and thinly sliced
2 large carrots, peeled and coarsely grated
100 ml (4 fl oz) single cream

100 ml (4 fl oz) milk
8.75 ml (1¾ level tsp) salt
5 ml (1 level tsp) dried basil
pinch cayenne pepper
4 eggs, beaten

For the garnish:
vegetable shapes, page 327 or watercress sprigs

1. Put the spinach in a colander in the sink and press it firmly with the back of a wooden spoon to drain out the liquid. Then squeeze it by hand to remove any remaining moisture. Chop the drained spinach very finely.
2. Grease a 450-g (1-lb) loaf tin and line the base with foil. Melt the fat, add the spring onions and carrots and cook, stirring frequently, for about 5 minutes, until the onions are soft but not coloured. Stir in the spinach, cream, milk, salt, basil and cayenne. Bring to the boil, then remove the saucepan from the heat and stir in the eggs.
3. Spoon the mixture into the prepared loaf tin, spreading it evenly, and cover with foil. Stand the tin in a roasting tin and add hot water to come 2.5 cm (1 in) up the sides of the loaf tin. Bake at 190°C (375°F) mark 5 for 1¼ hours or until a knife inserted through the foil, into the centre of the pâté, comes out clean.
4. Place the loaf tin on a wire rack to cool for 15 minutes, then place two heavy cans on top of the foil to weight it down. Chill overnight.
5. To serve, remove the weights and foil from the top of the pâté and loosen the pâté from the sides of the tin with a palette knife dipped in hot water. Turn the pâté out on to a flat plate and remove the foil. Garnish with vegetable shapes or watercress sprigs and cut the pâté into thick slices.

Duck Pâté in Aspic

*1.8–2.3-kg (4–5-lb) oven-
   ready duck
225 g (8 oz) lean pork
150 ml (¼ pint) dry sherry
100 g (4 oz) large
   mushrooms
40 g (1½ oz) butter or
   margarine
350 g (12 oz) chicken livers
2 spring onions, trimmed
   and sliced
100 g (4 oz) pork fat, diced
5 ml (1 level tsp) salt*

*2.5 ml (½ level tsp) pepper
50 g (2 oz) frozen peas,
   thawed
15 g (½ oz) aspic powder
283-g (10-oz) can
   condensed consommé*

Colour index page 19
10 first course servings

1 Remove all the meat
from the duck with a
sharp knife. Discard the
bones, skin and fat. Dice
the duck meat and the
pork, put them in a large
bowl, and toss together
with 50 ml (2 fl oz) dry
sherry; cover with cling
film and chill thoroughly
for about 2 hours. Reserve
one whole mushroom and
chop the remainder.

2 Heat the butter in a frying pan and gently fry
the chopped mushrooms,
chicken livers and spring
onions for 10 minutes,
until the livers are firm.

3 Put the mushroom and
liver mixture, pork fat,
salt and pepper in a
blender and blend to a
smooth purée.

4 Spread a third of the
mixture in a 900-g
(2-lb) loaf tin; spoon over
a third of the peas, then
top with a third of the duck
mixture. Repeat layering
twice and press down.

5 Stand the loaf tin in a
roasting tin and add
hot water to come 2.5 cm
(1 in) up the side. Bake at
180°C (350°F) mark 4 for
1¾ hours. Remove from
the oven, cover and weight
down. Chill.

6 Dissolve the aspic pow-
der in the remaining
sherry and consommé over
gentle heat; cool slightly.
Meanwhile, remove the
weights and foil from the
top of the pâté.

7 Loosen the pâté with a
warmed palette knife
and remove from the tin.
Pour a 0.3-cm (⅛-in) layer
of liquid aspic into the tin
and chill for about 20 minutes. Slice the reserved
mushroom thickly.

8 Arrange the mushroom
slices on top of the as-
pic and pour another thin
layer over the top; chill for
a further 20 minutes until
the aspic is set.

9 Return the pâté to the
tin on top of the aspic
layer; pour the remaining
liquid aspic around it.
Cover and chill until
completely set.

10 Loosen the pâté
from the sides of the
tin with a palette knife dipped in hot water. Turn out
on to a flat serving plate
and cut into slices to serve.

Spreads

Colour index page 19
Makes about 450 g (1 lb) or
12 first course servings

Pepper and Herb Cream Cheese

*568 ml (1 pint) single
   cream
568 ml (1 pint) milk
30 ml (2 tbsp) buttermilk
15 ml (1 tbsp) chopped
   fresh mixed herbs, eg.
   parsley, chervil, thyme*

*5 ml (1 level tsp) salt
30 ml (2 level tbsp) black
   peppercorns, coarsely
   crushed*

1 Put the cream and milk
in a saucepan and heat
gently to blood heat or
32–38°C (90–100°F); stir
in the buttermilk. Pour the
mixture into a bowl.

2 Cover the bowl with
cling film and leave it in
a warm place for 24–48
hours until the cream mixture turns to soft curds.
Line a colander with mus-
lin and place it in a sink.

3 Pour the curds into the
colander and drain for
10 minutes. Place the colander on a rack in a large
saucepan, cover with cling
film and chill for a further
18–24 hours.

4 Spoon the curds from
the colander into a
bowl and stir in the mixed
herbs and salt. Pour off the
whey from the saucepan.
Rinse the saucepan.

5 Line a small plastic
punnet or earthenware
cheese mould with a double
layer of damp cheesecloth,
leaving a 5-cm (2-in) overhang. Spoon in the curds
and fold the cheesecloth
over the top.

6 Place on a wire rack in
the large saucepan,
cover tightly with cling film
and chill for 18–24 hours.
Unmould the cheese on to
a plate, discard the cheesecloth and press the pepper
over the cheese.

Spreads

Rillettes de Porc

Colour index
page 18

6 first course
servings

900 g (2 lb) belly or
  shoulder of pork, rinded
  and boned
salt
450 g (1 lb) pork fat
1 clove garlic, skinned and
  bruised

bouquet garni
75 ml (5 tbsp) water.
freshly ground black pepper

To serve:
fresh bay leaves
toasted French bread

1. Rub the meat well with salt and leave it to stand for about 4–6 hours.
2. Cut the meat into strips along the grooves from where the bones were removed and cut the fat into strips. Put the meat and fat into an ovenproof dish with the garlic, bouquet garni and water and season with plenty of pepper. Cover and cook in the oven at 150°C (300°F) mark 2 for about 4 hours.
3. Remove from the oven, discard the bouquet garni and garlic and season the meat well. Strain off and discard the fat. Partly pound the meat then pull it into fine shreds with two forks.
4. Spoon the meat into an earthenware dish, packing it down well. Cover and chill until required.
5. Garnish with fresh bay leaves and serve with toasted French bread.

CHEESE SPREADS

Prepare these cheese spreads the day before they are needed and chill overnight in covered containers to allow the flavours to blend well. Serve them spread on savoury biscuits or bread.

PISTACHIO AND BLUE CHEESE SPREAD: Mix together *225 g (8 oz) crumbled Danish blue cheese, 50 g (2 oz) chopped pistachios* and *37.5 ml (2½ tbsp) milk.* Colour index page 18; 8–10 servings

ANCHOVY AND OLIVE CHEESE SPREAD: Soften *225 g (8 oz) Neufchâtel cheese* and stir in *12 finely chopped pimento-stuffed olives* and *20 ml (4 level tsp) anchovy paste.* 8–10 servings

PEPPERY CHEDDAR CHEESE SPREAD: Stir together *225 g (8 oz) finely grated Cheddar cheese, 60 ml (4 tbsp) mayonnaise* (page 462), *5 ml (1 level tsp) coarsely ground black pepper* and a *pinch of salt.* Colour index page 18; 8–10 servings

HAM AND GRUYERE CHEESE SPREAD: Stir together *100 g (4 oz) cooked ham,* finely chopped, *100 g (4 oz) Gruyère cheese,* finely grated, *100 ml (4 fl oz) soured cream, 30 ml (2 tbsp) chopped parsley, 7.5 ml (½ level tbsp) made mustard* and *1.25 ml (¼ level tsp) salt.* Colour index page 18; 8–10 servings

LAGER AND CHEDDAR CHEESE SPREAD: Stir together *225 g (8 oz) finely grated Cheddar cheese, 75 ml (3 fl oz) lager* or white wine and *1.25 ml (½ level tsp) salt.* 8–10 servings

CHEESE AND PIMENTO SPREAD: Beat together *150 g (5 oz) finely grated Cheddar cheese, 50 g (2 oz) drained, canned pimentos, 30 ml (2 tbsp) milk, 2.5 ml (½ tsp) Worcestershire sauce* and *1.25 ml (¼ level tsp) salt.* 8–10 servings

Dips

Guacamole

Colour index
page 18

Makes 400 ml
(¾ pint)

1 tomato
2 avocados
30 ml (2 tbsp) lemon juice
6.25 ml (1¼ level tsp) salt
½ small onion, skinned and
  finely chopped
1 clove garlic, skinned and
  crushed
2.5–5 ml (½–1 level tsp)
  chilli powder

To serve:
fresh coriander leaves,
  optional
potato crisps

1 Skin and chop the tomato. Cut the avocados in half, remove the stones and peel.

2 Mash the avocado with the lemon juice and stir in the salt, chopped tomato, onion, garlic and chilli powder to taste.

3 Spoon into a bowl. Garnish with coriander leaves if you wish. Serve with potato crisps.

Peppery Mayonnaise Dip

Colour index
page 19

Makes 225 ml
(8 fl oz)

225 ml (8 fl oz)
  mayonnaise, page 462
30 ml (2 tbsp) grated
  onion
10 ml (2 tsp) tarragon
  vinegar
10 ml (2 tsp) chopped
  chives
10 ml (2 tsp) mild chilli
  sauce

2.5 ml (½ level tsp) curry
  powder
2.5 ml (½ level tsp) salt
1.25 ml (¼ level tsp)
  pepper

To serve:
cauliflower florets
carrot sticks

1. Mix together all the ingredients, cover and chill.
2. Spoon the mixture into a bowl, place in the centre of a plate and surround with raw vegetables.

Blue Cheese Dip

Colour index
page 19

Makes 400 ml
(¾ pint)

225 ml (8 fl oz) soured
  cream
75 ml (5 tbsp) milk
100 g (4 oz) Danish blue
  cheese, crumbled

3 dashes Tabasco sauce
2.5 ml (½ tsp)
  Worcestershire sauce

Mix all the ingredients together in a small bowl; cover and chill thoroughly.

Spring Onion Dip

Colour index
page 19

Makes 225 ml
(8 fl oz)

225 ml (8 fl oz) soured
  cream
5 ml (1 level tsp) instant
  beef stock powder

60 ml (4 tbsp) thinly sliced
  spring onions
5 ml (1 tsp) Worcestershire
  sauce

Mix all the ingredients together in a small bowl; cover and chill.

Yogurt and Cream Cheese Dip

Colour index
page 19

Makes 350 ml
(12 fl oz)

225 g (8 oz) cream cheese,
  softened
100 ml (4 fl oz) plain
  yogurt

3.75 ml (¾ level tsp) salt
pinch dried dill weed

Beat the cream cheese until smooth and fluffy, then
gradually beat in the remaining ingredients until
well mixed.

Tuna Dip

Colour index
page 19

Makes 400 ml
(¾ pint)

210-g (7½-oz) can tuna,
  drained
225 ml (8 fl oz)
  mayonnaise, page 462
50-g (2-oz) can anchovy
  fillets, drained
30 ml (2 tbsp) lemon
  juice

1.25 ml (¼ level tsp) salt
pinch pepper
pinch paprika

For the garnish, optional:
15 ml (1 tbsp) capers

1. Put the tuna, mayonnaise, anchovy fillets, lemon
juice and seasoning into a blender and blend to a
smooth purée.
2. Pour the mixture into a bowl; cover and chill.
Garnish with capers if you wish.

Fresh Vegetables with Chilli-tomato Dip

Colour index
page 19

600 ml (1 pint)

798-g (28-oz) can
  tomatoes, drained
1 small onion, skinned
60 ml (4 tbsp) chopped
  parsley
60 ml (4 tbsp) chopped
  mild green chillies
1 clove garlic, skinned
15 ml (1 tbsp) white
  vinegar
5 ml (1 level tsp) dried
  oregano

2.5 ml (½ level tsp) salt

To serve:
1 head celery, washed and
  trimmed
3 courgettes, trimmed
450 g (1 lb) broccoli,
  trimmed
450 g (1 lb) large
  mushrooms

1. Cut the celery and courgettes into sticks. Cut the
broccoli into small florets and halve each mushroom. Wrap the prepared vegetables separately and
chill them.
2. Put all the ingredients for the dip into a blender
and blend until smooth or press through a sieve.
Pour into a small bowl, cover and chill.
3. Just before serving, line a large basket with foil,
place the bowl of dip in the centre of the basket and
surround with the vegetables.

Preparing the vegetables:
Cut the celery and cour-
gettes into sticks, cut the
broccoli into florets and
halve the mushrooms.

Serving the dip: Line a
large basket with foil,
place the dip in the centre
and surround with the
prepared vegetables.

Bagna Cauda

Colour index
page 19

12 first course
servings

400 ml (¾ pint) double
  cream
40 g (1½ oz) butter
1 clove garlic, skinned and
  crushed
50-g (2-oz) can anchovy
  fillets, drained and
  mashed
5 ml (1 level tsp) salt
5 ml (1 level tsp) thyme
5 ml (1 level tsp) dried
  oregano
pinch sugar

To serve:
1 Cos lettuce, washed

1 bunch spring onions,
  trimmed
1 head celery, trimmed and
  washed
6 red or green peppers,
  seeded and quartered
450 g (1 lb) broccoli, cut
  into florets
3 courgettes, cut into
  wedges
450 g (1 lb) mushrooms,
  quartered
450 g (1 lb) small tomatoes
breadsticks

1 Arrange the prepared
vegetables in a large,
shallow dish and place the
dish in a basket. Cover
and chill.

2 Put the cream in a
saucepan, bring to the
boil; simmer, stirring, for
20 minutes, until reduced
to about 300 ml (½ pint).
Remove from heat.

3 Melt the butter, add the
garlic and cook for
1 minute. Stir in the
anchovies, salt, thyme,
oregano and sugar. Cook,
stirring, for 10 minutes.

4 Remove from the heat
and gradually stir in
the hot cream with a wire
whisk until smooth.

5 Pour into a fondue pot
or flameproof dish;
place over a spirit burner.
Serve with chilled vege-
tables and breadsticks.

Hors d'oeuvre variés

A mixed hors d'oeuvre can be one of the most attractive appetisers, with colour and contrasting shapes playing as much part as flavour in the choice of ingredients.

Try to include five or six different dishes. It is usual to include at least one meat and one fish dish, which can be bought ready-made – sliced cooked ham or continental sausage and a canned or pickled fish. Add one or two salads or vegetable dishes (below and right) and perhaps a pickle or relish to add piquancy.

Serve hors d'oeuvre variés in a series of small dishes, or choose a large tray, line it with lettuce leaves and arrange the dishes on the lettuce.

Marinated Green Beans

Colour index page 21

450 g (1 lb) green beans, trimmed
100 g (4 oz) onion, skinned and chopped
100 ml (4 fl oz) olive oil
100 ml (4 fl oz) cider vinegar
50 g (2 oz) sugar
7.5 ml (1½ level tsp) salt

1. Cook the beans in boiling salted water until just tender and drain well.
2. Mix the remaining ingredients and spoon them over the warm beans. Cover and chill.

Marinated Aubergine

Colour index page 21

100 ml (4 fl oz) olive oil
1 aubergine, cubed
2 red peppers, seeded and cut into thin strips
1 small clove garlic, skinned and crushed
50 g (2 oz) onion, skinned and chopped
60 ml (4 tbsp) water
10 ml (2 level tsp) salt
5 ml (1 level tsp) sugar
5 ml (1 level tsp) dried thyme

Heat the oil in a large frying pan and add the remaining ingredients. Cook for about 15 minutes or until the vegetables are tender, stirring from time to time. Spoon the mixture into a dish, cover and chill.

Marinated Tuna and Red Cabbage

Colour index page 21

210-g (7½-oz) can tuna
175 g (6 oz) red cabbage, finely chopped
30 ml (2 tbsp) capers
15 ml (1 tbsp) wine vinegar
1.25 ml (¼ level tsp) salt
pinch coarsely ground black pepper

Flake the tuna in its oil and mix in remaining ingredients. Spoon into a dish. Cover and chill.

Marinated Cauliflower

Colour index page 21

1 large cauliflower
175 ml (6 fl oz) olive oil
100 ml (4 fl oz) cider vinegar
15 ml (1 level tbsp) sugar
15 ml (1 tbsp) chopped parsley
6.25 ml (1¼ level tsp) salt
2.5 ml (½ level tsp) dried basil
pinch pepper

Break the cauliflower into florets and put them in a dish with the remaining ingredients. Mix well, cover and chill, stirring occasionally.

Tiny Pâté-stuffed Tomatoes

Colour index page 20

450 g (1 lb) small tomatoes
156-g (5½-oz) can pâté
30 ml (2 tbsp) soured cream
30 ml (2 tbsp) creamed horseradish
parsley sprigs

1. Cut a thin slice from the top of each tomato; scoop out seeds and flesh. Drain shells upside down.
2. Mix the pâté with the soured cream and horseradish and spoon some of the mixture into each tomato. Chill. Garnish with parsley sprigs.

Herbed Mushrooms

Colour index page 20

225 g (8 oz) button mushrooms
60 ml (4 tbsp) cider vinegar
15 ml (1 tbsp) vegetable oil
3.75 ml (¾ level tsp) dried mixed herbs
3.75 ml (¾ level tsp) sugar
2.5 ml (½ level tsp) salt
50 g (2 oz) canned pimentos, drained and diced

1. Wipe the mushrooms clean with a damp cloth and trim any tough ends from the stems.
2. Mix the remaining ingredients, add the mushrooms and stir together gently until well mixed. Cover and chill for 8–12 hours, stirring occasionally.

Spicy Carrots

Colour index page 20

450 g (1 lb) carrots, peeled
45 ml (3 tbsp) vegetable oil
3 cloves garlic, skinned and finely chopped
15 ml (1 tbsp) chopped onion
60 ml (4 tbsp) vinegar
15 ml (1 tbsp) mixed pickling spice
2.5 ml (½ level tsp) dry mustard
7.5 ml (1½ level tsp) salt
pinch pepper
1 onion, skinned and thinly sliced

1. Cut the carrots diagonally into thin slices. Heat the oil, add the garlic and onion and fry gently for 5 minutes. Add the carrots and vinegar.
2. Tie the pickling spice in a square of muslin and add to the pan with the mustard, salt and pepper. Cover and simmer for about 5 minutes, then discard the muslin bag.
3. Spoon the carrot mixture into a shallow dish and top with the raw onion slices. Cover and chill, stirring occasionally. Discard marinade and onions before serving.

Cocktail Onions

Colour index page 20

700 g (1½ lb) small pickling onions
15 ml (1 tbsp) mixed pickling spice
2.5 ml (½ level tsp) crushed red pepper
400 ml (¾ pint) cider vinegar
100 g (4 oz) sugar
100 ml (4 fl oz) water
7.5 ml (1½ level tsp) salt

1. Skin the onions, leaving a little of the root in place. Tie the pickling spice and crushed red pepper in a square of muslin.
2. Put the onions and spice bag in a saucepan with the remaining ingredients. Bring to the boil; cover and simmer for 10 minutes. Discard spice bag.
3. Spoon the onions and their liquid into a large bowl; cover and chill. Drain the onions and serve them within 1 week.

SOUPS

Some people tend to think of soup exclusively in terms of the first course, or as a light main dish, but soups are far more versatile than that, particularly in winter. For example, a mug of hot soup makes a change as an after-school snack on a cold day. Or you can offer guests a cup of hot soup instead of coffee or tea. On the other hand, a cup of ice-cold fruit soup makes a refreshing dessert after a mid-summer lunch served out of doors.

Most important of all, remember that while many soups may be equally good served hot or cold, none benefit from being served lukewarm. When serving a hot soup the bowls should be warmed beforehand if possible, but if you are planning to serve a cold soup, make sure that the bowls as well as the soup are thoroughly chilled when brought to the table.

The flavours of fish, meat and chicken soups may be enriched and varied by adding small amounts of white wine, sherry, vermouth or lemon juice.

THICKENING SOUPS

Some soups thicken naturally as their ingredients soften and dissolve in cooking. They can then be left as they are, rubbed through a sieve, or puréed in a blender for a smoother texture. But for cream soups a thickener, usually in the form of starch (flour or cornflour) or eggs, is used. In both cases, it is a good idea to add the thickener with the pan off the heat to avoid the danger of lumping (starch) or curdling (eggs). Use flour for soups which are to be served hot. Cornflour, which gives a lighter texture, is sometimes used for cold soups. In a small bowl, blend the flour or cornflour to a smooth, thin paste with a few tablespoons of cold water. Stir some of the hot soup into the cold paste, then stir this into the soup. Bring slowly to the boil, stirring all the time, and simmer gently until it has thickened and any taste of uncooked flour disappears.

If using eggs, beat the whole eggs or yolks together before adding a few tablespoons of the hot soup. When thoroughly blended, pour the mixture into the pan, stirring vigorously. The soup may still be hot enough for the egg mixture to thicken it without further heating, but if not, return the pan to a very low heat and stir the soup constantly until it has thickened. Do not on any account allow it to come to boiling point, or the egg will curdle and spoil the texture of the finished soup.

STORING SOUPS

For short-term storage keep the soup in a covered container in the refrigerator for up to 2 or 3 days. It can be stored in the freezer, but if you plan to freeze it for over a week keep the following tips in mind.

Seasonings are affected by freezing – some become stronger while others lose their potency, so it is always a good idea to keep seasonings mild and leave final adjustments until after thawing. Some ingredients do not freeze well and are best left out until the soup is to be reheated – these include potatoes, which should be cooked separately and added to the soup after thawing. Soup thickened with flour will separate when frozen over a long period, so use cornflour for preference.

To freeze soup, chill it thoroughly, then pour it into a rigid freezer container, leaving 2 cm headspace per litre (½ in per pint) to allow for expansion. Seal tightly and label. Soups can be frozen for up to 3 months.

Soups can either be reheated gently from frozen, or first thawed in the refrigerator, then reheated. If thawing and reheating a thick purée or cream soup, the danger of scorching can be avoided by using a heavy pan over very low heat and stirring occasionally, or by reheating in a double saucepan. A little stock can be used to dilute the soup if it is too thick. This is also the time to enrich a thawed soup with milk, cream or egg yolks, or to add any extra ingredients specified in a particular recipe. Finally, adjust the seasoning before serving the soup.

STOCK SUBSTITUTES

There are numerous ready-made stock substitutes with which you can quickly make a soup, ranging from stock cubes and powders to cans of concentrated consommé. Use these in exactly the same way as your own stocks, but remember that they are often very highly seasoned and that the finished soup may be salty if you are too free with your own additional seasonings – generally, it is wisest to dilute the stock cube with extra water and to leave seasoning until you have checked the final flavour after the soup is cooked.

Beware of making all your soups on the same stock substitute base – the characteristic flavour will predominate in the finished soup and will be instantly recognisable. Choose one with a strength of flavour to match the particular soup you are making.

Stocks

A good rich stock is the foundation of nearly all home-made soups. Few cooks these days will want to maintain a stock pot continually, but it makes sense to use scraps such as a chicken carcass and giblets, or fish trimmings, or the bones from a roast joint with some bacon rinds and fresh vegetables, for occasional stock making. Any of these stocks will keep for 2 or 3 days in the refrigerator and if boiled up every other day can be kept for a week or more. In the freezer, of course, they will keep much longer and make a convenient stand-by. A pressure cooker helps reduce cooking times.

Basic Bone Stock

Makes about
1.1 litres
(2 pints)

900 g (2 lb) meat bones,
fresh or from cooked
meat, chopped
2 litres (3½ pints) water
2 onions, skinned and
chopped
2 sticks celery, washed
and chopped

2 carrots, peeled and
chopped
5 ml (1 level tsp) salt
3 peppercorns
bouquet garni

1. Put the bones in a large saucepan and add the cold water. Bring to the boil and remove any scum that forms with a slotted spoon.
2. Add the remaining ingredients.
3. Bring the stock back to the boil, cover tightly and simmer for 5–6 hours.
4. Strain the stock and when cold remove all traces of fat with a spoon or kitchen paper towel.

PRESSURE COOKER METHOD
1. Follow steps 1–2 as above, using the pressure cooker instead of a saucepan, but reduce the amount of cold water to 1.4 litres (2½ pints), or 1.7 litres (3 pints) if you are using marrow bones.
2. Bring to high (15 lb) pressure and cook for 1–1¼ hours, or 2 hours if you are using marrow bones. Reduce pressure at room temperature.
3. After cooking finish as above.

White Stock

Makes about
1.7 litres
(3 pints)

900 g (2 lb) knuckle of
veal, chopped
2.3 litres (4 pints) water
little lemon juice

1 onion, skinned and sliced
2 carrots, peeled and sliced
bouquet garni
5 ml (1 level tsp) salt

1. Put the bones in a large saucepan. Add the water and lemon juice and bring to the boil. Remove any scum that rises with a slotted spoon.
2. Add the remaining ingredients.
3. Bring the stock back to the boil, cover tightly and simmer for 5–6 hours.
4. Strain the stock and when cold remove all traces of fat with a spoon or kitchen paper towel.

PRESSURE COOKER METHOD
1. Follow steps 1–2 as above, using the pressure cooker instead of a saucepan, but reduce the amount of cold water to 1.4 litres (2½ pints).
2. Bring to high (15 lb) pressure and cook for 1–1¼ hours. Reduce pressure at room temperature.
3. After cooking finish as above.

Brown Stock

Makes about
1.4 litres
(2½ pints)

450 g (1 lb) marrow bones
or knuckle of veal,
chopped
450 g (1 lb) shin of beef,
cut into pieces
1.7 litres (3 pints) cold
water
1 carrot, peeled and
sliced

1 onion, skinned and
sliced
1 stick celery, washed and
trimmed
bouquet garni
2.5 ml (½ level tsp) salt

1. Brown the bones and meat in the oven to give a good flavour and colour to the stock (the exact temperature is not important).
2. Put the bones in a large saucepan with the water and remaining ingredients. Bring to the boil and remove any scum.
3. Cover and simmer for 5–6 hours.
4. Strain and when cold remove all traces of fat with a spoon or kitchen paper towel.

PRESSURE COOKER METHOD
1. Follow steps 1–2 as above, using the pressure cooker instead of a saucepan, but reduce the amount of cold water to 1.4 litres (2½ pints).
2. Bring to high (15 lb) pressure and cook for 1–1¼ hours. Reduce pressure at room temperature.
3. After cooking finish as above.

Chicken Stock

Makes about
1.1–1.4 litres
(2–2½ pints)

carcass, bones and scraps
from a carved roast
chicken
1.4–1.7 litres (2½–3 pints)
cold water

1 small onion, skinned and
sliced
2 carrots, peeled and sliced
bouquet garni

1. Break down the carcass and bones of the chicken and put them in a large saucepan with any skin and meat attached to the carcass.
2. Add the water and remaining ingredients.
3. Cover and simmer for 3 hours. Strain and when cold remove all traces of fat.

PRESSURE COOKER METHOD
1. Follow steps 1–2 as above, using the pressure cooker instead of a saucepan, but reduce the amount of cold water to 1.1 litres (2 pints).
2. Bring to high (15 lb) pressure and cook for 45–60 minutes. Reduce pressure at room temperature.
3. After cooking finish as above.

Fish Stock

Makes about
900 ml
(1½ pints)

1 cod's head or fish bones
and trimmings
900 ml (1½ pints) cold
water

salt
bouquet garni
1 onion, skinned and sliced

1. Clean the cod's head or wash the fish trimmings.
2. Put them in a large saucepan, cover with the measured cold water and add a little salt.
3. Bring to the boil and remove any scum.
4. Reduce the heat and add the bouquet garni and onion. Cover, simmer for 20 minutes and strain. Use on the same day or store, covered, in the refrigerator for no longer than 2 days.

First course soups

A first course soup should stimulate the appetite without satisfying it, creating enthusiasm for what is to follow. For this reason, the soup course should always be planned along with the other dishes in the menu. Avoid repeating flavours, textures, even colours if possible. For example, gazpacho is scarcely the best prelude to a main dish dressed with tomato sauce, though its sharp, refreshing flavour may be just the right start for a meal centred around a creamy main course.

Many chilled soups are also delicious hot and if the weather changes unexpectedly you can act accordingly. But leave final seasoning adjustments until you have decided how the soup is to be served. The balance of flavours alters quite noticeably depending on whether it is hot or chilled. As a general rule, chilling will reduce the intensity of flavour.

For a first course serving, allow about 150–200 ml (¼ -⅓ pint) soup for each person.

Chilled Cucumber Soup

Colour index
page 25

6 servings

50 g (2 oz) butter or margarine
100 g (4 oz) spring onions, trimmed and chopped
450 g (1 lb) cucumber, peeled and chopped
25 g (1 oz) plain flour

1 litre (1¾ pints) chicken stock
salt and pepper
100 ml (4 fl oz) single cream or top of the milk
cucumber slices

1 Melt the fat in a frying pan, add the spring onions and cucumber and cook until the onions are tender. Stir in the flour.

2 Gradually add the chicken stock and bring to the boil, stirring until the sauce thickens. Season to taste with salt and pepper.

3 Reduce the heat, cover and simmer for 10 minutes, stirring occasionally. Cool quickly and chill.

4 When the mixture is well chilled, purée it a little at a time in a blender.

5 When smooth, sieve the soup into a large bowl, to remove all the seeds from the cucumber.

6 Stir in the cream and check the seasoning. Serve in a chilled tureen, garnished with cucumber.

Gazpacho

Colour index
page 25

4–6 servings

1 medium cucumber
450 g (1 lb) tomatoes
100 g (4 oz) green peppers, seeded
50–100g (2–4 oz) onions, skinned
1 clove garlic, skinned
45 ml (3 tbsp) oil
45 ml (3 tbsp) wine vinegar

425-g (15-oz) can tomato juice
30 ml (2 level tbsp) tomato paste
1.25 ml (¼ level tsp) salt

To serve:
cucumber sticks

1. Wash and roughly chop the cucumber, tomatoes, peppers, onions and garlic.
2. Mix the chopped vegetables with the remaining ingredients in a large bowl.
3. Purée the mixture in small amounts in a blender, or rub through a sieve.
4. Return the purée to the bowl. Serve chilled, accompanied with cucumber sticks.

Jellied Consommé

Colour index
page 25

4–6 servings

1.1 litres (2 pints) brown stock, cold
100 g (4 oz) lean shin of beef, shredded
150 ml (¼ pint) cold water
1 carrot, peeled and quartered
1 small onion, skinned and quartered
bouquet garni

1 egg white
salt
10 ml (2 tsp) dry sherry, optional

For the garnish:
seedless grapes
chopped onion

1. Remove any fat from the stock with a spoon.
2. Soak the meat in the water for 15 minutes.
3. Put the meat and water, stock, vegetables and bouquet garni in a large saucepan. Finally, add the egg white to the mixture.
4. Heat the soup gently, whisking continuously until a thick froth begins to form. Stop whisking and bring to the boil.
5. Reduce the heat immediately, cover and simmer for 2 hours. Do not boil the liquid too rapidly, or the froth will break and cloud the consommé.
6. Pour the soup through a scalded clean cloth or jelly bag into a bowl, keeping the froth back with a spoon. Then let the froth slide out on to the cloth and filter the soup again, this time through the egg white as well as the cloth.
7. Add salt to taste and, if you like, a little sherry. Leave the soup to cool and set.
8. Serve the consommé broken up, in individual dishes, and garnish with grapes and a little onion.

First course soups

Chicken and Rice Soup

Colour index page 25

4–6 servings

1.1 litres (2 pints) chicken stock
50 g (2 oz) long grain rice
salt and freshly ground pepper

2 egg yolks, beaten
juice of 1 lemon

For the garnish:
lemon slices

1. Bring the stock to the boil, add the rice and seasoning and cook until just tender.
2. Remove from the heat and allow to cool slightly.
3. Pour the stock and rice over the egg yolks, gently whisking all the time.
4. Add the lemon juice and serve at once, garnished with lemon slices.

Crème Vichyssoise

Colour index page 25

4–6 servings

50 g (2 oz) butter
4 leeks, sliced and washed
1 onion, skinned and sliced
1 litre (1¾ pints) white stock
2 potatoes, peeled and thinly sliced

salt
freshly ground pepper
200 ml (7 fl oz) cream

For the garnish:
chopped chives

1. Melt the butter in a large saucepan and sauté the sliced leeks and onion for about 10 minutes, until soft but not coloured.
2. Add the stock and potatoes. Season, cover and cook until the vegetables are soft.
3. Purée the soup in a blender or rub it through a fine meshed sieve into a large bowl.
4. Stir in the cream, check the seasoning, adding salt and pepper if necessary. Pour the soup into a large tureen or individual bowls and chill.
5. Sprinkle with chives before serving.

Cream of Green Pea Soup

Colour index page 25

4–6 servings

1 small onion, skinned and chopped
25 g (1 oz) butter
400 ml (¾ pint) white stock
900 g (2 lb) peas, shelled or 450 g (1 lb) frozen peas
600 ml (1 pint) béchamel sauce, pouring consistency, page 461

30 ml (2 tbsp) single cream or creamy milk
pinch sugar
salt
pepper

For the garnish, optional:
mint sprigs

1. Sauté the onion in the butter for about 5 minutes, until soft but not coloured. Gradually add the white stock and bring to the boil.
2. Reserve a few peas for the garnish. Add the rest of the peas to the soup. Cover and cook until soft (20–30 minutes for shelled peas, or as directed on the packet for frozen peas).
3. Purée the soup in a blender or rub it through a sieve. Add it to the béchamel sauce and heat through gently, stirring until evenly blended.
4. Stir in the cream. Add the sugar and adjust seasoning if necessary.
5. For the garnish, either chop the mint finely or cook the reserved peas with the sprig of mint until just tender and drain well. Sprinkle the mint or peas over the soup just before serving.

French Onion Soup

Colour index page 25

4–6 servings

50 g (2 oz) butter
225 g (8 oz) onions, skinned and sliced
30 ml (2 level tbsp) plain flour
900 ml (1½ pints) brown stock
salt and pepper
bay leaf
French bread
Gruyère cheese, sliced or grated

1 Melt the butter in a large saucepan and fry the onions for 5–10 minutes, until browned.

2 Stir in the flour, mixing well. Cook, stirring, for 1–2 minutes.

3 Pour in the stock gradually. Season, add the bay leaf and bring to the boil. Cover and simmer for 30 minutes.

4 Cut the French loaf into diagonal slices about 1 cm (½ in) thick and toast them lightly on both sides.

5 Ladle the soup into individual ovenproof soup bowls, removing the bay leaf. Place a slice of toasted French bread in each soup bowl to float on top of the soup.

6 Cover each slice of bread with a slice of Gruyère cheese, folded in half, or with a thick layer of grated cheese.

7 Stand the bowls on a baking sheet or in a roasting tin and put in the hot oven or under the grill until the cheese is melted.

Cream of Mushroom Soup

Colour index
page 25

4–6 servings

225 g (8 oz) button
    mushrooms
75 g (3 oz) butter
175 g (6 oz) onions,
    skinned and chopped
40 g (1½ oz) plain flour
900 ml (1½ pints) chicken
    stock
300 ml (½ pint) milk
salt and pepper
pinch garlic salt
lemon juice

To serve, optional:
croûtons, right

1 Remove the stalks from the mushrooms and cut off the tough ends. Slice the mushroom caps thinly.

2 Melt the butter in a large saucepan and sauté the sliced mushroom caps until they are just tender. Remove from the pan with a slotted spoon and reserve.

3 In remaining butter sauté mushroom stalks and onion until tender. Stir in the flour and cook for 3 minutes, continuing to stir.

4 Slowly add the stock, stirring all the time. Bring to the boil and simmer gently for 20 minutes, until the vegetables are soft.

5 Purée the cooled mixture in a blender, or rub through a sieve with a wooden spoon until smooth. Return mixture to the saucepan.

6 Add the milk, salt and pepper, garlic salt and lemon juice to taste. Simmer for 10 minutes, but do not allow to boil.

7 Return the reserved mushroom slices to the soup and heat through. Serve immediately, with croûtons if you wish.

SOUP GARNISHES

A well chosen garnish such as a sprinkling of finely chopped parsley or egg, a slice of lemon or a few paper-thin slices of cucumber can turn an otherwise ordinary, everyday soup into something quite special. A more decorative garnish is a tablespoon of cream or soured cream swirled lightly into each bowl to marble the surface, or a few flaked almonds sprinkled over the soup just before serving.

HARD-BOILED EGG

LEMON SLICES

MEATBALLS

CROUTONS

CAULIFLOWER

CREAM OR SOURED CREAM

CARROT OR CELERY MATCHSTICKS

GRATED CHEESE

CHOPPED BACON

FLAKED ALMONDS

Croûtons should be passed around in a separate bowl to be added to each bowl of soup at the last moment; otherwise they may go soggy. Use any bread which is on the stale side.

Trim the crusts off the bread slices and cut them into 0.5–1-cm (¼–½-in) cubes.

Fry in oil, butter and oil, bacon fat or lard, until crisp and golden. Keep stirring the croûtons while they are frying.

Fish soups

A smooth creamy bisque is perhaps the most luxurious of soups, a perfect start to a special dinner. Other fish soups, especially chowders, lend themselves to less formal occasions, less extravagant budgets. Canned or frozen fish can often be used, with very good results, when fresh fish is not available or too expensive.

Lobster Bisque

Colour index page 25

4–6 servings

1 hen lobster, cooked
1 small carrot, peeled and
   sliced
1 small onion, skinned and
   sliced
1 litre (1³/₄ pints) fish stock
   or water
bay leaf
parsley sprig
salt and pepper

25 g (1 oz) butter
45 ml (3 level tbsp) plain
   flour
squeeze lemon juice
little cream
¹/₂ glass white wine

For the lobster butter:
coral from lobster, butter,
   pepper

1. Scrub the lobster shell thoroughly. Cut the lobster in half and detach the tail meat. Crack the claws and remove the meat (page 168).
2. Cut the meat into neat pieces and reserve the coral for the lobster butter. Break up the shell.
3. Put the lobster shell and vegetables in a saucepan with the stock, herbs and seasoning, cover and cook for ³/₄–1 hour. Strain off the liquid.
4. To make the lobster butter, wash the cooked coral and dry it in a cool oven, without allowing it to change colour. Pound it in a mortar with double its weight in butter. Season to taste with salt and pepper and rub the mixture through a fine sieve.
5. Melt the 25 g (1 oz) butter, stir in the flour and cook for 2–3 minutes. Remove from the heat and stir in the lobster stock. Bring to the boil and cook until it thickens, stirring. Cook for 3 minutes.
6. Remove from the heat and add the lemon juice, cream and wine. Check the seasoning. Add the pieces of lobster meat and whisk in the lobster butter until it has blended into the soup.

Prawn Soup

Colour index page 26

4–6 servings

450 g (1 lb) shelled prawns
1 onion, skinned and
   chopped
900 ml (1¹/₂ pints) water
grated rind and juice of
   1 lemon
pinch dried mixed herbs

50 g (2 oz) butter
25 g (1 oz) plain flour
little grated nutmeg
salt and pepper
3 egg yolks
150 ml (¹/₄ pint) single
   cream

1. Chop the prawns roughly.
2. Put them in a saucepan with the onion, water, lemon rind and herbs. Simmer for about 5 minutes and strain. Reserve the stock.
3. Melt the butter in a separate pan, add the flour and cook for 2–3 minutes, stirring. Gradually add the stock and bring to the boil, still stirring. Season with nutmeg, salt and pepper.
4. Stir in the lemon juice, prawns and onion and cook for 2–3 minutes. Remove from the heat.
5. Beat the egg yolks and cream together and mix with 30–45 ml (2–3 tbsp) of the soup. Return to the pan and heat through, but do not boil.

Fish Chowder

Colour index page 26

4–6 servings

450 g (1 lb) fresh haddock
knob of butter
1 onion, skinned and sliced
2 bacon rashers, rinded and
   chopped
3 potatoes, peeled and
   sliced

425-g (15-oz) can tomatoes
600 ml (1 pint) fish stock
salt and pepper
bay leaf
2 cloves

1. Skin the haddock and cut it into cubes.
2. Melt the butter and sauté the onion and bacon for 5 minutes. Add the potatoes and the fish.
3. Sieve the tomatoes with their juice and add the purée to the fish stock. Stir into the fish mixture and add the seasoning and flavourings.
4. Cover and simmer for 30 minutes, until the fish is soft but holds its shape. Remove bay leaf and cloves.

Curried Cod Chowder

Colour index page 26

4–6 servings

700 g (1¹/₂ lb) cod fillet
900 ml (1¹/₂ pints) cold
   water
salt and pepper
225 g (8 oz) potatoes,
   peeled and diced
50 g (2 oz) butter
175 g (6 oz) onions,
   skinned and chopped
175 g (6 oz) celery, washed
   and chopped

2.5 ml (¹/₂ level tsp) mild
   curry powder
45 ml (3 level tbsp) plain
   flour
300 ml (¹/₂ pint) creamy
   milk
bay leaf

For the garnish:
chopped parsley
chives

1. Wipe the fish with a damp cloth. Put it in a large saucepan, pour over the cold water and season. Bring it almost to the boil, remove from the heat and skim off the surface froth.
2. Using a fish slice, lift out the fish carefully and cool on a plate. Strain stock and reserve.
3. Remove the skin and bones and flake the fish into bite-sized pieces. Set aside.
4. Bring the potatoes to the boil in salted water and cook until tender. Drain and reserve.
5. Melt the butter and sauté the onions and celery until soft. Add the curry powder and flour and gradually stir in the fish stock and milk; add the bay leaf. Bring to the boil and cook for 2–3 minutes.
6. Reduce the heat to a simmer and add the potato and the fish pieces. Finally, check the seasoning.
7. Garnish with chopped parsley and chives.

Prawn Chowder

Colour index page 26

4–6 servings

knob of butter
1 large onion, skinned and
   sliced
200 ml (7 fl oz) boiling
   water
3 medium potatoes, peeled
   and diced
salt and pepper

225 g (8 oz) shelled
   prawns
568 ml (1 pint) milk
50 g (2 oz) cheese, grated

For the garnish:
chopped parsley

1. Melt the butter and sauté the onion for about 5 minutes, until soft but not coloured.
2. Add the boiling water, potatoes and seasoning. Cover and simmer gently for 15–20 minutes, or until the potatoes are just cooked.
3. Add the prawns and milk, heat through and stir in the cheese. Garnish with chopped parsley.

Fruit soups

Fruit soups make an unusual and refreshing first course or dessert for a summer meal. Most of them are purées, sweetened and diluted with wine, fruit juice or iced water. They can be made in minutes, using a blender or sieve, and involve little or no cooking.

Strawberry and Rhubarb Soup

Colour index
page 99

4–6 servings

275 g (10 oz) strawberries,
   hulled
450 g (1 lb) rhubarb
300 ml (½ pint) fresh
   orange juice
about 100 g (4 oz) sugar
1 orange

1 Slice the strawberries and set aside 4–6 of the best slices for garnishing.

2 Trim the rhubarb and cut the stalks into small bite-sized chunks.

3 Put the fruit and orange juice in a saucepan and heat to boiling. Simmer uncovered for 1 minute.

4 Remove the pan from the heat, cool and stir in the sugar to taste.

5 Purée soup half at a time in blender; sieve to remove seeds. Pour into bowl.

6 Peel the orange; chop the flesh. Add it to the soup. Cover and chill.

7 Serve in chilled bowls, garnished with remaining strawberry slices.

Strawberry Soup

Colour index
page 99

4–6 servings

450 g (1 lb) strawberries,
   hulled
175 ml (6 fl oz) white wine
45 ml (3 tbsp) lemon juice

100 g (4 oz) sugar
15 ml (1 level tbsp) grated
   lemon rind

1. Reserve 6 strawberries for the garnish. Purée remaining ingredients in a blender and sieve to remove seeds, or rub through a sieve until smooth.
2. Transfer the soup to a large serving bowl, cover and chill until required.
3. Slice reserved strawberries and use to garnish soup.

Cold Raspberry Soup

Colour index
page 99

6 servings

1.1 kg (2½ lb) fresh or
   frozen and thawed
   raspberries
400 ml (¾ pint) port or
   sweet sherry
25–50 g (1–2 oz) sugar
4 short sticks cinnamon

10 ml (2 level tsp) cornflour
100 ml (4 fl oz) water

For the garnish, optional:
   whipped cream or soured
   cream

1. Put the raspberries, port or sherry, sugar and cinnamon sticks in a large saucepan. Bring to the boil, reduce heat and simmer gently for 10 minutes.
2. Remove the cinnamon sticks and rub the mixture through a sieve to remove the seeds.
3. Blend the cornflour and water and slowly stir into the soup. Cook until thickened, stirring all the time. Cool and refrigerate. If you wish, serve with whipped or soured cream swirled through the soup.

Red Cherry Soup

Colour index
page 99

4–6 servings

450 g (1 lb) cherries
1.1 litres (2 pints) water
15 ml (1 level tbsp)
   cornflour
25 g (1 oz) sugar

lemon juice
a little red wine, optional

For the garnish, optional:
   whipped cream, mint leaves

1. Wash and stem the cherries. Stone a few for the garnish and reserve them. Put the remainder in a saucepan with the water and simmer until tender.
2. Rub the cooked fruit and water through a sieve and reheat to boiling point.
3. Mix the cornflour and sugar with a little water, add to the soup and cook for a further 10 minutes.
4. Add the stoned cherries, lemon juice and, if you wish, a little red wine. Cool. Garnish with cream and mint leaves if you wish.

Blackcurrant Soup

Colour index
page 99

6 servings

700 g (1½ lb)
   blackcurrants
1.4 litres (2½ pints) water
15 g (½ oz) cornflour

100 g (4 oz) sugar
10 ml (2 tsp) lemon juice
30 ml (2 tbsp) white wine
lemon slices, optional

1. Wash and top and tail blackcurrants. Put into a pan with the water and simmer until tender.
2. Rub blackcurrants and water through a sieve, return to the pan and reheat to boiling point.
3. Mix cornflour and sugar with a little water, slowly stir into the soup and cook for a further 10 minutes until thickened. Add the lemon juice and wine to the soup. Refrigerate until required. If you wish, serve garnished with lemon slices.

Main dish soups

Some soups contain such a large quantity of vegetables, meat or fish that they make a substantial meal in themselves. They make a good informal lunch or family supper, served in larger portions than a first course soup with crusty bread and butter, and with a salad or crisp fresh vegetables to complete the menu.

Many of the soup recipes in this section are based on traditional European dishes, originally contrived to make use of commonly available ingredients and as a means of using up leftovers from other meals. If a particular ingredient is not available, it is often possible to find an alternative with a similar flavour and texture.

Beef and Beetroot Soup

Colour index
page 27

4 servings

700 ml (1¼ pints) hot water
450 g (1 lb) shin of beef, cut into 2.5-cm (1-in) chunks
3 beetroots, skinned
2 carrots, peeled and sliced
1 onion, skinned and sliced
1 stick celery, washed and cut into chunks

bay leaf
5–10 ml (1–2 level tsp) salt
75 ml (5 level tbsp) tomato paste
7.5 ml (1½ level tsp) sugar
½ small head cabbage, shredded
15 ml (1 tbsp) cider vinegar
100 ml (4 fl oz) soured cream

1 Put the water, beef, 2 sliced beetroots, carrots, onion, celery, bay leaf and half the salt in a large saucepan. Heat to boiling, cover and simmer for 2 hours.

2 Grate the remaining beetroot and add to the soup with the tomato paste, sugar and the remaining salt.

3 Cover and simmer for 20 minutes. Remove from the heat and discard the bay leaf. Cool.

4 Refrigerate until about 20 minutes before serving, then remove the hardened fat from the soup.

5 Return the pan to the heat and bring to the boil. Add the cabbage and cook for about 10 minutes.

6 Stir in the vinegar and serve in wide soup bowls, garnishing with swirls of soured cream.

German Lentil Soup

Colour index
page 26

4–6 servings

3 rashers streaky bacon, rinded and diced
1 large onion, skinned and sliced
1 large carrot, peeled and sliced
75 g (3 oz) celery, washed and sliced
1 ham bone, soaked overnight
350 g (12 oz) lentils, soaked overnight

5 ml (1 level tsp) salt
1.25 ml (¼ level tsp) pepper
2.5 ml (½ level tsp) dried thyme
2 bay leaves
1.4 litres (2½ pints) hot water
15 ml (1 tbsp) lemon juice

1. In a large saucepan, fry the bacon in its own fat until lightly browned. Remove and drain on kitchen paper towel. Fry the sliced vegetables in the same fat for about 5 minutes, until the onion is tender.
2. Return the bacon to the pan and add the ham bone, lentils, seasonings, herbs and water. Cover and bring to the boil; reduce heat and simmer for about 1 hour, until the lentils are tender. Remove and discard the bay leaves.
3. Remove the ham bone and allow to cool slightly. Cut off any meat and add it to the soup.
4. Add the lemon juice and check the seasoning.

Old Fashioned Beef and Vegetable Soup

Colour index
page 27

4–6 servings

30 ml (2 tbsp) vegetable oil or melted dripping
700 g (1½ lb) stewing beef, cut into chunks
1 small onion, skinned and finely chopped
2 sticks celery, washed and sliced
1 large carrot, peeled and sliced
½ small head cabbage, shredded
1 courgette, thickly sliced
4 medium potatoes, peeled

700 ml (1¼ pints) water
396-g (14-oz) can tomatoes
225 g (8 oz) frozen or canned green beans
225 g (8 oz) frozen or canned broad beans
1 beef stock cube, crumbled
10 ml (2 level tsp) salt
2.5 ml (½ level tsp) pepper
2.5 ml (½ level tsp) basil

1. Heat the oil in a very large saucepan, add the beef and fry for 5 minutes until brown.
2. Add the onion, celery, carrot, cabbage and courgette and fry for about 10 minutes until the vegetables are lightly browned, stirring frequently.
3. Meanwhile, grate one of the potatoes and cut the remainder into 2.5-cm (1-in) cubes. Add the grated potato to the fried beef and vegetables, together with the water and the tomatoes.
4. Bring the soup to the boil. Reduce the heat, cover, simmer for 1 hour. Add the remaining ingredients and simmer for a further 25–30 minutes, until potatoes are tender.

Split Pea Soup

*1 leftover ham bone with
  meat scraps*
*450 g (1 lb) dried split
  peas, soaked overnight*
*2 carrots, peeled and thinly
  sliced*
*1 medium onion, skinned
  and chopped*
1.6 litres (2¾ pints) water
6 whole allspice berries
12 black peppercorns
bay leaf
salt

Colour index
page 27

4–6 servings

1 Put the ham bone, peas
and their soaking liquid,
carrots, onion and water in
a pan. Bring to the boil.

2 Tie the allspice, peppercorns and bay leaf in a
piece of muslin.

3 Add to the pan. Reduce
the heat, cover and sim-
mer for about 1 hour.
Discard herbs; season.

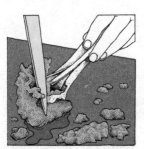

4 Remove the bone, cut
off any meat and cut it
into bite-sized pieces.

5 Return the meat to the
soup and discard the
bone. Heat through.

SOUP ACCOMPANIMENTS

Make a soup into a main dish by serving it with a salad or
sticks of crisp fresh vegetables such as celery or carrot. Pass
crusty bread, melba toast, crispbread or rolls and butter as
well. Making your own melba toast is a good way of using up
slightly stale bread: follow the instructions given below.

Melba toast: Cut 0.5-cm (¼-in)
slices of bread or use ready cut
thin-sliced bread. Cut off the
crusts and halve diagonally if
you wish. Toast the bread, split
slices through the middle and
toast the uncooked surfaces
until slices are crisp and brown.

Minestrone

Colour index
page 27

4–6 servings

*1 stick celery, washed and
  trimmed*
3 runner beans
1 carrot, peeled
1 turnip, peeled
½ leek
¼ cabbage
1 onion, skinned
1 clove garlic, skinned
25 g (1 oz) butter
1 litre (1¾ pints) stock
*45 ml (3 tbsp) short-cut
  macaroni*

45 ml (3 tbsp) frozen peas
*5 ml (1 level tsp) tomato
  paste or 4 tomatoes,
  skinned and diced*
*1–2 rashers bacon, rinded,
  chopped and fried*
salt and pepper

To serve:
grated Parmesan cheese

1. Thinly slice the celery and runner beans, and cut
the carrot and turnip into thin strips. Shred and
wash the leek and cabbage. Chop the onion finely
and crush the garlic.
2. Melt the butter and sauté the leek, onion and
garlic for 5–10 minutes until soft.
3. Add the stock, bring to the boil and add the
carrot, turnip, celery and macaroni. Simmer,
covered, for 20–30 minutes.
4. Add the cabbage, beans and peas. Cover and
simmer for a further 20 minutes.
5. Stir in the tomato paste (or tomatoes) and bacon.
Season to taste and bring back to the boil.
6. Serve with the grated Parmesan cheese in a
separate dish, for each person to help himself.

Goulash Soup

Colour index
page 26

4–6 servings

*700 g (1½ lb) silverside
  or lean chuck
  steak*
*10 ml (2 level tsp) salt
pepper*
25 g (1 oz) butter
*225 g (8 oz) onions,
  skinned and
  chopped*
*1 small green pepper,
  seeded and chopped*
*4 tomatoes, skinned
  and quartered*
*141-g (5-oz) can tomato
  paste*

*600 ml (1 pint) rich beef
  stock*
*15 ml (1 level tbsp)
  paprika*
*450 g (1 lb) potatoes,
  peeled*
*150 ml (¼ pint) soured
  cream*

For the garnish, optional:
chopped parsley

1. Wipe the meat with a damp cloth. Remove any
excess fat or gristle and cut the meat into small
pieces. Season well.
2. Melt the butter in a large saucepan, add the
onions and green pepper and sauté until tender.
3. Add the meat pieces, tomatoes, tomato paste,
stock and paprika. Stir well and bring to the boil.
4. Reduce the heat, cover and simmer for 2½ hours,
stirring occasionally.
5. Half an hour before the end of cooking, cut the
potatoes into bite-sized pieces, bring to the boil in
salted water and simmer until cooked. Drain well
and add to the soup.
6. Check the seasoning and stir in 30 ml (2 tbsp) of
the soured cream.
7. Garnish with chopped parsley if you wish and
serve the remaining soured cream separately, for
each person to spoon into their soup.

Main dish soups

Mulligatawny Soup

Colour index
page 27

4–6 servings

*3 rashers streaky bacon
550 g (1¼ lb) chicken
  portions
600 ml (1 pint) chicken
  stock
1 carrot, peeled and sliced
1 stick celery, washed
  and chopped
1 apple, chopped
10 ml (2 level tsp) curry
  powder
4 peppercorns, crushed
1 clove
bay leaf
15 ml (1 level tbsp) flour
150 ml (¼ pint) milk*

*To serve: 50 g (2 oz) long
grain rice, cooked*

1 Remove and discard the bacon rind; chop the bacon into small pieces and fry it in a large pan until the fat begins to run. Do not allow the bacon to become brown.

2 Add the chicken and brown well. Drain the meat on kitchen paper towel and pour off the fat.

3 Return the bacon and chicken to the pan and add the chicken stock and next seven ingredients.

4 Cover the pan and simmer for about 30 minutes or until the chicken is tender. Remove chicken and allow to cool slightly.

5 Cut off the meat and return it to the soup. Discard clove and bay leaf. Heat the soup gently.

6 Mix the flour with a little cold water. Add to soup with milk. Reheat without boiling.

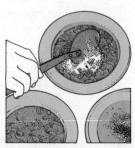

7 Ladle the soup into wide bowls, spoon a mound of rice into each one and serve immediately.

Chicken Soup with Dumplings

Colour index
page 26

4–6 servings

*1.1–1.4-kg (2½–3-lb)
  oven-ready chicken,
  skinned
1 medium onion, skinned
  and chopped
1 litre (1¾ pints) chicken
  stock
350 g (12 oz) carrots,
  peeled and sliced
1.25 ml (¼ level tsp)
  pepper
15 ml (1 level tbsp) salt*

*100 g (4 oz) celery with
  leaves, chopped*

*For the dumplings:
100 g (4 oz) self raising
  flour
50 g (2 oz) shredded suet
2.5 ml (½ level tsp) salt
water*

1. Put the chicken, onion, stock, carrots, pepper and salt into a large saucepan and bring to the boil. Reduce the heat, cover and simmer for about 1 hour, until the chicken is tender. Remove chicken; cool.
2. Mix together the flour, suet, salt and sufficient water to make a soft dough. Shape with your hands into 16 small dumplings.
3. Add the dumplings and celery to the simmering soup. Cook gently for about 20 minutes.
4. Carve the chicken off the bones and cut into small chunks. Stir into the soup and heat through.

Making the dough: Mix together the flour, suet and salt with enough water to give a soft dough.

Shaping the dumplings: Use your hands to shape the dough into 16 small, even-sized dumplings.

Creamy Cheddar Cheese Soup

Colour index
page 27

4–6 servings

*50 g (2 oz) butter or
  margarine
1 medium onion, skinned
  and chopped
50 g (2 oz) plain flour
700 ml (1¼ pints) chicken
  stock
700 ml (1¼ pints) milk
450 g (1 lb) Cheddar
  cheese, grated*

*2.5 ml (½ level tsp) salt
freshly ground white
  pepper*

*For the garnish:
3 slices pumpernickel
  bread, toasted and
  cubed*

1. Melt the fat in a large saucepan, add the onion and cook for about 5 minutes until soft and transparent, stirring occasionally.
2. Stir in the flour and cook for a few minutes. Gradually add the chicken stock and cook until slightly thickened, stirring all the time. Add the milk and bring to the boil, still stirring.
3. Purée the mixture a little at a time in a blender or rub through a sieve. When smooth, return to the saucepan and bring back to the boil.
4. Reduce the heat and stir in the cheese and seasoning. Heat gently just until the cheese has melted.
5. Serve with toasted pumpernickel cubes.

Haricot Bean and Bacon Soup

Colour index
page 27
4–6 servings

*350 g (12 oz) dried haricot
  beans, washed to remove
  grit*
*350 g (12 oz) streaky
  bacon, rinded*
*2 medium onions, skinned
  and chopped*
*2 sticks celery, washed and
  chopped*
*1.4 litres (2½ pints)
  water*
bay leaf
*3 chicken stock cubes,
  crumbled*
*1.25 ml (¼ level tsp)
  pepper*
pinch ground cloves
*396-g (14-oz) can
  tomatoes*

1 Soak the beans for 12 hours or overnight in enough cold water to cover.

2 Chop the bacon finely and fry it in its own fat until golden brown, stirring occasionally. Spoon off all but 60 ml (4 tbsp) fat from the pan and discard the surplus.

3 Add the onions and celery and cook them for about 10 minutes or until just tender, stirring occasionally.

4 Put the beans, soaking water and vegetable mixture in a large saucepan. Add the water, bay leaf, stock cubes, pepper and cloves, cover and simmer for 1½–2 hours.

5 Stir in the canned tomatoes with their juice, breaking the tomatoes into small pieces as you do so. Heat through the mixture just until it is gently simmering again.

6 Cover and cook for a further 30 minutes, stirring occasionally, until the beans are very tender and the soup has thickened. Remove the bay leaf and serve immediately.

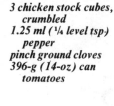

Bouillabaisse

Colour index
page 26
4–6 servings

*900 g (2 lb) mixed fish, eg.
  whiting, mackerel, bass,
  crab, prawns or eel*
*2–3 onions, skinned and
  sliced*
*1 stick celery, washed and
  chopped*
150 ml (¼ pint) olive oil
225 g (8 oz) tomatoes
*2 cloves garlic, skinned and
  crushed*
bay leaf
*2.5 ml (½ level tsp) dried
  thyme or fennel*
few parsley sprigs
*pared and finely shredded
  rind of ½ an orange*
salt and pepper
pinch saffron, optional

1 Clean and wash the firm-fleshed fish, pat it dry with kitchen paper towel. Skin and fillet it (page 171) if necessary, then cut it into fairly large, thick pieces.

2 If you are using shellfish, remove them from their shells.

3 Lightly fry the onions and celery in the oil for 5 minutes, until soft.

4 Skin and slice the tomatoes and stir them in with the garlic, herbs, orange rind, salt and pepper. Dissolve the saffron in a little water.

5 Put all the firm-fleshed fish in a layer over the vegetables. Add the saffron and just enough water to cover. Bring to the boil and simmer for 8 minutes.

6 Add the shellfish and cook for a further 5–8 minutes. The fish should be cooked but still hold their shape. Serve with French bread.

EGGS

The egg is a remarkable culinary ingredient–never out of season, economical and treasured by all the great cuisines of the world. In one form or another, eggs can be served in sweet and savoury courses and at any meal. Whole eggs can be used to bind mixtures such as stuffings and croquettes, as a raising agent in cakes and batters, or to glaze foods to a rich, golden colour. Egg yolks thicken sauces and custards and emulsify with oil to make dressings and mayonnaise. Egg whites can be beaten to make meringues, to raise soufflés and to lighten foamy desserts and icings.

No matter what the method, eggs should always be cooked at moderate to low temperatures. If the heat is too high they will become dry or rubbery; even at a low temperature they should not be cooked for too long. Saucepans made of stainless steel, glass, porcelain, enamel, or any metal with a non-stick finish, are all suitable to cook eggs in. When eggs are cooked in water in aluminium pans, the aluminium sometimes darkens. This is not harmful to either the pan or the eggs but it does spoil the look of the pan.

CHOOSING EGGS

A brown egg may look more wholesome and inviting than a white egg or vice versa, depending on personal preference, but the colour of the shell is of no culinary significance. It is dictated by the breed of hen that laid it.

What is important for the cook is that the egg be fresh. For good results, eggs which are to be eaten soft-boiled, fried or poached should be as fresh as possible. For cooking with other ingredients they can be older.

GRADING

Throughout the EEC eggs are graded by weight. Most recipes in this book use Size 3 eggs. If you use larger or smaller eggs in recipes where the proportion of egg to the other ingredients is important (eg. cakes, soufflés), adjust other quantities and cooking times accordingly.

EEC EGG GRADINGS			
Size 1	over 70 g	Size 5	50–55 g
Size 2	65–70 g	Size 6	45–50 g
Size 3 *	60–65 g	Size 7	below 45 g
Size 4	55–60 g	*Most commonly used in this book	

FRESH OR STALE?

A fresh egg will smell clean and faintly sweet, if at all, when opened, whereas the offensive smell of a bad egg is unmistakable. You can tell a lot by appearance, too. The white should be translucent, thick and firmly shaped, the yolk smooth and well rounded. If the yolk is flat and the white runs thinly all over the saucer, the egg is probably well past its best.

TO TEST FOR FRESHNESS

There is always a small air space inside an egg and this increases as the egg ages. The fresher the egg, therefore, the fuller it is, and that is the basis of the following test. Put the egg in a tumbler of cold water. If fresh and full it will lie flat at the bottom of the glass. If the egg tilts slightly it is probably not fresh enough to boil but will fry or scramble satisfactorily; if it floats it is probably bad – crack it open and smell before cooking.

STORING EGGS

Eggs keep well if stored in a cool place, but as you have no way of knowing how long ago they were laid, it is best to work on a maximum storage time of 2 weeks at home. Store them large end up to keep the yolks centred, either in egg boxes, or in the specially designed racks in the refrigerator for maximum protection. The shells are porous, so eggs should be kept well away from strong-smelling foods such as cheese and onions. When recipes call for beaten egg whites, the eggs should be separated when cold and the whites allowed to come to room temperature before use; this way they beat to a higher volume. Eggs to be fried or poached keep their shape better if they are chilled.

Leftover yolks or whites can be stored safely for a few days in the refrigerator in a tightly covered container. They can also be frozen; whites need no special treatment, but yolks should be mixed with a little salt or sugar before freezing – 2.5 ml (½ level tsp) per yolk. To cook leftover yolks, place them in a strainer and lower into a small saucepan with enough simmering water to cover. Cook leftover whites in a well greased shallow ovenproof dish, in an oven set at 170°C (325°F) mark 3 for approximately 10 minutes. Cooked egg yolks or whites can be used to make garnishes for hot or cold savoury dishes, following the ideas on page 140.

SEPARATING EGGS

It is easier to separate eggs if they are firm and chilled. To avoid ruining a bowlful of whites with a broken yolk or stale egg, crack each egg open separately over a small bowl or cup. Give it a sharp tap against the side of the bowl and follow the half-shell method shown below. Drop the yolk into another bowl. Take care not to puncture the yolk on the sharp edge of the shell. Remove any trace of egg yolk from the bowl of whites with a spoon or kitchen paper towel moistened in cold water.

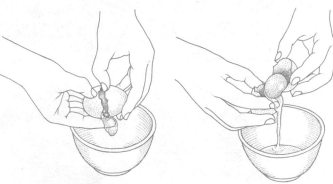

Half-shell method: Transfer the yolk carefully back and forth from one half-shell to the other, letting the white drop into the bowl and taking care not to break the yolk on the edge of the shell.

Removing a piece of eggshell: Use a spoon or piece of kitchen paper towel to remove any shell which may have fallen into the whites.

BEATING EGGS

In many recipes eggs are used as a raising agent. The rise is achieved by beating the raw egg to incorporate air, mixing it with other ingredients and then cooking. As it is heated, the air in the beaten egg expands and raises the whole mixture. When the egg sets, the pockets of air are trapped and the rise is fixed.

Whole eggs, egg yolks or whites may be beaten, according to the recipe. To beat lightly, for instance for an omelette, use a fork in a small basin. For beating to greater volume use a balloon or rotary whisk or electric mixer, in a large basin.

Egg whites reach their highest volume if beaten at room temperature, so separate eggs well ahead of time. Even a tiny trace of egg yolk will greatly reduce the bulk of the beaten whites, so separate the eggs carefully.

Since egg whites increase many times in volume when beaten, it is important to use a large bowl. Be sure that the bowl and beaters are perfectly clean as the slightest trace of grease will prevent the whites from beating to their fullest volume. For most recipes a hand whisk or electric mixer are equally suitable. However, for meringues the egg whites should be whisked by hand with a balloon or rotary whisk.

If the recipe calls for lightly beaten egg whites, the mixture should be foamy but still unstable; it will separate easily back into a liquid form. If the recipe calls for soft peaks, beat the whites until they are moist and shiny and form soft peaks when the beaters or whisk are raised. For stiff peaks, beat the whites until they are moist and glossy and form stiff, strong peaks when the beaters or whisk are raised.

If overbeaten, egg whites become too stiff and dry; when heat is applied, the whites collapse, as the cell walls no longer have the elasticity that allows them to expand.

FOLDING IN EGG WHITES

Stiffly beaten egg whites, as used in a soufflé for example, should be prepared and combined with the basic mixture at the very last moment. They should be folded rather than stirred or mixed in; incorporate them as lightly as possible so that the little bubbles of air beaten in will not break down. Start by stirring a small quantity of the whites into the heavier mixture; this will soften it, making it easier to achieve an even mix with the remainder. Then tip in the remaining whites and fold in.

To soften a heavier mixture: Gently stir in a small amount of the beaten egg whites to give a consistency that will blend evenly with the rest of the whites.

Folding in the whites: Cut down through the centre of the mixture, across the bottom and up the sides of the bowl. Turn the bowl and fold as lightly as possible just until the whites are evenly dispersed.

USING EGGS AS A THICKENER

Eggs, particularly the yolks, are often used to thicken and enrich sauces. The success of thickening with eggs depends on cooking the mixture below boiling point until the desired consistency is reached. Too high a heat, or heat applied for too long, will curdle the mixture. Some recipes suggest cooking sauces over simmering water in a double saucepan and custards are put in a pan of water to bake. Both these methods give you better control of the temperature. To help prevent curdled sauces, first stir a little of the hot mixture into the eggs to raise their temperature before stirring them back into the mixture; cook over low heat, stirring constantly, until the sauce has reached the desired consistency.

Boiled eggs

'Boiled' is a misnomer really, as eggs should be simmered rather than boiled. For a soft-boiled egg, if you are taking the eggs straight from the refrigerator, put them into cold water and bring slowly to the boil. They will then be lightly set. If the eggs are at room temperature they can be put into boiling water without fear of cracking; bring the water to the boil, lower in the eggs with a spoon, turn down the heat and cook for 3 minutes for a light set, up to 4½ minutes for a firmer set. Fresh eggs tend to take a little longer to cook than those which are a few days old.

For hard-boiled eggs, bring the water to the boil, put in the eggs and simmer for 10 – 12 minutes. As soon as they are cooked put the eggs under cold running water to cool them quickly; if allowed to overcook a discoloured rim may form round the outside of the yolk and the white will be tough. Cooling the egg quickly also makes it easier to remove the shell cleanly.

Soft-boiled eggs that are not served in the shell should also be plunged into cold water as soon as cooking is complete. If they are to be served warm, remove the shell as soon as it is cool enough to handle; for serving cold, leave the eggs in cold water for about 8 minutes, then carefully peel away the shell.

Very fresh eggs are hard to peel cleanly; the white clings obstinately to the shell. For dishes using shelled, boiled eggs, choose eggs that are at least a few days old.

Duck eggs are larger and richer than hens' eggs and need to be thoroughly cooked to be safe. To boil a duck egg, put it into boiling water, lower the heat and cook for at least 10 minutes. Turkey and goose eggs, although larger than hens' eggs, are not as rich as duck eggs; for soft-boiled eggs allow about 7 minutes.

SHELLING A BOILED EGG

To shell a boiled egg without breaking the white, gently crack the shell all over and remove the pieces of shell under cold running water, as shown below.

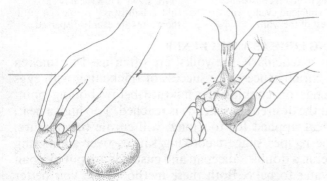

Cracking the shell: Gently tap the shell against a flat surface, taking care not to damage the egg inside. Crack the shell all over.

Removing the shell: Under running cold water, gently peel off the pieces of shell, beginning at the rounded end of the egg. Wash off any remaining fragments, taking care not to allow any of the white to come away with them.

Soft - boiled Eggs

Colour index page 28

1 Put the eggs in a pan large enough to hold them without crowding. Pour over enough cold water to cover them.

2 Place it over heat. Bring the water slowly to the boil. Eggs will then be lightly set.

3 For a firmer set, remove the pan from the heat, cover and leave for 1–2 minutes longer.

4 Drain as soon as the eggs are cooked. For eggs to be served without the shell, hold under cold running water until cool enough to handle.

EGG GARNISHES

Hard-boiled eggs make attractive garnishes. Sliced or cut in wedges, they can be arranged on salads and mousses or set in aspic to decorate cold dishes for more formal occasions. When cutting hard-boiled eggs, make sure your knife is very sharp and work carefully to avoid crumbling the yolk. Egg slicers are useful for cutting uniform shapes.

Using the yolks alone, make egg mimosa to sprinkle over sauces, soups and rice dishes. Using the whites only, cut out small decorative shapes and use them to garnish canapés, savouries, appetisers and snacks.

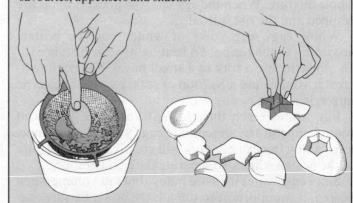

Making egg mimosa: Rub the yolks through a fine sieve with a spoon.

Cutting out shapes: Use small aspic or biscuit cutters to cut whites.

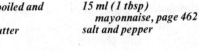

Stuffed Eggs

Colour index
page 23

4 servings

*4 eggs, hard-boiled and
cooled*
25 g (1 oz) butter

*15 ml (1 tbsp)
mayonnaise, page 462*
salt and pepper

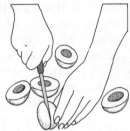

1 Shell the eggs and cut them in half lengthways with a sharp knife.

2 Keeping the whites whole, remove the yolks and put them in a small bowl.

3 Add the butter, mayonnaise and seasoning. Mix with a fork until smooth.

4 Pile the yolk mixture back into the whites with a spoon, or pipe it in using a forcing bag with a 1-cm (½-in) star nozzle.

STUFFED EGG VARIATIONS

Stir one of the following into the yolk mixture:

Colour index
page 23

BACON: Add *1 rasher streaky bacon,* rinded, fried until crisp and crumbled.

MEXICAN STYLE: Add extra *salt and pepper, 5 ml (1 level tsp) chilli seasoning* and *1 large ripe tomato,* skinned, finely chopped and drained.

PRAWN SALAD: Add *50 g (2 oz) shelled prawns* or shrimps, finely chopped, and *1 small stick celery,* trimmed and finely chopped.

CUCUMBER-DILL: Add *1.25 ml (¼ level tsp) dried dill weed, 2.5 ml (½ tsp) cider vinegar* and *60 ml (4 tbsp) finely chopped cucumber.*

TUNA: Add *45 ml (3 tbsp) flaked tuna* and *10 ml (2 tsp) lemon juice.*

PIZZA: Add *2.5 ml (½ level tsp) dried oregano,* a *pinch of garlic powder* and *10 ml (2 tsp) tomato ketchup or tomato paste.*

ANCHOVY: Add *5 ml (1 tsp) anchovy essence.*

RADISH: Add *45 ml (3 tbsp) chopped radishes.*

CAPERS: Add *10 ml (2 tsp) finely chopped capers.*

OLIVES: Add *3 pimento-stuffed olives,* finely chopped, and *5 ml (1 tsp) Dijon mustard.*

Eggs en Gelée

Colour index
page 23

4 first course
servings

4 eggs, hard-boiled
salt and pepper
50 g (2 oz) cream cheese
*15 ml (1 tbsp) chopped
chives*
*396-g (14-oz) can
consommé*
30 ml (2 tbsp) dry sherry
*5 ml (1 tsp)
Worcestershire sauce*
5 ml (1 tsp) lemon juice
*2.5 ml (½ level tsp)
powdered gelatine*
½ canned pimento
4 stoned olives

1 Halve the eggs and cream the yolks in a bowl with the seasoning, cheese and chives. Stuff the mixture into the egg whites and smooth over the tops.

2 Put the stuffed egg halves together again, removing any excess stuffing mixture.

3 Put the eggs into individual ramekins or foil dishes. Stand the dishes in a shallow roasting tin.

4 Put the consommé, sherry, Worcestershire sauce and lemon juice in a saucepan, sprinkle the gelatine over; heat gently to dissolve. Leave to cool.

5 Cut the pimento into decorative shapes and the olives into slivers.

6 Arrange the pimento shapes and cut olives on the stuffed eggs to make an attractive design.

7 Spoon the gelatine mixture over each egg until the dishes are almost full. Refrigerate until set.

Boiled eggs

Colour index
page 28

4 servings

Stuffed Eggs à la Mornay, with Broccoli

4 eggs, hard-boiled and shelled while still warm
25 g (1 oz) mushrooms, chopped
½ onion, skinned and chopped
20 g (¾ oz) butter

226-g (8-oz) packet frozen broccoli
300 ml (½ pint) mornay sauce, page 461
little extra grated cheese

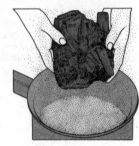

1 Halve the eggs lengthways; remove the yolks. Fry the mushrooms and onion in hot fat until golden . Mix with yolks and spoon into whites.

2 Cook the broccoli as directed on the packet and drain thoroughly.

3 Arrange the broccoli in a greased ovenproof dish, alternating with the stuffed egg halves.

4 Spoon the sauce over the broccoli, scatter with the remaining cheese and brown under a hot grill for a few minutes.

Creole Eggs

Colour index
page 28

4 servings

50 g (2 oz) butter or margarine
1 large onion, skinned and chopped
1 medium green pepper, seeded and chopped
1 clove garlic, skinned and crushed
5 ml (1 level tsp) salt
1.25 ml (¼ level tsp) rosemary

large pinch paprika
396-g (14-oz) can tomatoes
8 hard-boiled eggs, shelled and halved
75 g (3 oz) long grain rice

1. Melt the butter or margarine in a frying pan. Add the onion, pepper, garlic and seasonings and cook for about 5 minutes.
2. Add the tomatoes with their liquid and the hard-boiled eggs to the same frying pan. Cover and simmer for a further 10 minutes, stirring.
3. Meanwhile cook the rice and drain thoroughly. Serve the egg mixture spooned over the rice.

Poached eggs

Eggs which are to be poached in water should be as fresh and cold as possible. If an egg is stale, its white will start separating from it and coagulating in ragged shreds as soon as it hits the water.

The method shown below is the traditional way of poaching eggs. If you prefer to use a special egg poacher, half-fill the lower container with water, place a small piece of butter in each cup and put over the heat. When the water boils, break the eggs into the cups, season lightly and cover the pan. Simmer gently until the eggs are set and loosen them with a knife before turning out.

Poached Eggs

Colour index
page 29

1 Grease a shallow pan to prevent sticking and half-fill with water. Bring to the boil. Reduce the heat until the water is just simmering.

2 Break an egg into a saucer or cup and slip into the water. Repeat with the remaining eggs. Simmer gently until the eggs are lightly set.

3 Lift the eggs out one at a time with a slotted spoon or fish slice.

4 Drain thoroughly over kitchen paper towel before serving.

Eggs Bénédict

Colour index
page 29

4 servings

150 ml (¼ pint) hollandaise sauce, page 463
4 eggs
4 slices bread, cut from a round white loaf or 2 muffins, halved

4 thin slices lean cooked ham

For the garnish, optional:
parsley sprigs

1. Make the hollandaise sauce and keep warm.
2. Poach the eggs lightly in simmering water and toast the bread or muffins on both sides.
3. Fold the ham slices and place one on each piece of toast or muffin. Remove the poached eggs from the pan and drain; place on top of the ham.
4. Coat each poached egg lightly with hollandaise sauce. Garnish with parsley sprigs if you wish.

Baked eggs

Fried eggs

There are many variations on the baked egg, sometimes called shirred egg, theme. You can serve them just as they are with fingers of hot buttered toast, or you can dress them up a little by adding a garnish.

Always cook the eggs over low heat, or the whites will be crisp and toughened around the edges before the yolks are barely heated through to the centre.

The pan should be large enough for the eggs to stay separate, because once egg whites have joined together they can only be separated by cutting. Only the minimum of fat should be used, or the eggs will be greasy – dripping, lard or bacon fat are the usual choice. If the eggs are being served with bacon, fry that first, remove it from the pan and use the fat left behind for the eggs.

It is traditional to fry an egg on one side only, so that it is served 'sunny side up'. If you prefer, you can turn the egg over halfway through the cooking time.

Baked Eggs

Colour index page 28

1 Butter an individual ovenproof ramekin for each serving.

2 Break an egg into each dish, or for 2-egg servings use larger, 300-ml (1/2-pint) dishes; season.

3 Put the dishes on a baking sheet and bake the eggs at 180°C (350°F) mark 4 until they are just set – about 5–8 minutes.

4 Garnish with parsley sprigs, chives or a little chopped parsley and serve immediately.

BAKED EGG VARIATIONS: Add a little cream to the bottom of the ramekins before adding the eggs and stir in a little of one or more of the following: *chopped cooked ham, chopped sautéed mushrooms, chopped cooked asparagus tips, creamed spinach, flaked smoked fish, chopped fresh herbs, skinned and chopped tomato* or *grated Gruyère cheese.*

Eggs Baked in Cream

Colour index page 28

4 servings

knob of butter	salt and pepper
60 ml (4 tbsp) cream	8 eggs

1. Butter four small ovenproof dishes.
2. Put 5 ml (1 tsp) cream into the bottom of each dish and sprinkle lightly with salt and pepper.
3. Break 2 eggs into each dish, sprinkle with more salt and pepper and carefully spoon 10 ml (2 tsp) cream over the top of each one.
4. Place the dishes in a roasting tin and fill it with enough water to come halfway up their sides. Bake in the oven at 180°C (350°F) mark 4 for about 15 minutes, until the eggs are just set.
5. Garnish if you wish, with parsley sprigs, chopped cooked bacon, watercress, chives or cheese and serve with fresh brown bread and butter.

Fried Eggs

Colour index page 28

1 Melt a little dripping, lard or bacon fat in a frying pan.

2 Break each egg into a saucer and slide gently into the hot fat. Keep the eggs separate if possible.

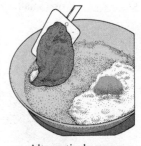

3 Cook gently and use a spoon to baste the eggs with the fat so that they cook evenly on top and underneath.

4 Alternatively, as soon as the eggs are firm enough, use a wide spatula or fish slice to turn them over and fry on the other side until cooked.

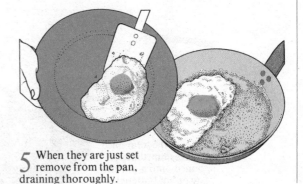

5 When they are just set remove from the pan, draining thoroughly.

Scrambled eggs

Opposite page
Omelette Fines Herbes (page 146

If they are to stay creamy, scrambled eggs must be cooked slowly. By mixing a little milk or water with the eggs – about 15 ml (1 tbsp) for each egg – you can slow the cooking and make them fluffier and more tender.

Scrambled eggs should not be stirred too often; frequent stirring breaks down the curds and the eggs will be dry and crumbly when they are cooked.

The size of pan you choose is important – the egg mixture should not be more than 2.5 cm (1 in) deep, otherwise the curds which form at the beginning will have toughened before the remaining mixture has had a chance to thicken. The pan should be made from a metal which conducts heat evenly.

Colour index
page 28

Scrambled Eggs

1 For each serving, put 2 eggs, 30 ml (2 tbsp) milk or water and some salt and pepper in a small basin and whisk together with a fork or a small wire whisk.

2 Melt a knob of butter in a pan and swirl round to coat sides and base thoroughly.

3 Pour in the egg mixture and stir slowly over gentle heat with a spatula until the mixture begins to thicken and set slightly.

4 Remove from the heat and stir until creamy. The egg will continue to cook in the heat of the pan.

5 Serve the scrambled eggs immediately, spooned onto a warmed plate or hot buttered toast.

Colour index
page 28
2 servings

Shrimp Scramble

4 eggs
30 ml (2 tbsp) milk
* or water*
salt and pepper
50 g (2 oz) shelled
* shrimps*
knob of butter

To serve, optional:
hot buttered toast, toasted
* rolls or muffins*

1 Lightly beat together the eggs, milk or water and seasoning. Rinse and drain the shrimps and add to the egg mixture. Stir in evenly with a fork.

2 Melt a little butter in a pan, add the egg and shrimp mixture and cook, stirring gently with a wooden spoon until just thickened and creamy.

3 Spoon over hot buttered toast, toasted roll muffins, or as required.

SCRAMBLED EGG VARIATIONS

Add to a basic 4-egg mixture:

MUSHROOM: *50 g (2 oz) sliced mushrooms,* lightly fried in *oil* or butter.

SMOKED FISH: *50 g (2 oz) Finnan haddock* or other smoked fish, cooked, boned and flaked.

CHEESE: *50–75 g (2–3 oz) grated cheese.*

HERB: *2.5 ml (½ level tsp) dried herbs* or 15 ml (1 tbsp) finely chopped mixed fresh herbs.

Colour index
page 23
4 servings

Scrambled Eggs Archiduchesse

90 g (3½ oz) butter
25 g (1 oz) mushrooms,
* sliced*
6 eggs, beaten
30–45 ml (2–3 tbsp) single
* cream*
salt

paprika
50 g (2 oz) cooked ham,
* chopped*
4 slices bread, fried
12 fresh or canned
* asparagus tips, cooked*
* and kept warm*

1. Melt 15 g (½ oz) butter and lightly fry the mushrooms. Set aside.
2. In a fresh pan, melt the remaining butter and add the eggs, cream, salt and paprika. Cook very slowly, stirring gently. Add the ham and mushrooms as the mixture starts to thicken.
3. Spoon on to the fried bread and serve topped with the cooked asparagus tips.

Omelettes

Opposite page
Painted Easter eggs

A plain omelette, sometimes known as a French omelette, should be shiny and golden on the outside, moist and creamy in the centre. It can be served plain, just lightly seasoned with salt and pepper, or with any one of the savoury fillings on page 146. A soufflé omelette has a drier, fluffier texture, achieved by whisking the egg whites separately and folding them into the yolk mixture. A soufflé omelette can be served with a savoury filling, just like a plain one, but is more commonly filled with something sweet, to serve as a dessert.

COOKING OMELETTES

Remember that eggs should always be cooked at a moderate to low temperature. A few minutes before you are ready to start cooking an omelette, place the pan over a gentle heat, to ensure that it is heated evenly right to the edges before the egg mixture goes in – a fierce heat would cause the pan to heat unevenly. When the pan is ready it will feel comfortably hot if you hold the back of your hand about 2.5 cm (1 in) away from the surface. For the most tender omelette use only 2 or 3 eggs at a time and serve it on a warmed plate as soon as it is cooked. The total cooking time should not be more than 2 minutes for a plain omelette; a soufflé omelette takes just a moment or two longer.

THE OMELETTE PAN

An omelette should be made in a good, heavy-based pan. Cast iron, copper, enamelled iron and aluminium are all suitable as long as the pan is thick, so that it will cook the egg evenly. The pan should be of such a size that the egg mixture is about 0.5 cm (¼ in) deep.

If the omelette is too thin it will be dry and tough, if too thick the outside will be over-cooked before the centre is ready. For a 2 or 3-egg omelette use a 15–18-cm (6–7-in) pan.

An omelette pan: Special omelette pans are obtainable, but any heavy-based frying pan with sloping sides and an easy-to-grip handle can be used.

If your pan does not have a non-stick finish, before use put 15 ml (1 level tbsp) salt in the pan, heat it slowly, then rub the salt well into the surface with paper. Tip away the salt and wipe the pan with fresh paper.

Plain Omelette

2 eggs
salt and pepper
15 ml (1 tbsp) water
knob of butter

Colour index page 28

1 serving

1 Break the eggs into a small bowl. Season lightly and add the water.

2 Whisk with a wire whisk or fork just enough to break down the eggs, as overbeating will spoil the texture of the finished omelette.

3 Place the omelette pan over gentle heat and when hot add a knob of butter to grease it lightly. Do not let the butter overheat and burn.

4 Pour the beaten eggs into the hot butter in the omelette pan.

5 Stir gently with a palette knife or the back of a fork, drawing setting mixture to centre and letting liquid run to sides.

6 When the egg is set, stop stirring and cook for another minute. Shake the pan a little; the omelette should move freely.

7 Lift the edge with a palette knife and look at underside. The omelette should be golden underneath and creamy on top.

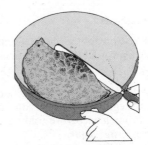

8 Tilt the pan slightly and use a palette knife to fold the omelette in half, taking care not to break it around the edges.

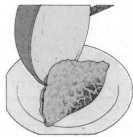

9 Turn the omelette on to a warmed plate, garnish if you wish and serve at once, to prevent the omelette from spoiling.

Omelettes

FLAVOURING A FOLDED OMELETTE

Plain and soufflé omelettes can be varied by adding flavouring ingredients to the egg mixture before cooking. Or you can add a separately prepared filling to the cooked omelette before folding it in half. Follow the method shown below, then slide the omelette on to a heated plate and serve immediately.

Adding the filling: Spread the prepared filling over half the omelette.

Folding the omelette: Fold the other half of the omelette over the filling.

SAVOURY FILLINGS

FINES HERBES: Add *5 ml (1 level tsp) mixed dried herbs* or 10 ml (2 tsp) finely chopped fresh herbs to the beaten egg before cooking. Parsley, chives and tarragon are all suitable.

CHEESE: Grate *40 g (1½ oz) cheese.* Mix 45 ml (3 tbsp) with the beaten egg mixture before cooking, and sprinkle the rest over the omelette just before it is folded over.

HAM OR TONGUE: Add *50 g (2 oz) chopped cooked ham* or tongue to the beaten egg mixture before cooking.

TOMATO: Skin and chop *1–2 tomatoes,* fry in a little *butter* for 5 minutes until soft and pulpy, and season. Put in the centre of the omelette just before folding it over.

MUSHROOM: Slice *50 g (2 oz) mushrooms* and sauté in *butter* for a few minutes. Put in the centre of the omelette just before folding it over.

FISH: Heat some *flaked, cooked fish* gently in a little *cheese sauce* and season. Put in the centre of the omelette just before folding it over.

SWEET FILLINGS

STRAWBERRY: Spread the cooked omelette with *sliced strawberries,* fold it over and serve sprinkled with *icing sugar.* (Colour index page 98)

APRICOT: Add the *grated rind of an orange* or tangerine to the egg yolks. Spread some *thick apricot pulp* over the omelette before folding it and serve sprinkled with *caster sugar.*

RUM: Substitute *15 ml (1 tbsp) rum* for half the water added to the egg yolks. Put the cooked omelette on a hot dish, pour *45–60 ml (3–4 tbsp) warmed rum* around it and ignite.

Soufflé Omelette

Colour index page 29

1 serving

2 eggs, separated
5 ml (1 level tsp) caster sugar, or salt and pepper

30 ml (2 tbsp) water
knob of butter

1 Whisk the whites with the sugar or seasonings until stiff but not dry. Whisk the yolks and water until creamy. Melt the butter over a low heat.

2 Turn the egg whites on to the yolks and fold in carefully, using a spoon or spatula. Do not overmix.

3 Swirl the butter round the pan to grease the sides and pour in the egg mixture. Preheat the grill.

4 Cook over a moderate heat until golden brown underneath and just firm to the touch in the centre. Place under the grill and cook until just set.

5 Run a knife round the edge and underneath the omelette and mark it across the middle.

6 Double the omelette over, slide it gently on to a hot plate and serve straight away.

SCORING A SOUFFLE OMELETTE

Just before serving, dredge the omelette with icing sugar.

Make a criss-cross pattern across top by pressing red-hot skewers on to sugar.

Pancakes

This pancake batter may be used at once or left to stand in a cool place. If it is left to stand it may be necessary to add a little extra milk before using.

Cooked pancakes keep for up to a week in the refrigerator, wrapped in polythene or foil, or up to 2 months in the freezer. To reheat frozen pancakes, thaw for 2–3 hours at room temperature then place the stack of pancakes, wrapped in foil, in the oven at 190°C (375°F) mark 5 for 20–30 minutes.

Pancakes

Makes 8 pancakes

125 g (4 oz) plain flour
pinch salt

1 egg
300 ml (½ pint) milk
lard

1 Mix the flour and salt, make a well in the centre and break in the egg. Add half the liquid and then gradually work in the plain flour.

2 Beat until smooth. Add the remaining liquid gradually and beat until well mixed and the surface is covered with bubbles.

3 Heat a little lard in an 18-cm (7-in) heavy based frying pan, running it round to coat the sides of the pan; pour off surplus.

4 Raise the handle side of the pan slightly and pour in a little batter from the raised side so the batter flows over the pan.

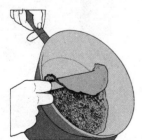 

5 Place over a moderate heat and cook until golden underneath. Turn with a palette knife and cook the other side.

6 Slide the pancake on to waxed paper. Repeat with the remaining batter, keeping the pancakes hot until they are all made.

Spinach Pancakes

Colour index page 29
4 servings

325 g (12 oz) frozen chopped spinach or 450 g (1 lb) fresh spinach, trimmed
25 g (1 oz) butter
20 g (¾ oz) plain flour
2.5–5 ml (½–1 level tsp) salt
pepper

150 ml (¼ pint) milk
45 ml (3 tbsp) single cream
75 g (3 oz) Gruyère cheese, grated
8 pancakes, left, kept hot

1. Cook the frozen spinach according to the instructions on the packet and drain well; or cook the fresh spinach (page 295), drain and chop finely.
2. Melt the butter in a large saucepan over low heat and stir in the flour, salt and pepper. Gradually add the milk and cream and cook until the sauce is thickened, stirring constantly.
3. Add the cooked spinach and grated cheese. Warm through until the cheese is melted.
4. Fill the pancakes as shown below, using about 60 ml (4 tbsp) mixture for each one.

Curried Shrimp Pancakes

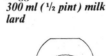

Colour index page 29
4 servings

2 small green peppers, seeded and diced
25 g (1 oz) butter
225 g (8 oz) potted shrimps
25 g (1 oz) plain flour
5 ml (1 level tsp) curry paste

300 ml (½ pint) single cream
120 ml (8 tbsp) milk
salt
freshly ground black pepper
8 pancakes, left, kept hot

1. Blanch the peppers in boiling water for 3 minutes and drain thoroughly.
2. Melt the butter in a frying pan, add the shrimps and heat gently, stirring occasionally.
3. Stir in the flour and curry paste; cook for 1–2 minutes, stirring constantly, then add the cream, the milk and the green pepper. Stir until thickened and season to taste with salt and pepper.
4. Fill the pancakes as shown below, using about 60 ml (4 tbsp) mixture for each one.

FILLING A PANCAKE

Spoon a little of the filling across the centre of the cooked pancake.

Fold one edge of the pancake over the filling and roll up carefully. Arrange the finished pancakes on a serving dish and keep hot in the oven while filling remaining pancakes.

Soufflés

A soufflé consists of a thick sauce of flour, butter, milk and egg yolks (known as a panada) combined with stiffly beaten egg whites. When making the panada, choose a saucepan large enough to hold not only the basic sauce mixture but also the beaten egg whites. Cook the flour and butter first, then add the liquid to form a smooth sauce. The panada should boil for a minute to avoid the raw, pasty taste of uncooked flour. Then beat the yolks in one at a time and add the flavouring.

Although you should separate your eggs when cold, let the whites warm to room temperature in a covered bowl so that they will beat to a greater volume. Fold the egg whites gently into the sauce, taking care not to stir the whites or they will lose their volume. Pour the mixture into a greased soufflé dish.

A soufflé should be served as soon as it is ready, but in an emergency it can be left in the oven, turned off, for about 10 minutes without coming to any great harm.

TESTING A SOUFFLE

If the soufflé doesn't seem done after the baking time called for in the recipe, gently insert a table knife into the puffy side of the soufflé; if it comes out clean the soufflé is done. Do not open the door before the end of the cooking time given in the recipe.

SOUFFLE DISHES

The traditional soufflé dish is round and of medium depth with straight sides, usually made of porcelain, earthenware or glass. Soufflés can be baked in casseroles; those with straight sides yield the greatest height. If you want your soufflé to look tall and impressive, there should be enough uncooked mixture to fill the dish almost three-quarters full so that it puffs up well above the rim as it rises.

SOUFFLE DISHES

SERVING THE SOUFFLE

Using a large serving spoon, reach down to the bottom of the dish. Each portion should include a piece of crust and some of the light centre. Take a large spoonful at a time so that you do not damage the delicate texture or appearance of the remaining soufflé in the dish.

Classic Cheese Soufflé

3 eggs
25 g (1 oz) butter
45 ml (3 level tbsp)
  plain flour
150 ml (¼ pint) milk
75 g (3 oz) mature cheese,
  finely grated
salt and pepper

Colour index page 29

4 servings

1 Separate the eggs and leave the whites to come to room temperature.

2 Melt the butter in a pan large enough to hold the entire soufflé mixture. Add the flour and cook gently for 2–3 minutes, stirring all the time.

3 Gradually stir in the milk and bring to the boil, stirring all the time.

4 Reduce the heat and stir in the cheese. Do not overheat or the cheese will separate and become stringy.

5 Cool slightly and add the egg yolks one at a time, beating well, and season. The sauce may now be covered and left to stand until needed.

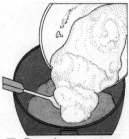

6 In a large bowl, whisk the egg whites until stiff, using an electric mixer or rotary whisk.

7 Pour the egg whites on to the sauce in the pan all at once; fold in gently with a large metal spoon until evenly blended. Do not stir the mixture.

8 Pour the mixture into a greased 1.1-litre (2-pint) soufflé dish and bake in the centre of the oven at 180°C (350°F) mark 4 for about 30 minutes.

9 When the soufflé has cooked and is golden brown, remove it from the oven and serve it at once from the dish while it is still at its full height.

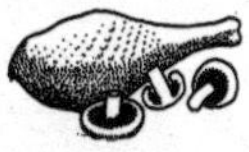

Chicken Soufflé

Colour index
page 29

4 servings

50 g (2 oz) butter	225 ml (8 fl oz) milk
100 g (4 oz) mushrooms, chopped	1 chicken stock cube
45 ml (3 tbsp) chopped onion	5 eggs, separated
	450 g (1 lb) cold cooked chicken, finely chopped
30 ml (2 level tbsp) plain flour	2.5 ml (½ level tsp) salt

1. Melt the butter in a large pan, add the mushrooms and onion and cook until tender. Blend in the flour.
2. Reduce the heat and add the milk and crumbled stock cube. Cook, stirring, until thickened.
3. Mix the egg yolks together and beat in a little of the hot sauce. Pour the egg mixture slowly into the sauce, stirring rapidly. Do not boil. Remove from the heat and stir in the chicken.
4. Whisk the egg whites and salt stiffly and fold into the mixture. Grease the bottom only of a 1.1-litre (2-pint) soufflé dish and pour in the chicken mixture. Bake in the oven at 170°C (325°F) mark 3 for 1 hour.

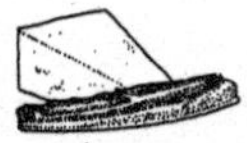

Cheese and Bacon Soufflé

Colour index
page 29

2 servings

40 g (1½ oz) butter	100 g (4 oz) Cheddar cheese, grated
30 ml (2 level tbsp) plain flour	3 eggs, separated
2.5 ml (½ level tsp) salt	2 rashers streaky bacon, rinded, chopped and fried
225 ml (8 fl oz) evaporated milk or milk	

1. Melt the butter in a large pan and blend in the flour and salt. Gradually stir in the milk and cook, stirring, until thickened. Stir in the grated cheese and remove from heat.
2. Mix the egg yolks together and beat in a little of the hot sauce. Slowly pour the egg mixture into the sauce, stirring rapidly. Cook over low heat for about 1 minute until thickened; do not boil. Set aside.
3. Whisk the egg whites stiffly and fold into the cheese mixture with the bacon pieces. Pour into a 1.5-litre (2½-pint) soufflé dish and bake at 180°C (350°F) mark 4 for 40–50 minutes.

Individual Asparagus Soufflés

Colour index
page 24

8 first course servings

225 g (8 oz) asparagus	2.5 ml (½ level tsp) white pepper
50 g (2 oz) butter	
60 ml (4 level tbsp) plain flour	5 ml (1 level tsp) dry mustard
5 ml (1 level tsp) salt	100 g (4 oz) Cheddar cheese, grated
350 ml (12 fl oz) milk	
6 eggs, separated	

1. Cook the asparagus in boiling salted water until just tender. Drain well and cut into small chunks.
2. Melt the butter and blend in the flour and salt. Gradually stir in milk and cook, stirring, until thick. Add the asparagus and remove pan from heat.
3. Mix the egg yolks together and beat in a little of the hot sauce. Slowly pour the egg mixture into the sauce, stirring rapidly. Stir in the pepper, mustard and cheese and set aside.
4. Whisk whites stiffly; fold into asparagus mixture.
5. Spoon into eight greased 150-ml (¼-pint) ramekins and bake in the oven at 170°C (325°F) mark 3 for about 30 minutes or until well risen and golden.

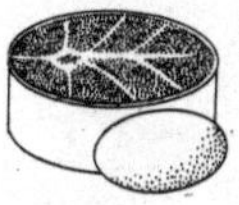

Salmon Puff

Colour index
page 29

4 servings

40 g (1½ oz) butter or margarine	225 ml (8 fl oz) milk
45 ml (3 level tbsp) plain flour	4 eggs, separated
	198-g (7-oz) can salmon, drained and flaked
5 ml (1 level tsp) salt	
2.5 ml (½ level tsp) dry mustard	
2.5 ml (½ tsp) Worcestershire sauce	

1. Melt the butter in a large saucepan and blend in the flour, salt, mustard and Worcestershire sauce. Gradually stir in the milk and cook, stirring, until thickened. Leave to cool for about 10 minutes.
2. Mix the egg yolks together and beat in a little of the warm sauce. Stirring rapidly, pour the egg mixture into the sauce.
3. Cook, stirring, until thickened, but do not boil, then stir in the flaked salmon.
4. Whisk the egg whites stiffly and fold into the salmon mixture with a metal spoon.
5. Pour into a greased 1.1-litre (2-pint) soufflé dish and cook in the oven at 190°C (375°F) mark 5 for 30–35 minutes until well risen and golden.

Spinach Soufflé

Colour index
page 29

6 servings

450 g (1 lb) fresh trimmed spinach or 2 226-g (8-oz) packets frozen chopped spinach	1.25 ml (¼ level tsp) cayenne pepper
	350 ml (12 fl oz) milk
40 g (1½ oz) butter or margarine	6 eggs, separated
40 g (1½ oz) onion, skinned and chopped	25 g (1 oz) Parmesan cheese, grated
25 g (1 oz) plain flour	
10–12.5 ml (2–2½ level tsp) salt	

1. Prepare and cook the spinach. If you are using fresh spinach, wash it well in several waters to remove all the grit. Pack into a saucepan with only the water that clings to the leaves. Heat gently, turning the spinach occasionally, then bring to the boil and cook for 5–10 minutes or until tender. Drain thoroughly and chop finely. For frozen spinach, cook according to the instructions on the packet label and drain thoroughly.
2. Melt the butter or margarine, add the onion and fry for 5 minutes. Stir in the flour, salt and cayenne and cook gently, stirring, until smooth. Slowly add the milk and cook, stirring, until thickened.
3. Mix the egg yolks together lightly and beat in a little of the hot sauce; slowly pour the egg mixture into the sauce, stirring rapidly. Cook over low heat, stirring, until thickened; do not boil. Remove the pan from the heat and stir in the spinach and cheese.
4. Whisk the egg whites until stiff then gently fold into the spinach mixture. Pour into a greased 1.8-litre (3¼-pint) soufflé dish and bake in the oven at 190°C (375°F) mark 5 for 40–45 minutes until well risen and golden brown.

CHEESE

Cheese is one of the tastiest savoury foods, whether eaten in its natural state or cooked and combined with other ingredients. It is a highly concentrated food and an important source of protein, fat and minerals.

Cheese is made by separating out the curds from the whey. The curds are then pressed and allowed to mature. The type and breed of animal which produced the milk is the prime factor differentiating one cheese from another and giving each its own characteristic flavour. In addition, local climate and vegetation influence the quality and fat content of the milk and storage conditions during ripening affect flavour and texture, so that no two cheeses will taste the same.

With so many determining factors, many cheeses are essentially local and cannot be produced in large quantities or under factory conditions. Other processes, notably the Cheddar process, lend themselves well to factory techniques, making possible large scale production of a relatively cheap but high quality cheese. Cheese blends and spreads add still further to the range.

CHOOSING CHEESE

Hard cheeses keep quite well and can be bought in quantities that will last a week or two, but soft cheeses deteriorate very quickly and should be bought only as required. It is a good idea to buy cheese you are not familiar with from a specialist who can advise you whether it is ready for eating, or whether it should be stored for a few days first.

Prepackaged cheese is always creamery cheese, that is, produced under factory conditions from the blended milk of many herds. Grading and quality control ensure the reliability of all creamery cheeses produced in the United Kingdom, New Zealand and EEC countries. Prepackaged cheese should always be bought from a refrigerated cabinet. Check the 'Sell By' or 'Eat By' date and do not buy if that date has passed; but if the date is many weeks ahead it may mean that the cheese is immature, and might not have the strength of flavour you would really like.

English Farmhouse cheeses and country cheeses from other parts of Europe are normally sold unwrapped and cut to order. These cheeses are made in small dairies, usually from the milk of a limited number of selected herds within a small area. They are the finest cheeses,

each with a character of its own. Check that the cut surface of the cheese looks clean and fresh. If it is dry, cracked and flaking, the cheese has been exposed to the air too long and is stale. On the other hand, it should not look wet or greasy; this suggests that the cheese has been stored at too high a temperature and humidity. A hard cheese should look firm and just moist, a soft one should give slightly to the touch of the knife.

SERVING CHEESE

Allow refrigerated cheese to come to room temperature before serving, except for cottage and cream cheeses which should be served chilled. On the other hand, do not unwrap and expose cheese to the air until you are ready to serve it and cover the cheese again as soon as possible after serving, to prevent it drying out.

For a snack meal nothing can beat a piece of good cheese with fresh bread and butter, a little salad or pickle and a glass of wine or beer. Served like this an adequate portion is normally about 50 g (2 oz). Any type of bread goes well with cheese, from the traditional English farmhouse crusty loaf to a dark continental rye bread. Cheese also makes a good filling for sandwiches.

CUTTING CHEESE

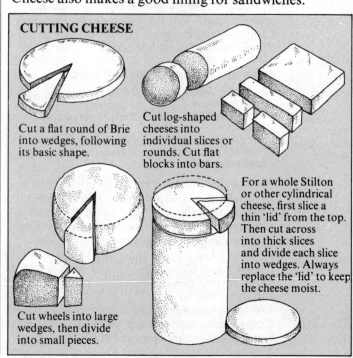

Cut a flat round of Brie into wedges, following its basic shape.

Cut log-shaped cheeses into individual slices or rounds. Cut flat blocks into bars.

For a whole Stilton or other cylindrical cheese, first slice a thin 'lid' from the top. Then cut across into thick slices and divide each slice into wedges. Always replace the 'lid' to keep the cheese moist.

Cut wheels into large wedges, then divide into small pieces.

SERVING CHEESE – THE CHEESE BOARD

For an after-dinner cheese board, choose a variety of cheeses to provide a balance of textures and flavours. A choice of hard and soft, mild and fully flavoured ones will tempt most palates. If you can ring the changes in shape and colour the cheese board will look more decorative and appealing.

How many different types of cheese you serve will depend on the number of guests, but try to offer at least four. It is usual to have at least one well known English hard cheese such as Cheddar or Cheshire and one of the popular soft French cheeses such as Brie or Camembert. Stilton, often known as the 'King of Cheeses', will usually be appreciated and after that consider your own favourites or try something new – perhaps a goat's milk cheese or one of the lesser known continental cheeses. Present rich cheeses in small quantities as a mouthful is often enough to satisfy the palate after a good dinner.

To go with the cheese you can offer fresh bread, rolls or a selection of plain and semi-sweet biscuits (a salty flavour in both biscuits and cheese may be too pronounced to round off a meal satisfactorily). Butter is not really necessary with a creamy, soft cheese but unsalted or lightly salted butter should be passed round for those eating a hard cheese, served either in a block or in individual pats or cubes.

Add to the cheese board small portions of crisp salad vegetables such as celery, radishes, wedges of lettuce heart, chicory or tiny tomatoes. These both garnish the board and are delicious to eat with the cheese. And always provide two or three cheese knives so that no-one has to cut the Brie with a knife that bears traces of Stilton or Roquefort.

Fruit is also an excellent accompaniment for cheese. In fact, a cheese board and bowl of fresh fruit can often replace a dessert. Offer a selection of freshly washed apples, pears, grapes, peaches or other fruits in season and provide small dessert knives for peeling the fruit. Nuts also offer an agreeable contrast of texture and a complementary flavour to cheese – try serving Brazil nuts, walnuts or hazel nuts with the cheese board.

STORING CHEESE

Keep cheese in the refrigerator or a cool larder, covered with cling film or foil. Wrap different types of cheese separately, so that one does not take on the flavour of another. For larder storage wrap the cheese loosely, but for refrigerator storage wrap each piece as closely as possible and keep it away from the coldest part of the refrigerator next to the ice compartment.

Hard cheeses will normally keep in good condition in the refrigerator for up to 2 weeks. Soft cheeses such as Brie and Camembert deteriorate very quickly once fully ripe and even in the refrigerator will keep in prime condition for only a day or two. Cottage cheese and cream cheese must be kept in the refrigerator and will keep for a maximum of 4–5 days. Vacuum-packed cheese will keep in the refrigerator until the 'Eat By' date stamped on the pack, which may be several weeks ahead; it should be kept in the coldest part of the refrigerator, next to the ice compartment, at about 5°C (40°F). Once opened, re-wrap it in cling film or foil and store as for freshly cut cheese.

If you are lucky enough to have a whole Stilton in the house, keep it in good condition by covering it with a piece of muslin which has been wrung out in salt water and storing in a cool, airy larder.

FREEZING CHEESE

Soft and cream cheeses store well in the freezer for up to 6 months wrapped in foil, freezer film or a polythene bag. Hard cheeses are inclined to become crumbly if stored for more than a few weeks, but the flavour remains good and they can always be used for cooking if the texture becomes unacceptable for serving on the cheese board. Cottage cheese deteriorates after 1–2 weeks in the freezer.

Thaw frozen cheese for 24 hours in the refrigerator and allow it to come to room temperature before serving. Crumble grated cheese straight from the freezer. Once thawed, cheese that has been frozen deteriorates much more quickly than fresh cheese. It should be eaten quickly and cannot safely be refrozen.

COOKING WITH CHEESE

When cooking cheese, remember that too fierce a heat can make it stringy; it needs to melt rather than cook. When you are preparing a sauce, it should not boil after you have added the cheese. For toasting, use a moderate rather than a fierce grill heat.

Cheese with a high fat content blends into a sauce better than a drier type: a small amount of mature Farmhouse Cheddar with plenty of 'bite' will give a better flavour than a large amount of humble creamery Cheddar. If using the latter you may need to ginger up the flavour a little with mustard or Worcestershire sauce. Among English cheeses, Cheddar is good for baking but the more crumbly Lancashire, Cheshire and Leicester are best for toasting. Many continental recipes suggest combining Gruyère or Emmenthal, which blend well into a sauce, with Parmesan, which gives a good kick to the flavour of a finished dish.

CHEESE LEFTOVERS

Scraps of cheese need never be wasted. Grate pieces of hard cheese and store in the refrigerator for use in cooking. To use up scraps of mixed cheeses, cream them with a little butter – about 15 g (½ oz) butter to 450 g (1 lb) cheese – and flavour the mixture with wine and freshly ground black pepper. Press into small pots and cover with melted butter to store.

British cheeses

CHEESE	CHARACTERISTICS	USE
Arran	A hard, yellow cheese, moist and close-textured. Made on the island of Arran in individual rindless packs weighing 1 kg (2¼ lb).	Use uncooked or cooked as for Cheddar.
Blue Dorset	A hard, white cheese with a slightly crumbly texture and blue veining; fairly strong in flavour.	Use uncooked.
Caboc	A very rich double cream cheese rolled in oatmeal.	Use uncooked.
Caerphilly	A white, close-textured, semi-hard cheese with a clean mild flavour.	Best uncooked.
Cheddar	Farmhouse Cheddar is a rich yellow cheese, with a close, hard texture. Creamery Cheddars come in all shades from very light yellow to orangey-red. Because the cheeses are usually sold young, the flavour tends to be mild, although some are matured to give them more bite. New Zealand Cheddar is mild in flavour and Canadian strongest of all.	Use uncooked or cooked. Cheddar is an ideal cheese for grating; use it melted on toast and in sauces. To sharpen the flavour of a dish made with mild Cheddar, add a little prepared mustard.
Cheshire	A white or red hard cheese with a loose, crumbly texture and mild or mellow flavour. Blue Cheshire is a rich creamy open-textured cheese with blue veining.	White and red Cheshires are good uncooked or cooked. Blue is best uncooked.
Cottage	A soft, white, unripened cheese with a rather lumpy texture, high moisture content and a very mild flavour. Available plain or flavoured with herbs or fruit, and generally sold in cartons.	Usually used uncooked, sometimes cooked in savoury dishes or cheesecakes.
Cream	A soft, white, unripened cheese with a rich, creamy flavour. Available plain or flavoured with herbs, nuts or fruit. Sold in small cartons, foil packages or from a bulk container.	Use uncooked or cooked, in savoury pies or cheese-cakes and other desserts.
Curd	A soft, slightly granular, unripened cheese with a clean, acid flavour. Usually sold from a bulk container.	Generally used in combination with other ingredients (eg. in savoury pies and cheesecakes).
Derby	A hard, close-textured, white cheese, mild when young but developing a full flavour as it matures. Sage Derby is a green-marbled cheese with a sharp tang and the flavour of sage.	White and Sage Derbies are best uncooked.

CHEESE	CHARACTERISTICS	USE
Double Gloucester	A hard, orangey-yellow cheese with a close, crumbly texture and a full, mellow flavour rather similar to mature Cheddar.	Use uncooked or crumble to cook in pies and sauces.
Dunlop	A hard, yellow, Scottish cheese, not unlike Cheddar, but more moist and with a closer texture.	Use uncooked or cook as for Cheddar.
Highland Crowdie	A finely ground cottage cheese, high in protein and low in fat, with a light, fresh flavour.	Use uncooked.
Hramsa	A soft cheese made from fresh double cream and delicately flavoured with wild garlic.	Use uncooked, plain or combined with other ingredients (eg. in dips and savoury spreads).
Islay	A miniature Dunlop, at its best when fairly mature.	An excellent melting cheese, good on toast and in sauces.
Lancashire	A white, open-textured, semi-hard cheese, inclined to crumble when cut. The flavour is mild, becoming very much stronger as the cheese matures.	Very good uncooked, but also an excellent toasting cheese.
Leicester	A hard, orangey-red cheese, slightly granular in texture. The flavour is fairly strong and sweet.	Another very good toasting cheese.
Orkney	A firm, white or red cheese, close-textured and with a mellow flavour; there is also a smoked variety with a more subtle flavour. Made as 454-g (1-lb) miniature cheeses.	Best uncooked.
Stilton	A semi-hard cheese with a crinkled greyish rind. When young it is white and slightly crumbly, with a light, mild flavour. It matures with abundant blue veining to a moister cheese with a rich mellow flavour. Made in large cylinders and sold whole or in wedges.	Excellent uncooked; Stilton is a favourite after-dinner cheese, often served with port.
Wensleydale	A white close-textured cheese with a clean, mild and slightly sweet flavour. Blue Wensleydale is a soft, creamy cheese with blue veining and a rich flavour.	Use white Wensleydale uncooked or cooked. Blue is best uncooked.
Windsor Red	A mature Cheddar cheese injected with English fruit wine to give a hard, yellow cheese with red veining. The texture is rather crumbly and the flavour rich and strong.	Usually eaten uncooked, but may be cooked as for Cheddar.

Continental cheeses

CHEESE	CHARACTERISTICS	USE
Bel Paese *(Italian)*	A semi-soft, even-textured cheese, creamy-white in colour and usually mild in flavour. Sold in segments and wheels.	Use uncooked or combine with a sharp cheese, such as Parmesan, for cooking.
Brie *(French)*	A soft, whitish cheese with a thin, edible, white to grey crust, made in large flat wheels. Ripens from a mild to a rich, creamy flavour, but then deteriorates quickly.	Use uncooked.
Camembert *(French)*	A soft, creamy-coloured cheese with an edible crust, made in small rounds. Ripens from a mild to a rich, pungent flavour, but then deteriorates quickly. Sold boxed or in individual foil-wrapped portions.	Excellent uncooked, served with French bread or unsalted biscuits.
Danish Blue *(Danish)*	A white, semi-soft cheese with blue veining and rather crumbly texture. The flavour is sharp and salty.	Use uncooked.
Edam *(Dutch)*	A firm, smooth, deep yellow cheese, made in balls weighing 450 g–2 kg (1–5 lb) and coated with bright red wax. Mild in flavour.	Use uncooked or cooked on toast and in sauces; a good melting cheese.
Emmenthal *(Swiss)*	A firm, rich cheese, light yellow in colour and with large holes. Mellow in flavour, similar to Gruyère.	Excellent uncooked, also a good melting cheese.
Feta *(Greek)*	A semi-soft, white, flaky cheese, preserved in brine, with a salty, sour flavour.	Good uncooked or cooked in Greek dishes.
Fontina *(Italian)*	A semi-soft, creamy-textured cheese, light yellow in colour, with a scattering of small holes. The flavour is delicate and nutty, becoming smoky as it matures.	Use uncooked or cooked, a good melting cheese.
Gjetost *(Norwegian)*	A hard, brown, unripened cheese with a pungent, sweetish flavour. Mysost and Primost are similar but without the genuine goat's milk flavour.	Use uncooked as a snack, served with wholemeal or rye bread or crispbread.
Gorgonzola *(Italian)*	A semi-soft, white cheese with blue-green veining and a rich, piquant flavour.	Use uncooked.
Gouda *(Dutch)*	A hard, yellow cheese with a mild flavour, becoming mellower with maturity.	Use uncooked or cooked; mature Gouda is good in sauces and savoury dishes.
Gruyère *(Swiss)*	A hard, pale yellow cheese with small holes. The distinctive flavour is mellow, sweetish and rich.	Use uncooked or cooked. A good melting cheese to combine with the stronger flavour of Parmesan.

CHEESE	CHARACTERISTICS	USE
Jarlsberg *(Norwegian)*	A semi-hard, pale yellow cheese with irregular holes and a smooth texture. The flavour is mild and slightly sweet.	Best uncooked, served with savoury breads and biscuits.
Limburger *(Belgian)*	A semi-hard, smooth-textured cheese, creamy white with a dark orange outside. It has a full flavour and is strong smelling.	Use uncooked.
Mozzarella *(Italian)*	A firm, soft, unripened cheese, creamy-coloured and mild in flavour.	Use uncooked or cooked, especially in pizza.
Münster *(French)*	A semi-soft cheese, rich and creamy, developing a red skin. It has a sharp flavour and strong smell.	Best used uncooked.
Parmesan *(Italian)*	A very hard, grainy, pale yellow cheese, full of tiny holes and with a strong flavour. Often sold grated.	Sprinkle uncooked on hot dishes or use cooked, mixed with softer cheeses.
Petit Suisse *(French)*	A soft, unsalted, unripened cream cheese with a very mild flavour. Sold in small, foil-wrapped packs.	Use uncooked, especially with soft fruit desserts.
Port Salut *(French)*	A semi-hard, very smooth-textured, golden cheese with orange rind and a mild, creamy flavour.	Use uncooked or cooked.
Provolone *(Italian)*	A hard, golden or light brown cheese, made in pear-shapes, balls and sausages. Matures from a mild to a sharp flavour.	Good uncooked when young or cooked when matured.
Raclette *(Swiss)*	A semi-hard, pale-coloured cheese with tiny holes and a thin, brownish rind.	Use uncooked or cooked.
Ricotta *(Italian)*	A soft, unripened whey cheese with a delicate, slightly sweet flavour.	Use uncooked or cooked, especially in sweet dishes.
Romano *(Italian)*	A hard, yellow cheese, rather like Parmesan, with a sharp flavour.	Use uncooked or cooked when young, or as a grating cheese when matured.
Roquefort *(French)*	A semi-soft, white cheese with blue-green veins. It is well matured, with a strong flavour and a characteristically pungent smell.	Use uncooked.
Samsoe *(Danish)*	A firm, light yellow cheese with holes and a delicate and slightly sweet flavour when young, becoming pungent as it matures.	Best uncooked; frequently used in open sandwiches.
Sapsago *(Swiss)*	A very hard green cheese. The colour and pungent flavour are produced by adding dried clover leaves.	Use grated in cooking.

Main course dishes

Welsh Rarebit

Colour index page 30
4 servings

4 slices white bread
225 g (8 oz) Cheddar cheese
60 ml (4 tbsp) brown ale
25 g (1 oz) butter or margarine
5 ml (1 level tsp) dry mustard
salt and pepper

1 Toast the bread slices in a toaster or under a grill and keep them warm until they are required.

2 Grate the cheese coarsely and put it in a heavy-based saucepan.

3 Add the ale and fat to the pan and heat the mixture very gently, stirring continuously.

4 Stir in the mustard and salt and pepper. Cook the mixture very gently until creamy, stirring all the time.

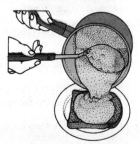

5 Pour the cheese mixture over the toast and put under a hot grill until golden and bubbling. Serve immediately.

Cheese on Toast

Colour index page 30
4 servings

225 g (8 oz) hard cheese, grated
5 ml (1 level tsp) dry mustard
salt and pepper
2.5–5 ml (½–1 tsp) Worcestershire sauce

milk to bind
4 slices white bread

For the garnish, optional: paprika

1. Mix the cheese with the mustard, salt, pepper and Worcestershire sauce and bind with enough milk to make a smooth paste.
2. Toast the bread on both sides, leaving one side only very lightly browned.
3. Spread the cheese mixture thickly on the lightly browned sides of the toast and cook under a hot grill until the cheese mixture is golden and bubbling. Sprinkle lightly with paprika if you wish.

Italian Cheese Toast

Colour index page 30
4 servings

150 ml (¼ pint) single cream
150 ml (¼ pint) milk
½ 60-g (2-oz) can anchovy fillets, drained
15 ml (1 tbsp) vegetable oil
5 ml (1 level tsp) cornflour
2.5 ml (½ level tsp) paprika
15 ml (1 tbsp) capers
French bread

225 g (8 oz) Mozzarella or Bel Paese cheese, thinly sliced

For the garnish:
15 ml (1 tbsp) chopped parsley or chopped fresh marjoram

1. Put the cream, milk, anchovy fillets, oil, cornflour and paprika in a saucepan and bring to the boil, stirring all the time. Boil for 1 minute, then reduce the heat and stir in the capers. Cover and keep warm while you toast the bread.
2. Cut eight 2.5-cm (1-in) thick diagonal slices from the French bread and toast them until golden on both sides. Arrange them in a single layer in a large flameproof dish (or divide between four individual flameproof dishes).
3. Place the cheese slices, overlapping slightly, on the bread and grill until just melted. Spoon the cream mixture over evenly. Garnish with the chopped parsley and serve immediately.

Raclette

Colour index page 30
4 servings

450 g (1 lb) Raclette cheese

pepper or paprika

1. Using a sharp knife, cut the rind from the cheese and slice the cheese thinly.
2. Place the slices, overlapping slightly, in a shallow ovenproof dish and bake at 190°C (375°F) mark 5 for 4–6 minutes, until the cheese has just melted and the surface is smooth.
3. Sprinkle with freshly ground pepper or paprika and serve in the cooking dish to keep hot. It can be eaten by itself or may be served with hot boiled potatoes, pickled cucumbers and cocktail onions.

Swiss Cheese and Tomato Bake

Colour index page 30
4 servings

3 thick slices white bread
30 ml (2 tbsp) vegetable oil
3 medium tomatoes, thinly sliced
225 g (8 oz) Gruyère or Emmenthal cheese, grated
2 eggs

350 ml (12 fl oz) milk
5 ml (1 level tsp) salt
2.5 ml (½ level tsp) paprika
2.5 ml (½ level tsp) dry mustard

1. Trim the crusts from the slices of bread, cut the bread into cubes and fry quickly in the oil until crisp and golden on all sides.
2. Grease a 23-cm (9-in) pie dish. Arrange the croûtons in the dish and place the tomato slices over them. Sprinkle evenly with the grated cheese.
3. Beat the eggs, milk, salt and flavourings with a fork or whisk and pour the mixture over the cheese. Bake at 180°C (350°F) mark 4 for 40 minutes, or until browned. Serve at once.

Swiss Fondue

Colour index page 30

4 servings

1 clove garlic, halved
300 ml (½ pint) dry white
* wine*
squeeze lemon juice
225 g (8 oz) Gruyère
* cheese*
225 g (8 oz) Emmenthal
* cheese*
20 ml (4 level tsp) cornflour
pepper
grated nutmeg
2 liqueur glasses kirsch

To serve:
crusty bread

1 Rub the inside of a flameproof dish with the garlic clove. Discard the garlic after use.

2 Pour in the wine and lemon juice and warm through. Place the dish over gentle heat.

3 Grate the cheeses. Blend the cornflour, pepper and grated nutmeg to a smooth cream with the measured kirsch.

4 Add the cheese gradually to the wine and lemon juice and heat gently, stirring, until the cheese has melted. Stir in the cornflour mixture.

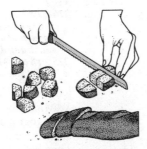

5 Continue cooking for 2–3 minutes until the mixture is thick and creamy. Cut bread into chunks for dipping into the fondue.

6 Keep the fondue hot on a table-top burner. Each person spears chunks of bread on a long fork and dips into the fondue.

Cheddar and Cider Fondue

Colour index page 30

4 servings

1 clove garlic, skinned and
* halved*
300 ml (½ pint) cider
squeeze lemon juice
450 g (1 lb) Cheddar
* cheese, cut into thin*
* strips*
20 ml (4 level tsp) cornflour

2 liqueur glasses brandy
pepper
grated nutmeg

To serve:
crusty bread

1. Rub the inside of a flameproof dish with the garlic clove. Put the cider and lemon juice in the dish and heat gently to simmering point.
2. Add the cheese and continue to heat gently, stirring well until the cheese has melted and begun to cook. Do not allow to boil.
3. Blend the cornflour, brandy and seasonings to a smooth paste and stir into the cheese mixture. Cook for a further 2–3 minutes until it is thick and creamy. Cut the bread into chunks for dipping into the cheese fondue.
4. Keep the fondue hot on a table-top burner. Each person spears chunks of bread on a long fork and dips into the fondue.

Cheese Pudding

Colour index page 30

4 servings

4–6 slices white bread,
* weighing 100 g (4 oz)*
60 ml (4 tbsp) dry white
* wine, optional*
25 g (1 oz) butter,
* melted*

2 eggs, beaten
300 ml (½ pint) milk
salt and pepper
100 g (4 oz) mature cheese,
* grated*

1. Grease a 900-ml (1½-pint) capacity ovenproof dish. Cut the bread into cubes and arrange them in the bottom of the dish. Moisten with the wine (if it is being used) and the melted butter.
2. Mix the eggs and milk, season well and pour over the bread mixture. Sprinkle with the grated cheese and bake at 190°C (375°F) mark 5 for about 30 minutes, until golden and well risen. Serve at once.

SAVOURY CHEESE PUDDING: Halve *6–8 thin slices buttered bread* and layer them in a greased pie dish. Beat together *2 eggs*, a *little made mustard, salt, pepper*, a *skinned and chopped onion* and *10 ml (2 tsp) tomato ketchup*. Add *75 g (3 oz) grated cheese* and *568 ml (1 pint) milk.* Pour the mixture over the bread and leave to stand for 10–15 minutes. Mix a further *25 g (1 oz) grated cheese* with *25 g (1 oz) fresh white breadcrumbs* and sprinkle it over the top. Bake at 180°C (350°F) mark 4 for about 45 minutes, until set and golden brown on top.

INDIVIDUAL CHEDDAR AND TOMATO PUDDINGS: Drain and purée a *397-g (14-oz) can tomatoes.* Heat the purée gently and add *50 g (2 oz) fresh white breadcrumbs* and *100 g (4 oz) Cheddar cheese,* grated; blend the mixture into *3 egg yolks,* lightly beaten. Whisk *3 egg whites* stiffly, fold them into the tomato mixture and season to taste with *salt* and *pepper.* Divide the mixture between four greased individual ovenproof dishes and place them in a tin of hot water. Bake at 180°C (350°F) mark 4 for 45 minutes–1 hour, until set.

Quiches, pies and patties

Quiche Lorraine

Colour index
page 31

4 servings

**shortcrust pastry made with
150 g (5 oz) flour,
page 343**
**75–100 g (3–4 oz) lean
streaky bacon,
rinded**
2 eggs
**150 ml (¼ pint) single
cream or creamy
milk**
**75–100 g (3–4 oz) Gruyère
or Emmenthal cheese,
grated**
2.5 ml (½ level tsp) salt
freshly ground black pepper

1 Roll out the pastry thinly on a lightly floured surface to a 25-cm (10-in) circle. Lift the pastry with a rolling pin and lower it into a 20.5-cm (8-in) flan dish or tin placed on a baking sheet. Lightly ease the pastry to fit the tin, pressing it into the sides with one finger. Do not stretch the pastry. Trim round the top of the flan dish or tin with a sharp knife, or roll a rolling pin over the top, to remove surplus pastry.

2 Fry the bacon gently in its own fat until it is browned and crisp.

3 Drain bacon well on kitchen paper towel and crumble into pieces.

4 Spread the crumbled bacon pieces in the prepared flan case.

5 Beat together the eggs and cream. Add grated cheese and season well.

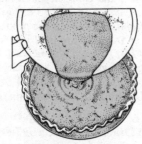

6 Pour the egg mixture into the flan case. Bake at 200°C (400°F) mark 6 for about 30 minutes.

7 When the quiche is cooked, a knife inserted in the centre should come out clean.

CHEDDAR CHEESE QUICHE: Prepare the quiche as above, but omit the bacon and add **75–100 g (3–4 oz) lightly boiled onion rings**, and use **Cheddar cheese**. Bake at 200°C (400°F) mark 6.

4–6 servings

HERBED QUICHE: Make *shortcrust pastry* (page 343) with 225 g (8 oz) flour, roll it out thinly on a lightly floured surface and use it to line a 23-cm (9-in) flan dish or tin placed on a baking sheet. Bake blind (page 350) at 200°C (400°F) mark 6 for 15 minutes, until the pastry is just set. Mix *150 g (5 oz) Gruyère cheese* or Emmenthal cheese, grated, with *2.5 ml (½ level tsp) dried basil* and *2.5 ml (½ level tsp) dried marjoram*. Sprinkle over the base of the pastry case. Beat together *2 eggs, 225 ml (8 fl oz) double cream* or whipping cream, *5 ml (1 level tsp) salt* and *pepper* to taste. Pour the egg mixture into the flan case and bake at 200°C (400°F) mark 6 for 15–20 minutes until well risen and golden.

ROQUEFORT QUICHE: Make *shortcrust pastry* (page 343) with 150 g (5 oz) flour, roll it out thinly on a lightly floured surface and use it to line a 20.5-cm (8-in) flan dish or tin placed on a baking sheet. Bake blind (page 350) at 200°C (400°F) mark 6 for 15 minutes, until the pastry is just set. Cream *75 g (3 oz) Roquefort cheese* or other blue cheese with *175 g (6 oz) cream cheese*, stir in *2 beaten eggs, 150 ml (¼ pint) single cream, 15 ml (1 tbsp) chopped chives* and season to taste. Pour the mixture into the flan case and bake at 190°C (375°F) mark 5 for 30 minutes or until well risen and golden.

Colour index
page 31

4–6 servings

Cheese, Sausage and Spinach Pie

**225 g (8 oz) sausages,
chopped**
3 eggs
**226-g (8-oz) packet
frozen chopped
spinach, thawed
and drained well**
**225 g (8 oz) Mozzarella
or Bel Paese cheese,
grated**
100 g (4 oz) curd cheese
1.25 ml (¼ level tsp) salt
pepper
pinch garlic salt
**shortcrust pastry made
with 200 g (7 oz) flour,
page 343**

1. Make the filling for the pie. Fry the chopped sausages for about 10 minutes or until well browned, stirring frequently. Remove and drain well. Reserve 1 egg yolk. Mix the remaining eggs with the sausage, spinach, cheeses, salt, pepper and garlic salt.
2. Divide the pastry into two pieces, one slightly larger than the other. Roll out the larger piece and use to line an 18-cm (7-in) flan dish or tin, or deep pie plate, leaving a 2.5-cm (1-in) rim. Spoon the filling on to the pastry.
3. Roll out the remaining pastry to a 20.5-cm (8-in) circle and cut a small hole in the centre. Place the pastry over the filling and trim top and bottom crusts together to leave a 1-cm (½-in) rim. Seal the edges firmly together then pinch the rim to make a stand-up decorative edge.
4. Cut slits in the pastry top with a sharp knife. Use the pastry trimmings to make leaf shapes, decorate the pie with them and glaze with the reserved egg yolk beaten with a little water.
5. Bake at 190°C (375°F) mark 5 for 1¼ hours, or until the pastry is golden and well glazed. Leave the pie to stand for at least 10 minutes to set slightly before slicing it. Serve hot or cold.

Cheese and Onion Quiche

Colour index
page 31
4 servings

shortcrust pastry made with
175 g (6 oz) flour,
page 343
25 g (1 oz) butter or
margarine
450 g (1 lb) onions,
skinned and sliced into
rings
1 egg, beaten
150 ml (¼ pint) single
cream or creamy milk

salt and pepper
175 g (6 oz) Gruyère or
Emmenthal cheese,
grated

For the garnish, optional:
chopped parsley
red pepper rings

1. Roll out the pastry thinly on a lightly floured surface and use it to line a 20.5-cm (8-in) flan dish or tin placed on a baking sheet. Bake the pastry case blind (page 350) at 200°C (400°F) mark 6 for 15 minutes, or until the pastry is just set.
2. Meanwhile, melt the butter or margarine in a large frying pan, add the onion rings and cook them gently, covered, for 15 minutes or until tender but not browned. Drain well. Spread the onion rings evenly over the base of the pastry case.
3. Beat together the egg and cream and season with salt and pepper. Stir in half the grated cheese and pour the mixture over the onions in the pastry case. Sprinkle the remaining cheese over the top.
4. Bake at 190°C (375°F) mark 5 for about 20 minutes, until well risen and golden; a knife inserted in the centre should come out clean.
5. Garnish the quiche with chopped parsley and red pepper rings, if you wish.

Italian Cheese and Ham Pie

Colour index
page 31
4–6 servings

shortcrust pastry made
with 200 g (7 oz) flour,
page 343
beaten egg yolk
to glaze
225 g (8 oz) cottage or
Ricotta cheese
225 g (8 oz) curd cheese
50 g (2 oz) Parmesan or
Romano cheese,
grated

225 g (8 oz) cooked ham,
diced
2 eggs, beaten
5 ml (1 level tsp) Italian
seasoning
1.25 ml (¼ level tsp)
salt
1.25 ml (¼ level tsp)
pepper

1. Roll out two thirds of the pastry to a 25-cm (10-in) circle, 0.3 cm (⅛ in) thick and use it to line a 20.5-cm (8-in) spring-release cake tin. Trim the pastry to the top edge of the tin and brush it with some of the beaten egg yolk to glaze.
2. Mix the cheeses, ham, eggs, Italian seasoning, salt and pepper together. Spoon the mixture into the pastry case and fold the edges over the filling. Brush with more beaten egg yolk.
3. Roll out the remaining pastry to a 20.5-cm (8-in) circle and cut a decorative design in it if you wish. Place it over the filling, sealing the edge by pressing lightly on to the rim of the pastry base. Brush the top with the remaining egg yolk.
4. Bake the pie at 190°C (375°F) mark 5 for 1 hour. When cooked, a knife inserted in the centre of the pie should come out clean. Leave the pie to stand for 10 minutes before cutting into wedges, or leave to cool completely before cutting it if you are serving it cold.

Fried Cheese Patties

Colour index
page 31
6 servings

65 g (2½ oz) butter or
margarine
5 ml (1 level tsp) made
mustard
2.5 ml (½ level tsp) salt
1.25 ml (¼ level tsp)
pepper
plain flour
350 ml (12 fl oz) milk
225 g (8 oz) Gruyère,
Emmenthal or Jarlsberg
cheese, grated
15 ml (1 tbsp) grated
onion

2 egg yolks
1 egg
50 g (2 oz) dried
breadcrumbs
100 ml (4 fl oz) vegetable
oil

To serve, optional:
tomato sauce, page 337

1 Melt the butter or margarine in a saucepan and stir in the mustard, salt, pepper and 75 g (3 oz) flour. Cook, stirring, for 2 minutes. Slowly stir in the milk and cook, stirring constantly, until the sauce has thickened. Add the grated cheese and onion and cook for a further 2–3 minutes, stirring until the cheese has melted and the sauce is smooth again. Remove the saucepan from the heat and leave to cool slightly. Beat the egg yolks.

2 Stir a little hot sauce into the egg yolks. Slowly pour the egg mixture into the sauce and cook, stirring, until thickened. Do not boil.

3 Cover and refrigerate for at least 6 hours or overnight. Beat the egg and put the breadcrumbs and a little flour on separate sheets of greaseproof paper.

4 On the floured paper, with floured hands, shape the cheese mixture into cakes about 1 cm (½ in) thick. Coat with egg, then breadcrumbs.

5 Heat the oil in a large frying pan. Add the patties a few at a time and cook on one side for about 2 minutes until browned. Turn the patties and cook for a further 2 minutes.

6 Drain the cooked patties on kitchen paper towel and keep them warm while the rest are being cooked. Serve the patties with tomato sauce, if you wish.

Cheese desserts

Cheese pies and cakes make an elegant finale to lunch or dinner. Pies made with cream cheese will be rich and smooth, those made with cottage cheese light and fluffy with a less pronounced cheese flavour. It is traditional to make cheesecakes on a crust of pastry or biscuit crumbs, and they are frequently served with fruit. A tart cherry or blackcurrant topping is particularly good.

Store leftovers, closely wrapped in cling film, in the refrigerator and serve within a day or two. Cheesecakes freeze well, whether set with gelatine or by baking. Freeze in the tin, then turn out and wrap in freezer film or foil.

Baked Rich Cheesecake

550 g (1¼ lb) cream cheese
200 g (7 oz) granulated sugar
2 eggs
1 egg yolk
20 ml (4 level tsp) plain flour
30 ml (2 tbsp) double or whipping cream
15 ml (1 level tbsp) grated orange rind
pinch salt

For the crust:
150 g (5 oz) plain flour
175 g (6 oz) butter
50 g (2 oz) sugar
1 egg yolk
grated rind of 1 lemon

To serve:
150 ml (¼ pint) soured cream

Colour index page 98

8 servings

1 Make the crust. Beat together the flour, butter, sugar, egg yolk and lemon rind until well mixed. Cover and refrigerate for 1 hour.

2 Press one third of the dough on to the base of a 20.5-cm (8-in) spring-release cake tin and bake at 200°C (400°F) mark 6 for 8 minutes. Cool.

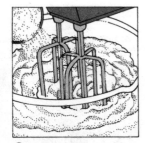

3 In a large bowl, beat the cream cheese until smooth (this is easier with an electric mixer). Slowly beat in the sugar until evenly blended.

4 Add all the remaining ingredients and continue beating until the mixture is really smooth.

5 Press the remaining dough firmly round the sides of the cake tin, to within 2.5 cm (1 in) of the top. Increase the oven temperature to 240°C (475°F) mark 9.

6 Pour cheese mixture into tin; bake for 12 minutes. Bake for a further 35 minutes at 150°C (300°F) mark 2. Turn off oven but leave cheesecake in oven 30 minutes. Cool.

7 Refrigerate until required. To serve, remove sides of tin and loosen cake from the base with a palette knife. Slide it on to a plate and spread the top with soured cream.

Colour index page 98

8 servings

Chocolate Cheesecake

550 g (1¼ lb) cream cheese
200 g (7 oz) sugar
20 ml (4 level tsp) plain flour
1 egg yolk
2 eggs
30 ml (2 tbsp) milk
1.25 ml (¼ level tsp) salt

100 g (4 oz) plain chocolate, melted

For the crust:
150 g (5 oz) plain flour
175 g (6 oz) butter
50 g (2 oz) sugar
1 egg yolk

1. Using a mixer on low speed, beat all the ingredients for the crust together. Chill for 1 hour.
2. Remove one third of the dough from the refrigerator and press it over the base of a 20.5-cm (8-in) spring-release cake tin. Bake in the oven at 200°C (400°F) mark 6 for 8 minutes. Allow to cool.
3. Using a mixer, beat the cream cheese until just smooth. On low speed, gradually add the remaining ingredients and beat until well mixed. Turn the mixer to high speed and beat for 5 minutes.
4. Press the remaining dough round the sides of the tin to within 2.5 cm (1 in) of the top. Pour the cream cheese mixture into the tin and bake at 240°C (475°F) mark 9 for 12 minutes. Turn the oven down to 150°C (300°F) mark 2 and bake for a further 50 minutes. Turn off the oven but leave the cheesecake in it for another 30 minutes.
5. Cool in tin for 30 minutes, then cover and chill.
6. Just before serving, remove the sides of the tin, loosen the cheesecake from the base and slide it on to a plate. Swirl with whipped cream if you wish.

Colour index page 98

8 servings

Cherry Cheesecake

450 g (1 lb) cream cheese
225 g (8 oz) sugar
4 eggs
300 ml (½ pint) soured cream
20 ml (4 level tsp) cornflour
15 ml (1 tbsp) lemon juice
5 ml (1 tsp) vanilla essence

For the crust:
150 g (5 oz) digestive biscuits

50 g (2 oz) walnuts, finely chopped
50 g (2 oz) sugar
65 g (2½ oz) butter or margarine, melted

For the topping:
396-g (14-oz) can cherry pie filling
15 ml (1 tbsp) grated lemon rind
2.5 ml (½ tsp) lemon juice

1. Crush the digestive biscuits and mix with the remaining ingredients for the crust. Press firmly on to the base and sides of a 20.5-cm (8-in) spring-release cake tin, to within 4 cm (1½ in) of the top edge.
2. Beat the cream cheese with the sugar. Gradually beat in the remaining ingredients for the filling.
3. Pour the mixture into the crust and bake at 180°C (350°F) mark 4 for 1 hour. Turn off the oven but leave the cheesecake in it for 30 minutes. Cool in the tin, then cover and chill until required.
4. Remove the sides of the tin, loosen the cake from the base and slide it on to a plate. Mix the ingredients for the topping and spoon over the cake.

Unbaked Cheesecake

225 ml (8 fl oz) milk
225 g (8 oz) granulated
    sugar
2 eggs, separated
pinch salt
20 ml (4 level tsp)
    powdered gelatine
15 ml (1 tbsp) lemon
    juice
5 ml (1 tsp) grated
    lemon rind
450 g (1 lb) cottage
    cheese
2.5 ml (½ tsp) vanilla
    essence
150 ml (¼ pint) double or
    whipping cream

For the crust:
225 g (8 oz) wheatmeal
    or plain biscuits,
    crushed
100 g (4 oz) butter,
    melted

To serve:
fresh fruit, canned fruit
    or chopped nuts

Colour index page 98

6–8 servings

1 Put the milk and sugar in a saucepan and heat gently, stirring all the time, until the milk is warm and the sugar has dissolved. Meanwhile, beat the egg yolks. Pour the warm milk mixture slowly on to the beaten egg yolks, stirring well. Return the mixture to the pan with the salt and heat gently, stirring constantly until the mixture coats the back of a spoon. Do not allow to boil. Remove the custard from the heat and cool slightly.

2 Dissolve the gelatine in the lemon juice in a bowl over a pan of hot water. Stir into custard with lemon rind. Cool.

3 Press the cottage cheese through a sieve into a large bowl to remove any lumps.

4 Stir the vanilla essence and custard into the sieved cheese. Refrigerate for about 30 minutes, stirring frequently, until just beginning to set.

5 Meanwhile, make crust. Mix biscuit crumbs with butter. Press half on to base of a 20.5-cm (8-in) spring-release cake tin.

6 Whisk the egg whites until stiff peaks form and spoon them on to the cheese mixture in the bowl.

7 Whip the cream lightly and spoon on to the whites. Gently fold the whites and cream into the cheese mixture.

8 Pour the cheese mixture into the crumb-lined tin and level the top gently with a palette knife or the back of a spoon.

9 Spread the remaining crumb mixture evenly on top of the cheesecake and chill it until firm or until required.

10 To serve, remove side of tin and loosen cake from base. Slide on to a plate and decorate with fruit or chopped nuts.

Colour index page 98

6 servings

Cream Cheese and Rhubarb Pie

shortcrust pastry made
    with 225 g (8 oz) flour,
    page 343
700 g (1½ lb) rhubarb,
    washed and chopped into
    2.5-cm (1-in) pieces
350 g (12 oz) sugar
45 ml (3 level tbsp)
    cornflour

1.25 ml (¼ level tsp) salt
225 g (8 oz) cream cheese
2 eggs

To serve:
150 ml (¼ pint) soured
    cream
25 g (1 oz) blanched
    almonds

1. Roll out the pastry, use it to line a 20.5-cm (8-in) flan dish or tin and bake blind (page 350) at 200°C (400°F) mark 6 for 15 minutes. Put the chopped rhubarb, 225 g (8 oz) sugar, cornflour and salt into a saucepan and cook until the mixture comes to the boil and thickens, stirring frequently.
2. Pour the rhubarb mixture into the pastry case and bake at 220°C (425°F) mark 7 for 10 minutes.
3. Beat the cream cheese, eggs and remaining sugar until smooth and pour over the rhubarb mixture. Bake at 180°C (350°F) mark 4 for 30–35 minutes, or until set. Cool the pie and refrigerate until required.
4. Before serving, spread the soured cream over the cheese pie and garnish with the almonds.

Colour index page 98

6–8 servings

Luxury Cheese Flan

350 g (12 oz) cream cheese,
    softened
2 eggs, beaten
100 g (4 oz) sugar
2.5 ml (½ tsp) vanilla
    essence

For the crust:
150 g (5 oz) digestive
    biscuits

25 g (1 oz) brown sugar
2.5 ml (½ level tsp) ground
    cinnamon
65 g (2½ oz) butter, melted

To serve:
150 ml (¼ pint) soured
    cream

1. Prepare the crust. Crush the biscuits and stir in the remaining ingredients. Grease a 20.5-cm (8-in) flan dish or tin and press the crumb mixture on to the base and sides with the back of a spoon.
2. Beat the cheese with the eggs, sugar and vanilla essence until well mixed and smooth. Pour into the biscuit crumb crust.
3. Bake at 180°C (350°F) mark 4 for 35 minutes, or until the filling is set. When the flan is completely cool, spread the soured cream over the top and refrigerate it until required.

PEACH CHEESE FLAN: Prepare the flan as above, omitting the soured cream topping. Meanwhile, drain well an 822-g (29-oz) can sliced cling peaches, dry the slices with kitchen paper towel and chill them while the flan is cooling. Melt 45 ml (3 tbsp) apricot jam with 5 ml (1 tsp) lemon juice, mixing well. Arrange the peach slices on the flan in overlapping rows and brush with the apricot glaze.

159

SHELLFISH

Shellfish fall into two groups, crustaceans and molluscs. Crustaceans have an external skeleton which forms a jointed but rather fragile shell; this group includes prawns, crabs and lobsters. Although sometimes found on the seashore, crustaceans are mainly inhabitants of deep water. Molluscs, invertebrates usually protected by a strong shell, are estuary or shore dwelling creatures and include mussels, oysters, cockles, winkles, whelks and clams. Opening the shell, or separating the animal from it, kills a mollusc instantly.

Shellfish should be eaten absolutely fresh, so always buy from a reliable source and take care to clean all types thoroughly before cooking.

While it is unwise to freeze your own shellfish – since the temperature required for satisfactory preservation of shellfish is lower than that normally obtainable in any domestic freezer – commercially frozen shellfish are useful when the type you require is out of season. You can also freeze very fresh shellfish in made-up dishes such as soups, fish pies and quiches. Some shellfish are available canned and are another useful standby to have in the store cupboard.

Mussels

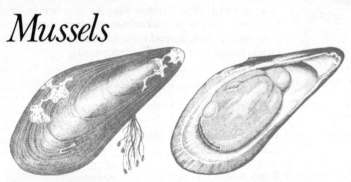

Mussels are in season in the autumn and winter. They must be alive when bought, their shells tightly closed; discard any with gaping shells or whose shells remain open when tapped lightly with the fingers. Always eat mussels on the day that you buy them.

Mussels on the commercial market are collected from waters known to be clean, but they need to be carefully washed before cooking. Wash them thoroughly in several changes of water and discard any that remain open or floating in the water. Scrub each shell individually and remove any barnacles and weed. Cut off the beards, or tufts of hair, which protrude from the closed shell with a pair of kitchen scissors or sharp knife. The final washing water should be clean.

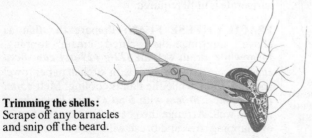

Trimming the shells:
Scrape off any barnacles and snip off the beard.

Colour index
page 24
4 servings

Moules à la Marinière

4 dozen mussels, about 3.4 litres (6 pints)
butter
4 shallots or 1 onion, skinned and finely chopped

½ bottle dry white wine
2 sprigs thyme, optional
bay leaf
pepper
chopped parsley
10 ml (2 level tsp) flour

1. Clean the mussels thoroughly (left).
2. Melt a large knob of butter in a saucepan and sauté the shallots until soft but not coloured. Add the wine, thyme, bay leaf, pepper and a small handful of chopped parsley. Cover and simmer for about 10 minutes.
3. Drain the mussels and add to the pan. Cover and steam for 5 minutes or until the shells are open, shaking the pan often. Remove them from the pan with a slotted spoon.
4. Remove the top shells and place the mussels on the half shell in warmed soup plates. Keep warm.
5. Strain the liquid and boil until reduced by half. Blend a small knob of butter with the flour and whisk into the liquid in small pieces. Adjust the seasoning. When thickened, pour over the mussels.
6. Sprinkle with chopped parsley before serving.

Cooking mussels: Steam mussels until the shells open; remove from the pan.

Arranging in plates: Place the mussels, on their shells, in wide soup plates.

Oysters

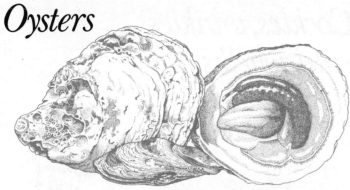

Like mussels, oysters are in season in the coldest months of the year. Some imported frozen oysters are available all year round, but this is mainly for the restaurant trade. Before they are marketed, oysters are kept alive for 2–3 days in purification tanks, with water washing through them to ensure the removal of any pollution. Always buy oysters from a reputable source and eat them on the day that you buy them.

Until the 19th century oysters were everyday fare, but indiscriminate gathering has depleted the oyster beds and they have become something of a luxury. English Natives are generally recognised as the finest oysters in the world and are best served 'au naturel', but the smaller Portuguese and Pacific varieties also grown here are quite adequate for cooked dishes.

OPENING OYSTERS

Oysters may be eaten raw or cooked. Scrub them under cold running water to remove the sand. Discard any that are open and remain open when tapped.

Work the point of the knife into the hinge linking the shells and cut through the ligament.

With deeper shell downwards, insert a knife between shells and cut round to hinge.

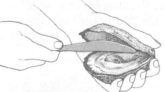

Prise the shells apart carefully, twisting with the knife to separate them.

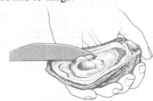

Discard the top shell, scrape off the beard and loosen the oyster. Retain as much liquid as possible.

Serving oysters 'au naturel':
Serve the oysters raw in the deeper half-shell with their liquid, on cracked ice. Season with cayenne or black pepper and, if you wish, serve with thin brown bread, butter and lemon. Allow 6 oysters per person for an hors d'oeuvre. (Colour index page 23)

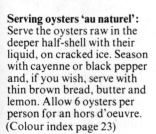

Baked Oysters with Spinach

Colour index page 24

6 first course servings

40 g (1½ oz) butter or
  margarine
150 g (5 oz) frozen
  chopped spinach,
  thawed
15 ml (1 tbsp) finely
  chopped onion
15 ml (1 tbsp) chopped
  parsley
bay leaf
2.5 ml (½ level tsp) salt
pinch cayenne pepper
25 g (1 oz) dried
  breadcrumbs

1½ dozen large or 2 dozen
  small oysters, on the
  half-shell
rock salt, optional
2 rashers bacon, rinded and
  chopped
grated Parmesan cheese,
  optional

For the garnish:
lemon wedges

1. Melt the fat, add the spinach, onion, parsley, bay leaf and seasonings and cook, stirring, until the spinach is hot; remove the bay leaf. Stir in the breadcrumbs and set the mixture aside.
2. Place the oysters in an ovenproof dish (if you wish, put enough rock salt in the bottom of the dish to prevent the oyster shells tipping over). Spoon the spinach mixture over them and sprinkle with the bacon, and cheese if you wish.
3. Bake at 220°C (425°F) mark 7 for 10 minutes, or until the bacon is crisp. Garnish with lemon wedges.

Fried Oysters

Colour index page 24

6 first course servings

2 dozen fresh or 350 g
  (12 oz) frozen shelled
  oysters
75 g (3 oz) salt biscuit
  crumbs

45 ml (3 tbsp) vegetable oil
40 g (1½ oz) butter

To serve:
lemon slices

1 Drain the oysters and dry them thoroughly with kitchen paper towel.

2 Spread half the biscuit crumbs on a piece of waxed paper and lay the oysters on them.

3 Sprinkle the remaining biscuit crumbs over the oysters and turn them until they are thoroughly coated with the crumbs, keeping the oysters as flat as possible: do not squash them.

4 Heat oil and butter in a frying pan. Add half the oysters and fry for about 5 minutes or until golden, turning once. Repeat with remaining oysters. Serve with lemon slices.

Clams

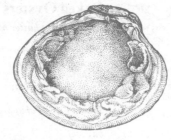

Clams are obtainable in certain areas all year round, although they are at their best in autumn. They are sold live in the shell, which may be hard or soft. Wash the clams well before cooking and discard any which have broken or gaping shells.

Clams are often eaten raw, like oysters (allow 12 clams per person), but they may be cooked according to any recipe for oysters or mussels.

OPENING AND SHELLING CLAMS

Cleaning clams: Scrub the shells thoroughly under cold running water with a stiff brush.

Opening clams: Prise the shell open with a knife and sever the hinge. Discard the top shell.

Shelling the clam: If you want to remove the clam from the shell, insert the point of the knife between the clam and the shell and cut the clam free. Remove any pieces of broken shell.

Steamed Clams

6 dozen clams	15 ml (1 tbsp) chopped
225 g (8 oz) butter, melted	parsley
salt and pepper	

Colour index page 34

6 servings

1. Scrub the clams thoroughly under cold running water until free of sand.
2. Put enough water in a large steamer or fish kettle to just cover the bottom and bring to the boil. Put the clams on the rack and lower into the pan. Cover tightly and steam for 5–10 minutes, just until the shells have opened.
3. Serve the clams in soup bowls with an individual dish of melted butter for each person. Pour the broth into mugs, season and sprinkle with parsley.
4. To eat them, pull clams from the shells by the neck, dip each one into the broth to remove any sand and then into the butter; all except the tough skin of the neck may be eaten. When the sand settles to the bottom, the broth may be drunk.

Cockles, winkles and whelks

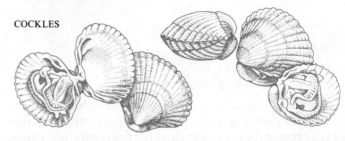

COCKLES

Cockles are at their best in winter. They are usually sold cooked, with or without the shell. Traditionally they are eaten plain with vinegar, but can be used in dishes in place of mussels or oysters.

If fresh cockles are available, the tightly closed shells should be left in a bucket of lightly salted water for about 1 hour to remove the sand. To prepare them, wash and scrub the shells thoroughly under cold running water, then cook in a large pan with a little water. Heat gently, shaking the pan, for about 5 minutes or until the shells have opened. Drain well and serve.

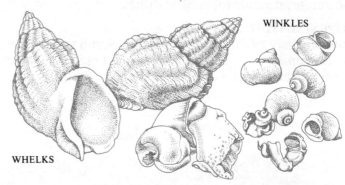

WINKLES

WHELKS

Winkles and whelks resemble each other in shape, but winkles are much smaller. They are available all year, but are at their best in the winter months. Although normally sold cooked, they can be bought live; to prepare live winkles or whelks, simmer them in boiling water for about 5 minutes. Whelks are shelled before serving and winkles are left in the shell; serve them with vinegar and plenty of salt and pepper.

To eat winkles: Remove each winkle from its shell with a pin. Sprinkle with vinegar and season to taste with salt and pepper.

Scallops

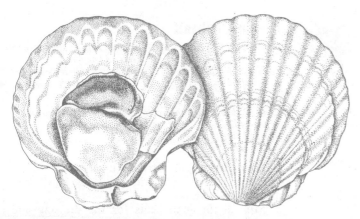

Scallops are at their best during the coldest months, although they are available all through the winter. Select those with tightly closed shells.

To prepare fresh scallops, rest the hinge of the shell on a flat surface and insert a small knife into one of the openings on either side of the shell, just above the hinge. Prise open slightly and, keeping the knife close against the flat shell, sever the muscle attaching the meat to the shell. Remove the meat and discard the black sac and remaining muscle. Scrub the shells to use as dishes.

Coquilles St. Jacques

*8 large fresh scallops,
   prepared, or 450 g (1 lb)
   scallop meat*
bouquet garni
*150 ml (¼ pint) dry white
   wine*
150 ml (¼ pint) water
100 g (4 oz) butter
*30 ml (2 tbsp) lemon
   juice*
*100 g (4 oz) button
   mushrooms, sliced*
*50 g (2 oz) onion, skinned
   and chopped*
*75 ml (5 level tbsp) plain
   flour*
1 egg yolk

*60 ml (4 tbsp) double
   cream*
salt and pepper
*25 g (1 oz) fresh white
   breadcrumbs*

For the garnish, optional:
parsley sprigs
lemon slices

Colour index page 24
4 first course servings

1 Put the scallops in a pan with the bouquet garni and pour over the wine and water. Bring to the boil, cover and simmer for 10–15 minutes until the scallops are tender.

2 Drain scallops, remove bouquet garni and reserve stock. Cut large scallops into pieces. Brush shells or ovenproof dishes with melted butter.

3 Melt 25 g (1 oz) butter with 15 ml (1 tbsp) lemon juice, add the mushrooms and onion. Cover and cook gently, without browning, for 10 minutes.

4 Add half remaining butter, stir in the flour and cook for 1–2 minutes without colouring. Stir in stock and simmer for 3 minutes. Remove from the heat.

5 Blend the egg yolk and cream; stir in a little hot sauce. Stir the mixture into the bulk of the sauce and carefully fold in the hot cooked scallops.

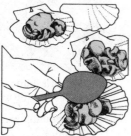

6 Season and reheat without boiling. Divide the mixture between the buttered shells or oven-proof dishes. Place them on a large baking sheet.

7 Melt remaining butter, stir in breadcrumbs and lemon juice. Sprinkle the mixture over the scallops and grill under medium heat until well browned.

Colour index page 24
4 first course servings

Scallops and Bacon

*8 fresh scallops, prepared, or
   450 g (1 lb) scallop meat*
salt and pepper
lemon juice
8 rashers streaky bacon

To serve:
*watercress sprigs, trimmed
   lemon wedges*

1. Sprinkle the scallops with salt, pepper and a little lemon juice to moisten them.
2. Rind the bacon and wrap a rasher round each scallop. Secure with wooden cocktail sticks.
3. Grill them under a moderate heat for about 5 minutes on each side, or until cooked through. Arrange on a serving dish and garnish with watercress and lemon wedges.

Colour index page 35
4 servings

Scallops Bonne Femme

*40 g (1½ oz) butter or
   margarine*
*1 small onion, skinned and
   chopped*
*8 fresh scallops, prepared,
   or 450 g (1 lb) scallop
   meat*
*225 g (8 oz) mushrooms,
   sliced*
*100 ml (4 fl oz) dry white
   wine*
15 ml (1 tbsp) lemon juice
100 ml (4 fl oz) water

*45 ml (3 level tbsp) plain
   flour*
5 ml (1 level tsp) salt
*225 ml (8 fl oz) single
   cream or half cream and
   half milk*

To serve:
4 slices toast
*30 ml (2 level tbsp) grated
   Parmesan cheese*
*30 ml (2 tbsp) chopped
   parsley*

1. Melt the butter or margarine in a large frying pan, add the chopped onion and sauté for about 5 minutes, until tender.
2. Add the scallops, mushrooms, wine, lemon juice and water. Cover and cook gently for about 15 minutes, or until the scallops are tender.
3. Blend the flour, salt and cream together and gradually stir into the scallop mixture. Cook until it thickens, stirring all the time.
4. Remove the crusts from the toast and cut into triangles. To serve, spoon the scallop mixture on to a warmed serving dish. Sprinkle with cheese and parsley and surround with toast triangles.

Prawns and shrimps

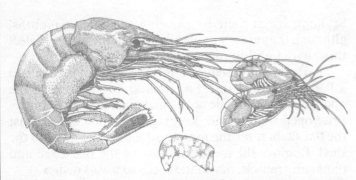

Prawns and shrimps range in size from the giant Dublin Bay prawns, of which half a dozen make an ample starter portion, to tiny shrimps about 1 cm (½ in) long. Dublin Bay prawns are most commonly available frozen; the tail meat is served as scampi, cooked and served hot in a variety of dishes. Smaller prawns and shrimps are sold fresh, usually boiled, either in the shell or ready shelled; they are also available frozen or canned. The best quality prawns come from the cold waters of the North Atlantic; warm water prawns do not have the same fullness of flavour.

Shrimps may also be bought potted in butter, to be served as a starter. These can be warmed slightly to bring out the full flavour of the shrimps and spices and may be served with brown bread, or toast, and butter.

SHELLING PRAWNS AND SHRIMPS

Tiny shrimps and small prawns are shelled most easily with the fingers. Larger varieties need the help of kitchen scissors or a knife (below).

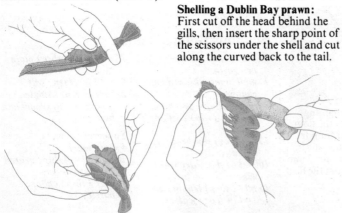

Shelling a Dublin Bay prawn:
First cut off the head behind the gills, then insert the sharp point of the scissors under the shell and cut along the curved back to the tail.

Peel back the shell with your fingers and gently begin lifting out the body of the prawn, starting at the head end.

Hold the tip of the tail firmly with one hand and hold the prawn close to the tail with the other; pull the tail free of the shell.

COOKING PRAWNS AND SHRIMPS

If you buy prawns or shrimps uncooked, simmer them in salted water until they are pink and opaque and then leave to cool in the cooking liquid. Small shrimps and prawns will take about 3 minutes to cook, but Dublin Bay prawns need to be cooked for 10–15 minutes. The stock may be used in a soup or sauce if you wish.

Colour index page 23

4 first course servings

Prawn Cocktail

100–175 g (4–6 oz) shelled prawns
½ lettuce, washed and shredded

For the dressing:
30 ml (2 tbsp) mayonnaise, page 462
30 ml (2 tbsp) tomato ketchup

30 ml (2 tbsp) single cream
salt and pepper
squeeze lemon juice or dash Worcestershire sauce

For the garnish:
cucumber slices, capers or lemon wedges

1. If using frozen prawns, thaw and drain them well. Line four glasses or individual serving bowls with the shredded lettuce.
2. Mix all the ingredients for the dressing and combine with the prawns.
3. Pile the mixture into the glasses and garnish with cucumber slices, capers or lemon wedges.

Colour index page 34

4 servings

Grilled Prawns with Garlic Butter

450 g (1 lb) shelled Dublin Bay prawns
3 large cloves garlic, skinned
75 g (3 oz) butter
15 ml (1 tbsp) lemon juice
5 ml (1 level tsp) salt
pinch pepper

2.5 ml (½ level tsp) dried oregano

To serve:
60 ml (4 tbsp) chopped parsley
lemon wedges

1 If you are using frozen prawns, thaw and drain them well. Spread them in a single layer in the bottom of the grill pan.

2 Crush the garlic cloves and put them into a small saucepan. Add the butter, lemon juice, salt, pepper and oregano. Heat through to melt butter.

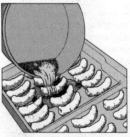 

3 Pour the garlic butter over the prawns, turning them to coat well. Grill for 5–8 minutes until the prawns are hot.

4 Transfer the prawns to a hot serving dish, pour over any butter from the pan and garnish with parsley and lemon wedges.

BUTTERFLY GRILLED PRAWNS: Prepare the prawns as above, but use *900 g (2 lb) unshelled prawns* and butterfly them (opposite); place them tail side up in grill pan before coating with butter.

Stir-fried Prawns

Colour index
page 34

4 servings

450 g (1 lb) shelled prawns	50 g (2 oz) mange tout,
350 g (12 oz) Chinese	trimmed or shelled peas
cabbage, washed	15 ml (1 level tbsp) salt
6 spring onions, trimmed	2.5 ml (½ level tsp) ground
75 ml (5 tbsp) water	ginger
30 ml (2 level tbsp)	2.5–5 ml (½–1 level tsp)
cornflour	paprika
20 ml (4 tsp) soy sauce	226-g (8-oz) can straw
5 ml (1 level tsp) sugar	mushrooms, or 120-g
60 ml (4 tbsp) oil	(4¼-oz) can whole
25–50 g (1–2 oz) blanched	mushrooms, drained
almonds	30 ml (2 tbsp) dry sherry

1. If using frozen prawns, thaw and drain them well. Cut the cabbage into 5-cm (2-in) pieces and the spring onions into 2.5-cm (1-in) pieces.
2. Mix the water, cornflour, soy sauce and sugar; reserve. Heat 30 ml (2 tbsp) oil in a large frying pan and fry the almonds until lightly browned, stirring frequently. Remove and drain well.
3. Stir-fry (page 266) the cabbage, spring onions and mange tout with 5 ml (1 level tsp) salt in the oil remaining in the pan for 2 minutes, or until the vegetables are tender but still slightly crisp.
4. Stir 15 ml (1 tbsp) of the cornflour mixture into the vegetables; cook until it thickens and coats the vegetables. Remove to a serving dish and keep hot.
5. Put the remaining 30 ml (2 tbsp) oil in the pan and add the prawns, ginger, paprika and remaining 10 ml (2 level tsp) salt. Stir-fry for 3–4 minutes until the prawns are heated through, then add the mushrooms, sherry and remaining cornflour mixture. Stir-fry for a further 3–4 minutes until the mixture thickens and coats the prawns.
6. Spoon the prawn mixture over the vegetables and sprinkle with the almonds.

Prawn Curry

Colour index
page 34

3–4 servings

350 g (12 oz) shelled	300 ml (½ pint) chicken
prawns	stock
25 g (1 oz) butter	15 ml (1 tbsp) sweet
2 onions, skinned and	chutney
chopped	15 ml (1 level tbsp) tomato
1 cooking apple, peeled and	paste
chopped	pinch cayenne pepper
15 ml (1 level tbsp) curry	lemon juice
powder	salt
5 ml (1 level tsp) curry	30–45 ml (2–3 tbsp) single
paste	cream, optional
15 ml (1 level tbsp) plain	
flour	

1. If using frozen prawns, thaw and drain them well.
2. Melt the butter in a large saucepan, add the onion and apple; fry gently for 5–8 minutes without browning. Add the curry powder and paste and cook for 5 minutes, stirring occasionally.
3. Stir in the flour and cook for 1 minute. Gradually add the stock and bring to the boil, continuing to stir. Add the chutney, tomato paste, cayenne pepper and a squeeze of lemon juice. Cover and simmer for about 45 minutes.
4. Add the prawns to the sauce and heat through. Check the seasoning and stir in a little cream if you prefer a slightly milder flavour.

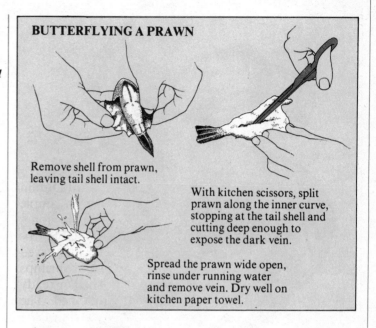

BUTTERFLYING A PRAWN

Remove shell from prawn, leaving tail shell intact.

With kitchen scissors, split prawn along the inner curve, stopping at the tail shell and cutting deep enough to expose the dark vein.

Spread the prawn wide open, rinse under running water and remove vein. Dry well on kitchen paper towel.

Paella

Colour index
page 34

6–8 servings

225 g (8 oz) Italian	1.25 ml (¼ level tsp)
sausages	pepper
45 ml (3 tbsp) olive oil	1 dozen mussels, fresh or
4 chicken legs, divided	bottled
into drumsticks and	1.25 ml (¼ level tsp)
thighs	saffron
1 large green pepper, seeded	30 ml (2 tbsp) hot water
and sliced	275 g (10 oz) long grain
1 clove garlic, skinned and	rice
crushed	50 g (2 oz) pimentos,
825-g (1 lb 12-oz) can	sliced
tomatoes	450 lb (1 lb) prawns,
2.5 ml (½ level tsp) ground	shelled
cinnamon	275 g (10 oz) frozen peas,
7.5 ml (1½ level tsp) salt	thawed

1. Cook the sausages in a little water in a covered pan for about 5 minutes. Cook uncovered for a further 20 minutes until the sausages are very well browned. Remove them from the pan, leave to cool and then cut into 1-cm (½-in) slices.
2. Heat the oil in a paella dish or large, deep frying pan and fry the chicken until well browned on all sides. Add the pepper and garlic and cook for a further 2 minutes, until the pepper has softened.
3. Stir in the tomatoes with their liquid, the cinnamon and seasonings and bring to the boil. Reduce the heat, cover and simmer for 30 minutes or until the chicken is tender, stirring occasionally. Meanwhile, if you are using fresh mussels, clean them thoroughly (page 160).
4. Mix the saffron and water together and add to the dish with the rice and pimentos. Bring to the boil, reduce the heat, cover the pan and simmer gently for a further 15 minutes.
5. Stir in the sausage, prawns and peas, and place the mussels on the top. Cover again and simmer for 5–10 minutes until the mussels are heated through, the rice is tender and all of the liquid has been absorbed. If you are using fresh mussels, the shells should have opened. Serve from the dish.

Crabs

Crab is at its best during the summer. Unless you are buying direct from a fisherman, crabs are usually sold ready-boiled; most fishmongers will also dress them for you. Choose one that is heavy for its size and shake it to check that the shell does not contain a lot of water. The best crabs are the males, as they have larger claws; it is the claws that contain the fine white meat. The body contains only a small amount of dark, moist meat. A 900-g (2-lb) crab should yield about 325 g (12 oz) meat, which should be sufficient to serve two people.

A high quality crab is excellent eaten cold, with mayonnaise, but there are many hot crab dishes that are delicious and lesser quality crabs make a luxurious soup. Frozen and canned crab are also available and make a reasonable substitute for fresh crab in cooked dishes.

BOILING A CRAB

Choose a crab that is lively and clean looking. Wash it under cold running water and put it into a pan of cold salted water. Cover and bring slowly to the boil; boil fairly quickly for 10–15 minutes per 450 g (1 lb). Do not overcook the crab or the flesh will become hard and thready: leaving it to cool in the water will help to keep the flesh tender and moist.

Dressed Crab

1.4–1.6-kg (3–3½-lb)
  crab, cooked
juice of 1 lemon
salt and pepper
25 g (1 oz) fresh white
  breadcrumbs
45 ml (3 tbsp) thick
  mayonnaise, page 462
5 ml (1 level tsp) tomato
  paste

For the garnish: *paprika,*
1 hard-boiled egg yolk,
sieved, chopped parsley,
lemon wedges

Colour index page 34

4–6 first course servings;
3–4 main dish servings

1 After washing the crab thoroughly under cold running water, lay it shell side down on the work surface and twist off the legs and claws where they join the body.

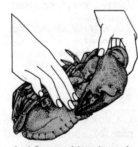

2 With the tail flap towards you, hold the shell firmly and push body section upwards from beneath the tail flap; ease it out with your thumbs, until body is detached.

3 Pull off the grey feather-like gills (known as dead men's fingers) from the body section and discard them. Make sure none are left in the top shell.

4 Scrape out the dark flesh from the top shell with a fork or teaspoon and put into a bowl. Discard the stomach bag attached to the shell just below the head.

5 Scrape the dark meat from the body section into the same bowl then work the white meat from the leg sockets with a skewer. Keep white and dark meats in separate bowls.

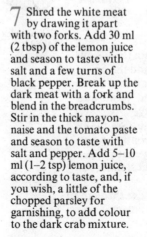

6 Crack the larger limbs with a lobster cracker or small hammer and pick out meat with a skewer. Remove any bits of shell or cartilage and add meat to the white meat bowl.

7 Shred the white meat by drawing it apart with two forks. Add 30 ml (2 tbsp) of the lemon juice and season to taste with salt and a few turns of black pepper. Break up the dark meat with a fork and blend in the breadcrumbs. Stir in the thick mayonnaise and the tomato paste and season to taste with salt and pepper. Add 5–10 ml (1–2 tsp) lemon juice, according to taste, and, if you wish, a little of the chopped parsley for garnishing, to add colour to the dark crab mixture.

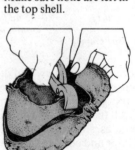

8 Wash and dry the shell and, using pliers, remove the thin under-shell, following the natural line. Rinse and dry well. Rub the shell with a little oil to give it gloss.

9 Arrange dark meat in centre of shell and white meat at either end. Garnish with paprika, egg yolk and parsley. Surround with lemon wedges and crab legs.

Crab Imperial

Colour index page 35
4 servings

450 g (1 lb) crab meat, flaked
25 g (1 oz) butter or margarine
1 small green pepper, seeded and chopped
25 g (1 oz) plain flour
5 ml (1 level tsp) dry mustard
2.5 ml (½ level tsp) salt

2.5 ml (½ tsp) Worcestershire sauce
pinch paprika
pinch pepper
400 ml (¾ pint) milk
30 ml (2 tbsp) lemon juice
1 egg, beaten

1. If using frozen crab meat, thaw it and drain well. Melt the butter or margarine and sauté the green pepper gently for about 5 minutes until tender.
2. Add the flour, mustard, salt, Worcestershire sauce, paprika and pepper. Mix well.
3. Gradually stir in the milk and cook gently until the mixture thickens and boils, stirring all the time. Remove from the heat and stir in the lemon juice.
4. Blend a little of the hot sauce with the beaten egg, and then slowly pour the mixture back into the bulk of the sauce, stirring constantly. Stir in the crab meat and mix well.
5. Grease a 900-ml (1½-pint) capacity casserole and spoon in the mixture. Bake at 180°C (350°F) mark 4 for 1 hour or until golden.

Crab Cakes

Colour index page 35
4 servings

450 g (1 lb) crab meat
25 g (1 oz) fresh white breadcrumbs
30 ml (2 tbsp) mayonnaise, page 462
10 ml (2 tsp) finely chopped parsley
5 ml (1 tsp) Worcestershire sauce
2.5 ml (½ level tsp) salt
2.5 ml (½ level tsp) dry mustard

pepper
1 egg
40 g (1½ oz) butter or margarine

To serve:
tartare sauce, page 185
lemon wedges

1. If using frozen crab meat, thaw it and drain well. Flake the crab meat with a fork and add the remaining ingredients, except for the fat. Mix well and divide into eight equal portions.
2. Melt the butter or margarine in a large frying pan. Spoon in the eight portions and flatten them into cakes. Fry them until golden underneath, turn and repeat on the other side.
3. Serve with tartare sauce and lemon wedges.

Adding mixture to the pan: When the fat has melted, spoon in the portions of crab mixture.

Forming the cakes: Use a fish slice or spatula to flatten the portions into neat, round cakes.

Crab Gratiné

Colour index page 35
4 servings

700-g (1½-lb) crab, cooked, to give 225 g (8 oz) crab meat
50 g (2 oz) fresh white breadcrumbs
100 g (4 oz) cheese, grated
dash Worcestershire sauce
1.25 ml (¼ level tsp) dry mustard
2.5 ml (½ level tsp) salt
1.25 ml (¼ level tsp) pepper

2.5 ml (½ level tsp) cayenne pepper
about 45 ml (3 tbsp) single cream or creamy milk

For the garnish:
watercress sprigs, trimmed
2 bananas, peeled and sliced
knob of butter

1. Remove crab meat as for dressed crab (opposite). Wash and dry the shell and, using pliers, remove the thin undershell, following the natural line. Rinse and dry well. Rub the shell with a little oil to give it a gloss. Reserve the small legs for garnishing.
2. With a fork, flake the white and dark crab meat together in a bowl and mix well. Add the breadcrumbs, grated cheese, flavourings and seasonings. Stir in enough cream to bind the mixture to a fairly soft consistency.
3. Spoon the mixture into the shell; bake at 200°C (400°F) mark 6 for 20 minutes. When the crab is nearly cooked, fry the banana slices in butter until lightly browned, turning once.
4. Arrange the shell and claws on a bed of watercress and garnish with the banana slices.

Flaking the crab meat: Use a fork to flake the white and dark meats together and mix well.

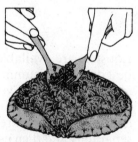

Filling the crab shell: Spoon the crab and cheese mixture into the washed and oiled shell.

Crab Toasts

Colour index page 34
4 servings

100 g (4 oz) crab meat
25 g (1 oz) butter
25 g (1 oz) fresh white breadcrumbs
45 ml (3 tbsp) creamy milk
salt and pepper

15 ml (1 tbsp) sherry

To serve:
4 slices toast
butter

1. If using frozen crab meat, thaw it and drain well. Melt the butter in a saucepan. Flake the crab meat and add it to the pan. Add the breadcrumbs and stir to mix well.
2. Stir in the milk and cook for a few minutes, stirring all the time. Season well with salt and pepper and add the sherry.
3. Remove the crusts from the toast, cut it into triangles and spread with butter. Pile the crab meat mixture on to the pieces of toast.

Lobsters

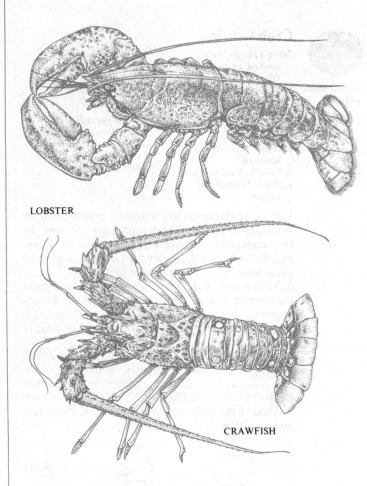

LOBSTER

CRAWFISH

REMOVING THE MEAT

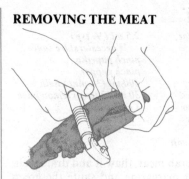

Break the claws and legs off lobster and crack the large claws with a lobster cracker or hammer. Remove meat.

Twist off the head from the tail and use kitchen scissors to cut away the thin underside of the tail shell. Gently pull the meat out.

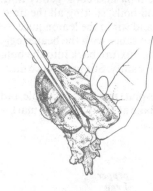

Cut along the rounded back of the meat, about 0.5 cm (¼ in) deep, to expose the dark vein. Remove the vein and discard. Reserve the red roe (coral) to make lobster butter or sauce, or to use as a garnish. Add the greenish liver to the meat.

Lift out the bony portion from the head shell and pick out any further pieces of roe or liver. Use a lobster pick or the point of a knife to pick the meat out of the head. Discard the stomach sac and the greyish spongy gills from the top of the head.

Break bony portion into several pieces and remove the meat with a pick or fork.

Lobsters are available most of the year but are at their best during the summer months. They are generally sold ready-boiled, but if you buy a live lobster it should seem clean and active. The female has the more tender flesh, and the coral-coloured roe under its tail can be cooked separately and then used to make lobster butter or sauce. Fresh lobster meat is delicious served plainly dressed, with melted butter or mayonnaise. Frozen or canned lobster meat is a useful substitute for fresh in hot dishes.

Crawfish do not have large claws as lobsters do, but they are prepared and cooked in similar ways. Crawfish tails are usually bought ready cooked, fresh or frozen.

BOILING A LOBSTER

To cook a live lobster, tie the large claws with rubber bands, then place it in a pan of cold salted water. Bring slowly to the boil, cover and cook for 15–25 minutes, until the shell is bright red. Leave it to cool in the water.

Both head and body shells, if not broken, can be used as containers for the lobster meat.

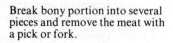

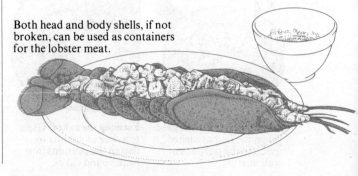

Lobster Thermidor

Colour index
page 35

2 servings

*2 small lobsters or 1 large
  lobster, cooked*
50 g (2 oz) butter
*15 ml (1 tbsp) chopped
  shallot*
*10 ml (2 tsp) chopped
  parsley*
*5–10 ml (1–2 tsp) chopped
  tarragon*

*60 ml (4 tbsp) dry white
  wine*
*300 ml (½ pint) béchamel
  sauce, page 461*
*45 ml (3 tbsp) grated
  Cheddar cheese*
mustard, salt and paprika

1. For small lobsters, remove the meat and leave the shells whole (opposite). For a large lobster, split it in half, as for grilled lobster with shrimp sauce (right) and serve the meat in the half-shells. Chop the claw and head meat; slice the tail meat thickly.
2. Melt half the butter in a saucepan and add the shallot, parsley and tarragon. Cook gently for a few minutes then add the wine; simmer for 5 minutes. Stir in the béchamel sauce and simmer until reduced to a creamy consistency.
3. Add the lobster meat, with 30 ml (2 level tbsp) cheese and the remaining butter in small pieces. Season with mustard, salt and paprika.
4. Arrange the lobster mixture in the shells, sprinkle with remaining cheese and brown under a hot grill.

Making the filling: Simmer the sauce until it is thick, then add the lobster meat.

Filling the shells: Spoon the lobster sauce into the shells; sprinkle with cheese.

Grilled Crawfish Tails

Colour index
page 35

2 servings

*4 crawfish tails, fresh or
  frozen*

To serve:
melted butter

1. If the crawfish tails are frozen, thaw for several hours or overnight in the refrigerator.
2. Use kitchen scissors to cut away the thin under-side shell of each tail and insert a skewer lengthways through the meat so that the tail will lie flat. Brush with melted butter.
3. Put the tails shell side up on the rack of the grill pan. Grill under medium heat for about 5 minutes, turn and grill for a further 5–10 minutes depending on size, basting occasionally with melted butter. When the tails are cooked the meat should be opaque. Serve with melted butter.

GRILLED CRAWFISH TAILS AND MUSTARD BUTTER: Beat *100 g (4 oz) softened butter* with *30 ml (2 level tbsp) Dijon mustard*, *10 ml (2 tsp) lemon juice*, *15 ml (1 tbsp) chopped chives* and *salt* and *pepper* to taste and chill. Grill the crawfish tails as above, but top each with a slice of the butter just before the end of cooking time. Serve immediately.

Grilled Lobster with Shrimp Sauce

Colour index
page 35

2 servings

900-g (2-lb) cooked lobster
vegetable oil
butter
salt
cayenne pepper, optional
*300 ml (½ pint) shrimp
  sauce, page 185*

For the garnish, optional:
parsley sprigs
cooked and shelled shrimps
lemon wedges

1 Remove the claws and legs, then using a strong, pointed knife, split the lobster in half right down the middle of the body from head to tail.

 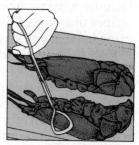

2 Place them flesh side up in the grill pan and brush the flesh with oil. Grill under high heat for 8–10 minutes.

3 Turn the lobster halves over carefully with kitchen tongs and grill the shell side for 5 minutes.

 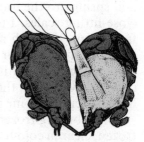

4 Remove the dark intestinal vein, the stomach sac and the grey, spongy gills and discard.

5 Place the lobster halves flesh side down and brush the shells generously all over with oil.

6 Place on a warmed serving dish and dot the flesh with small pieces of butter. Sprinkle with a little salt and, if you wish, cayenne pepper.

7 Spoon the hot shrimp sauce over the lobster halves. If you wish, garnish with parsley sprigs, lemon wedges or a few cooked shelled shrimps.

FISH

Fish are usually divided into two categories, according to whether the flesh is white or oily. The first group, including, for instance, cod, plaice, sole and haddock, has white flesh and a low fat content. In oily fish the flesh is much richer and usually darker in colour. This group includes herring, mackerel, trout and salmon. In most recipes one type of fish may be substituted for another, provided that you stay within these two main categories.

Fish is more or less equivalent to meat in protein value and is also a good source of vitamins and minerals. White fish, with its low fat content, therefore makes an ideal slimmers' food and also forms an important part of the regular diet for invalids and old people because it is nourishing and easily digestible.

CHOOSING FISH
Really fresh fish has clear, bulging eyes and bright red gills. Avoid any with sunken, cloudy eyes and faded pink or grey gills. The body of the fish should be firm and springy to the touch, with shining skin and bright, close-fitting scales. Fish fillets and steaks should look freshly cut, the flesh moist and firm-textured, showing no signs of dryness or discoloration. The bones should be firmly embedded in the flesh; if they are loose and coming away from the flesh this indicates that the fish has been cut for some time and is past its best.

When buying frozen fish, make sure that it is solidly frozen, clear in colour and free of ice crystals. Any smell should be mild and clean, exactly as for fresh fish. Breadcrumb or batter coatings on frozen fish portions should be crisp and dry looking. Avoid frozen fish that has a brownish tinge or that is in any way damaged.

HOW MUCH FISH TO BUY FOR EACH SERVING	
Whole white fish	275–350 g (10–12 oz)
Whole white fish, cleaned and head removed	225–275 g (8–10 oz)
Whole oily fish	200–225 g (7–8 oz)
Whole oily fish, cleaned and head removed	175–200 g (6–7 oz)
Fish steaks	175–225 g (6–8 oz)
Fish fillets	100–175 g (4–6 oz)
Fish portions	100–175 g (4–6 oz)

STORING FISH
Store fresh fish loosely wrapped in the refrigerator and cook it within 24 hours of purchase. Store frozen fish in the freezer or frozen food compartment in its original wrapping. Commercially frozen fish will often be marked with recommended storage times: if not, you may normally assume that white fish will keep for up to 3 months and oily fish for up to 2 months. Cooked fish dishes which you have prepared and frozen yourself will retain their quality for up to 2 months.

THAWING FROZEN FISH
In most cases fish can be cooked from frozen – simply follow a recipe for fresh fish and add a little extra cooking time. Fish portions frozen in breadcrumbs or batter should always be cooked from frozen as thawing will make the coating soggy. Large fish such as salmon should be thawed before cooking, otherwise the outside will be done long before the fish is cooked in the centre. You will also need to thaw fish that is to be stuffed or coated with breadcrumbs or batter, as the coating will not stick to a frozen surface.

Thaw fish in its wrapping in the refrigerator until it is just pliable enough to handle. Allow about 6 hours per 450 g (1 lb). If you are short of time, submerge the package in cold water to hasten the thaw without affecting the quality of the fish. Thawed fish should be drained well, dried on kitchen paper towel and used immediately. It should never be refrozen.

CLEANING FISH
Fish is usually sold cleaned and cut into steaks or fillets ready for cooking. However, you may occasionally have to deal with a fish straight from the water, so cleaning instructions are given on the opposite page.

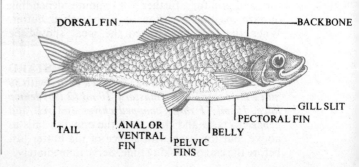

DORSAL FIN — BACKBONE — GILL SLIT — PECTORAL FIN — BELLY — PELVIC FINS — ANAL OR VENTRAL FIN — TAIL

SCALING FISH

Fish scales come off most easily when the fish is wet, so soak it in cold water for a few minutes. Then lay it flat on a work surface, hold the fish firmly at the tail end and scrape off the scales with the back of a firm-bladed knife, holding it almost at right angles to the body of the fish and working from the tail towards the head. Turn the fish over and remove the scales from the other side. Rinse the fish thoroughly during and after scaling to wash off any scales that remain clinging to its body.

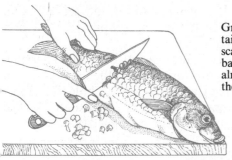

Grip the fish firmly by the tail and scrape off the scales, working with the back of the knife held almost at right angles to the body of the fish.

GUTTING A FISH

Slit the belly of the fish open from the vent (anal opening) to the head. Remove the entrails and rinse the cavity clean. If there is a line of blood on the backbone, it can be dislodged by rubbing with a little salt. For a flat fish, slit the fish behind the gills, squeeze out the entrails and rinse thoroughly.

REMOVING HEAD, TAIL AND FINS

If the fish is to be served whole, remove the head, tail and fins. Large whole fish are often served with the head and tail on: simply remove the eyes.

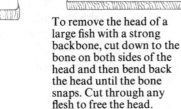

Use a large sharp knife to cut around the pelvic fins and remove them. Then cut off the head with the pectoral fins, and the tail.

To remove the head of a large fish with a strong backbone, cut down to the bone on both sides of the head and then bend back the head until the bone snaps. Cut through any flesh to free the head.

To remove the dorsal fin, make a deep incision on either side of it with a sharp knife and pull the fin out firmly to bring the root bones with it. Give the fish a final thorough rinse in cold water and pat it dry with kitchen paper towel.

FILLETING AND SKINNING FISH

A sharp knife with a thin, flexible blade is essential for filleting. Leave on the head and tail and if the fillets are to be skinned (below) do not scale the fish.

Round fish: Work with the knife held almost flat and parallel to the body of the fish.

Cutting a fillet: Slit fish along backbone from tail to head, cutting right down to the bone.

Working your way from head to tail, cut the fillet away from the bones with clean, even strokes, taking care not to cut into the flesh. Lift off the fillet in one piece.

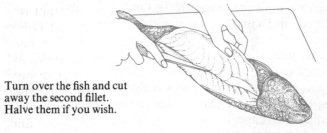

Turn over the fish and cut away the second fillet. Halve them if you wish.

Flat fish: It is easier to skin a flat fish before filleting it: follow the instructions given below. To fillet the fish, cut along the backbone, making sure that you cut right down to the bone. Insert the knife under the flesh on one side of the bone and, working from head to tail, remove the fillet with long clean strokes. Cut off the second fillet on the same side, working from tail to head. Turn over the fish and cut off the remaining two fillets.

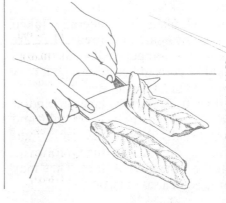

Skinning: Lay the fillet or fish skin side down and, with the tip of the knife, loosen enough skin at the tail end to give a good grip. Holding the loosened skin down with one hand, cut the flesh free from the skin. For a whole flat fish, turn it over and repeat on the other side.

Canned and smoked fish

CANNED FISH

Many types of fish are available canned, chiefly the oily-fleshed varieties and also some smoked and cured fish. The following are the most widely available.

Salmon is available in two qualities. Red salmon is the best quality, with a good, rich colour and firm texture. Use it for salads and dishes where flavour and appearance are of prime importance. Pink salmon is lighter in texture and flavour as well as colour; it is suitable for sandwiches, soups and dishes where the fish is to be mixed with other ingredients.

Tuna is another firm-fleshed fish, useful for sandwiches, cold dishes and casseroles.

Sardines are small fish of the herring family, canned whole in oil or tomato sauce. The canning process softens the bones so that they can be eaten whole. Serve in appetisers or in sandwiches.

Pilchards are larger members of the same family, also packed in oil or tomato sauce. They can be used in made-up dishes such as fish cakes.

Mackerel fillets are available plain or smoked, packed in oil or tomato sauce. They are useful for hors d'oeuvre, sandwich fillings and snacks.

Kipper fillets from cans can be cooked just as fresh kippers or eaten cold, without further cooking.

Anchovies are the tiniest of the herring family. They are filleted and cured, then canned in oil or brine. The flavour is very strong and they are generally used in small quantities as a savoury addition to lightly flavoured dishes. They can also be used for canapés, pizza toppings, sauces and sandwich fillings, or as the basis of a spread for toast. Anchovies are available rolled and stuffed with capers.

SMOKED FISH

Smoking is a traditional method of preserving fish; the extent of the smoking decides the length of time the fish will keep. Fish that have been smoked at a high temperature for a long time will need no further cooking and make a delicious savoury snack just as they are. They are often served as an appetiser, with buttered bread. Lightly smoked fish need cooking as well and are usually poached or grilled. Smoked fish are also excellent in savoury pies and tarts.

Smoked haddock and cod fillets are generally taken from large fish and may be coarse-textured. They are frequently dyed to a bright orangey-yellow. Although smoked, the fish should be cooked before eating: it may be grilled, poached or used in a savoury pie.

Finnan haddock are named after the village of Findon near Aberdeen. Before smoking, the fish are split and lightly brined but not usually dyed. They are a light straw colour after smoking and darken during cooking. The flesh should be tender, the flavour light. They may be poached, grilled or used in a savoury pie.

Smokies are haddock and whiting with the heads cut off and the bodies left round. They are hot-smoked and therefore already cooked, but are nicest reheated. Brush them with butter and heat in the oven or under the grill. Split them and add a piece of butter, then close and reheat until the butter melts.

Golden fillets are small haddock which have been split, boned and had the heads removed before smoking. They should be cooked like Finnan haddock, with the time adjusted to their size.

Smoked cod's roe needs no further cooking, though it may be reheated. It is usually sliced and served as an appetiser on a bed of lettuce, accompanied by lemon wedges and fingers of toast.

Kippers are the most popular variety of smoked herring. The fish are split, lightly brined and then smoke-cured over wood chips. They can be bought whole, filleted or in boil-in-the-bag packs. Kippers are usually served poached or grilled, or they may be jugged (below).

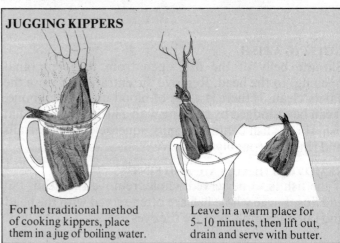

JUGGING KIPPERS

For the traditional method of cooking kippers, place them in a jug of boiling water.

Leave in a warm place for 5–10 minutes, then lift out, drain and serve with butter.

Buckling are whole smoked herrings. They are smoked for a longer time and at a higher temperature than kippers, so that the flesh becomes lightly cooked during smoking. They are usually served cold as an appetiser.

Bloaters are lightly smoked, dry salted, whole herrings. They do not keep as long as other types of smoked herring and they should be cooked and served within 24 hours of buying. They should be cooked like kippers.

Red herrings are heavily smoked and highly salted. They make an excellent cold snack or hors d'oeuvre.

Mackerel are smoked whole and ready for eating. Smoked fillets are also available but tend to be dry.

Trout are also smoked whole and ready for eating. They are often served as an appetiser.

Smoked salmon is ready for eating and is served very thinly sliced. It can be bought fresh, frozen or canned and should be moist and a deep pink colour. Scottish smoked salmon is the best quality, Canadian and Pacific smoked salmon being slightly drier.

Cooking fish

Fish needs very little cooking – it is ready as soon as it loses its translucent appearance and turns opaque and milky-looking all the way through. Beware of over-cooking as this will spoil both the texture and the flavour: the fish will become tough and the natural juices will be lost. Start testing the fish halfway through the cooking time suggested in the recipe. Insert a fork deep into the thickest part of the flesh and gently divide it; if the fish is done it should come up in thick flakes or layers. With a whole fish or a steak, the flesh should come away cleanly from the backbone when tested at the end of cooking time with a fork.

GRILLED FISH

Thin fillets or steaks need grilling on one side only. Thick pieces and whole fish should be turned once during grilling to ensure that the fish is cooked through. With a round fish such as mackerel, it helps the heat to penetrate the flesh if you make three or four diagonal cuts on each side of the body. Oily fish will not always need any additional fat, but white fish should be brushed with oil or melted butter to prevent the surface drying out. Cook under a moderate heat, allowing 4–5 minutes for thin fillets, 10–15 minutes for thicker pieces.

STEAMED FISH

Steaming is really only suitable for thin fillets of white fish such as sole or plaice. Wash and dry the fish and place it on a greased heatproof plate. Dot with a little butter and add 15 ml (1 tbsp) milk and a little seasoning. Cover tightly with foil and place over a pan of boiling water. Cook for 10–15 minutes. If you wish, you can use the liquid from the cooked fish in a béchamel sauce (page 461) to serve with it, or simply pour a little liquid over the fish on the serving dish.

POACHED FISH

Poaching is suitable for most fish, from the smallest fillets and steaks to a large whole salmon, though it is not usually used for the coarser oily fish such as herring or mackerel. Simmer the fish on top of the stove or in the oven in a lightly seasoned liquid such as the court bouillon used for poached salmon (page 176), milk, white wine or cider. A stock made by cooking fish bones in salted water flavoured with parsley sprigs, lemon juice, a bay leaf, peppercorns and pieces of onion and carrot can also be used and will give a good flavour to the fish. Allow about 10–15 minutes per 450 g (1 lb) or 5–10 minutes for steaks. The liquid should completely cover the fish and must not be allowed to boil as this will spoil the texture of the fish. If the fish is to be served cold, it may be left to cool in the poaching liquid. This will retain the maximum moisture and flavour in the flesh. Cooking time remains the same. The cooking liquid is often strained and poured over the fish, or used as the basis of a sauce to serve with the fish.

BAKED FISH

Small whole fish, fillets, or steaks cut from a larger fish can all be baked in the oven at 180°C (350°F) mark 4. Put the fish in an ovenproof dish with seasoning and a little liquid, such as milk or wine. Cover it with a lid or foil and bake until tender. Unless you are following a specific recipe, allow about 10–12 minutes for fillets, 20 minutes for steaks and 25–30 minutes for small whole fish. A large stuffed fish may need up to 1 hour.

SHALLOW FRIED FISH

Fillets, steaks, small whole fish and fish cakes are all suitable for shallow frying. Coat the fish with seasoned flour or with egg and breadcrumbs and fry gently in hot oil, turning carefully when the first side is browned to cook the other side. Fish cooked à la meunière is coated in flour and cooked in butter. Drain on kitchen paper towel to remove any excess fat before serving. Allow about 10 minutes frying time, depending on the thickness of the fish.

DEEP FRIED FISH

Oil, lard or clarified dripping are all suitable for deep frying but the fat must be clean and free from moisture. It should come about halfway up the side of the pan. Heat the oil or fat to 177–188°C (350–370°F): test the temperature with a thermometer or by dropping in a 2.5-cm (1-in) cube of bread; if the oil is the correct temperature for frying the bread should turn golden brown in 1 minute.

Coat the fish with egg and breadcrumbs or with seasoned flour and batter. Lower the fish into the hot oil, using a wire basket for pieces coated with egg and breadcrumbs, but tongs or a fish slice for battered fish. Do not overfill the pan as this will lower the temperature of the oil and prevent the fish cooking quickly enough. Cook the fish for 5–10 minutes until golden brown, then lift it out and drain well on kitchen paper towel. Keep hot while cooking any remaining fish. The oil may be strained into a clean basin and kept for frying fish again. Do not use for other foods as it will taste fishy.

Dipping in egg: After dusting the fish with flour, dip it into beaten egg or egg yolks mixed with a little cold water.

Coating with crumbs: Press the breadcrumbs in firmly. For a thicker coating, dip the fish in egg and bread-crumbs again before frying.

Whole fish

Grilled Sesame Trout

Colour index
page 36

6 servings

**6 small trout, cleaned
100 ml (4 fl oz) lemon
   juice
20 ml (4 level tsp) salt
1.25 ml (¼ level tsp)
   pepper
25 g (1 oz) sesame
   seeds
175 g (6 oz) butter**

1 With a sharp knife,
make three light slashes
in both sides of each fish,
not cutting too deeply.

2 Mix the lemon juice,
salt and pepper in a
large, shallow dish. Add
the fish and turn to coat
thoroughly. Cover and re-
frigerate for 3 hours, turning the fish occasionally.

3 Put the sesame seeds in
a saucepan and cook
them until golden, stirring
gently. Add the butter and
heat until melted.

4 Put the fish on a rack
in the grill pan and
pour the marinade into the
sesame seed mixture. Stir
to mix well.

5 Spoon the sesame seed
mixture over the fish
and grill for about 5 minutes on each side, basting
frequently with the juices
from the grill pan.

6 Test with a fork. The
fish are cooked when
the flesh flakes easily and
comes away from bones.

7 Lift the fish carefully
on to a warm serving
plate and spoon the cook-
ing juices over them.

Grilled Herrings

Colour index
page 35

4 servings

**4 herrings
salt and pepper
vegetable oil or melted
   butter**

**To serve:
mustard sauce, page 185
or horseradish cream,
page 185**

1. Remove the heads and fins from the herrings
Clean them but leave the fish whole, then wash and
wipe them with kitchen paper towel.
2. Make two or three diagonal cuts in the flesh of
both sides of the fish. Sprinkle with salt and pepper
and brush with oil or melted butter. Grease the gril
rack and put the fish on it.
3. Grill the herrings under a moderate heat, turning
them once, for 10–15 minutes or until thoroughly
cooked; test with a fork. Serve with mustard sauce
or horseradish cream.

GRILLED MULLET: Follow the recipe above
using **whole cleaned mullet** instead of herrings, bu
marinate the fish before cooking for about an hour
in **60 ml (4 tbsp) oil** and **60 ml (4 tbsp) vinegar**
mixed with a little **finely chopped onion,** a few
peppercorns and **half a bay leaf.** Serve with **tomato
sauce (page 337)** or **mustard sauce (page 185).**

CARVING A LARGE COOKED FISH

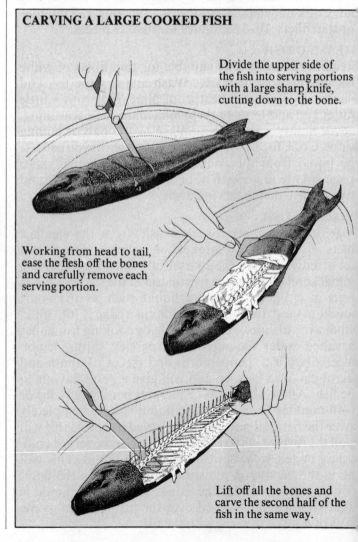

Divide the upper side of
the fish into serving portions
with a large sharp knife,
cutting down to the bone.

Working from head to tail,
ease the flesh off the bones
and carefully remove each
serving portion.

Lift off all the bones and
carve the second half of the
fish in the same way.

Fried Whitebait

Colour index
page 24

first course
servings

450 g (1 lb) whitebait
30–45 ml (2–3 level tbsp)
  plain flour
oil or fat for deep
  frying
salt

To serve:
lemon wedges
brown bread and butter

1 Put the fish in a colander and wash under running cold water. Drain them and dry carefully with a cloth without crushing them.

2 Put the flour in a dry cloth or polythene bag and toss the whitebait in it a few at a time, to coat. Heat the frying oil.

3 Test the temperature of the oil by dropping in a 2.5-cm (1-in) cube of bread. At the correct temperature of 177–188°C (350–370°F) it will take 1 minute to brown.

4 Put half the whitebait in a frying basket and immerse in the hot fat. Fry for 2–3 minutes until lightly browned.

5 Tip the fish on to a plate lined with kitchen paper towel to drain. Keep hot while frying the remaining whitebait.

6 Sprinkle liberally with salt and garnish with lemon wedges. Serve with brown bread and butter.

Trout and Almonds

Colour index
page 36

4 servings

4 trout, weighing 100–150 g
  (4–5 oz) each
seasoned flour
175 g (6 oz) butter
50 g (2 oz) almonds,
  blanched and flaked
  or slivered

juice of ½ lemon

For the garnish:
lemon wedges

1. Clean the trout but leave the heads on them. Wash the fish and wipe them with kitchen paper towel, then coat them with the seasoned flour.
2. Melt 100 g (4 oz) butter in a large frying pan, add two of the trout and fry for about 6–7 minutes on each side until the fish are tender and golden and the flesh flakes easily when tested with a fork. Drain the fish, place them in a warm serving dish and keep hot. Repeat with the remaining trout.
3. Wipe the pan clean with kitchen paper towel, and melt the remaining butter. Add the almonds and cook gently until browned. Add the lemon juice to the pan and pour over the fish. Serve at once with lemon wedges.

Wiping the pan clean: Use kitchen paper towel to wipe any sediment from the pan before melting the remaining butter.

Frying the almonds: Add the almonds to the pan and cook gently until browned, turning occasionally to prevent them burning.

Sole Meunière

Colour index
page 36

4 servings

4 small soles, skinned
seasoned flour
75 g (3 oz) butter
15 ml (1 tbsp) chopped
  parsley

juice of 1 lemon

For the garnish:
lemon slices

1. If necessary, cut the fins off the soles. Wipe the fish and coat with seasoned flour.
2. Heat 50 g (2 oz) butter in a large frying pan. Put in the fish so that the side to be served uppermost goes into the fat first. Fry gently for about 5 minutes until browned. Turn over the fish carefully and fry for a further 5 minutes until tender and golden. Drain on kitchen paper towel, place on a warm serving dish and keep hot.
3. Wipe the pan clean with kitchen paper towel, melt the remaining butter and heat until lightly browned. Add the parsley and lemon juice and pour over the fish at once. Garnish with lemon slices.

FILLETS MEUNIERE: Although it is more traditional to cook the fish on the bone, **sole fillets** may be prepared as above. Other white fish, such as plaice and perch, may also be cooked à la meunière.

Whole fish

Colour index page 35
3–4 servings

Opposite page
From top left: sea bass, salmon trout (*right*
plaice (*centre*); *left and right:* sea bas
Dover sole, rainbow trout, mussels, oyster
scallops, clams

Baked Stuffed Red Snapper

1 large red snapper or
  bream, cleaned and scaled
melted butter
salt and pepper

For the forcemeat:
75 g (3 oz) lean bacon
100 g (4 oz) lean veal
1 small onion, skinned
1 stick celery, washed and
  trimmed
25 g (1 oz) butter

75 g (3 oz) fresh white
  breadcrumbs
1 large mushroom,
  chopped
5 ml (1 level tsp) finely
  chopped parsley
salt and pepper
ground mace
1 egg, beaten
little milk, optional

Poached Salmon

1 salmon, cleaned

For the court bouillon:
2 litres (3½ pints) water or
  dry white wine and water
1 small carrot, peeled and
  sliced
1 small onion, skinned and
  sliced
1 small stick celery, washed
  and chopped, optional
30 ml (2 tbsp) white
  vinegar or lemon juice
few parsley sprigs
bay leaf
6–8 peppercorns
20 ml (4 level tsp) salt

To serve:
15 ml (1 level tbsp)
  powdered gelatine
lemon slices
parsley sprigs
green mayonnaise,
  page 185

Colour index page 36
3–4 servings per 450 g (1 lb)
dressed fish

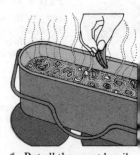

1 Put all the court bouillon ingredients into a
fish kettle or large deep
pan and bring to the boil.
Reduce heat to simmering.

1 Brush the cleaned fish
with melted butter and
sprinkle all over with salt
and pepper. Generously
butter a roasting tin and
lay the buttered fish in it.

2 Make the forcemeat.
Rind the bacon. Mince
the veal and bacon twice,
then beat well in a bowl.
Chop the onion and celery
and fry lightly in a little
butter until softened but
not coloured. Add the
cooked onion and celery
to the veal and bacon with
the remaining forcemeat
ingredients and mix well
together with a wooden
spoon, binding with the egg
and adding a little milk if
the mixture is too stiff.

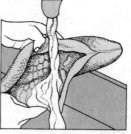

2 Rinse fish, cut off head
if you wish and add to
court bouillon. Lay the fish
carefully on the rack out of
the fish kettle.

3 Lower fish into liquid
and simmer for 5–10
minutes per 450 g (1 lb),
until tender. Cool in the
cooking liquid if you wish.

4 Lift the rack out of the
kettle and drain
thoroughly. Transfer the
fish to a large serving dish,
cover and refrigerate.

3 Spoon the forcemeat
into the stomach of the
fish. Do not pack it tightly
or the stomach will burst.

4 Fasten the stomach of
the fish securely with
wooden cocktail sticks.
Cover with foil.

5 Line a sieve with mus-
lin and use to strain the
poaching liquid thorough-
ly. Discard the vegetables
and flavourings.

6 Measure 600 ml (1 pint)
fish stock into a sauce-
pan and leave to cool.

7 Sprinkle the gelatine
over the cooled stock
then heat gently, stirring,
until completely dissolved.
Pour into a shallow dish
and chill until lightly set.

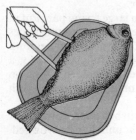

5 Bake at 180°C (350°F)
mark 4 for 45 minutes –
1 hour or until tender. Lift
the cooked fish carefully
on to a heated serving dish.
Remove the wooden
cocktail sticks.

6 Cut one side of the fish
just down to the bone
into portions and serve
each piece with some stuffing. Lift off the bones and
divide the second side of
the fish in the same way.

8 With a sharp knife,
carefully cut the skin
round the top half of the
salmon and lift off the skin.
Carefully turn over salmon
and repeat on other side.

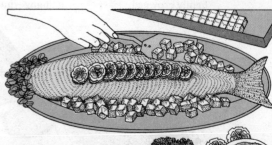

9 Garnish the fish with
lemon slices and the as-
pic jelly, cut into cubes.
Finish with parsley sprigs.
Serve accompanied by
green mayonnaise.

Fish fillets

Opposite page
Paella (page 165)

Colour index
page 37

4 servings

Tarragon Fish

*60 ml (4 tbsp) vegetable
  oil
15 ml (1 tbsp) lemon juice
2.5 ml (½ level tsp) dried
  tarragon or 7.5 ml
  (1½ tsp) chopped fresh
  tarragon
2.5 ml (½ level tsp) salt
pinch pepper
700 g (1½ lb) white fish
  fillets*

For the garnish:
*lemon wedges or lemon
  slices
parsley sprigs or
  chopped parsley*

1 Mix together the oil,
  lemon juice, tarragon,
  salt and pepper.

2 Lay the fish in the grill
  pan and spoon the tar-
ragon mixture generously
over the fillets. Turn them
over to coat both sides.

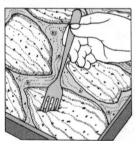

3 Grill under high heat
  for 5–8 minutes, or
until the fish flakes easily
when tested with a fork.

4 Lift the fillets on to a
  serving plate. Garnish
with lemon wedges or slices
and a little parsley.

Grilled Fish with Courgettes

Colour index
page 36

4 servings

*700 g (1½ lb) cod or
  haddock fillets
100 g (4 oz) large button
  mushrooms
4 small courgettes, washed
  and trimmed
melted butter*

*salt and pepper
30 ml (2 level tbsp) grated
  Parmesan cheese
barbecue sauce, page 185*

1. Cut the fillets crossways into serving pieces.
Grease a large flameproof dish and put the fish in it.
2. Remove the stems from the mushrooms and place
the caps beside the fish. Halve the courgettes lengthways and score the cut surfaces with a fork; place
them, cut side up, next to the mushrooms.
3. Brush the vegetables with the melted butter.
Season lightly. Sprinkle the cheese over the courgettes and spoon the barbecue sauce over the fish.
4. Grill under medium heat for 10–12 minutes,
basting the mushrooms occasionally with the melted
butter, until the courgettes are tender and the fish
flakes when tested with a fork.

Colour index
page 37

4 servings

Deep Fried Fish Fillets

*125 g (4 oz) plain
  flour
pinch salt
1 egg
150 ml (¼ pint) milk or
  milk and water
oil or fat for deep
  frying
700 g (1½ lb) white fish
  fillets
seasoned flour*

1 Mix together the flour
  and salt, make a well in
the centre and break in the
egg. Add the liquid grad-
ually as for a batter,
beating until smooth.

2 Heat the oil or fat to
  177–188°C (350–370°F).
Test with a thermometer
or by dropping in a bread
cube, which should brown
in 1 minute.

3 When the oil is hot,
  coat each piece of fish
with seasoned flour and
then with batter.

4 Lower gently into the
  fat, cooking two at a
time to avoid lowering the
temperature. Cook 5–10
minutes, until golden.

5 Remove the fish pieces
  and drain thoroughly on
kitchen paper towel. Keep
hot while you cook the
remaining pieces.

USING A FRYING BASKET

To deep fry fish with a delicate coating, such as egg and breadcrumbs, use a wire frying basket.

Choose a frying basket to
fit your largest saucepan.
Dip the basket in the hot fat
before adding the fish, to
preheat the metal. Fry only
two fillets at a time to
avoid lowering the temp-
erature of the oil or fat.

Fish fillets

Colour index
page 37
4 servings

Fried Fish alla Margherita

30 ml (2 tbsp) olive or
vegetable oil
25 g (1 oz) butter or
margarine
700 g (1½ lb) sole or
plaice fillets
396-g (14-oz) can tomatoes
15 ml (1 level tbsp) tomato
paste
30 ml (2 tbsp) chopped
parsley

5 ml (1 level tsp) dried
oregano
5 ml (1 level tsp) caster
sugar
1.25 ml (¼ level tsp) salt
freshly ground black
pepper

1. Heat the oil and butter in a large frying pan and fry the fillets for 2–3 minutes on each side, until the fish is tender and flakes when tested with a fork.
2. Purée the tomatoes in a blender or by rubbing through a sieve and stir in the remaining ingredients. Pour over the fish. Reduce the heat, cover and simmer for about 5 minutes, occasionally basting the fish with the sauce.
3. Serve the fish in the pan, or transfer the fish to a heated serving dish and pour the tomato sauce evenly over the top.

Colour index
page 36
4 servings

Mediterranean Cod with Vegetables

75 ml (5 tbsp) vegetable oil
2 cloves garlic, skinned and
sliced
1 small aubergine, cut into
chunks
2 onions, skinned and
roughly chopped
1 green pepper, seeded and
roughly chopped
5 ml (1 level tsp) salt
1.25 ml (¼ level tsp)
pepper
75 ml (5 tbsp) water
700 g (1½ lb) cod fillets

150 g (5 oz) fresh white
breadcrumbs
30 ml (2 tbsp) chopped
fresh dill weed
2 eggs, beaten
2 tomatoes, cut into wedges

For the garnish, optional:
chopped parsley

1. Heat 30 ml (2 tbsp) of the oil in a large saucepan and fry 1 clove of garlic for 3–4 minutes, or until golden. Discard the garlic. Add the aubergine and onions and fry gently, stirring frequently, for about 5 minutes or until well browned.
2. Add the green pepper, half the salt, the pepper and the water. Cover and cook for 5 minutes, stirring occasionally, then uncover and continue to cook until all the liquid has evaporated.
3. Meanwhile cut the cod into four equal portions and sprinkle with the remaining salt. Mix the breadcrumbs and chopped dill weed together on a sheet of greaseproof paper.
4. Dip the fish in the beaten egg and then coat in the breadcrumbs, pressing them in firmly. Repeat to make a substantial coating.
5. Put the remaining oil and second garlic clove in a frying pan and heat for 3–4 minutes. Discard the garlic. Add the fish and fry for 10 minutes or until tender, turning once. Transfer the pieces to a serving dish and keep hot.
6. Add the tomatoes to the vegetable mixture and cook gently to heat them thoroughly. Spoon on to the serving dish with the fish. Garnish with a little chopped parsley if you wish.

Colour index
page 36
4 servings

Sole au Gratin

8 sole fillets, skinned
25 g (1 oz) butter, melted
salt and pepper
300 ml (½ pint) milk or
milk and water
pinch paprika
25 g (1 oz) mature cheese,
grated, optional

For the sauce:
milk, optional
25 g (1 oz) butter
45 ml (3 level tbsp) flour
75–100 g (3–4 oz) mature
cheese, grated
salt and pepper
pinch dry mustard

1 Wash and dry the fillets and brush them with the melted butter. Season the fillets lightly on both sides with a little salt and pepper to taste.

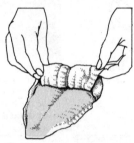

2 Roll up the fillets and place seam side down in a flameproof dish.

3 Add milk or milk and water to half cover fish. Bring to the boil, remove from heat, cover and leave for 5 minutes.

4 Carefully spoon off all the cooking liquor from the fish into a measuring jug. If necessary make it up to 300 ml (½ pint) with milk.

5 Make the sauce. Melt the butter, stir in the flour and gradually add the fish liquid.

6 Stir over gentle heat until thickened, then add the cheese and seasonings and stir until the cheese has melted.

7 Pour sauce over fish and sprinkle with paprika and, if you wish, grated cheese. Grill under high heat until golden.

Colour index
page 37
4 servings

Baked Fillets with Lemon Sauce

700 g (1½ lb) sole or plaice
 fillets, skinned
2.5 ml (½ level tsp) salt
1.25 ml (¼ level tsp)
 pepper
25 g (1 oz) butter

150 ml (¼ pint) chicken
 stock
15 ml (1 tbsp) lemon juice
1 egg yolk
5 ml (1 tsp) water
salt and pepper

For the sauce:
15 g (½ oz) butter or
 margarine
15 ml (1 level tbsp) plain
 flour

For the garnish:
4 stuffed olives, sliced

1. Grease a large ovenproof dish and arrange the fillets in it. Sprinkle them with the salt and pepper and dot with the butter.
2. Bake the fish at 180°C (350°F) mark 4 for 10 minutes or until tender. Spoon off any cooking liquid and discard it.
3. Meanwhile, make the sauce. Melt the fat in a small saucepan and stir in the flour. Cook gently for 2–3 minutes. Gradually add the chicken stock and lemon juice and cook until the sauce thickens slightly, stirring all the time.
4. Beat the egg yolk with the water and add a little of the hot sauce, stirring rapidly. Pour the mixture slowly back into the bulk of the sauce and cook without boiling until it has thickened, stirring all the time. Adjust the seasoning to taste.
5. Pour the sauce over the baked fish and garnish with the sliced olives.

Colour index
page 37
4 servings

Stuffed Plaice Moulds

198-g (7-oz) can mussels or
 shrimps
50 g (2 oz) butter or
 margarine
1 stick celery, washed and
 chopped
½ onion, skinned and
 chopped
salt
75 g (3 oz) bread, cubed

1 egg, beaten
pinch dried thyme
450 g (1 lb) plaice fillets,
 skinned

For the garnish:
parsley sprigs

1. Grease four 9-cm (3½-in) ramekins. Drain the mussels or shrimps and reserve 30 ml (2 tbsp) of the liquid for the stuffing.
2. Melt the fat, add the celery, onion and 2.5 ml (½ level tsp) salt and cook gently for about 5 minutes, until the celery is tender. Stir in the mussels or shrimps and their reserved liquid with the bread cubes, beaten egg and thyme and beat until thoroughly mixed. Remove the pan from the heat and allow the stuffing to cool slightly.
3. Sprinkle the fish fillets with salt and line the ramekins with the fillets, cutting them to fit if necessary. Divide the stuffing between the four fillet-lined dishes; do not press down too firmly as the stuffing will expand during cooking.
4. Bake at 180°C (350°F) mark 4 for 25–30 minutes until the fish is tender and the stuffing thoroughly heated and lightly set.
5. With two spoons, gently lift the stuffed fillets out of the ramekins and place them on a heated serving plate. Garnish with the parsley sprigs.

Colour index
page 37
4 servings

Poached White Fish with Hollandaise Sauce

700 g (1½ lb) white fish
 fillets
300 ml (½ pint) hollandaise
 sauce, page 463

For the court bouillon:
600 ml (1 pint) water
½ small carrot, peeled and
 sliced
½ small onion, skinned and
 sliced
½ small stick celery,
 washed and chopped

10 ml (2 tsp) white vinegar
 or lemon juice
parsley sprigs
½ bay leaf
2–3 peppercorns
5 ml (1 level tsp) salt
½ lemon, sliced

For the garnish:
chopped parsley
lemon wedges

1 Put the court bouillon ingredients in a large frying pan or flameproof casserole and bring to the boil. Cover, reduce heat and simmer gently for about 30 minutes.

2 Remove the flavouring vegetables and herbs with a slotted spoon and discard them.

3 Cut the fish into serving pieces and arrange in a single layer in the pan of court bouillon.

4 Cover and simmer very gently for 10–15 minutes until the fish is just cooked and flakes when tested with a fork. Do not allow the bouillon to boil or the fish will break up.

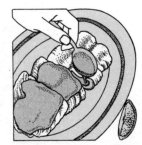

5 Transfer the pieces of fish carefully to a hot serving plate, draining them well. Discard the court bouillon.

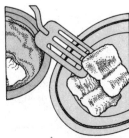

6 Spoon the hollandaise sauce over the fish pieces to coat them and garnish with chopped parsley and lemon wedges.

Fish fillets

Sole Stuffed with Prawns

Colour index
page 37

6 servings

50 g (2 oz) butter
*175 g (6 oz) shelled
  prawns, chopped*
*100 g (4 oz) mushrooms,
  chopped*
*25 g (1 oz) dried
  breadcrumbs*
*2.5 ml (½ level tsp) dried
  dill weed*
5 ml (1 level tsp) salt
6 sole fillets, skinned
225 ml (8 fl oz) white wine
100 ml (4 fl oz) water
*15 ml (1 level tbsp)
  cornflour*
100 ml (4 fl oz) cream
1 egg

1 Melt the butter and
cook the prawns and
mushrooms gently for
about 5 minutes. Stir in the
breadcrumbs, dill and
2.5 ml (½ level tsp) salt.

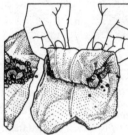

2 Spoon some prawn
mixture on to each fillet
and roll up. Secure with
wooden cocktail sticks.

3 Put them in a pan with
the wine, water and re-
maining salt. Bring to the
boil then reduce heat.

4 Cover the pan and sim-
mer for 12–15 minutes
or until cooked. Remove
the fillets to a warm plate
and remove the cocktail
sticks. Keep hot.

5 Blend the cornflour and
cream and stir grad-
ually into the poaching
liquid. Cook, stirring, until
sauce boils and thickens.
Remove the sauce from the
heat and cool slightly.

6 Beat the egg lightly and
add a little hot sauce.
Beat well, then pour into
the bulk of the sauce, stirring all the time.

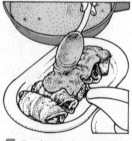

7 Cook, stirring, until
thickened, but do not
boil. Spoon some of the
sauce over the fish and
serve the rest separately.

Stuffed Mackerel Fillets

Colour index
page 37

4 servings

4 large mackerel fillets
5 ml (1 level tsp) arrowroot
*5–10 ml (1–2 level tsp)
  sugar*
150 ml (¼ pint) apple juice

For the stuffing:
*175 g (6 oz) cooking apples,
  peeled and cored*
75 g (3 oz) celery
25 g (1 oz) butter
4 medium gherkins, chopped

*2.5 ml (½ level tsp) dried
  thyme*
5 ml (1 tsp) vinegar
*45 ml (3 level tbsp) fresh
  white breadcrumbs*
salt and pepper

For the garnish:
sliced gherkins

1. Make the stuffing. Chop the apples and celery.
Melt the butter and cook the apple and celery until
the apple is pulpy. Add the remaining stuffing
ingredients and mix well.
2. Spread the stuffing over the fillets and fold each
one in half. Arrange them in an ovenproof dish and
bake uncovered at 180°C (350°F) mark 4 for 25–30
minutes or until tender.
3. Blend the arrowroot and sugar with a little apple
juice. Warm the remaining apple juice and stir in the
arrowroot mixture. Bring to the boil and cook,
stirring, until thickened.
4. Garnish the mackerel fillets with sliced gherkins
and glaze them with some of the sauce. Serve the
remaining sauce separately.

Creamed Finnan Haddie

Colour index
page 37

4 servings

*700 g (1½ lb) Finnan
  haddock fillets*
25 g (1 oz) butter
*15 ml (1 level tbsp) plain
  flour*
300 ml (½ pint) milk
*150 ml (¼ pint) double
  cream*

2 hard-boiled eggs, shelled

To serve:
*chopped parsley, optional
  biscottes or toast
  triangles*

1. Cut the fish into large pieces.
2. Melt the butter in a large frying pan and stir in the
flour. Gradually add the milk and cream and cook,
stirring, until the sauce thickens.
3. Add the fish to the sauce, cover and simmer for 15
minutes or until the fish is tender. Chop the hard-
boiled eggs, reserving one yolk.
4. Flake the cooked fish into the sauce and stir in the
chopped eggs. Pour the mixture into a warmed
serving dish and sieve the reserved egg yolk over the
top. Garnish with chopped parsley if you wish, and
serve with biscottes or toast triangles.

Flaking the fish: Flake the
cooked fish into the sauce
with the back of a fork.

Garnishing: Press the egg
yolk through a coarse sieve
over the creamed haddock.

Fish steaks

Halibut Steak with Aubergine Sauce

Colour index page 38

servings

1 green pepper
1 large onion, skinned
1 large aubergine, weighing about 350 g (12 oz)
15 ml (1 tbsp) oil
396-g (14-oz) can tomatoes
100 ml (4 fl oz) dry white wine
1 clove garlic, skinned and crushed
bay leaf
5 ml (1 level tsp) sugar
50 g (2 oz) butter
30 ml (2 tbsp) lemon juice
salt and pepper
700-g (1½-lb) halibut steak

1 Seed the pepper and cut it into 1-cm (½-in) strips; slice the onion. Peel the aubergine and cut it into cubes.

2 Heat the oil in a frying pan, add pepper and onion and sauté gently for 10 minutes. Add aubergine, cover and sauté 5 minutes.

3 Add the tomatoes and the next four ingredients. Mix well and simmer, uncovered, for about 15 minutes.

4 Brush the grill pan rack with a little oil or melted butter to prevent the fish sticking.

5 Melt the butter in a small saucepan, stir in the lemon juice and season with salt and pepper.

6 Put fish on rack and brush generously with butter mixture. Grill under high heat for 7 minutes. Turn fish and brush again with butter mixture.

7 Grill for 7 minutes more, or until the fish flakes easily when tested with a fork. Serve the halibut steak with the hot aubergine sauce.

Salmon Steaks with Cucumber Salad

Colour index page 38

6 servings

6 salmon steaks
court bouillon, page 176
1 large cucumber
15 ml (1 level tbsp) salt
1 small onion, skinned and thinly sliced
100 ml (4 fl oz) wine vinegar
30 ml (2 level tbsp) sugar
1.25 ml (¼ level tsp) white pepper

To serve:
lettuce leaves
lemon wedges
green mayonnaise, page 185

1 Put three steaks in a deep frying pan and cover with court bouillon. Cover and bring to boiling point. Reduce heat.

2 Simmer gently for 5–10 minutes. Pierce the thickest flesh with a fork; if cooked it should offer no resistance.

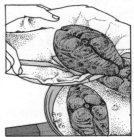

3 Remove steaks with a fish slice; drain on kitchen paper towel. Repeat with remaining steaks. Cover and chill.

4 Slice cucumber thinly into a colander, sprinkle with salt and leave 30 minutes; drain. Press out excess liquid with the back of a spoon.

5 Tip the cucumber into a bowl and add the onion, vinegar, sugar and pepper. Mix thoroughly. Cover and chill.

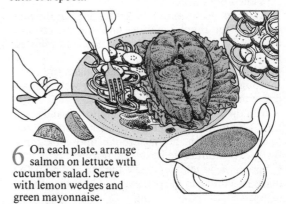

6 On each plate, arrange salmon on lettuce with cucumber salad. Serve with lemon wedges and green mayonnaise.

Fish steaks

Colour index page 38
4 servings

Marinated Halibut Steaks

2 350-g (12-oz) halibut
  steaks

For the marinade:
75 ml (5 tbsp) vegetable oil
75 ml (5 tbsp) tarragon
  vinegar
2 bay leaves
30 ml (2 tbsp) chopped
  parsley

1.25 ml (¼ level tsp) dried
  tarragon
5 ml (1 tsp) Worcestershire
  sauce
10 ml (2 level tsp) salt
1.25 ml (¼ level tsp)
  pepper

1. Put the halibut steaks in a shallow dish large enough to take the fish steaks in a single layer.
2. Mix the oil and vinegar, add the herbs, Worcestershire sauce and seasonings and stir well. Pour the marinade over the steaks, turning them to coat well on both sides.
3. Cover the dish with foil and refrigerate for at least 3 hours, turning the fish occasionally.
4. Place the fish steaks on the grill rack and grill for 15 minutes or until the fish is tender, basting occasionally with the marinade. The flesh should flake easily when tested with a fork.

Colour index page 38
4 servings

Cod Steak with Mushrooms and Spinach

100 g (4 oz) butter
700-g (1½-lb) cod, halibut
  or hake steak
2.5 ml (½ level tsp) salt
225 g (8 oz) mushrooms,
  sliced
30 ml (2 tbsp) lemon juice

275 g (10 oz) spinach

For the garnish:
lemon wedges

1. Melt the butter in a large frying pan, add the fish and sprinkle it with salt. Cook gently for 5 minutes, then turn the fish and cook for a further 4–5 minutes or until the thickest flesh flakes easily when tested with a fork.
2. Transfer the fish to a large serving dish with a fish slice and keep warm.
3. Add the mushrooms and lemon juice to the pan and cook for about 5 minutes until the mushrooms are tender. Remove them from the pan with a slotted spoon and reserve.
4. Trim any coarse stalks from the spinach and wash thoroughly to remove any grit. Drain well and pat dry with kitchen paper towel.
5. Add the spinach to the juices in the pan and cook for 2–3 minutes or until tender, stirring occasionally. Stir in the mushrooms and cook for a further few minutes to heat them through.
6. Spoon the vegetables round the fish and pour the juices remaining in the pan over it. Garnish with the lemon wedges before serving.

Minced fish

Quenelles with Cream Sauce

450 g (1 lb) white fish
  fillets, eg. cod, haddock
  or hake
50 g (2 oz) butter or
  margarine
50 g (2 oz) plain flour
120 ml (8 tbsp) creamy
  milk
30 ml (2 tbsp) single
  cream
2 eggs, beaten
salt and pepper
100 g (4 oz) Gruyère or
  Emmenthal cheese,
  grated
For the sauce:
45 ml (3 level tbsp) plain
  flour

25 g (1 oz) butter, softened
200 ml (7 fl oz) double
  cream
100 ml (4 fl oz) dry
  vermouth
5 ml (1 tsp) lemon juice
1.25 ml (¼ level tsp) salt
pinch pepper

Colour index page 36
4–6 servings

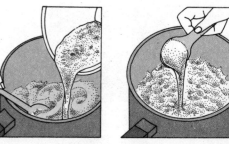

1 Cut the fish into chunks and dry them with kitchen paper towel, pressing out as much liquid as possible, then mince the fish finely to a paste.

2 Melt the butter, stir in the flour and cook for 2–3 minutes, stirring.

3 Remove the pan from the heat and gradually stir in the milk. Return to the heat and stir until the sauce thickens. Remove from the heat again.

4 Stir in the cream, beaten eggs and fish. Season generously. Grease a large frying pan, half fill it with water and heat to simmering point.

5 Using two wetted tablespoons, shape the fish mixture into egg-shaped or oval pieces.

6 Spoon the quenelles gently into the water and simmer uncovered for 10 minutes, basting well.

7 When the quenelles are swollen and just set, lift out with a slotted spoon and drain on kitchen paper towel. Reserve liquid.

8 Arrange the drained quenelles in a flame-proof dish large enough to take them in a single layer.

9 For the sauce, measure 450 ml (¾ pint) poaching liquid into a pan and boil rapidly until reduced by half. Blend together the flour and butter and whisk into the liquid. Cook over gentle heat, stirring, until slightly thickened. Add the cream, vermouth, lemon juice, salt and pepper. Cook for about 5 minutes, stirring all the time, until the sauce is thick and smooth. Spoon the sauce over the quenelles.

10 Sprinkle with grated cheese and grill under high heat until melted and golden.

Flaked fish

Fish Mousse

225 g (8 oz) white fish
fillets, eg. cod, haddock
or hake
2.5 ml (½ level tsp) pepper
45 ml (3 tbsp) lemon
juice
150 ml (¼ pint)
mayonnaise, page 462
2.5 ml (½ level tsp) celery
salt
15 ml (1 level tbsp)
powdered gelatine
150 ml (¼ pint)
double or whipping
cream

For the garnish:
lettuce leaves
lemon wedges
stoned olives, sliced
½ canned pimento,
sliced

Colour index page 24

4 servings

1 Put the fish in a pan with enough water to cover and poach until tender. Drain the fish and reserve 300 ml (½ pint) stock.

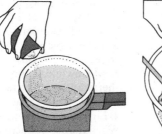

2 Remove the skin and bones from the fish and discard them. Flake the flesh with the back of a fork, add the pepper, lemon juice, mayonnaise and celery salt and mix.

3 Sprinkle the gelatine on to 45 ml (3 tbsp) stock in a small basin and dissolve completely over a pan of hot water. Stir into the remaining stock.

4 Add the stock to the fish and stir well until evenly blended; refrigerate the mixture until it is just beginning to set.

5 When the fish mixture is almost set, whip the double cream until it just holds its shape and fold it gently into the fish mixture until evenly blended.

6 Lightly oil a 600-ml (1-pint) capacity fish mousse mould and pour in the fish mixture. Level the surface and refrigerate for 5–6 hours or until set.

7 To loosen the mousse before turning it out, dip the mould into hot water for a few seconds.

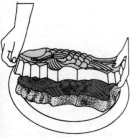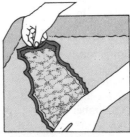

8 Invert it on to a flat serving dish and carefully lift the mould off the mousse, shaking gently if necessary.

9 Arrange lettuce leaves and lemon wedges round mousse; garnish with sliced olives and pimento to mark fins, spine and eye.

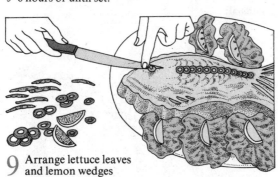

Colour index page 38

6 servings

Country Fish Pie

700 g (1½ lb) mixed white
fish and salmon
pinch salt
milk or water
50 g (2 oz) butter
100 g (4 oz) button
mushrooms
90 ml (6 level tbsp) plain
flour
300 ml (½ pint) milk

60 ml (4 tbsp) chopped
parsley
salt and pepper
2 hard-boiled eggs, shelled
and chopped
flaky pastry made with
100 g (4 oz) flour, page
344 or 212-g (7½-oz)
packet puff pastry
beaten egg to glaze

1. Put the fish in a saucepan with a pinch of salt and just enough milk or water to cover. Cover pan, bring slowly to the boil, remove from the heat and leave covered for a further 5 minutes. Drain the fish, reserving 300 ml (½ pint) of the cooking liquid. Skin and flake the fish, discarding any bones.
2. Melt the butter and sauté the mushrooms. Stir in the flour and cook for 2–3 minutes. Stir in the fish liquid and the 300 ml (½ pint) milk, bring to the boil and cook, stirring, until the sauce has thickened.
3. Mix half the sauce with the flaked fish, parsley, salt, pepper and chopped egg and pour into a 20.5-cm (8-in) round pie dish.
4. Roll out the pastry to make a circle 0.3 cm (⅛ in) thick and large enough to cover the dish leaving a 2.5-cm (1-in) rim. Place the pastry over the filling, fold under the rim and pinch to make a stand-up edge. Cut slits in the pastry and decorate with leaves made from the trimmings. Glaze with beaten egg.
5. Bake at 200°C (400°F) mark 6 for 30 minutes, or until golden. Serve the remaining sauce separately.

Colour index page 38

4 servings

Fish Cakes

450 g (1 lb) potatoes,
peeled
25 g (1 oz) butter
225 g (8 oz) cooked or
canned fish, drained
15 ml (1 tbsp) chopped
parsley
salt and pepper

little milk or beaten egg
1 egg, beaten
dried breadcrumbs
vegetable oil

To serve, optional:
tomato sauce, page 337 or
hollandaise sauce, page 463

1. Boil the potatoes, drain them and mash with the butter. Flake the fish and add to the potatoes with the parsley. Season to taste and bind if necessary with a little milk or egg. Shape into a roll on a floured board.
2. Cut the roll into eight slices and form into cakes. Dip them in the egg, then coat with the bread-crumbs, patting them on well.
3. Heat the oil in a large frying pan and fry the cakes until crisp and golden. Drain well. If you wish, serve them with tomato sauce or, for a more substantial dish, place each cake on a toasted bun or muffin and coat with hollandaise sauce.

Canned fish

Colour index
page 38

4–6 servings

Tuna Loaf with Cucumber Sauce

150 ml (¼ pint) milk
2 eggs, lightly beaten
100 g (4 oz) dried
  breadcrumbs
2 198-g (7-oz) cans tuna,
  drained
75 g (3 oz) celery, finely
  chopped
30 ml (2 tbsp) grated onion
7.5 ml (1½ level tsp) salt
large pinch pepper

For the sauce:
1 cucumber, peeled, seeded
  and chopped

25 g (1 oz) butter
15 ml (1 level tbsp) plain
  flour
5 ml (1 level tsp) salt
5 ml (1 tsp) grated lemon
  rind
10 ml (2 tsp) lemon juice
1 egg yolk

For the garnish:
chopped fresh dill weed or
  parsley
cucumber slices

1. Mix the milk, eggs and dried breadcrumbs. Leave
to stand for 5 minutes, stirring occasionally.
Meanwhile, grease well a 15 × 10 × 7.5 cm (6 × 4 ×
3 in) loaf tin.
2. Flake the tuna with a fork and add to the
breadcrumb mixture with the chopped celery, grated onion and salt and pepper. Stir the mixture well
until evenly blended, pour into the loaf tin and bake
at 180°C (350°F) mark 4 for 1 hour, or until a knife
or skewer inserted in the centre comes out clean.
Leave the tuna loaf to cool slightly.
3. Meanwhile, make the sauce. Simmer the cucumber in water to cover until just tender. Remove the
cucumber, reserve the cooking liquid and make it up
to 300 ml (½ pint) with water.
4. Melt the butter in a saucepan and stir in the flour.
Gradually add the reserved liquid and cook, stirring, until the sauce thickens slightly.
5. Add the salt, lemon rind, lemon juice and cucumber and bring to the boil. Beat the egg yolk and stir in
a little of the hot sauce. Return the mixture to the
pan and stir over gentle heat, without boiling, until
the sauce thickens.
6. Loosen the tuna loaf with a spatula and turn it out
on to a serving dish. Pour some sauce over the loaf
and garnish with the dill or parsley and cucumber
slices. Serve the remaining sauce separately.

Colour index
page 38

4 servings

Tuna and Spaghetti Bake

100 g (4 oz) short-cut
  spaghetti
15 g (½ oz) butter
50 g (2 oz) button
  mushrooms, sliced
198-g (7-oz) can tuna,
  drained
300 ml (½ pint) béchamel
  sauce, page 461

75 g (3 oz) Cheddar cheese,
  grated
salt and pepper

For the topping, optional:
25 g (1 oz) dry
  breadcrumbs

1. Cook the spaghetti in boiling salted water for
8–12 minutes, until tender. Drain well.
2. Melt the butter and sauté the sliced mushrooms
for a few minutes. Flake the tuna and add to the
béchamel sauce with the cheese and mushrooms, or
add only 50 g (2 oz) cheese and reserve the rest for a
topping. Stir in the spaghetti and season.
3. Pour into a greased ovenproof dish. Sprinkle with
the reserved cheese and breadcrumbs, if you wish.
Bake at 180°C (350°F) mark 4 for 20–30 minutes.

Colour index
page 38

6–8 servings

Salmon Mousse

300 ml (½ pint) béchamel
  sauce, page 461
200 ml (7 fl oz) boiling
  water
40 ml (2½ level tbsp) aspic
  jelly powder
185-g (6½-oz) can salmon
30 ml (2 tbsp) dry sherry
finely grated rind and juice
  of 1 lemon
5 ml (1 level tsp) dried
  chervil

5 ml (1 level tsp) salt
white pepper
150 ml (¼ pint) double
  cream

For the garnish:
2 peppercorns
lemon slices
trimmed watercress or
  1 bunch radishes,
  thinly sliced

1. Cover the béchamel sauce to prevent a skin
forming and leave to cool.
2. Pour the boiling water into a measuring jug,
sprinkle on the aspic jelly powder and stir until it has
completely dissolved. Make up to 300 ml (½ pint)
with cold water and leave until just beginning to set.
Stir the aspic into the cooled béchamel sauce and
cover. Leave again until it is on the point of setting.
3. Meanwhile, drain the salmon. Mash it with the
sherry and add the next four ingredients. Oil a 1.4-
litre (2½-pint) capacity fish mould.
4. Lightly whip the cream until it just holds its shape.
When the aspic sauce is on the point of setting, stir in
the salmon mixture and fold in the cream evenly.
Turn into the oiled mould and refrigerate for 5–6
hours or until set.
5. Remove the mousse from the refrigerator 30
minutes before serving and unmould on to a large
serving dish. Place the peppercorns on the fish as
eyes, arrange the lemon slices on the dish and
garnish with watercress. For a more elaborate presentation decorate with radish slices, as shown below.

DECORATING THE MOUSSE

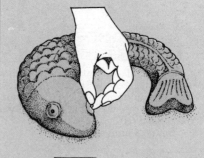

Place the two
peppercorns on the
mousse as eyes on
the head of the fish.

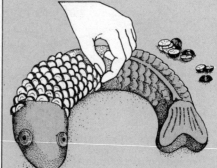

Cut the radish slices
in half and arrange
them on the mousse,
pressing them in
lightly in neatly
overlapping rows, to
resemble scales on
the body of the fish.
Arrange the lemon
slices on the serving
dish round the fish.

Fish sauces

Makes 225 ml
(8 fl oz)

Horseradish Cream

30 ml (2 tbsp) grated fresh horseradish	pinch dry mustard, optional
10 ml (2 tsp) lemon juice	150 ml (¼ pint) double cream
10 ml (2 level tsp) sugar	

1. Mix the horseradish with the lemon juice, sugar and pinch of mustard.
2. Whip the cream lightly, then fold in the horseradish mixture. Serve with trout or mackerel.

Makes 300 ml
(½ pint)

Mustard Sauce

15 ml (1 level tbsp) dry mustard	15 ml (1 tbsp) vinegar
10 ml (2 level tsp) sugar	300 ml (½ pint) béchamel sauce, page 461

1. Blend the dry mustard, sugar and vinegar to a smooth cream.
2. Stir the mixture into the sauce. If you wish, use fish stock as half the liquid for the béchamel sauce. Serve with steamed and poached fish.

ANCHOVY SAUCE: Prepare the sauce as above, but omit the mustard, sugar and vinegar and add *5–10 ml (1–2 tsp) anchovy essence.*

EGG SAUCE: Prepare the sauce as above, but omit the mustard, sugar and vinegar and add *1 hard-boiled egg, shelled and chopped.*

Makes 300 ml
(½ pint)

Barbecue Sauce

2 small onions, skinned and thinly sliced	10 ml (2 level tsp) dry mustard
30 ml (2 tbsp) diced celery	5 ml (1 level tsp) salt
30 ml (2 tbsp) vegetable oil	15 ml (1 tbsp) Worcestershire sauce
226-g (8-oz) can tomatoes	10 ml (2 tsp) lemon juice
15 ml (1 level tbsp) tomato paste	1.25 ml (¼ level tsp) pepper
20 ml (4 level tsp) soft light brown sugar	

1. Sauté the onion and celery in the oil for 5 minutes or until soft. Add the tomatoes and simmer gently for 5 minutes.
2. Add all the remaining ingredients. Cover and simmer gently for 15–20 minutes, stirring frequently. Spoon over fish before grilling.

Watercress Sauce

Makes 225 ml
(8 fl oz)

50 g (2 oz) butter or margarine	2 bunches watercress, washed
1 onion, skinned and thinly sliced	60 ml (4 tbsp) white wine
1 small clove garlic, skinned	30 ml (2 tbsp) stock
	5 ml (1 level tsp) sugar

1. Melt the fat in a small saucepan, add the onion and garlic and fry gently for about 10 minutes or until the onion is tender but not browned. Discard the garlic.
2. Trim the stems from the watercress, chop the leaves and add to the onion. Stir in the wine, stock and sugar and cook the mixture for about 3 minutes, until the watercress is tender.
3. Purée the mixture in a blender or rub it through a sieve to make a smooth sauce. Heat through gently Serve with baked and steamed fish.

Makes 200 ml
(7 fl oz)

Tartare Sauce

5 ml (1 tsp) chopped fresh tarragon or chives	10 ml (2 tsp) chopped gherkins
10 ml (2 tsp) chopped parsley	150 ml (¼ pint) mayonnaise, page 462
10 ml (2 tsp) chopped capers	15 ml (1 tbsp) lemon juice or tarragon vinegar

1. Add the chopped herbs, capers and gherkins to the mayonnaise and stir in the lemon juice or vinegar. Mix well.
2. Leave the sauce for at least 1 hour before serving so that the flavours have a chance to blend. Serve with fried fish.

Makes 300 ml
(½ pint)

Shrimp Sauce

300 ml (½ pint) béchamel sauce, page 461, flavoured with pared rind of 1 lemon and a small bay leaf	50 g (2 oz) frozen, canned or potted shrimps salt and pepper

1. Use fish stock as half the liquid for the béchamel sauce if you wish.
2. When the sauce has thickened, stir in the shrimps and seasoning to taste. Reheat gently. Serve with poached, steamed or grilled fish.

Makes 450 ml
(¾ pint)

Cucumber and Lemon Dressing

½ cucumber	300 ml (½ pint) béchamel sauce, page 461
10 ml (2 tsp) lemon juice	salt and pepper

1. Peel the cucumber and quarter it lengthways. Remove the seeds, chop the flesh roughly and blanch in boiling salted water for 5 minutes. Drain. Rinse the cucumber in cold water and drain again.
2. Add the cucumber and the lemon juice to the béchamel sauce. Season to taste and heat through the sauce. Serve with poached and baked fish.

Makes 600 ml
(1 pint)

Green Mayonnaise

1 bunch watercress, washed	400 ml (¾ pint) thick mayonnaise, page 462
1–2 sprigs fresh tarragon or chervil	30 ml (2 tbsp) double cream, lightly whipped
15 ml (1 tbsp) chopped parsley	

1. Trim the stems from the watercress. Chop the watercress leaves and fresh tarragon or chervil sprigs very finely.
2. Just before serving, mix the herbs, mayonnaise and cream. Serve with chilled fish dishes.

Makes 300 ml
(½ pint)

Sharp Gooseberry Sauce

225 g (8 oz) gooseberries, topped and tailed	30–60 ml (2–4 level tbsp) sugar
25 g (1 oz) butter	

1. Wash the fruit and stew it in as little water as possible, until soft and pulped, stirring occasionally. Purée the mixture in a blender or rub it through a sieve until smooth.
2. Stir in the butter and sugar to taste and heat through. Serve with baked or grilled mackerel.

MEAT

Meat plays an extremely important part in our diet. It supplies large quantities of high quality protein, iron and several vitamins, especially those of the B group that are not readily available in other foods. Apart from that, of course, most of us find a good appetising meat dish one of the most satisfying meals.

BUYING MEAT

When choosing meat, it helps to bear in mind the cooking method that you intend using. If you want something to cook quickly by a dry heat method such as grilling or roasting, it must be a lean, tender cut from a prime quality animal and will inevitably be expensive. Slower cooking with added moisture is suitable for one of the tougher, probably fattier cuts that will be cheaper. The nutritional quality of the cheaper cuts is just as high as that of the dearer cuts and they will be just as tasty if cooked properly. Generally speaking, choose meat which has no undue amount of fat; what fat there is should be firm and free from dark marks or discoloration. Lean meat should be finely grained, firm and slightly elastic; a fine marbling of fat is no disadvantage.

Whether you choose fresh or frozen meat, home reared or imported, is a matter mainly of personal preference, but always be prepared to ask advice of a butcher because carcasses are carefully graded on the wholesale market and he should know precisely the quality of the meat he is offering. Many prepackaged meat cuts carry labels suggesting suitable methods of cooking, and these too should be given due regard.

The most satisfactory way of buying meat is to use one or two regular sources, so that you are able to buy meat of a consistent quality and have access to consistently reliable advice.

HOW MUCH TO BUY

If the meat is boneless, plan to use 100–150 g (4–5 oz) per serving. If it has a little bone, allow 175–225 g (6–8 oz) per serving. For cuts with a high proportion of bone, you may need as much as 350 g (12 oz) per serving.

STORING MEAT

Put meat in the refrigerator as soon as possible after buying. Remove any paper wrappings, rewrap the meat loosely in polythene or foil, leaving an end open for ventilation, and place the package on a plate in case it drips. If the meat is prepackaged in polythene or cling film, just loosen the wrapping to allow air to circulate. Most fresh meat can be stored in the refrigerator for up to 3 or 4 days; minced meat and offal are more perishable and should be used within 24 hours. Cooked meat should be cooled quickly, wrapped in foil or polythene and, if possible, put into the refrigerator within 1½–2 hours of cooking. Store for up to 4 days.

Frozen meat should be left in its wrappings and stored in the freezer or frozen food compartment of the refrigerator. For use, put it in the refrigerator to thaw, allowing about 6 hours per 450 g (1 lb).

FREEZING MEAT

Freeze only meat that is fresh, well hung and of top quality. If you buy direct from a farm or slaughterer, make sure that the meat is chilled immediately after killing. Pork and veal should then be cut up and frozen as quickly as possible. Beef and lamb should be hung for 6–12 days to ensure that the meat will be tender. If possible employ a butcher to cut up the carcass for you. Have it cut up into suitable quantities for your serving requirements and, as far as possible, have bones removed to save space. Trim off any excess fat as this will turn rancid before the lean meat. Pack the meat carefully in heavy duty polythene bags, separating individual chops or steaks with sheets of polythene or waxed paper. Where bones are left in, pad them with foil to prevent them puncturing the polythene. Lower the temperature in the freezer as far as possible by using the 'fast freeze' switch if you have one, and freeze no more than one-tenth of your freezer's total capacity in any 24 hours – or follow manufacturer's directions.

If you are buying meat in bulk from a butcher, he will usually freeze the meat for you, cut to your requirements. Then all you have to do is repack as necessary and put it into the freezer for storage.

COOKING MEAT

There are two basic ways of cooking meat. The most tender cuts are best cooked quickly by dry heat, either roasting, grilling or dry-frying; sautéing is a variation on this process, using only a little moisture in the form of fat. Less tender cuts need added liquid and longer, slower cooking; methods include braising, pot roasting, stewing and boiling.

Roasting: Meat is traditionally roasted in a hot oven – 220°C (425°F) mark 7, so that the joint is seared quickly, giving a good brown outside and a dryish texture to the meat. The flavour of meat roasted by this method is excellent, but only the most tender cuts should be used. It is much more common to roast at a lower temperature, usually 190°C (375°F) mark 5. This leaves the joint more moist, is inclined to tenderise the meat more and there is less shrinkage, but the 'roast' flavour may be less pronounced. The low temperature method is more suitable for smaller joints and if you are uncertain of the quality of the meat.

Place the joint in the roasting tin with the largest cut surfaces exposed and the thickest fat on top. If the joint is exceptionally lean, add a little dripping for basting. As the joint cooks and the fat melts, baste the joint with the fat and juices that form in the tin. You can place the joint on a roasting rack so that it does not stand in the fat during cooking.

Roasting meat in foil or in a covered tin helps retain moisture, as well as keep the oven clean, but the flavour and colour of the meat are not as good as if it is open-roasted. Open the foil or remove the lid from the tin for the final 30 minutes of cooking to allow the outside of the meat to brown. Roasting wraps and bags serve much the same purpose as foil but some are designed to allow the meat to brown; follow the manufacturer's instructions, as some bags should be pierced before cooking starts.

Rôtisserie cooking: Any cut suitable for roasting can be cooked on a spit, either in front of an open grill, in the oven or in a separate rôtisserie cooker. As the spit turns, the meat bastes itself and therefore needs little attention during cooking.

Joints that are to be cooked on a rôtisserie must be as uniform in shape and thickness as possible, so that the spit will turn evenly. Temperatures used and cooking times vary according to the manufacture of the cooker. If you wish to coat the joint with a spicy or sweet sauce, do not add it before the last 30 minutes of cooking time or it may burn.

Grilling: This method is suitable only for the most tender cuts such as steaks and chops. The meat should be cut to an even thickness of 1–2 cm (½–¾ in); some cuts may be thicker. When cooking ham or bacon, snip the fat at intervals round the edge to prevent it curling. Always grill under or over a fierce heat, to sear the meat well on the outside first, then regulate the cooking by moving the grill rack further from the source of heat rather than by moderating the heat. Preheat a gas or electric grill for about 5 minutes

before use. On an outdoor grill, let the charcoal burn for at least 30 minutes before starting to cook. Cook until the meat is well browned on the outside, turning once, and season the meat well with salt and pepper before serving.

Dry frying: This method is suitable only for tender cuts or for minced meat recipes such as hamburgers and sausages. Preheat a heavy frying pan or griddle and brush it very lightly with oil or rub it with a piece of fat trimmed from the meat. There should be only enough oil just to grease the surface and prevent sticking; with a non-stick pan no oil is necessary. If much fat runs from the meat during cooking, spoon it off and discard it. Cook the meat quickly until well browned on both sides, turning once, and season well.

Sautéing: Many good quality cuts can be sautéed, if they are not too fatty. Use sufficient fat to cover the bottom of the pan. Start with a moderately high heat and brown the meat quickly on both sides; then reduce the heat and continue cooking more slowly until the meat is cooked through. A light sauce is often made in the same pan, using the cooking juices as a base, or the meat may first be coated with egg and breadcrumbs to give a crisp finish to the outside.

Braising: This method is suitable for less tender cuts. The meat may be left as whole joints or cut into smaller steaks or chunks as preferred. First, brown the meat quickly on all sides in a little hot fat in a frying pan or flameproof casserole on top of the stove. Add liquid and cover and cook slowly, either on top of the stove or in the oven, until the meat is tender. Flavouring vegetables are usually part of the dish and the cooking liquid is thickened to serve as a sauce.

Pot roasting: Similar to braising, this method is used for whole joints only. The meat is browned, then flavouring vegetables and a very little liquid are added. The pan is then covered tightly and cooking continues on top of the stove or in the oven. As very little liquid is added, check occasionally that it has not boiled dry.

Boiling: This method is used for tougher joints that need long, moist cooking to break down the fibres. Just cover the joint with cold water, bring it slowly to the boil and add flavouring ingredients. Cover the pan, reduce the heat and simmer the meat on top of the stove until tender. The joint is then drained and carved and the flavouring vegetables are usually discarded. The cooking liquid may be used for a sauce or gravy or as a base for soups.

Stewing: This method is used for tough cuts that can be cut into small pieces. The meat may be browned first or not, as required. Barely cover it with water or stock, add flavourings and simmer in the oven or on top of the stove until tender. The cooking liquid and flavouring vegetables are served with the meat.

USING A MEAT THERMOMETER

A meat thermometer is a useful extra check that roasted meat is cooked as you wish; it is essential if you are cooking a joint from frozen as the outside of the meat may appear cooked before the middle has reached a safe temperature. Insert the thermometer into the thickest part of the joint, so that the tip will be in the centre; take care that the tip does not touch bone and, if possible, ensure it does not go into a layer of fat. Normally, you would insert the thermometer before starting to cook; with a frozen joint, insert the thermometer part way through the cooking time, when the joint is sufficiently thawed. When the thermometer registers the required internal temperature (see chart below), the meat is correctly cooked.

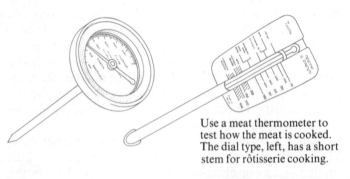

Use a meat thermometer to test how the meat is cooked. The dial type, left, has a short stem for rôtisserie cooking.

MEAT THERMOMETER TEMPERATURES		
Meat	**Temperature**	**Result**
Beef: Rare	60°C (140°F)	Very rare when hot; ideal for carving cold.
Beef: Medium	75°C (160°F)	Brown meat, but with bloody juices; pale pinkish tinge when cold.
Beef: Well done	77°C (170°F)	Well cooked; tends to be dry when cold.
Veal	82°C (180°F)	Moist, pale meat.
Lamb	82°C (180°F)	Moist, brown meat.
Pork	89°C (190°F)	Moist, pale meat.

MAKING GRAVY

Remove the joint from the roasting tin. For thin gravy, pour off all the fat from the meat juices, leaving behind the sediment. Season with salt and pepper and add 300 ml (½ pint) hot stock. Stir until all the sediment is scraped from the tin and the gravy is a rich brown. Return the tin to the heat, or pour the gravy into a small saucepan, and boil for 2–3 minutes.

For thick gravy, pour off most of the fat, but spoon 30 ml (2 tbsp) fat into a saucepan. Add 15 ml (1 level tbsp) plain flour, blend it into the fat and cook, stirring, until it turns brown. Add hot stock to the meat juices to make 300 ml (½ pint), stir it into the browned roux and boil for 2–3 minutes. Season well and strain.

Beef

CUTS OF BEEF

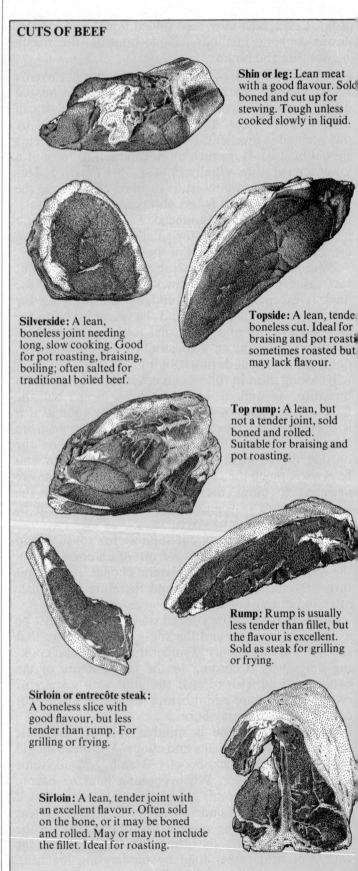

Shin or leg: Lean meat with a good flavour. Sold boned and cut up for stewing. Tough unless cooked slowly in liquid.

Silverside: A lean, boneless joint needing long, slow cooking. Good for pot roasting, braising, boiling; often salted for traditional boiled beef.

Topside: A lean, tender boneless cut. Ideal for braising and pot roasting; sometimes roasted but may lack flavour.

Top rump: A lean, but not a tender joint, sold boned and rolled. Suitable for braising and pot roasting.

Rump: Rump is usually less tender than fillet, but the flavour is excellent. Sold as steak for grilling or frying.

Sirloin or entrecôte steak: A boneless slice with good flavour, but less tender than rump. For grilling or frying.

Sirloin: A lean, tender joint with an excellent flavour. Often sold on the bone, or it may be boned and rolled. May or may not include the fillet. Ideal for roasting.

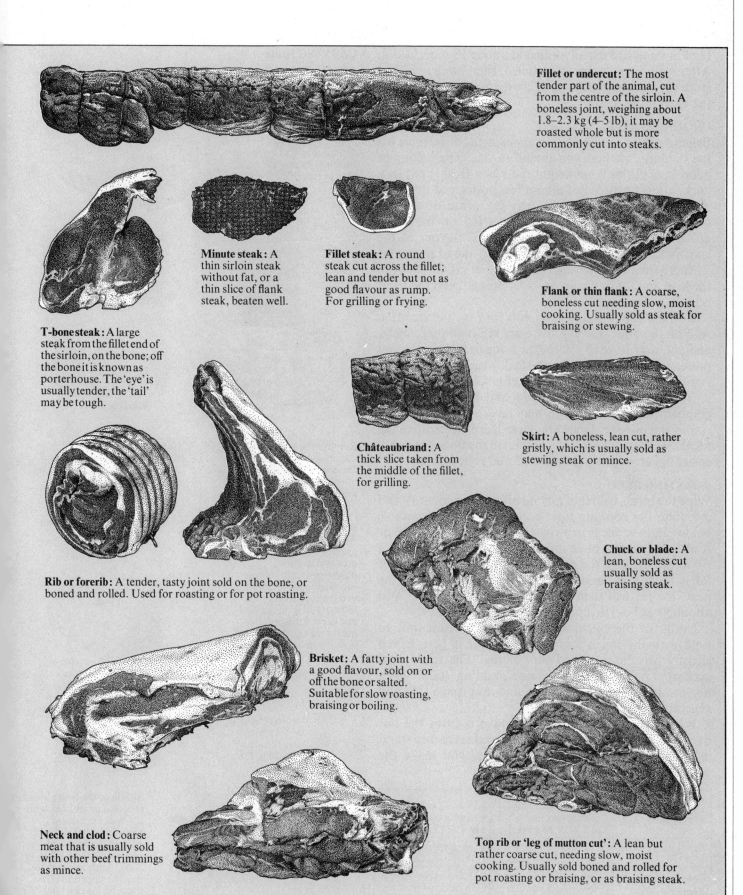

Fillet or undercut: The most tender part of the animal, cut from the centre of the sirloin. A boneless joint, weighing about 1.8–2.3 kg (4–5 lb), it may be roasted whole but is more commonly cut into steaks.

Minute steak: A thin sirloin steak without fat, or a thin slice of flank steak, beaten well.

Fillet steak: A round steak cut across the fillet; lean and tender but not as good flavour as rump. For grilling or frying.

Flank or thin flank: A coarse, boneless cut needing slow, moist cooking. Usually sold as steak for braising or stewing.

T-bone steak: A large steak from the fillet end of the sirloin, on the bone; off the bone it is known as porterhouse. The 'eye' is usually tender, the 'tail' may be tough.

Châteaubriand: A thick slice taken from the middle of the fillet, for grilling.

Skirt: A boneless, lean cut, rather gristly, which is usually sold as stewing steak or mince.

Rib or forerib: A tender, tasty joint sold on the bone, or boned and rolled. Used for roasting or for pot roasting.

Chuck or blade: A lean, boneless cut usually sold as braising steak.

Brisket: A fatty joint with a good flavour, sold on or off the bone or salted. Suitable for slow roasting, braising or boiling.

Neck and clod: Coarse meat that is usually sold with other beef trimmings as mince.

Top rib or 'leg of mutton cut': A lean but rather coarse cut, needing slow, moist cooking. Usually sold boned and rolled for pot roasting or braising, or as braising steak.

Beef

Beef animals are usually killed at about 18 months old. After slaughter the meat is chilled, then hung in a cold store for about 10 days to relax the muscles and make the meat more tender.

CHOOSING BEEF

Be guided by your butcher in choosing a cut suitable for the cooking method you intend to use. The colour of good beef varies from bright red when freshly cut to a dark, almost brown red after a few hours, but this does not affect quality. The fat may be white or yellow, depending whether the animal was fed on barley or grass, but this again does not affect the flavour of the lean meat, so buy a fatty cut only if you like to eat the fat – otherwise it may be wasteful. A line of gristle between the lean and fat indicates an older animal, and the meat is likely to be tough.

Rib, aitchbone and sirloin joints for roasting are often sold on the bone, though there are regional preferences and you may have to ask for the bone to be left in if you prefer it that way; a T-bone steak also includes bone. Apart from these joints, most beef is sold without bone; if for roasting, it will be rolled and tied into a neat, compact shape. Lean joints may have a piece of fat tied round the outside. Once you have learnt to remove the meat cleanly from the bone, joints on the bone are much easier to carve neatly than boned and rolled joints.

ROASTING BEEF

Wipe the meat, trim it of any surplus fat if necessary and calculate the cooking time according to the timetable below. Put the meat in a roasting tin, on a wire rack or resting on its own bone if the joint is suitable, such as a rib joint. Arrange the meat so that the thickest layer of fat is uppermost and the cut sides are exposed to the heat; the fat will then baste the meat as it melts. Add about 50 g (2 oz) dripping if the joint is very lean.

Cook for the calculated time, basting from time to time with the juices from the tin. Beef is best served slightly rare, and carved very thinly. The traditional accompaniments are Yorkshire pudding (page 191), horseradish cream (page 185), thin gravy (page 188) and vegetables as required.

When the meat is cooked, remove it from the hot oven, put it on a heated serving dish and leave it to stand in a warm place for 15 minutes while you make the gravy, to make it easier to carve.

TIMETABLE FOR ROASTING BEEF		
Type of joint	Roasting time at 220°C (425°F) mark 7	Roasting time at 190°C (375°F) mark 5
Joints on the bone	20 minutes per 450 g (1 lb), plus 20 minutes	27 minutes per 450 g (1 lb), plus 27 minutes
Boned and rolled joints	25 minutes per 450 g (1 lb), plus 25 minutes	33 minutes per 450 g (1 lb), plus 33 minutes

CARVING BEEF

Rib of beef: Place the beef on a carving board or dish with the flat side down and the rib bones to your left. Insert the fork, prongs down, between the top and second ribs. Cut across the meat, taking as thin a slice as possible.

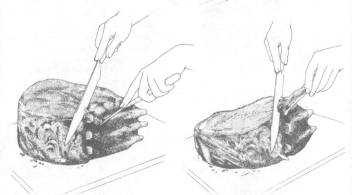

Remove the knife and, with the tip, cut along the side of the bone to free the slice. Lift it off supporting the slice with knife and fork.

Continue cutting thin slices, removing each rib bone as it becomes exposed.

Boned and rolled joints: Always carve against the grain. For a long joint it is easiest to carve downwards, removing each string just before you get to it. For a small joint, stand it on one end and carve horizontally, taking the thinnest possible slices.

Sirloin on the bone: Stand the joint on its back with the fillet uppermost. Carve out the flank, then remove the fillet and carve both these into slices. Turn the joint so that the uppercut is on top, and make a long slice against the backbone.

Roast and baked beef

Roast Rib of Beef with Yorkshire Pudding

Colour index page 50

6 servings

2-kg (4½-lb) rib of beef, on the bone, chine bone removed
salt and pepper

For the Yorkshire pudding:
125 g (4 oz) plain flour
pinch of salt
1 egg
300 ml (½ pint) milk or two-thirds milk and one-third water

To serve:
thin gravy, page 188
horseradish cream, page 185

1 Wipe the meat, place it fat side up in the roasting tin and season.

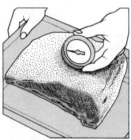

2 Insert a meat thermometer into thickest part, making sure the tip is in the centre of meat, not resting on bone or fat.

3 Roast at 220°C (425°F) mark 7 for 20 minutes per 450 g (1 lb) plus 20 minutes, basting from time to time with the juices in the tin. For rare meat, the thermometer will read 60°C (140°F); continue cooking until the thermometer reads 75°C (160°F) for medium, or 77°C (170°F) for well done. When the meat is cooked, leave it to stand for 15 minutes in a warm place, to make carving easier.

4 Mix the flour and salt in a bowl, add the egg and half the liquid and beat well until completely smooth, then beat in the remaining liquid.

5 About 30 minutes before the end of cooking time, spoon off 30 ml (2 tbsp) dripping and divide it between six 7.5-cm (3-in) Yorkshire pudding tins.

6 Heat them in the oven for 5 minutes then divide the batter between them. Bake above the meat for 15–20 minutes.

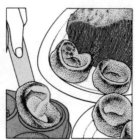

7 Place the beef on a heated serving dish; surround with puddings. Serve with thin gravy and horseradish cream.

ROTISSERIED RIB OF BEEF: Buy the beef boned and rolled. Insert the spit through the centre of the joint and tighten the holding prongs. Make sure the joint is balanced on the spit; test by turning the spit slowly in your hands. Roast according to the manufacturer's instructions, basting occasionally with the melted fat. Test that the meat is cooked by inserting a meat thermometer (see chart page 188), making sure it does not touch the spit. Remove the holding prongs and spit and put the joint on a heated serving dish. Keep hot while you make the gravy.

Vegetable-topped Roast Beef

Colour index page 51

6–8 servings

1.4-kg (3-lb) piece boned and rolled sirloin
15 ml (1 level tbsp) made mustard
freshly ground black pepper
6.25 ml (1¼ level tsp) salt
100 g (4 oz) carrots, peeled and grated
25 g (1 oz) celery leaves, finely chopped
5 ml (1 level tsp) dried thyme
175 ml (6 fl oz) water
45 ml (3 tbsp) red wine

1. Put the beef on a rack in a roasting tin and spread the mustard over the top. Sprinkle with the pepper and 5 ml (1 level tsp) of the salt. Mix together the grated carrots, chopped celery leaves and dried thyme and spread all but 45 ml (3 tbsp) of the mixture over the joint, pressing it well into the mustard with your hands.
2. Insert a meat thermometer into the centre of the joint, making sure it is not resting on fat, and roast at 190°C (375°F) mark 5 for 1 hour.
3. Cover the beef loosely with foil, leaving the thermometer uncovered, and roast for a further 1 hour, or until the thermometer registers 60°C (140°F) for rare meat or 75°C (160°F) for medium, according to how well done you like your beef.
4. Transfer the joint to a heated serving dish, sprinkle the reserved vegetable mixture over the top and keep hot.
5. Remove the rack from the roasting tin and spoon off any fat from the juices in the tin. Pour the water and wine into the tin, add the remaining 1.25 ml (¼ level tsp) salt and stir well to loosen the sediment on the bottom. Bring to the boil on top of the stove, stirring, and pour into a heated sauce boat.
6. Serve the gravy with the roast beef.

Adding the vegetables: Spread over the mustard, then press the vegetable mixture evenly over the joint with your hands.

Covering the joint: To prevent the topping burning, make a tent of foil over the joint, leaving the thermometer uncovered.

Roast and baked beef

Individual Beef Wellingtons

350 g (12 oz) mushrooms
50 g (2 oz) butter or
margarine
1 onion, skinned and finely
chopped
100 g (4 oz) fresh white
breadcrumbs
10 ml (2 level tsp) salt
2.5 ml (½ level tsp) freshly
ground black pepper
1.25 ml (¼ level tsp) dried
thyme
1.4 kg (3 lb) fillet of beef
flaky pastry made with
350 g (12 oz) flour,
page 344

1 egg, separated
20 ml (4 tsp) water

For the garnish:
endive leaves or watercress
sprigs, washed and
trimmed

Colour index page 52
8 servings

1 Remove the stems from 8 mushrooms and reserve the caps. Chop the stems and the remaining mushrooms finely.

2 Melt the butter in a large frying pan and add the chopped mushrooms and onion. Cook gently until the onion is soft but not coloured.

3 Stir in the breadcrumbs, 5 ml (1 level tsp) of the salt, the pepper and dried thyme. Mix well and remove from the heat.

4 Cut the meat in half lengthways, then slice each half crossways into four equal pieces. Dry the pieces of meat with kitchen paper towel.

5 Divide pastry into four pieces. Roll out one piece to a 35.5 × 28 cm (14 × 11 in) rectangle, halve and trim each half to 16 × 25.5 cm (6½ × 10 in).

6 Put 60 ml (4 tbsp) of the mushroom mixture in the middle of one pastry rectangle. Place a piece of beef on top and sprinkle it with the remaining salt.

7 Top the beef with a whole mushroom cap. Beat the egg white with 10 ml (2 tsp) water and brush this along the edges of the pastry rectangle.

8 Fold pastry over meat and mushroom, overlapping edges; press lightly to seal. Place on a baking sheet. Prepare remainder.

9 Roll out pastry trimmings and cut out decorative shapes. Brush one side with egg white mixture and arrange on pastry cases.

10 Chill the prepared beef Wellingtons until you are ready to cook them. Beat the egg yolk with 10 ml (2 tsp) water and brush this glaze over the pastry. Bake at 200°C (400°F) mark 6, allowing 25 minutes for rare beef or 27 minutes for medium-cooked beef. Transfer the Wellingtons to a large heated serving dish or plate and garnish with endives or watercress. Serve with French and English mustards, if you wish.

Pot roast beef

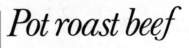

Colour index page 54
6–8 servings

Country Pot Roast

1.4-kg (3-lb) piece
topside or silverside
2 cloves garlic, skinned and
crushed
25 g (1 oz) plain flour
45 ml (3 tbsp) vegetable oil
225 ml (8 fl oz) tomato
juice
2 carrots, peeled and sliced
2 onions, skinned and
chopped
100 g (4 oz) celery,
trimmed and sliced

5 ml (1 level tsp) dried
oregano
15 ml (1 level tbsp) salt
1.25 ml (¼ level tsp)
pepper

For the garnish:
celery leaves

1 Rub the meat with the crushed garlic and coat it all over with flour.

2 Heat the oil in a large flameproof casserole and fry the meat, turning, until it is well browned on all sides.

3 Add the tomato juice, carrots, onions, celery, oregano and seasoning and bring to the boil.

4 Cover and simmer for 3 hours or until the meat is tender, turning it occasionally. Remove the meat to a heated serving dish and keep hot.

5 Purée the cooking liquid and vegetables in a blender or by pushing them through a sieve with a wooden spoon to make a thick, smooth gravy.

6 Return the gravy to the casserole and bring to the boil. Garnish the meat with the celery leaves and serve with the gravy spooned round it.

Colour index page 52
6 servings

Simple Beef Pot Roast

*1.6-kg (3½-lb) piece
topside or brisket
salt and pepper
25 g (1 oz) lard
2–3 cloves*

*1 onion, skinned
300 ml (½ pint) water
300 ml (½ pint) beef
stock*

1. Sprinkle the meat all over with salt and pepper. Melt the lard in a flameproof casserole and fry the meat until lightly browned all over.
2. Stick the cloves into the onion, add it to the meat with the water. Bring to the boil, then cover and simmer over a gentle heat for about 3 hours, or until the meat is tender, turning it occasionally. Alternatively, cook the meat in the oven at 150°C (300°F) mark 2. Remove the meat to a heated serving dish and keep it hot. Leave the cooking liquid to cool slightly.
3. Discard the onion and cloves. Spoon off and discard all the fat from the surface of the cooking liquid. Add the stock to the casserole and bring to the boil, stirring to loosen any sediment on the bottom of the pan. Season the gravy well and serve with the beef.

Colour index page 55
6–8 servings

Beef Pot Roast with Broad Beans

*1.4-kg (3-lb) piece topside
1 large onion, skinned and
sliced
1 clove garlic, skinned and
crushed
30 ml (2 tbsp)
Worcestershire sauce
20 ml (4 level tsp) salt*

*5 ml (1 level tsp) sugar
1.25 ml (¼ level tsp)
pepper
400 ml (¾ pint) water
4 parsnips, peeled and cut
into chunks
700 g (1½ lb) shelled broad
beans*

1. Put the meat in a large casserole with the onion, garlic, Worcestershire sauce, salt, sugar, pepper and water. Cover and cook in the oven at 180°C (350°F) mark 4 for 2 hours.
2. Add the parsnips and beans and return to the oven for a further 1–1½ hours, until the vegetables and meat are tender, turning the meat occasionally.
3. Put the meat on a heated serving dish and remove the strings; arrange the vegetables around it and keep them hot. Skim off and discard the fat from the cooking juices, bring them back to the boil and spoon the hot cooking juices over the meat and vegetables on the serving dish.

POT ROAST WITH MIXED VEGETABLES:
Prepare the beef as above but use *4 onions,* skinned and thickly sliced, and replace the parsnips and broad beans with *3–4 carrots,* peeled and thickly sliced, *1 small turnip,* peeled and quartered, and *2 sticks celery,* trimmed and sliced. When adding the vegetables, remove the meat from the pan first then replace it on top of the vegetables.

Sauerbraten

*1.4-kg (3-lb) piece
silverside
30 ml (2 level tbsp) plain
flour
1.25 ml (¼ level tsp)
pepper
10 ml (2 level tsp) salt
60 ml (4 tbsp) vegetable oil
1 onion, skinned and sliced
2 carrots, peeled and sliced
60 ml (4 level tbsp)
gingernut crumbs
100 ml (4 fl oz) soured
cream*

For the marinade:
*2 onions, skinned and
sliced
1 carrot, peeled and sliced*

*2 large sticks celery,
trimmed and sliced
400 ml (¾ pint) red wine
45 ml (3 tbsp) red wine
vinegar
300 ml (½ pint) water
2 bay leaves
6 peppercorns
1.25 ml (¼ level tsp)
mustard seed*

Colour index page 54
6–8 servings

1 Put all the ingredients for the marinade in a saucepan and bring to the boil, stirring occasionally. Reduce the heat, cover the pan and simmer gently for 10 minutes.

2 Pour the marinade into a large bowl, cover and cool. Add the meat, turning to coat it thoroughly. Cover and refrigerate for 2–3 days, turning the meat each day.

3 Remove the meat, dry it with kitchen paper towel; coat with the flour, mixed with the pepper and 5 ml (1 level tsp) salt. Strain the marinade and reserve the liquid.

4 Heat the oil in a large flameproof casserole, add the meat and brown well on all sides. Remove the meat; drain off and discard all but 15 ml (1 tbsp) of the drippings.

5 Add the onion and carrots to the casserole and cook gently for 3 minutes. Return meat to casserole.

6 Add marinade and bring to the boil. Cover and simmer for 2½ hours, turning meat occasionally.

7 Remove the meat to a heated serving dish and keep it hot. Skim off the fat from the gravy.

8 Stir in the gingernut crumbs and remaining salt. Simmer, stirring, until thick Remove from heat.

9 Whisk in the soured cream and stir over gentle heat until heated through (do not boil).

10 Spoon some of the gravy over the meat and serve the rest separately in a sauce boat.

Pot roast beef

Beef Pot Roast with Sweet and Sour Cabbage

Colour index page 51

6–8 servings

30 ml (2 tbsp) vegetable oil
1.4-kg (3-lb) piece boneless top rib or 'leg of mutton cut', cut 5 cm (2 in) thick
2 onions, skinned and sliced
100 ml (4 fl oz) red wine vinegar
25 ml (5 level tsp) salt
20 ml (4 level tsp) soft light brown sugar

5 ml (1 level tsp) caraway seed
2.5 ml (½ level tsp) coarsely ground black pepper
120 ml (8 tbsp) water
900-g (2-lb) red cabbage
30 ml (2 level tbsp) plain flour

1. Heat the oil in a flameproof casserole and brown the meat all over.
2. Stir in the onions, vinegar, salt, brown sugar, caraway seed, pepper and 60 ml (4 tbsp) water. Bring to the boil then reduce the heat, cover and simmer for 2½ hours or until the meat is tender, turning the meat occasionally.
3. Meanwhile, coarsely shred the cabbage, discarding any tough stalks.
4. When the meat is cooked put it on a heated serving dish and keep hot. Skim off the fat from the cooking liquid.
5. Add the cabbage to the casserole and bring to the boil. Reduce the heat, cover and simmer for about 30 minutes, until tender, stirring occasionally.
6. Blend the flour with the remaining water, gradually stir it into the cabbage and cook, stirring, until the sauce thickens. Spoon the cabbage round the meat on the serving dish.

Beef Pot Roast with Peppers

Colour index page 53

6–8 servings

30 ml (2 tbsp) vegetable oil
3 large red or green peppers, seeded and cut lengthways into 1-cm (½-in) strips
1.4-kg (3-lb) piece chuck steak, cut 4 cm (1½ in) thick

1 onion, skinned and thinly sliced
100 ml (4 fl oz) dry sherry
30 ml (2 tbsp) soy sauce
15 ml (1 level tbsp) cornflour
5 ml (1 level tsp) sugar

1. Heat the oil in a large flameproof casserole and cook the peppers for about 3 minutes, stirring, until just tender. Remove the peppers from the pan.
2. Brown the beef in the oil remaining in the pan, then add the onion, sherry, soy sauce and 30 ml (2 tbsp) water. Bring to the boil, cover and simmer for 2–2½ hours until the meat is tender, turning the meat occasionally. Add a little more water if necessary during the cooking.
3. Put the beef on a heated serving dish and keep hot. Pour the cooking liquid into a measuring jug and leave to stand for a few seconds. Skim off 15 ml (1 tbsp) fat from the top and put it in the casserole; skim off and discard the rest of the fat. Add water if necessary to make the liquid up to 350 ml (12 fl oz).
4. Blend the cornflour and sugar into the fat in the casserole and gradually stir in the cooking liquid. Cook, stirring, until thickened. Return the peppers to the casserole and heat through.
5. To serve, spoon the peppers round the beef and pour the sauce over the top.

Mexican Beef Pot Roast

Colour index page 52

6–8 servings

15 ml (1 tbsp) vegetable oil
3 garlic cloves, skinned and halved
1.4-kg (3-lb) piece chuck or blade steak, cut 4 cm (1½ in) thick
2–4 fresh chillies, seeded and chopped
2 onions, skinned and chopped
425-g (16-oz) can tomatoes, puréed

60 ml (4 tbsp) red wine vinegar
15 ml (1 level tbsp) sugar
15 ml (1 level tbsp) salt
5 ml (1 level tsp) dried oregano
4 green peppers, seeded and quartered
2 226-g (8-oz) packets frozen sweetcorn kernels

1 Heat the oil in a large pan and fry the garlic until lightly browned; discard the garlic.

2 Add the steak and fry it in the garlic-flavoured oil until well browned all over. Remove it from the pan, set aside and keep warm.

3 Add the chillies and onions to the oil remaining in the pan and cook for 10 minutes or until tender, stirring them frequently.

4 Return the meat to the pan and add the tomato purée, vinegar, sugar, salt and oregano; bring to the boil, stirring. Reduce the heat, cover and simmer for 1½ hours.

5 Add the green peppers, cover the pan again and simmer for a further hour or until the meat is tender. Skim off and discard the fat from the surface of the cooking liquid.

6 Add the sweetcorn and bring back to the boil, then reduce the heat, cover again and simmer for a further 5 minutes or until the corn is heated through and tender.

Fried and grilled beef

Boeuf en Daube

Colour index
page 50

6 servings

*1.1-kg (2½-lb) piece top
  rump
25 g (1 oz) butter
30 ml (2 tbsp) vegetable oil
225 g (8 oz) onions,
  skinned and thinly sliced
450 g (1 lb) carrots, peeled
  and thinly sliced
225 g (8 oz) salt pork,
  rinded and cubed
300 ml (½ pint) dry white
  wine*

*150 ml (¼ pint) beef stock
5 ml (1 level tsp) dried
  basil
2.5 ml (½ level tsp) dried
  rosemary
bay leaf
2.5 ml (½ level tsp) ground
  mixed spice
salt and pepper
6 stoned black olives*

1. Tie the beef firmly with string. Heat the butter and oil together in a frying pan and fry the meat until it is just browned and sealed all over. Remove it from the pan, drain on kitchen paper towel and place it in a flameproof casserole.
2. Fry the vegetables and salt pork in the fat remaining in the pan until golden brown. Drain well and spoon around the beef.
3. Pour over the wine and stock and stir in the herbs, spice and seasoning. Bring to the boil, cover the casserole and cook in the oven at 170°C (325°F) mark 3 for about 2½ hours. Turn the meat occasionally while cooking.
4. Stir in the olives, cover again and cook for a further 30 minutes or until the beef is tender.
5. To serve, remove the meat from the pan, cut away the string and slice the meat thickly. Skim off the fat from the cooking juices and return the meat slices to the casserole.

Fruited Beef Pot Roast

Colour index
page 55

6–8 servings

*25 g (1 oz) lard
1.4-kg (3-lb) piece
  silverside or boned
  brisket
2 onions, skinned and
  sliced
225 ml (8 fl oz) cider
15 ml (1 level tbsp) soft
  light brown sugar
5 ml (1 level tsp) salt
2.5 ml (½ level tsp) freshly
  ground black pepper*

*1.25 ml (¼ level tsp)
  ground cloves
175 g (6 oz) dried apricots,
  soaked overnight
175 g (6 oz) stoned prunes,
  soaked overnight
15 g (½ oz) plain flour,
  optional
60 ml (4 tbsp) water,
  optional*

1. Melt the lard in a flameproof casserole, add the beef and brown it all over.
2. Add the onions, cider, sugar, salt, pepper and cloves and bring to the boil. Lower the heat, cover and simmer for 2½ hours or until the meat is almost cooked, turning it occasionally and adding more cider if necessary.
3. Add the apricots and prunes to the casserole and cook for a further 30 minutes or until the meat is tender. Remove the meat and fruit from the casserole with a slotted spoon, put them on a heated serving dish and keep hot.
4. Skim off and discard the fat from the cooking juices. If you prefer a thicker gravy, blend the flour with the water until smooth, then gradually stir it into the cooking juices. Cook, stirring constantly, until the gravy has thickened and serve it with the meat and fruit.

Fillet Steak with Mustard-caper Sauce

Colour index
page 51

6 servings

*40 g (1½ oz) butter or
  margarine
6 fillet steaks, cut 4 cm
  (1½ in) thick*

For the sauce:
*100 ml (4 fl oz) dry
  vermouth
30 ml (2 tbsp) chopped
  spring onions
100 ml (4 fl oz) water
100 ml (4 fl oz) double
  cream
30 ml (2 tbsp) capers*

*12.5 ml (2½ level tsp)
  made mustard
5 ml (1 level tsp) salt
2.5 ml (½ level tsp) freshly
  ground black pepper
1 beef stock cube,
  crumbled*

For the garnish:
*watercress sprigs, trimmed
  and washed*

1. Melt the butter or margarine in a large frying pan, add the steaks three at a time and fry them for about 4 minutes, until they are browned underneath. Turn them and fry the other side according to taste: allow 5 minutes for rare steak, 7 minutes for medium-cooked and 10 minutes for well done.
2. Put the steaks on a heated serving dish as they are cooked and keep them hot while you make the mustard-caper sauce.
3. Add the vermouth and spring onions to the fat remaining in the pan and cook for about 2 minutes, stirring to loosen the sediment on the bottom. Add the remaining ingredients, stirring, and bring the sauce to the boil.
4. Garnish the steaks with watercress and serve the sauce separately.

Châteaubriand

Colour index
page 55

4 servings

*8 large artichokes
900-g ((2-lb) piece
  châteaubriand or
  fillet steak*

*5 ml (1 level tsp) salt
béarnaise sauce, page 463*

1. Prepare the artichokes (page 277). Cook them, cool slightly and remove the inner leaves and choke. Keep the prepared artichokes hot.
2. Sprinkle the steak with salt, place it on the rack in the grill pan and grill according to taste, allowing 25 minutes for rare steak, 30 minutes for medium-cooked, and turning the meat once.
3. Cut the steak into thick slices and arrange them on a heated serving dish. Spoon some béarnaise sauce into the artichokes and arrange around the steak. Serve the remaining sauce separately.

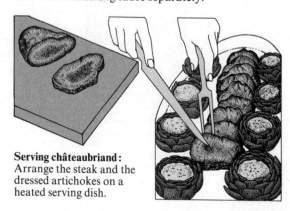

Serving châteaubriand:
Arrange the steak and the dressed artichokes on a heated serving dish.

Fried and grilled beef

London Grill

Colour index
page 51

4 servings

700-g (1½-lb) piece
   entrecôte or rump
   steak
10 ml (2 level tsp)
   seasoning salt
1.25 ml (¼ level tsp)
   freshly ground black
   pepper
2 tomatoes
French dressing, page 326
6 large mushrooms

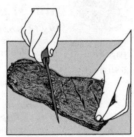

1 Wipe the steak with kitchen paper towel, then score it in diamond shapes on both sides with a sharp knife. Put it on a rack in the grill pan.

2 Sprinkle with 5 ml (1 level tsp) seasoning salt and half the pepper. Cut the tomatoes in half.

3 Brush the tomatoes with dressing and arrange, cut sides up, around the steak. Cook under a hot grill for 5 minutes. Slice the mushrooms.

4 Turn the steak and sprinkle second side with the remaining seasoning salt and pepper.

5 Arrange the mushroom slices overlapping on the rack and brush with French dressing.

6 Grill for a further 5–6 minutes, according to taste; to check whether the steak is cooked, make a small cut in the centre with a sharp knife.

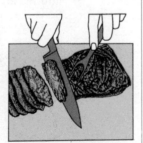

7 Carve the steak in thin crossways slices, on a slant, and serve with the grilled vegetables. Spoon over the juices from the grill pan, if you wish.

Entrecôte Mirabeau

Colour index
page 52

4 servings

6 anchovy fillets
45 ml (3 tbsp) milk
4 entrecôte steaks, cut
   about 1 cm (½ in) thick
150 ml (¼ pint)
   well-flavoured beef stock

For the anchovy butter:
100 g (4 oz) butter,
   softened

2.5 ml (½ tsp) anchovy
   essence

For the garnish:
watercress sprigs, trimmed
   and washed

1. Make the anchovy butter. Cream the butter and mix in the anchovy essence. Shape it into a neat roll, wrap it and chill until firm.
2. Put the anchovy fillets on a saucer, spoon the milk over them and leave for 5–10 minutes. Drain them, pat them dry with kitchen paper towel and cut them into narrow strips.
3. Put the steaks on a rack in the grill pan and brush with stock. Cook under a hot grill for 5–10 minutes according to taste, brushing with stock from time to time and turning the steaks once.
4. Arrange strips of anchovy in a lattice pattern over each steak, brush with more stock and grill for a further 1–2 minutes until the anchovies are heated through. Put on a heated serving dish, and garnish with watercress. Cut the roll of anchovy butter into pats and serve with the steaks.

Steak Diane

Colour index
page 52

4 servings

4 entrecôte steaks, cut
   about 1 cm (½ in) thick
salt
pepper
50 g (2 oz) butter
60 ml (4 tbsp) brandy

2 small shallots, finely
   chopped
45 ml (3 tbsp) chopped
   chives
120 ml (8 tbsp) dry sherry

1. Beat the steaks until they are about 0.5 cm (¼ in) thick, turning occasionally. Sprinkle each one with salt and pepper.
2. Melt 15 g (½ oz) of the fat in a chafing dish or frying pan and sauté one steak just until both sides are browned. Pour 15 ml (1 tbsp) brandy over the steak and ignite. When the flames die down, remove the steak from the pan and cook the remaining steaks in the same way. Keep hot.
3. Add the shallots and chives and cook, stirring constantly, until the shallots are tender. Add the sherry and heat through.
4. Place each steak on a hot plate, pour over some sauce and serve immediately.

Beating the steaks: Use a meat mallet to pound the steaks to even thickness.

To flambé the steaks: Pour over the brandy and ignite it with a taper.

Devilled Porterhouse Steak

Colour index
page 54
6 servings

*1.1–1.4-kg (2¹⁄₂–3-lb)
  piece porterhouse steak,
  cut 5 cm (2 in) thick
75 g (3 oz) butter, softened
15 ml (1 tbsp)
  Worcestershire sauce
5 ml (1 level tsp) dry
  mustard*

*2.5 ml (¹⁄₂ level tsp) curry
  powder
1.25 ml (¹⁄₄ level tsp) salt
1.25 ml (¹⁄₄ level tsp)
  pepper
100 g (4 oz) dried
  breadcrumbs*

1. Trim any excess fat from the steak and put the meat on a rack in the grill pan. Grill under high heat according to taste: allow about 25 minutes for rare steak, 35 minutes for medium-cooked, or 45 minutes for well done. Turn the steak from time to time during cooking.
2. Cream the butter and mix in the Worcestershire sauce, mustard, curry powder, salt and pepper.
3. Spread one side of the cooked steak with half of the devilled butter mixture and sprinkle with half the breadcrumbs, pressing them in well. Turn and repeat with the remaining butter mixture and breadcrumbs on the other side.
4. Grill the steak for a further 3–5 minutes on each side until the breadcrumbs are golden.

BARBECUE VARIATION: Prepare the steak as above, but light the charcoal at least 30 minutes before you start to cook. Grill the meat to taste and finish with the butter mixture and breadcrumbs as for devilled porterhouse steak above.

ROSEMARY PORTERHOUSE STEAK: Grill the steak as in step 1 (above). Meanwhile, melt *50 g (2 oz) butter* in saucepan and add *2 large onions*, skinned and sliced, and *1 clove garlic*, skinned and crushed; fry them gently for 5 minutes until soft but not coloured. Stir in *60 ml (4 tbsp) red wine, 5 ml (1 level tsp) tomato paste*, a little *salt and pepper* and *sprig of rosemary*. Cover the pan and simmer for 15 minutes. Discard the rosemary. Spread the wine mixture over the cooked steak and grill for a further 3–5 minutes on each side.

Carpet Bag Steak

Colour index
page 55
4 servings

*700–900-g (1¹⁄₂–2-lb) piece
  rump or fillet steak, cut
  5 cm (2 in) thick
1 dozen oysters,
  shelled*

*50 g (2 oz) mushrooms,
  thinly sliced
salt
cayenne pepper
olive oil or melted butter*

1. Slit the steak almost through horizontally and open it out like a book. Lay the oysters and mushrooms evenly over one side and sprinkle with salt and cayenne pepper.
2. Fold over the other side and sew up the cut edges with a trussing needle and fine string so that the filling cannot escape.
3. Brush the steak on both sides with oil, put it on a rack in the grill pan and cook under a hot grill for 5–6 minutes on each side.
4. Lower the heat and grill for a further 3–5 minutes, according to taste.
5. Remove the string and cut the steak into four pieces before serving.

Steak Medici

Colour index
page 53
4 servings

*50 g (2 oz) butter or
  margarine
4 sirloin steaks, cut
  about 2 cm (³⁄₄ in)
  thick
225 g (8 oz) mushrooms,
  sliced
3.75 ml (³⁄₄ level tsp)
  seasoning salt
60 ml (4 tbsp) port*

For the garnish:
chopped parsley

1 Melt half the butter or margarine in a large frying pan. When it is very hot, add the steaks, two at a time, and brown them on both sides.

2 Continue to fry according to taste (allow 5–6 minutes on each side for medium-cooked steak) then remove them to a heated plate and keep hot.

3 Reduce the heat slightly and add the remaining fat to the pan.

4 Stir in the sliced mushrooms and seasoning salt. Cook, stirring, until the mushrooms are tender but still firm.

5 Add the port, stirring to loosen any sediment on the bottom of the pan.

6 Spoon the mushroom and port mixture over the steaks and garnish with chopped parsley. Serve the steaks immediately.

Fried and grilled beef

Steak Sauternes

Colour index page 50

4 servings

100 g (4 oz) mushrooms
50 g (2 oz) cooked ham
75 g (3 oz) butter or
    margarine
60 ml (4 tbsp) Sauternes or
    other sweet white wine
60 ml (4 tbsp) stock or
    water
4 fillet steaks, cut about
    5 cm (2 in) thick
4 slices white bread

For the garnish:
watercress sprigs, washed
    and trimmed

1 Reserve 4 whole mushrooms and slice the remainder. Chop the cooked ham finely.

2 Melt 25 g (1 oz) of the butter or margarine in a small saucepan and add the wine and stock or water. Bring to the boil.

3 Add the sliced mushrooms and the ham to the pan and simmer gently for 8–10 minutes or until thickened, stirring.

4 Melt the remaining butter in a large frying pan. Add the steaks and fry, turning once; allow 5–6 minutes on each side for medium cooked steaks.

5 Add the whole mushrooms to the fillet steaks for the last 3 minutes of the cooking time.

6 Meanwhile cut the bread slices into circles the same size as the steaks and toast them. Arrange the toast circles on a heated serving dish.

7 Place each steak on a circle of toast, top with a whole mushroom and spoon some of the Sauternes sauce over the top. Garnish with watercress.

Minute Steaks with Fresh Tomato Sauce

Colour index page 53

6–8 servings

60 ml (4 tbsp) vegetable oil
6–8 minute steaks
6 tomatoes, skinned
100 ml (4 fl oz) water
60 ml (4 tbsp) chopped
    spring onions
30 ml (2 level tbsp) sugar
10 ml (2 level tsp) salt
10 ml (2 level tsp) dried
    basil
30 ml (2 level tbsp)
    cornflour

1. Heat the oil in a large frying pan, add two or three of the steaks and fry them for 2–3 minutes on each side, according to taste. Place on a heated serving dish and keep hot while you cook the remaining steaks in the same way.
2. Slice three tomatoes and chop the rest.
3. Add half the water, the chopped tomatoes, spring onions, sugar, salt and basil to the pan. Blend the remaining water with the cornflour, gradually stir it into the tomato mixture and cook, stirring, until the sauce is thickened.
4. Add the sliced tomatoes to the sauce and cook gently until heated through. Spoon the sauce over the steaks and serve immediately.

Teriyaki Beef Kebabs

Colour index page 53

6 servings

900-g (2-lb) piece rump
    steak, cut about 2.5 cm
    (1 in) thick
1 small pineapple, peeled,
    cored and cut into 2.5-cm
    (1-in) chunks
30 ml (2 tbsp) lemon juice
15 ml (1 tbsp) vegetable
    oil
1.25 ml (¼ level tsp)
    ground ginger
1 clove garlic, skinned and
    crushed

For the marinade:
40 g (1½ oz) soft light
    brown sugar
60 ml (4 tbsp) soy sauce

1. Trim any excess fat from the steak and cut the meat into 2.5-cm (1-in) cubes.
2. Make the marinade. Mix together the sugar, soy sauce, lemon juice, oil, ginger and garlic. Stir in the beef cubes, cover and refrigerate for at least 3 hours, stirring frequently.
3. Just before cooking, drain the meat and thread the beef and pineapple chunks alternately on to long metal skewers (if done earlier, the pineapple will make the meat mushy).
4. Cook under a hot grill according to taste, allowing about 15 minutes for medium-cooked kebabs. Baste occasionally with the marinade and turn once during cooking.

Marinating the beef: Stir the meat into the marinade and refrigerate for 3 hours.

Threading the skewers: Just before grilling, thread the meat and pineapple on to skewers.

Braised beef

Carbonnade of Beef

Colour index page 51

5–8 servings

1.4-kg (3-lb) piece chuck
    or blade steak, cut
    2.5 cm (1 in) thick
65 g (2½ oz) butter or
    margarine
4 large onions, skinned
    and thinly sliced
1 clove garlic, skinned
    and crushed
175 ml (6 fl oz) beer
1 beef stock cube, crumbled
2.5 ml (½ level tsp) dried
    thyme

5 ml (1 level tsp) salt
pinch pepper
30 ml (2 level tbsp) plain
    flour
60 ml (4 tbsp) water

For the garnish, optional:
chopped parsley or
    watercress

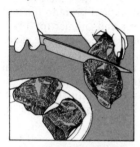

1 Trim the meat and cut it into six or eight pieces. Melt 40 g (1½ oz) of the butter or margarine in a large frying pan with a lid or a flameproof casserole.

2 When the fat is hot, add the steak, three or four pieces at a time, and fry until browned all over. Remove the pieces from the pan as they brown. Reduce the heat.

3 Melt the remaining butter or margarine, add the onions and garlic and cook, stirring, for about 10 minutes or until the onions are soft but not coloured.

4 Add the beer, stock cube, thyme, salt and pepper, stirring to loosen any sediment from the bottom of the pan.

5 Return the meat to the pan and bring to the boil. Reduce the heat, cover and simmer for 1¾ hours or until tender, turning the meat once.

6 Arrange the pieces of steak on a heated serving dish and keep hot while you make the gravy. Blend the flour to a smooth paste with the water and stir it into the cooking liquid in the pan. Cook, stirring constantly, until the liquid thickens. Spoon some of the gravy over the meat and serve the remainder separately in a sauce boat. If you wish, garnish the carbonnade of beef with chopped parsley or a few sprigs of watercress before serving.

Chunky Beef with Celery

Colour index page 54

4 servings

25 g (1 oz) lard
700 g (1½ lb) top rib, cut
    into four
225 g (8 oz) celery, washed
    and trimmed
100 g (4 oz) onion, skinned
    and sliced

50 g (2 oz) red kidney
    beans, soaked overnight
400 ml (¾ pint) beef stock
30 ml (2 tbsp) sherry
salt and pepper
30 ml (2 level tbsp)
    cornflour

1. Melt the lard in a flameproof casserole, add the pieces of beef and brown them all over. Remove from the pan.

2. Cut the celery into 5-cm (2-in) lengths. Add them with the onion to the fat remaining in the casserole and fry until lightly browned. Drain the red kidney beans and add them to the casserole; discard the soaking liquid.

3. Place the beef on top of the vegetables in the casserole, and pour over the stock and sherry. Season well and bring to the boil. Cover and cook in the oven at 180°C (350°F) mark 4 for about 2 hours or until the beef is tender. Strain off the liquid into a small saucepan.

4. Blend the cornflour with a little cold water and gradually stir it into the liquid in the saucepan. Bring to the boil, stirring, and cook until thickened. Adjust the seasoning.

5. Arrange the beef and vegetables on a heated serving dish and spoon a little of the sauce over the top. Serve the remaining sauce separately.

Marinated Beef Casserole

Colour index page 54

6 servings

900-g (2-lb) piece chuck or
    blade steak, cut into six
    pieces
30 ml (2 tbsp) wine vinegar
2 cloves garlic, skinned
40 g (1½ oz) plain flour
50 g (2 oz) dripping
100 g (4 oz) button onions,
    skinned
100 g (4 oz) button
    mushrooms
100 g (4 oz) streaky bacon,
    rinded and diced

600 ml (1 pint) well-
    flavoured beef stock
bay leaf
15 ml (1 level tbsp) tomato
    paste
bouquet garni

For the garnish:
chopped parsley

1. Put the meat in a shallow dish, add the vinegar and garlic and mix well. Cover and leave the meat to marinate overnight.

2. Drain the meat and pat dry; strain and reserve the marinade, discarding the garlic. Coat the meat with the flour. Melt the dripping in a flameproof casserole, add the pieces of meat and brown them all over; remove them from the pan.

3. Add the onions, mushrooms and bacon to the fat remaining in the pan and fry for 5 minutes. Pour in the stock and reserved marinade and stir to loosen any sediment. Add the bay leaf, tomato paste and bouquet garni and bring to the boil. Return the browned meat to the casserole.

4. Cover the casserole tightly and cook in the oven at 170°C (325°F) mark 3 for about 1½–2 hours until the meat is tender.

5. Discard the bay leaf and bouquet garni and serve the casserole garnished with chopped parsley.

Braised beef

Swiss Steak with Pepper-tomato Sauce

Colour index
page 55

6 servings

1.1–1.4-kg (2½–3-lb) piece chuck steak, cut about 4 cm (1½ in) thick
30 ml (2 level tbsp) plain flour
45 ml (3 tbsp) vegetable oil
2 large onions, skinned and sliced
225 ml (8 fl oz) tomato sauce, page 337
1 clove garlic, skinned and finely chopped

5 ml (1 level tsp) salt
1.25 ml (¼ level tsp) pepper
bay leaf
2 small green peppers, seeded and chopped

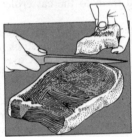

1 Trim any excess fat from the meat and pound one side well with a meat mallet.

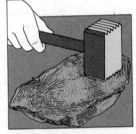

2 Turn the meat over and pound the other side until it is an even thickness. Sprinkle 15 ml (1 level tbsp) flour evenly over each side of the steak.

3 Heat the oil in a large frying pan, add the meat and cook until well browned on both sides. Remove from the pan.

4 Add the onions to the fat remaining in the pan and cook, stirring frequently, for about 5 minutes, until the onions are lightly browned.

5 Add the tomato sauce, garlic, salt, pepper and bay leaf and return the meat to the pan. Reduce the heat, cover and simmer for about 2¾ hours, turning the meat once.

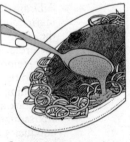

6 Add the green peppers and cook for a further 45 minutes until the beef is tender. Discard the bay leaf and skim off the fat. Serve the meat with the sauce spooned over.

Oriental Aniseed Beef

Colour index
page 53

6 servings

1 bunch spring onions
100 ml (4 fl oz) dry sherry
60 ml (4 tbsp) soy sauce
15 ml (1 level tbsp) sugar
10 ml (2 level tsp) aniseed
2.5 ml (½ level tsp) ground ginger

120 ml (8 tbsp) water
1.1-kg (2½-lb) piece chuck or blade steak, cut 4 cm (1½ in) thick
10 ml (2 level tsp) cornflour

1. Trim the spring onions and cut them into 2.5-cm (1-in) pieces. Place half in a large frying pan, then stir in the sherry, soy sauce, sugar, aniseed, ginger and 60 ml (4 tbsp) of the water.
2. Add the steak and bring to the boil, then reduce the heat, cover and simmer for 1¾ hours or until tender, turning once. Place the steak on a heated serving dish, and keep hot.
3. Blend the cornflour with the remaining water and gradually stir it into the liquid in the pan. Cook, stirring constantly, until thickened. Stir in the remaining spring onions, reheat the sauce and pour over the steak.

Creamed Beef and Noodles

Colour index
page 50

6 servings

1.1-kg (2½-lb) piece chuck or blade steak, cut 2.5 cm (1 in) thick
15 ml (1 tbsp) vegetable oil
75 ml (5 tbsp) water
1 beef stock cube, crumbled
2.5 ml (½ level tsp) salt
pinch pepper
175 g (6 oz) noodles

225 ml (8 fl oz) soured cream
2.5 ml (½ level tsp) dried dill weed

For the garnish:
watercress sprigs, trimmed and washed

1. Cut the steak into six pieces. Heat the oil in a large frying pan or flameproof casserole and brown the steaks on both sides. Stir in the water, crumbled stock cube, salt and pepper and bring to the boil, stirring, then cover and simmer for 1¾ hours or until tender, turning once.
2. Cook the noodles in boiling salted water until just tender, drain well and place on a heated serving dish. Place the steaks on top and keep hot.
3. Stir the soured cream and dill into the cooking juices and cook, stirring constantly, until slightly thickened; do not boil. Spoon some sauce over the steaks and noodles and serve the rest separately. Garnish with watercress.

To serve the steaks:
Spoon some of the sauce over the meat and noodles and serve the rest in a sauce boat.

Caesar Style Braised Steak

Colour index
page 51

4 servings

75 ml (5 tbsp) olive or
  vegetable oil
2 cloves garlic, skinned and
  sliced
4 fillet or rump steaks, cut
  2.5 cm (1 in) thick
50-g (2-oz) can anchovies,
  drained
15 ml (1 tbsp)
  Worcestershire sauce
5 ml (1 tsp) lemon juice

1.25 ml (¼ level tsp) dry
  mustard
150 ml (¼ pint) water
15 ml (1 level tbsp) plain
  flour
4 slices French bread, cut
  diagonally, 1 cm (½ in)
  thick

For the garnish:
chopped parsley

1. Heat 15 ml (1 tbsp) of the oil in a large frying pan, add the garlic and fry just until browned. Remove the garlic and set aside. Add the steaks and fry until well browned on both sides. Chop four of the anchovy fillets finely.
2. Add to the steaks with the Worcestershire sauce, lemon juice, mustard and 75 ml (5 tbsp) water. Bring to the boil, then cover and simmer for 1¼ hours or until tender, turning once.
3. Blend the flour with the remaining water and gradually stir it into the liquid in the pan. Cook, stirring constantly, until thickened.
4. Heat the remaining oil in another large frying pan, add the reserved garlic and cook for 5 minutes.
5. Discard the garlic, add the bread to the pan and cook until golden brown on both sides, adding more garlic-flavoured oil if necessary. Remove the bread to a heated serving dish and keep warm.
6. Place a steak on each slice of bread, spoon some of the sauce over the steaks and serve the rest separately. Garnish the steaks with chopped parsley and the remaining anchovies.

Beef with Soured Cream and Mushrooms

Colour index
page 54

6 servings

1.1-kg (2½-lb) piece chuck
  or blade steak, cut about
  2.5 cm (1 in) thick
15 g (½ oz) butter
1 onion, skinned and sliced
5 ml (1 level tsp) salt
pinch pepper
120 ml (8 tbsp) water
225 g (8 oz) button
  mushrooms

225 g (8 oz) noodles
15 ml (1 level tbsp) plain
  flour
150 ml (¼ pint) soured
  cream

For the garnish:
chopped parsley

1. Cut the steak into six pieces. Melt the fat in a large frying pan, add the steaks and onion and fry for about 10 minutes until the steaks are well browned on both sides.
2. Add the salt, pepper and 60 ml (4 tbsp) water and bring to the boil. Cover and simmer for 1¾ hours or until tender. Add the mushrooms and heat through.
3. Cook the noodles in boiling salted water until just tender. Drain and place in a heated serving dish. Put the steaks on top and keep hot.
4. Blend the flour with the remaining water, stir it gradually into the liquid in the pan and cook, stirring constantly, until thickened. Stir in the soured cream and heat through gently; do not allow to boil. Spoon the sauce over the steaks and noodles and garnish with parsley.

Celery-stuffed Beef Steak

Colour index
page 51

6 servings

1.4-kg (3-lb) piece flank
  steak, boned
50 g (2 oz) fresh white
  breadcrumbs
4 sticks celery, washed,
  trimmed and chopped
25 g (1 oz) onion, skinned
  and chopped

40 g (1½ oz) butter
salt and pepper
pinch thyme
plain flour
15 ml (1 level tbsp)
  cornflour
1.25 ml (¼ level tsp)
  ground ginger

1. Trim any excess fat from the steak and score it in a diamond pattern on both sides, then cut it in half horizontally with a sharp knife.
2. Mix together the breadcrumbs, celery, onion, 15 g (½ oz) melted butter, a pinch each of salt, pepper and thyme and 30 ml (2 tbsp) water. Spread the mixture evenly over one piece of steak, and place the second piece on top.
3. Sew the two pieces together with a trussing needle and string at 2.5-cm (1-in) intervals; cut the sandwiched steak in half if necessary. Sprinkle with pepper, then with flour.
4. Melt the remaining butter in a flameproof casserole and brown the meat all over. Add 225 ml (8 fl oz) water and bring to the boil. Reduce the heat, cover and simmer for 2½ hours or until the meat is tender, stirring the liquid occasionally and adding more water if necessary. Place the meat on a heated serving dish, remove the strings and keep hot while you make the sauce.
5. Blend the cornflour and ginger with 30 ml (2 tbsp) cold water and 1.25 ml (¼ level tsp) salt and stir into the liquid in the casserole. Cook, stirring constantly, until thickened. Serve the sauce with the steak.

Scoring the steak: Use a sharp knife to score both sides of the steak in a diamond pattern.

Stuffing the steak: Spread the stuffing on one piece of steak, top with the other piece and sew up.

Serving the meat: Cut the stuffed steak in slices and serve with the sauce, passed in a sauce boat.

Stewed beef and beef pies

Beef Stew

Colour index
page 54

6 servings

25 g (1 oz) plain flour
1.1 kg (2½ lb) stewing
    steak, cut into chunks
75 ml (5 tbsp) vegetable oil
1 large onion, skinned and
    chopped
1 clove garlic, skinned and
    finely chopped
700 ml (1¼ pints) stock
2.5 ml (½ tsp)
    Worcestershire sauce
salt and pepper
700 g (1½ lb) potatoes,
    peeled and cut into
    chunks
450 g (1 lb) carrots, peeled
    and cut into chunks
225 g (8 oz) frozen peas

1 Spread the flour on a sheet of greaseproof or waxed paper and coat the pieces of meat with it; reserve any leftover flour. Heat the oil in a flameproof casserole.

2 Add the pieces of meat a few at a time and cook until browned on all sides, removing them as they brown. Reduce the heat.

3 Add the onion and garlic to the fat remaining in the pan. Cook until the onion is almost tender. Stir in any reserved flour.

4 Gradually stir in the stock, Worcestershire sauce, salt and pepper and cook, stirring, until slightly thickened.

5 Return the meat to the pan and bring to the boil. Reduce the heat, cover and simmer for 2½ hours until almost tender.

6 Add the potatoes and carrots, stir well and bring back to the boil. Reduce the heat, cover and simmer for 20 minutes.

7 Stir in the frozen peas, cover again and simmer for a further 5–10 minutes until the beef and all the vegetables are tender.

Boeuf Bourguignon

Colour index
page 53

6 servings

225 g (8 oz) streaky bacon,
    rinded and cut into
    2.5-cm (1-in) pieces
12 shallots, skinned
900 g (2 lb) lean stewing
    steak, cut into 5-cm
    (2-in) cubes
75 ml (5 level tbsp) plain
    flour
1 large carrot, peeled and
    chopped
1 large onion, skinned and
    chopped
60 ml (4 tbsp) brandy
2 cloves garlic, skinned and
    crushed

10 ml (2 level tsp) salt
2.5 ml (½ level tsp) dried
    thyme
1.25 ml (¼ level tsp)
    pepper
bay leaf
700 ml (1¼ pints) red
    Burgundy
50 g (2 oz) butter or
    margarine
450 g (1 lb) mushrooms,
    sliced

For the garnish, optional:
chopped parsley

1. Fry the bacon in its own fat in a flameproof casserole until it is lightly browned. Remove with a slotted spoon and drain on kitchen paper towel. Set aside. Drain off all but 45 ml (3 tbsp) of the fat from the casserole.

2. Add the shallots and cook until they are lightly browned, stirring occasionally. Remove the shallots and reserve them.

3. Sprinkle the pieces of meat with 45 ml (3 level tbsp) of the flour. Add them to the casserole, a few at a time and fry until they are well browned on all sides; remove the pieces as they brown and set aside on a plate.

4. Add the carrot and onion to the casserole and cook, stirring frequently, for 5 minutes or until tender. Return the beef to the casserole, pour over the brandy and ignite it with a long taper. Leave until the flames die down.

5. Add the fried bacon, garlic, salt, thyme, pepper, bay leaf and wine. Mix together well and bring to the boil. Cover and cook in the oven at 170°C (325°F) mark 3 for 1½ hours.

6. Meanwhile, melt half the butter or margarine in a frying pan, add the mushrooms and cook for about 7 minutes until golden.

7. Cream the remaining butter or margarine and mix with the remaining flour until smooth. Stir it into the casserole, a little at a time until well blended. Add the shallots and mushrooms, cover and cook for a further hour or until the meat is tender.

8. Serve in the casserole, garnished with a little chopped parsley if you wish.

To flambé the meat: Pour the brandy over the beef and vegetables and ignite the liquid.

Thickening the sauce: Stir the butter and flour mixture into the casserole, 2.5 ml (½ tsp) at a time.

Colour index page 50

6 servings

Californian Beef Stew

3 rashers streaky bacon,
  rinded and chopped
900 g (2 lb) stewing steak,
  cubed
300 ml (½ pint) stock
225 ml (8 fl oz) red wine
2 cloves garlic, skinned and
  crushed
25 g (1 oz) onion, skinned
  and chopped

10 ml (2 level tsp) salt
1.25 ml (¼ level tsp) dried
  thyme
small piece orange rind
18 small onions, skinned
350 g (12 oz) mushrooms
30 ml (2 level tbsp)
  cornflour
350 g (12 oz) frozen peas
75 g (3 oz) black olives

1. Fry the bacon in its own fat in a flameproof
casserole until crisp, then push it to one side of the
pan. Add the pieces of meat a few at a time and fry
until well browned, removing them as they brown.
2. Add 225 ml (8 fl oz) of the stock, the wine, garlic,
onion, salt, thyme and orange rind. Add the
browned meat, and bring to the boil. Cover and
simmer for 2½ hours or until the meat is tender.
3. Meanwhile, cook the onions in boiling salted
water in a covered saucepan for about 10 minutes.
Add the mushrooms, cook for 5 minutes, then drain.
4. Blend the cornflour with the remaining stock, stir
it into the casserole and cook, stirring, until
thickened. Add the onions, mushrooms, peas and
olives. Cover and cook for 10 minutes until the peas
are tender. Discard the rind before serving.

Colour index page 52

6 servings

Pressure-cooked Beef Stew

100 ml (4 fl oz) red wine
30 ml (2 tbsp) vegetable oil
900 g (2 lb) stewing steak,
  cut into chunks
100 g (4 oz) salt pork, cut
  into 1-cm (½-in) cubes
425-g (15-oz) can tomatoes
1 large onion, skinned and
  finely chopped
1 large carrot, peeled and
  finely chopped
1 stick celery, washed,
  trimmed and chopped

½ clove garlic, skinned and
  finely chopped
bay leaf
7.5 ml (1½ level tsp) salt
5 ml (1 level tsp) dried
  thyme
3 sprigs parsley
12 stuffed olives, halved
30 ml (2 level tbsp)
  cornflour
45 ml (3 tbsp) water
100 g (4 oz) button
  mushrooms

1. Mix the wine and oil in a bowl and add the beef.
Cover and chill for 4 hours, turning the meat
occasionally. Drain the meat, reserve the marinade.
2. Fry the salt pork in its own fat in the pressure
cooker until golden. Add the beef and brown.
3. Add the reserved marinade and all the remaining
ingredients except the cornflour, water and mushrooms. Cover and bring to high (15 lb) pressure.
Cook under pressure for 20 minutes, then remove
from the heat and reduce the pressure quickly.
4. Blend the cornflour to a smooth paste with the
water and add to the cooker with the mushrooms.
Bring to the boil, stirring, and cook until thickened.
Discard the parsley and bay leaf before serving.

Steak and Kidney Pie

225 g (8 oz) lamb, pig or
  ox kidney
25 g (1 oz) plain flour
900 g (2 lb) stewing steak,
  cut into 2.5-cm (1-in)
  chunks
vegetable oil
1 large onion, skinned and
  chopped
100 ml (4 fl oz) red wine or
  beer
225 ml (8 fl oz) beef stock
10 ml (2 tsp)
  Worcestershire sauce
5 ml (1 level tsp) salt

1.25 ml (¼ level tsp)
  pepper
shortcrust or flaky pastry
  made with 225 g (8 oz)
  flour, pages 343 or 344
1 egg yolk, beaten with 5 ml
  (1 tsp) water

Colour index page 53

6 servings

1 Wash the kidney and
remove the membrane
and hard white core. Cut
the kidney into 2.5-cm
(1-in) chunks.

2 Spread the flour on
waxed paper and coat
the kidney and steak with
it. Heat 45 ml (3 tbsp) oil in
a large flameproof
casserole or saucepan.

3 Add the pieces of meat
to the pan a few at a
time and cook until brow-
ned all over; remove the
pieces as they brown, adding more oil as necessary.

4 When all the meat is
browned, reduce the
heat and add the onion to
the fat remaining in the pan.
Cook until it is almost
tender, stirring occasionally.

5 Stir in the wine or beer,
stock, Worcestershire
sauce, salt and pepper.

6 Add the browned meat
and bring to the boil.
Reduce the heat, cover and
simmer for 2 hours or until
the meat is tender.

7 Spoon into a 1.1-litre
(2-pint) pie dish and
place a pie funnel in the
centre. Roll out the pastry
to a circle 5 cm (2 in) larger
all round than the dish.

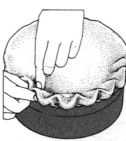

8 Cut a 2.5-cm (1-in)
strip from pastry edge
and lay on dampened edge
of dish. Lay the pastry circle
on top; trim and flute.

9 Brush the pastry with
the egg yolk and water
glaze and make a slit in the
centre with the point of a
knife for steam to escape.

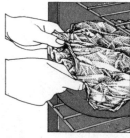

10 Bake at 200°C
(400°F) mark 6 for
about 40 minutes. Cover
loosely with foil if pastry
browns too quickly.

Stewed beef and beef pies

Queues de Boeufs aux Olives Noires

2 oxtails, jointed
30–45 ml (2–3 tbsp) olive oil
90 ml (6 tbsp) brandy
200 ml (7 fl oz) dry white wine
bouquet garni: bay leaves, thyme, parsley, orange rind, and a clove of garlic skinned and crushed, tied together in a piece of muslin
stock or water
225 g (8 oz) stoned black olives
350–450 g (12–16 oz) long grain rice

25 g (1 oz) butter or margarine
15 ml (1 level tbsp) plain flour
salt and pepper

Colour index page 53
6–8 servings

1 Put the oxtail in a bowl, cover with cold water and leave for 2 hours. Drain and dry the oxtail with kitchen paper towel.

2 Heat the oil in a flame-proof casserole, add the pieces of oxtail a few at a time and brown them well on all sides.

3 Warm the brandy in a small saucepan, ignite it and pour it over the oxtail in the casserole.

4 When the flames have died down, add the wine and let it bubble rapidly, stirring to remove any sediment.

5 Add the bouquet garni and sufficient stock to cover the meat. Cover and cook in the oven at 150°C (300°F) mark 2 for 3 hours.

6 Spoon off the liquid into a bowl and remove the bouquet garni. Refrigerate the meat and liquid separately overnight.

7 Remove the fat from the liquid. Pour the liquid into a saucepan, bring to the boil and pour over the meat in the casserole.

8 Add the olives, cover the casserole and cook on top of the stove for a further 1–1½ hours, until the meat comes easily away from the bone.

9 Meanwhile, cook the rice in boiling salted water until tender; drain and keep hot. Cream the butter and blend with the flour to a smooth paste.

10 Whisk the paste a little at a time into the cooking liquid. Adjust the seasoning and serve the meat and sauce spooned over the rice.

Colour index page 55
6–8 servings

Oxtail Ragout

45 ml (3 tbsp) vegetable oil
2 oxtails, cut into 6.5-cm (2½-in) pieces
2 298-g (10½-oz) cans condensed tomato soup
400 ml (¾ pint) water
50 g (2 oz) sugar
15 ml (1 level tbsp) salt

1.25 ml (¼ level tsp) pepper
10 large carrots, peeled and halved crossways
6 small onions, skinned and halved
225 g (8 oz) shelled broad beans

1. Heat the oil in a flameproof casserole, add the oxtail a few pieces at a time and fry until the meat is well browned all over, removing the pieces as they are browned.
2. Return the meat to the casserole, add the soup, water, sugar, salt and pepper; bring to the boil. Cover and simmer for 2¼ hours, stirring the ragout occasionally.
3. Add the halved carrots and cook for 40 minutes, then stir in the halved onions; cover and cook for 30 minutes more. Finally, stir in the beans, cover again and cook for a further 10 minutes. Skim off the surface fat before serving the ragout.

Colour index page 54
6 servings

Beef and Chestnut Casserole

50 g (2 oz) seasoned flour
1.1–1.4 kg (2½–3 lb) chuck or blade steak, cut into 5-cm (2-in) pieces
50 g (2 oz) lard
1 onion, skinned and sliced
425-g (15-oz) can tomatoes
100-g (4-oz) can pimentos, drained and sliced
150 ml (¼ pint) well-flavoured beef stock

150 ml (¼ pint) red wine
75-g (3-oz) packet sliced garlic sausage
12 canned whole chestnuts, drained
butter

For the garnish:
chopped parsley

1. Spread the seasoned flour on waxed paper and use it to thoroughly coat the pieces of beef; reserve any leftover flour.
2. Melt the lard in a frying pan. Add the pieces of beef to the lard a few at a time and fry until well browned all over, then remove them to a casserole as they brown.
3. Add the onion to the pan and fry gently until golden. Stir in the excess flour and gradually add the tomatoes with their juice, and the sliced pimentos, stock and wine to the frying pan and bring to the boil, stirring.
4. Cut the sausage into strips, add to the casserole and pour over the tomato and wine sauce. Cover and cook in the oven at 170°C (325°F) mark 3 for about 3 hours.
5. Just before serving, sauté the chestnuts in a little hot butter until browned and add to the casserole. Garnish with the chopped parsley.

Boiled beef

Minced beef

Boiled Beef with Winter Vegetables

*1.4-kg (3-lb) piece lean
    boneless brisket*
1 clove garlic, skinned
bay leaf
*1.25 ml (¼ tsp)
    peppercorns*
1 swede, peeled
1 cabbage
6–8 carrots, peeled
*6–8 small potatoes,
    peeled*

For the garnish, optional:
chopped parsley

1 Put the beef, garlic, bay
    leaf and peppercorns in a
flameproof casserole or
saucepan; cover with water.
Bring to the boil, skimming
off any scum that rises.

2 Reduce the heat, cover
    and simmer for 3–3½
hours until the meat is
tender. Remove the meat
and keep hot.

3 Cut the swede and cab-
    bage into wedges, leave
the rest of the vegetables
whole and add them all to
the cooking liquid in the
casserole or saucepan.

4 Bring back to the boil,
    then reduce the heat,
cover and simmer for 30
minutes or until the vegetables are tender.

5 To serve, slice the beef
    and arrange on a large
heated serving dish with
the vegetables. Garnish
with parsley, if you wish.

SPICED BRISKET: Soak a *1.8–2.2-kg (4–5-lb)
piece salted brisket* in cold water for several hours or
overnight, then drain and put it in a pan with fresh
water, garlic, bay leaf and *peppercorns*. Boil it as in
steps 1 and 2 above, then leave the meat to cool in
the cooking liquid. Drain the meat and put it in a
roasting tin. Stick *8 cloves* into the fat. Mix together
*100 g (4 oz) soft brown sugar, 2.5 ml (½ level tsp)
dry mustard, 5 ml (1 level tsp) ground cinnamon* and
the *juice of 1 orange* and spread the mixture evenly
over the meat. Bake at 180°C (350°F) mark 4 for
about 45 minutes–1 hour, basting from time to time
with the juices in the tin. Serve the brisket hot or
cold. 8 servings

Butcher's mince generally consists of meat scraps
trimmed from all parts of the carcass, wherever there
has been a certain amount of waste in cutting up large
joints. This type of minced beef has as high a nutritional
content as any cut of beef. Avoid minced beef that
contains an excessive amount of fat, its protein content
will be lower, the flavour will not be so good and there
will be excessive shrinkage during cooking. For minced
beef recipes where there are few added flavourings, it is
worth asking the butcher to mince a specific cut of lean
meat, such as chuck or blade steak; this will be more
expensive but will give a better flavour to the dish.

Hamburgers

*450 g (1 lb) lean minced
    beef*
*30 ml (2 tbsp) finely
    chopped onion*
5 ml (1 level tsp) salt
*1.25 ml (¼ level tsp)
    pepper*

To serve, optional:
*hamburger toppings, see
    grilled hamburgers,
    below*

*plain or toasted hamburger
    buns, toasted muffins,
    sliced rye bread or
    toasted white bread*

1 Put the beef, onion and
    seasonings in a bowl
and mix together.

2 Shape the mixture into
    four patties, each about
2.5 cm (1 in) thick.

3 Heat a frying pan or
    griddle until very hot
and cook the hamburgers
for 3–4 minutes each side.

4 Serve the hamburgers
    plain, with a topping,
or in buns, muffins or
bread if you wish.

GRILLED HAMBURGERS: Prepare the minced
beef mixture as above, shape it into thick patties and
place them on a rack in the grill pan. Cook under a
hot grill for about 8 minutes, turning once. If you
wish, top with one of the following during the last
minute of the grilling time: *a slice of Cheddar or
processed cheese; ketchup; chilli, soy* or *barbecue
sauce; crumbled blue cheese.*

Minced beef

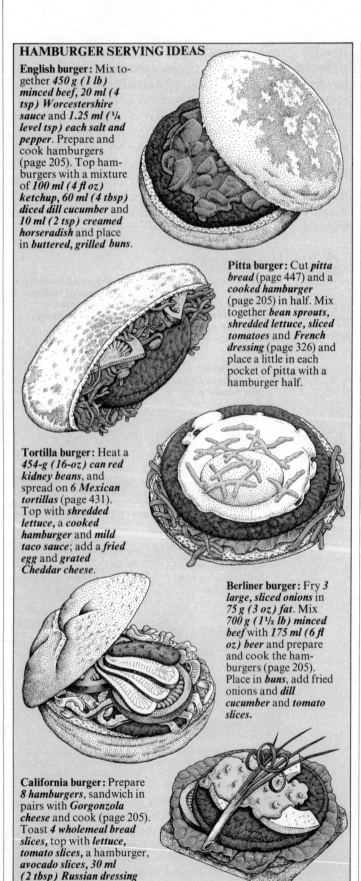

HAMBURGER SERVING IDEAS

English burger: Mix together *450 g (1 lb) minced beef, 20 ml (4 tsp) Worcestershire sauce* and *1.25 ml (¼ level tsp) each salt and pepper*. Prepare and cook hamburgers (page 205). Top hamburgers with a mixture of *100 ml (4 fl oz) ketchup, 60 ml (4 tbsp) diced dill cucumber* and *10 ml (2 tsp) creamed horseradish* and place in *buttered, grilled buns*.

Pitta burger: Cut *pitta bread* (page 447) and a *cooked hamburger* (page 205) in half. Mix together *bean sprouts, shredded lettuce, sliced tomatoes* and *French dressing* (page 326) and place a little in each pocket of pitta with a hamburger half.

Tortilla burger: Heat a *454-g (16-oz) can red kidney beans*, and spread on *6 Mexican tortillas* (page 431). Top with *shredded lettuce*, a *cooked hamburger* and *mild taco sauce*; add a *fried egg* and *grated Cheddar cheese*.

Berliner burger: Fry *3 large, sliced onions* in *75 g (3 oz) fat*. Mix *700 g (1½ lb) minced beef* with *175 ml (6 fl oz) beer* and prepare and cook the hamburgers (page 205). Place in *buns*, add fried onions and *dill cucumber* and *tomato slices*.

California burger: Prepare *8 hamburgers*, sandwich in pairs with *Gorgonzola cheese* and cook (page 205). Toast *4 wholemeal bread slices*, top with *lettuce, tomato slices*, a hamburger, *avocado slices, 30 ml (2 tbsp) Russian dressing* and a *spring onion*.

Colour index page 51

6–8 servings

Meat Loaf

900 g (2 lb) lean minced beef
100 g (4 oz) fresh white or wholemeal breadcrumbs
225 ml (8 fl oz) milk
2 eggs

50 g (2 oz) onion, skinned and finely chopped
10 ml (2 level tsp) salt
1.25 ml (¼ level tsp) pepper

1 Put all the ingredients in a large bowl and mix thoroughly together.

2 Spoon into a 900-g (2-lb) loaf tin and level. Bake at 180°C (350°F) mark 4 for 1½ hours.

3 Leave to stand at room temperature for 5 minutes, then pour off and discard the excess fat.

4 Loosen the loaf from the tin and turn it out on to a heated plate. Serve cut into slices.

 GERMAN MEAT LOAF: Prepare the meat loaf as above, but omit the milk and add *2.5 ml (½ level tsp) caraway seeds* to the breadcrumbs. Add a *226-g (8-oz) can sauerkraut*, drained. Make the sauerkraut liquid up to 100 ml (4 fl oz) with water and stir into the mixture. Cook and serve as above.

 CHEESE AND TOMATO MEAT LOAF: Prepare the meat loaf as above, but add *2.5 ml (½ level tsp) dried oregano* to the mixture. Spread half the mixture in a loaf tin, arrange *2½ processed cheese slices* on top, then top with the remaining mixture. Cook as above, but remove from the oven 10 minutes before the end of the cooking time. Cover with another *2½ processed cheese slices*, then top with a skinned and *sliced tomato* and finish cooking.

 PINEAPPLE MEAT LOAF: Prepare the meat loaf as above, but replace the milk with the *juice drained from a 226-g (8-oz) can sliced pineapple*. Shape into a 28 × 12.5 cm (11 × 5 in) oval loaf; top with *pineapple slices*. Wrap in foil and cook for 1 hour. Colour index page 51

 CURRIED MEAT LOAF: Prepare the meat loaf as above, but add *175 g (6 oz) apple*, peeled, cored and grated, *50 g (2 oz) celery*, finely chopped and *15 ml (1 level tbsp) curry powder*.

FILLED MEAT LOAVES: Prepare the meat loaf mixture (opposite). Spread half the mixture in a loaf tin, top with *one of the fillings below* and finish with the remaining meat mixture. Cook and serve as for meat loaf (opposite). Some suggested fillings are: 4 or 5 whole mushrooms; 100 g (4 oz) mushrooms, chopped; 225-g (8-oz) packet frozen leaf spinach, thawed and drained; 100 g (4 oz) Mozzarella cheese, grated; 4 hard-boiled eggs; 2 frankfurters, cut lengthways in four; 4 or 5 slices cheese.

SPINACH AND CHEESE MEAT LOAF: Prepare the meat loaf mixture (opposite), but omit the milk and add *225 g (8 oz) cottage cheese*. In a bowl, mix *225 g (8 oz) frozen chopped spinach*, thawed and drained, *1 onion*, skinned and finely chopped, *2.5 ml (½ level tsp) salt, pinch ground nutmeg* and *1 egg*. Spread half the meat mixture in an ovenproof dish, cover with the spinach mixture, then top with the remaining meat mixture. Cook for 1½ hours as for meat loaf (opposite).

MEAT LOAF ADDITIONS: Prepare meat loaf, (opposite), but add one of the following: *1 clove garlic*, skinned and crushed; *2.5 ml (½ level tsp) dried oregano*; *15 ml (1 level tbsp) chilli powder*.

Individual Lemon Barbecued Meat Loaves

Colour index
age 52

servings

700 g (1½ lb) minced beef
100 g (4 oz) fresh white
   breadcrumbs
60 ml (4 tbsp) lemon juice
1 small onion, skinned and
   finely chopped
1 egg, beaten
10 ml (2 level tsp) salt

For the sauce:
100 ml (4 fl oz) tomato
   ketchup

50 g (2 oz) soft dark brown
   sugar
5 ml (1 level tsp) dry
   mustard
1.25 ml (¼ level tsp)
   ground allspice
1.25 ml (¼ level tsp)
   ground cloves
6 thin lemon slices

1. Mix together the beef, breadcrumbs, lemon juice, onion, egg and salt in a large bowl, using your fingers to combine the ingredients thoroughly. Shape into six individual loaves and place in an ovenproof dish. Bake at 180°C (350°F) mark 4 for 15 minutes.

2. Combine all the ingredients for the sauce and spoon it over the loaves. Top each one with a lemon slice. Cook for a further 30 minutes, basting occasionally with the sauce in the tin.

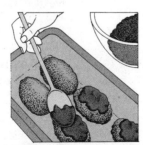

Shaping the meat loaves: With your hands, form into six loaves.

Adding the sauce: Spoon over loaves then top each one with a lemon slice.

Chilled Meat Loaf

Colour index
page 52

6–8 servings

30 ml (2 tbsp) vegetable
   oil
1 onion, skinned and
   chopped
1 stick celery, trimmed and
   chopped
2 slices white bread
900 g (2 lb) minced beef
1 carrot, peeled and finely
   chopped
7.5 ml (1½ level tsp) salt
1.25 ml (¼ level tsp)
   pepper
1 egg

225 ml (8 fl oz) tomato
   sauce, page 337
15 ml (1 level tbsp) soft
   light brown sugar
15 ml (1 tbsp) cider vinegar
15 ml (1 level tbsp) made
   mustard

1 Heat the oil in a saucepan, add the onion and celery and cook for about 10 minutes or until soft and lightly browned, stirring occasionally. Remove from the heat.

2 Tear the bread into small pieces and put them in a large bowl. Add the onion and celery.

3 Add the beef, chopped carrot, salt, pepper, egg and half the tomato sauce to the bread and onion mixture; stir them together with a spoon or fork to mix thoroughly.

4 Turn the beef mixture into an ovenproof dish and shape into a loaf measuring about 20.5 × 10 cm (8 × 4 in).

5 Put the soft light brown sugar, cider vinegar, made mustard and the remaining tomato sauce in a jug and stir briskly until well mixed.

6 Spoon the sauce over the loaf. Bake at 180°C (350°F) mark 4 for 1½ hours. Cool slightly in the dish then cover and chill thoroughly before serving.

Minced beef

Opposite page
Left to right: Barbecued Lamb Kebabs (page 228); rump steak; Barbecued Pork and Onion Kebabs (page 213)

Dilled Meatballs

Colour index
page 53

6 servings

700 g (1½ lb) lean minced
  beef
75 g (3 oz) quick-cooking
  oats
1 egg
5 ml (1 level tsp) salt
1.25 ml (¼ level tsp)
  pepper
12.5 ml (2½ level tsp)
  dried dill weed
30 ml (2 tbsp) vegetable
  oil
225 ml (8 fl oz) beef stock
225 ml (8 fl oz) soured
  cream

1 Mix together the beef, oats, egg, salt, pepper and 2.5 ml (½ level tsp) dried dill weed.

2 Using floured hands, shape the mixture into small meatballs about 2.5 cm (1 in) in diameter.

3 Heat the oil in a large frying pan and cook the meatballs a few at a time until browned all over, turning them gently with a slotted spoon.

4 As they brown, remove the meatballs to a large bowl. When they are all browned, pour off any remaining fat from the frying pan and discard it.

5 Return the meatballs to the pan and add the stock. Bring to the boil.

6 Reduce the heat, cover and simmer for 15 minutes, stirring occasionally, until the meatballs are cooked through.

7 Stir in the soured cream and remaining dill and heat through gently, stirring occasionally; do not allow to boil.

Mushroom and Cheese Meatballs

Colour index
page 53

6 servings

75 ml (5 tbsp) vegetable oil
1 small onion, skinned and
  finely chopped
½ green pepper, seeded and
  finely chopped
700 g (1½ lb) lean minced
  beef
1 egg, beaten
3.75 ml (¾ level tsp) salt
1.25 ml (¼ level tsp)
  pepper

225 g (8 oz) mushrooms,
  sliced
30 ml (2 level tbsp) plain
  flour
400 ml (¾ pint) stock or
  water
225 g (8 oz) sliced
  processed cheese,
  diced
30 ml (2 tbsp) dry sherry

1. Heat 30 ml (2 tbsp) of the oil in a frying pan, add the onion and green pepper and cook for about 5 minutes until the onion is soft but not coloured.
2. Mix the vegetables with the beef, egg, salt and pepper in a large bowl. With floured hands, shape the mixture into 2.5-cm (1-in) meatballs.
3. Heat the remaining oil in the pan, add the meatballs a few at a time and cook them until well browned all over; remove them from the pan as they brown. Pour off and discard all but 30 ml (2 tbsp) fat from the pan.
4. Add the sliced mushrooms and cook for about 5 minutes until tender.
5. Blend the flour with the stock or water. Return the meatballs to the pan, stir in the flour mixture and the diced cheese and bring to the boil.
6. Cover and simmer for 15 minutes, stirring occasionally, until the cheese has melted. Add the sherry and heat through.

Burgundied Meatballs

Colour index
page 53

4 servings

450 g (1 lb) lean minced
  beef
75 g (3 oz) dried
  breadcrumbs
175 ml (6 fl oz) milk
1 egg, beaten
1 small onion, skinned and
  finely chopped
2.5 ml (½ level tsp) salt
60 ml (4 tbsp) vegetable oil

30 ml (2 level tbsp) plain
  flour
225 ml (8 fl oz) beef stock
225 ml (8 fl oz) red
  Burgundy
3.75 ml (¾ level tsp)
  sugar

1. Mix together the beef, breadcrumbs, milk, egg, onion and salt in a large bowl. With floured hands, shape the mixture into 2.5-cm (1-in) meatballs.
2. Heat the oil in a frying pan, add the meatballs, a few at a time, and cook them until well browned all over, removing them from the pan as they brown.
3. Stir the flour into the fat remaining in the pan until blended. Gradually stir in the stock, wine and sugar and cook, stirring constantly, until thickened. Return the meatballs to the pan and bring to the boil, then cover and simmer for 15 minutes.

DEEP FRIED MEATBALLS: Prepare the meatballs as in step 1 above, but omit the remaining ingredients. Coat the meatballs with *1 beaten egg* and *100 g (4 oz) fresh white breadcrumbs*. Half fill a saucepan with oil and heat it to 170°C (325°F); deep fry the meatballs a few at a time for 7–8 minutes. Drain them on kitchen paper towel and keep hot until all are cooked. Serve with *tomato sauce* (page 337) or horseradish cream (page 185).

Opposite page

Clockwise from top left: Chinese Fried Rice (page 341); Stir-fried Chicken and Mushrooms (page 266); Oriental Aniseed Beef (page 200); Pork Chops Orientale (page 214); Stir-fried Mixed Vegetables (page 299); fresh kiwi fruit (page 307)

Colour index page 51

4–6 servings

Macaroni Bake

225 g (8 oz) short-cut macaroni
350 g (12 oz) minced beef
275 g (10 oz) cottage cheese
50 g (2 oz) Parmesan cheese, grated
45 ml (3 tbsp) chopped parsley
1 egg, beaten
3.75 ml (¾ level tsp) salt
1.25 ml (¼ level tsp) pepper
900 ml (1½ pints) tomato sauce, page 337
175 g (6 oz) Mozzarella cheese, grated

1. Cook the macaroni in boiling salted water until just tender and drain well.
2. Place the beef in a large frying pan and cook gently in its own fat for about 10 minutes until well browned, stirring occasionally. Remove the pan from the heat and stir in the cottage and Parmesan cheeses, parsley, egg, salt, pepper and half the tomato sauce until well mixed. Add the macaroni and toss gently to coat well.
3. Spoon the mixture into a large ovenproof dish, pour over the remaining tomato sauce and sprinkle with the Mozzarella cheese. Bake at 180°C (350°F) mark 4 for 20 minutes or until heated through and the cheese on top is melted and bubbling.

Colour index page 52

6 servings

Chilli Con Carne

15 ml (1 tbsp) vegetable oil
700 g (1½ lb) minced beef
1 onion, skinned and chopped
1 green pepper, seeded and chopped
2 cloves garlic, skinned and crushed
425-g (15-oz) can tomatoes or 450 g (1 lb) tomatoes, skinned and chopped
15 ml (1 level tbsp) chilli powder
5 ml (1 level tsp) salt
425-g (15-oz) can red kidney beans

To serve, optional:
salt crackers or other accompaniments (see below)

1. Heat the oil in a large flameproof casserole, add the beef, onion, green pepper and garlic and cook for about 10 minutes, stirring, until the onion and green pepper are tender and the beef is browned.
2. Stir in the tomatoes with their liquid, chilli powder and salt and bring to the boil. Lower the heat, cover and simmer for 1 hour, stirring occasionally.
3. Stir in the beans with their liquid and heat through. Serve in soup bowls with salt crackers or other accompaniments (see below), if you wish.

ACCOMPANIMENTS: Grated Cheddar cheese, shredded lettuce, finely chopped onion, chopped green pepper, potato crisps, French bread.

TEXAS-STYLE CHILLI: Replace the minced beef with *700 g (1½ lb) chuck or blade steak*, cut into 1-cm (½-in) cubes. Cook as in steps 1 and 2 above, but simmer for 1½ hours or until tender. Omit the beans and serve as above. 4 servings

Whole Stuffed Cabbage

798-g (28-oz) can tomatoes
salt and pepper
141-g (5-oz) can tomato paste
15 ml (1 level tbsp) brown sugar
2.5 ml (½ tsp) Worcestershire sauce
pinch ground allspice
1 large cabbage
450 g (1 lb) minced beef
1 onion, skinned and chopped
1 clove garlic, skinned and finely chopped
75 g (3 oz) long grain rice, cooked

Colour index page 54

6 servings

2 Discard tough outer leaves from cabbage. Remove two large leaves and reserve them. Cut out stem and centre of cabbage, leaving a 2.5-cm (1-in) thick shell.

3 Discard the hard core and roughly chop the rest of the cabbage removed from the middle.

4 Put the beef, onion, garlic, pepper, 5 ml (1 level tsp) salt and 75 g (3 oz) chopped cabbage into a large flame-proof casserole and cook for about 15 minutes.

1 Put the tomatoes, with their liquid, 2.5 ml (½ level tsp) salt, tomato paste, brown sugar, Worcestershire sauce and allspice into a pan. Bring to the boil, stirring; reduce the heat, cover and simmer for 20 minutes, stirring occasionally.

5 Add the rice and 225 ml (8 fl oz) of the tomato sauce and stir with a slotted spoon to blend well. Remove the casserole from the heat.

6 Spoon the beef mixture into the cabbage shell and cover the top with the two large reserved leaves.

7 Tie the cabbage with string to hold the leaves firmly in position.

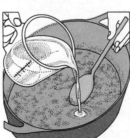

8 Pour 600 ml (1 pint) water into the pan used for the beef mixture, stirring to loosen sediment. Add the remaining chopped cabbage and tomato sauce. Stir well.

9 Put the cabbage, stem down, in the sauce. Bring to the boil, reduce the heat, cover and simmer for 2 hours, basting the cabbage with sauce occasionally.

10 To serve, put the cabbage stem down in a heated serving dish. Remove the string. Spoon over the tomato sauce and cut the cabbage into wedges for serving.

Pork

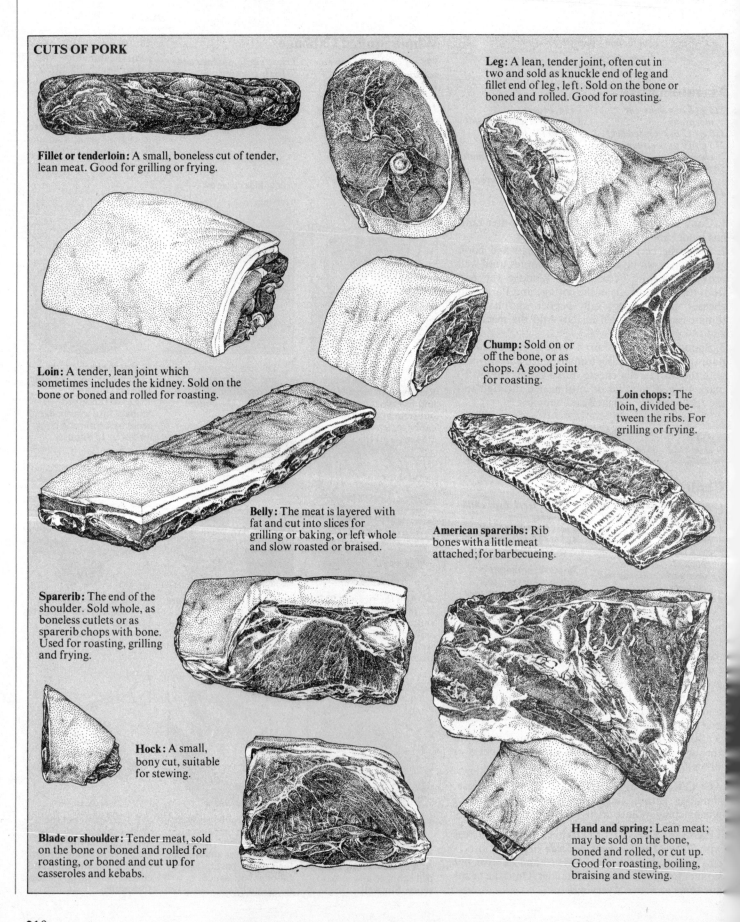

CUTS OF PORK

Fillet or tenderloin: A small, boneless cut of tender, lean meat. Good for grilling or frying.

Loin: A tender, lean joint which sometimes includes the kidney. Sold on the bone or boned and rolled for roasting.

Leg: A lean, tender joint, often cut in two and sold as knuckle end of leg and fillet end of leg, left. Sold on the bone or boned and rolled. Good for roasting.

Chump: Sold on or off the bone, or as chops. A good joint for roasting.

Loin chops: The loin, divided between the ribs. For grilling or frying.

Belly: The meat is layered with fat and cut into slices for grilling or baking, or left whole and slow roasted or braised.

American spareribs: Rib bones with a little meat attached; for barbecueing.

Sparerib: The end of the shoulder. Sold whole, as boneless cutlets or as sparerib chops with bone. Used for roasting, grilling and frying.

Hock: A small, bony cut, suitable for stewing.

Blade or shoulder: Tender meat, sold on the bone or boned and rolled for roasting, or boned and cut up for casseroles and kebabs.

Hand and spring: Lean meat; may be sold on the bone, boned and rolled, or cut up. Good for roasting, boiling, braising and stewing.

CUTS OF BACON

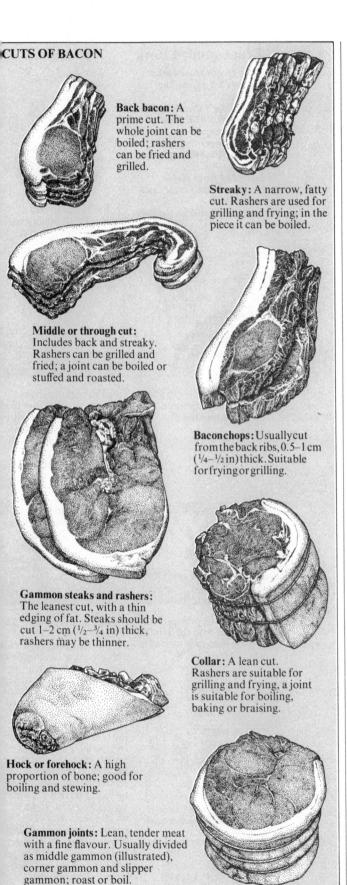

Back bacon: A prime cut. The whole joint can be boiled; rashers can be fried and grilled.

Streaky: A narrow, fatty cut. Rashers are used for grilling and frying; in the piece it can be boiled.

Middle or through cut: Includes back and streaky. Rashers can be grilled and fried; a joint can be boiled or stuffed and roasted.

Bacon chops: Usually cut from the back ribs, 0.5–1 cm (¼–½ in) thick. Suitable for frying or grilling.

Gammon steaks and rashers: The leanest cut, with a thin edging of fat. Steaks should be cut 1–2 cm (½–¾ in) thick, rashers may be thinner.

Collar: A lean cut. Rashers are suitable for grilling and frying, a joint is suitable for boiling, baking or braising.

Hock or forehock: A high proportion of bone; good for boiling and stewing.

Gammon joints: Lean, tender meat with a fine flavour. Usually divided as middle gammon (illustrated), corner gammon and slipper gammon; roast or boil.

CHOOSING PORK

Pork is a rich meat so it is as well to choose cuts which look lean for their type, indicating a young animal. The flesh should be finely grained and pale pink and the fat firm and creamy white.

ROASTING PORK

Wipe the meat, trim off any excess fat then calculate the cooking time according to the timetable below. To make the crackling crisp, score the skin with a sharp knife then rub it with oil, salt and pepper. Put the joint in the roasting tin, standing on the bone if it is a loin joint, but otherwise on a rack, with the thickest fat uppermost and the cut sides exposed. Cook for the calculated time, basting occasionally with the juices that run into the tin. Serve pork well done.

When the meat is cooked, put it on a heated serving dish and leave it in a warm place for 15 minutes, to make it easier to carve. Carve in thick slices and serve with traditional accompaniments, including apple sauce (page 463) or gooseberry sauce (page 185), sage and onion stuffing (page 253) and thickened gravy.

TIMETABLE FOR ROASTING PORK		
Type of joint	**Roasting time at 220°C (425°F) mark 7**	**Roasting time at 190°C (375°F) mark 5**
Joints on the bone	25 minutes per 450 g (1 lb), plus 25 minutes	30–35 minutes per 450 g (1 lb), plus 25 minutes
Boned and rolled joints		30–35 minutes per 450 g (1 lb), plus 35 minutes

CARVING PORK

Loin of pork: Stand the joint on a carving dish or board on its shortest side, with the rib bones upwards. Remove and discard the chine bone first. Anchor the joint firmly with the fork, then cut down between each bone, dividing the joint into chops. Or remove the chine bone, then stand the joint on the ribs with the fat side up, and carve downwards into thick slices.

Leg of pork: Use the point of the knife to cut through and remove the crackling. Divide it into portions to serve with each portion of meat. To carve the meat, begin by cutting a wedge-shaped slice from the centre of the meatier side of the joint, then carve thick slices from either side of the cut, gradually slanting the knife to make larger slices and ending cutting parallel to the bone. Turn the joint over, remove the fat and carve in long, flat slices along the leg.

Boned and rolled joints: Cut away the string from each part of the joint as it is carved. Remove the crackling half way down the joint and divide it into portions for serving with the meat. Stand the meat on one end and cut thick horizontal slices or, for a very long roll, lay it on its side and carve downwards. Remove more crackling as necessary.

Roast and grilled pork joints

Roast Loin of Pork

*2.3–2.8-kg (5–6-lb) loin
of pork, on the bone
30 ml (2 tbsp) vegetable
oil
10 ml (2 level tsp) salt
1.25 ml (¼ level tsp)
pepper
25 g (1 oz) plain flour*

1 Place the joint in a
roasting tin, fat side up,
rub the rind with the oil
and sprinkle with the salt
and pepper.

2 Insert a meat thermo-
meter into centre of
meat. Roast at 220°C
(425°F) mark 7 for 2½–
2¾ hours or until thermo-
meter reads 89°C (190°F).

3 Remove the joint, put it
on a heated serving
dish and keep hot; pour
the juices into a measuring
jug and leave to stand until
the fat separates.

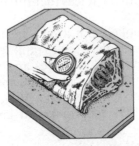

4 Spoon off 45 ml (3
tbsp) fat from the
juices into a saucepan.
Skim off and discard the
rest of the fat.

5 Add a little water to the
roasting tin and stir
well to loosen any
sediment from the bottom
of the tin. Add this to the
roasting juices in the
measuring jug, then make
up to 700 ml (1¼ pints)
with water. Add the flour
to the fat in the saucepan
and cook for 1–2 minutes,
stirring until browned,
then pour in the roasting
juices. Bring to the boil
and cook, stirring, until
thickened. Season with
salt and pepper.

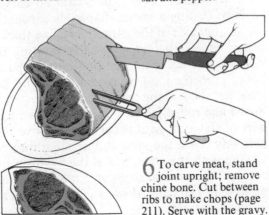

6 To carve meat, stand
joint upright; remove
chine bone. Cut between
ribs to make chops (page
211). Serve with the gravy.

Prune-stuffed Pork

*175 g (6 oz) stoned prunes
225 ml (8 fl oz) boiling
water
2.1–2.3-kg (4½–5-lb) loin
of pork, on the bone
salt and pepper
ground ginger
45 ml (3 level tbsp) plain
flour
100 ml (4 fl oz) single
cream or half cream and
half milk
5 ml (1 tsp) redcurrant jelly*

1 Put the prunes in a
bowl with boiling water
and soak for 30 minutes.

2 Drain the prunes and
dry thoroughly on
kitchen paper towel.

3 Pierce through the
centre of the joint from
one end to the other with a
long, narrow, sharp knife,
twisting the knife slightly
to make a slit right
through the meat.

4 Force the prunes into
the slit with the handle
of a wooden spoon or with
your fingers.

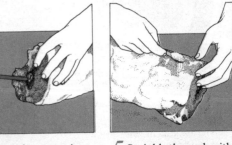

5 Sprinkle the pork with
salt, pepper and 5 ml
(1 level tsp) ginger and rub
them into the fat. Place the
joint, fat side up, in a
roasting tin.

6 Insert a meat thermo-
meter; roast at 190°C
(375°F) mark 5 for 30–35
minutes per 450 g (1 lb)
plus 25 minutes, until
reading is 77°C (170°F).

7 Place joint on a heated
serving dish and keep
hot. Pour juices from tin
into a measuring jug and
leave until fat separates.
Spoon 45 ml (3 tbsp) fat
back into tin; discard
remaining fat. Make juices
up to 225 ml (8 fl oz) with
water. Add flour to fat in
tin and cook for 1–2
minutes, then stir in juices.
Bring to the boil, stirring;
add cream, jelly and ginger
and salt to taste and cook
gently, stirring, until
thickened. Serve the pork
with the sauce.

Fried pork

Roast Pork with Piquant Sauce

Colour index
page 57
6–8 servings

2-kg (4½-lb) blade of
pork, on the bone

For the sauce:
226-g (8-oz) can tomatoes,
puréed
40 g (1½ oz) soft light
brown sugar
60 ml (4 tbsp) water

60 ml (4 tbsp) cider vinegar
60 ml (4 level tbsp) golden
syrup
15 ml (1 level tbsp)
cornflour
2.5 ml (½ level tsp) salt
pinch pepper

1. Place the pork, fat side up, on a rack in a roasting
tin. Insert a meat thermometer into the centre of the
joint, being careful not to touch bone. Roast at
190°C (375°F) mark 5 for 2¼–2½ hours.
2. Meanwhile, put all the sauce ingredients in a
saucepan and cook, stirring, until thickened.
3. Brush the pork liberally with the sauce. Roast for
a further 30 minutes or until the thermometer reads
77°C (170°F), brushing occasionally with sauce.
4. Place the meat on a heated serving dish, remove
the bone and leave for 15 minutes to make carving
easier. Serve the remaining sauce separately.

Marinated Pork and Onion Kebabs

Colour index
page 57
4 servings

900 g (2 lb) boneless pork
sparerib
3 small onions, skinned and
quartered

For the marinade:
60 ml (4 tbsp) soy sauce
30 ml (2 level tbsp) honey

30 ml (2 tbsp) mild chilli
sauce
15 ml (1 tbsp) vegetable oil
15 ml (1 tbsp) finely
chopped spring onion
5 ml (1 level tsp) curry
powder

1. Trim any excess fat from the pork, then cut the
meat into 2.5-cm (1-in) cubes.
2. Mix all the marinade ingredients in a bowl. Stir in
the pork cubes, cover and refrigerate for at least 3
hours, stirring occasionally. Drain the pork well and
reserve the marinade.
3. Thread the pork cubes and onion quarters alternately on to long metal skewers. Place on a rack in
the grill pan and grill for 20 minutes or until tender,
basting frequently with the reserved marinade and
turning occasionally.

BARBECUED PORK AND ONION KEBABS:
Prepare the kebabs as above, but light the charcoal
in the barbecue at least 30 minutes before you start
cooking. Lay the kebabs on the barbecue grill and
cook as above.

Threading the skewers:
Thread pork cubes and
onion quarters
alternately on to long
metal skewers.

Basting the kebabs: Use
the reserved marinade to
baste the kebabs, turning
them occasionally while
they are cooking.

Breaded Pork Fillet

Colour index
page 56
4–6 servings

2 225–350-g (8–12-oz)
pork fillets
2 eggs
60 ml (4 tbsp) water
5 ml (1 level tsp) salt
2.5 ml (½ level tsp) dried
rosemary
pinch pepper

175 g (6 oz) dried
breadcrumbs
60 ml (4 tbsp) vegetable
oil

1. Cut each fillet almost in half lengthways, taking
care not to cut all the way through; open it out and
pound it with a meat mallet until about 0.5 cm (¼
in) thick. Cut each fillet crossways into two or three
even pieces.
2. Beat the eggs with the water, salt, rosemary and
pepper. Dip the pieces of meat into the mixture, then
coat in the breadcrumbs. Repeat to make a double
coating. Chill for 30 minutes.
3. Heat half the oil in a large frying pan, add half the
pieces of pork and fry them for about 10 minutes or
until well browned and tender, turning once.
Arrange on a heated serving dish and keep hot while
you fry the remaining pork.

Preparing the fillets: Cut
each fillet lengthways
almost in half, and open
out like a book.

Pounding the meat: Beat
out the pork evenly with
a meat mallet until it is
0.5 cm (¼ in) thick.

Stir-fried Pork and Vegetables

Colour index
page 57
6 servings

60 ml (4 tbsp) soy sauce
15 ml (1 tbsp) dry sherry
12.5 ml (2½ level tsp)
cornflour
6.25 ml (1¼ level tsp) sugar
2.5 ml (½ tsp) finely
chopped fresh ginger or
1.25 ml (¼ level tsp)
ground ginger
2 350-g (12-oz) pork fillets,
thinly sliced

150 ml (¼ pint) vegetable
oil
450 g (1 lb) asparagus or
broccoli, washed,
trimmed and cut into
chunks
225 g (8 oz) mushrooms,
sliced
1.25 ml (¼ level tsp) salt
30 ml (2 tbsp) water

1. Mix the soy sauce, sherry, cornflour, sugar and
ginger in a bowl; add the pork and toss well.
2. Heat 60 ml (4 tbsp) of the oil in a flameproof
casserole and add the asparagus, mushrooms and
salt. Fry quickly, stirring, until the vegetables are
coated with oil. Add the water and continue to stir-
fry until the asparagus is tender but still crisp. Place
the vegetables and liquid on a heated serving dish
and keep hot.
3. Heat the remaining oil in the casserole until very
hot. Add the meat mixture and stir-fry for about 2
minutes until the meat is browned. Return the
vegetables to the casserole and heat through.

Pork chops and steaks

Braised Pork Chops

Colour index page 57

4 servings

4 pork chops
2.5 ml (½ level tsp) salt
1.25 ml (¼ level tsp) pepper
175 ml (6 fl oz) water
15 ml (1 level tbsp) plain flour, blended with 60 ml (4 tbsp) water, optional

1 Trim a piece of fat from the edge of one chop; heat a frying pan and rub the fat over the base of the pan to grease it. Discard the piece of fat.

2 Add the pork chops to the frying pan and brown them well on both sides. Season the chops with salt and pepper.

3 Add the water, cover and simmer for 45 minutes. Skim off the fat and, if you wish, thicken the gravy with the blended flour and water.

BRAISED PORK CHOP VARIATIONS

APPLE CHOPS: Prepare the chops as above, but replace 100 ml (4 fl oz) water with *apple juice* and use *3.75 ml (¾ level tsp) salt*. Top each chop with a *slice of cooking apple*, peeled and cored, 5 minutes before the end of cooking time.

SPANISH CHOPS: Prepare the chops as above, but replace 100 ml (4 fl oz) water with *vegetable juice;* top each chop with a *green pepper ring* and a *slice of onion* 5 minutes before the end of cooking time.

MUSHROOM AND BASIL CHOPS: Drain and slice a *113-g (4-oz) can mushrooms* and make the liquid up to 175 ml (6 fl oz) with water. Prepare the chops as above, but replace the water with the mushroom liquid, omit the pepper and add *2.5 ml (½ level tsp) dried basil* and *5 ml (1 tsp) Worcestershire sauce* with the liquid; stir in the mushrooms 5 minutes before the end of cooking time.

PLUM CHOPS: Drain a *454-g (16-oz) can plums;* add *45 ml (3 tbsp) cider vinegar* to *75 ml (5 tbsp) plum syrup.* Prepare the chops as above, but replace 120 ml (4½ fl oz) water with the syrup mixture. Add the plums 5 minutes before the end of cooking time.

TOMATO AND THYME CHOPS: Prepare the chops as above, but add a *pinch of dried thyme* with the water and top each chop with a *thick tomato slice sprinkled with salt* 5 minutes before the end of cooking time.

Pork Chops Orientale

Colour index page 57

6 servings

6 pork chops

For the marinade:
50 ml (2 fl oz) soy sauce
50 ml (2 fl oz) dry sherry or sake
30 ml (2 tbsp) vegetable oil
1 clove garlic, skinned and crushed
5 ml (1 level tsp) ground ginger

For the garnish:
spring onions

1 Mix the soy sauce, sherry or sake, oil, garlic and ginger together in a large shallow dish.

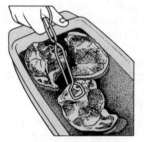

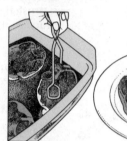

2 Add the pork chops and turn to coat them evenly with the marinade. Cover and chill for at least 4 hours, turning the pork chops occasionally.

3 Remove the chops from the marinade and drain slightly. Trim a piece of fat from the edge of one of the chops.

4 Heat a frying pan and rub the piece of pork fat over the base of the pan. Discard the fat.

5 Fry the chops for 15–20 minutes, until tender and browned on both sides, then garnish with spring onions.

Pork Baps with Barbecue Sauce

Colour index page 56

6 servings

30 ml (2 tbsp) vegetable oil
6 boneless pork steaks, cut 0.5 cm (¼ in) thick
5 ml (1 level tsp) salt
1.25 ml (¼ level tsp) pepper

6 baps or rolls, halved
120 ml (8 tbsp) tomato ketchup
30 ml (2 level tbsp) black treacle
15 ml (1 tbsp) lemon juice

1. Heat the oil in a large frying pan, add the pork steaks and fry for 15–20 minutes until well browned, turning once and sprinkling with salt and pepper. Remove from the pan and place in the baps. Keep hot.
2. Add the remaining ingredients to the fat in the pan and bring to the boil. Simmer, stirring constantly, until the sauce has thickened. Spoon a little sauce over the meat in each bap.

Colour index page 57
6 servings

Orange Pork Chops

6 pork chops
175 ml (6 fl oz) water
2.5 ml (½ level tsp)
  paprika
1.25 ml (¼ level tsp)
  pepper
6.25 ml (1¼ level tsp) salt
1 orange

225 ml (8 fl oz) orange
  juice
100 g (4 oz) sugar
15 ml (1 level tbsp)
  cornflour
2.5 ml (½ level tsp) ground
  cinnamon
12 whole cloves

1. Trim several pieces of fat from the pork chops. Place them in a large frying pan and fry gently until they are lightly browned, rubbing them over the base of the pan. Discard the fat.
2. Add the chops to the pan and fry over high heat until well browned on both sides.
3. Add the water, paprika, pepper and 5 ml (1 level tsp) salt to the pan and bring to the boil. Reduce the heat, cover and simmer for about 40 minutes or until the chops are tender, turning once.
4. Meanwhile, grate 15 ml (1 tbsp) rind from one end of the orange and cut 6 thin slices from the other end with a serrated knife.
5. Put the orange rind and juice, sugar, cornflour and spices in a small saucepan and cook, stirring, until thickened. Add the orange slices, remove from the heat, cover and keep hot.
6. Put the chops in a heated serving dish and spoon the orange slices and sauce over them.

Colour index page 57
6 servings

Grilled Pork Chops with Pineapple

425-g (15-oz) can
  pineapple rings
100 ml (4 fl oz) soy sauce
75 ml (5 tbsp) vegetable oil
1 small onion, skinned and
  finely chopped

½ clove garlic, skinned and
  crushed
15 ml (1 level tbsp) soft
  light brown sugar
6 pork chump chops

1. Drain the pineapple rings and spoon 60 ml (4 tbsp) of the syrup into a roasting tin. Add the soy sauce, oil, onion, garlic and sugar and mix well. Add the pork chops and turn to coat with the marinade; cover and refrigerate for at least 3 hours, turning the chops once.
2. Remove the chops from the marinade and drain well. Place the chops on a rack in the grill pan and grill for 10 minutes, brushing with the marinade once. Meanwhile, dip 6 pineapple rings in the reserved marinade, turning them so that they are completely coated.
3. Turn the chops over and grill them on the other side for 10 minutes, brushing once with the remaining marinade.
4. Place a pineapple ring on each chop and grill for a further 3–5 minutes, until the pineapple is heated through and the pork is tender.

Pork Chops with Prune and Apple Stuffing

4 pork chops

For the stuffing:
25 g (1 oz) dried prunes
15 g (½ oz) long grain rice
1 cooking apple
15 g (½ oz) shredded suet
15 g (½ oz) finely chopped
  almonds
2.5 ml (½ level tsp) salt
1.25 ml (¼ level tsp)
  pepper
15 ml (1 tbsp) lemon juice
15 ml (1 tbsp) grated lemon
  rind
½ egg, beaten

For the garnish:
lemon wedges
apple rings brushed
  with lemon juice,
  optional
watercress, optional

Colour index page 56
4 servings

1 Put the prunes in a bowl, cover them with water and leave them to soak overnight.

2 Cook the rice in boiling salted water until tender but still firm. Drain thoroughly, then leave to cool. Separate the grains gently with a fork.

3 Drain the prunes, remove the stones and cut the fruit into quarters.

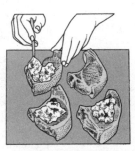

4 Peel the cooking apple thinly, core it and roughly chop the flesh.

5 Mix the quartered prunes with the cooked rice, chopped apple, suet, chopped almonds and the salt and pepper.

6 Add the lemon juice and grated rind to the stuffing and bind together with the beaten egg.

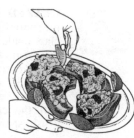

7 Trim the excess fat from the chops and place a spoonful of stuffing on the top of each one.

8 Arrange the stuffed pork chops in a single layer in a greased roasting tin and cover them loosely with foil or greased greaseproof paper.

9 Bake the chops at 200°C (400°F) mark 6 for 1 hour or until they are tender when tested with a fork, and the stuffing is set and lightly browned.

10 Transfer the chops to a heated serving dish and garnish with lemon wedges. Surround with apple rings and watercress, if you wish.

Braised and grilled pork

Barbecued Spareribs

Colour index page 56

4 servings

1.8 kg (4 lb) American pork spareribs
1 onion, skinned and sliced

For the sauce:
350 ml (12 fl oz) tomato juice
45 ml (3 tbsp) cider vinegar
30 ml (2 level tbsp) clear honey
10 ml (2 level tsp) salt
5 ml (1 level tsp) paprika
3.75 ml (¾ level tsp) chilli powder

1 Divide the spareribs into portions of two or three ribs each.

2 Put them all in a large flameproof casserole or saucepan, add the onion and cover with cold water.

3 Bring to the boil, reduce the heat, cover and simmer for 1 hour or until almost tender. Drain the ribs, cover and chill until ready to barbecue.

4 Light the barbecue 30 minutes before you want to start cooking. Put all the remaining ingredients in a bowl and mix together to make a sauce.

5 Put the spareribs on the barbecue and brush with sauce. Cook for 20 minutes until tender; brush with sauce and turn occasionally. Heat remaining sauce to serve separately.

GLAZED BARBECUED SPARERIBS: Prepare the spareribs as above, but replace the sauce with a glaze made from *275 g (10 oz) redcurrant jelly, 100 ml (4 fl oz) lemon juice, 45 ml (3 level tbsp) cornflour, 15 ml (1 level tbsp) salt, 15 ml (1 tbsp) grated lemon rind* and *1 clove garlic*, skinned and crushed. Heat the ingredients gently in a small saucepan, stirring, until the jelly has melted and the glaze thickened. Brush spareribs with the glaze during cooking.

GRILLED SPARERIBS: Prepare the spareribs as above, but cook them indoors, grilling under a high heat for 20–30 minutes or until the meat is tender, basting frequently with the sauce or glaze and turning the ribs occasionally.

Country Spareribs

Colour index page 56

4 servings

900 g (2 lb) small pork sparerib chops
25 g (1 oz) plain flour
15 ml (1 tbsp) vegetable oil
175 ml (6 fl oz) apple juice
10 ml (2 level tsp) salt
1.25 ml (¼ level tsp) pepper
450 g (1 lb) small potatoes, peeled

225 g (8 oz) carrots, peeled and cut into 5-cm (2-in) pieces
225 g (8 oz) small onions, skinned
1 small cabbage, trimmed, shredded and washed

1. Coat the pork chops with the flour, reserving any leftover flour. Heat the oil in a large flameproof casserole and brown the chops a few at a time, removing them from the pan as they brown.
2. Stir the reserved flour into the fat remaining in the pan and gradually add the apple juice. Return the chops to the casserole, add the salt and pepper and bring to the boil.
3. Cover and cook in the oven at 180°C (350°F) mark 4 for 30 minutes. Add the potatoes, carrots and onions. Stir well, then cover the casserole again and cook for a further 30 minutes.
4. Skim off the excess fat, then add the shredded cabbage. Cover and continue cooking for 45–60 minutes more until the meat and all the vegetables are tender, stirring occasionally.

Pork Spareribs with Sauerkraut

Colour index page 56

6 servings

1.1 kg (2½ lb) American pork spareribs
15 ml (1 tbsp) vegetable oil
350 ml (12 fl oz) lager
5 ml (1 level tsp) salt
2 600-g (1 lb 6-oz) cans sauerkraut, drained

30 ml (2 level tbsp) soft dark brown sugar

For the garnish:
chopped parsley

1. Divide the spareribs into portions of two or three ribs each. Heat the oil in a large frying pan, add the ribs a few at a time and brown well on all sides, removing them from the pan as they brown. Pour off the fat from the pan.
2. Return all the ribs to the pan, add the lager and half the salt and bring to the boil. Cover and simmer for 30 minutes.
3. Stir in the sauerkraut, sugar and remaining salt. Cover and simmer for a further hour or until the ribs are tender, stirring occasionally. Garnish with chopped parsley.

Browning the spareribs: Add the ribs to the pan, a few at a time, and brown well on all sides.

Adding the sauerkraut: Stir in the sauerkraut and simmer the ribs for 1 hour more or until tender.

Stewed pork

Pork Hocks with Haricot Beans

Colour index
page 57
5 servings

700 g (1½ lb) dried haricot
  beans
4 pork hocks or spring
  joints
1.25 ml (¼ level tsp)
  pepper
2 cloves garlic, skinned and
  crushed
bay leaf
4 cloves
450 g (1 lb) button onions,
  skinned
450 g (1 lb) carrots, peeled
  and cut into chunks
30 ml (2 tbsp) lemon juice
30 ml (2 level tbsp) salt

1 Put the beans in a
  colander and rinse them
thoroughly under running
cold water; discard any
that are shrivelled or
discoloured and drain.

2 Put the beans into
  boiling water, cook for
2 minutes then remove
from the heat and leave to
soak for about 2 hours.

3 Put the hocks in a large
  saucepan with the
pepper, herbs and 1.1 litres
(2 pints) water; bring to
the boil. Reduce the heat,
cover and simmer for 1½
hours, skimming.

4 Drain the beans and
  add them to the meat;
simmer for 30 minutes.
Add the cloves, onions and
carrots to the pan and
bring to the boil.

5 Cover and simmer for
  45 minutes then add the
lemon juice and salt and
simmer for another 15
minutes or until the meat
and vegetables are tender.

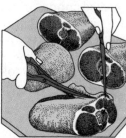

6 Remove the hocks; cut
  off and discard the skin
and bones.

7 Cut the meat into neat
  pieces, return them to
the pan and heat through.

Pork Ragout

Colour index
page 57
4 servings

60 ml (4 tbsp) vegetable oil
2 onions, skinned and
  sliced
900 g (2 lb) shoulder pork,
  boned and cubed
2 small green peppers,
  seeded and sliced
2 cloves garlic, skinned and
  crushed
150 ml (¼ pint) red wine
150 ml (¼ pint) stock or
  water

1.25 ml (¼ level tsp) chilli
  seasoning
5 ml (1 level tsp) celery salt
bay leaf
salt and pepper
45 ml (3 level tbsp) long
  grain rice
450 g (1 lb) sage and onion
  stuffing, page 253

1. Heat the oil in a large saucepan or flameproof
casserole and fry the onions gently for about 5
minutes; remove them from the pan.
2. Add the cubes of meat, a few at a time, to the oil
remaining in the pan and brown them well, removing them as they brown. Pour off the fat from the
pan and reserve it.
3. Return the onions and meat to the pan with the
green peppers, garlic, wine, stock or water, chilli
seasoning, celery salt, bay leaf, salt and pepper.
Bring to the boil, then cover and simmer for 1½
hours or until the meat is tender.
4. Just before the end of cooking time, cook the rice
in boiling salted water until it is tender but still firm
and drain it thoroughly.
5. Shape the sage and onion stuffing into 12 small
balls. Heat the reserved fat in a frying pan and fry
the stuffing balls for 3–4 minutes or until cooked
through. Add the rice and stuffing balls to the meat
just before serving.

Burritos

Colour index
page 57
6 servings

vegetable oil
225 g (8 oz) boneless,
  shoulder pork, cut into
  1-cm (½-in) chunks
450 g (1 lb) beef stewing
  steak, cut into 1-cm
  (½-in) cubes
100 g (4 oz) onions,
  skinned and chopped
1 clove garlic, skinned and
  finely chopped

5 ml (1 level tsp) salt
5 ml (1 level tsp) chilli
  powder
350 ml (12 fl oz) water
425-g (15-oz) can red
  kidney beans, drained
25 g (1 oz) Cheddar cheese,
  grated
Mexican tortillas,
  page 431

1. Heat a little oil in a large saucepan, add the pieces
of pork and beef a few at a time and brown them
well, removing them as they brown. Return all the
meat to the pan.
2. Add the onion, garlic, salt, chilli powder and
water and bring to the boil. Reduce the heat, cover
and simmer for 2 hours or until the meat is so tender
that it is beginning to fall apart.
3. When the meat is cooked, flake it with a fork.
Continue cooking, uncovered, until the liquid has
evaporated and the mixture has thickened.
4. Meanwhile, mix together the beans and cheese in
a small saucepan and stir over gentle heat until the
cheese has melted.
5. To make up a burrito, spread about 30 ml (2 tbsp)
of the bean and cheese mixture over a tortilla, spoon
on about 30 ml (2 tbsp) of the meat mixture and fold
the sides over.

Bacon and ham

Pigs for bacon are specially bred to have small bones, long backs, small shoulders and large, plump hind legs. Cured meat keeps better than fresh pork and has a distinctive flavour. Ham is the leg only, cut away from the carcass and cured and matured individually.

BACON CURES

'Green' or unsmoked bacon: This is cured by a combination of dry salting and brine injection, followed by immersion in brine and a period of maturation.

Smoked bacon: The meat is cured by the same method as green bacon, but then goes through the additional process of smoking.

Special cures: In addition to the traditional cures there are other, mostly regional, variations, often known as 'tender cure' or 'sweet cure'. These are generally mild and should be cooked as for green bacon.

CHOOSING BACON

Rashers, chops and steaks: Green bacon should have pale pink flesh and a pale rind. The flesh should look firm and moist, the fat white or cream but with no greenish tinges. Smoked bacon has a darker flesh and golden rind, keeps rather better than green bacon and has a more pronounced flavour.

Vacuum-packed bacon: Bacon is widely available in vacuum-sealed packets, which are hygienic and convenient, and though usually more expensive than the equivalent cuts bought loose, keep longer. Always buy vacuum-packed bacon from a refrigerated counter, and check the 'sell by' or 'eat by' date marked on the packet.

Bacon joints: Large joints may be bought on the bone, but smaller joints are more commonly boned and rolled before sale. There is very little waste, as amounts of fat are small and leftover cooked bacon is good hot or cold, alone or included in dishes with other meats and savoury ingredients.

Boil-in-the-bag bacon packs: Joints are sometimes sold packed in film bags with special instructions for cooking without removing the bag. This helps to retain the shape of the joint and prevents the natural juices and flavour being lost into the cooking liquid. Unlike vacuum packs, the film bags do not extend the life of the contents.

Bath chap: The half-head of the bacon pig is divided into two, giving the upper jaw and eye piece, which is very fat, and the lower jaw with half the tongue, which is more meaty and is known as the bath chap. This cut is cured and often smoked and is usually sold ready cooked for serving cold alongside chicken, turkey or ox tongue. If it is not cooked when you buy it, soak it overnight and boil until tender, as for a bacon joint.

HAM CURES

York ham: This is dry-salt cured and lightly smoked, cut next to the oyster bone and rounded off. The average weight of a ham is about 7–9 kg (16–24 lb).

Wiltshire ham: This is a long cut of ham, straw-coloured and mild cured.

Bradenham ham: This is a small ham, processed in molasses instead of brine; this turns the skin black and the meat rather red.

Irish peat-cured ham: Cured in a similar way to York ham but finished with peat smoke.

Jambon de Paris: Similar to York ham, this is available unsmoked or very lightly smoked.

Jambon de Bayonne: Salted and then smoked with herbs, jambon de Bayonne should be eaten raw or used in cooking; never boil it.

Mainz, Westphalian and Parma ham: These are smoked hams, usually cut wafer thin and eaten raw or used in cooking; never boil them.

CHOOSING HAM

Most ham is sold ready cooked. Look for moist, fresh-looking, pink meat with a narrow edging of white fat. Avoid any that looks dry or dark-coloured. Ham cut freshly from the bone always has the best flavour but is expensive. Precut slices are usually of a good quality and more reasonable price. Vacuum-packed slices should always be bought from a refrigerated counter; check the 'eat by' or 'sell by' date.

When selecting a ham or joint to cook yourself, choose a short, thick leg without too much fat and with a thin rind. A bloom on the rind is often a sign of a ham with a good flavour.

STORING BACON AND HAM

Remove any paper wrapping and wrap bacon closely in foil or cling film, to exclude as much air as possible from the surface of the bacon. Store in the coolest part of the refrigerator for a maximum of 10 days. Wrap cooked ham slices closely in foil or cling film and store in the refrigerator for no more than 3 days.

Vacuum-packed ham or bacon can be stored in the unopened pack until the 'eat by' date but once opened, should be rewrapped and treated as for ham or bacon slices bought loose.

FREEZING BACON AND HAM

Freeze only perfectly fresh bacon or it will deteriorate quickly during storage. For the best results, freeze commercially vacuum-packed joints or rashers, which will store well for up to 4 months. Otherwise wrap the bacon closely in freezer film and overwrap with a thick polythene bag. Smoked joints and rashers wrapped this way should keep for up to 8 weeks, unsmoked joints or rashers for about 3 weeks. Thaw bacon in the refrigerator and, once thawed, use it up quickly.

Freeze cooked ham in small quantities, preferably no more than 225 g (8 oz) per package. Wrap it tightly in freezer film, overwrap with polythene and store for no more than about 2 months.

COOKING BACON AND HAM

Rashers, steaks and chops: Some bacon is sold without rind, but otherwise cut off the rind thinly with kitchen scissors or a sharp knife. Remove any bone from rashers before cooking. Snip the fat edge at intervals so that the bacon does not curl during cooking. If you suspect that chops or steaks may be salty, soak them for a few hours, or poach them in water for a few minutes, before cooking. Rashers, steaks and chops are usually grilled, fried or occasionally braised.

Bacon and ham joints: Fresh joints bought from a butcher usually need soaking before cooking, to remove excess salt. Ask your butcher's advice, but small joints should usually be soaked for 2–3 hours, larger ones for up to 8 hours. Alternatively, put the joint in a large pan, cover with cold water, bring to the boil and throw away the water; then start again with fresh water. Many mild cures, especially prepacked joints, will not require any soaking.

To calculate the cooking time for an average-sized joint, allow 20–25 minutes per 450 g (1 lb) plus 20 minutes extra; for a joint over 4.5 kg (10 lb) allow 15–20 minutes per 450 g (1 lb), plus 15 minutes.

Boiling: Put the joint in a large pan, skin side down, cover with cold water and bring slowly to the boil, skimming off any scum that forms. When the water is boiling, add any flavouring vegetables or herbs, reduce the heat, cover and start to time the cooking from this point. When the joint is cooked the rind should peel away easily; if it is difficult to remove the rind, return the joint to the hot water for further cooking. If the joint is to be served cold, remove the pan from the heat but leave the joint to cool in the liquid. If it is not too salty, the cooking liquid can be saved and used as a basis for soups or stews.

Baking: To bake a bacon joint or ham, calculate the cooking time as above and boil for half the calculated time. Then drain the joint, wrap it in foil and put it in a roasting tin; continue cooking in the oven at 180°C (350°F) mark 4. About 30 minutes before the end of the cooking time, raise the oven temperature to 220°C (425°F) mark 7; open the foil, remove the rind and score the fat. Stud the fat with cloves, sprinkle with brown sugar, or use one of the glazes suggested on page 223, and continue cooking the joint until the fat is a rich, golden brown.

CARVING HAM

For carving a whole or half ham on the bone, it helps to have a ham stand, shaped to hold the ham firmly while you carve. This is not essential, however, and an ordinary large carving dish or board can be used. If possible, though, exchange your normal carving knife for a ham knife with a long, thin, straight-sided blade.

CARVING HAM AND BACON

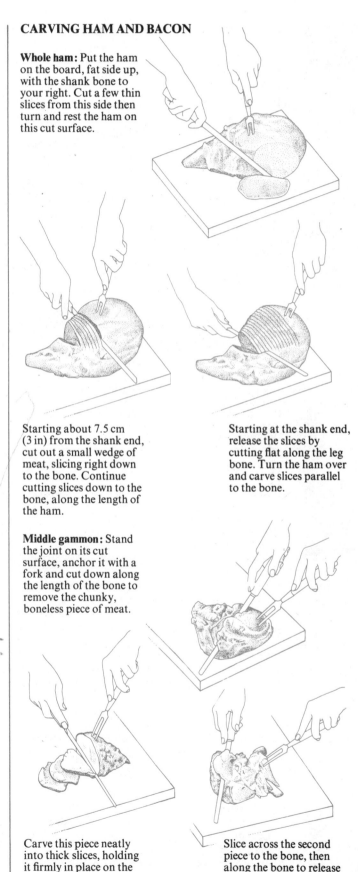

Whole ham: Put the ham on the board, fat side up, with the shank bone to your right. Cut a few thin slices from this side then turn and rest the ham on this cut surface.

Starting about 7.5 cm (3 in) from the shank end, cut out a small wedge of meat, slicing right down to the bone. Continue cutting slices down to the bone, along the length of the ham.

Starting at the shank end, release the slices by cutting flat along the leg bone. Turn the ham over and carve slices parallel to the bone.

Middle gammon: Stand the joint on its cut surface, anchor it with a fork and cut down along the length of the bone to remove the chunky, boneless piece of meat.

Carve this piece neatly into thick slices, holding it firmly in place on the board with the fork.

Slice across the second piece to the bone, then along the bone to release the meat from each side.

Bacon and ham

Pineapple-glazed Baked Ham

Colour index page 59

12–15 servings

2.3–3.2-kg (5–7-lb) piece ham, on the bone
566-g (20-oz) can crushed pineapple, drained well

175 g (6 oz) soft dark brown sugar

1. Soak the ham in cold water for 8 hours; drain. Put it in a large saucepan, cover with fresh cold water and bring to the boil, skimming off the scum as it rises. Cover and simmer for 1¼–1½ hours. Drain.
2. Wrap the ham in foil and place in a roasting tin. Insert a meat thermometer into the centre of the joint. Bake at 180°C (350°F) mark 4 for 45 minutes.
3. Mix the pineapple and sugar. Remove ham from oven, remove foil and place the meat on a rack in the roasting tin; cut off the skin. Spoon the pineapple mixture over and bake uncovered for 30 minutes until thermometer reads 71°C (160°F).

Removing the skin: Cool the ham slightly, then cut away any tough skin before glazing.

Adding the glaze: Spoon the pineapple glaze mixture evenly over the ham and pat it on gently.

Roast Gammon

Colour index page 59

10 servings

1.8-kg (4-lb) piece boneless gammon
50 g (2 oz) demerara sugar
150 g (5 oz) marmalade

10 ml (2 level tsp) made mustard
2 oranges
cloves

1. Soak the gammon in cold water for 2–3 hours. Drain well. Put it in a large saucepan, skin side down, cover with fresh cold water and add the sugar. Bring slowly to the boil, skimming off the scum as it rises. Reduce the heat, cover and simmer for 50 minutes–1 hour. Top up with extra boiling water when necessary.
2. Drain the joint. Carefully cut off the rind and score the fat into squares. Wrap the joint in foil, place in a roasting tin and roast at 180°C (350°F) mark 4 for 40 minutes.
3. Put the marmalade and mustard together in a small saucepan and stir over gentle heat until the marmalade is melted. Remove the gammon from the oven, remove the foil and brush with glaze.
4. Raise the temperature to 220°C (425°F) mark 7 and cook uncovered for a further 20 minutes.
5. Slice the oranges very thinly and halve the slices. Arrange them in rows, overlapping slightly, over the gammon; fasten them in place with cloves. Brush the remaining warm marmalade glaze gently over the orange slices.
6. Return the gammon to the oven for 10 minutes or until the orange slices are heated through.

Barbecued Bacon and Peaches

Colour index page 58

4 servings

700-g (1½-lb) piece boil-in-the-bag bacon
50 g (2 oz) sugar
50 ml (2 fl oz) mild chilli sauce
15 ml (1 tbsp) lemon juice
5 ml (1 tsp) Worcestershire sauce

1.25 ml (¼ level tsp) chilli powder
50 ml (2 fl oz) water
2–3 peaches, peeled, halved and stoned

1. Leave the bacon joint covered as directed on the label and place in an ovenproof dish. Cook in the oven at 190°C (375°F) mark 5 for 1 hour.
2. Meanwhile, put the sugar, chilli sauce, lemon juice, Worcestershire sauce, chilli powder and water in a large saucepan and bring to the boil, stirring occasionally. Remove from the heat, add the peaches and stir gently to coat well.
3. Remove the bacon from the oven. Cut off the wrapping and insert a meat thermometer into the centre of the joint.
4. Spoon the peaches into the dish and pour the remaining sauce over the bacon. Bake for about 20 minutes until the thermometer reaches 60°C (140°F), basting occasionally with the sauce.
5. Place the bacon on a heated serving dish and arrange the peaches around it.

Braised Bacon

Colour index page 58

8 servings

1.4-kg (3-lb) piece boneless gammon or collar bacon
45 ml (3 tbsp) vegetable oil
1 onion, skinned and sliced
4 carrots, peeled and sliced

½ turnip, peeled and sliced
2 sticks celery, trimmed and sliced
stock
bouquet garni
salt and pepper

1. Soak the bacon in cold water for 2–3 hours. Drain well. Place it in a large saucepan, skin side down, cover with fresh cold water and bring to the boil, skimming off the scum as it rises. Reduce the heat, cover and simmer for 30–40 minutes; drain.
2. Heat the oil in a frying pan and lightly fry the vegetables for 3–4 minutes. Place them in a casserole, put the bacon on top and add enough stock to cover the vegetables. Add the bouquet garni, salt and pepper; cover and cook in the oven at 180°C (350°F) mark 4 for 20 minutes.
3. Cut off the rind, return the bacon to the oven and cook, uncovered, for a further 30 minutes. Remove the bouquet garni before serving.

CIDER-BRAISED BACON: Cook the bacon as above, replacing half the stock with *cider*. To serve, remove the bacon from the casserole and slice it thickly. Place it in a heated serving dish with the vegetables and keep it hot. Blend together in a small bowl *15 ml (1 level tbsp) softened butter* and *15 ml (1 level tbsp) flour*. Pour the cooking juices from the casserole into a small saucepan and bring to the boil. Whisk in the blended butter and flour a little at a time, until the sauce is just thickened. Cook for 1–2 minutes, stirring, then adjust the seasoning and spoon it over the bacon. Serve with *apple jelly*.

Whole Boiled Ham

*4.5–5.4-kg (10–12-lb)
ham, on the bone
clear honey*

To serve:
*bread, crispbreads and
rolls*

Colour index
page 58

30–36 servings

1 Put the ham skin side down in a large saucepan and add enough cold water to cover the ham completely. Leave to soak at room temperature for 12 hours or overnight. Drain the ham.

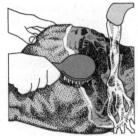

2 Scrub the ham with a vegetable brush and rinse well. Return it to the saucepan and cover with fresh water; bring to the boil, skimming off scum.

3 Cover and simmer for 20 minutes per 450 g (1 lb), or until the bone at the knuckle end protrudes about 2.5 cm (1 in) and begins to feel loose.

4 Drain ham and place on a rack in a large roasting tin. Cool for 20 minutes; cut off skin and trim fat to 0.5 cm (¼ in).

5 Brush the fat all over with honey and bake at 170°C (325°F) mark 3 for 15 minutes or until the ham is glazed. Chill.

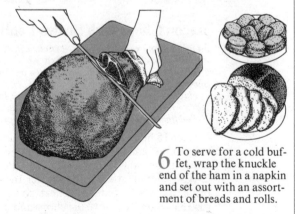

6 To serve for a cold buffet, wrap the knuckle end of the ham in a napkin and set out with an assortment of breads and rolls.

TO SERVE HOT: When the ham is cooked, remove it from the cooking liquid, remove the skin and put the joint on a heated carving dish; leave it to stand in a warm place for 15 minutes. Carve in thick slices and serve with **creamed parsnips, broad beans** and **parsley sauce**, page 267.

Gammon Steak Hawaii

*75 g (3 oz) soft light brown
sugar
50 g (2 oz) butter or
margarine
60 ml (4 tbsp) red wine
vinegar
700-g (1½-lb) smoked
gammon steak, cut 1–2
cm (½–¾ in) thick
4 firm bananas*

For the garnish, optional:
watercress

Colour index
page 59

6 servings

1 Heat the sugar, butter or margarine and vinegar in a large frying pan until the sugar has dissolved and the butter melted, stirring frequently.

2 Add the gammon steak to the pan. Cook for 5 minutes on each side, or until cooked through.

3 Remove the steak to a heated serving dish and keep it hot while you prepare the bananas.

4 Peel the bananas and cut them into 4-cm (1½-in) pieces. Add to the sugar and vinegar syrup in the frying pan.

5 Cook the bananas for about 5 minutes or until heated through, spooning the syrup over them all the time.

6 Spoon the bananas around the gammon steak on the heated serving dish and pour the remaining sauce over the steak and fruit. Serve hot, garnished with watercress if you wish.

Bacon and ham

Lemony Gammon Steaks

Colour index
page 59
6–8 servings

100 g (4 oz) soft light
  brown sugar
45 ml (3 level tbsp) made
  mustard
30 ml (2 tbsp) lemon juice
2.5 ml (½ tsp) grated
  lemon rind

1 lemon, thinly sliced
2 450-g (1-lb) gammon
  steaks, cut about 2 cm
  (¾ in) thick

1. Mix together the sugar, mustard, lemon juice and rind. Cut the lemon slices in half.
2. Snip the fat at intervals round the gammon steaks, put them in the grill pan and cook under a hot grill for 2–3 minutes. Brush with some of the lemon glaze and grill for a further 5 minutes. Turn the steaks and grill for 2–3 minutes more.
3. Arrange the lemon slices over the steaks, brush generously with the remaining glaze and grill for 5 minutes or until the glaze is bubbling and the steaks are cooked through.

Gammon Rashers with Fruit Sauce

Colour index
page 59
6 servings

6 gammon rashers, cut
  about 1 cm (½ in) thick
175 g (6 oz) prunes, stoned
175 g (6 oz) dried apricots
400 ml (¾ pint) orange
  juice

50 g (2 oz) sugar
15 ml (1 level tbsp)
  cornflour
30 ml (2 tbsp) water

1. Trim a little of the fat from one of the gammon rashers. Place the piece of fat in a large frying pan and cook until lightly browned, rubbing it over the bottom of the pan to grease it; discard the fat.
2. Snip the fat around the edge of each rasher four or five times. Cook the rashers, two at a time, until lightly browned on each side, removing them from the pan as they brown.
3. Add the prunes, apricots, orange juice and sugar. Return the rashers to the pan, overlapping them to fit. Spoon a little juice over each one, then bring to the boil. Lower the heat, cover and simmer for 20 minutes or until the apricots are tender.
4. Place the gammon rashers on a heated serving dish and keep hot.
5. Blend the cornflour and water, add it to the pan and cook, stirring constantly, until thickened. Serve the sauce with the gammon.

Cheese-topped Gammon Rashers

Colour index
page 59
4 servings

4 gammon rashers, cut
  about 1 cm (½ in) thick
2 green eating apples

a little melted butter
175 g (6 oz) Cheddar
  cheese, thinly sliced

1. Cut the rind off the gammon and snip the fat on each rasher in four or five places. Lay the gammon rashers side by side in the grill pan and cook under a hot grill for 4–5 minutes, turning once half way through the cooking time.
2. Wipe and core the apples but do not peel them; slice them thinly across into rounds. Arrange the apple slices over the gammon. Brush with melted butter and grill for 2–3 minutes.
3. Lay the cheese slices over the apple and return to the grill for a further minute.

Choucroute Garni

Colour index
page 59
6–8 servings

450–700-g (1–1½-lb) piece
  boneless collar bacon
450–700-g (1–1½-lb) piece
  pork shoulder, boned and
  rolled
300 ml (½ pint) dry white
  wine
300 ml (½ pint) chicken
  stock

4 juniper berries or 15 ml
  (1 tbsp) gin
3 onions, skinned
3 potatoes, peeled
350 g (12 oz) frankfurters
  or bratwurst
450 g (1 lb) sauerkraut,
  well drained

1. Put the bacon, pork, wine, stock and juniper berries or gin in a large saucepan. Bring to the boil, then reduce the heat, cover and simmer gently for about 1 hour.
2. Place the onion halves and then the potato halves over the top in layers. Add the whole frankfurters or bratwurst and cover with a thick layer of sauerkraut. Cover tightly and simmer for a further 25–30 minutes, until the bacon, pork, sausage and vegetables are all tender.
3. To serve, transfer the sauerkraut, frankfurters or bratwurst, potatoes and onions to a large heated serving dish. Remove the bacon and pork from the saucepan, cut into slices and arrange them over the vegetables and sausages. Strain the cooking juices and skim off the fat. Pour the juices into a sauce boat and spoon a little over each serving.

Serving the choucroute:
Spoon a little of the
cooking juices over each
plate of choucroute.

Bacon Chops with Brown Lentils

Colour index
page 58
4 servings

30 ml (2 tbsp) vegetable oil
4 lean bacon chops, cut
  about 1 cm (½ in) thick
about 600 ml (1 pint)
  chicken stock
100 g (4 oz) onion, skinned
  and finely sliced

3 sticks celery, trimmed and
  sliced
100 g (4 oz) mushrooms,
  sliced
175 g (6 oz) large brown
  lentils, soaked overnight
salt and pepper

1. Heat 15 ml (1 tbsp) oil in a frying pan and fry the chops until golden on both sides. Spoon off all the fat from the pan.
2. Add enough stock just to cover the chops, and bring to the boil. Reduce the heat, cover and simmer for 15 minutes. Remove the chops and keep hot.
3. Heat remaining oil in a large saucepan and sauté onion, celery and mushrooms for 2 minutes. Drain the lentils and add them with cooking liquid from the chops and salt and pepper to taste. Cover and simmer for 15 minutes or until the lentils are tender.
4. Spoon the lentils and vegetables on to a heated serving dish and arrange the chops on top.

IDEAS FOR LEFTOVER HAM

HAM DIP: Mix finely chopped *cooked ham* with *soured cream, mayonnaise, Worcestershire sauce* and *salt* and serve with *fresh vegetables* and *crisps*.

HAM AND GRUYERE SPREAD: Mix minced *cooked ham* with grated *Gruyère cheese*, softened *cream cheese, milk* and a *few drops Tabasco sauce*. Spread on *salt biscuits* or use as a filling for sandwiches.

HAM CHEF SALAD: Arrange chunks or slivers of *cooked ham, tomato slices, olives, cucumber sticks* and *sliced radishes* over *cooked macaroni* or potato salad. Colour index page 59

GLAZED KEBABS: Thread chunks of *cooked ham* and thick *wedges of apple* alternately on to skewers. Brush with *marmalade* mixed with *lemon juice* and grill until glazed. Colour index page 59

HAM AND WATERCRESS SOUP: Bring well-flavoured *chicken stock* to the boil, add a few *sliced mushrooms*, slivers of *cooked ham* and trimmed *watercress sprigs*. Bring back to the boil, season with *salt* and *pepper* to taste and serve immediately.

HAM CASSEROLE: Mix drained, canned *red kidney beans* with *tomato ketchup, brown sugar, mustard*, diced *green pepper* and chunks of *cooked ham*; bake until heated through. Colour index page 59

HAM PATTIES: Mix minced *cooked ham* with a *beaten egg, dried breadcrumbs*, a *pinch of ground sage* and a *pinch of pepper*. Shape into small patties and fry in butter. Serve in hamburger buns.

CREAMED HAM AND VEGETABLES: Stir chunks or julienne strips of *cooked ham* into *béchamel sauce* (page 461) and pour over *cooked cauliflower*, leeks, fennel or courgettes.

HAM, NUT AND FRUIT SALAD: Mix diced *cooked ham* with *chopped walnuts* or almonds and *sliced celery*. Moisten with *mayonnaise* and serve in a halved *avocado* . Colour index page 59

GLAZES FOR BAKED HAM OR BACON

SPICED MARMALADE AND HONEY GLAZE: Blend together *60 ml (4 level tbsp) fine shred marmalade, 75 ml (5 level tbsp) clear honey* and *4–5 drops Tabasco sauce*. Brush about one third of the glaze over the joint 30 minutes before the end of the cooking time. Bake for 10 minutes then brush with another third of the glaze; bake for 10 minutes and repeat with the last of the glaze. Do not use the glaze that has run into the tin as this will dull the shine. Makes enough to glaze a 2-kg (4½-lb) joint

SHARP HONEY GLAZE: Warm together *15 ml (1 level tbsp) clear honey* and *30 ml (2 tbsp) vinegar* in a small saucepan. Strip the rind off the bacon and pour the glaze over the fat. Sprinkle with *50 g (2 oz) brown sugar* and *50 g (2 oz) fresh white breadcrumbs*, mixed. Return the joint to the oven and baste frequently until cooked. Makes enough to glaze a 2-kg (4½-lb) joint

Glazed Ham Loaf

Colour index page 59

4 servings

450 g (1 lb) cooked ham, minced
1 large carrot, peeled and grated
1 small onion, skinned and finely chopped
2 eggs
30 ml (2 tbsp) chopped parsley
10 ml (2 level tsp) made mustard
225-g (8-oz) can pineapple slices

30 ml (2 level tbsp) soft light brown sugar
10 ml (2 level tsp) cornflour
25 g (1 oz) butter or margarine
15 ml (1 tbsp) lemon juice

1 Mix together the ham, carrot, onion, eggs, parsley and mustard. Grease a small roasting tin.

2 Spoon the ham mixture into the tin and shape it into a loaf about 18 × 7.5 cm (7 × 3 in); or spoon it into a 450-g (1-lb) loaf tin. Bake at 180°C (350°F) mark 4 for 30 minutes.

3 Meanwhile, drain the pineapple juice into a small saucepan. Blend in the sugar and cornflour and cook gently, stirring constantly, until the mixture is thickened.

4 Remove from the heat and stir in the butter or margarine and lemon juice until well blended.

5 Remove the ham loaf from the oven and brush it generously all over with the pineapple and lemon juice glaze, reserving a little glaze.

6 Arrange the pineapple slices on top, slightly overlapping; bake for a further 30 minutes, brushing occasionally with the remaining glaze.

Lamb

LAMB CUTS

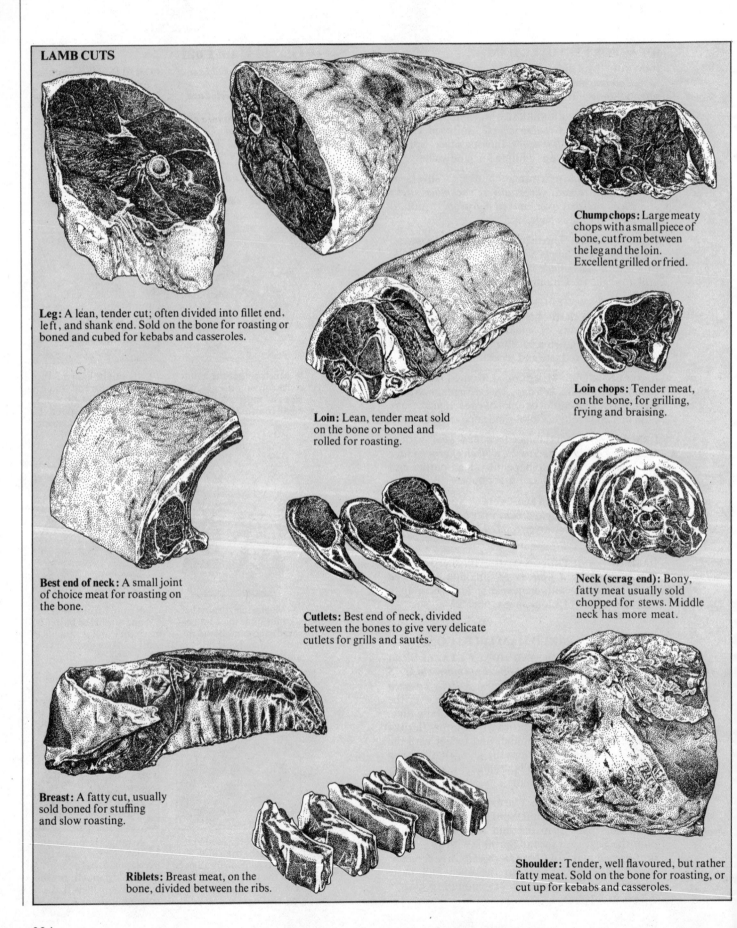

Leg: A lean, tender cut; often divided into fillet end, left, and shank end. Sold on the bone for roasting or boned and cubed for kebabs and casseroles.

Chump chops: Large meaty chops with a small piece of bone, cut from between the leg and the loin. Excellent grilled or fried.

Loin: Lean, tender meat sold on the bone or boned and rolled for roasting.

Loin chops: Tender meat, on the bone, for grilling, frying and braising.

Best end of neck: A small joint of choice meat for roasting on the bone.

Cutlets: Best end of neck, divided between the bones to give very delicate cutlets for grills and sautés.

Neck (scrag end): Bony, fatty meat usually sold chopped for stews. Middle neck has more meat.

Breast: A fatty cut, usually sold boned for stuffing and slow roasting.

Riblets: Breast meat, on the bone, divided between the ribs.

Shoulder: Tender, well flavoured, but rather fatty meat. Sold on the bone for roasting, or cut up for kebabs and casseroles.

Sheep are usually killed for meat between 4 and 12 months of age. After slaughter the carcasses are chilled and are hung in cold store for a period of 4–6 days in order to tenderise the meat.

CHOOSING LAMB

The meat from young English lambs is fine and pale, with a small amount of creamy fat. The joints are very small and the meat is expensive, but it is always tender. Older animals, native and imported, give larger joints and chops and slightly coarser, darker meat; this should still be tender if the meat has been hung correctly.

With the exception of middle neck and scrag, which need slow, moist cooking, all lamb cuts can be roasted, grilled or fried. Joints are normally sold on the bone, except for breast which is sometimes boned and rolled. Most butchers will bone the meat if asked in advance.

ROASTING LAMB

Wipe the meat, trim it if necessary and calculate the cooking time according to the timetable below. Put the meat in a roasting tin, on a rack if you wish, with the thickest layer of fat on top. If the joint is very lean, add a little dripping. Cook for the calculated time, basting occasionally with the juices from the tin. Lamb is usually served medium to well done and the traditional accompaniments are mint sauce (page 463) or redcurrant jelly, and thick gravy. Onion or caper sauce may also be served with roast lamb.

TIMETABLE FOR ROASTING LAMB		
Type of joint	Roasting time at 220°C (425°F) mark 7	Roasting time at 180°C (350°F) mark 4
Joints on the bone	20 minutes per 450 g (1 lb), plus 20 minutes	30–35 minutes per 450 g (1 lb)
Boned and rolled joints	25 minutes per 450 g (1 lb), plus 25 minutes	40–45 minutes per 450 g (1 lb)

CARVING LAMB

Leg of lamb: Put the meat on the carving dish with the meatiest side uppermost. Start in the centre of the thickest meat and cut a wedge right down to the bone. Carve slices from either side of this cut, gradually slanting the knife to get larger slices and ending parallel to the bone. Turn the joint over and carve the other side in long flat slices along the leg.

Shoulder of lamb: Cut a long, thick slice down to the bone from the centre of the meatier side of the joint. Carve small slices from each side of the hump on the blade bone down to the shank until the whole surface is clean. Turn the joint over, remove the fat and carve in horizontal slices.

An alternative method of preparing a shoulder of lamb for easy carving is to insert a knife and ease the meat away from the blade bone before cooking. After roasting, twist and remove this bone. Carve downwards

until the bone is reached, then turn the joint over and continue carving the other side.

Best end of neck of lamb: First remove the chine bone and set it aside, then carve down into single or double rib portions, between the rib bones.

CARVING LAMB

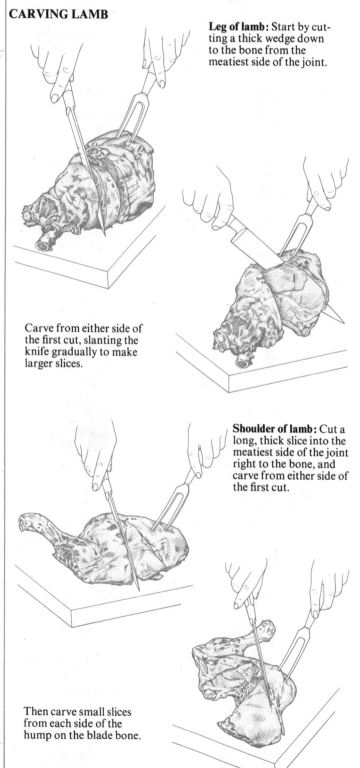

Leg of lamb: Start by cutting a thick wedge down to the bone from the meatiest side of the joint.

Carve from either side of the first cut, slanting the knife gradually to make larger slices.

Shoulder of lamb: Cut a long, thick slice into the meatiest side of the joint right to the bone, and carve from either side of the first cut.

Then carve small slices from each side of the hump on the blade bone.

Roast lamb

Roast Leg of Lamb

Colour index
page 60

6–8 servings

3 juniper berries
10 ml (2 level tsp) dry
mustard
10 ml (2 tsp) water
salt and pepper
1.8–2.2-kg (4–5-lb) leg of
lamb
8 large potatoes, peeled

For the sauce:
60 ml (4 tbsp) gin, optional
175 g (6 oz) redcurrant
jelly
30 ml (2 level tbsp)
cornflour
1.25 ml (¼ level tsp) salt

1 Crush the juniper berries with the mustard, water and seasoning to taste. Spread over lamb.

2 Put the lamb on a rack in a roasting tin and insert a meat thermometer into the thickest part, being careful it does not touch bone. Roast at 180°C (350°F) mark 4 for 2¼–2½ hours, until the thermometer reads 82°C (180°F). Meanwhile, cut the potatoes into slices about 2.5 cm (1 in) thick. About 1 hour before the meat is done, sprinkle the potato slices with 5 ml (1 level tsp) salt.

3 Put potatoes on rack round meat; cook until tender, basting. Put lamb and potatoes on a heated serving dish. Keep hot.

4 Pour the juices from the roasting tin into a measuring jug; leave to stand until the fat separates, then skim off and discard the fat.

5 Add 300 ml (½ pint) water to tin and bring to the boil, stirring to loosen sediment. Add to jug with the gin. Add water to make 400 ml (¾ pint).

6 Tip into a saucepan and add jelly. Bring to the boil, stirring. Blend cornflour to a smooth paste with the salt and 60 ml (4 tbsp) water.

7 Stir the blended cornflour into the hot liquid in the saucepan and cook, stirring, until thickened. Carve lamb and serve with potatoes and sauce.

Marinated Boned Leg of Lamb

Colour index
page 61

6–8 servings

1.8–2.3-kg (4–5-lb) leg of
lamb
30 ml (2 tbsp) black
peppercorns
100 ml (4 fl oz) red wine
60 ml (4 tbsp) olive or
vegetable oil
10 ml (2 level tsp) salt

10 ml (2 level tsp) dried
oregano
2 cloves garlic, skinned and
sliced

For the garnish, optional:
parsley sprigs

1. Bone the leg of lamb as shown in the drawings below, then weigh it.
2. Pound the peppercorns with a meat mallet or grind them very coarsely in a peppermill, then mix them with the wine, oil, salt, oregano and garlic in a shallow dish. Add the meat and turn to coat it well with the marinade. Cover and refrigerate for 12–24 hours, turning the meat occasionally.
3. Drain the lamb, reserving the marinade. Place the meat on a rack in a roasting tin and roast at 220°C (425°F) mark 7 for 25 minutes per 450 g (1 lb) plus 25 minutes or until tender, basting it occasionally with the marinade.
4. Remove the lamb to a carving board or a heated serving dish and serve garnished with parsley sprigs, if you wish.

BONING A LEG OF LAMB

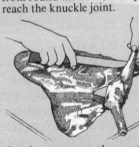

Place the joint meaty side down. With a sharp knife, cut through the meat, parallel to the bone to expose the leg bone.

Holding the knife blade against the bone, scrape all the meat from round the bone, until you reach the knuckle joint.

Turn the leg slightly and cut round the knuckle joint.

Continue to scrape the meat from the bone until the entire bone is exposed. Remove bone.

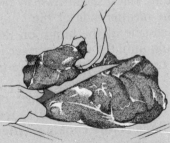

Cut the thicker muscles almost in half and open them out to make the meat a more even thickness. Trim off any excess fat.

Marinated Leg of Lamb

Colour index
page 60

6 servings

1.8-kg (4-lb) leg of lamb
45 ml (3 level tbsp) plain
flour
1.25 ml (¼ level tsp) salt

For the marinade:
10 ml (2 level tsp) salt
100 ml (4 fl oz) orange
juice
100 ml (4 fl oz) red wine
100 ml (4 fl oz) mild chilli
sauce

30 ml (2 tbsp) vegetable oil
1 small onion, skinned and
finely chopped
1 clove garlic, skinned and
crushed
30 ml (2 level tbsp) sugar
10 ml (2 level tsp) chilli
powder
5 ml (1 level tsp) dried
basil

1. Mix the marinade ingredients in a large shallow dish, add the lamb and turn to coat. Cover and refrigerate for 12–24 hours, turning occasionally.
2. Drain the lamb, reserving the marinade. Place the meat, fat side up, on a rack in a roasting tin. Insert a meat thermometer into the centre of the meat, being careful it does not touch bone. Roast at 180°C (350°F) mark 4 for about 2 hours, until the thermometer reaches 82°C (180°F), basting occasionally with the reserved marinade. Place on a heated serving dish and keep hot.
3. Pour the juices from the tin into a measuring jug and leave to stand until the fat separates. Skim off 45 ml (3 tbsp) of the fat and return it to the roasting tin. Skim off and discard the remaining fat in the jug. Heat the fat in the roasting tin, stir in the flour and salt until blended and cook, stirring, until golden.
4. Add 350 ml (12 fl oz) water and the meat juices to the roasting tin; cook over medium heat, stirring, until the sediment is loosened and the gravy thickened. Add more water if necessary. Serve the gravy with the lamb.

Rôtisseried Leg of Lamb

Colour index
page 61

6–8 servings

1.8–2.3-kg (4–5-lb) leg of
lamb, boned and rolled

For the marinade:
100 ml (4 fl oz) vegetable
oil
100 ml (4 fl oz) white wine
100 ml (4 fl oz) red wine
vinegar
1 clove garlic, skinned and
crushed

10 ml (2 level tsp) salt
2.5 ml (½ level tsp) dried
sage
2.5 ml (½ level tsp) ground
ginger
1.25 ml (¼ level tsp)
pepper

1. Mix the marinade ingredients in a large shallow dish, add the lamb and turn to coat. Cover and refrigerate for 12–24 hours, turning occasionally.
2. Drain the lamb, reserving the marinade. Insert the spit through the centre of the joint and tighten the holding prongs. Insert a meat thermometer into the centre of the lamb, being careful it does not touch the spit, heating element or oven as it turns.
3. Roast on the high setting for 15 minutes to seal the meat, then reduce the temperature to low and continue cooking for 2–3 hours, according to the manufacturer's instructions or until the thermometer reaches 82°C (180°F), brushing frequently with the marinade. Remove the spit and strings and leave the meat to stand in a warm place for 15 minutes to make carving easier.

Roast Rack of Lamb with Apricot Glaze

Colour index
page 61

4 servings

3.75 ml (¾ level tsp) garlic
salt
1.25 ml (¼ level tsp) salt
pinch pepper
1.1-kg (2½-lb) best end
of neck of lamb,
chined
75 g (3 oz) apricot jam
10 ml (2 tsp) lemon
juice

1 Mix together the garlic salt, salt and pepper and rub them all over the joint. Place the lamb, fat side up, in a roasting tin.

2 Insert a meat thermometer into the centre of the meat, being careful it does not touch bone. Roast at 180°C (350°F) mark 4 for 45 minutes.

3 Meanwhile gently heat the apricot jam and lemon juice, stirring, until the jam has melted.

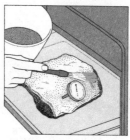

4 Brush lamb with apricot glaze and roast for 30 minutes or until thermometer reads 82°C (180°F), basting with glaze.

5 Place the lamb on a heated serving dish and leave to stand for 15 minutes. Remove the chine bone and discard.

6 To serve, hold the lamb securely with a carving fork and carve between every other rib, allowing two ribs per serving.

Grilled lamb

Barbecued Lamb Kebabs

Colour index
page 61

4 servings

25 g (1 oz) butter or
  margarine
50 g (2 oz) chopped onion
1 small green pepper,
  seeded and finely
  chopped
1 stick celery, trimmed,
  washed and chopped
1 clove garlic, skinned and
  crushed
226-g (8-oz) can tomatoes
141-g (5-oz) can tomato
  paste
30 ml (2 level tbsp) soft
  light brown sugar
7.5 ml (1½ tsp) vinegar

2.5 ml (½ level tsp) salt
1.25 ml (¼ level tsp)
  pepper
2.5 ml (½ tsp) Tabasco
  sauce
60 ml (4 tbsp) water
1 aubergine
2 green or red peppers,
  seeded
900 g (2 lb) boned leg or
  shoulder of lamb, cubed

1 Melt the fat in a saucepan and cook the onion, green pepper, celery and garlic for about 10 minutes or until tender.

2 Add tomatoes and their liquid, the tomato paste, sugar, vinegar, salt, pepper, Tabasco and water. Bring to the boil; simmer for 5 minutes. Cool.

3 Cut the aubergine lengthways in half, then crossways into 2.5-cm (1-in) slices. Cut the peppers into 5-cm (2-in) pieces.

4 When the tomato mixture is cool, add the lamb cubes, aubergine and peppers and mix well. Cover and chill for 4 hours.

5 Prepare the barbecue about 1 hour before serving. Drain the lamb and vegetables; thread them alternately on to long skewers. Spoon the marinade into a saucepan.

6 Place the skewers over the hot coals and barbecue, turning frequently, for about 30 minutes. Heat the marinade in the saucepan on the barbecue grill to serve with the lamb.

Lamb Chops à l'Orange

Colour index
page 61

4 servings

150 g (5 oz) orange
  marmalade
15 g (½ oz) butter or
  margarine
15 ml (1 tbsp) dry sherry
1 small clove garlic, skinned
  and finely chopped

5 ml (1 level tsp) salt
4 chump lamb chops

For the garnish, optional:
orange slices
parsley

1. Heat the marmalade, butter or margarine, sherry, garlic and salt in a small saucepan, stirring occasionally, until the marmalade is melted.
2. Place the chops on a greased rack in the grill pan and grill under medium heat for 10–15 minutes, turning them once and brushing them occasionally with the marmalade mixture.
3. Transfer the chops to a heated serving dish and spoon over any remaining marmalade sauce. If you wish, garnish the chops with orange slices and sprigs of parsley.

Roquefort Lamb Chops

Colour index
page 61

8 servings

100 g (4 oz) Roquefort
  cheese
5 ml (1 level tsp) salt
5 ml (1 tsp) Worcestershire
  sauce
pinch pepper

8 loin lamb chops, cut about
  6.5 cm (2½ in) thick
298-g (10½-oz) can
  condensed consommé

1. With a fork, stir and mash the cheese in a small bowl with the salt, Worcestershire sauce and pepper until well mixed.
2. Trim the chops, leaving only a thin layer of fat. Place the chops on a rack in the grill pan. Grill for 8–10 minutes on each side.
3. Hold each chop with tongs and spread the Roquefort mixture evenly over the outer edge of the chops, over the fat, or over one flat side. Arrange the chops in a shallow flameproof dish, pour over the undiluted consommé and grill for a further 2–3 minutes or until the cheese has melted and is bubbling and the sauce is hot.

Gingered Lamb Chops

Colour index
page 61

6 servings

30 ml (2 tbsp) vegetable oil
1.25 ml (¼ level tsp) salt
7.5 ml (1½ level tsp)
  ground ginger
2.5 ml (½ level tsp) garlic
  salt

6 loin or chump lamb chops,
  cut about 2.5 cm (1 in)
  thick
225 g (8 oz) mushrooms

1. Mix together the oil, salt, ginger and garlic salt in a small bowl.
2. Place the chops on a greased rack in the grill pan and brush one side with a little of the ginger mixture. Grill for 6 minutes.
3. Remove the stems from the mushrooms. Turn the chops and arrange the mushroom caps around them. Brush the meat and mushrooms with the remaining ginger mixture and grill for a further 6 minutes or until tender.
4. Transfer the chops to a heated serving dish and spoon the mushrooms into the centre. Pour any ginger mixture remaining in the grill pan over the meat and mushrooms.

Baked lamb

Colour index
page 60
4–6 servings

Lamb Cutlets with Fruit Sauce

salt and freshly ground
  black pepper
6 lamb cutlets, trimmed
1 egg, beaten
50 g (2 oz) fresh white
  breadcrumbs
50 g (2 oz) butter
225 g (8 oz) gooseberries,
  topped and tailed

450 g (1 lb) eating apples,
  peeled, cored and sliced
15 ml (1 level tbsp) sugar

For the garnish:
6 cutlet frills
6 sprigs mint

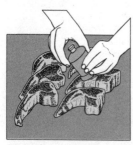

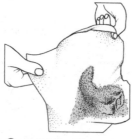

1 Season the cutlets. Put the beaten egg in a shallow dish and spread the breadcrumbs on a sheet of greaseproof paper.

2 Dip each cutlet in egg and coat with the breadcrumbs, using the paper to help you. Place the cutlets on a greased rack in the grill pan.

3 Cook under a hot grill for a few seconds to brown the crumbs. Reduce the heat and grill for 20 minutes more, turning the cutlets once.

4 Meanwhile, melt the butter in a saucepan, add the fruit, cover and cook gently until soft.

5 Purée the stewed fruit in a blender or press it through a sieve with a wooden spoon. Stir in the sugar and spread the sauce on a heated serving dish.

6 Put a cutlet frill on the end of each bone and arrange the cutlets on the sauce. Garnish with a sprig of mint on each cutlet.

FRIED LAMB CUTLETS BORDELAISE: Coat the cutlets as above, but fry them in shallow fat for about 8 minutes, turning them occasionally. Drain well on kitchen paper towel and serve with *bordelaise sauce* (page 462).

Barbecued Breast of Lamb

Colour index
page 60
4 servings

1.4-kg (3-lb) breast of
  lamb, on the bone
3 oranges
100 ml (4 fl oz) mild chilli
  sauce
30 ml (2 level tbsp) clear
  honey
5 ml (1 level tsp) salt
1.25 ml (¼ level tsp)
  pepper
5 ml (1 tsp) Worcestershire
  sauce

1 Cut the lamb into portions. Grate 15 ml (1 tbsp) rind and squeeze 60 ml (4 tbsp) juice from one orange.

2 Mix orange rind and juice with the chilli sauce, honey, salt, pepper and Worcestershire sauce.

3 Put the lamb in a roasting tin and pour the chilli sauce mixture over the top of each portion.

4 Bake at 180°C (350°F) mark 4 for 2–2½ hours until tender, basting with sauce occasionally. Slice the remaining oranges.

5 About 15 minutes before the end of cooking time, add the orange slices to the portions of lamb to heat through.

Lamb Riblets with Pineapple

Colour index
page 61
6 servings

454-g (16-oz) can
  pineapple chunks
60 ml (4 level tbsp) clear
  honey
45 ml (3 tbsp) white wine
  vinegar

15 ml (1 level tbsp) salt
5 ml (1 tsp) Worcestershire
  sauce
1.25 ml (¼ level tsp)
  ground ginger
2.7 kg (6 lb) lamb riblets

1. Drain the pineapple chunks and reserve them; mix the liquid with the honey, vinegar, salt, Worcestershire sauce and ginger in a roasting tin.
2. Add the lamb, turning the riblets to coat them in the sauce. Cover the tin tightly with foil and bake at 180°C (350°F) mark 4 for 2 hours or until tender. About 10 minutes before the end of cooking time, add the pineapple chunks to the lamb mixture to heat through.

Braised and stewed lamb

Lancashire Hot-pot

Colour index
page 60

4 servings

900 g (2 lb) middle neck
   lamb chops
2 lamb's kidneys, optional
225 g (8 oz) onions,
   skinned and sliced
450 g (1 lb) potatoes,
   peeled and sliced

salt and pepper
300 ml (½ pint) stock
25 g (1 oz) lard or
   dripping

1. Trim any excess fat from the chops and put them in a casserole. Skin the kidneys and chop them, removing any membrane and white core.
2. Add the onions, kidneys and potatoes to the casserole in layers, ending with a layer of potatoes. Season well with salt and pepper.
3. Pour over the stock and brush the top of the potatoes with melted lard or dripping.
4. Cover and cook in the oven at 170°C (325°F) mark 3 for 2 hours or until the meat and potatoes are tender when tested with a fork.
5. Remove the lid, turn the oven temperature up to 220°C (425°F) mark 7 and cook for a further 20 minutes to brown the potatoes.

HOT-POT WITH OYSTERS: Prepare the Lancashire hot-pot as above, but add **8 shelled oysters** in a layer on top of the lamb chops, and omit the kidneys. Cut the potatoes into chunks rather than slices and cook as above.

Braised Neck of Lamb

Colour index
page 60

4 servings

900 g (2 lb) middle neck
   lamb chops
45 ml (3 level tbsp) plain
   flour
15 ml (1 tbsp) vegetable
   oil
225 ml (8 fl oz) water
175 g (6 oz) stoned prunes,
   soaked overnight
30 ml (2 level tbsp) sugar
30 ml (2 tbsp) cider vinegar

6.25 ml (1¼ level tsp) salt
1.25 ml (¼ level tsp)
   pepper
1.25 ml (¼ level tsp)
   ground cinnamon
1.25 ml (¼ level tsp)
   ground allspice

1. Trim any excess fat from the chops and coat them all over with the flour.
2. Heat the oil in a large frying pan and cook the chops a few at a time until well browned all over, removing them from the pan as they brown. Skim the excess fat from the frying pan.
3. Return the chops to the pan, add the water and bring to the boil. Reduce the heat, cover and simmer for 45 minutes.
4. Turn the lamb and add the prunes. Cover and simmer for a further 10 minutes. Stir in the remaining ingredients, cover again and simmer for 5 minutes more or until the meat is tender.
5. Spoon the lamb and cooking liquid on to a heated serving dish and serve at once.

CARAWAY BRAISED NECK OF LAMB: Flour and brown the lamb as above. Add **350 ml (12 fl oz) beef stock, 5 ml (1 level tsp) caraway seeds, 5 ml (1 level tsp) salt** and a **pinch of pepper**. Bring to the boil, then reduce the heat; cover and simmer for 1 hour or until the meat is tender, turning it once.

Middle East Lamb Stew

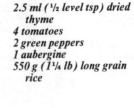

Colour index
page 61

6–8 servings

1.4 kg (3 lb) lean boneless
   lamb
25 g (1 oz) plain flour
60 ml (4 tbsp) vegetable oil
400 ml (¾ pint) water
2 onions, skinned and
   chopped
2 cloves garlic, skinned and
   finely chopped
30 ml (2 level tbsp)
   seasoning salt
2.5 ml (½ level tsp) freshly
   ground black pepper

2.5 ml (½ level tsp) dried
   thyme
4 tomatoes
2 green peppers
1 aubergine
550 g (1¼ lb) long grain
   rice

1 Cut the meat into 4-cm (1½-in) chunks and coat them with the flour.

2 Heat the oil in a flame-proof casserole or a large saucepan and brown the lamb a few pieces at a time, removing the pieces from the saucepan as they brown.

3 Return the meat to the pan and stir in the water, onions, garlic, seasoning salt, pepper and thyme. Bring to the boil, reduce the heat, then cover and simmer for 2 hours.

4 Skin the tomatoes and cut them into wedges; seed the green peppers and trim the aubergine; cut them both into chunks.

5 Add the vegetables to the lamb and cook for a further 30 minutes, stirring occasionally. Cook the rice in boiling salted water; drain and keep it hot.

6 When both meat and vegetables are tender, remove from the heat. Spread out the rice on a heated serving dish and spoon the stew over the top.

Minced lamb

Lamb Curry

Colour index
page 60

6 servings

*900 g (2 lb) lean boneless
lamb, cut into 2.5-cm
(1-in) cubes*
25 g (1 oz) plain flour
30 ml (2 tbsp) vegetable oil
2 onions, skinned and sliced
*1 clove garlic, skinned and
crushed*
*15–45 ml (1–3 level tbsp)
curry powder*
10 ml (2 level tsp) salt
*1.25 ml (¼ level tsp)
ground cinnamon*
*1.25 ml (¼ level tsp)
ground cloves*
*pinch coarsely ground black
pepper*

225 ml (8 fl oz) beef stock
*100 ml (4 fl oz) tomato
juice*

To serve:
*350 g (12 oz) long grain
rice*
mango chutney, optional
*banana slices brushed with
lemon juice, optional*
lime pickle, optional
*grated fresh or desiccated
coconut, optional*
seedless raisins, optional
tomato wedges, optional
fried onion rings, optional

1. Toss the lamb in the flour to coat. Heat the oil in a large frying pan, add the meat a few pieces at a time and brown on all sides, removing the pieces from the pan as they are browned.
2. Add the onions, garlic and curry powder to the oil remaining in the pan and cook over a low heat for about 5 minutes, stirring frequently, until the onions are soft but not coloured.
3. Return the meat to the pan and stir in the salt, cinnamon, cloves, pepper and stock. Bring to the boil, then reduce the heat, cover the pan and simmer gently for 2 hours or until the meat is tender, stirring occasionally to prevent sticking.
4. Meanwhile, cook the rice in boiling salted water until tender; drain and keep hot.
5. Stir the tomato juice into the curry and heat through. Serve with boiled rice and a selection of curry accompaniments.

Lamb Stew Rosé

Colour index
page 61

6 servings

15 ml (1 tbsp) vegetable oil
*900 g (2 lb) lean boneless
lamb, cubed*
225 ml (8 fl oz) rosé wine
*2 cloves garlic, skinned and
finely chopped*
7.5 ml (1½ level tsp) salt
*1.25 ml (¼ level tsp)
pepper*
*1.25 ml (¼ level tsp) dried
rosemary*

*550 g (1¼ lb) long grain
rice, optional*
450 g (1 lb) small tomatoes
*75 g (3 oz) almond or
pimento-stuffed olives*

For the garnish, optional:
chopped parsley

1. Heat the oil in a heavy saucepan or flameproof casserole and fry the meat a few pieces at a time until well browned all over, removing the pieces from the pan as they brown.
2. Return all the meat to the pan and stir in the wine, garlic, salt, pepper and rosemary. Bring to the boil then reduce the heat; cover and simmer gently for about 2½ hours until the meat is tender, stirring occasionally to prevent sticking.
3. Meanwhile, if you are serving the stew with rice, cook the rice in boiling salted water until tender. Drain and keep hot.
4. Add the whole tomatoes and olives to the stew and heat through for 5 minutes. Serve with the rice and garnish with parsley, if you wish.

Persian Lamb with Almonds

Colour index
page 60

4 servings

15 ml (1 tbsp) vegetable oil
*50 g (2 oz) almonds,
slivered*
700 g (1½ lb) minced lamb
*2 onions, skinned and
chopped*
1 beef stock cube, crumbled
3.75 ml (¾ level tsp) salt
*2.5 ml (½ level tsp) garlic
salt*
*1.25 ml (¼ level tsp)
pepper*
*30 ml (2 tbsp) lime or
lemon juice*
*10 ml (2 level tsp) dried
mint*
spinach leaves
2 tomatoes, cut into wedges

1 Heat the oil in a frying pan and cook the almonds, stirring constantly, until they are golden brown. Remove them from the pan.

2 Add the lamb, onions, stock cube and seasonings to the oil remaining in the pan and cook, stirring, for 10–15 minutes until browned.

3 Return the almonds to the pan and add the lime or lemon juice and mint. Stir to blend well.

4 Line the serving dish with spinach leaves and spoon the lamb mixture into the centre. Garnish with the tomatoes.

Lamb Patties

Colour index
page 61

6 servings

700 g (1½ lb) minced lamb
*15 ml (1 tbsp) grated lemon
rind*
15 ml (1 tbsp) lemon juice
*15 ml (1 tbsp) chopped
parsley*

small bay leaf, crushed
pinch dried rosemary
salt and pepper
*6 rashers streaky bacon,
rinded*

1. Mix the lamb, lemon rind and juice, herbs and seasoning and shape into six round patties. Wrap a rasher of bacon round each patty and secure with wooden cocktail sticks.
2. Place the patties on a greased rack in the grill pan and cook under a hot grill for 5 minutes on each side.

Veal

CUTS OF VEAL

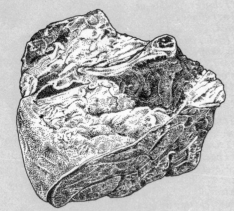

Leg: This is a prime cut; usually roasted. It is often boned and stuffed before cooking.

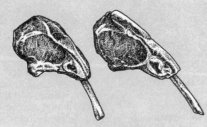

Chops: Chops are usually taken from the loin, with the bone in. Chump chops are from the bottom end of the loin. Suitable for grilling and frying.

Fillet: A boneless roasting cut, but more commonly sliced thinly into escalopes and sautéed.

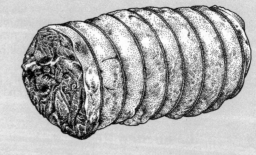

Loin: A roasting cut sold on the bone or boned and rolled.

Cutlets: These are from the neck end of the loin. Suitable for grilling, frying, braising or sautés.

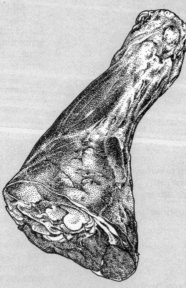

Best end of neck: There is a high proportion of bone in this cut but it is suitable for roasting, braising or stewing.

Knuckle: A bony cut usually used for boiling and stewing; or the whole knuckle can be boned, stuffed and braised.

Shoulder: An awkwardly shaped joint, usually cut up for stews and pies although the meat is suitable for roasting if boned and rolled.

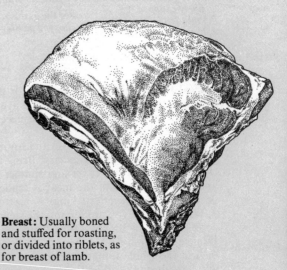

Pie veal: Usually consists of trimmings and small pieces of shoulder, breast, neck or knuckle, cut up and ready for pies and stews.

Breast: Usually boned and stuffed for roasting, or divided into riblets, as for breast of lamb.

Veal comes from specially bred calves, killed between the ages of 2 and 10 months. The best quality veal is from milk-fed calves; when they leave the mother, they may be killed immediately or they may be fed on enriched dried milk calf-feed products, with no solid foods, until they reach the required weight.

Rather lower quality veal is produced from calves that have been grass fed after weaning. The meat is darker and not of such a fine, tender quality as that of the milk-fed animals.

After slaughter veal is chilled but, unlike beef, does not need hanging to tenderise it.

CHOOSING VEAL

Veal deteriorates quickly and many butchers do not sell it in large quantities, so be sure always to buy from a reputable source.

Look for moist, pale pink, fine-textured meat. There should be very little fat, but what there is should be firm, satiny and creamy white; in the best quality veal there should be a faint smell of milk. Avoid meat with a sour smell. The bones should be very red.

While the lean surfaces should appear moist, avoid meat that looks wet or flabby. Any brownish or bluish tinges in the lean suggest an older animal, and the meat will not be as tender as it should be. This is less important for braised dishes, but for roast and sautéed veal choose the best you can find.

COOKING VEAL

Veal is a delicate meat, with a subtle flavour and texture. Because it comes from such a young animal it is generally tender, but it does require careful cooking to ensure that the quality and flavour are not lost before it reaches the table. As there is little natural fat on any veal joint, adding liquid or fat during cooking will help to keep the meat soft and tender. Cook veal slowly whenever possible, to minimise the shrinkage and loss of moisture, and always ensure that the meat is cooked through: underdone veal is indigestible.

ROASTING VEAL

Wipe the joint, trim it and tie it into a compact shape if necessary, then weigh it and calculate the cooking time according to the chart below; if the joint is stuffed, include the weight of the stuffing. Season it well and place it in the roasting tin.

TIMETABLE FOR ROASTING VEAL		
Type of joint	Roast at 230°C (450°F) mark 8 then at	180°C (350°F) mark 4
Joints on the bone	15–20 minutes	35 minutes per 450 g (1 lb)
Boned and rolled joints (weight including any stuffing)	15–20 minutes	40 minutes per 450 g (1 lb)

Place it on a rack or, for a loin or best end of neck, rest it on its bones. If you wish, cover the joint with strips of streaky bacon to add moisture and flavour. Cook the joint for the calculated time, basting well with the juices from the tin. Seal the surface of the meat quickly in a hot oven, then lower the heat and cook at a moderate temperature to retain maximum moisture. When the meat is cooked, put it on a heated serving dish and leave it in a warm place for 15 minutes to make it easier to carve. Serve well done and carved in thick slices. Veal needs a tasty stuffing and sauce to counteract the bland flavour of the meat. The traditional accompaniments are bacon rolls, veal forcemeat and thick gravy; lemon is a popular flavouring.

CARVING VEAL

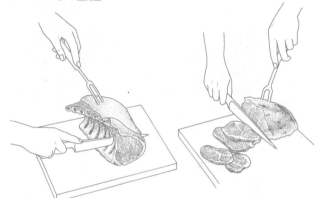

Loin of veal: Cut out the chine bone and discard it. Turn the joint so that the rib bones face you and cut down on either side of each rib keeping the knife close to the bone; one slice will contain a bone, the next will be boneless.

Boneless joints: Place the roasted joint on the carving board or dish and remove the strings. Anchor the joint with the fork and cut downwards into thick, even slices.

Fillet end of leg: Stand the joint on its cut surface, anchor it with the fork and cut down along the bone to remove the boneless half of the joint. Carve this piece into neat, even slices.

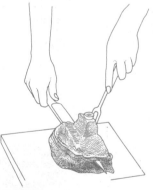

Hold the remaining half of the joint with the fork; slice across to the bone. Then cut neatly down along the bone to release a slice of meat and continue until the bone is clean.

Roast and pot roast veal

Lemon Tarragon Veal Roast

Colour index
page 62

6–8 servings

10 ml (2 level tsp) salt
10 ml (2 tsp) grated lemon
  rind
5 ml (1 level tsp) dried
  tarragon
1.4-kg (3-lb) piece
  boneless shoulder
  of veal
400 ml (³⁄₄ pint) beef stock
25 g (1 oz) plain flour

For the garnish, optional:
lemon slices

1 Stir together the salt,
  grated lemon rind and
dried tarragon until they
are well mixed.

2 Make about 2 dozen
  slits, about 6 cm (2½
in) deep, over the top and
sides of the veal joint with
the tip of a knife, being careful not to cut strings.

3 Force a little of the tarragon mixture into each
of the slits with a spoon.

4 Sprinkle any remain-
  ing tarragon mixture
generously over the veal.
Put the veal on a rack in a
roasting tin.

5 Insert a meat thermo-
  meter into the thickest
part of the veal joint.
Roast at 230°C (450°F)
mark 8 for 15 minutes,
then at 180°C (350°F)
mark 4 for 1¾ hours.

6 Put the veal on a heated
  serving dish and leave
to stand for 15 minutes to
make it easier to carve.
Remove the strings.

7 Meanwhile, make the
  gravy. Skim off any fat
from the juices in roasting
tin. Stir 350 ml (12 fl oz)
stock into the juices and
stir well to loosen any sediment. Blend the remaining
stock with the flour until
smooth and gradually stir
into the liquid in the tin.
Bring to the boil, stirring,
and cook until thickened.
Cut the meat into thick
slices and serve with the
gravy. Garnish the veal
with lemon slices,
if you wish.

Roast Loin of Veal Marsala

Colour index
page 62

6–8 servings

1.8 kg (4 lb) loin of veal
5 ml (1 level tsp) salt
1.25 ml (¼ level tsp)
  pepper
1.25 ml (¼ level tsp) dried
  thyme
bay leaf, finely crumbled
300 ml (½ pint) water

100 g (4 oz) mushrooms,
  thinly sliced
1 shallot, skinned and finely
  chopped
30 ml (2 level tbsp) plain
  flour
100 ml (4 fl oz) dry
  Marsala

1. Stand the loin on its rib bones in a roasting tin.
Mix together salt, pepper and herbs; rub into meat.
2. Insert a meat thermometer into the centre of the
thickest part of the meat, taking care that it does not
touch bone. Roast at 230°C (450°F) mark 8 for 15
minutes, then at 180°C (350°F) mark 4 for 2¼ hours
or until the meat thermometer reads 82°C (180°F).
Cut out the chine bone and discard it. Put the meat
on a heated serving dish and keep hot.
3. Spoon 30 ml (2 tbsp) fat from the roasting tin into
a small saucepan. Skim off and discard the remaining fat. Pour the water into the roasting tin and stir.
4. Add the mushrooms and shallot to the fat in the
saucepan and fry gently until tender. Blend in the
flour, then gradually stir in the liquid from the
roasting tin and the Marsala. Bring slowly to the
boil, stirring, and boil for 1 minute or until thickened. Carve the meat and serve it with the sauce.

Seasoning the veal: Rub
the salt, pepper, thyme
and crumbled bay leaf
well into the meat.

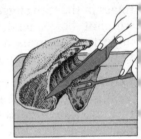

Carving the veal: When
the meat is cooked, cut
out the chine bone and
carve the meat into slices.

Country Veal Pot Roast

Colour index
page 63

6–8 servings

1.8-kg (4-lb) piece fillet
  end of leg of veal, boned
3 carrots, peeled and diced
1 onion, skinned and
  chopped
298-g (10½-oz) can
  condensed cream of
  mushroom soup
150 ml (¼ pint) water

5 ml (1 level tsp) salt
1.25 ml (¼ level tsp)
  pepper
1.25 ml (¼ level tsp) dried
  marjoram
bay leaf

1. Brown the veal well all over in its own fat, in a
flameproof casserole. Push the meat to one side, add
the carrots and onion to the fat in the casserole and
fry them for about 5 minutes or until the onions are
tender. Spoon off any excess fat.
2. Add the undiluted soup, water, salt, pepper,
marjoram and bay leaf and bring to the boil,
stirring. Reduce the heat, cover the casserole and
simmer for 2½–3 hours or until the veal is tender.
3. Put the meat on a heated serving dish, discard the
bay leaf and serve the sauce separately.

Sautéed veal

Colour index
page 62

6–8 servings

Spiced Leg of Veal

30 ml (2 tbsp) vegetable oil
1.8-kg (4-lb) piece fillet
end of leg of veal
1 onion, skinned and
chopped
5 ml (1 level tsp) curry
powder
400 ml (¾ pint) apple juice
12.5 ml (2½ level tsp) salt
1.25 ml (¼ level tsp)
pepper

15 ml (1 tbsp) mixed
pickling spice
5 small red apples
45 ml (3 level tbsp) plain
flour
75 ml (5 tbsp) water

For the garnish:
celery leaves

1. Heat the oil in a large flameproof casserole and brown the veal well all over. Remove it from the casserole and set aside.
2. Add the onion and curry powder to the fat remaining in the casserole and fry gently, stirring, for 5 minutes or until the onion is tender.
3. Stir in the apple juice, salt and pepper. Tie the pickling spice in a small square of muslin and add to the casserole.
4. Return the browned veal to the casserole and bring to the boil. Reduce the heat, cover the casserole and simmer for 2½–3 hours or until the veal is tender, turning the meat occasionally. Place the veal on a heated serving dish and keep hot. Discard the pickling spice bag.
5. Wipe and core the apples but do not peel them. Cut them into thick wedges and add them to the cooking juices in the casserole.
6. Blend the flour with the water and gradually stir it into the cooking juices. Simmer gently, stirring constantly, until the apples are tender and the sauce has thickened.
7. Spoon the apples round the meat, garnish with celery leaves and serve the sauce separately.

Colour index
page 63

6–8 servings

Tomato-paprika Veal

30 ml (2 tbsp) vegetable oil
1.8-kg (4-lb) piece fillet
end of leg of veal
100 g (4 oz) onion, skinned
and chopped
225 ml (8 fl oz) tomato
juice
30 ml (2 level tbsp) paprika

10 ml (2 level tsp) salt
1.25 ml (¼ level tsp) chilli
seasoning
30 ml (2 level tbsp)
cornflour
60 ml (4 tbsp) water
100 ml (4 fl oz) soured
cream

1. Heat the oil in a flameproof casserole and brown the veal all over; remove it from the pan.
2. Add the onion to the oil remaining in the casserole and fry gently for about 5 minutes until tender. Stir in the tomato juice, paprika, salt and chilli seasoning. Return the meat to the casserole and bring to the boil. Reduce the heat, cover the casserole and simmer for 2½–3 hours or until the meat is tender, turning it occasionally. Put the meat on a heated serving dish and keep hot.
3. Blend the cornflour with the water and gradually stir it into the cooking juices. Cook, stirring, until the sauce is thickened, then stir in the soured cream and heat through gently, stirring constantly. Do not allow the sauce to boil.
4. Carve the veal into thick slices and serve it with the sauce spooned over the top.

Colour index
page 63

8 servings

Veal and Peppers

2 cloves garlic, skinned
2 onions, skinned
3 green peppers, seeded
3 red peppers, seeded
75 ml (5 tbsp) vegetable oil
30 ml (2 tbsp) red wine
vinegar
5 ml (1 level tsp) dried basil
2.5 ml (½ level tsp) dried
oregano
salt and pepper
8 veal escalopes, cut about
0.5 cm (¼ in) thick
75 ml (5 level tbsp) plain
flour
40–75 g (1½–3 oz) butter
or margarine

1 Slice garlic and vegetables. Heat oil in a large frying pan, fry garlic until browned and discard. Add onions and peppers; cook for 2 minutes, stirring.

2 Stir in vinegar, herbs, 10 ml (2 level tsp) salt and 1.25 ml (¼ level tsp) pepper. Reduce heat, cover; cook for 10 minutes, stirring occasionally.

3 Remove the vegetables to a bowl with a slotted spoon and keep hot.

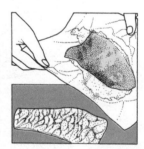

4 Meanwhile, pound the escalopes with a meat mallet to about 0.3 cm (⅛ in) thick. Season with salt and pepper.

5 Spread flour on a sheet of greaseproof paper and coat escalopes lightly with it. Melt 40 g (1½ oz) fat in the frying pan.

6 Fry the escalopes, two at a time, until lightly browned on both sides; add more fat if necessary. Transfer to a serving dish.

7 Spoon the hot cooked peppers and onions evenly over the centre of the veal escalopes and serve immediately.

Sautéed veal

Wiener Schnitzel

Colour index page 63

6 servings

6 veal escalopes, cut about
* 0.5 cm (¼ in) thick*
2 eggs
6.25 ml (1¼ level tsp) salt
2.5 ml (½ level tsp)
* coarsely ground*
* black pepper*
75 ml (5 level tbsp) plain
* flour*
175 g (6 oz) dried
* breadcrumbs*
50–100 g (2–4 oz) butter or
* margarine*

For the garnish:
lemon wedges
chopped parsley
anchovy fillets, optional
capers, optional

1 Pound the escalopes with a meat mallet until about 0.3 cm (⅛ in) thick.

2 Beat eggs, salt and pepper together in a dish. Spread flour on a sheet of greaseproof paper and the crumbs on another.

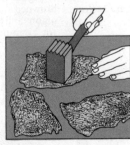

3 Coat the escalopes in flour, then dip them in egg and coat well with the breadcrumbs. Melt 50 g (2 oz) fat in a large frying pan.

4 Fry the escalopes, two at a time, for 3–4 minutes on each side until well browned, adding more fat to the pan if necessary. Transfer to a heated serving dish.

5 Serve garnished with lemon wedges and parsley, adding anchovies and capers if you wish.

VEAL A LA HOLSTEIN: Prepare the veal escalopes as above, but top each one with a *fried egg* as well as the other garnishes. Colour index page 63

Saltimbocca

Colour index page 62

4 servings

4 veal escalopes, cut about
* 0.5 cm (¼ in) thick*
50 g (2 oz) butter or
* margarine*
60 ml (4 tbsp) medium
* sherry*

100 g (4 oz) prosciutto or
* cooked ham, thinly sliced*
225 g (8 oz) Gruyère or
* Emmenthal cheese,*
* coarsely grated*

1. Pound escalopes to about 0.3 cm (⅛ in) thick.
2. Melt the fat in a frying pan; lightly brown the escalopes on both sides. Transfer them to a large ovenproof dish.
3. Add the sherry to the pan and heat, stirring, to loosen any sediment; pour over the meat. Cut the ham into thin strips and arrange over the veal. Cook in the oven at 180°C (350°F) mark 4 for 5 minutes.
4. Sprinkle with cheese and cook for a further 4–5 minutes, until the cheese has melted.

Veal Escalopes with Lemon

Colour index page 62

4 servings

4 veal escalopes, cut about
* 0.5 cm (¼ in) thick*
salt and pepper
45 ml (3 level tbsp) plain
* flour*
45–60 ml (3–4 tbsp) olive
* or vegetable oil*
25–50 g (1–2 oz) butter or
* margarine*

100 ml (4 fl oz) chicken
* stock*
75 ml (3 fl oz) dry white
* wine*
juice of 1 lemon

For the garnish:
1 lemon, sliced
parsley sprigs

1. Pound escalopes to about 0.3-cm (⅛-in) thickness. Sprinkle with 5 ml (1 level tsp) salt and 1.25 ml (¼ level tsp) pepper. Coat lightly with flour.
2. Heat oil and fat in a frying pan; lightly brown the escalopes, two at a time. Remove from the pan.
3. Reduce heat and stir in the stock, wine and 2.5 ml (½ level tsp) salt, stirring well to loosen any sediment. Return the veal to the pan, cover and simmer for 15 minutes or until the meat is tender.
4. Arrange the escalopes, overlapping, on a large heated serving dish; keep hot. Stir lemon juice into cooking juices, bring to the boil and spoon over veal. Garnish with lemon slices and parsley sprigs.

Veal Parmigiana

Colour index page 62

6 servings

100 g (4 oz) dried
* breadcrumbs*
5 ml (1 level tsp) salt
pinch pepper
6 veal escalopes, cut 0.5 cm
* (¼ in) thick*
2 eggs, beaten
75 g (3 oz) butter or
* margarine*

5 ml (1 level tsp) sugar
400 ml (¾ pint) tomato
* sauce, page 337*
225 g (8 oz) Mozzarella
* cheese, cut into 6 slices*
25 g (1 oz) Parmesan
* cheese, grated*

1. Mix the breadcrumbs with salt and pepper. Dip the escalopes in the eggs, then in the breadcrumbs.
2. Melt half the fat in a frying pan, add three escalopes and fry them for 3–4 minutes on each side until well browned. Remove them from the pan and cook the remaining escalopes in the same way.
3. Return the first three escalopes to the pan. Mix the sugar with the tomato sauce, spoon some over each escalope, top with a slice of Mozzarella and sprinkle with Parmesan cheese. Cover and cook for a further 5 minutes or until the cheese has melted.

Stewed veal

Colour index page 63
6 servings

Blanquette de Veau

1 stick celery, trimmed and
  chopped
1 carrot, peeled and
  chopped
2 whole cloves
bay leaf
700 g (1½ lb) lean veal, cut
  into 4-cm (1½-in)
  chunks
100 ml (4 fl oz) dry
  vermouth or white wine
10 ml (2 level tsp) salt
12 button onions, skinned

350 g (12 oz) button
  mushrooms
2 egg yolks
60 ml (4 tbsp) double or
  whipping cream

To serve:
350 g (12 oz) noodles,
  cooked, optional
350 g (12 oz) long grain
  rice, cooked, optional
chopped fresh dill weed

1 Put the celery, carrot, cloves and bay leaf on a square of muslin and tie into a bag with string to make a bouquet garni.

2 Put the bouquet garni, veal, vermouth or wine and salt in a large flame-proof casserole or sauce-pan and bring to the boil. Reduce the heat, cover and simmer for 1½ hours.

3 Add the button onions and mushrooms, bring back to the boil, then cover again and simmer for a further 30 minutes or until the veal is tender. Discard the bouquet garni.

4 Whisk together the egg yolks and cream, then whisk in a little of the hot cooking juices.

5 Slowly pour the egg yolk and cream mixture into the casserole, stirring rapidly to prevent lumps forming. Reduce the heat until very low.

6 Cook gently, stirring constantly, until the sauce has thickened, do not allow to boil. Serve with hot noodles or rice, garnished with dill.

Veal Paprika

Colour index page 62
6 servings

40 g (1½ oz) butter or
  margarine
900 g (2 lb) pie veal, cubed
2 large onions, skinned and
  chopped
15 ml (1 level tbsp) paprika
7.5 ml (1½ level tsp) salt
225 g (8 oz) noodles

15 ml (1 level tbsp) plain
  flour
100 ml (4 fl oz) soured
  cream

For the garnish:
chopped parsley

1. Melt the fat in a large flameproof casserole and brown the veal a few pieces at a time, adding more fat to the casserole if necessary. Remove the pieces as they brown.
2. Reduce the heat, add the onions and paprika to the fat remaining in the casserole and cook, stirring occasionally, for about 10 minutes or until the onions are tender.
3. Return the veal to the casserole; add the salt and 100 ml (4 fl oz) water and bring to the boil. Reduce the heat, cover and simmer for 1¼ hours or until the meat is tender.
4. Just before the end of the cooking time, cook the noodles in boiling salted water for 8–10 minutes until just tender and drain well. Spread the noodles on a heated serving dish and keep hot.
5. Blend the flour with 45 ml (3 tbsp) water, gradually stir it into the juices in the casserole and cook, stirring, until thickened and smooth. Stir in the soured cream and heat through; do not allow to boil. Serve the veal spooned over the noodles and garnished with parsley.

Veal Milanese

Colour index page 62
6 servings

30–60 ml (2–4 tbsp) olive
  or vegetable oil
900 g (2 lb) pie veal, cubed
1 large onion, skinned and
  chopped
1 large carrot, peeled and
  chopped
1 large stick celery,
  trimmed, washed and
  chopped
1 clove garlic, skinned and
  finely chopped
75 ml (5 tbsp) dry white
  wine

425-g (15-oz) can tomatoes
10 ml (2 level tsp) salt
1.25 ml (¼ level tsp) pepper
2.5 ml (½ level tsp) dried
  basil
bay leaf
1 chicken stock cube,
  crumbled

For the garnish:
15 ml (1 tbsp) chopped
  parsley
7.5 ml (1½ tsp) grated
  lemon rind

1. Heat 30 ml (2 tbsp) oil in a large flameproof casserole and brown the veal a few pieces at a time, removing the pieces as they brown and adding more oil if necessary.
2. Add the onion, carrot, celery and garlic to the fat remaining in the casserole and fry gently for 5 minutes until lightly browned, stirring occasionally. Stir in the wine, tomatoes with their liquid, salt, pepper, basil, bay leaf and stock cube, breaking up the tomatoes.
3. Return the meat to the pan and bring to the boil. Reduce the heat, cover and simmer for 1¼ hours or until the veal is tender, stirring occasionally.
4. Spoon the veal into a heated serving dish and remove the bay leaf. Garnish with chopped parsley and grated lemon rind.

Offal

LIVER

Ox liver: This is inclined to be tough, but the flavour is excellent in stews and casseroles.

Calf's liver: This is the most delicately flavoured and most expensive liver. It is very tender and can be grilled or fried; serve lightly cooked as it may be dry.

Lamb's liver: This has a stronger flavour than calf's liver and is suitable for grilling and frying. It also makes good casseroles and stews.

Pig's liver: This has a pronounced flavour and soft texture; use in pâtés, braise or stew.

KIDNEY

Ox kidney: This has a strong flavour and needs slow, moist cooking to make it tender. It is ideal for a steak and kidney pie, casseroles or stews.

Veal kidney: This is more delicate in flavour than ox kidney, but still needs long cooking to make it tender.

Lamb's kidney: This is small, tender and delicately flavoured, suitable for grilling and frying.

Pig's kidney: This is not as tender as lamb's kidney. It is suitable for grilling and frying and for casseroles.

HEART

Ox heart: This is large and rather tough and is usually cut up for braising, or par-boiled, stuffed and roasted.

Veal heart: This is smaller and more tender, but still needs slow cooking. Roast, braise or stew.

Lamb's heart: This is the most tender and has the finest flavour. It is usually stuffed and then roasted or braised.

SWEETBREADS

Ox sweetbreads: These have a good flavour but are inclined to be tough, so need slow, moist cooking.

Veal sweetbreads: These are more tender than ox sweetbreads, but still need slow cooking for the best results.

Lamb's sweetbreads: These are the finest, with a delicate flavour and fine texture. Fry or casserole.

TRIPE

'Blanket' tripe: This is smooth textured and comes from the first stomach of the ox. It should be thick, firm, white and clean looking. Usually sold partially cooked, it can be finished in a stew, or sliced and deep fried.

'Honeycomb' tripe: This is heavily textured and comes from the second stomach. There is little difference in quality from blanket tripe and is prepared the same way.

TONGUE

Ox tongue: This is the most commonly available and is usually sold salted for boiling, pressing and serving cold.

Veal tongue: This can be cooked as for an ox tongue and several tongues pressed together, or it may be braised.

Lamb's tongue: This is small and is usually braised.

BRAINS

Calf's brains: These are the most tender, and have the finest flavour; serve poached, with a sauce.

Lamb's brains: These may be poached or braised.

Colour index page 65

4 servings

Fried Liver and Bacon

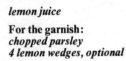

8 rashers streaky bacon, rinded
450 g (1 lb) calf's or lamb's liver, sliced about 0.5 cm (¼ in) thick
30 ml (2 level tbsp) plain flour
1.25 ml (¼ level tsp) salt

lemon juice

For the garnish:
chopped parsley
4 lemon wedges, optional

1 Fry the bacon in a frying pan in its own fat until crisp, drain on kitchen paper towel and keep hot. Pour off all but 30 ml (2 tbsp) fat.

2 Trim any membrane from the liver and coat the slices with flour.

3 Reheat the bacon fat in the pan and fry the liver for 4 minutes, turning once; it should be crisp and browned on the outside and still pink on the inside.

4 Add the salt and a squeeze of lemon juice. Arrange liver and bacon on a heated dish and sprinkle with parsley. Garnish with lemon wedges, if you wish

Liver Jardinière

Colour index page 65

4 servings

450 g (1 lb) ox liver, sliced
30 ml (2 level tbsp) plain flour
100 g (4 oz) streaky bacon, rinded

2 onions, skinned and sliced
2 large green peppers, seeded and thinly sliced
226-g (8-oz) can tomatoes
salt and pepper

1. Lightly coat the liver slices with flour.
2. Fry the bacon in its own fat until crisp; drain, crumble and set aside. Pour off all but 45 ml (3 tbsp) fat from the pan and reserve it.
3. Reheat the fat in the pan and fry the liver a few pieces at a time until lightly browned on both sides, removing the pieces as they brown.
4. Add 30 ml (2 tbsp) reserved bacon fat to the pan and lightly brown onions and green peppers. Drain juice from tomatoes and add it to pan; season.
5. Place liver on top of vegetables, cover and cook gently for 25 minutes or until liver is tender. Towards end of cooking time, add the tomatoes to heat through. Serve sprinkled with crumbled bacon.

Colour index
page 65
3–4 servings

Sweetbreads Meunière

450 g (1 lb) veal
   sweetbreads
salt
lemon juice
vinegar or dry sherry,
   optional
1.25 ml (¼ level tsp)
   ground ginger, optional

100 g (4 oz) butter or
   margarine
25 g (1 oz) dried
   breadcrumbs

For the garnish:
chopped parsley

1. Wash the sweetbreads and put them in a saucepan with hot water to cover. For every 900 ml (1½ pints) water, add 5 ml (1 level tsp) salt and 15 ml (1 tbsp) lemon juice, or vinegar or sherry. Add the ginger if you wish. Bring to the boil, reduce the heat, cover tightly and simmer for 20 minutes.
2. Drain the sweetbreads and place in cold water to cool, then remove the membrane, veins and thick connective tissue. Slice in half lengthways.
3. Melt the fat in a small saucepan. Dip sweetbreads in fat, then in breadcrumbs; reserve remaining fat.
4. Place the sweetbreads on a greased rack in the grill pan and grill for 8–10 minutes until lightly browned, turning once. Remove to a heated serving dish.
5. Reheat fat, stir in 30 ml (2 tbsp) lemon juice and pour over sweetbreads. Garnish with parsley.

Colour index
page 65
8–10 servings

Boiled Ox Tongue

1 salted ox tongue,
   weighing about 1.6 kg
   (3½ lb)
1 onion, skinned and halved
1 carrot, peeled and sliced

1 turnip, peeled and sliced
6 peppercorns
bouquet garni

1. Soak tongue in water for several hours; drain.
2. Put it in a pan with fresh cold water to cover and bring to the boil; drain again.
3. Add remaining ingredients, cover with fresh cold water and bring to the boil again. Cover and simmer for 2½–3 hours, skimming off scum.
4. Plunge tongue into cold water, then skin it and remove bones and pieces of gristle from the base.
5. Serve hot, or fit into a tongue press or cake tin, fill up with stock, weight down and leave to cool and set. Turn out and cut into slices to serve.

REMOVING SKIN, BONES AND GRISTLE FROM TONGUE

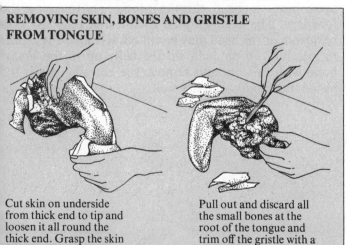

Cut skin on underside from thick end to tip and loosen it all round the thick end. Grasp the skin firmly and pull it off.

Pull out and discard all the small bones at the root of the tongue and trim off the gristle with a sharp knife.

Colour index
page 65
4 servings

Sautéed Veal Kidneys

2 veal kidneys, weighing
   about 450 g (1 lb)
40 g (1½ oz) butter,
   margarine or
   bacon fat
100 g (4 oz) mushrooms,
   sliced
2 spring onions, trimmed
   and sliced
100 ml (4 fl oz) chicken
   stock

30 ml (2 tbsp) Madeira or
   dry Marsala
1.25 ml (¼ level tsp) salt
4 slices bread, crusts
   removed

For the garnish:
chopped parsley

1. Cut the kidneys into 2.5-cm (1-in) cubes, removing the membrane and the hard white core with a sharp knife.
2. Melt the fat in a frying pan. Add the mushrooms and spring onions and cook for about 5 minutes until tender. Remove from the pan and set aside.
3. Cook the kidneys in the fat remaining in the pan for about 3 minutes until lightly browned, stirring occasionally. Add the mushroom mixture, stock, Madeira or Marsala and salt and bring to the boil. Cover and simmer for 30 minutes or until the kidneys are tender.
4. Meanwhile, toast the bread and cut each slice in half to form eight triangles. Serve the kidneys on the toast, garnished with parsley.

Colour index
page 65
4 servings

Kidneys Madeira

8 lamb's kidneys
30 ml (2 tbsp) Madeira
2 cloves garlic, skinned and
   crushed
75 g (3 oz) butter or
   margarine, softened
1 small onion, skinned and
   finely chopped
45 ml (3 tbsp) chopped
   parsley

5 ml (1 tsp) Worcestershire
   sauce
2.5 ml (½ level tsp) dry
   mustard
1.25 ml (¼ level tsp) garlic
   salt
freshly ground pepper
4 slices bread

1. Skin and core the kidneys, keeping each of them in one piece. Open them out flat and place, cut side up, on a greased rack in the grill pan. Sprinkle with the Madeira.
2. Mix the crushed garlic with the fat, onion, parsley, Worcestershire sauce, mustard, garlic salt and pepper and spoon over the kidneys.
3. Grill the kidneys for 6–10 minutes, according to taste. Toast the bread and cut each slice in half to form eight triangles. Place a kidney on each piece of toast and spoon over some of the pan drippings.

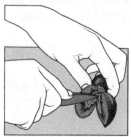

Preparing kidneys:
Remove membrane; cut out the hard core.

Adding Madeira:
Sprinkle the kidneys with Madeira before grilling.

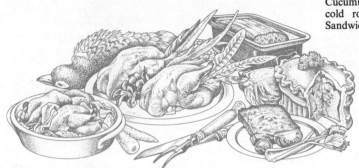

Opposite page

Clockwise from top left: Herring Salad (page 324); assorted rolls and breads; Danish Cucumber Salad (page 319); platters of sliced cold roast beef, turkey and ham; Open Sandwiches (page 458)

GAME

Game is the term used for wild birds and animals that may be hunted and killed for food or for sport, but which are protected by law during the breeding season and while rearing their young. The most common game birds are pheasant, partridge and grouse and various varieties of wild duck and goose. In this country, hare and venison are the only other animals that come within the term, although most venison is farmed these days. Rabbit and pigeon are prepared and cooked much like game, although they are not protected. Guinea fowl are cooked as game, though they are farmed as poultry.

For precise information about the availability of different types of game, check with your local supplier.

GAME BIRDS

Game birds are often sold by the pair or brace. Buy young birds with soft, even feathers, smooth, pliable legs, short spurs and a firm, plump breast.

If you are buying a bird from a poulterer, it will probably be sold oven-ready. But you may be offered a freshly killed bird which has to be hung for a time before it is plucked and drawn. This allows the flesh to develop a mature flavour and become tender: the time required varies with the bird, weather and strength of flavour you like in game meat. Hang the bird by the neck in a cool, airy place, well protected from flies; 2–3 days is usually long enough in mild weather, but up to 3 weeks may be necessary in a period of heavy frost. For most people the bird is sufficiently mature when the tail or breast feathers can be plucked out easily.

Plucking: Always work over a sheet of newspaper or an old cardboard box. Holding the bird firmly, take two or three feathers at a time and pull them sharply towards the head, against the natural direction of growth. Be particularly careful with the breast feathers or you may tear the skin. You may need pliers to get a good grip on the tiny wing feathers. Remove any down left on after the feathers have been plucked by singeing it off.

Drawing: Tiny birds such as quail, snipe and woodcock are often not drawn before cooking, but most others should have the entrails removed first. Again, work over newspaper to avoid a mess. Cut off the feet at the first leg joint. Then cut off the head; slip back the neck skin and cut off the neck close to the body, leaving the flap of skin to tuck underneath when you truss. Carefully loosen the windpipe and gullet with your fingers. Cut round the vent at the tail end with scissors or a sharp knife, taking care not to puncture the entrails. Make a hole large enough to get two or three fingers inside the body as far as you can reach and gently work the gizzard and entrails loose. Draw out all the entrails including lungs, windpipe and gullet. If you wish, reserve the heart, gizzard and liver for stock. Wash the inside of the bird thoroughly, dry and truss as for poultry (page 248).

GAME ANIMALS

Rabbits should be hung by the feet for about 24 hours, then skinned, paunched and cooked straight away. Hares should be hung for 3–7 days depending on the weather; tie a cup under the muzzle to catch the blood.

To skin a hare or rabbit, first cut the skin from vent to breast, along the belly. Then cut off the feet at the first joint and work the hind legs out of the skin. Pull the skin up towards the head, turning it inside out to release the fore legs. The head may be left on and only the eyes removed, or the head may be cut off. Remove any bluish membrane. To paunch, slit the belly up to the breast bone with scissors and remove the entrails. Wash inside thoroughly and dry well.

Plucking a pheasant: Pull feathers towards the head, against the natural growth.

Skinning a hare: Turn the skin inside out to release the legs.

Roast game

Opposite page
Selection of continental sausages

Always choose a young bird or animal, as an older one is likely to be tough. Even young game is inclined to be dry, so it is usual to bard it with fat bacon and to baste it with extra melted fat during roasting.

Roast Pheasant

Colour index page 64

servings

1 brace oven-ready
  pheasants
50 g (2 oz) streaky bacon,
  rinded
50 g (2 oz) butter
30 ml (2 level tbsp) plain
  flour
300 ml (½ pint) stock

salt and pepper
For the garnish:
100 g (4 oz) fresh white
  breadcrumbs
25 g (1 oz) butter
watercress

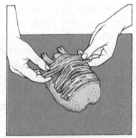

1 Truss the birds and cover the breasts with bacon; put them side by side in a roasting tin. Soften the butter and spread over legs and wings.

2 Roast at 230°C (450°F) mark 8 for 10 minutes, then at 200°C (400°F) mark 6 for 15–20 minutes, basting frequently with the butter in the tin.

3 Remove from oven, discard bacon and sprinkle the breasts with flour. Baste with butter; cook for a further 15 minutes.

4 Fry the breadcrumbs in the butter until they are golden brown, stirring them occasionally to ensure even browning.

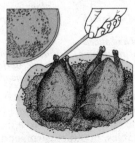

5 Put the pheasants on a heated serving dish and remove the trussing strings. Spoon the fried crumbs round the birds, garnish with watercress and keep hot.

6 Skim the fat from the cooking juices. Add the stock and stir to loosen any sediment. Boil for 2–3 minutes and season to taste. Serve the gravy with the pheasants.

ROAST GROUSE: Prepare as left, but replace the pheasants with *1 brace oven-ready grouse*. Season and put a *knob of butter* inside each bird before trussing, then place each bird on a *slice of toast* in the roasting tin. Roast at 200°C (400°F) mark 6 for 40 minutes. Serve on the toast. 2 servings

Roast Loin of Venison

Colour index page 64

8 servings

1.8-kg (4-lb) loin of venison
60 ml (4 tbsp) vegetable
  oil
45 ml (3 level tbsp) plain
  flour
salt and pepper
watercress
redcurrant jelly

For the marinade:
6 peppercorns

parsley stalks
bay leaf
3 blades mace
2 carrots, peeled and
  chopped
2 small onions, skinned and
  chopped
1 stick celery, trimmed and
  chopped
red wine

1. Put marinade flavourings and vegetables in a large bowl; add the venison and enough wine to half cover it. Marinate for 12 hours, turning occasionally.
2. Remove the meat, place it in a roasting tin and brush with oil. Cover with foil and roast at 170°C (325°F) mark 3 for 1 hour 20 minutes.
3. Remove the foil, dredge the joint with 30 ml (2 level tbsp) flour and roast for a further 20 minutes. Place on a heated serving dish and keep hot.
4. Boil the marinade until reduced by half, then strain. Skim off all but 30 ml (2 tbsp) fat from the roasting tin, stir in the remaining flour and heat gently until browned. Stir in the marinade and boil for 1–2 minutes; season and strain.
5. Garnish the venison with watercress and serve with the gravy and redcurrant jelly.

Roast Baron of Hare

Colour index page 65

4 servings

1 oven-ready baron of hare,
  back and hind legs
  in 1 piece
50 g (2 oz) streaky bacon
25 g (1 oz) dripping
hot potato crisps

For the forcemeat:
heart, liver and kidneys
  from hare
100 g (4 oz) lean veal
75 g (3 oz) lean bacon,
  rinded

1 small onion, skinned and
  finely chopped
25 g (1 oz) butter
75 g (3 oz) fresh white
  breadcrumbs
1 large mushroom, chopped
5 ml (1 tsp) chopped
  parsley
salt and pepper
pinch cayenne
pinch ground mace
1 egg, beaten

1. For the forcemeat, put heart, liver and kidneys in a pan of cold water; bring to the boil. Drain and chop.
2. Mince the veal and bacon together twice. Fry the onion in a little of the butter until soft and add to the meat. Mix in the remaining butter, forcemeat ingredients and the heart, liver and kidney.
3. Stuff the hare, sew it up, and place, breast side up, in a roasting tin. Cover with bacon and add the dripping. Cover with foil and roast at 180°C (350°F) mark 4 for 1¼–1¾ hours, basting frequently.
4. Remove foil and bacon; cook the hare for a further 15 minutes until browned. Remove the string and place the hare on a heated serving dish, surrounded by hot potato crisps.

Braised game

Braising is an ideal way of cooking older game birds and animals. They are first browned in a little hot fat then cooked in the oven with a small amount of liquid and flavouring vegetables, herbs and spices. The slow cooking makes them tender and the added liquid overcomes any tendency to dryness. If you are doubtful about the age of game, choose this method in preference to roasting.

Colour index
page 64
6 servings

Braised Partridge with Cabbage

Colour index
page 64

4 servings

50 g (2 oz) butter or bacon fat	1 carrot, peeled and roughly chopped
1 brace oven-ready partridges	1 onion, skinned and stuck with 2–3 cloves
1 firm cabbage	bouquet garni
175 g (6 oz) streaky bacon	about 600 ml (1 pint) chicken stock
salt and pepper	

1 Melt the fat in a frying pan, add the partridges and brown them well on all sides.

2 Trim, quarter and wash the cabbage. Cook in boiling salted water for 5 minutes, then drain well.

3 Line a casserole with the bacon rashers and lay half the cabbage over it. Season with salt and pepper to taste.

4 Place the partridges on top with the rest of the cabbage, the remaining vegetables, bouquet garni and more salt and pepper.

5 Bring the stock to the boil and pour enough into the casserole to cover the birds. Cover and cook at 180°C (350°F) mark 4 for 1–1½ hours.

6 Halve the partridges and chop the cabbage. Arrange the cabbage on a heated serving dish, place partridges on top and surround with bacon.

Casserole of Rabbit with Juniper Berries

105–135 ml (7–9 tbsp) vegetable oil	5 ml (1 level tsp) mixed dried herbs
1.1-kg (2½-lb) oven-ready rabbit, jointed	2 bay leaves
60 ml (4 level tbsp) plain flour	5 ml (1 level tsp) salt
	pinch pepper
30 ml (2 level tbsp) tomato paste	8 juniper berries
	1 clove garlic, skinned and crushed
300 ml (½ pint) well-flavoured brown stock	225 g (8 oz) back bacon rashers, rinded
150 ml (¼ pint) red wine	4 slices white bread

1. Heat 45 ml (3 tbsp) oil in a large frying pan and brown the rabbit joints on all sides. Put them in a large casserole.
2. Add the flour and tomato paste to the oil remaining in the pan and cook for 1–2 minutes, stirring. Stir in the stock, wine, herbs, salt and pepper. Lightly crush the juniper berries and add to the pan with the garlic. Boil for 2 minutes.
3. Pour the sauce over the rabbit, cover and cook at 170°C (325°F) mark 3 for 2–2½ hours.
4. Meanwhile, stretch the bacon rashers with the back of a knife, halve them and roll up. Thread on to skewers; grill until crisp. Remove from skewers.
5. Add the bacon rolls to the casserole and cook for a further 30 minutes.
6. Trim the crusts from the bread, then cut into triangles. Heat the remaining oil and fry the bread triangles until crisp. Arrange them around the edge of the casserole.

CASSEROLE OF PIGEON: Prepare as above, but replace the rabbit with *4 oven-ready pigeons*. After browning the pigeons, fry *50 g (2 oz) bacon*, rinded and chopped, *2 carrots*, peeled and sliced, and *1 onion*, skinned and chopped, in the oil remaining in the pan; place in casserole with pigeons. Finish as above, but replace the wine with extra *stock* and omit bacon rolls and toast triangles. 4 servings

Jugged Hare

Colour index
page 65

6 servings

25 g (1 oz) lard or dripping	about 900 ml (1½ pints) stock
50 g (2 oz) bacon, rinded and chopped	juice of ½ lemon
1 oven-ready hare, jointed, with blood	45 ml (3 level tbsp) plain flour
1 onion, skinned and stuck with 2 cloves	45 ml (3 tbsp) water
1 carrot, peeled and sliced	15 ml (1 tbsp) redcurrant jelly
1 stick celery, trimmed and sliced	150 ml (¼ pint) port or red wine, optional
bouquet garni	salt and pepper

1. Melt the lard or dripping in a large frying pan and brown the bacon pieces and the hare joints.
2. Transfer the hare and bacon to a deep casserole; add the vegetables, bouquet garni, enough stock to cover the joints and the lemon juice. Cover and cook in the oven at 170°C (325°F) mark 3 for 3–4 hours.
3. Blend the flour with the water, stir in the blood of the hare and gradually add to the casserole, stirring until thickened. Stir in jelly and wine, if used. Adjust seasoning; reheat without boiling.

Game pies and terrines

The pronounced flavour of most game makes it ideal for pie fillings and terrines. Used on its own or mixed with other meats, game makes a delicious filling either for a traditional cold raised pie, made with a thick case of hot water crust pastry, or for a lighter hot pie of braised meats with a top crust of short or flaky pastry.

Terrines and potted meats are among the oldest style of preserved meats. The meat is generally minced or puréed and seasoned before it is packed into a terrine for baking. Larger chunks of meat may be included to give the dish added texture. Sealed well with a layer of clarified butter or fat bacon a terrine will keep for several weeks in the refrigerator.

Raised Game Pie

350 g (12 oz) pork sausagemeat
100 g (4 oz) lean cooked ham, cubed
175 g (6 oz) lean beef chuck steak, cubed
cold meat from 1 cooked pheasant or 2 pigeons, boned and cut into small pieces
salt and pepper
150–300 ml (¼–½ pint) well-flavoured brown stock

For the hot water crust pastry:
350 g (12 oz) plain flour
7.5 ml (1½ level tsp) salt
75 g (3 oz) lard
150 ml (¼ pint) milk or milk and water
beaten egg to glaze

Colour index page 64
6 servings

1 Make the pastry. Mix the flour and the salt. Melt the lard in the liquid, bring to the boil and pour on to the dry ingredients. Working quickly, beat to make a soft dough. Lightly pinch together with one hand; knead until smooth. Cover with cling film and leave to rest for 20–30 minutes. Cut off three quarters of the pastry and roll out to an oval 0.5 cm (¼ in) thick.

2 Place an 18-cm (7-in) hinged pie mould on a baking sheet and lift the rolled pastry into it. Press carefully into the mould and trim to stand 0.5 cm (¼ in) above the rim.

3 Using the back of a spoon, gently press the sausagemeat over the bottom and sides of the pie crust.

4 Mix together the ham, chuck steak and game, season well and pack into the centre of the pie.

5 Roll out the remaining pastry and position over the filling. Damp the edges, pinch them together and flute. Cut a hole in the centre of the pastry lid and brush the pastry with beaten egg.

6 Bake at 220°C (425°F) mark 7 for 15–20 minutes, then at 180°C (350°F) mark 4 for 1 hour until tender when tested through hole with skewer. Remove sides of tin, brush pie with egg.

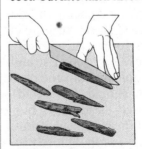

7 Bake pie for 30 minutes more, then cool slightly. Pour cold stock through the hole in the pastry lid; leave to cool completely. Top up with stock, if necessary, to fill the pastry shell.

Colour index page 65
4 servings

Poacher's Pie

4 rabbit joints, chopped
3–4 rashers bacon, rinded and chopped
2 potatoes, peeled and sliced
1 leek, trimmed, sliced and washed
salt and pepper
15 ml (1 tbsp) chopped parsley

1.25 ml (¼ level tsp) mixed dried herbs
stock or water
shortcrust pastry made with 200 g (7 oz) flour, page 343
beaten egg to glaze

1. Fill a 1.1-litre (2-pint) capacity pie dish with alternate layers of rabbit, bacon, potatoes and leek, sprinkling each layer with the seasoning and herbs.
2. Half fill the dish with stock or water.
3. Roll out the pastry 2.5 cm (1 in) larger than the pie dish, and cut off a thin strip all round. Damp edge of dish, press strip in position and damp it. Lift pastry over the pie; seal and decorate edge. Make a hole in the centre; decorate with pastry trimmings.
4. Brush with beaten egg and bake at 220°C (425°F) mark 7 for 15–20 minutes until the pastry is set, then at 170°C (325°F) mark 3 for 1¼ hours.

Colour index page 64
6 servings

Hare Terrine

1 oven-ready hare, jointed and boned
225 g (8 oz) pork sausagemeat
1 small onion, skinned and grated
2 egg yolks

1 small carrot, peeled and grated
100 g (4 oz) seedless raisins
30 ml (2 tbsp) stock
salt and pepper
225 g (8 oz) streaky bacon, rinded

1. Cut the best pieces of hare meat into neat fillets and mince the rest. Mix the minced hare with all the remaining ingredients, except the bacon.
2. Line a 450-g (1-lb) terrine with overlapping bacon rashers, leaving at least 5 cm (2 in) hanging over each side. Fill with alternate layers of the minced hare mixture and pieces of hare meat.
3. Wrap the bacon over the top and bake at 180°C (350°F) mark 4 for 1¼ hours. Pour off the excess fat; cool. Cut into thick slices to serve.

Preparing the hare: Cut the best of the hare into neat fillets; mince the rest.

Filling the terrine: Layer the hare and minced meats in the bacon-lined dish.

POULTRY

Poultry is the term used for all birds reared specially for the table. These birds are always in season and can be cooked in different ways to suit any occasion, from a festive dinner to a quick supper or cold lunch. Chicken, duck and turkey are generally available in portions as well as whole. Poultry provides high quality protein in the diet but where chicken and turkey are light, easily digestible meats, duck and goose are much richer.

Modern poultry production methods ensure a moist, tender-fleshed bird. Prompt freezing also guarantees freshness, so you can expect high quality from any of the well-known brands of frozen poultry. Traditionally reared farmyard birds are inclined to have more flavour.

Larger birds generally give the best value as the proportion of meat to bone is higher and the extra meat leftover from the first meal, particularly chicken and turkey, is excellent cold or made up in another dish. Remember that packaged poultry, frozen or fresh, is sold by oven-ready weight, but a fresh bird bought from a traditional poulterer or butcher will probably be sold at 'plucked weight' – plucked but not drawn. The butcher will draw it for you, but after weighing and pricing. You will need to allow for this in estimating the size of bird you require.

Choose a fresh bird that looks plump and well rounded. The skin should be free from blemishes and bruising. In a young chicken the tip of the breast bone will be soft and flexible; if it is hard and rigid the bird is probably too old to roast satisfactorily, although it will be suitable for steaming or boiling.

STORING FRESH POULTRY

Remove the giblets from inside the bird as soon as you get it home. Remove any tight packaging, cover the bird loosely with a bag that will allow the air to circulate and store in the refrigerator for a maximum of 3 days. The giblets should preferably be cooked straight away, as they deteriorate more quickly than the rest of the bird, but in any case they should be stored separately. Stuffings can be prepared in advance, but store them separately too and stuff the bird just before cooking.

To freeze fresh poultry, wrap it closely in freezer film or a polythene bag and seal tightly, expelling as much air as possible. Freeze the giblets separately.

FROZEN POULTRY

Frozen chicken will keep in good condition in the freezer for up to a year, but the giblets will start to deteriorate after about 2 months. Commercially frozen chicken, packed with the giblets in the body cavity, should therefore be cooked within 1–2 months of purchase. Frozen stuffed poultry can be stored for a maximum of 2 months from the time of purchase.

Turkey with the giblets removed stores well for about 6 months, duck or goose for 4–5 months.

THAWING POULTRY

Frozen poultry must be thawed completely before cooking. Once thawed, it should not be left too long before cooking, as deterioration will set in quite quickly. Experience will tell you how long it takes to thaw a bird in the normal temperature of your kitchen or refrigerator; the figures below will serve as a guide.

A 1.4-kg (3-lb) oven-ready chicken takes about 15 hours to thaw in the refrigerator or 8–10 hours to thaw at room temperature; chicken portions generally take about 6 hours in the refrigerator or 3 hours at room temperature. Because turkey takes so long to thaw, it is safest to use the refrigerator; allow 2 days for a small bird and 3–4 days for a large one. Duck and geese take 1–1½ days in the refrigerator or 12 hours at room temperature if you prefer.

Thaw the bird in its polythene bag, but open the end and remove the giblets as soon as possible. It is best to thaw frozen poultry gradually, preferably in the refrigerator, as it loses less of its natural moisture this way and will be more tender when cooked. Thawing at room temperature is next best, but if you are really desperate to hasten the thaw you can immerse the package in cold water. If the bird is almost thawed but still icy inside, hold it under cold running water for a few minutes until the limbs move freely at the joint.

STORING COOKED POULTRY

Leftover cooked poultry can be stored for use in other dishes. It will keep for 2–3 days if covered and refrigerated as soon as it is cool. It also freezes well and will keep for up to 2 months: for a roast stuffed bird, spoon out the stuffing and remember to freeze it separately, as stuffings will keep for only about 1 month.

TYPES OF POULTRY

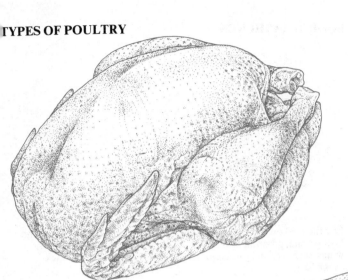

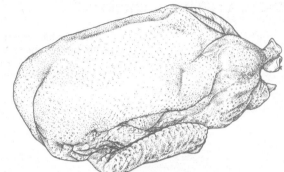

Geese weigh from 2.6–6.3 kg (6–14 lb). Allow about 350–400 g (12–14 oz) for each portion.

Turkeys range in weight from about 2.6–14 kg (6–30 lb). A 4-kg (9-lb) oven-ready turkey is equivalent to one of about 5.4 kg (12 lb) undressed weight. Allow 275–350 g (10–12 oz) for each portion.

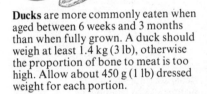

Ducks are more commonly eaten when aged between 6 weeks and 3 months than when fully grown. A duck should weigh at least 1.4 kg (3 lb), otherwise the proportion of bone to meat is too high. Allow about 450 g (1 lb) dressed weight for each portion.

Broilers are small birds weighing 1.1–1.6 kg (2½–3½ lb); one serves 3–4 people. They are suitable for all methods of cooking.

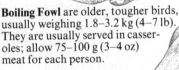

Boiling Fowl are older, tougher birds, usually weighing 1.8–3.2 kg (4–7 lb). They are usually served in casseroles; allow 75–100 g (3–4 oz) meat for each person.

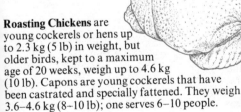

Roasting Chickens are young cockerels or hens up to 2.3 kg (5 lb) in weight, but older birds, kept to a maximum age of 20 weeks, weigh up to 4.6 kg (10 lb). Capons are young cockerels that have been castrated and specially fattened. They weigh 3.6–4.6 kg (8–10 lb); one serves 6–10 people.

Spring Chickens are small broilers weighing 900 g– 1.1 kg (2–2½ lb), 6–8 weeks old; one serves 2–3 people.

Poussins are baby chickens, weighing 350–450 g (12 oz–1 lb); one serves 1–2 people. A double poussin weighs 550–900 g (1¼–2 lb) and will serve 3–4.

OTHER WAYS OF BUYING POULTRY

When a whole bird is too large for your requirements, buy poultry portions. There is a wide selection on the market, ranging from boned and rolled joints ready for roasting and easy slicing, through halved and quartered birds, down to individual serving portions. Boneless chicken breast is a luxury cut of white meat, delicious for sautés and grills. It is often known as a 'suprême'. Cold cooked chicken suprêmes are excellent with a salad, and are ideal for packed meals.

The breast and wing are either sold separately or as one joint.

A leg portion includes drumstick and thigh, or it may be divided and sold as two separate joints.

Turkey breast is often sold boned and rolled ready for roasting. Turkey portions are available either with or without the bones.

CUTTING UP A TURKEY OR CHICKEN

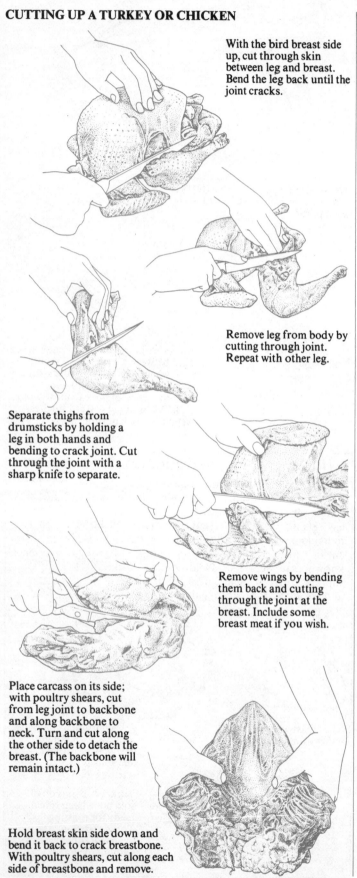

With the bird breast side up, cut through skin between leg and breast. Bend the leg back until the joint cracks.

Remove leg from body by cutting through joint. Repeat with other leg.

Separate thighs from drumsticks by holding a leg in both hands and bending to crack joint. Cut through the joint with a sharp knife to separate.

Remove wings by bending them back and cutting through the joint at the breast. Include some breast meat if you wish.

Place carcass on its side; with poultry shears, cut from leg joint to backbone and along backbone to neck. Turn and cut along the other side to detach the breast. (The backbone will remain intact.)

Hold breast skin side down and bend it back to crack breastbone. With poultry shears, cut along each side of breastbone and remove.

BONING A CHICKEN

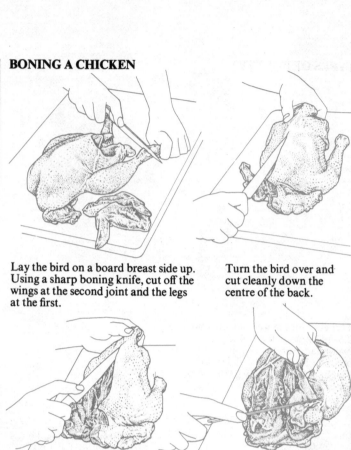

Lay the bird on a board breast side up. Using a sharp boning knife, cut off the wings at the second joint and the legs at the first.

Turn the bird over and cut cleanly down the centre of the back.

Keeping the knife close to the carcass and slightly flattened to avoid damaging the flesh, carefully work the flesh off the rib cage until the wing joints are exposed.

Take hold of the severed end of one wing joint. Scrape the knife over the bone backwards and forwards, working the flesh from the bone. When wing and socket are exposed, sever ligaments and draw out bone. Repeat for second wing.

Continue working the flesh off the carcass until the leg joint is exposed. Sever the ligaments attaching the bone to the body flesh and break the leg joint by twisting it firmly (use a cloth to get a good grip).

Hold the end of the leg firmly and scrape away all flesh, working from inside of leg. Scrape thigh bone clean, then drumstick; pull bone free. Repeat with other leg.

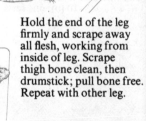

Continue working the flesh cleanly off the body, being careful not to break the skin and keeping the two halves of the breast attached to each other.

HALVING A CHICKEN

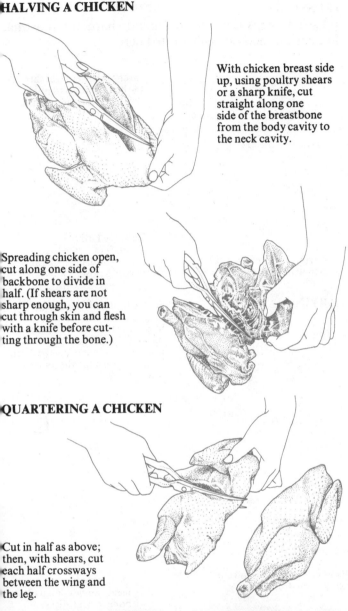

With chicken breast side up, using poultry shears or a sharp knife, cut straight along one side of the breastbone from the body cavity to the neck cavity.

Spreading chicken open, cut along one side of backbone to divide in half. (If shears are not sharp enough, you can cut through skin and flesh with a knife before cutting through the bone.)

QUARTERING A CHICKEN

Cut in half as above; then, with shears, cut each half crossways between the wing and the leg.

BONING A CHICKEN OR TURKEY BREAST

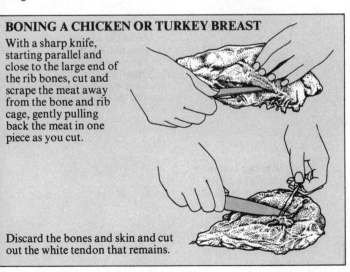

With a sharp knife, starting parallel and close to the large end of the rib bones, cut and scrape the meat away from the bone and rib cage, gently pulling back the meat in one piece as you cut.

Discard the bones and skin and cut out the white tendon that remains.

QUARTERING A DUCK

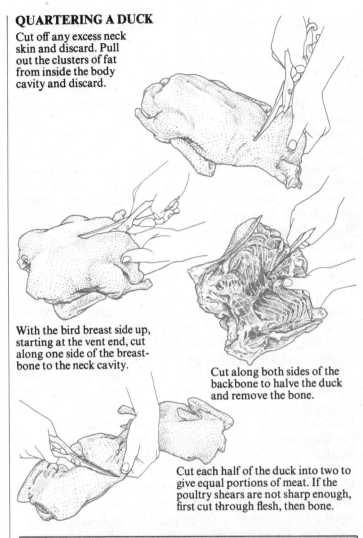

Cut off any excess neck skin and discard. Pull out the clusters of fat from inside the body cavity and discard.

With the bird breast side up, starting at the vent end, cut along one side of the breastbone to the neck cavity.

Cut along both sides of the backbone to halve the duck and remove the bone.

Cut each half of the duck into two to give equal portions of meat. If the poultry shears are not sharp enough, first cut through flesh, then bone.

TESTING WHETHER POULTRY IS COOKED

Use either of the methods shown below to test that poultry is thoroughly cooked.

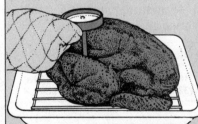

Insert a meat thermometer into the thickest part of the meat between the breast and thigh, making sure that the tip of the thermometer does not touch the bone. It should read 88°C (190°F).

Insert a skewer into the thickest part of the meat between thigh and breast. The bird is cooked when the juices are clear not pink.

Roast chicken and turkey

Roast poultry is the traditional dinner for Christmas and many other celebrations. It is also popular as an alternative to a roast joint for Sunday lunch. The presentation may be as elaborate or simple as you like, but the technique remains the same. The meat is also good served cold, either carved or dressed more formally with a chaudfroid sauce or aspic.

Always wash the inside of the bird and dry it thoroughly with kitchen paper towel before stuffing and trussing. A large chicken is usually stuffed at the neck end; with a small one it is often easier to stuff the body cavity. A turkey often has a different flavoured stuffing at each end. If the body cavity is not stuffed, add extra flavour by putting an onion, a thick wedge of lemon or a knob of butter inside.

Brush the skin with melted butter or oil and season with salt and pepper. A few strips of streaky bacon laid over the breast will help to prevent it becoming too dry, or a piece of greaseproof paper laid over the breast towards the end of the cooking time will stop over-browning. Roast chicken at 200°C (400°F) mark 6 for 20 minutes per 450 g (1 lb), plus 20 minutes. For a turkey, either roast slowly at 170°C (325°F) mark 3 or roast quickly at 230°C (450°F) mark 8, calculating the time according to the chart below. If you prefer to roast in foil, cook at the higher temperature allowing the same cooking time, but open the foil for the last 15–20 minutes to allow the skin to brown. Do not use foil when using the slow cooking method, but if the bird fills the oven it is wise to protect the legs and breast with foil as they will brown too quickly and may burn. The flat-breasted birds often produced today are best started off breast side down for even cooking; turn after about 1 hour.

To roast an older boiling fowl, steam or boil it for about 2 hours on the day ahead to make it tender. Allow the chicken to become completely cold before you stuff it. Then roast it for 30–45 minutes at 200°C (400°F) mark 6 to make the skin crisp and well browned.

ROASTING TIMETABLE FOR TURKEY		
Oven-ready weight (including stuffing if used)	Hours at 170°C (325°F) mark 3	Hours at 230°C (450°F) mark 8
2.7–3.6 kg (6–8 lb)	3–3½	2¼–2½
3.6–4.5 kg (8–10 lb)	3½–3¾	2½–2¾
4.5–5.4 kg (10–12 lb)	3¾–4	2¾
5.4–6.3 kg (12–14 lb)	4–4¼	3
6.3–7.3 kg (14–16 lb)	4¼–4½	3–3¼
7.3–8.2 kg (16–18 lb)	4½–4¾	3¼–3½
8.2–9 kg (18–20 lb)	4¾–5	3½–3¾
9–10 kg (20–22 lb)	5–5¼	3¾–4

TRUSSING

Trussing keeps the bird in a good shape for roasting. The easiest method is illustrated here.

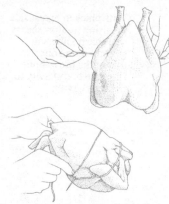

Insert a skewer right through the body of the bird just below the thigh bone, and turn the bird over on its breast.

Pass string under ends of skewer, catch in wing tips; cross it over.

Turn the bird over and tie the ends of string together round the drumsticks and parson's nose.

CARVING

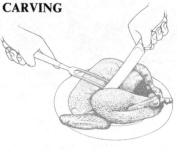

Set the bird with the breast diagonally towards you. Steadying the bird with the flat of the knife, prise the leg outwards with the fork, exposing the thigh joint. Cut through the joint to sever the leg.

Bend back the joint and cut thigh from drumstick.

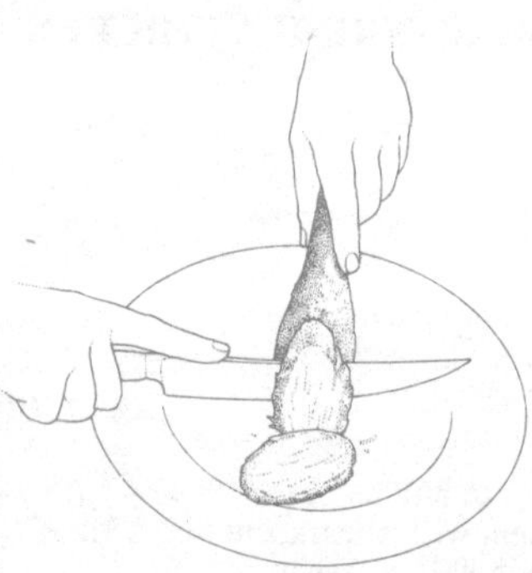

On a large bird the thigh meat can be carved off the bone in neat slices.

Hold the wing with the fork and cut through the outer layer of the breast into the joint. Ease wing from body and cut through gristle.

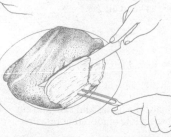

Cut the breast in thin slices parallel with the breastbone. Repeat with the other side of the bird. Stuffing can be sliced from the front of the breast or scooped with a spoon from the vent.

Roast Stuffed Turkey

*4.5–5.5-kg (10–12-lb)
oven-ready turkey
chestnut stuffing, page 253
450 g (1 lb) sausagemeat,
or sausage and apple
stuffing, page 253; for a
larger bird increase the
quantity of stuffing in
proportion
melted dripping or butter
salt and pepper*

Colour index page 39

18–20 servings

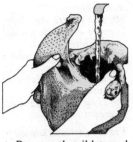

1 Remove the giblets and wash the inside of the bird with cold running water. Drain well and dry with kitchen paper towel.

2 Stuff the neck end with chestnut stuffing. Do not pack it too tightly. Cover the stuffing smoothly with the neck skin.

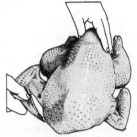

3 With the bird breast side up, fold the wing tips neatly under the body, catching in the neck skin.

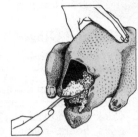

4 Spoon the sausage-meat or sausage and apple stuffing into the body cavity.

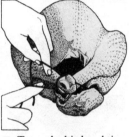

5 Truss the bird and tie the legs together. Make the body as plump and even in shape as possible.

6 Put the bird breast side up on a rack in a roasting tin. Brush with the melted fat and season well.

7 Insert a meat thermo-meter between breast and thigh. The tip should not touch bone.

8 Cover the bird with foil; roast at 230°C (450°F) mark 8 for calculated cooking time (opposite).

9 Remove foil and baste 30 minutes before end of cooking time. Thermometer should read 88°C (190°F).

Rich Gravy

*turkey giblets (gizzard,
heart and neck)
1 small onion
1 small carrot, peeled
1 stick celery, washed and
cut into chunks
bacon rinds
salt and pepper
1.1 litres (2 pints) water
15 ml (1 level tbsp) plain
flour
turkey liver
butter*

Colour index page 39

Makes 600 ml (1 pint)

1 Put the giblets in a saucepan with the vege-tables, a few bacon rinds, seasoning and water. Bring to the boil, cover and sim-mer for about 2 hours.

2 Strain the giblet stock into a basin. Discard the vegetables and bacon rinds and, if you wish, set aside the cooked giblets for use in another dish.

3 When cooked, remove turkey to a warm plate and pour off most of the fat from the tin, leaving behind sediment and about 30 ml (2 tbsp) fat.

4 Blend the flour into the fat in the roasting tin. Cook until it turns brown, stirring continuously and scraping any sediment from the bottom of the tin.

5 Slowly stir in 600 ml (1 pint) giblet stock. Bring to the boil, stirring.

6 Meanwhile, sauté the liver in a knob of butter until just cooked.

7 Remove the liver from the pan, drain well and chop it into small pieces.

8 Add chopped liver to gravy and simmer for 2–3 minutes to heat.

9 Check the seasoning. Pour into gravy boat and keep hot until needed.

Roast chicken and turkey

Colour index page 39
12 servings

Rolled and Glazed Turkey Roast

1.8 kg (4 lb) boned and rolled turkey meat   *melted butter, optional glaze, below*

1. Put the turkey in a roasting tin and insert a meat thermometer into the centre of it.
2. Cook in the oven at 170°C (325°F) mark 3 for 2½–2¾ hours, basting or brushing occasionally with the roasting juices or melted butter. When the turkey is cooked the thermometer should register 88°C (190°F).
3. While the turkey is roasting prepare one of the glazes below. Brush or spoon the warm glaze over the meat several times during the last 20 minutes of the cooking time.

GLAZES

APPLE: Mix together *275–350 g (10–12 oz) apple purée* and *2.5 ml (½ level tsp) salt* in a small saucepan. Heat gently, stirring, until warm.

TANGY TOMATO: Put *150 ml (¼ pint) tomato purée* or ketchup in a small saucepan with *2.5 ml (½ level tsp) meat extract* or vegetable extract and the *grated rind and juice of ½ lemon.* Heat the mixture gently, stirring frequently, until the mixture is well blended.

REDCURRANT: Put *225 ml (8 fl oz) redcurrant jelly* in a small saucepan with *25 g (1 oz) butter, 10 ml (2 level tsp) ground cinnamon* and *5 ml (1 level tsp) ground cloves.* Stir over gentle heat until the jelly has melted and the mixture is well blended.

APRICOT: Soak *75 g (3 oz) dried apricots* overnight. Drain, then chop and put into a small saucepan with *275–350 g (10–12 oz) apricot jam.* Heat gently, stirring frequently until well blended.

SULTANA: Pour *100 ml (4 fl oz) boiling water* over *40 g (1½ oz) sultanas* and leave on one side for 15–20 minutes or until the sultanas are plump. Drain and put them in a small saucepan with *150–175 g (5–6 oz) redcurrant jelly.* Heat the mixture gently, stirring frequently, until the jelly has melted and the mixture is well blended.

Chicken Galantine

1.8-kg (4-lb) oven-ready chicken, boned
225 g (8 oz) pork sausagemeat
225 g (8 oz) lean pork, minced
2 shallots, skinned and chopped
salt and pepper
60 ml (4 tbsp) Madeira
75 g (3 oz) cooked ham, sliced
75 g (3 oz) cooked tongue, sliced
50 g (2 oz) bacon fat, sliced
15 g (½ oz) pistachio nuts, blanched
6 black olives, stoned

melted butter
600 ml (1 pint) aspic jelly, made with aspic powder and chicken stock
5 ml (1 level tsp) powdered gelatine
400 ml (¾ pint) béchamel sauce, page 461
30–45 ml (2–3 tbsp) double cream

For the garnish: 2 small tomatoes, 1 spring onion, few large black olives, stoned, 1 carrot, peeled

Colour index page 40
6–8 servings

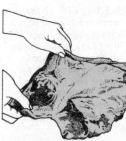

1 Lay the boned chicken skin side down on a board and turn the legs and wings inside out. In a bowl, work together the next four ingredients until evenly blended.

2 Moisten with Madeira and spread half the mixture over the chicken.

3 Cut ham, tongue and bacon fat into long strips 0.5 cm (¼ in) wide. Lay nuts, olives and meat strips over mixture.

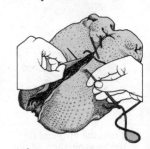

4 Cover with the remaining mixture, draw the sides of the chicken together and sew up, using a trussing needle and string.

5 Place the galantine in a roasting tin, brush with melted butter, season and roast at 190°C (375°F) mark 5 for 1¾ hours. Remove the outside skin.

6 Put galantine on a plate; cover with another plate and weight down. When completely cold remove string. Prepare the aspic jelly.

7 Dissolve the gelatine in 100 ml (4 fl oz) prepared aspic and stir into the béchamel sauce with the cream. Strain and beat the sauce well.

8 Put the galantine on a rack in a roasting tin. Coat with the cream sauce and chill well.

9 Garnish with sliced vegetables; spoon over aspic to glaze. Chill chicken and remaining aspic.

10 Lift the galantine on to a serving plate. Chop the aspic jelly and arrange around galantine.

Boned and Stuffed Turkey

Colour index
page 39

25–30
servings

4.5-kg (10-lb) oven-ready
turkey, boned,
about 2.7 kg (6 lb)
meat
apricot and ginger stuffing,
page 253, in treble
quantities
100 g (4 oz) softened
butter
salt and pepper

For the garnish, optional:
watercress sprigs, washed
and trimmed

1 Lay the boned turkey skin side down on a board or work surface, and pound to even thickness with a meat mallet or a rolling pin.

2 Cover the meat with the apricot and ginger stuffing and carefully roll it up. Do not roll up too tightly or the stuffing will burst out during cooking.

3 Tie the roll at intervals with string, or sew up using a trussing needle and fine string or thread.

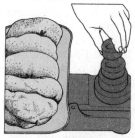

4 Weigh the stuffed roll and calculate the cooking time, allowing 35–40 minutes for every 450 g (1lb) prepared weight.

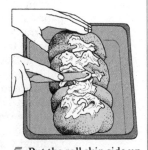

5 Put the roll skin side up in a roasting tin and spread the softened butter over it with a knife.

6 Cover with foil and roast at 170°C (325°F) mark 3, until 30 minutes before cooking time ends.

7 Remove the foil and baste the turkey well with the juices in the tin. Increase the oven temperature to 220°C (425°F) mark 7. Pour off the excess fat and return the tin to the oven to roast for a further 30 minutes. To serve, place the boned and stuffed turkey roll on a serving plate and remove the string. Garnish with sprigs of watercress if you wish and serve hot or cold, cut into neat slices.

Roast Chicken

Colour index
page 43

4 servings

1.6–1.8-kg (3½–4-lb)
oven-ready chicken
herb stuffing, page 253
1 onion, skinned, optional
1 thick lemon wedge,
optional

knob of butter, optional
oil or melted butter
salt and pepper
streaky bacon, optional

1. If the bird is frozen, thaw and remove giblets. Wash the inside of the bird and stuff it at the neck end before tucking under the neck skin. To add flavour you can put an onion, lemon wedge or knob of butter in the body of the chicken.

2. Brush the bird with oil or melted butter, sprinkle it with salt and pepper and put it in a shallow roasting tin. Streaky bacon laid over the breast will prevent it becoming too dry. Cook in the oven at 200°C (400°F) mark 6, basting from time to time and allowing 20 minutes per 450 g (1 lb), plus 20 minutes. Put a piece of greaseproof paper over the breast if the skin becomes too brown. Alternatively, wrap the chicken in foil before roasting; allow the same cooking time but open the foil for the final 15–20 minutes to allow the chicken to brown.

3. Serve with bacon rolls, forcemeat balls, small sausages, bread sauce (page 276) and thin gravy.

French Roast Capon

Colour index
page 41

8 servings

75 g (3 oz) butter
salt and pepper
5–6 sprigs tarragon or
parsley
3.6-kg (8-lb)
oven-ready capon

melted butter
2 rashers bacon, rinded
300 ml (½ pint) chicken
stock

1. Cream the butter with a good sprinkling of salt and pepper and put inside the capon with the herbs. Truss the capon firmly.

2. Brush the breast with melted butter and cover with the rashers of bacon. Put the capon in a roasting tin and add the stock.

3. Bake at 190°C (375°F) mark 5, basting with stock every 15 minutes, for 3 hours. Remove bacon during the last 15 minutes of cooking to brown the breast.

Barbecued Roast Chicken

Colour index
page 43

4 servings

1.7–1.8-kg (3¾–4-lb)
oven-ready chicken
25 g (1 oz) butter, melted

For the sauce:
75 ml (5 tbsp) red wine
60 ml (4 tbsp) chicken
stock
5 ml (1 tsp) soy sauce
30 ml (2 tbsp) red wine
vinegar

5 ml (1 tsp) Worcestershire
sauce
5 ml (1 level tsp) tomato
paste
5 ml (1 level tsp) French
mustard
15 ml (1 level tbsp) sugar

1. Truss the chicken, put it in a roasting tin and brush with melted butter. Cook in the oven at 200°C (400°F) mark 6 for 1 hour.

2. Meanwhile, mix the sauce ingredients in a saucepan and boil until reduced by half.

3. Brush the chicken with the sauce and cook for a further 1 hour, basting every 15 minutes. Cover with foil if it starts to over-brown.

Baked chicken

Poultry can be baked whole or in portions. To vary the flavour marinate the meat first, using the recipes on page 262, or baste with a spicy sauce during cooking. Coating portions with egg and breadcrumbs can add variety of texture and stuffings help extend small portions to make a more satisfying meal.

Baked Chicken

Colour index
page 44

6 servings

6 chicken portions, skinned
25 g (1 oz) seasoned plain flour
1 egg, beaten, optional

100 g (4 oz) fresh white breadcrumbs, optional
50–75 g (2–3 oz) butter or bacon fat

1 Coat the chicken portions with seasoned flour, then dip in the beaten egg and coat with breadcrumbs if you wish.

2 Melt the butter or bacon fat in a roasting tin and put in the joints in a single layer. Baste with the hot fat.

3 Bake at 200°C (400°F) mark 6, turning once and basting occasionally.

4 Cook for about 45 minutes, until tender when tested with a fork.

Chicken Baked in Wine

Colour index
page 46

4 servings

2 900-g (2-lb) oven-ready chickens, halved

For the marinade:
175 ml (6 fl oz) dry white wine
30 ml (2 tbsp) vegetable oil

▸ 30 ml (2 tbsp) chopped parsley
30 ml (2 tbsp) chopped spring onions
10 ml (2 level tsp) salt

1. Prick the chicken skin all over with a fork.
2. Mix marinade ingredients. Add chicken and coat well. Cover and leave to marinate for 4 hours.
3. Put chickens flesh side down in an ovenproof dish and pour marinade over. Bake at 190°C (375°F) mark 5 for 1 hour or until tender, basting occasionally and turning chickens once.
4. Pour the cooking juices into a bowl, skim off the fat and discard. Spoon remaining liquid over the baked chicken and serve immediately.

Nut-Stuffed Chicken Breasts

Colour index
page 41

6 servings

12 chicken breasts, boned and skinned
100 g (4 oz) butter or margarine
5 ml (1 level tsp) paprika
7.5 ml (1½ level tsp) salt
30 ml (2 level tbsp) plain flour
1 chicken stock cube, crumbled
300 ml (½ pint) milk

For the stuffing:
25 g (1 oz) butter
½ clove garlic, skinned and crushed
½ small onion, skinned and chopped

75 ml (5 tbsp) salted peanuts, finely chopped
60 ml (4 tbsp) finely chopped parsley
2.5 ml (½ level tsp) salt
pepper

For the garnish:
parsley
fine strips of canned pimento, optional

1. Make the stuffing. Melt the butter in a small saucepan and sauté the garlic and onion together for 5 minutes until soft but not coloured. Stir in the remaining ingredients for the stuffing until they are well blended.
2. Using a meat mallet or rolling pin, beat out the chicken breasts to about 0.5-cm (¼-in) thickness.
3. Working with two chicken breasts at a time, overlap the pieces by about 2.5 cm (1 in). Sprinkle a generous spoonful of the peanut stuffing to within 1 cm (½ in) of the edges. Turn in the two long edges and roll up the breasts in the opposite direction. Secure the rolls with wooden cocktail sticks, or tie them with pieces of fine string.
4. Repeat with the remaining chicken breasts and nut stuffing to make six rolls in all.
5. Melt the butter in a roasting tin and stir in the paprika and 5 ml (1 level tsp) salt until well mixed.
6. Arrange the stuffed chicken breasts seam side down in the tin and brush with the butter mixture. Bake at 200°C (400°F) mark 6 for 40 minutes or until tender, basting occasionally with the butter mixture and juices in the tin.
7. Spoon 45 ml (3 tbsp) of the fat from the tin into a small saucepan. Heat gently and stir in the flour, crumbled stock cube and the remaining salt. Gradually stir in the milk and cook, stirring constantly, until thickened.
8. To serve, remove the cocktail sticks and arrange the chicken breasts on a warmed serving dish. Spoon over the gravy and garnish with parsley and strips of pimento, if you wish.

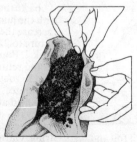 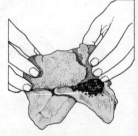

Enclosing the stuffing: Fold the long sides of the chicken over the stuffing.

Forming the rolls: Roll up the chicken breasts to make a neat parcel.

Stuffings

Stuffing poultry helps to keep the meat moist during cooking and adds extra flavour. Chicken is usually stuffed at the neck end (although it may be more convenient to stuff the vent end of a very small bird), while both duck and goose are stuffed at the vent end. Turkey traditionally has a different stuffing at each end; for example, chestnut stuffing in the neck and sausage-meat stuffing in the body. Do not pack the neck of a bird too tightly as the stuffing will swell during cooking.

Do not mix stuffing ingredients with the liquid and egg or stuff the bird until you are ready to start cooking.

For a 1.8-kg (4-lb) chicken

Herb Stuffing

50 g (2 oz) bacon, rinded and chopped
45 ml (3 tbsp) shredded suet
100 g (4 oz) fresh white breadcrumbs
15 ml (1 tbsp) chopped parsley

10 ml (2 level tsp) dried mixed herbs or 30 ml (2 tbsp) chopped fresh mixed herbs
grated rind of ½ lemon
1 small (size 6) egg, beaten
salt and pepper
milk or stock to bind

1. Fry the bacon in its own fat without browning and drain it on kitchen paper towel.
2. Mix it with the remaining ingredients, moistening with enough milk or stock to bind the mixture. Double the given quantities for a turkey.

For a 4.5-kg (10-lb) turkey

Chestnut Stuffing

50 g (2 oz) bacon, rinded and chopped
225 g (8 oz) unsweetened chestnut purée
100 g (4 oz) fresh white breadcrumbs

5 ml (1 tsp) chopped parsley
25 g (1 oz) butter, melted
grated rind of 1 lemon
salt and pepper
1 egg, beaten

1. Fry the bacon gently in its own fat until crisp and drain well on kitchen paper towels.
2. Combine with the remaining ingredients.

For a 4.5-kg (10-lb) turkey

Sausage and Apple Stuffing

450 g (1 lb) sausagemeat
3 cooking apples, peeled, cored and chopped
1 onion, skinned and chopped
2 sticks celery, chopped

225 g (8 oz) fresh white breadcrumbs
2 eggs, beaten
7.5 ml (1½ level tsp) salt
pinch pepper

1. Brown the sausagemeat and remove from the pan. Pour off all but 60 ml (4 tbsp) fat.
2. Add the apples, onion and celery and cook until tender. Stir in sausagemeat and remaining ingredients.

For a 1.8-kg (4-lb) duck

Sage and Onion Stuffing

2 large onions, skinned and chopped
25 g (1 oz) butter
salt and pepper

100 g (4 oz) fresh white breadcrumbs
10 ml (2 level tsp) dried sage

1. Put the onions in a pan and cover with cold water. Bring to the boil and cook for about 10 minutes.
2. Drain and mix with the other ingredients. Double the given quantities for a goose.

For a 1.8-kg (4-lb) duck

Rice Stuffing

1 chicken liver
1 small onion, skinned
50 g (2 oz) almonds, blanched
30 ml (2 tbsp) chopped parsley

50 g (2 oz) raisins
50 g (2 oz) long grain rice, cooked
salt and pepper
25 g (1 oz) butter
1 egg, beaten, optional

1. Chop the chicken liver, onion and almonds.
2. Combine all the dry ingredients and season well. Melt the butter and use it to bind the mixture. Add a beaten egg if you wish.

For a 4.5–5.4-kg (10–12-lb) turkey

Corn and Bacon Stuffing

100 g (4 oz) streaky bacon rashers, rinded
1 small onion, skinned
½ small green pepper, seeded
50 g (2 oz) butter
326-g (11½-oz) can sweetcorn kernels

100 g (4 oz) fresh white breadcrumbs
30 ml (2 tbsp) chopped parsley
salt and pepper
1 small (size 6) egg, beaten

1. Chop the bacon and onion and finely chop the green pepper.
2. Melt the butter and sauté the bacon and onion together for a few minutes.
3. Drain the sweetcorn and add it to the pan with the green peppers. Cook for a few more minutes.
4. Remove from the heat. Stir in the breadcrumbs, parsley and seasoning and mix well. Add enough of the beaten egg to bind the mixture.

For a 1.8-kg (4-lb) duck

Apricot and Ginger Stuffing

225 g (8 oz) canned apricot halves, drained, or 100 g (4 oz) dried apricots, soaked overnight in water
4 pieces stem ginger

100 g (4 oz) fresh white breadcrumbs
50 g (2 oz) shredded suet
1 large (size 2) egg, beaten
salt and pepper

1. Chop the apricots and stem ginger finely.
2. Mix the breadcrumbs with the suet and add the ginger and apricots.
3. Bind with the egg and season to taste. Double the given quantities for a goose.

For a 4–4.5-kg (9–10-lb) turkey

Nut Stuffing

50 g (2 oz) shelled walnuts
45 ml (3 tbsp) shelled cashew nuts
6 Brazil nuts, shelled
50 g (2 oz) butter
2 small onions, skinned and finely chopped
100 g (4 oz) mushrooms, finely chopped

pinch dried mixed herbs
15 ml (1 tbsp) chopped parsley
175 g (6 oz) fresh white breadcrumbs
1 large (size 2) egg, beaten
giblet stock, optional
salt and pepper

1. Chop the nuts finely.
2. Melt the butter in a saucepan and sauté the onion for 5 minutes, add the mushrooms and sauté together for a further 5 minutes.
3. Mix the chopped nuts, mixed herbs, parsley and breadcrumbs with the mushroom mixture. Bind with the beaten egg and moisten with a little stock if necessary. Season to taste.

Braised and stewed chicken and turkey

Braising and stewing are methods of cooking slowly in liquid, suitable for small whole birds and for poultry joints. These methods are especially good for tougher boiling fowl as the flavour of these is often exceptionally good and the slow cooking tenderises the meat. The meat is usually browned first in a little hot fat, then flavouring vegetables and liquid are added and cooking continues in a tightly covered pot. For braising, very little liquid is used and the meat cooks in the heat of the steam; for stewing, the meat is totally immersed in the simmering liquid. Cooking may be carried out on top of the stove or in the oven.

PRESSURE COOKING METHOD

Cooking can be speeded by the use of a pressure cooker. Brown the poultry first in a little hot fat in the pressure cooker (do not use the trivet). Then add the vegetables and liquid, browning the vegetables in the cooker first, if you wish, and filling the pressure cooker no more than two-thirds full. Bring the cooker to high (15 lb) pressure and cook for 15–20 minutes. Remove the cooker from the heat and reduce the pressure to normal before uncovering. If the poultry is not fully cooked return the cooker to pressure for a few minutes longer. Thicken the cooking liquid with beurre manié (page 493) for a sauce.

Arroz con Pollo

Colour index
page 44

4 servings

1.4-kg (3-lb) oven-ready chicken
salt and pepper
30 ml (2 level tbsp) plain flour
60 ml (4 tbsp) vegetable oil
1 onion, skinned and chopped
396-g (14-oz) can tomatoes
170-g (6-oz) can pimentos, drained and sliced
2 chicken stock cubes, crumbled

8 stuffed olives
175 g (6 oz) long grain rice
225 g (8 oz) pork chipolata sausages, cut into 1-cm (½-in) slices
100 g (4 oz) frozen peas

For the garnish, optional:
watercress sprigs, washed and trimmed

1 Cut the chicken into 8 pieces, season and coat with flour. Heat the oil in a pan, brown chicken on all sides and remove. Add onion and fry until golden brown.

2 Put the chicken back in the pan. Drain the tomatoes and make the juice up to 400 ml (¾ pint) with water. Add to the pan with tomatoes and next five ingredients. Season.

3 Cover the pan tightly and simmer gently for 45 minutes, forking gently through the rice occasionally to prevent it sticking and to mix with other ingredients.

4 Add the peas to the pan, cover again and simmer for a further 30 minutes until the chicken is tender. Before serving, garnish with the sprigs of watercress, if you wish.

Chicken Paprika with Spaetzles

Colour index
page 41

4 servings

1.4-kg (3-lb) oven-ready chicken, jointed
salt and pepper
50 g (2 oz) plain flour
50 g (2 oz) dripping
450 g (1 lb) onions, skinned and sliced
1 green pepper, seeded and sliced
15 ml (1 level tbsp) paprika
1 clove garlic, skinned and crushed
396-g (14-oz) can tomatoes

300 ml (½ pint) chicken stock
bay leaf
150 ml (¼ pint) soured cream

For the spaetzles:
2.5 ml (½ level tsp) salt
225 g (8 oz) plain flour
100 ml (4 fl oz) water
3 eggs, beaten

1. Season the chicken joints and toss in the flour. Melt the dripping in a frying pan and fry two joints at a time until golden brown. Transfer the joints to a casserole large enough to take them in a single layer.
2. Add the onions and green pepper and cook until soft. Stir in the paprika, garlic and any remaining flour. Cook gently, stirring, for a few minutes. Add the tomatoes with their juice, the stock and bay leaf. Season and bring to the boil. Pour over chicken. Cover tightly and cook at 170°C (325°F) mark 3 for about 1½ hours. Remove and discard bay leaf.
3. Make the spaetzles. Bring a large pan of salted water to the boil. Beat together the salt, flour, water and eggs to make a smooth batter. Holding a colander over the saucepan, press the batter through the holes into the water. Boil for 5 minutes, or until tender but firm. Drain and add to the chicken.
4. Gently heat soured cream; stir into chicken. Arrange on a heated serving dish.

To make spaetzles with a colander: Press the batter through the holes with a spatula or wooden spoon.

To cook spaetzles: Stir the water gently so that the spaetzles will not stick together in a lump.

Pollo Cacciatore

Colour index
page 42
4 servings

45 ml (3 tbsp) vegetable
  oil
25 g (1 oz) butter
1.5-kg (3¼-lb) oven-ready
  chicken, skinned and
  jointed
12 small whole onions,
  skinned
1 clove garlic, skinned and
  crushed
396-g (14-oz) can tomatoes
1 green pepper, seeded and
  sliced

30 ml (2 tbsp) chopped
  parsley
1.25 ml (¼ level tsp) dried
  basil
2.5 ml (½ level tsp) salt
pepper
150 ml (¼ pint) red wine

For the garnish, optional:
chopped parsley

1. Heat the oil and butter in a large saucepan and fry the chicken pieces, a few at a time, until golden brown all over. Remove the chicken pieces and keep them on one side.
2. Put the onions in the same pan and fry them until golden brown. Add the garlic, tomatoes with their juice, green pepper, parsley, basil, salt and pepper. Stir until all the ingredients are well mixed and then bring the mixture slowly to the boil.
3. Return the chicken joints to the pan, add the wine and bring back to the boil. Cover and reduce the heat to simmering.
4. Cook for 40–45 minutes until the chicken is tender. Transfer to a heated serving dish and serve sprinkled with chopped parsley if you wish.

*Cooked 13-1-95 - Split 9 Self 6 thigh jods
small czu tomatoes. 2 V. good. 2
3 portions +*

Deep South Chicken Curry

Colour index
page 41
4–6 servings

1.6-kg (3½-lb) oven-ready
  chicken, jointed
75 ml (5 level tbsp) plain
  flour
45 ml (3 tbsp) vegetable
  oil
2 cloves garlic, skinned
2 onions, skinned and thinly
  sliced
1 green pepper, seeded and
  chopped
50 g (2 oz) celery, washed
  and chopped
15 ml (1 level tbsp) curry
  powder

10 ml (2 level tsp) salt
822-g (29-oz) can tomatoes

To serve:
knob of butter
50 g (2 oz) blanched
  almonds
225 g (8 oz) long grain rice
  cooked and kept hot
75 g (3 oz) seedless raisins
  or sultanas
chopped parsley

1. Coat the chicken with flour. Heat the oil in a large saucepan and fry the joints a few pieces at a time until golden brown all over. Remove the chicken joints from the pan.
2. Add the garlic, onion, pepper, celery, curry powder and salt and cook for 5 minutes, stirring occasionally. Stir in the tomatoes with their juice.
3. Add the chicken joints and bring the mixture to the boil. Reduce the heat, cover and simmer for 30 minutes, or until the chicken is tender.
4. Meanwhile, melt the butter in a frying pan and sauté the almonds until lightly browned, shaking the pan occasionally. Mix together the rice and raisins.
5. Arrange the rice mixture and the chicken joints on a large heated serving dish. Discard the garlic cloves and spoon the sauce over the chicken. Sprinkle the chicken and rice with the sautéed almonds and the chopped parsley.

Braised Chicken with Soured Cream Sauce

Colour index
page 41
4 servings

45 ml (3 tbsp) vegetable
  oil
1.1–1.4-kg (2½–3-lb)
  oven-ready chicken,
  jointed
20 ml (4 level tsp)
  salt
1.25 ml (¼ level tsp)
  pepper
100 ml (4 fl oz) water
225 g (8 oz) celery, washed
  and diagonally sliced

225 g (8 oz) carrots, peeled
  and diagonally sliced
150 ml (¼ pint) soured
  cream

To serve:
225g (8 oz) long
  grain rice, cooked and
  kept hot

1. Heat the oil in a large saucepan, add the chicken joints and fry them until they are brown all over. Sprinkle with salt and pepper and add the water. Bring to the boil, then reduce the heat, cover and simmer gently for 20 minutes.
2. Add the celery and carrot slices, cover and simmer for a further 15 minutes or until the chicken and vegetables are tender, stirring occasionally.
3. Remove the chicken and vegetables, arrange on a warm serving dish and keep hot.
4. To make the sauce, skim the fat off the juices remaining in the pan and stir in the soured cream. Warm through the sauce without allowing it to boil and pour over the chicken and vegetables. Serve with the hot cooked rice.

Chicken with Cucumber

Colour index
page 42
4 servings

30 ml (2 tbsp) vegetable oil
1.1–1.4-kg (2½–3-lb)
  oven-ready chicken,
  quartered
100 g (4 oz) mushrooms,
  sliced
1 clove garlic, skinned and
  crushed
45 ml (3 level tbsp) plain
  flour

60 ml (4 tbsp) dry sherry
350 ml (12 fl oz) chicken
  stock
7.5 ml (1½ level tsp) salt
1 large cucumber
150 ml (¼ pint) soured
  cream

1. Heat the oil in a large saucepan, add the chicken quarters and fry them until brown all over. Remove the chicken from the pan.
2. Add the mushrooms and garlic and cook them in the same oil for about 2 minutes.
3. Stir in the flour, then gradually add the sherry, stock and salt. Cook the sauce until slightly thickened, stirring all the time.
4. Return the chicken to the pan and bring the sauce to the boil. Reduce the heat, cover and simmer for 30 minutes, stirring occasionally. Peel three quarters of the cucumber and cut it into large chunks. Cut the remaining cucumber into very thin slices and reserve for the garnish.
5. Add the cucumber chunks to the chicken and cook for a further 15–20 minutes, until the chicken is tender and the cucumber cooked but still slightly crisp. Stir the soured cream into the sauce and warm through without allowing to boil.
6. Arrange the chicken on a warm serving dish, surround with the cucumber chunks and pour over the sauce. Garnish with the cucumber slices.

255

Braised and stewed chicken and turkey

Chicken with Lemon Sauce

Colour index
page 43

4 servings

1.4-kg (3-lb) oven-ready
  chicken
salt and pepper
75–100 g (3–4 oz) butter

For the sauce:
1 clove garlic, skinned
5 ml (1 level tsp) salt
2.5 ml (½ level tsp) pepper

45 ml (3 tbsp) olive oil
juice of 4 lemons
1 onion, skinned

For the garnish:
chopped parsley
lemon wedges

1. Make the sauce. Crush the garlic and mix with the salt, pepper, oil and lemon juice. Grate the onion and add to the mixture. Leave for several hours so that the flavours are well blended.
2. Quarter the chicken and sprinkle the pieces with salt and pepper.
3. Melt the butter in a flameproof casserole large enough to take the chicken pieces in a single layer, add the chicken pieces and fry until they are well browned all over.
4. Turn the chicken skin side up and pour over the lemon sauce. Cover and simmer very gently for 1 hour or until tender, basting occasionally with sauce.
5. Just before serving, sprinkle the chicken with the parsley and garnish with the lemon wedges.

Chicken Chorizo

Colour index
page 42

6 servings

30 ml (2 tbsp) olive or
  vegetable oil
3 small cloves garlic,
  skinned and finely
  chopped
1.6–1.8-kg (3½–4-lb)
  oven-ready chicken,
  jointed
100 g (4 oz) cooked ham,
  cubed
2 chorizo sausages or
  100 g (4 oz) pork
  sausages, cut into 0.5-cm
  (¼-in) slices
100 ml (4 fl oz) chicken
  stock

50 g (2 oz) soft dark brown
  sugar
75 ml (5 tbsp) red wine
  vinegar
5 ml (1 level tsp) salt
2.5 ml (½ level tsp)
  pepper
7.5 ml (1½ level tsp)
  cornflour
30 ml (2 tbsp) water

For the garnish, optional:
black olives

1. Heat the oil in a flameproof casserole, add the garlic and fry the chicken pieces a few at a time for about 15 minutes. Remove the chicken pieces to a plate and set aside.
2. Add the ham and sliced chorizo sausages to the casserole and fry in the same oil, stirring frequently, until lightly browned.
3. Spoon off any remaining oil from the casserole, leaving behind the chorizo mixture. Add the chicken stock, brown sugar and wine vinegar, stirring well to loosen any meat sediment.
4. Add the chicken pieces and the seasoning. Bring to the boil, reduce the heat and cover. Simmer for 25–30 minutes, or until the chicken is tender. Transfer the cooked meat to a heated serving dish and keep it hot.
5. Blend the cornflour with the water and gradually stir into the cooking juices in the casserole. Cook the sauce until it has thickened, stirring all the time. Pour the sauce over the chicken, garnish with black olives if you wish, and serve immediately.

Chicken Seville

Colour index
page 41

6 servings

50 ml (2 fl oz) olive oil
1.6–1.8-kg (3½–4-lb)
  oven-ready chicken,
  jointed and skinned
2 medium green peppers,
  seeded and cut
  into strips
1 large onion, skinned and
  sliced
100 g (4 oz) cooked ham,
  finely chopped
2 cloves garlic, skinned and
  finely chopped
2 396-g (14-oz) cans
  tomatoes, drained

5 ml (1 level tsp) salt
1.25 ml (¼ level tsp)
  pepper
large pinch fennel seeds
large pinch dried
  marjoram
large pinch dried thyme
50 g (2 oz) large stoned
  olives
50 g (2 oz) pimento-
  stuffed olives

1. Heat the oil in a large pan and fry the chicken pieces a few at a time for about 15 minutes, until lightly browned all over. Remove.
2. Add the green pepper, onion, ham and garlic to the pan and cook in the same oil for 5 minutes, stirring occasionally. Spoon off the oil, leaving behind the vegetable mixture.
3. Add the chicken joints, drained tomatoes, seasonings and herbs and bring the mixture to the boil. Reduce the heat, then cover and simmer for 30 minutes, or until the chicken is tender.
4. Meanwhile halve the olives. Add them to the pan and cook for a further 5 minutes. Remove the chicken joints, arrange on a warmed serving dish and keep them hot.
5. Raise the heat and cook the vegetable mixture for about 5 minutes, stirring occasionally, until it has thickened and reduced by half. To serve, spoon the mixture over the chicken.

Saucy Chicken with Avocado

Colour index
page 45

4 servings

25 g (1 oz) butter or
  margarine
1.1–1.4-kg (2½–3-lb)
  oven-ready chicken,
  jointed
150 ml (¼ pint) dry
  sherry
30 ml (2 level tbsp) plain
  flour
5 ml (1 level tsp) salt
large pinch paprika

150 ml (¼ pint) single
  cream
175 ml (6 fl oz) milk
1 large avocado

For the garnish:
watercress sprigs, washed
  and trimmed

1. Melt the butter or margarine in a large pan and fry the chicken pieces for 20 minutes, or until they are golden brown all over.
2. Add the sherry and bring to the boil. Reduce the heat, cover and simmer gently for 25 minutes, or until the chicken joints are tender. Remove the chicken joints from the pan, arrange them on a warmed serving dish and keep hot.
3. Stir the flour, salt and paprika into the cooking juices left in the pan. Gradually add the cream and milk and cook gently until the sauce is thickened, stirring all the time.
4. Peel the avocado and cut into slices, add to the pan and heat through.
5. Spoon the sauce over the chicken pieces and garnish with the watercress.

Coq au Vin

Colour index
page 44

4 servings

*15 ml (1 tbsp) vegetable oil
knob of butter
75 g (3 oz) bacon, rinded
and chopped
175 g (6 oz) mushrooms
16 button onions, skinned
1 roasting chicken, jointed
60 ml (4 tbsp) brandy
45 ml (3 level tbsp) flour
400 ml (³/₄ pint) red wine
150 ml (¹/₄ pint) chicken
stock
15 ml (1 level tbsp) sugar
bouquet garni
pinch grated nutmeg
salt and pepper*

1 Heat the oil and butter in a flameproof casserole and fry the bacon, mushrooms and onions for 3–4 minutes, until browned. Remove from the pan.

2 Add the chicken pieces and fry for 8–10 minutes until golden brown.

3 Pour the brandy over the chicken, remove from heat and ignite the liquid. When the flames die down, remove the chicken.

4 Stir the flour into the fat remaining in the casserole and cook for 2–3 minutes.

5 Gradually add wine and stock, bring to the boil and stir until thickened. Add the sugar, bouquet garni and seasonings.

6 Return the chicken pieces, bacon, mushrooms and onions to the casserole and fold them gently into the sauce until well mixed.

7 Cover and cook in the oven at 180°C (350°F) mark 4 for 45 minutes–1 hour, until tender. Remove and discard the bouquet garni before serving.

Chicken en Cocotte with Apples and Cream

Colour index
page 43

4 servings

*50 g (2 oz) butter or
margarine
1.4-kg (3-lb) oven-ready
chicken
100 g (4 oz) onion, skinned
and chopped
175 g (6 oz) celery, washed
and sliced
350 g (12 oz) cooking
apples, peeled
and cored*

*45 ml (3 level tbsp) plain
flour
150 ml (¹/₄ pint) dry cider
300 ml (¹/₂ pint) chicken
stock
salt and pepper
150 ml (¹/₄ pint) double
cream*

1. Melt the butter or margarine in a large frying pan and fry the chicken, turning until brown all over. Transfer it to a large flameproof casserole.

2. Add the onion and celery to the pan and sauté in the remaining juices until the onion is transparent. Cut the apple into thick wedges and add to the vegetables in the pan.

3. Stir in the flour and cook for a few minutes. Gradually add the cider and stock, stirring well, and season to taste. Pour the sauce over the chicken, cover and cook at 190°C (375°F) mark 5 for 1¼ hours or until the chicken is tender.

4. Remove the casserole from the oven and skim off the surface fat from the liquid.

5. Carve the chicken, arrange the pieces on a warm serving dish and keep hot. Stir the cream into the cooking juices, adjust the seasoning and heat gently without boiling. To serve, pour the sauce over the chicken pieces.

Party Chicken and Prawns

Colour index
page 42

6 servings

*50 g (2 oz) butter or
margarine
100 g (4 oz) onion, skinned
and chopped
1 small clove garlic, skinned
and finely chopped
227-g (8-oz) can tomatoes
6 chicken breasts
10 ml (2 level tsp) salt
2.5 ml (¹/₂ level tsp) pepper*

*50 ml (2 fl oz) port
5 ml (1 level tsp) dried basil
60 ml (4 tbsp) chopped
parsley
1.25 ml (¹/₄ level tsp) sugar
225 g (8 oz) shelled prawns*

1. Melt half the fat in a saucepan and cook the onion and garlic for about 5 minutes, until tender. Add the tomatoes and cook for about 10 minutes until a thick purée is formed.

2. Meanwhile, rub the chicken breasts with salt and pepper. Heat the remaining fat in a frying pan and cook the chicken breasts for 15 minutes, until golden brown on all sides. Drain on kitchen paper towel and set aside.

3. Stir the port, basil, 45 ml (3 tbsp) parsley and sugar into the tomato mixture, season and bring to the boil; add the chicken. Reduce the heat, cover the pan and simmer for 10 minutes or until tender.

4. Add the prawns and bring to the boil. Reduce the heat and simmer for 5 minutes to heat through the prawns, stirring all the time.

5. Skim off the fat and spoon the mixture into a deep serving dish. Sprinkle the chicken with the remaining parsley to garnish.

Braised and stewed chicken and turkey

Chicken in a Pot

225 g (8 oz) carrots
225 g (8 oz) small onions
100 g (4 oz) streaky bacon
25 g (1 oz) butter
1 lemon
large pinch thyme
1 clove garlic, skinned
1.8-kg (4-lb) oven-ready
  chicken
salt and pepper
450 g (1 lb) Jerusalem
  artichokes

For the garnish:
chopped parsley

Colour index page 43
6 servings

1 Peel and slice the carrots with a small, sharp knife, then skin the onions. Rind the bacon and cut it into small pieces.

2 Using a flameproof casserole a little larger than the chicken, melt the butter and sauté the carrots, onions and bacon for 10 minutes until browned.

3 Pare the lemon and add rind to the pan. Stir in the thyme and garlic. Remove mixture from pan.

4 Put the chicken in the casserole, spoon the vegetables around it and season lightly.

5 Cover and cook in the oven at 150°C (300°F) mark 2 for about 2 hours.

6 Just before the end of the cooking time, peel the artichokes, putting them in salted water to prevent discoloration.

7 When all the artichokes are peeled, drain them and add to the casserole, mixing them gently with the other vegetables.

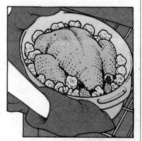

8 Return the casserole to the oven without its lid, and cook for a further 30 minutes, until tender.

9 Remove from the oven; transfer the chicken to a warmed serving dish and spoon the vegetables around it. Keep hot while you reduce the juices.

10 Discard the garlic and lemon rind from the casserole; skim the fat from the juices in the casserole and bring the juices to the boil.

11 Spoon the reduced cooking juices over the chicken and vegetables on the serving dish and garnish generously with the chopped parsley.

Colour index page 41
4–6 servings

Chicken in Port

25 g (1 oz) butter
1 small onion, skinned and
  chopped
225 g (8 oz) mushrooms,
  thinly sliced
40 g (1½ oz) flour
10 ml (2 level tsp) salt
1.25 ml (¼ level tsp)
  pepper
2.5 ml (½ level tsp) grated
  nutmeg
8 chicken breasts, skinned
  and boned
150 ml (¼ pint) chicken
  stock
75 ml (5 tbsp) port
150 ml (¼ pint) double
  cream

1. Melt the fat and cook the onion and mushrooms for 5 minutes. Remove the vegetables and set aside.
2. Sift the flour and seasonings and use to coat the chicken. Reheat the fat in the pan and cook the chicken for about 15 minutes, until brown all over. Stir in the stock, port and vegetables and bring to the boil. Cover; simmer for 20–25 minutes, until tender.
3. Add the cream and reheat without boiling.

Colour index page 44
4 servings

Chicken Imperial

4 chicken breasts, skinned
75 ml (5 level tbsp) flour
50 g (2 oz) butter
225 g (8 oz) button
  mushrooms, quartered
15 ml (1 tbsp) finely
  chopped onion
150 ml (¼ pint) double or
  whipping cream
45 ml (3 tbsp) dry sherry
2.5 ml (½ level tsp) salt
pinch pepper

1. Coat the chicken breasts with flour. Melt the butter and cook the chicken until lightly browned. Remove the chicken and set aside.
2. Add the mushrooms and onion to the pan and cook for 5 minutes, stirring. Stir in the cream, sherry, salt and pepper. Add the chicken, cover and simmer for 20 minutes or until tender. Remove to a heated serving dish and keep hot.
3. Blend any remaining flour with a little water. Gradually stir into the liquid in the pan and cook until thickened. Spoon the sauce over the chicken.

Colour index page 39
4 servings

Saucy Turkey Wings

900 g (2 lb) turkey wings
15 ml (1 tbsp) vegetable oil
298-g (10½-oz) can
  condensed cream of
  celery soup
2.5 ml (½ level tsp) salt
1.25 ml (¼ level tsp)
  paprika
pinch pepper

1. Divide the turkey wings at the joints and remove the wing tips. (They can be used for stock.)
2. Heat the oil in a large frying pan and fry the turkey wings a few at a time until browned all over. Transfer to a casserole.
3. Mix the undiluted soup with the salt, paprika and pepper and spoon over the turkey. Cover and bake at 180°C (350°F) mark 4 for 2 hours, or until tender.

Chicken in White Wine

Colour index
page 43
4 servings

30 ml (2 tbsp) olive oil
1 clove garlic, skinned and
    quartered
4 chicken breasts
450 g (1 lb) pork
    sausages
300 ml (½ pint) light dry
    white wine

100 g (4 oz) mushrooms,
    sliced
2.5 ml (½ level tsp) salt
toast slices
20 ml (4 level tsp) cornflour
45 ml (3 tbsp) water

1. Heat the oil in a large pan, add the garlic and cook until golden. Discard the garlic.
2. Add the chicken pieces and sausages a few at a time to the garlic flavoured oil and fry gently until the chicken pieces are lightly browned and the sausages are well browned all over.
3. Spoon off all but about 30 ml (2 tbsp) of the drippings. Add the wine, mushrooms and salt. Bring to the boil, cover and simmer for 30 minutes or until the chicken is tender, basting occasionally.
4. Halve the toast slices diagonally, arrange them on a warm serving dish and spoon the chicken breasts over them. Keep warm.
5. Blend the cornflour with the water and gradually stir into the pan juices. Heat gently, stirring until thickened. Spoon some sauce over the chicken and serve the rest separately.

Chicken Avgolemono

Colour index
page 43
4 servings

25 g (1 oz) butter
1 clove garlic, skinned and
    sliced
4 chicken breasts, boned
2 courgettes, sliced
100 ml (4 fl oz) water
2 egg yolks
10 ml (2 level tsp) cornflour
5 ml (1 level tsp) salt
pinch cayenne pepper
150 ml (¼ pint) chicken
    stock

45 ml (3 tbsp) lemon juice

For the pilaf:
65 g (2½ oz) butter
225 g (8 oz) long grain
    rice
700 ml (1¼ pints) boiling
    chicken stock

For the garnish, optional:
chopped parsley

1. Make the pilaf. Melt 50 g (2 oz) of the butter in a large pan and fry the rice gently for about 5 minutes, stirring all the time until it looks transparent. Add the stock slowly. Stir well, cover and leave over a very low heat for 15–20 minutes, until the liquid is absorbed and the grains are just soft. Remove the lid and cover the rice with a cloth; replace the lid and leave for at least 15 minutes to dry out.
2. Melt the 25 g (1 oz) butter in a large pan, and cook the garlic until brown. Discard the garlic. Add the chicken breasts and brown them on all sides, then add the courgettes and cook for 2–3 minutes. Pour in the water, bring to the boil, then cover and simmer for 10 minutes or until the chicken and courgettes are just tender.
3. Meanwhile, in a saucepan, whisk together the next four ingredients. Add stock and cook gently, stirring, for about 10 minutes or until the sauce has thickened (do not boil). Add the lemon juice.
4. Arrange the chicken mixture in a warm serving dish and spoon the sauce over it. Add the remaining 15 g (½ oz) butter to the pilaf and serve separately. Garnish with chopped parsley if you wish.

Turkey Cordon Bleu

Colour index
page 41
6 servings

6 175-g (6-oz) slices turkey
    breast
6 slices Gruyère or
    Emmenthal cheese
6 slices cooked ham
45 ml (3 level tbsp) plain
    flour
5 ml (1 level tsp) paprika
75 g (3 oz) butter

100 ml (4 fl oz) dry white
    wine
1 chicken stock cube,
    crumbled
15 ml (1 level tbsp)
    cornflour
150 ml (¼ pint) double or
    whipping cream

1. Beat out the turkey slices and place a slice of cheese and then a slice of ham over each one, folding in the edges to fit. Fold the slices in half, securing the edges with wooden cocktail sticks. Mix the flour and paprika and use to coat the turkey.
2. Melt the butter in a large pan, add the turkey and fry gently for 10 minutes until brown all over. Add the wine and crumbled stock cube. Reduce the heat, cover the pan and simmer gently for 30 minutes, or until the turkey parcels are tender. Transfer the turkey parcels to a warmed serving dish, remove the wooden cocktail sticks and keep hot.
3. Blend the cornflour and cream until smooth and gradually stir into the liquid in the pan. Cook gently until thickened, then pour over the turkey parcels.

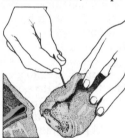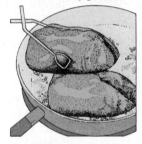

Securing the edges: Use a cocktail stick to hold the edges together.

Browning the turkey: Fry the turkey in butter until lightly browned.

Chicken Breasts with Artichoke Hearts

Colour index
page 44
6 servings

6 chicken breasts
90 ml (6 level tbsp) plain
    flour
30 ml (2 tbsp) vegetable oil
25 g (1 oz) butter
5 ml (1 level tsp) salt
pinch white pepper
350 ml (12 fl oz) chicken
    stock

45 ml (3 tbsp) brandy
10 ml (2 tsp) lemon juice
225 ml (8 fl oz) soured
    cream
396-g (14-oz) can
    artichoke hearts,
    drained

1. Coat the chicken pieces in 60 ml (4 level tbsp) flour and fry in hot oil for 10 minutes, or until lightly browned all over. Transfer the chicken pieces to an ovenproof casserole.
2. Melt the butter and stir in 30 ml (2 level tbsp) flour, the salt and pepper. Gradually stir in the stock, brandy and lemon juice. Cook, stirring constantly, until thickened.
3. Gradually whisk in the soured cream and pour the mixture over the chicken pieces. Cover and bake at 180°C (350°F) mark 4 for 45 minutes.
4. Add the artichoke hearts, cover again and cook for a further 15 minutes or until the chicken and artichoke hearts are just tender.

Braised and stewed chicken and turkey

Turkey in Cider

Colour index
page 40

4–6 servings

15 ml (1 tbsp) vegetable
 oil
1.1–1.4 kg (2½–3 lb)
 turkey legs
400 ml (¾ pint) chicken
 stock
1 large onion, skinned and
 thinly sliced
7.5 ml (1½ level tsp) salt
1.25 ml (¼ level tsp)
 pepper
40 g (1½ oz) plain flour

150 ml (¼ pint) single
 cream
25 g (1 oz) butter
175 g (6 oz) mushrooms,
 sliced
75 ml (5 tbsp) finely
 chopped parsley
300 ml (½ pint) dry cider

To serve, optional:
bread slices

1. Heat the oil in a large saucepan and fry the turkey legs until well browned all over. Add the stock, onion, salt and pepper and bring to the boil. Reduce the heat, cover and simmer for 1½–2 hours, or until the meat is tender.
2. Remove the turkey pieces from the pan and allow to cool slightly. Discard the skin, carve the meat off the bones and cut into 2.5-cm (1-in) pieces. Meanwhile, boil the turkey stock rapidly until it is reduced to 175 ml (6 fl oz).
3. Blend the flour with half the cream and gradually add to the turkey stock, stirring all the time until smooth. Stir in the remaining cream and cook the sauce over a gentle heat until it boils and thickens, stirring well all the time.
4. Melt the butter and sauté the sliced mushrooms until tender. Add them to the sauce with the turkey meat and 60 ml (4 tbsp) of the chopped parsley. Stir in the cider and heat through the sauce.
5. Spoon the turkey mixture into a warmed serving dish and garnish with the remaining parsley. If you prefer a more formal presentation, serve with toast flowers. To make toast flowers, cut shapes from sliced bread with a decorative biscuit cutter and bake in a hot oven for 5 minutes, until golden.

Apricot-Glazed Turkey Drumsticks

Colour index
page 40

4 servings

4 turkey drumsticks,
 weighing 1.8 kg (4 lb)
2 sticks celery, washed and
 halved
1 medium onion, skinned
 and halved
15 ml (1 level tbsp) salt

2.5 ml (½ level tsp)
 peppercorns, crushed
100 g (4 oz) apricot jam

For the garnish:
410-g (14½-oz) can
 apricot halves, drained

1. Put the turkey, celery, onion, salt and peppercorns in a large saucepan. Cover with hot water. Bring to the boil, then reduce the heat, cover tightly and simmer for 1½ hours, or until the turkey drumsticks are tender.
2. Remove the turkey, drain well and reserve 150 ml (¼ pint) of the stock. Pull the tendons from the end of the drumsticks, using kitchen paper towel to help you grip them. Melt the jam in a small saucepan with the reserved stock.
3. Arrange the drumsticks in an ovenproof dish and brush them with the apricot jam glaze. Garnish with the drained apricot halves and brush them lightly with the remaining warm jam glaze.
4. Bake at 200°C (400°F) mark 6 for 10 minutes, until the drumsticks are glazed.

Turkey-Tamale Casserole

Colour index
page 40

6 servings

60 ml (4 tbsp) vegetable oil
700 g (1½ lb) uncooked
 turkey meat
100 ml (4 fl oz) water
1 small onion, skinned and
 chopped
2 sticks celery, washed and
 chopped
425-g (15-oz) can tomatoes
439–454-g (15½–16-oz)
 can red kidney beans
10 ml (2 level tsp) chilli
 powder
5 ml (1 level tsp) salt
1.25 ml (¼ level tsp)
 pepper

For the topping:
100 g (4 oz) cornmeal
25 g (1 oz) plain flour
7.5 ml (1½ level tsp)
 baking powder
2.5 ml (½ level tsp) salt
2.5 ml (½ level tsp) dried
 sage
1 egg
100 ml (4 fl oz) milk
30 ml (2 tbsp) vegetable oil

1. Heat 30 ml (2 tbsp) of the oil in a large saucepan, add the turkey meat and fry it until well browned.
2. Add the water and bring to the boil. Reduce the heat, cover and simmer for 1½ hours, or until the turkey is tender, adding more water if it evaporates too much during cooking.
3. Remove the turkey from the pan and allow to cool slightly. Cut the meat into 1-cm (½-in) pieces.
4. Heat the remaining 30 ml (2 tbsp) oil in a flameproof casserole, add the onion and celery and sauté for about 5 minutes or until soft but not coloured, stirring occasionally.
5. Add the turkey meat, tomatoes with their juice, kidney beans with their liquid, chilli powder, salt and pepper. Bring to the boil, stirring occasionally.
6. Meanwhile, prepare the tamale topping. Mix the cornmeal, flour, baking powder, salt and sage in a large bowl. Mix the egg, milk and oil with a fork and stir into the flour mixture until just blended.
7. Pour the batter over the turkey mixture and bake at 200°C (400°F) mark 6 for 20 minutes, or until a wooden cocktail stick inserted in the middle of the topping comes out clean.

Festive Chicken with Asparagus

Colour index
page 42

6 servings

6 chicken breasts
30 ml (2 level tbsp) plain
 flour
45 ml (3 tbsp) vegetable oil
60 ml (4 tbsp) dry white
 wine
25 g (1 oz) blue cheese,
 crumbled

286-g (10¾-oz) can
 condensed cream of
 chicken soup
2.5 ml (½ level tsp) salt
1.25 ml (¼ level tsp)
 pepper
450 g (1 lb) asparagus

1. Coat the chicken breasts in flour and fry in the hot oil until lightly browned all over.
2. Meanwhile, in a shallow casserole, mix the wine, cheese, undiluted soup, salt and pepper. Arrange the chicken in the mixture and spoon some over the pieces to coat them. Bake at 190°C (375°F) mark 5 for 30 minutes.
3. Cut the asparagus spears in half and rinse. Cook in boiling salted water for 5 minutes; drain. Remove the casserole from the oven and arrange the asparagus between the chicken pieces. Cover the casserole tightly and bake for a further 30 minutes or until the chicken is tender and the asparagus is cooked but still firm.

Grilled chicken and turkey

Poultry pieces are good for grilling as the tender meat responds well to quick cooking. To prevent the meat drying out, brush it well with melted butter or oil before and during cooking, or marinate it first to add extra juiciness and flavour. Always preheat the grill to give the meat a good, crisp outside.

Rôtisserie cooking achieves a similar effect to grilling for whole birds or large joints. Open cooking by direct, radiant heat gives chicken a flavour that many people prefer to that of an oven-roasted bird. Many gas and electric cookers can be fitted with a rôtisserie or you can buy a separate, electrically operated model.

Rôtisseried Chicken

Colour index
page 42

A 1.6-kg
(3½-lb)
chicken gives
4 servings

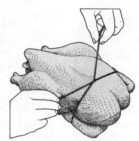 

1 Remove giblets. Fold neck skin over the back and skewer it in position. Tie wings close to body.

2 Insert spit through body and tighten holding prongs. Make sure bird is balanced on spit.

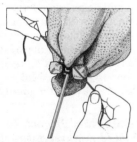 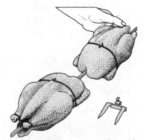

3 Tie the parson's nose and then the drumsticks securely on to the rôtisserie rod.

4 If cooking more than one bird, thread on to rod in opposite directions to balance evenly. Test by turning spit slowly.

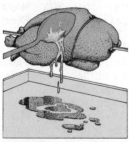 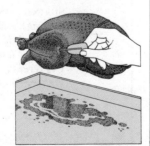

5 Cook the chicken, basting occasionally with melted fat. If you are using a basting sauce, use it only during the last 20 minutes of cooking time.

6 Test the chicken by inserting a meat thermometer in the thigh (do not hit the bone); it is cooked when the thermometer reaches 88°C (190°F).

Tandoori Chicken

Colour index
page 46

8 servings

8 chicken joints
salt and pepper

For the marinade:
225 ml (8 fl oz) plain
　yogurt
5 ml (1 level tsp) pepper
10 ml (2 level tsp) salt
7.5 ml (1½ level tsp) chilli
　powder

pinch ground ginger
pinch ground coriander
1 large clove garlic, skinned
　and crushed
juice of 1½ lemons

For the garnish, optional:
lemon wedges
chopped fresh coriander
　leaves.

1. Wipe the chicken joints and prick the skin with a fork. Season with salt and pepper.
2. Combine the yogurt with all of the remaining ingredients for the marinade; mix well. Add the chicken pieces, turning to coat well. Cover and leave to stand for 3–4 hours, turning occasionally.
3. Place the chicken, skin side down, in a grill pan and baste with some of the marinade. Grill for 25 minutes; turn and baste with the remaining marinade. Grill for a further 15 minutes or until the chicken is tender.
4. Transfer the chicken to a heated serving dish and garnish with lemon wedges and coriander if you wish.

BARBECUE VARIATION: Marinate the chicken as above. Prepare an outdoor grill; pour a little melted butter on each chicken joint and place on the barbecue grid over very hot coals. Brown quickly on all sides then remove from the grid and place each joint on a 38-cm (15-in) square piece of foil. Wrap round the chicken and seal the edges securely. Place each packet on the grid and cook for a further 20 minutes, turning once. Heat the marinade and serve separately as a sauce.

Savoury Chicken

Colour index
page 42

4 servings

1.4–1.6-kg (3–3½-lb)
　oven-ready chicken,
　quartered

For the marinade:
10 medium garlic cloves,
　skinned
175 ml (6 fl oz) tarragon
　vinegar

25 g (1 oz) sugar
15 ml (1 tbsp) vegetable
　oil
15 ml (1 tbsp)
　Worcestershire sauce
10 ml (2 level tsp) dry
　mustard
5 ml (1 level tsp) salt

1. Crush the garlic cloves and put into a dish large enough to take the chicken pieces in one layer. Add the remaining ingredients for the marinade and mix together until well blended.
2. Prick the skin of the chicken pieces with a fork and add to the marinade, turning to coat evenly. Cover and refrigerate for at least 2 hours, turning the chicken occasionally.
3. Place the chicken, skin side down, in a grill pan and baste with the marinade. Grill for 40 minutes, or until the chicken is tender, turning once and basting with the marinade during cooking.

BARBECUE VARIATION: Marinate the chicken as above. Prepare an outdoor grill and, when the coals are very hot, place the chicken pieces on the barbecue grid. Cook for 35 minutes, or until the chicken is tender, turning frequently and basting occasionally with the marinade.

Grilled chicken and turkey

Made for dinner for
Geoff Robin & Self. 4-1-95. using.
Chicken thighs - 2 each.
excellent. good flavour.

Buttery Garlic Chicken

Colour index
page 45

4 servings

4 chicken joints
4 medium tomatoes

For the sauce:
75 g (3 oz) butter
30 ml (2 tbsp) malt vinegar
30 ml (2 level tbsp) honey
2 cloves garlic, skinned and
   crushed
10 ml (2 level tsp) salt
2.5 ml (½ level tsp) dried
   marjoram
2.5 ml (½ level tsp) dry
   mustard
pepper

For the garnish, optional:
grated lemon rind

1 Warm the butter in a small saucepan until just melted. Add vinegar, honey, garlic, salt, marjoram, mustard and a few turns of pepper, then stir until evenly blended.

2 Arrange the chicken joints in a flameproof dish or foil-lined grill pan, fleshy side down.

3 Spoon sauce over the chicken joints and leave for 30 minutes. Grill under a high heat for 5 minutes.

4 Reduce heat and cook joints 10 minutes on each side. Cut each tomato nearly through into 6 wedges and open gently.

5 Add tomatoes to grill pan, cover pan with foil and grill for a further 15 minutes until tender.

6 Lift the foil and baste the chicken joints and tomatoes with the pan juices occasionally during the cooking.

7 Pierce with a skewer to check chicken juices run clear. Sprinkle with grated lemon rind before serving, if you wish.

Chicken with Chilli Marinade

Colour index
page 46

4 servings

1.4-kg (3-lb) oven-ready
  chicken, quartered or
  jointed

For the marinade:
350-g (12-oz) bottle mild
  chilli relish
5 ml (1 level tsp) salt

10 ml (2 level tsp) dried
  horseradish
1 clove garlic, skinned and
  quartered
100 ml (4 fl oz) wine
  vinegar

1. Prick the chicken skin all over with a fork.
2. Mix all the marinade ingredients in a large dish. Add the chicken pieces and coat well. Cover and refrigerate for at least 2 hours, turning occasionally.
3. Arrange the chicken in a single layer in the grill pan. Grill for 35–45 minutes, turning frequently and basting with the marinade.

Coating with marinade:
Turn chicken pieces in marinade to coat well on all sides and chill.

Grilling chicken: Use kitchen tongs or a fork to turn the chicken occasionally during cooking.

MARINADES

Marinating both flavours and helps to tenderise meat, so that it is ideal for use in conjunction with quick cooking methods like grilling. Try the following marinades for chicken, using the method from the recipe above. A simple marinade of wine or sherry with flavouring herbs, seasonings and vegetables also gives a light, subtle flavour to poultry. Make sure that the chicken is evenly coated before leaving it to marinate.

LIME MARINADE: Mix *100 ml (4 fl oz) lime juice* with *45 ml (3 tbsp) vegetable oil.* Add *15 ml (1 level tbsp) grated lime rind, 20 ml (4 level tsp) salt* and *1.25 ml (¼ level tsp) crushed peppercorns* and stir until well blended. Spoon over the chicken and marinate for at least 2 hours.

SPRING ONION AND SOY MARINADE: Mix *100 ml (4 fl oz) soy sauce* and *30 ml (2 tbsp) dry sherry.* Add *50 g (2 oz) thinly sliced spring onion, 30 ml (2 level tbsp) soft light brown sugar, 2.5 ml (½ level tsp) salt* and *2.5 ml (½ level tsp) ground ginger.* Blend well. Spoon over the chicken and marinate for at least 2 hours.

ORANGE HERB MARINADE: Mix *150 ml (¼ pint) white wine* or dry vermouth with *45 ml (3 tbsp) olive oil* and the *juice of 2 oranges.* Add *5 ml (1 level tsp)* each of *chopped fresh rosemary, thyme* and *marjoram* and a *crushed clove of garlic* and stir until well blended. Spoon over the chicken, marinate for at least 2 hours.

Fried chicken

Colour index page 44
6 servings

Cheese and Anchovy Grilled Chicken Breasts

50-g (2-oz) can anchovy fillets	6 chicken breasts vegetable oil
30 ml (2 tbsp) finely chopped onion	225 g (8 oz) Mozzarella cheese, sliced
5 ml (1 tsp) lemon juice	

1. Drain 15 ml (1 tbsp) anchovy oil into a small saucepan. Chop the anchovies finely.
2. Heat the anchovy oil, add the anchovies and onion and cook for about 5 minutes, until a paste forms. Stir in the lemon juice and leave to cool.
3. Lift the skin from each chicken breast and rub 5 ml (1 tsp) of the anchovy mixture on to the flesh, underneath the skin.
4. Put the chicken pieces skin side down on the grill-pan rack and grill under medium heat for 35–45 minutes until tender, turning chicken once. Brush with oil occasionally during cooking.
5. Cover the chicken breasts with slices of cheese and grill for a further 5 minutes, or until the cheese begins to bubble.

Flavouring the meat: Rub flavourings well into the flesh under the skin.

Adding the cheese: Lay the cheese slices carefully over the chicken breasts.

Colour index page 39
6 servings

Turkey and Sausage Kebabs

	For the marinade:
1.1–1.4 kg (2½–3 lb) turkey meat	75 ml (5 tbsp) soy sauce
225 g (8 oz) sausages	75 ml (5 tbsp) dry sherry
3 large spring onions	15 ml (1 level tbsp) sugar
226-g (8-oz) can pineapple chunks	45 ml (3 tbsp) vegetable oil

1. Cut the turkey into 2.5-cm (1-in) chunks.
2. Put the marinade ingredients in a bowl and mix well. Add the turkey pieces and coat with the marinade. Refrigerate for 30 minutes.
3. Meanwhile, halve the sausages crossways, trim and cut the spring onions into 4-cm (1½-in) pieces. Drain the pineapple chunks very well.
4. Thread chunks of turkey, sausage, pineapple and spring onion alternately on to kebab skewers. Cook under a hot grill for 20–25 minutes until the meat is tender, turning the kebabs and basting frequently with the reserved marinade.

Individual portions of chicken or turkey are ideal for frying. If they are to be fried without a coating, the pieces must be completely dry before being placed in the hot fat. A coating of flour or breadcrumbs will help hold the juices in the meat, making it crisp outside but soft and moist inside. If there is time, let the coated pieces dry for about 15 minutes before cooking; this will help the coating adhere better.

Frying in the oven achieves a similar effect but with less handling, which means that the coating is less likely to be dislodged. Remember that the side which is fried first will always look best. Use vegetable oil or butter, or a combination of the two: meat fried in oil sticks less, but adding butter gives a good flavour.

Fried Chicken with Parsley Sauce

1.1–1.4-kg (2½–3-lb) oven-ready chicken, jointed
salt and pepper
plain flour
vegetable oil

For the sauce:
15 ml (1 level tbsp) flour
150 ml (¼ pint) milk
150 ml (¼ pint) chicken stock
salt and pepper
15–30 ml (1–2 tbsp) chopped parsley

Colour index page 44
4 servings

1 Season the chicken pieces with salt and pepper and coat them all over with flour.

2 Using a large frying pan, pour in enough oil to cover the bottom of the pan. Heat the oil and fry the chicken, turning the pieces, until brown.

3 Reduce the heat and cook the chicken for 15 minutes on each side. Remove from the pan, arrange the chicken pieces on a warmed serving dish and keep hot.

4 Drain off all but 30 ml (2 tbsp) oil and sprinkle in 15 ml (1 level tbsp) flour. Cook over medium heat, stirring all the time, until the mixture is well browned.

5 Blend in the liquid. Bring sauce to the boil, stirring all the time, and boil for 2–3 minutes or until thickened. Adjust seasoning, add parsley and pour sauce over chicken.

CHICKEN IN A BASKET

Skin an onion and seed a green pepper. Slice the onion and green pepper thinly into rings.

Pile the fried chicken pieces in a napkin-lined basket and garnish with the onion and pepper rings.

Fried chicken

French Fried Chicken

Colour index
page 41
4 servings

1.1–1.4-kg (2½–3-lb)
oven-ready chicken
100 g (4 oz) plain flour
pinch salt
1 egg

150 ml (¼ pint) milk
15 g (½ oz) butter, melted
vegetable oil
tomato sauce, page 337,
optional

1. Joint the chicken. Mix the flour and salt in a bowl, make a well in the centre and break in the egg. Add half the milk and beat until smooth. Gradually beat in the remaining milk and melted butter.
2. Heat the oil in a large frying pan. Dip the chicken pieces into the batter and fry until golden brown.
3. Finish cooking in the oven at 180°C (350°F) mark 4 for about 30 minutes, until the chicken is tender. Serve with tomato sauce if you wish.

Crunchy Drumsticks

Colour index
page 46
4 servings

1.4 kg (3 lb) chicken
drumsticks, skinned
115 g (4½ oz) flaked oats
50 g (2 oz) butter or
margarine

For the marinade:
225 ml (8 fl oz) orange
juice
15 ml (1 tbsp) vegetable oil
15 ml (1 level tbsp) salt
1.25 ml (¼ level tsp)
pepper

1 Mix together all the ingredients for the marinade. Add the chicken and coat well. Cover and chill for at least 4 hours, turning occasionally.

3 Melt the butter or margarine in a large frying pan and fry the chicken pieces, a few at a time, for about 15–20 minutes on each side until crisp and golden. Alternatively, line a roasting tin with foil, add the fat and melt it in the oven.

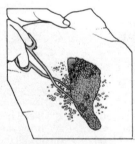

2 Put the oats on to a piece of waxed paper. Roll the chicken pieces in the oats to coat evenly.

4 Put the chicken in one layer in the tin, turning to coat with the fat.

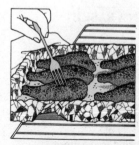

5 Bake at 200°C (400°F) mark 6, for 40–50 minutes, turning once.

Chicken Maryland

Colour index
page 45
4 servings

1–1.4-kg (2¼–3-lb)
oven-ready chicken,
jointed
45 ml (3 level tbsp)
seasoned flour

1 egg, beaten
dried breadcrumbs
50 g (2 oz) butter
15–30 ml (1–2 tbsp)
vegetable oil

1. Discard the skin from the chicken joints. Divide the chicken joints into fairly small portions. Coat each one with seasoned flour, dip into the beaten egg and finally coat with breadcrumbs, patting the crumbs firmly on to the chicken. Leave the coated chicken pieces to dry for 15 minutes.
2. Heat the butter and oil together in a large frying pan, add the chicken pieces and fry until lightly browned. Reduce the heat and fry the pieces gently, turning them once, for a further 20 minutes, or until the chicken is tender.
3. Drain the chicken pieces and serve with fried bananas and corn fritters (below).

FRIED BANANAS: Peel the *bananas,* and slice them lengthways. Fry gently in a *little hot butter* or the chicken fat for 3 minutes, or until lightly browned. (Allow 1 banana per person.)

CORN FRITTERS: Mix *100 g (4 oz) plain flour* and a *pinch salt* in a bowl. Break in *1 egg* and add *75 ml (3 fl oz) milk*; beat until smooth. Gradually beat in a further *75 ml (3 fl oz) milk.* Fold in a *312-g (11-oz) can sweetcorn kernels,* drained. Fry in spoonfuls in a little hot fat for 5 minutes until crisp and golden, turning once.

Lemon Chicken on Spinach Leaves

Colour index
page 46
6 servings

6 chicken breasts, boned
and skinned
5 ml (1 level tsp) salt
40 g (1½ oz) plain
flour
100 ml (4 fl oz) vegetable
oil
150 g (5 oz) fresh spinach,
washed

For the sauce:
225 ml (8 fl oz) chicken
stock

65 g (2½ oz) sugar
75 ml (5 tbsp) lemon juice
15 ml (1 tbsp) dry sherry
7.5 ml (1½ tsp) soy sauce
30 ml (2 level tbsp)
cornflour
30 ml (2 tbsp) water

For the garnish , optional:
lemon wedges

1. For the sauce, in a small saucepan heat together the chicken stock, sugar, lemon juice, sherry and soy sauce. Meanwhile, blend the cornflour with the water to make a smooth paste.
2. Add a little of the hot sauce to the cornflour mixture and then stir into the sauce. Bring to the boil, stirring, until the sauce is smooth and thickened. Keep warm.
3. Sprinkle the chicken breasts with the salt and coat them with the flour. Heat the oil in a large frying pan and cook the chicken for about 15–20 minutes, until lightly browned and just tender.
4. Shred the spinach coarsely and arrange it on a warmed serving dish. Arrange the chicken on the spinach and pour over some of the sauce. Serve the remaining sauce separately. Garnish the chicken with lemon wedges if you wish.

Chicken Kiev

175 g (6 oz) butter,
  softened
grated rind of ½ lemon
15 ml (1 tbsp) lemon juice
salt and pepper
15 ml (1 tbsp) chopped
  parsley
1 clove garlic, skinned and
  crushed
6 large chicken breasts,
  boned and skinned
25 g (1 oz) seasoned
  flour
1 egg, beaten

100 g (4 oz) fresh white
  breadcrumbs
oil for deep frying

For the garnish, optional:
lemon wedges
parsley sprigs

Colour index page 44
4 servings

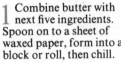

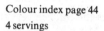

1 Combine butter with next five ingredients. Spoon on to a sheet of waxed paper, form into a block or roll, then chill.

2 Place the chicken breasts on a flat surface and pound them to an even thickness with a meat mallet or rolling pin.

3 Cut the butter into six pieces and place one piece on the centre of each chicken breast.

4 Roll up, folding the ends in to enclose the butter completely.

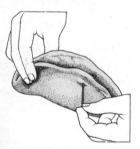

5 Secure the rolls with wooden cocktail sticks, then coat each one with seasoned flour.

6 Dip the rolls in the beaten egg. Finally coat them with breadcrumbs, patting the crumbs firmly on to the chicken.

7 Place the rolls on a baking sheet, cover lightly with waxed or greaseproof paper and refrigerate for 2 hours or until required, to allow the coating to dry.

8 Heat the oil to 160°C (325°F). Carefully lower in two chicken rolls at a time. Fry for 15 minutes.

9 The chicken is cooked when it is browned and firm when pressed with a fork. Do not pierce.

10 Drain on kitchen paper towel and re-move the cocktail sticks. Garnish if you wish.

Colour index page 46
4 servings

Chicken Roulades

4 chicken breasts, boned
  and skinned
4 slices lean cooked
  ham
150 g (5 oz) Gruyère
  cheese, grated
few fresh rosemary
  leaves
100 g (4 oz) fresh white
  breadcrumbs
2 eggs, beaten

75 g (3 oz) butter
15 ml (1 tbsp) vegetable oil

To serve, optional:
tomato sauce, page 337
  or hollandaise sauce,
  page 463
few sprigs fresh
  rosemary
tomato wedges

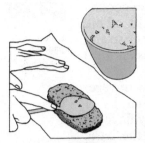

1 Place the chicken breasts on a flat surface and pound them to an even thickness with a meat mallet or rolling pin.

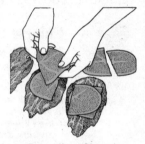

2 Cut a slice of ham in half and place the two halves on a chicken breast, folding in the ham so that it does not overhang the edges. Repeat with remaining ham and chicken.

3 Take 75 g (3 oz) of the cheese and divide it be-tween the chicken breasts, sprinkling it over the ham.

4 Place a little rosemary on the top of each chicken breast and roll up neatly; secure with wooden cocktail sticks. Mix the breadcrumbs with the re-maining grated cheese.

5 Brush each roulade with egg, then coat well in the breadcrumb mix-ture. Pat the coating on to the roulades firmly.

6 Melt the butter with the vegetable oil in a frying pan. Add the roulades and fry quickly until evenly browned all over, then re-duce the heat and cook slowly for about 15 minutes until cooked right through. Drain the roul-ades on kitchen paper towel and remove the cocktail sticks. Serve plain, or with a tomato or hol-landaise sauce, if you wish. If not serving with a sauce, garnish with sprigs of rose-mary or tomato wedges.

Stir-fried chicken

Stir-frying is the traditional Chinese way of cooking high quality meats. Very thin slices of meat are cooked and stirred over high heat in a small amount of oil. Cooking is very quick and the result should be crisp and tender. Chicken is fine-fleshed and lean and is an ideal meat for stir-fried dishes.

Stir-fried recipes invariably include a variety of vegetables, which serve both to extend a small quantity of expensive meat and to give the blend of many flavours that is typical of Chinese foods. When all the basic ingredients have been stir-fried separately, they are blended together and a liquid is added for the final few minutes of cooking to make the sauce.

Chinese Chicken with Vegetables

Colour index page 45

3–4 servings

450 g (1 lb) chicken meat
45 ml (3 tbsp) oil
5 ml (1 level tsp) salt
30 ml (2 tbsp) soy sauce
2–3 sticks celery, washed
½ green pepper, seeded
270-g (9½-oz) can bean sprouts, drained
50 g (2 oz) mushrooms
100 g (4 oz) water chestnuts, drained
150 ml (¼ pint) chicken stock
15 ml (1 level tbsp) cornflour
salt and pepper
50 g (2 oz) flaked almonds, toasted

1 Carefully slice the uncooked chicken into thin strips, about 0.5 cm (¼ in) wide across the grain of the meat.

2 Heat the oil in a large frying pan and add the chicken and salt. Stir-fry for 3–5 minutes.

3 Add the soy sauce and blend well. Slice the celery and green pepper into thin strips.

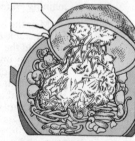

4 Add the bean sprouts, celery, pepper, mushrooms, chestnuts and stock to the chicken in the pan; cover and simmer for 15 minutes until tender.

5 Blend the cornflour with a little water and stir into the chicken. Bring slowly to the boil, stirring. Season and sprinkle with toasted almonds.

Stir-fried Chicken and Mushrooms

Colour index page 45

4 servings

4 chicken breasts, boned and skinned
15 ml (1 level tbsp) cornflour
30 ml (2 tbsp) dry sherry
1.25 ml (¼ level tsp) ground ginger
pinch monosodium glutamate
10 ml (2 level tsp) salt
75 ml (5 tbsp) vegetable oil
75 g (3 oz) shelled walnuts

400-g (15-oz) can Chinese straw mushrooms, drained or 283-g (10-oz) can whole mushrooms, drained
283-g (10-oz) can bamboo shoots, drained and sliced
100 g (4 oz) mange tout or snow peas

1. Slice the chicken very thinly across the grain of the meat. Mix with the cornflour, sherry, ginger, monosodium glutamate and 7.5 ml (1½ level tsp) salt; set the coated chicken aside.
2. Heat the oil in a large frying pan and cook the walnuts for about 3 minutes until lightly browned, stirring constantly. Remove and drain on kitchen paper towel. Reheat the oil and add the mushrooms, bamboo shoots, peas and 2.5 ml (½ level tsp) salt. Stir-fry for 3–5 minutes until the peas are just tender. Remove the vegetables with a slotted spoon.
3. Reheat the remaining oil, add the chicken mixture and stir-fry for 5 minutes or until the chicken is tender; stir in the vegetables.
4. Spoon the chicken and vegetables into a serving dish and sprinkle with the walnuts.

Chicken Szechuan Style

Colour index page 45

4 servings

1 carrot, peeled
6 large chicken breasts, boned and skinned
30 ml (2 tbsp) soy sauce
30 ml (2 tbsp) dry sherry
8 spring onions, cut into 5-cm (2-in) pieces
5 ml (1 level tsp) peeled and finely chopped root ginger or 1.25 ml (¼ level tsp) ground ginger
1.25 ml (¼ level tsp) pepper

15 ml (1 level tbsp) cornflour
2.5 ml (½ level tsp) sugar
2.5 ml (½ level tsp) salt
175 ml (6 fl oz) orange juice
60 ml (4 tbsp) vegetable oil

1. Slice the carrot lengthways very thinly. Blanch for 5 minutes in boiling, salted water. Drain well.
2. Cut the chicken into 4-cm (1½-in) pieces. Mix with the soy sauce, sherry, spring onion, ginger and pepper. Cover and refrigerate.
3. Mix the cornflour, sugar, salt and orange juice. Cover and refrigerate separately.
4. Heat the oil in a large frying pan and stir-fry the carrot strips for about 2 minutes, until crisp and slightly browned. Remove and drain on kitchen paper towel.
5. Reheat the oil, add the chicken mixture and stir-fry for about 4 minutes, until the chicken loses its pink colour and is just tender.
6. Stir the orange juice mixture until blended, add to the chicken and stir-fry for 5 minutes until the mixture is slightly thickened and coats the chicken. Spoon on to a warmed serving plate and sprinkle with the carrot strips.

Boiled chicken and turkey

Although 'boiled' is the traditional term for poultry cooked at length in plenty of liquid, 'simmered' would really be a more accurate description. Fast boiling toughens connective tissues and dries out the meat. For a tender, succulent bird, bring the water or stock to boiling point, then reduce the heat and maintain it at no more than a gentle, bubbling simmer. Vegetables and herbs add extra flavour to the bird and the stock, which is often strained and used in making a sauce to serve with the meat. A boiling fowl gives the best flavour but you can cook a broiler or roasting chicken following the same method; simply reduce the cooking time.

Boiled Chicken with Parsley Sauce

Colour index
page 44

6 servings

1.8-kg (4-lb) oven-ready
chicken
½ lemon
salt
1 onion, skinned and stuck
with 3–4 cloves
1 carrot, peeled
bouquet garni

For the sauce:
20 g (¾ oz) butter
30 ml (2 level tbsp) plain
flour
150 ml (¼ pint) milk
15–30 ml (1–2 tbsp)
chopped parsley
salt and pepper

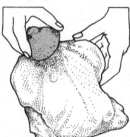

1 Truss the chicken, making sure that the legs are tied together firmly, and rub with a lemon half to preserve the white colour.

2 Put it in a large pan with the flavouring ingredients and water to cover. Bring to the boil, cover and simmer about 3 hours for a boiling fowl, 1 hour for a younger bird.

3 Drain the chicken, remove the trussing string and keep hot while making the sauce. Strain the stock and reserve.

4 For the sauce, melt the butter in a small saucepan and blend in the flour. Cook over a gentle heat, stirring, until the mixture begins to bubble. Gradually stir in the milk and 150 ml (¼ pint) of the chicken stock. Bring to the boil, stirring, and cook for 1–2 minutes, stirring, until smooth and thickened. Add the parsley to the sauce, but do not re-boil or the sauce may turn green.

5 Adjust seasoning, pour into a sauceboat and serve with the chicken.

Chicken Fricassee

Colour index
page 45

4 servings

1.1-kg (2½-lb) oven-ready
boiling fowl, jointed
2 onions, skinned and
chopped
2 carrots, peeled and sliced
100 g (4 oz) mushrooms,
sliced
bouquet garni
salt and pepper
50 g (2 oz) butter

50 g (2 oz) plain flour
1 egg yolk
45 ml (3 tbsp) cream
juice of ½ lemon

For the garnish:
4 rashers streaky bacon,
rinded, rolled and grilled
parsley sprigs

1. Put the chicken and vegetables in a large pan with enough water to cover. Add the bouquet garni, salt and pepper. Bring slowly to the boil and simmer gently for 1 hour, or until the chicken is tender.
2. Strain the stock; reserve the vegetables and stock separately. If you wish, remove the skin from the chicken, carve the meat and cut it into cubes.
3. Melt the butter, stir in the flour and cook for 2–3 minutes. Remove from the heat and gradually add 600 ml (1 pint) stock. Bring to the boil and cook until the sauce thickens, stirring constantly. Add the meat and vegetables; remove from the heat.
4. Beat the egg yolk and cream, add a little sauce and blend well. Return the mixture to the sauce and heat through without boiling. Add the lemon juice.
5. Pour into a serving dish and garnish with the grilled bacon rolls and parsley sprigs.

Turkey Mole

Colour index
page 39

4 servings

900-g (2-lb) turkey breast,
skinned
15 ml (1 tbsp) vegetable oil
45 ml (3 level tbsp) sesame
seeds
1 small onion, skinned and
chopped
1 clove garlic, skinned and
crushed
15 g (½ oz) plain chocolate
25 g (1 oz) raisins
15 g (½ oz) slivered
almonds
298-g (10½-oz) can
enchilada sauce

2 taco shells, crumbled,
optional
1 slice white bread, cubed
2.5 ml (½ level tsp) salt
1.25 ml (¼ level tsp)
ground cinnamon
1.25 ml (¼ level tsp)
ground coriander
1.25 ml (¼ level tsp) anise
seeds, crushed
pinch ground cloves
pinch pepper
1 avocado

1. Put the turkey in a large pan, cover with water and simmer for 1½ hours or until tender. Drain and reserve the stock. Slice meat and keep warm.
2. Heat the oil in a large frying pan, add the sesame seeds and fry until lightly browned. Remove and drain on kitchen paper towels. Add the onion and garlic to the remaining oil and cook until tender. Stir in the chocolate and heat until melted.
3. Spoon the mixture into a blender, add 15 ml (1 level tbsp) toasted sesame seeds and all the remaining ingredients except the avocado. Blend until smooth. Return the mixture to the frying pan and stir in 400 ml (¾ pint) stock. Bring the sauce to the boil, stirring constantly.
4. Arrange the turkey slices on a warmed serving plate and garnish with slices of peeled and stoned avocado. Spoon over some of the sauce and sprinkle with the remaining sesame seeds. Serve the remaining sauce separately.

Boiled chicken and turkey

Simmered Chicken with Pasta

1.6-kg (3½-lb) oven-ready
  chicken
1 onion, skinned and stuck
  with 3–4 cloves
1 carrot, peeled
salt and pepper
50 g (2 oz) butter
350 g (12 oz) onion,
  skinned and chopped
30 ml (2 level tbsp) flour
396-g (14-oz) can tomatoes
30 ml (2 level tbsp) tomato
  paste
2 cloves garlic, skinned

15 ml (1 level tbsp) dried
  basil
100 g (4 oz) lasagne sheets
100 g (4 oz) mushrooms,
  sliced
600 ml (1 pint) well
  flavoured béchamel
  sauce, page 461
25–50 g (1–2 oz) grated
  Parmesan cheese

Colour index page 45

4–6 servings

1 Put the chicken, onion
  and carrot in a large
saucepan with the salt and
pepper and enough water
to cover. Bring slowly to
the boil and cover. Reduce
the heat and simmer gently
for about 40 minutes until
the chicken is tender.
Remove the chicken from
the saucepan, using two
large slotted spoons, drain
over the pan for a few
seconds and allow to cool.

2 Strain the chicken
  stock and measure out
300 ml (½ pint) for the
tomato sauce.

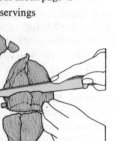

3 When the chicken has
  cooled, carve the meat
and discard the skin and
bones. Cut the meat into
fairly thick strips and set
them on one side.

4 Melt the butter in a
  large saucepan, add
the onion and sauté until it
is transparent. Do not
allow it to brown.

5 Stir in the flour and
  cook gently for 1
minute, stirring constantly.

6 Stir in the reserved
  stock, add the tomatoes
with their juice and the
tomato paste. Crush the
garlic and add it to the
mixture with the basil.
Adjust the seasoning.

7 Add the chicken pieces.
  Bring the mixture to
the boil, then reduce the
heat and simmer for 10
minutes until the flavours
are well blended.

8 Cook the lasagne in a
  large saucepan of boil-
ing salted water. Drain
well. Add the mushrooms
to the béchamel sauce and
mix in thoroughly.

9 Layer the lasagne,
  chicken mixture and
mushroom sauce in a
large, buttered, ovenproof
dish, finishing with a layer
of mushroom sauce.

10 Sprinkle with the
   Parmesan cheese and
bake at 200°C (400°F)
mark 6 for about 30 min-
utes, until golden brown
and bubbling.

Colour index page 46
4–6 servings

Chicken Pot Pie

1.1-kg (2½-lb) oven-ready
  chicken, jointed
1.25 ml (¼ level tsp) dried
  marjoram
bay leaf
400 ml (¾ pint) water
salt and pepper
2 large carrots, peeled and
  sliced
1 large stick celery, washed
  and sliced
175 g (6 oz) button onions,
  skinned

225 g (8 oz) broad beans
45 ml (3 level tbsp) plain
  flour
60 ml (4 tbsp) double cream
150 ml (¼ pint) milk
100 g (4 oz) mushrooms,
  halved
25 g (1 oz) butter
shortcrust pastry made with
  175 g (6 oz) flour,
  page 343
1 egg yolk, beaten with 5 ml
  (1 tsp) water

1. Put the chicken in a large saucepan with the
marjoram, bay leaf, water, 15 ml (1 level tbsp) salt
and 1.25 ml (¼ level tsp) pepper. Bring to the boil,
reduce the heat, cover and simmer for 35 minutes or
until the chicken is tender. Strain and reserve 150 ml
(¼ pint) chicken stock.
2. Cool the chicken. Remove the bones and skin and
discard them. Cut meat into 2.5-cm (1-in) pieces.
3. Put the reserved stock in a saucepan with the
carrots, celery, onions and broad beans. Cover and
simmer for 10 minutes or until the vegetables are
almost tender. Remove them with a slotted spoon,
reserving the stock for the sauce.
4. Blend the flour with the cream until smooth.
Gradually stir it into the stock in the pan and add the
milk. Cook over a gentle heat until the sauce has
thickened, stirring all the time.
5. Sauté the mushrooms in the butter for 5 minutes;
drain off any liquid. Stir the mushrooms into the
sauce with the cooked chicken and vegetables, 2.5 ml
(½ level tsp) salt and a little pepper. Spoon into a
1.1-litre (2-pint) capacity pie dish.
6. Roll out the pastry to about 2.5 cm (1 in) larger
than the pie dish all round.
7. Place the pastry loosely over the filling and trim
the edges, leaving a 2.5-cm (1-in) rim. Fold the rim
under and pinch to make a stand-up edge. Use the
trimmings to make leaves and decorate the pie.
8. Brush the pastry with the egg yolk mixture and
bake at 180°C (350°F) mark 4 for about 45 minutes,
or until the pastry is golden brown and the filling is
completely heated through.

Trimming the edges: Cut
the pastry with kitchen
scissors or a knife.

Shaping pie edge: Pinch all
around the pie to form a
stand-up edge.

Cooked chicken and turkey

Colour index page 40
4–6 servings

Chicken or Turkey Salad

150 ml (¼ pint)
mayonnaise, page 462
30 ml (2 tbsp) cider vinegar
5 ml (1 level tsp) salt
700–900 g (1½–2 lb) cold
cooked chicken or
turkey, chopped
100 g (4 oz) celery, washed
and sliced
100 g (4 oz) green pepper,
seeded and chopped
10 ml (2 level tsp) grated
onion
lettuce leaves

1 Mix together the mayonnaise, vinegar and salt in a large bowl.

2 Stir in the chicken or turkey, celery, green pepper and onion. Cover and refrigerate.

3 Arrange the lettuce leaves on a chilled serving plate and lightly pile the salad in the centre.

Colour index page 43

CHICKEN SALAD VARIATIONS

TOASTED WALNUT AND CHICKEN SALAD: Prepare the chicken salad as above, then melt a *knob of butter* in a small saucepan, add *50 g (2 oz) chopped walnuts* with a *large pinch of salt* and cook them for 3 minutes, until crisp. Cool the walnuts and add to the chicken mixture before refrigerating it.

HAM, PINEAPPLE AND CHICKEN SALAD: Prepare the salad as above, but replace half the chicken with the same weight of *cooked ham,* cut into chunks. Add *100 g (4 oz) fresh, or canned and drained, pineapple chunks* to the mixture.

CHICKEN WALDORF SALAD: Prepare chicken salad as above, but add *100 g (4 oz) unpeeled, diced red apples* and *50 g (2 oz) chopped shelled walnuts* to the chicken mixture.

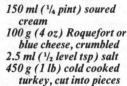

Colour index page 40
4 servings

Turkey Roquefort Salad

150 ml (¼ pint) soured
cream
100 g (4 oz) Roquefort or
blue cheese, crumbled
2.5 ml (½ level tsp) salt
450 g (1 lb) cold cooked
turkey, cut into pieces

lettuce or endive leaves,
washed and trimmed
6 canned peach halves,
drained

For the garnish, optional:
chopped chives

1. Mix the soured cream, Roquefort and salt. Add the turkey and coat well with the dressing. Cover and chill until required.
2. To serve, arrange the lettuce leaves and the peach halves on a serving dish. Spoon the turkey mixture over the peach halves; sprinkle with chives if wished.

Colour index page 45
4 servings

Chicken Vol-au-Vents

50 g (2 oz) butter
100 g (4 oz) mushrooms,
sliced
½ green pepper, seeded and
chopped
40 g (1½ oz) plain flour
100 g (4 oz) cooked diced
carrot
400 ml (¾ pint) milk and
chicken stock, mixed

225–350 g (8–12 oz) cold
cooked chicken, diced
salt and pepper
paprika or ground nutmeg
15–30 ml (1–2 tbsp) sherry

To serve:
vol-au-vent cases, page 344
or 225 g (8 oz) long grain
rice, cooked and kept hot

1 Melt the butter and fry the mushrooms and pepper until soft. Stir in flour and cook for 2–3 minutes. Add the carrot.

2 Reduce the heat and stir in the milk and stock gradually. Bring to the boil and continue to stir until thickened.

3 Add the chicken and heat through, stirring. Add the salt, pepper and nutmeg; stir in sherry.

4 Serve mixture spooned into hot vol-au-vent cases or, if you prefer, with hot cooked rice.

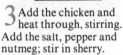

Creamy Chicken Hash

25 g (1 oz) butter or
margarine
1 small onion, skinned and
chopped
15 ml (1 level tbsp) plain
flour
5 ml (1 level tsp) salt
75 ml (5 tbsp) single cream
75 ml (5 tbsp) milk

350 g (12 oz) cooked
potato, diced
450 g (1 lb) cold cooked
chicken, diced

For the garnish:
chopped parsley

Colour index page 46
4 servings

1. Melt the butter or margarine in a large saucepan and sauté the onion for 5 minutes or until tender, stirring occasionally.
2. Remove from the heat and stir in the flour and salt. Gradually add the cream and milk, return the pan to a gentle heat and cook until thickened, stirring all the time. Do not boil.
3. Add the diced potato and chicken to the mixture. Reduce the heat, cover the pan and simmer for 10 minutes to heat through the hash, stirring occasionally to prevent sticking.
4. Serve garnished with the chopped parsley.

Cooked chicken

Soured Cream Chicken Enchiladas

Colour index
page 42
6 servings

*400 ml (³/₄ pint) soured
 cream
150 ml (¹/₄ pint) milk
vegetable oil
100 g (4 oz) mushrooms,
 chopped
2 green chillis, chopped
1 medium onion, skinned
 and chopped
450 g (1 lb) cold cooked
 chicken, chopped*

*5 ml (1 level tsp) chilli
 powder
2.5 ml (¹/₂ level tsp) garlic
 powder
2.5 ml (¹/₂ level tsp) salt
1.25 ml (¹/₄ level tsp)
 pepper
12 tortillas, page 431
150 g (5 oz) Cheddar
 cheese, grated*

1. Stir the soured cream and milk together. Spread half the mixture over the base of a roasting tin.
2. Heat 15 ml (1 tbsp) oil in a large saucepan and cook the mushrooms, chillis and onion for about 10 minutes. Add the chicken, 50 ml (2 fl oz) of the soured cream mixture and the seasonings. Cook gently to warm the mixture.
3. Heat 1 cm (¹/₂ in) vegetable oil in a large frying pan. To make an enchilada, fry a tortilla quickly on either side until soft, remove from the pan and spread 30 ml (2 tbsp) chicken mixture down the centre. Fold the tortilla over the filling. Place the enchilada seam side down in the roasting tin. Repeat with the remaining tortillas and chicken mixture.
4. Spread the remaining soured cream over the enchiladas and sprinkle with the cheese. Bake at 230°C (450°F) mark 8 for 10–12 minutes, until the cheese is melted and bubbling and the enchiladas are thoroughly heated.

Chicken Croquettes

Colour index
page 46
4 servings

*350 g (12 oz) cold cooked
 chicken or turkey,
 minced
300 ml (¹/₂ pint) white
 sauce, page 461
30 ml (2 tbsp) chopped
 parsley
15 ml (1 tbsp) chopped
 onion*

*2.5 ml (¹/₂ tsp) lemon juice
1.25 ml (¹/₄ level tsp) salt
25 g (1 oz) plain flour
1 egg, beaten with 15 ml
 (1 tbsp) water
50 g (2 oz) dried
 breadcrumbs
oil for deep frying*

1. Mix the first six ingredients, stirring well. Chill.
2. Divide mixture into eight and shape into rolls or cork shapes. Roll each one in flour, then in beaten egg and water and finally breadcrumbs.
3. Heat the oil to 150°C (300°F) and deep fry the croquettes for 8–10 minutes until golden. Drain on kitchen paper towel and serve with a mushroom or cheese sauce, if you wish.

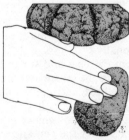

Forming the croquettes:
Use your hands to make rolls or cork shapes.

Coating with breadcrumbs:
Roll croquettes in breadcrumbs until well coated.

Chicken livers

Chicken Liver Sauté

Colour index
page 47
4 servings

*50 g (2 oz) butter
700 g (1¹/₂ lb) chicken
 livers
1 onion, skinned and
 roughly chopped
25 g (1 oz) plain flour
400 ml (³/₄ pint) chicken
 stock
50 ml (2 fl oz) dry or
 medium sherry
7.5 ml (1¹/₂ level tsp) salt*

To serve:
toast triangles

For the garnish:
chopped parsley

1 Melt the butter and sauté the chicken livers and onion for about 10 minutes, stirring all the time.

2 Remove the chicken livers and the onion, leaving the cooking juices behind in the pan.

3 Add the flour to the pan, stir well into the cooking juices and cook for a few minutes.

4 Gradually add the stock and cook, stirring, until sauce thickens.

5 Stir in sherry, salt and livers; heat through. Garnish, serve with toast.

Chicken Livers Aloha

Colour index
page 47
4 servings

*50 g (2 oz) butter
100 g (4 oz) celery, washed
 and chopped
50 g (2 oz) onion, skinned
 and chopped
1 medium or large
 green pepper, seeded
 and sliced
700 g (1¹/₂ lb) chicken
 livers*

*439-g (15¹/₂-oz) can
 pineapple chunks,
 drained
30 ml (2 level tbsp) soft
 brown sugar
15 ml (1 level tbsp)
 cornflour
7.5 ml (1¹/₂ level tsp) salt
175 ml (6 fl oz) water
30 ml (2 tbsp) cider vinegar*

1. Melt the butter in a large frying pan. Add the celery, onion and pepper and sauté for about 5 minutes, until tender but still slightly crisp.
2. Add the chicken livers and cook for a further 10 minutes, stirring frequently. Add the pineapple.
3. Mix the brown sugar, cornflour and salt in a bowl and stir in the water and vinegar. Gradually add to the chicken livers and cook until thickened, stirring.

Poussin and spring chicken

Poussins with Red Sultana Sauce

Colour index page 47
4 servings

4 450-g (1-lb) oven-ready
    poussins
salt and pepper
100 g (4 oz) breadcrumbs
50 g (2 oz) wheatgerm
50 g (2 oz) celery, washed
    and chopped
100 ml (4 fl oz) stock
15 ml (1 tbsp) grated
    lemon rind
15 ml (1 tbsp) chopped
    parsley
5 ml (1 level tsp) sugar

1 clove garlic, skinned and
    crushed
75 g (3 oz) butter, melted

For the sauce:
275-g (10-oz) jar
    redcurrant jelly
75 g (3 oz) sultanas
50 g (2 oz) butter
10 ml (2 tsp) lemon juice
large pinch allspice

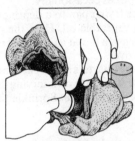

1 Sprinkle the body cavity of each poussin with salt and pepper. Twist the wing tips back under each bird, tucking the neck skin under the wings to hold it securely in place.

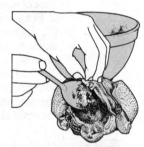

2 Mix the next eight ingredients well; add 25 g (1 oz) of the butter and season well. Spoon the stuffing into the body cavity of each poussin.

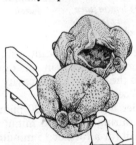

3 Tie together the legs and tail of each poussin. Brush with remaining butter and place on a rack in a roasting tin. Roast at 220°C (425°F) mark 7 for 45 minutes.

4 Meanwhile, prepare the red sultana sauce. Put all the ingredients into a saucepan and cook gently for about 10 minutes, stirring occasionally to blend well.

5 Cut the strings tying together the legs of each bird and brush the skin generously all over with the hot red sultana sauce.

6 Continue roasting the poussins for 10–15 minutes, until a leg will move freely. Serve the remaining hot red sultana sauce separately.

Spring Chicken Casserole

Colour index page 47
3–4 servings

1.1-kg (2½-lb) oven-ready
    spring chicken
25 g (1 oz) lard .
100 g (4 oz) onion, skinned
    and sliced
45 ml (3 level tbsp) plain
    flour
396-g (14-oz) can tomatoes
600 ml (1 pint) chicken
    stock
salt and pepper
450 g (1 lb) small carrots,
    peeled

For the dumplings:
150 g (5 oz) self raising
    flour
pinch salt
65 g (2½ oz) shredded suet
finely grated rind of
    ½ lemon
30 ml (2 tbsp) chopped
    parsley
cold water

1. Cut the chicken into eight pieces and remove the skin. Melt the lard in a large pan. Add the chicken pieces and fry them until browned on all sides. Remove and set on one side.
2. Add the onion to the fat and fry quickly. Stir in the flour. Drain the tomatoes and add their liquid to the pan with the stock. Cook until slightly thickened, stirring all the time. Season to taste.
3. Put chicken pieces in a 1.7-litre (3-pint) capacity casserole and tuck the tomatoes and carrots between them. Add the tomato sauce, cover and cook in the oven at 190°C (375°F) mark 5 for about 50 minutes, or until tender.
4. Meanwhile make the dumplings. Combine the flour, salt, suet, lemon rind and parsley with enough cold water to make an elastic dough. Divide into eight and shape into balls. Add to the casserole and cook for a further 20 minutes.

Poussins Marsala

Colour index page 48
6 servings

3 800-g (1¾-lb)
    oven-ready poussins,
    halved
50 g (2 oz) butter
150 ml (¼ pint) Marsala
    or sherry
150 ml (¼ pint) double
    cream
1.25 ml (¼ level tsp)
    paprika
1 clove garlic, skinned and
    crushed

100 g (4 oz) Cheddar
    cheese, grated
salt and pepper
chopped parsley

For the garnish, optional:
rosemary sprigs

1. Fry the poussin halves two at a time in butter for about 5 minutes, until golden brown. Remove each pair from the pan as they are browned.
2. Drain off the excess fat and replace the poussin halves flesh side down. Pour over the Marsala or sherry and bring to the boil.
3. Cover with a tightly fitting lid or foil and simmer gently for about 40 minutes, or until the juices run clear when the thickest part of the chicken flesh is punctured with a fork.
4. Whip the cream and fold in the paprika, garlic and cheese. Season lightly.
5. Transfer the poussin halves and juices to a flameproof serving dish and spoon over the whipped cream and cheese topping.
6. Grill under high heat until the cheese melts and browns. Sprinkle with chopped parsley and garnish with sprigs of rosemary if you wish.

Poussin and spring chicken

Poussins with Apricot Stuffing

Colour index
page 47

4 servings

2 450–700-g (1–1½-lb)
  oven-ready poussins
50 g (2 oz) butter or
  margarine, melted

For the stuffing:
75 g (3 oz) dried apricots
25 g (1 oz) sultanas
75 g (3 oz) fresh white
  breadcrumbs
25 g (1 oz) shelled walnuts,
  finely chopped
1.25 ml (¼ level tsp)
  ground mixed spice
1.25 ml (¼ level tsp) salt

1.25 ml (¼ level tsp)
  pepper
15 ml (1 tbsp) lemon juice
5 ml (1 tsp) grated
  lemon rind
25 g (1 oz) butter, melted
1 egg, beaten

For the glaze:
30 ml (2 level tbsp) golden
  syrup or clear honey
10 ml (2 tsp) medium
  sherry

1. Soak the apricots and sultanas in cold water for 8 hours or overnight.
2. Place the poussins breast side up on a rack in a roasting tin and brush with the melted butter. Roast at 190°C (375°F) mark 5 for about 1½ hours or until cooked, basting occasionally.
3. Drain off the liquid from the apricots and sultanas and chop the fruit finely. Stir in the remaining stuffing ingredients and bind with the egg. Spread the stuffing evenly in a small ovenproof dish and bake alongside the poussins for the last 30 minutes of the roasting time.
4. Mix together the golden syrup and sherry and brush the mixture over the poussins to glaze them, 10 minutes before the end of cooking time. Finish roasting the poussins and serve them on a heated serving dish with the stuffing.

Lemon Glazed Poussins

Colour index
page 47

4 servings

2 700–900-g (1½-2-lb)
  oven-ready poussins
30 ml (2 tbsp) vegetable oil
10 ml (2 level tsp) salt
large pinch pepper

For the glaze:
75 ml (5 tbsp) water
30 ml (2 tbsp) lemon juice

75 ml (5 level tbsp) sugar
30 ml (2 tbsp) apple juice
15 ml (1 tbsp) grated
  lemon rind
large pinch salt

For the garnish, optional:
grated lemon rind

1. Rinse and drain the birds well and fold the neck skin over the back of each one. Insert the rôtisserie skewer lengthways through the poussins, ensuring that the skewer passes through the fleshy part, so that the poussins will balance evenly and turn without slipping.
2. Tie the wings close to the bodies, then bring the string down and fasten the legs and tail together tightly. Brush the poussins with oil and sprinkle with salt and pepper.
3. Position the poussins on the skewer as close to the heating element as possible without allowing them to touch the element as they turn. Cook for 1¼ hours, or until tender.
4. Meanwhile, place the glaze ingredients in a saucepan, heat gently until the sugar dissolves and then boil for 5 minutes. Brush the poussins frequently with the glaze during the last 20 minutes of cooking time. Take the poussins off the skewer, remove the strings and serve on a warmed dish. Garnish with a little grated lemon rind if you wish.

Honeyed Spring Chicken

Colour index
page 48

2–3 servings

175 ml (6 fl oz) soy sauce
75 ml (5 tbsp) dry sherry
4 spring onions, trimmed
  and finely chopped
2.5 ml (½ level tsp) ground
  ginger
1.1-kg (2½-lb) oven-ready
  spring chicken, quartered
vegetable oil

60 ml (4 level tbsp) clear
  honey

To serve:
1 small lettuce, washed and
  shredded
chopped chives, optional

1. Mix together the first four ingredients in a large dish, add the chicken quarters and turn to coat well. Cover and refrigerate for at least 6 hours, turning the chicken pieces occasionally.
2. Fill a large frying pan to a depth of about 0.5 cm (¼ in) with vegetable oil. Heat the oil and fry the chicken quarters a few at a time until tender and well browned all over.
3. When all the quarters are cooked, brush the pieces with honey and arrange on a serving dish on a bed of coarsely shredded lettuce. Sprinkle the lettuce with chopped chives if you wish.

Grilled Poussin Halves

Colour index
page 47

2 servings

1 550–700-g (1¼–1½-lb)
  oven-ready poussin
2.5 ml (½ level tsp) salt
pinch pepper
25 g (1 oz) butter or
  margarine
30 ml (2 tbsp) lemon juice
225-g (8-oz) can pineapple
  slices, drained

15 ml (1 level tbsp) soft
  light brown sugar
100–175 g (4–6 oz) long
  grain rice, cooked and
  kept hot
15 ml (1 tbsp) chopped
  parsley

1. Halve the poussin with poultry shears or a sharp knife. Season and place skin side down in the grill pan. Put half the butter in each cavity and pour over the lemon juice.
2. Grill under high heat for 20 minutes, brushing with butter during the first 5 minutes, as it melts. Turn and grill for a further 15 minutes. Brush with the pan juices from time to time during cooking.
3. Arrange the pineapple slices around the poussin halves in the grill pan and sprinkle the pineapple evenly with brown sugar. Grill for a further 5 minutes or until the poussin is cooked and the pineapple is golden.
4. Mix the cooked rice and parsley together and arrange in a hot serving dish with the poussin halves and pineapple slices. Spoon the cooking juices over the poussin halves.

Arranging the pineapple:
Fit slices around poussin.

Adding the sugar: Sprinkle sugar evenly over slices.

Duck and goose

Ducks and geese have more fat than other poultry, so the cook's efforts are concentrated on drawing off as much of the fat as possible. The meat itself has a stronger flavour than chicken or turkey and is both richer and darker. Allow 450 g (1 lb) of duck and 350–400 g (12–14 oz) of goose per person.

When roasting duck or goose, prick the skin with a sharp fork, so that the fat can escape, basting the bird as it rolls down the sides. Always use a rack – otherwise the bird will end up frying in its own fat. Duck should be roasted at 190°C (375°F) mark 5 until the meat thermometer registers 88°C (190°F). The procedure is the same for goose, with the oven set either at 200°C (400°F) mark 6 for quick roasting a young bird, or at 180°C (350°F) mark 4 for slow roasting an older bird. A sour apple in the roasting tin adds flavour to the gravy.

Roast Duck

15 ml (1 tbsp) vegetable oil
duck giblets
600 ml (1 pint) water
1 stick celery, cut up
1 onion, skinned
1 bay leaf
sage and onion stuffing, page 253
1.8-kg (4-lb) oven-ready duck
salt and pepper
15 ml (1 level tbsp) plain flour

Colour index page 49
6 servings

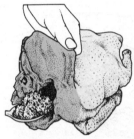

1 Heat the oil in a saucepan and brown the gizzard and heart. Add the water, vegetables, bay leaf and liver. Bring to the boil, cover and simmer gently for 45 minutes.

2 Spoon the stuffing into the duck and truss it. Weigh it and calculate cooking time, allowing 20 minutes per 450 g (1 lb).

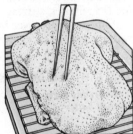

3 Put the duck on a wire rack in a roasting tin and sprinkle the breast liberally with a mixture of salt and pepper. Rub the seasoning thoroughly into the skin.

4 Prick skin all over with a sharp fork or skewer to allow fat to escape. Roast at 190°C (375°F) mark 5 for calculated cooking time, basting occasionally with fat in tin.

5 When cooked, a skewer pushed into the meat should release clear, not pink, juices. Transfer to a warm plate, remove trussing string and keep hot.

6 Strain the giblet stock into a bowl, return it to the pan and bring back to the boil. Boil rapidly until reduced to about 300 ml (½ pint). Cool and skim the fat off the surface.

7 Drain the fat from the roasting tin and stir the flour into the remaining juices. Cook over moderate heat until it bubbles, stirring all the time to prevent sticking.

8 Gradually stir in the reduced stock. Cook the gravy for about 10 minutes, stirring until smooth and thickened. Season to taste and serve with the duck.

Colour index page 48
6 servings

Roast Goose

1 oven-ready goose	For the garnish, optional:
salt	1 apple, cored and cut into
sour apple, optional	rings, lemon juice, oil

1. Sprinkle the bird with salt and put it on a rack in a roasting tin. Cover the goose with the fat taken from inside, then with greased greaseproof paper. Place a sour apple in the roasting tin if you wish.
2. To cook by the fast method, roast the goose at 200°C (400°F) mark 6 for 15 minutes per 450 g (1 lb), plus 15 minutes. To cook by the slow method, roast at 180°C (350°F) mark 4 for 25–30 minutes per 450 g (1 lb). Remove the paper during the last 30 minutes to allow the bird to brown.
3. Spoon off the fat from the tin and make rich gravy (page 249) with the remaining juices. Serve the goose with gravy and, if you wish, with apple rings that have been dipped in lemon juice, brushed with oil and lightly grilled. The goose may also be served with apple sauce (page 463).

Colour index page 48
8–10 servings

Bohemian Roast Goose

2 566-g (1¼-lb) cans sauerkraut	5 ml (1 level tsp) salt
4–5-kg (9–11-lb) oven-ready goose	2.5 ml (½ level tsp) caraway seeds
225 g (8 oz) peeled and cored apples, cut into cubes	

1. Put the sauerkraut with its liquid in a large saucepan and bring to the boil. Reduce the heat, cover and simmer for 30 minutes. Drain and rinse with cold water; drain again.
2. Prick the skin of the goose with a fork in several places. Add the apples, salt and caraway seeds to the sauerkraut and spoon into the goose. Skewer the neck skin to the back of the goose and truss.
3. Put the goose breast side up on a rack in a roasting tin and roast in the oven at 180°C (350°F) mark 4 for 4–4½ hours or until tender. When cooked, a meat thermometer should register 88°C (190°F). Let the goose stand at room temperature for 15 minutes, so that it is easier to carve.

Duck and goose

Shanghai Duck

Colour index
page 48

4 servings

8 medium leeks
2–2.3-kg (4½–5-lb)
  oven-ready duck
100 ml (4 fl oz) dry sherry
100 ml (4 fl oz) soy sauce
2.5 ml (½ level tsp) sugar
0.5-cm (¼-in) piece root
  ginger, peeled or 1.25 ml
  (¼ level tsp) ground
  ginger
300 ml (½ pint) water
3 small carrots, cut
  lengthways into strips

1 Prepare the leeks. Trim the roots, discard the tough outer leaves and cut about 15 cm (6 in) from the thick white root section. Rinse thoroughly under running water and drain. Cover and refrigerate. Cut the remaining leaves across into 1-cm (½-in) slices and wash. Put them into a saucepan which is large enough to hold the duck.

2 Remove the giblets. Trim as much fatty skin as possible from around the neck and body cavity of the duck. Rinse the duck and giblets well and pat dry with kitchen paper towel.

3 Place the duck, breast side down, on the leeks in the pan and tuck the giblets around it.

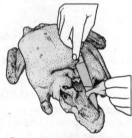

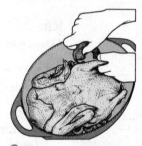

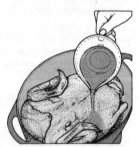

4 Add the sherry, soy sauce, sugar, ginger and water to the pan. Bring to the boil, reduce the heat, cover and simmer for about 30 minutes.

5 Carefully turn the duck over, cover and cook for a further hour, basting occasionally with the cooking liquid.

6 Skim the fat from the cooking liquid and discard, then arrange the carrots and reserved leeks around the duck. Bring to the boil. Cover and simmer for a further 20 minutes.

7 Baste occasionally during cooking, until the duck and vegetables are tender when tested with a fork or skewer. Skim any fat from the sauce and serve the duck immediately.

Duck à l'Orange

Colour index
page 49

4 servings

1 oven-ready duck
knob of butter
salt and pepper
150 ml (¼ pint) white wine
3 oranges (use Seville
  oranges when
  available)
1 lemon
15 ml (1 level tbsp) sugar

15 ml (1 tbsp) vinegar
30 ml (2 tbsp) brandy
15 ml (1 level tbsp)
  cornflour

For the garnish:
1 orange, sliced
1 bunch watercress,
  trimmed

1. Rub the breast of the duck with the butter and sprinkle with salt and pepper. Put the duck and wine in a roasting tin and cook in the oven at 190°C (375°F) mark 5 for 30 minutes per 450 g (1 lb) basting occasionally.
2. Pare the rind from one of the oranges and shred it finely. Squeeze the juice from all three oranges and from the lemon.
3. Dissolve the sugar in a pan with the vinegar and heat until it is a dark brown caramel. Add the brandy, orange juice and lemon juice to the caramel and simmer gently for 5 minutes.
4. When the duck is cooked, remove it from the roasting tin, joint it and place the pieces on a heated serving dish. Keep hot.
5. Spoon the excess fat from the roasting tin and add the shredded rind and the orange sauce to the sediment and juices remaining in the tin. Blend the cornflour with a little water, stir it into the juices and return the tin to the heat. Bring to the boil and cook for 2–3 minutes, stirring. Season.
6. Pour the sauce over the duck joints and garnish with the orange slices and watercress.

Duck with Cherries

Colour index
page 49

4 servings

1 oven-ready duck
knob of butter
salt
300 ml (½ pint) stock
3–4 sugar lumps
1 orange
40 g (1½ oz) caster sugar

1 wine glass port
450 g (1 lb) red cherries,
  stoned
600 ml (1 pint) espagnole
  sauce, page 462 or well-
  flavoured gravy

1. Rub the breast of the duck with the butter and sprinkle with salt. Put it in the roasting tin with the stock and cook in the oven at 190°C (375°F) mark 5 for 30 minutes per 450 g (1 lb), basting occasionally with the stock in the tin.
2. Meanwhile, rub the sugar lumps over the orange skin to obtain the zest. Put the sugar lumps in a pan with the caster sugar and port.
3. Squeeze the orange, add the juice to the sugar in the pan and allow the sugar to dissolve slowly. Add the cherries, cover and simmer gently for about 5 minutes until just tender.
4. The duck should still be slightly pink when cooked. Remove from the oven and cut into quarters. Place them on a serving dish and keep hot.
5. Drain the cherries and keep them warm. Add the strained syrup to the hot espagnole sauce and mix together thoroughly. Spoon some of the sauce over the duck. Arrange the cherries on the serving dish and serve the remaining sauce separately.

Peking Duck with Thin Pancakes

*2.3-kg (5-lb) oven-ready
    duck
4.5 litres (8 pints) boiling
    water
15 ml (1 level tbsp) salt
15 ml (1 tbsp) dry sherry
thin pancakes, right
60 ml (4 tbsp) maple-
    flavoured syrup
100 ml (4 fl oz) hoisin
    sauce (can be bought at
    Chinese speciality shops
    or good delicatessens)
4 spring onions, cut into
    5-cm (2-in) pieces*

Colour index page 48

4 servings or 16 pancakes

1 Early on the day
ahead, rinse the duck
and drain on a rack in
the sink. Pour the boiling
water slowly over the duck
until skin whitens. Drain well.

2 Gently pat dry the skin and body
cavity with kitchen paper towel. Rub
the body cavity with salt and the sherry.

3 Put the duck breast side down on a
rack in a roasting tin and
refrigerate until the evening. Do not
cover. Meanwhile, make the thin
pancakes (right).

4 Early that evening, brush the duck
all over with the maple syrup. Leave
it on the rack, breast side up, and refrigerate uncovered until the next day.

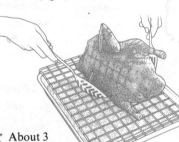

5 About 3
hours before
serving, put the
duck, breast down on its rack, in the
tin and cook in the oven at 190°C
(375°F) mark 5 for 1½ hours. Turn the
duck breast up and cook for a further
1–1½ hours until the skin is golden
and crisp. About 15 minutes before the
duck is done, reheat the thin pancakes.

6 To serve, slice the duck
thinly into pieces about
5 × 2.5 cm (2 × 1 in) and
arrange on a warmed
plate. Put the hoisin sauce
in a small bowl and the
spring onions on a small
plate. Pass round the duck,
hoisin sauce, onions and
pancakes for each person
to help himself, keeping
the duck and pancakes
hot while you eat.

Thin Pancakes

*275 g (10 oz) plain
    flour
2.5 ml (½ level tsp) salt*   *225 ml (8 fl oz) boiling
    water
vegetable oil*

1. Sift the flour and salt into a large bowl. Gradually
add the boiling water, blending it in with a fork.
2. Press the dough into a ball, place on a lightly
floured surface and knead for about 5 minutes to
make a soft smooth dough. Shape into a roll about
40 cm (16 in) long and slice it crossways into 16
pieces. Cover with a damp cloth.
3. Take two pieces of dough at a time and put them
on a lightly floured surface. With your fingers, flatten
them into circles about 7.5 cm (3 in) across and
brush the tops generously with vegetable oil. Place
them one on top of another, oiled surfaces together.
With a lightly floured rolling pin, roll from the
centre to form a 20-cm (8-in) circle, turning over the
dough to roll both sides evenly.
4. Heat an ungreased frying pan. Add the circle of
dough and cook each side for 2–3 minutes or until
light brown. Remove it to an ovenproof plate and
separate the two layers. Stack them, browned side
up, and cover with foil. Repeat to make 16 pancakes.
5. Put the plate of pancakes over a pan of water,
cover with foil and bring the water to the boil.
Reduce the heat and simmer for about 10 minutes,
until the pancakes are soft and hot. Or put the whole
plate inside a steamer, cover lightly and steam until
the pancakes are hot.

Forming a pancake: Put
the dough circles together,
oiled surfaces touching,
before rolling out.

Separating a pancake:
Carefully pull apart the
cooked layers to make two
thin pancakes.

TO ASSEMBLE EACH PORTION

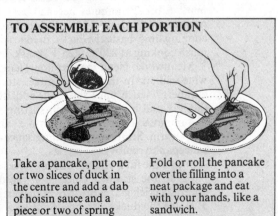

Take a pancake, put one
or two slices of duck in
the centre and add a dab
of hoisin sauce and a
piece or two of spring
onion according to taste.

Fold or roll the pancake
over the filling into a
neat package and eat
with your hands, like a
sandwich.

Duck and goose

**Colour index
page 49**

4 servings

Plum Glazed Duck

1.8–2.3-kg (4–5-lb)
  oven-ready duck,
  quartered
garlic salt
25 g (1 oz) butter
1 medium onion, skinned
  and roughly chopped
396-g (14-oz) can Victoria
  plums
50 g (2 oz) soft light brown
  sugar
45 ml (3 tbsp) chilli sauce
30 ml (2 tbsp) soy sauce

30 ml (2 tbsp) lemon juice
2.5 ml (½ level tsp) salt
2.5 ml (½ level tsp) ground
  ginger
5 ml (1 level tsp) made
  mustard
2.5 ml (½ tsp)
  Worcestershire sauce

For the garnish, optional:
red eating plums, washed
  and halved

1. Prick duck skin all over and sprinkle with garlic salt. Place the pieces skin side up on a rack in a roasting tin and cook at 170°C (325°F) mark 3 for 2½ hours, or until tender.
2. Meanwhile melt the butter and cook the onion gently until soft but not coloured.
3. Drain the plum liquid into a blender. Stone the fruit and add to the blender with the butter, onion and remaining ingredients. Blend until smooth then pour the mixture into a saucepan and simmer for 25 minutes, stirring occasionally.
4. When the duck is cooked, remove from the oven and turn the temperature to 200°C (400°F) mark 6. Spoon the fat from the roasting tin and brush the duck pieces with some sauce. Roast for a further 15 minutes, brushing with some sauce. Garnish with plum halves if you wish; serve with remaining sauce.

**Colour index
page 49**

4 servings

Roast Duck with Cranberry Glaze

2 1.6-kg (3½-lb) oven-
  ready ducks
175 ml (6 fl oz) water
salt
flour for dredging
30 ml (2 level tbsp)
  cornflour
30 ml (2 tbsp) lemon juice

60 ml (4 tbsp) red wine
396-g (14-oz) jar whole
  berry cranberry sauce

For the garnish:
watercress sprigs, washed
  and trimmed

1. Put the duck giblets and water in a saucepan. Cover and simmer for 1 hour.
2. Prick the ducks' skin and rub well with salt. Place on a rack in a roasting tin; roast at 200°C (400°F) mark 6 for 20 minutes per 450 g (1 lb), basting occasionally. About 15 minutes before the end of cooking time, baste the ducks, dredge with flour and finish cooking at 220°C (425°F) mark 7.
3. Meanwhile, blend the cornflour, lemon juice and wine and stir in the strained giblet stock. Heat the cranberry sauce until softened, add the cornflour mixture and bring to the boil, stirring. Simmer for 3–4 minutes. Pour two thirds into a sauceboat and keep warm. Strain the remaining sauce into a clean saucepan to remove the berries.
4. Spoon the fat from the roasting juices and add the juices to the strained sauce; boil rapidly until reduced to a rich glaze. Brush over the ducks in the tin.
5. Halve the ducks, arrange them on a serving dish and pour any remaining glaze over them. Garnish with watercress and serve with cranberry sauce.

Poultry sauces

**Makes about
400 ml
(¾ pint)**

Bread Sauce

2 cloves
1 medium onion, skinned
400 ml (¾ pint) milk
salt
few peppercorns

½ small bay leaf
knob of butter
75 g (3 oz) fresh white
  breadcrumbs

1. Stick the cloves into the onion and put it into a saucepan with the milk, salt, peppercorns and bay leaf. Bring almost to the boil, remove from the heat and leave covered in a warm place for 20 minutes.
2. Remove the peppercorns and bay leaf. Add the butter and breadcrumbs and cook very slowly for about 15 minutes, stirring from time to time. Remove the onion. Serve with roast chicken or turkey.

**Makes about
400 ml
(¾ pint)**

Cranberry Sauce

225 g (8 oz) sugar
300 ml (½ pint) water
225 g (8 oz) cranberries

port, optional

1. Dissolve the sugar in the water over gentle heat, then boil for 5 minutes.
2. Add the cranberries and a little port if you wish. Simmer gently for 10 minutes, or until the berries burst. Cool before serving. Serve with roast turkey.

**Makes about
225 ml
(8 fl oz)**

Currant-Mint Jelly

250–350 g (10–12 oz)
  redcurrant jelly
30 ml (2 tbsp) grated
  orange rind

30 ml (2 tbsp) chopped
  mint or 10 ml (2 level
  tsp) dried mint

Mix the redcurrant jelly with the orange rind and mint, stirring until well blended. Serve with hot or cold roast poultry.

**Makes about
300 ml
(½ pint)**

Lemon Sauce

juice and pared rind of
  1 lemon
300 ml (½ pint) béchamel
  sauce, page 461, using
  half milk and half
  chicken stock

5–10 ml (1–2 level tsp)
  sugar
salt and pepper
15–30 ml (1–2 tbsp) single
  cream, optional

1. Put the lemon rind in a saucepan with the milk and stock and simmer for 5 minutes. Strain the liquid and use for a béchamel sauce.
2. When the sauce has thickened, stir in the lemon juice and sugar. Season to taste. For a less sharp flavour, stir in some single cream just before serving. Serve with chicken.

**Makes about
300 ml
(½ pint)**

Velouté Sauce

15 g (½ oz) butter
30 ml (2 level tbsp) flour
400 ml (¾ pint) chicken
  stock

30–45 ml (2–3 tbsp) single
  cream
few drops lemon juice
salt and pepper

1. Melt the butter, stir in the flour and cook gently, stirring, until fawn. Stir in the stock.
2. Bring to the boil, stirring. Simmer until slightly reduced and syrupy, then remove from the heat and add the cream, lemon juice and seasoning.

VEGETABLES

Fresh vegetables are full of the vitamins, minerals and fibres that are essential to our diet and are delicious cooked or raw. Remember that simple recipes are often best for bringing out the natural flavour and preserving the goodness of vegetables. However you are preparing them, keep the cooking time as brief as possible and use a minimum of liquid. The cooking liquid can often be used to make a sauce, so none of the goodness is lost.

Careful storage helps to keep vegetables in good condition for as long as possible. The best place is usually the bottom of the refrigerator. Trim away any damaged parts and wrap the vegetables in polythene before refrigerating. Root vegetables, including onions, should be stored in a drier, more moderate atmosphere.

Artichokes

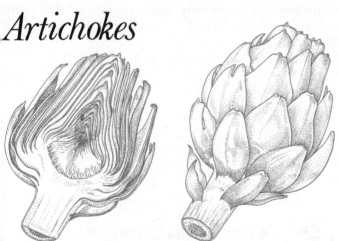

Season: Imported globe artichokes are available all year, domestic varieties only in the summer.

To buy: Choose heads with tightly closed leaves, showing no signs of browned or dry edges. There should be no sign of swelling at the base of the artichoke.

To prepare: Wash globe artichokes well under running cold water, or soak for about 30 minutes in a bowl of cold water acidulated with a little lemon juice, to remove insects. Cut off the stem and, if you wish, trim the leaves. If you are using the hearts only, remove all the leaves and trim the stem as close as possible to the base of the artichoke. Carefully remove all the hairy 'choke', pulling it away from the heart with your fingers or scraping it off gently with a knife or a spoon. This can be done either before or after the basic cooking, depending on the recipe you are following.

Basic cooking: Place the heads in a large pan of boiling salted water and simmer for 35–40 minutes, until a leaf will pull out easily. Drain upside down in a colander. Serve hot with melted butter or hollandaise sauce (page 463) or cold with French dressing (page 326).

Seasonings: Dill, parsley, bay leaf, garlic, oregano.

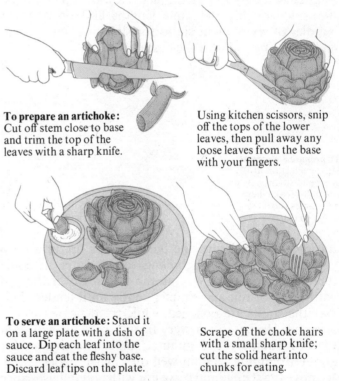

To prepare an artichoke: Cut off stem close to base and trim the top of the leaves with a sharp knife.

Using kitchen scissors, snip off the tops of the lower leaves, then pull away any loose leaves from the base with your fingers.

To serve an artichoke: Stand it on a large plate with a dish of sauce. Dip each leaf into the sauce and eat the fleshy base. Discard leaf tips on the plate.

Scrape off the choke hairs with a small sharp knife; cut the solid heart into chunks for eating.

ARTICHOKES WITH BEARNAISE SAUCE

Remove inner leaves and choke from each cooked artichoke, but leave outer leaves intact. Spoon some béarnaise sauce (page 463) into the centre of each one and serve immediately.
Colour index page 51

Asparagus

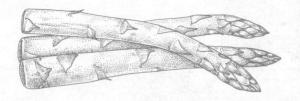

Season: The domestic asparagus season lasts only for about 1 month–6 weeks in late spring and early summer. However, imported asparagus is available throughout the summer months and often late into the autumn.

To buy: Choose firm, fresh-looking stalks. Whether they are green or white depends on variety rather than quality, but avoid any that look at all droopy or have thin, wrinkled or woody stems. Since asparagus needs to be eaten really fresh, the further it has travelled, the less likely it is still to be of the best quality.

To prepare: Rinse each stalk gently and break or cut off the end if it is tough and woody. Scrape or shave the length of each stalk, starting just below the tip. Trim the stalks to roughly the same lengths and tie them in bundles of six to eight stalks for steaming, tying them under the tips and near the base of the stalks.

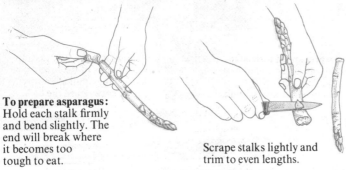

To prepare asparagus: Hold each stalk firmly and bend slightly. The end will break where it becomes too tough to eat.

Scrape stalks lightly and trim to even lengths.

Basic cooking: Wedge the bundles, tips up, in a deep saucepan with enough boiling salted water to come three quarters of the way up the stalks. Cover the tips with a cap of foil and simmer gently until tender. This way the stalks are poached, while the delicate tips are steamed. Home-grown, very fresh asparagus will need to cook for only 3–5 minutes; otherwise simmer for about 10 minutes. Drain well on kitchen paper towel. Remove the strings and serve hot with hollandaise sauce (page 463) or melted butter. (Colour index page 21.) To serve cold, refresh cooked asparagus in cold water; drain. Serve with French dressing (page 326).

Seasonings: Dill, tarragon, parsley, mustard, coriander.

Stir-fried Asparagus

700 g (1½ lb) asparagus, washed and trimmed

30 ml (2 tbsp) vegetable oil
2.5 ml (½ level tsp) salt

Colour index page 70

6 side dish servings

1. Cut the asparagus diagonally into pieces.
2. Heat the oil in a large frying pan, add the asparagus and stir to coat with the oil.
3. Sprinkle with the salt and stir-fry (page 266) for a further 3 minutes, until the asparagus is just tender.

Aubergines

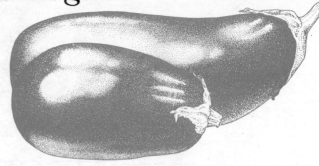

Season: Imported aubergines are available all year.

To buy: Look for firm, smooth aubergines with tight, shiny skins. Size makes no difference to flavour.

To prepare: Remove the stalk and leaves, then peel if you wish. To remove any bitterness and make the vegetable more easily digestible, slice fairly thickly, put the slices in a colander and sprinkle with salt. Leave for 30 minutes to drain, then rinse thoroughly and pat dry.

Basic cooking: Coat aubergine slices with flour and fry gently in melted butter for 5 minutes on each side or until golden. Alternatively, brush the floured slices with melted butter and cook under a hot grill for 5–10 minutes, turning once.

Seasonings: Garlic, caraway, mint.

To prepare an aubergine: Cut off stalk and leaves then slice the aubergine thickly. If you wish, sprinkle with salt and leave for 30 minutes to drain bitter juices.

Colour index page 69

4 side dish servings

Aubergine with Caraway Seeds

30 ml (2 tbsp) vegetable oil
175 g (6 oz) streaky bacon, rinded and finely chopped
1 medium onion, skinned and sliced

5 ml (1 level tsp) caraway seeds
10 ml (2 tsp) vinegar
2.5 ml (½ level tsp) salt
1 small aubergine

1. Heat the oil in a large frying pan. Add the bacon with the onion, caraway seeds, vinegar and salt and fry gently for about 10 minutes, until the bacon and onion are lightly browned.
2. Cut the aubergine into cubes and add them to the pan. Cover and cook for a further 5 minutes or until the aubergine is tender.

Sautéed Aubergine Slices

450 g (1 lb) aubergines
75 ml (5 tbsp) olive or vegetable oil
25 g (1 oz) butter or margarine

175 ml (6 fl oz) water
5 ml (1 level tsp) salt
pinch pepper

Colour index page 69

4 side dish servings

1. Cut the aubergines into 1-cm (½-in) slices; halve each slice. Heat the oil and fat in a large frying pan, add the aubergine and fry over high heat, stirring constantly, until lightly browned.
2. Stir in the water and seasoning; cook for a further 5 minutes, stirring frequently.

Beans, broad

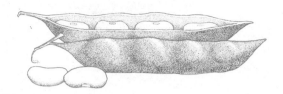

Season: Broad beans are available during the summer.
To buy: Choose smallish, full-looking pods if possible, as these are likely to be the youngest and most tender. If you have your own garden and can grow your own, you can pick them when only 5–7.5 cm (2–3 in) long and cook them whole, in the pod.
To prepare: Tiny pods need trimming only. Larger ones should be split and the beans removed.
Basic cooking: Cook in boiling salted water until just tender; 5 minutes for really young, fresh beans and 15–20 minutes for older ones. When cooked, slip any large beans out of their skins, as these may be tough. Large, mature beans should be puréed. Cook in boiling salted water as above, remove the outer skins and purée in a blender, or rub through a sieve; then add 25–50 g (1–2 oz) butter and some chopped fresh herbs.
Seasonings: Thyme, lemon juice, dill, parsley, chives.

To remove beans: Snap off one end of pod, open it with your thumbs and squeeze out beans.

Or, cut a thin strip from the inner edge of the pod to open it, then remove beans.

Broad Beans with Soured Cream

Colour index page 68

4 side dish servings

900 g (2 lb) young broad beans, shelled
100 ml (4 fl oz) soured cream
45 ml (3 tbsp) chopped chives

25 g (1 oz) canned pimentos, diced
1.25 ml (¼ level tsp) garlic salt
1.25 ml (¼ level tsp) salt
1.25 ml (¼ level tsp) pepper

1. Cook the beans in boiling salted water for 15–20 minutes until just tender. Drain well.
2. Toss beans lightly with the remaining ingredients until well mixed. Reheat gently without boiling.

Broad Beans with Water Chestnuts

Colour index page 68

4 side dish servings

900 g (2 lb) broad beans, shelled
141-g (5-oz) can water chestnuts, drained and sliced

60 ml (4 tbsp) French dressing, page 326
3.75 ml (¾ level tsp) dried dill weed

1. Cook the broad beans in boiling salted water for 15–20 minutes until just tender. Drain well.
2. Toss with the water chestnuts, French dressing and dill weed until well mixed. Cover and chill.

Beans, dried

BLACK-EYE BEANS　　RED KIDNEY BEANS ✱　　BUTTER BEANS

These include haricot beans, red kidney beans, flageolets, butter beans and black-eye beans, but many other varieties are available from specialist shops.
To buy: If you are buying packaged beans, the brand name should be some guarantee of quality. If you are buying loose beans, go to a shop that has a fast turnover to ensure that the beans will be young and fresh. Stale beans rarely soften, however long the cooking time.
To prepare: Rinse the beans and soak overnight in cold water, or cover with cold water, bring to the boil, then leave to stand in the hot water for about 2 hours. Dried peas and lentils are prepared in much the same way.
Basic cooking: Drain the soaked beans, cover with fresh water and add herbs, vegetables, bacon or a ham bone for flavouring. Bring to the boil, cover and simmer until soft, following the cooking times given below.
✱ Boil red kidney beans vigorously for at least 10 minutes.
Seasonings: Dried beans are seasoned by the flavouring ingredients used in the basic cooking. Add salt 10 minutes before cooking is complete.

COOKING DRIED BEANS, PEAS AND LENTILS			
Type of bean	**Cooking time after soaking**	**Type of bean**	**Cooking time after soaking**
Aduki beans	30–40 minutes	Foule beans	1 hour
Black beans	1 hour	Haricot beans	1 hour
Black-eye beans	1 hour	Peas	40–50 minutes
Brown lentils	10–15 minutes	Red kidney beans	1 hour ✱
Butter beans	1½ hours	Red lentils	10–15 minutes
Cannellini beans	1 hour	Rose cocoa beans	1 hour
Chick peas	30–40 minutes	Split peas	1 hour
Flageolets	1 hour	Soya beans	1½ hours

Boston Baked Beans

Colour index page 68

4 side dish servings

250–350 g (9–12 oz) haricot beans, soaked overnight
225 g (8 oz) salt belly pork
2 onions, skinned and halved
7.5 ml (1½ level tsp) dry mustard

5 ml (1 level tsp) salt
large pinch pepper
15 ml (1 level tbsp) sugar
30 ml (2 level tbsp) black treacle
30 ml (2 tbsp) cider vinegar
pinch ground cinnamon
pinch ground cloves

1. Drain the beans, reserving the soaking liquid. Cut the pork into 2.5-cm (1-in) cubes, if you wish. Put the beans in a large ovenproof casserole and tuck in the salt pork and onions. Add enough soaking liquid to cover the beans and stir in the remaining ingredients until well mixed. Reserve the rest of the soaking liquid.
2. Cover the casserole and cook at 150°C (300°F) mark 2 for 8–9 hours, stirring occasionally. Add more of the soaking liquid if the beans dry out too much during cooking.

Beans, dried

Colour index
page 68

4–6 side dish
servings

Southern Style Black-eye Beans

225 g (8 oz) black-eye
beans, soaked overnight
1 litre (1³/₄ pints) cold
water

225 g (8 oz) salt belly pork
salt and pepper

1. Drain the black-eye beans well and place in a saucepan with the water.
2. Slice the salt pork or cut it into chunks, add to the pan and bring to the boil.
3. Reduce the heat, cover and simmer for 1¼ hours or until the salt pork is tender, stirring occasionally. Season with salt and pepper to taste.

Colour index
page 68

6 side dish
servings

Spicy Beans and Sweetcorn

450 g (1 lb) red kidney
beans, cooked
326-g (11½-oz) can
sweetcorn kernels
175 ml (6 fl oz) cider
vinegar
100 g (4 oz) sugar
2 onions, skinned and sliced

5 ml (1 level tsp) salt
5 ml (1 level tsp) mustard
seeds
2.5 ml (½ level tsp) pepper
20 ml (4 level tsp) cornflour
100 ml (4 fl oz) water

1. Mix the beans with the sweetcorn and its liquid in a large serving bowl.
2. Put the vinegar, sugar, onions, salt, mustard seeds and pepper in a saucepan and bring to the boil. Cover and cook for 5 minutes.
3. Blend the cornflour with the water and stir it into the vinegar mixture. Bring to the boil, stirring constantly, and boil for 1 minute.
4. Pour the mixture over the beans and sweetcorn and stir until well mixed. Cool slightly, cover and chill for at least 4 hours before serving, stirring occasionally so that the flavours will blend evenly.

Colour index
page 33

6 main dish
servings

Puerto Rican Beans and Rice

450 g (1 lb) rose cocoa
beans, soaked
overnight
1.5 litres (2½ pints) water
50 g (2 oz) salt belly
pork, diced
1 large onion, skinned and
chopped
1 large green pepper, seeded
and chopped
226-g (8-oz) can tomatoes
2.5 ml (½ level tsp) dried
oregano

1.25 ml (¼ level tsp) garlic
salt
10 ml (2 level tsp) salt
1.25 ml (¼ level tsp)
pepper
To serve:
300 g (10 oz) long grain
rice, cooked and kept hot

1. Drain the beans, place them in a large saucepan with the water and bring to the boil. Reduce the heat, cover the saucepan and simmer for about 40 minutes, stirring occasionally.
2. Meanwhile, fry the salt pork gently in its own fat for 10 minutes or until well browned. Add the onion and green pepper and cook until the vegetables are tender, stirring occasionally.
3. Stir the salt pork mixture and the remaining ingredients into the beans and cook for a further 40–50 minutes, until the beans are tender and the mixture has thickened.
4. Arrange the rice on a heated serving dish and spoon the beans over the top.

Beans, French

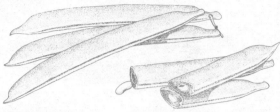

Season: French beans are available all year round, but are at their best in early summer and midsummer.

To buy: Look for firm, strong beans with a bright green colour. They should break with a crisp snap. Avoid any that are limp or have brown patches.

To prepare: Wash beans in cold water, top and tail them and trim into even lengths or cut in half. If wilted, refresh them by chilling in the refrigerator.

Basic cooking: Cook in boiling salted water for 5–10 minutes or steam for 15–20 minutes, until just tender but still crisp. Toss in a little melted butter or reheat with a little cream. For serving cold in salads, drain the cooked beans well and refresh in cold water; this helps to retain their bright green colour and will also keep them crisp. Toss in French dressing (page 326) and chill thoroughly before serving.

Seasonings: Marjoram, basil, oregano, bay leaf, dill, thyme, garlic, paprika.

To prepare French beans: Wash in cold water and snap off the ends with your fingers.

Using a small sharp knife, trim the beans to even lengths or halve them if very long.

Colour index
page 68

4 side dish
servings

French Beans with Thyme

25 g (1 oz) butter
1 onion, skinned and thinly
sliced
4 rashers streaky bacon,
rinded and chopped
700 g (1½ lb) French
beans, topped and tailed

5 ml (1 level tsp) dried
thyme
2.5 ml (½ level tsp) salt
large pinch pepper
90 ml (6 tbsp) cold water

1. Melt the butter in a large saucepan, add the onion and bacon and fry them together for 10 minutes.
2. Add the beans to the pan with the thyme, seasoning and water. Cover and simmer for 10–15 minutes, until the beans are just tender.

FRENCH BEANS PAPRIKA: Prepare as above, but omit the bacon; replace the thyme with *2.5 ml (½ level tsp) paprika* and the water with *chicken stock*. When the beans are cooked, stir in *150 ml (¼ pint) soured cream* and reheat gently.

DILLED FRENCH BEANS: Prepare as above, but add *75 ml (5 tbsp) wine vinegar, 7.5 ml (1½ level tsp) dill seed* and *7.5 ml (1½ level tsp) seasoned salt* to the onion and bacon and simmer for 20 minutes. Cook the beans separately and stir in just before serving.

Beans, runner

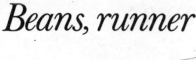

Season: Available from midsummer to autumn.

To buy: Runner beans need to be eaten very young and fresh. To test a runner bean for freshness, snap it in two; it should break with a crisp snap and the inside should be fresh and juicy. Avoid large, dark green beans, which are likely to be tough and stringy.

To prepare: Wash the beans in cold water. Top and tail them and remove the strings from the sides with the help of a small sharp knife. Slice the beans into 5-7.5 cm (2–3 in) lengths and then cut them lengthways into thin slivers or diagonally into 2.5-cm (1-in) lengths.

Basic cooking: Cook in boiling salted water for 5-10 minutes or steam for 15-20 minutes, according to age and size, until tender but still crisp. Drain well and toss in a little melted butter.

Seasonings: Marjoram, basil, dill, sage.

To prepare runner beans: Use a small knife to pull off strings.

Cut beans lengthways into thin slivers or slice diagonally.

Runner Beans with Sage Butter

Colour index page 67

4 side dish servings

700 g (1½ lb) runner beans, strings removed	**50 g (2 oz) butter**
4 spring onions, trimmed and chopped	**15 ml (1 tbsp) chopped fresh sage**
	salt and pepper

1. Cut beans into strips and cook in boiling salted water for 5–10 minutes until just tender. Drain well.
2. Sauté the spring onions in the butter for 5–10 minutes until soft. Stir in the sage and seasoning and cook for 1 minute more. Add the beans and toss lightly until well coated.

Runner Beans with Cheesy Topping

Colour index page 67

4 side dish servings

700 g (1½ lb) runner beans, strings removed	**50 g (2 oz) butter**
50 g (2 oz) fresh white breadcrumbs	**salt and pepper**
	50 g (2 oz) Cheddar cheese, grated

1. Cut beans into strips and cook in boiling salted water for 5–10 minutes until just tender. Drain well.
2. Sauté the breadcrumbs in half the butter until golden and season with salt and pepper. Add the remaining butter to the beans; toss until well coated.
3. Just before serving, sprinkle the beans with the cheese and breadcrumbs.

Beetroots

Season: Beetroots are available all year round.

To buy: Look for firm, smallish beetroots. The tops, if any, should be crisp and fresh-looking.

To prepare: Scrub carefully, taking care not to damage the skin or the colour and flavour will 'bleed' away during cooking. Twist off the roots about 2.5 cm (1 in) from the end and trim any tops.

Basic cooking: Place in a pan of cold salted water, bring to the boil and simmer gently for 1–3 hours, according to size. To test if beetroots are cooked, remove one from the pan and rub the skin gently; it should slide off easily. To bake beetroots, scrub and wrap in foil or place in a covered ovenproof dish. Bake at 180°C (350°F) mark 4 for 2–3 hours, according to size. Remove the skin and slice or dice the beetroots. To serve hot, toss in melted butter and sprinkle with plenty of herbs, salt and pepper. Or, chill thoroughly and serve in a salad or with French dressing (page 326).

Seasonings: Fennel, caraway, dill, parsley; for cold salads use horseradish, tarragon, savory, mint.

To prepare beetroots: Twist off the root, trim tops and clean thoroughly with a vegetable brush, being careful not to damage the skin.

After cooking the beetroots, allow them to cool slightly. Scrape off the skins with a sharp knife and slice or dice as required.

Sweet and Sour Beetroots

Colour index page 68

6 side dish servings

15 g (½ oz) butter or margarine	**2.5 ml (½ level tsp) salt**
30 ml (2 tbsp) chopped onion	**75 ml (5 tbsp) vinegar**
50 g (2 oz) sugar	**700 g (1½ lb) cooked beetroots, skinned and sliced**
15 ml (1 level tbsp) cornflour	

1. Melt the fat in a saucepan and sauté the onion for 5 minutes. Stir in the sugar, cornflour, salt and vinegar and cook, stirring, until thickened.
2. Reduce the heat, add the beetroots and heat through, stirring occasionally. Serve hot or cold.

BEETROOTS IN ORANGE SAUCE: Prepare as above, but omit vinegar and onion; add **100 ml (4 fl oz) orange juice** and **5 ml (1 tsp) grated orange rind.** Serve hot or cold.

Broccoli

Season: Sprouting broccoli is available from mid-winter to early spring; heading varieties in autumn and winter.
To buy: Broccoli may be green, purple or white. Sprouting varieties should have strong stalks and heads. In heading varieties look for closely packed heads.
To prepare: For sprouting varieties, trim the stalks and leaves, halve shoots if large, then tie in small bundles. Prepare heading varieties as cauliflower (page 284).
Basic cooking: Simmer bundles of sprouting broccoli upright in boiling salted water for 10–15 minutes or steam for 20 minutes. Toss in melted butter. Cook heading varieties as for cauliflower.
Seasonings: Parsley, marjoram, dill, nutmeg.

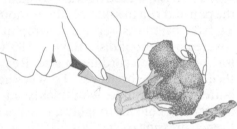

To prepare broccoli:
Trim the stems and remove any small leaves. Divide larger stalks of broccoli lengthways into two or three pieces with a sharp knife.

Stir-fried Broccoli

Colour index page 72

4–6 side dish servings

700 g (1½ lb) broccoli, trimmed	50 ml (2 fl oz) water
45 ml (3 tbsp) vegetable oil	2.5 ml (½ level tsp) salt
	1.25 ml (¼ level tsp) sugar

1. With a sharp knife, cut the head and stalk of the broccoli into 5-cm (2-in) pieces.
2. Heat the oil in a large frying pan, add the broccoli and fry quickly over high heat, stirring, until evenly coated with the oil.
3. Add the water, salt and sugar and reduce the heat. Cover and cook for 2 minutes, then uncover and stir-fry (page 266) for a further 5–6 minutes, until the broccoli is tender but still crisp.

Baked Broccoli with Gruyère

Colour index page 72

6 side dish servings

450 g (1 lb) broccoli, trimmed	45 ml (3 tbsp) chopped onion
40 g (1½ oz) butter or margarine	300 ml (½ pint) milk
30 ml (2 level tbsp) plain flour	225 g (8 oz) Gruyère cheese, grated
7.5 ml (1½ level tsp) salt	2 eggs, beaten

1. Chop the broccoli roughly. Cook in 2.5 cm (1 in) boiling salted water for 10 minutes. Drain well.
2. Melt the fat and stir in the flour and salt. Add the onion and cook for 1 minute. Gradually stir in the milk and cook until the sauce boils and thickens, stirring constantly. Remove from the heat.
3. Stir the cheese into the sauce until it melts. Beat in the eggs and stir in the broccoli.
4. Pour the mixture into a greased ovenproof dish and bake at 190°C (375°F) mark 5 for 30 minutes.

Brussels sprouts

Season: Brussels sprouts are available throughout the winter and in spring.
To buy: Choose small, evenly sized sprouts that look closely packed and solid. Avoid any with wilted leaves.
To prepare: Wash the sprouts thoroughly in cold water. Trim off any damaged outer leaves and the stem. Cut a small cross in the base of the sprout to help the thick stem cook at the same speed as the leaves. Sprouts can also be served raw in salads: shred them finely.
Basic cooking: Cook in boiling salted water for 10–15 minutes or steam for 15–20 minutes. Drain well, pressing if necessary to remove all excess water. Serve tossed in melted butter or mornay sauce (page 461).
Seasonings: Fennel, marjoram, parsley, mustard, nutmeg, mace.

To prepare Brussels sprouts:
Trim the stem and pull off any damaged outer leaves with your fingers.

Cut a small cross in the base of the sprout so stem and leaves will finish cooking at the same time.

Brussels Sprouts with Buttered Crumbs

Colour index page 71

4 side dish servings

700 g (1½ lb) Brussels sprouts, washed and trimmed	salt and pepper
50 g (2 oz) butter	45 ml (3 tbsp) chopped parsley, optional
50 g (2 oz) fresh white breadcrumbs	15 ml (1 tbsp) chopped fresh marjoram, optional

1. Cut a cross in the base of each Brussels sprout and cook them in boiling salted water for 10–15 minutes until just tender. Drain well.
2. Meanwhile, melt the butter in a small pan, add the breadcrumbs and cook until golden brown. Add the seasoning and, if you wish, the herbs.
3. Stir in the Brussels sprouts and reheat gently.

Brussels Sprouts with Bacon

Colour index page 71

4–6 side dish servings

175 g (6 oz) streaky bacon, rinded and finely chopped	30 ml (2 tbsp) wine vinegar
½ onion, skinned and finely chopped	15 ml (1 level tbsp) sugar
700 g (1½ lb) Brussels sprouts, washed and trimmed	3.75 ml (¾ level tsp) salt
	1.25 ml (¼ level tsp) dry mustard
	pinch pepper

1. Fry the bacon with the onion until browned. Remove and drain on kitchen paper towel.
2. Cut a cross in the base of each Brussels sprout. Add them to the bacon fat with the vinegar, sugar and seasonings. Cook for 10 minutes or until tender but still crisp, stirring occasionally.
3. Add the bacon and onion and mix well.

Cabbages

SAVOY CABBAGE

WHITE CABBAGE

Season: Different types are available all year.
To buy: The leaves of green cabbage should be fresh and crisp looking; avoid any that show signs of yellowing. White and red cabbages should be round, closely packed and heavy for their size. Chinese cabbage should have a good, fresh colour and a closely packed heart.
To prepare: Discard any damaged leaves. Cut the cabbage into wedges or shred on a grater; wash in cold water. Crisp varieties such as Dutch, Savoy and Chinese cabbage make good salad vegetables. Shred finely for use in coleslaw (page 319).
Basic cooking: Place shredded cabbage in boiling salted water and cook for 5–10 minutes or steam for 10–15 minutes, until tender but still crisp. Cabbage wedges will cook in 15 minutes. Add 15 ml (1 tbsp) vinegar to the water before cooking red cabbage, then boil for 15–20 minutes. Drain well, toss with butter and season to taste.
Seasonings: Nutmeg, fennel, marjoram, caraway.

To prepare cabbage: Discard any wilted or discoloured leaves before cutting or shredding.

Using a strong sharp knife, cut the cabbage in half and then quarters. Rinse thoroughly.

Cut away most of the tough stalk, leaving just enough to hold the leaves in wedges.

Or, shred the cabbage with a sharp knife or grater, discarding stalk. Rinse well.

Fried Cabbage

Colour index page 69

4–6 side dish servings

700 g (1½ lb) white cabbage, trimmed and quartered
8 rashers streaky bacon, rinded and diced

50 g (2 oz) onion, skinned and finely chopped
10 ml (2 level tsp) salt

1. Shred the cabbage and wash it thoroughly.
2. Fry the bacon and onion together for 5 minutes or until the onion is soft but not coloured.
3. Add the cabbage and salt and cook for 10 minutes or until the cabbage is tender, stirring occasionally.

Sweet and Sour Red Cabbage Casserole

Colour index page 69

4 side dish servings

900 g (2 lb) red cabbage, trimmed and quartered
2 onions, skinned and sliced
2 cooking apples, peeled, cored and chopped
10 ml (2 level tsp) sugar

salt and pepper
bouquet garni
30 ml (2 tbsp) red wine vinegar
30 ml (2 tbsp) water
25 g (1 oz) butter

1. Shred the cabbage and wash it thoroughly.
2. Layer the cabbage, onions, apples, sugar and seasoning in a casserole. Place the bouquet garni in the centre and spoon over the vinegar and water.
3. Cover and bake at 150°C (300°F) mark 2 for 2½ hours. Dot with butter before serving and stir well.

Cabbage Braised in Cider

Colour index page 69

4 side dish servings

1 green cabbage, trimmed and quartered
25 g (1 oz) butter
1 onion, skinned and chopped
30 ml (2 level tbsp) plain flour

300 ml (½ pint) cider
150 ml (¼ pint) chicken stock
salt and pepper
225 g (8 oz) cooking apples, peeled, cored and chopped

1. Cut the thick centre stalk out of the cabbage quarters and blanch them in boiling salted water for 5 minutes. Drain and arrange in an ovenproof dish.
2. Melt the butter, add the onion and sauté for 5 minutes or until soft. Stir in the flour and cook for 1 minute. Gradually stir in the cider and stock and bring to the boil, stirring.
3. Add seasoning and the apples; pour over the cabbage. Cover and bake at 180°C (350°F) mark 4 for 1½–1¾ hours.

Marinated Cabbage

Colour index page 69

4–6 side dish servings

350 g (12 oz) green cabbage, trimmed, shredded and washed
1 large green pepper, seeded and chopped
1 large red pepper, seeded and chopped
1 onion, skinned and thinly sliced

For the marinade:
175 ml (6 fl oz) white vinegar
175 ml (6 fl oz) water
10 ml (2 level tsp) salt
75 ml (5 level tbsp) sugar
15 ml (1 level tbsp) mustard seeds

1. Put all the ingredients for the marinade into a saucepan; bring to the boil. Reduce the heat and simmer for 5 minutes, stirring occasionally. Leave to cool until lukewarm.
2. Mix all the vegetables in a large salad bowl. Pour the marinade over them and mix well together. Cover and chill thoroughly before serving.

Carrots

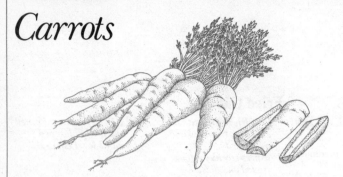

Season: Carrots are available all year round.

To buy: Choose brightly coloured, evenly sized carrots with smooth skins. Avoid soft or shrivelled carrots.

To prepare: For new carrots, remove stalks, scrub thoroughly and leave whole. For larger carrots, cut a slice from each end and scrape or peel thinly. Slice, dice or cut lengthways into matchsticks. Remove core if it is woody. Grate young, raw carrots into salads.

Basic cooking: Cook in boiling salted water for 8–10 minutes if sliced or diced, or for 10–12 minutes if whole or quartered. Alternatively, steam for 20–25 minutes. Drain well, toss in melted butter and sprinkle with fresh herbs. Purée very large carrots or use for soups.

Seasonings: Parsley, marjoram, basil, savory, thyme, chives, cloves, cinnamon, dill, ginger, nutmeg.

To prepare carrots: Wash thoroughly in cold water. Scrape with a small knife or peel thinly using a vegetable peeler. Cut them into even slices, dice or matchsticks, or grate for use in salads.

Glazed Carrots

Colour index page 68

4 side dish servings

700 g (1½ lb) carrots, peeled
50 g (2 oz) butter
30 ml (2 level tbsp) sugar
10 ml (2 level tsp) ground nutmeg

1. Cut the carrots into chunks or slices and cook in boiling salted water for 8–10 minutes. Drain well.
2. Melt the butter in a saucepan, add the sugar and cook until lightly browned. Add the carrots and nutmeg and cook over a low heat for 5 minutes until tender and glazed.

Spiced Carrots

Colour index page 68

4–6 side dish servings

700 g (1½ lb) carrots, peeled
50 g (2 oz) seedless raisins
50 g (2 oz) butter or margarine
45 ml (3 tbsp) finely chopped onion
5 ml (1 level tsp) salt
5 ml (1 level tsp) ground cinnamon
75 ml (3 fl oz) water
15 g (½ oz) soft light brown sugar

1. Slice the carrots and place in a large saucepan with all the ingredients except the sugar. Cook for 15 minutes or until the carrots are tender, stirring the mixture occasionally.
2. Add the sugar to the carrot mixture and continue to cook until the sugar has completely dissolved.

Cauliflowers

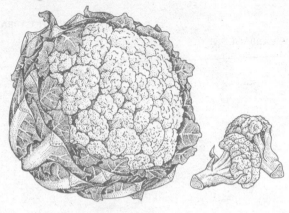

Season: Cauliflowers are available all year round.

To buy: Look for fresh green leaves surrounding a firm white head free of blemishes. The 'curd', made up of tiny flowers, should be tightly curled and closely packed.

To prepare: Cut away the green outside leaves. Trim base of stem and cut a cross in it. Cut away any damaged parts of the head and wash thoroughly. If you wish, cut the head into florets, discarding the centre stem.

Basic cooking: Cook a whole cauliflower, stem down, in 2–5 cm (1–2 in) boiling salted water for about 10–15 minutes, until the stalk is tender but still firm. Cook florets for only 5–10 minutes. Drain well and serve with béchamel sauce (page 461), mornay sauce (page 461) or dill butter (page 296).

Seasonings: Marjoram, savory, parsley, chervil, cloves, nutmeg, dill, thyme, curry powder.

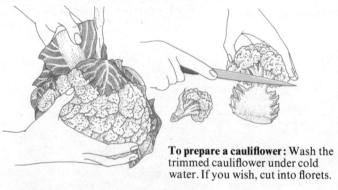

To prepare a cauliflower: Wash the trimmed cauliflower under cold water. If you wish, cut into florets.

Cauliflower Polonaise

Colour index page 67

6 side dish servings

1 cauliflower, trimmed and washed
25 g (1 oz) butter
25 g (1 oz) fresh white breadcrumbs
1 hard-boiled egg, shelled and chopped
15 ml (1 tbsp) chopped parsley
15 ml (1 tbsp) lemon juice
1.25 ml (¼ level tsp) salt

1. Cook the whole cauliflower, stem downwards, in boiling salted water for 10–15 minutes, until the stalk is tender but still crisp. Drain well.
2. Meanwhile, melt the butter in a small saucepan and sauté the breadcrumbs until golden. Add the chopped egg, parsley, lemon juice and salt and stir together until well mixed.
3. Place the whole cauliflower in a heated serving dish and sprinkle with the breadcrumb mixture.

Celery

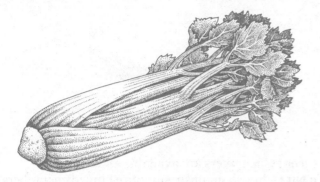

Chicory

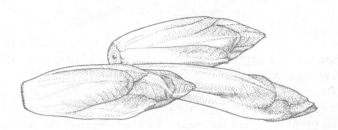

Season: Celery is available all year round.
To buy: Celery should look crisp and whole heads should have plenty of small inner stalks and 'heart'. Avoid over-large heads as these may be stringy. Self-blanching varieties have clean, light green stalks. Winter celery has a sweet flavour and tender stalks.
To prepare: Trim leaves and root. Separate stalks and scrub well. Save tough stalks and leaves to use as a flavouring. Celery is often eaten raw in salads.
Basic cooking: Cut celery into 2.5-cm (1-in) lengths. Cook in butter for 5 minutes, add stock to cover and simmer for 15–20 minutes, until the stalks are tender but still crisp. Drain well and sprinkle with herbs.
Seasonings: Chives, parsley, bay leaf, basil, dill, mustard, tarragon, thyme, lemon juice.

Season: Chicory is available all year round.
To buy: Look for compact heads with white leaves and yellow-green edges. Those with green tips are likely to be too bitter for salads, although the bitterness may be lessened by cooking.
To prepare: Wash in cold water if necessary and trim the root end and any damaged leaves. Separate each leaf, or leave the head whole and quarter it or slice it crossways. Chicory is usually eaten raw in salads.
Basic cooking: Blanch the whole heads in boiling salted water for 5 minutes and drain well. Cook in a very little fresh water with lemon juice, a knob of butter and seasoning for 20–30 minutes until just tender. Sprinkle with chopped parsley or paprika before serving.
Seasonings: Parsley, chives, marjoram, paprika, nutmeg, lemon juice, tarragon.

To prepare celery: Cut off the leaves and reserve to use as a flavouring. Trim root end.

Scrub celery stalks thoroughly under running cold water to remove all traces of soil.

To prepare chicory: Wash the chicory in cold water if it is dirty and trim the root end with a sharp knife.

Remove any wilted or damaged leaves before cooking the head whole or separating it into leaves to serve raw.

Sautéed Celery

Colour index page 71

4 side dish servings

1 small head celery	*2 bay leaves*
30 ml (2 tbsp) vegetable oil	*2.5 ml (½ level tsp) salt*
3.75 ml (¾ level tsp) dried thyme	*1.25 ml (¼ level tsp) pepper*

1. Trim the leaves and root from the celery. Wash thoroughly and cut diagonally into thin slices.
2. Heat the oil in a frying pan, add the celery and remaining ingredients; cook, stirring, for 15 minutes until celery is tender but crisp. Discard bay leaves.

SAUTEED CELERY WITH SPRING ONIONS: Prepare as above, but cut the celery into 7.5-cm (3-in) matchsticks and add *1 bunch spring onions*, trimmed and cut into 7.5-cm (3-in) pieces.

CELERY AU GRATIN: Prepare as above, but fry the celery with *1 chopped onion*. Put into an oven-proof dish; cover with *300 ml (½ pint) cheese sauce* (page 461). Sprinkle over *75 g (3 oz) grated Cheddar cheese* mixed with *50 g (2 oz) fresh breadcrumbs*. Bake at 190°C (375°F) mark 5 for 20–25 minutes.

Chicory au Gratin

Colour index page 69

6 side dish servings

6 small heads chicory, trimmed and washed	*50 g (2 oz) butter*
175 g (6 oz) Gruyère cheese, grated	*salt and pepper*
	75 ml (5 tbsp) single cream

1. Cook the chicory in boiling salted water for about 10 minutes and drain well.
2. Arrange chicory in a flameproof dish; sprinkle with the cheese. Dot with butter and season lightly.
3. Pour the single cream over the top and bake at 180°C (350°F) mark 4 for 10–15 minutes, until the cheese has melted then grill for 3 minutes.

CHICORY AND HAM AU GRATIN: Prepare as above, but wrap each head of chicory in a slice of *cooked ham* before arranging in the dish. Season and pour over the cream. Mix the cheese with *25 g (1 oz) fresh white breadcrumbs* and sprinkle on top. Bake at 200°C (400°F) mark 6 for 15 minutes.

Courgettes

Season: Courgettes are in season all year round. Cheaper, domestic supplies are available in summer.

To buy: Look for small courgettes with blemish-free skins as the larger ones will tend to have tough skins.

To prepare: Trim the ends and wash or wipe the skins with a damp cloth. Slice or cook whole. Larger courgettes may need salting, as for cucumbers (right), to remove bitter juices. Young courgettes are good raw.

Basic cooking: Steam whole courgettes for 5–8 minutes, until they are just tender. Toss in butter and season. Or, slice courgettes thickly and cook gently in butter in a covered pan for 5–10 minutes until tender.

Seasonings: Basil, marjoram, mint, thyme, garlic.

To prepare courgettes: Cut a thin slice off both ends of the courgettes before washing or wiping the skin with a damp cloth to remove any dirt.

Cut the trimmed courgettes into thick slices for cooking, or leave whole if you are going to steam them.

Stir-fried Courgettes

Colour index page 67

4 side dish servings

4 courgettes, trimmed and washed	60 ml (4 tbsp) water
15 ml (1 tbsp) vegetable oil	7.5 ml (1½ level tsp) salt
	2.5 ml (½ level tsp) sugar

1. Cut the courgettes into diagonal slices about 0.5 cm (¼ in) thick with a small sharp knife.

2. Heat the oil in a large frying pan. Add the courgettes and fry quickly, stirring all the time, until the slices are coated with the oil.

3. Add the water, salt and sugar and stir-fry (page 266) for 7–8 minutes, until courgettes are tender.

Courgettes in Soured Cream

Colour index page 67

4 side dish servings

4 courgettes, trimmed and washed	150 ml (¼ pint) soured cream
50 g (2 oz) plain flour	10 ml (2 tsp) lemon juice
2.5 ml (½ level tsp) salt	salt and pepper
50 g (2 oz) butter	chopped parsley
1 clove garlic, skinned	

1. Slice the courgettes diagonally. Mix the flour with the salt and coat the courgette slices with it.

2. Melt the butter in a large frying pan. Add the courgettes with the garlic and cook for 5 minutes on each side until golden. Drain well on kitchen paper towel, place in a serving dish and keep hot.

3. Remove the garlic from the pan and stir in the soured cream, lemon juice and seasoning. Heat through without boiling, pour over the courgettes and garnish with the chopped parsley.

Cucumbers

Season: Cucumbers are available all year round.

To buy: Choose smallish, smooth-skinned cucumbers as larger ones tend to be less tender, with bitter, indigestible seeds and rather tough skins.

To prepare: Small cucumbers need only wiping and cutting into slices, dice or chunks. Larger ones are better peeled. If bitter, peel and slice or dice the cucumber, put in a colander and sprinkle with salt. Leave to stand for 30 minutes–1 hour, then drain off the juice, rinse the cucumber and pat dry with kitchen paper towel. Cucumber is usually eaten raw as a salad vegetable.

Basic cooking: Steam or cook in boiling salted water for 5–10 minutes, then drain and toss in butter. To sauté, cook in butter for 5–10 minutes, add a little lemon juice and serve sprinkled with chopped fresh herbs.

Seasonings: Chervil, dill, chives, fennel, parsley, mint, paprika, lemon juice.

Buttery Cucumber Rings

Colour index page 70

4 side dish servings

1 large cucumber	2.5 ml (½ level tsp) salt
25 g (1 oz) butter	

1. Peel the cucumber thinly and cut it crossways into slices about 0.5 cm (¼ in) thick. Cut the seeds from each slice to form rings.

2. Melt the butter in a frying pan and add the cucumber rings and salt. Sauté for about 10 minutes or until the cucumber is tender but still crisp, stirring occasionally. Serve hot.

CUCUMBER GARNISHES

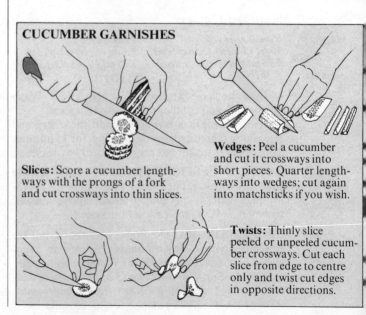

Slices: Score a cucumber lengthways with the prongs of a fork and cut crossways into thin slices.

Wedges: Peel a cucumber and cut it crossways into short pieces. Quarter lengthways into wedges; cut again into matchsticks if you wish.

Twists: Thinly slice peeled or unpeeled cucumber crossways. Cut each slice from edge to centre only and twist cut edges in opposite directions.

Fennel

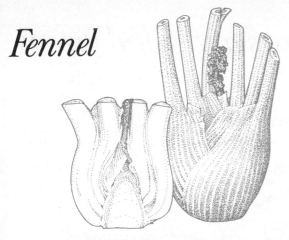

Season: Imported fennel is available all year round.
To buy: Select white or pale green bulbs, as dark green ones are likely to be slightly bitter.
To prepare: Trim off the root end and stalks, reserving any feathery leaves to use as a garnish. Leave the bulb whole, quarter it or slice it thinly, according to the recipe. Drop cut fennel into water acidulated with a little lemon juice to prevent discoloration.
Basic cooking: Place whole or cut fennel in a pan of cold salted water or chicken stock. Bring to the boil and simmer for 30–40 minutes. Drain, slice and serve tossed in melted butter. Alternatively, blanch the whole heads briefly in boiling salted water, then drain and sauté in butter for 5–10 minutes until golden.
Seasonings: Parsley, lemon juice, basil.

To prepare fennel: Using a small sharp knife, cut off the root end and the leaves.

Leave the bulb whole, cut it into quarters or slice it thinly, as you wish.

Braised Fennel

Colour index page 68

4 side dish servings

2 large heads fennel, trimmed
400 ml (³/₄ pint) chicken stock

25 g (1 oz) butter, softened
15 ml (1 level tbsp) plain flour

1. Cut each fennel in half lengthways. Chop any feathery leaves and reserve them for the garnish.
2. Put the fennel halves and stock in a saucepan and bring to the boil. Reduce the heat, cover and simmer for 15 minutes or until the fennel is just tender. Remove the fennel with a slotted spoon, arrange it on a serving dish and keep hot.
3. Blend the butter with the flour and whisk it into the stock in the pan. Cook, stirring, until the sauce boils and has thickened slightly. Spoon the sauce over the fennel, garnish with the chopped fennel leaves and serve at once.

BRAISED FENNEL RINGS: Prepare the fennel as above, but slice the bulbs carefully into rings instead of halving them lengthways and simmer for only 7–10 minutes or until just tender. Remove the rings carefully and finish as above.

Jerusalem artichokes

Season: Jerusalem artichokes are available from mid-autumn to early spring.
To buy: Look for hard Jerusalem artichokes and avoid any that are soft or have wrinkled skins. Choose smooth, even sized artichokes, as this makes their preparation much easier and less wasteful.
To prepare: Scrub, then leave the skins on for boiling or steaming; the skins can be peeled off before serving. Alternatively, peel and remove the most knobbly lumps before cooking. Drop peeled artichokes into acidulated water as they discolour quickly.
Basic cooking: Steam artichokes for 20–25 minutes or cook in boiling salted water for 15–20 minutes. A slice of lemon in the cooking water improves the flavour and helps keep the artichokes white. Drain well, toss in melted butter and sprinkle with chopped fresh herbs. Alternatively, coat with béchamel sauce (page 461), mornay sauce (page 461) or hollandaise sauce (page 463). Jerusalem artichokes can also be blanched for 5–10 minutes, then either sautéed gently in butter until golden or roasted in the fat around a joint of meat, as for parsnips (page 291).
Seasonings: Dill, parsley, nutmeg, lemon juice, thyme.

Jerusalem Artichokes in Lemon Cream

Colour index page 71

4 side dish servings

700 g (1¹/₂ lb) Jerusalem artichokes, washed and peeled
1 lemon
50 g (2 oz) butter

150 ml (¹/₄ pint) single cream
salt
white pepper
pinch ground nutmeg

1. Put the artichokes in a saucepan with a slice of lemon and cover with cold salted water. Bring to the boil, simmer gently for about 10 minutes and drain the artichokes well.
2. Melt the butter in a clean saucepan and add the artichokes and a little lemon juice. Cover and cook for 8–10 minutes, shaking the pan occasionally.
3. Remove from the heat and add the cream, seasoning and nutmeg. Heat through gently for about 5 minutes.

PUREE OF JERUSALEM ARTICHOKES: Prepare the artichokes as above, but mash well to make a thick purée before adding the cream, seasoning and nutmeg.

JERUSALEM ARTICHOKES POLONAISE: Prepare the artichokes as above, but omit the cream and nutmeg. While they are cooking, melt *25 g (1 oz) butter*, add *50 g (2 oz) fresh white breadcrumbs* and cook until golden brown. Chop the white and sieve the yolk of *1 hard-boiled egg*. Spoon the breadcrumbs, chopped egg white, sieved yolk and a little *chopped parsley* in rows over the artichokes.

Leeks

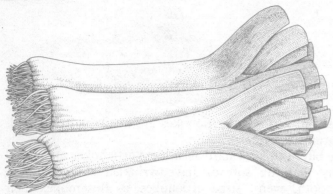

Season: Leeks are available from autumn to spring.

To buy: Look for small, tender leeks, well blanched at the root end and with crisp, green tops.

To prepare: Cut off the root and as much of the green tops as look tough. Cut a lengthways slit halfway through the leeks or cut very large leeks lengthways in half and wash. Or slice and wash in a colander.

Basic cooking: Steam sliced leeks for 5–7 minutes, or tie pieces in bundles and cook in boiling salted water for 10–15 minutes. Drain well; serve with melted butter and chopped fresh herbs or béchamel sauce (page 461).

Seasonings: Basil, sage, tarragon, thyme, parsley.

To prepare leeks: Trim roots and coarse green leaves. Slit small leeks or halve large leeks lengthways.

Wash the leeks thoroughly under running cold water to remove all the dirt.

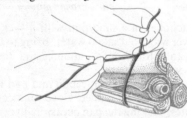

Cut the leeks into even sized pieces and tie loosely into bundles with string. Cook in boiling salted water. Remove the string before serving.

Leeks au Gratin

Colour index page 70

4 side dish servings

4 leeks, trimmed and washed	salt and white pepper
100 g (4 oz) Cheddar cheese, grated	300 ml (½ pint) béchamel sauce, page 461
2.5 ml (½ level tsp) dry mustard	50 g (2 oz) fresh white breadcrumbs

1. Cook the leeks in boiling salted water for 15 minutes until tender but still firm. Drain well.
2. Stir half the cheese and the seasonings into the béchamel sauce; heat gently until cheese has melted.
3. Arrange leeks in a greased flameproof dish and pour over sauce. Mix remaining cheese and breadcrumbs, spoon over leeks; brown under a hot grill.

Lettuces and salad greens

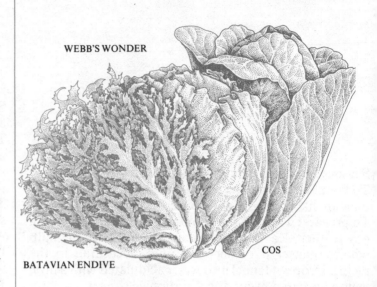

WEBB'S WONDER

BATAVIAN ENDIVE

COS

Season: Different varieties of lettuce are available throughout the year.

To buy: Webb's Wonder, Cos or similar crisp, firm-hearted varieties of lettuce have more flavour than the soft-leaved round lettuce, although all varieties are interchangeable. Look for fresh, strong leaves without brown or damaged patches; drooping lettuces can rarely be revived. When winter lettuces are in poor condition, look for alternatives among the following greens.

Batavian endive is crisp and curly-leaved. The flavour is very similar to that of lettuce, though perhaps slightly more bitter. Prepare and use in salads as for crisp varieties of lettuce.

Celtuce looks like a lettuce on a stalk and is rich in vitamin C. The leafy tops can be eaten raw, like lettuce, or cooked and eaten like spinach. The stem can be peeled and eaten raw, or cooked like celery.

Corn salad or lamb's lettuce has succulent, fleshy leaves with a good flavour. It is rarely grown commercially but is a good garden crop for over-wintering. Prepare and use in salads as for lettuce.

Dandelion leaves, either wild or cultivated, are good if blanched and eaten when young and tender. The flavour is slightly peppery and adds variety to a mixed green salad; in cooked dishes it combines well with fried bacon.

Sorrel, either wild or cultivated, can also be used in salads. Choose the youngest possible leaves and use sparingly, as the flavour is quite pronounced. Sorrel is also good cooked, particularly made into a soup.

To prepare: Follow the instructions on page 317 for cleaning and preparing lettuce and other salad greens.

Basic cooking: Lettuce wedges or small whole lettuces can be blanched in boiling salted water for 1 minute and then braised in well-seasoned chicken stock for 25–30 minutes until tender. Crisp lettuce leaves are good sautéed in butter or oil for 2–3 minutes, stirring all the time, until they are just beginning to soften.

Marrows

Season: Marrows are available in summer and autumn.
To buy: Look for small marrows that weigh only about 1 kg (2¼ lb).
To prepare: Peel marrows thinly, scoop out the seeds and cut into chunks or slices. If you wish, sprinkle cut-up marrow with salt and leave to drain for 30 minutes. Rinse well and pat dry.
Basic cooking: Steam for 20–40 minutes, according to age, or sauté in a little butter for 5–10 minutes.
Seasonings: Basil, marjoram, mint, thyme, nutmeg.

To prepare marrow: Halve, peel thinly and scoop out seeds.

If you wish, sprinkle marrow pieces with salt; leave to drain.

Spiced Marrow

Colour index page 72

4 side dish servings

1 onion, skinned and chopped
1 clove garlic, skinned and crushed
15 ml (1 tbsp) vegetable oil
25 g (1 oz) butter
15 ml (1 level tbsp) paprika
15 ml (1 level tbsp) tomato paste
pinch ground nutmeg

salt and pepper
15 ml (1 level tbsp) plain flour
150 ml (¼ pint) beef stock
4 large tomatoes, skinned and chopped
1 marrow, weighing about 1 kg (2¼ lb), peeled, seeded and cubed

1. Cook the onion and garlic in the oil and butter for 5 minutes. Add the next five ingredients; cook for 1–2 minutes more, stirring. Add the stock and tomatoes and simmer gently for 15 minutes.
2. Add the marrow and cook for about 10–15 minutes or until tender.

Marrow Fritters

Colour index page 72

4 side dish servings

1 marrow, weighing about 1 kg (2¼ lb), peeled, seeded and cubed
60 ml (4 level tbsp) seasoned flour
2 eggs, beaten

100 g (4 oz) fresh white breadcrumbs
45 ml (3 tbsp) vegetable oil
salt
tomato sauce, page 337

1. Coat the marrow with the seasoned flour, egg and finally the breadcrumbs. Heat the oil and fry the marrow for 6–8 minutes, turning once, until golden.
2. Sprinkle with salt and serve with tomato sauce.

Mushrooms

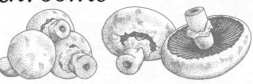

Season: Cultivated mushrooms are available all year round, field mushrooms in the late summer.
To buy: Look for button mushrooms when appearance is important. For flavour, buy flat or field mushrooms. Eat as soon as possible after purchase.
To prepare: Wipe with a damp cloth if necessary; do not peel unless the skin is damaged. Trim off any earthy root. Very fresh button mushrooms can be eaten raw.
Basic cooking: Poach in a little salted water and lemon juice for 3–5 minutes, then drain well. Steam whole or sliced mushrooms for 5–10 minutes until just tender.
Seasonings: Marjoram, mint, tarragon, lemon juice, thyme, chives, nutmeg, garlic, coriander.

To prepare mushrooms: Wipe with a damp cloth if dirty.

Mushrooms can be left whole or sliced thinly.

Sautéed Mushrooms

Colour index page 69

4 side dish servings

50 g (2 oz) butter or margarine
30 ml (2 tbsp) finely chopped onion
450 g (1 lb) button mushrooms

5 ml (1 tsp) lemon juice
2.5 ml (½ level tsp) salt
pinch pepper

To serve, optional:
toast slices

1. Melt the fat in a large saucepan, add the onion and fry gently for about 5 minutes or until tender. Slice the mushrooms and add to the pan. Cover and cook for a further 10 minutes, stirring occasionally.
2. Add the lemon juice, salt and pepper to the saucepan and stir until well mixed. For a more substantial dish, serve the mushrooms on toast.

DEVILLED MUSHROOMS: Prepare the mushrooms as above, but add *15 ml (1 level tbsp) tomato paste, 5 ml (1 tsp) Worcestershire sauce, 2.5 ml (½ tsp) vinegar* and a *pinch of ground nutmeg*.

Mushrooms in Soured Cream

Colour index page 69

6 first course servings

50 g (2 oz) butter
450 g (1 lb) mushrooms
450 g (1 lb) spring onions, trimmed and chopped
2.5 ml (½ level tsp) salt

1.25 ml (¼ level tsp) pepper
50 ml (2 fl oz) soured cream

1. Melt the butter in a large frying pan. Slice the mushrooms and add to the pan with the spring onions, salt and pepper. Cook the mushrooms gently, stirring frequently, for about 10 minutes or until tender.
2. Stir in the soured cream and heat through without boiling. Spoon into a heated serving dish and serve immediately, or chill thoroughly and serve cold.

Okra

Season: Imported okra is available all year round.

To buy: The ribbed pods are best when no more than about 7.5–10 cm (3–4 in) long. A brown tinge indicates staleness, so look for clean, dark green pods.

To prepare: Top and tail the pods and, if the ridges look tough or damaged, scrape them. Slice or leave whole, according to the recipe.

Basic cooking: Cook in boiling salted water for 5 minutes or sauté in oil for 5–10 minutes until tender.

Seasonings: Oregano, parsley, chives, garlic.

To prepare okra: Top and tail the okra and scrape the ridges if they are tough. Slice the okra cross-ways with a small sharp knife if you wish.

Okra Vinaigrette

Colour index page 69

6 side dish servings

700 g (1½ lb) okra
25 g (1 oz) red pepper
lettuce leaves

For the dressing:
75 ml (5 tbsp) vinegar
100 ml (4 fl oz) olive oil
1.25 ml (¼ level tsp) sugar

2.5 ml (½ level tsp) dry mustard
2.5 ml (½ level tsp) dried thyme
1 large clove garlic, skinned and crushed
salt and pepper

1 Top and tail the okra; trim any damaged pods. Place the okra in 2.5 cm (1 in) boiling salted water and cook for 5 minutes or until tender.

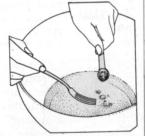

2 To make the dressing, put the vinegar and oil into a large bowl and add the sugar, mustard, thyme, garlic and a little salt and pepper. Stir well.

3 Seed and dice the red pepper. Add to the dressing with the cooked okra and mix together well. Chill for 4 hours, stirring occasionally.

4 To serve, arrange a few lettuce leaves on individual plates or dishes and divide the chilled okra vinaigrette equally between the plates.

Onions

Season: Onions are available all year round.

To buy: Look for clean, firm onions with dry, papery skins. Large Spanish onions have a mild, sweetish flavour; the smaller domestic varieties are stronger.

To prepare: Cut a thin slice off the top of the onion. Remove the dry papery skin and peel off any slightly soft, outer layers. Hold the onion by the root and slice, or cut in half and chop. Discard the root.

Basic cooking: Cook whole onions in boiling salted water for 30–40 minutes, depending on size. Drain and serve with butter. Steam whole onions for 40 minutes and sliced onions for 15 minutes.

Seasonings: Basil, sage, tarragon, thyme, cloves, dill, nutmeg, paprika, parsley, mint.

To prepare an onion: Cut a thin slice from the top of the onion and pull off the dry outer skin.

To chop an onion: Halve it and cut parallel slices down to the root. Turn and slice again, then cut across at right angles so the pieces fall away in neat dice.

Jacket Baked Onions

Colour index page 67

4 side dish servings

4 large onions
25 g (1 oz) butter
50 g (2 oz) Cheddar cheese, grated

15 ml (1 tbsp) chopped parsley
salt and pepper

1. Wash the onions and trim the base, leaving on the skin. Place in a roasting tin and bake at 180°C (350°F) mark 4 for 1–1½ hours until tender.
2. Scoop out the centre and chop finely. Mix with remaining ingredients and spoon mixture back into each onion. Bake for a further 10–15 minutes.

Glazed Onions

Colour index page 67

4 side dish servings

450 g (1 lb) small onions, skinned
50 g (2 oz) butter

10 ml (2 level tsp) sugar
salt and pepper
chopped parsley, optional

1. Put onions in a saucepan; cover with cold water. Bring to the boil; blanch for 10 minutes. Drain well.
2. Melt the butter and add the sugar, seasoning and onions. Cover and cook for 15 minutes, stirring occasionally, until the onions are tender and glazed.
3. Turn the onions into a heated serving dish and sprinkle with parsley if you wish.

Parsnips

Colour index page 67

4 side dish servings

Fried Onions

60 ml (4 tbsp) vegetable oil
4 large onions, skinned and sliced

1.25 ml (¼ level tsp) dried thyme
salt and pepper

1. Heat the oil in a frying pan and add the onions with the thyme. Fry them gently for about 5–10 minutes or until they are soft and golden brown, stirring occasionally.
2. Drain well on kitchen paper towel and season with salt and pepper before serving.

Crispy Fried Onions

Colour index page 67

4 side dish servings

4 large onions, skinned and cut into 0.5-cm (¼-in) slices
milk
seasoned flour

oil or fat for deep frying
salt and pepper

1. Separate the onion slices into rings. Dip them into the milk and then into the seasoned flour until they are evenly coated.
2. Heat the oil in a deep saucepan until an onion ring dropped into it rises to the surface surrounded by bubbles. Add the onion rings to the oil a few at a time and fry them for about 2–3 minutes or until golden brown.
3. Drain well on kitchen paper towel and season with salt and pepper before serving.

Onions in Cream Sauce

Colour index page 67

4 side dish servings

450 g (1 lb) small onions, skinned
300 ml (½ pint) chicken stock
large pinch paprika or cayenne pepper

For the sauce:
150 ml (¼ pint) single cream
300 ml (½ pint) béchamel sauce, page 461
salt and pepper

1. Put the onions and the stock in a saucepan, bring to the boil and simmer gently for 10 minutes. Drain well and cool slightly.
2. Stir the single cream into the béchamel sauce until evenly blended and add the onions. Season with salt and pepper to taste.
3. Reheat gently without boiling. Sprinkle with paprika or cayenne pepper before serving.

SPRING ONIONS AND SHALLOTS

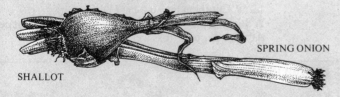

SPRING ONION

SHALLOT

Spring onions are small, immature onions, with a narrow white bulb and tender green shoots. Follow the instructions on page 316 for their preparation. They are usually served raw in salads; the green leaves can be chopped and used as a garnish. Shallots produce a cluster of cloves rather than a single large bulb. They have a milder flavour than onions and are useful for sauces and subtly flavoured dishes.

Season: Available from early autumn to spring.
To buy: Young parsnips are the most tender and the flavour is best after several frosts. Look for firm, clean roots without side shoots or soft brown blemishes.
To prepare: Scrub well. Trim top and root end and peel thinly. Leave whole, slice or quarter as required. Cut out the core from older, coarser parsnips.
Basic cooking: Steam sliced parsnips for 10 minutes. Parsnip quarters may be blanched in boiling salted water for 1–2 minutes, then drained well and either sautéed or roasted around a joint of meat. To sauté them, cook in melted butter for 10–12 minutes until golden and tender. To roast them, place in the roasting tin around the joint of meat and cook at 200°C (400°F) mark 6 for 40 minutes.
Seasonings: Basil, marjoram, thyme, parsley, ginger.

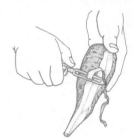

To prepare parsnips: Scrub parsnips well in cold water, then trim tops and bottoms.

Peel the parsnips thinly with a vegetable peeler.

Leave the parsnips whole, slice them or quarter them lengthways.

Creamed Parsnips

Colour index page 68

4 side dish servings

450 g (1 lb) parsnips, washed and trimmed
2.5 ml (½ level tsp) salt
225 ml (8 fl oz) water
chopped parsley

For the sauce:
30 ml (2 level tbsp) plain flour

100 ml (4 fl oz) milk
pinch pepper
2.5 ml (½ level tsp) salt
5 ml (1 tsp) grated orange rind

1. Peel the parsnips and cut crossways into 0.3-cm (⅛-in) slices. Put in a saucepan with the salt and water. Cook for 10 minutes or until tender; drain well. Reserve 100 ml (4 fl oz) of the cooking liquid.
2. Put the flour in a small saucepan and gradually stir in the milk. Add the reserved cooking liquid and seasonings and cook, stirring, until thickened.
3. Stir in the grated orange rind and the parsnips and heat through. Sprinkle with chopped parsley.

Peas

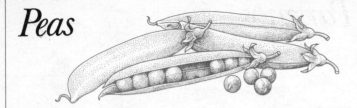

Season: Peas are in season in summer.

To buy: Look for crisp, young, well-filled pods, with a little air space left between the individual peas. Overfull pods may give tough, hard peas. Home or locally grown ones are often the best because they are more likely to be freshly picked.

To prepare: Shell the peas, discarding any that are blemished or discoloured and wash in running cold water. Peas need to be eaten very fresh indeed, so use them as soon as possible.

Basic cooking: Cook in lightly salted boiling water, with a sprig of fresh mint, for 10–15 minutes or until just tender. Alternatively, steam them for 3–5 minutes. Drain well and add a knob of butter if you wish.

Seasonings: Mint, basil, summer savory, chives.

To prepare peas: Press the pods between your thumb and forefinger to open and push the peas out with your thumb. Rinse well under running cold water and cook as soon as possible.

Peas Amandine

Colour index
page 70

4 side dish
servings

900 g (2 lb) peas, shelled
150 g (5 oz) streaky bacon, rinded and chopped
25 g (1 oz) onion, skinned and finely chopped

50 g (2 oz) blanched almonds, slivered
5 ml (1 level tsp) salt
100 ml (4 fl oz) double cream

1. Wash the peas in running cold water. Cook them in boiling salted water for about 5 minutes or until tender. Drain well.
2. Fry the bacon and onion together in a large saucepan for about 10 minutes or until lightly browned. Add the drained peas to the pan with the almonds and salt and heat through gently.
3. Stir in the double cream until evenly blended and reheat without boiling.

MANGE TOUT

The flat, undeveloped pods of mange tout, or snow peas, are eaten whole before the peas start to swell in their pods. They are in season early in the summer and should be eaten as soon as possible after picking. Rinse the pods and trim the ends. Mange tout can be eaten raw in salads, steamed, stir-fried (page 266) or sautéed gently in butter.

Peppers

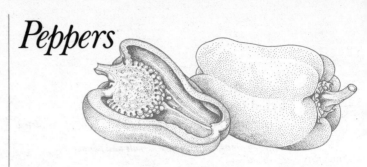

Season: Imported peppers are available all year round.

To buy: Look for firm, shiny peppers. The flavours of green, red and yellow peppers are similar.

To prepare: Rinse under running cold water, slice off the stem end and scrape out seeds and membrane. Use whole for stuffing or slice as required. Raw peppers are more digestible if skinned; grill until charred all over, plunge into cold water and rub off the skin.

Basic cooking: Steam whole peppers for 12 minutes. Use sliced in casseroles, mixed vegetable dishes or salads.

Seasonings: Basil, marjoram, rosemary, garlic.

To prepare a pepper: Slice off stem; remove seeds and membranes.

If you wish, slice the pepper into rings or strips.

Herb Sautéed Green Peppers

Colour index
page 70

4 side dish
servings

3 large green peppers, washed and seeded
25 g (1 oz) butter

2.5 ml (½ level tsp) salt
7.5 ml (1½ level tsp) dried marjoram or oregano

1. Cut the peppers into 1-cm (½-in) strips.
2. Melt the butter; sauté the peppers with the salt and herbs for 10 minutes or until just tender.

Marinated Peppers

Colour index
page 70

6 side dish
servings

6 large green peppers

For the marinade:
75 ml (5 tbsp) mayonnaise, page 462
60 ml (4 tbsp) white wine vinegar

10 ml (2 level tsp) sugar
5 ml (1 level tsp) salt
1.25 ml (¼ level tsp) white pepper

1. Char the peppers, skin them and scoop out the seeds. Cut them into 0.5-cm (¼-in) strips.
2. Stir together all the ingredients for the marinade. Add the peppers, toss well and chill.

CHILLI PEPPERS

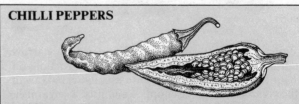

A chilli is a hot variety of pepper, rarely used on its own but often added to sauces and made-up dishes. Trim stems, halve lengthways and scoop out seeds; wash hands after handling.

Potatoes

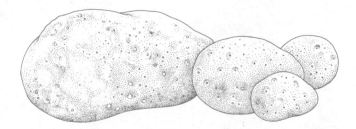

Season: Different varieties of potato are available all year round. New potatoes are in season in summer.

To buy: Look for smooth, evenly sized, firm potatoes, free of blemishes and sprouts. New potatoes should have skins so soft that they will rub off with your thumb.

To prepare: Scrape new potatoes or peel old ones very thinly. Cut large potatoes into even pieces, or scrub potatoes and cook them in their skins. Either eat the potatoes in their skins, which contain most of the goodness, or peel them after cooking.

Basic cooking: Place in cold salted water and bring to the boil. Cook new potatoes for 10–15 minutes and old potatoes for 15–20 minutes, until tender. Drain well, toss in melted butter and add chopped mint or parsley.

Seasonings: Chives, mint, parsley, dill, tarragon, fennel.

To prepare potatoes: Scrub thoroughly. Scrape new potatoes or peel old ones as thinly as possible, as most of the vitamins are contained in the skin or just underneath it. Cook immediately after peeling or the potato will discolour.

Baked Potatoes

Colour index page 71

4 side dish servings

4 large potatoes, well scrubbed
vegetable oil or melted butter

To serve:
soured cream, butter or grated Cheddar cheese

1. Dry the potatoes with kitchen paper towel and prick them all over with a fork. Brush the skins with a little oil or melted butter. Bake at 200°C (400°F) mark 6 for 1–1¼ hours, until soft.
2. Cut the potatoes in half lengthways or cut a cross in each one and serve topped with soured cream, butter or cheese.

Creamed Potatoes

Colour index page 71

4 side dish servings

700–900 g (1½–2 lb) potatoes, peeled
knob of butter

little hot milk
salt and pepper

1. Cut any large potatoes into small pieces. Place the potatoes in cold salted water and bring to the boil. Cook for 15–20 minutes or until tender and drain.
2. Mash the potatoes to a smooth purée with a fork or a potato masher and quickly beat in the butter, a little hot milk and salt and pepper to taste. Reheat gently, beating until fluffy.

Chip Potatoes

Colour index page 71

4 side dish servings

700–900 g (1½–2 lb) potatoes, peeled

oil or fat for deep frying
salt

1. Cut potatoes into 0.5–1-cm (¼–½-in) slices, then 0.5–1-cm (¼–½-in) sticks with a knife or crinkle cutter. Soak in cold water for 30 minutes; pat dry.
2. Heat the oil to 190°C (375°F): a chip dropped into it should rise immediately, surrounded by bubbles.
3. Quarter fill the basket with chips and lower into the oil. Cover and cook for 6–7 minutes. Drain on kitchen paper towel. Repeat with remaining chips.
4. Reheat oil; fry chips for 3 minutes more until golden and crisp. Drain well; sprinkle with salt.

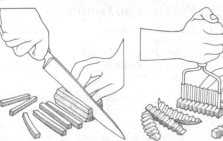

Cutting the chips: Using a large knife, cut the potato slices into neat sticks.

Using a crinkle cutter: For crinkle chips, cut the sticks with a special cutter.

Roast Potatoes

Colour index page 71

4 side dish servings

700–900 g (1½–2 lb) potatoes, peeled

lard or dripping
finely chopped parsley

1. Cut the potatoes into evenly sized pieces, place them in cold salted water and bring to the boil. Cook for 2–3 minutes and drain well.
2. Heat a little lard or dripping in a roasting tin in the oven. Add the potatoes, baste with the fat and cook at 220°C (425°F) mark 7, turning them once or twice, for 45 minutes or until golden brown. Or roast them around a joint. Sprinkle with parsley.

Sauté Potatoes

Colour index page 71

4 side dish servings

700–900 g (1½–2 lb) potatoes, washed
50 g (2 oz) butter or 60 ml (4 tbsp) vegetable oil

salt
freshly ground black pepper

1. Cook the potatoes in boiling salted water for 15 minutes or until just tender. Drain well and remove the skins. Cut the potatoes into 0.5-cm (¼-in) slices with a sharp knife.
2. Heat the butter or oil in a large frying pan and add the potato slices. Cook until golden brown and crisp all over. Drain well on kitchen paper towel and sprinkle with salt and pepper before serving.

CHATEAU POTATOES: Wash and scrape *700 g (1½ lb) small new potatoes*. Melt *50 g (2 oz) butter* in a frying pan and add the potatoes. Cover and cook gently, shaking the pan occasionally, for 15 minutes or until the potatoes are golden brown. Season well with *salt* and *freshly ground black pepper* and garnish with *chopped parsley* or chives.

Potatoes

Potato Hash

Colour index
page 71

6 side dish
servings

5-6 medium potatoes,
  peeled
100 g (4 oz) butter or
  margarine
5 ml (1 level tsp) salt

1.25 ml (¼ level tsp)
  pepper
2.5 ml (½ level tsp)
  paprika

1. Dice or coarsely grate the potatoes. Melt the fat in a large frying pan and add the potatoes; cover and cook for about 10 minutes.
2. Sprinkle with the salt, pepper and paprika and cook, uncovered, for a further 15 minutes or until the potatoes are tender and well browned, stirring occasionally. Serve at once.

Potatoes au Gratin

Colour index
page 71

6 side dish
servings

4–5 medium potatoes,
  peeled
7.5 ml (1½ level tsp) salt
25 g (1 oz) butter or
  margarine

100 g (4 oz) Cheddar
  cheese, grated
25 g (1 oz) fresh white
  breadcrumbs

1. Thinly slice the potatoes. Sprinkle them with salt and toss together until well mixed. Arrange them in even layers in a greased ovenproof dish.
2. Melt the fat and pour over the potatoes. Sprinkle evenly with the grated cheese and the breadcrumbs and bake at 220°C (425°F) mark 7 for about 1 hour until golden brown and bubbling.

Potatoes Anna

Colour index
page 71

4 side dish
servings

700 g (1½ lb) waxy
  potatoes, peeled
50–75 g (2–3 oz) butter,
  melted

salt and pepper

For the garnish, optional:
chopped parsley

1. Grease a round ovenproof dish or cake tin and line the base with greased greaseproof paper.
2. Slice the potatoes thinly and arrange them in layers, overlapping the slices and sprinkling each layer with melted butter and salt and pepper. Press the layers down well.
3. Cover with greaseproof paper or foil and bake at 190°C (375°F) mark 5 for about 1 hour until golden brown. Add a little more butter during cooking if the potatoes begin to look dry.
4. Loosen the potato cake with a palette knife or spatula and unmould on to a heated serving plate. Cut into wedges with a sharp knife. Sprinkle with a little chopped parsley if you wish.

Adding butter: Pour a little melted butter evenly over each layer of potato slices. Press down well.

Loosening the potatoes: Use a palette knife to loosen the cake before turning it out.

Radishes

Season: Radishes are available all year round.
To buy: Look for firm, brightly coloured radishes, free from blemishes. Red is the most common colour, but yellow, white and black varieties are available.
To prepare: Cut off any stalk or leaves and trim the root. Wash in cold water. Radishes are usually eaten raw.
Basic cooking: Cook in boiling salted water for 5–10 minutes, according to size. Drain; toss in melted butter.
Seasonings: Chives, parsley, mint, caraway.

To prepare radishes: Rinse in running cold water and trim the root and stem end with a sharp knife. If you wish, leave a little stalk on raw radishes and serve with a vegetable dip. If you are making radish garnishes, cut as desired and chill thoroughly.

Radish Spread

Colour index
page 18

Makes 400 ml
(¾ pint)

100 g (4 oz) radishes,
  trimmed and washed
225 ml (8 fl oz)
  mayonnaise, page 462
2.5 ml (½ level tsp) salt

50 ml (2 fl oz) soured
  cream
pumpernickel bread slices
radish slices

1. Grate the radishes and mix with the mayonnaise, salt and soured cream until well blended.
2. Spread on pumpernickel bread slices and top each one with a few radish slices.

RADISH GARNISHES

Radish lantern: Wash a large radish in cold water. Using a small sharp knife, trim the root and stem end. With the tip of the knife, cut out petal-shaped wedges, 0.3 cm (⅛ in) deep, around one end of the radish. Repeat around the other end, cutting each wedge under a space in the first row. Chill in iced water.

Radish rose: Wash a radish, including the stalk and leaves, in cold water. Using a small sharp knife, trim the root end neatly. Make five small cuts across the radish in a row around the stalk end. Make five more cuts into the radish just above the first row. Chill in iced water, until the 'petals' of the rose open.

Spinach

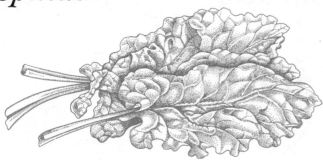

Season: Spinach is in season all year round.

To buy: Look for bright green, tender leaves. Avoid spinach that is yellowed or wilted. Buy plenty, as spinach reduces greatly in bulk during cooking.

To prepare: Wash well in several changes of water to remove all grit. For winter spinach or perpetual spinach, remove coarser stalks and centre ribs. For summer spinach, trim the base of the stalks and keep the leaves whole. Summer spinach is good served raw in a salad.

Basic cooking: Steam for 5-10 minutes in the water that remains on the leaves after washing, lightly salting the leaves first. Coarser spinach may require a little extra water. Drain well and sprinkle with ground nutmeg.

Seasonings: Nutmeg, marjoram, mint, lemon juice.

To prepare spinach: Wash leaves thoroughly in cold water.

Trim off any coarse stalks and centre ribs with a small knife.

Baked Creamed Spinach

Colour index page 67

4–6 side dish servings

900 g (2 lb) spinach, washed and trimmed
1 small onion, skinned and chopped
25 g (1 oz) butter or margarine
30 ml (2 level tbsp) plain flour
5 ml (1 level tsp) salt
pinch pepper
225 ml (8 fl oz) milk or single cream
2 eggs, separated

1. Cook the spinach in a large saucepan for 10 minutes. Drain well and chop finely.

2. Sauté the chopped onion in the fat for about 5 minutes or until tender.·

3. Stir in the flour, salt and pepper until well blended. Gradually add the milk or cream and cook, stirring, until the sauce has boiled and thickened.

4. Beat the egg yolks and stir in a small amount of sauce. Pour the mixture back into the bulk of the sauce; cook until the sauce has thickened, stirring constantly. Remove from heat and stir in spinach.

5. Beat the egg whites until stiff and fold them gently into the spinach mixture. Pour into a greased ovenproof dish and bake at 180°C (350°F) mark 4 for 20-25 minutes until a knife inserted into the centre comes out clean.

Swedes

Season: Swedes are in season in autumn and winter.

To buy: Select smaller swedes where possible, avoiding those that have been damaged during lifting.

To prepare: Scrub and peel swedes thickly to remove all tough skin and roots. Cut into even pieces or slices and keep covered with water. Cook as soon as possible after preparation as swedes discolour quickly. The green tops can be used as a vegetable if young and tender; cook in boiling salted water for about 5 minutes, until just tender.

Basic cooking: Place prepared swedes in cold salted water, bring to the boil and cook for about 20 minutes. Alternatively, steam for 15–20 minutes. Drain and serve as pieces or mash with a little butter and seasoning. Swedes can also be roasted in the fat around a joint of meat; allow 1–1¼ hours at 200°C (400°F) mark 6.

Seasonings: Parsley, marjoram, chives, ginger, nutmeg.

To prepare swedes: Using a stiff vegetable brush, scrub the swedes thoroughly in running cold water to remove dirt.

Peel thickly with a vegetable peeler or knife, remove the roots and cut into evenly sized pieces for cooking.

Butter-basted Swedes

Colour index page 72

4 side dish servings

700 g (1½ lb) small swedes, scrubbed and peeled
75 g (3 oz) butter, melted
2.5 ml (½ level tsp) salt
75 g (3 oz) fresh wholemeal breadcrumbs

1. Cut each swede into eight or ten pieces and score them with a knife.

2. Brush an ovenproof dish with a little of the butter, arrange the swedes in it and pour over most of the butter. Sprinkle with the salt, cover and bake at 200°C (400°F) mark 6 for 45 minutes, basting the swedes occasionally with the butter in the dish.

3. Stir the breadcrumbs into the remaining butter and spoon them evenly over the swedes. Bake uncovered for a further 15 minutes or until the breadcrumbs are golden brown.

Sweetcorn

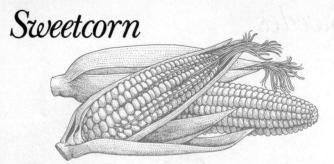

Season: Sweetcorn is available in summer and autumn.

To buy: Choose medium-sized cobs with leaves wrapped tightly around them. When the leaves are parted, the corn kernels should show plump and pale yellow.

To prepare: Cut off the stalk and remove the outer leaves and silk. If you want to remove the kernels, hold the cob upright and cut the kernels off the lower half of the cob with a strong sharp knife, working downwards and away from you. Reverse the cob and cut the kernels from other end in the same way.

Basic cooking: Plunge cobs into plenty of unsalted boiling water. Cook for 5–15 minutes, according to size and age, until a kernel can be removed easily from the base. Drain well; serve with melted butter and coarse salt and pepper. Cook kernels in a little unsalted boiling water for 5–10 minutes until tender; drain. Serve tossed in melted butter or cooled and stirred into a salad.

Seasonings: Parsley, marjoram, chives, mint, thyme.

To prepare corn on the cob: Just before cooking, remove the stalk, leaves and silk.

Use a stiff vegetable brush to clear any silk left clinging to the kernels.

Hold the cob upright and, working downwards and away from you, cut the kernels from the lower half with a strong, sharp knife. Reverse cob and repeat.

Colour index page 70

FLAVOURED BUTTERS FOR SWEETCORN

CHILLI BUTTER: Beat *100 g (4 oz) softened butter* with *10 ml (2 level tsp) salt, 5 ml (1 level tsp) chilli powder* and *1.25 ml (¼ level tsp) pepper* until evenly blended.

CHIVE BUTTER: Prepare as above, but omit the chilli powder and add *10 ml (2 tsp) chopped chives.*

DILL BUTTER: Prepare as above, but omit the chilli powder and add *5 ml (1 tsp) chopped dill weed.*

Tomatoes

Season: Tomatoes are available all year round, but they are at their best from late spring to autumn.

To buy: Look for firm, unblemished, light red tomatoes. Dark red tomatoes may be over-ripe.

To prepare: Halve, slice or cut into wedges, as required. To skin a tomato, scald it in boiling water for 1–2 minutes, then plunge in cold water; or hold the tomato over a low gas flame until the skin has blistered; the skin will peel off easily. Tomatoes are often served raw.

Basic cooking: Halve tomatoes and fry in hot oil for 3–6 minutes or grill for 4–5 minutes. To bake tomatoes, cut a cross in one end, add a little butter and seasoning and bake at 180°C (350°F) mark 4 for 15 minutes.

Seasonings: Basil, marjoram, sage, parsley, savory, chervil, thyme, chives.

To skin a tomato: Scald a whole tomato in boiling water for 1–2 minutes; or hold it on a fork over a low flame.

Carefully pull away the loosened, blistered skin with a sharp knife.

Fried Green Tomatoes

Colour index page 72

4–6 side dish servings

700 g (1½ lb) green tomatoes	*5 ml (1 level tsp) salt pinch pepper*
75 g (3 oz) plain flour	*30 ml (2 tbsp) vegetable oil*

1. Slice the tomatoes thickly. Mix the flour with the seasonings and use to coat the tomato slices.
2. Heat the oil in a frying pan and fry the tomato slices, a few at a time, until golden. Drain well.

Stuffed Tomatoes

Colour index page 72

4 side dish servings

4 large tomatoes	*2.5 ml (½ tsp) chopped parsley*
25 g (1 oz) cooked ham	
5 ml (1 tsp) chopped onion	*salt and pepper*
knob of butter	*30 ml (2 tbsp) grated Cheddar cheese, optional*
30 ml (2 tbsp) fresh white breadcrumbs	

1. Cut a small round lid from the top of each tomato and scoop out the seeds and flesh; reserve.
2. Chop the ham and fry with the onion in the butter for 3 minutes. Stir in the remaining filling ingredients and tomato pulp. Spoon mixture into tomatoes, put on lids and bake at 200°C (400°F) mark 6 for 10–15 minutes.

Turnips

Herby Baked Tomatoes

Colour index page 72

4 side dish servings

4 tomatoes
2.5 ml (¹/₂ level tsp) salt
2.5 ml (¹/₂ level tsp) dried rosemary
2.5 ml (¹/₂ level tsp) dried basil
25 g (1 oz) butter or margarine

1. Cut the tomatoes in half as for tomato lilies (below) and carefully separate the halves.
2. Mix the salt with the herbs and sprinkle the mixture over the cut surfaces of the tomatoes. Dot them with the fat and bake at 180°C (350°F) mark 4 for 15 minutes or until thoroughly heated.

Scalloped Tomatoes

Colour index page 72

6 side dish servings

50 g (2 oz) butter or margarine
1 small onion, skinned and chopped
100 g (4 oz) fresh white breadcrumbs
5 ml (1 level tsp) salt
1.25 ml (¹/₄ level tsp) pepper
2.5 ml (¹/₂ level tsp) dried basil
20 ml (4 level tsp) sugar
5 tomatoes, skinned and sliced

1 Melt the fat in a saucepan and sauté the onion for 5 minutes or until tender. Stir in the breadcrumbs, seasoning, basil and sugar.

2 Arrange a quarter of the tomato slices in a casserole and sprinkle some of the breadcrumb mixture on top. Repeat the layering three times, ending with breadcrumbs.

3 Cover the casserole and bake at 190°C (375°F) mark 5 for about 30 minutes or until bubbling. Uncover for the last 5 minutes of cooking time so crumbs turn golden brown.

TOMATO GARNISHES

Tomatoes can be cut in a variety of shapes to make attractive garnishes for hot and cold dishes. For tomato lilies, choose firm, evenly sized tomatoes.

Using a small, sharp knife, make a series of 'V'-shaped cuts round the middle of each tomato, cutting right through to the centre. Carefully pull the halves apart with your fingers.

Season: Turnips are available all year round.
To buy: Look for turnips with clean, unblemished skins. Buy tender, early turnips with white or pale green skins in spring and early summer. Main crop turnips are less tender, with creamy-coloured skins.
To prepare: Trim early turnips and peel thinly for eating raw; leave the skins on for cooking. Peel main crop turnips thickly and cut into pieces or slices before cooking.
Basic cooking: Cook early turnips whole in boiling salted water for 20-30 minutes, then drain and rub off the skins. Toss in melted butter or coat in cheese sauce (page 461). Cook prepared main crop turnips in boiling salted water for 20-30 minutes. Drain them well and mash with milk and butter. Turnips may also be cut into large dice and steamed for 15 minutes, or added to stews, casseroles or soups. Use them with care as they are strongly flavoured.
Seasonings: Chives, fennel, parsley, cloves, mustard.

Turnip Purée

Colour index page 68

4 side dish servings

700 g (1¹/₂ lb) turnips, trimmed and peeled
300 ml (¹/₂ pint) chicken stock
25 g (1 oz) butter
60 ml (4 tbsp) single cream or top of the milk

salt and pepper

For the garnish:
parsley sprig

1. Cut the turnips into small pieces. Put them into a saucepan with the stock and simmer gently for 20–30 minutes, until the turnips are tender and the stock is absorbed. Drain well.
2. Mash the turnip to a smooth purée with the butter. Stir in the cream and seasoning and reheat gently. Serve the turnip purée garnished with a sprig of parsley.

TURNIPS IN MUSTARD SAUCE: Cook the turnips as above. Melt the butter in a separate pan, stir in **45 ml (3 level tbsp) flour** and cook over a gentle heat for 1–2 minutes. Remove the pan from the heat and gradually stir in **300 ml (¹/₂ pint) milk**. Bring to the boil, stirring, and cook for 1–2 minutes. Blend **15 ml (1 level tbsp) dry mustard** and **10 ml (2 level tsp) sugar** with **15 ml (1 tbsp) vinegar** until smooth. Stir the mixture into the sauce and reheat. Drain the turnips, add to the mustard sauce, season to taste and reheat gently.

MIXED ROOT VEGETABLE PUREE: Prepare the turnips as above and mix with equal quantities of **puréed carrot**, parsnip or potato.

Mixed vegetable dishes

Ratatouille

Colour index
page 67

4–6 side dish
servings

100 ml (4 fl oz) olive oil
1 large onion, skinned and
  chopped
1 large clove garlic, skinned
  and halved
450 g (1 lb) aubergines, cut
  into small pieces
1 large red pepper, seeded
  and chopped
450 g (1 lb) courgettes,
  washed and sliced
100 ml (4 fl oz) water
15 ml (1 level tbsp) salt
15 ml (1 level tbsp) dried
  oregano
5 ml (1 level tbsp) sugar
2 large tomatoes, skinned
  and cut into wedges

1 Heat the olive oil in a
large flameproof
casserole and add the
onion and garlic. Cook for
10 minutes or until tender,
stirring occasionally.
Remove the garlic.

2 Add the aubergine and
the red pepper and
cook for a further 5 min-
utes, stirring frequently.

3 Stir in the courgettes,
water, salt, oregano
and sugar. Bring to the
boil, cover and simmer for
30 minutes or until the
vegetables are tender,
stirring occasionally.

4 Stir in tomato wedges
and continue cooking
for 10–15 minutes more.

5 If you wish to serve the
ratatouille cold, cover
and chill thoroughly.

Ribbon Vegetables

Colour index
page 71

4 side dish
servings

225 g (8 oz) courgettes,
  washed and grated
225 g (8 oz) carrots,
  peeled and grated
225 g (8 oz) parsnips or
  turnips, peeled
  and grated
60 ml (4 tbsp) water

25 g (1 oz) butter or
  margarine
5 ml (1 level tsp) sugar
5 ml (1 level tsp) salt

1. Put all the ingredients in a large saucepan and
bring slowly to the boil.
2. Cover the saucepan and simmer gently for about
5 minutes or until all the vegetables are tender but
still crisp.

Summer Vegetable Bowl

Colour index
page 69

6 side dish
servings

4 rashers streaky bacon,
  rinded
12 button onions, skinned
1 green pepper, seeded and
  diced
400 ml (3/4 pint) water
450 g (1 lb) French beans,
  topped and tailed
6 sweetcorn cobs, cut into
  chunks

15 ml (1 level tbsp) salt
1.25 ml (1/4 level tsp) white
  pepper
10 ml (2 level tsp) sugar
6 small courgettes, washed
  and trimmed
2 large sticks celery,
  washed
tomato wedges

1. Fry bacon in its own fat until crisp. Drain well.
2. Sauté the onions and pepper in the bacon fat until
the onions are golden. Add the water to the pan with
the beans, sweetcorn, seasoning and sugar and bring
to the boil. Cover and simmer for 10 minutes.
3. Cut the courgettes and celery into 2.5-cm (1-in)
slices and add to the pan. Cover and cook for about
8–10 minutes more, until the vegetables are just
tender. Drain them well and arrange on a large
serving dish. Crumble the bacon and sprinkle over
the top. Garnish with tomato wedges.

Serving the vegetables:
Sprinkle crumbled bacon
over the top and garnish
with tomato wedges.

Simmered Carrots and Celery

Colour index
page 70

4–6 side dish
servings

30 ml (2 tbsp) vegetable oil
450 g (1 lb) carrots, peeled
  and diagonally sliced
5 ml (1 level tsp) salt
1.25 ml (1/4 level tsp) sugar

50 ml (2 fl oz) water
6 sticks celery, washed and
  diagonally sliced

1. Heat the oil in a large saucepan, add the carrots,
salt, sugar and water and bring to the boil. Reduce
the heat, cover and simmer for 7 minutes.
2. Add the celery and cook uncovered for a further
5–7 minutes, stirring frequently, until the vegetables
are tender but still crisp.

Braised Mixed Vegetables

Colour index
page 69

4–6 side dish
servings

225 g (8 oz) French beans,
  topped and tailed
225 g (8 oz) carrots, peeled
  and cut into matchsticks
100 g (4 oz) mushrooms,
  sliced

5 ml (1 level tsp) salt
2.5 ml (1/2 level tsp) dried
  thyme
40 g (1 1/2 oz) butter or
  margarine

1. Cut the beans into 2.5-cm (1-in) pieces. Put in a
large saucepan with the remaining ingredients.
2. Cover and cook for about 15 minutes, stirring
occasionally, until the vegetables are just tender.

Stir-fried Cabbage and Courgettes

Colour index
page 69

4 side dish
servings

45 ml (3 tbsp) vegetable oil
1 large clove garlic, skinned
    and sliced
225 g (8 oz) white cabbage,
    trimmed, shredded and
    washed
2 courgettes, washed and
    thinly sliced
10 ml (2 level tsp) salt
5 ml (1 level tsp) sugar

1 Heat the oil in a large
casserole, add the garlic
and cook until browned.
Discard the garlic.

2 Add the cabbage and
the courgettes and stir-
fry (page 266) until they
are well coated with oil.

3 Add salt and sugar, and
stir-fry for 7–8 minutes
more, until vegetables are
tender but still crisp.

French Beans with Courgettes and Bacon

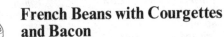

Colour index
page 67

6 side dish
servings

250 g (9 oz) French beans,
    topped and tailed
4 rashers streaky bacon,
    rinded
50 g (2 oz) butter or
    margarine

1 small onion, skinned and
    finely chopped
2 medium courgettes,
    trimmed and sliced
3.75 ml (¾ level tsp) salt
pinch pepper

1. Cut the beans into 2.5-cm (1-in) pieces. Cook in boiling salted water for 10 minutes and drain well.
2. Fry the bacon in its own fat until crisp. Drain well and crumble finely.
3. Melt the fat and sauté the onion until soft but not coloured. Add the courgettes and stir-fry them (page 266) until just tender.
4. Stir in the crumbled bacon, beans and seasoning and cook for a further minute to heat through the beans and bacon.

Stir-fried Mixed Vegetables

Colour index
page 70

6 side dish
servings

45 ml (3 tbsp) vegetable oil
2 carrots, peeled and cut
    into matchsticks
1 head broccoli, trimmed
    and cut into florets

1 onion, skinned and sliced
3.75 ml (¾ level tsp) salt
2.5 ml (½ level tsp) sugar
100 g (4 oz) button
    mushrooms

1. Heat the oil in a large frying pan and add the carrots, broccoli and onion. Stir-fry for 3–4 minutes until the vegetables are evenly coated with oil.
2. Add the salt, sugar and mushrooms. Cover and cook for 5–6 minutes more, stirring occasionally, until the vegetables are tender but still crisp.

Pepper and Tomato Sauté

Colour index
page 70

4-6 side dish
servings

30 ml (2 tbsp) vegetable oil
3 large green peppers,
    seeded and roughly
    chopped
1 onion, skinned and
    chopped

3 large tomatoes, skinned
    and cut into large
    chunks
7.5 ml (1½ level tsp) salt
5 ml (1 level tsp) dried
    basil

1. Heat the vegetable oil in a large frying pan. Add the chopped peppers and onion. Fry gently, stirring, for about 10 minutes or until the onion is soft and the peppers are tender.
2. Add the tomatoes to the pan with the salt and basil. Cover and simmer for about 15 minutes.

Aubergine Parmigiana

Colour index
page 33

6 main dish
servings

60 ml (4 tbsp) olive oil
1 clove garlic, skinned and
    crushed
1 large onion, skinned and
    chopped
2 396-g (14-oz) cans
    tomatoes
10 ml (2 level tsp) sugar
2.5 ml (½ level tsp) dried
    oregano
2.5 ml (½ level tsp) dried
    basil
2.5 ml (½ level tsp) salt
1 large aubergine, cut into
    1-cm (½-in) slices

2 eggs, beaten with 30 ml
    (2 tbsp) water
100 g (4 oz) dried
    breadcrumbs
50 g (2 oz) grated
    Parmesan cheese
225 g (8 oz) Mozzarella
    cheese, cut into 0.5-cm
    (¼-in) slices

1 Heat half the oil in a
large frying pan, add the
garlic and onion and cook
until tender. Add the next
five ingredients, reduce the
heat, cover and simmer for
30 minutes.

2 Dip the aubergine slices
in beaten egg, then coat
evenly with breadcrumbs.
Repeat to give a substan-
tial coating on both sides.

3 Heat the remaining oil
in a frying pan and fry
the aubergine slices a few
at a time until golden
brown, adding more oil if
necessary. Drain well on
kitchen paper towel.

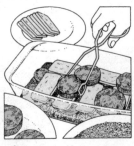

4 Layer half the auber-
gine, tomato mixture,
Parmesan and Mozzarella
cheeses in a greased ovenproof dish; repeat. Bake at
180°C (350°F) mark 4 for
25 minutes.

Mixed vegetable dishes

Caponata

Colour index
page 20

6 first course
servings

75 ml (5 tbsp) olive or
vegetable oil
450 g (1 lb) aubergines, cut
into chunks
450 g (1 lb) courgettes,
washed and cut into
chunks
100 g (4 oz) button
mushrooms, thickly sliced
1 small onion, skinned and
chopped
4 sticks celery, washed and
sliced
1 clove garlic, skinned and
crushed

45 ml (3 tbsp) red wine
vinegar
15 g (½ oz) capers
15 ml (1 level tbsp) caster
sugar
5 ml (1 level tsp) salt
pinch pepper
2 large tomatoes, cut into
small chunks
50 g (2 oz) pimento-stuffed
olives, halved

1. Heat the oil in a large saucepan and add the aubergines, courgettes, mushrooms, onion, celery and garlic. Cook over high heat for about 10 minutes, stirring occasionally.
2. Add the vinegar with the capers, sugar and seasoning and stir together until well mixed. Reduce the heat, cover and simmer for 5–10 minutes until the vegetables are just tender. Stir in the tomatoes and olives and bring to the boil.
3. Leave to cool, then cover and chill for at least 3 hours before serving.

Stuffed Green Peppers

Colour index
page 70

4 side dish
servings

2 green peppers
50 g (2 oz) long grain rice
50 g (2 oz) mature Cheddar
cheese, grated
salt
pinch pepper

15 ml (1 tbsp) chopped
parsley
175 g (6 oz) sweetcorn
kernels or mixed
vegetables

1. Cut the peppers in half lengthways, scoop out the seeds and cut away the membrane. Cook them in boiling salted water for 5 minutes or until they are tender but still firm. Drain well.
2. Cook the rice for 10–12 minutes in boiling salted water and drain well. Add the cheese with the seasoning and parsley while the rice is still hot and stir together until well mixed.
3. Meanwhile, cook the corn kernels or the mixed vegetables in boiling salted water for about 5–10 minutes and drain well.
4. Spoon the rice mixture into the base of the peppers and top with the corn or mixed vegetables.

To prepare peppers: Slice the peppers in half lengthways, then use a small sharp knife to remove stem, seeds and membrane.

To add stuffing: Spoon rice into the base of the blanched peppers and top with the sweetcorn kernels or the mixed vegetables.

Sauces

Butter Sauce

Makes 100 ml
(4 fl oz)

150 ml (¼ pint) vegetable
cooking liquid
15 g (½ oz) butter, melted

30 ml (2 level tbsp) plain
flour
salt and pepper

1. Place the vegetable cooking liquid in a small saucepan. Blend the butter and flour to a smooth paste and stir or whisk into the liquid.
2. Cook until the sauce has thickened, stirring gently, and season to taste.

Herb Butter Sauce

Makes 150 ml
(¼ pint)

60 ml (4 tbsp) white wine
vinegar
1 shallot or small onion,
skinned and finely
chopped
15 ml (1 tbsp) chopped
parsley

15 ml (1 tbsp) chopped
fresh mixed herbs
175 g (6 oz) butter, melted
salt and pepper

1. Place the vinegar, shallot and herbs in a small saucepan, bring to the boil and boil quickly for 3–5 minutes until reduced to 15 ml (1 tbsp). Strain the vinegar and discard the flavourings.
2. Add the vinegar to the melted butter, heat through gently and season to taste.

Lemon Parsley Sauce

Makes 300 ml
(½ pint)

25 g (1 oz) butter
45 ml (3 level tbsp) plain
flour
150 ml (¼ pint) chicken
stock
60 ml (4 tbsp) milk
salt and white pepper
1 egg yolk

30 ml (2 tbsp) single
cream
grated rind and juice of
½ lemon
15 ml (1 tbsp) chopped
parsley

1. Melt the butter in a small saucepan, add the flour and cook for 1 minute. Gradually stir in the stock, bring to the boil and cook for 1–2 minutes, stirring constantly. Stir in the milk and seasoning.
2. Beat the egg yolk and cream. Stir 45 ml (3 tbsp) sauce into the cream and return to the bulk of the sauce. Cook over a very low heat, stirring constantly, until the sauce has thickened.
3. Stir in the lemon rind and juice and the chopped parsley before serving.

Soured Cream and Mustard Sauce

Makes 225 ml
(8 fl oz)

225 ml (8 fl oz) soured
cream
15 ml (1 tbsp) finely
chopped onion
15 ml (1 level tbsp) made
mustard
1.25 ml (¼ level tsp) salt

pinch pepper

To serve:
15 ml (1 tbsp) chopped
parsley or finely chopped
chives

1. In a saucepan over gentle heat, stir together the soured cream with the onion, mustard and seasoning. Do not allow the mixture to boil.
2. Sprinkle with the chopped parsley or chives before serving.

YOGURT AND MUSTARD SAUCE: Prepare the soured cream and mustard sauce as above, but replace the soured cream with **natural yogurt**.

FRUIT

Most freshly picked, ripe fruit is best eaten in its natural state; it can be served this way as a delicious and healthy snack or as a perfect dessert for any meal. However, some fruits (notably currants and some varieties of berry), are too tart or hard to be enjoyed raw and are always cooked before being eaten. Cooking will also improve fruit that is imperfect or not quite ripe, or can help vary the ways of serving a fruit that is over-abundant after a good crop.

Careful buying is most important if you are to enjoy fruit to the full, so as much guidance as possible is given to help you choose only the best.

Apples

Season: Different varieties of dessert and cooking apples are available all year round.

To buy: Look for firm, well-coloured fruit with un-blemished skins. For eating raw or in salads, choose a dessert variety: the best known are Cox's Orange Pippin, Newton Wonder, Laxton Superb, Granny Smith, Golden Delicious, James Grieve, Worcester Pearmain and Jonathan. Other varieties may be locally available. For baking, stewing and puréeing, choose Bramley's Seedling, Lord Derby or Grenadier, but for cooking in flans and pies where you want the apple to retain its shape as well as have a good flavour when cooked, choose a dessert variety such as Cox's Orange Pippin or Newton Wonder.

To store: Keep apples in a cool, dry place. Bramley's Seedling and Cox's Orange Pippin store well for several months, but other varieties deteriorate more quickly and should be used within a few weeks. Apples stored at room temperature should be used within 1–2 weeks.

To prepare: Apples to be eaten with their skins on should be wiped or washed. For cooking, quarter the apples, core them and peel them as thinly as possible; then cut them into wedges or slices as required. Once they are prepared, either use them immediately or brush the cut surfaces with lemon juice to prevent browning. Soaking the apples in salt water will also stop dis-coloration but this is inclined to affect the flavour.

Stewed Apples

Colour index
page 101
4 dessert
servings

75–100 g (3–4 oz) sugar
300 ml (½ pint) water
450 g (1 lb) cooking apples,
  peeled, cored and thinly
  sliced

squeeze lemon juice
small piece lemon rind
1–2 cloves

1. Make a syrup by dissolving the sugar in the water over a gentle heat, stirring occasionally.
2. Add the apples, lemon juice, lemon rind and cloves to the syrup and simmer gently until the apples are soft but still hold their shape. Discard the lemon rind and cloves before serving.

Baked Apples

Colour index
page 101
4 dessert
servings

4 medium cooking apples,
  wiped
60 ml (4 tbsp) water
demerara sugar or
  mincemeat

25 g (1 oz) butter

To serve:
whipped cream

1. Core the apples and peel off the top third of the skin. Place them in an ovenproof dish and pour the water around them.
2. Stuff the central cavities of the apples with the sugar or the mincemeat and place a small knob of butter on the top of each one.
3. Bake at 180°C (350°F) mark 4 for 30–45 minutes, or until apples are soft. Serve with whipped cream.

Fried Apple Wedges

Colour index
page 72
4 side dish
servings

2 red dessert apples, wiped
  and cored
25 g (1 oz) butter or
  margarine

150–175 g (5–6 oz) apple
  jelly

1. Cut the apples into wedges about 1 cm (½ in) thick with a sharp knife.
2. Melt the butter in a frying pan and add the apple wedges. Fry them gently for about 5–7 minutes, turning them once, until they are just tender.
3. Stir in the apple jelly and heat through gently. Serve with baked ham or grilled poultry.

Apples

Apricots

Colour index
page 106

Makes 6–8
toffee apples

Toffee Apples

6–8 medium dessert apples
6–8 short wooden sticks,
 eg. ice lolly sticks
450 g (1 lb) demerara
 sugar
50 g (2 oz) butter
10 ml (2 tsp) vinegar
150 ml (¼ pint) water
15 ml (1 level tbsp) golden
 syrup

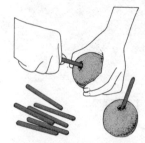

1 Wipe the apples with a damp cloth and push a wooden stick firmly into the core of each one.

2 To make the toffee mixture, heat the remaining ingredients gently in a large heavy-based saucepan until the sugar has completely dissolved, then bring to the boil.

3 Boil steadily without stirring for about 5 minutes, until the temperature reaches 143°C (290°F), soft crack stage (page 414).

4 Brush the sides of the pan occasionally with a brush dipped in water, to prevent crystals forming.

5 Remove the pan from the heat, tilt it slightly and dip an apple into the toffee mixture.

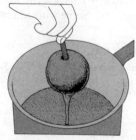

6 Lift out the apple and twirl it over the saucepan for a few seconds until evenly coated with toffee. Repeat with remaining apples, working quickly.

7 Place the toffee apples on a buttered baking sheet, or on waxed paper, and leave them until the toffee has hardened before serving or wrapping.

Season: Apricots are available in late winter and during the summer months.

To buy: The skin should be velvety, yellow to orange in colour and free of blemishes. Under-ripe apricots are hard and sour, but over-ripe fruit quickly becomes soft and tasteless; if in doubt, buy under-ripe fruit and keep it until it is ready for eating.

To store: Keep under-ripe apricots at room temperature. Refrigerate ripe fruit and use it within 2–3 days.

To prepare: Wash the apricots, cut them in half and remove the stone; peel if you wish. If the apricots are not to be used immediately, brush the cut surfaces, or all over if peeled, with lemon juice to prevent browning.

Cinnamon Apricots in Cream

Colour index
page 100

4 dessert
servings

450 g (1 lb) apricots,
 washed, halved and
 stoned
75 ml (5 tbsp) water
65 g (2½ oz) sugar

2.5 ml (½ level tsp) ground
 cinnamon
45 ml (3 tbsp) double
 cream

1. Place the apricots in an ovenproof dish.
2. Mix the water, sugar and cinnamon and pour over the apricots. Bake at 190°C (375°F) mark 5 for 20 minutes, until the apricots are tender.
3. Pour cream over and bake for 5 minutes more.

DRIED FRUIT

It is often convenient to buy packets of ready-mixed dried fruit, especially if you only need a small quantity, but fruit sold separately is usually of a much higher quality.

Currants, raisins and sultanas may be bought ready-washed, but always check that there are no stones or grit left in them. Unwashed fruits are cheaper, but need a little more preparation. Wash them well in cold water, drain them and spread them out to dry on muslin, or blotting paper, over a wire rack. They will probably take about 24 hours to dry properly; never try to speed up the drying by direct heat, as it will harden the fruit. Seeded or stoned raisins are much larger and juicier than the small seedless raisins and have a better flavour. Remove any stones which have been left in the fruit by dipping your fingers in water and working the raisins between your fingertips to squeeze out the stones.

Dried apricots, prunes, figs, pears and apples should all be rinsed in cold water, then soaked for several hours, or overnight, in fresh water. Cook them in the soaking water, adding 100–175 g (4–6 oz) sugar and a small piece of lemon rind to every 600 ml (1 pint) water. Stew gently until soft and serve hot or cold with egg custard sauce (page 359).

Avocados

Season: Avocados are available all year round.
To buy: The skin of an avocado can be smooth and bright green or rough, dark and purplish-black. A ripe avocado should feel soft and yielding all over.
To store: Keep under-ripe fruit at room temperature or warmer to aid ripening. Store ripe avocados in the refrigerator and use them as soon as possible.
To prepare: Halve the avocado lengthways, separate the halves and remove the stone. If necessary, peel thinly. Brush flesh immediately with lemon juice or French dressing (page 326) to prevent browning. Avocados are usually served raw, in the shell or sliced in salads.

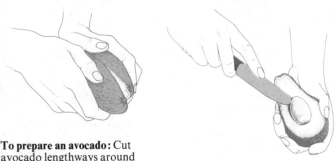

To prepare an avocado: Cut avocado lengthways around the stone, then twist the halves gently to separate.

To remove the avocado stone, flick or ease it out gently with a round bladed knife, being careful not to damage the flesh.

Serve the avocado half in the shell with French dressing (page 326), or peel it thinly and slice the flesh as required for use in salads.

Appetiser Avocados

Colour index page 21

6 first course servings

3 medium avocados
4 rashers streaky bacon, rinded, fried and crumbled

For the sauce:
25 g (1 oz) sugar
30 ml (2 tbsp) white vinegar
30 ml (2 tbsp) water
30 ml (2 tbsp) Worcestershire sauce
45 ml (3 tbsp) mild chilli sauce
25 g (1 oz) butter or margarine

1. Put all the ingredients for the sauce into a saucepan and bring to the boil. Simmer for 15 minutes.
2. Peel and slice the avocados and arrange the slices on six individual plates. Spoon the hot sauce over the top and sprinkle with the crumbled bacon.

Bananas

Season: Bananas are available all year round.
To buy: Look for firm, evenly yellowed skins. Greenish, unripe bananas are very indigestible, but blackened patches indicate over-ripe fruit.
To store: Keep bananas at room temperature.
To prepare: Peel back the skin from the stem end and slice the banana as required. Brush the fruit with lemon juice to prevent browning if it is not going to be eaten immediately; do not add it to a fruit salad until just before serving. Bananas can be eaten raw, baked or fried.

Baked Bananas

Colour index page 72

4 side dish or 2 dessert servings

40 g (1½ oz) butter or margarine
4 firm bananas, peeled
large pinch salt or 5 ml (1 level tsp) sugar

To serve, optional:
single cream

1. Put the fat in an ovenproof dish and place in a warm oven until the fat has melted.
2. Roll bananas in the fat. Sprinkle lightly with salt for a savoury dish, or with sugar for a dessert.
3. Bake at 230°C (450°F) mark 8 for 10–12 minutes until the bananas are tender. Serve with hot or cold ham dishes, or with cream as a dessert.

Flambéed Bananas in Orange Sauce

Colour index page 101

6 dessert servings

8 large firm bananas, peeled
25 g (1 oz) butter
45 ml (3 level tbsp) soft light brown sugar
30 ml (2 tbsp) rum
coarsely grated rind and juice of 2 oranges
30 ml (2 tbsp) lemon juice

To decorate:
1 medium orange

To serve:
single cream

1. Cut each banana crossways into four equal pieces.
2. Melt the butter in a large frying pan. Add the bananas and stir until evenly coated. Sprinkle sugar over the top and fry gently, turning occasionally, until the bananas are golden and just softening.
3. Pour rum over the top, set it alight and shake gently until the flames subside. Add the rind and fruit juices, cover and simmer for 5 minutes.
4. Meanwhile, cut off narrow strips of rind, free from pith, at 1-cm (½-in) intervals around the orange, working downwards from the stem end. Slice the orange thinly and remove the pips.
5. Arrange the bananas on a hot serving dish and decorate with the orange slices. Spoon the juices over the top and serve immediately with cream.

Berries and currants

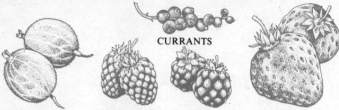

CURRANTS

GOOSEBERRIES   RASPBERRIES BLACKBERRIES STRAWBERRIES

These include blackberries, bilberries, cranberries, elderberries, gooseberries, loganberries, mulberries, raspberries, strawberries, black, red and white currants.
Season: Berries and currants ripen mainly in midsummer, although some ripen in late summer and early autumn (blackberries, bilberries and elderberries). Imported cranberries are available in winter.
To buy: Look for plump, fresh, evenly coloured fruit. Avoid any that look bruised, are over-ripe or have leaked juice. Mulberries, bilberries and elderberries are rarely on sale, but mulberries are a delicious garden crop and bilberries and elderberries grow wild.
To store: Refrigerate the fruit without washing it; use as soon as possible. Gooseberries will keep for 2–3 days.

To hull strawberries: Pull the stem firmly from the fruit.

To wash firm berries and currants: Place in a colander and wash in cold water; drain thoroughly. Discard any bruised or over-ripe fruit.

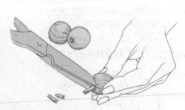

To top and tail gooseberries: Snip off the stem and flower ends.

To string currants: Remove them from the stalks with a fork to avoid bruising.

To prepare: Wash and pick over the fruit to remove stalks, leaves or damaged fruit; watch raspberries and loganberries carefully for fruit grubs. Pull hulls from strawberries and top and tail currants and gooseberries with kitchen scissors or a small sharp knife. Raspberries and strawberries are best served raw, with caster sugar and whipped cream; other berries and currants are better cooked. They can simply be stewed gently with a little water and sugar to taste and served with cream or egg custard sauce (page 359). Elderberries are commonly used for making wine and for jelly. Many of the summer fruits are traditionally cooked together in a summer pudding, mixed fruit compôte or pie; include at least one variety of currant to sharpen the flavour.

Colour index page 100

4–6 dessert servings

Mixed Berry Compôte

450 g (1 lb) strawberries, washed and hulled
100 g (4 oz) raspberries
150 g (5 oz) blackcurrants or blueberries, washed and cooked

50 g (2 oz) sugar
900 ml (1½ pints) vanilla ice cream, softened
30 ml (2 tbsp) grated orange rind

1. Pick over the raw fruits. Halve the strawberries and gently toss them with the sugar; cover and chill for about 2 hours, tossing occasionally.
2. Spoon the strawberries, raspberries and black-currants alternately into a large bowl.
3. Mix the ice cream with the orange rind and spoon a little over the berries. Serve the remaining ice cream in a separate bowl.

Colour index page 100

4 dessert servings

Summer Pudding

450–500 g (1–1¼ lb) mixed blackcurrants, blackberries, raspberries and redcurrants
30 ml (2 tbsp) water
150 g (5 oz) sugar
100–175 g (4–6 oz) white bread, thinly sliced

To serve:
whipped cream or egg custard sauce made with 300 ml (½ pint) milk, page 359

1. Wash and pick over the fruits, string the currants and top and tail them. Put the water and sugar in a large saucepan and bring slowly to the boil. Add the fruits and stew them gently until they are soft but still hold their shape.
2. Cut the crusts off the bread and discard them. Line a 900-ml (1½-pint) capacity pudding basin with some of the slices, pour in the stewed fruit mixture and cover with the remaining bread.
3. Place a saucer smaller in diameter than the top of the basin on top of the pudding; weight it down and leave overnight in a cool place. Turn out and serve with whipped cream or egg custard sauce.

Colour index page 100

Makes 600 ml (1 pint)

Bilberry Sauce

450 g (1 lb) bilberries, washed
225 ml (8 fl oz) water
15 ml (1 level tbsp) cornflour

175 g (6 oz) caster sugar
pinch salt
5 ml (1 tsp) lemon juice

1. Trim the bilberries. Bring the water to the boil, add the berries and bring back to the boil.
2. Meanwhile, mix the cornflour to a smooth paste with a little cold water. Stir it into the bilberries with the sugar and salt and cook until the mixture has thickened, stirring constantly. Add the lemon juice. Serve with ice cream or pancakes.

GOOSEBERRY SAUCE: Put *50 g (2 oz) sugar* and *300 ml (½ pint) water* in a large saucepan and heat gently until the sugar has completely dissolved. Add *225 g (8 oz) gooseberries*, washed and trimmed, and simmer until they are just tender. Mix the *juice of 1 orange* with *15 ml (1 level tbsp) cornflour*, stir in a little of the gooseberry juice and pour the mixture into the sauce, stirring well. Bring to the boil and simmer for 1–2 minutes until sauce has thickened.

Strawberries Romanoff

Colour index
page 100

6 dessert
servings

450 g (1 lb) strawberries,
washed and hulled
60 ml (4 tbsp) port
22.5 ml (1½ level tbsp)
caster sugar
225 ml (8 fl oz) double
cream

22.5 ml (1½ tbsp) milk
vanilla sugar

For the feuilles royales,
optional: 175 g (6 oz)
icing sugar, 1 egg white

1. Reserve six strawberries for decoration if you wish. Slice the rest, place them in a bowl with the port and sugar, toss and leave for at least 1 hour.
2. To make the feuilles royales, stir the icing sugar into the egg white and beat well. Pipe the mixture on to foil in leaf shapes, starting with the outline and then filling in the leaf. Leave to dry for 1 hour, then pipe on the centre vein.
3. Grill the feuilles royales under low heat for 10 minutes. Remove from the foil, turn them over and grill for a little longer. Cool on a wire rack.
4. Spoon strawberries into individual glasses. Whip the cream with the milk and vanilla sugar to taste. Spoon into the glasses; decorate with whole strawberries and feuilles royales if you wish.

Gooseberry Fool

Colour index
page 100

4 dessert
servings

450 g (1 lb) gooseberries,
washed
30 ml (2 tbsp) water
100 g (4 oz) sugar
150 ml (¼ pint) double
cream
15 ml (1 level tbsp) custard
powder

15 ml (1 level tbsp) caster
sugar
150 ml (¼ pint) milk

To serve:
grated chocolate

1. Top and tail the gooseberries and put them in a saucepan with the water and sugar. Cook until the fruit is completely soft, then sieve to a smooth purée.
2. Mix the custard powder and sugar to a smooth paste with 30 ml (2 tbsp) of the milk and heat the rest of the milk until boiling. Pour on to the custard powder mixture and stir to blend well. Return the sauce to the pan and cook, stirring, until it has thickened. Leave to cool, stirring occasionally.
3. Fold the custard and then the cream into the gooseberry purée. Chill thoroughly.
4. To serve, divide the fool between four sundae glasses and sprinkle with a little grated chocolate.

Cranberry and Apple Relish

Colour index
page 72

Makes 700 g
(1½ lb)

225 g (8 oz) cranberries,
washed
350 g (12 oz) cooking
apples
30 ml (2 tbsp) cider vinegar
225 g (8 oz) demerara
sugar

2.5 ml (½ level tsp) ground
mixed spice
grated rind of 1 orange
60 ml (4 tbsp) water

1. Top and tail the cranberries. Peel and core the apples and slice them thickly.
2. Put the fruit into a saucepan with the vinegar, sugar, spice and orange rind. Cover and simmer, stirring occasionally, for 20 minutes or until pulpy.
3. Add the water and cook for a further 2 minutes. Leave to cool. Serve with poultry or ham.

Cherries

Season: Cherries are available throughout the summer.
To buy: Look for large white, red or black cherries for eating raw, but small, dark-skinned May Duke and Morello cherries for cooking, as they give more flavour.
To store: Refrigerate ripe cherries and use them within 3 days. Keep unripe cherries at room temperature.
To prepare: Remove the stems, place the cherries in a colander and wash under running cold water. If you want to stone them, use a special cherry stoner or the tip of a pointed knife to scoop out the stone from the stem end. Cherries may be eaten raw, just as they are or in salads, or can be cooked in pies, jams and sauces.

To stone cherries: Cut into the centres with the point of a knife and scoop out the stones.

Alternatively, you can remove the stones by using a rounded cherry stoner.

Brandied Cherry Sauce

Colour index
page 100

Makes 400 ml
(¾ pint)

450 g (1 lb) cherries,
washed and stoned
100 ml (4 fl oz) brandy
100 g (4 oz) sugar

10 ml (2 level tsp) cornflour
5 ml (1 tsp) almond
essence

1. Put the cherries into a large saucepan with the brandy, sugar and cornflour and cook, stirring all the time, until the mixture has thickened and just begins to boil.
2. Remove from the heat and stir in the almond essence. Serve the sauce hot or cold, spooned over ice cream, pancakes or waffles.

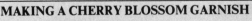

MAKING A CHERRY BLOSSOM GARNISH

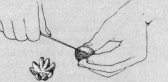

Using a sharp knife, cut a glacé cherry three quarters of the way through into six or eight sections. Spread out sections to make petals.

Cut slices from green glacé cherries and arrange them around the cut cherry to make the leaves.

Coconuts

Season: The best quality coconuts are available in autumn and early winter, although supplies are generally available most of the year.

To buy: Look for coconuts that feel heavy for their size; shake them and listen for a good quantity of milk. Avoid any in which the eyes are wet or mouldy.

To store: Refrigerate coconuts and use within a week of purchase. Fresh shredded coconut and coconut milk will keep in the refrigerator for 1–2 days.

To prepare: Crack open carefully and drain off the milk into a cup. Prise the flesh away from the shell with a small sharp knife and shred if required.

To prepare a coconut: Puncture the shell at the eyes with a screwdriver and hammer.

Drain off all the coconut milk into a jug or small bowl; store, covered, in the refrigerator. It can be served chilled as a drink, or used in recipes.

Crack the shell right open, by hitting hard with a hammer all around the widest part of the coconut. Separate the halves.

Carefully separate the flesh from the shell with a small sharp knife.

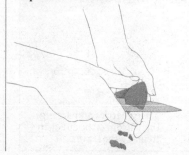

To shred and toast coconut: Peel off the rough brown skin with a sharp knife and shred the white flesh on a coarse grater. To toast, spread the shredded flesh evenly in a shallow roasting tin and roast at 180°C (350°F) mark 4 until golden brown.

Grapes

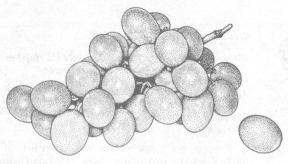

Season: Grapes are available all year round.

To buy: Look for plump grapes, with fruits that are firmly attached to the stems. Bruised grapes rot quickly. Black and white grapes have equally good flavour, although black tend to colour the syrup in a fruit salad.

To store: Refrigerate grapes and use within 3–4 days.

To prepare: Wash and dry grapes. To remove pips, halve fruit and flick out pips with point of a knife, or leave fruit whole and scoop pips out from stem end. To skin grapes, remove stalks and place fruit in boiling water for 20 seconds. Drain and peel off skin with a knife. Do not peel black grapes as all the colour is in the skin.

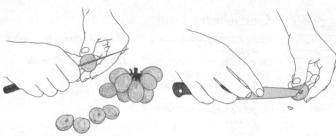

To remove pips from grapes: Carefully cut each grape in half lengthways.

Scoop out the pips from the inside of the halved grapes with the tip of a sharp knife.

To frost grapes: Dip a small bunch of grapes, on the stalk, into some beaten egg white and then dip them in caster sugar.

Remove the grapes from the sugar and leave them to dry on a wire rack. Use as a garnish for desserts.

Minted Grapes

450 g (1 lb) seedless white grapes

For the marinade:
120 ml (8 level tbsp) honey

30 ml (2 tbsp) lime juice
30 ml (2 tbsp) finely chopped fresh mint

Colour index page 101

4 dessert servings

1. Wash the grapes and remove the stalks. Divide the fruit between four individual bowls or dishes.

2. Mix all the ingredients for the marinade and divide equally between the bowls. Chill thoroughly.

Grapefruit

Season: Grapefruit are available all year round, but are at their best in the winter months.
To buy: Look for fruit that feel heavy for their size, with evenly coloured skin. The most common varieties are yellow-skinned, others are tinged with green or pink.
To store: Keep grapefruit at room temperature for 3–4 days or refrigerate, wrapped, for up to 2 weeks.
To prepare: Cut the fruit in half and use a curved grapefruit knife to cut round the circumference, between the flesh and the skin. Then cut the segments free from the membrane and remove the white pithy centre.

To prepare a grapefruit: Cut round the edge of the fruit with a grapefruit knife to free the flesh from the skin. Cut between each of the segments, separating the flesh from the membrane.

Cut out the coarse pithy centre with a sharp knife and remove the pips if you wish.

Grilled Grapefruit

Colour index page 23

4 first course servings

2 grapefruit
30 ml (2 level tbsp) soft brown sugar

30 ml (2 tbsp) medium or sweet sherry

1. Halve the grapefruit, cut the segments free from the skin and membrane and remove the pips.
2. Sprinkle the halves with the brown sugar and sherry and grill until the sugar has melted.

BAKED GRAPEFRUIT: Prepare the grapefruit as above, but place the halves on a baking sheet and bake at 230°C (450°F) mark 8 for 20 minutes.

SPICED GRILLED GRAPEFRUIT: Prepare as above, but sprinkle with a little *grated nutmeg*.

Grapefruit Ambrosia

Colour index page 100

4 dessert servings

3 large grapefruit
40 g (1½ oz) desiccated or fresh shredded coconut

60 ml (4 level tbsp) clear honey

1. Peel the grapefruit, removing all the pith, and cut the segments free from the flesh and membrane.
2. Place the segments in a large bowl with the coconut and the honey; stir to mix well.

Kiwi fruit

These are also known as Chinese gooseberries.
Season: Available from midsummer to late winter.
To buy: Look for egg-shaped fruit about 5 cm (2 in) long, with brown, hairy skin. When ripe, the fruit should yield slightly if gently pressed.
To store: Keep the fruit at room temperature until ripe. Once ripe, refrigerate it and use within 1–2 days.
To prepare: Peel off the skin and slice as required.

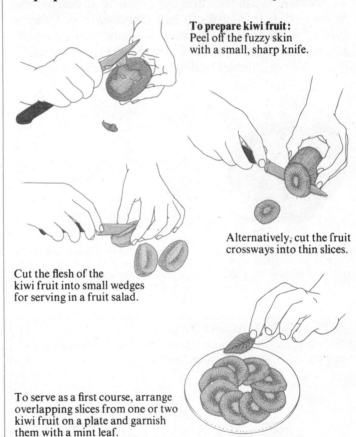

To prepare kiwi fruit: Peel off the fuzzy skin with a small, sharp knife.

Alternatively, cut the fruit crossways into thin slices.

Cut the flesh of the kiwi fruit into small wedges for serving in a fruit salad.

To serve as a first course, arrange overlapping slices from one or two kiwi fruit on a plate and garnish them with a mint leaf.

Gingered Kiwi Fruit

Colour index page 101

4 dessert servings

45 ml (3 level tbsp) sugar
45 ml (3 tbsp) water
30 ml (2 level tbsp) finely chopped crystallised ginger

1.25 ml (¼ tsp) vanilla essence
4 large kiwi fruit
2 oranges

1. Put the sugar, water and crystallised ginger in a saucepan and bring to the boil, stirring constantly. Boil for about 3 minutes, until the mixture becomes a thin syrup. Remove from the heat, stir in the vanilla essence and leave to cool.
2. Peel and slice the kiwi fruit. Remove the pith and peel from the oranges (page 311) and segment them.
3. Pour the ginger syrup into a large bowl, add the fruit and stir to mix well. Chill thoroughly.

Kumquats

Season: Kumquats are available all year round.

To buy: Kumquats should be small, bright orange and heavy for their size, with smooth, shiny (edible) skins. Avoid any fruit that is blemished or shrivelled.

To store: Keep kumquats at room temperature for 1–2 days, or store them in the refrigerator for up to a week.

To prepare: Wash the kumquats, remove any stems and drain well. Cut the fruit in half lengthways and slice it thinly for use as a dessert fruit, in salads or as a garnish. Kumquats can also be cooked and used for marmalade (page 468) or candied peel (page 311), as for oranges.

To prepare kumquats: Wash them in a colander under cold water and remove the stems. Drain well.

Serve raw kumquats whole, or cut them in half lengthways and remove the seeds with the tip of a small sharp knife.

Lemons and limes

Season: Lemons and limes are available all year round, although limes are less widely available than lemons.

To buy: Look for fruit that feel heavy for their size, with smooth skins free from blemishes. Avoid any that look shrivelled or soft. Lemons are slightly larger than limes and are bright yellow in colour. The skin of a lime will be green when under-ripe, but can turn almost as yellow as a lemon when it is fully ripened.

To store: Keep lemons and limes for a few days at room temperature, or refrigerate them and use within 2 weeks.

To prepare: To extract the juice, halve the fruit and use a lemon squeezer or electric juicer. To slice the fruit, use a serrated stainless steel knife.

To prepare lemons and limes: Cut the fruit in half crossways for squeezing. As a garnish for food or drinks, they may be cut into thin slices or wedges with a small serrated knife. If you wish, remove the seeds with the tip of a small sharp knife.

PREPARING CITRUS RIND

Use the rinds from lemons, limes and oranges as a flavouring or garnish for sweet or savoury dishes.

Grated rind: Wash and dry the fruit. Grate the rind on the finest grater available, turning the fruit frequently to avoid grating any of the bitter white pith.

Shredded rind: Score peel into quarters and remove from the fruit with your fingers. With the tip of a spoon, scrape pith from the inside. Stack two or three pieces on a cutting board and slice thinly.

Chopped rind: Prepare shredded rind as above, then chop finely with a small sharp knife.

LEMON AND LIME GARNISHES

Twists: Cut the fruit into thin slices, then cut each slice from the centre to the edge once; open the cut and twist each side in opposite directions.

Wheels: Cut thin slices and notch the edges at intervals with a small knife.

Roses: Using a potato peeler or a small sharp knife, thinly pare off the rind of the fruit, being careful to remove it in one long strip.

Roll up the strip tightly and secure the end with a cocktail stick.

Boats: Halve the fruit lengthways. Cut out the flesh and scrape the shell clean. Make a jagged edge and cut a thin slice from the base, so that the boat can stand steadily.

Mangoes

Season: Available from midwinter to early autumn.

To buy: Mangoes come in varying shapes and sizes. When they are ripe, the tough skins are either yellow or orange in colour and should yield slightly if gently squeezed. Unripe mangoes are hard and have a very poor flavour. Avoid any that look soft or shrivelled.

To store: Allow mangoes to ripen at room temperature, then refrigerate them and use within 2–3 days.

To prepare: Cut a thick lengthways slice on either side of the stone and scoop out or cube the flesh. Repeat with the flesh on the stone. Serve plain or in fruit salads.

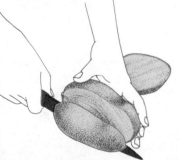 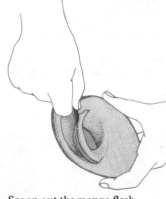

To prepare a mango: Cut a lengthways slice from each side of the fruit with a sharp knife, slicing as close as possible to the stone. Reserve the mango stone and flesh which is left attached to it.

Scoop out the mango flesh with a spoon to make long curved slices.

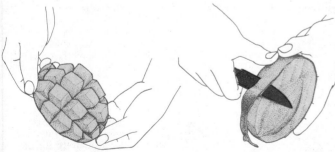

Alternatively, score the flesh on each slice lengthways and then crossways, without cutting through skin. Gently push out the flesh with your fingers.

Using a sharp knife, peel the skin from the reserved middle section of the mango and carefully cut the flesh away from the stone. Divide it into neat slices or chunks.

Melons

Season: Different varieties of imported melon are available all year round, except for watermelons, which are in season only during the summer and early autumn.

To buy: A ripe melon should yield to fingertip pressure round the stem end, but the body of the fruit should be firm and unyielding. Soft patches on the rind indicate bruising rather than ripeness. Buy slices or wedges only if they have been kept with the cut surface closely covered with cling film.

Canteloup melons are almost round in shape, with a dark green, segmented rind and pinkish-yellow flesh. One canteloup melon serves 4–6 people.

Charentais melons are small and round. They have a yellowish-green rind and deep yellow flesh which has quite a pronounced, distinctive flavour and a slightly perfumed smell. One melon serves 1–2 people.

Honeydew melons are oval in shape, with a dark green, yellow or pale greenish-white rind. The flesh is light greenish-yellow and very sweet. One honeydew melon serves 4–6 people.

Ogen melons are small and round, with a lightly striped orangey rind; the flesh is yellow and very sweet. One ogen melon serves 1–2 people.

Tiger melons are segmented and similar to canteloup melons, with striped or spotted green and yellow rind. One tiger melon serves 4–6 people.

Watermelons are very large, oval or round in shape with dark green or lightly striped rind. Because of their size, watermelons are often sold in portions, displaying the dark pink flesh and large, flat seeds. The flesh is crisp, watery and sweet. In a ripe watermelon, the seeds will be dark brown or black. One melon serves 12–16 people.

To store: Keep melons at room temperature until they are ripe, then refrigerate them and use within 2–3 days. Always cover the cut surfaces of any remaining slices or wedges closely with cling film.

To prepare: Wipe the rind with a damp cloth, cut melon in half lengthways, or cut into wedges, and scoop out the seeds from the centre. Serve in wedges with a little caster sugar or ground ginger as a dessert or first course, or peel and cut up the flesh for use in salads. Melons can also be used in jams and other preserves.

Melons

To serve round melons: Cut them in half crossways and scoop out the seeds with a spoon. If you want to make a decorative edge, you can cut a zig-zag pattern in the shell (see watermelon bowl, below right). Chill thoroughly and serve on a bed of ice.

To make melon rings: Halve the fruit crossways, scoop out seeds and cut slices with a sharp knife.

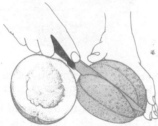

To make melon wedges: Halve the fruit lengthways, scoop out seeds and cut into wedges.

To make melon balls: Scoop out the melon flesh with a melon baller.

Gingered Melon Wedges

Colour index page 23

4–6 first course servings

1 medium honeydew melon
30 ml (2 level tbsp) icing sugar

2.5 ml (½ level tsp) ground ginger

1. Cut the melon in half lengthways, scoop out the seeds and discard them. Slice each melon half into two or three wedges. Cut the flesh free from the rind, but leave it in place; divide it into neat cubes.
2. Mix the sugar and ginger and sprinkle it over the melon. Cover and chill thoroughly.

Canteloup Water Ice

Colour index page 101

Makes 1.2 litres (2 pints)

2 medium canteloup melons
100 g (4 oz) sugar

30 ml (2 tbsp) lemon juice
2.5 ml (½ level tsp) salt

1. Cut the melons in half lengthways, scoop out the seeds and discard them. Remove the rind and cut the flesh into 2.5-cm (1-in) cubes.
2. Put a few of the melon cubes in a blender with the sugar, lemon juice and salt and blend until smooth. Add the remaining melon and blend for a further few seconds until smooth again.
3. Pour the purée into a Swiss roll tin or large shallow roasting tin and freeze for about 2 hours, until partially frozen and slushy.
4. Spoon the mixture into a large chilled bowl and beat well with a rotary whisk, or beat it in a mixer at high speed, until fluffy. Pour it back into the tin and freeze again until completely firm.

Marinated Watermelon

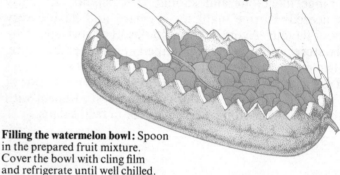

Colour index page 101

4–6 dessert servings

225 g (8 oz) cranberries
50 g (2 oz) sugar
300 ml (½ pint) water
30 ml (2 tbsp) lemon juice

30 ml (2 level tbsp) golden syrup
1 small honeydew melon
1.4-kg (3-lb) watermelon

1. Wash and trim the cranberries. Simmer with the sugar and 150 ml (¼ pint) water for 10 minutes; purée in a blender. Stir in the remaining water, lemon juice and golden syrup.
2. Halve the honeydew melon, discard seeds and scoop out flesh with a melon baller. Make a melon bowl (below) from the watermelon.
3. Mix the melon pieces and cranberry mixture. Spoon into the watermelon bowl. Cover and chill.

PARTY MARINATED WATERMELON: Prepare as above, but use a *4.5-kg (10-lb) watermelon* and triple quantities of remaining ingredients.

Filling the watermelon bowl: Spoon in the prepared fruit mixture. Cover the bowl with cling film and refrigerate until well chilled.

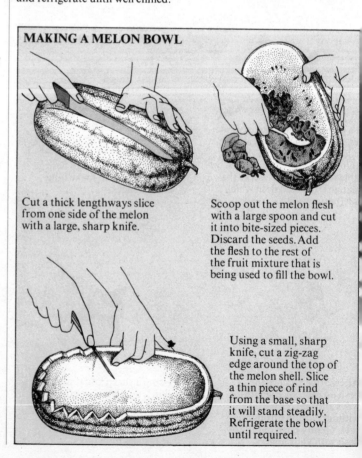

MAKING A MELON BOWL

Cut a thick lengthways slice from one side of the melon with a large, sharp knife.

Scoop out the melon flesh with a large spoon and cut it into bite-sized pieces. Discard the seeds. Add the flesh to the rest of the fruit mixture that is being used to fill the bowl.

Using a small, sharp knife, cut a zig-zag edge around the top of the melon shell. Slice a thin piece of rind from the base so that it will stand steadily. Refrigerate the bowl until required.

Nectarines

Season: Home-grown and imported nectarines are available from midsummer to early autumn; imported ones are also available from early winter to late spring.

To buy: Look for plump, rich-coloured fruit with a slight softening along the indentation. Some varieties are yellowish, but the more common ones are dark yellow to red. Avoid hard, very soft or shrivelled fruit.

To store: Ripen nectarines at room temperature, then refrigerate them and use within 3–5 days.

To prepare: Wash the nectarines, peel them if you wish, then cut them in half lengthways and remove the stone. If the cut fruit is not to be eaten immediately, brush the flesh with a little lemon juice to prevent discoloration.

To peel nectarines: Peel the skin away from the flesh with a sharp knife. If necessary, you can scald the fruit first as for peeling peaches (page 312).

Colour index page 101

4 dessert servings

Nectarines Brûlées

4 large nectarines, peeled and stoned
30 ml (2 level tbsp) soft dark brown sugar
2.5 ml (½ level tsp) ground cinnamon

300 ml (½ pint) soured cream
60 ml (4 level tbsp) caster sugar

1. Halve and slice the nectarines; arrange in four individual flameproof soufflé dishes or ramekins.
2. Mix the brown sugar with the cinnamon and sprinkle over the nectarines. Spoon over the soured cream and sprinkle each one with 15 ml (1 level tbsp) caster sugar.
3. Grill under high heat until the sugar melts and caramelises to form a crust. Chill thoroughly.

Colour index page 72

16 side dish servings

Spiced Nectarine Slices

350 ml (12 fl oz) water
10 cloves
1.25 ml (¼ level tsp) ground cinnamon
1.25 ml (¼ level tsp) ground ginger

1.25 ml (¼ level tsp) salt
4 large nectarines, peeled, stoned and thinly sliced
100 g (4 oz) sugar
45 ml (3 tbsp) lemon juice

1. Put the water, cloves, cinnamon, ginger and salt in a small saucepan; boil for 2 minutes.
2. Add nectarine slices; cook until tender, stirring. Add sugar and lemon juice just before the end of the cooking time.
3. Chill thoroughly. Serve with ham or poultry.

Oranges

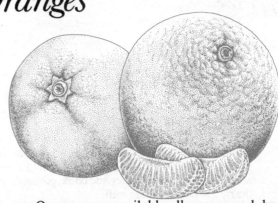

Season: Oranges are available all year round, but are at their best from early winter to late spring. Seville oranges are in season briefly in midwinter.

To buy: Look for firm oranges that are heavy for their size. Avoid any with blemished, dry or hard looking skins. All sweet varieties are good eaten raw or cooked. Seville oranges are bitter, but make good marmalade.

To store: Keep oranges at room temperature for 3–4 days, or refrigerate them, wrapped, for up to 2 weeks.

To prepare: Remove the peel and pull the sections apart. For use in desserts, remove all the pith as well as the rind. Slice between the segments or slice the fruit into rings.

To prepare skinned orange segments: Peel the skin from the orange in one long spiral, cutting right down to the flesh to remove all the pith.

Carefully cut down both sides of each dividing membrane, freeing the orange segments.

Candied Orange Peel

2–3 oranges
350 g (12 oz) sugar

Colour index page 103

Makes 225 g (8 oz) peel

1. Wash the oranges thoroughly, halve them and remove the pulp. Scrape the halves clean.
2. Simmer the peel in a little water for 1–2 hours. Remove the peel with a slotted spoon and drain well.
3. Make the cooking liquid up to 300 ml (½ pint) with water. Add 225 g (8 oz) sugar and heat gently until completely dissolved, then bring to the boil. Remove from the heat, add peel and leave for 2 days.
4. Drain off the syrup and dissolve the remaining sugar in it. Add the peel to the syrup and simmer until the peel is semi-transparent. Remove from the heat. Leave the peel in the syrup for about 2 weeks.
5. Drain off the syrup and place the peel on a wire rack. Cover and leave to dry before storing.

CRYSTALLISED MIXED PEEL: Prepare the candied peel as above, but use *1 orange, 1 lemon and 1 grapefruit* and change the water two or three times while simmering the peel. For the crystallised finish, take each piece of candied peel and dip it into boiling water. Drain well and sprinkle with *caster sugar*. Cover and leave until completely dry before storing.

Oranges

Colour index
page 100

4–6 dessert
servings

Oranges à la Turque

6 juicy oranges
275 ml (9 fl oz) water
2 cloves

For the caramel:
350 g (12 oz) caster sugar

1. Thinly pare the rind from half the oranges and cut it into very thin julienne strips. Put them in a small saucepan. Cover with water and cook, covered, until the rind is tender. Drain well.
2. Remove the pith from the rinded oranges and the rind and pith from the remaining fruit, holding them over a bowl to catch the juice.
3. Put the sugar, 200 ml (⅓ pint) water and the cloves in a saucepan. Heat gently until the sugar has completely dissolved, then boil steadily, without stirring, until the mixture is caramel coloured.
4. Remove from the heat, add the remaining water and return to a very gentle heat until the caramel has dissolved. Stir in the orange juice.
5. Arrange the oranges in a single layer in a serving dish. Place the julienne strips on top and spoon over the caramel syrup. Chill for several hours, turning the oranges occasionally.
6. To serve, leave the oranges whole, or slice them and then reassemble into whole orange shapes.

Orange Praline Mousse

Colour index
page 100

12 dessert
servings

100 g (4 oz) lump sugar
2 large juicy oranges
6 eggs, separated
10 ml (2 level tsp)
cornflour
900 ml (1½ pints) milk
25 g (1 oz) powdered
gelatine

For the praline:
100 g (4 oz) caster sugar

To serve:
whipped cream
skinned orange segments
ratafia biscuits

1. Rub two or three sugar lumps over the skins of the oranges to extract the zest. Squeeze the oranges and, if necessary, add a little water to the juice to make it up to 90 ml (6 tbsp).
2. Beat the egg yolks in a large bowl and blend them with the cornflour. Heat the sugar lumps and milk gently to just below boiling point and pour on to the egg yolk mixture, stirring constantly. Return the mixture to the pan and cook gently without boiling, stirring until the custard has thickened.
3. Dissolve the gelatine in the orange juice in a small basin over a pan of hot water. Mix into the custard and leave to cool until almost set.
4. Meanwhile, make the praline. Grease a baking sheet. Place the caster sugar in a pan and heat very gently until it turns into a syrup. Raise the heat and continue to cook until it has formed a golden brown caramel. Pour on to the baking sheet and when cold, crush firmly with a rolling pin.
5. Beat the egg whites until they are stiff but not dry and fold them into the orange custard with half the praline. Pour the mixture into a 20.5-cm (8-in) spring-release cake tin and refrigerate until set.
6. To serve, turn the mousse out on to a flat serving plate. Pipe whirls of whipped cream over the top and decorate with the skinned orange segments, ratafia biscuits and the remaining praline.

Peaches

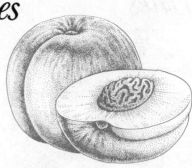

Season: Peaches are at their best in the summer months, although they are available all year round.
To buy: Ripe fruit should be slightly soft, with yellow or slightly orangey skin, often tinged with red. Avoid greenish, bruised or over-soft fruit.
To store: Keep peaches at room temperature and use within 1–2 days, or wrap and refrigerate for up to 5 days.
To prepare: To peel peaches, first dip them in boiling water to loosen the skin. Plunge quickly into cold water, then remove the skin. If you wish, halve lengthways to remove stone. If cut fruit is not to be used immediately, brush with lemon juice to prevent discoloration.

To peel a peach: Dip the peach into boiling water for 15 seconds, then dip into cold water to cool.

Using a small sharp knife, carefully peel the loosened skin away from the flesh.

Poached Peaches

Colour index
page 100

6 dessert
servings

6 peaches, peeled
175 ml (6 fl oz) water
50 g (2 oz) sugar
4 cloves

1. Halve and stone the peaches.
2. Put the water, sugar and cloves into a large saucepan and bring to the boil.
3. Add the peaches and bring back to the boil. Cover the pan, reduce the heat and simmer gently for 10 minutes or until the peaches are tender.

Buttery Baked Peaches

Colour index
page 100

6 dessert
servings

6 peaches, peeled
225 ml (8 fl oz) water
100 g (4 oz) sugar
30 ml (2 tbsp) lemon juice
25 g (1 oz) butter or
margarine

1. Halve and stone the peaches.
2. Put the water, sugar, lemon juice and fat into a saucepan. Bring to the boil; simmer for 5 minutes.
3. Place the peaches in an ovenproof dish and pour the syrup over them. Cover and bake at 170°C (325°F) mark 3 for 30 minutes, or until the peaches are tender but still hold their shape.
4. Serve immediately with the cooking juices.

SHERRIED PEACHES: Prepare the peaches as above, but omit the lemon juice and add *30 ml (2 tbsp) dry sherry* to the sugar syrup.

Pears

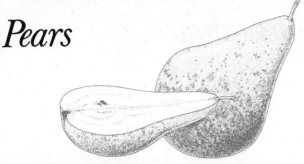

Season: Pears are available all year round.
To buy: Look for well formed, firm pears. When ripe, they should yield slightly to pressure at the stalk end. Avoid any that are bruised or over-ripe. Choose Williams, Conference, Comice and Laxton's for eating raw. Most varieties are good poached in a light syrup.
To store: Ripen pears at room temperature, then re-frigerate them and use them within 2–3 days.
To prepare: Wash or peel the fruit. If you wish, remove the core and slice as required. Alternatively, use a pear wedger to slice the fruit quickly. If the fruit is not to be eaten immediately, brush cut surfaces with lemon juice.

Using a pear wedger: Press the cutter down firmly from the top and the pear will separate into neat wedge-shaped slices, leaving the core in the centre.

Pears in White Wine

Colour index page 101

6 dessert servings

3 large pears   *50 g (2 oz) sugar*
100 ml (4 fl oz) white wine

1. Peel, halve and core the pears.
2. Bring 1 cm (½ in) water to the boil in a wide pan, add pears and bring back to boiling point. Reduce heat, cover and simmer until pears are tender.
3. Remove the pears with a slotted spoon and place them in a serving dish.
4. Add the wine and sugar to the cooking liquid. Bring to the boil, reduce heat and simmer for 8 minutes. Pour syrup over pears, cover and chill.

Pears in Chocolate Sauce

Colour index page 101

4 dessert servings

4 ripe eating pears, chilled   *50 g (2 oz) plain chocolate*
                     60 ml (4 tbsp) milk
For the sauce:
100 g (4 oz) sugar   **To serve:**
60 ml (4 tbsp) brandy   *whipped cream*
2 egg yolks
pinch salt

1. Peel and core the pears, but do not remove the stems. Place them in a shallow dish.
2. Mix the sugar with the brandy, egg yolks and salt. Heat the chocolate and milk in a double saucepan over hot water and stir until the chocolate has melted. Gradually add the sugar mixture and cook for about 5 minutes, stirring all the time, until the sauce has thickened.
3. Pour sauce over pears and chill until required.
4. Spoon some whipped cream on to each plate, place a pear on top and carefully pour over any remaining chocolate sauce.

Pineapples

Season: Pineapples are available all year round.
To buy: Choose a firm fruit, heavy for its size, with a sweet aroma. If ripe, a leaf will pull easily from the crown.
To store: Keep at room temperature until ripe.
To prepare: Cut off the crown of leaves and cut the pineapple crossways into thick slices with a sharp knife. Cut off the rough, stringy skin to leave a clean circle. Remove the central woody core with a small pastry cutter or a sharp knife.

To cut rings and chunks: Using a strong knife, cut off the leafy crown of the pineapple and then cut into slices 1 cm (½ in) thick.

Trim off the rough, stringy skin around the edge to leave a clean ring.

Cut out all the eyes with the tip of a small sharp knife.

Remove the central core with a small pastry cutter. Leave in rings or cut into chunks.

To serve wedges: Halve the pineapple lengthways from the bottom to the crown, then cut it into quarters, leaving on the leafy crown for decoration. Cut out the central core. With a curved serrated knife, loosen the fruit from the rough skin and cut each wedge crossways into slices. Stagger the slices on the skin before serving.

Plums

Season: Different varieties are available from late spring to early autumn; damsons are in season in early autumn.
To buy: Look for plump fruit that yields to gentle pressure. The colour varies from yellow or green to light red or almost black, depending on the variety. Avoid hard, shrivelled or split fruit. Choose sweet varieties for eating raw; all types may be cooked.
To store: Keep at room temperature; use within 4 days.
To prepare: Wash; halve and remove stones if you wish. The kernels give an almond flavour to cooked fruit.

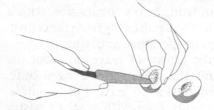

To stone plums: Wash in cold running water, halve lengthways and remove the stone with the tip of a sharp knife.

Stewed Plums

Colour index page 100

4 dessert servings

450 g (1 lb) plums, washed   *300 ml (½ pint) water*
75–100 g (3–4 oz) sugar   *few almonds, optional*

1. Halve the plums, remove the stones and crack them open to extract the kernels if you wish.
2. Put the sugar and water in a saucepan and heat gently until the sugar has completely dissolved.
3. Add the plums, with the kernels or almonds for flavouring, and simmer gently until the fruit is soft but still holds its shape. Remove the kernels or almonds before serving.

Creamy Plum Sauce

Colour index page 100

Makes 400 ml (¾ pint)

4 eating plums, washed   *225 g (8 oz) cream cheese,*
100 g (4 oz) icing sugar   *softened*

1. Halve and stone the plums. Put them in a blender with the sugar and blend until smooth, or rub through a sieve to remove the skins. Add the cream cheese and beat until well blended.
2. Cover and chill until required. Serve with fresh fruit salads or compôtes.

Plums in Port

Colour index page 100

6 dessert servings

900 g (2 lb) small plums,   *1 stick cinnamon*
*   washed*   *7.5 ml (1½ tsp) grated*
400 ml (¾ pint) port   * orange rind*
6 whole cloves   *225 g (8 oz) sugar*

1. Halve and stone the plums. Put them in a large saucepan with the port, cloves, cinnamon and orange rind and bring to the boil. Cover and simmer gently for 3–5 minutes until the plums are tender. Remove the cloves and cinnamon.
2. Add the sugar and stir until it has completely dissolved. Spoon the plum mixture into a large bowl, cover and chill thoroughly.

Pomegranates

Season: Pomegranates are available in the autumn.
To buy: Look for clean fruit with a hard, russet-coloured skin. The seeds should be red and juicy.
To store: Refrigerate and use within a week.
To prepare: Cut off a slice at the stem end and cut the rest of the fruit into segments. Peel back the skin, freeing the fleshy seeds for eating or making juice.

To prepare a pomegranate: Cut a thin slice off the rough stem end of the pomegranate with a small sharp knife.

Remove the slice to reveal the juicy red seeds.

Divide the fruit into sections, cutting just through the skin.

Carefully separate the sections with your fingers.

Bend back the skin and push off the seeds.

To extract the juice, place the seeds in a sieve and crush with the back of a spoon.

Rhubarb

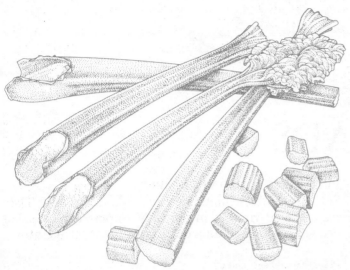

Season: Forced rhubarb is available in winter and early spring, outdoor rhubarb in spring and early summer.

To buy: Forced rhubarb should look pink and tender and the stems slender and clean. It will have a fairly sweet flavour. Outdoor rhubarb is stronger and darker in colour, with thicker stems and a more acid flavour.

To store: Keep rhubarb in a cool place or refrigerate it and use within 3–4 days.

To prepare: Trim off the leaves and root ends and scrub each stem clean. Remove any strings and cut the rhubarb into 2.5-cm (1-in) chunks ready for cooking.

Stewed Rhubarb

Colour index page 101

4 dessert servings

450 g (1 lb) rhubarb, trimmed and scrubbed	piece root ginger, stick cinnamon, lemon rind or orange rind
75–100 g (3–4 oz) sugar	
300 ml (½ pint) water	

1. Using a small sharp knife, cut the prepared rhubarb into even-sized chunks.
2. Put the sugar and water in a saucepan and heat gently until the sugar has completely dissolved.
3. Add the prepared fruit and the ginger, cinnamon, lemon or orange rind for flavour. Simmer gently until the fruit is soft but still holds its shape.
4. Remove the flavourings before serving.

Rhubarb Crumble

Colour index page 101

4 dessert servings

700 g (1½ lb) rhubarb, trimmed and scrubbed	75 g (3 oz) butter or margarine
225 g (8 oz) sugar	175 g (6 oz) plain flour

1. Using a small sharp knife, cut the prepared rhubarb into even-sized chunks and layer it with 175 g (6 oz) of the sugar in a 900 ml–1.1-litre (1½–2-pint) capacity ovenproof dish.
2. Rub the fat into the flour with your fingertips until the mixture resembles fine breadcrumbs, then stir in the remaining sugar. Sprinkle flour mixture on top of the prepared fruit in the dish.
3. Bake at 200°C (400°F) mark 6 for 30–40 minutes. (If you are using stewed rhubarb instead of fresh fruit, reduce the cooking time to 20 minutes.)

Tangerines and satsumas

Season: Imported tangerines and satsumas are available throughout the winter months.

To buy: Look for small, loose-skinned tangerines with a clean, bright orange colour. Clementines, which are a form of tangerine, are seedless and have a closer skin. Satsumas are also seedless, with sweeter flesh and a thicker skin. Avoid any that look dry, are damaged or have patches of soft skin.

To store: Keep at room temperature and use within a few days, or store in a cool place and use within 10 days.

To prepare: Remove the thin skin and divide the fruit into its natural segments for eating raw and in salads. If you want to use the segments for garnishing, skin them with a small sharp knife and remove the pips from tangerines. Grate the rind and squeeze the juice for use as a flavouring in puddings and cakes, or use cooked in marmalades and preserves.

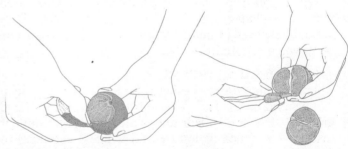

To prepare tangerines and satsumas: Peel off the loose skin with your hand and remove any pith on the fruit.

Divide the fruit into its natural segments for eating raw or mixing into fruit salads. If there are any pips, discard them.

Zesty Tangerine Salad

Colour index page 77

4 side dish servings

6 tangerines or clementines	50 ml (2 fl oz) French dressing, page 326
4 sticks celery, thinly sliced	
30 ml (2 tbsp) sliced pimento	**To serve:**
2.5 ml (½ level tsp) salt	lettuce leaves

1. Peel the tangerines and divide the fruit into segments. Remove any pips.
2. Mix the celery, pimento and salt with the French dressing. Add the tangerine segments and toss together gently until evenly coated.
3. Line a salad bowl with the lettuce leaves and spoon the tangerine and celery salad into the bowl.

SALADS

Salads are a delicious way of introducing variety into both summer and winter meals. There are a few classic recipes that should be part of any cook's repertoire, but the possibilities are endless and limited only by the cook's imagination and the availability of fresh fruit and vegetables. Salads have the added advantage of being quick to prepare, because they generally involve little or no cooking. They are also easy to make up and serve in large quantities for a cold buffet.

Side salads are a light combination of vegetables tossed in a dressing. The most popular is the classic green salad tossed in French dressing, which offers a crispness and mildness of flavour that complements a rich meat, poultry or fish dish perfectly.

Main dish salads are usually more elaborate, containing a greater variety of vegetables and also some form of protein, such as meat, fish or cheese; sometimes they include a more filling ingredient, such as pasta or potatoes, or fruit for contrasting texture and flavour.

Jellied and fruit salads, or salads based on marinated vegetables, make appetising first course dishes. They should be served in small portions. Fruit salads can also be served more traditionally as desserts.

CHOOSING SALAD GREENS
There are many greens other than lettuce leaves which can be used in salads. Try to combine sharply flavoured greens (such as spinach and watercress) with milder tasting ones (such as lettuce and Chinese cabbage) to give a pleasing variety of texture and flavour, and mix dark and light greens together for colour. Although your choice will generally be guided by seasonal availability, aim to serve a selection from the following in a green salad: lettuce (Cos, Webb or round), endive, chicory, kale, cabbage (white, red or Chinese), leafy broccoli, summer spinach, Swiss chard, blanched dandelion leaves, sorrel or watercress. In early summer you can use the leafy tops from beetroot and spinach beet.

Be sure that the greens are crisp, fresh and free from wilted or discoloured leaves. (For details of choosing lettuce and other greens, see page 288.) The darker green, outer leaves of a lettuce carry more nutritional value than the pale, crisp heart. As long as they are not wilted, damaged or too discoloured, add them to the salad bowl or use them as a garnish for cold dishes.

PREPARING SALAD VEGETABLES
Salad vegetables should be trimmed and washed. They may then be wrapped in cling film, or placed in the salad drawer, and stored for a day or two in the refrigerator.

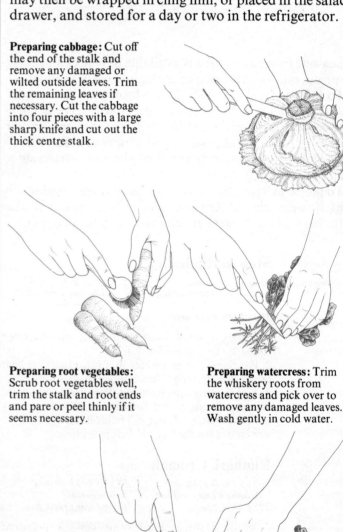

Preparing cabbage: Cut off the end of the stalk and remove any damaged or wilted outside leaves. Trim the remaining leaves if necessary. Cut the cabbage into four pieces with a large sharp knife and cut out the thick centre stalk.

Preparing root vegetables: Scrub root vegetables well, trim the stalk and root ends and pare or peel thinly if it seems necessary.

Preparing watercress: Trim the whiskery roots from watercress and pick over to remove any damaged leaves. Wash gently in cold water.

Preparing spring onions: Trim the roots and tops of the onions to leave about 5–7.5 cm (2–3 in) green leaf. Peel away the outer skin if it is discoloured or looks at all damaged.

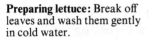

Preparing lettuce: Break off leaves and wash them gently in cold water.

Place the leaves in a colander to drain, then dry gently with kitchen paper towel, or shake in a salad basket or clean tea towel.

CLEANING OTHER SALAD GREENS

Wash all greens thoroughly in cold water. Drain well, pat dry or shake well in a salad basket and trim off any tough ribs or stems.

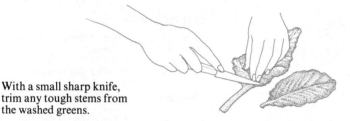

With a small sharp knife, trim any tough stems from the washed greens.

CRISPING SALAD GREENS

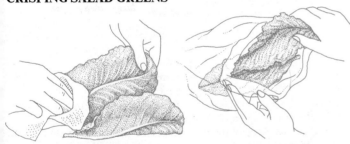

If lettuce is a little wilted, dry it gently with kitchen paper towel or a clean tea towel, taking care not to bruise the leaves.

Transfer it to a polythene bag and chill in the bottom of the refrigerator for about 30 minutes, or until crisp.

DRESSING SALADS

As a general rule, light oil and vinegar dressings go best with tender-leafed green salads, while creamy, spicy or mayonnaise-based dressings go with crisper, more strongly flavoured vegetables. In a slimmer's diet, cut down on oil and toss the greens in lemon juice, or use a yogurt dressing instead of a rich mayonnaise. Always choose a good quality vegetable or olive oil for dressings, and try to use a wine, cider or herb-flavoured vinegar rather than a strong malt vinegar.

If possible, mix a dressing well in advance to give the flavours time to blend, but do not dress a green salad until just before you take it to the table. If you wish, mix the dressing in the bottom of the salad bowl, cross the

servers over it and place the salad on top; it is then simple to toss the greens and dressing together at the table. On the other hand, a salad of cooked vegetables will absorb the flavour of the dressing better if it is added while the vegetables are still warm – it may then be chilled or served just tepid, depending on the rest of the meal and how soon you want to serve the salad.

Leftover dressings keep well. Store mayonnaise and creamy dressings in a covered bowl in the refrigerator. Store French dressing or other oil dressings in a screw-topped jar in the kitchen cupboard – chilling them is not necessary and will solidify the oil.

JELLIED SALADS

Shimmering jellied salads, shaped in decorative moulds, add a colourful touch to any cold table. They should be well chilled and only lightly gelled – excess gelatine will spoil the texture. They should also be served the day they are made, as a jelly becomes rubbery if it is allowed to stand for too long. Follow the instructions below for unmoulding jellied salads cleanly.

Use individual moulds for first course or side salads and large ones for buffet salads. If you want a dramatic effect, use richly coloured ingredients, such as tomatoes and beetroot. On the other hand, a pale-coloured, lightly flavoured cucumber jelly makes a good accompaniment to chilled fish dishes and light summer food.

UNMOULDING JELLIED SALADS

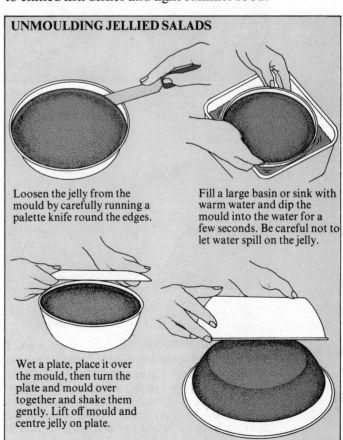

Loosen the jelly from the mould by carefully running a palette knife round the edges.

Fill a large basin or sink with warm water and dip the mould into the water for a few seconds. Be careful not to let water spill on the jelly.

Wet a plate, place it over the mould, then turn the plate and mould over together and shake them gently. Lift off mould and centre jelly on plate.

Tossed salads

Caesar Salad

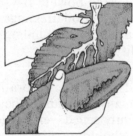

Colour index
page 75

4 side dish
servings

*1 head Cos or Webb
lettuce
175 ml (6 fl oz) French
dressing made with
olive oil, page 326
squeeze lemon juice
50 g (2 oz) grated
Parmesan cheese*

*50-g (2-oz) can anchovy
fillets, drained well
and chopped
1 raw or very lightly boiled
egg, beaten
garlic croûtons, below*

1 Break off individual
lettuce leaves and wash
them thoroughly in cold
water. Drain well and dry
gently with kitchen paper
towel or shake well in a
salad basket.

2 Tear the lettuce leaves
into shreds and put
them in a large salad bowl.
Cover and chill until
ready to serve.

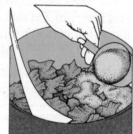

3 Mix the French dressing with the lemon juice
and pour over the lettuce.
Toss gently until it is
evenly coated.

4 Add the Parmesan
cheese, anchovies and
raw egg to the bowl and
toss together with the
lettuce until well mixed.

5 Just before serving, mix
the garlic croûtons
lightly into the salad.

GARLIC CROUTONS: Trim the crusts from *3
slices of French bread* and cut the bread into 1-cm
(½-in) cubes. Heat a little *vegetable oil* in a frying
pan with *2 cloves garlic*, skinned and halved.
Discard the garlic cloves. Add the bread cubes and
fry them until they are golden brown. Remove the
croûtons from the frying pan and drain them well
on kitchen paper towel.

Spinach Salad with Lemon and Mustard Dressing

Colour index
page 75

4–6 side dish
servings

*225 g (8 oz) spinach
1 medium head lettuce
1 small head chicory
100 g (4 oz) mushrooms*

For the dressing:
*5 ml (1 tsp) grated lemon
rind
45 ml (3 tbsp) lemon juice*

*100 ml (4 fl oz) olive or
vegetable oil
5 ml (1 level tsp) sugar
5 ml (1 level tsp) salt
2.5 ml (½ level tsp) dry
mustard
5 ml (1 tsp) chopped chives
pinch pepper*

1. Wash the spinach and lettuce thoroughly; drain
well and dry gently with kitchen paper towel. Shred
the leaves and put them in a large salad bowl.
2. Cut the chicory head crossways in half, separate
the top leaves and cut the bottom halves into
wedges. Thinly slice the mushrooms. Add the
chicory and mushrooms to the salad and toss gently.
3. Mix all the ingredients for the dressing, pour over
the salad and toss together until well mixed.

Mixed Green Salad Bowl

Colour index
page 75

4–6 side dish
servings

*150 g (5 oz) frozen peas
1 small head Webb lettuce
1 small head Cos lettuce
1 small cucumber, thinly
sliced
3 spring onions, trimmed
and chopped
1 stick celery, washed and
sliced*

For the dressing:
60 ml (4 tbsp) vegetable oil

*75 ml (5 tbsp) white wine
vinegar
15 ml (1 level tbsp) sugar
15 ml (1 tbsp) chopped
parsley
2.5 ml (½ level tsp) garlic
salt
2.5 ml (½ level tsp) salt
1.25 ml (¼ level tsp) dried
oregano
large pinch pepper*

1. Put the peas in a bowl, pour over enough boiling
water to cover them and leave to stand for 5 minutes.
Drain well and leave to cool.
2. Wash the lettuces thoroughly, drain well and dry
gently with kitchen paper towel. Shred the leaves
and put them in a large salad bowl with the cucumber, spring onion, celery and peas.
3. Mix all the ingredients for the dressing, pour over
the salad and toss together until well mixed.

California Salad

Colour index
page 75

4–6 side dish
servings

*1 small head Webb lettuce
1 small head Cos lettuce
2 avocados*

For the dressing:
*60 ml (4 tbsp) vegetable oil
15 ml (1 level tbsp) sugar
30 ml (2 tbsp) white wine
vinegar
10 ml (2 tsp) finely chopped
parsley*

*2.5 ml (½ level tsp) garlic
salt
2.5 ml (½ level tsp) salt
1.25 ml (¼ level tsp) dried
oregano
large pinch pepper*

For the garnish:
50 g (2 oz) shelled walnuts

1. Mix all the ingredients for the dressing in a large
salad bowl until well blended.
2. Wash the lettuces thoroughly, drain well and dry
gently with kitchen paper towel. Shred the leaves
and add them to the salad bowl.
3. Peel, stone and slice the avocados and add to the
bowl. Toss the salad with the dressing until well
mixed. Garnish with the walnuts.

Vegetable salads

Coleslaw

Colour index
page 76
4 side dish
servings

*about 75 ml (5 tbsp) salad
cream or mayonnaise,
page 462*
*5 ml (1 level tsp) caster
sugar*
2.5 ml (½ level tsp) salt
large pinch pepper
*few drops vinegar or lemon
juice*
*450 g (1 lb) white cabbage,
trimmed*
½ small green pepper

*2 sticks celery, washed and
trimmed*
1 large carrot
*15 ml (1 tbsp) grated or
finely chopped onion,
optional*

1 Mix the salad cream or
mayonnaise with the
sugar, salt, pepper and
vinegar or lemon juice
to sharpen the flavour.

2 With a sharp knife,
shred the cabbage
finely. Remove the seeds
from the green pepper and
slice it very thinly.

3 Slice the celery thinly
with a sharp knife.
Scrub and trim the carrot,
then peel it and grate it
quite coarsely.

4 Put the prepared
vegetables and onion
in a large salad bowl, add
the dressing and toss
together well. Chill.

COLESLAW BOWL

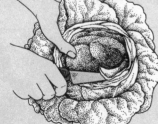

With a sharp knife, carefully
cut out the centre from a
Savoy cabbage, leaving the
outer leaves as a bowl. Wash
between leaves and dry with
kitchen paper towel.

After removing the cabbage
centre, wash it thoroughly
in cold water, shred it and
use to make coleslaw. Pile
the prepared salad into the
cabbage bowl to serve.

Cucumbers in Soured Cream

Colour index
page 75
6 side dish
servings

3 small cucumbers

For the dressing:
*225 ml (8 fl oz) soured
cream*
30 ml (2 tbsp) lemon juice

*45 ml (3 tbsp) finely
chopped onion or chives*
*7.5 ml (1½ level tsp) salt
pinch pepper*

1. Wipe the cucumbers with a damp cloth; peel them
and then slice them thinly.
2. Mix all the ingredients for the dressing in a salad
bowl until well blended.
3. Add the cucumber slices to the dressing and stir
together until well mixed. Cover and chill thoroughly.
Stir again just before serving.

Danish Cucumber Salad

Colour index
page 75
4 side dish
servings

2 small cucumbers
5 ml (1 level tsp) salt

For the dressing:
*100 ml (4 fl oz) white
vinegar*

50 g (2 oz) sugar
*30 ml (2 tbsp) chopped
fresh dill weed*
*1.25 ml (¼ level tsp) white
pepper*

1. Wipe the cucumbers and slice them very thinly.
Sprinkle with the salt and leave to stand for 1 hour.
Drain well, rinse and pat dry.
2. Mix all the ingredients for the dressing, add to the
cucumbers and stir together until well mixed. Cover
and chill thoroughly before serving.

Tomatoes Vinaigrette

Colour index
page 75
4 first course
or side dish
servings

4 tomatoes
salt and pepper

For the dressing:
*finely chopped chives or
spring onion*

*100 ml (4 fl oz) French
dressing, page 326*

For the garnish, optional:
chopped parsley

1. Wipe the tomatoes, skin them if you wish (page
296) and slice them thinly.
2. Arrange the slices in overlapping rows in a serving
dish and sprinkle with salt and pepper.
3. Stir the chopped chives into the French dressing
and pour it over the tomatoes. Garnish with chopped parsley if you wish.

Marinated Artichoke Hearts
and Mushrooms

Colour index
page 20
6 first course
servings

*396-g (14-oz) can
artichoke hearts, drained*
*350 g (12 oz) mushrooms,
sliced*
*30 ml (2 tbsp) diced red or
green pepper*

For the dressing:
*175 ml (6 fl oz) vegetable
oil*
100 ml (4 fl oz) lemon juice

15 ml (1 level tbsp) sugar
10 ml (2 level tsp) salt
*5 ml (1 level tsp) dry
mustard*
2.5 ml (½ level tsp) pepper
*2.5 ml (½ level tsp) dried
basil*
*1 small clove garlic, skinned
and crushed*

1. Mix all the ingredients for the dressing in a large
salad bowl until well blended.
2. Add the artichoke hearts, mushrooms and red or
green pepper to the dressing in the salad bowl and
toss together until well mixed. Cover and chill
thoroughly until required, stirring occasionally.

Vegetable salads

Greek Salad

Colour index
page 77

6 side dish
or first course
servings

1 small head endive
1 small head Cos lettuce
1 cucumber
2 large tomatoes
175 g (6 oz) stoned black
  olives
100 g (4 oz) feta cheese,
  crumbled
50-g (2-oz) can anchovy
  fillets, drained, optional
2 spring onions, trimmed
  and chopped

30 ml (2 tbsp) capers

For the dressing:
100 ml (4 fl oz) olive or
  vegetable oil
45 ml (3 tbsp) red wine
  vinegar
5 ml (1 level tsp) dried
  oregano
2.5 ml (½ level tsp) salt
large pinch pepper

1. Wash the endive and lettuce thoroughly, drain
well and dry gently with kitchen paper towel. Shred
the leaves and put them in a large salad bowl.
2. Wipe the cucumber, pare off alternating strips of
the skin and slice the flesh thinly. Cut the tomatoes
into small wedges.
3. Add the cucumber slices, tomato wedges, olives,
cheese, anchovy fillets, spring onions and capers to
the salad bowl.
4. Mix all the ingredients for the dressing, pour over
the salad and toss together until well mixed.

Preparing the cucumber:
Peel off strips of skin with
a sharp knife, then slice
the cucumber thinly.

Assembling the salad:
Add all the ingredients to
the bowl before tossing
with the dressing.

Mixed Vegetable Salad

Colour index
page 75

4 side dish
servings

1 cucumber
1.25 ml (¼ level tsp) salt
4 medium potatoes, scrubbed
226-g (8-oz) packet frozen
  peas and carrots, cooked
  and drained

For the dressing:
225 ml (8 fl oz) mayonnaise,
  page 462

75 ml (5 tbsp) milk
1.25 ml (¼ level tsp)
  pepper
7.5 ml (1½ level tsp) salt

To serve:
lettuce leaves

1. Wipe the cucumber and slice it thinly into a
colander. Sprinkle with the salt and leave to stand.
2. Meanwhile, cook the potatoes in their skins in
boiling salted water for 20–25 minutes until just
tender. Drain well and cool slightly.
3. Peel the potatoes and cut them into 1-cm (½-in)
cubes. Add the peas, carrots and all the ingredients
for the dressing; toss together until well mixed.
4. Wash the lettuce leaves and dry gently with
kitchen paper towel. Drain the cucumber slices well,
then rinse them and pat them dry.
5. Line a serving dish with the lettuce, pile the salad
in the centre and arrange the cucumber on top.

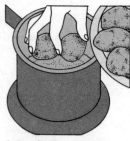

Hot Potato Salad

Colour index
page 75

4 side dish
servings

450 g (1 lb) potatoes,
  scrubbed
4 rashers streaky bacon,
  rinded and chopped
1 small onion, skinned and
  chopped
15 ml (1 level tbsp) plain
  flour
15 ml (1 level tbsp) sugar
5 ml (1 level tsp) salt
freshly ground black pepper
105 ml (7 tbsp) water
90 ml (6 tbsp) cider vinegar

For the garnish:
chopped parsley

1 In a large saucepan over
a high heat, cook the
potatoes in their skins in
boiling salted water for
20–25 minutes until they
are tender. Drain well and
cool slightly.

2 When the potatoes are
cool enough to handle,
peel them and cut them
into bite-sized cubes.

3 Fry the bacon gently in
its own fat until crisp;
remove from the pan and
drain thoroughly on kitchen
paper towel.

4 Add the onion to the
bacon fat in the pan
and fry gently for about 5
minutes, until just beginning to turn golden.

5 Stir in the flour and the
sugar. Add the salt and
freshly ground black pep-
per to taste.

6 Gradually blend in the
water and the vinegar;
bring to the boil and cook
for about 2 minutes, stirring constantly, until the
mixture has thickened.

7 Add the potatoes and
the bacon to the frying
pan. Mix together gently
and heat for about 10 minutes, stirring occasionally.
Garnish with parsley.

Celery Hearts Vinaigrette

Colour index page 20

6 first course servings

3 small heads celery
400 ml (³/₄ pint) chicken stock
lettuce leaves

For the marinade:
¹/₂ small green pepper
75-g (3-oz) can pimentos, drained and chopped

150 ml (¹/₄ pint) white wine vinegar
50 ml (2 fl oz) vegetable oil
5 ml (1 level tsp) sugar
5 ml (1 level tsp) salt
5 ml (1 level tsp) dry mustard
2.5 ml (¹/₂ level tsp) pepper

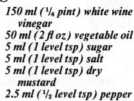

1 Trim the leaves and roots from the celery and remove the coarse outer stalks. Cut each head of celery in half lengthways and wash in cold water.

2 Bring the chicken stock to the boil, add the halved celery hearts and cook them for about 15 minutes, or until just tender but still firm.

3 Meanwhile, seed and finely chop the green pepper and mix together all the ingredients for the marinade in a large shallow dish.

4 Drain celery and arrange in a single layer in the dish, turning to coat well. Cover and chill for several hours, turning the celery occasionally.

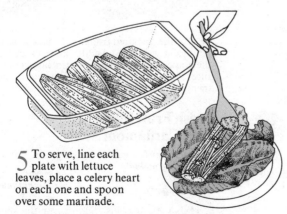

5 To serve, line each plate with lettuce leaves, place a celery heart on each one and spoon over some marinade.

FRENCH BEANS VINAIGRETTE: Prepare the salad as above, but replace the celery heads with *700 g (1¹/₂ lb) French beans.* Trim and wash them, then cook in boiling salted water for 5–10 minutes before marinating them; omit the green pepper from the marinade and add *100 g (4 oz) mushrooms,* sliced.

BRAISED LEEKS VINAIGRETTE: Prepare the salad as left, but replace the celery with *6 medium leeks.* Trim them, cut each one in half crossways and then halve the root ends lengthways; rinse them well under cold running water to remove any grit. Cook in boiling *chicken stock* for 30 minutes or until tender before marinating. (Colour index page 76)

Mixed Bean Salad

Colour index page 76

6 side dish servings

275 g (10 oz) mixed dried beans, soaked overnight, eg. aduki, red kidney, black, haricot
50 g (2 oz) onion, skinned and thinly sliced
salt and pepper

For the dressing:
100 ml (4 fl oz) French dressing, page 326
2.5 ml (¹/₂ level tsp) ground coriander

1. Cook the beans in boiling salted water for about 1 hour or until tender, or pressure cook at high (15 lb) pressure for 15–20 minutes. If you are using aduki beans, add them halfway through the cooking time. Drain the beans well.
2. Put the French dressing in a large salad bowl and stir in the ground coriander. Add the warm beans and toss together until well mixed. Leave to cool.
3. Add the onion to the beans and adjust the seasoning. Cover and chill thoroughly.

Turkish Bean Salad

Colour index page 76

4–6 side dish servings

225 g (8 oz) dried haricot beans, soaked overnight
750 ml (1¹/₄ pints) chicken stock
bay leaf
75 g (3 oz) stoned black olives, halved
2 large tomatoes, chopped

60 ml (4 tbsp) lemon juice
45 ml (3 tbsp) chopped fresh mint or 15 ml (1 level tbsp) dried mint
10 ml (2 level tsp) salt
10 ml (2 level tsp) sugar
pinch white pepper

For the dressing:
60 ml (4 tbsp) olive or vegetable oil

For the garnish:
mint leaves

1. Put the beans in a large saucepan with the stock and bay leaf and bring to the boil. Cover and simmer for about 1 hour, stirring occasionally, until tender but still firm. Drain well and discard bay leaf.
2. Put the beans, olives and tomatoes in a large salad bowl. Mix all the ingredients for the dressing, pour over the salad and toss together until well mixed. Leave to cool. Cover and chill thoroughly.
3. To serve, garnish the salad with mint leaves.

German Sauerkraut Salad

Colour index page 76

4–6 side dish servings

566-g (1¹/₄-lb) can sauerkraut
2 red apples, cored

10 ml (2 level tsp) sugar
2.5 ml (¹/₂ level tsp) freshly ground black pepper

For the dressing:
75 ml (5 tbsp) olive oil

1. Drain the sauerkraut very well and put it in a large salad bowl.
2. Grate the apples and add them to the sauerkraut.
3. Mix all the ingredients for the dressing, pour over the salad and toss together until well mixed. Cover and chill thoroughly before serving.

Fruit salads

Waldorf Salad

Colour index
page 77

4–6 side dish
servings

450 g (1 lb) red apples
6–8 sticks celery, washed,
trimmed and thinly sliced
50 g (2 oz) chopped
walnuts
100 g (4 oz) seedless raisins

For the dressing:
150 ml (¼ pint) mayonnaise,
page 462
50 ml (2 fl oz) lemon juice

To serve:
lettuce leaves, washed

1 Put the mayonnaise in a
large bowl and stir in the
lemon juice.

2 Halve and core the
apples, but do not peel
them. With a sharp knife,
chop into bite-sized cubes.

3 Add the apples to the
mayonnaise dressing
and stir until the pieces are
well coated.

4 Add the celery, wal-
nuts and raisins to the
bowl and toss together
gently until well mixed.

5 Arrange the lettuce
leaves on a large serv-
ing plate and spoon the
salad on to the centre.

Lemon Fruit Salad

Colour index
page 21

4 first course
servings

2 lemons
1 orange
30 ml (2 level tbsp) caster
sugar
15 ml (1 tbsp) chopped
fresh tarragon

150 ml (¼ pint) French
dressing, page 326

For the garnish:
small crisp lettuce leaves

1. Dip the lemons and the orange into boiling water
and peel them, being careful to remove all the pith.
Using a sharp knife, cut the flesh into thin slices.
2. Arrange the lemon and orange slices in layers in a
shallow dish, sprinkling each layer with a little sugar
and chopped tarragon.
3. Pour the French dressing over the salad and leave
to stand for a short time.
4. Wash the lettuce leaves thoroughly in cold water
and dry gently with kitchen paper towel. Use the
lettuce leaves to garnish the salad.

Mediterranean Fruit Bowl

Colour index
page 101

4–6 dessert
servings

225 g (8 oz) sugar
300 ml (½ pint) water
30 ml (2 tbsp) lemon juice
15 ml (1 level tbsp) anise
seed
1.25 ml (¼ level tsp) salt
1 small pineapple
½ honeydew melon
1 small canteloup melon
2 oranges
2 nectarines or 4 apricots
2 dark-skinned eating
plums
100 g (4 oz) seedless white
grapes
1 lime, sliced, optional

1 Put the sugar, water,
lemon juice, anise seed
and salt in a heavy-based
saucepan. Heat gently to
dissolve sugar; bring to
boil and boil 15 minutes.
Cool slightly, then chill.

2 Remove rough skin
and core from pine-
apple and rind and seeds
from melons; peel oranges.
Cut fruit into small pieces.

3 Remove the stones
from the nectarines and
the plums; cut the flesh
into wedges or slices.

4 Put the prepared fruits
in a large bowl and add
the grapes and the lime
slices if you are using
them. Stir together gently.

5 Strain the chilled syrup
over the fruit and stir
the salad to mix well.
Cover and chill thoroughly
before serving.

Fresh Fruit Salad
with Cardamom Sauce

Colour index
page 101

4 dessert
servings

1 small honeydew melon
1 canteloup melon
3 peaches
6 eating plums

2 pears

To serve:
cardamom sauce, page 326

1. Halve the melons. Scoop out the seeds, cut the
flesh free from the rind and cut it into bite-sized
pieces. Peel the peaches, remove the stones and slice
the fruit. Remove the stones from the plums and
core the pears and slice them.
2. Put all the fruit in a large bowl and toss together
gently. Serve with the cardamom sauce.

Jellied and moulded salads

Tomato Jelly Ring

450 g (1 lb) firm tomatoes
2 small onions, skinned and chopped
1 small clove garlic, skinned and crushed
5 ml (1 level tsp) sugar
2.5 ml (½ level tsp) salt
pinch celery salt
pinch grated nutmeg
bay leaf
5 ml (1 tsp) peppercorns
15 ml (1 level tbsp) powdered gelatine
45 ml (3 tbsp) lemon juice

15 ml (1 tbsp) tarragon vinegar
lettuce leaves

For the dressing:
225 ml (8 fl oz) natural yogurt
30 ml (2 tbsp) chopped fresh dill
5 ml (1 tsp) grated lemon rind

Colour index page 76

4 side dish servings

1 Skin the tomatoes (page 296) and then cut them into small wedges.

2 Put the tomatoes in a pan with the onions, garlic, sugar, salts and nutmeg. Tie the bay leaf and peppercorns in muslin; add to pan. Cook over low heat until onion is tender. Cool.

3 Dissolve the gelatine in a little water in a small bowl over a pan of hot water. Leave to cool.

4 Meanwhile, spoon the cooked tomato mixture from the saucepan into a blender and blend to make a smooth purée.

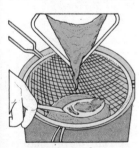

5 Rub the puréed mixture through a sieve to remove the tomato seeds and put the purée into a measuring jug. Add the lemon juice and the vinegar and stir to mix well.

6 Add water if necessary to make the tomato mixture up to 600 ml (1 pint), then stir in the dissolved gelatine.

7 Pour the mixture into a wetted 600-ml (1-pint) capacity ring tin and refrigerate for about 1 hour, or until set.

8 Mix together the natural yogurt, chopped fresh dill and grated lemon rind in a small bowl; cover and chill.

9 Turn the jelly out on to a flat plate (page 317) and garnish with lettuce leaves. Serve with the yogurt dressing.

Colour index page 76
4–6 side dish servings

Perfection Salad

600 ml (1 pint) water
30 ml (2 level tbsp) powdered gelatine
100 g (4 oz) sugar
5 ml (1 level tsp) salt
90 ml (6 tbsp) cider vinegar
30 ml (2 tbsp) lemon juice
175 g (6 oz) white cabbage, finely shredded

3 sticks celery, washed and sliced
100 g (4 oz) canned pimentos, sliced

For the garnish:
lettuce leaves

1. Bring 150 ml (¼ pint) of the water to the boil. Mix the gelatine with the sugar and the salt and add to the boiling water, stirring until the gelatine and sugar have completely dissolved.
2. Add the vinegar, lemon juice and remaining water to the gelatine mixture and refrigerate until it is just beginning to set.
3. Fold in the cabbage, celery and pimentos with their liquid; spoon into a wetted 1.1-litre (2-pint) capacity bowl. Cover and refrigerate for about 2 hours or until set.
4. To serve, turn the salad out on to a flat plate (page 317) and garnish with lettuce leaves.

Colour index page 76
4–6 side dish servings

Curried Pasta Ring

75 g (3 oz) pasta shells or short-cut macaroni
5 ml (1 level tsp) concentrated curry sauce or paste
75 ml (5 level tbsp) thick mayonnaise, page 462
75 g (3 oz) lean cooked ham, chopped
1 stick celery, washed and chopped
1 red eating apple, cored and chopped

30 ml (2 tbsp) chopped parsley

For the garnish:
1 red eating apple, cored
30 ml (2 tbsp) lemon juice
watercress sprigs, washed and trimmed

1. Cook the pasta shapes in boiling salted water for 10–12 minutes, until tender but still firm. Drain and rinse in cold water; leave to cool.
2. In a large bowl, stir together the concentrated curry sauce or paste and the mayonnaise until they are evenly blended.
3. Fold the ham, celery, apple, parsley and cooled pasta into the mayonnaise mixture and toss gently together until they are well mixed.
4. Spoon the mixture into a lightly oiled 900-ml (1½-pint) ring tin. Press down in the tin very firmly, using the back of the spoon, and level off the top.
5. For the garnish, slice the apple into thin wedges and brush the cut surfaces with lemon juice to prevent discoloration.
6. To serve, turn the pasta ring carefully out on to a flat plate and centre it on the plate. Garnish the salad with the apple slices and the watercress sprigs.

Main dish salads

Chef's Salad

Colour index
page 66

6 main dish
servings

1 clove garlic, halved
1 large head Cos or
  Webb lettuce
225 g (8 oz) cold cooked
  chicken or turkey
225 g (8 oz) Gruyère
  cheese, sliced
175 g (6 oz) cooked ham,
  sliced
2 tomatoes

1 hard-boiled egg,
  shelled
225 ml (8 fl oz) French
  dressing, page 326 or
  garlic French dressing,
  page 326

1 Rub each half of the
garlic clove over the in-
side of a large salad bowl;
discard the garlic.

2 Wash the lettuce well
and dry it gently with
kitchen paper towel. Tear
into shreds; place in bowl.

3 Cut the chicken, cheese
and ham into thin
strips. Cut the tomatoes
into wedges and quarter
the hard-boiled egg with a
very sharp knife to avoid
breaking the yolk.

4 Pour the French dress-
ing over the lettuce and
toss gently until it is evenly
coated. Arrange chicken,
cheese, ham, tomato and
egg attractively over the
top of the lettuce.

Herring Salad

Colour index
page 66

4 main dish
servings

225 ml (8 fl oz) double or
  whipping cream
2 potatoes, cooked, skinned
  and diced
450 g (1 lb) pickled
  beetroots, drained and
  sliced
1 medium apple, cored and
  diced
450 g (1 lb) smoked herring
  or mackerel, coarsely
  flaked

60 ml (4 tbsp) chopped
  gherkins
60 ml (4 tbsp) finely
  chopped onion
7.5 ml (1½ level tsp) salt
1.25 ml (¼ level tsp)
  pepper

For the garnish:
2 hard-boiled eggs, shelled
  and cut into wedges
parsley sprigs

1. Whip the cream in a large bowl until soft peaks
form. Carefully fold in the potatoes, beetroots,
apple, herring or mackerel, gherkins, chopped onion
and seasoning until well mixed. Cover and chill for
at least 6 hours, or until required.
2. Spoon the salad on to a large serving dish and
arrange the egg wedges and parsley sprigs around
the edge or over the top of the salad.

Salade Niçoise

Colour index
page 66

4 main dish
servings

3 medium potatoes,
  scrubbed
3 eggs
2 tomatoes
2 212-g (7½-oz) cans tuna,
  drained well
1 medium head Cos or
  Webb lettuce
450 g (1 lb) French beans,
  cooked or 411-g
  (14½-oz) can French
  beans, drained well
50-g (2-oz) can anchovy
  fillets, drained well

225 ml (8 fl oz) classic
  French dressing, page
  326 or garlic French
  dressing, page 326 or
  mixed herb French
  dressing, page 326

For the garnish:
175 g (6 oz) stoned black
  olives

1 Cook the potatoes in
their skins in boiling
salted water for 20 – 30
minutes until tender; drain
well and cool. Meanwhile,
hard-boil the eggs.

2 When the potatoes are
cool enough to handle,
peel them and cut them
into bite-sized pieces.

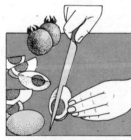

3 Shell the hard-boiled
eggs under running
cold water, being careful
not to peel any of the white
away with the shell. Cut
the eggs into quarters and
the tomatoes into wedges.

4 Flake the tuna into
bite-sized pieces with
the prongs of a fork. Separate the anchovy fillets
carefully.

5 Wash the lettuce
thoroughly in cold
water; dry gently with kitchen paper towel. Tear the
lettuce leaves into shreds;
put in a large salad bowl.

6 Arrange the prepared
potatoes, tuna, eggs,
tomatoes, beans and
anchovies on the lettuce;
garnish with olives. Serve
with the French dressing.

Pineapple and Cheese Salad

Colour index page 66

4 main dish servings

1 large pineapple
225 g (8 oz) Cheddar cheese
225 g (8 oz) Gruyère cheese
2 sticks celery, washed and sliced
½ medium green pepper, seeded and diced

For the dressing:
175 ml (6 fl oz) mayonnaise, page 462
30 ml (2 tbsp) milk
2.5 ml (½ level tsp) salt

1. Cut the pineapple lengthways into four equal wedges, with some leaves attached to each wedge.
2. Remove the core from each wedge and cut out the fruit, leaving a 1-cm (½-in) shell. Cover shells and chill. Cut the fruit into small pieces.
3. Grate 50 g (2 oz) of the Cheddar cheese and reserve for garnishing. Cut the remaining Cheddar and the Gruyère into small pieces.
4. Mix all the ingredients for the dressing; stir in the pineapple, cheese, celery and green pepper.
5. Serve in pineapple shells and sprinkle with cheese.

Crab Louis

Colour index page 66

4 main dish servings

350 g (12 oz) crab meat

For the dressing:
150 ml (¼ pint) mayonnaise, page 462
30 ml (2 tbsp) tomato ketchup
15 ml (1 tbsp) chopped spring onion
10 ml (2 tsp) Worcestershire sauce
5 ml (1 tsp) lemon juice

10 ml (2 tsp) red wine vinegar
salt and pepper

For the garnish:
lettuce leaves
2 hard-boiled eggs, shelled and sliced
1 tomato, sliced
1 cucumber, sliced

1. If using frozen crab meat, thaw and drain well.
2. Mix all the ingredients for the dressing in a small bowl, cover and chill well.
3. Pile the crab on a large plate, surround with lettuce leaves and garnish with egg, tomato and cucumber slices. Serve with the dressing.

Prawn Salad

Colour index page 66

6 main dish servings

450 g (1 lb) shelled prawns
6 sticks celery, washed and sliced
25 g (1 oz) stuffed olives, sliced
50 g (2 oz) shelled walnuts, chopped, optional
lettuce leaves

For the dressing:
100 ml (4 fl oz) mayonnaise, page 462
60 ml (4 tbsp) French dressing, page 326
5 ml (1 tsp) finely chopped onion

1. If using frozen prawns, thaw and drain them well. Mix with the celery, olives and walnuts in a bowl.
2. Mix all the ingredients for the dressing, pour over the salad and toss together until well mixed. Cover and chill. Serve spooned on to lettuce leaves.

TUNA SALAD: Prepare the salad as above, but replace the prawns with *2 198-g (7-oz) cans tuna*, drained and coarsely flaked.

SALMON SALAD: Prepare the salad as above, but replace the prawns with *2 198-g (7-oz) cans salmon*, drained and coarsely flaked. Omit the walnuts and add *2 hard-boiled eggs*, shelled and chopped.

Rice Salad

Colour index page 66

6 main dish servings

75 ml (5 tbsp) vegetable oil
1 onion, skinned and chopped
200 g (7 oz) long grain rice
375 ml (13 fl oz) chicken stock
60 ml (4 tbsp) tomato ketchup
5 ml (1 level tsp) dried thyme

450 g (1 lb) cooked ham, diced
1 green pepper, seeded and finely chopped
60 ml (4 tbsp) red wine vinegar

To serve:
lettuce leaves

1. Heat the oil in a large saucepan, add the onion and cook until soft but not coloured.
2. Stir in the rice, stock, ketchup and thyme and bring to the boil. Reduce the heat, cover and simmer gently for 25 minutes or until the rice is tender.
3. Stir in the remaining ingredients gently with a fork. Cover and chill. Serve on lettuce leaves.

Chunky Egg Salad

Colour index page 66

4 main dish servings

6 hard-boiled eggs, shelled
4 sticks celery, washed and sliced
30 ml (2 tbsp) finely chopped green pepper

For the dressing:
60 ml (4 tbsp) mayonnaise, page 462
15 ml (1 tbsp) cider vinegar
6.25 ml (1¼ level tsp) salt

5 ml (1 tsp) finely chopped onion
2.5 ml (½ tsp) Worcestershire sauce
pinch pepper

To serve:
lettuce leaves
chopped parsley

1. Mix all the ingredients for the dressing.
2. Cut the eggs into large chunks; place them in a large salad bowl with the celery and green pepper. Add the dressing to the bowl and toss together gently until well mixed; cover and chill.
3. Serve spooned on to lettuce; garnish with parsley.

Buffet Salad

Colour index page 66

6 main dish servings

175 g (6 oz) Gruyère cheese, grated
175 g (6 oz) mature Cheddar cheese, grated
350 g (12 oz) cooked ham, sliced
4 medium tomatoes
1 large head lettuce
parsley sprigs, optional

For the dressing:
225 ml (8 fl oz) mayonnaise, page 462
60 ml (4 tbsp) made mustard
2.5 ml (½ level tsp) sugar
2.5 ml (½ level tsp) salt
1.25 ml (¼ level tsp) paprika

1. Line a 2.4-litre (4-pint) capacity bowl with cling film. Mix the grated cheeses and press in an even layer over the bottom and sides of the bowl.
2. Cut the ham into 2.5-cm (1-in) strips and thinly slice the tomatoes. Reserve 4 – 6 large lettuce leaves and tear the remaining leaves into shreds.
3. Arrange one third each of the ham, shredded lettuce and tomato slices in separate layers over the cheese, pressing each layer down firmly. Repeat twice. Cover the bowl and chill.
4. Mix the mayonnaise with the remaining ingredients for the dressing. Cover and chill.
5. To serve, turn the salad out from the lined bowl, tuck the reserved lettuce leaves around it and garnish with parsley sprigs if you wish. Cut into wedges and serve with the chilled dressing.

Salad dressings and sauces

Makes 175 ml
(6 fl oz)

French Dressing

3.75 ml (³/₄ level tsp) salt
1.25 ml (¼ level tsp) pepper
3.75 ml (³/₄ level tsp) dry mustard

3.75 ml (³/₄ level tsp) sugar
60 ml (4 tbsp) vinegar
120 ml (8 tbsp) olive or vegetable oil

1. Put the salt, pepper, mustard and sugar in a bowl, add the vinegar and stir well until the sugar has completely dissolved.
2. Gradually beat in the oil with a fork. If the dressing separates, whisk it immediately before use until well blended.

ANCHOVY FRENCH DRESSING: Add *30 ml (2 tbsp) finely chopped anchovies* to the dressing.

GARLIC FRENCH DRESSING: Add *2 cloves of garlic*, skinned and crushed, to the dressing.

BLUE CHEESE FRENCH DRESSING: Add *50 g (2 oz) crumbled blue-veined cheese* to the dressing.

MIXED HERB FRENCH DRESSING: Add *15 ml (1 tbsp) chopped parsley, 2.5 ml (½ level tsp) dried marjoram* and a *pinch of dried thyme* to the dressing.

OLIVE FRENCH DRESSING: Add *30 ml (2 tbsp) chopped stuffed olives* to the dressing.

Makes 300 ml
(½ pint)

Thousand Island Dressing

225 ml (8 fl oz) mayonnaise, page 462
30 ml (2 tbsp) mild chilli sauce
30 ml (2 tbsp) finely chopped green pepper

15 ml (1 tbsp) chopped parsley
5 ml (1 tsp) grated or finely chopped onion

Mix the mayonnaise with the remaining ingredients and stir until well blended.

Makes 350 ml
(12 fl oz)

Poppy Seed Dressing

75 ml (5 tbsp) cider vinegar
50 g (2 oz) sugar
5 ml (1 level tsp) dry mustard
15 ml (1 tbsp) grated or finely chopped onion
5 ml (1 level tsp) salt

15 ml (1 level tbsp) poppy seeds
225 ml (8 fl oz) vegetable oil

1. Place the vinegar, sugar, mustard, onion, salt and poppy seeds in a blender and blend at low speed until well mixed.
2. Turn to high speed and slowly pour in the oil through the hole in the lid. Blend until well mixed.

Makes 225 ml
(8 fl oz)

Green Goddess Dressing

175 ml (6 fl oz) mayonnaise, page 462
2 anchovy fillets, finely chopped
15 ml (1 tbsp) chopped parsley
15 ml (1 tbsp) chopped chives

15 ml (1 tbsp) chopped spring onion
3.75 ml (³/₄ level tsp) dried tarragon
15 ml (1 tbsp) tarragon vinegar

Mix the mayonnaise with the remaining ingredients and stir until thoroughly blended.

Makes 300 ml
(½ pint)

Blender Mayonnaise

2 egg yolks
2.5 ml (½ level tsp) salt
1.25 ml (¼ level tsp) dry mustard
1.25 ml (¼ level tsp) pepper

1.25 ml (¼ level tsp) sugar
300 ml (½ pint) vegetable or olive oil
15 ml (1 tbsp) vinegar or lemon juice

1. Place the egg yolks, salt, dry mustard, pepper and sugar in blender; blend at high speed for 10 seconds.
2. Turn to medium speed and very slowly pour in the oil through the hole in the lid. Continue blending until well mixed.
3. Add the vinegar or lemon juice and blend again at medium speed just until the mayonnaise is smooth.

Makes 175 ml
(6 fl oz)

Soured Cream Dressing

150 ml (¼ pint) soured cream
30 ml (2 tbsp) white vinegar
5 ml (1 tsp) grated onion

2.5 ml (½ level tsp) sugar
5 ml (1 level tsp) salt
pinch pepper

Mix the soured cream with the remaining ingredients and stir until well blended.

Makes 150 ml
(¼ pint)

Foamy Mayonnaise

2 egg yolks
salt and pepper
150 ml (¼ pint) vegetable oil

30 ml (2 tbsp) lemon juice
1 egg white

1. Cream the egg yolks and seasonings and the oil drop by drop, stirring hard all the time until the mayonnaise has thickened.
2. Stir in the lemon juice until well blended.
3. Just before serving, whisk the egg white stiffly and fold it into the mayonnaise.

Makes 150 ml
(¼ pint)

Garlic and Pimento Dressing

4 pimentos or 184-g (6½-oz) can pimentos
60 ml (4 tbsp) olive oil
60 ml (4 tbsp) white vinegar

2 cloves garlic, skinned and crushed

Blend or sieve the pimentos, then stir in the oil, vinegar and garlic until well blended.

Makes 225 ml
(8 fl oz)

Cardamom Sauce

350 g (12 oz) cream cheese, softened
100 ml (4 fl oz) milk
45 ml (3 level tbsp) sugar

2.5 ml (½ level tsp) ground cardamom

Place all the ingredients for the sauce in a bowl and beat until well blended and smooth.

Makes 450 ml
(³/₄ pint)

Lemon Chive Dressing

225 g (8 oz) cottage cheese
15 ml (1 tbsp) lemon juice
15 ml (1 tbsp) vegetable oil
salt and pepper

15 ml (1 tbsp) chopped chives

Blend or sieve the cheese, then add the remaining ingredients and stir until well blended.

Decorative ideas

GARNISHES

Cucumber slices: Run a sharp-pronged fork down the length of an unpeeled cucumber to score it, and cut crossways into slices.

Radish fans: Cut each radish crossways into thin slices, being careful not to cut all the way through. Chill in iced water; drain.

Curled spring onions: Trim green tops; thinly slice remaining green lengthways to the bulb. Chill in iced water; drain.

Melon clusters: Peel, halve crossways and seed a firm canteloup melon. Slice into rings; cut one side.

Roll each ring round to form a cone and fasten the ends in position with a cocktail stick.

Put some parsley into each cone. Secure three cones with cocktail sticks to form a cluster.

Pepper chains: Slice red or green peppers thinly into rings. Snip each ring once and link to make a chain.

Celery curls: Cut celery into pieces 7.5 cm (3 in) long. Slit each piece into narrow strips, almost to the end. Chill in iced water until ends curl. Drain well.

Cheese balls: Using softened cream cheese, form small balls with your hands, then roll them in chopped nuts to cover completely.

Vegetable shapes: Thinly slice a peeled turnip or swede crossways and cut out shapes with canapé cutters. To make flower shapes, cut notches around the edge of a circle; trim corners to form rounded petals. For carrots, cut out the shapes with small biscuit cutters or use a small sharp knife.

CUCUMBER FLOWER

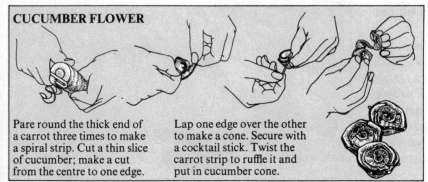

Pare round the thick end of a carrot three times to make a spiral strip. Cut a thin slice of cucumber; make a cut from the centre to one edge.

Lap one edge over the other to make a cone. Secure with a cocktail stick. Twist the carrot strip to ruffle it and put in cucumber cone.

SALAD SHELLS

These fruit and vegetable shells make attractive serving dishes for salads.

Apple flower cup: Slice the top off a dessert apple and scoop out inside; leave a shell 0.5 cm (¼ in) thick. Mark petals, then cut with a sharp knife. Brush cut surfaces with lemon juice.

Avocado half: Halve avocado lengthways; remove stone. Cut a thin slice from base so avocado will stand steadily. Brush cut surfaces with lemon juice.

Grapefruit or orange waterlily: Remove the flesh from a grapefruit or orange half and cut a zig-zag edge around the top.

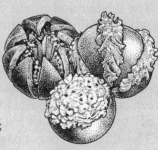

Tomato shells: Slice top off tomato and scoop out centre; or cut tomato into lengthways wedges, leaving them joined at the bottom; spoon in filling. Or cut three slices part way through tomato; fill between slices.

Pepper flower cup: Slice the stem end from a small pepper; remove and discard the seeds and membrane. Cut petal edge as for apple cup (above).

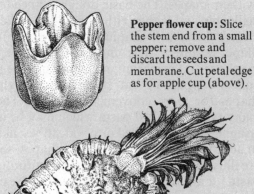

Pineapple boat: Halve a pineapple lengthways and cut out the fruit from the inside. Cut a thin slice from the base so boat will stand steadily.

PASTA

Fresh home-made Italian pasta is the best in the world. It is made from finely ground, hard durum wheat which is mixed with water to a soft dough and then kneaded, shaped and cooked on the same day. In this country we generally use dried, packeted pastas, which are also of excellent quality. They are widely available and have the advantage of keeping almost indefinitely in a dry cupboard. Try making your own pasta dough; although it is not quite the same made with British flour, the flavour and texture of fresh pasta makes the effort well worthwhile.

The flavour and colour of pasta dough can be varied by adding salt, oil or other ingredients. Eggs give the dough added richness and food value, as well as a creamier colour; a really yellow pasta may have been tinted with turmeric. Lasagne is often coloured with spinach, or with a dye made from spinach, to give it a green colour, while pasta made from wholemeal flour is a rich brown colour.

The different types of pasta are traditionally identified by their shapes. The basic dough is kneaded to make it malleable and is then either moulded, rolled and cut or forced through a shaping machine, according to the shape required. The most well known shapes are spaghetti and macaroni; macaroni may be made in long hollow lengths or cut short into straight or curved shapes for more convenient cooking. Then there are many types of rolled pasta which may be used flat, like lasagne sheets, or rolled into wide tubes, like cannelloni. In addition, there are decorative shapes, some of which are illustrated (right). If you are substituting one type of pasta for another in a recipe, try to choose one of similar thickness to give the dish the same texture.

The quantity of pasta you serve will depend on whether the pasta is the main ingredient or a side dish and on what else is served with the meal, but as a rough guide 450 g (1 lb) pasta will generally serve four people for a main course. A much smaller portion is adequate when pasta is being served as a first course or side dish; allow 50–75 g (2–3 oz) pasta per person. If you are judging the quantity by eye, remember that pasta will roughly double in bulk when cooked.

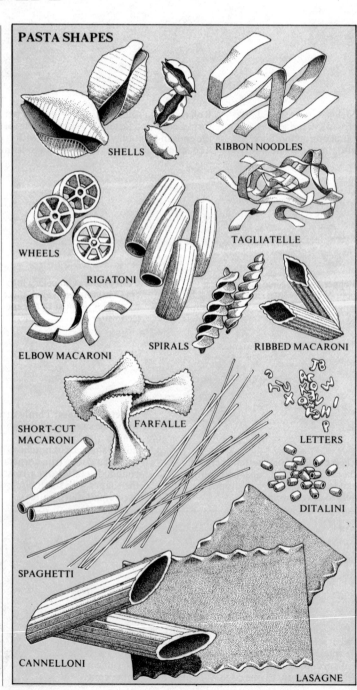

PASTA SHAPES

SHELLS

RIBBON NOODLES

WHEELS

RIGATONI

TAGLIATELLE

ELBOW MACARONI

SPIRALS

RIBBED MACARONI

SHORT-CUT MACARONI

FARFALLE

LETTERS

SPAGHETTI

DITALINI

CANNELLONI

LASAGNE

COOKING PASTA

For cooking pasta you will need a large saucepan of boiling salted water – about 2 litres (4 pints) water and 10 ml (2 level tsp) salt for every 450 g (1 lb) pasta. A little oil or butter can also be added to the water to prevent the pasta sticking together during cooking. Add the pasta gradually, so that the water does not stop boiling, and keep it boiling steadily throughout cooking. It is best not to cover the pan to avoid the water boiling over. For long shapes that will not fit into the pan, hold the pasta in one hand and put one end into the pan first; as the pasta softens, coil it round the side of the pan.

Cook all pasta until it is 'al dente' – that is, tender but still firm if tested with your teeth or your finger nail; it should never be served soft. The cooking time will also vary according to the thickness of the pasta; thin ribbon noodles such as tagliatelle will cook more quickly than spaghetti, while vermicelli cooks in next to no time. Dried pasta needs much longer cooking than fresh and wholemeal pasta takes a little longer still. As a rough guide you can estimate that fresh spaghetti will cook in approximately 5 minutes and dried in 10–12 minutes; wholemeal spaghetti will need about 15 minutes. If you are using dried pasta follow the cooking time suggested on the pack, but begin testing just before the time is up.

Cooking spaghetti: Hold the spaghetti in a bunch with one end in the boiling water and coil the strands round the side of the pan as they soften.

When the pasta is cooked, drain it immediately in a colander and rinse with boiling water to remove any excess starch. Rinsing is not necessary if you have added oil or butter to the cooking water. Cooked pasta can be kept hot without further softening if it is drained and returned to the pan with sufficient warm water to cover it; the water should be cool enough that you can just hold your hand in it. Cover the pan and leave it in a warm place until the pasta is required.

If you are making lasagne or one of the other dishes in which cooked pasta is stuffed or layered with other ingredients, the pasta may be cooked a few hours in advance. After cooking, place it in a bowl of salted cold water. Remove and pat dry just before using.

SERVING PASTA

Always serve pasta on really hot plates. The simplest way of serving spaghetti, noodles or tagliatelle is 'al burro', with butter and Parmesan cheese. After draining the hot pasta, return it to the saucepan with a large lump of butter and a generous sprinkling of freshly ground black pepper. As the butter melts, toss the pasta until each strand is glossy. Add some Parmesan cheese and serve with more cheese passed in a separate dish. Any pasta shapes that are not to be layered or stuffed with other ingredients will benefit from being tossed with butter, or olive oil, and black pepper before serving. If you are serving the pasta with a sauce, spoon the sauce generously over the top.

STORING PASTA

Fresh pasta should be used within 24 hours, before it begins to dry out. Unopened packets of dried pasta will keep almost indefinitely in a cool, dry cupboard.

Leftover cooked pasta without a sauce should be cooled and stored in a covered container in the refrigerator or freezer. To reheat it, drop it into boiling water and simmer gently until just heated through. Leftover pasta with sauce is likely to be soft if reheated.

PASTA MACHINES

Many pasta shapes can be made easily from home-made pasta dough (below) with the help of a rolling pin and a sharp knife. A pastry wheel will give flat shapes a decorative edge. However, if you make pasta often you may like to invest in a pasta machine, which cuts larger quantities more evenly and quickly than you can by hand. Various shapes can be made, including spaghetti, macaroni and flat noodles. Choose a good, sturdy machine which will withstand hard use.

Home-made Pasta Dough

Makes 450 g (1 lb) dough

250–275 g (9–10 oz) plain flour
75 ml (5 tbsp) water
2 eggs, beaten
1 egg yolk
15 ml (1 tbsp) olive or vegetable oil
5 ml (1 level tsp) salt

1. Put 100 g (4 oz) flour in a large bowl with the remaining ingredients and beat well with a wooden spoon. Stir in enough of the remaining flour to make a soft and manageable dough.
2. Turn the dough on to a floured surface and knead for about 10 minutes until smooth and not sticky. Wrap in waxed paper and leave to rest for about 30 minutes before shaping as required.

Kneading the dough: With floured hands fold the dough towards you, then push it away with the heel of your hand in a rolling motion. Give the dough a quarter turn and repeat the kneading until the dough is smooth.

Noodles

Home-made Noodles

*home-made pasta dough
made with 125–150 g
(4½–5 oz) flour,
page 329
1.5 litres (2½ pints)
chicken stock
15 g (½ oz) butter*

*To serve:
butter
freshly ground black
pepper
tomato sauce, page 337,
optional*

Colour index
page 74

6 side dish
servings

1 Knead the dough on a
floured surface for
about 10 minutes, until
smooth, elastic and no
longer sticky. Wrap in
waxed paper; leave to
rest for 30 minutes.

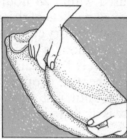

2 Roll out the dough on a
floured surface to a
51 × 35.5 cm (20 × 14 in)
rectangle. Flour it lightly,
then fold in half crossways,
bringing the long sides
together. Repeat folding.

3 Cut it crossways into
0.3-cm (⅛-in) strips for
narrow noodles, 0.5-cm
(¼-in) strips for medium
noodles or 1-cm (½-in)
strips for wide noodles.

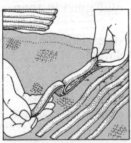

4 Open out the strips
and spread them in a
single layer on floured tea
towels. Leave the noodles
to dry for at least 2 hours
before cooking them.

5 To cook the noodles,
put the stock and
butter in a large saucepan
and bring to the boil.
Break the noodles into
smaller lengths if required
and add them gradually to
the pan; bring back to the
boil and cook for 10–12
minutes, until the noodles
are tender but still firm.
Drain well and place in a
heated serving dish. Serve
tossed with more butter
and freshly ground black
pepper and, if you wish,
with tomato sauce.

Colour index
page 74

6 side dish
servings

NOODLE RING: Cook *225 g (8 oz) egg noodles* or
home-made noodles (above) in a large saucepan of
boiling salted water until they are tender but still
firm. Drain the noodles well, then return them to the
saucepan and toss with *50 g (2 oz) butter* and *1.25 ml
(¼ level tsp) salt*. Spoon them into a 1.1-litre (2-
pint) capacity ring tin, pressing the noodles down
lightly with the back of a spoon. Stand it in a
roasting tin and pour in boiling water to come halfway up the sides of the tin. Bake at 190°C (375°F)
mark 5 for 20 minutes, turn out on to a heated
serving dish and serve immediately.

Home-made Spinach Noodles

Colour index
page 74

8 servings

*350 g (12 oz) spinach
7.5 ml (1½ level tsp) salt
2 eggs, beaten
275–350 g (10–12 oz) plain
flour*

*15 ml (1 tbsp) vegetable oil
100 g (4 oz) butter
freshly ground black
pepper*

1. Wash the spinach thoroughly and trim the leaves
and stalks if necessary. Cover the base of a large
saucepan with water, add 2.5 ml (½ level tsp) of the
salt and bring to the boil. Add the spinach, bring
back to the boil, cover and cook for 3 minutes.
Drain well and pat dry with kitchen paper towel.
Purée the spinach in a blender or by rubbing it
through a sieve with a spoon.
2. Stir in the eggs, 275 g (10 oz) of the flour and the
remaining salt until the mixture resembles coarse
breadcrumbs. Shape into a ball.
3. Knead the dough on a floured surface until
smooth, elastic and no longer sticky, kneading in a
little more flour if necessary. Wrap it in waxed paper
and leave to rest for 30 minutes.
4. Cut the dough in half. Roll out one half on a
floured surface to a 51 × 35.5 cm (20 × 14 in)
rectangle, then cut the dough lengthways into 1 cm
(½ in) wide strips. Spread the noodles in a single
layer on floured tea towels. Repeat with the remaining dough and leave to dry for 2 hours.
5. To cook the noodles, add them with the oil to a
large saucepan of boiling salted water. Bring back to
the boil and cook for 8 minutes, until tender but still
firm. Drain well and place in a heated serving dish.
Add butter and pepper and toss well to coat noodles.

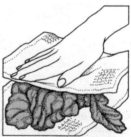

Drying cooked spinach:
Press out any surplus
liquid between sheets of
kitchen paper towel, to
dry the spinach thoroughly.

Puréeing the spinach:
Spoon the dried spinach
into blender to purée it,
or rub it through a sieve
with a wooden spoon.

Tagliatelle Alfredo

Colour index
page 74

4 servings

*225 g (8 oz) tagliatelle or
home-made noodles, left
50 g (2 oz) butter, melted
25 g (1 oz) Parmesan
cheese, grated*

*30 ml (2 tbsp) creamy milk
salt and pepper*

*To serve:
Parmesan cheese, grated*

1. Cook the noodles in a large saucepan of boiling
salted water until tender but still firm. Drain well.
2. Meanwhile, mix the butter with the cheese and
milk in a heated serving dish and season to taste.
3. Add the hot noodles to the cheese mixture and
toss well until the noodles are coated. Serve immediately with a little extra grated cheese.

Spaghetti

Spaghetti and Meatballs

Colour index
page 32

6 servings

700 g (1½ lb) minced beef
50 g (2 oz) fresh white breadcrumbs
2.5 ml (½ level tsp) dried oregano
pinch pepper
10 ml (2 level tsp) salt
1 egg
45 ml (3 tbsp) vegetable oil
900 ml (1½ pints) tomato sauce, page 337
450 g (1 lb) spaghetti

To serve:
Parmesan cheese, grated

1 Mix together the beef, breadcrumbs, oregano, pepper and salt until well blended. Bind with the egg to make a firm mixture that will hold together.

2 With your hands, shape the beef mixture into neat balls about 2.5 cm (1 in) in diameter.

3 Heat 30 ml (2 tbsp) oil in a frying pan and fry the meatballs until they are well browned all over. Spoon off the excess fat from the pan.

4 Add the tomato sauce to the frying pan and bring it to the boil, stirring occasionally. Reduce the heat, cover and simmer for 10 minutes.

5 Meanwhile, cook the spaghetti in a large saucepan of boiling salted water until it is tender but still firm.

6 Drain the spaghetti well and toss it with the remaining oil. Place in a heated serving dish.

7 Spoon the meatballs and sauce evenly over the spaghetti. Serve with grated Parmesan cheese.

Spaghetti alla Carbonara

Colour index
page 32

4–6 servings

450 g (1 lb) spaghetti
4 oz (100 g) streaky bacon, rinded and chopped
4 eggs
15 ml (2 tbsp) single cream
50 g (2 oz) Parmesan cheese, grated
ground black pepper

1. Cook the spaghetti in a large saucepan of boiling salted water for about 8 minutes until tender but still firm.
2. Meanwhile, fry the bacon in its own fat until crisp. Beat the eggs in a bowl and add the cream and half the cheese; season with black pepper.
3. Drain the cooked spaghetti and return it to the pan. Quickly stir in the bacon. Immediately add the eggs and toss well together. (The heat of the spaghetti will be enough to cook the eggs.) Serve at once, sprinkled with the remaining cheese.

Spaghetti con Formaggio

Colour index
page 32

4 servings

225 g (8 oz) spaghetti
25 g (1 oz) butter or margarine
15 ml (1 level tbsp) plain flour
350 ml (12 fl oz) single cream or creamy milk
100 g (4 oz) Fontina or Edam cheese, grated
100 g (4 oz) Mozzarella cheese, grated
50 g (2 oz) Provolone or smoked cheese, grated
25 g (1 oz) Parmesan cheese, grated
salt and pepper
30 ml (2 tbsp) chopped parsley

1. Cook the spaghetti in a large saucepan of boiling salted water until tender but still firm. Drain well.
2. Meanwhile, melt the fat in a large saucepan, stir in the flour and cook for about 30 seconds. Gradually add the cream and bring to the boil, stirring constantly until the cream has thickened slightly. Stir in the cheeses, season to taste and cook gently, continuing to stir until the cheese has melted.
3. Put the spaghetti into a heated serving dish. Pour the sauce over the top and add the parsley. Toss together until the spaghetti is coated.

Spaghetti with Ham and Peas

Colour index
page 32

4 servings

225 g (8 oz) spaghetti
50 g (2 oz) butter or margarine
15 ml (1 level tbsp) plain flour
1.25 ml (¼ level tsp) salt
1.25 ml (¼ level tsp) pepper
350 ml (12 fl oz) single cream or creamy milk
225-g (8-oz) packet frozen peas, thawed
100 g (4 oz) Fontina or Edam cheese, grated
100 g (4 oz) Mozzarella cheese, grated
100 g (4 oz) cooked ham, cut into strips

1. Cook the spaghetti in a large saucepan of boiling salted water until tender but still firm. Drain well.
2. Meanwhile, melt the fat in a large saucepan over gentle heat. Stir in the flour, salt and pepper, then gradually add the cream and cook until the mixture has thickened, stirring constantly. Add the peas and cheeses and cook gently, stirring, until the cheese melts. Stir in the ham and heat through.
3. Put the spaghetti in a heated serving dish. Add the cheese mixture and toss together until well mixed.

Pasta shapes

The recipes shown here use short-cut macaroni and home-made cavatelli, but you can adapt them for any short pasta shapes by adjusting the cooking time to the type and thickness of the pasta.

Baked Macaroni Cheese

Colour index page 32
4 servings

225 g (8 oz) short-cut macaroni
50 g (2 oz) butter or margarine
40 g (1½ oz) fresh white breadcrumbs
1 small onion, skinned and finely chopped
15 ml (1 level tbsp) plain flour
5 ml (1 level tsp) salt
1.25 ml (¼ level tsp) dry mustard
pinch pepper
350 ml (12 fl oz) milk
225 g (8 oz) mature Cheddar cheese, grated

1 Cook the macaroni in a large saucepan of boiling salted water until tender but still firm, then drain well in a colander. Generously grease a large ovenproof dish.

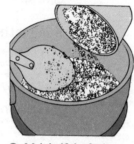

2 Melt half the fat in a small saucepan, add the breadcrumbs and mix well. Remove from the heat.

3 Melt the remaining fat in another saucepan, add the chopped onion and cook gently for about 5 minutes, until it is soft but not coloured.

4 Blend in the flour, salt, mustard and pepper and stir in the milk. Cook, stirring, until sauce has thickened. Remove from heat and stir in cheese.

5 Put the macaroni in the greased ovenproof dish and pour over the sauce.

6 Top with breadcrumbs; bake at 180°C (350°F) mark 4 for 20 minutes.

One-pan Macaroni Cheese

Colour index page 32
4 servings

100 g (4 oz) butter
225 g (8 oz) short-cut macaroni
1 small onion, skinned and finely chopped
½ green pepper, seeded and finely chopped
5 ml (1 level tsp) salt
1.25 ml (¼ level tsp) dry mustard
400 ml (¾ pint) water
225 g (8 oz) Cheddar cheese, grated
10 stuffed green olives, sliced

1. Melt the butter and cook the macaroni, onion, green pepper and seasonings for 5 minutes.
2. Add the water and bring to the boil. Reduce the heat, cover and simmer gently for 10–15 minutes until the macaroni is tender, stirring occasionally.
3. Remove from the heat and stir in the cheese and olives until the cheese has melted.

Cavatelli with Italian Meat Sauce

Colour index page 32
4 servings

home-made pasta dough made with 250–275 g (9–10 oz) flour, page 329
15 ml (1 tbsp) vegetable oil
900 ml (1½ pints) Italian meat sauce, page 337

To serve:
Parmesan cheese, grated

1 Cut dough into eight pieces. With floured hands, roll them to 38-cm (15-in) ropes.

2 Cut ropes into 1 cm (½- in) pieces. Press a finger into each piece to flatten; draw finger towards you to curl sides.

3 Spread cavatelli in a single layer on floured tea towels and leave to dry for about 2 hours.

4 Add cavatelli and oil to a large saucepan of boiling salted water; cook until tender but still firm. Meanwhile heat sauce.

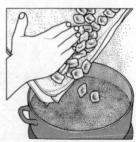

5 Drain pasta; place in a heated serving dish. Spoon the meat sauce over the pasta. Serve with the Parmesan cheese.

Stuffed pasta

Stuffed pasta dishes take longer to prepare than simple pasta shapes, but are well worth the extra effort. Ravioli and tortellini are stuffed raw and then boiled, but most other shapes are cooked first, then stuffed or layered and baked. All are finished with a savoury sauce. Serve as a main dish, or in smaller portions as a first course.

Ravioli

Colour index page 32
4 servings

home-made pasta dough made with 250–275 g (9–10 oz) flour, page 329 cheese, meat or spinach filling, right

15 ml (1 tbsp) vegetable oil 900 ml (1½ pints) tomato sauce, page 337 25 g (1 oz) Parmesan cheese, grated

1 Halve the dough. Roll out each piece on a floured surface to a 51 × 35.5 cm (20 × 14 in) rectangle. Spoon small mounds of filling in lines over one piece of dough.

2 Brush around each mound with water. Cover with the second piece of dough. Seal around each mound by pressing with finger, then cut around mounds.

3 If you wish, make a decorative edge around the ravioli by pressing three or four sides with the prongs of a fork dipped in flour.

4 Spread the filled ravioli in a single layer on floured tea towels. Leave to dry for at least 30 minutes before cooking.

5 Add the ravioli and oil to a large saucepan of boiling salted water. Bring back to the boil and simmer for 5 minutes, until tender but still firm.

6 Drain well in a colander. Place on a heated serving dish and spoon over the hot tomato sauce. Sprinkle with the Parmesan cheese.

Jumbo Ravioli

Colour index page 32
4 servings

home-made pasta dough made with 250–275 g (9–10 oz) flour, page 329 cheese, meat or spinach filling, below

900 ml (1½ pints) tomato sauce, page 337 15 ml (1 tbsp) vegetable oil 25 g (1 oz) Parmesan cheese, grated

1. Cut the pasta dough into four pieces. Roll out one piece on a floured surface to a 38 × 15 cm (15 × 6 in) rectangle and cut it crossways into five 15 × 7.5 cm (6 × 3 in) strips.
2. Spread some filling over half the surface of a pasta strip to within 0.5 cm (¼ in) of the edges. Fold the dough over the filling, bring the edges together neatly and press them firmly together with a fork dipped in flour. Spread in a single layer on floured tea towels. Repeat with the remaining pasta and filling and leave them to dry for 30 minutes.
3. Meanwhile, heat through the tomato sauce.
4. Add a few of the ravioli and the oil to a large saucepan of boiling salted water and cook them for 10 minutes, or until tender but still firm. Drain well and keep hot while you cook the remaining ravioli. Arrange them in a heated serving dish. Spoon the hot tomato sauce over the ravioli and sprinkle with the grated Parmesan cheese.

Making the ravioli: Fold dough over filling, with the edges meeting neatly.

Sealing the ravioli: Press edges together with a fork dipped in flour.

RAVIOLI FILLINGS

CHEESE FILLING: Mix well *225 g (8 oz) Ricotta cheese*, cream cheese or curd cheese with *45 ml (3 tbsp) chopped parsley, 30 ml (2 level tbsp) grated Parmesan cheese, 1 egg white, 1.25 ml (¼ level tsp) salt* and a *pinch of pepper*. Stir until evenly blended.

MEAT FILLING: Cook *225 g (8 oz) minced beef* with *50 g (2 oz) onion*, finely chopped and *1 clove garlic*, skinned and finely chopped, until the meat is browned. Remove from heat, spoon off juices and mix in *1 egg*, beaten, *15 g (½ oz) chopped parsley, 30 ml (2 level tbsp) grated Parmesan cheese* and *2.5 ml (½ level tsp) salt*. Stir until evenly blended.

SPINACH FILLING: Thaw and drain well *225 g (8 oz) frozen spinach* and mix in *40 g (1½ oz) grated Parmesan cheese, 2 egg yolks*, beaten, *15 g (½ oz) butter*, softened, *1.25 ml (¼ level tsp) salt*, a *few turns of freshly ground black pepper* and a *pinch of ground nutmeg*. Stir until evenly blended.

Stuffed pasta

Manicotti

50 g (2 oz) plain flour
2 eggs, beaten
15 ml (1 tbsp) vegetable or
    olive oil
2.5 ml (½ level tsp) salt
100 ml (4 fl oz) cold
    water

For the sauce:
15 g (½ oz) butter
225 g (8 oz) lean veal
    or turkey meat,
    minced
400 g (¾ pint) tomato
    sauce, page 337

For the filling:
225 g (8 oz) Ricotta or
    cottage cheese
15 ml (1 level tbsp) grated
    Parmesan cheese
pinch pepper
pinch salt
1 egg, beaten
100 g (4 oz) Mozzarella
    cheese, coarsely
    grated

Colour index page 33

4 servings

1 Beat together the flour, eggs, oil and salt with a wooden spoon until they are well blended. Add the water gradually and beat the batter until smooth.

2 Brush a small frying pan lightly with oil and place over moderate heat.

3 Pour about 30 ml (2 tbsp) batter into the pan; tip it so that the batter coats the bottom evenly.

4 Cook for about 30 seconds until the top is set and dry and the underside browned. Repeat with remaining batter.

5 Melt the butter in a large frying pan, add the meat and cook it until it is well browned, stirring occasionally. Stir in the tomato sauce.

6 Heat through the meat sauce, then spoon one third of it evenly over the base of a roasting tin or ovenproof dish. Keep the remaining sauce hot.

7 Mix together the Ricotta and Parmesan cheeses, add the pepper, salt and egg and stir well.

8 Spoon some of the cheese mixture down the centre of each pancake and sprinkle over some of the Mozzarella cheese.

9 Fold the pancake sides over the filling, so that it is completely enclosed. Arrange the manicotti seam side down in rows in the tin.

10 Spoon the remaining sauce over the top and bake at 190°C (375°F) mark 5 for 30 minutes or until hot and bubbling.

Colour index page 33

4 servings

Cheese-stuffed Pasta

225 g (8 oz) large pasta
    shells or 100 g (4 oz)
    cannelloni, cooked and
    drained well
400 ml (¾ pint) tomato
    sauce, page 337
25 g (1 oz) Parmesan
    cheese, grated

100 g (4 oz) Mozzarella
    cheese, grated
1 egg, beaten
25 g (1 oz) dried
    breadcrumbs
30 ml (2 tbsp) chopped
    parsley
2.5 ml (½ level tsp) salt
pinch pepper

For the filling:
350 g (12 oz) Ricotta or
    cottage cheese

1. Mix together all the ingredients for the filling. Spoon a heaped tablespoonful into each shell.
2. Spread 150 ml (¼ pint) of tomato sauce in a large ovenproof dish and arrange the cheese-filled shells open side down on the sauce. Pour the remaining sauce over the top and sprinkle evenly with the grated Parmesan cheese.
3. Bake at 180°C (350°F) mark 4 for 30 minutes.

Colour index page 33

4 servings

Stuffed Pasta in Meat Sauce

100 g (4 oz) cannelloni or
    rigatoni, cooked and
    drained well
Parmesan cheese, grated

For the sauce:
225 g (8 oz) Italian
    sausages
150 ml (¼ pint) water
225 g (8 oz) minced beef
1 onion, skinned and
    chopped
396-g (14-oz) can
    tomatoes, puréed
63-g (2¼-oz) can tomato
    paste
2.5 ml (½ level tsp) salt

2.5 ml (½ level tsp) sugar
2.5 ml (½ level tsp) dried
    basil
pinch pepper

For the filling:
450 g (1 lb) cottage cheese
100 g (4 oz) Mozzarella
    cheese, chopped
15 ml (1 tbsp) chopped
    parsley
2.5 ml (½ level tsp) dried
    basil
pinch salt

1. Make the sauce. Place sausages and 50 ml (2 fl oz) of the water in large saucepan, cover and cook for 5 minutes. Continue to cook them uncovered until they are well browned. Remove and drain well.
2. Spoon off the fat, add the beef and onion and cook until well browned. Stir in the remaining sauce ingredients, cover and simmer for 45 minutes. Cut the sausages into small chunks, add to the pan and cook for 15 minutes, stirring occasionally.
3. Mix all the ingredients for the filling. Spoon a heaped tablespoonful into each cannelloni.
4. Spread half the meat sauce in an ovenproof dish and arrange half the stuffed pasta on top. Spoon all but 100 ml (4 fl oz) of the remaining sauce over the pasta and top with the remaining stuffed pasta. Spoon the reserved sauce over the top and sprinkle with the grated Parmesan cheese. Bake at 190°C (375°F) mark 5 for about 30 minutes.

FILLING PASTA SHAPES

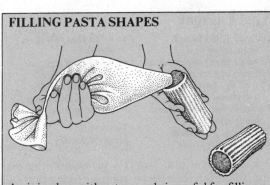

A piping bag without a nozzle is useful for filling a large number of pasta shapes quickly and neatly. Spoon the filling into the bag and squeeze some gently into each of the cooked shapes.

Colour index page 23
4–6 servings

Tortellini in Cream Sauce

*home-made pasta dough
    made with 250–275 g
    (9–10 oz) flour, page 329
15 ml (1 tbsp) vegetable oil
100 g (4 oz) butter
225 ml (8 fl oz) double
    cream
100 g (4 oz) Parmesan
    cheese, grated*

For the filling:
15 ml (1 tbsp) vegetable oil

*4 chicken breasts, boned,
    skinned and finely
    chopped
100 g (4 oz) prosciutto,
    mortadella or cooked
    ham, chopped
1 egg, beaten
pinch pepper
pinch ground nutmeg
salt*

1. Make the filling. Heat the oil in a large frying pan and cook the chicken for about 5 minutes or until tender, stirring frequently. Remove from the heat and cool slightly. Put the chicken, prosciutto, egg, pepper, nutmeg and salt to taste in a blender. Blend to a smooth paste.
2. Cut the prepared dough into three pieces. Roll out one on a floured surface to a 66 × 23 cm (26 × 9 in) rectangle; keep the other pieces covered. Cut out rounds with a 5-cm (2-in) pastry cutter, reserving the trimmings to make more tortellini.
3. To make up the tortellini, place 2.5 ml (½ level tsp) of the chicken filling on each round, brush the edges with water and fold in half, with edges not quite meeting. Press the edges firmly together with a fork dipped in flour, then fold each semicircle in half to form a fan shape and press to seal at the corners. Repeat with the remaining pasta, re-rolling all the trimmings to make more tortellini. Spread them in a single layer on floured tea towels and leave to dry for at least 30 minutes before cooking.
4. Add the oil to a large saucepan of boiling salted water and then add the tortellini a few at a time, stirring so that they do not stick together. Cook for 5 minutes or until tender but still firm. Drain well.
5. Melt the butter in the same saucepan, add the tortellini and the cream. Bring to the boil, stirring gently until the cream has thickened slightly. Stir in the cheese and spoon into a heated serving dish.

Cannelloni

*home-made pasta dough
    made with 125–150 g
    (4½–5 oz) flour,
    page 329
15 ml (1 tbsp) vegetable oil
400 ml (¾ pint) Parmesan
    sauce, page 461
chopped parsley*

For the filling:
*25 g (1 oz) butter
15 ml (1 tbsp) chopped
    spring onion
100 g (4 oz) frozen chopped
    spinach, cooked and
    drained
pinch pepper*

*50 g (2 oz) cooked ham,
    finely chopped
25 g (1 oz) Parmesan or
    Romano cheese,
    grated
1 egg, beaten
15 ml (1 tbsp) dry or
    medium sherry
100 g (4 oz) cooked
    chicken, finely chopped*

Colour index page 33
4 servings

1 Halve the dough with a sharp knife and roll out one piece on a floured surface to a 40 × 20 cm (16 × 8 in) rectangle.

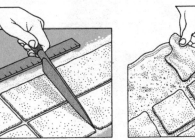

2 With a sharp knife, cut the rectangle into eight 10-cm (4-in) squares.

3 Spread the squares in a single layer on floured tea towels. Repeat with the remaining dough and leave the squares to dry for at least 1 hour.

4 Melt the butter in a saucepan and cook the onion until soft but not coloured. Stir in the remaining ingredients for the filling. Heat through.

5 Lightly brush a small roasting tin or oven-proof dish with a little oil or melted butter.

6 Add a few pasta squares and the oil to a large saucepan of boiling salted water and cook them until they are tender but still firm.

7 Remove the cooked pasta with a slotted spoon and drain well in a colander. Keep warm while you cook the remaining squares.

8 Place a heaped tablespoonful of the meat filling on each warm pasta square and spread it evenly over the centre.

9 Roll up a square and place it seam side down in the greased tin. Repeat with the remaining squares and arrange them in rows.

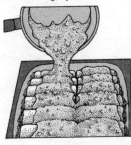

10 Pour over the sauce; sprinkle with parsley. Bake at 170°C (325°F) mark 3 for 20 minutes, then brown under grill.

Lasagne

Opposite page

From top, left to right: spirals, spaghetti, rigatoni, farfalle, tortellini, wheels, ditalini, shells, ribbed macaroni

Lasagne

Colour index
page 33

4 servings

450 g (1 lb) minced beef
1 small onion, skinned and
  chopped
396-g (14-oz) can tomatoes
63-g (2¼-oz) can tomato
  paste
10 ml (2 level tsp) sugar
5 ml (1 level tsp) salt
1.25 ml (¼ level tsp) dried
  oregano
1.25 ml (¼ level tsp) dried
  thyme
1.25 ml (¼ level tsp)
  cayenne pepper

1.25 ml (¼ level tsp) garlic
  salt
bay leaf
175 g (6 oz) lasagne
1 egg, beaten
225 g (8 oz) Ricotta or
  cream cheese
225 g (8 oz) Mozzarella
  cheese, diced

1 Cook the minced beef and onion in a large saucepan until the beef is browned, stirring. Add the tomatoes with their liquid, tomato paste, sugar, salt, herbs and spices.

2 Bring to the boil, stirring. Reduce the heat, cover and simmer for 30 minutes, stirring occasionally. Discard the bay leaf.

3 Tilt the pan and spoon off any fat from the sauce. Meanwhile, cook the lasagne in a large saucepan of boiling salted water. Drain well.

4 Arrange half the lasagne sheets in a greased roasting tin or ovenproof dish, carefully overlapping them to fit the dish neatly.

5 Mix the beaten egg with the Ricotta cheese and stir well. Spoon half of the mixture over the top of the lasagne and spread it out evenly to the edges, to cover the lasagne.

6 Sprinkle over half the Mozzarella and top with half the meat sauce. Repeat layers, finishing with meat sauce. Bake at 190°C (375°F) mark 5 for about 45 minutes.

Veal Lasagne

Colour index
page 33

4–6 servings

700 g (1½ lb) boned
  shoulder of veal
15 ml (1 tbsp) vegetable oil
175 g (6 oz) lasagne
50 g (2 oz) butter or
  margarine
1 large onion, skinned and
  finely chopped
25 g (1 oz) plain flour
568 ml (1 pint) milk

45 ml (3 tbsp) medium
  sherry
10 ml (2 level tsp) salt
pinch white pepper
pinch ground nutmeg
50 g (2 oz) Parmesan
  cheese, grated

To serve:
chopped parsley

1. Cut the veal into 1-cm (½-in) cubes, trim and discard the fat. Heat the oil in a large frying pan, add the veal and cook it until it is lightly browned, stirring occasionally.
2. Meanwhile, cook the lasagne in a large saucepan of boiling salted water until it is tender but still firm. Drain well.
3. Melt the fat in a large saucepan and cook the onion gently for 5 minutes or until soft but not coloured, stirring occasionally. Stir in the flour until well blended, gradually add the milk and continue cooking until thickened, stirring all the time.
4. Remove the cooked veal from the frying pan with a slotted spoon and stir it into the sauce with the sherry and seasonings.
5. Arrange one third of the lasagne sheets lengthways in a large greased ovenproof dish and top with half the meat mixture. Repeat the layers and finish with a final layer of lasagne. Cover tightly with foil and bake at 180°C (350°F) mark 4 for 30 minutes. Remove from the oven, sprinkle with the cheese and bake uncovered for a further 15 minutes or until lightly browned. Sprinkle with parsley and leave to stand for 10 minutes before serving.

Aubergine Lasagne

Colour index
page 33

4 servings

100 g (4 oz) lasagne
50 g (2 oz) dried
  breadcrumbs
1.25 ml (¼ level tsp) salt
pinch pepper
1 egg, beaten
15 ml (1 tbsp) water
1 medium aubergine, cut
  into 1-cm (½-in) slices

30–45 ml (2–3 tbsp)
  vegetable oil
225 g (8 oz) Mozzarella
  cheese, thinly sliced
600 ml (1 pint) tomato
  sauce, page 337
25 g (1 oz) Parmesan
  cheese, grated

1. Cook the lasagne in a large saucepan of boiling salted water until tender but still firm. Drain well.
2. Meanwhile, mix the breadcrumbs with the salt and pepper. Beat the egg and the water together. Dip the aubergine in the egg mixture, then in the seasoned breadcrumbs.
3. Heat 30 ml (2 tbsp) oil in a large frying pan and fry the aubergine gently a few slices at a time until tender, adding more oil as necessary. Drain the slices well on kitchen paper towel.
4. Arrange half the lasagne sheets in a greased ovenproof dish. Layer half the aubergine slices and Mozzarella cheese over the lasagne and pour half the tomato sauce over the top. Repeat the layers with the remaining ingredients and sprinkle with the Parmesan cheese. Bake at 180°C (350°F) mark 4 for 30 minutes, or until bubbling.

Pasta sauces

Opposite page
Left to right: Aubergine Lasagne (page 336);
Cannelloni (page 335)

Bolognese Sauce

*Makes about
500 ml
1 pint)*

knob of butter
*50 g (2 oz) bacon, rinded
and chopped*
*1 small onion, skinned and
chopped*
*1 carrot, peeled and
chopped*
*1 stick celery, washed and
chopped*
225 g (8 oz) minced beef

*100 g (4 oz) chicken livers,
chopped*
*15 ml (1 level tbsp) tomato
paste*
*150 ml (¼ pint) dry white
wine*
300 ml (½ pint) beef stock
salt and pepper

1. Melt the butter in a large saucepan, add the bacon and fry for 2–3 minutes. Add the onion, carrot and celery and fry for 5 minutes until just browned.
2. Add the beef and brown lightly, then stir in the chopped chicken livers and cook for a further 3 minutes. Add the tomato paste and wine and simmer for a few minutes more.
3. Stir in the remaining ingredients and simmer for 30–40 minutes, until the meat is tender.

Italian Meat Sauce

*Makes about
900 ml
(1½ pints)*

30 ml (2 tbsp) vegetable oil
450 g (1 lb) minced beef
*1 onion, skinned and
chopped*
*1 clove garlic, skinned and
crushed*
396-g (14-oz) can tomatoes
*20 ml (4 level tsp)
sugar*

*141-g (5-oz) can tomato
paste*
*10 ml (2 level tsp) dried
oregano*
7.5 ml (1½ level tsp) salt
pinch cayenne pepper
bay leaf, crumbled

1. Heat the oil in a large saucepan, add the beef, onion and garlic and fry until the meat is well browned, stirring occasionally.
2. Spoon off the excess fat. Stir in the tomatoes with their liquid and the remaining ingredients. Reduce the heat, cover and simmer for 35 minutes.

Tomato Sauce

*Makes about
900 ml
(1½ pints)*

30 ml (2 tbsp) vegetable oil
*1 onion, skinned and
chopped*
*1 clove garlic, skinned and
crushed*
*2 425-g (15-oz) cans
tomato juice*
*141-g (5-oz) can tomato
paste*

*10 ml (2 level tsp) brown
sugar*
*30 ml (2 tbsp) chopped
parsley*
*5 ml (1 level tsp) dried
oregano*
5 ml (1 level tsp) salt
pinch pepper
bay leaf

1. Heat the oil in a large saucepan, add the onion and garlic and fry for 10 minutes, stirring frequently.
2. Add the remaining ingredients and bring the mixture to the boil. Reduce the heat, partially cover and cook for 30 minutes. Remove the bay leaf.

Pesto

*Makes about
100 ml
(4 fl oz)*

75 ml (5 tbsp) olive oil
*25 g (1 oz) Parmesan
cheese, grated*
5 ml (1 level tsp) salt
*60 ml (4 tbsp) chopped
parsley*

*1 clove garlic, skinned and
quartered*
*30 ml (2 level tbsp) dried
basil*
*1.25 ml (¼ level tsp)
ground nutmeg*

Place all the ingredients in a blender and blend at medium speed until well mixed. Toss with hot pasta.

Prawn Marinara Sauce

*Makes about
900 ml
(1½ pints)*

15 ml (1 tbsp) olive oil
*1 clove garlic, skinned and
crushed*
*425-g (15-oz) can tomato
juice*
*141-g (5-oz) can tomato
paste*
*30 ml (2 tbsp) chopped
parsley*

15 ml (1 level tbsp) sugar
*2.5 ml (½ level tsp) dried
oregano*
2.5 ml (½ level tsp) salt
*1.25 ml (¼ level tsp)
pepper*
*450 g (1 lb) shelled frozen
prawns*

1. Heat the olive oil in a saucepan and lightly brown the garlic. Add the remaining ingredients except for the prawns, cover and simmer gently for 10 minutes.
2. Add the frozen prawns and cook for about 8 minutes until heated through, stirring occasionally.

Italian Anchovy Sauce

*Makes about
100 ml
(4 fl oz)*

60 ml (4 tbsp) olive oil
*1 clove garlic, skinned and
halved*
*50-g (2-oz) can anchovy
fillets, drained and
chopped*

*30 ml (2 tbsp) chopped
parsley*
*30 ml (2 level tbsp) grated
Parmesan cheese*
5 ml (1 tsp) lemon juice

1. Heat the oil in a small saucepan, brown the garlic and then remove it.
2. Remove the pan from the heat and stir in the remaining ingredients until well mixed.

Clam Sauce

*Makes about
750 ml
(1¼ pints)*

60 ml (4 tbsp) olive oil
*1 clove garlic, skinned and
crushed*
2 283-g (10-oz) cans clams
30 ml (2 tbsp) white wine

*25 g (1 oz) parsley,
chopped*
5 ml (1 level tsp) dried basil
2.5 ml (½ level tsp) salt

1. Heat the oil and fry the garlic until tender.
2. Drain the clams, reserving the juice. Add the juice to the pan with the wine, parsley, basil and salt and cook for 10 minutes, stirring occasionally.
3. Stir in the clams and heat through.

Spinach Sauce

*Makes about
600 ml
(1 pint)*

50 g (2 oz) butter
*225 g (8 oz) frozen chopped
spinach*
5 ml (1 level tsp) salt
60 ml (4 tbsp) milk

*225 g (8 oz) Ricotta or
cream cheese*
*25 g (1 oz) Parmesan
cheese*
pinch ground nutmeg

1. Melt the butter in a saucepan, add the spinach and salt and cook for 10 minutes.
2. Reduce the heat, stir in the remaining ingredients until well mixed and heat through.

Walnut Sauce

*Makes about
300 ml
(½ pint)*

*50 g (2 oz) butter or
margarine*
*100 g (4 oz) shelled
walnuts, roughly
chopped*

100 ml (4 fl oz) milk
*30 ml (2 tbsp) chopped
parsley*
5 ml (1 level tsp) salt

1. Melt the fat in a small frying pan, add the walnuts and cook them for about 5 minutes until lightly browned, stirring occasionally.
2. Stir in the remaining ingredients; heat through.

RICE

Always cook rice until the grains are tender, but firm and separated. Choose a saucepan with a tightly fitting lid to prevent the steam escaping and avoid lifting the lid or stirring the rice while it is cooking. When the rice is cooked, the liquid should be absorbed and a grain squeezed between your fingers should retain its shape in the centre. Serve as soon as possible.

Allow about 50 g (2 oz) rice per person for plain rice dishes. Leftover rice can be covered and refrigerated for up to a week without deterioration.

Boiled Rice

Colour index page 73

3–4 servings

600 ml (1 pint) water
225 g (8 oz) long
grain rice
5 ml (1 level tsp) salt

25 g (1 oz) butter,
optional

1 Put the water and rice into a large saucepan with a tightly fitting lid, but do not cover. Add the salt and bring quickly to a fast boil.

2 Stir the rice well with a fork and reduce the heat until the water is just simmering gently.

3 Cover the saucepan with a tightly fitting lid and simmer, without stirring, for about 15 minutes or until the water has been absorbed and the rice is tender but still firm.

4 Spoon the cooked rice into a heated serving dish and separate the grains gently with a fork. If you wish, stir in 25 g (1 oz) butter with a fork until melted. Serve immediately.

ALTERNATIVE METHOD FOR BOILED RICE: Bring a large pan of salted water to a fast boil and add the rice. Stir, bring back to the boil and boil rapidly for 12–15 minutes, or until rice is tender but firm. Drain, rinse with hot water; drain again.

BOILED RICE VARIATIONS

BOILED BROWN RICE: Prepare the rice as left, but use *750 ml (1¼ pints) water* and simmer for about 40 minutes, or until the water has been absorbed and the rice is tender.

BOILED WILD RICE: Prepare the rice as left, but wash and drain the rice before cooking it. Simmer for 40–45 minutes, or until the water has been absorbed and the rice is tender. (Colour index page 73)

CHICKEN- OR BEEF-FLAVOURED BOILED RICE: Prepare the rice as left, but replace the water with the same quantity of *chicken or beef stock*.

HERB-FLAVOURED BOILED RICE: Prepare the rice as left, but add a *pinch of dried mixed herbs*, sage or marjoram when you add the water and salt.

BOILED RICE WITH PEPPERS: Prepare the rice as left; but sauté *½ green pepper*, seeded and chopped, *½ red pepper*, seeded and chopped and *60 ml (4 tbsp) chopped spring onions* in *25 g (1 oz) butter* for a few minutes before adding the rice, water and salt. (Colour index page 73)

REHEATED BOILED RICE: Put about *1 cm (½ in) water* in a saucepan with a *large pinch of salt*; bring to the boil and add the cooked rice. Cover the saucepan with a tightly fitting lid, reduce the heat and simmer very gently for 5 minutes or until heated through. Drain thoroughly before serving.

Buttery Baked Rice

Colour index page 73

4 servings

200 g (7 oz) long grain rice
5 ml (1 level tsp) salt
25 g (1 oz) butter

400 ml (¾ pint) boiling
water

1. Grease a 1.1-litre (2-pint) capacity ovenproof dish or casserole.

2. Put the rice in the dish and stir in the salt until well mixed. Dot with butter.

3. Pour over the boiling water. Cover and bake at 180°C (350°F) mark 4 for 30 minutes or until the water has been absorbed and the rice is tender.

Rice side dishes

Colour index
page 73

6 servings

Pilaf with Bacon and Peas

*4 rashers streaky bacon,
rinded and chopped
1 small onion, skinned and
finely chopped
200 g (7 oz) long grain rice
350 g (12 oz) frozen peas
200 ml (7 fl oz) chicken
stock
200 ml (7 fl oz) water
5 ml (1 level tsp) salt
freshly ground black
pepper*

1 In a large frying pan, fry the bacon gently in its own fat until crisp; remove from the pan with a slotted spoon and drain on kitchen paper towel.

2 Pour off all but 60 ml (4 tbsp) bacon fat from the frying pan.

3 Add the chopped onion and fry gently for about 5 minutes until soft but not coloured.

4 Stir in the remaining ingredients and bring to the boil. Reduce heat, cover and simmer for 15–20 minutes or until the liquid has been absorbed and the rice is tender.

5 Add the reserved fried bacon to the rice mixture and stir gently with a slotted spoon or fork until well mixed. Spoon the pilaf into a heated serving dish.

Curried Rice

Colour index
page 74

3–4 servings

*25 g (1 oz) butter or
margarine
2 small onions, skinned and
sliced
2.5 ml (½ level tsp) curry
powder*

*2.5 ml (½ level tsp) salt
pinch ground nutmeg
175 g (6 oz) long grain rice,
cooked
100 ml (4 fl oz) single
cream or creamy milk*

1. Melt the butter or margarine in a saucepan and add the onions with the curry powder, salt and nutmeg. Fry gently for about 7 minutes, stirring frequently, until the onions are soft and golden.
2. Stir in the rice and cream and heat through without boiling. Spoon into a heated serving dish.

Risotto alla Milanese

Colour index
page 74

4 servings

*75 g (3 oz) butter
1 onion, skinned and finely
chopped
225 g (8 oz) medium or
long grain rice
150 ml (¼ pint) white wine*

*600 ml (1 pint) boiling
chicken stock
pinch powdered saffron
salt and pepper
30–45 ml (2–3 level tbsp)
grated Parmesan cheese*

1 Melt 50 g (2 oz) butter; add the chopped onion and fry gently for about 5 minutes until golden.

2 Add the rice and continue frying, stirring constantly, until the rice looks transparent.

3 Pour in the wine and boil rapidly until well reduced. Add stock, saffron and seasoning. Cover; cook for 15–20 minutes or until the rice is tender.

4 Add the remaining butter and the cheese and stir them into the rice with a fork until the cheese melts. Spoon into a heated serving dish.

TYPES OF RICE

Long grain white rice has clean, white-coloured grains that are fluffy and separate when cooked, with a bland flavour. It is the rice most commonly used in savoury dishes.

Medium grain white rice (or Italian rice) has a slightly chewy texture and a creamier colour. It is also used for savoury dishes and is the traditional rice used in risottos.

Short grain white rice gives a smooth, creamy texture, suitable for rice pudding and other sweet dishes.

Brown rice may be long, medium or short grain. It is a less heavily milled version of the grains described above, with only the inedible husk and a small amount of bran removed. Brown rice has a high nutritional content and distinctive flavour and can be used as a replacement to highly polished white rice.

Wild rice is not technically rice, but the seeds of a wild grass. It is expensive and not widely available, but delicious for special savoury dishes.

Pre-cooked or instant rice is completely cooked and then dehydrated; it is very quick to prepare.

Rice side dishes

Casseroled Rice with Mushrooms

*100 g (4 oz) long grain
rice*
*50 g (2 oz) butter or
margarine*
*100 g (4 oz) mushrooms,
sliced*
*50 g (2 oz) onion, skinned
and chopped*

*50 g (2 oz) celery, washed
and chopped*
300 ml (½ pint) beef stock
*2.5 ml (½ level tsp) salt
pinch dried thyme*

For the garnish:
fresh thyme sprigs

1 Cook the rice in a frying
pan without any fat for
5 minutes or until golden,
stirring constantly. Pour
into a small casserole.

2 Melt half the fat in the
frying pan and add the
mushrooms with the onion
and celery. Fry gently for 5
minutes or until tender.
Add stock, salt and thyme
and bring to the boil.

3 Pour mixture over rice.
Cover casserole; bake
at 180°C (350°F) mark 4
for 30 minutes or until the
liquid has been absorbed
and the rice is tender.

4 Add the remaining
fat to the rice and
mushroom mixture and
stir gently with a fork until
it has melted. Garnish with
fresh thyme.

Baked Rice and Noodles

50 g (2 oz) butter
*1 onion, skinned and
chopped*
200 g (7 oz) long grain rice
*100 g (4 oz) mushrooms,
sliced*
pinch pepper

*1.25ml (¼ level tsp) curry
powder*
*600 ml (1 pint) chicken
stock*
5 ml (1 level tsp) salt
50 g (2 oz) noodles

1. Melt half the butter, add the onion and fry gently
for about 5 minutes, until golden.
2. Add the rice with the sliced mushrooms, pepper
and curry powder; cook gently for a further 5
minutes, stirring frequently.
3. Add the stock, salt and remaining butter and
bring to the boil; stir in the noodles. Pour into a 1.5-
litre (2½-pint) capacity casserole.
4. Cover and bake at 180°C (350°F) mark 4 for
35–40 minutes or until the liquid has been absorbed
and the rice and noodles are tender. Separate the
grains and noodles gently with a fork before serving.

Spanish Rice

*4 rashers streaky bacon,
rinded*
*100 g (4 oz) onion, skinned
and chopped*
*75 g (3 oz) green pepper,
seeded and chopped*
425-g (15-oz) can tomatoes
*225 ml (8 fl oz) tomato
sauce, page 337*
10 ml (2 level tsp) sugar
5 ml (1 level tsp) salt
250 g (9 oz) long grain rice
*50 g (2 oz) Cheddar cheese,
grated, optional*

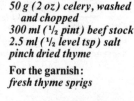

1 In a large frying pan, fry
the bacon gently in its
own fat until crisp; remove
from the pan and drain
well on kitchen paper
towel. Pour off all but
30 ml (2 tbsp) bacon fat.

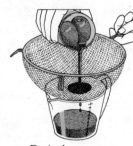

2 Add the onion and
green pepper to the pan
and fry gently for about 5
minutes or until the onion
is soft but not coloured.

3 Drain the tomatoes
and make the juice up to
400 ml (¾ pint) with water.
Roughly chop the tomatoes.

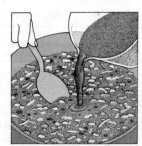

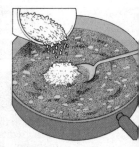

4 Add the tomato liquid,
chopped tomatoes,
tomato sauce, sugar and
salt to the frying pan and
bring to the boil.

5 Stir in rice; pour into a
casserole or ovenproof
dish. Cover; bake at 180°C
(350°F) mark 4 for 30
minutes until rice is tender.

6 Sprinkle with cheese if
you wish and bake for a
further 5 minutes. Crumble
bacon over the top.

Rice desserts

Herbed Orange Rice

50 g (2 oz) butter
2 sticks celery, washed and chopped
30 ml (2 tbsp) grated onion
15 ml (1 tbsp) grated orange rind

350 ml (12 fl oz) water
225 ml (8 fl oz) orange juice
5 ml (1 level tsp) salt
pinch dried thyme
200 g (7 oz) long grain rice

1. Melt the butter in a saucepan and add the celery and onion. Fry gently for about 5 minutes, stirring occasionally, until the onion is golden.
2. Add the next five ingredients; bring to the boil.
3. Stir in rice. Cover and simmer for 15–20 minutes or until the liquid has been absorbed and the rice is tender. Spoon into a heated serving dish.

Rice Ring

425 g (15 oz) long grain rice, cooked and kept hot
40 g (1½ oz) butter

60 ml (4 tbsp) chopped parsley

1. Toss the rice with the butter and parsley. Pack into a greased 1.1-litre (2-pint) capacity ring tin.
2. Leave to stand for 1 minute. Loosen the edges of the ring with a palette knife and turn it out on to a heated serving plate.

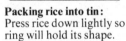

Packing rice into tin: Press rice down lightly so ring will hold its shape.

Turning out rice ring: Invert the tin carefully on to the heated plate.

RICE RING WITH VEGETABLES: Mix *225 g (8 oz) long grain rice*, cooked and kept hot, with *100 g (4 oz) French beans*, cooked and chopped, *100 g (4 oz) frozen peas*, cooked, and *10 ml (2 tsp) chopped chives*. Pack into a 1.5-litre (2½-pint) capacity ring tin and turn out on to a heated serving plate.

Chinese Fried Rice

6 eggs
1.25 ml (¼ level tsp) salt
75 ml (5 tbsp) vegetable oil
200 g (7 oz) long grain rice, cooked and chilled
15 ml (1 tbsp) soy sauce

225 g (8 oz) streaky bacon, rinded, fried and crumbled
30 ml (2 tbsp) chopped spring onions

1. Beat together the eggs and the salt. Heat 45 ml (3 tbsp) of the oil in a frying pan. Scramble the eggs (page 144) until they leave the sides of the pan. Reduce the heat and push the eggs to one side.
2. Add the rice and remaining oil to the pan and stir with a fork until the rice is well coated. Stir in the soy sauce, bacon and scrambled eggs and heat through gently. Spoon into a heated serving dish and sprinkle with chopped spring onions.

Creamed Rice

50 g (2 oz) short grain rice
30 ml (2 level tbsp) caster sugar
568 ml (1 pint) creamy milk

5 ml (1 tsp) vanilla essence
1.25 ml (¼ level tsp) ground nutmeg

1 Put the rice and sugar into a heavy-based saucepan and add the creamy milk.

2 Cook the mixture over a very low heat, stirring frequently, until bubbles begin to form round the edge of the pan.

3 Reduce heat, cover and simmer for about 30 minutes or until the rice is tender and creamy.

4 Remove the rice mixture from the heat and stir in the vanilla essence.

5 Spoon into serving dishes and sprinkle with nutmeg. Serve hot, or cover and chill.

LEMON AND CINNAMON CREAMED RICE: Prepare as above, but add the *thinly pared rind of 1 lemon* with the milk; discard after cooking. Stir in *3 beaten egg yolks*. Reheat rice without boiling; cool. Sprinkle with *15 ml (1 level tbsp) caster sugar* mixed with *1.25 ml (¼ level tsp) ground cinnamon*.

BAKED RICE PUDDING: Prepare as above, but put the rice, sugar and milk into a buttered 900-ml (1½-pint) capacity ovenproof dish, dot with *butter* and sprinkle with nutmeg. Bake at 150°C (300°F) mark 2 for 2 hours, stirring well after 30 minutes.

PASTRY AND SWEET PIES

The basic shortcrust, flaky and puff pastries can all be used for both sweet and savoury dishes. For savoury pies, look for individual references in the index.

Most pastries should be made in cool working conditions; aim to keep your hands, the tools and the work surface cool. If your hands are inclined to be warm, it helps to use a pastry blender for rubbing the fat into short pastries to avoid your hands coming into contact with the dough. Water used for mixing should be very cold, except for choux pastry (page 366); measure it into a jug before you start mixing and chill it in the refrigerator or in a bowl containing ice cubes until you are ready to use it. If there is time, refrigerate the dough after mixing and before rolling it, to let it rest, and keep rolled pastry in the refrigerator if it has to wait while you prepare a filling.

INGREDIENTS
Flour: Plain flour is recommended for most pastries, although self raising flour can be used for shortcrust pastry to give a slightly softer, more crumbly texture.
Fats: Butter, margarine and lard are the most commonly used fats, although blended white vegetable fat is sometimes used; with the latter, follow the manufacturer's instructions carefully regarding quantities, as it may give different results. For shortcrust pastry, use 25 g (1 oz) fat for every 50 g (2 oz) flour; for flaky pastry use a slightly higher proportion of fat, and for puff pastry, use equal weights of each.
Liquid: Always add as little water as possible to pastry dough – only just enough to make the dough bind. A sticky dough will end up as hard pastry. As a rule, use 5 ml (1 tsp) liquid for every 25 g (1 oz) flour in short pastries and 15 ml (1 tbsp) liquid for every 25 g (1 oz) flour in flaky pastries.

ROLLING PASTRY
Roll pastry lightly and evenly, using as little flour as possible on the work surface and rolling pin. Short pastries are usually rolled about 0.3 cm (1/8 in) thick; flaky and puff pastries up to 0.5 cm (1/4 in) thick. Roll pastry in one direction only, away from you, and rotate it frequently to keep it an even shape. Lessen the pressure on the rolling pin slightly as you get to the edges of the pastry or they will be thinner than the centre.

LINING A FLAN CASE
If you are using a flan ring, place it on a baking sheet; otherwise use a flan tin with a removable base, or an ovenproof earthenware or glass flan dish. Roll out the pastry 2.5 cm (1 in) larger all round than the case, then lift it into tin or dish, pressing pastry against the sides of the tin or dish without stretching it.

With a fluted flan tin, press your finger into each flute to ensure a good finish; there should be no air left between tin and pastry. Trim the pastry on a rimmed tin or dish with scissors or a sharp knife to make an even edge, leaving a little for shrinkage, or make one of the decorative edges (opposite). For a neat finish on a rimless tin, roll the rolling pin across top of tin.

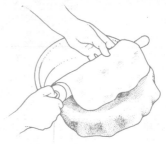

Lining a flan case: Use the rolling pin to help you lift the pastry from the work surface to the dish.

MAKING A COVERED PIE
For a double crust pie, divide the pastry into two pieces, one slightly larger than the other. Roll out the larger piece to a circle about 2.5 cm (1 in) larger all round than the inverted pie dish. Lift the pastry into the dish, unfold it and ease it gently into place without stretching. Place a pie funnel in the centre to support the pastry. Add the filling, mounding it in the centre. Then roll out the second piece of pastry to a circle about 1 cm (1/2 in) larger than the dish. Brush the edge of the lower crust with water and lift the lid into position. Either fold the upper rim under the lower one and pinch up into a decorative edge (opposite), or press the edges firmly together and trim with a sharp knife against the edge of the dish. Cut a slit in the centre of the top crust to allow the steam to escape.

For a pie with a top crust only, first cut a 2.5-cm (1-in) wide strip of pastry and place it on the dampened rim of the dish; brush the strip with water. Cover the pie with the remaining pastry, pressing it lightly to the rim to seal. Trim and decorate as for a double crust pie.

MAKING A DECORATIVE EDGE

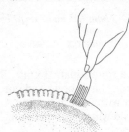

Forked edge: Trim the pastry to leave a 1-cm (½-in) rim, then press all round the edge with the back of a floured fork.

Fluted edge: Place your forefinger on the inside of the edge and pinch the pastry round it with the thumb and forefinger of the other hand, to make curved flutes at 0.5-cm (¼-in) intervals.

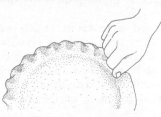

Rope edge: Press your thumb into the edge at an angle and pinch pastry between it and the knuckle of your index finger. Repeat, placing your thumb each time in indentation made by index finger.

Forked fluted edge: Make a fluted edge but pinch the flutes at 1-cm (½-in) intervals and flatten slightly with the back of a fork.

Cut edge: Make cuts about 1 cm (½ in) deep at 1-cm (½-in) intervals with scissors or a sharp knife. Fold alternate pieces inwards, not breaking the pastry, and press to flatten well.

Scalloped edge: Place your thumb and forefinger about 3 cm (1¼ in) apart on the outside of the edge and press the pastry outwards between them with a floured spoon. Repeat, pinching the points between the scallops.

STORING AND FREEZING PASTRY

All pastry doughs can be stored in the refrigerator for a day or so before cooking, wrapped in waxed paper, polythene or foil, or rolled and shaped ready for filling and cooking at the last minute.

For freezing, wrap unshaped pastry in polythene; to use, thaw at room temperature for 3–4 hours or overnight in the refrigerator. Freeze pastry cases cooked or uncooked in foil containers or freezer-proof earthenware or glass. Bake pastry cases from frozen, adding about 5 minutes to the normal baking time. Uncooked, frozen pastry can be stored for 3–4 months; cooked pastry will keep up to 6 months.

Short pastries

Shortcrust Pastry

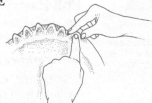

200 g (7 oz) plain flour
pinch salt
100 g (3½ oz) fat, half lard and half margarine or butter
about 35 ml (7 tsp) cold water

Makes one 23-cm (9-in) flan case, or 25.5-cm (10-in) top crust, or 18-cm (7-in) top and bottom crusts, or 12 deep tart cases, or 24 shallow patty cases

1 Sift the flour with the salt into a large bowl. Cut the fat into small pieces and add to the flour.

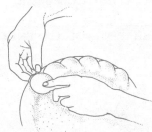

2 With both hands, rub the fat into the flour between fingertips and thumb or cut it in with a pastry blender. After 2–3 minutes the mixture will look like fresh breadcrumbs.

3 Add the water and stir with a round-bladed knife until the dough begins to stick together in lumps.

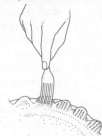

4 Collect together with one hand and knead quickly and lightly for a few seconds, to give a smooth, firm dough.

5 Wrap the dough loosely in greaseproof paper and leave it to rest in the refrigerator for about 15 minutes, or wrap it in polythene and refrigerate for up to 2 days. Roll the dough out on a lightly floured surface with a lightly floured rolling pin and shape as required in recipe. Bake at 200–220°C (400–425°F) mark 6–7 or as the recipe directs. For baking blind, see page 350.

Sweet Flan Pastry

200 g (7 oz) plain flour
pinch salt
150 g (5 oz) fat, half butter or margarine and half lard
10 ml (2 level tsp) caster sugar

1 egg, beaten
about 30 ml (2 tbsp) cold water

Makes one 23-cm (9-in) flan case

1. Sift the flour with the salt, then cut or rub in the fat with your fingertips. Stir in the sugar. Beat the egg and water together and stir into the flour. Knead lightly for a few seconds.

2. Roll out and shape as required. Bake at 200°C (400°F) mark 6 or as the recipe directs.

Flaky pastries

Flaky Pastry

150 g (5 oz) butter or
   butter and lard
200 g (7 oz) plain flour
pinch salt

about 105 ml (7 tbsp)
   cold water
squeeze of lemon juice
beaten egg to glaze

Makes one
25.5-cm (10-in)
top crust, or
12 7.5-cm (3-in)
vol-au-vent
cases,
or 25 4-cm
(1½- in)
bouchée cases

1 Soften the fat with a knife then divide it into four pieces. Sift the plain flour with the salt into a large bowl.

2 Rub one piece of fat into the flour. Add the water and lemon juice and mix to make a soft dough.

3 Roll out the dough on a floured surface, to a rectangle three times as long as it is wide.

4 Spread a second piece of the fat over two thirds of the dough in evenly spaced dots.

5 Fold the dough into thirds, making sure the unbuttered section is in the middle.

6 Seal the edges by pressing with a rolling pin and turn dough through 90°.

7. Repeat the rolling, buttering and folding twice more. Wrap in greaseproof paper and chill for at least 30 minutes. Roll out, using as little flour as possible and shape as required.

8. Brush with beaten egg before baking and bake at 220°C (425°F) mark 7 or as the recipe directs.

ROUGH PUFF PASTRY: Prepare the pastry as above, but cut the fat into small cubes and stir them gently into the dry ingredients. Mix to a fairly stiff dough with the water and the lemon juice, then roll and fold the dough four times. Leave to rest for about 30 minutes, then roll out and bake as for flaky pastry (above).

Puff Pastry

200 g (7 oz) butter
200 g (7 oz) plain flour
pinch salt
squeeze of lemon juice

about 105 ml (7 tbsp) cold
   water
beaten egg to glaze

Makes one
23-cm (9-in)
top crust

1. Soften the butter with a round-bladed knife. Sift the flour with the salt into a large bowl and cut or rub in a knob of the butter with your fingertips. Add the lemon juice and the cold water and mix to make a soft, elastic dough.

2. Form the rest of the butter into a rectangle. Roll out the dough on a floured surface to a square about twice the size of the butter. Place the block of butter on one half of the dough, then fold over the other half and seal the edges by pressing them together with the rolling pin.

3. Turn the dough so that the fold is to the side and roll out to a rectangle three times as long as it is wide. Fold the bottom third up and the top third down and seal the edges again by pressing with the rolling pin. Wrap the dough loosely in greaseproof paper or cling film and leave to rest in the refrigerator for at least 20 minutes.

4. Repeat the rolling, folding and resting of the dough five more times.

5. Roll out the puff pastry using as little flour as possible and shape as required. Brush lightly with beaten egg or milk before baking to glaze it. Bake the pastry at 230°C (450°F) mark 8 or as the recipe directs.

SHAPING VOL-AU-VENT CASES

Roll out puff pastry 0.5–1 cm (¼–½ in) thick or more thinly for ready-made frozen pastry. Cut out 6–8 rounds with a 7.5-cm (3-in) plain cutter and place them on a greased baking sheet.

Cut part of the way through the pastry in the centre of each round with a 5-cm (2-in) plain round cutter to mark the lid.

Brush the tops with beaten egg and bake at 230°C (450°F) mark 8 for about 10 minutes, or until golden.

Remove the lids with the point of a knife, scoop out any soft pastry from the centres and cool the cases and lids on a wire rack.

Sweet pie crusts

Baked Crumb Crust

175 g (6 oz) unsweetened biscuits
75 g (3 oz) butter, melted
50 g (2 oz) sugar

Makes one 23-cm (9-in) flan case

1 Break the biscuits into a blender and blend to make fine crumbs, or put the biscuits in a strong polythene bag and crush with a rolling pin.

2 Mix the crumbs with the melted butter and sugar; stir well. If you wish, reserve 45 ml (3 level tbsp) mixture to sprinkle over the filling.

3 Press the rest of the mixture firmly and evenly over the bottom and sides of a 23-cm (9-in) round pie dish with the back of a spoon.

4 Bake at 190°C (375°F) mark 5 for 8 minutes. Cool on a wire rack.

5 Fill crust as required; sprinkle reserved crumbs over top, if you wish.

BAKED CRUMB CRUST VARIATIONS

BAKED SPICED CRUMB CRUST: Prepare the crust as above, but add *5–10 ml (1–2 level tsp) mixed spice.*

BAKED COCONUT CRUMB CRUST: Prepare the crust as above, but replace 25 g (1 oz) of the crumbs with *25 g (1 oz) desiccated coconut.*

BAKED LEMON CRUMB CRUST: Prepare the crust as above, but add the *grated rind of 1 lemon.*

BAKED NUT CRUMB CRUST: Prepare the crust as above, but replace 25 g (1 oz) of the crumbs with *25 g (1 oz) shelled walnuts* or hazel nuts, finely chopped.

BAKED GINGER CRUMB CRUST: Prepare the crust as above, but replace the unsweetened biscuits with *ginger biscuits.*

Unbaked Crumb Crust

175 g (6 oz) digestive biscuits
75 g (3 oz) butter, melted

Makes one 23-cm (9-in) flan case

1. Crush the biscuits in a blender or in a strong polythene bag with a rolling pin and mix with the melted butter.
2. Press the crumbs firmly and evenly over the bottom and sides of a greased 23-cm (9-in) round pie dish with the back of a spoon. Chill until set.

UNBAKED CHOCOLATE CRUMB CRUST: Prepare the crust as above, but replace 75 g (3 oz) butter with a *large knob of butter*, melted, and *75–100 g (3–4 oz) plain chocolate*, melted.

Pâte Sucrée

200 g (7 oz) plain flour
pinch salt
100 g (3½ oz) caster sugar
100 g (3½ oz) butter, cut into small pieces
3–4 egg yolks

Makes 12 deep tart cases or one 23-cm (9-in) flan case

1. Sift the flour and salt into a pyramid on a working surface. Make a well in the centre and add the sugar, butter and egg yolks.
2. Flip the flour over the egg yolks with a palette knife and work the mixture together with your fingertips until all the flour is incorporated. Knead the dough lightly for a few seconds.
3. Wrap the pastry in greaseproof paper and leave to rest in the refrigerator for 1 hour. To make tart cases, cut the dough into 12 pieces.

4 Roll out the pieces to rounds slightly larger than tops of tart cases.

5 Ease each one into a case; lightly press the pastry against the sides.

6 Carefully trim edge of case with a sharp knife or kitchen scissors to remove surplus pastry.

7 Prick the bases with a fork. Bake at 200°C (400°F) mark 6 for 10–15 minutes. Cool completely.

PATE SUCREE FLAN CASE: Prepare the pastry as above, but use it to line a 23-cm (9-in) flan case (page 342); bake blind (page 350) at 200°C (400°F) mark 6 for 15–20 minutes.

Fruit pies

Fruits that have a firm shape and texture and a tart flavour cook best in pies. Use soft fruits uncooked in cold flans and tarts, or mix them with a hard fruit – try apple and raspberry, for instance, as a change from the more common apple and blackberry pie. Mixing soft fruit with apple also gives the apple a better flavour and more attractive colour.

For a covered apple pie choose a well-flavoured cooking apple such as a Bramley to give a good bulky filling, but for an open flan in which you want the fruit slices to retain their shape, use a crisp dessert apple such as Cox's Orange Pippin or Worcester Pearmain. A pear pie is best made with firm, slightly unripe fruit, and a cherry pie will have more flavour if it is made with Morello or May Duke cherries rather than the sweet white-heart or black-heart varieties. Use canned or frozen fruit if there is no cheap fresh fruit available, but sharpen the flavour of those packed in syrup by adding lemon juice or mixing in a few fresh or frozen blackcurrants, redcurrants or blackberries. The flavour can also be varied with spices and other flavourings such as lemon rind.

Fruit pies can be served either hot or cold with cream or custard, and any leftover wedges are good plain for packed lunches. All fruit pies will freeze well if not required immediately.

Apple Pie

shortcrust pastry made with 350 g (12 oz) plain flour, page 343
150–175 g (5–6 oz) sugar
30 ml (2 level tbsp) plain flour
2.5 ml (½ level tsp) ground cinnamon
1.25 ml (¼ level tsp) ground nutmeg
2.5 ml (½ tsp) grated lemon rind
5–10 ml (1–2 tsp) lemon juice

900 g (2 lb) cooking apples, peeled, cored and thinly sliced
15 g (½ oz) butter or margarine
milk to glaze

Colour index page 86
6 servings

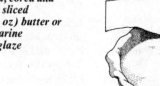

1 Roll out half the pastry and use to line a 23-cm (9-in) round pie dish.

2 Mix the sugar with the flour, ground cinnamon and nutmeg, lemon rind and lemon juice.

3 Put half the sliced apples in the pie dish and sprinkle with half the sugar mixture. Top with the rest of the apples, then the sugar mixture.

4 Dot the butter or margarine evenly over the pie filling.

5 Roll out the remaining pastry to a circle 2.5 cm (1 in) larger all round than the pie dish and use a decorative cutter to make a design in the top.

6 Damp the edges of the pie and cover with the lid, pressing the edges well together. Trim the edge, pinch to seal and make a decorative edge.

7 Brush the top lightly with milk and bake at 220°C (425°F) mark 7 for 40–50 minutes or until the pastry is golden brown. Serve hot or cold.

Colour index page 86
6 servings

BLACKBERRY PIE: Prepare as left, but make filling with *700 g (1½ lb) blackberries, 175 g (6 oz) sugar, 25 g (1 oz) plain flour, 2.5 ml (½ tsp) grated lemon rind, 2.5 ml (½ level tsp) ground cinnamon, 1.25 ml (¼ level tsp) ground nutmeg* and a *pinch of salt*. Dot with 15 g (½ oz) butter. Cover pie, brush with milk and bake as for apple pie (left).

Colour index page 86
6 servings

CHERRY PIE: Prepare as left, but make filling with *900 g (2 lb) stoned cherries, 225 g (8 oz) sugar, 25 g (1 oz) cornflour* and *2.5 ml (½ level tsp) salt*. Dot with 15 g (½ oz) butter. Cover pie, cut parallel slashes in top, brush with milk and bake at 220°C (425°F) mark 7 for 50–60 minutes.

6 servings

RHUBARB PIE: Prepare as left, but make filling with *700 g (1½ lb) rhubarb*, cut into chunks, *350 g (12 oz) sugar, 25 g (1 oz) plain flour, 15 ml (1 tbsp) grated orange rind* and *1.25 ml (¼ level tsp) salt*. Dot with *25 g (1 oz) butter*. Cover pie, cut parallel slashes or a design in the top and finish as for apple pie (left).

Colour index page 87
6 servings

BLUEBERRY PIE: Prepare as left, but make filling with *700 g (1½ lb) blueberries, 150–175 g (5–6 oz) sugar, 25 g (1 oz) plain flour, 10 ml (2 tsp) lemon juice, 2.5 ml (½ tsp) grated lemon rind, 2.5 ml (½ level tsp) ground cinnamon, 1.25 ml (¼ level tsp) ground nutmeg* and a *pinch of salt*. Dot with 15 g (½ oz) butter. Cover pie, cut cross in centre of lid; fold back points to make a square opening and press points to secure. Brush with milk; bake at 220°C (425°F) mark 7 for 50 minutes.

Peach Pie

Colour index page 88

6 servings

shortcrust pastry made with 350 g (12 oz) plain flour, page 343
900 g (2 lb) peaches, peeled, stoned and sliced
175–225 g (6–8 oz) sugar
75 ml (5 level tbsp) plain flour

15 ml (1 tbsp) lemon juice
2.5 ml (½ tsp) grated lemon rind
2.5 ml (½ level tsp) ground cinnamon
milk to glaze

1 Roll out half the pastry and use it to line a 23-cm (9-in) round pie dish.

2 Toss the sliced peaches in a large bowl with all the remaining ingredients except the milk, and spoon into the pie dish.

3 Roll out the remaining pastry to a circle 2.5 cm (1 in) larger all round than the pie dish, and cut it into six strips.

4 Lay the strips parallel to each other across the filling. Twist each one and press the ends firmly on to the pie rim.

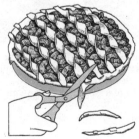

5 Trim edge, leaving a 2.5-cm (1-in) rim, damp rim; fold up over strips. Scallop edge (page 343).

6 Brush the strips with milk and bake at 220°C (425°F) mark 7 for 45–50 minutes or until golden.

PEAR PIE: Prepare the pie as above, but make the filling with *5–6 pears*, peeled, cored and sliced, *175 g (6 oz) sugar, 45 ml (3 level tbsp) tapioca, 30 ml (2 tbsp) lemon juice, 25 g (1 oz) butter* or margarine, melted, *5 ml (1 tsp) grated lemon rind, 2.5 ml (½ level tsp) ground nutmeg, 2.5 ml (½ level tsp) ground cinnamon* and *1.25 ml (¼ level tsp) salt.* Bake at 220°C (425°F) mark 7 for 50–60 minutes.

Streusel-topped Pear Pie

Colour index page 88

8 servings

4–5 medium pears, peeled, cored and thickly sliced
100 g (4 oz) sugar
25 g (1 oz) plain flour
1.25 ml (¼ level tsp) salt
30 ml (2 tbsp) lemon juice

For the pastry:
225 g (8 oz) plain flour
5 ml (1 level tsp) salt
175 g (6 oz) butter or margarine
45 ml (3 tbsp) water
75 g (3 oz) soft light brown sugar

5 ml (1 level tsp) ground cinnamon
1.25 ml (¼ level tsp) ground nutmeg
1.25 ml (¼ level tsp) ground cloves
50 g (2 oz) butter or margarine
50 g (2 oz) Cheddar cheese, grated

1. Make the pastry. Mix the flour with the salt in a large bowl. Rub in the fat until the mixture resembles coarse breadcrumbs. Reserve 100 g (4 oz) for the topping. Add the water to the remaining flour mixture, a spoonful at a time to make a soft dough. Collect it together with one hand and knead lightly for a few seconds.
2. Roll out the pastry and use it to line a 23-cm (9-in) round pie dish.
3. Mix the sliced pears with the sugar, plain flour, salt and lemon juice in a large bowl and spoon the mixture into the pie dish.
4. Make the topping. Mix the reserved flour mixture with the brown sugar and spices. Rub in the extra fat until the mixture resembles coarse breadcrumbs and stir in the cheese. Sprinkle the topping evenly over the pears.
5. Bake at 220°C (425°F) mark 7 for 40 minutes, then cover with foil and bake for a further 20 minutes until golden brown.

Prune, Apricot and Nut Flan

Colour index page 86

8 servings

23-cm (9-in) shortcrust pastry case, page 343, baked blind
350 g (12 oz) stoned prunes, soaked
175 g (6 oz) dried apricots, soaked
800 ml (29 fl oz) water
25 g (1 oz) shelled mixed nuts, roughly chopped
45 ml (3 level tbsp) cornflour

50 g (2 oz) sugar
15 ml (1 tbsp) grated lemon rind
5 ml (1 level tsp) ground cinnamon
pinch salt

1. While the case is cooling, put the prunes and apricots in a saucepan with 700 ml (25 fl oz) water and bring to the boil. Reduce the heat and simmer for 15 minutes or until tender.
2. Spread the chopped nuts on a baking sheet and toast at 190°C (375°F) mark 5 for 8–10 minutes until lightly browned.
3. Blend the cornflour with the remaining 100 ml (4 fl oz) water; stir into the simmering fruit. Cook, stirring constantly, until the mixture has thickened. Stir in the remaining ingredients.
4. Spoon the filling into the pastry case, sprinkle with the toasted nuts and leave to cool.

Fruit pies

Colour index page 86
6 servings

Deep Dish Peach Pie

*shortcrust pastry made with
350 g (12 oz) plain flour,
page 343
1.1 kg (2½ lb) peaches
25 g (1 oz) butter
100 g (4 oz) sugar*

*15 g (½ oz) cornflour
1.25 ml (¼ level tsp)
ground cinnamon
pinch salt
milk to glaze*

1. Roll out three quarters of the pastry; use to line a
25.5 × 20.5 cm (10 × 8 in) rectangular ovenproof
dish. Trim edge, leaving a 2.5-cm (1-in) rim.
2. Peel, stone and slice the peaches, then arrange
them on the pastry and dot with butter. Mix the
sugar with the cornflour, cinnamon and salt and
sprinkle over the peaches.
3. Roll remaining pastry to a 23 × 15 cm (9 × 6 in)
rectangle; cut lengthways into six 2.5-cm (1-in) wide
strips. Lay them parallel to each other across
peaches. Twist each one and press ends firmly on to
pastry rim. Damp rim, fold it up over ends of strips
and flute edge (page 343). Brush strips with milk.
4. Bake at 220°C (425°F) mark 7 for 50 minutes.

Colour index page 87
6 servings

Deep Dish Plum Pie

*shortcrust pastry made with
350 g (12 oz) plain flour,
page 343
900 g (2 lb) plums, washed
1.25 ml (¼ tsp) almond
essence*

*25 g (1 oz) butter or
margarine
175 g (6 oz) sugar
40 g (1½ oz) plain flour
milk to glaze*

1. Roll out three quarters of the pastry; use to line a
25.5 × 20.5 cm (10 × 8 in) rectangular ovenproof
dish. Trim edge, leaving a 2.5-cm (1-in) rim.
2. Halve and stone the plums and arrange on pastry.
Sprinkle with almond essence and dot with butter.
Mix the sugar with the flour; sprinkle over plums.
3. Roll out the remaining pastry to a 28 × 12.5 cm
(11 × 5 in) rectangle and cut it lengthways into ten
1-cm (½-in) wide strips. Lay them across plums to
make a lattice, press ends firmly on to pastry rim and
trim. Damp rim, fold it up over ends of strips; make
a rope edge (page 343). Brush with milk.
4. Bake at 220°C (425°F) mark 7 for 45–50 minutes.

PREVENTING PIE EDGES BURNING

If the pie edges become
too brown before the filling
is cooked, cover them with
strips of foil to prevent
them burning.

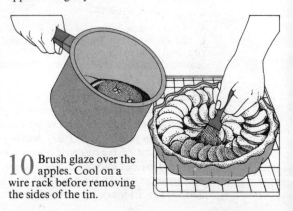

French Apple Flan

*3 dessert apples
5 ml (1 tsp) lemon juice
sugar
900 g (2 lb) cooking apples
75 ml (5 tbsp) water
350 g (12 oz) apricot jam*

For the pastry:
*200 g (7 oz) plain flour
pinch salt
100 g (3½ oz) caster sugar
100 g (3½ oz) butter
3–4 egg yolks*

Colour index page 88
8 servings

1 Sift the flour with
the salt and work in
the sugar, butter and
egg yolks. Knead lightly
to make a smooth dough,
then wrap in foil and
chill for 1 hour.

2 Pat the pastry over the
base and sides of a
23-cm (9-in) fluted flan tin
with a removable base; or
roll out and use to line tin.

3 Cut the dessert apples
into quarters with a
sharp knife, then peel, core
and thinly slice them.

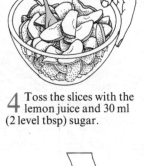

4 Toss the slices with the
lemon juice and 30 ml
(2 level tbsp) sugar.

5 Peel and core the cook-
ing apples and cut them
into chunks. Put them in a
saucepan with 60 ml
(4 tbsp) water and cook
gently for about 20
minutes, stirring to make a
smooth purée. Add 150 g
(5 oz) apricot jam and 50 g
(2 oz) sugar and bring to
the boil. Reduce the heat
and simmer, uncovered,
for a further 10 minutes or
until the purée is very
thick, stirring constantly.

6 Spoon the apple purée
into the prepared
pastry case and spread it
out evenly.

7 Arrange the dessert
apple slices on top in
overlapping circles. Bake
at 200°C (400°F) mark 6
for 45 minutes until the
apples are lightly browned.

8 Press the remaining
apricot jam through a
sieve into a saucepan and
stir in 15 ml (1 tbsp) water.

9 Bring to the boil and
boil for about 2 min-
utes, until the glaze coats
the back of a spoon.

10 Brush glaze over the
apples. Cool on a
wire rack before removing
the sides of the tin.

Custard pies

Unbaked egg custard poured into an uncooked pastry case is inclined to make the pastry soggy; to prevent this, rub the pastry first with butter or margarine, or brush with beaten egg white. Avoid spilling any mixture by placing the pie dish on the oven rack before pouring in the filling, then push the rack back into place.

Many custard fillings are cooked separately, added to a cooked pastry case or biscuit crust and chilled. Decorate with chopped nuts, whipped cream, toasted coconut or chocolate curls or top with meringue.

Custard Tart

Colour index page 88

6 servings

shortcrust pastry, made with 200 g (7 oz) flour, page 343
small knob of butter, softened
3 eggs
45 ml (3 level tbsp) sugar
400 ml (¾ pint) milk

To decorate:
chopped nuts, toasted coconut or whipped cream

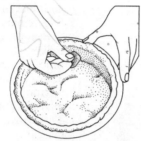

1 Roll out the pastry, use it to line a 23-cm (9-in) pie dish and flute the edge (page 343), if you wish. Rub with the butter.

2 Whisk the eggs with the sugar. Warm the milk; whisk into the egg mixture.

3 Place the pie dish on the oven shelf; pour custard into the pastry.

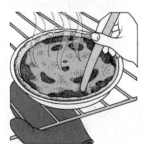

4 Bake at 220°C (425°F) mark 7 for 10 minutes, then at 180°C (350°F) mark 4 for 20 minutes, until knife inserted comes out clean.

5 Leave the tart to cool completely. Just before serving, decorate it with chopped nuts, toasted coconut or cream.

NUTMEG CUSTARD TART: Prepare as above, but sprinkle *2.5 ml (½ level tsp) ground nutmeg* over the top before baking.

Pumpkin Pie

Colour index page 86

6 servings

shortcrust pastry made with 200 g (7 oz) flour, page 343
3 eggs, separated
425-g (15-oz) can pumpkin
225 ml (8 fl oz) evaporated milk
225 g (8 oz) sugar
5 ml (1 level tsp) ground cinnamon
2.5 ml (½ level tsp) ground ginger
1.25 ml (¼ level tsp) ground nutmeg
1.25 ml (¼ level tsp) salt

To serve:
whipped cream

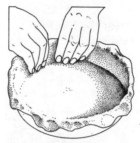

1 Roll out the pastry and use it to line a 23-cm (9-in) pie dish; flute the edge (page 343).

2 Whisk the egg whites with a mixer or a rotary whisk until soft peaks form.

3 In another bowl, using the same beaters, lightly beat the egg yolks, pumpkin, evaporated milk, sugar, spices and salt until well blended.

4 Gently fold the whisked egg whites into the pumpkin mixture with a wire whisk or metal spoon.

5 Place the pie dish on the oven shelf and pour the pumpkin mixture into the pastry case. Push the shelf back into place.

6 Bake at 190°C (375°F) mark 5 for 45 minutes until a knife inserted in the filling comes out clean. Serve hot with cream.

FRESH PUMPKIN PIE: Prepare as above but, to make pumpkin purée, cut *450 g (1 lb) fresh pumpkin* into pieces, remove seeds and membrane; cut off skin. Steam pieces between two plates over a pan of boiling water for 15–20 minutes; drain and purée. Cool before mixing with the filling ingredients.

Custard pies

Cream-topped Chocolate Pie

*23-cm (9-in) shortcrust
pastry case, page 343,
baked blind, or baked
crumb crust, page 345*
100 g (4 oz) sugar
50 g (2 oz) plain flour
1.25 ml (¼ level tsp) salt
400 ml (¾ pint) milk
*50 g (2 oz) plain
chocolate, broken into
small pieces*
3 egg yolks, beaten
*40 g (1½ oz) butter or
margarine*
5 ml (1 tsp) vanilla essence

For the topping:
*225 ml (8 fl oz) double or
whipping cream*

To decorate, optional:
*chocolate curls (page 394)
or grated chocolate*

Colour index page 86
8 servings

1 While the pastry case is
cooling, mix the sugar
with the flour and salt in a
large saucepan and stir in
the milk.

2 Add the chocolate and
heat gently until the
chocolate is melted, stirring continuously.

3 Whisk until the choco-
late and milk are
blended, then increase the
heat and cook for about
10 minutes, stirring
constantly. Remove the
saucepan from the heat.

4 Beat the egg yolks and
whisk in small amount
of the hot chocolate sauce.

5 Slowly pour the egg
mixture into the sauce-
pan, stirring rapidly. Cook
over low heat, stirring until
the mixture is very thick
and creamy. Do not
allow to boil.

6 Remove from the heat.
Stir in the butter and
vanilla essence and pour
into the pastry case. Cover
to prevent a skin forming
and chill for about 4 hours
until set.

7 Just before serving,
whip the cream lightly
and spread it evenly over
the chocolate filling. If you
wish, decorate the top with
chocolate curls or grated
chocolate.

BAKING BLIND

Many recipes require a pastry case that has been baked 'blind', or without a
filling. Use dried beans, rice or pasta to weight down paper before baking.

To bake blind: Line the shaped
pastry with greased greaseproof
paper or the wrapper from a block
of fat, greased side down, and half
fill it with uncooked, dried beans.
Bake at 200°C (400°F) mark 6 for
10–15 minutes, remove paper and
beans and bake 5–10 minutes more.

Colour index page 89
8 servings

Cream-topped Vanilla Pie

*23-cm (9-in) shortcrust
pastry case, page 343,
baked blind or baked
crumb crust, page 345*
100 g (4 oz) caster sugar
40 g (1½ oz) plain flour
1.25 ml (¼ level tsp) salt

500 ml (18 fl oz) milk
4 egg yolks
*15 g (½ oz) butter or
margarine*
10 ml (2 tsp) vanilla essence
*225 ml (8 fl oz) double or
whipping cream*

1. While the pastry case is cooling, mix the sugar
with the flour and salt in a large saucepan and stir in
the milk. Cook over medium heat for about 10
minutes, stirring all the time, until the mixture boils
and thickens. Boil for 1 minute, stirring constantly,
then remove the saucepan from the heat.
2. Beat the egg yolks and whisk in a little of the hot
milk mixture. Slowly pour the yolk mixture into the
saucepan, stirring rapidly.
3. Cook over low heat, stirring constantly, until the
mixture is very thick and creamy. Do not boil. The
mixture should mound when dropped from a spoon.
4. Remove from the heat. Stir in the butter or
margarine and vanilla essence and pour into the
pastry case. Cover to prevent a skin forming and
chill for about 4 hours until set.
5. Just before serving, whip the cream lightly and
spread it over the filling.

CREAMY BANANA PIE: Prepare the pastry case
and filling as above, but cover the filling and chill
separately for about 2 hours until cool. Peel and slice
4 bananas and arrange the slices from 3 over the base
of the pastry case. Pour in the vanilla filling, chill for
about 2 hours until set and top with the whipped
cream. Decorate the flan with *grated lemon rind* and
remaining banana slices which have been tossed in
lemon juice. Brush the banana slices with a little
heated *apricot jam*. Colour index page 89

CREAMY LEMON PIE: Prepare the pie as above,
but use *150 g (5 oz) sugar* and *400 ml (¾ pint) milk*;
omit the vanilla essence and add *60 ml (4 tbsp)
lemon juice* and *5 ml (1 tsp) grated lemon rind* to the
filling before pouring it into the pastry case.

CREAMY BUTTERSCOTCH PIE: Prepare the
pie as above, but use *175 g (6 oz) soft light brown
sugar, 400 ml (¾ pint) milk* and *40 g (1½ oz) butter*
or margarine.

CREAMY COCONUT PIE: Prepare the pie as
above, but add *50 g (2 oz) desiccated coconut* to the
vanilla filling before pouring it into the pastry case.

MERINGUE-TOPPED PIE: Prepare the cream-
topped chocolate or vanilla pie, but omit the whipped cream and do not cool the pie after filling. Make
a *meringue topping* (opposite) and spread it over the
filling, forming it into peaks with the back of a
spoon. Bake at 200°C (400°F) mark 6 for 10 minutes, then chill before serving.

Meringue pies

Lemon Meringue Pie

Colour index
page 89

6 servings

**23-cm (9-in) shortcrust
 pastry case, page 343,
 baked blind**
40 g (1½ oz) cornflour
225 g (8 oz) caster sugar
pinch salt
**350 ml (12 fl oz) tepid
 water**
grated rind of 1 lemon
100 ml (4 fl oz) lemon juice
4 egg yolks
15 g (½ oz) butter

For the meringue:
4 egg whites
100 g (4 oz) caster sugar

1 While the pastry case is cooling, mix the cornflour with the caster sugar and salt in a large heavy-based saucepan.

2 Stir in the water, lemon rind and juice and heat gently, stirring, until the mixture thickens. Remove from the heat.

3 Beat the egg yolks in a small bowl and whisk in a small amount of the hot sauce.

4 Slowly pour the egg mixture into the sauce, stirring rapidly. Cook, stirring, until the mixture has thickened; do not allow to boil.

5 Add the butter or margarine and stir until it has melted into the lemon mixture.

6 Pour the filling into the pastry case. Make a meringue topping (right) with the egg whites and remaining sugar.

7 Spread the meringue over the filling and bake at 200°C (400°F) mark 6 for 10 minutes or until lightly browned.

MAKING A MERINGUE PIE TOPPING

A meringue pie topping should be soft in the centre with a crisp, lightly browned crust. Pipe the meringue on top of the filling to create a decorative effect, or spread it out evenly to completely cover the pie. The following method can be adapted for any quantity of meringue, using 25 g (1 oz) caster sugar for every egg white.

Whisk the egg whites lightly with a rotary whisk or mixer until soft peaks form. Be careful not to over-whisk the whites or they will become dry and the meringue will crumble.

Whisk in half the sugar until the mixture is thick and glossy and no longer feels grainy; then carefully fold in the remaining sugar with a large metal spoon.

Spoon the meringue on top of the filling, then spread it out evenly to completely cover the pie. Form peaks with back of a spoon. Bake at 200°C (400°F) mark 6 for 10 minutes or until golden.

MERINGUE PIE VARIATIONS

LEMON SNOW PIE: Prepare the pie as left, but fold the meringue into the hot filling before pouring it into the flan case.

ORANGE MERINGUE PIE: Prepare the pie as left, but use **65 g (2½ oz) sugar** and **30 ml (2 tbsp) lemon juice**; replace 225 ml (8 fl oz) water with **orange juice** and replace the lemon rind with the **grated rind of 1 orange**.

LIME MERINGUE PIE: Prepare the pie as left, but replace the lemon juice and lemon rind with **lime juice** and **lime rind**. For decoration, thinly pare a **few strips of lime rind**, shred it finely and blanch in boiling water for 1 minute. Drain well and sprinkle over the pie before baking it.

PINEAPPLE MERINGUE PIE: Drain a **226-g (8-oz) can crushed pineapple**. Prepare the pie as left, but use **100 g (4 oz) sugar** and **15 ml (1 tbsp) lemon juice**; replace the water with **pineapple syrup** made up to 350 ml (12 fl oz) with water. Stir drained pineapple into the filling before pouring into flan case.

Chiffon and cream pies

A cold pie or flan with a light, fluffy filling is often known as a chiffon pie. The texture is usually achieved with whisked egg whites and most fillings are set with gelatine; they may also be enriched with whipped cream. Chiffon and cream pies are ideal for a party dessert as they can be made a day ahead and stored in the refrigerator; they do not freeze well.

When using gelatine, dissolve it completely in a little liquid, stirring constantly, before adding it to the filling. If the filling is hot stir a little into the gelatine, so that both mixtures are the same temperature, before blending it evenly through the mixture. The smooth, flat tops of these pies can be elaborately decorated for parties and formal occasions. Shredded or grated citrus peel (page 308) looks attractive and emphasises the flavour of any lemon, lime or orange juice in the filling. Sugar-dipped blackcurrants or redcurrants, or sliced fresh fruit add a contrast of texture as well as colour. There are many store-cupboard decorations – try angelica, candied fruits, chocolate curls or crystallised flowers. Piped whipped cream or meringue rosettes are also attractive decorations (page 399).

A crumb crust sometimes sticks to the serving dish. To prevent this happening, dip a cloth in warm water, wring it out and wrap it round the dish. The heat will loosen the crust so that the slices come out easily.

Lemon Chiffon Pie

23-cm (9-in) shortcrust pastry case, page 343, baked blind
15 ml (1 level tbsp) powdered gelatine
60 ml (4 tbsp) lemon juice
4 eggs, separated
75 ml (5 tbsp) water
15 ml (1 tbsp) grated lemon rind
190 g (6½ oz) caster sugar

shredded lemon rind, page 308, or crystallised lemon slices

To decorate:
100 ml (4 fl oz) double or whipping cream, whipped

Colour index page 87
8 servings

1 While the pastry case is cooling, dissolve the gelatine in lemon juice in a basin over hot water.

2 Whisk together the egg yolks, water, lemon rind and 65 g (2½ oz) sugar in a small saucepan and stir in the dissolved gelatine.

3 Heat gently, stirring, until the mixture has thickened and coats the back of the spoon. Remove the pan from the heat.

4 Whisk the egg whites stiffly with a mixer or rotary whisk and whisk in 50 g (2 oz) sugar. Fold in the remaining sugar with a large metal spoon until evenly blended.

5 Add the lemon mixture to the egg whites and fold in gently until evenly blended.

6 Spoon the lemon mixture into the cooled pastry case and chill thoroughly until set.

7 Just before serving, spoon whipped cream round the edge of the pie; sprinkle with lemon rind.

LIME SWIRL PIE: Prepare the pie as left, but omit the sugar from the egg mixture; replace the lemon juice with *lime juice* and the lemon rind with *lime rind*. Swirl the whipped cream through the filling in the flan case, then chill the pie thoroughly until set. To decorate, arrange *shredded lime rind* (page 308) over the top of the pie.

Colour index page 88
8 servings

Orange Chiffon Pie

23-cm (9-in) shortcrust pastry case, page 343, baked blind, or unbaked crumb crust, page 345
15 ml (1 level tbsp) powdered gelatine
30 ml (2 tbsp) water
90 ml (6 tbsp) frozen orange juice, thawed but not diluted
3 eggs, separated
45 ml (3 tbsp) curaçao

50 g (2 oz) caster sugar
75 ml (5 tbsp) double or whipping cream, lightly whipped

To serve:
1 orange
225 ml (8 fl oz) double or whipping cream
25 g (1 oz) sugar

1. While the pastry case is cooling, dissolve the powdered gelatine in the water with 45 ml (3 tbsp) of the orange juice in a small heatproof basin over a pan of hot water.
2. Whisk together the egg yolks, curaçao and caster sugar until thick and pale in colour. Stir in the lightly whipped cream, the remaining orange juice and the dissolved gelatine.
3. Cover and chill the mixture for about 45 minutes, stirring occasionally, until it mounds when dropped from a spoon.
4. Whisk the egg whites until stiff peaks form and fold them gently into the chilled orange mixture until evenly blended. Spoon the filling into the cooled pastry case and chill thoroughly for about 30 minutes until set.
5. To serve, cut the rind and pith from the orange (page 311) and divide the flesh into segments. Put the double cream and sugar into a bowl. Whisk together until soft peaks form and spread evenly over the top to completely cover the pie. Arrange the orange segments on top.

Old English Eggnog Pie

Colour index
page 87

6 servings

*23-cm (9-in) sweet flan
  pastry case, page 343,
  baked blind*
*15 ml (1 level tbsp)
  powdered gelatine*
45 ml (3 tbsp) rum
2 egg yolks
*90 ml (6 level tbsp) caster
  sugar*
300 ml (½ pint) milk
1 egg white
*90 ml (6 tbsp) double
  cream*
*1.25 ml (¼ level tsp)
  ground nutmeg*

To decorate:
grated chocolate

1 While the pastry case is cooling, dissolve the gelatine in the rum in a small heatproof basin over a pan of hot water.

2 Whisk together the egg yolks, half the sugar and the milk in a small saucepan and stir in the gelatine.

3 Heat very gently, stirring, until the custard has thickened and coats the back of the spoon. Remove from heat.

4 Cover and chill the custard for about 40 minutes until it mounds when dropped from a spoon, then whisk until completely smooth.

5 Whisk the egg white stiffly and gradually whisk in the remaining sugar. Lightly whip the cream until thick.

6 Gently fold the egg white and cream into the custard mixture until evenly blended and smooth.

7 Pour into the pastry case, sprinkle with nutmeg and chill. Decorate with grated chocolate.

EGG NOG PIE VARIATIONS

COFFEE EGG NOG PIE: Prepare the pie as left, but omit the cream and add *30 ml (2 level tbsp) instant coffee powder* to the egg whites before whisking them. To decorate, melt *100 g (4 oz) plain chocolate* in a small heatproof basin over a pan of hot water. Stir in *60 ml (4 tbsp) hot water* and drizzle it over the flan. Colour index page 87

STRAWBERRY EGG NOG PIE: Prepare the pie as left, but fold *100 g (4 oz) sliced strawberries* into the filling before spooning into pastry case. Decorate the top of the pie with whole or halved *strawberries*. Colour index page 87

COCONUT EGG NOG PIE: Prepare the pie as left, but omit the nutmeg and add *50 g (2 oz) desiccated coconut* or fresh grated coconut to the custard before folding in the egg white and cream.

CRANBERRY-TOPPED EGG NOG PIE: Prepare the pie as left, but omit the nutmeg and decoration. For the topping, stir *15 ml (1 level tbsp) cornflour* into the contents of a *454-g (16-oz) jar whole cranberry sauce* and cook until it has cleared and thickened; leave to cool. Spread over the flan before serving.

NUT EGG NOG PIE: Prepare the pie as left, but add *100 g (4 oz) chopped walnuts* to the custard mixture. Sprinkle *cocoa powder* over the top.

Chocolate Cream Pie

Colour index
page 87

8 servings

*unbaked chocolate crumb
  crust, page 345*
*15 ml (1 level tbsp)
  powdered gelatine*
225 ml (8 fl oz) water
3 eggs, separated
225 g (8 oz) caster sugar
*50 g (2 oz) plain
  chocolate, broken into
  small pieces*

*2.5 ml (½ tsp) vanilla
  essence*
*1.25 ml (¼ level tsp) cream
  of tartar*

To decorate:
whipped cream

1. While the crumb crust is setting, dissolve the gelatine in 45 ml (3 tbsp) of the water in a small basin over a pan of hot water.

2. Whisk together the egg yolks, remaining water and 175 g (6 oz) of the sugar in a small saucepan. Stir in the pieces of chocolate and the dissolved gelatine and heat gently, stirring constantly, until the chocolate has melted and the mixture has thickened and will coat the back of spoon. Remove from the heat and stir in the vanilla essence.

3. Pour the mixture into a large bowl and whisk with a mixer or rotary whisk for 1–2 minutes. Cover and chill the mixture for about 45 minutes until it mounds when dropped from a spoon.

4. Whisk the egg whites stiffly with the cream of tartar and add the remaining sugar a little at a time, whisking well after each addition, until thick and glossy. Beat the chilled chocolate mixture with a mixer or rotary whisk for about 2 minutes or until fluffy, then gently fold in the egg whites.

5. Spoon the filling into the crumb crust and chill for at least 2 hours, until set. Decorate with whipped cream before serving.

Chiffon and cream pies

Raspberry Ribbon Flan

Colour index
page 89

8 servings

23-cm (9-in) shortcrust
pastry case, page 343,
baked blind
1 packet raspberry jelly
50 g (2 oz) caster sugar
350 ml (12 fl oz) boiling
water
275 g (10 oz) frozen
raspberries
15 ml (1 tbsp) lemon
juice
75 g (3 oz) cream cheese
40 g (1½ oz) icing sugar,
sifted

pinch salt
5 ml (1 tsp) vanilla
essence
225 ml (8 fl oz) double
cream

To decorate:
fresh or frozen, thawed
raspberries or whipped
cream

1 While the pastry case is cooling, dissolve the jelly and sugar in the boiling water, then add raspberries and lemon juice

2 Leave to stand until the raspberries are thawed, then cover and chill the mixture, stirring occasionally, until it mounds when dropped from a spoon.

3 Beat the cream cheese with a wire whisk to soften it, then whisk in the icing sugar, salt and vanilla essence until the mixture is evenly blended and smooth.

4 Whip the cream lightly, then fold the cream cheese mixture into the whipped cream very lightly, with a wire whisk or metal spoon.

5 Spread half the cream cheese mixture in the pastry case, then spoon over half the raspberry jelly mixture.

6 Repeat with the remaining cheese mixture and jelly. Chill for 1–2 hours then decorate with raspberries or cream.

Coffee Liqueur Flan

Colour index
page 89

8 servings

23-cm (9-in) unbaked
chocolate crumb crust,
page 345
10 ml (2 level tsp)
powdered gelatine
60 ml (4 tbsp) water

2 eggs, separated
30 ml (2 tbsp) Tia Maria
75 g (3 oz) caster sugar
30 ml (2 level tbsp) instant
coffee powder

1. While the crumb crust is setting, dissolve the gelatine in 30 ml (2 tbsp) water in a small basin over a pan of hot water.
2. Whisk the egg yolks with the Tia Maria and sugar until thick and pale in colour. Blend the instant coffee with the remaining water and stir it into the egg yolk mixture with the dissolved gelatine.
3. Cover and chill the mixture for about 45 minutes, stirring occasionally, until it mounds when dropped from a spoon.
4. Whisk the egg whites stiffly and fold them gently into the chilled coffee mixture until evenly blended.
5. Spoon the filling into the crumb crust and chill for about 2 hours or until set.

Spiced Pumpkin Chiffon Pie

Colour index
page 88

8–10 servings

15 ml (1 level tbsp)
powdered gelatine
100 ml (4 fl oz) milk
3 eggs, separated
3.75 ml (¾ level tsp)
ground cinnamon
2.5 ml (½ level tsp) ground
nutmeg
2.5 ml (½ level tsp) salt
175 g (6 oz) sugar
350 ml (12 fl oz) pumpkin
purée, page 349

For the crumb crust:
100 g (4 oz) grated fresh or
desiccated flaked
coconut
20 g (¾ oz) finely crushed
digestive biscuit crumbs
75 g (3 oz) butter, melted
30 ml (2 level tbsp) sugar

To decorate:
whipped cream

1. Make the crust. Spread the coconut on a baking sheet and toast at 190°C (375°F) mark 5 for 8–10 minutes until lightly browned. Reserve 30 ml (2 tbsp) coconut and mix the rest with the biscuit crumbs, butter and sugar. Press firmly over the base and sides of a 23-cm (9-in) round pie dish with the back of a spoon and bake at 190°C (375°F) mark 5 for 6–8 minutes or until golden.
2. While the crust is cooling, dissolve the gelatine in 45 ml (3 tbsp) of the milk in a small basin over a pan of hot water.
3. Whisk together the egg yolks, remaining milk, spices, salt and 100 g (4 oz) sugar in the top of a double saucepan and stir in the dissolved gelatine and the pumpkin purée. Cook the mixture over hot water for 20 minutes, stirring frequently, until it has thickened. Do not boil.
4. Cover and chill the mixture until it mounds when dropped from a spoon.
5. Whisk the egg whites stiffly, then add the remaining sugar a little at a time, whisking well after each addition until thick and glossy. Fold the whisked egg whites gently into the chilled pumpkin mixture until evenly blended.
6. Spoon the filling into the crumb crust and chill for 1–2 hours until set. Decorate with the whipped cream and reserved toasted coconut before serving.

Christmas Rum Flan

Colour index page 89

8 servings

23-cm (9-in) unbaked crumb crust, page 345
15 ml (1 level tbsp) powdered gelatine
300 ml (½ pint) milk
4 eggs, separated
1.25 ml (¼ level tsp) salt
90 g (3½ oz) sugar
15 ml (1 tbsp) rum

5 ml (1 tsp) grated lemon rind
100 g ((4 oz) mixed crystallised fruit, finely chopped
150 ml (¼ pint) double or whipping cream

To decorate:
crystallised fruit

1. While the crumb crust is setting, dissolve the gelatine in 45 ml (3 tbsp) of the milk in a small heatproof basin over a pan of hot water.
2. Whisk together the egg yolks, milk, salt and 40 g (1½ oz) of the sugar in a small saucepan and stir in the dissolved gelatine. Heat gently, stirring constantly, until the mixture has thickened. Remove from the heat and stir in the rum and the lemon rind until evenly blended.
3. Cover and chill the mixture, stirring occasionally, until it mounds when dropped from a spoon.
4. Whisk the egg whites stiffly, then gradually whisk in the remaining sugar until thick and glossy. Fold the egg whites into the chilled custard with the crystallised fruit. Spoon into the crumb crust; chill for 1–2 hours until set.
5. Just before serving, lightly whip the cream and use to decorate the filling. Cut the crystallised fruit into slivers and arrange on top.

Chocolate and Rum-layered Flan

Colour index page 89

8 servings

23-cm (9-in) baked ginger crumb crust, page 345
15 ml (1 level tbsp) powdered gelatine
45 ml (3 tbsp) water
3 eggs, separated
300 ml (½ pint) milk
10 ml (2 level tsp) cornflour

100 g (4 oz) caster sugar
40 g (1½ oz) plain chocolate
5 ml (1 tsp) vanilla essence
15 ml (1 tbsp) white rum
whipped cream
grated chocolate

1. While the crumb crust is cooling, dissolve the gelatine in the water in a small heatproof basin over a pan of hot water.
2. Whisk together the egg yolks, milk, cornflour and half the sugar in a small saucepan and stir in the dissolved gelatine. Heat gently, stirring occasionally, until thickened. Remove from the heat; pour equal quantities into two separate bowls.
3. Break the chocolate into small pieces and melt in a small heatproof basin over a pan of hot water. Cool slightly, then stir into half the custard mixture with the vanilla essence, beating until smooth. Cover and chill until the custard mounds slightly when dropped from a spoon.
4. Spoon the chocolate custard into the crumb crust and chill for 1–2 hours until set. Meanwhile, whisk the egg whites stiffly, then gradually whisk in the remaining sugar until thick and glossy. Fold the egg whites and rum gently into the chilled plain custard and spoon it over the chocolate layer to fill the crumb crust. Chill until set.
5. Decorate with the cream and chocolate.

Cherry and Kirsch Flan

Colour index page 88

8 servings

almond pastry, page 356 or pâte sucrée made with 200 g (7 oz) plain flour, page 345
15 ml (1 level tbsp) powdered gelatine
60 ml (4 tbsp) kirsch
3 egg yolks
100 g (4 oz) caster sugar
300 ml (½ pint) single cream
150 ml (¼ pint) milk
100 ml (4 fl oz) double or whipping cream, whipped
450 g (1 lb) cherries

1 Roll out the almond pastry or pâte sucrée and use it to line a 25.5-cm (10-in) fluted flan tin with a removable base. Bake blind at 200°C (400°F) mark 6 for about 10–15 minutes, then remove the paper and the beans and bake the pastry for a further 5–10 minutes. Cool the pastry in the tin on a wire rack while you make the filling.

2 Dissolve the gelatine in kirsch in a small basin over a pan of hot water. Whisk together the egg yolks, sugar, single cream and milk; heat gently, stirring until thickened.

3 Whisk a little of the hot custard into the dissolved gelatine until evenly blended.

4 Whisk the gelatine mixture into the custard, then remove the saucepan from the heat and continue whisking the custard for a further 1–2 minutes.

5 Leave the custard to cool. Cover and chill the custard, stirring frequently, until it mounds slightly when dropped from a spoon.

6 Gently fold the whipped cream into the chilled custard then pour into the pastry case.

7 Stone the cherries; arrange them on top and chill for 1–2 hours or until set.

Nut pies

Nut-filled pies make unusual desserts served plain, with whipped cream or with ice cream. Serve only small portions as the high protein and fat content of nuts make the pies rich and substantial. Walnuts, peanuts and pecans are the fillings most frequently used.

You can achieve an interesting contrast in texture if you serve a nut crust with a creamy filling or with a fruit filling such as apple or pear. Nut crusts can be substituted for pastry or crumb crusts to vary pie recipes.

Pecan Pie

Colour index
page 86
6–8 servings

shortcrust pastry made with 200 g (7 oz) flour, page 343
3 eggs
15 ml (1 tbsp) milk
175 g (6 oz) demerara sugar

150 g (5 oz) maple or golden syrup
50 g (2 oz) butter, softened
2.5 ml (½ tsp) vanilla essence
175 g (6 oz) shelled pecans or walnuts, halved

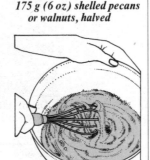

1 Roll out the pastry and use it to line a 23-cm (9-in) pie dish; flute the edge.

2 Whisk together the eggs and milk. Dissolve the sugar in the syrup then boil for 3 minutes.

3 Stir in the butter and vanilla essence. Slowly whisk the syrup mixture into the eggs and milk.

4 Arrange the halved nuts in the pastry case, covering the bottom of the case completely.

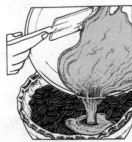

5 Pour in filling. Bake at 220°C (425°F) mark 7 for 10 minutes, then at 170°C (325°F) mark 3.

6 Bake for a further 45 minutes, or until a knife inserted in the filling comes out clean.

Peanut Pie

Colour index
page 88
8 servings

23-cm (9-in) shortcrust pastry case, page 343, baked blind
3 eggs
75 g (3 oz) golden syrup
75 g (3 oz) black treacle
100 g (4 oz) sugar

100 g (4 oz) peanut butter
2.5 ml (½ tsp) vanilla essence
100 g (4 oz) salted peanuts

To serve:
whipped cream

1. While the pastry case is cooling, put the eggs, golden syrup, black treacle, sugar, peanut butter and vanilla essence in a large bowl and beat with a wooden spoon until smooth. Stir in the peanuts.
2. Pour the mixture into the pastry case and bake at 180°C (350°F) mark 4, for 45–60 minutes or until a knife inserted in the filling comes out clean. Leave to cool and serve with whipped cream.

Fudgy Nut Pie

Colour index
page 88
8 servings

23-cm (9-in) shortcrust pastry case, page 343, baked blind
50 g (2 oz) plain chocolate, broken into small pieces
50 g (2 oz) butter
175 g (6 oz) sugar
75 g (3 oz) soft light brown sugar
100 ml (4 fl oz) milk
75 g (3 oz) corn syrup or golden syrup

5 ml (1 tsp) vanilla essence
1.25 ml (¼ level tsp) salt
3 eggs
100 g (4 oz) chopped mixed nuts

To serve:
vanilla, coffee or chocolate ice cream

1. While the pastry case is cooling, melt the chocolate and butter together in a large bowl over hot water. Remove from the heat.
2. Add the remaining ingredients except for the chopped nuts and beat with a wooden spoon until well mixed. Stir in the nuts.
3. Pour the filling into the pastry case and bake at 180°C (350°F) mark 4 for 45–60 minutes or until puffy and golden. Serve with the ice cream.

NUT CRUSTS

HAZEL NUT PASTRY: Sift *200 g (7 oz) plain flour* and rub in *90 g (3½ oz) butter*. Stir in *50 g (2 oz) caster sugar* and *50 g (2 oz) ground hazel nuts*. Bind with *3 beaten egg yolks* and a little *cold water*. Press firmly over the base and sides of a 23-cm (9-in) pie dish. Bake blind at 190°C (375°F) mark 5 until golden.

ALMOND PASTRY: Sift *175 g (6 oz) plain flour* and rub in *100 g (4 oz) butter* or margarine. Stir in *90 g (6 level tbsp) caster sugar* and *45 ml (3 level tbsp) ground almonds*. Bind with *1 egg yolk* beaten with *15 ml (1 tbsp) water*. Roll out, shape as required and bake at 200°C (400°F) mark 6 until golden or as the recipe directs.

GROUND NUT CRUST: Mix *175 g (6 oz) finely ground shelled Brazil nuts*, walnuts, almonds or peanuts with *45 ml (3 tbsp) sugar* and *25 g (1 oz) butter*, softened. Press firmly over the base and sides of a 23-cm (9-in) pie dish and bake at 200°C (400°F) mark 6 for about 8 minutes until golden.

Small tarts

Fruit Cream Tarts

Colour index
page 87

Makes
12 tarts

*12 pâte sucrée tart cases,
page 345, baked blind
50 g (2 oz) caster sugar
45 ml (3 level tbsp)
cornflour
1.25 ml (¼ level tsp) salt
225 ml (8 fl oz) milk
1 egg
5 ml (1 tsp) vanilla essence
225 ml (8 fl oz) double or
whipping cream,
whipped*

*cherries, raspberries, whole
or halved strawberries,
peach slices, apricot
halves, mandarin
orange sections*

For the glaze, optional:
*300–350 g (10–12 oz)
redcurrant jelly
15 ml (1 tbsp) water*

1 While the tart cases are cooling, mix the sugar with the cornflour, salt and milk in a saucepan. Bring slowly to the boil and boil for 1 minute, stirring constantly.

2 Beat the egg lightly with a fork, then stir in a little of the hot sauce.

3 Slowly pour the egg mixture into the sauce, stirring briskly. Reheat gently, stirring, until mixture has thickened; do not boil.

4 Cover the surface of the custard with waxed or damp greaseproof paper; chill. When cold, stir in the vanilla essence, then gently fold in the whipped cream.

5 Spoon the filling into the tart cases; top with prepared fruit. If you wish, melt the jelly with the water, cool slightly; spoon over the fruit to glaze. Chill thoroughly.

Walnut Tarts

Colour index
page 87

pâte sucrée ... *essence*
(7 ... ...ed
 ...oughly
 ...ped
 ...pped cream*

... the pâte sucrée and use it to line 12 deep ...ases. Place them on a baking sheet.
2. Put the eggs in a bowl with the remaining ingredients except for the walnuts and cream and mix well.
3. Spread walnuts in cases; pour in syrup mixture. Bake at 180°C (350°F) mark 4 for 25–30 minutes. Cool in tins for 10 minutes, then remove from tins and cool on a wire rack. Serve with whipped cream.

Mince Tarts

Colour index
page 89

Makes 12 tarts

*175 g (6 oz) shelled walnuts
500 g (1 lb 2 oz) spicy
mincemeat, page 470, or
454-g (1-lb) jar
mincemeat
2 large cooking apples,
cored, peeled and diced
75 g (3 oz) soft light brown
sugar*

*60 ml (4 tbsp) brandy,
optional
15 ml (1 tbsp) lemon juice
shortcrust pastry, made
with 200 g (7 oz) flour,
page 343
brandy butter, page 375*

1. Roughly chop the walnuts. Mix with the mincemeat, apples, sugar, brandy and lemon juice. Cover and leave to stand in a cool place overnight.
2. Roll out the pastry and use it to line 12 deep tart cases. Place them on a baking sheet.
3. Divide the mincemeat between the tart cases and bake at 220°C (425°F) mark 7 for 15–20 minutes until golden. Serve hot or cold with brandy butter.

MINCE PIES: Prepare the filling as above. Roll out pastry until 0.3 cm (⅛ in) thick; cut out 15 rounds with a 7.5-cm (3-in) fluted cutter and 15 rounds with a 5.5-cm (2¼-in) fluted cutter. Line 6.5-cm (2½-in) patty tins with large rounds; fill with mincemeat. Damp edges of small rounds; place on top. Make a slit in each one; bake at 220°C (425°F) mark 7 for 15–20 minutes. Serve hot or cold, dusted with *sugar*.

Peach Meringue Tarts

Colour index
page 89

Makes 12
tarts

*900 g (2 lb) ripe peaches,
peeled and stoned
15 ml (1 level tbsp)
cornflour
30 ml (2 tbsp) lemon juice
2.5 ml (½ tsp) almond
essence*

*100 g (4 oz) sugar
pâte sucrée made with 200 g
(7 oz) flour, page 345*

For the topping:
*2 egg whites
25 g (1 oz) caster sugar*

1. Slice the peaches and toss with the cornflour, lemon juice, almond essence and sugar. Leave to stand for 20 minutes. Roll out the pastry; use it to line 12 tart cases. Place them on a baking sheet.
2. Spoon the peach mixture into the cases. Bake them at 190°C (375°F) mark 5 for 35–40 minutes.
3. Make a meringue topping (page 351) with the egg whites and sugar. Spoon some meringue on to each cooked tart; bake for 4 minutes more.

DESSERTS

When your guests leave the table, their final impression of the meal may well depend on the dessert, so always plan it carefully to balance with the other dishes. If the main course you serve is rich and filling, choose a light, refreshing dessert, but if it is comparatively light, round off the meal with a more substantial pudding.

COOKING EGG CUSTARDS

Care is needed when you are cooking dishes that contain whole eggs, as they may curdle or go lumpy if cooked too quickly or over too high a temperature. For the very best results use a double saucepan, or choose an ordinary saucepan with a small heatproof basin that fits snugly into it, and make sure that the base of the upper pan or basin does not touch the water below. If you do cook over direct heat, always use a heavy-based saucepan. Stir the custard constantly and watch it carefully as it thickens.

Testing consistency: The custard is cooked when it is thick enough to coat the back of the spoon thoroughly.

USING GELATINE

Many dessert recipes use gelatine for thickening and this requires careful handling. Never sprinkle powdered gelatine directly into hot liquid as it is likely to go lumpy and give the finished dish a stringy texture. Instead, spoon a small quantity of the cold liquid into a heatproof basin and wedge the basin over a saucepan containing about 1 cm (½ in) hot water, being careful that the bottom does not touch the water. Place the pan over low

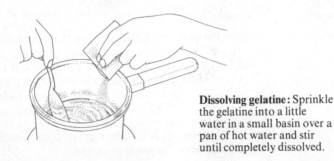

Dissolving gelatine: Sprinkle the gelatine into a little water in a small basin over a pan of hot water and stir until completely dissolved.

heat, add the gelatine to the basin and stir until it has completely dissolved and the liquid has become clear. Remove the basin from the saucepan and leave the gelatine to cool while you prepare remaining ingredients. The dissolved gelatine should then blend evenly into a liquid at the same temperature. In some recipes using a large quantity of liquid it is possible to sprinkle the gelatine directly on to the full quantity of cold liquid and heat them gently together, stirring until the gelatine is dissolved.

Sometimes it is necessary to chill liquid containing gelatine until it is just beginning to set before mixing it with flavouring ingredients, whipped cream or whisked egg whites; this ensures even mixing. To test that the consistency is right, lift a spoonful of the gelatine liquid and allow it to drop back into the basin; it should form a small mound that does not quickly blend back into the bulk of the mixture.

To speed up the setting of a gelatine mixture, place it for a short time in a bowl containing ice cubes, or in the freezer or frozen food compartment of the refrigerator, just until it begins to stiffen. After final mixing, leave the dessert to set at normal refrigerator temperature; leaving it for too long at too low a temperature may lead to the formation of ice crystals, which will collapse when the dessert returns to room temperature.

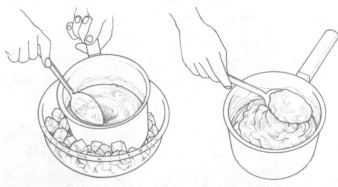

Chilling gelatine: Place the pan or basin of gelatine mixture in a bowl of ice to speed up the setting.

Testing consistency: The gelatine mixture should form a mound when dropped from a spoon.

FREEZING DESSERTS

Pastries and meringues freeze well, but are best filled after thawing. Gelatine desserts can be frozen as long as you allow them to set completely before putting them in the freezer. Do not attempt to freeze custard or cream desserts as these will separate when thawed.

Custards

Egg custard dishes are delicious and simple to prepare if you follow the recipe directions and avoid overheating. Cook baked egg dishes in a bain marie or water bath, and use a double saucepan for dishes cooked on top of the stove to prevent the eggs curdling.

Crème Brûlée with Fresh Fruit

Colour index page 97
4–6 servings

300 ml (½ pint) double cream
300 ml (½ pint) single cream
1 vanilla pod
75–90 ml (5–6 level tbsp) caster sugar
4 egg yolks

To serve:
sliced strawberries, bananas, pineapple chunks and mandarin orange sections

1 Heat the creams very gently with the vanilla pod to scalding point. Remove the pod.

2 In another pan, whisk 15 ml (1 level tbsp) sugar with the egg yolks. Whisk in the hot cream.

3 Heat very gently until the mixture thickens enough to coat the back of the spoon, stirring all the time; do not boil. Strain the custard.

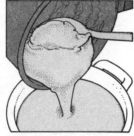

4 Pour it into a flame-proof dish in a shallow tin with hot water halfway up sides. Bake at 150°C (300°F) mark 2 for 15–20 minutes. Chill.

5 Sift the remaining sugar evenly over the top and place under a hot grill until it caramelises. Chill again for 2–3 hours or overnight.

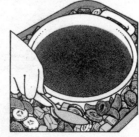

6 Place the dish of crème brûlée in the centre of a large tray and surround with the prepared fruit. Serve the crème brûlée with the fruit.

Crème Caramel

Colour index page 96
6 servings

125 g (4½ oz) sugar
150 ml (¼ pint) water
4 eggs
568 ml (1 pint) milk
2.5 ml (½ tsp) vanilla essence

1 Dissolve 100 g (4 oz) sugar in the water in a small pan, stirring all the time. Boil without stirring until it caramelises.

2 Meanwhile, place six heated 150-ml (¼-pint) custard cups or dariole moulds in a shallow tin. Quickly pour the caramel into the cups or moulds.

3 Lightly whisk the eggs and remaining sugar. Warm the milk and vanilla and pour on to the egg mixture, whisking well. Strain the custard.

4 Divide between cups; add hot water to tin to come halfway up sides. Bake at 170°C (325°F) mark 3 for 45 minutes, until a knife inserted in custard comes out clean.

5 Leave in the custard cups overnight or until quite cold, then gently turn the crème caramels out on to individual plates or dishes before serving.

Egg Custard Sauce

Colour index page 96
Makes 300 ml (½ pint)

300 ml (½ pint) milk
few strips thinly pared lemon rind or ½ vanilla pod, split

1½ eggs or 3 egg yolks
15 ml (1 level tbsp) sugar

1. Warm the milk with the lemon rind to just below boiling point and leave to infuse for 10 minutes.
2. Whisk the eggs and sugar lightly in a bowl. Pour the milk on to the egg mixture, stirring all the time, and strain into the top of a double saucepan.
3. Cook gently without boiling, stirring constantly until the sauce thickens and coats the spoon.

Custards

Colour index
page 95
8 servings

Apricot Cream Flan

100 g (4 oz) plain flour
75 g (3 oz) shelled walnuts,
finely ground
1.25 ml (¼ level tsp)
ground cinnamon
1.25 ml (¼ level tsp) salt
75 g (3 oz) butter or
margarine
45 ml (3 level tbsp) sugar
2 egg yolks, beaten

50 g (2 oz) sugar
1.25 ml (¼ level tsp) salt
6 egg yolks
3.75 ml (¾ tsp) almond
essence
454-g (16-oz) can apricot
halves, drained, or 7
large apricots, washed,
halved and stoned
60 ml (4 tbsp) apricot jam,
melted

For the filling:
400 ml (¾ pint) milk
25 g (1 oz) cornflour

1. Make the crust. Mix the flour, ground walnuts, cinnamon and salt together and cut or rub in the fat with your fingertips until the mixture resembles fine breadcrumbs. Mix in the sugar and add the beaten egg yolks, stirring until the ingredients begin to stick together, then kneading lightly with your hands to give a smooth, soft dough.
2. Press the mixture into a 25.5-cm (10-in) fluted flan tin or spring-release cake tin, pressing it over the base and 2.5 cm (1 in) up the sides of the tin with your fingers. Prick the base with a fork and bake at 200°C (400°F) mark 6 for 20 minutes or until golden brown. Cool in the tin.
3. Meanwhile, make the filling. Mix 60 ml (4 tbsp) milk with the cornflour, sugar and salt in a basin and stir until smooth. Bring the remaining milk to the boil, pour it on to the cornflour mixture, stirring, then return it to the saucepan. Cook gently for about 5 minutes or until the mixture thickens and boils, stirring all the time. Remove the pan from the heat.
4. Beat the egg yolks in a large bowl and stir in a little of the thickened milk mixture. Return this to the bulk of the mixture in the pan, stirring all the time to prevent lumps forming.
5. Cook gently, stirring all the time, until the custard thickens and coats the back of a spoon. Stir in the almond essence; remove the pan from the heat, cover and chill for about 30 minutes or until cool but not completely set.
6. Pour the custard into the cooled crust and chill for about 4 hours or until set. To serve, remove the sides of the tin, loosen the flan from the base and slide it on to a serving plate. Arrange the apricot halves over the custard filling and brush with melted apricot jam.

Colour index
page 97
4 servings

Zabaglione

6 egg yolks, beaten
50 g (2 oz) caster sugar
75 ml (5 tbsp) Marsala

To serve, optional:
macaroons or sponge
fingers

1. Place the beaten egg yolks, caster sugar and Marsala in a deep basin or top of a double saucepan over a pan of hot but not boiling water.
2. Whisk continuously, with a whisk or electric mixer, until the mixture becomes thick and creamy, then pour into small glasses or dessert dishes.
3. Serve the zabaglione immediately, with macaroons or sponge fingers, if you wish.

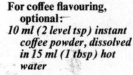

Colour index
page 95
6–8 servings

Bavarois

400 ml (¾ pint) milk
1 vanilla pod
3 size 2 eggs, separated
75 g (3 oz) caster
sugar
22.5 ml (1½ level tbsp)
powdered gelatine
75 ml (5 tbsp) water
175 ml (6 fl oz) double
cream, lightly whipped

**For chocolate flavouring,
optional:**
75 g (3 oz) plain chocolate
or chocolate dots, melted

**For coffee flavouring,
optional:**
10 ml (2 level tsp) instant
coffee powder, dissolved
in 15 ml (1 tbsp) hot
water

To serve:
mixed fruit, sliced

1 In a heavy-based saucepan heat the milk and vanilla pod very gently just to boiling point. Meanwhile, whisk together the egg yolks and the sugar until pale and fluffy. Remove the vanilla pod from the milk. Ladle about one third of the warm milk on to the whisked yolks, stirring and scraping down the sides of the bowl with a spatula until well blended.

2 Blend the egg mixture with the remaining milk in the saucepan and stir over gentle heat until the egg custard is thick enough to coat the back of the spoon thoroughly.

3 Dissolve the gelatine in the water in a small heatproof basin over a pan of hot water and cool; stir a little of the custard into the gelatine.

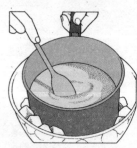

4 Stir blended gelatine and flavouring into the custard. Place in a bowl of ice cubes and stir until starting to thicken. Whisk the egg whites stiffly.

5 Blend the whipped cream into the custard; gently fold in the whisked egg whites with a wire whisk or metal spoon.

6 Pour into a lightly oiled 1.5-litre (2½-pint) mould and chill until set. Unmould on to a plate and serve with the fruit.

Cold soufflés and mousses

Soufflés and mousses, lightened with whisked egg whites, set with gelatine and flavoured with fruit or chocolate, are some of the most popular desserts. To achieve the characteristic height of a soufflé, support the mixture as it sets with a foil or paper collar wrapped around the dish (below right). Always use a straight sided dish to give the maximum effect.

A rich cream mousse like pots de crème is served in traditionally shaped china cups. Make it in one flavour only, the most popular being chocolate, or offer a variety of flavours such as vanilla, coffee or mocha for a special buffet.

Strawberry Soufflé

350 g (12 oz) strawberries, washed and hulled
30 ml (2 level tbsp) powdered gelatine
60 ml (4 level tbsp) caster sugar
20 ml (4 tsp) lemon juice
3 egg whites
pinch salt
200 ml (7 fl oz) double or whipping cream

1 Reserve six strawberries for decoration. Purée the remainder in a blender or by rubbing them through a nylon sieve.

Colour index page 94
4–6 servings

2 Put the gelatine and 15 ml (1 level tbsp) sugar in a small saucepan, stir in about one third of the purée and stir over very gentle heat until the gelatine has dissolved.

3 Remove from the heat, stir in the remaining purée and the lemon juice and pour into a bowl. Chill until the mixture mounds slightly when dropped from a spoon.

4 Prepare a foil or paper collar for a 600-ml (1-pint) soufflé dish (right) and place the dish on a baking sheet for easier handling. In a large bowl, whisk the egg whites and the salt together with a whisk or electric mixer until soft peaks form. Add the remaining caster sugar a little at a time, whisking well after each addition until the sugar has completely dissolved and stiff peaks form.

5 Beat the chilled strawberry mixture in a mixer or with a rotary whisk until fluffy. Whip the cream until stiff peaks form.

6 Add the strawberry mixture and whipped cream to the stiffly whisked egg whites and fold them in carefully.

7 Spoon the soufflé mixture into the prepared dish and smooth the top. Chill for about 4 hours until completely set.

8 Carefully peel off the collar from the soufflé dish. Decorate the top of the soufflé with the reserved strawberries.

Colour index page 96
4 servings

Chocolate and Cherry Soufflé

425-g (15-oz) can black cherries, drained and stoned
45 ml (3 tbsp) kirsch
2 eggs, separated
225 ml (8 fl oz) milk
75 g (3 oz) sugar
50 g (2 oz) plain chocolate, grated

15 ml (1 level tbsp) powdered gelatine
175 ml (6 fl oz) double cream

To decorate:
30 ml (2 tbsp) double cream, whipped

1. Prepare a foil or paper collar for a 600-ml (1-pint) soufflé dish (below) and place the dish on a baking sheet for easier handling.
2. Reserve three whole cherries for decoration and cut the remainder in half. Place the halved cherries in a bowl with half the kirsch, stir well and leave to soak while you make the soufflé mixture.
3. Put the egg yolks, milk and 50 g (2 oz) of the sugar in a heavy-based saucepan and whisk together until well mixed. Add the chocolate, then sprinkle the gelatine over the top. Cook gently for about 15 minutes, stirring all the time, until the gelatine has completely dissolved, the chocolate has melted and the mixture coats the back of the spoon. Stir in the remaining kirsch, then cover the saucepan and chill the mixture until it mounds slightly when dropped from a spoon.
4. Whisk the egg whites stiffly, then add the remaining sugar a little at a time, whisking well after each addition until the sugar has dissolved. Whip the cream until soft peaks form.
5. Gently fold the chocolate mixture, egg whites and cherry halves into the cream with a large metal spoon or wire whisk until they are evenly mixed. Turn the mixture into the prepared dish and chill for about 4 hours or until set.
6. Just before serving, remove the foil or paper collar and decorate the soufflé with whipped cream and the reserved cherries.

MAKING A COLLAR

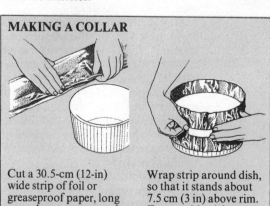

Cut a 30.5-cm (12-in) wide strip of foil or greaseproof paper, long enough to wrap around the soufflé dish with a 5-cm (2-in) overlap. Fold the foil or paper strip in half lengthways.

Wrap strip around dish, so that it stands about 7.5 cm (3 in) above rim. Fasten with sticky tape or string. To remove, run a heated knife round soufflé between layers of foil. Peel off foil.

Cold soufflés and mousses

Lime Soufflé Milanaise

Colour index
page 97

4–6 servings

grated rind of 3 limes
90 ml (6 tbsp) lime juice
100 g (4 oz) caster sugar
4 eggs, separated
few drops green food
　colouring, optional
15 ml (1 level tbsp)
　powdered gelatine
45 ml (3 tbsp) cold water

175 ml (6 fl oz) double
　cream

To decorate:
grated lime rind

1. Prepare a foil or paper collar for a 900-ml (1½-pint) soufflé dish (page 361) and place the dish on a baking sheet for easier handling.
2. Put the lime rind into a deep heatproof bowl with the lime juice, sugar and egg yolks. Place the bowl over a saucepan of hot but not boiling water and whisk for about 10 minutes, until the mixture is pale and will coat the back of a spoon. Remove from the heat, add the food colouring if you wish and whisk until cool.
3. Dissolve the gelatine in the water in a small heatproof basin over a pan of hot water; cool.
4. Stir a little of the soufflé mixture into the gelatine, then whisk this into the bulk of the mixture. Chill until the mixture mounds slightly when dropped from a spoon.
5. Whip the cream until soft peaks form; whisk the egg whites until they are stiff. Fold the cream into the lime mixture, then fold in the egg whites. Turn into the prepared dish and chill for 4 hours until set.
6. Just before serving, remove the collar. Decorate the soufflé with a little lime rind.

Cranberry Soufflé

Colour index
page 98

6–8 servings

350 g (12 oz) cranberries
300 ml (½ pint) water
juice of 1 orange
350 g (12 oz) caster sugar
20 g (¾ oz) powdered
　gelatine
4 egg whites
1.25 ml (¼ level tsp) salt

225 ml (8 fl oz) double
　cream

To decorate:
15 cranberries
1 egg white
sugar

1. Prepare a foil or paper collar for a 1.1-litre (2-pint) soufflé dish (page 361) and place the dish on a baking sheet for easier handling.
2. If you are using frozen cranberries, thaw and drain them well. Put the cranberries, water, orange juice and 225 g (8 oz) of the sugar in a large saucepan and cook for about 10 minutes until tender. Sprinkle with the gelatine and cook for a further 7 minutes. Chill for about 25–30 minutes until the mixture mounds when dropped from a spoon.
3. Whisk the egg whites and salt until soft peaks form. Add the remaining sugar a little at a time, whisking well until stiff peaks form. Whip the cream until soft peaks form.
4. Gently fold the egg whites and cream into the chilled cranberry mixture until evenly blended. Turn into the prepared dish and chill for about 4 hours.
5. Meanwhile, dip the cranberries for decoration into the egg white, coat them in sugar and leave to dry on a wire rack. Before serving, remove the collar and decorate with the sugared cranberries.

Pots de Crème

Colour index
page 94

6 servings

400 ml (¾ pint) single
　cream
100 g (4 oz) plain chocolate
6 egg yolks, beaten
50 g (2 oz) sugar
2.5 ml (½ level tsp) salt
10 ml (2 tsp) vanilla essence

For mocha flavouring,
optional:
15 ml (1 level tbsp) instant
　coffee powder, dissolved
　in 10 ml (2 tsp) hot
　water

To decorate:
50 ml (2 fl oz) double
　cream
30 ml (2 level tbsp) icing
　sugar
1.25 ml (¼ tsp) vanilla
　essence

1 In a small saucepan, heat the cream gently until bubbles begin to form round the edge of the pan; do not allow the cream to boil. Remove the saucepan from the heat. Break the chocolate into small pieces and place in the top of a double saucepan or a small basin over a pan of hot water. Melt the chocolate, stirring constantly, until it is completely smooth. Remove the saucepan from the heat and cool slightly, stirring occasionally.

2 When the chocolate has cooled, beat in the egg yolks until the mixture is smooth, using a rubber spatula or wooden spoon. Stir in the sugar and salt until completely dissolved.

3 Gradually stir the cream into the chocolate mixture until well blended. Replace the double saucepan or basin over hot water.

4 Cook for 5 minutes more or until the mixture coats the back of the spoon, stirring all the time. Stir in the vanilla essence, or dissolved coffee for a mocha flavouring.

5 Pour the mixture into six pots de crème cups, individual dessert glasses or deep dishes and chill for 4 hours or until the mixture is just set.

6 Whip the cream with the icing sugar and vanilla essence until soft peaks form; spoon a little on to each pot de crème just before serving them.

Hot soufflés

A hot soufflé will rise without the help of a foil or paper collar but take care to choose the right size of soufflé dish for the amount of mixture used; the dish should be about two-thirds full before baking. A cooked soufflé collapses quickly after it is removed from the oven, so prepare the soufflé dish and make the basic sauce in advance, but for perfect results whisk the egg whites and fold them in only just before the soufflé goes into the oven. Once cooked, the oven can be switched off and the soufflé left to stand in it for a maximum of 10 minutes before serving.

Hot Chocolate Soufflé

60 ml (4 level tbsp) plain
* flour*
350 ml (12 fl oz) milk
100 g (4 oz) sugar
75 g (3 oz) plain chocolate,
* grated*
5 eggs, separated
1.25 ml (¼ level tsp) salt
10 ml (2 tsp) vanilla
* essence*

1 Put the flour and milk in a large saucepan, add 50 g (2 oz) sugar and blend well.

2 Cook over medium heat stirring constantly until the mixture has thickened and started to boil; cook for a further minute. Remove from heat and stir in the chocolate.

Colour index page 95
6–8 servings

3 Cool the chocolate mixture slightly; beat egg yolks and add all at once. Beat well until smooth, then leave to cool until lukewarm, stirring from time to time.

4 Butter a 1.8-litre (3-pint) soufflé dish and lightly sprinkle it with a little extra sugar.

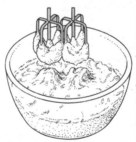

5 Put the egg whites and salt in a large bowl and whisk until soft peaks form.

6 Gradually whisk in the remaining 50 g (2 oz) sugar, whisking well after each addition until the sugar has completely dissolved and the egg whites form stiff peaks.

7 Gradually and gently fold the cooled chocolate mixture and the vanilla essence into the beaten egg whites, using a wire whisk or metal spoon, until evenly mixed.

8 Turn into the soufflé dish and make a crown with the back of a spoon. Bake at 190°C (375°F) mark 5 for 35–40 minutes until well risen and firm. Serve at once.

Colour index page 95
6 servings

Individual Chocolate Soufflés

75–100 g (3–4 oz)
* chocolate chips*
30 ml (2 tbsp) water
400 ml (¾ pint) milk
50 g (2 oz) caster
* sugar*
60 ml (4 level tbsp) plain
* flour*
knob of butter

3 egg yolks, beaten
4 egg whites

To serve:
icing sugar, optional
whipped cream

1. Butter six 300-ml (½-pint) individual soufflé dishes or ramekins.
2. Put the chocolate chips and the water in a small heatproof basin. Place the basin over a pan of hot water and heat, stirring, until the chocolate is completely melted and smooth.
3. Heat all but 45 ml (3 tbsp) milk with the sugar until the sugar has dissolved and pour it on to the melted chocolate, stirring well. Blend the reserved milk with the flour to make a smooth paste and stir in the chocolate mixture.
4. Return the mixture to the saucepan, bring it to the boil and cook for a further 2 minutes, stirring all the time. Stir in the butter a little at a time, then remove the saucepan from the heat and leave the mixture to cool until lukewarm.
5. Beat in the egg yolks all at once. Whisk the egg whites until stiff peaks form and fold them into the mixture until evenly mixed.
6. Turn the mixture into the soufflé dishes and bake at 180°C (350°F) mark 4 for about 45 minutes, until well risen and firm to the touch. Dust with a little icing sugar, if you wish, and serve at once with the whipped cream.

COOKING WITH CHOCOLATE

To melt chocolate: Break it into small pieces and place them in the top of a double saucepan over hot, but not boiling, water, or in a heatproof basin wedged over a pan of hot water. Alternatively, put the chocolate in an ovenproof bowl and leave in a cool oven until just melted. If you do melt chocolate over direct heat use a heavy-based saucepan and stir constantly with a wooden spoon to prevent the chocolate burning.

To thin melted chocolate: If the melted chocolate thickens or curdles because it has become too hot, add a little blended white vegetable fat (do not use butter or margarine). Break the fat into small pieces and stir into the mixture until it reaches the desired consistency.

To substitute cocoa for chocolate: If you run out of plain chocolate, use 45 ml (3 level tbsp) cocoa powder and 15 ml (1 level tbsp) softened blended white vegetable fat or vegetable oil (do not use butter or margarine) for every 25 g (1 oz) of chocolate used in the recipe.

Hot soufflés

Orange Liqueur Soufflé

Colour index
page 97

6 servings

50 g (2 oz) butter
40 g (1½ oz) plain flour
pinch salt
350 ml (12 fl oz) milk
40 g (1½ oz) sugar
4 egg yolks, beaten
15 ml (1 tbsp) grated
orange rind

75 ml (5 tbsp) curaçao
4 egg whites
1.25 ml (¼ level tsp) cream
of tartar

To serve:
whipped cream

1. Butter a 2.5-litre (4½-pint) soufflé dish and sprinkle with a little extra sugar.
2. Melt the butter in a large saucepan. Stir in the flour and salt until well blended and gradually add the milk. Cook, stirring constantly, until the sauce thickens, then remove from the heat and leave to cool slightly.
3. Stir the sugar into the sauce, then stir a small amount of the hot sauce into the egg yolks. Mix well, then pour back into the bulk of the sauce. Stir in the orange rind and curaçao.
4. Whisk together the egg whites and cream of tartar until stiff peaks form and fold them into the sauce until evenly mixed.
5. Turn the mixture into the soufflé dish and make a crown about 2.5 cm (1 in) from the edge of the dish with the back of a spoon. Bake at 190°C (375°F) mark 5 for about 35 minutes or until well risen and firm to the touch. Serve the soufflé at once with the whipped cream.

Banana Soufflé

Colour index
page 95

4 servings

3 large bananas
15 ml (1 tbsp) lemon juice
65 g (2½ oz) sugar
15 ml (1 level tbsp)
cornflour
2.5 ml (½ level tsp) ground
nutmeg
1.25 ml (¼ tsp) grated
lemon rind
pinch salt

175 ml (6 fl oz) milk
3 eggs, separated
30 ml (2 tbsp) melted
butter
7.5 ml (1½ tsp) vanilla
essence

To serve:
whipped cream

1. Butter a 1.5-litre (2½-pint) soufflé dish and sprinkle with a little extra sugar.
2. Peel and slice the bananas. Mash them with lemon juice or purée together in a blender until creamy.
3. Mix the sugar, cornflour, nutmeg, lemon rind and salt in a small bowl and stir in a little cold milk until well blended. Heat the rest of the milk and pour it on to the cornflour mixture, stirring. Return the sauce to the saucepan and cook over gentle heat until thickened, stirring constantly. Remove the saucepan from the heat.
4. Beat the egg yolks well. Stir in a little of the hot sauce, mix well, then pour the yolk mixture back into the bulk of the sauce, stirring rapidly to prevent lumping. Stir in the butter, vanilla essence and the puréed bananas.
5. Whisk the egg whites until stiff peaks form. Fold them into the banana mixture until evenly mixed.
6. Turn the mixture into the soufflé dish and bake at 170°C (325°F) mark 3 for 50–60 minutes or until well risen and golden. Serve the soufflé at once with the whipped cream.

Meringues

A meringue is a light, sugary confection that may form either the base or the topping for a dessert. For the fluffiest meringues, use a balloon whisk or a hand-held rotary whisk: an electric mixer works faster and produces a closer-textured meringue.

Meringue Nests

Makes 6 nests

3 large (size 2) egg whites
75 g (3 oz) granulated
sugar and 75 g (3 oz)
caster sugar or 175 g
(6 oz) caster sugar

To serve:
whipped cream or ice cream

1. Grease a baking sheet or line it with kitchen foil or non-stick paper.
2. Whisk the egg whites very stiffly with a balloon or rotary whisk. Gradually add 75 g (3 oz) granulated or caster sugar, whisking well after each addition until stiff peaks form.
3. Fold in the remaining sugar very lightly with a metal spoon. Spoon the meringue into six mounds, spaced well apart on the prepared baking sheet, hollowing out the centres with the back of a spoon.
4. Dry out the meringues in the oven at 130°C (250°F) mark ¼ for about 2½–3 hours, until they are firm and crisp, but still white. If they begin to brown, prop the oven door open a little. Remove from the baking sheet and cool on a wire rack. Serve filled with whipped cream or ice cream.

Shaping the meringue:
Spoon six heaps on to the prepared baking sheet.

Making the nests:
Hollow out the centres with the back of a spoon.

MAKING A MERINGUE BASKET

Prepare the meringue mixture as for meringue nests above, then shape it into a basket as described and shown below. Bake as for meringue nests.

Grease a 23-cm (9-in) pie dish and spoon in the meringue.

Pile meringue high round sides of dish to make basket.

Walnut Chiffon Pie

3 egg whites
pinch salt
225 g (8 oz) caster sugar
5 ml (1 tsp) vanilla
* essence*
50 g (2 oz) shelled walnuts,
* chopped*
50 g (2 oz) biscuit
* crumbs*
5 ml (1 level tsp) baking
* powder*

For the filling:
225 ml (8 fl oz) double
* cream*
25 g (1 oz) caster sugar
5 ml (1 tsp) vanilla
* essence*

To serve:
1 small pineapple

1. Grease a 23-cm (9-in) flan tin and line it with greased foil or non-stick paper.
2. Whisk the egg whites with the salt until soft peaks form. Add the sugar a little at a time, whisking well after each addition until stiff peaks form. Fold in the vanilla essence with the nuts, biscuit crumbs and baking powder.
3. Spread the walnut chiffon mixture evenly in the prepared tin and bake at 180°C (350°F) mark 4 for 35 minutes, or until light golden. Leave to cool in the tin for 2 hours.
4. Remove the pie from the tin, using the foil to lift it out, and chill for at least 1 hour. Remove the foil and place the pie on a serving dish.
5. Whip the cream stiffly with the sugar and vanilla essence and spoon it over the chilled pie.
6. Cut the pineapple into thick slices, trim off the rough outer skin, cut out the eyes and remove the central core. Cut the fruit into cubes. Arrange on the filling or serve separately.

Strawberry Meringues

550 g (1¼ lb) strawberries,
* washed and hulled*
65 g (2½ oz) caster sugar
6 meringue nests, left

900 ml (1½ pints) vanilla
* ice cream*

1. Thinly slice the strawberries into a bowl, stir in the sugar and chill.
2. Just before serving, top each meringue nest with a scoop of ice cream and spoon on some strawberries and juice.

Chocolate Meringue Flan

50 g (2 oz) plain chocolate,
* grated*
45 ml (3 tbsp) water
3 egg yolks, beaten
50 g (2 oz) sugar
pinch salt

300 ml (½ pint) double
* cream*
5 ml (1 tsp) vanilla
* essence*
1 meringue basket,
* left*

1. Place the chocolate, water, egg yolks, sugar and salt in the top of a double saucepan over hot, but not boiling water, or in a heavy-based saucepan over low heat. Cook for about 5 minutes, stirring all the time, until the chocolate melts and the mixture is very thick and coats the back of the spoon. Remove from the heat and chill.
2. Just before serving, whip the cream with the vanilla essence until soft peaks form and carefully fold in the chocolate mixture. Spoon into the meringue basket and smooth over the top.

Floating Islands

1 egg white
75 ml (5 level tbsp) sugar

For the custard:
5 egg yolks, beaten
400 ml (¾ pint) milk
1.25 ml (¼ level tsp) salt
175 g (6 oz) sugar
2.5 ml (½ tsp) vanilla
* essence*

1 First prepare the custard. Put the beaten egg yolks, milk, salt and sugar in the top of a double saucepan over hot water, or in a heavy-based saucepan over low heat. Cook gently for about 15 minutes, stirring constantly, until the mixture thickens and coats the back of the spoon. Stir in the vanilla essence.

2 Divide the custard between four stemmed glasses or dessert dishes. Cover and chill for 1 hour.

3 Meanwhile, whisk the egg white in a mixer or with a rotary whisk until stiff peaks form. Add 30 ml (2 level tbsp) sugar and whisk again until the sugar is dissolved.

4 Put some cold water into a shallow tin and spoon on the meringue in four even mounds. Bake at 180°C (350°F) mark 4 for 7–10 minutes until just set and lightly browned.

5 Remove the meringues with a slotted spoon, drain for a minute on kitchen paper towel and spoon on to the custards.

6 Put the remaining sugar into a heavy-based saucepan and cook, stirring constantly, for about 3 minutes or until it forms a golden syrup.

7 Remove from the heat and leave for 2 minutes to cool slightly, then drizzle a little of the warm syrup over the top of each meringue

Choux pastries

Cream puffs and éclairs are universal favourites but there are many other more unusual and decorative desserts you can also make with the same choux pastry.

Cream Puffs

Colour index
page 95

Makes
8–10 puffs

For the choux paste:
50 g (2 oz) butter
about 150 ml (¼ pint)
water
65 g (2½ oz) plain flour,
sifted
2 size 2 eggs, beaten

To serve:
300 ml (½ pint)
confectioners' custard,
right, or double cream,
whipped
icing sugar or melted
plain chocolate

1 Put the butter and water in a saucepan, heat gently to melt the butter and bring to the boil. Remove from the heat.

2 Quickly tip in all the flour and beat to a smooth paste with a wooden spoon until it forms a ball in the centre of the pan. Leave for 1–2 minutes to cool slightly.

3 Add the beaten eggs a little at a time, beating vigorously until there is a sheen on the paste.

4 Spoon the paste into eight or ten large mounds 7.5 cm (3 in) apart on two dampened baking sheets, lifting the top of each one into a peak.

5 Bake at 200°C (400°F) mark 6 for 45–50 minutes. Split the puffs in half horizontally with a sharp knife to release the steam and leave to cool completely on a wire rack.

6 When the puffs are cold, fill them with the confectioners' custard or whipped cream and dust with sifted icing sugar or dip the tops in melted plain chocolate.

FILLINGS AND GLAZES

CONFECTIONERS' CUSTARD: Cream *2 egg yolks* with *50 g (2 oz) caster sugar* until really thick and pale in colour. Beat in *30 ml (2 level tbsp) plain flour*, *30 ml (2 level tbsp) cornflour* and a little cold milk taken from *300 ml (½ pint) milk* to make a smooth paste. Heat the remaining milk until almost boiling and pour on to the egg mixture, stirring all the time. Return the mixture to the saucepan, stir over a low heat until the mixture boils and remove from the heat. Whisk *1 egg white* stiffly and fold it into the custard. Return to the heat again, add *vanilla essence* to taste and cook for a further 2–3 minutes. Cool before using. Makes 400 ml (¾ pint).

CHOCOLATE SATIN ICING: Put *50 g (2 oz) chocolate* and *25 g (1 oz) butter* in a heavy-based saucepan and heat gently until the chocolate melts, stirring all the time. Stir in *125 g (4½ oz) icing sugar* and *45 ml (3 tbsp) milk* until the icing is smooth. Makes 225 ml (8 fl oz).

Chocolate Eclairs

Colour index
page 97

Makes about
12 éclairs

choux paste, made with 65 g (2½ oz) flour, left
150 ml (¼ pint) confectioners' custard, above or 150 ml (¼ pint) double cream, whipped

chocolate satin icing, above, or melted chocolate

1. Drop the paste in tablespoonfuls on a dampened baking sheet and shape into neat rectangles with a palette knife. Alternatively, put the choux paste into a piping bag fitted with a plain round 1-cm (½-in) nozzle. Pipe 9-cm (3½-in) fingers on to the baking sheet, keeping the lengths very even, and cut off the paste with a wet knife against the edge of the nozzle.
2. Bake at 200°C (400°F) mark 6 for about 35 minutes, until well risen, crisp and golden brown. Remove the éclairs from the baking sheet, slit each one down one side to allow the steam to escape and cool on a wire rack.
3. When the éclairs are cold, cut a lid from each one and fill the base with confectioners' custard or whipped cream. Replace the lids and spread chocolate satin icing over the éclairs, or dip the lids in melted chocolate.

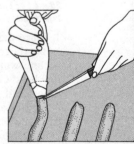

Shaping the éclairs: Spread the paste into rectangles with a small palette knife.

Or, pipe the paste into fingers, cutting off each length with a wet knife.

Cream Puff Ring

Colour index
page 94

6–8 servings

*choux paste made with
65 g (2½ oz) flour, left
confectioners' custard,
opposite
chocolate satin icing,
opposite
350 g (12 oz) strawberries,
washed and hulled*

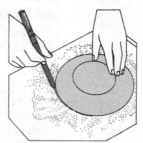

1 Put an 18-cm (7-in)
plate on a greased and
lightly floured baking
sheet; trace a circle around
it with a knife. Or draw the
circle on greaseproof paper
on a baking sheet.

2 Drop heaped table-
spoons of the choux
paste just inside the circle
to form a ring and bake at
200°C (400°F) mark 6 for
40 minutes or until golden
brown and crisp. Cool.

3 When the choux pastry
is cold, split the ring
horizontally with a large
sharp knife.

4 Use a spoon to scrape
out any soft uncooked
paste inside the ring to
leave a hollow shell.

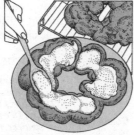

5 Fill the base of the ring
with the confectioners'
custard. Replace the top
half of the ring.

6 Spread the chocolate
satin icing evenly over
the ring with a spatula.
Leave the icing to set.

7 Just before serving,
spoon the strawberries
into the centre of the
custard-filled ring.

Swan Eclairs

Colour index
page 95

Makes
12 swans

*choux paste made with 65 g
(2½ oz) flour, left*

For the filling:
*15 ml (1 level tbsp)
  powdered gelatine
100 g (4 oz) sugar*

*15 g (½ oz) plain flour
4 egg yolks
225 ml (8 fl oz) milk
5 ml (1 tsp) vanilla essence
225 ml (8 fl oz) double
  cream*

1. Put some of the choux paste into a small piping
bag fitted with a plain round 0.3-cm (⅛-in) nozzle.
Pipe twelve 5-cm (2-in) gently curved question
mark shapes on to a greased baking sheet to make
the swans' necks, with a small blob at the beginning of each one for the head.

2. Put remaining paste into a piping bag fitted with
a plain round 1-cm (½-in) nozzle and pipe twelve
4 × 2.5 cm (1½ × 1 in) teardrop shapes 2.5 cm (1
in) apart to make the bodies.

3. Bake the necks at 190°C (375°F) mark 5 for 10
minutes and the bodies at same temperature for
30–35 minutes until golden. Cool on a wire rack.

4. Mix together the gelatine, sugar and flour in a
large saucepan. Beat the egg yolks and milk well
and stir into the gelatine mixture. Cook the mixture gently without boiling for 10 minutes, stirring
all the time until it is very thick and coats the back
of a spoon well. Remove from the heat and stir in
the vanilla essence. Cover and chill for about 45
minutes, until cold but not set. Whip the cream
and fold it into the custard.

5. Cut lids from the swans' bodies. Put the filling
into a piping bag fitted with a large star nozzle and
pipe some into each body. Cut the lids in half
lengthways and push gently into the filling to form
wings; place the necks in position in the same way.

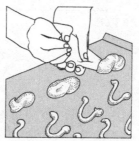

Piping choux paste: Pipe
slender curved shapes to
form the necks and teardrop
shapes for the bodies.

Adding filling: Cut out
lids from the swans' bodies
and pipe some of the filling into each one.

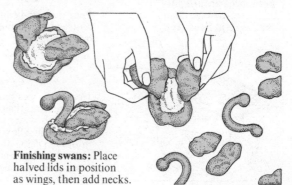

Finishing swans: Place
halved lids in position
as wings, then add necks.

Sweet pancakes

Opposite page
Ice cream sundaes (page 377)

Crêpes Suzette

For the pancakes:
175 g (6 oz) plain flour
pinch salt
grated rind of 1 lemon
2 eggs
400 ml (¾ pint) milk
25 g (1 oz) butter,
  melted
butter for frying

For the sauce:
5–6 sugar lumps
3 large oranges
100 g (4 oz) butter
75 g (3 oz) caster sugar
30 ml (2 tbsp) orange juice
30 ml (2 tbsp) curaçao
60 ml (4 tbsp) brandy

Colour index
page 94

6 servings

1. Make the pancake batter (page 147), but add half the melted butter with the milk. Melt a knob of butter in a heavy-based 18-cm (7-in) frying pan and make 12 pancakes. Stack the cooked pancakes on a plate as you make them, with a sheet of grease-proof paper between each one. Cover and keep the pancakes warm.
2. Make the sauce. Rub the sugar lumps over the oranges to extract the zest from the rind. Crush the lumps in a bowl and add the butter and the caster sugar. Beat together until soft and creamy. Work in the orange juice and curacao.
3. Heat the orange butter gently in a heavy-based saucepan. Pour half into a heated chafing dish or heatproof serving dish and keep it hot over a spirit burner or gentle heat.
4. Fold a pancake into quarters and place in the dish; spoon plenty of sauce over it then move it to one side of the dish. Repeat with the remaining pancakes and sauce, making sure that they are well soaked with the sauce and arranging them in the dish as you make them.
5. Measure the brandy into a small jug, heat the base with a lighted match and pour the warmed brandy into centre of dish. Ignite and serve immediately.

SERVING CREPES SUZETTE

Fold each pancake into quarters. Arrange them in the chafing dish. Heat gently.

Pour the brandy into the centre of the chafing dish but do not stir.

Heat the crêpes gently for a few minutes then ignite the brandy with a taper or long match. Allow the brandy to flame, then serve the crêpes and the brandy sauce immediately.

Pancakes with Soured Cream and Orange Sauce

100 g (4 oz) plain flour
10 ml (2 level tsp) icing
  sugar
pinch salt
1 egg
400 ml (¾ pint) milk
knob of butter, melted
butter for frying

For the sauce:
50 g (2 oz) butter
190 g (6½ oz) icing
  sugar

75 ml (5 tbsp) orange
  juice
30 ml (2 tbsp) grated
  orange rind

To serve:
225 ml (8 fl oz) soured
  cream
2 oranges, peeled and
  chopped

Colour index
page 94

6 servings

1. Sift the flour, icing sugar and salt into a large bowl. Make a well in the centre and break in the egg. Add half the liquid and gradually work in the flour, beating well. Add the remaining milk and the melted butter, beat until the batter is smooth.
2. Melt a knob of butter in a frying pan, tilting the pan so that the melted butter coats the base and sides. Pour in enough batter to cover the base of the pan and cook for about 3 minutes until golden underneath. Toss or turn the pancake and cook the second side until golden. Repeat with the remaining batter to make 12 pancakes in all, brushing the pan with more butter as necessary. Stack the cooked pancakes on a plate as you make them, with a sheet of greaseproof paper between each one. Cover and keep warm.
3. To make the sauce, melt the butter in a saucepan, add the icing sugar, orange juice and rind and cook gently, stirring frequently, until the sauce is smooth and hot.
4. Spread a little soured cream over each of the pancakes, roll them up and arrange on a heated serving dish. Spoon the sauce over them and arrange the chopped orange on top.

Strawberry Blintzes

12 pancakes, page 147,
  kept hot
25 g (1 oz) butter
275 g (10 oz)
  strawberries, washed
  and hulled

For the filling:
225 g (8 oz) cottage cheese
75 g (3 oz) cream cheese
50 g (2 oz) caster sugar
2.5 ml (½ tsp) vanilla
  essence

Colour index
page 98

6 servings

1. Put the cottage cheese, cream cheese, caster sugar and vanilla essence in a bowl and beat well with a wooden spoon until smooth.
2. Spoon 15 ml (1 tbsp) filling on to each pancake, then fold in the sides and roll up.
3. Melt the butter in an ovenproof dish. Arrange the blintzes in it in a single layer and bake at 180°C (350°F) mark 4 for 10 minutes or until they are heated through.
4. Arrange the strawberries over the top and serve.

CHERRY BLINTZES: Prepare as above, but omit the strawberries. Prepare *cherry sauce* (page 464) or brandied cherry sauce (page 305), pour it into a shallow flameproof pan or dish and add the filled pancakes. Simmer over a low heat for 10 minutes or until the blintzes are heated through.

Party desserts

Opposite page

Clockwise from top: Strawberries Romanoff (page 305); Individual Strawberry Shortcakes (page 369); strawberries with sugar and cream; Fruit Cream Tarts (page 357)

Strawberry Shortcake

Colour index page 97

8 servings

225 g (8 oz) self raising flour
5 ml (1 level tsp) baking powder
1.25 ml (¼ level tsp) salt
75 g (3 oz) butter or margarine
75 g (3 oz) sugar
1 egg, beaten

15–30 ml (1–2 tbsp) milk, optional

For the filling:
450 g (1 lb) strawberries
60 ml (4 level tbsp) caster sugar
150 ml (¼ pint) double or whipping cream

1. Grease a 20.5-cm (8-in) sandwich tin. Sift together the flour, baking powder and salt and rub in the fat. Stir in the sugar and add the egg a little at a time, stirring until the mixture begins to stick together, and using a little milk if necessary. Knead lightly.
2. Turn the dough on to a floured board, form it into a round and roll out to a 20.5-cm (8-in) circle. Press it evenly into the prepared tin and bake at 190°C (375°F) mark 5 for 20 minutes, or until golden and firm. Turn on to a wire rack and cool.
3. Make the filling. Wash and hull the strawberries and drain them well. Reserve a few whole berries for decoration and crush the rest with a fork in a basin, sprinkling them with 30–45 ml (2–3 level tbsp) of the sugar. Whip the cream with the remaining sugar.
4. When the shortcake is nearly cold, split it in half and spread with half the crushed strawberries. Replace the top, spread the remaining crushed berries over it and top with the whipped cream. Decorate with the reserved whole strawberries.

Splitting the shortcake: Cut the cooled cake in half horizontally with a long sharp knife.

Adding the strawberries: Spoon the crushed strawberries on to the top and spread over the cake.

INDIVIDUAL STRAWBERRY SHORTCAKES:
Prepare the dough as above, but divide it into eight equal portions, roll out to small circles, and bake for only 12 minutes. Finish as above.

Everlasting Syllabub

Colour index page 94

4 servings

grated rind and juice of 1 lemon
75 g (3 oz) caster sugar
15–30 ml (1–2 tbsp) brandy
30 ml (2 tbsp) sweet sherry

300 ml (½ pint) double cream

To serve:
grated lemon rind
sponge fingers, optional

1. Soak the lemon rind in the juice for 2–3 hours, then stir in the sugar, brandy and sherry.
2. Whip the cream and mix in the lemon mixture. Spoon into chilled glasses and sprinkle with lemon rind. Serve with sponge fingers if you wish.

Summer Sponge Gâteau

Colour index page 94

12 servings

4 eggs, separated
1.25 ml (¼ level tsp) cream of tartar
175 g (6 oz) caster sugar
100 g (4 oz) plain flour
7.5 ml (1½ level tsp) baking powder
2.5 ml (½ tsp) vanilla essence
75 ml (5 tbsp) water
60 ml (4 tbsp) vegetable oil

For the filling:
275 g (10 oz) strawberries or raspberries
300 ml (½ pint) double cream, whipped

1. Whisk the egg whites and cream of tartar until soft peaks form, then add 50 g (2 oz) of the sugar a little at a time, whisking well after each addition until the sugar has completely dissolved and stiff peaks form.
2. Sift the flour and baking powder into a large bowl and stir in the remaining sugar. Make a well in the centre, add the egg yolks, vanilla essence, water and oil and beat with a wooden spoon until well blended. Fold in the egg whites.
3. Pour the mixture into a 23-cm (9-in) ring or savarin tin and bake at 170°C (325°F) mark 3 for 1 hour until golden. Leave the sponge to cool in the tin, then turn it out and halve it horizontally.
4. Meanwhile, prepare the fruit. If you are using strawberries, wash, hull and drain them and cut them in half lengthways. If you are using raspberries, pick over them carefully.
5. Spread the bottom layer of the cake with half the whipped cream, spoon on one third of the fruit and replace the top cake layer. Spread the remaining cream over; decorate with the remaining fruit.

YOGURT DESSERTS

Natural and flavoured yogurts are useful for making quick, delicious desserts. Fold in whisked egg whites or whipped cream and set the dessert with gelatine, if you wish.

Add clear honey to natural yogurt or sprinkle whole fresh berries or other fresh fruit over the top.

Layer coffee-flavoured yogurt with chopped nuts or biscuit crumbs and serve topped with chocolate sauce (page 464).

Place layers of plain or sweetened yogurt and fresh or canned fruit in sundae glasses or stemmed dessert dishes and reserve a piece of fruit for the top.

Party desserts

Colour index page 95
8 servings

Chocolate Cups with Strawberry Cream

175 g (6 oz) plain chocolate
15 g (½ oz) lard

For the filling:
225 g (8 oz) strawberries

150 ml (¼ pint) double cream
25 g (1 oz) icing sugar

1. Break half the chocolate into small pieces and put them in the top of a double saucepan over hot but not boiling water, or in a large heavy-based saucepan over low heat. Heat the chocolate with half the lard for about 5 minutes or until they have melted and are completely smooth, stirring occasionally to blend well.
2. Put out eight paper cases. Holding one case at an angle, drizzle some chocolate into it, a teaspoonful at a time, until the whole of the inside is thinly coated. Repeat with the remaining cases. Chill for about 30 minutes, until set. Repeat with the remaining chocolate and lard until all the cases have a thick, smooth coating.
3. Remove one paper case at a time from the refrigerator and gently but quickly peel off the paper, leaving a chocolate cup. Stand the cups on a chilled serving plate and put them back into the refrigerator until they are required.
4. To make the filling, wash and hull the strawberries and pat them dry with kitchen paper towel. Using a small sharp knife, slice them thinly and reserve about 16 slices for decoration.
5. Whip the cream and icing sugar until stiff peaks form and gently fold in the strawberries. Divide the mixture between the chocolate cups and decorate with the reserved strawberry slices.

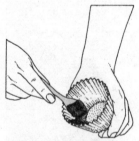
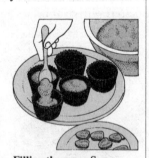

Making the cups: Tilt a paper case; drizzle some chocolate over the inside until it is thinly coated.

Filling the cups: Spoon in the strawberry cream; decorate with the reserved sliced strawberries.

CHOCOLATE CUPS WITH ORANGE CREAM:
Prepare as above, but use *100 ml (4 fl oz) cream*. Fold *50 ml (2 fl oz) confectioners' custard* (page 366) and *30 ml (2 tbsp) curaçao* into the whipped cream mixture. Spoon into cups and sprinkle with *cocoa*.

CHOCOLATE CUPS WITH COCOA CREAM:
Prepare as above, but omit the strawberries and add *25 g (1 oz) cocoa powder* to the cream. If you wish, decorate the tops with *small chocolates*.

Apple Strudel

For the pastry:
225 g (8 oz) strong white flour
2.5 ml (½ level tsp) salt
1 egg, lightly beaten
30 ml (2 tbsp) oil
1.25 ml (¼ level tsp) lemon juice
90 ml (6 tbsp) lukewarm water
25 g (1 oz) butter, melted

For the filling:
450 g (1 lb) cooking apples, peeled, cored and thinly sliced

75 g (3 oz) raisins
50 g (2 oz) shelled walnuts, chopped
65 g (2½ oz) caster sugar
2.5 ml (½ level tsp) ground cinnamon
1.25 ml (¼ level tsp) ground nutmeg
100 g (4 oz) dry white breadcrumbs
50 g (2 oz) butter

To serve: *whipped cream*

Colour index page 94

8 servings

1 To make the pastry, mix together flour and salt in a large bowl. Make a well in the centre and pour in egg, oil, and lemon juice. Gradually add water to make a soft, sticky dough. Knead the dough in bowl until it leaves sides clean. Turn on to a lightly floured surface and knead for 15 minutes until smooth. Return dough to bowl, cover with a damp tea towel and leave to rest for 30 minutes.

2 To make the filling, mix together the first six ingredients with half the breadcrumbs. Grease a 38 × 25-cm (15 × 11-in) Swiss roll tin.

3 Place the dough on a floured teacloth and roll out to a rectangle 0.3-cm (⅛-in) thick, lifting to prevent sticking. Brush with butter.

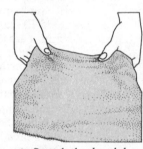

4 Stretch the dough by carefully lifting it on to the palms of hand and fingertips and pulling it out from the centre to the edge.

5 Lift and stretch the dough until it is paper thin and measures a minimum of 50 × 30 cm (20 × 16 in). Trim the with scissors.

6 Brush pastry with half the melted butter. Sprinkle with the reserved breadcrumbs.

7 Spoon the apple mixture on to the pastry leaving a 7.5-cm (3-in) border on three sides, placing the filling to the edge of one long side.

8 Fold over borders and roll up lengthways from the filled edge. Place seam down in the tin.

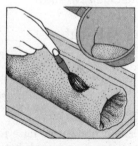

9 Brush with remaining melted butter. Bake at 190°C (375°F) mark 5 for 40 minutes until golden.

10 Cool in the tin for about 30 minutes. Cut into slices and serve with cream.

Colour index
page 96

Makes
20 pieces

Baklava

225 g (8 oz) shelled
  walnuts, ground
50 g (2 oz) soft brown sugar
2.5 ml (½ level tsp)
  ground cinnamon

450-g (1-lb) bought phyllo
  or strudel pastry
150 g (5 oz) butter
175 g (6 oz) clear honey

1. Grease a 24 × 18-cm (9½ × 7½-in) roasting tin. Mix the walnuts, sugar and cinnamon together.
2. Halve each sheet of pastry to measure 25 × 25 cm (10 × 10 in). Fit one sheet of pastry into the bottom of the tin, allowing it to come up the sides and brush with melted butter. Repeat with five more pastry sheets. Sprinkle with 50 g (2 oz) of walnut mixture.
3. Fit one sheet over the walnut mixture and brush with a little melted butter. Repeat with five more pastry sheets. Sprinkle with another 50 g (2 oz) of the walnut mixture.
4. Repeat layering of pastry and walnuts three more times producing five pastry and walnut layers. Top with remaining pastry and trim all the sheets to fit the tin. Mark the surface into 20 squares with a sharp knife.
5. Bake at 220°C (425°F) mark 7 for 15 minutes, then at 180°C (350°F) mark 4 for 10–15 minutes, until golden brown. Meanwhile warm the honey in a saucepan over a low heat, spoon over the cooked baklava, and cool. Cut out the marked squares.

PUFF PASTRY VARIATION: Replace the phyllo pastry with **386-g (13-oz) packet bought puff pastry.** Cut into six equal pieces and roll out very thinly to a 24 × 18-cm (9½ × 7½-in) rectangle. Layer the pastry with the walnut mixture as above, using only 50 g (2 oz) of melted butter. Bake and finish as above.

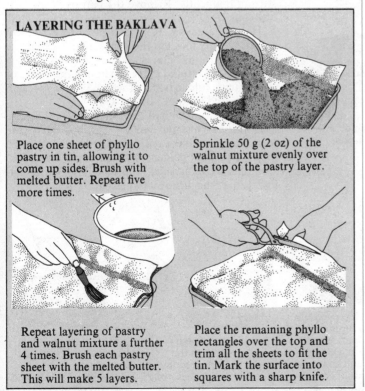

LAYERING THE BAKLAVA

Place one sheet of phyllo pastry in tin, allowing it to come up sides. Brush with melted butter. Repeat five more times.

Sprinkle 50 g (2 oz) of the walnut mixture evenly over the top of the pastry layer.

Repeat layering of pastry and walnut mixture a further 4 times. Brush each pastry sheet with the melted butter. This will make 5 layers.

Place the remaining phyllo rectangles over the top and trim all the sheets to fit the tin. Mark the surface into squares with a sharp knife.

Colour index
page 96

Makes
20 pieces

Galatoboureko

450 ml (¾ pint) milk
200 ml (7 fl oz) double
  cream
65 g (2½ oz) cornflour
50 g (2 oz) caster sugar
3 egg yolks
5 ml (1 tsp) vanilla
  essence

225 g (8 oz) bought
  phyllo or strudel pastry
25 g (1 oz) butter, melted
For the syrup:
175 g (6 oz) caster sugar
75 ml (5 tbsp) water
15 ml (1 tbsp) lemon
  juice

1. Grease a 24 × 18-cm (9½ × 7½-in) roasting tin. Bring the milk and cream to the boil. Mix the cornflour with a little water to make a smooth paste. Stir in the sugar and gradually add to the milk mixture, stirring all the time. Bring to the boil, then reduce the heat and cook for 5–10 minutes, or until the mixture thickens, stirring constantly. Remove from the heat.
2. Beat the egg yolks and vanilla essence together and gradually beat into the cornflour mixture. Cover the mixture and leave until cold.
3. Cut each sheet of pastry in half to measure 25 × 25 cm (10 × 10 in). Fit one sheet of the pastry in the bottom of the tin, allowing it to come slightly up the sides, and brush with a little melted butter. Repeat with seven more sheets, and pour the cooled custard over the top.
4. Fit another pastry sheet over the custard, and brush with a little melted butter. Repeat with the remaining pastry and butter. Mark the top into 20 squares with a sharp knife.
5. Bake at 190°C (375°F) mark 5 for 35 minutes or until golden brown and puffy. Meanwhile, make the syrup. Heat the sugar and water, stirring occasionally, until the sugar is dissolved. Bring to the boil, reduce the heat and simmer for 8 minutes, until syrupy. Stir in the lemon juice.
6. Pour the hot lemon syrup over the cooked galatoboureko, and leave to cool in the tin for at least 30 minutes, then place in the refrigerator.
7. Before serving, chill thoroughly, then cut along the marked lines through the pastry base.

PUFF PASTRY VARIATION: Replace the phyllo pastry with **386-g (13-oz) packet bought puff pastry.** Halve the pastry and roll out each piece to measure 24 × 18 cm (9½ × 7½ in). Fit one piece into the base of the tin, cover with custard, and top with other half of pastry.

Cutting the pastry: Cut each sheet of pastry in half to measure 25 × 25 cm (10 × 10 in).

Dividing the dessert: Cut through the top pastry layers to mark into squares before baking.

Party desserts

Sherry Trifle

raspberry or strawberry
 jam
150 ml (¼ pint) medium
 sherry
6 macaroons, crushed
400 ml (¾ pint) egg
 custard sauce,
 page 359
300 ml (½ pint) double
 cream, whipped

For the sponge:
2 eggs
50 g (2 oz) caster
 sugar
75 g (3 oz) plain flour

To decorate:
glacé cherries
toasted slivered almonds
angelica, optional
crystallised violets,
 optional

Colour index page 97
4–6 servings

1 Make the sponge. Grease a 20.5-cm (8-in) sandwich tin and dust it with flour and caster sugar. Put the eggs and sugar in a large heatproof bowl, stand it over a pan of hot water and whisk until light and creamy; the mixture should be stiff enough to hold the impression of the whisk for a few seconds. Remove the bowl from the pan of hot water and continue whisking until cold. Sift the flour on to a sheet of greaseproof paper.

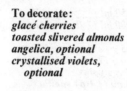

Colour index page 98
Makes 8 turnovers

Apple Turnovers

200 g (7 oz) plain flour
pinch salt
150 g (5 oz) butter
about 105 ml (7 tbsp)
 cold water
squeeze lemon juice

15 ml (1 level tbsp)
 cornflour
5 ml (1 tsp) lemon juice
1.25 ml (¼ level tsp)
 ground cinnamon

For the filling:
2 cooking apples, peeled
 cored and sliced
100 g (4 oz) sugar

To glaze:
1 egg
30 ml (2 tbsp) water
50 g (2 oz) icing sugar

1. Mix together the flour and salt. Soften the butter by working it with a knife on a plate and divide it into four equal portions. Rub a quarter of the butter into the flour and mix to a soft, elastic dough with the water and lemon juice.
2. Roll out the pastry on a lightly floured surface to a rectangle three times as long as it is wide. Dab another quarter of the fat in small pieces over the top two thirds of the pastry; fold the unbuttered third of the pastry down and the buttered third over it. Give the pastry a quarter turn so that the folds are at the side and seal the edges by pressing firmly with a floured rolling pin.
3. Repeat the rolling, buttering and folding twice. Wrap the pastry loosely in greaseproof paper and chill for about 30 minutes.
4. Meanwhile, put the apples, sugar, cornflour, lemon juice and ground cinnamon in a saucepan and cook over low heat until the apples are tender, stirring frequently. Remove the pan from the heat and chill.
5. Halve the pastry. Roll each piece to a 30.5-cm (12-in) square, then cut them into quarters to make eight 15-cm (6-in) squares.
6. Place a spoonful of apple mixture in the centre of each square, fold in half and seal the edges. Place on an ungreased baking sheet and chill.
7. Beat the egg with half the water. Brush the glaze over the turnovers and make two or three cuts in the top of each one. Bake at 230°C (450°F) mark 8 for 20 minutes or until golden, then cool on a wire rack. Combine the icing sugar and remaining water and drizzle over the turnovers when cold.

2 Sprinkle the flour over the whisked egg mixture and fold it in gently.

3 Pour the mixture into the tin, spread it evenly to the edges and bake at 190°C (375°F) mark 5 for 20–25 minutes.

4 When the sponge is cooked, the top should spring back when lightly pressed with a finger. Remove from the tin and cool on a wire rack.

5 Cut the sponge horizontally in half and spread the cut surface of the bottom half with jam; reassemble the halves.

6 Cut the sponge into small pieces and arrange in a shallow glass serving dish.

7 Pour over the sherry and leave to soak for 30 minutes. Sprinkle with the crushed macaroons.

8 Make the egg custard sauce and leave for a few minutes to cool slightly. Stir occasionally during the cooling to prevent a skin forming on the top of the custard.

9 Pour the warm custard over the sponge pieces, then cover the glass dish tightly with cling film to prevent a skin forming. Chill for about 2 hours or until quite cold.

10 Spoon the cream into a piping bag fitted with a rosette nozzle and pipe over custard. Decorate with cherries and almonds, adding angelica or crystallised violets, if you wish.

Adding butter to pastry: Using a quarter of the butter, dot it in portions over the top two thirds of the pastry rectangle.

Folding the pastry: Fold the unbuttered third of the pastry to the centre and fold the opposite end down over that.

Colour index
page 96

10–12 servings

Chocolate and Cinnamon Torte

350 g (12 oz) butter or
  margarine
450 g (1 lb) caster sugar
2 eggs, beaten
300 g (11 oz) plain flour
30 ml (2 level tbsp)
  ground cinnamon

900 ml (1½ pints) double
  cream
75 g (3 oz) cocoa powder
75 g (3 oz) plain
  chocolate

1. Cut out fourteen 23-cm (9-in) circles of grease-proof paper. Place one on each of two dampened baking sheets.
2. Cream the butter or margarine and sugar together until light and fluffy and beat in the eggs, one at a time, beating well after each addition. Sift together the flour and cinnamon and gradually stir into the creamed mixture to make a soft dough.
3. Spread a scant 75 ml (5 tbsp) dough in a thin layer on each circle of greaseproof paper and bake at 190°C (375°F) mark 5 for 8–12 minutes, until lightly browned around the edges. Leave the biscuit rounds to cool on the baking sheets for 5 minutes, then carefully transfer them to a wire rack until they are completely cold. Do not remove the greaseproof paper backing.
4. Repeat with the remaining dough to make a total of 14 biscuit rounds, allowing the baking sheets to cool between use and stacking the cooled rounds carefully on a flat plate. If you wish, the biscuit rounds may be stored at this stage. They will stay crisp for 2–3 days if placed in an airtight container.
5. To make the filling, whip the cream with the cocoa powder until soft peaks form, then coarsely grate the plain chocolate.
6. Assemble the torte 30 minutes before serving. Carefully peel the paper from one biscuit round, place it on a flat serving plate and spread 100 ml (4 fl oz) of the cocoa cream over it. Top with another biscuit round. Repeat with the remaining biscuits and cocoa cream, finishing with the cream. Pile the grated chocolate on the top.

CHOCOLATE AND GINGER TORTE: Make the biscuit rounds as above using *30 ml (2 level tbsp) ground ginger* in place of the cinnamon. Omit the cocoa powder and whip the cream with *30 ml (2 level tbsp) sifted icing sugar* and *60 ml (4 tbsp) brandy* to layer between the biscuit rounds. Finish with grated chocolate as above.

Spreading the dough:
Spread the dough very thinly on the circles of greaseproof paper on the baking sheets.

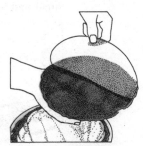

Adding biscuit rounds:
Peel back the greaseproof paper as you place the biscuit rounds over the cocoa cream on the torte.

DECORATIONS AND SAUCES FOR COLD DESSERTS

Chocolate leaves: Melt some cooking chocolate and spread it thinly over a sheet of waxed paper. When firm but not brittle, cut out leaf shapes using a leaf as a guide.

Leave them to harden. Pull the paper down over the edge of a table and ease the chocolate leaves off one at a time. Use them to decorate soufflés, mousses and meringues.

Candied peel: Cut the peel (page 311) into slivers and use it to decorate cold soufflés and mousses.

Chopped nuts: Coarsely chop nuts and serve them raw or toasted, sprinkled over cold desserts just before serving.

WHIPPED CREAM ROSETTES AND SHELLS: Whip double cream until it is just stiff enough to hold its shape. Spoon it into a piping bag fitted with a 1-cm (½-in) rosette nozzle, and pipe rosettes or shells on to the dessert.

To freeze whipped cream rosettes or shells, pipe them on to waxed paper on a baking sheet and freeze unwrapped until firm. Transfer to rigid containers, with waxed paper between each layer and seal tightly (they will keep for up to 9 months). To use the frozen decorations, carefully peel off wrapping, arrange decorations on the dessert and leave to thaw in the refrigerator for 1–2 hours before serving.

CREME CHANTILLY: Whip *300 ml (½ pint) double cream* until thick but not too stiff. Fold in a *stiffly whisked egg white, 25 g (1 oz) sifted icing sugar* and a few drops of *vanilla essence*. Makes about 600 ml (1 pint).

COFFEE CREAM SAUCE: Dissolve *10 ml (2 level tsp) instant coffee powder* in *5 ml (1 tsp) hot water*. Cool slightly and put in a small bowl with *150 ml (¼ pint) double cream, 15 ml (1 tbsp) milk, 30 ml (2 level tbsp) caster sugar* and a few drops of *vanilla essence*. Whisk just until the cream begins to hold its shape. Makes about 200 ml (7 fl oz).

ALMOND PRALINE: Heat *50 g (2 oz) caster sugar* in a small saucepan until it turns a deep amber colour. Stir in *50 g (2 oz) chopped, toasted almonds* and pour the mixture on to an oiled baking sheet. When it is completely cold, crush it with a rolling pin. Use as a topping or flavouring for whipped cream, mousses, soufflés, creamy desserts and ice cream desserts. Makes about 100 g (4 oz).

Puddings

English puddings are the traditional way of rounding off a meal on a cold day. Sponge puddings are steamed or boiled in a basin; try the variations below or serve them with hot sauce (page 375). When you want to serve something more substantial, make the traditional suet pastry into a roly-poly.

Jam Sponge Pudding

Colour index page 96

4 servings

100 g (4 oz) butter or
*   margarine*
100 g (4 oz) caster
*   sugar*
2 eggs, beaten
few drops vanilla
*   essence*
175 g (6 oz) self raising
*   flour*
milk to mix
30 ml (2 tbsp) jam

To serve:
egg custard sauce,
*   page 359*

1 Grease a 900-ml (1½-pint) pudding basin. Half fill a steamer or large saucepan with water and bring to the boil.

2 Cream together the fat and sugar until pale and fluffy. Add the beaten eggs and vanilla essence a little at a time, beating well after each addition.

3 Sift half the flour over the beaten mixture, and fold in with a metal spoon. Then fold in the rest, adding just enough milk to give a soft, dropping consistency.

4 Put the jam in the bottom of the pudding basin; spoon the mixture on top. Cover with foil or greased greaseproof paper; secure with string.

5 Put the basin into the boiling water; cover pan; steam 1½ hours. Turn pudding on to heated serving plate. Serve with egg custard sauce.

LEMON SPONGE PUDDING: Prepare the sponge as above, but add the ***grated rind of 1 lemon*** to the creamed mixture and replace the milk with ***lemon juice***. Serve with ***lemon sauce***, opposite.

CASTLE PUDDINGS: Prepare the sponge mixture as left, but divide the sponge mixture between four greased dariole moulds, filling each one only two-thirds full, and steam for only 30–45 minutes. Serve with ***jam sauce,*** right. Colour index page 96

GINGER SPONGE PUDDING: Prepare the sponge mixture as left, but sift ***2.5 ml (½ level tsp)*** ***ground ginger*** with the flour or add 2 pieces preserved ginger, finely chopped, and 10 ml (2 tsp) ginger syrup. Serve with ***syrup sauce***, right.

Apple and Ginger Roly-poly

Colour index page 96

4–6 servings

225 g (8 oz) self raising
*   flour*
2.5 ml (½ level tsp) salt
100 g (4 oz) shredded suet
about 120 ml (8 tbsp) cold
*   water*

For the filling:
450 g (1 lb) cooking
*   apples, peeled and cored*
50 g (2 oz) sultanas

2.5 ml (½ level tsp)
*   ground ginger*
50 g (2 oz) demerara sugar

To serve:
caster sugar
egg custard sauce,
*   page 359*

1. Mix the flour with the salt and suet in a large bowl. Add enough cold water to make a light elastic dough and knead very lightly until smooth. Roll out to a rectangle about 0.5 cm (¼ in) thick.
2. Half fill a steamer or large saucepan with water and bring the water to the boil.
3. Meanwhile, slice the apples evenly, but not too thinly, into a large bowl. Add the sultanas, ginger and demerara sugar and mix well.
4. Spread the apple mixture evenly over the pastry to within 1 cm (½ in) of the edges. Turn in the edges to contain the filling and brush them lightly with water.
5. Roll up the pastry from the longest side like a Swiss roll. Enclose the roll in greased foil, making a tight seam and twisting the ends of the foil to seal well: the foil must prevent the water coming into contact with the pastry.
6. Place the roll in the steamer or place a heatproof plate upside down in the saucepan and lower the roll into the boiling water. Cover and steam for about 1½ hours, adding more boiling water as necessary to keep the roll covered.
7. Lift the roll carefully from the saucepan. Allow it to stand for a minute or two, then remove the foil and put the roll on a hot serving dish. Dredge with sugar and serve with egg custard sauce.

Shaping the roly-poly: Spread the filling evenly over the pastry rectangle and roll up.

Wrapping in foil: Seal the foil tightly to prevent any water from reaching the pastry.

Christmas Pudding with Brandy Butter

350 g (12 oz) fresh white breadcrumbs
350 g (12 oz) plain flour
5 ml (1 level tsp) salt
2.5 ml (½ level tsp) ground mace
2.5 ml (½ level tsp) ground ginger
2.5 ml (½ level tsp) ground nutmeg
2.5 ml (½ level tsp) ground cinnamon
350 g (12 oz) shredded suet
225 g (8 oz) caster sugar
225 g (8 oz) soft brown sugar

175 g (6 oz) mixed candied peel, very finely chopped
275 g (10 oz) currants
225 g (8 oz) sultanas
450 g (1 lb) seedless raisins
175 g (6 oz) almonds, blanched and chopped
225 g (8 oz) apples, peeled, cored and chopped
grated rind and juice of 1 lemon
grated rind and juice of 1 orange
60 ml (4 tbsp) brandy

3 large (size 2) eggs, beaten
150 ml (¼ pint) milk

Brandy butter to serve with each pudding:
75 g (3 oz) butter
75 g (3 oz) caster sugar
90 ml (6 tbsp) brandy

Colour index page 96

Makes 2 puddings

6–8 servings each pudding

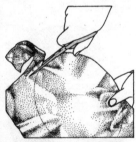  

1 Mix together the dry ingredients. Add the peel, dried fruit, almonds, apples and rinds; mix well.

2 Mix the fruit juices and brandy with the beaten eggs and add them to the bowl.

3 Add enough milk to give a soft dropping consistency. Cover lightly and leave overnight.

4 Grease two 1.1-litre (2-pint) pudding basins. Cut a circle of greaseproof paper and foil for each one, about 2.5 cm (1 in) larger all round than the basin. Grease the paper.

5 Stir the mixture, spoon it into the prepared basins and cover with greaseproof paper and foil; secure with string.

6 Put each basin into a large saucepan half filled with boiling water, cover and steam for 9 hours. Top up with more boiling water from time to time.

7 Remove the pudding basins from the pans; leave to cool. Remove foil, leaving greaseproof paper in place. Cover again with fresh foil, secure with string and store the puddings in a cool place. When a pudding is required, steam it again for 3 hours. Remove foil and greaseproof paper covers and turn the pudding out on to a heated serving dish. Cover with the basin until ready to serve.

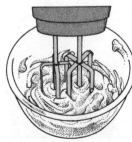 

8 Cream together the butter and sugar. Beat in 45 ml (3 tbsp) brandy a few drops at a time. Leave to harden.

9 Warm the remaining brandy, pour it over the pudding and ignite. When flames subside, serve with the brandy butter.

Hot sauces

Makes about
225 ml
(8 fl oz)

Jam Sauce

60 ml (4 tbsp) jam, sieved
150 ml (¼ pint) juice drained from a can of fruit
10 ml (2 level tsp) arrowroot

30 ml (2 tbsp) cold water
squeeze of lemon juice, optional

1. Warm the jam with the fruit juice and simmer gently for 5 minutes, stirring to blend well. Blend the arrowroot and cold water to a smooth cream and stir in the jam mixture.
2. Return to the pan and heat gently until it thickens and clears, stirring constantly. Add the lemon juice, if using. Serve hot with steamed and baked puddings or cold over ice cream.

THICK JAM SAUCE: Omit the fruit juice and arrowroot. Heat the jam gently in a heavy-based saucepan until just melted and stir in a little *lemon juice*. Makes 100 ml (4 fl oz)

Makes about
350 ml
(12 fl oz)

Lemon Sauce

juice and grated rind of 1 large lemon
15 ml (1 level tbsp) cornflour
30 ml (2 level tbsp) sugar

knob of butter
1 egg yolk, optional

1. Make up the lemon juice to 300 ml (½ pint) with water. Add the lemon rind. Blend a little of the liquid with the cornflour and the sugar until smooth and creamy.
2. Bring the remaining liquid to the boil and stir it into the creamed cornflour. Return all the liquid to the pan and bring to the boil, stirring until the sauce thickens and clears. Add the butter.
3. Cool, beat in the egg yolk if used and reheat without boiling, stirring all the time. Serve hot with steamed and baked puddings and ice creams or cold over ice creams, meringue desserts or cold soufflés.

ORANGE SAUCE: Prepare as above, but use the *juice and rind of an orange* instead of a lemon.

Makes about
150 ml
(¼ pint)

Syrup Sauce

60–75 ml (4–5 level tbsp) golden syrup

45 ml (3 tbsp) water
juice of ½ lemon

1. Put the syrup and water in a saucepan, stir over gentle heat until blended, then simmer for 2–3 minutes. Add the lemon juice.
2. Serve with steamed or baked sponge puddings.

ICE CREAMS AND ICED DESSERTS

Ice creams are not difficult to make at home, and are always popular with the family. You can either buy a special ice cream churn that freezes and beats at the same time or make them in the freezer, taking the mixture out several times while it is freezing to beat out ice crystals; an electric mixer gives the best results.

Small ice cream makers are designed to be plugged into an electric socket and then placed in the frozen food compartment of the refrigerator, with the flex wedged in the door; these make up to about 1 litre (1¾ pints) ice cream fairly simply and quickly. But most people like to keep a stock of ice cream in the freezer ready for quick desserts, and to make a large amount easily you need a churn-type freezer. These larger ice cream makers have a central churn for the ice cream mixture, with an outer container that you fill with ice and rock salt. A dasher, or paddle, fits into the central churn and you can either operate this by hand or attach a small electric motor to work it automatically. These make up to about 2.7 litres (5 pints) ice cream at a time.

Apart from simple ice creams and water ices, you can make delicious party desserts, moulding or shaping ice creams into bombes and gâteaux. They require a little time and attention in the making, but are not technically difficult; use either your own home-made ice creams, or the ready-made varieties. By mixing different textures and flavouring ingredients you can achieve some unusual and attractive effects.

Ice creams

Vanilla Ice Cream

450 g (1 lb) sugar
75 g (3 oz) plain flour
5 ml (1 level tsp) salt
1.6 litres (2¾ pints) milk
6 eggs, beaten
400 ml (¾ pint) single cream
30 ml (2 tbsp) vanilla essence
ice cubes
rock salt

Colour index page 102

Makes 2.7 litres (5 pints) or 12 servings

1 Mix the sugar with the plain flour and the salt in a large saucepan. Mix together 1.1 litres (2 pints) milk and the beaten eggs and beat well, then stir them into the sugar mixture until well blended and smooth. Place the pan over low heat and cook, stirring constantly, for about 30–45 minutes until the custard thickens and coats the back of the spoon. Remove the saucepan from the heat.

2 Cover the surface of the custard with damp greaseproof or waxed paper. Let the saucepan cool; put in the refrigerator and chill for about 2 hours.

3 Pour the remaining milk, the cream and vanilla essence into the ice cream churn and add the chilled custard.

4 Put the dasher in the churn, put on the lid and place the churn in the bucket. Attach the motor or hand crank.

5 Half fill the bucket with ice; sprinkle with 60 ml (4 level tbsp) rock salt. Repeat to just below the churn lid.

6 Freeze according to the manufacturer's instructions, for 35–45 minutes, adding more ice and rock salt as necessary.

7 Remove motor or hand crank, wipe the churn lid; remove lid and dasher. Pack down the ice cream with the back of a spoon.

8 Cover the top of the churn with waxed paper and replace the lid, then put a cork in the hole in the centre.

9 Add more ice and salt to cover the churn lid. Leave for 2–3 hours to harden ice cream, adding ice and salt as necessary.

Ice creams

ICE CREAM VARIATIONS

Colour index
page 102

HOME-FREEZER METHOD: Prepare custard as left, but use *225 g (8 oz) sugar, 45 ml (3 level tbsp) plain flour, 2.5 ml (½ level tsp) salt, 568 ml (1 pint) milk* and *3 eggs,* beaten; cook for 15 minutes; chill. Stir in *400 ml (¾ pint) double cream* or whipping cream and *25 ml (5 tsp) vanilla essence.* Pour into a rigid freezer container, cover and freeze for 3–4 hours. Spoon mixture into a chilled bowl and beat hard until smooth but still frozen. Return to freezer container, cover and freeze until firm. Makes 1.5 litres (2½ pints) or 6 servings

Colour index
page 102

CHOCOLATE ICE CREAM: Prepare custard as left, but use *900 ml (1½ pints) milk.* Melt *225 g (8 oz) plain chocolate* in a small saucepan and stir in *175 g (6 oz) sugar* and *225 ml (8 fl oz) water;* chill. Put the chocolate mixture in the ice cream churn with the custard, *400 ml (¾ pint) milk,* the single cream and vanilla essence. Freeze as left. Makes 2.7 litres (5 pints) or 12 servings

Colour index
page 102

PEACH ICE CREAM: Prepare custard as left. Peel, stone and chop *10–12 ripe peaches,* then purée them in a blender with *100 g (4 oz) sugar.* Stir the peach purée, custard, *225 ml (8 fl oz) milk, 225 ml (8 fl oz) single cream* and *3.75 ml (¾ tsp) almond essence* into the ice cream churn. Freeze as left. Makes 3.1 litres (5½ pints) or 14 servings

Colour index
page 102

STRAWBERRY ICE CREAM: Prepare as for vanilla ice cream, left. Crush *450 g (1 lb) strawberries,* washed and hulled, and add *225 g (8 oz) sugar* and *30 ml (2 tbsp) lemon juice;* leave for 1 hour. Stir the custard, remaining milk, single cream, hulled strawberries and *1.25 ml (¼ tsp) red food colouring* into the ice cream churn. Freeze as left. Makes 3.6 litres (6½ pints) or 16 servings

Colour index
page 102

PISTACHIO ICE CREAM: Prepare custard as left, but use *225 g (8 oz) sugar, 45 ml (3 level tbsp) flour, 2.5 ml (½ level tsp) salt, 568 ml (1 pint) milk* and *3 eggs,* beaten; cook for 15 minutes; chill. In step 3, use only *225 ml (8 fl oz) milk* and *225 ml (8 fl oz) single cream;* replace the vanilla essence with a few drops of *green food colouring* and *1.25 ml (¼ tsp) almond essence.* Freeze for 20 minutes. Chop *175 g (6 oz) salted green pistachios.* Remove dasher; stir in nuts. Cover churn as left; leave to harden. Makes 1.5 litres (2½ pints) or 6 servings

Colour index
page 102

SPICED BANANA ICE CREAM: Prepare custard as left, but use *225 g (8 oz) sugar, 45 ml (3 level tbsp) flour, 2.5 ml (½ level tsp) salt, 568 ml (1 pint) milk* and *3 eggs,* beaten; cook for 15 minutes; chill. Dissolve *15 ml (1 level tbsp) ascorbic acid* in *60 ml (4 tbsp) water;* put in a blender with *6 firm, ripe, bananas,* peeled and cut up, *75 ml (5 level tbsp) sugar* and *7.5 ml (1½ level tsp) ground cinnamon;* blend until smooth. Pour the banana mixture, the custard, *225 ml (8 fl oz) milk* and *225 ml (8 fl oz) single cream* into the ice cream churn; omit the vanilla essence. Freeze for about 20 minutes. Makes 2.2 litres (4 pints) or 10 servings

Peppermint Rock Ice Cream

Colour index
page 102

Makes 2.7
litres
(5 pints) or
12 servings

120 g (4½ oz) coarsely crushed peppermint rock
568 ml (1 pint) milk
350 ml (12 fl oz) single cream

3 196-g (7-oz) cans sweetened condensed milk
22.5 ml (1½ tbsp) vanilla essence
100 ml (4 fl oz) water

1. Stir half the rock and the remaining ingredients into the ice cream churn. Cover; chill for 1 hour.
2. Prepare the ice cream as in steps 4–9 of vanilla ice cream, left, but in step 7, stir in the remaining peppermint rock before packing down ice cream.

HOME-FREEZER METHOD: Stir together a *496-g (14-oz) can sweetened condensed milk, 225 ml (8 fl oz) water, 15 ml (1 tbsp) vanilla essence* and *75 ml (5 tbsp) crushed peppermint rock;* fold in *400 ml (¾ pint) double cream,* whipped. Pour into a freezer container, cover and freeze for 1 hour. Spoon into a bowl and beat hard. Fold in *75 ml (5 tbsp) crushed peppermint rock.* Return to the container, cover and freeze. Makes 1.5 litres (2½ pints) or 6 servings

ICE CREAM SUNDAES

Sundaes are layers of ice cream and fruit, sweet sauce, chocolate, jelly or nuts. Serve in tall glasses or attractive dishes.

For a chocolate sundae, layer vanilla ice cream and chocolate sauce, page 464. Decorate with whipped cream and grated chocolate or chopped nuts.

For a fruit cocktail sundae, alternate layers of vanilla ice cream and chilled canned fruit cocktail mixed with seedless grapes and grated orange rind.

For a raspberry sundae, alternate layers of vanilla ice cream and raspberries. Crumble a few macaroons and spoon them over the top of each serving.

Ice creams

Strawberry Milk Ice

Colour index
page 102

Makes
1.8 litres
(3¼ pints) or
6 servings

15 ml (1 level tbsp)
  powdered gelatine
45 ml (3 tbsp) water
900 ml (1½ pints) milk
10 ml (2 tsp) vanilla
  essence
175 g (6 oz) sugar

1.25 ml (¼ level tsp) salt
350 g (12 oz) strawberries,
  washed and hulled
6 drops red food colouring,
  optional

1 Dissolve the gelatine in the water in a small heatproof basin over a pan of hot water and leave until cool.

2 Warm the milk with the vanilla essence, sugar and salt, and stir in the dissolved gelatine.

3 Pour into a shallow freezer container, cover with foil and freeze for 3 hours, until frozen but still soft. Crush the strawberries to a pulp.

4 Put half the frozen milk mixture into a blender; blend until smooth. Pour into a chilled bowl. Repeat with remaining frozen milk mixture.

5 Pour the strawberries and the red food colouring into the milk mixture and stir together until well blended.

6 Return to freezer container; freeze for 2 hours. Leave at room temperature for 10 minutes before serving.

PEACH MILK ICE: Prepare milk mixture as above; but replace vanilla essence with **2.5 ml (½ tsp) almond essence;** omit strawberries and colouring. Peel, stone and chop **700 g (1½ lb) peaches,** and purée with **60 ml (4 tbsp) lemon juice** in a blender; stir into milk mixture. Pour into freezer container; freeze for 3 hours. Spoon into a bowl; beat until smooth. Return to freezer container; freeze for 2 hours. Beat again; freeze until firm.

Ice cream desserts

Baked Alaska

Colour index
page 102

4–6 servings

18 sponge fingers, split
  lengthways
37.5 ml (2½ tbsp) curaçao
150 g (5 oz) frozen
  raspberries, partially
  thawed
700 ml (1¼ pints) vanilla
  ice cream, slightly
  softened
2 egg whites
pinch salt
pinch cream of tartar
65 g (2½ oz) caster
  sugar

1 Line a 16.5-cm (6½-in) pie dish with two thirds of sponge fingers; allow to extend over rim. Sprinkle with half the curaçao.

2 Crush the raspberries to a pulp with a potato masher or fork.

3 Stir ice cream and spoon over the raspberry pulp. Cut it through the ice cream with a knife.

4 Spoon half the mixture into the pie dish. Arrange remaining sponge fingers on top; sprinkle with remaining curaçao. Spoon over remaining ice cream. Freeze.

5 About 20 minutes before serving, whisk the egg whites with the salt and cream of tartar until soft peaks form.

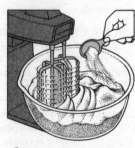

6 Whisk in the caster sugar, 30 ml (2 level tbsp) at a time, and continue whisking until stiff peaks form.

7 Quickly spread meringue over ice cream, swirling it into peaks. Bake at 240°C (475°F) mark 9 for 3–4 minutes. Serve at once.

Praline Bombe

700 ml (1¼ pints)
  vanilla or coffee ice
  cream
400 ml (¾ pint)
  strawberry ice cream or
  raspberry sorbet
50 g (2 oz) almond
  praline, page 373

To decorate:
100 ml (4 fl oz) double or
  whipping cream
15 ml (1 level tbsp) caster
  sugar
few drops vanilla
  essence
strawberries, washed

For the chocolate sauce:
75 g (3 oz) granulated
  sugar or golden syrup
15 g (½ oz) cocoa powder
60 ml (4 tbsp) double
  or whipping cream
25 g (1 oz) butter or
  margarine
3.75 ml (¾ tsp) vanilla
  essence

Colour index page 103
6 servings

1 Soften the vanilla ice cream in the refrigerator then spread it evenly over the sides and base of a 1.1-litre (2-pint) capacity bombe mould or a freezer-proof bowl.

2 Cover and freeze for 30 minutes until firm. Meanwhile soften the strawberry ice cream in the refrigerator.

3 Spread the strawberry ice cream evenly over the vanilla, leaving a well in the centre. Cover; freeze again until firm.

4 Spoon the praline into the well in the centre of the moulded ice cream.

5 Fill the sink with warm water. Dip the mould quickly into the water for a few seconds.

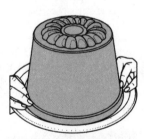

6 Invert a large plate on top of mould; invert mould and plate. Lift off mould. Freeze bombe.

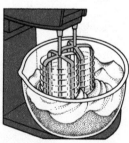

7 Whip the cream, sugar and the vanilla essence until stiff peaks form.

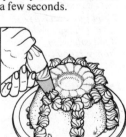

8 Spoon the whipped cream into a piping bag fitted with a large star nozzle and pipe it over the bombe; freeze.

9 For the chocolate sauce, put the sugar, cocoa powder, cream and butter or margarine in a heavy-based saucepan and heat gently until the mixture is smooth and comes to the boil. Remove the saucepan from the heat and stir in the vanilla essence. Keep hot. Remove the praline bombe from the freezer and decorate it with strawberries. Leave the bombe to stand at room temperature for 10 minutes before serving.

10 Cut the bombe into wedges; spoon some of the almond praline from the centre over each wedge. Serve with chocolate sauce.

Colour index page 102
6 servings

Nesselrode Ice Cream Mould

25 g (1 oz) candied orange
  peel, chopped, page 311
25 g (1 oz) glacé cherries,
  chopped
25 g (1 oz) sultanas,
  chopped
25 g (1 oz) black walnuts,
  chopped

700 ml (1¼ pints) vanilla
  ice cream, slightly
  softened
40 g (1½ oz) sponge
  fingers
45 ml (3 tbsp) brandy

1. Mix together the orange peel, cherries, sultanas, walnuts and ice cream; spoon one third of the mixture into a 900-ml (1½-pint) capacity mould. Split one third of the sponge fingers and press lightly into the ice cream mixture; drizzle with 15 ml (1 tbsp) brandy. Repeat the layering twice, then cover and freeze.

2. About 1 hour before serving, loosen the edges of the mixture from the mould with a palette knife dipped in hot water. Fill a large basin with warm water; dip mould into the water for a few seconds. Turn out on to a freezerproof plate; return to freezer.

3. Leave at room temperature for 10 minutes before serving; cut into wedges with a sharp knife.

ALTERNATIVE FLAVOURINGS: Prepare as above, but replace the candied orange peel, glacé cherries and sultanas with **225 g (8 oz) mixed glacé fruits**, chopped; replace the black walnuts with ordinary **walnuts** and the brandy with **rum**.

Colour index page 103
6 servings

Rainbow Ice Cream Gâteau

400 ml (¾ pint) chocolate
  ice cream
400 ml (¾ pint) chocolate
  and peppermint ice
  cream
400 ml (¾ pint) strawberry
  ice cream
400 ml (¾ pint) vanilla
  ice cream

175 g (6 oz) gingernut
  biscuits, finely crushed
50 g (2 oz) butter or
  margarine, melted
½ 425-g (15-oz) can
  stoned black cherries,
  drained
25 g (1 oz) shelled walnuts,
  chopped

1. Soften the ice creams in the refrigerator for about 30 minutes. Meanwhile, mix together the biscuit crumbs and butter and press the mixture firmly into the bottom of a 20.5-cm (8-in) spring release cake tin. Chill in the freezer for 10 minutes.

2. Layer the chocolate ice cream, chocolate and peppermint ice cream, cherries, strawberry ice cream and vanilla ice cream on top of the crumb crust. Sprinkle the walnuts over the ice cream. Cover and freeze again until firm.

3. Loosen the edges of the gâteau from the tin with a palette knife dipped in hot water. Remove the sides of the tin and leave to stand at room temperature for 10 minutes before serving. Cut the gâteau into wedges with a sharp knife.

Sherbets and and mousses

Pineapple Sherbet

175 g (6 oz) granulated
sugar
100 ml (4 fl oz) water
1 large pineapple
45 ml (3 tbsp) lemon
juice
2 egg whites, at room
temperature

Colour index
page 102

Makes
1.1 litres
(2 pints) or
10 servings

1 Stir the sugar and water over gentle heat until the sugar has dissolved, then bring to the boil, still stirring. Remove the syrup from the heat.

2 Slice the ends off the pineapple, remove the rough skin and cut out the eyes with a sharp knife. Quarter the fruit and remove the core then cut the fruit into small chunks.

3 Put the pineapple chunks into a blender and blend until smooth. Strain purée into a large bowl, pressing out all the juice. Discard the pulp.

4 Stir the syrup and lemon juice into the pineapple purée. Whisk the egg whites until stiff peaks form.

5 Fold the egg whites into the pineapple mixture; pour into a shallow freezer container. Cover; freeze for 3 hours.

6 Spoon the mixture into a large, chilled bowl and beat, preferably with an electric mixer, until fluffy. Return to the freezer container, then cover and freeze again for about 2 hours, or until frozen but still soft. Spoon the mixture into a large, chilled bowl and beat again as before. Return to the freezer container, then cover and freeze again until firm.

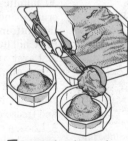

7 Leave the pineapple sherbet to stand at room temperature for 10 minutes before serving.

Minted Sherbet Ring

Colour index
page 103

4–6 servings

700 ml (1¼ pints)
pineapple sherbet, left,
slightly softened
37.5 ml (2½ tbsp) crème de
menthe

450 g (1 lb) strawberries,
washed and hulled

To decorate:
shredded coconut

1. Beat the pineapple sherbet and the crème de menthe until smooth; spoon into a 700-ml (1¼-pint) capacity ring mould. Cover with foil and freeze.
2. Loosen the edges of the mixture from the mould with a palette knife dipped in hot water. Dip the mould into a sink or large basin filled with warm water for a few seconds. Turn out on to a flat serving plate; fill the centre of the ring with strawberries. Decorate with the shredded coconut.

Iced Canteloup Mousse

Colour index
page 102

Makes
1.8 litres
(3¼ pints) or
12 servings

350 g (12 oz) sugar
250 ml (9 fl oz) water
1 small, very ripe canteloup
melon
700 ml (1¼ pints) milk
30 ml (2 level tbsp)
powdered gelatine

3.75 ml (¾ level tsp) salt
3 drops yellow food
colouring
1 drop red food colouring

1. Stir together 225 g (8 oz) sugar and 150 ml (¼ pint) water, and heat gently until the sugar is dissolved. Bring to the boil and boil steadily, without stirring, for 5 minutes.
2. Cut the melon in half, scoop out the seeds, remove the rind and cut the flesh into chunks. Put the chunks in a blender with 225 ml (8 fl oz) milk and blend until smooth.
3. Dissolve the gelatine in the remaining water in a small heatproof bowl over a pan of hot water, then blend it into the rest of the milk. Stir this into the melon mixture with the sugar syrup and remaining ingredients. Pour the mixture into a shallow freezer container; freeze for 3 hours, stirring occasionally.
4. Spoon the mixture into a chilled bowl and beat hard, until smooth but still frozen. Return to the freezer container; freeze again for 3 hours. Leave at room temperature for 10 minutes before serving.

Iced Orange Mousse

Colour index
page 102

Makes
1.8 litres
(3¼ pints) or
12 servings

15 ml (1 level tbsp)
powdered gelatine
45 ml (3 tbsp) water
1.1 litres (2 pints) milk
350 g (12 oz) sugar
225 ml (8 fl oz) orange
juice

60 ml (4 tbsp) grated
orange rind
60 ml (4 tbsp) lemon juice
3.75 ml (¾ level tsp) salt
1.25 ml (¼ tsp) yellow
food colouring
1 drop red food colouring

1. Dissolve the gelatine in the water, in a small heatproof basin over a pan of hot water, then blend into the milk. Stir into the remaining ingredients.
2. Pour the mixture into a shallow freezer container, cover with foil and freeze for 3 hours, stirring occasionally, until frozen but still soft.
3. Spoon the mixture into a chilled bowl and beat hard, until smooth but still frozen. Return to the freezer container, cover and freeze until firm.
4. Leave the mousse to stand for 10 minutes at room temperature before serving.

Water ices

Lemon Water Ice

6 large lemons
225 g (8 oz) granulated
  sugar
500 ml (18 fl oz) water
15 ml (1 level tbsp)
  powdered gelatine

To decorate:
mint sprigs

Colour index page 103

Makes 900 ml (1½ pints)
or 6 servings

1 Cut off one third of each lemon and grate the rind from the small pieces of lemon only.

2 Squeeze the juice from all of the lemons to make about 175 ml (6 fl oz).

3 Remove all the crushed pulp and membrane to make large lemon cups and cut a thin slice from the base of each one so they will stand level. Wrap in cling film; chill.

4 Dissolve sugar in 400 ml (¾ pint) water over gentle heat. Dissolve gelatine in remaining water in a basin over hot water. Remove both from heat; stir gelatine into sugar syrup.

5 Stir the lemon juice and grated lemon rind into the syrup mixture.

6 Pour the mixture into a shallow freezer container, cover with foil; freeze for 3 hours until frozen but still soft.

7 Spoon the mixture into a chilled bowl and beat hard, preferably with an electric mixer, until smooth but still frozen.

8 Return the beaten mixture to the freezer container, then cover and freeze again until frozen but still soft.

9 Spoon into a chilled bowl and beat again as in step 7. Return to the freezer container; cover and freeze again.

10 Leave to stand at room temperature for 10 minutes before serving. Scoop into the lemon cups; decorate with mint.

Makes 900 ml (1½ pints)
or 6 servings

ORANGE WATER ICE: Dissolve *100 g (4 oz) sugar* in *175 ml (6 fl oz) water* over gentle heat, then dissolve *15 ml (1 level tbsp) powdered gelatine* in *50 ml (2 fl oz) water* in a small heatproof basin over a pan of hot water. Remove both from the heat, stir the gelatine into the sugar syrup and add *400 ml (¾ pint) orange juice, 5 ml (1 tsp) grated lemon rind* and *15 ml (1 tbsp) lemon juice*. Freeze as in steps 6–9 of lemon water ice, left. Serve the orange water ice in small chilled dishes.

Colour index page 103

1.1 litres (2 pints) or 10 servings

Strawberry-orange Ice

60 ml (4 tbsp) lemon juice　　*175 g (6 fl oz) orange juice*
30 ml (2 tbsp) curaçao　　　*225 g (8 oz) sugar*
450 g (1 lb) strawberries,
  washed and hulled

1. Put the lemon juice, curaçao, strawberries, orange juice and sugar in a blender and blend until smooth. Pour the mixture into a shallow freezer container. Cover with foil and freeze for about 4 hours, until the mixture is frozen but still soft.
2. Spoon the mixture into a chilled bowl and beat hard, preferably with an electric mixer, until smooth but still frozen. Return it to the freezer container; cover and freeze again until firm.
3. Leave to stand at room temperature for 10 minutes before serving.

Colour index page 103

Makes 1.1 litres (2 pints) or 10 servings

Watermelon Ice

½ small watermelon,　　　*45 ml (3 level tbsp) sifted*
  rinded, seeded and　　　　*icing sugar*
  cut into 2.5-cm (1-in)　　*15 ml (1 tbsp) lemon juice*
  chunks, to make about　　*1.25 ml (¼ level tsp) salt*
  700 g (1½ lb) prepared
  fruit

1. Put 100 g (4 oz) of the watermelon chunks in a blender with the icing sugar, lemon juice and salt and blend until smooth. Add the remaining watermelon chunks and blend again for a few seconds longer, until smooth.
2. Pour the watermelon mixture into a shallow freezer container and freeze for about 2 hours until frozen but still soft.
3. Spoon the mixture into a chilled bowl and beat hard, preferably with an electric mixer, until fluffy. Return it to the freezer container, then cover and freeze again until firm.
4. Leave to stand at room temperature for 10 minutes before serving.

CAKES

Nothing can equal the flavour and texture of a home-made cake, whether it is a simple sandwich cake or an elaborate gâteau. Know what the different ingredients contribute and follow the recipe to learn techniques.

TECHNIQUES

Rich cakes containing a high proportion of fat are made by first creaming the fat and sugar together with a wooden spoon or mixer. The egg is then beaten in and the flour folded in lightly. A high proportion of egg may curdle the creamed mixture, but this can be corrected by adding 15–30 ml (1–2 level tbsp) flour with the egg.

Plainer cakes with a lower proportion of fat are made by rubbing the fat into the flour with your fingertips. The lightest cakes are sponges, for which the eggs and sugar are whisked together until really thick, or the egg whites whisked separately and folded in at the end.

INGREDIENTS

Flour: Self raising flour is popular for many cakes because the raising agents are blended with it during manufacture, eliminating the possibility of error in the kitchen. Self raising flour is mixed with plain flour for some cakes because the amount of raising agent would be too great if self raising flour were used alone.

Raising agents: A cake rises because either air, carbon dioxide or steam is introduced into the mixture, causing it to expand. This is done by hand during creaming or beating, for example, or by including a raising agent in the mixture. Baking powder is the most commonly used raising agent; it consists of bicarbonate of soda and an acid-reacting chemical such as cream of tartar. With moisture and heat these react together to produce carbon dioxide. During baking, the bubbles enlarge and the cake rises; then the heat dries and sets the mixture, giving the cake its characteristic texture.

Eggs: Eggs help the raising process in two ways. Firstly, the whisking of eggs produces thousands of tiny air bubbles which are then incorporated into the mixture. The egg white whisked alone is more effective than whole egg; egg yolk tends to decrease the foaming action. Secondly, the moisture contained in the egg produces steam during cooking and as the mixture cools, the egg yolk 'sets', holding the trapped air in suspension. For baking, always use eggs at room temperature. A size 4–5 egg weighing 50–60 g (2 oz) is suitable for most baking and should be used for the recipes in this section, except where stated otherwise.

Fats: Butter and margarine are the fats most commonly used in cake making, although others, such as blended white vegetable fat and oil, may also be used. Butter and margarine are interchangeable, although butter gives a better flavour: as a general rule, use block margarine for rubbed-in mixtures and soft tub margarine for creamed. Butter and block margarine should be at room temperature for creaming and rubbing in.

Sugars: Caster sugar should be used for creamed mixtures and whisked sponges. Granulated sugar may be used for creamed mixtures with fairly good results, although it will give rather less volume, a more open texture and sometimes a speckly appearance. For rubbed-in mixtures, granulated sugar is acceptable.

Soft brown sugars, whether dark or light, have more flavour than white sugar, with a caramel taste and a slightly finer grain. They will give just as good a volume if used instead of caster sugar in sandwich cakes; soft brown sugars also cream well. Demerara sugar is coarser in grain than granulated sugar, but can be used for rubbed-in mixtures. It is unsatisfactory for creamed mixtures because its large crystals do not break down when mixed. Barbados sugar is a very dark, treacle-coloured, unrefined sugar. It is too strong in flavour for light cake mixtures, but will give a good flavour and colour to rich fruit cakes and gingerbreads.

PREPARING CAKE TINS

Tins with a non-stick finish generally do not need greasing or lining, but do be sure to follow manufacturer's instructions for use and general care. All other cake tins should be lightly greased before use. The quickest method is to brush them with melted fat or oil. As an additional precaution against sticking, coat the greased tin with a little flour. For sponge cakes, dust with a little mixed flour and caster sugar.

Fruit cakes and some sponges should be baked in lined tins. Use greased greaseproof paper or a non-stick paper, which does not require greasing. Follow the instructions opposite for lining a deep tin and on page 391 for a Swiss roll tin.

LINING A CAKE TIN

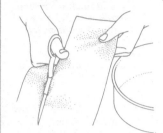

Cut a strip of paper 5 cm (2 in) wider than the depth of the tin and long enough to go right round the tin and overlap by about 2.5 cm (1 in).

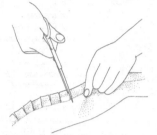

Fold lengthways about 2.5 cm (1 in) from the edge, then snip edge at intervals as far as the fold. Fit the strip of paper round inside of tin.

Place the tin on another sheet of paper, draw round the base and cut out. Fit the base piece in, to cover the snipped edges and make a neat lining. For some cakes, line only the base of the tin.

BAKING

A prepared cake mixture should go straight into a hot oven or it will spoil; turn the oven on before starting to mix. Always bake cakes in the centre of the oven.

TESTING WHETHER A CAKE IS COOKED

It is important not to remove a cake from the oven before it is fully cooked. Small cakes should be well risen, golden brown and just firm to the touch. They should begin to shrink from the sides of the tin when taken out of the oven. The following tests are helpful for larger cakes.

Insert a fine skewer or wooden cocktail stick into the centre of the cake. It should come out perfectly clean. If any mixture is sticking to it, the cake requires more cooking. Never use a cold knife.

If you are baking a light mixture, press the top of the cake very lightly with your fingertips. The cake should be spongy and should give only slightly to the pressure. When your fingertip is removed, the surface should rise again immediately, retaining no impression.

If you are baking a fruit cake, lift it gently from the oven and listen to it, putting it close to your ear. A continued sizzling sound indicates that the cake is not cooked in the centre.

COOLING

Leave cakes to cool for a few minutes before turning them out; during this time they will shrink away from the sides of the tin and will be easier to remove. If necessary, ease the cake away from the sides of the tin with a round-bladed knife, then turn it out, very gently,

upside down on to a wire rack. Remove any paper, place a second rack over it and invert both racks so that the cake is now right side up. Take away the top rack and leave to cool completely before decorating or storing.

STORING AND FREEZING

Most cakes are best eaten fresh, but fruit cakes and gingerbreads improve with keeping and should be stored for at least 24 hours before being cut. To store a cake, cool it completely and then place it in a tin with a tightly fitting lid. If it is to be stored for any length of time, wrap in greaseproof paper or foil first. Really rich cakes, such as Christmas or wedding fruit cakes, should be given plenty of time to mature – at least a month, preferably 2 or 3 months – stored in a cool, dry place.

Most undecorated cakes – creamed, sponge or light fruit cakes – will freeze for up to 6 months. Frosted or iced cakes will keep for only about 2 months, so it is often a good idea to freeze the separated layers of a cake undecorated, adding any icing or filling after thawing. Do not freeze a cake filled with jam as it will go soggy.

Wrap undecorated cakes well in freezer wrap, excluding as much air as possible, and seal with freezer tape. To freeze a decorated cake, freeze unwrapped until firm, then cover with freezer wrap and place in a rigid box.

To thaw plain cakes, leave them in their freezer wrapping at room temperature for 1–2 hours. For decorated cakes, remove the wrapping as soon as you take the cake from the freezer or it may stick to the icing as it thaws. An iced layer cake will take about 4 hours to thaw at room temperature.

CAKE TIN SIZES

If you do not have the tin suggested for a cake recipe, you can use any tin with the same liquid capacity. The chart below shows the liquid capacity of round and square tins based on an average finished cake depth of 7.5 cm (3 in); it consequently excludes sandwich and other shallow tins.

If you wish to use an unusually shaped tin, check the liquid capacity in the same way but be particularly careful that the cake mixture comes to approximately the same depth as it would have done in the original tin.

LIQUID CAPACITY OF ROUND AND SQUARE TINS		
Liquid capacity	Round tin	Square tin
1.1 litres (2 pints)	18 cm (7 in)	12.5 cm (5 in)
1.7 litres (3 pints)	20.5 cm (8 in)	18 cm (7 in)
2.3 litres (4 pints)	23 cm (9 in)	20.5 cm (8 in)
3.4 litres (6 pints)	25.5 cm (10 in)	23 cm (9 in)
4.5 litres (8 pints)	28 cm (11 in)	25.5 cm (10 in)
5.7 litres (10 pints)	30.5 cm (12 in)	28 cm (11 in)
6.8 litres (12 pints)	33 cm (13 in)	30.5 cm (12 in)

Creamed cakes

Victoria Sandwich Cake

175 g (6 oz) butter
175 g (6 oz) caster
*   sugar*
3 eggs, beaten
175 g (6 oz) self raising
*   flour*
butter cream made with
*   275 g (10 oz) icing*
*   sugar, page 400*

Colour index
page 92

Makes one
20.5-cm (8-in)
sandwich cake

1 Grease two 20.5-cm
(8-in) sandwich tins and
base line them with
greased greaseproof paper.

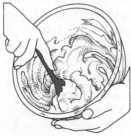

2 Beating by hand with
a wooden spoon or
using an electric mixer,
cream together the butter
and the caster sugar until
the mixture is light
and fluffy.

3 Add the eggs a little
at a time, beating well
after each addition.

4 Sift and lightly fold in
half the flour with a
metal spoon or spatula,
then lightly fold in the rest
of the flour.

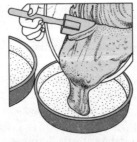

5 Divide the mixture be-
tween the prepared tins
and level the tops with a
knife. Bake both on same
shelf at 190°C (375°F)
mark 5 for 20 minutes.

6 When the cakes are well
risen and firm to the
touch, turn them out on to
a wire rack to cool.

7 Sandwich the layers
together with butter
cream and coat the top and
sides as well, if you wish.

Pineapple Upside-down Cake

Colour index
page 92

Makes one
33 × 23 cm
(13 × 9 in)
cake

50 g (2 oz) butter or
*   margarine*
50 g (2 oz) brown sugar
411-g (14½-oz) can
*   pineapple chunks,*
*   drained well*
6 maraschino cherries,
*   drained well*

Victoria sandwich mixture
*   made with 225 g (8 oz)*
*   self raising flour, left*

To serve:
whipped cream or vanilla
*   ice cream*

1. Grease a 33 × 23 cm (13 × 9 in) oblong tin and
base line it with greased greaseproof paper.
2. Put the butter or margarine in the tin and place it
in the oven at 190°C (375°F) mark 5. Heat until the
fat has melted.
3. Remove the tin from the oven and sprinkle the
sugar evenly over the base. Arrange the pineapple
chunks on top to make six flower shapes and place a
maraschino cherry in the centre of each one.
4. Spoon the cake mixture carefully into the tin and
bake for 30 minutes, or until well risen, golden and
firm to the touch. Cool in the tin on a wire rack for a
few minutes, then turn the cake out on to the rack to
cool completely.
5. Serve with whipped cream or vanilla ice cream.

Adding the sugar:
Sprinkle the sugar in
an even layer over the
melted fat.

Making the flowers:
Arrange the pineapple
chunks and cherries to
make flowers.

Devil's Food Cake

Colour index
page 90

Makes one
20.5-cm (8-in)
sandwich cake

275 g (10 oz) plain flour
10 ml (2 level tsp)
*   bicarbonate of soda*
pinch salt
75 g (3 oz) butter
250 g (9 oz) soft light
*   brown sugar*
4 large (size 2) eggs

100 g (4 oz) unsweetened
*   chocolate, melted*
200 ml (7 fl oz) milk
5 ml (1 tsp) vanilla essence
rich chocolate frosting
*   made with 190 g*
*   (6½ oz) icing sugar,*
*   page 400*

1. Grease and line two 20.5-cm (8-in) sandwich
tins, so that the greaseproof paper stands above
the rims. Sift together the flour, soda and salt.
2. Cream together the butter and sugar until pale
and fluffy, then gradually add the eggs, one at a
time, beating well after each addition.
3. Add the melted chocolate and beat well. Carefully fold in the flour alternately with the milk and
vanilla essence.
4. Divide the mixture evenly between the tins and
level the surfaces. Bake in the oven at 180°C (350°F)
mark 4 for about 40 minutes, until firm to the touch.
Turn out on to a wire rack to cool, then sandwich
together and coat with chocolate frosting.

Colour index
page 90

Makes one
20.5-cm (8-in)
sandwich cake

Silver-white Sandwich Cake

*3 egg whites
pinch salt
350 g (12 oz) caster
    sugar
100 g (4 oz) blended white
    vegetable fat
225 g (8 oz) self raising
    flour
25 g (1 oz) cornflour
175 ml (6 fl oz) milk
5 ml (1 tsp) vanilla
    essence*

*1.25 ml (¼ tsp) almond
    essence
chocolate butter cream
    made with 275 g (10 oz)
    icing sugar, page 400 or
    lemon curd and lemon
    butter cream made with
    175 g (6 oz) icing sugar,
    page 400*

1. Grease two deep 20.5-cm (8-in) sandwich tins and base line them with greased greaseproof paper.

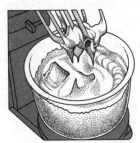

2 Whisk the egg whites and salt with a mixer or rotary whisk until stiff peaks form.

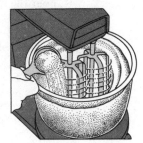

3 Gradually whisk in 175 g (6 oz) of the caster sugar until stiff peaks form again.

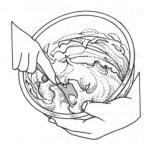

4 Cream the fat and remaining sugar. Sift the flour and cornflour and beat into the creamed mixture with the milk and essences, until smooth.

5 Fold the whisked egg whites carefully into the cake mixture and divide evenly between the prepared tins.

6. Bake at 190°C (375°F) mark 5 for about 25 minutes, until well risen and firm to the touch. Cool in the tins on a wire rack for several minutes, then turn out on to the rack to cool completely.

7. When the layers are cold, sandwich them together and coat with chocolate butter cream; or fill with lemon curd and coat with lemon butter cream.

WALNUT SANDWICH CAKE: Prepare and cool the cake as above. Sieve *120 ml (8 tbsp) apricot jam* or raspberry jam, sandwich the cake layers with a little of it and brush the rest over the sides of the cake. Spread *50 g (2 oz) chopped walnuts* on a sheet of greaseproof paper; holding the cake on its side, roll it on the chopped walnuts until the sides are evenly coated. Coat the top with *glacé icing* made with 100 g (4 oz) icing sugar (page 400), and decorate with *walnut halves* as the icing is setting.

Colour index
page 93

Makes 24 cup
cakes

Chocolate Cup Cakes

*75 g (3 oz) blended white
    vegetable fat
200 g (7 oz) caster sugar
2 eggs, beaten
2.5 ml (½ tsp) vanilla
    essence
100 g (4 oz) plain flour
50 g (2 oz) cocoa powder
2.5 ml (½ level tsp)
    bicarbonate of soda*

*1.25 ml (¼ level tsp)
    baking powder
50 ml (2 fl oz) milk
coffee cream cheese
    frosting, made with 450 g
    (1 lb) icing sugar, page
    401 or chocolate glacé
    icing made with 175 g
    (6 oz) icing sugar,
    page 400*

1 Arrange 24 paper cake cases in deep 7.5-cm (3-in) patty tins.

2 Cream the fat with the sugar until light and fluffy. Gradually beat in the eggs and vanilla essence.

3 Sift together the dry ingredients and beat into the creamed mixture alternately with the milk until the mixture is well blended and smooth.

4 Divide between the paper cases and bake at 190°C (375°F) mark 5 for 30–35 minutes, until the cakes are well risen and firm to the touch.

5 Cool in the tins on wire racks for a few minutes, turn out on to the racks to cool completely.

6 When the cakes are cold, dip or spread the top of each one with cream cheese or glacé icing.

CHOCOLATE CAKE: Grease two 20.5-cm (8-in) sandwich tins; base line with greased greaseproof paper. Prepare cake mixture as above, but divide between the tins and bake at 180°C (350°F) mark 4 for 30–35 minutes. When cake layers are cold, sandwich together and coat the top and sides with an icing or frosting or your choice. Makes one 20.5-cm (8-in) round sandwich cake. Colour index page 93

Creamed cakes

Marble Cake

Colour index
page 90

Makes one
23-cm (9-in)
round cake

50 g (2 oz) plain chocolate
15 ml (1 tbsp) water
5 ml (1 tsp) vanilla
*   essence*
175 g (6 oz) butter
175 g (6 oz) caster sugar
3 eggs, beaten
250 g (9 oz) plain flour
10 ml (2 level tsp) baking
*   powder*
2.5 ml (½ level tsp) salt
30 ml (2 tbsp) milk
5 ml (1 tsp) orange essence
25 g (1 oz) icing sugar

1 Grease and base line a 23-cm (9-in) spring-release cake tin. In a small saucepan over very low heat, melt the chocolate in the water, then add the vanilla essence and cool.

2 Put the butter in a bowl and cream it with the caster sugar until the mixture is light and fluffy, then add the beaten eggs a little at a time. Beat well after each addition. Sift together the plain flour, baking powder and salt. Fold the dry ingredients into the creamed mixture alternately with the milk and the orange essence until the mixture is well blended and smooth.

3 Remove two thirds of the cake mixture to a separate bowl; add the cooled, melted chocolate to the remainder of the mixture and stir in until evenly blended.

4 Place large spoonfuls of the plain and chocolate mixtures alternately into the prepared tin.

5 Cut through the mixture several times with a knife; bake at 180°C (350°F) mark 4 for 1 hour.

6 Cool in tin for a few minutes; remove sides of tin to cool completely.

7 When the cake is cold, dredge the top with sifted icing sugar.

Madeira Cake

Colour index
page 90

Makes one
18-cm (7-in)
round cake

175 g (6 oz) butter
175 g (6 oz) caster sugar
5 ml (1 tsp) vanilla
*   essence*
3 eggs, beaten
110 g (4 oz) plain flour
110 g (4 oz) self raising
*   flour*
15–30 ml (1–2 tbsp) milk
2–3 thin slices citron peel,
*   optional*

1. Grease an 18-cm (7-in) round cake tin or 900-g (2-lb) loaf tin; line with greased greaseproof paper.
2. Cream the butter with the sugar and vanilla until light and fluffy, then beat in the eggs.
3. Sift together the flours and fold into the creamed mixture until smooth, adding enough milk to give a dropping consistency.
4. Pour the mixture into the tin and bake at 180°C (350°F) mark 4 for about 1 hour, placing the citron peel on the top halfway through baking time, if you wish. Cool in the tin on a wire rack for a few minutes, then turn out to cool completely.

RICH SEED CAKE: Prepare the cake as above, but omit the vanilla essence; add *10 ml (2 level tsp) caraway seeds* with the flour. Dredge with *granulated sugar* before baking.

Deluxe Coconut Cake

Colour index
page 92

Makes one
20.5-cm (8-in)
round layer
cake

100 g (4 oz) blended white
*   vegetable fat*
225 g (8 oz) caster sugar
2.5 ml (½ tsp) vanilla
*   essence*
2 eggs, beaten
200 g (7 oz) plain flour
10 ml (2 level tsp) baking
*   powder*
2.5 ml (½ level tsp) salt
50 ml (2 fl oz) milk
American frosting made
*   with 450 g (1 lb) sugar,*
*   page 400*

175 g (6 oz) thread
*   coconut*
crystallised orange slices

For the filling:
4 egg yolks
50 g (2 oz) cornflour
100 g (4 oz) caster sugar
425 ml (16 fl oz) milk
45 ml (3 tbsp) curaçao
75 g (3 oz) thread
*   coconut*

1. Grease two 20.5-cm (8-in) sandwich tins and base line them with greased greaseproof paper.
2. Cream the fat with the sugar and vanilla essence until light and fluffy; gradually beat in the eggs.
3. Sift the flour, baking powder and salt. Fold into the creamed mixture alternately with the milk.
4. Divide the mixture between the prepared tins and bake at 190°C (375°F) mark 5 for 25–30 minutes, until well risen and firm to the touch. Cool slightly in the tins, then turn out to cool completely.
5. Meanwhile, make the custard filling. Whisk the egg yolks with the cornflour and sugar in a bowl. Warm the milk and pour it on to the egg mixture, stirring all the time. Strain the custard into the top of a double saucepan, stir in the curaçao and cook gently, stirring, for about 10 minutes or until thickened. Cool and stir in the coconut.
6. When the cakes are cold, cut them in half horizontally with a long-bladed knife. Sandwich the four layers together with the custard filling.
7. Coat the top and sides of the cake with American frosting and sprinkle with the coconut. Decorate the top with crystallised orange slices.

Treacle Spice Cake

Colour index page 90

Makes one 23-cm (9-in) square cake

100 g (4 oz) blended white vegetable fat
100 g (4 oz) caster sugar
350 g (12 oz) black treacle
1 egg, beaten
275 g (10 oz) plain flour
7.5 ml (1½ level tsp) bicarbonate of soda
5 ml (1 level tsp) each ground cinnamon and ground ginger
1.25 ml (¼ level tsp) ground cloves
3.75 ml (¾ level tsp) salt
225 ml (8 fl oz) double or whipping cream, whipped

1 Grease a 23-cm (9-in) square tin and base line the tin with greaseproof paper.

2 Cream the fat with the sugar until light and fluffy, then beat in the treacle. Add the egg a little at a time, beating well after each addition. Sift together the flour, bicarbonate of soda, ground cinnamon, ginger and cloves and the salt and beat into the creamed mixture alternately with 225 ml (8 fl oz) boiling water until the mixture is well blended.

3 Pour the mixture into the prepared tin and level the surface. Tap the tin gently to remove any air bubbles.

4 Bake in the oven at 180°C (350°F) mark 4 for 55–60 minutes.

5 Cool in the tin on a wire rack. To serve, top with whipped cream.

Light Spice Cake

Colour index page 91

Makes one 20.5-cm (8-in) sandwich cake

100 g (4 oz) blended white vegetable fat
175 g (6 oz) caster sugar
75 g (3 oz) brown sugar
2 eggs, beaten
225 g (8 oz) plain flour
12.5 ml (2½ level tsp) baking powder

5 ml (1 level tsp) each salt, ground cinnamon and allspice
2.5 ml (½ level tsp) each ground cloves, nutmeg
175 ml (6 fl oz) milk
5 ml (1 tsp) vanilla essence
whipped cream

1. Grease two 20.5-cm (8-in) sandwich tins and base line them with greased greaseproof paper.
2. Cream the fat with the sugars; gradually beat in the eggs. Sift the dry ingredients and beat into the creamed mixture with the milk and vanilla essence.
3. Divide the mixture between the prepared tins; bake at 190°C (375°F) mark 5 for 35 minutes. Cool.
4. Sandwich and coat layers with whipped cream.

Chocolate and Walnut Layer Cake

Colour index page 92

Makes one 18-cm (7-in) round layer cake

175 g (6 oz) butter or margarine
100 g (4 oz) caster sugar
5 ml (1 tsp) vanilla essence
6 eggs, separated
100 g (4 oz) plain chocolate, melted
75 g (3 oz) shelled walnuts, ground
75 g (3 oz) plain flour

For the filling:
50 g (2 oz) plain chocolate, melted
50 g (2 oz) shelled walnuts, ground

25 g (1 oz) icing sugar
50 g (2 oz) butter or margarine
5 ml (1 tsp) vanilla essence

For the icing:
100 g (4 oz) plain chocolate
25 g (1 oz) butter or margarine
30 ml (2 level tbsp) golden syrup
15 ml (1 tbsp) milk
walnut halves

1. Grease three 18-cm (7-in) sandwich tins and base line them with greased greaseproof paper.
2. Cream the fat with 75 g (3 oz) of the caster sugar and the vanilla essence until light and fluffy. Beat the egg yolks and gradually beat them into the creamed mixture. Add the melted chocolate and walnuts and beat again.
3. Whisk the egg whites with a mixer or rotary whisk until soft peaks form. Gradually add the remaining caster sugar until the egg-white mixture is soft and glossy.
4. Sift the flour and fold it into the creamed mixture until the mixture is smooth. Gently fold in the whisked egg whites and sugar mixture using a metal spoon.
5. Divide the mixture between the prepared tins and bake at 180°C (350°F) mark 4 for 25 minutes. Cool in the tins on wire racks for a short time, then turn on to the racks to cool separately.
6. Meanwhile, make the filling. Melt the chocolate in the top of a double saucepan over hot, not boiling water. Stir in the walnuts and sugar. Add the fat and vanilla essence. Remove from the heat and cool.
7. When the cake layers are cold, sandwich them together with the filling.
8. Make the icing. Melt the chocolate and the fat in the top of a double saucepan over hot boiling water. Remove from the heat and beat in the golden syrup and milk.
9. Coat the top and sides of the cake with icing and decorate with walnut halves.

Icing the cake: Spread the icing over the top and sides of the cake.

Creamed and rubbed-in mixtures

Banana Cake

100 g (4 oz) butter
275 g (10 oz) caster sugar
2 eggs, beaten
350 g (12 oz) self
  raising flour
2.5 ml (½ level tsp)
  baking powder
2.5 ml (½ level tsp)
  bicarbonate of soda
2.5 ml (½ level tsp) salt
5 ripe bananas
5 ml (1 tsp) vanilla
  essence
75 ml (3 fl oz) buttermilk
400 ml (¾ pint) double
  cream, whipped
30 ml (2 tbsp) lemon juice

Colour index
page 92

Makes one
20.5-cm (8-in)
sandwich cake

1 Grease the bottom and sides of two deep 20.5-cm (8-in) sandwich tins and dust them with a little flour. Shake out any excess flour.

2 Put the butter in a bowl and cream it with the caster sugar until the mixture is light and fluffy, then add the beaten eggs a little at a time. Beat well after each addition. Sift together the self raising flour, baking powder, bicarbonate of soda and salt. Fold the dry ingredients into the creamed mixture, a third at a time, until the mixture is well blended.

3 Mash three of the bananas and stir in the vanilla essence and buttermilk until mixed. Gradually beat the banana mixture into the cake mixture.

4 Divide the cake mixture between the tins and bake at 180°C (350°F) mark 4 for about 30 minutes, or until well risen and firm to the touch.

5 Cool in the tins on a wire rack for a short time, then turn the cakes out on to the rack to cool completely.

6 When the cake layers are cold, sandwich them together and coat top and sides with cream.

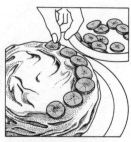

7 Slice the remaining bananas, dip in lemon juice and use to decorate the top of the cake.

Cherry Cake

225 g (8 oz) self raising
  flour
pinch salt
100 g (4 oz) butter
100g (4 oz) sugar
100–175 g (4–6 oz) glacé
  cherries, washed, dried
  and quartered

1 egg, beaten
2.5 ml (½ tsp) vanilla
  essence
75–90 ml (5–6 tbsp) milk
glacé icing made with
  100–175 g (4–6 oz)
  sugar, page 400, optional

Colour index
page 90

Makes one
21.5 × 11 cm
(8½ × 4½ in)
cake

1. Grease a 700-g (1½-lb) loaf tin and base line it with greased greaseproof paper.
2. Put the flour and salt in a large bowl and rub in the fat until the mixture resembles fine breadcrumbs. Stir in the sugar and cherries.
3. Make a well in the centre and pour in the beaten egg, vanilla essence and 75 ml (5 tbsp) of the milk. Gradually work the dry ingredients into the liquid, adding more milk if necessary to give the mixture a dropping consistency.
4. Pour the mixture into the tin and level the top. Bake at 180°C (350°F) mark 4 for about 1¼ hours, until well risen and firm to the touch.
5. Cool in the tin on a wire rack for a few minutes, then turn out of the tin on to the rack to cool completely. When the cake is cold, coat the top with glacé icing if you wish.

LEMON CAKE: Grease and base line a 15-cm (6-in) round cake tin. Prepare the mixture as above, but omit the cherries and vanilla essence and use *90–120 ml (6–8 tbsp) milk,* add the *grated rind of 1 lemon* with the sugar and add the *juice of 1 lemon* with the egg yolk and the milk. Makes one 15-cm (6-in) round cake

Moist Apple Cake

225 g (8 oz) plain flour
2.5 ml (½ level tsp) salt
2.5 ml (½ level tsp)
  bicarbonate of soda
100 g (4 oz) butter or
  margarine
225 g (8 oz) caster sugar
2 medium cooking apples,
  peeled, cored and diced

50 g (2 oz) shelled walnuts,
  chopped
50 g (2 oz) seedless
  raisins
2 eggs, beaten
5 ml (1 tsp) vanilla
  essence
icing sugar

Colour index
page 91

Makes 20.5-cm
(8-in) square
cake

1. Grease a shallow 20.5-cm (8-in) square tin and base line it with greased greaseproof paper.
2. Sift the flour with the salt and bicarbonate of soda and rub in the fat until the mixture resembles fine breadcrumbs. Stir in the sugar, apples, walnuts and the seedless raisins.
3. Make a well in the centre, pour in the beaten egg and vanilla essence and gradually work the dry ingredients into the liquid.
4. Pour the mixture into the prepared tin and bake at 170°C (325°F) mark 3 for about 1½ hours, or until the cake is golden brown. Cool in the tin on a wire rack for a short time, then turn out on to the rack to cool completely.
5. When the cake is cold, place a paper doily on top and dredge with sifted icing sugar to make a pattern. Remove the doily carefully without disturbing any of the icing sugar.

Sponge cakes

Whisked Sponge Cake

Colour index
page 90

Makes one
18-cm (7-in)
sandwich cake

3 large (size 2) eggs
100 g (4 oz) caster
sugar
75 g (3 oz) plain flour
icing sugar, optional

For the filling:
75 ml (3 fl oz) double or
whipping cream,
whipped

1 Grease two 18-cm (7-in) sandwich tins and dust them with a mixture of flour and caster sugar. Shake out any excess.

2 Put the eggs and sugar in a deep bowl, stand the bowl over a pan of hot water and whisk until light and creamy. (No heat is necessary if you use an electric mixer.)

3 Whisk until the mixture is stiff enough to retain the impression of the whisk for a few seconds. Remove from the heat and continue to whisk until the mixture is cool.

4 Sift half the flour over the whisked mixture and fold it in lightly with a metal spoon. Add the remaining flour and fold it in lightly.

5 Divide between the tins and bake at 190°C (375°F) mark 5 for 20–25 minutes, until well risen and the top springs back when lightly touched.

6. Turn out on to a wire rack to cool. When the cake layers are cold, sandwich them together with whipped cream; dust top with icing sugar, if you wish.

SPONGE FINGERS: Grease a sponge finger tray and dust it with a mixture of flour and sugar. Prepare the mixture as above, using *1 large (size 2) egg, 60 ml (4 level tbsp) caster sugar* and *60 ml (4 level tbsp) plain flour.* Spoon enough mixture into each hollow in the tray to reach the top and bake at 200°C (400°F) mark 6 for 10 minutes, until golden. Remove from the tray and cool on a wire rack. Dip the ends in *melted chocolate* if you wish. Makes 12

Walnut Sponge Ring Cake

Colour index
page 90

Makes one
20.5-cm (8-in)
ring cake

3 large (size 2) eggs,
separated
1.25 ml (¼ level tsp) cream
of tartar
175 g (6 oz) caster
sugar
50 ml (2 fl oz) vegetable
oil
2.5 ml (½ tsp) vanilla
essence

2.5 ml (½ tsp) almond
essence
75 ml (3 fl oz) cold water
150 g (5 oz) plain flour
5 ml (1 level tsp) baking
powder
50 g (2 oz) shelled walnuts,
finely chopped

1. Whisk the egg whites and cream of tartar until stiff peaks form. Gradually whisk in 50 g (2 oz) sugar until glossy and stiff peaks form again.
2. Beat the egg yolks with the oil, vanilla essence, almond essence and water. Sift together the flour and baking powder and stir in the remaining sugar. Make a well in the centre, add the liquid and beat well for 2–3 minutes.
3. Beat in the walnuts, then fold in the egg whites with a metal spoon until evenly blended.
4. Spoon into an ungreased 20.5-cm (8-in) ring tin and bake at 170°C (325°F) mark 3 for 1 hour 15 minutes, until the top springs back when lightly touched. Invert the tin on to a bottle neck, funnel or wire rack to cool upside down. When the cake is cold, loosen it with a palette knife and turn out.

Chocolate Feather Sponge Cake

Colour index
page 92

Makes one
20.5-cm (8-in)
ring cake

3 large (size 2) eggs,
separated
1.25 ml (¼ level tsp) cream
of tartar
200 g (7 oz) caster sugar
50 ml (2 fl oz) vegetable oil
2.5 ml (½ tsp) vanilla
essence

75 ml (3 fl oz) water
100 g (4 oz) plain flour
25 g (1 oz) cocoa powder
1.25 ml (¼ level tsp)
baking powder
1.25 ml (¼ level tsp) salt
25 g (1 oz) icing sugar

1. Whisk the egg whites and cream of tartar until stiff peaks form. Gradually whisk in 50 g (2 oz) sugar until glossy and stiff peaks form again.
2. Beat the egg yolks with the oil, vanilla essence and water. Sift together the flour, cocoa powder, baking powder and salt and stir in the remaining caster sugar. Make a well in the centre, add the liquid and beat well for 2–3 minutes.
3. Fold in the egg whites with a metal spoon.
4. Pour into an ungreased 20.5-cm (8-in) ring tin or 18-cm (7-in) round cake tin and bake at 180°C (350°F) mark 4 for about 1 hour, until the top springs back when lightly touched. Invert the tin on to a bottle neck, funnel or wire rack to cool upside down. When the cake is cold, loosen it with a palette knife and turn out. Dredge the top with icing sugar.

CHOCOLATE AND STRAWBERRY FEATHER SPONGE CAKE: Prepare the cake as above. When it is cold, slice it in half horizontally and scoop out a shallow hollow in each half. Sprinkle the cut surfaces with *the juice of 1 orange* and *30 ml (2 tbsp) curaçao.* Sandwich the cake halves together with *300 ml (½ pint) whipped cream* and *225 g (8 oz) strawberries*, hulled and sliced. Dredge the top with *icing sugar* and sprinkle with *grated chocolate.*

Sponge cakes

Angel Food Cake

75 g (3 oz) icing sugar
50 g (2 oz) plain flour
5 large (size 2) egg whites
5 ml (1 level tsp) cream of tartar
5 ml (1 tsp) vanilla essence
pinch salt
1.25 ml (¼ tsp) almond essence
175 g (6 oz) caster sugar

Colour index page 91

Makes one 20.5-cm (8-in) ring cake

1 Sift the icing sugar and place in a small bowl. Stir in the plain flour until evenly mixed.

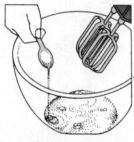

2 Put the egg whites, cream of tartar, vanilla essence, salt and almond essence in a large bowl and whisk with an electric mixer or rotary whisk until stiff peaks form.

3 Whisk in the caster sugar a little at a time and continue whisking until smooth and glossy and stiff peaks form again.

4 Add the flour and sugar mixture about a quarter at a time and fold in lightly with a spatula or metal spoon until blended.

5 Pour into an ungreased 20.5-cm (8-in) ring tin and cut through the mixture with a knife to break any air bubbles.

6 Bake at 190°C (375°F) mark 5 for about 45 minutes, until the top springs back when lightly touched with your finger.

7 To cool, invert the tin on to a funnel, bottle neck or wire rack. When cold, loosen with a knife and turn out.

Orange and Lemon Genoese Sponge Ring

40 g (1½ oz) butter
65 g (2½ oz) plain flour
15 ml (1 level tbsp) cornflour
3 large (size 2) eggs
75 g (3 oz) caster sugar
grated rind of 1 lemon

For the crème au beurre:
175 g (6 oz) caster sugar
10 ml (2 tsp) lemon juice
10 ml (2 tsp) orange juice

120 ml (8 tbsp) water
4 egg yolks
225-350 g (8-12 oz) unsalted butter
grated rind of ½ lemon
grated rind of ½ orange

To decorate, optional:
½ lemon
50 g (2 oz) caster sugar

Colour index page 93

Makes one 20.5-cm (8-in) ring cake

1. Grease and flour a 20.5-cm (8-in) ring tin. Shake out any excess flour.

2. Heat the butter gently until it has just melted, remove it from the heat and leave to stand for a few minutes. Sift together the flour and cornflour.

3. Put the eggs and sugar in a large, deep bowl and whisk over a pan of hot water until light, creamy and stiff enough to hold the impression of the whisk for a few seconds. (If you are using an electric mixer, no heat is necessary.) Remove the bowl from the heat and whisk until cool.

4. Re-sift the flour and cornflour and fold half of it into the whisked egg mixture with a metal spoon. Pour the cooled, but still liquid, butter a little at a time round the edge of the mixture, keeping back the salt and sediment, then lightly fold it in alternately with the rest of the sifted flour, the cornflour and the grated lemon rind.

5. Spoon the mixture into the prepared tin and bake at 190°C (375°F) mark 5 for about 30 minutes, until well risen and firm to the touch. Invert the tin on to a bottle neck, funnel or wire rack to cool upside down. When the cake is cold, loosen it gently with a palette knife and turn out.

6. Make the crème au beurre. Place the sugar, lemon juice, orange juice and water in a small saucepan and heat gently, stirring frequently, until the sugar has dissolved. Bring to the boil and boil steadily, without stirring, until it reaches 107°C (225°F). To test, dip your fingers in cold water, then in the syrup; the syrup should slide smoothly over your fingertips.

7. Remove the sugar syrup from the heat. As soon as the bubbles subside, pour the syrup on to the egg yolks in a thin stream, whisking continuously, until the mixture is thick.

8. Put the butter in a large bowl and cream until very soft. Gradually beat in the egg mixture, then stir in the lemon and orange rinds.

9. To decorate, cut the lemon half into four slices about 0.5 cm (¼ in) thick and cut each slice into quarters. Poach them in a little water until the skin is tender. Drain off nearly all the water, add the caster sugar, and heat gently until the sugar has dissolved. Boil until reduced to a glaze, turning the slices to coat well. Leave to cool.

10. When the cake is cold, coat it thickly with the crème au beurre. Swirl the crème au beurre into peaks and decorate with the quartered, glazed lemon slices, if you wish.

Swiss Roll

Colour index page 91

Makes one 33-cm (13-in) roll

3 large (size 2) eggs
100 g (4 oz) caster sugar
100 g (4 oz) plain flour
15 ml (1 tbsp) hot water
sifted icing or caster sugar

warmed raspberry, strawberry or apricot jam
whipped cream, optional

1 Grease a 33 × 22.5 cm (13 × 9 in) Swiss roll tin. Cut a 43 × 33 cm (17 × 13 in) rectangle of greaseproof paper. Place the tin in the centre and, at each corner, make a diagonal cut in one edge of the paper, just as far as the corner of the tin. Put the paper in the tin, over-lapping the corners so that it fits closely over the base and sides and brush it with oil or melted fat.

2 Put the eggs and sugar in a large deep bowl, stand it over a pan of hot water and whisk until thick, light and creamy. Remove from the heat and whisk until cool. (If you are using an electric mixer, no heat is necessary.) Sift half the flour over the mixture and fold it in very lightly using a metal spoon. Add the remaining flour in the same way. Lightly stir in the water.

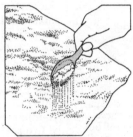

3 Pour into the tin and spread evenly. Bake at 220°C (425°F) mark 7 for 7–9 minutes until risen.

4 Meanwhile, sprinkle a tea towel or sheet of greaseproof paper with icing or caster sugar.

5 Turn the cooked sponge quickly out on to the towel, peel off the lining paper and trim off the crusty edges.

6 Spread the warm sponge with jam and roll up with the aid of the towel. Dredge with sifted icing or caster sugar.

7 Or, for cream filling, roll up cake and towel together, without filling.

8 When cake is cold, spread with jam and cream and re-roll.

Mocha Cream Roll

Colour index page 91

Makes one 33-cm (13-in) roll

3 large (size 2) eggs
100 g (4 oz) caster sugar
90 g (3½ oz) plain flour
15 g (½ oz) cocoa powder
15 ml (1 tbsp) hot water

For the filling:
300 ml (½ pint) double cream
50 g (2 oz) cocoa powder
50 g (2 oz) icing sugar
30 ml (2 tbsp) Tia Maria

For the chocolate icing:
175 g (6 oz) plain chocolate
25 g (1 oz) butter
30 ml (2 level tbsp) golden syrup
45 ml (3 tbsp) milk

For the white icing:
75 g (3 oz) icing sugar
15 ml (1 tbsp) water

1. Grease a 33 × 22.5 cm (13 × 9 in) Swiss roll tin and line with greased greaseproof paper or with non-stick paper (left).
2. Put the eggs and sugar in a large deep bowl, stand it over a pan of hot water and whisk until thick, light and creamy. Remove the bowl from the heat and whisk until cool. (If you are using an electric mixer, no heat is necessary.)
3. Mix the flour with the cocoa powder, sift half over the mixture and fold it in very lightly with a metal spoon. Add the remaining flour and cocoa in the same way and lightly stir in the hot water.
4. Pour the mixture into the tin, and tilt it backwards and forwards to spread the mixture evenly. Bake at 220°C (425°F) mark 7 for 7–9 minutes, until well risen and spongy. Meanwhile, sprinkle a sheet of greaseproof paper with cocoa powder.
5. Turn the cooked sponge quickly out on to the paper, gently peel off the lining paper and trim off the crusty edges of the sponge with a sharp knife. Carefully roll up the cake and paper together from the narrow end and leave to cool on a wire rack.
6. Whip the cream with the sifted cocoa, icing sugar and Tia Maria until soft peaks form.
7. When the cake is cold, unroll and spread cream over it, almost to the edges. Re-roll without the paper and place, seam side down, on a serving dish.
8. Make the chocolate icing. Melt the chocolate with the butter in the top of a double saucepan over hot, not boiling, water; remove from the heat and beat in the syrup and milk until smooth. Spread the warm icing over the roll.
9. Blend the icing sugar and water until smooth and drizzle white icing decoratively over the roll.

YULE LOG: Prepare the sponge as above. Make *chocolate butter cream*, using 350 g (12 oz) icing sugar (page 400). Mix one third of the butter cream with *50 g (2 oz) seedless raisins* and *15 ml (1 tbsp) brandy.* Unroll the cold sponge, spread with the chocolate and raisin butter cream and roll up again. Cut a thick diagonal slice from one end of the roll and secure it, halfway along one side of the roll, with butter cream, to represent a branch on the log. Spoon the remaining butter cream into a piping bag fitted with a star nozzle. Pipe lines of butter cream over the log, with one or two swirls to represent knots in the wood. Pipe butter cream over the ends of the log and branch if you wish. Dredge the yule log lightly with *sifted icing sugar* and decorate it with *holly leaves* and *berries.*

Sponge cakes

Petits Fours

6 large (size 2) eggs
175 g (6 oz) caster
sugar
150 g (5 oz) plain flour
30 ml (2 level tbsp)
cornflour
75 g (3 oz) butter, melted
and cooled but still
liquid
apricot glaze, page 401
almond paste made
with 100 g (4 oz)
ground almonds,
page 401
glacé or fondant icing made
with 350 g (12 oz) icing
sugar, pages 400, 401

few drops red, green or
yellow food colouring,
optional

To decorate :
glacé cherries, crystallised
flowers, silver dragées

Colour index page 91
Makes 30 petits fours

1 Grease and base line a 35.5 × 25.5 cm (14 × 10 in) tin. Whisk the eggs and sugar in a bowl over hot water until light, creamy and stiff enough to hold impression of whisk. Remove from the heat and whisk until cool. Sift flour and cornflour twice; fold half into the egg mixture. Pour melted butter round the edge, keeping back the salt and sediment. Fold in alternately with the rest of the flour and spread evenly in the tin.

2 Bake at 190°C (375°F) mark 5 for 20–25 minutes, until well risen and firm to the touch. Turn out on to a wire rack, peel off the paper and cool. Trim off crusty edges.

3 Brush some warm apricot glaze over the cake and cut the cake crossways into two pieces measuring 18 × 25.5 cm (7 × 10 in).

4 Place the almond paste between two sheets of waxed paper and roll out to about the same size. Peel off the top sheet of paper.

5 Invert the almond paste on to one piece of cake and peel off the second sheet of paper.

6 Top with the second piece of cake, glazed side down, and press the layers firmly together.

7 Cut lengthways into six even strips, and then crossways into five strips to make 30 small cakes.

8 Brush the cut surfaces of each small cake with the remaining apricot glaze. Place on wire racks over greaseproof paper.

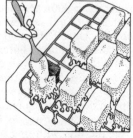

9 Tint the icing with colouring if you wish and spoon it over each cake, letting excess drip through. Leave to dry.

10 Just before the icing dries, decorate each cake with cherries, flowers and dragées, or with piped glacé icing.

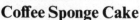

Colour index page 92
Makes one 20.5-cm (8-in) ring cake

Coffee Sponge Cake

3 large (size 2) eggs,
separated
1.25 ml (¼ level tsp) cream
of tartar
225 g (8 oz) caster sugar
100 ml (4 fl oz) cold coffee
2.5 ml (½ tsp) vanilla
essence

100 g (4 oz) plain flour
1.25 ml (¼ level tsp)
baking powder
1.25 ml (¼ level tsp) salt
50 g (2 oz) shelled walnuts,
finely chopped
sifted icing sugar, optional

1. Whisk the egg whites and cream of tartar until stiff peaks form. Gradually whisk in 50 g (2 oz) of the sugar until mixture is smooth and glossy and stiff peaks form again.
2. Beat the egg yolks with the coffee and vanilla essence. Sift together the flour, baking powder and salt and stir in the remaining sugar. Make a well in the centre, add the coffee mixture and beat until the mixture is light and fluffy.
3. Stir in the walnuts, then fold in the whisked egg whites with a metal spoon until evenly blended.
4. Spoon into an ungreased 20.5-cm (8-in) ring tin or 18-cm (7-in) round cake tin and bake at 180°C (350°F) mark 4 for 1 hour–1 hour 10 minutes, or until the top springs back when lightly touched with your fingertips.
5. Invert the tin on to a bottle neck, funnel or wire rack to cool upside down. When the cake is cold, loosen it gently with a palette knife and turn it carefully out of the tin. Dredge the cake with sifted icing sugar, if you wish.

COFFEE AND WALNUT SPONGE CAKE: Prepare the cake as above. When it is cold, slice it in half horizontally. Make coffee butter cream, using *275 g (10 oz) icing sugar* (page 400); sandwich the layers together with about a fifth of it, then coat the sides of the cake thinly. Spread *50 g (2 oz) chopped walnuts* on a sheet of greaseproof paper; holding the cake on its side, roll it on the chopped walnuts until the sides are evenly coated. Divide the remaining butter cream in half and spread one half over the cake, making sure that the inside of the ring is covered. Put the remainder in a piping bag with a star nozzle and pipe rosettes round the top and bottom edges of the cake.

Loosening the cake: Run a palette or round-bladed knife around the sides.

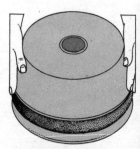

Turning out the cake: Turn the tin upside down over a plate; shake gently.

Fruit cakes

Christmas Cake

400 g (14 oz) plain flour
5 ml (1 level tsp) ground
  mixed spice
5 ml (1 level tsp) ground
  cinnamon
grated rind of ¼ lemon
350 g (12 oz) butter
350 g (12 oz) caster sugar
6 large (size 2) eggs,
  beaten
625 g (1 lb 6 oz) currants
225 g (8 oz) sultanas
225 g (8 oz) seedless
  raisins, chopped
175 g (6 oz) glacé cherries,
  quartered

100 g (4 oz) almonds,
  blanched and chopped
100 g (4 oz) chopped mixed
  peel
brandy

To finish:
almond paste made with
  400 g (14 oz) ground
  almonds, page 401
royal icing made with 900 g
  (2 lb) icing sugar,
  page 401

Colour index page 93

Makes one 20.5-cm (8-in)
square cake

1 Grease a 20.5-cm (8-in)
square cake tin; line it
with greased greaseproof
paper. Tie double brown
paper round the outside.

2 Sift the flour and spices
together into a large
bowl and stir in the grated
lemon rind.

3 Cream the butter in a
large mixing bowl and
gradually beat in the sugar
until light and fluffy.

4 Add eggs a little at a
time, beating well after
each addition. If mixture
curdles, beat in a little flour.

5 Lightly fold in the
sifted flour alternately
with the fruit, nuts and
mixed peel, until they are
evenly distributed. Stir in
30 ml (2 tbsp) brandy.

6 Spoon the mixture into
the prepared tin and
level the surface; hollow
out the centre with the
back of a spoon so cake
will be level when cooked.

7 Cover and leave in a
cool place overnight, if
you wish. Place on a
double thickness of brown
paper and bake at 150°C
(300°F) mark 2 for 4 hours.

8 When the cake is
cooked, a skewer
inserted in the centre
should come out clean.
Cool in the tin for 1 hour,
then turn out on to a wire
rack. Remove paper.

9 When cold, prick at
intervals with a fine
skewer and spoon a little
brandy evenly over
surface. Invert the cake
and wrap in fresh
greaseproof paper.

10 Store the cake in an
airtight tin for at
least 1 month before covering with almond paste.
Leave to dry, then flat or
rough ice with royal icing;
decorate as you wish.

Colour index page 91

Makes one 25.5-cm (10-in) ring cake

or one 20.5-cm (8-in) round cake

Rich Dark Fruit Ring

225 g (8 oz) plain flour
2.5 ml (½ level tsp) each
  ground ginger and mace
225 g (8 oz) butter
225 g (8 oz) soft dark
  brown sugar
4 large (size 2) eggs,
  beaten
grated rind of 1 lemon
225 g (8 oz) currants
225 g (8 oz) sultanas

100 g (4 oz) small glacé
  cherries, halved
50 g (2 oz) almonds,
  chopped
100 g (4 oz) chopped mixed
  peel
15–30 ml (1–2 tbsp)
  brandy

To serve, optional:
apricot glaze, page 401

1. Grease a 25.5-cm (10-in) ring tin and line it with
greased greaseproof paper. Tie a double thickness of
brown paper round the outside of the tin.
2. Sift together the flour and spices. Cream the
butter with the sugar until light and fluffy.
3. Gradually beat in the eggs. If the mixture begins
to curdle, beat in some of the sifted flour.
4. Lightly fold in the sifted flour alternately with the
lemon rind, fruit, nuts and mixed peel, until evenly
distributed. Stir in the brandy.
5. Spoon the mixture into the prepared tin and level
the surface. Stand the tin on a double thickness of
brown paper and bake at 150°C (300°F) mark 2 for
about 3¾ hours. If the cake is browning too quickly,
cover with a sheet of greaseproof paper 1 hour
before the end of cooking time.
6. Cool in the tin on a wire rack for 1 hour, then turn
out on to the rack to finish cooling. Remove the
paper, wrap in fresh greaseproof paper and store in
an airtight tin or wrapped in foil.
7. Just before serving brush the top of the cake with
apricot glaze if you wish.

Colour index page 92

Makes one 25.5 × 15 cm (10 × 6 in) cake

Brazil Nut and Fruit Loaf

450 g (1 lb) shelled Brazil
  nuts
275 g (10 oz) stoned dates
2 175-g (6-oz) jars
  maraschino cherries,
  drained
75 g (3 oz) plain flour
2.5 ml (½ level tsp) baking
  powder

2.5 ml (½ level tsp) salt
175 g (6 oz) caster
  sugar
3 eggs
5 ml (1 tsp) vanilla
  essence

1. Grease and line a 900-g (2-lb) loaf tin.
2. Mix the Brazil nuts with the dates and cherries in a
large bowl. Sift together the flour, baking powder
and salt and stir in the sugar. Stir with the nuts and
fruit until they are evenly coated.
3. Whisk the eggs and vanilla essence until foamy;
stir into the nut mixture until evenly mixed.
4. Spoon into the prepared tin and level the surface.
Bake at 150°C (300°F) mark 2 for 2½ hours. Cool in
the tin on a wire rack for at least 1 hour, then turn
out on to the wire rack to cool completely.

Gâteaux and Torten

Sachertorte

Colour index page 90

Makes one 23-cm (9-in) round cake

100 g (3½ oz) shelled hazel
 nuts
100 g (3½ oz) butter
150 g (5 oz) caster sugar
5 large (size 2) eggs,
 separated
75 g (3 oz) plain chocolate
15 ml (1 tbsp) rum
60 ml (4 level tbsp) dried
 white breadcrumbs
pinch ground cloves
275 g (10 oz) apricot jam

For the icing:
50 g (2 oz) cooking
 chocolate
30 ml (2 tbsp) water
5 ml (1 tsp) glycerine
about 75 g (3 oz) icing
 sugar, sifted

To serve:
whipped cream

1. Grease a 23-cm (9-in) spring-release cake tin and line it with greased greaseproof paper.
2. Lightly brown the hazel nuts under the grill, place them in a paper bag and rub between your hands to remove the skins. Grind them finely.
3. Cream the butter and sugar; beat in the egg yolks.
4. Put the chocolate and rum in the top of a double saucepan and melt the chocolate over hot, not boiling, water. Cool slightly; fold into the creamed mixture with the nuts, breadcrumbs and cloves.
5. Whisk the egg whites until stiff peaks form and fold them carefully into the mixture with a metal spoon until evenly blended.
6. Pour the mixture into the tin and bake at 200°C (400°F) mark 6 for 30 minutes, or until well risen and firm to the touch. Cool in the tin on a wire rack, then remove sides of tin to cool completely.
7. When the cake is cold, cut it in half horizontally and sandwich the layers together with the jam.
8. Put the chocolate and water in the top of a double saucepan over hot, not boiling, water, and stir until the chocolate has melted. Add the glycerine and stir in enough of the sugar to give a coating consistency.
9. Coat the top and sides of the cake with the icing and serve with whipped cream.

ASSEMBLING THE SACHERTORTE

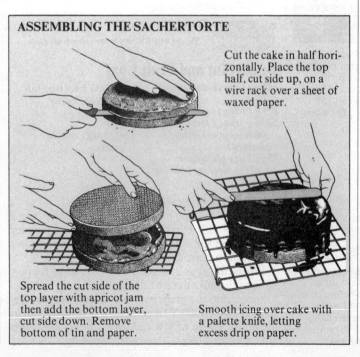

Cut the cake in half horizontally. Place the top half, cut side up, on a wire rack over a sheet of waxed paper.

Spread the cut side of the top layer with apricot jam then add the bottom layer, cut side down. Remove bottom of tin and paper.

Smooth icing over cake with a palette knife, letting excess drip on paper.

MAKING CHOCOLATE CURLS

Soften the chocolate with the heat of your hands or in a cool oven. Slowly and firmly pull a vegetable peeler across the chocolate to shave it off in curls.

Alternatively, melt the chocolate over hot water, spread in a thick layer on non-stick or waxed paper and leave until just on the point of setting. Using a sharp knife held at an angle of 45° and a light, sawing movement , scrape off very thin layers of chocolate, which will form curls.

Chocolate curls will keep in an airtight tin, but look better if freshly made. Curls kept in the refrigerator will look slightly grey.

Eggnog Gâteau

Colour index page 93

Makes one 20.5-cm (8-in) round cake

3 eggs
225 g (8 oz) caster sugar
175 g (6 oz) plain flour
7.5 ml (1½ level tsp)
 baking powder
1.25 ml (¼ level tsp)
 ground nutmeg
1.25 ml (¼ level tsp) salt
300 ml (½ pint) double
 cream

1.25 ml (¼ tsp) rum
 essence
100 g (4 oz) plain chocolate
chocolate butter cream
 made with 550 g (1¼ lb)
 icing sugar, page 400, or
 rich chocolate frosting
 made with 375 g (13 oz)
 icing sugar, page 400

1. Grease and flour three 20.5-cm (8-in) sandwich tins. Shake out any excess flour.
2. Put the eggs and sugar in a large deep bowl, stand it over a pan of hot water and whisk until thick, light and creamy. The mixture should be stiff enough to hold the impression of the whisk for a few seconds. Remove the bowl from the heat and whisk until cool. (If you are using an electric mixer, no heat is necessary while whisking.)
3. Sift together the flour, baking powder, nutmeg and salt. Whip the cream with the rum essence until stiff peaks form. Fold the dry ingredients and cream into the whisked egg mixture.
4. Divide the mixture between the tins and bake at 180°C (350°F) mark 4 for 25–30 minutes, or until a wooden toothpick inserted in the centre of each cake comes out clean. Cool in the tins on wire racks for about 10 minutes, then turn out on to the racks to cool completely.
5. When the cake layers are cold, cut them in half horizontally with a long-bladed knife. Sandwich the six layers together with some of the chocolate butter cream or rich chocolate frosting, finishing with the top surface of one of the layers uppermost. Coat the top and sides of the gâteau with the remaining butter cream or frosting. Chill until required.
6. Meanwhile, make chocolate curls (above) with the plain chocolate.
7. Just before serving, pile the chocolate curls on top of the gâteau, lifting them on with wooden cocktail sticks to prevent them melting.

Black Forest Cherry Torte

2 425-g (15-oz) cans stoned
  Morello cherries,
  drained
120 ml (8 tbsp) kirsch
6 eggs
225 g (8 oz) caster
  sugar
2.5 ml (½ tsp) vanilla
  essence
75 g (3 oz) plain flour
50 g (2 oz) cocoa
  powder
100 g (4 oz) butter,
  warmed until very soft
300 ml (½ pint) double
  cream

150 ml (¼ pint) single
  cream
50 g (2 oz) icing sugar,
  sifted
75 g (3 oz) plain chocolate
12 maraschino cherries,
  drained

Colour index page 92

Makes one 23-cm (9-in)
round cake

1 Put the cherries in a bowl with 90 ml (6 tbsp) kirsch and leave at room temperature for 2½ hours, stirring occasionally.

2 Grease and base line a 23-cm (9-in) round cake tin. Put the eggs, sugar and vanilla essence in a bowl. Stand it over a pan of hot water and whisk until thick. Remove from the heat and whisk until cool. Sift together the flour and cocoa and fold into the whisked mixture. Fold in the butter. Pour into the tin and bake at 180°C (350°F) mark 4 for about 40 minutes, or until the top springs back when lightly touched. Cool the cake, then cut into three layers.

3 Prick the top of each cake layer with a fork, then drain the cherries and sprinkle the reserved liquid over the cakes.

4 Whip the double and single creams together. Add the icing sugar and remaining 30 ml (2 tbsp) kirsch and whip again until stiff peaks form.

5 Put the first cake layer on a flat plate and spread with a quarter of the whipped cream; spoon half the cherries over top.

6 Put a second cake layer on top and spread with another quarter of cream and remaining cherries; top with the third layer.

7 Cover the sides of the cake with half the remaining cream. Grate 25 g (1 oz) chocolate.

8 Gently press the grated chocolate on to the cream all round the sides of the cake with a spoon or spatula.

9 Pipe the remaining whipped cream in whirls round the top of the cake; top each whirl with a maraschino cherry.

10 Make chocolate curls (opposite) with the remaining chocolate and pile them in the centre. Chill until required.

Colour index page 91
Makes one 23-cm (9-in) round cake

Hazel Nut Gâteau

175 g (6 oz) butter
175 g (6 oz) caster
  sugar
3 large (size 2) eggs,
  beaten
150 g (5 oz) self raising
  flour
25 g (1 oz) ground hazel
  nuts

400 ml (¾ pint) double or
  whipping cream
30 ml (2 level tbsp) sifted
  icing sugar
50 g (2 oz) hazel nuts,
  shelled and finely
  chopped

1. Lightly grease a 23-cm (9-in) round cake tin and base line it with greased greaseproof paper.
2. Cream the butter with the sugar until light and fluffy, then add the eggs a little at a time, beating well after each addition. If the mixture curdles, add a little of the flour.
3. Sift the flour over the mixture and fold it in with the ground hazel nuts.
4. Pour the mixture into the prepared tin, level the surface and bake at 180°C (350°F) mark 4 for about 40 minutes, until the top springs back when lightly touched with your fingertips. Cool in the tin on a wire rack for 10 minutes, then turn out on to the rack to cool completely.
5. Meanwhile, whip the cream with the icing sugar until stiff peaks form.
6. When the cake is cold, cut it in half horizontally with a long-bladed knife. Sandwich the cake layers together with about a quarter of the sweetened cream. Spread half the remaining cream over the sides and lightly press in the chopped hazel nuts with your hand or a spatula.
7. Place the remaining cream in a piping bag fitted with a large star nozzle and pipe decoratively over the top of the cake.

DECORATING THE HAZEL NUT GATEAU

Sandwich the cake layers together and then coat the sides of the gâteau with sweetened whipped cream; press in chopped nuts with your hand or with a spatula.

Pipe the remaining whipped cream decoratively around the edge and over the top of the hazel nut gâteau.

Tiered cakes

Three-tier Rose Sponge Cake

Colour index page 93

Makes one three-tier cake with 30.5-cm (12-in) base

10 eggs
950 g (2 lb 2 oz) caster
* sugar*
425 ml (16 fl oz) milk
10 ml (2 tsp) vanilla
* essence*
550 g (1 lb 4 oz) plain flour
25 ml (5 level tsp) baking
* powder*
7.5 ml (1½ level tsp) salt
275 g (10 oz) butter,
* softened*
lemon butter cream made
* with 450 g (1 lb) icing*
* sugar, page 400*

To decorate:
vanilla butter cream made
* with 1.1 kg (2½ lb)*
* icing sugar, page 400 or*
* glacé icing made with*
* 700 g (1½ lb) icing*
* sugar, page 400*
red food colouring
piped roses and leaves,
* page 399*

1. Grease a 30.5-cm (12-in) round cake tin, 23-cm (9-in) round cake tin and 15-cm (6-in) round cake tin; base line them with greased greaseproof paper.

2. Separate the eggs and place the whites in a very large bowl. Put the yolks in another bowl.

3. Whisk the egg whites with a mixer or rotary whisk until stiff peaks form, then gradually whisk in 175 g (6 oz) of the sugar until the mixture is smooth and glossy and stiff peaks form again.

4. Beat the egg yolks with the milk and vanilla essence. Sift together the flour, baking powder and salt into a very large bowl and stir in the remaining sugar. Make a well in the centre, add the egg yolk mixture and beat together.

5. Beat in the softened butter until light and fluffy. Fold in the whisked egg whites with a metal spoon until evenly blended.

6. Divide the mixture between the prepared cake tins and bake at 190°C (375°F) mark 5, with the largest cake on the lower shelf of the oven and the smaller cakes on the top shelf. Put the 15-cm (6-in) cake at the front of the oven.

7. Bake the 15-cm (6-in) cake for about 45 minutes, the 23-cm (9-in) cake for about 1 hour and the 30.5-cm (12-in) cake for about 1 hour 20 minutes, removing the smaller cakes quickly from the oven to avoid draughts. A wooden cocktail stick or fine skewer inserted in the centre of each cake should come out clean when the cake has finished cooking. Cool each cake in its tin on a wire rack for a short time, then turn the cakes out on to the racks to cool completely.

8. When the cakes are cold, cut each one in half horizontally with a long-bladed knife. Fill and assemble them (right) on a large cake plate or drum, using the lemon butter cream for the filling and placing a cake board between each layer.

9. Reserve a little of the vanilla butter cream or glacé icing and tint the rest with red food colouring to a delicate pink colour. Ice the cake with the pink butter cream or glacé icing (opposite) and pipe the reserved white butter cream decoratively over it with a star and plain nozzle. Decorate with the piped roses and leaves.

10. To cut the cake, start with the top tier and remove each thin cake board as it is exposed. Use a long-bladed knife and cut with a sawing action.

ASSEMBLING THE CAKE

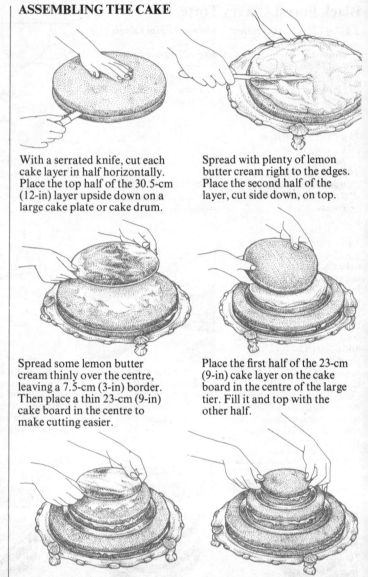

With a serrated knife, cut each cake layer in half horizontally. Place the top half of the 30.5-cm (12-in) layer upside down on a large cake plate or cake drum.

Spread with plenty of lemon butter cream right to the edges. Place the second half of the layer, cut side down, on top.

Spread some lemon butter cream thinly over the centre, leaving a 7.5-cm (3-in) border. Then place a thin 23-cm (9-in) cake board in the centre to make cutting easier.

Place the first half of the 23-cm (9-in) cake layer on the cake board in the centre of the large tier. Fill it and top with the other half.

Spread lemon butter cream thinly over the centre of the second tier; place a thin 15-cm (6-in) cake board on top.

Place half the 15-cm (6-in) layer in the centre of this cake board. Fill with lemon butter cream and top with the other half.

PIPING BORDERS

Shell border: Using a piping bag fitted with a star nozzle, pipe a series of well-formed shells, linking them in a line. Release the pressure as you form each point so that each shell is quite distinct in shape, with a broad head and pointed tail.

Alternating shell border: Pipe over the top edge of the cake so that the head of one shell is piped on the top, and the head of the next shell is on the side of the cake. Round the base of the cake, pipe one shell on the cake board, the other on the side of the cake.

Zig-zag border: Using a piping bag fitted with a star nozzle, pipe in a continuous line, moving the nozzle evenly from side to side.

String border: (Royal icing only) Using a piping bag fitted with a plain nozzle, pipe two rows of dots. Link the dots in pairs with diagonal strings of icing.

ICING THE CAKE

Spread sides of each layer smoothly with pink icing.

Leave icing to dry, then smooth pink icing over the top of each layer.

Using a piping bag and plain nozzle, pipe a looped edge round the top of each tier, attaching icing at the top and lifting the nozzle away from the sides of the cake to form loops.

Using a piping bag and small star nozzle, make a border round the top and bottom edge of each tier with white vanilla butter cream or glacé icing. Leave the icing to dry.

ICING FRUIT CAKES WITH ROYAL ICING

1. Cover the cake with almond paste and leave to dry for 1 week.
2. Secure the cake to the centre of a cake board with a small spoonful of icing and place it on an icing turntable.
3. Spread about half the icing round sides of cake and smooth it roughly with a palette knife. Hold knife or an icing comb upright and at an angle of 45° to the side of the cake; draw it towards you to smooth surface, rotating turntable with your other hand. Neaten edges and remove any surplus icing. Leave for 24 hours. (For a square cake, ice two opposite sides; leave for 24 hours before icing other sides.)
4. Spoon remaining icing on top of cake and spread evenly, removing air bubbles. Take an icing ruler or palette knife longer than the width of the cake and, without applying any pressure, draw it across top of cake at an angle of 30°. Neaten edges and remove surplus. Leave for 48 hours before adding decorations.
5. For a cake with pillars, sketch your design on paper first, marking spaces for the pillars. Ice each cake separately and leave to harden. Fix pillars in position with a little icing and leave for 1 week to dry. Assemble just before needed.

THREE-TIER WEDDING CAKE

For a cake to serve approximately 150 people, make a cake with round tiers measuring 30.5 cm (12 in), 23 cm (9 in) and 15 cm (6 in). Use the method given for Christmas cake (page 393) with the following quantities of ingredients. Bake the large cake for about 8 hours, the middle cake for 4 hours and the small cake for 2½–3 hours. A skewer inserted in the centre of the cakes should come out clean when the cakes are cooked.

QUANTITIES OF INGREDIENTS FOR THE CAKE			
Ingredient	30.5 cm (12 in)	23 cm (9 in)	15 cm (6 in)
Plain flour	825 g (1 lb 13 oz)	400 g (14 oz)	175 g (6 oz)
Mixed spice	12.5 ml (2½ level tsp)	5 ml (1 level tsp)	1.25 ml (¼ level tsp)
Cinnamon	12.5 ml (2½ level tsp)	5 ml (1 level tsp)	1.25 ml (¼ level tsp)
Lemon rind	½ lemon	¼ lemon	a little
Butter	800 g (1 lb 12 oz)	350 g (12 oz)	150 g (5 oz)
Sugar	800 g (1 lb 12 oz)	350 g (12 oz)	150 g (5 oz)
Size 2 eggs	14	6	2½
Currants	1.5 kg (3 lb 2 oz)	625 g (1 lb 6 oz)	225 g (8 oz)
Sultanas	525 g (1 lb 3 oz)	225 g (8 oz)	100 g (4 oz)
Raisins	525 g (1 lb 3 oz)	225 g (8 oz)	100 g (4 oz)
Glacé cherries	350 g (12 oz)	175 g (6 oz)	50 g (2 oz)
Almonds	250 g (9 oz)	100 g (4 oz)	25 g (1 oz)
Mixed peel	250 g (9 oz)	100 g (4 oz)	25 g (1 oz)
Brandy	60 ml (4 tbsp)	30 ml (2 tbsp)	15 ml (1 tbsp)
Almond paste	1.1 kg (2½ lb)	800 g (1 lb 12 oz)	350 g (12 oz)
Royal icing	1.4 kg (3 lb)	900 g (2 lb)	450 g (1 lb)

CUTTING A THREE-TIER CAKE
Use a long, thin knife and, with a sawing action, cut the cake into 150 servings following this guide.

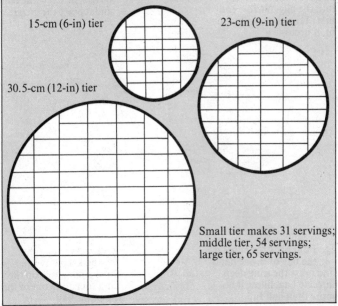

15-cm (6-in) tier

23-cm (9-in) tier

30.5-cm (12-in) tier

Small tier makes 31 servings; middle tier, 54 servings; large tier, 65 servings.

Piped decorations

To decorate a cake with a professional touch you simply need the basic equipment and a little practice. With a piping bag and a selection of nozzles and icing nails you can make a wide range of shapes and designs. Practise new shapes on an upturned plate, scraping up the icing while it is still soft to use on the cake when you have perfected the piping technique.

Butter cream, stiff glacé icing and royal icing can all be piped successfully. Use butter cream or glacé icing for sponge cakes and royal icing for the formal decoration of fruit cakes. Whichever icing you are using, it must be free of any lumps that might block the piping nozzle. It must also be of a consistency that can be forced easily through the nozzle without strong pressure, yet still retain its shape.

Our instructions are for right-handed cooks. If you are left-handed, read 'left' for 'right' and vice versa.

Make flowers ahead and freeze them. Butter cream flowers will keep for a week in the freezer, while royal icing flowers keep for months.

BASIC EQUIPMENT

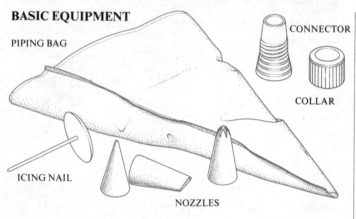

PIPING BAG

CONNECTOR

COLLAR

ICING NAIL

NOZZLES

FITTING AND FILLING THE BAG

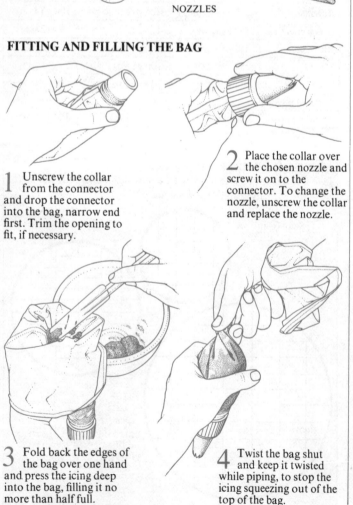

1 Unscrew the collar from the connector and drop the connector into the bag, narrow end first. Trim the opening to fit, if necessary.

2 Place the collar over the chosen nozzle and screw it on to the connector. To change the nozzle, unscrew the collar and replace the nozzle.

3 Fold back the edges of the bag over one hand and press the icing deep into the bag, filling it no more than half full.

4 Twist the bag shut and keep it twisted while piping, to stop the icing squeezing out of the top of the bag.

HOLDING THE PIPING BAG

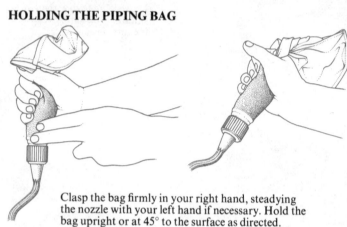

Clasp the bag firmly in your right hand, steadying the nozzle with your left hand if necessary. Hold the bag upright or at 45° to the surface as directed.

TYPES OF NOZZLE

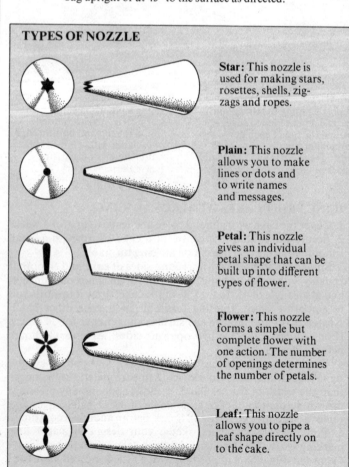

Star: This nozzle is used for making stars, rosettes, shells, zig-zags and ropes.

Plain: This nozzle allows you to make lines or dots and to write names and messages.

Petal: This nozzle gives an individual petal shape that can be built up into different types of flower.

Flower: This nozzle forms a simple but complete flower with one action. The number of openings determines the number of petals.

Leaf: This nozzle allows you to pipe a leaf shape directly on to the cake.

PIPING WITH A STAR NOZZLE

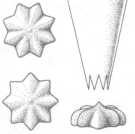

Stars: With the nozzle held upright and just above surface, squeeze and lift slightly, keeping the tip in the icing. Stop pressure; pull away.

Rosettes: Position nozzle as for stars, but as you squeeze, move nozzle in a circle, enclosing the middle. Stop pressure; pull away sharply.

Shells: With nozzle held at 45° and touching surface, squeeze; lift slightly as icing fans out. Stop pressure and pull to right to form a point.

PIPING WITH A PLAIN NOZZLE

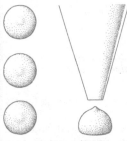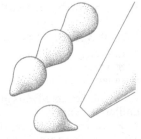

Dots: With the nozzle held upright and touching the surface, squeeze to form a dot, and lift slightly, keeping the tip in icing. Stop pressure; pull nozzle away.

Beads: With the nozzle held at 45°, follow technique for shells (above), slightly overlapping beads by starting each bead on the point of the preceding one.

Writing: Use slightly thinned icing that will flow smoothly. Holding nozzle at 45° and touching surface at the start to secure the icing, squeeze lightly, then lift nozzle away as you begin to form letters. Use even pressure and guide piping bag with entire arm. Stop pressure and lower nozzle to surface, 1 cm (½ in) before end of last letter.

PIPING WITH A PETAL NOZZLE

Scallop edge: With nozzle at 45°, touch surface at wide end of opening but keep narrow end slightly lifted; squeeze gently, moving in a series of curves.

Scalloped ribbon edge: Position the nozzle as for a scallop edge, but as you complete each curve, move the nozzle up and down in three short strokes.

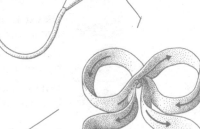

Bow: Work with bag pointing towards you. With nozzle held at 45°, and touching surface at wide end of opening, hold bag so the opening is vertical. Squeeze and make a loop to left, then stop pressure as you cross starting point. Repeat to make a loop to right of starting point, then make two streamers from the centre point.

MAKING A ROSE

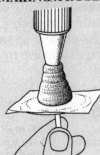

Attach a small square of non-stick or waxed paper to an icing nail with a dab of icing; hold the nail with the thumb and forefinger of your left hand. With a plain nozzle held upright, pipe a mound of icing to form the centre of the rose.

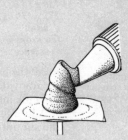

With petal nozzle at 45°, touch just below top of mound at wide end; hold bag so opening is vertical. Turn nail to left as you pipe a band of icing up, round and down to starting point to make bud.

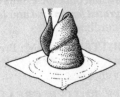

Touch wide end to base so opening is vertical; move up and down in arc. Make two more petals.

With the narrow end outwards, opening at a slight slant, pipe a row of four petals under first row.

With the opening at a greater slant, pipe a final row of five or seven petals under the previous row. Lift paper off nail and leave rose to dry.

MAKING LEAVES

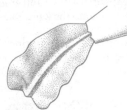

Flat leaf: With a leaf nozzle at 45° and touching the surface, squeeze until the icing fans out, then draw leaf to a point, gradually relaxing the pressure.

Stand-up leaf: With a leaf nozzle at 90° and touching the surface, squeeze until icing fans out, then raise nozzle and draw the point of the leaf up, gradually relaxing the pressure.

Icings and fillings

Opposite page
Piped cake decorations (pages 398–399)

Birthday, Christmas and other special occasion cakes are usually iced and decorated, but any cake will taste and look a little better with a smooth icing or fluffy butter cream or frosting. Use glacé icing to give a pretty gloss to cup cakes and sponges and use royal icing for a rich fruit cake.

Vanilla Butter Cream

To fill and coat one 20.5-cm (8-in) sandwich cake or coat one 20.5-cm (8-in) ring cake

150 g (5 oz) butter
275 g (10 oz) icing sugar, sifted
few drops vanilla essence

15–30 ml (1–2 tbsp) milk or warm water
few drops food colouring, optional

1. Put the butter in a bowl and cream until soft.
2. Gradually beat the icing sugar, vanilla essence and milk into the butter until smooth.
3. Add a few drops of food colouring if you wish, and stir until the butter cream is evenly coloured.
4. Spread over cooled cake layers as a filling, or over the top and sides of a cake as an icing.

LEMON BUTTER CREAM: Prepare the butter cream as above, but omit the vanilla essence and add a little *finely grated lemon rind* and *lemon juice*. Beat well to avoid curdling.

WALNUT BUTTER CREAM: Prepare the butter cream as above, but add *30 ml (2 level tbsp) shelled walnuts,* finely chopped.

CHOCOLATE BUTTER CREAM: Prepare the butter cream as above, but add *25–40 g (1–1½ oz) plain chocolate*, melted and cooled, or 15 ml (1 level tbsp) cocoa powder, dissolved in a little hot milk taken from the measured amount.

COFFEE BUTTER CREAM: Prepare the butter cream as above, but omit the vanilla essence and add *15 ml (1 tbsp) coffee essence* or 10 ml (2 level tsp) instant coffee dissolved in a little hot milk or water taken from the measured amount.

Glacé Icing

To top one 20.5-cm (8-in) cake or 18 small cakes

100–175 g (4–6 oz) icing sugar, sifted
15–30 ml (1–2 tbsp) warm water

few drops food colouring, optional

1. Put the icing sugar in a bowl and gradually add the water, beating well, until the icing is smooth and will coat the back of the spoon.
2. Add a few drops of food colouring if you wish.
3. Pour the icing on to the cake and spread evenly or, for small cakes, dip the top of each cake into the icing. Leave to set for about 1 hour.

LEMON GLACÉ ICING: Prepare the icing as above, but replace 15 ml (1 tbsp) water with *strained lemon juice.*

CHOCOLATE GLACÉ ICING: Prepare the icing as above, but add *10 ml (2 level tsp) cocoa powder* dissolved in a little warm water taken from the measured amount.

American Frosting

To coat one 23-cm (9-in) cake

450 g (1 lb) granulated sugar
60 ml (4 tbsp) water

pinch cream of tartar
1 egg white

1. Put the sugar, water and cream of tartar in a small heavy-based saucepan and heat gently, stirring frequently, until the sugar has dissolved.
2. Bring the mixture to the boil and boil steadily without stirring until it reaches 120°C (240°F), hard ball stage (page 414). Meanwhile, whisk the egg white until stiff peaks form.
3. Remove the sugar syrup from the heat and, as soon as the bubbles subside, pour it on to the egg whites in a thin stream, whisking continuously, until the frosting is thick and just beginning to go dull around the edges.
4. Pour the frosting immediately on to a cake and, working as quickly as possible, spread it evenly over the top and sides. Make swirls with the back of a spoon. Serve the cake within 24 hours.

Seven Minute Frosting

To fill and coat one 20.5-cm (8-in) sandwich cake

350 g (12 oz) caster sugar
2 egg whites
pinch salt

60 ml (4 tbsp) water
pinch cream of tartar

1. Put all the ingredients in a bowl and whisk lightly until well blended.
2. Place the bowl over hot water and continue whisking for about 7 minutes, or until the mixture thickens sufficiently to form peaks.
3. Spoon the frosting on to a cake, spreading it evenly over the top and sides, and make swirls with the back of a spoon.
4. Serve the cake within 24 hours.

AMERICAN AND SEVEN MINUTE FROSTING VARIATIONS

LEMON FROSTING: Prepare frosting as above, but add a little *lemon juice* while you are whisking.

ORANGE FROSTING: Prepare frosting as above, but add a little *orange juice* while you are whisking.

CARAMEL FROSTING: Prepare frosting as above, but replace the white sugar with *demerara sugar*.

COFFEE FROSTING: Prepare the frosting as above, but add *5 ml (1 tsp) coffee essence*.

Rich Chocolate Frosting

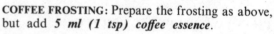
To fill and coat one 20.5-cm (8-in) sandwich cake

175 g (6 oz) plain chocolate, broken into small pieces
25 g (1 oz) blended white vegetable fat

190 g (6½ oz) icing sugar, sifted
50 ml (2 fl oz) milk

1. Put the chocolate and fat in the top of a double saucepan and heat gently over hot, not boiling, water until melted.
2. Stir in the icing sugar and milk. Remove from the heat and beat until smooth.
3. Spread the frosting over cooled cake layers as a filling, or use to coat the top and sides of the cake.

Opposite page

Clockwise from top: Citrus Pinwheels (page 411); Spice Biscuits (page 413); Shrewsbury Biscuits (page 412); Walnut Clusters (page 407); Chocolate Rum Truffles (page 420); Marzipan Fruits (page 419)

DECORATIVE IDEAS

The surface of soft or fluffy icings can very quickly be patterned with a fork or palette knife.

For a spiral, place cake on an icing turntable and lightly press palette knife blade into icing at centre; turn cake in one direction, drawing knife towards edge.

For a trellis pattern, draw the prongs of a fork over the icing in straight or wavy lines. Repeat at right angles to form a trellis.

Cream Cheese Frosting

To fill and coat one 20.5-cm (8-in) sandwich cake or top 24 small cakes

175 g (6 oz) cream cheese
30 ml (2 tbsp) evaporated milk
pinch salt

5 ml (1 tsp) vanilla essence
450 g (1 lb) icing sugar, sifted

1. Beat the cream cheese with the milk until smooth, then beat in the salt, vanilla essence and sugar.
2. Spread over cake layers as a filling or over the top and sides of a cake as an icing. For small cakes, dip the top of each into the frosting.

COFFEE CREAM CHEESE FROSTING: Prepare the frosting as above, but add *5 ml (1 level tsp) instant coffee powder* with the salt and sugar.

Fudge Filling

To fill and top one 20.5-cm (8-in) sandwich cake

350 g (12 oz) granulated sugar
100 ml (4 fl oz) single cream

25 g (1 oz) butter
5 ml (1 tsp) vanilla essence

1. Put the sugar, cream and butter into a heavy-based saucepan and heat gently, stirring frequently, until the sugar has dissolved.
2. Bring to the boil and boil steadily, stirring occasionally, until it reaches 112°C (234°F). Remove the saucepan from the heat, add the vanilla essence and beat until the mixture thickens. Spread the filling over cooled cake layers.

Fondant Icing

To coat one 18-cm (7-in) cake

fondant made with 450 g (1 lb) sugar, page 417

few drops food colouring, optional

1. Put the fondant in a bowl, place over hot water and heat very gently, stirring just until melted.
2. Dilute the fondant with cold water until the mixture just coats the back of the spoon and stir in a few drops of food colouring, if you wish.
3. Pour the icing quickly all over the cake to coat smoothly; do not touch with a knife or the glossy finish will be spoilt. Dip the tops of small cakes in the icing. Leave to set.

Satin Frosting

To coat one 20.5-cm (8-in) round cake

75 g (3 oz) butter
350 g (12 oz) icing sugar, sifted

45 ml (3 tbsp) single cream
few drops vanilla essence

1. Cream the butter until smooth, and gradually beat in the icing sugar and single cream. Flavour with vanilla essence.
2. Spread over the top and sides of the cooled cake.

Royal Icing

Makes 450 g (1 lb) to coat one 15-cm (6-in) round cake

2 egg whites
450 g (1 lb) icing sugar, sifted

10 ml (2 tsp) lemon juice
5 ml (1 tsp) glycerine

1. Whisk the egg whites until slightly frothy.
2. Beat in about a quarter of the icing sugar with a wooden spoon, then continue adding the sugar gradually, beating well after each addition, until about three quarters has been added.
3. Beat in the lemon juice and continue beating for about 10 minutes, until the icing is smooth, glossy and white.
4. Beat in the remaining sugar and glycerine to the required consistency. For flat icing, a wooden spoon placed upright in the icing will fall slowly to one side; do not overbeat. Cover the bowl with a damp cloth and leave for 24 hours to allow the air bubbles to rise to the surface.
5. To ice a Christmas cake, spread the icing over the top and sides of the cake and smooth it roughly with a palette knife. Draw the icing up into peaks all over the cake, or around the sides and in a border round the top of the cake only. To flat ice a formal cake follow the instructions on page 397.

Almond Paste

Makes 450 g (1 lb), to coat one 18-cm (7-in) round cake

100 g (4 oz) icing sugar, sifted
100 g (4 oz) caster sugar
225 g (8 oz) ground almonds

5 ml (1 tsp) lemon juice
few drops almond essence
1 egg or 2 egg yolks, beaten

1. Put the sugars and almonds in a large bowl.
2. Add the lemon juice, almond essence and enough egg to make a firm but manageable dough.
3. Turn the almond paste on to a working surface dusted with sifted icing sugar and knead with your hands until smooth.
4. To cover a cake with almond paste, first brush with apricot glaze (below). Roll out the paste and cut pieces to fit the sides and top of the cake; apply to the cake and seal the joins with a rolling pin. Leave for 2–5 days before icing.

Apricot Glaze

Makes 225 g (8 oz)

225 g (8 oz) apricot jam   *30 ml (2 tbsp) water*

1. Place the apricot jam and the water in a heavy-based saucepan and heat gently until the jam softens. Sieve the mixture.
2. Return the sieved jam to the saucepan, then bring it to the boil and boil gently until the glaze is of a coating consistency.

BISCUITS AND COOKIES

Most biscuits and cookies are easy to make and are an excellent introduction to the more complicated techniques of cake making. They require accurate measurement of ingredients and a minimum of handling, but are otherwise almost foolproof. For each basic recipe there are a dozen others you can invent by varying the flavourings, shapes or decoration.

Originally, biscuits were simply a substitute for bread. They were made of flour and water and baked twice (hence the French name 'bis cuit') to make them really dry so that they would keep a long time. They constituted part of the staple diet in situations where regular baking was not possible, such as on board ship: in fact, ship's biscuit was a part of naval rations right through to the present century. The nearest modern equivalent to this original biscuit is a water biscuit, usually served with cheese. Much more common are biscuits made from the sweetened and enriched mixtures that were developed to vary the original. As well as flour or other cereal and water, they include butter, sugar, flavourings, sometimes eggs and sometimes a chemical raising agent. Even in this enriched form true biscuits are thin and crisp and will keep well if properly stored.

Cookies are produced by much the same methods as traditional biscuits, but they have a softer and in some cases almost a cake-like texture. The distinction between biscuits and cookies has become blurred until the two words are now almost interchangeable.

PREPARATION

Always weigh biscuit and cookie ingredients accurately, to give a mixture of the correct consistency. Where butter is listed in the ingredients, substitute block margarine if you wish, but do not use soft tub margarine, as this gives a mixture of a different texture. Roll all dough to the same thickness for even browning and cut or shape biscuits to the same size so that they cook through evenly. Always choose a flat baking sheet with hardly any sides, as high sides will prevent proper browning, and if you need extra baking sheets use the bottoms of upturned roasting tins, but adjust the position of the oven shelves to accommodate the extra height. Grease the baking sheets or tins only if the recipe directs; if the recipe tells you to line a baking tin, follow the instructions on page 383.

TYPES OF BISCUIT AND COOKIE

Bar cookies can be crisp or soft and cake-like. They are very easy to make; you simply spoon or pour the mixture into a tin, bake it in one large piece and cut into bars or squares when cool.

Drop cookies are made from a soft mixture, which is too sticky to knead or roll and is placed by the spoonful on the baking sheet. Some mixtures spread to become thin, brittle biscuits during baking, while others retain their mounded shape so that the centre cooks to a cake-like texture.

Shaped biscuits and cookies are made from a soft mixture, which should not be too sticky as it is shaped by hand. Handle the mixture quickly, damping your hands if the mixture sticks. A shaped cookie may also be made by baking a much softer mixture in decorative patty tins.

Pressed or piped cookies are attractive and quick to make. The mixture must be smooth to flow through a biscuit press or piping nozzle, but firm enough to hold its shape during baking.

Refrigerator cookies are crisp, thin biscuits made from a rich mixture that improves with several days storage in the refrigerator. It makes an excellent stand-by for fresh biscuits in a hurry. Chill the mixture until it is firm enough to cut neatly, then slice off thin biscuits for baking. If you freeze the mixture, thaw it slightly before slicing and allow a little extra baking time.

Rolled biscuits are traditional crisp biscuits. The mixture is rolled out thinly and cut into shapes with a knife or biscuit cutter, so it must be firm and pliable. Chill it slightly and roll out thinly between sheets of waxed paper. Avoid adding extra flour to stop the mixture sticking as this toughens biscuits.

BAKING

Always turn on the oven early, so that it is preheated to the correct temperature by the time you are ready to bake. If you are baking one sheet of biscuits at a time, put it in the centre of the oven or just above; for two sheets, space the shelves evenly. Take care not to overcook biscuits by checking them just before the minimum baking time is up. If they are slow to brown, move them higher in the oven for the remaining baking time.

COOLING

You should normally transfer cookies to a wire rack for cooling as soon as they come out of the oven. But some, especially those sweetened with syrup or honey, are still soft after baking and should be left on the baking sheets for a few moments to harden slightly. Don't overlap the warm cookies or they will bend and become misshaped as they cool and harden on the racks.

STORING AND FREEZING

Most cookies and biscuits keep well in an airtight container for up to 2 weeks. Line the bottom of the container with waxed paper and layer them in, placing a sheet of waxed paper between each layer for soft cookies or between every two layers for crisp biscuits. Secure the lid firmly and make sure that the lid is replaced properly after any are taken out. To save space, store bar cookies in their baking tin, covered tightly with foil.

If you are storing cookies, do not decorate them until just before serving. Store soft and crisp cookies in separate containers so that the crisp cookies don't absorb any moisture. If plain biscuits lose their crispness, freshen them in the oven at 170°C (325°F) mark 3 for about 5 minutes.

Biscuits and cookies keep well in the freezer for several months. Pack fragile ones in rigid boxes but just wrap others in foil or freezer film. Spread in a single layer, they will thaw at room temperature in 30 minutes.

DECORATING

Biscuits and cookies can be topped with melted chocolate, a soft icing or a sugar glaze, or you can pipe on a design with stiff glacé icing (page 400) or royal icing (page 401). Use nuts, glacé fruit or jam for additional decoration, or simply dredge with caster or icing sugar.

The correct tools make decorating easy: use a small board and a sharp knife for chopping, a wire rack for drying biscuits, a palette knife for spreading icings and a pastry brush to dust away crumbs. Other useful tools are a piping bag, with writing and decorative nozzles for icing and wooden cocktail sticks or tweezers, to handle tiny decorations.

DECORATIVE IDEAS

Biscuits can be transformed into something special with just a little inspiration. You can buy cake decorations such as vermicelli, dragées and hundreds and thousands, but you can also make your own from glacé cherries, angelica, nuts or the children's favourite sweets. Here are some ideas that you can adapt to suit the available ingredients.

Double star: Ice two star-shaped biscuits and press them together so that all the points show. Sprinkle with vermicelli, hundreds and thousands or dragées.

Chequerboard: Coat an oblong biscuit with white icing. Using a fine writing nozzle, pipe on a chequerboard outline in chocolate icing, then fill in alternate squares with it.

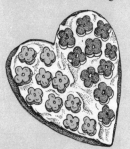

Valentines: Using a piping bag fitted with a star or plain nozzle, pipe icing over a heart-shaped biscuit. Decorate the two halves with contrasting sugar flowers, sugar strands or dragées.

Pine cone: Ice an oval biscuit and press in sliced hazel nuts or almonds in overlapping rows to resemble a pine cone.

Letter biscuit: Using a piping bag fitted with a star nozzle, pipe on rippled lines of icing in two or three contrasting colours, following the shape of the letter.

Doughnut biscuit: Ice the top of a doughnut-shaped biscuit and coat with sugar strands, vermicelli or hundreds and thousands.

Bar cookies

Boston Brownies

75 g (3 oz) butter
50 g (2 oz) plain chocolate
175 g (6 oz) caster sugar
2 eggs, beaten
75 g (3 oz) self raising
  flour
1.25 ml (¼ level tsp)
  salt
2.5 ml (½ tsp) vanilla
  essence
50 g (2 oz) shelled walnuts,
  roughly chopped

Colour index
page 104

Makes
12 cookies

1 Grease and flour a shal-low 20.5-cm (8-in) square tin. Melt the butter and chocolate in a sauce-pan over very low heat, stirring constantly to pre-vent the mixture sticking.

2 Remove the pan from the heat, add the sugar all at once and stir in well to dissolve. Allow the mix-ture to cool slightly.

3 Add the eggs and beat into the mixture until well blended. Sift the flour with the salt into a bowl.

4 Beat the flour and the vanilla essence into the chocolate mixture.

5 Add the chopped nuts, stir to mix well then beat until smooth.

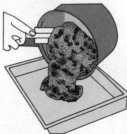 

6 Pour the mixture into the tin and bake at 180°C (350°F) mark 4 for 35–40 minutes, until it has risen and is beginning to leave the sides of the tin.

7 The brownies are cook-ed when a wooden cocktail stick or skewer inserted in the centre comes out clean. Cool in the tin, then cut into squares.

Almond and Coconut Bars

Colour index
page 104

Makes
12 cookies

100 g (4 oz) butter
100 g (4 oz) soft light
  brown sugar
50 g (2 oz) rolled oats
25 g (1 oz) wheat germ,
  toasted
75 g (3 oz) plain flour
15 ml (1 tbsp) grated
  orange rind

For the topping:
2 eggs, beaten
50 g (2 oz) soft light
  brown sugar
50 g (2 oz) desiccated
  coconut
100 g (4 oz) blanched
  almonds, halved

1. Grease well and base line a shallow 20.5-cm (8-in) square baking tin.
2. Cream the butter and sugar together until light and fluffy. Stir in the oats, wheat germ, flour and orange rind to make a fairly dry mixture. Press the mixture into the tin.
3. To make the topping, whisk the eggs and sugar well and stir in the coconut and almonds. Spread evenly over the mixture in the tin.
4. Bake at 180°C (350°F) mark 4 for 35 minutes. Cool in the tin, then cut into bars or squares.

Luscious Apricot Squares

Colour index
page 105

Makes
16 cookies

100 g (4 oz) butter
50 g (2 oz) caster sugar
100 g (4 oz) plain flour
icing sugar for dredging

For the topping:
150 g (5 oz) dried apricots
175 g (6 oz) soft light
  brown sugar
50 g (2 oz) plain flour

2 eggs, beaten
2.5 ml (½ level tsp) baking
  powder
2.5 ml (½ tsp) vanilla
  essence
1.25 ml (¼ level tsp) salt
50 g (2 oz) shelled walnuts,
  chopped

1. Grease well and base line a shallow 20.5-cm (8-in) square baking tin.
2. Cream the butter and sugar until light and fluffy and work in the flour to give a crumbly mixture. Press the mixture evenly into the tin and bake at 180°C (350°F) mark 4 for 25 minutes.
3. Put the apricots in a small saucepan with enough water to cover them, cover with a lid and cook for 15 minutes. Drain and chop them finely. Mix well with the remaining topping ingredients. Pour the mixture over the baked biscuit layer.
4. Return to the oven for a further 25 minutes. Cool in the tin and cut into squares. Dredge with icing sugar before serving.

Walnut Bars

Colour index
page 105

Makes
20 cookies

225 g (8 oz) butter
225 g (8 oz) caster sugar
5 ml (1 tsp) vanilla essence
1 egg, separated

200 g (7 oz) plain flour
50 g (2 oz) shelled walnuts,
  chopped

1. Grease well and base line two shallow 25 × 18 cm (10 × 7 in) oblong baking tins.
2. Cream the butter and sugar together until light and fluffy, and mix in the vanilla essence, egg yolk and flour. Press half the mixture into each tin.
3. Whisk the egg white lightly, brush it over the mixture and sprinkle the walnuts over the top.
4. Bake at 180°C (350°F) mark 4 for 45 minutes or until golden. Cut into bars and cool on a wire rack. Store for 3–4 days before serving.

Shortbread

Colour index
page 104

Makes
12 wedges

350 g (12 oz) plain flour or
225 g (8 oz) plain flour
mixed with 100 g (4 oz)
rice flour
pinch salt
225 g (8 oz) butter

100 g (4 oz) caster
sugar
caster sugar for
dredging

1 Grease and base line a
30.5-cm (12-in) round
sandwich tin. Sift the flour
and salt, rub in the butter
and add the sugar. Knead
lightly to mix.

2 Roll out the mixture to
a circle and press it
evenly into the tin.

3 Bake at 170–180°C
(325–350°F) mark 3–4,
for 1–1¼ hours, until coloured. Dredge with sugar.

4 Cut into portions while
still warm and leave to
cool in the tin on a wire
rack; then remove from tin.

Marbled Fudge Bars

Colour index
page 104

Makes
36 cookies

225 g (8 oz) butter
100 g (4 oz) plain chocolate
450 g (1 lb) caster sugar
3 eggs, beaten
100 g (4 oz) plain flour
2.5 ml (½ level tsp) salt
100 g (4 oz) shelled
walnuts, chopped
5 ml (1 tsp) vanilla essence

For the topping:
225 g (8 oz) cream cheese
100 g (4 oz) caster sugar
1 egg, beaten
5 ml (1 tsp) vanilla essence

1. Grease well and base line a shallow 33 × 23 cm
(13 × 9 in) oblong baking tin.
2. Melt the butter and chocolate in a heavy-based
saucepan over gentle heat. Whisk in the sugar and
eggs until well blended. Stir in the flour, salt,
chopped walnuts and vanilla essence. Spread the
chocolate dough in the tin.
3. Beat together the cream cheese, sugar, egg and
vanilla essence until well mixed. Spoon the mixture
roughly over the chocolate dough and make a criss-
cross pattern over the top with the tip of a knife.
4. Bake at 180°C (350°F) mark 4 for 40–45 minutes.
Cool in the tin and then cut into bars or squares.
Store in the refrigerator, wrapped in polythene.

Prune Ribbon Cookies

Colour index
page 105

Makes
27 cookies

175 g (6 oz) butter
275 g (10 oz) soft light
brown sugar
1 egg, beaten
5 ml (1 tsp) vanilla essence
225 g (8 oz) plain flour
5 ml (1 level tsp) baking
powder
2.5 ml (½ level tsp) salt

For the filling:
350 g (12 oz) dried stoned
prunes
300 ml (½ pint) water
60 ml (4 level tbsp) honey
¼ large lemon

1. Grease well and base line a shallow 23-cm (9-in)
square baking tin.
2. Cream together the butter and sugar until light
and fluffy, then beat in the egg and vanilla essence.
Stir in the flour, baking powder and salt, mixing well
until blended and smooth.
3. Put the prunes in a saucepan with the water and
bring to the boil. Reduce the heat and simmer for
3 minutes. Drain well. Purée the prunes, honey and
lemon wedge in a blender until smooth.
4. Press one third of the biscuit mixture into the tin
and spoon over half the prune filling. Repeat and
spread the remaining biscuit mixture over the top.
5. Bake at 180°C (350°F) mark 4 for 1 hour. Cool in
the tin and then cut into 7.5 × 2.5 cm (3 × 1 in) bars.

Linzer Cookies

Colour index
page 105

Makes
30 cookies

75–100 g (3–4 oz) ground
almonds
1 egg, beaten
225 g (8 oz) plain flour
225 g (8 oz) sugar
175 g (6 oz) butter,
softened

5 ml (1 level tsp) ground
cinnamon
5 ml (1 tsp) grated lemon
rind
pinch ground cloves
175 g (6 oz) raspberry jam

1. Grease a shallow 28 × 18 cm (11 × 7 in) tin.
2. Place all the ingredients, except for the jam, in a
large bowl and beat together well until thoroughly
mixed to form a dryish dough. Chill for about 30
minutes until easy to handle.
3. Press half the chilled dough evenly into the tin.
Spread the jam over the top.
4. Knead remaining dough and divide in half. Cut
one half into six equal pieces and roll each to a 28-cm
(11-in) rope. Place lengthways on the jam, 2.5 cm
(1 in) apart. Cut second half into eight equal pieces
and roll each to an 18-cm (7-in) rope. Arrange
crossways to form a lattice pattern.
5. Bake at 180°C (350°F) mark 4 for 40 minutes.
Cool in the tin and cut into 5 × 2.5 cm (2 × 1 in)
bars. The cookies may be served while still warm.

Making the ropes: Using
both hands, roll the pieces
of dough into long ropes.

Making the lattice pattern:
Arrange ropes crossways
to form a lattice pattern.

Drop cookies

Chocolate Cookies

Colour index
page 104

Makes
20 cookies

75 g (3 oz) butter
75 g (3 oz) granulated
  sugar
75 g (3 oz) soft light brown
  sugar
few drops vanilla essence
1 egg, beaten
175 g (6 oz) self raising
  flour
pinch salt
50–100 g (2–4 oz)
  chocolate chips
50 g (2 oz) shelled walnuts,
  chopped

1 Grease two baking
sheets. Cream the butter
with the sugars and vanilla
essence until light and
fluffy. Beat in the egg.

2 Sift the flour and salt
into the bowl and fold
into the creamed mixture.

3 Add the chocolate
chips and nuts and stir
to mix them thoroughly.

4 Drop spoonfuls on to
the baking sheets.
Bake at 180°C (350°F)
mark 4 for 12–15 minutes.

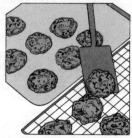

5 Cool on the baking
sheets for 1 minute then
transfer the cookies to a
wire rack to finish cooling.

Ginger and Cinnamon Cookies

Colour index
page 105

Makes
30 cookies

100 g (4 oz) blended white
  vegetable fat
100 g (4 oz) caster sugar
90 ml (6 level tbsp) black
  treacle or golden syrup
1 egg, beaten
275 g (10 oz) plain flour
10 ml (2 level tsp)
  bicarbonate of soda

5 ml (1 level tsp) ground
  ginger
5 ml (1 level tsp) ground
  cinnamon
1.25 ml (¼ level tsp) salt
75 ml (5 tbsp) water
seedless raisins

1. Grease three baking sheets. Cream the fat with the
sugar until light and fluffy. Beat in the syrup, egg and
remaining ingredients, except for the raisins.
2. Drop dessertspoonfuls of the mixture at least 5 cm
(2 in) apart on to the baking sheets and decorate
each one with a few raisins.
3. Bake at 200°C (400°F) mark 6 for 8 minutes.
Remove from the baking sheets; cool on a wire rack.

Double Chocolate Drops

Colour index
page 104

Makes
36 cookies

100 g (4 oz) butter
175 g (6 oz) caster sugar
50 g (2 oz) plain chocolate,
  melted
1 egg, beaten
5 ml (1 tsp) vanilla essence
200 g (7 oz) plain flour
5 ml (1 level tsp) salt
2.5 ml (½ level tsp)
  bicarbonate of soda
30 ml (2 tbsp) milk

For the icing:
50 g (2 oz) butter
40 g (1½ oz) plain
  chocolate, melted
175 g (6 oz) icing sugar,
  sifted
few drops vanilla essence,
  optional
50 g (2 oz) shelled pecans
  or walnuts, halved

1. Grease four baking sheets. Cream the butter with
the sugar and chocolate until fluffy. Beat in the egg
and vanilla essence. Add the remaining ingredients
for the cookie mixture and stir until smooth.
2. Drop teaspoonfuls of the mixture about 2.5 cm
(1 in) apart on to the baking sheets.
3. Bake at 200°C (400°F) mark 6 for 8–10 minutes
until the biscuits are slightly puffy. Remove from the
baking sheets and cool on a wire rack.
4. To make the icing, cream the butter with the
melted chocolate, then gradually beat in the icing
sugar until the mixture is smooth and creamy. If you
wish, add a few drops of vanilla essence. When the
biscuits are cold, decorate each one with a little icing
and half a pecan or walnut.

Toasted Oat and Raisin Cookies

Colour index
page 105

Makes
48 cookies

100 g (4 oz) butter
75 g (3 oz) caster sugar
75 g (3 oz) soft dark
  brown sugar
1 egg, beaten
175 g (6 oz) plain flour
2.5 ml (½ level tsp) salt
2.5 ml (½ level tsp)
  bicarbonate of soda

2.5 ml (½ tsp) vanilla
  essence
75 g (3 oz) toasted oats
75 g (3 oz) seedless raisins
50 g (2 oz) shelled unsalted
  peanuts, roughly
  chopped

1. Grease three baking sheets. Cream the butter and
sugars together until light and fluffy. Beat in the egg.
Sift together the flour, salt and bicarbonate of soda
and fold into the creamed mixture with the remaining ingredients.
2. Drop heaped teaspoonfuls of the mixture about
5 cm (2 in) apart on to the baking sheets, allowing
plenty of room for the biscuits to spread.
3. Bake at 180°C (350°F) mark 4 for 12–15 minutes
until lightly browned. Remove from the baking
sheets and cool on a wire rack.

TOASTED OAT AND CHOCOLATE COOKIES:
Prepare the mixture as above, but omit the raisins
and add *75 g (3 oz) chocolate chips* to the mixture.
Bake and cool the cookies as above.

TOASTED OAT AND DATE COOKIES: Prepare
the mixture as above, but omit the raisins and add
75 g (3 oz) stoned dates, chopped, to the mixture.
Bake and cool the cookies as above.

TOASTED OAT AND SULTANA COOKIES:
Prepare the mixture as above, but omit the raisins
and peanuts and add *75 g (3 oz) sultanas* and *50 g
(2 oz) chopped walnuts.* Bake and cool as above.

Colour index
page 105

Makes
20 biscuits

Brandy Snaps

100 g (4 oz) butter
100 g (4 oz) caster sugar
60 ml (4 level tbsp) golden syrup
100 g (4 oz) plain flour, sifted
5 ml (1 level tsp) ground ginger
10 ml (2 tsp) brandy, optional
grated rind of 1 lemon

1 Grease three baking sheets and some wooden spoon handles. Melt the butter, sugar and syrup. Stir in the remaining ingredients over low heat.

2 Drop spoonfuls 10 cm (4 in) apart on baking sheets. Keep rest warm. Bake biscuits at 180°C (350°F) for 7 minutes.

3 Allow the biscuits to cool on the sheets for 1–2 minutes, then loosen with a fish slice or palette knife.

4 Roll biscuits, smooth side in, round spoon handle; leave to set. Soften in oven if hard to roll.

5 Gently slide biscuits off spoon handles and cool on a wire rack. Repeat with remaining mixture.

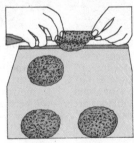

Colour index
page 104

Makes
36 cookies

Oat Cookies

100 g (4 oz) blended white vegetable fat
50 g (2 oz) caster sugar
100 g (4 oz) soft light brown sugar
2.5 ml (½ tsp) vanilla essence
1 egg, beaten

90 g (3½ oz) plain flour
2.5 ml (½ level tsp) salt
2.5 ml (½ level tsp) bicarbonate of soda
75 g (3 oz) rolled oats
50 g (2 oz) shelled walnuts, chopped

1. Grease three baking sheets. Cream the fat and sugars until light and fluffy. Beat in the vanilla essence, egg and remaining ingredients.
2. Drop teaspoonfuls of the mixture 2.5 cm (1 in) apart on to the baking sheets. Bake at 190°C (375°F) mark 5 for 12 minutes. Cool on a wire rack.

Colour index
page 104

Makes
36 cookies

Walnut Clusters

50 g (2 oz) butter
100 g (4 oz) caster sugar
40 g (1½ oz) plain chocolate, melted
1 egg, beaten
7.5 ml (1½ tsp) vanilla essence
50 g (2 oz) plain flour

2.5 ml (½ level tsp) salt
1.25 ml (¼ level tsp) baking powder
175 g (6 oz) shelled walnuts, chopped
icing sugar for dredging

1. Grease three baking sheets. Cream the butter with the sugar and chocolate until fluffy. Beat in the egg and vanilla essence. Sift together the flour, salt and baking powder and fold into the butter mixture with the walnuts.
2. Drop heaped teaspoonfuls of the mixture about 1 cm (½ in) apart on to the baking sheets.
3. Bake at 180°C (350°F) mark 4 for 10 minutes. Cool on a wire rack. Dredge with icing sugar.

Colour index
page 104

Makes
36 cookies

Chocolate Peanut Drops

100 g (4 oz) blended white vegetable fat
50 g (2 oz) plain chocolate, melted
100 g (4 oz) caster sugar
1 egg, beaten
5 ml (1 tsp) vanilla essence
100 g (4 oz) plain flour
5 ml (1 level tsp) salt

For the topping:
25 g (1 oz) butter
90 ml (6 level tbsp) peanut butter
100 g (4 oz) soft light brown sugar
30 ml (2 level tbsp) plain flour

1. Grease three baking sheets. Cream the fat with the chocolate and sugar until fluffy and then beat in the egg and vanilla essence. Sift together the flour and salt and stir into the chocolate mixture until smooth.
2. To make the topping, cream the butter and peanut butter with the sugar. Mix in the flour.
3. Drop teaspoonfuls of the chocolate dough 2.5 cm (1 in) apart on to the baking sheets and top each one with 2.5 ml (½ level tsp) of the peanut butter mixture. Dip a fork in a little flour and press lines on the top of each biscuit if you wish.
4. Bake at 170°C (325°F) mark 3 for 12 minutes. Cool on a wire rack.

Colour index
page 104

Makes
25 cookies

Orange and Raisin Cookies

150 g (5 oz) plain flour
100 g (4 oz) sugar
100 g (4 oz) butter, softened
1 egg, beaten
2.5 ml (½ level tsp) baking powder
2.5 ml (½ level tsp) salt

2.5 ml (½ tsp) vanilla essence
100 g (4 oz) seedless raisins
15 ml (1 tbsp) grated orange rind

1. Grease three baking sheets. Place all the ingredients except for the raisins and grated orange rind in a large bowl and beat lightly until just mixed. Stir in the raisins and orange rind.
2. Drop heaped dessertspoonfuls of the mixture about 5 cm (2 in) apart on to the baking sheets.
3. Bake at 190°C (375°F) mark 5 for 15 minutes or until the cookies are golden brown. Remove from the baking sheets and cool on a wire rack.

Drop cookies

Shaped cookies

Nut Rocks

Colour index
page 105

Makes
24–26
cookies

175 g (6 oz) blanched
almonds
250 g (9 oz) icing sugar,
sifted
4 egg whites
few drops almond or
vanilla essence

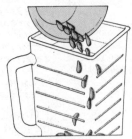

1 Line a baking sheet with
foil. Chop the almonds
finely in a blender or with
a sharp knife.

2 Whisk the sugar and
egg whites over boiling
water until stiff.

3 Remove from the heat
and stir in the almond
essence and chopped nuts.

4 With a teaspoon, drop
small mounds of mix-
ture on to prepared baking
sheet. Bake at 150°C
(300°F) mark 2 for 20–30
minutes until crisp outside
and soft inside.

5 Remove from the oven
and transfer the foil to
a wire rack. When cool,
peel the cookies off the foil
and store them in a con-
tainer with a tightly
fitting lid.

Coconut Meringue Cookies

Colour index
page 104

Makes
24 cookies

4 egg whites
275 g (10 oz) sugar
275 g (10 oz) shredded
coconut

few drops red or green food
colouring, optional

1. Grease two baking sheets and line with rice paper.
2. Whisk the egg whites stiffly and use a metal spoon
to fold in the sugar and coconut. If you wish to
colour the cookies, tint the mixture pink or green
with a little food colouring.
3. With a teaspoon, drop small mounds of the
mixture on to the baking sheets.
4. Bake at 140°C (275°F) mark 1 for 45 minutes
–1 hour until the cookies are just beginning to colour.
Transfer to a wire rack and leave to cool.

Peanut Butter Cookies

Colour index
page 105

Makes
25–30
cookies

45 ml (3 level tbsp) peanut
butter
grated rind of ½ orange
50 g (2 oz) caster
sugar
45 ml (3 level tbsp) soft
light brown sugar

50 g (2 oz) butter
1 egg, beaten
100 g (4 oz) self raising
flour

1 Cream the peanut but-
ter, orange rind, sugars
and butter together until
the mixture is light and
fluffy. Beat in the egg and
stir in the flour to make a
fairly firm mixture.

2 Using both your hands,
roll the mixture into
small balls about the size
of a walnut and place them
well apart on an ungreased
baking sheet.

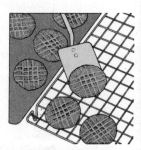

3 Dip a fork in a little
flour and press criss-
cross lines on the top of
each cookie. Bake at 180°C
(350°F) mark 4 for about
25 minutes, until they are
risen and golden brown.

4 Remove the cookies
from the baking sheet
and transfer them to a wire
rack to cool: do not allow
them to overlap, or they
will bend as they cool.

Hazel Nut Drops

Colour index
page 105

Makes
24 cookies

100 g (4 oz) blended white
vegetable fat
50 g (2 oz) caster
sugar
1 egg, separated
5 ml (1 tsp) grated orange
rind

2.5 ml (½ tsp) grated
lemon rind
1.25 ml (¼ level tsp) salt
100 g (4 oz) plain flour
75 g (3 oz) shelled hazel
nuts, ground

1. Grease two baking sheets. Cream the fat with the
sugar until light and fluffy and beat in the egg yolk.
Add the grated orange and lemon rinds and salt. Stir
in the flour until well blended. Refrigerate the
mixture until it is easy to handle.
2. With your hands, shape the mixture into balls
about 2.5 cm (1 in) in diameter and roll them first in
egg white and then in the ground hazel nuts. Place
them about 2.5 cm (1 in) apart on the baking sheets.
3. Bake at 180°C (350°F) mark 4 for 18–20 minutes
until just firm. Remove from the baking sheet
immediately and cool on a wire rack.

Danish Almond Cookies

Colour index
page 104

Makes
35 cookies

100 g (4 oz) butter
75 g (3 oz) blended white
vegetable fat
100 g (4 oz) sugar
1 egg, beaten
200 g (7 oz) plain flour
15 ml (1 level tbsp) ground
cinnamon
2.5 ml (½ level tsp) ground
cardamom
2.5 ml (½ level tsp)
baking powder

75 g (3 oz) blanched
almonds, chopped and
toasted
1 egg yolk, lightly beaten
15 ml (1 tbsp) water

To decorate:
blanched almonds, halved

1. Grease four baking sheets. Cream the fats with the sugar until light and fluffy and beat in the egg. Sift together the flour, spices and baking powder and stir into the creamed mixture with the nuts. Refrigerate the mixture for 2 hours or until it is easy to handle.
2. With your hands, shape the mixture into balls about 2.5 cm (1 in) in diameter. Place them about 5 cm (2 in) apart on the baking sheets and flatten evenly, using the bottom of a glass covered with a damp cloth (below).
3. Mix the egg yolk with water and brush over the tops of the cookies to glaze them. Decorate each one with an almond half.
4. Bake at 190°C (375°F) mark 5 for 10 minutes or until golden. Remove from the baking sheets immediately and cool on a wire rack.

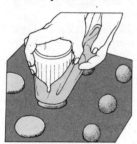 

Shaping the cookies: Use the bottom of a glass covered with a damp cloth to flatten the cookies to an even thickness.

Decorating the cookies: Press an almond half lightly on to each of the shaped and glazed cookies for decoration.

Cardamom Cookies

Colour index
page 105

Makes
30 cookies

225 g (8 oz) butter,
softened
75 g (3 oz) icing sugar,
sifted
225 g (8 oz) plain flour
5 ml (1 tsp) almond essence

2.5 ml (½ level tsp)
ground cardamom
pinch salt
50 g (2 oz) shelled walnuts,
chopped
icing sugar to dredge

1. Grease two or three baking sheets. Put the butter in a large bowl with the icing sugar and flour. Add the almond essence, cardamom, salt and walnuts and beat them all together until well blended to give a firm mixture.
2. With your hands, shape the mixture into 2.5-cm (1-in) balls and place them 5 cm (2 in) apart on the prepared baking sheets.
3. Bake at 180°C (350°F) mark 4 for 20 minutes, until lightly browned. Cool on a wire rack. Dredge with icing sugar before serving.

Shell Cookies

Colour index
page 105

Makes
12 cookies

50 g (2 oz) plain flour
2 eggs
pinch salt
75 g (3 oz) caster sugar

5 ml (1 tsp) grated lemon
rind
50 g (2 oz) butter, melted
and cooled

1. Grease well and flour 12 shell-shaped or fluted patty tins. Sift the flour.
2. Whisk the eggs and salt with a rotary whisk until thick enough to retain the impression of the whisk. Gradually add the sugar and whisk until the mixture is thick and pale. Using a metal spoon, carefully fold in the flour and lemon rind. Gradually add the melted butter, folding it into the mixture carefully.
3. Three-quarters fill the tins with the mixture.
4. Bake at 200°C (400°F) mark 6 for 8 minutes or until golden. Remove the cookies from the tins and cool on a wire rack.

ALMOND SHELL COOKIES: Prepare the shell cookies as above, but add *25 g (1 oz) ground almonds* and *1.25 ml (¼ level tsp) almond essence* to the mixture when you are folding in the flour.

Christmas Wreaths

Colour index
page 104

Makes
24 cookies

100 g (4 oz) butter
50 g (2 oz) caster sugar
1 egg yolk, beaten
5 ml (1 tsp) grated orange
rind
175 g (6 oz) plain flour
pinch salt

For the topping:
1 egg white, beaten
sugar
green and red glacé
cherries

1. Grease two baking sheets. Cream the butter with the sugar until light and fluffy. Beat in the egg yolk and grated orange rind. Stir in the flour and salt to give a dryish mixture.
2. Take a heaped teaspoonful of the mixture and roll it into a rope 15 cm (6 in) long. Repeat with the remaining mixture. On the baking sheets, shape each rope into a circle with slightly overlapping ends, to make a wreath.
3. Brush the wreaths with the beaten egg white and sprinkle them with sugar. Decorate each one with pieces of cherry.
4. Bake at 200°C (400°F) mark 6 for 10–12 minutes. Remove the cookies from the baking sheets, transfer to a wire rack and leave to cool.

 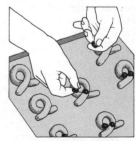

Shaping the wreaths: Shape each rope into a circle, leaving a 1-cm (½-in) overlap where the ends cross over each other.

Decorating the cookies: To decorate each wreath, lightly press small pieces of green and red glacé cherry over the top.

Shaped and pressed cookies

Vienna Cookies

150 g (5 oz) butter
75 g (3 oz) caster sugar
1 egg yolk, beaten
225 g (8 oz) plain flour
30 ml (2 tbsp) orange juice

Colour index page 106
Makes 36 cookies

1 Grease three or four baking sheets. Cream together the butter and sugar until light and fluffy then beat in the egg yolk. Sift the flour and fold it into the creamed mixture. Add the orange juice and mix until well blended. Cover and refrigerate for 1 hour, until the mixture is firm and easy to handle. Fill a biscuit press fitted with a bar plate, or a piping bag with a large rosette nozzle, with the mixture; press it down to force out any air.

2 Press or pipe the mixture out into long strips about 2.5 cm (1 in) apart, running lengthways down the prepared baking sheets.

3 Cut each strip across at 6.5-cm (2½-in) intervals with a sharp knife. Bake at 190°C (375°F) mark 5 for 8 minutes or until the cookies are light golden.

4 Remove the baking sheet from the oven and cut again between the biscuits, along the marked divisions, to separate them from each other.

5 Remove the biscuits from the baking sheets immediately and place on wire racks; leave to cool completely. Store in a tightly covered container.

RASPBERRY THUMBPRINTS

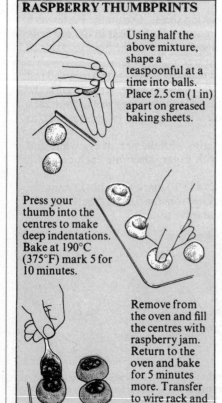

Using half the above mixture, shape a teaspoonful at a time into balls. Place 2.5 cm (1 in) apart on greased baking sheets.

Press your thumb into the centres to make deep indentations. Bake at 190°C (375°F) mark 5 for 10 minutes.

Remove from the oven and fill the centres with raspberry jam. Return to the oven and bake for 5 minutes more. Transfer to wire rack and cool. Makes 36.

RINGLETS

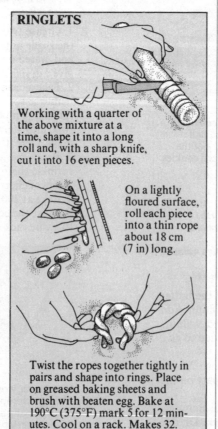

Working with a quarter of the above mixture at a time, shape it into a long roll and, with a sharp knife, cut it into 16 even pieces.

On a lightly floured surface, roll each piece into a thin rope about 18 cm (7 in) long.

Twist the ropes together tightly in pairs and shape into rings. Place on greased baking sheets and brush with beaten egg. Bake at 190°C (375°F) mark 5 for 12 minutes. Cool on a rack. Makes 32.

Colour index page 106
Makes 27 cookies

Chocolate Dipped Butter Cookies

75 g (3 oz) butter
50 g (2 oz) caster sugar
1 egg yolk, beaten
30 ml (2 tbsp) soured cream
1.25 ml (¼ tsp) almond essence
150 g (5 oz) plain flour
pinch salt

For the glaze:
75 g (3 oz) sugar
10 ml (2 level tsp) golden syrup
15 g (½ oz) butter
30 ml (2 tbsp) water
50 g (2 oz) chocolate chips

1. Cream the butter with the sugar until light and fluffy and beat in the egg yolk, soured cream and almond essence.
2. Mix in the flour and salt to make a smooth dough.
3. Fill a biscuit press with a Christmas tree plate, or a piping bag fitted with a large rosette nozzle. Press into shapes or pipe into bars on to three ungreased baking sheets so that the shapes or bars are about 1 cm (½ in) apart.
4. Bake at 190°C (375°F) mark 5 for 12–15 minutes until lightly browned around the edges. Transfer to a wire rack and leave to cool.
5. To make the glaze, put the sugar, golden syrup, butter and water in a saucepan. Heat gently until the sugar dissolves and bring to the boil. Remove from the heat and add the chocolate chips. Stir until the chocolate has melted and the glaze is smooth, then keep the chocolate glaze warm over a very low heat while you dip the cookies.
6. When the cookies are completely cool lower them into the glaze on a fork, allowing the glaze to come 0.3 cm (⅛ in) up the side. Drain off the excess glaze before placing the cookies, chocolate side up, on a wire rack to dry.

Glazing with chocolate: Use a fork to lower the biscuits into the chocolate, then drain well.

Drying the biscuits: Carefully turn the biscuits chocolate side up on a wire rack and leave to dry.

ORANGE GLAZED BUTTER COOKIES: Make the biscuits as above, but remove them from the oven 3–4 minutes before the end of cooking time. Combine *45 ml (3 level tbsp) sifted icing sugar* with *15 ml (1 tbsp) orange juice*. Brush each cookie with a little sieved *apricot jam*, then with the orange mixture; return to the oven for a further 5 minutes, until the sugar glaze begins to crystallise slightly.

Refrigerator cookies

Colour index
page 102

Makes
45 cookies

Refrigerator Cookies

175 g (6 oz) plain flour
5 ml (1 level tsp) baking
   powder
pinch salt

90 g (3½ oz) butter
90 g (3½ oz) sugar
1 egg yolk, beaten
5 ml (1 tsp) vanilla essence

1. Sift together the flour, baking powder and salt.
2. Cream the butter and sugar together until light and fluffy then beat in the egg yolk and vanilla essence. Stir in the dry ingredients.
3. Shape into a neat roll about 4 cm (1½ in) in diameter and refrigerate for about 1 hour, until firm.
4. Cut the roll into 0.5-cm (¼-in) thick slices and place the slices on a baking sheet.
5. Bake at 200°C (400°F) mark 6 for 5–10 minutes. Cool on a wire rack.

Colour index
page 105

Makes
48 cookies

Citrus Pinwheels

recipe quantity refrigerator
   cookie mixture, above
icing sugar
1.25 ml (¼ tsp) lemon
   essence
few drops yellow food
   colouring

2.5 ml (½ tsp) orange
   essence
few drops red food
   colouring

1. Divide the refrigerator cookie mixture into four equal pieces. Sift a layer of icing sugar on to four sheets of waxed paper.
2. With a lightly sugared rolling pin, roll out one portion of the mixture on the sugared paper to a 30.5 × 15 cm (12 × 6 in) rectangle.
3. Put a second portion into a small bowl and mix in the lemon essence and a little yellow food colouring. On another sheet of sugared paper, roll it out to the same size as the first rectangle.
4. Invert the lemon mixture on to the plain mixture and peel off the top paper. Trim the edges neatly and roll up like a Swiss roll, peeling back the waxed paper as you roll. Wrap in the waxed paper and chill.
5. Roll out the third portion of the mixture to a 30.5 × 15 cm (12 × 6 in) rectangle. Put the final portion of mixture into a bowl and add the orange essence. Tint with a few drops each of red and yellow food colouring. Roll out, invert on to the plain mixture and roll up as before. Wrap and chill.
6. Slice the rolls 0.5 cm (¼ in) thick and lay the slices on baking sheets 2.5 cm (1 in) apart.
7. Bake at 180°C (350°F) mark 4 for 12–15 minutes, until light brown. Cool on wire racks.

Layering the mixtures: Lay the flavoured mixture on top of the plain one.

Making the roll: Peel back the paper as you roll up the mixture from the long edge.

Neapolitan Cookies

Colour index
page 105

Makes
64 cookies

recipe quantity refrigerator
   cookie mixture, left
2.5 ml (½ tsp) almond
   essence
2 drops red food colouring
25 g (1 oz) plain chocolate
50 g (2 oz) shelled walnuts,
   chopped

1 Divide the mixture between three small bowls. Add the almond essence and red food colouring to one portion and mix well until evenly coloured.

2 Melt the chocolate and mix into the second portion. Mix the walnuts into the third. Line a 20.5 × 10 × 6.5 cm (8 × 4 × 2½ in) loaf tin with waxed paper.

3 Spread the almond mixture evenly in the bottom of the tin. Layer the walnut and then the chocolate mixture on top.

4 Cover the layered mixture in the tin with waxed paper and place it in the refrigerator for several hours, until firm.

5 Turn out the chilled mixture and peel off the waxed paper.

6 With a sharp knife, cut the mixture lengthways in half then slice each half crossways into 0.5-cm (¼-in) slices.

7 Place 2.5 cm (1 in) apart on a baking sheet; bake at 180°C (350°F) mark 4 for 10–12 minutes. Cool on a rack.

Rolled biscuits

Shrewsbury Biscuits

Colour index
page 105

Makes
20–24
biscuits

125 g (4 oz) butter
150 g (5 oz) caster
*   sugar*
1 egg yolk, beaten
225 g (8 oz) plain
*   flour*
grated rind of 1 lemon
1 egg white, lightly
*   beaten with 15 ml*
*   (1 tbsp) water*

To decorate:
sugar for dredging
chopped nuts

shredded coconut
cut-up gumdrops
sugar strands
butterscotch pieces
silver dragées
hundreds and thousands
chocolate vermicelli

1 Grease two large baking sheets. Cream together the butter and sugar until light and fluffy, add the egg yolk and beat well. Stir in the flour and the grated lemon rind.

2 Knead lightly and shape into a ball. Wrap in non-stick paper and chill slightly to make it firm and easier to roll.

3 Roll out half the mixture at a time, keeping the rest refrigerated. Roll on a lightly floured surface or between sheets of non-stick paper to about 0.5 cm (¼ in) thick.

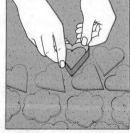

4 Cut out a variety of shapes with biscuit cutters. Knead the trimmings lightly together, re-roll and cut out more biscuits. Brush away any excess flour on the biscuits.

5 Put the biscuits on to the prepared baking sheets, spaced slightly apart so that they are not touching, and brush with the beaten egg white and water to glaze the tops.

6 Sprinkle with the decorations of your choice and bake at 180°C (350°F) mark 4 for about 15 minutes until light brown. Remove from baking sheets; cool on wire racks.

Sandwich Biscuits

Colour index
page 106

Makes
36 biscuits

175 g (6 oz) butter
175 g (6 oz) caster sugar
2 egg yolks, beaten
30 ml (2 tbsp) milk
5 ml (1 tsp) vanilla
*   essence*
250 g (9 oz) plain flour
1.25 ml (¼ level tsp) salt

For the filling:
50 g (2 oz) butter
225 g (8 oz) icing sugar,
*   sifted*
30 ml (2 tbsp) milk
few drops red, yellow and
*   green food colouring*

1. Grease three baking sheets. Cream the butter with the sugar until light and fluffy and beat in the egg yolks, milk and vanilla essence. Mix in the flour and salt to make a smooth dough.
2. Roll out the mixture on a lightly floured surface to about 0.3-cm (⅛-in) thickness and stamp out circles, using a 6-cm (2¼-in) round fluted or plain cutter. Cut out the centres of half the rounds with a 1-cm (½-in) fluted or plain cutter.
3. Knead lightly and re-roll the removed centres and trimmings and cut out more rounds. Place the rounds 1 cm (½ in) apart on the baking sheets.
4. Bake at 190°C (375°F) mark 5 for 8–10 minutes or until lightly browned. Lift on to wire racks and leave until completely cool.
5. Meanwhile make the filling. Cream the butter until soft and gradually stir in the sifted icing sugar and milk and beat until smooth. Divide the butter cream into three equal parts and use the food colouring to tint them pink, yellow and green.
6. To make up each cookie, spread a little pink, yellow or green butter cream over the bottom of a whole biscuit and top with a biscuit with a hole cut out of the centre. Repeat with the remaining biscuits and butter cream fillings.

Almond Butter Biscuits

Colour index
page 105

Makes
32 biscuits

175 g (6 oz) butter
50 g (2 oz) sugar
5 ml (1 tsp) almond
*   essence*
200 g (7 oz) plain flour
pinch salt

For the topping:
50 g (2 oz) caster sugar

pinch ground cinnamon
50 g (2 oz) blanched
*   almonds, chopped*
*   and toasted*
1 egg white, slightly
*   beaten*

1. Grease three baking sheets. Cream the butter with the sugar until light and fluffy. Add the almond essence, flour and salt and mix well (the mixture will remain slightly crumbly). Refrigerate for about 1 hour to make the mixture easier to roll.
2. Gather the mixture into a ball with your hands to make a smooth, firm dough, then roll out on a lightly floured surface to a 30.5 × 20.5 cm (12 × 8 in) rectangle and cut into bars measuring 7.5 × 2.5 cm (3 × 1 in), using a sharp knife or pastry wheel. Place them slightly apart on the baking sheets.
3. Make the topping. Mix the sugar with the cinnamon and chopped almonds.
4. Brush each biscuit with the beaten egg white and then sprinkle with the almond mixture. Bake at 170°C (325°F) mark 3 for 15 minutes or until golden brown. Remove from the baking sheets immediately and cool on a wire rack.

Gingerbread Men

350 g (12 oz) plain
   flour
5 ml (1 level tsp)
   bicarbonate of soda
10 ml (2 level tsp) ground
   ginger
100 g (4 oz) butter
50 g (2 oz) currants,
   optional
175 g (6 oz) soft light
   brown sugar
60 ml (4 level tbsp) golden
   syrup
1 egg, beaten

To decorate:
currants
glacé cherries, thinly
   sliced, optional
royal icing made with
   100 g (4 oz) icing sugar,
   page 401 or glacé icing
   made with 50 – 75 g
   (2 – 3 oz) icing sugar,
   page 400

Colour index page 104

Makes 18 biscuits

1 Grease three or four baking sheets. Sift together the flour, bicarbonate of soda and ginger and rub in the butter with the fingertips. Stir in the currants, if used. Add the sugar and mix well. Warm the golden syrup slightly until it is easy to pour and stir into the ginger mixture with the beaten egg until well blended. Knead thoroughly together until the gingerbread mixture is smooth and pliable.

2 Roll out the mixture on a lightly floured surface to about 0.3-cm (⅛-in) thickness.

3 Using a traditional gingerbread man cutter, cut out the shapes. Lift them on to the baking sheets, placed well apart. Re-roll and cut trimmings.

4 Decorate using currants for the buttons and eyes and a currant or a slice of cherry for the mouth. Or, pipe on the decorations after baking.

5 Bake at 190°C (375°F) mark 5 for 10–15 minutes, until evenly coloured. Cool completely on a wire rack before icing.

6 Outline the feet and sleeve ends with white icing and draw buttons and a ruff collar or bow tie at the neck.

MAKING A PAPER PATTERN

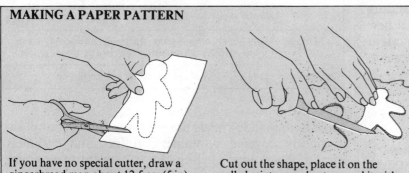

If you have no special cutter, draw a gingerbread man about 12.5 cm (5 in) high and 10 cm (4 in) wide on greaseproof or waxed paper.

Cut out the shape, place it on the rolled mixture and cut around it with a sharp pointed knife, holding the blade vertical to give straight sides.

Colour index page 105

Makes 36 biscuits

Spice Biscuits

100 g (4 oz) butter
200 g (7 oz) caster sugar
1 egg, beaten
10 ml (2 tsp) milk
225 g (8 oz) plain flour
5 ml (1 level tsp)
   bicarbonate of soda

5 ml (1 level tsp) ground
   cinnamon
1.25 ml (¼ level tsp)
   ground nutmeg
pinch ground cloves
75 g (3 oz) currants

1. Grease three baking sheets. Cream the butter with 175 g (6 oz) of the sugar until light and fluffy and then beat in the egg and milk.
2. Stir in the remaining ingredients and mix well until smooth. Cover and refrigerate the mixture until it is firm enough to handle.
3. On a lightly floured surface roll out the mixture as thinly as possible. Sprinkle evenly with the remaining sugar and cut into diamond shapes about 5 cm (2 in) in length.
4. Place on the baking sheets. Bake at 190°C (375°F) mark 5 for 8 minutes or until lightly browned. Cool on a wire rack.

CHRISTMAS ANGELS: Roll out the dough to 0.3-cm (⅛-in) thickness. Cut out about 20 7.5 × 5 cm (3 × 2 in) rectangles and use the trimmings to make 1-cm (½-in) balls for the heads. Place the rectangles on the greased baking sheets; from the top corners cut two small triangles and replace to form upright wings. Press the heads in position on the bodies. Bake as for spice biscuits, cool on wire racks and decorate with *royal icing (page 401)*.

Colour index page 104

Makes 36 biscuits

Cinnamon Biscuits

50 g (2 oz) butter
100 g (4 oz) caster sugar
1 egg yolk, beaten
100 g (4 oz) plain flour
5 ml (1 level tsp) ground
   cinnamon

1.25 ml (¼ level tsp)
   baking powder
1.25 ml (¼ level tsp) salt
15 ml (1 tbsp) milk

1. Cream the butter, beat in the sugar and egg yolk and stir in the remaining ingredients. Refrigerate for 2–3 hours to make the mixture easier to roll.
2. Divide the mixture in half and with a lightly floured rolling pin roll out each piece on a cold baking sheet to an even 0.3-cm (⅛-in) thickness.
3. Use a floured 6-cm (2¼-in) plain cutter to stamp out rounds, spaced about 2.5 cm (1 in) apart. Refrigerate for a further 1 hour.
4. Remove the mixture between the rounds from the baking sheet. Knead lightly and re-roll to 0.3-cm (⅛-in) thickness on another cold baking sheet. Cut out more rounds.
5. Bake at 180°C (350°F) mark 4 for 15 minutes, transfer the cookies immediately to a wire rack and leave to cool completely.

CONFECTIONERY

Sweets are great fun to make at home, either to pass round with coffee or to gift wrap and give away as presents. The simple, uncooked sweets are ideal for children to make, but take care with those that require boiling sugar as the temperatures involved are very high and can cause a bad scald.

SUGAR BOILING

Choose a heavy-based saucepan, preferably made of cast aluminium. Enamelled or non-stick pans are not suitable, as a high temperature may crack the lining; stainless steel pans may burn in patches on the base. Because boiling sugar rises considerably, use a large pan that will be no more than half full when all the ingredients for the syrup are added. Use a wooden spoon or spatula for stirring, as a metal one will get too hot to hold comfortably.

Heat the liquid gently, stirring occasionally, until the sugar is completely dissolved or the syrup will become grainy. Brush any crystals on the sides of the pan into the syrup with a pastry brush dipped in warm water and tap the bottom of the pan occasionally with your spoon to collect together any remaining sugar crystals without swirling the syrup up the sides of the pan.

When the sugar is completely dissolved, turn up the heat and do not stir again unless the recipe specifically says that you should. Bring the syrup to a full, foaming boil and keep it boiling steadily until it reaches the temperature you require. If you try to regulate the amount of foaming by alternately raising and lowering the heat, the sweets will not set properly.

USING A SUGAR THERMOMETER

Choose a thermometer that is easy to read, with a sliding clip that fits over the side of the pan. To season a new one, place it in cold water, bring to the boil and leave it in the water to cool. Always wash the thermometer after use.

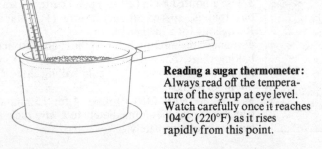

Reading a sugar thermometer: Always read off the temperature of the syrup at eye level. Watch carefully once it reaches 104°C (220°F) as it rises rapidly from this point.

TESTING WITHOUT A THERMOMETER

Many simple sweets can be made without a thermometer. You can estimate the approximate temperature of the syrup by carrying out the tests on the chart (below). Have ready a jug of very cold but not iced water, and test about 2.5 ml (½ tsp) syrup at a time. Always remove the saucepan from the heat while you are testing, in case the syrup overheats.

For recipes that call for a mixture to be cooled until it is lukewarm, let it stand off the heat until the bottom of the pan feels lukewarm to the touch. Never beat the mixture while it is hot or large sugar crystals will form.

When the mixture is ready for pouring out, do it quickly, holding the saucepan close to the tin. Do not scrape the sides of the saucepan, as the mixture clinging to the sides may be sugary. Always allow sweets to cool before cutting or breaking them into pieces, then leave them until they are completely cold before storing.

TEMPERATURE GUIDE FOR SUGAR BOILING		
Stage	Temperature	Appearance
Smooth	102–104°C (215–220°F)	Dip your fingers into water, then quickly in syrup; thumb will slide smoothly over fingers but sugar clings to the fingers.
Soft ball	113–118°C (235–245°F)	Syrup dropped into cold water forms a soft ball which flattens on removal from water.
Hard ball	118–130°C (245–265°F)	Syrup dropped into cold water forms a ball which holds its shape on removal from water.
Soft crack	132–143°C (270–290°F)	Syrup dropped into cold water separates into hard but not brittle threads.
Hard crack	149–154°C (300–310°F)	Syrup dropped into cold water separates into brittle threads.
Caramel	174°C (345°F)	Syrup turns golden brown.

STORING

Most home-made sweets are best stored in a cool place in tightly covered containers; toffees and caramels should be wrapped in cling film to prevent them going soft. Store different types of sweets separately until you are ready to gift wrap or serve them, to avoid the individual flavours mixing.

Fudges

Walnut and Chocolate Fudge

Colour index
page 106

Makes 700 g
(1½ lb)

450 g (1 lb) granulated
  sugar
150 ml (¼ pint) milk
100 g (4 oz) plain chocolate
50 g (2 oz) honey
150 g (5 oz) butter or
  margarine
100 g (4 oz) shelled
  walnuts, chopped

25 g (1 oz) shelled
  walnuts, halved,
  optional

1 Grease a 20.5 × 15 cm
(8 × 6 in) tin. Put the
sugar, milk, chocolate and
honey in a 2.8-litre (5-pint)
heavy-based saucepan
over gentle heat.

2 Stir constantly over low
heat until the sugar has
dissolved. Bring to the boil
and boil, without stirring,
to 116°C (240°F), soft ball
stage. Remove the saucepan
from the heat.

3 Add the butter to the
sugar mixture and leave
the pan to stand on a cool
surface for 5 minutes,
without stirring.

4 Then beat the mixture
until it is thick, creamy
and beginning to 'grain'.

5 Add the chopped nuts
all at once and stir with
a wooden spoon until they
are evenly mixed into the
fudge. Immediately pour
into the greased tin.

6 Press in the walnut
halves, if you wish.
Leave until completely
cold, then cut the fudge
into squares and remove
from the tin.

PEANUT AND CHOCOLATE FUDGE: Prepare
as above, but substitute **60 ml (4 level tbsp) smooth
peanut butter** for the butter and use **salted peanuts**
instead of walnuts.

Nutty Butterscotch Fudge

Colour index
page 106

Makes 700 g
(1½ lb)

100 g (4 oz) marshmallows
50 ml (2 fl oz) water
150 ml (¼ pint) evaporated
  milk
200 g (7 oz) sugar
50 g (2 oz) butter or
  margarine
3.75 ml (¾ level tsp) salt

350 g (12 oz) caramel
  chocolate, broken into
  small pieces
2.5 ml (½ tsp) vanilla
  essence
75 g (3 oz) salted peanuts,
  chopped

1. Grease a 20.5 × 15 cm (8 × 6 in) tin. Put the
marshmallows, water and milk in a saucepan. Heat
gently until smooth, stirring occasionally.
2. Add the sugar, fat and salt and bring to the boil.
Boil steadily for 5 minutes, stirring constantly.
3. Remove the pan from the heat and quickly stir in
the chocolate pieces and vanilla essence until the
mixture is smooth. Stir in the chopped peanuts.
4. Pour the mixture quickly into the tin and leave to
cool. When it is completely cold, cut into squares
with a sharp knife and remove from the tin.

Pecan Penuche

Colour index
page 107

Makes 900 g
(2 lb)

350 g (12 oz) soft light
  brown sugar
400 g (14 oz) granulated
  sugar
250 ml (9 fl oz) milk
75 g (3 oz) butter or
  margarine

7.5 ml (1½ tsp) vanilla
  essence
90 g (3½ oz) shelled
  pecans or walnuts,
  roughly chopped

1. Grease a 20.5-cm (8-in) square tin. Put the sugars
and milk in a saucepan, place over gentle heat and
bring slowly to the boil, stirring constantly. Boil
steadily, without stirring, until it reaches 116°C
(240°F), soft ball stage.
2. Remove from the heat and add the fat and vanilla
essence. Cool, without stirring, until the bottom of
the pan feels lukewarm to the touch.
3. Beat the mixture with a wooden spoon until it
becomes thick and begins to lose its gloss, then
quickly stir in the nuts.
4. Pour into the tin and leave to cool. When it is
completely cold, cut into squares with a sharp knife
and remove from the tin.

Vanilla Kisses

Colour index
page 106

Makes 350 g
(12 oz)

175 g (6 oz) soft light
  brown sugar
90 g (3½ oz) granulated
  sugar
90 ml (6 tbsp) evaporated
  milk
45 ml (3 level tbsp) corn
  syrup or golden syrup

25 g (1 oz) butter or
  margarine
5 ml (1 tsp) vanilla essence
150 g (5 oz) shelled
  walnuts, chopped

1. Cover two wire racks with waxed paper. Put the
sugars, milk and corn syrup in a large saucepan and
heat gently, stirring constantly. Bring to the boil;
boil steadily, stirring all the time, for 3 minutes
until it reaches 113°C (235°F), soft ball stage.
2. Remove from the heat and beat in the fat, vanilla
essence and nuts with a wooden spoon.
3. Working quickly, drop teaspoonfuls of the mixture on to the waxed paper and leave to cool.

Mixed sweets

Toffee

325 ml (11 fl oz) condensed milk
45 ml (3 level tbsp) golden syrup
large pinch salt

Colour index page 107

Makes 350 g (12 oz)

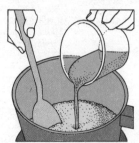

1 Grease a 20.5-cm (8-in) square tin or large plate. Put all the ingredients into a large saucepan and bring to the boil, stirring occasionally.

2 Boil the toffee mixture steadily, stirring constantly, for about 20 minutes until it reaches 118°C (245°F), hard ball stage.

3 Remove the saucepan from the heat and quickly pour the toffee mixture into the greased tin or plate. Leave the toffee until it is just cool enough to handle.

4 Pull the toffee with buttered fingers until it becomes shiny and a light golden colour.

5 Then twist the toffee into a long rope, about 2 cm (¾ in) thick.

6 Cut the rope into 2.5-cm (1-in) pieces with kitchen scissors and cool. Wrap in cling film.

Orange and Almond Caramels

600 g (1 lb 5oz) sugar
50 ml (2 fl oz) boiling water
250 ml (9 fl oz) evaporated milk
pinch salt
10 ml (2 tsp) grated orange rind
100 g (4 oz) slivered almonds

Colour index page 107

Makes 700 g (1½ lb)

1. Put 200 g (7 oz) of the sugar in a large heavy-based saucepan and heat gently, stirring constantly, until it has completely dissolved and turned a deep golden caramel colour.
2. Slowly add the boiling water and cook to a smooth syrup, stirring all the time. Stir in the remaining sugar, evaporated milk and salt.
3. Continue boiling the mixture steadily over medium heat, stirring constantly, until it reaches 115°C (238°F), soft ball stage.
4. Remove from the heat, add the orange rind and stir until the mixture cools slightly. Add 90 g (3½ oz) of the nuts and continue stirring until a teaspoonful of the mixture dropped on to waxed paper retains its shape and loses its gloss.
5. Drop heaped teaspoonfuls of the caramel mixture on to waxed paper, press the remaining slivered almonds on top of them and leave them to cool. When the caramels are completely cold, remove them from the waxed paper.

HAZEL NUT - RAISIN CARAMELS : Prepare as above, but omit the orange rind and stir *25 g (1 oz) seedless raisins* and *65 g (2½ oz) coarsely chopped hazel nuts* into the caramel. Press a hazel nut on to each finished caramel before leaving them to cool.

Nougat

3 egg whites
75 g (3 oz) honey
350 g (12 oz) sugar
150 ml (¼ pint) water
50 g (2 oz) glucose
2.5 ml (½ tsp) vanilla essence
50 g (2 oz) glacé cherries, chopped
25 g (1 oz) angelica, chopped
150 g (5 oz) almonds, chopped

Colour index page 107

Makes 550 g (1¼ lb)

1. Damp the inside of an 18-cm (7-in) square tin and line it with rice paper.
2. Whisk the egg whites until stiff peaks form. Melt the honey in a small basin over a pan of hot water; add the stiffly whisked egg whites and continue to whisk, preferably with a hand-held electric mixer, until the mixture is pale and thick.
3. Dissolve the sugar in the water in a small heavy-based saucepan. Add the glucose and boil, without stirring, to 118–130°C (245–265°F), hard ball stage. Pour this syrup on to the whisked honey mixture, add the vanilla essence and continue whisking with the electric mixer over hot water for about 25 minutes or until a little of the mixture forms a hard ball when tested in cold water.
4. Add the cherries, angelica and nuts and pour the mixture into the prepared tin. Cover with rice paper and weight down. Leave it until it is completely cold, then cut the nougat into 2.5-cm (1-in) squares with a sharp knife and remove from the tin. To store, wrap the nougat in waxed paper.

Lollipops

Colour index
page 106

Makes 12
lollipops

*12 200-ml (7-fl oz) paper
(not plastic) cups, with
7-cm (2¾-in) diameter
tops*
*36 2-cm (¾-in) long oval
boiled sweets*
*50 g (2 oz) small boiled
sweets or jelly tots*
400 g (14 oz) sugar
250 ml (9 fl oz) water
*175 ml (6 fl oz) corn syrup
or golden syrup*
*2.5 ml (½ tsp) lemon
essence*
*10 drops yellow food
colouring*
12 lollipop sticks

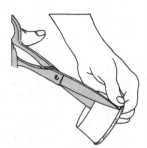

1 Cut off the top of each
cup to 4-cm (1½-in)
depth. Cut a slit in side of
each, down to, but not
through, rolled edge.

2 Grease moulds and two
baking sheets and
arrange moulds on sheets,
rim side down, leaving
space for lollipop sticks.

3 Make a flower pattern
in each mould with
three oval boiled sweets
and two clusters of small
boiled sweets or jelly tots.

4 Stir the sugar, water
and corn syrup over
gentle heat until the sugar
dissolves, brushing the
sides of the pan with a
damp pastry brush.

5 Bring to the boil and
boil steadily, without
stirring, until it reaches
149°C (300°F), hard crack
stage. Remove the pan
from the heat.

6 Stir in lemon essence
and food colouring.
Pour 50 ml (2 fl oz) mix-
ture into each mould, holding firm if necessary.

7 Press lollipop sticks
through slits and into
lollipops. Cool completely,
lift lollipops off baking
sheets and remove moulds.

White Clouds

Colour index
page 107

Makes 700 g
(1½ lb)

600 g (1 lb 5 oz) sugar
*90 ml (6 level tbsp) corn
syrup or golden syrup*

100 ml (4 fl oz) water
2 egg whites
5 ml (1 tsp) vanilla essence

1. Put the sugar, corn or golden syrup and water in a
saucepan and bring to the boil, stirring constantly
until the sugar has dissolved. Boil the mixture
steadily, without stirring, until it reaches 119°C
(248°F), hard ball stage.
2. Meanwhile, whisk the egg whites in a mixer until
stiff peaks form. Continue whisking at medium
speed and pour half the hot syrup slowly into the
whisked egg whites.
3. Heat the remaining syrup, without stirring, until it
reaches 133°C (272°F), soft crack stage. Meanwhile,
continue whisking the egg white mixture.
4. Pour the hot syrup slowly into the egg white
mixture, whisking all the time at medium speed. Add
the vanilla essence and continue to whisk until stiff,
glossy peaks form.
5. Working quickly, drop heaped teaspoonfuls of
the mixture on to waxed paper and leave to cool.
When the white clouds are completely cold, remove
them from the waxed paper.

NUT CLOUDS: Prepare as above, but add *100 g
(4 oz) chopped hazel nuts* with the vanilla essence.

Fondant Creams

Colour index
page 107

Makes 1.1 kg
(2½ lb)

For the fondant:
300 ml (½ pint) water
900 g (2 lb) sugar
*90 ml (6 level tbsp) glucose
or large pinch cream of
tartar*
*cream, evaporated milk or
melted butter*

To finish:
*few drops green, yellow or
red food colouring*
*few drops vanilla, almond,
fruit or peppermint
essence*
*plain chocolate, melted,
optional*

1. Put the water and sugar into a heavy-based
saucepan and heat gently, stirring constantly, until
the sugar has dissolved.
2. Bring the syrup to the boil, add the glucose or
cream of tartar and boil steadily, without stirring,
until it reaches 116°C (240°F), soft ball stage.
3. Sprinkle a little water over the sides of a large
bowl. Pour the syrup into it and leave to cool for 15
minutes. When a skin forms around the edges,
collect the mixture together with a spatula and turn
it, working it in a figure of eight movement.
Continue to work the mixture until it changes its
character and develops a grainy texture, becoming
opaque and thick.
4. Turn the fondant on to greaseproof paper and
knead it until the mixture is of an even texture.
5. Knead in a little cream, evaporated milk or melted
butter. Divide the mixture into portions and colour
and flavour as required.
6. Roll out the fondant to the required thickness on a
surface sprinkled with a little icing sugar and cut out
shapes with a pastry cutter or knife. Alternatively,
model the fondant by hand into different shapes.
The fondants may be coated in melted plain chocolate, if you wish.

Mixed sweets

Fondant Bonbons

Colour index
page 107

Makes 1.1 kg
(2½ lb)

*fondant made with 900 g
(2 lb) sugar, page 417*
*2.5 ml (½ tsp) vanilla,
almond, fruit or
peppermint essence*

*few drops green, yellow or
red food colouring*

1. Divide the fondant in half. Wrap one piece in cling
film and reserve it. Knead the flavouring into the
second piece and shape into 2-cm (¾-in) balls.
Leave them to dry until a light crust forms, then
transfer them to a wire rack to dry underneath.
2. Melt the reserved piece of fondant with the food
colouring in the top of a double saucepan until the
mixture is hot and thin, stirring constantly to prevent a crust forming.
3. Lower a fondant ball into the melted fondant on a
fork and allow the excess fondant to drip back into
the saucepan. Place the bonbons rounded side up on
waxed paper, pulling the top into a slight peak or
curl with the fork. Repeat with the remaining balls,
stirring the melted fondant occasionally.
4. Leave the bonbons to dry for at least an hour
before removing them from the waxed paper.

FONDANT FRUITS: Prepare the fondant as for
fondant creams (page 417). Place it in a basin over a
pan of hot water, or in a double saucepan. Add a
little water or sugar syrup to make the fondant liquid
and a *few drops of food colouring*, if you wish. Dip
cubes of *crystallised ginger, glacé pineapple* or *fresh
fruits* into the fondant and leave to dry.

FONDANT NUTS: Prepare a liquid fondant as
above and flavour it with a *little coffee*. Dip *halved
walnuts* and *whole Brazil nuts* into it and leave to dry.

Popcorn Balls

Colour index
page 106

Makes 12
balls

*165 g (5½ oz) popping
corn and 50 ml (2 fl oz)
vegetable oil or 225 g
(8 oz) popped corn*
*225 g (8 oz) glacé cherries,
halved*
*400 ml (¾ pint) corn syrup
or golden syrup*

*15 ml (1 tbsp) white
vinegar*
5 ml (1 level tsp) salt
*10 ml (2 tsp) vanilla
essence*

1. If you are using popping corn, heat half the oil in a
large saucepan over high heat. Add half the corn,
cover the pan and cook, shaking the pan occasionally, until the corn stops popping. Cook the
remaining corn in the same way.
2. Put the popped corn and cherries in a large
greased saucepan and toss together until well mixed.
3. Put the syrup, vinegar and salt in another saucepan. Bring to the boil and boil, without stirring,
until it reaches 121°C (250°F), hard ball stage.
4. Remove from the heat, stir in the vanilla essence
and slowly pour the syrup over the popped corn
mixture, tossing until the corn is well coated.
5. With buttered hands, shape the mixture into 7.5-
cm (3-in) balls, using as little pressure as possible so
that the balls will not be too compact. If the mixture
becomes hard, warm it gently over low heat until it
becomes pliable. Leave to cool and harden.

Peanut Brittle

Colour index
page 106

Makes 900 g
(2 lb)

*350 g (12 oz) unsalted
peanuts, chopped*
*400 g (14 oz) granulated
sugar*
*175 g (6 oz) soft light
brown sugar*
*175 g (6 oz) corn syrup or
golden syrup*

150 ml (¼ pint) water
50 g (2 oz) butter
*1.25 ml (¼ level tsp)
bicarbonate of soda*

1. Grease a 30.5 × 10 cm (12 × 4 in) or an 18-cm (7-
in) square tin. Put the nuts in the oven at 110°C
(225°F) mark ¼ until they are just warm.
2. Put the sugars, corn syrup and water in a large
heavy-based saucepan and heat gently, stirring all
the time, until the sugar has dissolved.
3. Add the butter to the mixture, stir until it has
melted, then bring it to the boil and boil very gently,
without stirring, until it reaches 149°C (300°F), hard
crack stage.
4. Quickly stir in the bicarbonate of soda and the
slightly warmed nuts. Pour the mixture into the
greased tin immediately and leave to cool. Mark
into bars with a sharp knife when almost set and
break into pieces when completely cold.

Walnut Crunch

Colour index
page 107

Makes 700 g
(1½ lb)

200 g (7 oz) shelled walnuts
250 g (9 oz) sugar
*150 g (5 oz) butter or
margarine*
7.5 ml (1½ level tsp) salt
50 ml (2 fl oz) water

*2.5 ml (½ level tsp)
bicarbonate of soda*
*50 g (2 oz) plain chocolate,
melted*

1. Grease a 38 × 25.5 cm (15 × 10 in) tin. Chop 150 g
(5 oz) of the walnuts roughly and the remaining
walnuts finely. Keep them separate.
2. Put the sugar, fat, salt and water in a heavy-based
saucepan; bring to the boil, stirring frequently.
Continue to boil steadily, still stirring, until it
reaches 143°C (290°F), soft crack stage.
3. Remove from the heat and stir in the bicarbonate
of soda and the roughly chopped walnuts. Pour the
mixture into the tin immediately.
4. Spread the melted chocolate over the walnut
mixture in the tin and sprinkle with the finely
chopped walnuts. Leave to cool, then break into
small pieces when completely cold.

Testing the mixture: Drop
a little mixture into a
jug of cold water. It
should separate into hard
but not brittle threads,
the soft crack stage.

Adding the chocolate: Use
a spatula to spread the
melted chocolate over the
walnut mixture in the tin,
then sprinkle with the
finely chopped walnuts.

Peppermint Patties

*397-g (14-oz) can sweetened
    condensed milk*
*10 ml (2 tsp) peppermint
    essence*
*12 drops red or green food
    colouring*

*700–900 g (1½ –2 lb) icing
    sugar, sifted*
*150 g (5 oz) shelled pecans
    or walnuts, halved*

1. Mix the condensed milk with peppermint essence and food colouring. Stir in 700 g (1½ lb) sugar. On a surface sprinkled with icing sugar, knead in enough extra sugar to give a smooth, firm mixture.
2. Roll out the mixture to the required thickness and cut out circles with a small round pastry cutter.
3. Lightly press a nut half on to each patty. Leave them to dry for at least 1 hour.

Marzipan Fruits

450 g (1 lb) lump sugar
150 ml (¼ pint) water
pinch cream of tartar
*350 g (12 oz) ground
    almonds*
2 egg whites
*75 g (3 oz) icing sugar,
    sifted*

*red, yellow or green food
    colouring*

For the glaze:
1 kg (2¼ lb) sugar
225 ml (8 fl oz) water

1. Put the lump sugar and water into a saucepan; heat gently, stirring constantly, until the sugar has dissolved. Bring to the boil, add the cream of tartar and continue to boil steadily, without stirring, until it reaches 116°C (240°F), soft ball stage. Remove from the heat and stir rapidly until the mixture develops a grainy texture. Add the almonds and egg whites; cook gently for a few minutes, stirring well.
2. Pour the mixture on to an oiled surface, add the icing sugar and work with a palette knife, lifting the edges and pressing them into the centre. When the mixture is cool enough to handle, knead until smooth, adding extra icing sugar if necessary.
3. Divide the marzipan into portions. Colour it appropriately, mould into fruits and decorate (right).
4. Dissolve the sugar in the water over gentle heat; boil steadily, without stirring, until the syrup reaches 106°C (223°F). Remove from the heat and leave to cool.
5. Place the marzipan fruits in a tin on a wire rack. Remove any crystallised sugar from the glaze and spoon the glaze over the fruits. Leave for 12 hours or overnight to dry completely.

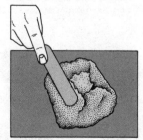

Working the marzipan: Pour the almond mixture on to an oiled surface and work with a palette knife until smooth.

Glazing the fruits: Spoon the cooled sugar syrup over the marzipan fruits to form a glaze.

SHAPING MARZIPAN FRUITS

APPLES: Knead a little green food colouring into the marzipan, divide it into small pieces and shape into apples. Stick clove stems into the tops of the apples to represent the stalks and paint on a little red food colouring diluted with water to give the colour of the skin. Leave to dry.

Making the stalks: Push a clove stem into the top of each shaped marzipan apple to form a stalk.

Painting the skins: Use a clean fine brush to tint the apples with diluted red food colouring.

BANANAS: Knead a little yellow food colouring into the marzipan, divide it into small pieces and shape into bananas. Paint brown lines with diluted food colouring lengthways down the bananas as their skin markings. Leave to dry.

PEARS: Knead a little yellow and green food colouring into the marzipan, divide it into small pieces and shape into pears. Stick a needle of dried rosemary into the top of each one to represent the stalk. Leave to dry.

ORANGES: Knead a little yellow and red food colouring into the marzipan and divide into small pieces. Shape into oranges and roll them over the fine cutter of a grater to make the rind. Leave to dry.

STRAWBERRIES: Divide three quarters of the marzipan into small pieces and shape them into strawberries. Roll them over the fine cutter of a grater to give the texture of the skin and paint on diluted red food colouring with a fine brush. Knead a little green food colouring into the remaining marzipan and roll it out 0.3 cm (⅛ in) thick on a surface lightly sprinkled with icing sugar. Cut out small stars with a star-shaped pastry cutter and press them on to the large ends of the strawberries to represent the leaves. Leave to dry.

 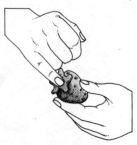

Marking the skin: Roll the strawberry over a grater to make the holes in the skin.

Adding the leaves: Press a green star on to the end of each strawberry.

Chocolates

Meltaway Chocolate Mints

Colour index
page 107

Makes 450 g
(1 lb)

450 g (1 lb) plain chocolate
30 ml (2 level tbsp)
    softened blended white
    vegetable fat
150 ml (¼ pint) double
    cream

15 ml (1 tbsp) peppermint
    essence
cocoa powder

1. Line a 20.5-cm (8-in) square tin with waxed paper.
2. Bring some water almost to the boil in the bottom of a double saucepan. Meanwhile, break the chocolate into small pieces and place them with the fat in the top of the double saucepan off the heat.
3. Remove the water from the heat, place the top of the double saucepan over it and melt the chocolate and fat, stirring constantly, until the mixture reaches 54°C (130°F) and is completely smooth.
4. Replace the hot water in the bottom of the double saucepan with cold water. Put the top in place again and cool the chocolate, stirring constantly, until it reaches 30°C (83°F) and thickens slightly.
5. Bring the cream to the boil. Remove from the heat and add the chocolate and peppermint essence. Beat until well blended, then beat for 2 minutes more.
6. Pour into the tin; leave for 2 hours until firm.
7. Loosen the mixture from the tin with a spatula; turn it out and peel back the waxed paper. Dust a sharp knife with cocoa powder; cut the mixture into diamonds or squares.

Chocolate Rum Truffles

Colour index
page 107

Makes 450 g
(1 lb)

100 g (4 oz) plain chocolate
275 g (10 oz) icing sugar,
    sifted
100 g (4 oz) unsalted butter
30 ml (2 tbsp) rum

To finish:
cocoa powder or chocolate
    vermicelli

1. Bring some water almost to the boil in the bottom of a double saucepan. Meanwhile, break the chocolate into small pieces and place them in the top of the double saucepan off the heat.
2. Remove the water from the heat, place the top of the double saucepan over it and melt the chocolate, stirring constantly, until it reaches 54°C (130°F) and is completely smooth.
3. In a bowl, beat together the chocolate, icing sugar, butter and rum.
4. Form the mixture into small balls, roll them in cocoa powder or chocolate vermicelli and leave them to harden for a few hours.

Shaping the truffles: Form the mixture into small balls with your fingers.

Finishing the truffles: Roll each one in cocoa powder or chocolate vermicelli.

Chocolate-dipped Fruit and Nuts

Colour index
page 107

Makes 60
dipped fruits
and 12 nut
clusters

2 large oranges
700 g (1½ lb) strawberries
450 g (1 lb) plain
    chocolate

200 g (7 oz) salted
    peanuts

1. Prepare the fruit. Peel the oranges, being careful to remove all the pith, and divide the fruit into segments. Rinse the strawberries under running cold water and pat them dry gently with kitchen paper towel; do not remove the stems or the leaves. Keep the fruit at room temperature. Lay out some sheets of waxed paper.
2. Bring some water to the boil in the bottom of a double saucepan. Meanwhile, grate the chocolate into the top of the double saucepan off the heat.
3. Remove the water from the heat, place the top of the double saucepan over it and melt the chocolate, stirring constantly, until it reaches 54°C (130°F) and is completely smooth.
4. Replace the hot water in the bottom of the double saucepan with cold water. Put the top in place again and cool the chocolate, stirring constantly, until it reaches 30°C (83°F) and thickens slightly.
5. Replace the cold water in the bottom of the double saucepan with warm water to keep the chocolate a good dipping consistency while you are working with it.
6. Dip each piece of fruit into the melted chocolate, leaving part of the fruit uncovered, and hold over the saucepan for a few moments to allow any excess chocolate to drip back into the pan. Place the fruit on the waxed paper and leave them for about 10 minutes or until the chocolate is completely cool, dry and set.
7. Add the peanuts to the leftover chocolate in the pan and stir them in quickly. Drop the mixture in tablespoonfuls on to the waxed paper and leave to dry for about 10 minutes.
8. Serve the chocolate-dipped fruit on the same day. The nut clusters will store in a tightly covered container for up to a week.

DIPPING THE FRUIT

Dip the fruits one by one in the melted chocolate, leaving part of each one uncovered. Allow any surplus chocolate to drip back into the saucepan. Place the fruits on sheets of waxed paper and leave them to dry.

SIMPLE BAKING

Scones and toasted muffins, Scotch pancakes and buttered teabreads are traditional tea-time fare. They are raised with a chemical raising agent, either baking powder or a mixture of bicarbonate of soda and cream of tartar, and baked quickly in the oven or on a griddle over direct heat. The same techniques can also be used to make plain 'soda' or 'quick' breads, which can be eaten in place of ordinary bread made with yeast. Serve them spread with butter, or at tea spread with butter and jam, honey or syrup. Pancakes, popovers, doughnuts and waffles can also be served as a dessert or the American way, for breakfast.

In some parts of the world it is more common to use breads that are not raised at all and some of these flat bread recipes are also included. Serve plainer breads as an accompaniment to spicy foods and savoury ones as appetisers or snacks with drinks.

RAISING AGENTS
Baking powder usually consists of a mixture of bicarbonate of soda and an acid-reacting chemical such as cream of tartar. If you are using baking powder with self raising flour for scones and soda breads, allow 5 ml (1 level tsp) for every 225 g (8 oz) flour; if you are using plain flour increase the proportion to 15 ml (1 level tbsp) baking powder for every 225 g (8 oz) flour. As an alternative, you can use bicarbonate of soda and cream of tartar: allow 2.5 ml (½ level tsp) bicarbonate of soda and 5 ml (1 level tsp) cream of tartar for every 225 g (8 oz) plain flour with ordinary milk, or 2.5 ml (½ level tsp) bicarbonate of soda and only 2.5 ml (½ level tsp) cream of tartar with soured milk or buttermilk, as these contain an acid that will encourage the raising action.

MAKING SCONES AND SODA BREADS
Be sure to preheat the oven or griddle and prepare baking sheets and tins before you start to mix a dough, as it must be baked immediately after mixing and shaping. Always measure ingredients accurately because the proportion of liquid to dry ingredients affects the texture of the finished product. The right proportion of raising agent is important, too; the bread will be flat and hard if there is not enough, but too much will cause it to rise quickly and then collapse. Make sure the raising agent is evenly distributed through the dry ingredients to prevent irregular rising. If fat is to be added, rub it in as for shortcrust pastry (page 343). Alternatively, you can use a pastry blender, which is particularly helpful for keeping the dough cool.

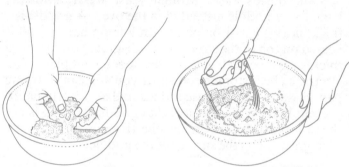

Adding the fat: Rub in the fat, using the finger and thumb tips of both hands.

Using a pastry blender: Cut the fat into the flour until it resembles fine breadcrumbs.

Adding the liquid activates the raising agent, so it is important to work quickly from this stage onwards. Many soda doughs can simply be spooned into a tin for baking as soon as they are mixed. However, if the bread is to be baked on a flat baking sheet it should be stiff enough to hold its shape. In these cases, mix the dough in the bowl, just until it comes away from the sides, then turn it out on to a lightly floured surface. It will be sticky, but avoid adding extra flour as this will harden the dough. Knead it quickly and lightly to form it into a manageable ball; six or eight times will usually be enough. Then roll the dough gently and cut or shape it as required. Press any trimmings together lightly and cut or shape them, but do not knead again as this may cause your scones or soda breads to be tough. Place the shaped dough in the preheated oven straight away before the activity of the raising agent is over.

BATTER MIXTURES
Scotch pancakes (also known as drop scones), waffles and popovers are made with a pouring batter. Like oven scones, they can be made with baking powder or bicarbonate of soda and cream of tartar, and the milk used may be fresh or soured. Batters can be made in advance and stored, covered, in the refrigerator. Stir thoroughly before using and add a little extra milk if the batter has thickened while standing.

BAKING EQUIPMENT

For scones, choose a baking sheet that will leave a 5-cm (2-in) gap between the edges of the sheet and the oven sides, to allow the hot air to circulate properly. If the sheet is too large, the heat will be deflected downwards, resulting in scones that are over-cooked on the bottom, but pale and doughy on the top. Loaf or cake tins should be of the correct size; if they are too large the loaf will bake flat and hard. If you have to use a smaller tin than that stated in the recipe, do not fill it more than two-thirds full and bake any leftover mixture separately in a small foil dish. Grease baking sheets and tins very lightly as too much fat will cause the dough to spread before it has time to set in shape.

Some breads made without yeast are traditionally baked on a griddle instead of in the oven. A griddle is a thick, heavy, cast-iron plate with a hoop handle and is heated on top of the stove. As a substitute you can use a thick, heavy-based frying pan or the solid hot plate of an electric or heat storage cooker. If you are using a frying pan, be sure that the base is thick and absolutely flat to prevent burning. Remember that griddle cooking is not the same as frying; there must be virtually no fat, just a light greasing on the surface of the griddle.

COOLING

As soon as scones are cooked, remove them from the oven and transfer them to a wire rack to cool. Loaves baked in a tin should be left to cool in the tin on a wire rack for up to 10 minutes, during which time they will shrink away from the sides, making it easier to turn them out cleanly. Finish cooling them on the wire rack.

Muffins should be turned out and preferably served at once or they will become soggy with steam. If they are to be served warm, but not immediately after cooking, lift them half out of their tins and leave them tilted to allow the steam to escape. Scotch pancakes, on the other hand, should be soft and moist, so try to contain the steam by stacking them and covering them with a clean tea towel while you cook the rest of the batch. Doughnuts and beignets, which are fried, should be drained well on kitchen paper towel to remove all excess fat before they are sprinkled with sugar.

SERVING

Most scones or breads raised with baking powder or soda are best eaten fresh from the oven or griddle, or at least the same day. Split or slice them and spread with butter. You can also add a savoury topping such as grated cheese or cream cheese flavoured with garlic, poppy seeds or caraway and toast them under a grill.

Loaves enriched with fruit should be kept for a day before serving so they will mellow in flavour and slice more easily. Serve waffles and popovers absolutely fresh, while they are still hot.

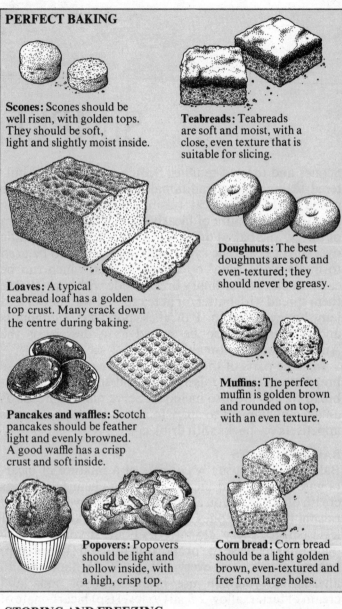

PERFECT BAKING

Scones: Scones should be well risen, with golden tops. They should be soft, light and slightly moist inside.

Teabreads: Teabreads are soft and moist, with a close, even texture that is suitable for slicing.

Loaves: A typical teabread loaf has a golden top crust. Many crack down the centre during baking.

Doughnuts: The best doughnuts are soft and even-textured; they should never be greasy.

Pancakes and waffles: Scotch pancakes should be feather light and evenly browned. A good waffle has a crisp crust and soft inside.

Muffins: The perfect muffin is golden brown and rounded on top, with an even texture.

Popovers: Popovers should be light and hollow inside, with a high, crisp top.

Corn bread: Corn bread should be a light golden brown, even-textured and free from large holes.

STORING AND FREEZING

To store scones and soda breads, wrap them tightly in cling film or foil and keep at room temperature. If stale, some of the original freshness can be restored by wrapping in foil and reheating in the oven at 190°C (375°F) mark 5 for about 20 minutes.

All the recipes in this chapter freeze well and can be stored for up to 6 months. Pack scones and muffins in bulk, in large polythene bags or well-sealed boxes. Wrap loaves and flat breads in foil, then overwrap with a polythene bag and freeze. Cook waffles which are to be frozen until only lightly browned and just set.

Scones, Scotch pancakes and muffins will thaw at room temperature in 1 hour or can be reheated in the oven at 200°C (400°F) mark 6 in about 10 minutes. Thaw loaves in their wrappings at room temperature for 2–3 hours and thaw waffles under the grill or in a toaster.

Scones

Scones

225 g (8 oz) self raising flour
2.5 ml (½ level tsp) salt
5 ml (1 level tsp) baking powder
25–50 g (1–2 oz) butter or margarine
150 ml (¼ pint) milk

To glaze, optional:
beaten egg or milk

Colour index
page 85

Makes
10–12
scones

1 Preheat a baking sheet in the oven. Sift the flour, salt and baking powder into a large bowl, then cut or rub in the fat until the mixture resembles fine breadcrumbs.

2 Make a well in the centre of the dry ingredients and stir in milk to make a soft dough.

3 Turn the dough on to a floured surface and knead quickly and lightly to remove any cracks.

4 Roll out the dough lightly with a rolling pin or pat it out evenly with your hand until it is about 2 cm (¾ in) thick.

5 Using a floured 5-cm (2-in) cutter, cut out dough rounds as close to each other as possible.

6 Place the rounds carefully on the hot baking sheet and, if you wish, brush them with beaten egg or milk to glaze.

7 Press the trimmings together and re-roll to make more rounds. Bake at 230°C (450°F) mark 8 for 8–10 minutes.

SCONE VARIATIONS

RICH AFTERNOON TEA SCONES: Prepare the scones as left, but add *15–30 ml (1–2 level tbsp) caster sugar* to the dry ingredients and replace the milk with *1 egg*, beaten, and *75 ml (5 tbsp) water* or milk.

FRUIT SCONES: Prepare the scones as left or above, but add *50 g (2 oz) currants*, sultanas, seedless raisins, chopped dates or mixed dried fruit to the dry ingredients before stirring in the liquid.

SCONE SHAPES: Prepare the scones as left, but cut the rolled dough into squares, triangles or diamonds with a sharp knife or biscuit cutter.

CHEESE SCONES: Prepare the scones as left, but add *50 g (2 oz) finely grated mature Cheddar cheese* and *5 ml (1 level tsp) dry mustard* to the dry ingredients and sprinkle the glazed scones with *50 g (2 oz) finely grated mature Cheddar cheese*. Bake at 220°C (425°F) mark 7 for 8–10 minutes until golden brown and well risen.

GRIDDLE SCONES: Prepare the dough as left, but use *225 g (8 oz) plain flour, 5 ml (1 level tsp) salt, 5 ml (1 level tsp) bicarbonate of soda, 10 ml (2 level tsp) cream of tartar, a large knob of butter* or lard and *150 ml (¼ pint) milk;* add *30 ml (2 level tbsp) caster sugar* to the rubbed-in mixture. Shape dough into two 0.5-cm (¼-in) thick rounds and cut each one into eight triangles with a floured knife. Cook for about 5 minutes on a lightly greased, hot griddle, then turn and cook for a further 5 minutes until the other side is browned and the centre dry.

WHOLEMEAL SCONE ROUND: Prepare the dough as left, but replace self raising flour with *175 g (6 oz) wholemeal flour* and *50 g (2 oz) plain flour* and increase the baking powder to 15 ml (1 level tbsp). Stir 50 g (2 oz) caster sugar into the rubbed-in mixture. Shape into a 15-cm (6-in) round, place on a baking sheet and mark into wedges with a floured knife. Bake for 15 minutes or until the top is a rich brown.

SCONE SHAPES

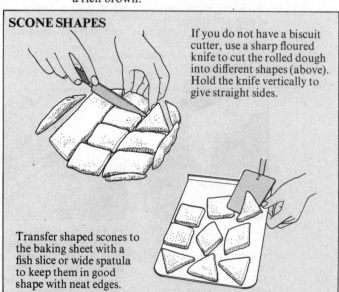

If you do not have a biscuit cutter, use a sharp floured knife to cut the rolled dough into different shapes (above). Hold the knife vertically to give straight sides.

Transfer shaped scones to the baking sheet with a fish slice or wide spatula to keep them in good shape with neat edges.

Muffins

Quick Muffins

225 g (8 oz) plain flour
30 ml (2 level tbsp) caster
*   sugar*
15 ml (1 level tbsp) baking
*   powder*
2.5 ml (½ level tsp) salt
1 egg
225 ml (8 fl oz) milk
50 ml (2 fl oz) vegetable oil

Colour index
page 85

Makes
12 muffins

1 Brush twelve 6.5-cm (2½-in) muffin tins with oil or melted butter until they are well greased.

2 Put the flour, sugar, baking powder and salt into a large bowl and stir to mix well.

3 Beat the egg lightly with a fork in a small bowl and then stir in the milk and vegetable oil.

4 Add the egg mixture to the dry ingredients all at once and stir lightly until the flour is just moistened. Do not overbeat: the mixture should still be slightly lumpy.

5 Spoon the mixture into the greased muffin tins wiping off any mixture spilt on the tin surrounds.

6 Bake at 200°C (400°F) mark 6 for 20–25 minutes until well risen. When cooked, a skewer inserted in the centre should come out clean.

7 Turn the muffins out on to a wire rack and serve them at once, split and buttered. Or, allow them to cool and split and toast them before serving.

Colour index
page 85

MUFFIN VARIATIONS

ORANGE MUFFINS: Prepare the muffins as left, but use 50 g (2 oz) caster sugar and 175 ml (6 fl oz) milk; add *50 ml (2 fl oz) orange juice* and *15 ml (1 tbsp) grated orange rind* to the egg mixture.

BLACKCURRANT MUFFINS: Prepare the muffins as left, but use 100 g (4 oz) caster sugar and add *75 g (3 oz) blackcurrants* to the egg mixture.

WHOLEMEAL MUFFINS: Prepare the muffins as left, but replace 100 g (4 oz) of the plain flour with *wholemeal flour*, and use 50 g (2 oz) caster sugar and 20 ml (4 level tsp) baking powder.

Bran Muffins

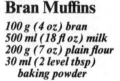

Colour index
page 85

Makes
20 muffins

100 g (4 oz) bran	*5 ml (1 level tsp) salt*
500 ml (18 fl oz) milk	*50 g (2 oz) butter*
200 g (7 oz) plain flour	*60 ml (4 level tbsp)*
30 ml (2 level tbsp)	* caster sugar*
* baking powder*	*2 eggs, beaten*

1. Grease well twenty 6.5-cm (2½-in) muffin tins.
2. Soak the bran in the milk for 5 minutes. Sift the flour, baking powder and salt into a large bowl.
3. Cream the butter and sugar. Beat in the eggs and then the bran mixture. Add the egg mixture to the dry ingredients all at once and stir until the flour is just moistened.
4. Spoon the mixture into the muffin tins until two-thirds full. Bake at 200°C (400°F) mark 6 for 25 minutes or until browned. Turn out on to a wire rack and serve at once, split and buttered.

BUTTER SHAPES

Butter shapes take a little time to make but can be kept in a bowl of iced water in the refrigerator for several days or in a box in the freezer for up to 3 months.

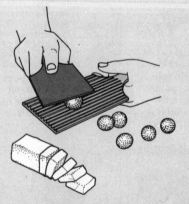

Butter balls: Chill the butter pats well in iced water. Cut a firm but not hard block of butter into 0.5-cm (¼-in) slices. Place one of them between the pats and roll into a ball, holding the lower pat steady. Repeat, dropping finished balls into iced water.

Butter curls: Heat the butter curler in hot water for 10 minutes. Halve a firm but not hard block of butter lengthways. Draw the curler lightly down the block of butter to make curls, dipping curler into hot water each time. Drop finished curls into iced water.

Doughnuts

Quick doughnuts and beignets are easier to make than traditional doughnuts made with yeast and are just as delicious. Serve them as soon as possible after they have been fried and drained, while they are still warm.

The dough for quick doughnuts should be kneaded and shaped lightly and quickly or the doughnuts will be tough; cut them closely together to reduce the amount of trimmings for re-rolling. Use a large saucepan, electric frying pan or thermostatically controlled deep-fat fryer for frying doughnuts and beignets. If you are using a saucepan, fill it no more than half full with oil and use a frying thermometer to check the temperature.

Quick Ring Doughnuts

Colour index page 85

Makes 20 doughnuts

225 g (8 oz) plain flour
2.5 ml (½ level tsp) bicarbonate of soda
5 ml (1 level tsp) cream of tartar
pinch ground cinnamon
25 g (1 oz) butter
50 g (2 oz) caster sugar
1 egg, beaten
milk
oil for deep frying

To serve, optional:
icing or caster sugar

1 Sift the flour, bicarbonate of soda, cream of tartar and cinnamon into a large bowl and cut or rub in the butter with your fingertips. Stir in the sugar. Make a well in the centre, pour in the beaten egg and gradually work it into the dry ingredients to make a stiff dough, adding a little extra milk if necessary. Turn on to a floured surface and knead quickly and lightly to remove any cracks.

2 Roll out the dough on a floured surface until it is about 1 cm (½ in) thick.

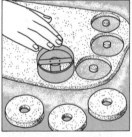

3 Cut out rings as close to each other as possible, using a floured doughnut cutter or a large and a small pastry cutter.

4 Heat the oil to 182°C (360°F). Lower in a few of the doughnuts with a fish slice or spatula and fry them until they are a light golden brown, turning them frequently.

5 Lift out the doughnuts with a slotted spoon and drain on kitchen paper towel while you fry the remaining doughnuts. Serve while still warm, plain or sprinkled with sugar.

QUICK DOUGHNUT VARIATIONS

QUICK WHOLEMEAL DOUGHNUTS: Prepare the doughnuts as left, but replace 100 g (4 oz) plain flour with *wholemeal flour*. Make a glaze by mixing *175 g (6 oz) clear honey* with *100 g (4 oz) sifted icing sugar* until evenly blended and spread it over the doughnuts while they are still warm.

QUICK NUT DOUGHNUTS: Prepare the doughnuts as left, but add *50 g (2 oz) roughly chopped shelled walnuts* to the dough with the sugar.

QUICK CHOCOLATE DOUGHNUTS: Prepare the doughnuts as left, but use 75 g (3 oz) sugar and add *5 ml (1 tsp) vanilla essence* and *40 g (1½ oz) chocolate*, melted in a small bowl over hot water, to the mixture with the egg. Sprinkle the doughnuts with icing sugar or leave them to cool completely and ice the tops with chocolate satin icing (page 366).

QUICK ROUND DOUGHNUTS: Prepare the dough as left or above, but shape small dessertspoonfuls of the dough into balls before frying them.

DOUGHNUT 'HOLES': Use the centres cut from the doughnuts or cut all the dough into small round circles using a plain round biscuit cutter. Serve plain or sprinkled with sugar.

Beignets

Colour index page 85

Makes 30 beignets

75 g (3 oz) plain flour
25 g (1 oz) caster sugar
50 g (2 oz) butter
150 ml (¼ pint) water
2 eggs, beaten

oil for deep frying

To serve:
icing sugar
hot dessert sauce, optional

1. Sift the flour with the sugar. Heat the butter and water in a small saucepan until the butter has melted, then bring the mixture to the boil.
2. Remove from the heat and add the flour mixture all at once. Beat well with a wooden spoon just until the paste is smooth and forms a ball in the centre of the saucepan. Remove from the heat.
3. Beat in the eggs, a little at a time, with a wooden spoon or a hand-held electric mixer, beating vigorously until the paste is smooth and glossy. Chill for about 30 minutes.
4. Heat the oil to 182°C (360°F). Drop a few heaped teaspoonfuls of the paste in the oil and fry for 2–3 minutes, turning them once, until they are puffed and golden. Drain well on kitchen paper towel and keep hot while you fry the remaining beignets.
5. Sprinkle the beignets with sifted icing sugar and serve immediately. If you wish, serve them with a hot dessert sauce (page 375).

GINGER BEIGNETS: Prepare the beignets as above, but sift *5 ml (1 level tsp) ground ginger* with the flour. Serve with *syrup sauce* (page 375).

CHEESE BEIGNETS: Prepare the beignet paste as above, but omit the caster sugar and beat in *50 g (2 oz) grated Cheddar cheese* before adding the eggs. Season the paste well with *salt, pepper* and *cayenne* and fry as above. Serve the beignets hot, sprinkled with *grated Parmesan cheese*.

Batters

Basic batter mixtures can be varied by adding whole-meal flour, nuts, potatoes, fruit, spices or herbs. Serve pancakes, waffles and popovers hot, with butter and golden syrup, maple syrup or honey, or cold with cream and jam or fresh fruit. If you prefer them plain, simply sprinkle them lightly with icing sugar.

To cook waffles, use an old-fashioned waffle iron on top of the stove or an electrically heated model. If the iron is not an automatic one, remember to turn it halfway through the cooking time, so both sides of the waffle will brown evenly. Always wait until the iron stops steaming before opening it.

Scotch Pancakes

100 g (4 oz) self raising
*   flour*
15–25 g (½-1 oz) sugar
1 egg
about 150 ml (¼ pint) milk

To serve:
butter
jam, honey or golden syrup,
*   optional*

Colour index
page 84

Makes about
10 large 10-cm
(4-in) or 15
small
5-cm (2-in)
pancakes

1 Mix the flour and sugar in a bowl, add the egg and half the milk and beat well until smooth. Add the remaining milk and beat well again until bubbles form on the surface.

2 Preheat a heavy-based frying pan or griddle and brush it very lightly with vegetable oil.

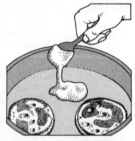

3 Drop on spoonfuls of batter to make 10-cm (4-in) or 5-cm (2-in) round pancakes.

4 When bubbles form on the surface, turn the pancakes and cook for a further ½–1 minute until golden brown.

5 Remove from the pan, stack and cover with a tea towel while you cook the remainder. Serve with butter and jam.

Potato Pancakes

1.4 kg (3 lb) large
*   potatoes, peeled*
1 small onion, skinned
2 eggs, beaten
75 ml (5 level tbsp) plain
*   flour*
15 ml (1 level tbsp) salt
pinch pepper
30 ml (2 tbsp) vegetable oil

For the garnish, optional:
parsley sprigs or
*   chopped parsley*

Colour index
page 84

Makes
16 pancakes

1 Coarsely grate the potatoes and the onion into a large bowl half filled with cold water.

2 Drain the potato and onion mixture through a colander lined with a clean tea towel or muslin.

3 Wrap the mixture tightly in the towel and squeeze hard to remove as much water as possible.

4 Mix the drained potato and onion mixture with the beaten eggs, flour, salt and pepper and stir until the ingredients are evenly blended together.

5 Heat the oil in a large frying pan and drop in four large mounds of the potato batter, spacing them well apart.

6 Flatten the pancakes with a fish slice or spatula and cook them for about 4 minutes until golden brown underneath. Turn them and cook until the other side is golden.

7 Remove from the frying pan and keep hot on a baking sheet lined with kitchen paper towel while you cook the remaining potato batter. Garnish with parsley.

Waffles

125 g (4 oz) self raising
   flour
pinch salt
15 ml (1 level tbsp) caster
   sugar
1 egg, separated
30 ml (2 tbsp) melted
   butter
2.5 ml (½ tsp) vanilla
   essence, optional
150 ml (¼ pint) milk

Colour index
page 84

Makes
6 waffles

1 Mix the flour with the salt and sugar in a large bowl and stir in the egg yolk, melted butter and vanilla essence.

2 Add the milk and whisk to make a smooth batter. Whisk the egg white stiffly and fold in.

3 Lightly grease and heat waffle iron. Pour in batter to cover to within 2.5 cm (1 in) of the edge.

4 Cook for 2–3 minutes, turning the iron halfway through if it is not an electrically heated type.

5 Loosen the waffle with a fork and turn it out. Reheat the iron before cooking the next waffle.

WAFFLE VARIATIONS

SPICE WAFFLES: Prepare the waffles as above, but add *2.5 ml (½ level tsp) ground mixed spice* to the dry ingredients.

PINEAPPLE WAFFLES: Prepare the waffles as above, but add *100 g (4 oz) drained crushed pineapple* to the mixture just before baking and serve the waffles with a sauce made by boiling *150 ml (¼ pint) pineapple syrup* with *50 g (2 oz) sugar*.

AMERICAN WAFFLES: Prepare the waffles as above and serve them immediately with *butter* and *maple syrup* or golden syrup, heated if you wish.

FRESH FRUIT WAFFLES: Prepare the waffles as above and serve cold, layered with *whipped cream* and whole or sliced *strawberries*, raspberries or skinned and sliced peaches.

Popovers

225 g (8 oz) plain flour
5 ml (1 level tsp) salt
6 eggs, beaten
75 g (3 oz) butter or
   margarine, melted
   and cooled
400 ml (¾ pint) milk

To serve:
butter

Colour index
page 85

Makes
8 popovers

1 Grease eight 200-ml (7-fl oz) ovenproof ramekins or soufflé dishes.

2 Put the ramekins or soufflé dishes on a baking sheet or in a roasting tin.

3 Mix the flour with the salt. Stir in the eggs and melted fat with a spoon until evenly mixed.

4 Add the milk and beat until smooth but bubbling on the surface.

5 Pour the batter into the ramekins, until about three-quarters full.

6 Bake at 190°C (375°F) mark 5 for 1 hour. Slit them; bake 10 minutes.

7 Turn out from ramekins and serve piping hot, with butter.

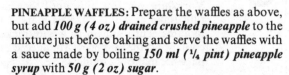
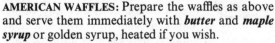

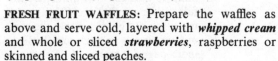

SAVOURY POPOVERS: Prepare as above, but add *225 g (8 oz) finely chopped mushrooms, 225 g (8 oz) finely chopped, lean cooked ham* or corned beef and a sprinkling of chopped *fresh mixed herbs*. Bake as above and sprinkle the popovers with a little finely chopped *parsley* before serving.

427

Teabreads

Nut Bread

350 g (12 oz) plain flour
150 g (5 oz) shelled
 walnuts, chopped
25 ml (5 level tsp) baking
 powder
275 g (10 oz) caster sugar

7.5 ml (1½ level tsp) salt
3 eggs
300 ml (½ pint) milk
60 ml (4 tbsp) vegetable
 oil

Colour index
page 84

Makes one
900-g (2-lb)
loaf

1 Grease a 900-g (2-lb) loaf tin. Mix the flour with the walnuts, baking powder, sugar and salt.

2 Beat eggs lightly, mix in milk and oil and add to the dry ingredients all at once, stirring until the flour is just moistened.

3 Pour into the tin. Bake at 180°C (350°F) mark 4 for 1 hour 25 minutes or until golden and shrinking away from sides of tin.

4 Cool in the tin on a wire rack for 10 minutes, then turn out on to the rack and leave to cool completely.

Lemon Teabread

Colour index
page 84

Makes one
900-g (2-lb)
loaf

250 g (9 oz) plain flour
7.5 ml (1½ level tsp)
 baking powder
3.75 ml (¾ level tsp) salt
350 g (12 oz) caster sugar
175 g (6 oz) butter
15 ml (1 tbsp) grated
 lemon rind

3 eggs
175 ml (6 fl oz) milk

For the glaze:
75 ml (5 tbsp) lemon juice
25 g (1 oz) caster sugar

1. Grease a 900-g (2-lb) loaf tin.
2. Sift the flour with the baking powder, salt and sugar. Cut or rub in the butter with your fingertips and stir in the lemon rind.
3. Beat the eggs lightly, then mix in the milk. Add the liquid to the dry ingredients all at once and stir until the flour is just moistened.
4. Pour mixture into the tin. Bake at 180°C (350°F) mark 4 for 1¼ hours or until a skewer inserted in the centre comes out clean. Cool in the tin on a wire rack for 10 minutes, then turn out on to the rack.
5. Make the glaze. Bring the lemon juice and sugar to the boil and boil for about 3 minutes, stirring frequently, until it has thickened slightly. Brush the warm loaf with the glaze and leave to cool completely.

Corn Bread

Colour index
page 84

Makes one
450-g (1-lb)
loaf

100 g (4 oz) plain flour
100 g (4 oz) corn meal
45 ml (3 level tbsp) caster
 sugar
15 ml (1 level tbsp) baking
 powder
5 ml (1 level tsp) salt

1 egg
150 ml (¼ pint) milk
75 g (3 oz) butter, melted
 and cooled

1 Grease a 20.5-cm (8-in) square cake tin. Mix the flour with the corn meal, sugar, baking powder and salt in a large bowl.

2 Beat the egg lightly in a small bowl and mix in the milk and the melted butter. Add the egg mixture to the dry ingredients all at once.

3 Stir together until the flour is just moistened and then pour the egg and flour mixture into the prepared cake tin.

4 Spread the mixture evenly in the tin and bake at 220°C (425°F) mark 7 for about 25 minutes or until golden.

CORN BREAD VARIATIONS

CORN BREAD RING: Prepare the mixture as above, but spoon it into a greased 1.1-litre (2-pint) capacity ring tin. Bake at 220°C (425°F) mark 7 for about 25 minutes or until the ring is golden. Turn out on to a wire rack and leave to cool. Serve the ring warm or leave to cool completely.   10 servings

CORN MUFFINS: Prepare the mixture as above, but spoon it into 12 greased 6.5-cm (2½-in) muffin or Yorkshire pudding tins until they are two-thirds full. Bake at 220°C (425°F) mark 7 for about 20 minutes. Turn out on to a wire rack and leave to cool. Serve the muffins warm or cold. Colour index page 85; makes 12 muffins

CORN STICKS: Prepare the mixture as above. Grease well a 14-hole corn stick tray, or an 18-hole sponge finger or éclair tray, with vegetable oil. Spoon the mixture into the tins until they are three-quarters full. Bake at 220°C (425°F) mark 7 for 15–20 minutes until golden. Serve the sticks warm or turn out on to a wire rack and leave to cool. Colour index page 84; makes 14–18 sticks

Colour index
page 84

Makes one
900-g (2-lb)
loaf

Chocolate, Date and Nut Loaf

175 ml (6 fl oz) boiling
   water
175 g (6 oz) stoned dates,
   sliced
275 g (10 oz) plain flour
50 g (2 oz) caster sugar
7.5 ml (1½ level tsp) salt
5 ml (1 level tsp) baking
   powder

5 ml (1 level tsp)
   bicarbonate of soda
175 g (6 oz) plain chocolate
50 g (2 oz) butter
1 egg
175 ml (6 fl oz) milk
5 ml (1 tsp) vanilla essence
175 g (6 oz) shelled
   walnuts, roughly chopped

1. Grease a 900-g (2-lb) loaf tin.
2. Pour the boiling water over the dates and leave to stand. Meanwhile, sift the flour, sugar, salt, baking powder and bicarbonate of soda into a large bowl. Melt the chocolate with the butter.
3. Beat the egg with the milk and vanilla essence. Add to the dry ingredients all at once with the walnuts, dates with their soaking water and melted chocolate and stir until just blended.
4. Pour the mixture quickly into the tin. Bake at 180°C (350°F) mark 4 for 1 hour 10 minutes. Cool in the tin on a wire rack for 10 minutes and then turn out on to the rack and leave to cool completely.

Colour index
page 83

Makes one
1.3-kg (2¾-lb)
loaf

Raisin and Caraway Soda Bread

450 g (1 lb) plain flour
45 ml (3 level tbsp) caster
   sugar
15 ml (1 level tbsp) baking
   powder
5 ml (1 level tsp) salt
3.75 ml (¾ level tsp)
   bicarbonate of soda

75 g (3 oz) butter
225 g (8 oz) seedless
   raisins
15 ml (1 level tbsp)
   caraway seeds
2 eggs
300 ml (½ pint) buttermilk

1. Grease a 19-cm (7½-in) diameter shallow casserole
2. Sift the flour, sugar, baking powder, salt and bicarbonate of soda into a large bowl. Cut or rub in the butter, then stir in the raisins and caraway seeds.
3. Beat the eggs, reserving 15 ml (1 tbsp). Mix the rest of the egg with the buttermilk, add to the dry ingredients all at once and stir until the flour is just moistened and the dough sticky.
4. Turn on to a floured surface and knead about 10 times. Shape into a ball and place in the casserole. Cut a 10-cm (4-in) cross, about 0.5 cm (¼ in) deep, with a sharp knife. Brush with egg.
5. Bake at 180°C (350°F) mark 4 for 1 hour 40 minutes. Cool in the casserole on a wire rack for 10 minutes, then turn out on to the rack. Leave to cool.

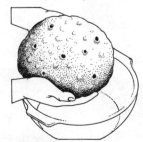

Shaping the loaf: Form the dough into a ball and place it in the casserole.

Cutting the cross: Use a sharp knife to cut the cross, about 0.5 cm (¼ in) deep.

Colour index
page 85

Makes two
450-g (1-lb)
loaves

Boston Brown Bread

100 g (4 oz) wholemeal
   flour
100 g (4 oz) rye flour
175 g (6 oz) corn meal
7.5 ml (1½ level tsp)
   bicarbonate of
   soda
7.5 ml (1½ level tsp) salt
400 ml (¾ pint)
   buttermilk
225 g (8 oz) black treacle
175 g (6 oz) seedless
   raisins, optional

1 Line two 450-g (1-lb) coffee tins or pudding basins with foil and cut foil lids for the tops. Grease the foil well.

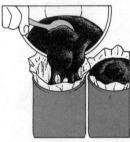

2 Measure all the ingredients into a large bowl and stir to mix.

3 Pour into the prepared tins, cover with foil and secure with string.

4 Place the tins on a trivet in a large, deep saucepan and add boiling water to come halfway up the tins. Cover saucepan.

5 Simmer gently for 2 hours or until a skewer inserted into the centre comes out clean; turn out on to a wire rack and cool.

Colour index
page 83

Makes two
700-g (1½-lb)
loaves

Courgette Bread

350 g (12 oz) plain flour
350 g (12 oz) caster sugar
22.5 ml (1½ level tbsp)
   baking powder
5 ml (1 level tsp) salt
175 g (6 oz) shelled
   walnuts, roughly
   chopped

4 eggs, lightly beaten
150 ml (¼ pint) vegetable
   oil
350 g (12 oz) courgettes,
   grated
10 ml (2 tsp) grated lemon
   rind

1. Grease two 700-g (1½-lb) loaf tins.
2. Sift the flour, sugar, baking powder and salt into a bowl and stir in the walnuts. Mix the eggs, oil, courgettes and lemon rind. Add to the dry ingredients all at once and stir until just moistened.
3. Spread mixture evenly in tins. Bake at 180°C (350°F) mark 4 for 1 hour. Cool in the tins for 10 minutes, then turn out and leave to cool completely.

Teabreads

Cherry Teabread

Colour index page 85

Makes one 1.3-kg (2¾-lb) loaf

150 g (5 oz) plain flour
100 g (4 oz) caster sugar
1.25 ml (¼ level tsp) baking powder
1.25 ml (¼ level tsp) bicarbonate of soda
1.25 ml (¼ level tsp) salt
100 g (4 oz) butter
1 egg, beaten
100 ml (4 fl oz) milk
5 ml (1 tsp) vanilla essence

For the topping:
25 g (1 oz) butter
50 g (2 oz) plain flour
50 g (2 oz) caster sugar
550 g (1¼ lb) cherry pie filling
1.25 ml (¼ tsp) lemon juice

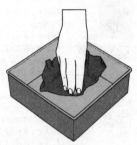

1 Grease and flour a 23-cm (9-in) square cake tin. Sift the flour, caster sugar, baking powder, bicarbonate of soda and salt into a large bowl. Melt and cool the butter.

2 Add the egg, milk, butter and vanilla essence to the dry ingredients. Mix well.

3 Pour the mixture into the tin and spread it evenly over the base.

4 Make the topping. Melt and cool the butter. Mix the flour, sugar and butter together until the mixture resembles coarse breadcrumbs.

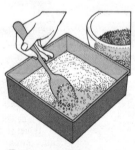

5 Spoon half the crumb topping in a layer over the mixture in the tin.

6 Mix the cherry pie filling with the lemon juice and spread it gently over the crumb topping.

7 Sprinkle with rest of topping. Bake at 180°C (350°F) mark 4 for 1 hour. Cool and cut into squares.

Peach-filled Teabread

Colour index page 85

Makes one 700-g (1½-lb) loaf

75 g (3 oz) plain flour
5 ml (1 level tsp) baking powder
pinch salt
100 g (4 oz) butter
100 g (4 oz) caster sugar
2 eggs
5 ml (1 tsp) grated lemon rind

411-g (14½-oz) can sliced peaches, drained

For the topping:
50 g (2 oz) butter
50 g (2 oz) plain flour
25 g (1 oz) caster sugar
2.5 ml (½ tsp) grated lemon rind

1. Grease well and base line an 18-cm (7-in) square cake tin.
2. Sift the flour, baking powder and salt into a large bowl. Cream the butter and sugar until light and fluffy, beat in the eggs and lemon rind and fold in the sifted dry ingredients.
3. Spread the mixture evenly in the tin and arrange the peaches over the top.
4. Make the crumble topping. Melt the butter, remove it from the heat and stir in the flour, sugar and lemon rind. Spoon it evenly over the peaches.
5. Bake at 180°C (350°F) mark 4 for 45–50 minutes or until golden. Cool in the tin on a wire rack and cut into squares or slices.

Nut-layered Teabread

Colour index page 85

Makes one 900-g (2-lb) loaf

225 g (8 oz) plain flour
5 ml (1 level tsp) baking powder
5 ml (1 level tsp) bicarbonate of soda
100 g (4 oz) butter
225 g (8 oz) caster sugar
2 eggs, beaten
5 ml (1 tsp) vanilla essence

225 ml (8 fl oz) soured cream

For the filling:
75 g (3 oz) shelled walnuts, finely chopped
100 g (4 oz) caster sugar
5 ml (1 level tsp) ground cinnamon

1. Grease a 23-cm (9-in) ring tin.
2. Sift the flour, baking powder and bicarbonate of soda into a large bowl. Cream the butter and sugar and beat in the eggs and vanilla essence until evenly blended. Carefully fold in the flour mixture and the soured cream with a spoon.
3. Mix together all the ingredients for the nut filling. Spread half the cake mixture in the tin and sprinkle with half the filling. Repeat the layering.
4. Bake at 180°C (350°F) mark 4 for 60–65 minutes. Cool in the tin on a wire rack for 10 minutes, then turn out on to the rack and leave to cool completely. Cut into slices to serve.

Making the layers: Spread alternate layers of the creamed mixture and nut filling in the prepared tin.

Cooling the teabread: Leave the teabread in the tin for 10 minutes before turning it on to the rack.

Flat breads

Mexican Tortillas

Colour index page 109

Makes 12 tortillas

250 g (9 oz) masa harina (fine corn meal; can be bought at shops specialising in Mexican and Spanish food and in good delicatessens)
2.5 ml (½ level tsp) salt
225 ml (8 fl oz) tepid water

1 Mix the masa harina with the salt in a large bowl. Gradually add the tepid water, mixing lightly with a fork to make a dough that is just moist enough to hold together. If necessary add more water, 15 ml (1 tbsp) at a time. Gather the dough lightly into a ball.

2 Knead the dough quickly and lightly in the bowl with one hand until it is smooth and free from cracks.

3 Divide the dough into 12 equal pieces and shape each one into a small ball. Keep the dough balls covered to prevent them drying while you roll each one out.

4 Flatten each ball until 0.5-cm (¼-in) thick, then place between two sheets of waxed paper. Roll out to 15-cm (6-in) rounds and leave between the waxed paper.

5 Remove the top sheet from one round and invert it on to a hot, ungreased frying pan. Peel off the second sheet of paper. Cook for 30 seconds or until the edges curl up.

6 Turn the tortilla over and press gently with a fish slice or spatula until bubbles form underneath it. Turn it again and cook for a further minute or until the underside is speckled with brown.

7 Remove from the frying pan. Place the tortilla on foil and wrap it to keep hot while you cook the remainder, stacking them in the foil as they are cooked. Serve with chilli con carne (page 209).

Indian Puris

Colour index page 85

Makes 8 puris

100 g (4 oz) wholemeal flour
knob of butter or ghee
salt and pepper
45 ml (3 tbsp) water
oil for deep frying

1. Put the flour in a small bowl, rub in the fat and season with salt and pepper. Gradually add the water, working it in to make a pliable dough.
2. Knead the dough in the bowl until smooth and no longer sticky. Cover and chill for 1 hour.
3. Roll out the dough between sheets of waxed paper until it is wafer-thin. Peel back the top sheet of waxed paper and cut out 7.5-cm (3-in) diameter rounds from the dough.
4. Remove the trimmings, re-roll them between waxed paper and cut out more rounds. Cover them with a damp cloth until they are to be fried.
5. Heat the oil in a large deep pan to 177–188°C (350–370°F) or until a cube of bread will brown in 1 minute. Add one of the rounds and fry it for about 30 seconds, pressing lightly with a fish slice or spatula to hold it under until it puffs up.
6. Remove carefully from the frying pan, drain on kitchen paper towel and keep hot while you fry the remaining rounds. Serve with curries.

SHALLOW-FRIED PURIS: Prepare the puris as above, but shallow-fry them in only 45 ml (3 tbsp) oil for about 15 seconds on each side.

Onion Crackers

Colour index page 85

Makes 16 crackers

100 g (4 oz) plain flour
50 g (2 oz) corn meal
15 ml (1 level tbsp) caster sugar
1.25 ml (¼ level tsp) bicarbonate of soda
1.25 ml (¼ level tsp) salt
25 g (1 oz) butter
35 ml (7 tsp) water
15 ml (1 tbsp) cider vinegar
25 g (1 oz) dried onion flakes

1. Mix the flour with the corn meal, sugar, bicarbonate of soda and salt in a large bowl. Cut or rub in the butter until the mixture resembles coarse breadcrumbs. Gradually add the water and vinegar, and stir lightly until the flour is just moistened and the dough sticky.
2. Shape the dough into a ball and knead it a few times in the bowl until it is smooth. Divide it into 32 equal pieces and form each into a ball. Cover the balls with cling film and leave them covered while you roll the dough into rounds.
3. Roll out one ball on a floured surface with a floured rolling pin to an 11.5-cm (4½-in) diameter round, with slightly ragged edges. Sprinkle 2.5 ml (½ tsp) of the onion flakes over the top and roll again to press in the onion. Transfer to an ungreased baking sheet. Repeat with five or six more balls until the baking sheet is full.
4. Bake the rounds at 190°C (375°F) mark 5 for 10 minutes, remove from the baking sheet immediately and cool the onion crackers on a wire rack. Repeat the rolling and baking until all the dough balls are used up. Store the crackers in an airtight tin and serve them with salads or appetisers.

YEAST BAKING

Yeast baking can give you everything from plain but delicious everyday bread to coffee cakes, fancy breads, buns, pizzas and some delightful desserts. Whatever the recipe, the basic skills and processes are the same. Pay particular attention to the kneading and rising of the dough, as these are the most crucial stages. There is a world of difference between the volume and texture of bread that has been well kneaded and allowed to rise properly and bread that has not.

INGREDIENTS

Yeast: Both fresh and dried yeast are widely available and there is nothing to choose between them as far as the taste and texture of the end product is concerned. Fresh yeast is rather like putty in both colour and texture and should crumble easily when broken. Although it will store for up to a month in the refrigerator, wrapped in cling film or foil, it will give the best results when used absolutely fresh, so buy it in small quantities, as required. Fresh yeast is usually blended with the liquid, then added to the dry ingredients all at once. Alternatively, the dough may be formed by mixing some of the dry ingredients into the yeast liquid to give a batter; this is left to ferment before mixing to a dough with the remaining ingredients. There are two types of dried yeast, the traditional granular type and the almost powder fine, easy blend type. Traditional dried yeast must be activated before it is mixed with the flour. Using 5 ml (1 level tsp) sugar to every 300 ml (½ pint) liquid in the recipe, dissolve the sugar in tepid liquid, sprinkle the yeast granules over the surface and leave for about 15 minutes, or until the surface is frothy, before adding the liquid to the dry ingredients. Easy blend dried yeast must be mixed directly with the flour before the liquid is added. The recipes in this chapter can all be made with granular or easy blend dried yeast. *Use 15 ml (1 level tbsp) of either type of dried yeast for every 700 g (1½ lb) flour.*
Flour: It is the flour used that gives bread its characteristic flavour and texture. For most white breads, the best results are obtained by using a strong flour because it has a high gluten content which forms the frame of the risen bread: ordinary flour gives a smaller rise and closer-textured bread with a pale crust.

White flour contains 70–72 per cent of the wheat. The bran and wheatgerm which give both wholemeal and wheatmeal flour their colour are removed, resulting in the flour used to make fine-textured white bread.

Wheatmeal flour contains 80–90 per cent of the wheat, but has some of the bran removed. It is more absorbent than white flour, giving a texture that is denser than white bread, but not as coarse as wholemeal bread.

Wholemeal (or wholewheat) flour contains 100 per cent of the wheat; the entire grain is milled. Bread made with this flour is brown in colour, has a nutty taste and is often coarse-textured.

Stoneground flour takes its name from a specific grinding process which heats the flour and gives it a slightly roasted, nutty flavour. Both wholemeal and wheatmeal flours can be stoneground.

Granary flour contains malt and crushed wheat and gives a crunchy, rough-textured bread.

Rye flour used on its own produces rather dense, heavy bread. When baking at home, the best results are obtained by combining it with a strong wheat flour.
Salt: Salt improves the flavour of the bread. It should be measured accurately; if there is not enough salt the dough will rise too quickly, but if too much is used it will kill the yeast and give the bread an uneven texture.
Fat: The addition of fat will enrich bread and give a moist loaf with a soft crust. Lard, butter and block margarine are the most commonly used fats.
Liquid: The amount of liquid used will vary according to the absorbency of the flour, brown flours usually being more absorbent than white. Too much liquid will give the bread a spongy and open texture, so measure it accurately. Water is most suitable for plain bread, giving a loaf with an even texture and crisp crust. Milk will give a softer crust and help the bread to stay fresh.

MAKING A YEAST DOUGH
All the ingredients and equipment for bread making should be at room temperature or slightly warmer. Liquids should be tepid, at approximately 43°C (110°F).

The yeast and liquid are usually added to the flour all at once and beaten in with a wooden spoon until they are well blended and leave the sides of the bowl clean. Yeast can also be rubbed directly into the flour or else mixed with some of the ingredients initially and then left to ferment to a batter before mixing with the remaining ingredients (see enriched white rolls, page 439).

KNEADING

Kneading is essential to strengthen the gluten in the flour, making the dough elastic in texture and enabling it to rise more easily. Turn the dough on to a floured surface, flour your hands and knead the dough firmly (as shown below) for about 10 minutes, until it is smooth, elastic and no longer sticky, or as the recipe directs. If you have a mixer with a dough hook attachment, it can take the hard work out of kneading. Follow the manufacturers' instructions and remember that you will get the best results with small amounts of dough.

With floured hands fold the dough towards you.

Push down and away with the heel of your hand.

Give the dough a quarter turn and knead until smooth.

RISING

The kneaded dough is now ready for rising. Unless otherwise stated, place it in a greased bowl and cover with a large sheet of polythene brushed with oil, to prevent a skin forming. The best results are obtained by allowing the covered dough to rise overnight or for up to 24 hours in the refrigerator. It must be allowed to return to room temperature before it is shaped. Allow about 2 hours for the dough to rise at room temperature, 18°C (65°F), or 45 minutes–1 hour if it is put in a warm place such as an airing cupboard.

KNOCKING BACK AND SHAPING

The best texture is obtained by kneading the dough a second time after rising, before it is shaped and baked. Turn the risen dough on to a lightly floured surface and knead for 2–3 minutes to knock out air bubbles and ensure an even texture, then shape as required.

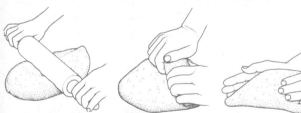

For a loaf tin: Roll or stretch dough to a rectangle the same width as the length of the tin.

Starting at the narrow end, fold or roll up the rectangle like a Swiss roll and pinch seam to seal.

Seal the ends by pressing with your hands and fold them under. Place seam side down in a greased loaf tin.

For a round loaf, knead the dough on a lightly floured surface until the underside is smooth. Turn it over, place on a lightly greased baking sheet and flatten slightly.

CHOOSING TINS

For a 450-g (1-lb) loaf, the appropriate size tin to use is 20.5 × 10 × 6.5 cm (8 × 4 × 2½ in) top measurements. For a 900-g (2-lb) loaf, use one with 23 × 13 × 7 cm (9 × 5 × 3 in) top measurements.

PROVING OR SECOND RISE

This is the last process before baking. Cover the shaped dough in the tin with oiled polythene and leave it at room temperature until it has doubled in size and will spring back when lightly pressed with a floured finger. The dough is now ready for baking.

BAKING

Plain breads are baked at 230°C (450°F) mark 8. Remove the bread from the tin for the last 5 minutes of cooking and return it to the oven to brown the sides and improve the crust. When cooked, the bread should be well risen and golden brown and should sound hollow when tapped underneath. Cool on a wire rack.

Testing the cooked bread: Tap the bottom of the loaf with your knuckles. If it is cooked the loaf should sound hollow, like a drum.

Cooling the bread: Transfer the cooked loaf to a wire rack immediately and allow it to cool completely before serving or storing it.

GLAZES

If you want a crusty finish for bread or rolls, brush them before baking with a glaze made by dissolving 10 ml (2 level tsp) salt in 30 ml (2 tbsp) water. For a soft crust, brush with oil and dust with flour, or alternatively brush with beaten egg or beaten egg and milk. To give breads and yeast buns a sticky finish, brush them as soon as they come out of the oven with warm honey or a sugar syrup. To make the syrup, dissolve 30 ml (2 level tbsp) sugar in 30 ml (2 tbsp) water and bring to the boil.

STORING

Bread that will be eaten within a few days can be stored in a polythene bag or an airtight tin. Baked loaves and rolls generally freeze well for up to 4 weeks, but the length of storage time will depend on the crust. Bread with a very crisp crust stores well for only about a week before the crust begins to shell off, while enriched breads and soft rolls freeze well for up to 6 weeks. Leave bread to thaw in the sealed freezer bag to prevent it drying out, either at room temperature or, if it is more convenient, overnight in the refrigerator.

Basic breads

Bread is one of the oldest baked foods. Man has been making it since time immemorial and it is still a staple food in most countries. It is genuinely good for you, being rich in vitamins (particularly the B group), calcium, iron and trace elements; it is also a useful source of protein. The bran in wholemeal and wheatmeal flour can provide the roughage needed in our diet, so that bread made from them is especially beneficial.

Choose your everyday bread from recipes in this section and ring the changes between a fine white flour and a coarse rye or wholemeal. Home-baked bread has an unbeatable flavour but an attractive shape can add to its appeal. Choose a simple tin shape when you are making bread for sandwiches and toast, but go to town with rounds, plaits, flowerpots and batons when you don't need a neat shape to slice evenly. To refresh bread that has gone slightly stale, wrap it in foil and heat through at 190°C (375°F) mark 5 for 15 minutes. Then, for a crisp crust, unwrap the loaf and return it to the oven for a further 5 minutes.

White Bread

700 g (1½ lb) strong white
    flour
10 ml (2 level tsp) salt
knob of lard
15 g (½ oz) fresh yeast
400 ml (¾ pint) tepid
    water

Colour index page 78
Makes one 900-g (2-lb) loaf

1 Sift the flour and salt into a large bowl and rub in the lard. Make a well in the centre. Blend the yeast with the tepid water until smooth.

2 Add the yeast liquid to the dry ingredients all at once and stir in. Work it to a firm dough, adding extra flour if needed, until it leaves the sides of the bowl.

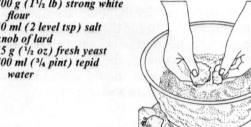

3 Turn the dough on to a floured surface and knead for about 10 minutes, until smooth, elastic and no longer sticky.

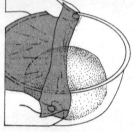

4 Shape the dough into a ball, put it in a large greased bowl and cover with oiled polythene to prevent a skin forming. Leave to rise until it has doubled in size.

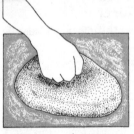

5 Turn the dough on to a floured surface, flatten it very firmly with your knuckles to knock out the air bubbles, then knead it again well. Grease a 900-g (2-lb) loaf tin.

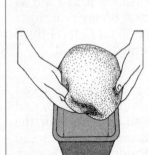

6 Stretch the dough to an oblong the same width as the length of the tin; roll up from narrow end. Tuck ends under and place in the tin, seam side down.

7 Cover again with oiled polythene and leave to prove until the dough has doubled in size. Bake at 230°C (450°F) mark 8 for 30–40 minutes.

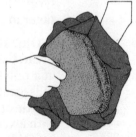

8 The cooked loaf should look well risen and golden brown and should sound hollow when you tap the bottom. Leave to cool on a wire rack.

Colour index page 78
Makes one 700-g (1½-lb) loaf

Quick Wheatmeal Bread

450 g (1 lb) wheatmeal
    flour or 225 g (8 oz)
    wheatmeal flour and
    225 g (8 oz) strong
    white flour
10 ml (2 level tsp) salt
10 ml (2 level tsp) sugar
knob of lard

15 g (½ oz) fresh yeast
300 ml (½ pint) tepid
    water
cracked wheat, optional

For the glaze:
milk or water

1. Stir together the flour, salt and sugar in a large bowl and rub in the lard with your fingertips. Make a well in the centre. Blend the yeast with the tepid water until smooth.
2. Add the yeast mixture to the dry ingredients all at once and mix well with a wooden spoon to make a soft dough that leaves the sides of the bowl clean.
3. Turn the dough on to a floured surface and knead well with floured hands for about 10 minutes, until smooth, elastic and no longer sticky.
4. Grease a 700-g (1½-lb) loaf tin.
5. Stretch or roll the dough to a rectangle the same width as the length of the tin and fold or roll up from the narrow end, like a Swiss roll. Tuck the ends under and place in the prepared tin, seam side down.
6. Cover the tin with lightly oiled polythene and leave to rise until the dough has doubled in size and will spring back when pressed with a floured finger.
7. Brush the top of the loaf lightly with milk or water to glaze and, if you wish, sprinkle with a little cracked wheat.
8. Bake at 230°C (450°F) mark 8 for 30–40 minutes, until well risen and a rich brown. Remove from the tin and cool on a wire rack.

WHEATMEAL COB: Prepare the bread as above, but shape the dough into a round loaf (page 433), place on a lightly greased baking sheet and sprinkle with cracked wheat before proving. Mark into wedges before baking if you wish.

WHEATMEAL FLOWERPOTS: Prepare the bread as above, but grease two clean clay flowerpots instead of a loaf tin and divide the dough between them for proving and baking. If you are using the flowerpots for the first time, grease them well and bake in a hot oven first for 30 minutes to prevent them cracking. (Makes two 350-g (12-oz) loaves.)

Colour index
page 78

Makes two
450-g (1-lb)
loaves

Light Rye Bread

700 g (1½ lb) white rye
 flour
10 ml (2 level tsp) sugar
2 25-mg ascorbic acid
 tablets, crushed
400 ml (¾ pint) tepid
 water
25 g (1 oz) fresh yeast
10 ml (2 level tsp) salt

30 ml (2 level tbsp)
 caraway seeds
knob of margarine

For the glaze:
5 ml (1 level tsp) cornflour

1. Mix 225 g (8 oz) of the flour with the sugar in a large bowl, add the ascorbic acid tablets and water and crumble in the yeast. Cover the mixture with oiled polythene and leave in a warm place for 1 hour, until it becomes a spongy batter. Mix the remaining flour and the salt in another large bowl, add the caraway seeds and rub in the margarine.
2. Add the yeast batter to the flour and caraway mixture and mix well with a wooden spoon to make a soft dough.
3. Turn the dough on to a floured surface and knead for about 5 minutes, until the dough is smooth, elastic and no longer sticky.
4. Put the dough into a large greased bowl, cover with oiled polythene and leave to rise until it has doubled in size. Grease a baking sheet.
5. Turn the dough on to a floured surface again and knead lightly for 2–3 minutes.
6. Divide the dough in half. Shape the two pieces into balls, by repeatedly drawing the sides down and folding them underneath to make a smooth top. Place them on the greased baking sheet and flatten them slightly into cobs. Alternatively, shape the pieces of dough by holding your hand flat, almost at table level, and moving it round in a circular motion. Gradually lift your palm to get a good round shape. Cover the loaves with oiled polythene and leave to prove, in a warm (if possible steamy) atmosphere, until the dough has doubled in size and will spring back when lightly pressed with a floured finger.
7. Bake at 180°C (350°F) mark 4 for 30 minutes. Remove the loaves and brush the tops with a glaze made by blending the cornflour with a little cold water and adding enough boiling water to clear and thicken it. Return the loaves to the oven for a further 20 minutes, until well risen and golden brown. Remove the loaves from the baking sheet and cool wrapped in a tea towel.

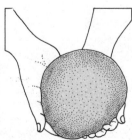

Shaping the dough: Draw down the sides of the dough and tuck them under to form a ball.

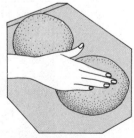

Flattening the loaves: Use your hand to flatten each ball slightly into a round, smooth cob loaf.

Colour index
page 78

Makes two
1.1-kg (2½-lb)
loaves

Marble Loaf

For the dark dough:
225 g (8 oz) wholemeal
 flour
225 g (8 oz) rye flour
350 g (12 oz) strong white
 flour
15 ml (1 level tbsp) sugar
15 ml (1 level tbsp) salt
500 ml (18 fl oz) water
40 g (1½ oz) margarine or
 lard
45 ml (3 level tbsp) black
 treacle
100 g (4 oz) corn meal
15 ml (1 level tbsp)
 caraway seeds
25 g (1 oz) fresh yeast

For the light dough:
700 g (1½ lb) strong white
 flour
12.5 ml (2½ level tsp) salt
45 ml (3 level tbsp) sugar
300 ml (½ pint) water
100 ml (4 fl oz) milk
40 g (1½ oz) margarine or
 lard
15 g (½ oz) fresh yeast

For the glaze:
1 egg white, beaten

1. Prepare the dark dough. Stir together the flours, sugar and salt in a large bowl. Make a well in the centre. Heat the water, margarine or lard, treacle and corn meal until tepid, add the caraway seeds and blend in the yeast until smooth.
2. Add the yeast mixture to the dry ingredients all at once and mix well with a wooden spoon to make a soft dough that leaves the sides of the bowl clean.
3. Turn the dough on to a floured surface and knead for about 10 minutes, until smooth, elastic and no longer sticky. Place it in a large greased bowl, cover with oiled polythene and leave to rise until it has doubled in size.
4. Meanwhile, prepare the light dough. Sift the flour, salt and sugar into a large bowl. Make a well in the centre. Heat the water, milk and margarine or lard until tepid and blend in the yeast until smooth.
5. Add the yeast mixture to the dry ingredients all at once and mix with a wooden spoon to make a soft dough that leaves the sides of the bowl clean.
6. Turn the dough on to a floured surface and knead for about 10 minutes, until smooth, elastic and no longer sticky. Place it in a large greased bowl, cover with oiled polythene and leave to rise until it has doubled in size. Grease two large baking sheets.
7. Turn the risen dark dough on to a floured surface and knead again lightly for 2–3 minutes. Repeat with the light dough. Cut each dough into two equal pieces with a sharp knife.
8. Take one piece of each dough and knead them together lightly on a floured surface for about 5 minutes, then roll out to a 40.5 × 23 cm (16 × 9 in) rectangle. Roll up very tightly from the long edge, like a Swiss roll. Pinch the seam together and place the loaf seam side down on one of the baking sheets. Press the ends lightly to seal them and tuck them under the loaf. Repeat with the remaining two pieces of dough to make a second loaf.
9. Cover the loaves again with oiled polythene and leave to prove at room temperature until the dough has doubled in size and will spring back when lightly pressed with a floured finger.
10. Brush the loaves with egg white and bake at 200°C (400°F) mark 6 for about 40 minutes until well risen and a rich brown. Remove from the baking sheets and cool on a wire rack.

435

Basic breads

French Bread

Colour index page 79

Makes two 350-g (12-oz) loaves

450 g (1 lb) strong white flour
6.25 ml (1¼ level tsp) salt
15 g (½ oz) fresh yeast
350 ml (12 fl oz) tepid water

For the glaze:
1 egg white
15 ml (1 tbsp) water

1. Sift the flour and salt into a large bowl. Make a well in the centre. Blend the yeast with 50 ml (2 fl oz) of the measured water until smooth.
2. Add the yeast liquid and the remaining water to the dry ingredients all at once and mix with a wooden spoon to make a soft dough.
3. Turn the dough on to a lightly floured surface and knead it for about 5 minutes. Leave the dough to rest for about 3 minutes, then knead it well again for a further 2 minutes, until it is smooth, elastic and no longer sticky.
4. Put the dough in a large greased bowl, cover with oiled polythene and leave to rise until it is about three times its original size.
5. Turn the dough on to a floured surface again and knead lightly for 2–3 minutes. Cover again with oiled polythene and prove at room temperature until it has returned to three times its original size and will spring back when lightly pressed with a floured finger. Grease a large baking sheet.
6. Divide the dough in half and rest for 5 minutes.

7 Roll out each piece of dough on a floured surface to a 38 × 25.5 cm (15 × 10 in) rectangle. Roll up tightly from the long edge, like a Swiss roll. Pinch the seams to seal.

8 Place the loaves seam side down on the baking sheet and taper the ends with your fingers. Cover with oiled polythene and leave to rise until the loaves have tripled in size.

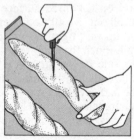

9 Cut three or four diagonal slashes across the top of each loaf with a sharp knife, then bake at 200°C (400°F) mark 6 for 25 minutes, until the loaves are golden brown.

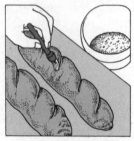

10 Beat the egg white well with the water, remove the loaves from the oven and brush them with the glaze. Return to oven and bake for 5 minutes more. Cool on a wire rack.

Wholemeal Bread

Colour index page 78

Makes two 900-g (2-lb) loaves

1.4 kg (3 lb) wholemeal flour
30 ml (2 level tbsp) sugar
20–25 ml (4–5 level tsp) salt
25 g (1 oz) lard
50 g (2 oz) fresh yeast
900 ml (1½ pints) tepid water

For the glaze:
1 egg white
15 ml (1 tbsp) water
5 ml (1 level tsp) caraway seeds

1. Stir together the flour, sugar and salt in a large bowl and rub in the lard with your fingertips. Make a well in the centre. Blend the yeast with 300 ml (½ pint) of the tepid water until smooth.
2. Add the yeast liquid all at once and mix well with a wooden spoon, adding enough of the remaining water to make a firm dough that leaves the sides of the bowl clean.
3. Turn the dough on to a floured surface and knead well for about 10 minutes, until it is smooth, elastic and no longer sticky.
4. Put the dough in a large greased bowl, cover it with oiled polythene and leave to rise until it has doubled in size.
5. Grease two large baking sheets or two 900-g (2-lb) loaf tins.
6. Turn the dough on to a floured surface again, flatten it with your knuckles to knock out any air bubbles and knead lightly.
7. Divide the dough in half. Shape each piece into an oval loaf, smooth the top and taper the ends. Place the loaves on the baking sheets. Or, if you are making tin loaves, stretch or roll each piece to a rectangle the same width as the length of the tin. Fold or roll up from the narrow end, like a Swiss roll; tuck the ends under and place the loaves seam side down in the tins.
8. Cover again with lightly oiled polythene and leave to prove at room temperature until the loaves have doubled in size and will spring back when lightly pressed with a floured finger.
9. Beat the egg white and the water together. Cut three diagonal slashes in each loaf, brush them with the egg white glaze and sprinkle the caraway seeds over the top. Bake at 230°C (450°F) mark 8 for 30 – 40 minutes, or until a rich brown. Remove the loaves from the baking sheets or tins immediately and cool on a wire rack.

Shaping the dough: Form each piece into an oval loaf with your hands, tapering the ends.

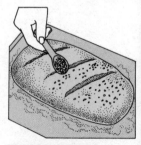

Finishing the loaves: Sprinkle caraway seeds over each glazed loaf just before baking.

Colour index
page 78

Makes one
900-g (2-lb)
loaf

Rye and Wholemeal Plait

For the rye dough:
150 g (5 oz) strong white
  flour
175 g (6 oz) rye flour
22.5 ml (1½ level tbsp)
  sugar
7.5 ml (1½ level tsp) salt
150 ml (¼ pint) water
25 g (1 oz) margarine or
  lard
45 ml (3 level tbsp) golden
  syrup
25 g (1 oz) plain chocolate
15 g (½ oz) fresh yeast

For the wholemeal dough:
200 g (7 oz) wholemeal
  flour

175 g (6 oz) strong white
  flour
10 ml (2 level tsp) sugar
10 ml (2 level tsp) salt
75 ml (5 tbsp) water
75 ml (5 tbsp) milk
25 g (1 oz) margarine
30 ml (2 level tbsp) honey
15 g (½ oz) fresh yeast

For the glaze:
1 egg yolk
10 ml (2 tsp) water
poppy seeds, optional

1. Prepare the rye dough. Mix the white and rye flours, sugar and salt together in a large bowl. Make a well in the centre.
2. Heat the water, margarine or lard, golden syrup and chocolate in a small saucepan until tepid and blend in the yeast until smooth.
3. Add the yeast mixture to the dry ingredients all at once and mix well with a wooden spoon to make a soft dough that leaves the sides of the bowl clean.
4. Turn the dough on to a floured surface and knead for about 7 minutes; the dough should be smooth and will still be slightly sticky. Place it in a large greased bowl, cover with oiled polythene and leave to rise until it has doubled in size.
5. Meanwhile, prepare the wholemeal dough. Stir together the wholemeal and white flours, sugar and salt in a large bowl.
6. Heat the water, milk, margarine and honey in a small saucepan until tepid and blend in the yeast.
7. Add the yeast mixture to the dry ingredients all at once and mix well with a wooden spoon to make a dough that leaves the sides of the bowl clean.
8. Turn the dough on to a floured surface and knead for about 10 minutes, until smooth, elastic and no longer sticky. Place it in a large greased bowl, cover with oiled polythene and leave to rise until it has doubled in size. Grease a large baking sheet.
9. Turn the rye dough on to a floured surface and knead lightly for 2–3 minutes to knock out any large air bubbles. Repeat with the wholemeal dough and divide it into two pieces.
10. Roll out the three pieces of dough to 51-cm (20-in) ropes; lay them next to each other on the baking sheet, with the rye dough in the centre. Plait the ropes (right), starting from the centre and working towards the ends. Pinch the ends together to seal and tuck under the ends. Cover again with oiled polythene and leave to prove at room temperature until the plait has doubled in size and will spring back when lightly pressed with a floured finger.
11. Beat the egg yolk with the water and brush it over the loaf. Sprinkle with poppy seeds if you wish. Bake at 180°C (350°F) mark 4 for 45 minutes, until well risen and brown. Remove from the baking sheet and cool on a wire rack.

Colour index
page 78

Makes one
700-g (1½-lb)
loaf

Plaited Herb Bread

450 g (1 lb) strong white
  flour
15 g (½ oz) fresh yeast
225 ml (8 fl oz) tepid milk
5 ml (1 level tsp) salt
7.5 ml (1½ level tsp) dried
  rosemary

50 g (2 oz) margarine
1 egg, beaten

For the glaze:
1 egg, beaten

1. Sift 150 g (5 oz) of the flour into a large bowl. Blend the yeast with the milk, stir it into the flour and leave in a warm place for about 20 minutes or until frothy. Sift the remaining flour and the salt into a large bowl, add the dried rosemary and rub in the margarine with your fingertips.
2. Add the dry ingredients and the egg to the yeast mixture and mix well to make a soft dough that leaves the sides of the bowl clean.
3. Turn it on to a floured surface and knead for 10 minutes, until smooth, elastic and no longer sticky.
4. Put the dough in a large greased bowl, cover with oiled polythene and leave to rise until it has doubled in size. Grease a large baking sheet.
5. Turn the dough on to a floured surface again and knead lightly for 2–3 minutes.
6. Divide the dough into three equal pieces and shape each one into a long rope. Place them on the baking sheet and plait them (below).
7. Brush the loaf with beaten egg. Cover again and leave to prove until it has doubled in size.
8. Bake at 190°C (375°F) mark 5 for 45–50 minutes until golden brown. Remove from the baking sheet and cool on a wire rack.

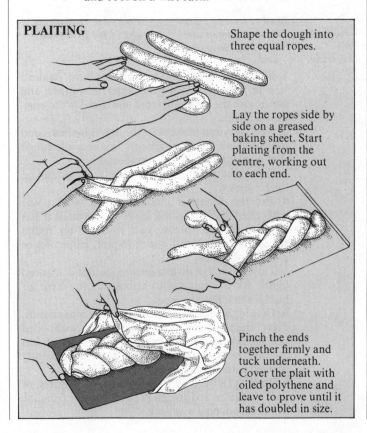

PLAITING

Shape the dough into three equal ropes.

Lay the ropes side by side on a greased baking sheet. Start plaiting from the centre, working out to each end.

Pinch the ends together firmly and tuck underneath. Cover the plait with oiled polythene and leave to prove until it has doubled in size.

Basic breads

Sesame Seed Bread

Colour index page 79

Makes two 450-g (1-lb) loaves

700 g (1½ lb) strong white flour
15 ml (1 level tbsp) salt
45 ml (3 level tbsp) sugar
200 ml (⅓ pint) water
225 ml (8 fl oz) milk
50 g (2 oz) margarine or lard

25 g (1 oz) fresh yeast
1 egg, beaten

For the glaze:
milk.
30 ml (2 level tbsp) sesame seeds

1. Sift the flour, salt and sugar into a large bowl. Make a well in the centre. Heat the water, milk and margarine or lard until tepid, stirring, and blend in the yeast until smooth.
2. Add the yeast liquid and the egg to the dry ingredients and mix well with a wooden spoon to make a soft dough.
3. Turn the dough on to a floured surface and knead for about 10 minutes, until smooth, elastic and no longer sticky. Grease two 23-cm (9-in) round cake tins or two 450-g (1-lb) loaf tins.
4. Divide the dough in half, shape into rounds or oblongs and press evenly into the tins. Cover with oiled polythene and leave to rise until the dough has doubled in size and will spring back when lightly pressed with a floured finger.
5. Brush the loaves with milk and sprinkle with the sesame seeds. Bake at 180°C (350°F) mark 4 for 40 minutes, until well risen and golden brown. Remove from the tins and cool on a wire rack.

Oatmeal Bread

Colour index page 79

Makes two 450-g (1-lb) loaves

700 g (1½ lb) strong white flour
10 ml (2 level tsp) salt
400 ml (¾ pint) water
15 g (½ oz) margarine or lard

175 g (6 oz) golden syrup
100 g (4 oz) rolled oats
25 g (1 oz) fresh yeast

1. Sift the flour and salt into a large bowl. Make a well in the centre. Heat the water, margarine and syrup with the oats until tepid and blend in the yeast until smooth.
2. Add the yeast mixture to the dry ingredients and mix well with a wooden spoon to make a soft dough that leaves the sides of the bowl clean.
3. Knead the dough until it is smooth, elastic and no longer sticky.
4. Put the dough in a large greased bowl, cover with oiled polythene and leave to rise until it has doubled in size. Grease two 18-cm (7-in) round cake tins, or shallow 1.1-litre (2-pint) casseroles or ovenproof dishes.
5. Turn the dough on to a floured surface and knead lightly for 2–3 minutes to knock out any large air bubbles that have formed.
6. Divide the dough in two and shape into rounds. Place them in the tins, cover again with oiled polythene and leave to prove until the dough has doubled in size and will spring back when lightly pressed with a floured finger.
7. Bake at 180°C (350°F) mark 4 for 40 minutes, or until well risen and golden brown. Remove from the tins and cool on a wire rack.

Cheese Casserole Bread

Colour index page 79

Makes one 900-g (2-lb) loaf

550 g (1¼ lb) strong white flour
30 ml (2 level tbsp) sugar
10 ml (2 level tsp) salt
350 ml (12 fl oz) milk
25 g (1 oz) fresh yeast

100 g (4 oz) Cheddar cheese, grated

For the glaze:
15 g (½ oz) margarine, melted

1. Sift the flour, sugar and salt into a large bowl. Heat the milk until tepid and blend in the yeast and the cheese until smooth.
2. Add the yeast mixture to the dry ingredients and mix well to make a firm dough.
3. Knead the dough well until it is smooth and elastic and leaves the sides of the bowl clean.
4. Put the dough in a large greased bowl, cover with oiled polythene and leave to rise until it has doubled in size. Grease well a 1.9-litre (3¼-pint) round casserole, cake tin or ovenproof dish with straight sides.
5. Turn the dough on to a floured surface and knead lightly for 2–3 minutes.
6. Shape the dough into a round and press it into the casserole evenly. Cover again with oiled polythene and leave to prove until it has doubled in size and will spring back when lightly pressed.
7. Brush with the margarine and bake at 190°C 375°F (mark 5) for 30–35 minutes, until well risen and golden brown. Remove from the casserole and cool on a wire rack.

Potato Bread

Colour index page 79

Makes two 1-kg (2¼-lb) loaves

900 g (2 lb) strong white flour
30 ml (2 level tbsp) sugar
20 ml (4 level tsp) salt
100 ml (4 fl oz) water
300 ml (½ pint) milk
50 g (2 oz) margarine
25 g (1 oz) fresh yeast

350 g (12 oz) potatoes, peeled, boiled and mashed
2 eggs, beaten

For the glaze:
milk

1. Sift the flour, sugar and salt into a large bowl. Heat the water, milk and margarine until tepid and blend in the yeast and the mashed potato.
2. Add the yeast mixture and the eggs to the dry ingredients and mix well to make a soft dough.
3. Turn the dough on to a floured surface and knead, until smooth, elastic and no longer sticky.
4. Put the dough in a large greased bowl, cover with oiled polythene and allow to rise until it has doubled in size. Grease two 18-cm (7-in) round cake tins or casseroles with shallow, straight sides.
5. Turn the dough on to a floured surface again and divide it in half.
6. Shape the pieces into rounds with your hands and place one in each cake tin. Cut two parallel slashes in the top of each loaf, cover again with oiled polythene and leave to prove until the dough has doubled in size and will spring back when lightly pressed with a floured finger.
7. Brush the loaves with milk and bake at 200°C (400°F) mark 6 for 40 minutes, or until well risen and a rich brown. Cool on a wire rack.

Rolls

Any bread dough can be used to make rolls, but the one given here is enriched with milk and eggs to give a moister bread with a softer crust. Cut the dough into pieces of equal weight before shaping the rolls, so that they are all the same size.

There are many ways of varying rolls made with the same basic dough. After glazing and before baking them, lightly sprinkle the tops with poppy, caraway or fennel seeds, or use sesame seeds, which are particularly good on soft baps. Cracked wheat goes well on wholemeal rolls and a mixture of crushed rock salt and caraway seeds is good on rolls to be eaten with cheese. Alternatively, try making some of the shaped rolls shown below and overleaf; it takes a little practice to make them evenly sized and shaped, but it is well worth the extra time and effort.

Enriched White Rolls

Colour index
page 83

Makes twelve
50-g (2-oz)
rolls

450 g (1 lb) strong white
flour
15 g (½ oz) fresh yeast
225 ml (8 fl oz) tepid milk

5 ml (1 level tsp) salt
50 g (2 oz) margarine
1 egg, beaten

1 Sift 150 g (5 oz) of the flour into a large bowl and make a well in the centre. Blend the yeast with the tepid milk until smooth, stirring until it has dissolved.

2 Stir the liquid into the flour and leave for 20 minutes, until frothy. Sift the remaining flour and salt into a bowl and rub in the margarine.

3 Add the dry ingredients and the egg to the yeast mixture. Mix well to make a soft dough that leaves the sides of the bowl clean.

4 Turn the dough on to a floured surface and knead for about 10 minutes, until smooth, elastic and no longer sticky.

5 Put in a greased bowl, cover with oiled polythene and leave to rise until it has doubled in size.

6 Turn the dough on to a floured surface again and knead well, then divide it into 50-g (2-oz) pieces and shape into neat rounds or roll shapes (right and overleaf). Place on greased baking sheets, cover and leave to prove until they have doubled in size. Bake at 190°C (375°F) mark 5 for 10–15 minutes, until well risen and golden brown. Remove from the baking sheets and cool on a wire rack.

DINNER ROLLS

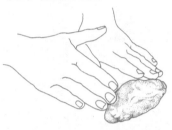

Shape the dough pieces into ovals, tapering the ends; place 5 cm (2 in) apart on greased baking sheets. Cover; prove until they have doubled in size.

With a sharp, floured knife, make a deep lengthways slash down the centre of each roll.

VIENNA ROLLS

Shape the dough as for dinner rolls, then brush with a glaze of 1 egg white beaten with 15 ml (1 tbsp) water.

Sprinkle lightly with caraway or fennel seeds.

TWISTS

Divide the dough pieces in half; roll out to ropes 15 cm (6 in) long. Pinch pairs of ropes firmly together at one end.

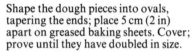

Carefully twist pairs of ropes and pinch the other ends to seal. Join ends underneath; place on greased baking sheets.

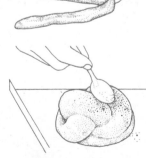

Cover and prove until they have doubled in size. Brush with beaten egg and sprinkle with a few sesame seeds.

Rolls

KNOTS

Roll out the pieces of dough to ropes 15 cm (6 in) long.

Tie ropes into knots; place on greased baking sheets. Cover; prove until they have doubled in size. Brush with melted butter.

CRESCENTS

Roll out all the dough to a circle; divide it into wedges. Brush with a little melted butter.

Roll up the wedges tightly, starting at the wide ends, and place them on greased baking sheets with points tucked under.

Curve the ends round to form crescents. Cover; prove until they have doubled in size.

BATCH ROLLS

With your hands, shape the dough pieces into 5-cm (2-in) balls.

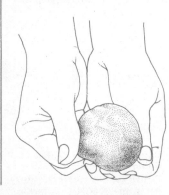

Melt some butter in a pan. Roll the balls in butter; place, just touching, in square tin. Cover; prove until they have doubled in size.

WINDMILLS

Roll out all the dough to a large rectangle; divide into 6.5-cm (2½-in) squares. Place 5 cm (2 in) apart on greased baking sheets. Cut from each corner towards centre, but not right through. Brush centres with water.

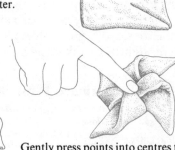

Fold alternate points into the centres of the squares.

Gently press points into centres to secure them and brush with melted butter. Cover; prove until they have doubled in size.

FAN ROLLS

Roll out all dough to a 0.3-cm (⅛-in) thick rectangle. Brush with melted butter and cut into strips 4 cm (1½ in) wide.

Stack six of the strips together and cut them into squares.

Place them, cut side up, in greased 6.5-cm (2½-in) patty tins. Cover and prove until they have doubled in size.

POPPIES

Shape dough pieces into balls and flatten slightly. Place on greased baking sheets.

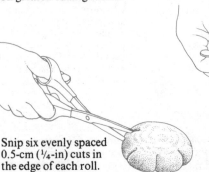

Snip six evenly spaced 0.5-cm (¼-in) cuts in the edge of each roll.

Brush rolls with beaten egg; sprinkle with poppy seeds. Cover; prove until they have doubled in size.

Sourdough bread

Colour index page 80

Makes 8 baps

Floury Baps

450 g (1 lb) strong white
flour
5 ml (1 level tsp) salt
50 g (2 oz) lard

15 g (½ oz) fresh yeast
300 ml (½ pint) tepid milk
and water, mixed
flour for dredging

1. Sift the flour and salt into a large bowl and rub in the lard with your fingertips. Blend the yeast with the tepid liquid until smooth.

2. Add the yeast liquid all at once to the dry ingredients and mix with a wooden spoon to make a firm dough, adding extra flour if needed, until it leaves the sides of the bowl clean.

3. Turn the dough on to a floured surface and knead for 5 minutes, until smooth, elastic and no longer sticky.

4. Put the dough in a greased bowl, cover with oiled polythene and leave to rise until it has doubled in size. Lightly flour a baking sheet.

5. Turn the dough on to a floured surface and knead lightly for 2–3 minutes.

6. Cut it into eight equal pieces and shape each piece into a ball. Place them on the floured baking sheet and flatten slightly. Cover again with oiled polythene and leave to prove until they have doubled in size.

7. Dredge the tops lightly with flour. Bake at 200°C (400°F) mark 6 for 15–20 minutes, until well risen. Cool on a wire rack.

Colour index page 80

Makes 36 rolls

Parkerhouse Rolls

450 g (1 lb) strong white
flour
5 ml (1 level tsp) salt
15 g (½ oz) fresh
yeast

about 300 ml (½ pint)
tepid water

For the glaze:
50 g (2 oz) butter

1. Sift the flour and salt into a large bowl. Make a well in the centre. Blend the yeast with the tepid water until smooth.

2. Add the yeast liquid all at once to the dry ingredients and mix with a wooden spoon to make an elastic dough, adding extra water if necessary.

3. Turn on to a floured surface and knead until smooth, elastic and no longer sticky.

4. Roll out the dough until it is about 1 cm (½ in) thick and cut out 6.5-cm (2½-in) rounds. Knead the trimmings, re-roll them and cut out more rounds.

5. Melt the butter in a roasting tin, dip both sides of the rounds in it and fold them in half. Arrange them closely in rows in the tin. Cover with oiled polythene and leave to prove until the dough has doubled in size and will spring back when lightly pressed with a floured finger.

6. Bake at 230°C (450°F) mark 8 for about 25 minutes, until well risen and golden brown. Remove from the tin and cool on a wire rack.

American Sourdough Bread

800–900 g (1¾–2 lb)
strong white flour
30 ml (2 level tbsp) caster
sugar
15 ml (1 level tbsp) salt
5 ml (1 level tsp)
bicarbonate of soda

For the glaze:
40 g (1½ oz) butter,
melted

For the sourdough starter:
15 g (½ oz) dried yeast
5 ml (1 level tsp) caster
sugar
450 ml (16 fl oz) tepid
water

225 g (8 oz) strong white
flour

For replenishing the starter:
100 g (4 oz) strong white
flour
225 ml (8 fl oz) tepid
water

Colour index page 79

Makes two 900-g (2-lb) loaves

1 Make starter: sprinkle yeast and sugar on to 150 ml (¼ pint) water; leave until frothy. Mix in remaining water and flour.

2 Cover with oiled polythene. Leave in a warm place for 48 hours; stir occasionally. It will rise and bubble, then separate. Stir well before using.

3 A day before required, mix together 225 ml (8 fl oz) starter, 350 g (12 oz) flour, the sugar, salt and bicarbonate of soda.

4 Mix well then cover with a tea towel or oiled polythene; leave to stand at room temperature, away from draughts, for at least 18 hours.

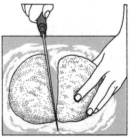

5 Mix in 450–550 g (1–1¼ lb) flour, enough to make a soft dough. Turn it on to a lightly floured surface and knead for 10 minutes.

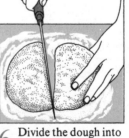

6 Divide the dough into two and shape into flat, round loaves about 18 cm (7 in) in diameter. Grease two baking sheets.

7 Put loaves on baking sheets and cover with tea towels or oiled polythene. Leave in a warm place for 1½ hours, until they have doubled in size.

8 Brush with water and cut 3–5 criss-cross slashes in each loaf. Bake at 220°C (425°F) mark 7 for 10 minutes.

9 Turn down oven to 200°C (400°F) mark 6; bake for 35–40 minutes more. Place on wire rack; brush with butter; cool.

To replenish the starter: If you make sourdough bread regularly, you will never need more yeast. Simply replenish the starter for the next batch of bread. Beat 100 g (4 oz) strong white flour with 225 ml (8 fl oz) tepid water until smooth. Stir this into 225 ml (8 fl oz) leftover starter. Leave at room temperature until the mixture begins to bubble. Cover loosely and re-frigerate. Prepare at least 3 days before required.

Sweet breads and yeast cakes

Many different sweet breads and buns can be made by adding extra ingredients, such as fruit, nuts and spices, to the basic sweet dough, or by varying the shape of the loaves. Wait until sweet breads have cooled slightly before adding any icing so that it does not melt.

Sweet breads and buns can be stored in the freezer in the same way as any ordinary bread. Wait until they have thawed completely before icing them.

Sweet Dough

Makes 1.8 kg (4 lb) dough

900 g (2 lb) strong white flour
225 g (8 oz) sugar
5 ml (1 level tsp) salt
225 g (8 oz) margarine
300 ml (½ pint) milk

150 ml (¼ pint) water
40 g (1½ oz) fresh yeast or 22.5 ml (1½ level tbsp) dried yeast and 10 ml (2 level tsp) sugar
2 eggs, beaten

1 Sift the flour, sugar and salt into a large bowl. Make a well in the centre. Put the margarine, milk and water into a small saucepan and heat through gently, stirring occasionally, until mixture is tepid. Crumble the fresh yeast into the tepid liquid and blend until smooth; if you are using dried yeast, sprinkle the yeast and the sugar on to the liquid and leave for 15 minutes, or until frothy.

2 Add the tepid yeast liquid and the beaten eggs to the sifted dry ingredients all at once.

3 Mix the liquid and the dry ingredients well with a wooden spoon to make a soft dough that leaves sides of bowl clean.

4 Turn the dough on to a floured surface and knead for about 10 minutes, until smooth, elastic and no longer sticky.

5 Put the dough in a large greased bowl and cover with oiled polythene. Leave to rise until it has doubled in size.

6 Turn the dough on to a floured surface again and knead lightly for 2–3 minutes. Shape, prove and bake as required.

Colour index page 81
Makes one 450-g (1-lb) turtle

TURTLE BREAD: Using *¼ recipe quantity sweet dough* (left), cut off a 150 g (5 oz) piece and reserve it. Shape the remaining piece into a neat oval and place it on a greased baking sheet. Roll the reserved dough into an 18-cm (7-in) rope. Cut a 5-cm (2-in) piece for the head and snip eyes and a mouth in it; cut four 2.5-cm (1-in) pieces as legs, then snip and shape toes on them. Make a pointed tail with the remaining dough. Assemble the body and shape the shell as shown below. Cover and prove until it has doubled in size. Beat *1 egg* with a little *water*, brush it over the turtle and bake at 190°C (375°F) mark 5 for 20–25 minutes. Cool on a wire rack.

Assembling turtle: Tuck head, legs and tail under body and pinch to seal.

Shaping the shell: Cut shell design and pinch wavy edges with fingers.

Hot Cross Buns

Colour index page 81
Makes 12 buns

450 g (1 lb) strong white flour
25 g (1 oz) fresh yeast
150 ml (¼ pint) tepid milk
60 ml (4 tbsp) tepid water
5 ml (1 level tsp) salt
2.5 ml (½ level tsp) each mixed spice, ground cinnamon and ground nutmeg
50 g (2 oz) caster sugar
50 g (2 oz) butter, melted and cooled but not firm

1 egg, beaten
100 g (4 oz) currants
30–45 ml (2–3 tbsp) chopped mixed peel
shortcrust pastry made with 50 g (2 oz) flour, page 343

For the glaze:
60 ml (4 tbsp) milk and water
45 ml (3 level tbsp) caster sugar

1. Sift 100 g (4 oz) of the flour into a large bowl. Blend the yeast with the milk and water, stir it into the flour and leave in a warm place for 15–20 minutes, until frothy. Sift remaining flour, salt, spices and sugar into a large bowl.
2. Add the butter, egg, flour mixture, fruit and peel to the yeast mixture and mix to a soft dough.
3. Turn on to a floured surface; knead until smooth.
4. Put in a large greased bowl, cover with oiled polythene; leave to rise until it has doubled in size.
5. Turn on to a floured surface and knead lightly.
6. Divide dough into 12 pieces. Using the palm of one hand, roll each piece into a ball, pressing down hard at first, then easing up as you turn and shape the buns. Arrange well apart on floured baking sheets, cover and leave to prove for 30 minutes.
7. Roll out the shortcrust pastry thinly; cut into 9-cm (3½-in) strips. Damp them and lay two on each bun to make a cross. Bake at 190°C (375°F) mark 5 for 15–20 minutes. Heat the milk and water with sugar. Brush the glaze over the hot buns twice; leave to cool on wire rack.

Kolacky

sweet dough made with 225 g (8 oz) flour, opposite   *kolacky toppings, below*

Colour index
page 81
6 servings

1. Grease a large baking sheet.
2. Roll out the dough on a floured surface to a 30-cm (12-in) circle. Place it on the baking sheet, cover with oiled polythene and leave to rise until it has nearly tripled in size. Meanwhile, prepare the kolacky toppings (below).
3. Flatten the centre of the risen dough with your knuckles, pressing firmly to within 1 cm (½ in) of the edge. With the back of a knife, lightly mark the dough into six wedges.
4. Spoon one of the toppings on to each section.
5. Bake at 190°C (375°F) mark 5 for 20–25 minutes. Cool on a wire rack.

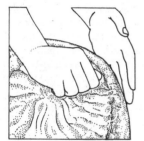

Shaping kolacky: Press out the dough with your knuckles to leave a flat centre with a raised edge.

Adding the toppings: Spoon a different topping on to each wedge-shaped section, leaving dividing spaces.

KOLACKY TOPPINGS

BLACKCURRANT: Spoon off *10 ml (2 tsp) juice* from a *396-g (14-oz) can blackcurrants*; blend with *12.5 ml (2½ level tsp) cornflour*. Boil remaining fruit and juice; pour on cornflour. Return to pan; cook 1 minute. Add *1.25 ml (¼ level tsp) grated lemon rind*.

CHERRY: Mix *60 ml (4 tbsp) canned cherry pie filling* and *15 ml (1 level tbsp) desiccated coconut*.

CREAM CHEESE: Mix *75 g (3 oz) softened cream cheese, 15 ml (1 level tbsp) sugar, 15 ml (1 tbsp) milk* and a *little finely grated lemon rind* or orange rind.

LEMON: Use *60 ml (4 tbsp) lemon curd*.

ORANGE: Use *60 ml (4 tbsp) orange marmalade*.

PINEAPPLE: Mix *60 ml (4 tbsp) pineapple jam, 15 ml (1 tbsp) chopped walnuts* and a *pinch of salt*.

Raisin Bread

sweet dough made with 450 g (1 lb) flour, opposite   *175 g (6 oz) raisins*

Colour index
page 81
Makes one
1.1-kg
(2½-lb) loaf

1. Roll out dough on a floured surface to a 30 × 23 cm (12 × 9 in) rectangle. Sprinkle the raisins over it and roll up from the longest edge. Pinch the seam and ends to seal and tuck under the ends.
2. Place seam side down in a greased 1.1-kg (2½-lb) loaf tin, cover with oiled polythene and leave to prove until it has doubled in size. Bake at 190°C (375°F) mark 5 for 1 hour. Cool on a wire rack.

Apricot Coffeecake

225 g (8 oz) dried apricots
300 ml (½ pint) water
50 g (2 oz) caster sugar
1.25 ml (¼ level tsp) ground cinnamon
sweet dough made with 225 g (8 oz) flour, opposite

Colour index
page 81
Makes one
800-g (1¾-lb)
cake

For the icing:
50 g (2 oz) icing sugar
1.25 ml (¼ tsp) vanilla essence
10 ml (2 tsp) water

1 Put the apricots in a saucepan, add the water and bring to the boil. Reduce the heat, then cover and simmer gently for 30 minutes. Cool.

2 Blend the apricots and their cooking water with the sugar and cinnamon to make a smooth purée, or rub through a sieve. Leave to cool.

3 Grease a large baking sheet. Roll out the dough on a floured surface to a 38 × 30 cm (15 × 12 in) rectangle and lift it on to the sheet.

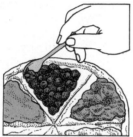

4 Spread the apricot mixture in a 10 cm (4 in) wide strip lengthways down the centre of the rolled dough.

5 Cut the dough on either side of the filling at 2.5-cm (1-in) intervals to make strips, and criss-cross them over the mixture.

6 Cover the coffeecake with oiled polythene and leave it to prove until it has doubled in size. Bake at 190°C (375°F) mark 5 for 25–30 minutes.

7 Cool on a wire rack for 15 minutes. Mix all the ingredients for the icing until smooth and drizzle over the top of the cake. Leave to cool completely.

Sweet breads and yeast cakes

Fruited Plait

Colour index
page 81

Makes one
1.3-kg
(2¾-lb)
loaf

sweet dough made with 450 g
 (1 lb) flour, page 442
175 g (6 oz) sultanas
150 g (5 oz) chopped mixed
 peel

15 ml (1 level tbsp) plain
 white flour
1 egg yolk, lightly beaten
50 g (2 oz) icing sugar
15 ml (1 tbsp) water

1. Cut the dough into three and roll out on a floured surface to 30 × 10 cm (12 × 4 in) strips.
2. Toss the sultanas with the peel and flour and spread lengthways down the centre of the dough strips. Brush the edges with egg yolk, fold them over the fruit to form a roll and pinch the edges to seal.
3. Place the rolls on a greased baking sheet and plait them (page 437). Cover and leave to prove.
4. Brush the loaf with egg yolk and bake at 180°C (350°F) mark 4 for 35 minutes. Cool on a wire rack. Mix the sugar and water and brush over the loaf while it is still warm.

Chelsea Buns

Colour index
page 81

Makes 9 buns

225 g (8 oz) strong white
 flour
15 g (½ oz) fresh yeast
100 ml (4 fl oz) tepid milk
2.5 ml (½ level tsp) salt
about 15 g (½ oz) butter
1 egg, beaten
melted butter

75 g (3 oz) dried fruit
30 ml (2 tbsp) chopped
 mixed peel
50 g (2 oz) soft dark brown
 sugar
clear honey

1. Sift 50 g (2 oz) of the flour into a large bowl. Blend the yeast with the tepid milk and add to the flour. Mix well and leave for 15–20 minutes in a warm place until frothy. Sift the remaining flour and the salt into a large bowl and rub in the fat.
2. Add the dry ingredients and egg to the frothy batter and beat to make a fairly soft dough.
3. Turn the dough on to a floured surface and knead for 5 minutes. Put in a greased bowl, cover with oiled polythene and leave to rise until doubled in size.
4. Knead the dough again, then roll out to a 30 × 23 cm (12 × 9 in) rectangle. Brush with melted butter. Mix together the fruit, peel and sugar and spread over dough. Roll up from longest edge and seal with water. Grease an 18-cm (7-in) square cake tin.
5. Cut the roll into nine equal slices and place them cut side down in the cake tin. Cover again and leave to prove until they have doubled in size. Bake at 190°C (375°F) mark 5 for 30 minutes. Brush the warm buns with honey and cool on a wire rack. Separate them when they are cold.

Arranging the buns: Put slices side by side in tin for proving and baking.

Separating the buns: When they are cool, pull buns apart gently with forks.

Lemon Ring

Colour index
page 81

Makes one
1-kg (2¼-lb)
loaf

700 g (1½ lb) strong white
 flour
5 ml (1 level tsp) salt
100 g (4 oz) sugar
225 ml (8 fl oz) milk
50 ml (2 fl oz) water
50 g (2 oz) margarine
25 g (1 oz) fresh yeast
2 eggs, beaten

For the topping:
100 g (4 oz) sugar
grated rind of 2
 lemons
1.25 ml (¼ level tsp)
 ground mace

1. Sift the flour, salt and sugar into a large bowl. Make a well in the centre . Heat the milk and water with 25 g (1 oz) margarine until tepid and blend in the yeast until smooth. Add the yeast liquid and the eggs to the dry ingredients and mix well to form a soft dough that leaves the sides of the bowl clean.
2. Turn the dough on to a lightly floured surface and knead for about 10 minutes, until smooth, elastic and no longer sticky.
3. Put the dough in a large greased bowl, cover with oiled polythene and leave to rise until it has doubled in size. Meanwhile, mix together all the topping ingredients and set aside. Melt the remaining margarine and set aside. Grease well a 25.5-cm (10-in) ring or savarin tin.
4. Turn the dough on to a floured surface again and knead lightly for 2–3 minutes.

5 Cut the dough into 32 even-sized pieces and roll each one into a small, smooth ball shape.

6 Place half the balls touching each other in the tin and brush with melted margarine.

7 Sprinkle half the lemon mixture evenly over the first layer of balls.

8 Add remaining balls to make a second layer, brush with margarine and sprinkle with the lemon mixture.

9. Cover again with oiled polythene and leave to prove until the balls have doubled in size and will spring back when pressed with a floured finger.
10. Bake at 180°C (350°F) mark 4 for 35 minutes. Cool in the tin for 5 minutes, before turning out to cool completely on a wire rack.

Wholemeal Sugar Bears

450 g (1 lb) wholemeal
flour
450 g (1 lb) strong white
flour
275 g (10 oz) sugar
7.5 ml (1½ level tsp) salt

400 ml (¾ pint) milk
225 g (8 oz) margarine
40 g (1½ oz) fresh yeast
2 eggs

Colour index
page 82

Makes three
700-g (1½-lb)
bears

1. Stir together the flours, sugar and salt in a large bowl. Heat the milk and margarine until tepid and blend in the yeast until smooth. Reserve one egg white, beat the remaining eggs together and add with the yeast liquid to the dry ingredients. Mix well with a wooden spoon to make a soft dough that will leave the sides of the bowl clean.
2. Turn the dough on to a floured surface and knead well for 10 minutes, until smooth, elastic and no longer sticky. Place in a greased bowl, cover with oiled polythene and leave to rise until it has doubled in size. Grease three baking sheets.
3. Turn the dough on to a floured surface again and knead lightly. Divide the dough into three equal pieces and shape each one into a bear as follows.
4. Cut the piece of dough in half and cut one of the halves in two again. Shape the large piece and one of the small ones into balls. Roll the remaining small piece into a thick rope, about 15 cm (6 in) long.
5. Place the large ball on a baking sheet and flatten it slightly for the body.

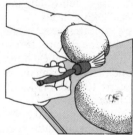

6 Brush one side of the small ball with some of the remaining egg white and tuck it slightly under the body, for the head.

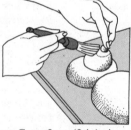

7 Cut a 5-cm (2-in) piece from the rope, brush the bottom with egg white and place on head as snout. Pinch up end for nose.

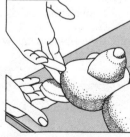

8 Cut two small pieces for ears, and four larger pieces for legs. Tuck under body and pinch to seal.

9 Snip fingers, toes, eyes, mouth and navel with kitchen scissors. Repeat for all three bears.

10. Cover with oiled polythene and prove until doubled in size. Brush with egg white and bake at 190°C (375°F) mark 5 for 25 minutes or until well browned. Cool on wire racks.

Apricot Butterfly Rolls

450 g (1 lb) strong white
flour
100 g (4 oz) sugar
5 ml (1 level tsp) salt
225 ml (8 fl oz) milk
100 g (4 oz) margarine
15 g (½ oz) fresh yeast
1 egg, beaten
10 ml (2 tsp) almond
essence

For the filling:
225 g (8 oz) dried apricots
600 ml (1 pint) water
175 g (6 oz) sugar
50 g (2 oz) butter, melted

For the glaze:
1 egg

Colour index
page 82

Makes
20 rolls

1. Sift the flour, sugar and salt into a large bowl. Heat the milk and margarine until tepid and blend in the yeast until smooth.
2. Add the yeast liquid with the egg and almond essence to the dry ingredients and mix to a soft dough.
3. Place the dough in a large greased bowl, cover with oiled polythene and leave to rise until it has doubled in size. Grease two baking sheets.
4. Meanwhile, prepare the filling. Bring the apricots and water to the boil, cover and simmer for about 15 minutes, until the apricots are tender. Purée the apricots in a blender, or rub through a sieve, and whisk in the sugar until thoroughly dissolved. Allow the mixture to cool.
5. Turn the dough on to a floured surface and knead lightly. Cut the dough in half.
6. Roll out one piece of dough on a floured surface to a 51 × 35.5 cm (20 × 14 in) rectangle and brush it with melted butter. Spread with half the filling to within 1 cm (½ in) of the edge and roll up from the longest edge like a Swiss roll. Pinch the seam and the ends firmly to seal.
7. Cut the roll crossways into ten wedges measuring about 2.5 cm (1 in) on the short side and 6.5 cm (2½ in) on the wide side. Repeat with the second piece of dough to make more wedges.
8. Place the wedges, with the wide side down, on the baking sheets and press your finger lightly across the top of each one to form the wedges into butterfly shapes with 'wings'. Cover with oiled polythene and leave to prove at room temperature until they have doubled in size and will spring back when lightly pressed with a floured finger.
9. Beat the egg for the glaze and brush the rolls with it. Bake at 180°C (350°F) mark 4 for about 20 minutes, until well risen and golden brown. Remove from the baking sheets and cool on a wire rack.

Cutting the rolls: Use a sharp knife to cut the filled rolls into even wedge shapes, making 20 wedges altogether.

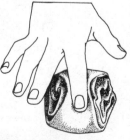

Forming the butterfly: Stand each wedge on its wide end and press in the centre with a finger to open out the 'wings'.

Special breads

In addition to everyday breads and rolls, there are many more fine yeast doughs to try. These are mainly rich doughs, many of them traditional national dishes in their countries of origin: muffins, for instance, are thoroughly English, but brioches and croissants are French, while pitta bread comes from the Middle East. Doughnuts are an American speciality and Danish pastries are genuinely Scandinavian in origin. At the end of the section is a group of loaves made to celebrate the major festivals in various parts of the world.

Cheese Bread Ring

Colour index page 31

Makes one 1.1-kg (2½-lb) ring

450 g (1 lb) strong white
    flour
17.5 ml (3½ level tsp)
    sugar
10 ml (2 level tsp) salt
100 g (4 oz) margarine or
    butter
225 ml (8 fl oz) milk
25 g (1 oz) fresh yeast

2 eggs, separated
700 g (1½ lb) Edam
    cheese, grated

For the garnish:
blanched almonds,
    sliced

1. Sift the flour, sugar and salt into a bowl. Heat the fat with the milk until tepid and then blend in the yeast until smooth.
2. Add the yeast liquid to the dry ingredients and mix with a wooden spoon to make a soft dough that leaves the sides of the bowl clean.
3. Turn the dough on to a floured surface and knead well for about 10 minutes, until smooth, elastic and no longer sticky.
4. Reserve an egg white. Beat the remaining eggs with the grated cheese. Grease a 23-cm (9-in) round cake tin.
5. Roll the dough out on a floured surface to a 61 × 15 cm (24 × 6 in) rectangle. Spoon the cheese mixture down the centre of the dough and form it into a neat sausage shape.

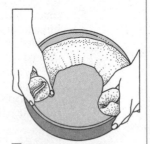

6 Brush the edges of the dough with egg white; fold them over the filling with an overlap of about 2.5 cm (1 in), to make a roll. Pinch the edges firmly together to seal.

7 Place the roll seam side down in the prepared cake tin, overlapping the ends slightly to form a ring. Damp and pinch the ends to seal.

8. Cover with oiled polythene and leave to prove at room temperature for 10 minutes. Brush with egg white, decorate with almonds and bake at 180°C (350°F) mark 4 for 1 hour. Remove from the tin and leave to stand for 15 minutes before cutting if you are serving it warm, or cool it on a wire rack.

Muffins

550 g (1¼ lb) strong white
    flour
5 ml (1 level tsp) salt
25 g (1 oz) sugar
300 ml (½ pint) milk
50 g (2 oz) margarine
15 g (½ oz) fresh yeast

1 egg, beaten
30 ml (2 level tbsp) corn
    meal
15 ml (1 tbsp) vegetable oil

To serve:
butter

Colour index page 83

Makes 18 muffins

1. Sift the flour, salt and sugar into a bowl. Make a well in the centre. Heat the milk and margarine until tepid and blend in the yeast until smooth.
2. Add the yeast liquid and the beaten egg to the dry ingredients all at once and mix well with a wooden spoon to make a soft dough.
3. Turn the dough on to a floured surface and knead for about 4 minutes, until smooth, elastic and no longer sticky.
4. Place the dough in a large greased bowl, cover with oiled polythene and leave to rise until it has doubled in size. Grease two baking sheets and place the corn meal on a large plate.
5. Turn the dough on to a floured surface and knead well until smooth, elastic and no longer sticky.
6. Roll out the dough until it is about 1 cm (½ in) thick and cut out 7.5-cm (3-in) circles, as close to each other as possible, with a floured cutter.
7. Dip both sides of the circles in the corn meal and place them on the prepared baking sheets.
8. Knead the trimmings together lightly, roll them out and cut out more rounds. Dip them in corn meal and place on the baking sheets.
9. Alternatively, for a more even shape, use muffin rings. Divide the dough into 18 even-sized pieces and shape into balls; flatten each piece slightly, dip in corn meal and place in a ring on the baking sheet. Continue as steps 10 and 11, leaving the rings in place around the muffins.
10. Cover the muffins with oiled polythene and leave to prove at room temperature until they have doubled in size and will spring back when lightly pressed with a floured finger.
11. Lightly brush a heavy-based frying pan or griddle with the oil and place over medium heat. When the pan is hot, add the muffins two at a time and cook for about 8 minutes on either side until golden brown. Remove from the pan immediately and cool on a wire rack.
12. To serve, split the muffins in half with the prongs of a fork, then toast and butter them.

Coating the muffins: Dip each one in corn meal until well coated.

Splitting the muffins: Break the muffins apart with the prongs of a fork.

Brioches

15 g (½ oz) fresh yeast
*22.5 ml (1½ tbsp) tepid
water*
*225 g (8 oz) strong white
flour*
pinch salt
*15 ml (1 level tbsp) caster
sugar*
2 eggs, beaten
50 g (2 oz) butter, melted

For the glaze:
beaten egg

Colour index page 82

Makes 12 small brioches
or 1 large brioche

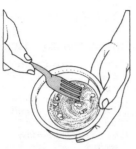

1 Blend the yeast with the tepid water in a small bowl until smooth, stirring until the yeast has completely dissolved.

2 Sift together the flour, salt and sugar into a large bowl. Make a well in the centre of the dry ingredients. Add the yeast liquid all at once and mix well with a wooden spoon.

3 Add the beaten eggs and melted butter and work to a soft dough, using a wooden spoon.

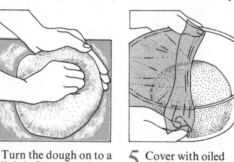

4 Turn the dough on to a lightly floured surface and knead for about 5 minutes, until smooth, elastic and no longer sticky.

5 Cover with oiled polythene and leave to rise until it has doubled in size and will spring back when lightly pressed.

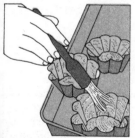

6 Brush 12 deep 7.5-cm (3-in) fluted patty tins with oil. Turn the dough on to a lightly floured surface and knead again.

7 Cut off about a quarter of the dough and set aside. Divide the remainder into 12 and shape each piece into a ball. Place in tins.

8 With one finger, make a hole in centre of each ball down to tin base. Cut reserved dough into 12; shape into small balls.

Making a large brioche:
Brush a 1.1-litre (2-pint) capacity fluted mould with oil. Shape three quarters of the kneaded dough into a ball and place in the mould. Make a hole in the centre as for small brioches, using the handle of a wooden spoon. Shape the remainder of the dough into a knob and put it on top of the larger piece. Finish as for the small brioches and bake at 230°C (450°F) mark 8 for 15–20 minutes.

9 Put a small ball on top of each larger one and press down lightly. Cover again; prove until dough nearly reaches tops of tins.

10 Brush the brioches with egg. Bake at 230°C (450°F) mark 8 for 10 minutes, until golden. Turn out; cool on a wire rack.

Colour index page 82

Makes 8 pitta breads

Pitta Bread

*450 g (1 lb) strong white
flour*
2.5 ml (½ level tsp) salt
15 g (½ oz) fresh yeast

*about 300 ml (½ pint)
tepid water*

1. Sift the flour and salt into a large bowl. Make a well in the centre. Blend the yeast with a little of the water and when smooth add the remaining water.
2. Add the yeast liquid to the dry ingredients all at once and mix well with a wooden spoon to make a firm, but not hard, dough that leaves the sides of the bowl clean.
3. Turn the dough on to a floured surface and knead with floured hands for about 10 minutes, until smooth, elastic and no longer sticky.
4. Shape the dough into a ball, place it in a large greased bowl, cover with oiled polythene and leave to rise until it has doubled in size and will spring back if lightly pressed with a floured finger.
5. Turn the dough on to a floured surface again and knead lightly for 2–3 minutes to knock out any large air bubbles that have formed.

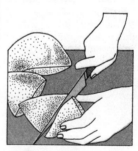

6 Divide the dough into eight equal pieces with a sharp knife and knead each one lightly. Shape each piece into a smooth ball with your hands.

7 On a lightly floured surface roll each ball out to a 0.5-cm (¼-in) thick oval. Place them on a baking sheet.

8 Cover the ovals and leave to prove until spongy. Meanwhile, heat two oiled baking sheets in the oven.

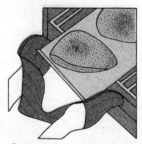

9 Put two ovals on to each baking sheet, brush them with a little cold water and bake at 230°C (450°F) mark 8 for about 10 minutes.

10. Remove from the baking sheets and cool on a wire rack while cooking the rest. Split each pitta down one side to make a pocket and fill with kebabs, or with Greek salad (page 320).

Special breads

Croissants

*450 g (1 lb) strong white
    flour*
10 ml (2 level tsp) salt
25 g (1 oz) lard
25 g (1 oz) fresh yeast
225 ml (8 fl oz) tepid water
1 egg, beaten
100–175 g (4–6 oz) butter

For the glaze:
1 egg, beaten
10 ml (2 tsp) water
*2.5 ml (¹/₂ level tsp) caster
    sugar*

Colour index page 82

Makes 12 croissants

1 Sift together the flour and salt and rub in the lard with your fingertips. Blend the yeast with the water. Add the yeast liquid and egg to the dry ingredients all at once and mix with a wooden spoon to make a soft dough. Turn on to a lightly floured surface and knead for 10–15 minutes, until smooth. Roll out into a 51 × 20.5 × 0.5 cm (20 × 8 × ¹/₄ in) strip, keeping the edges straight and the corners square.

2 Soften the butter and divide into three. Dot one portion over two-thirds of the dough, leaving a small border clear.

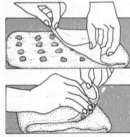

3 Fold the dough in three, folding in the unbuttered third first, then the buttered portion on top. Seal the edges firmly with a rolling pin.

4 Reshape to a long strip by gently pressing the dough at intervals with a rolling pin. Repeat steps 2 and 3 with the other two portions of butter.

5 Wrap folded dough in oiled polythene; chill 30 minutes. Roll out and fold three more times (without adding butter). Chill for at least 1 hour.

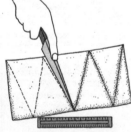

6 Roll out to a 55 × 33 cm (22 × 13 in) rectangle. Cover and leave for 10 minutes. Trim the edges and halve lengthways. Cut each strip into triangles.

7 To make the glaze, beat together the egg, water and sugar. Brush glaze over each of the triangles.

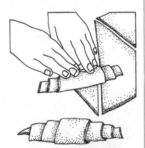

8 Roll up each triangle loosely, starting at the base and finishing with the tip underneath. Join the end pieces to make a triangle; glaze and roll up.

9 Put them on to ungreased baking sheets and curve into crescents. Brush tips with egg glaze.

10 Cover with oiled polythene and prove at room temperature for 30 minutes, until fluffy.

11 Brush with egg glaze. Bake at 230°C (450°F) mark 8 for 20 minutes. Cool on a wire rack.

Colour index page 83

Makes two 550-g (1¹/₄-lb) loaves

Poppy Seed Poticas

*450 g (1 lb) strong white
    flour*
100 g (4 oz) sugar
2.5 ml (¹/₂ level tsp) salt
175 ml (6 fl oz) tepid milk
15 g (¹/₂ oz) fresh yeast
*100 g (4 oz) margarine,
    melted*
1 egg, beaten
*10 ml (2 tsp) grated lemon
    rind*

50 g (2 oz) icing sugar
*100 g (4 oz) shelled
    walnuts, finely chopped*
*15 ml (1 tbsp) grated lemon
    rind*
*5 ml (1 level tsp) ground
    cinnamon*
2 egg whites

For the glaze:
1 egg yolk

For the filling:
100 g (4 oz) poppy seeds
*25 g (1 oz) butter or
    margarine*

1. Sift the flour, sugar and salt into a large bowl. Make a well in the centre. Blend the milk with the yeast until smooth.

2. Add the yeast mixture, margarine, egg and lemon rind to the flour and mix well to make a soft dough.

3. Turn the dough on to a floured surface and knead for about 8 minutes.

4. Place in a large greased bowl, cover with oiled polythene and leave to rise until it has doubled in size. Grease two baking sheets.

5. Make the filling. Grind the poppy seeds in a blender until finely ground. Melt the fat, stir in the ground poppy seeds and cook, stirring, for 2 minutes. Place in a bowl and add the icing sugar, walnuts, lemon rind and cinnamon. Whisk the egg whites until soft peaks form and fold into the poppy seed mixture.

6. Turn the dough on to a floured surface again and knead to knock out any large air bubbles. Divide the dough into two equal pieces.

7. Roll out one of the pieces on a floured surface to a 45.5 × 30 cm (18 × 12 in) rectangle and spread half the filling over it to within 1 cm (¹/₂ in) of the edges. Roll up from the longest edge, pinch the edges to seal and arrange seam side down in a flat coil on a baking sheet. Repeat with the remaining dough and filling to make a second loaf.

8. Cover the loaves and leave them to prove until they have doubled in size. Brush with the egg yolk and bake at 180°C (350°F) mark 4 for 25–30 minutes. Cool on a wire rack.

Rolling up dough: Roll up the dough tightly from the longest edge.

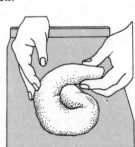

Arranging the roll: Wind the roll, seam side down, into a flat coil.

Colour index page 82

Makes 10–12 doughnuts

Jam Doughnuts

225 g (8 oz) strong white flour
2.5 ml (½ level tsp) salt
knob of butter or margarine
15 g (½ oz) fresh yeast
about 60 ml (4 tbsp) tepid milk
1 egg, beaten
oil for deep frying

To finish:
red jam
icing or caster sugar for dredging
ground cinnamon, optional

1. Sift the flour and salt into a large bowl and rub in the fat with your fingertips. Make a well in the centre. Blend the yeast with the milk until smooth.
2. Add the yeast liquid and egg to the dry ingredients all at once and mix with a wooden spoon to make a soft dough, adding a little more milk if necessary. Beat well until the dough is smooth and will leave the sides of the bowl clean.
3. Place the dough in a large greased bowl, cover with oiled polythene and leave to rise until it has doubled in size and will spring back if lightly pressed with a floured finger.
4. Grease two large baking sheets.
5. Turn the dough on to a floured surface and knead lightly for 2–3 minutes, to knock out any large air bubbles that have formed.
6. Roll out the dough to about 0.5-cm (¼-in) thickness and cut out circles as closely together as possible with a plain round biscuit cutter. Re-roll the trimmings and cut out more circles.

7 Place the circles on the baking sheets, cover with oiled polythene and leave to prove until they have doubled in size.

8 Heat the oil to 182°C (360°F) or until a 2.5-cm (1-in) bread cube will brown in 60 seconds. Fry doughnuts for 5 minutes, until golden brown.

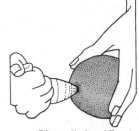

9 Drain them on kitchen paper towel and leave to cool. Make a deep hole in the side of each of the doughnuts with a sharp, thin-bladed knife.

10 Pipe a little stiff red jam into centre of each doughnut and sprinkle liberally with icing or caster sugar, mixed with a little cinnamon if you wish.

RING DOUGHNUTS: Prepare the dough as for jam doughnuts and cut out rings with a lightly floured ring doughnut cutter, re-rolling trimmings to use all the dough. When the doughnuts are cooked, drain them on kitchen paper towel. While they are still warm put them into a polythene bag containing *caster sugar* mixed with a little *ground cinnamon*. Shake the bag to coat the doughnuts.

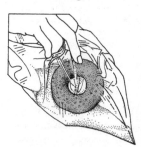

Shaping the doughnuts: Cut out the doughnuts as closely together as possible, re-roll the trimmings and cut out more.

Sugaring: Shake the warm doughnuts with sugar and ground cinnamon in a bag until well coated.

CREAM DOUGHNUTS: Prepare as for jam doughnuts but omit the jam. For the filling, use *thickly whipped cream* flavoured with *caster sugar* and, if you wish, a little *vanilla essence.*

PARTY DOUGHNUTS: Prepare as for cream doughnuts and then coat each one liberally with *white glacé icing (page 400)*, tinted with a few drops of *red or green food colouring* if you wish. Sprinkle with *hundreds and thousands*, chopped nuts or chocolate vermicelli. (Colour index page 82)

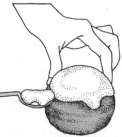

Coating with icing: Spoon glacé icing over the top of each filled doughnut.

Adding topping: Sprinkle the iced doughnuts with toppings to decorate.

DOUGHNUT TIES: Prepare the dough as for jam doughnuts and divide into eight or ten pieces. Shape each one into an 18-cm (7-in) roll and tie into a knot. Fry as for jam doughnuts, then toss in a mixture of *caster sugar* and *poppy seeds.*

ALTERNATIVE SHAPING METHOD FOR JAM DOUGHNUTS: Doughnuts can be cooked with the jam already inside them. Instead of rolling out the dough, cut it into 10 or 12 pieces with a knife. Shape each piece into a rough round and spoon *5 ml (1 tsp) fairly thick jam* into the centre. Draw up the edges to form a ball and press firmly to seal. Fry, drain and sprinkle with sugar as for jam doughnuts.

Special breads

Colour index page 82
Makes 16 babas or 1 savarin

Rum Babas

225 g (8 oz) strong white
  flour
90 ml (6 tbsp) tepid milk
25 g (1 oz) fresh yeast
2.5 ml (½ level tsp) salt
30 ml (2 level tbsp) caster
  sugar
4 eggs, beaten
100 g (4 oz) butter,
  softened
100 g (4 oz) currants or
  sultanas

For the syrup:
120 ml (8 level tbsp) clear
  honey
120 ml (8 tbsp) water
rum or rum essence
  to taste

To serve:
whipped cream
glacé cherries, optional

1. Sift 50 g (2 oz) flour into a large bowl. Blend the milk with the yeast until smooth, add to the flour and mix well with a wooden spoon. Leave in a warm place for about 20 minutes, until frothy. Grease 16 9-cm (3½-in) ring tins.

2. Add the remaining flour, salt, sugar, eggs, softened butter and currants and beat well for about 4 minutes.

3. Half fill the tins with the dough, cover with oiled polythene and leave to rise until the tins are two-thirds full.

4. Bake at 200°C (400°F) mark 6 for 15–20 minutes, until well risen and golden brown. Cool the babas in the tins for a few minutes, then turn them out on to a wire rack.

5. Make the rum syrup. Put the honey and water in a small saucepan, heat gently until thoroughly blended and add the rum or rum essence to taste.

6. Put a plate under the wire rack on which the babas are cooling. While they are still hot, spoon enough rum syrup over to soak them well. Leave babas to cool completely.

7. To serve, arrange the babas on a plate and spoon or pipe a little whipped cream into the centre of each one. Decorate each with a glacé cherry if you wish.

SAVARIN: Prepare the dough as above, but omit the currants and pour into a greased 20.5-cm (8-in) ring tin. Cover with oiled polythene and leave to rise until the tin is two-thirds full. Bake at 200°C (400°F) mark 6 for about 40 minutes or until golden and shrinking away from the sides of the tin. Turn out on to a wire rack and soak with the rum syrup and brush with a little *apricot jam*. To serve, place the savarin on a serving dish, spoon *fresh fruit salad* around it and top with *whipped cream.*

APRICOT SAVARIN: Soak *75 g (3 oz) dried apricots* overnight, drain and chop them. Prepare the savarin as above, but include the apricots in the dough. Make a brandy syrup. Put *90 ml (6 level tbsp) clear honey* and *90 ml (6 tbsp) water* in a small saucepan, heat gently until thoroughly blended and bring to the boil. While the savarin is still hot, spoon over the syrup until it is all absorbed. Place the savarin on a serving dish and, if you wish, fill the centre with more poached dried, fresh or canned *apricots*. Serve with *single cream.*

Danish Pastry Dough

25 g (1 oz) fresh yeast
about 150 ml (¼ pint)
  tepid water
450 g (1 lb) plain white
  flour
5 ml (1 level tsp) salt
50 g (2 oz) lard
30 ml (2 level tbsp) sugar
2 eggs, beaten
300 g (10 oz) butter

Makes about 1.1 kg
(2¼ lb) dough

1 Blend the yeast with the tepid water until smooth. Sift the flour and salt into a large bowl.

2 Rub the lard into the sifted dry ingredients with your fingertips, then stir in the sugar until it is evenly mixed. Make a well in the centre.

3 Add the yeast liquid and the beaten eggs to the flour mixture all at once and mix with a wooden spoon to make a smooth, elastic dough.

4 Knead lightly and cover with oiled polythene. Leave the dough to rest in the refrigerator for about 10 minutes.

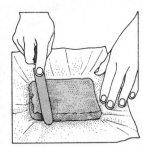

5 Work the butter with a knife until soft, then form it into an oblong on a piece of waxed paper.

6 Roll out the dough on a floured surface to an oblong three times the size of the butter. Put the butter in the centre.

7 Fold the dough over to enclose the butter, just overlapping the ends of the dough at the centre.

8 Seal the open sides by pressing them firmly together with a rolling pin.

9 Turn the dough so that the folds are to the sides and roll it out to a rectangle three times as long as it is wide.

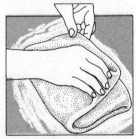

10 Carefully fold the top third of the dough down, then fold the remaining third on to the top of that.

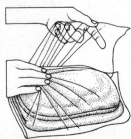

11 Wrap in oiled polythene; rest for 10 minutes. Turn dough and repeat steps 9 and 10 twice. Shape, prove and bake.

Danish Pastries

Colour index
page 82

Makes 16
pastries

*recipe quantity Danish
pastry dough, opposite
beaten egg to glaze
cinnamon butter, almond
paste, confectioners'
custard or jam, right*

*thin white glacé icing,
page 400
flaked or chopped blanched
almonds, toasted*

1. Roll out the dough thinly, cut it into 7.5-cm (3-in) squares and fill and shape as required (below and right). Place the shapes on greased baking sheets, cover with oiled polythene and leave to prove for 20–30 minutes.

2. Brush the pastries with beaten egg and bake at 220°C (425°F) mark 7 for about 20 minutes. Brush them with thin white glacé icing while they are still warm and sprinkle with toasted, flaked or chopped blanched almonds. Cool on a wire rack.

DANISH PASTRY FILLINGS

CINNAMON BUTTER: Cream *50 g (2 oz) butter* with *50 g (2 oz) caster sugar* and beat in *10 ml (2 level tsp) ground cinnamon* until evenly mixed.

ALMOND PASTE: Cream *15 g (½ oz) butter* with *75 g (3 oz) caster sugar.* Stir in *75 g (3 oz) ground almonds* and enough *beaten egg* to give a pliable consistency. Add a few drops of *almond essence*, if you wish, to bring out the almond flavour.

JAM: *Redcurrant jelly, apricot jam* and *apple jam* may all be used as fillings for the pastries.

CONFECTIONERS' CUSTARD: page 366.

IMPERIAL STARS

Make diagonal cuts from corners of the squares to within 1 cm (½ in) of centre.

Fold one corner of each cut section to the centre, securing tips with beaten egg.

To decorate the imperial stars, carefully spoon a little jam, almond paste or confectioners' custard on to the centre of each star where the tips meet.

FOLDOVERS

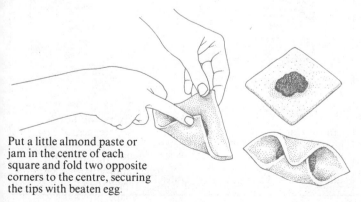

Put a little almond paste or jam in the centre of each square and fold two opposite corners to the centre, securing the tips with beaten egg.

CUSHIONS

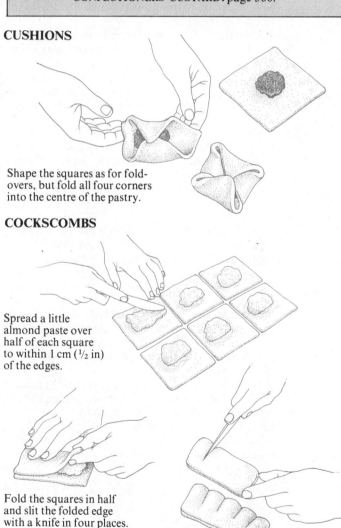

Shape the squares as for fold-overs, but fold all four corners into the centre of the pastry.

COCKSCOMBS

Spread a little almond paste over half of each square to within 1 cm (½ in) of the edges.

Fold the squares in half and slit the folded edge with a knife in four places.

Curve pastry to open into comb shape.

Special breads

Stollen

Colour index
page 83

Makes three
550-g (1¼-lb)
loaves

750 g (1 lb 10 oz) strong
white flour
100 g (4 oz) sugar
7.5 ml (1½ level tsp) salt
150 g (5 oz) butter or
margarine
175 ml (6 fl oz) milk
25 g (1 oz) fresh yeast
3 eggs, beaten
175 g (6 oz) glacé
cherries, chopped

100 g (4 oz) slivered
almonds, toasted
50 g (2 oz) sultanas
15 ml (1 level tbsp) icing
sugar for dredging

To decorate, optional:
candied or crystallised
peel, page 311

1. Sift the flour, sugar and salt into a large bowl.
Heat the fat and milk until tepid and blend in the
yeast until smooth.
2. Add the yeast liquid and the eggs to the dry
ingredients all at once and mix thoroughly with a
wooden spoon to make a soft dough that leaves the
sides of the bowl clean.
3. Turn the dough on to a floured surface and knead
well for about 10 minutes, until smooth, elastic and
no longer sticky.
4. Place the dough in a large greased bowl, cover
with oiled polythene and leave to rise until it has
doubled in size and will spring back if lightly pressed
with a floured finger.
5. Grease three baking sheets.
6. Mix the chopped cherries, toasted almonds and
sultanas together. Turn the dough on to a floured
surface and knead in the dried fruit mixture until
evenly distributed throughout the dough. Cut the
dough into three equal pieces; cover and refrigerate
two of the pieces.
7. Roll the third piece of dough out on a floured
surface to a 30 × 18 cm (12 × 7 in) oval. Make a
lengthways mark along the centre of the dough with
a rolling pin. Fold the dough in half along the mark
and place on a baking sheet. Repeat with a second
piece of dough.
8. Cover the loaves with oiled polythene and leave to
prove at room temperature until they have doubled
in size and will spring back when lightly pressed
with a floured finger. After 30 minutes, repeat with
the third piece of dough.
9. Bake the first two loaves at 180°C (350°F) mark 4
for 30 minutes or until well risen and golden brown,
remove from the baking sheets and cool on a wire
rack. Then bake the third loaf.
10. Dredge tops of loaves with icing sugar; decorate
with candied or crystallised peel if you wish.

Adding fruit and nuts:
Knead mixed fruit and
nuts evenly into dough.

Shaping the dough: Roll it
out to a neat oval and
fold in half lengthways.

Kulich

Colour index
page 83

Makes three
450-g (1-lb)
loaves

750 g (1 lb 10 oz) strong
white flour
100 g (4 oz) sugar
2.5 ml (½ level tsp) salt
1.25 ml (¼ level tsp)
ground cardamom
225 ml (8 fl oz) milk
100 g (4 oz) butter or
margarine
5 ml (1 tsp) vanilla essence
25 g (1 oz) fresh yeast
3 eggs, beaten
100 g (4 oz) sultanas

100 g (4 oz) chopped
mixed peel
25 g (1 oz) chopped
almonds, browned

For the icing:
175 g (6 oz) icing sugar
30 ml (2 tbsp) milk
2.5 ml (½ tsp) lemon juice

1. Sift the flour, sugar, salt and cardamom into a
large bowl. Heat the milk, fat and vanilla essence
until tepid and blend in the yeast until smooth.
2. Add the yeast mixture and the eggs to the flour
and mix well to make a soft dough.
3. Turn the dough on to a floured surface and knead
for 5 minutes. Add the sultanas, peel and almonds
and continue kneading for a further 5 minutes, until
the fruit, peel and nuts are evenly distributed
through the dough.
4. Shape the dough into a ball, place it in a large
greased bowl, cover with oiled polythene and leave
in a warm place to rise until it has doubled in size.
Line the inside of three 450-g (1-lb) coffee tins with
greased foil or non-stick paper.
5. Turn the dough on to a floured surface again,
knead it lightly and divide into three.
6. Shape the pieces to fit the coffee tins and place
them smooth side up in the tins. Using a double
thickness of greased foil or non-stick paper, make
collars for the coffee tins. Tie or fasten them with
sticky tape around the outside, with 5 cm (2 in)
extending above the rim all the way round.
7. Bake at 180°C (350°F) mark 4 for 50 minutes.
Remove from the tins and cool on a wire rack. When
the loaves are cold, mix together the icing sugar,
milk and lemon juice to make a smooth icing and
spoon it evenly over the tops of the loaves, allowing
a little to trickle down the sides.

PREPARING THE TINS

Line the coffee tins with
greased foil or non-stick
paper. Shape the pieces of
dough and place one in each
tin, smooth surface up.

Make firm collars for the tins
with a double thickness of
greased foil or non-stick paper.
Wrap around the tins, leaving
5 cm (2 in) extending above the
rims. Fold seams and secure.

Challah

Colour index
page 82

Makes two
450-g (1-lb)
loaves

800 g (1 lb 12 oz) strong
white flour
25 g (1 oz) caster sugar
7.5 ml (1½ level tsp) salt
350 ml (12 fl oz) tepid milk
25 g (1 oz) fresh yeast

75 g (3 oz) margarine,
melted and cooled but
not firm
6 eggs

1. Sift the flour, sugar and salt into a large bowl. Make a well in the centre.
2. Blend the tepid milk with the yeast until smooth, stirring until it has completely dissolved.
3. Add the yeast mixture and the melted fat to the dry ingredients. Reserve two egg yolks for glazing the loaf, beat the remaining eggs together well and add them to the mixture. Mix well with a wooden spoon to make a soft dough that leaves the sides of the bowl clean.
4. Turn the dough on to a floured surface and knead well for about 8 minutes, until smooth, elastic and no longer sticky.
5. Place the dough in a large greased bowl, cover it with oiled polythene and leave to rise until it has doubled in size.
6. Turn the dough on to a floured surface again and knead for about 8 minutes.
7. Cover with oiled polythene and leave to prove for about 15 minutes.
8. Grease two large baking sheets.
9. Cut the dough into three equal pieces with a sharp knife and shape it as follows.

Making a large plait: Cut one piece into thirds and roll each to a 40.5-cm (16-in) rope. Place them on a baking sheet and plait them, working from the centre to the ends.

Finishing large and small plaits: Pinch the ends of the plait to seal well. Repeat with second piece of dough. Cut the remaining dough into six pieces and roll each to a 43-cm (17-in) rope. Make into two smaller plaits.

Assembling the loaves: Place one smaller plait on top of each larger one and tuck the ends right under the loaf, stretching the top plait to fit, if necessary.

10. Cover the loaves again and leave to prove until they have doubled in size and the dough will spring back if lightly pressed with a floured finger.
11. Brush the top and sides of the loaves with the reserved egg yolk and bake at 220°C (450°F) mark 8 for 10 minutes; then bake at 190°C (375°F) mark 5 for a further 25 minutes. Cool on a wire rack.

Cardamom Christmas Wreath

Colour index
page 83

Makes one
1.4-kg (3-lb)
wreath

800 g (1 lb 12 oz) strong
white flour
5 ml (1 level tsp) ground
cardamom
225 g (8 oz) caster sugar
350 ml (12 fl oz) tepid milk
25 g (1 oz) fresh yeast
5 ml (1 level tsp) salt
225 g (8 oz) margarine,
melted

3 eggs
15 ml (1 tbsp) grated lemon
rind
2.5 ml (½ tsp) almond
essence
15 ml (1 tbsp) milk

1. Sift the flour and ground cardamom into a large bowl and add all except 5 ml (1 level tsp) sugar. Make a well in the centre.
2. Blend the tepid milk with the yeast until smooth, stirring until it has completely dissolved.
3. Add the yeast mixture and melted margarine to the flour all at once. Reserve one egg white for glazing, beat the remaining eggs and add them to the flour with the lemon rind and almond essence. Mix well with a wooden spoon to make a soft dough that leaves the sides of the bowl clean.
4. Turn the dough on to a floured surface and knead well for about 8 minutes, until smooth, elastic and no longer sticky.
5. Place the dough in a large greased bowl, cover with oiled polythene and leave to rise until it has doubled in size. Grease a baking sheet and the outside of an 18-cm (7-in) cake tin and place the tin in the middle of the baking sheet.
6. Turn the dough on to a floured surface again and knead well. Reserve a piece of dough about the size of a small apple.
7. Roll out the rest of the dough on a floured surface to a 63.5 × 25.5 cm (25 × 10 in) rectangle and roll up from the longest edge at a slight angle, like a Swiss roll. Wrap the roll around the tin, tucking the ends under and sealing them well.
8. Mix the reserved egg white with 15 ml (1 tbsp) milk. Roll the reserved piece of dough out to 0.3-cm (⅛-in) thickness; use to decorate the loaf as follows.

Cutting out the decorations: Cut out leaves with a cutter or sharp knife and roll the scraps into tiny balls, to represent the holly berries.

Arranging the decorations: Brush some egg white glaze on back of leaves and berries and decorate wreath with them. Cover and prove until doubled in size.

9. Brush wreath with egg white glaze and bake at 220°C (450°F) mark 8 for 10 minutes; then bake at 180°C (350°F) mark 4 for 50 minutes more. Cool on a wire rack and tie on a brightly coloured ribbon to decorate the wreath, if you wish.

Pizzas

Pizzas developed originally as a cheap way of making a meal from the odds and ends an Italian housewife might have in her kitchen. Leftover bread dough formed the base; the topping would be a tasty combination of tomatoes and herbs with scraps of cheese, salami or ham.

Nowadays, we enrich the dough with oil or extra butter to give a base that will cook crisply outside, but remain soft and moist inside. To cook it you can use a traditional pizza pan, which is a circular cast iron plate with an upturned lip all round, or an ordinary baking sheet, as we show opposite. If you want a very neat shape, you can place the dough in a large flan ring on a baking sheet for cooking. The oven temperature should always be high.

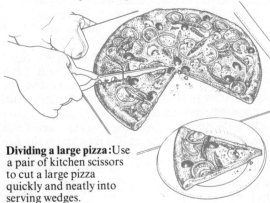

Dividing a large pizza: Use a pair of kitchen scissors to cut a large pizza quickly and neatly into serving wedges.

PIZZA TOPPINGS

Prepare cheese pizza (right) but use only *225 g (8 oz) Mozzarella cheese*, then add one of the following toppings. (Colour index page 31)

MUSHROOM: *225 g (8 oz) mushrooms*, sliced.

PEPERONI: *450 g (1 lb) peperoni* or chorizo sausages, thinly sliced.

ANCHOVY: *2 50-g (2-oz) cans anchovy fillets*, drained very well.

SAUSAGE: *450 g (1 lb) pork sausages*, cooked, drained well and cut into 1-cm (½-in) chunks.

ITALIAN SAUSAGE: *450 g (1 lb) sweet or spicy Italian sausages*, cooked, drained well and diced.

BEEF: *450 g (1 lb) lean minced beef*, cooked and drained very well.

OLIVE: *150–175 g (5–6 oz) green olives*, stoned or stuffed with pimentos.

GREEN PEPPER: *2 small green peppers*, seeded and thinly sliced.

ONION: *2 small onions*, skinned and chopped.

PIMENTO: *100 g (4 oz) canned pimentos*, drained well and chopped.

Cheese Pizza

225 g (8 oz) strong white flour
5 ml (1 level tsp) salt
small knob of lard
about 150 ml (¼ pint) water
15 g (½ oz) fresh yeast
vegetable oil

For the topping:
15 ml (1 tbsp) vegetable oil
1 onion, skinned and chopped
1 clove garlic, skinned and crushed
226-g (8-oz) can tomatoes

63-g (2¼-oz) can tomato paste
5 ml (1 level tsp) sugar
2.5 ml (½ level tsp) Italian seasoning
pinch paprika
2.5 ml (½ level tsp) salt
225 g (8 oz) Mozzarella cheese, grated

Colour index page 31

Makes one 30-cm (12-in) pizza

1 Sift together the flour and salt into a large bowl and rub in the lard with your fingertips. Make a well in the centre of the dry ingredients. Heat the water gently until tepid and blend in the yeast until smooth. Add the yeast liquid to the dry ingredients all at once. Beat well with a wooden spoon at first, then mix the dough by hand until it is smooth and leaves the sides of the bowl clean.

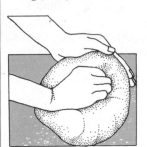

2 Turn it on to a floured surface and knead until smooth, elastic and no longer sticky. Cover with oiled polythene and leave to rise until it has doubled in size.

3 For the topping, heat the oil and cook the onion and garlic until soft but not coloured. Add the tomatoes with their liquid and the tomato paste. Stir well to break up tomatoes.

4 Add the sugar, herbs, paprika and salt and bring to the boil, stirring. Reduce the heat, partially cover the pan and simmer for 20 minutes. Cool until the dough is ready.

5 Turn the dough on to a floured surface, roll it out to a long strip and brush with vegetable oil.

6 Roll up the dough from the shortest edge like a Swiss roll, with the oiled side inside.

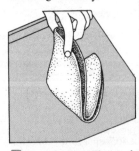

7 Repeat the rolling and oiling three times, then roll it out to a 32.5-cm (13-in) round. Grease a large baking sheet. Lift the dough carefully on to the baking sheet.

8 Pinch up the edges of the dough to form a round rim. Brush the top with vegetable oil again.

9 Sprinkle half the cheese on to the dough and spoon the tomato topping mixture over it.

10 Add the remaining cheese. Bake at 230°C (450°F) mark 8 for about 40 minutes.

SANDWICHES

Sandwiches may include anything from a light snack to a meal in themselves. For delicate party sandwiches, cut the bread thinly and remove the crusts, but choose crusty bread, cut thickly, or rolls for the more substantial recipes. Hot sandwiches, toasted, fried or oven-baked, are particularly good for a casual lunch or supper, especially if they are filled with a savoury meat mixture. For a change, use pitta bread or taco shells to make your sandwiches more interesting. Open sandwiches, originating in Scandinavia, have tremendous eye appeal and are good for buffet-style entertaining. Serve open sandwiches with a small knife and fork.

Hot sandwiches

Croque Monsieur

Colour index
page 108
8 servings

**16 thin slices white bread,
   crusts removed
made mustard
225 g (8 oz) Gruyère
   cheese, sliced**

**225 g (8 oz) cooked ham,
   thinly sliced
75 g (3 oz) butter or
   margarine, melted**

1 Spread half the slices of bread with mustard; trim the cheese slices to fit and put them on top.

2 Trim the ham slices to fit and put them on top of the cheese. Top with the remaining bread and put the sandwiches on a baking sheet.

3 Brush the sandwiches lightly with melted butter or margarine and toast in the oven at 230°C (450°F) mark 8 for about 5 minutes or until they are lightly browned.

4 Turn them, brush the other sides with butter and toast for a further 3 minutes. Cut the sandwiches in half and serve them hot, wrapped in small paper napkins.

Mozzarella Loaf

Colour index
page 108
6 servings

**1 long, crusty loaf, with
   sesame seeds
450 g (1 lb) Mozzarella
   cheese, sliced**

**75 g (3 oz) stoned olives,
   chopped
30 ml (2 tbsp) chopped
   parsley, optional**

1. Slice the crusty loaf at 2.5-cm (1-in) intervals without cutting through the bottom crust. Put a Mozzarella cheese slice and some chopped olives between each bread slice.
2. Put the loaf on a baking sheet and bake in the oven at 200°C (400°F) mark 6 for about 15 minutes or until the cheese is melted and the bread heated through. If you wish, sprinkle the Mozzarella loaf with chopped parsley before serving.

Barbecued Pork Rolls

Colour index
page 108
6 servings

**700 g (1½ lb) boneless
   shoulder of pork, cut into
   4-cm (1½-in) chunks
1 onion, skinned and
   chopped
1 green pepper, seeded and
   chopped
60 ml (4 level tbsp) tomato
   paste
25 g (1 oz) soft dark
   brown sugar
50 ml (2 fl oz) cider
   vinegar**

**50 ml (2 fl oz) water
15 ml (1 level tbsp) chilli
   powder
5 ml (1 level tsp) salt
5 ml (1 tsp)
   Worcestershire sauce
2.5 ml (½ level tsp) dry
   mustard
6 long crusty rolls
lettuce leaves
1 large tomato, chopped**

1. Put the pork in a large saucepan with the onion, pepper, tomato paste, sugar, vinegar, water and seasonings. Bring to the boil; cover and simmer for about 3 hours, stirring occasionally.
2. Skim off any fat and shred the cooked pork with two forks.
3. Slice each roll horizontally, without cutting all the way through. Line the rolls with lettuce leaves and fill with the pork mixture. Sprinkle with chopped tomato and serve immediately.

Hot sandwiches

Fried Salt Beef and Sauerkraut Sandwiches

Colour index
page 108
4 servings

100 ml (4 fl oz) mayonnaise, page 462	*225 g (8 oz) sauerkraut*
15 ml (1 tbsp) finely chopped green pepper	*75-g (3-oz) packet Gruyère or Emmenthal cheese slices*
15 ml (1 tbsp) mild chilli sauce	*225 g (8 oz) salt beef, sliced*
8 slices rye bread	*butter or margarine*

1. Mix mayonnaise, pepper and chilli sauce. Spread 15 ml (1 level tbsp) on each slice of bread.
2. Drain the sauerkraut and halve each slice of cheese. Place one piece of cheese on each of four slices of bread, top with a slice of salt beef, a quarter of the sauerkraut, another slice of cheese and another slice of bread, mayonnaise side down.
3. Melt 25 g (1 oz) butter in a large frying pan and brown the sandwiches on one side. Turn and brown the other side. Halve each sandwich before serving.

Layering the filling: Layer each sandwich with the mayonnaise mixture, cheese, salt beef, sauerkraut, and more cheese.

Cooking the sandwiches: Fry the sandwiches in butter until the bread is browned and the cheese is melted.

Bacon Burgers

Colour index
page 108
6 servings

450 g (1 lb) back bacon, rinded	*butter or margarine, softened*
6 hamburger buns	

1. Fry the bacon in its own fat until crisp. Split the buns, toast until golden and spread with butter.
2. Put two or three rashers of bacon on the bottom half of each bun. Replace the tops and halve each bacon burger before serving.

Omelette Sandwiches

Colour index
page 108
4 servings

40 g (1½ oz) butter	*6 eggs*
175 g (6 oz) cooked ham, shredded	*30 ml (2 tbsp) milk*
½ green pepper, seeded and chopped	*3.75 ml (¾ level tsp) salt*
½ onion, skinned and chopped	*8 slices white bread*

1. Melt the butter in a frying pan and cook the ham, pepper and onion for about 5 minutes.
2. Beat together the eggs, milk and salt and stir them into the ham mixture. Cover and cook over low heat for 12–15 minutes, until the top is set and the underside is lightly browned.
3. Toast the bread and keep hot. Quarter the omelette and serve each piece between slices of toast.

Sloppy Joes

Colour index
page 108
6 servings

450 g (1 lb) minced beef
1 green pepper, seeded and chopped
1 onion, skinned and chopped
425-g (15-oz) can baked beans and sausages
100 ml (4 fl oz) tomato ketchup
2.5 ml (½ level tsp) salt
2.5 ml (½ level tsp) chilli powder
6 long crusty rolls
lettuce leaves

1 Put the beef, pepper and onion in a frying pan and cook for 10 minutes until the beef is well browned. Skim off fat.

2 Stir in the beans and sausages, ketchup, salt and chilli powder; bring to the boil. Reduce heat; simmer for 10 minutes stirring occasionally.

3 Halve rolls horizontally. On bottom half of each one, arrange a lettuce leaf and large spoonful of meat mixture. Replace tops and serve.

Chicken Tacos

Colour index
page 109
6 servings

vegetable oil	*5 ml (1 level tsp) salt*
6 Mexican tortillas, page 431	*2.5 ml (½ level tsp) pepper*
For the filling:	**To finish:**
25 g (1 oz) butter	*shredded lettuce*
1 onion, skinned and chopped	*2 tomatoes, skinned and chopped*
450 g (1 lb) cooked chicken meat, diced	*100 g (4 oz) Cheddar cheese, grated*
2 tomatoes skinned and chopped	*Tabasco sauce*

1. Heat 1 cm (½ in) oil in a frying pan and fry a tortilla just until soft. With tongs, fold it in half, holding it open about 2.5 cm (1 in). Fry one side until crisp, then turn and fry the other side to make a taco shell. Drain; keep hot while you fry the rest.
2. Heat the butter in a clean frying pan and fry the onions until soft but not coloured. Stir in the chicken, tomatoes and seasoning; heat through.
3. Spoon 15–30 ml (1–2 tbsp) filling into each shell. Add a little lettuce, tomato and cheese and a few drops of Tabasco sauce; serve at once.

BEEF TACOS: Prepare the taco shells as above. For the filling, fry *450 g (1 lb) minced beef* and *1 onion,* skinned and chopped. Stir in *2 tomatoes,* skinned and chopped, *5 ml (1 level tsp) dried oregano, 5 ml (1 level tsp) salt, 2.5 ml (½ level tsp) pepper* and *1 clove garlic,* skinned and crushed; heat through. Spoon into the shells; finish as above.

Cold sandwiches

Curried Beef in Pitta Bread

Colour index page 108

6 servings

450 g (1 lb) lean minced beef
50 g (2 oz) onion, skinned and chopped
1 green dessert apple, wiped, cored and chopped
40 g (1½ oz) seedless raisins
6.25 ml (1¼ level tsp) salt

5 ml (1 level tsp) curry powder
3 pieces pitta bread, or pitta bread made with 175 g (6 oz) flour, page 447
225 ml (8 fl oz) plain yogurt

1. Fry the beef and onion, stirring occasionally, until the beef is well browned and the onion is tender; spoon off any excess fat. Add the apple, raisins, salt and curry powder. Reduce the heat, cover the pan and simmer for about 5 minutes or until the apple is just tender.
2. Halve the pitta bread crossways so that each piece makes two pockets. Fill each half with a large spoonful of the beef mixture and pass the yogurt separately to be spooned into each sandwich.

Italian Hero Sandwiches

Colour index page 109

4 servings

12 Italian sausages
60 ml (4 tbsp) water
30 ml (2 tbsp) olive or vegetable oil
2 onions, skinned and sliced

5 red or green peppers, washed, seeded and cut into strips
4 long crusty rolls

1. Put the sausages in a pan with the water; cover and simmer for 5 minutes. Remove the lid and continue to cook for about 15 minutes or until the sausages are browned, turning them occasionally.
2. Meanwhile, heat the oil in another pan and sauté the onions until soft but not coloured. Add the peppers and continue cooking, stirring occasionally, for about 10 minutes or until the peppers are tender. Add the cooked sausages.
3. Split the rolls in half lengthways. Spoon some of the pepper and onion mixture on to the bottom half of each roll; add three of the sausages, then replace the top half of the roll.
4. To serve, cut each roll crossways in half.

Open Steak Sandwiches

Colour index page 108

4 servings

4 slices white bread
butter or margarine
4 beef minute steaks
10 ml (2 level tsp) plain flour
175 ml (6 fl oz) beef stock

For the garnish:
watercress sprigs, washed and trimmed

1. Toast the bread and spread one side of each slice with butter or margarine; put each slice on a heated plate and keep hot.
2. Heat 40 g (1½ oz) butter or margarine in a frying pan and quickly fry the steaks for 1 minute on each side, or longer if you prefer. Put a steak on each slice of toast and keep hot.
3. Reduce the heat and stir in the flour. Cook for 1–2 minutes, stirring, then blend in the stock and cook, stirring, until thickened. Pour the gravy over the steaks and garnish with watercress sprigs.

Club Sandwiches

Colour index page 109

2 servings

6 rashers streaky bacon, rinded
6 slices white bread, toasted
mayonnaise, page 462
lettuce leaves

2 large slices cooked turkey
salt and pepper
1 large tomato, sliced

1 Fry the bacon in its own fat until crisp; drain on kitchen paper towel. Spread one side of each slice of toast with some of the mayonnaise.

2 Arrange lettuce on two slices of toast; top with turkey. Sprinkle with salt and pepper then add another slice of toast, mayonnaise side up.

3 Add more lettuce, half the tomato slices, and three rashers of bacon to each sandwich. Top with remaining toast slices, mayonnaise side down.

4 Cut the sandwiches diagonally into quarters and secure each one with a cocktail stick. Arrange, cut sides up, on individual plates.

VARIATIONS: Prepare the club sandwiches as above, but replace the turkey with *2 large slices cooked ham*, corned beef or roast beef and replace the bacon with *2 slices Gruyère* or Cheddar cheese.

Poor Boy

Colour index page 109

6 servings

450-g (1-lb) French loaf
60 ml (4 tbsp) Russian dressing
2 hard-boiled eggs, shelled and finely chopped
30 ml (2 tbsp) chopped spring onions
30 ml (2 tbsp) mayonnaise, page 462
pinch salt

freshly ground black pepper
½ cucumber, wiped and sliced
350 g (12 oz) cooked ham, sliced
225 g (8 oz) Gruyère or Cheddar cheese, sliced
1 large tomato, sliced

1. Cut the French loaf horizontally in half. Mix the Russian dressing with the chopped eggs, spring onions and mayonnaise. Season to taste.
2. Arrange the cucumber slices on the bottom half of the loaf and layer the remaining ingredients on top. Spread with the Russian dressing mixture and replace the top half of the loaf. Cut the loaf into slices before serving.

Open sandwiches

DANISH OPEN SANDWICHES

Open sandwiches can be served as a light meal or as part of a buffet lunch. The most popular breads to use are pumpernickel or rye. Butter the bread lightly and choose attractive toppings and garnishes. Colour index page 109

Marinated herring on lettuce, garnished with raw onion rings and a tomato wedge.

Slices of rare roast beef with a cucumber twist, a tomato wedge and chopped fried onions.

Slices of salami and cucumber twists.

Prawns tossed in mayonnaise, garnished with cucumber and lemon twists.

Lettuce leaves and slices of smoked salmon, garnished with lemon twists.

Sliced cold roast pork, garnished with an orange twist and crumbled fried bacon.

Slices of hard-boiled egg topped with black lumpfish roe and rings of red pepper.

Slices of Danish blue cheese topped with halved black grapes and a walnut half.

Colour index page 109
4 servings

Watercress and Walnut Sandwiches

small bunch watercress, washed and trimmed
25 g (1 oz) shelled walnuts, chopped

1.25 ml (¼ level tsp) salt
225 g (8 oz) Neufchâtel cheese, softened
4 slices pumpernickel

1. Chop enough watercress to make 75 ml (5 tbsp); reserve the rest for the garnish.
2. Mix the watercress with the chopped walnuts, salt and Neufchâtel cheese, then spread the mixture on the pumpernickel.
3. Cut each slice diagonally in half and garnish with 2–3 watercress sprigs.

SLIMMERS' SANDWICHES

CRUNCHY TUNA SANDWICH: Drain a *99-g (3½-oz) can tuna* and mix with a little *finely chopped celery, chopped nuts, salt* and a little *cottage cheese.* Spread on very thin slices of *sweet teabread.* Colour index page 109

CURRIED PRAWN SANDWICH: Drain a *92-g (3¼-oz) can prawns* and mix with *1 chopped apple, low-calorie mayonnaise* and *curry powder* to taste. Spread on *wholemeal bread.* Colour index page 109

CHICKEN LIVER SPECIAL SANDWICH: Mix *chopped, cooked chicken livers* with *chopped, stuffed olives.* Spread on *pumpernickel.*

MEAT AND PEPPER SANDWICH: Put *thinly sliced green pepper* and *slices of ham* or beef on *wholemeal bread* or white bread.

CHICKEN AND APPLE SANDWICH: Mix *cooked, diced chicken* with *grated apple* and *low-calorie mayonnaise.* Spread on *wholemeal bread.*

CHEESE AND PINEAPPLE SANDWICH: Mix *cottage cheese* with *chopped fresh pineapple* and *chopped onion.* Spread on *white bread.*

CARROT, CHEESE AND ONION SANDWICH: Grate *carrot, cheese* and *onion* and mix together. Spread on *wholemeal bread* or white bread.

SPICED CHEESE AND APPLE SANDWICH: Mix *cream cheese* with *grated apple* and a *pinch of mixed spice.* Spread on *white bread.*

EGG AND CHEESE SANDWICH: Mix *chopped, hard-boiled egg* with *grated cheese* and *low-calorie mayonnaise.* Spread on *wholemeal bread.*

SHRIMP AND CUCUMBER SANDWICH: Mix *diced cucumber* with *shrimps* and *low-calorie mayonnaise.* Spread on *white bread.*

KIPPER AND CHEESE SANDWICH: Marinate a *kipper fillet* overnight in *oil* and *lemon juice.* Butter slices of *granary bread,* line with *chicory,* spoon on *cottage cheese* and top with thin strips of kipper.

MIXED VEGETABLE SANDWICH: Chop *mushrooms, tomatoes* and *parsley.* Mix together, season to taste and spread on *starch-reduced white bread.*

COD'S ROE AND SALAD SANDWICH: Put *lettuce,* sliced *tomato* and *smoked cod's roe* on *starched-reduced brown bread* and sprinkle with *lemon juice.*

Party sandwiches

Sandwich fillings

Colour index
page 109

Makes 30
sandwiches

Pâté Pinwheels

156-g (5½-oz) can pâté
15 ml (1 tbsp) grated
orange rind
15 ml (1 level tbsp) made
mustard

10 ml (2 level tsp) creamed
horseradish
450-g (1-lb) white
sandwich loaf, crusts
removed

1. Put the pâté, grated orange rind, mustard and creamed horseradish into a bowl and mix together until well blended.
2. Cut five slices of bread lengthways, 0.5 cm (¼ in) thick. Spread some pâté mixture over each slice and roll up from the short side.
3. Cut each bread roll crossways into six slices to form pinwheels.

Spreading the filling:
Cover each slice of bread evenly with pâté filling.

Making the pinwheels:
Roll each slice up; cut crossways into pinwheels.

Ribbon Sandwiches

Colour index
page 109

Makes 50
sandwiches

100 g (4 oz) butter,
softened
45 ml (3 tbsp) finely
chopped parsley
275 g (10 oz) cooked
chicken, chopped
75 ml (5 tbsp) mayonnaise,
page 462

15 ml (1 tbsp) lemon juice
1.25 ml (¼ level tsp) salt
1.25 ml (¼ level tsp)
pepper
450-g (1-lb) white
sandwich loaf,
crusts removed

1. Mix butter and parsley. In another bowl, mix chicken, mayonnaise, lemon juice and seasoning.
2. Cut the bread lengthways into six 1-cm (½-in) slices. On the first slice, spread a quarter of the parsley butter. Place the second slice on top and spread with half the chicken mixture. Spread the third slice with parsley butter and place, butter side down, on the second slice. Wrap and repeat with remaining bread and fillings. Chill.
3. To serve, cut each loaf into 1-cm (½-in) thick slices and cut each slice crossways in half.

Making the layers: Spread fillings over the bread slices and layer neatly.

Cutting the sandwiches: Cut each layered loaf into slices and halve them.

The following fillings will each be enough for sandwiches from a 450-g (1-lb) sandwich loaf.

CHEESE AND RAISIN: Mix *350 g (12 oz) grated Cheddar cheese,* with *50 g (2 oz) seedless raisins* and bind with a little *mayonnaise.*

SALMON AND PARSLEY: Drain *two 210-g (7½-oz) cans salmon* and mix with *30 ml (2 tbsp) chopped parsley, 30 ml (2 tbsp) pineapple juice* and *1.25 ml (¼ level tsp) salt.*

TUNA SALAD: Drain a *210-g (7½-oz) can tuna* and mix with *50 g (2 oz) chopped celery, 75 ml (5 tbsp) mayonnaise, 30 ml (2 tbsp) finely chopped onion, 30 ml (2 tbsp) chutney, 1.25 ml (¼ level tsp) salt* and a *pinch of pepper.*

PRAWN SALAD: Mix *175 g (6 oz) chopped prawns,* with *2 chopped, hard-boiled eggs, 75 ml (3 fl oz) bottled sandwich spread, 25 g (1 oz) chopped celery, 15 ml (1 tbsp) milk, 1.25 ml (¼ level tsp) salt* and a *pinch of pepper.*

EGG SALAD: Mix *5 chopped, hard-boiled eggs,* with *25 g (1 oz) finely chopped onion, 75 ml (3 fl oz) mayonnaise, 30 ml (2 level tbsp) made mustard* and *2.5 ml (½ level tsp) salt.*

PINEAPPLE AND CREAM CHEESE: Drain a *376-g (13-oz) can crushed pineapple* and mix with *250 g (9 oz) softened cream cheese* and *15 ml (1 level tbsp) creamed horseradish.*

CHEESE AND ANCHOVY: Mix *225 g (8 oz) softened cream cheese,* with *90 ml (6 tbsp) single cream, 5 ml (1 tsp) Worcestershire sauce, 5 ml (1 level tsp) anchovy paste* and *25 g (1 oz) chopped stuffed olives.*

TURKEY AND CHUTNEY: Mix *225 g (8 oz) diced, cooked turkey,* with *75 g (3 oz) thinly sliced celery, 60 ml (4 tbsp) mayonnaise, 30 ml (2 tbsp) chutney, 5 ml (1 level tsp) grated onion* and *2.5 ml (½ level tsp) salt.*

TONGUE SALAD: Mix *225 g (8 oz) minced, cooked ox tongue,* with *100 ml (4 fl oz) mayonnaise, 5 ml (1 level tsp) creamed horseradish, 1.25 ml (¼ level tsp) salt* and a *pinch of pepper.*

SHARP SALMON: Drain and flake *two 210-g (7½-oz) cans salmon,* and mix with *75 ml (5 tbsp) mayonnaise, 15 ml (1 level tbsp) creamed horseradish, 15 ml (3 tbsp) capers* and *15 ml (1 tbsp) lemon juice.*

CHICKEN AND CRANBERRY: Mix *350 g (12 oz) chopped, cooked chicken,* with *30 ml (2 tbsp) whole berry cranberry sauce, 10 ml (2 tsp) orange juice* and *1.25 ml (¼ level tsp) salt.*

CHEESE SALAD: Mix *275 g (10 oz) diced Gruyère cheese,* or mature Cheddar cheese, with *150 ml (¼ pint) mayonnaise, 1 small green pepper,* seeded and diced, *5 ml (1 level tsp) mild chilli sauce* and a *pinch each of salt and pepper.*

SAUCES

A good sauce can bring life to your cooking and vary the flavour of all kinds of dishes, whether savoury or sweet. Certain basic techniques and recipes have become classics in their own right, and every aspiring cook should know how to prepare them; there is also scope for improvisation, so that you can give any dish an original flavour.

Recipes for sauces traditionally associated with certain foods and dishes, such as tomato sauce for spaghetti and gravy for roast beef, are given in the relevant chapters and may be found in the index. More versatile sauces that can be served with a variety of dishes are given in this chapter.

MAKING SAUCES

Most savoury sauces are thickened with plain flour, incorporated in the sauce in the form of a roux. This is made by melting a little butter or other fat, stirring in the flour and cooking for 1–2 minutes; the liquid is then blended carefully into the roux, brought to the boil and simmered for 2–3 minutes. For a white sauce, the roux should be no more than a light straw colour, but for a brown sauce, the roux may be cooked as long as 5 minutes until it turns a rich golden brown.

To thicken a sauce without making a roux, thoroughly blend the flour with a little cold water before mixing it gradually into the hot liquid; the sauce must then boil for 2–3 minutes until thickened. This method is also frequently used for sauces that are thickened with cornflour or with arrowroot.

If a sauce thickened with flour or cornflour turns lumpy it is usually possible to rescue it by removing the pan from the heat and beating the sauce vigorously. Alternatively, let the sauce cool slightly, pour it into a blender and blend until smooth.

Egg yolks are the other thickening agent used for sauces. To thicken and enrich a thin, roux-based sauce, beat the egg yolks lightly, mix in a little cream if you wish, and stir in a spoonful of the hot sauce; blend the mixture into the bulk of the sauce, beating rapidly to prevent lumping. The sauce must not boil again or it will curdle.

You can also use egg yolks in an emulsion with oil or melted butter to make mayonnaise or hollandaise sauce. The smooth, thick consistency of the sauce is achieved by whisking the two liquids evenly together. It is essential to add the oil or melted butter a little at a time, particularly in the early stages, or the sauce may curdle.

If mayonnaise curdles, start afresh with another egg yolk and slowly whisk the curdled sauce into the fresh yolk; the sauce will return to a smooth consistency and you can continue adding any remaining oil. If hollandaise sauce curdles, place 5 ml (1 tsp) lemon juice and 15 ml (1 tbsp) of the curdled sauce in a bowl. Whisk vigorously until the mixture is creamy and thickened, then gradually beat in the remaining curdled sauce, 15 ml (1 tbsp) at a time, making sure each spoonful has thickened before adding the next.

KEEPING SAUCES HOT

Many sauces are best made at the last minute and served absolutely fresh, but it is possible to keep them for a short while in a double saucepan over hot water or in an ordinary saucepan standing in a roasting tin of hot water. For egg-based sauces the water should be no more than warm or the sauce may curdle.

Preventing a skin forming: Cover the surface of the sauce with damp greaseproof paper or with waxed paper.

Or, dot the surface with tiny pieces of butter; just before serving, beat in the butter until the sauce is smooth.

FREEZING SAUCES

Many sauces freeze well and it is particularly useful to have béchamel and espagnole sauces in store, as they form the foundation of so many other sauces.

Cool the hot sauce quickly, then pour it into a freezer container, leaving 1 cm (½ in) space at the top. Pack large quantities in 300-ml (½-pint) portions. Seal tightly, chill and freeze. Reheat gently, stirring well, in a small saucepan or, for very thick sauces, a double saucepan. Egg-based sauces do not freeze successfully; other sauces store well for 2–3 months.

White sauces

White Sauce

Makes
300 ml (½ pint)

*20 g (¾ oz) butter or
margarine
30 ml (2 level tbsp) plain
flour
300 ml (½ pint) milk or
milk and stock
salt and pepper*

1 Put the fat into a small heavy-based saucepan; melt over gentle heat.

2 Add the flour and blend into the fat to make a smooth roux. Cook, stirring constantly, for 2–3 minutes.

3 Add the liquid gradually, stirring constantly; bring to the boil. Cook for 1–2 minutes, stirring. Season to taste.

WHITE SAUCE VARIATIONS

COATING CONSISTENCY WHITE SAUCE: Prepare the sauce as above, but use *25 g (1 oz) butter* or margarine and *45 ml (3 level tbsp) plain flour*.

CHEESE SAUCE: Prepare the sauce as above, then remove from the heat and stir in *50–100 g (2–4 oz) grated mature Cheddar cheese*, a *pinch of dry mustard* and a *pinch of cayenne pepper*, stirring until the cheese is melted.

ONION SAUCE: Simmer *2 skinned and chopped onions* in salted water for 10–15 minutes until soft; drain well. Prepare a white sauce as above, replacing 150 ml (¼ pint) milk with cooking liquid from the onions. Stir in the cooked onions and *grated rind of ½ lemon* when the sauce has thickened. Season to taste. Makes 350 ml (12 fl oz)

CURRY SAUCE: Prepare the sauce as above, but stir in *60 ml (4 tbsp) finely chopped onion, 10 ml (2 level tsp) curry powder, 3.75 ml (¾ level tsp) sugar* and a *pinch of ground ginger* with the flour. Just before serving, stir in *5 ml (1 tsp) lemon juice*.

HOT THOUSAND ISLAND SAUCE: Prepare the sauce as above, but mix together *60 ml (4 tbsp) mayonnaise* and *60 ml (4 tbsp) mild chilli sauce*. Stir into the white sauce before serving. Makes 350 ml (12 fl oz)

CAPER SAUCE: Prepare the sauce as above, but stir *15 ml (1 tbsp) capers* and *5–10 ml (1–2 tsp) vinegar* drained from the capers into the thickened white sauce. Season and reheat the sauce gently for 1–2 minutes before serving.

Béchamel Sauce

Makes
300 ml (½ pint)

*300 ml (½ pint) milk
1 shallot or small piece
onion, skinned and sliced
small piece carrot, peeled
and chopped
½ stick celery, washed and
chopped*

*½ bay leaf
3 peppercorns
25 g (1 oz) butter
45 ml (3 level tbsp) plain
flour
salt and pepper*

1. Put the milk, shallot, carrot, celery, bay leaf and peppercorns in a heavy-based saucepan; bring slowly to the boil. Remove from the heat, cover and leave to stand for 25 minutes. Strain the liquid and discard the flavourings.
2. Melt the butter in a small saucepan then stir in the flour and cook, stirring, for 1–2 minutes.
3. Add the flavoured milk gradually, stirring constantly. Bring to the boil, stirring, and cook for 1–2 minutes until thickened. Season to taste.

MORNAY SAUCE: Prepare as above, then remove from the heat. Stir in *50 g (2 oz) grated Gruyère cheese* and *25 g (1 oz) grated Parmesan cheese* or 75 g (3 oz) grated Cheddar cheese until melted.

Mushroom Sauce

Makes
300 ml (½ pint)

*40 g (1½ oz) butter or
margarine
30 ml (2 level tbsp) plain
flour*

*300 ml (½ pint) milk
50–75 g (2–3 oz) button
mushrooms, sliced
salt and pepper*

1. Melt half the fat in a small, heavy-based saucepan. Blend in the flour and cook, stirring constantly, for 1–2 minutes.
2. Add the milk gradually, stirring constantly. Bring to the boil, stirring, and cook for 2–3 minutes until thickened. Remove from the heat.
3. Lightly fry the mushrooms in the remaining fat until they are soft but not coloured. Fold them into the prepared sauce and season to taste.

Parmesan Sauce

Makes
400 ml (¾ pint)

*25 g (1 oz) butter
15 g (½ oz) plain flour
175 ml (6 fl oz) single
cream*

*175 ml (6 fl oz) water
1 chicken stock cube
25 g (1 oz) Parmesan
cheese, grated*

1. Melt the fat in a heavy-based saucepan, blend in the flour and cook, stirring, for 1–2 minutes.
2. Gradually stir in the cream and water; crumble in the stock cube. Cook, stirring, until thickened; remove from heat and stir in cheese until melted.

Peppery Blue Cheese Sauce

Makes about
225 ml (8 fl oz)

*15 g (½ oz) butter or
margarine
15 ml (1 level tbsp) plain
flour*

*175 ml (6 fl oz) milk
75 g (3 oz) blue cheese,
crumbled
salt and pepper*

1. Melt the fat in a small heavy-based saucepan, blend in the flour and cook, stirring constantly, for 1–2 minutes.
2. Gradually stir in the milk and cook, stirring constantly, until thickened. Remove from the heat, stir in the cheese until melted and season to taste.

Brown sauces

Bordelaise Sauce

Makes
300 ml (½ pint)

25 g (1 oz) butter or margarine
30 ml (2 level tbsp) plain flour
15 ml (1 tbsp) finely chopped onion
15 ml (1 tbsp) finely chopped parsley
bay leaf
1.25 ml (¼ level tsp) dried thyme
1.25 ml (¼ level tsp) salt

pinch coarsely ground black pepper
298-g (10½-oz) can condensed consommé, undiluted
60 ml (4 tbsp) red wine

1 Melt the fat over gentle heat, then blend in the flour and cook, stirring, for about 5 minutes or until the roux is just lightly browned.

2 Stir in the chopped onion and parsley, bay leaf, dried thyme and salt and pepper.

3 Gradually stir in the consommé and red wine until well blended.

4 Cook, stirring constantly, until thickened. Discard bay leaf.

Espagnole Sauce

Makes
300 ml (½ pint)

1 rasher streaky bacon, rinded and chopped
25 g (1 oz) butter
1 shallot, skinned and chopped
60 ml (4 tbsp) chopped mushroom stalks
1 small carrot, peeled and chopped

30–45 ml (2–3 level tbsp) plain flour
300 ml (½ pint) beef stock
bouquet garni
30 ml (2 level tbsp) tomato paste
salt and pepper

1. Fry the bacon in the butter for 2–3 minutes, then add the vegetables and fry for a further 3–5 minutes. Blend in the flour and cook, stirring until the mixture is well browned.
2. Remove from the heat and gradually add the stock, stirring constantly. Return the pan to the heat and cook, stirring, until the sauce thickens.
3. Add bouquet garni, tomato paste, salt and pepper. Simmer for 1 hour, stirring occasionally.
4. Strain the sauce, skim off any fat and reheat. Adjust the seasoning before serving.

Egg-based sauces

Mayonnaise

Makes about
400 ml (¾ pint)

3 egg yolks
7.5 ml (1½ level tsp) dry mustard
7.5 ml (1½ level tsp) salt
3.75 ml (¾ level tsp) pepper
7.5 ml (1½ level tsp) sugar
400 ml (¾ pint) vegetable oil
45 ml (3 tbsp) white vinegar or lemon juice

1 Put the egg yolks in a bowl with the seasonings and sugar and beat with a mixer or whisk.

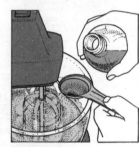

2 Continue beating and add 150 ml (¼ pint) of the oil, 2.5 ml (½ tsp) at a time, until the sauce is thick and smooth.

3 Add the white vinegar or the lemon juice, beating constantly.

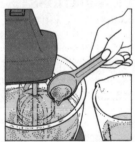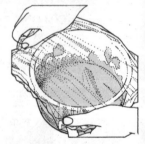

4 Add the remaining oil 15 ml (1 tbsp) at a time, beating until absorbed.

5 Cover with cling film or foil and refrigerate until ready to use.

MAYONNAISE VARIATIONS

TOMATO MAYONNAISE: Prepare as above, but add *1½ tomatoes*, skinned, seeded and diced, *3 spring onions*, trimmed and chopped, *3.75 ml (¾ level tsp) salt* and *15 ml (1 tbsp) vinegar* or lemon juice.

CUCUMBER MAYONNAISE: Prepare as above, but add *90 ml (6 tbsp) finely chopped cucumber* and *7.5 ml (1½ level tsp) salt.*

PIQUANT MAYONNAISE: Prepare as above, but add *15 ml (1 tbsp) tomato ketchup, 15 ml (1 tbsp) chopped olives* and a *large pinch of paprika*.

REMOULADE SAUCE: Prepare as above, but add *7.5 ml (1½ level tsp)* each of *made French* and *English mustards, 15 ml (1 tbsp)* each of *chopped capers, gherkin, parsley* and *chervil*, and *3 finely chopped anchovy fillets*.

Other savoury sauces

Hollandaise Sauce

Makes
200 ml (7 fl oz)

3 egg yolks
30 ml (2 tbsp) wine vinegar
100 g (4 oz) butter
1.25 ml (¼ level tsp) salt
pinch pepper

1 Put the egg yolks and vinegar in the top of a double saucepan and stir together until they are thoroughly mixed.

2 Place over the bottom of the double saucepan over hot, not boiling, water and heat gently, stirring, until the yolks are thickened.

3 Add a small piece of the butter to the egg yolks and whisk over gentle heat until the butter has melted.

4 Add the remaining butter a little at a time. Whisk sauce until thick.

5 Remove from the heat and stir in the salt and pepper. Serve warm.

Béarnaise Sauce

Makes
200 ml (7 fl oz)

60 ml (4 tbsp) wine or tarragon vinegar
1 shallot, skinned and chopped
5 ml (1 tsp) chopped tarragon

2 egg yolks, beaten
75 g (3 oz) butter
salt and pepper

1. Put the vinegar, shallot and tarragon in a saucepan; reduce by boiling to about 15 ml (1 tbsp).
2. Cool the mixture slightly and stir into the egg yolks in the top of a double saucepan.
3. Place over the bottom of the double saucepan containing hot, not boiling, water and stir gently until slightly thickened. Whisk in the butter a little at a time until it has melted and the mixture has thickened. Season to taste.

Sauce Maître d'Hôtel

Makes about
75 ml (5 tbsp)

50 g (2 oz) butter
15 ml (1 tbsp) lemon juice
15 ml (1 tbsp) chopped parsley

2.5 ml (½ level tsp) salt
pinch cayenne or few drops Tabasco sauce

Melt the butter in a small saucepan, then stir in the remaining ingredients.

MAITRE D'HOTEL BUTTER: Cream the butter until smooth, beat in the remaining ingredients and shape into small pats. Chill until required.

Cumberland Sauce

Makes about
225 ml (8 fl oz)

1 orange
1 lemon
60 ml (4 tbsp) redcurrant jelly
60 ml (4 tbsp) port

10 ml (2 level tsp) arrowroot
10 ml (2 tsp) water

1. Pare the rind thinly from the orange and lemon, cut it into fine strips and simmer in a little water for 5 minutes. Remove from the heat.
2. Squeeze the juice from the orange and lemon and put it in a pan with the redcurrant jelly. Heat gently, stirring, until the jelly has melted. Simmer for 5 minutes and add the port.
3. Blend the arrowroot with the water and slowly stir in redcurrant mixture. Return to the pan and reheat, stirring, until thickened and clear. Drain the strips of rind and add to the sauce.

Apple Sauce

Makes
300 ml (½ pint)

450 g (1 lb) cooking apples, peeled and cored
30–45 ml (2–3 tbsp) water

25 g (1 oz) butter
30–60 ml (2–4 level tbsp) sugar

1. Slice the apples and put them in a pan with the water. Cook gently for about 10 minutes, until soft.
2. Beat fruit well, then purée in a blender or press through a sieve.
3. Beat in the butter and sweeten to taste.

Mint Sauce

Makes
75 ml (5 tbsp)

small bunch of mint, finely chopped
10 ml (2 level tsp) sugar

15 ml (1 tbsp) boiling water
15–30 ml (1–2 tbsp) vinegar

1. Put the mint in a sauceboat with the sugar; add the water and stir until the sugar has dissolved.
2. Stir in vinegar to taste and leave for 1 hour.

Spicy Barbecue Sauce

Makes about
400 ml (¾ pint)

30 ml (2 tbsp) vegetable oil
1 onion, skinned and finely chopped
225 ml (8 fl oz) tomato sauce, page 337
75 g (3 oz) soft light brown sugar
60 ml (4 tbsp) white vinegar

15 ml (1 tbsp) Worcestershire sauce
20 ml (4 level tsp) chilli powder
10 ml (2 level tsp) salt
1.25 ml (¼ level tsp) dry mustard

Heat the oil in a pan, add the onion and cook for about 5 minutes until tender. Add the remaining ingredients and bring to the boil, stirring.

Sweet sauces

Caramel Sauce

Makes
600 ml (1 pint)

25 g (1 oz) butter or
  margarine
30 ml (2 level tbsp) plain
  flour
175 ml (6 fl oz) single
  cream
175 ml (6 fl oz) milk
115 g (4½ oz) soft light
  brown sugar
175 g (6 oz) granulated
  sugar
1.25 ml (¼ level tsp) salt

1 Melt the fat in a small, heavy-based saucepan over gentle heat; stir in the flour until well blended.

2 Stir in the single cream and milk gradually, and cook, stirring constantly, until the sauce is thick and smooth.

3 Add the sugars and salt and stir over gentle heat until dissolved. Serve warm or cover and chill.

Hot Butterscotch Sauce

Makes
225 ml (8 fl oz)

175 g (6 oz) soft light
  brown sugar
25 g (1 oz) butter or
  margarine
30 ml (2 level tbsp) golden
  syrup
60 ml (4 tbsp) single cream

Put all the ingredients in a small, heavy-based saucepan and bring to the boil, stirring occasionally. Serve the sauce warm.

NUTTY BUTTERSCOTCH SAUCE: Warm 25 g (1 oz) butter, 30 ml (2 level tbsp) brown sugar and 15 ml (1 level tbsp) golden syrup until blended. Boil for 1 minute, then stir in 45 ml (3 tbsp) chopped nuts and a squeeze of lemon juice, if you wish.

Hot Fudge Sauce

Makes about
400 ml (¾ pint)

350 g (12 oz) sugar
100 ml (4 fl oz) milk
75 ml (5 level tbsp) golden
  syrup
50 g (2 oz) plain chocolate
15 g (½ oz) butter or
  margarine
5 ml (1 tsp) vanilla essence
pinch salt

1. Put the sugar, milk, syrup and chocolate in a large heavy-based saucepan; bring to the boil, stirring constantly. Cook, stirring occasionally, until it reaches 109°C (228°F) on a sugar thermometer or until a small amount of the mixture dropped from a spoon into the pan spins a 0.5-cm (¼-in) thread.
2. Remove the saucepan from the heat and quickly add the fat, vanilla essence and salt, stirring until the sauce is smooth. Serve hot.

Chocolate and Marshmallow Sauce

Makes
350 ml (12 fl oz)

100 g (4 oz) small
  marshmallows
75 ml (5 tbsp) double or
  whipping cream
75 ml (5 level tbsp) honey
40 g (1½ oz) plain
  chocolate
pinch salt

Place all the ingredients in a heavy-based saucepan and heat gently, stirring constantly, until the marshmallows and chocolate have melted. Serve hot.

Chocolate Sauce

Makes about
100 ml (4 fl oz)

50 g (2 oz) plain chocolate
knob of butter
15 ml (1 tbsp) milk
5 ml (1 tsp) vanilla essence

Put the chocolate and butter in a small basin over a pan of hot water and stir until melted. Add the milk and vanilla essence and serve at once.

Sabayon Sauce

Makes about
150 ml (¼ pint)

50 g (2 oz) caster sugar
60 ml (4 tbsp) water
2 egg yolks
grated rind of ½ lemon
juice of 1 lemon
30 ml (2 tbsp) rum or
  sherry
30 ml (2 tbsp) single cream

1. Put the sugar and water in a heavy-based saucepan and heat gently, stirring, until the sugar has dissolved. Bring to the boil and boil for 2–3 minutes.
2. Beat the egg yolks in a basin and slowly pour on the hot syrup, whisking until pale and thick.
3. Add the lemon rind, lemon juice and rum and whisk for a further 2–3 minutes. Fold in the cream and leave to cool. Chill thoroughly.

Cherry Sauce

Makes about
400 ml (¾ pint)

150 ml (¼ pint) water
450 g (1 lb) dessert
  cherries, stoned
60 ml (4 level tbsp)
  granulated sugar

1. Put the water into a saucepan and bring to the boil. Add the cherries and simmer for 3 minutes.
2. Add the sugar and simmer for a further 2–3 minutes or until the cherries are tender. Serve hot.

Peach Sauce

Makes
300 ml (½ pint)

425-g (15-oz) can sliced
  peaches, drained
pinch ground nutmeg
1.25 ml (¼ tsp) almond
  essence

Purée all the ingredients in a blender or press them through a sieve with a wooden spoon. Serve cold.

Hot Fruit Sauce

Makes
900 ml
(1½ pints)

3 large nectarines, peeled
  and stoned
3 large plums, washed,
  peeled and stoned
100 ml (4 fl oz) orange
  juice
100 g (4 oz) granulated
  sugar
30 ml (2 tbsp) brandy,
  optional

1. Cut the nectarines and plums into wedges. Place in a saucepan with the orange juice and simmer for 10 minutes until tender.
2. Remove from the heat, add the sugar and brandy and stir until the sugar has dissolved.

Jams and jellies

If a jam or jelly is to set properly, there must be the correct balance of pectin, acid and sugar. Fruits rich in pectin and acid include currants, cooking apples, crab-apples, gooseberries, damsons and some plums; these will all set well in jam or jelly. Greengages, apricots and raspberries have a medium setting quality, but pears, melons, marrow, cherries and some varieties of strawberry need the addition of pectin or acid to help them set. If you are making a mixed jam, then the pectin required by one fruit may well be supplied by the other. If not, then lemon juice is an excellent source; add the juice of 1–2 lemons for every 1.8 kg (4 lb) fruit. Alternatively, buy bottled pectin and use it as directed. The yield of each jelly recipe cannot be given as this varies with the amount of juice extracted from the fruit.

Strawberry Jam

Colour index page 110

Makes about 2.3 kg (5 lb)

1.6 kg (3½ lb) strawberries, washed and hulled
1.4 kg (3 lb) sugar

45 ml (3 tbsp) lemon juice

1 Put the strawberries in a preserving pan with the lemon juice. Simmer them gently in their own juice for 20–30 minutes or until really soft.

2 Add the sugar and stir with a long-handled wooden spoon over a gentle heat until it has completely dissolved.

3 Bring to the boil. Boil rapidly until temperature reaches 105°C (221°F) or setting point is reached.

4 Leave to cool for 15–20 minutes. Stir, pour into warmed pots and cover in the usual way.

RASPBERRY JAM: Wash and hull *1.8 kg (4 lb) raspberries*; simmer gently in their own juice for 15–20 minutes. Add *1.8 kg (4 lb) sugar*; finish as above. Colour index page 110; makes 3 kg (6½ lb)

CHERRY JAM: Stone *1.8 kg (4 lb) tart cherries;* crack some stones and remove the kernels. Simmer fruit and kernels with the *juice of 3 lemons* until soft. Add *1.6 kg (3½ lb) sugar* and finish as above. Colour index page 110

Plum Jam

Colour index page 110

Makes about 4.5 kg (10 lb)

2.7 kg (6 lb) plums, washed
900 ml (1½ pints) water
2.7 kg (6 lb) sugar

1. Cut the plums in half and remove the stones. Crack some of the stones and remove the kernels. Put the plums, kernels and water in the preserving pan and simmer gently for about 30 minutes or until the fruit is really soft.
2. Add the sugar, stirring until it has dissolved. Bring to the boil and boil rapidly until setting point is reached. Pour the jam into warmed pots and cover in the usual way.

Blackberry and Apple Jam

Colour index page 110

Makes about 4.5 kg (10 lb)

1.8 kg (4 lb) blackberries, washed and hulled
300 ml (½ pint) water
700 g (1½ lb) sour apples, peeled and cored
2.7 kg (6 lb) sugar

1. Put the blackberries in a saucepan with 150 ml (¼ pint) water. Simmer until soft.
2. Slice the apples and put them in a preserving pan with the remaining water. Simmer until tender, then mash into a pulp with a spoon or potato masher.
3. Add the cooked blackberries and sugar to the apple pulp, stir over gentle heat to dissolve the sugar then bring to the boil and boil rapidly until setting point is reached, stirring frequently to prevent sticking. Pour the jam into warmed pots, using a wide-necked funnel, and cover in the usual way.

Gooseberry Jam

Colour index page 110

Makes about 4.5 kg (10 lb)

2.7 kg (6 lb) gooseberries, washed
1.1 litres (2 pints) water
2.7 kg (6 lb) sugar

1. Top and tail the gooseberries and put them in a preserving pan with the water. Simmer gently for about 30 minutes until the fruit is really soft, mashing it to a pulp with a spoon or potato masher and stirring occasionally to prevent the fruit from sticking to the pan.
2. Add the sugar, stirring until it has dissolved. Bring to the boil and boil rapidly until setting point is reached, stirring frequently to prevent sticking. Pour the jam into warmed pots, using a wide-necked funnel, and cover in the usual way.

Dried Apricot Jam

Colour index page 110

Makes about 2.3 kg (5 lb)

450 g (1 lb) dried apricots
1.7 litres (3 pints) water
juice of 1 lemon
1.4 kg (3 lb) sugar
50–75 g (2–3 oz) blanched almonds, optional

1. Wash the apricots thoroughly, cover them with the water and leave to soak for 24 hours. Put the fruit in a preserving pan with the soaking water and lemon juice and simmer for about 30 minutes until soft, stirring occasionally.
2. Add the sugar and blanched almonds to the apricots, stirring until the sugar has dissolved. Bring to the boil and boil rapidly until setting point is reached, stirring frequently to prevent sticking. Pour the jam into warmed pots, using a wide-necked funnel, and cover in the usual way.

Jams and jellies

Marmalades

Blackcurrant Jelly

1.8 kg (4 lb) blackcurrants, washed   **1.5 litres (2½ pints) water**
                                                 sugar

1 Pick over the currants but do not remove the stalks. Put them in a preserving pan with the water and simmer for about 1 hour until really soft.

2 Strain through a clean cloth or jelly bag. Do not press the fruit as the juice will become cloudy; leave the fruit to drip for several hours.

3 Measure the juice. Weigh out 450 g (1 lb) sugar for every 600 ml (1 pint) juice. Put the juice in a preserving pan, add the sugar and stir over gentle heat until dissolved.

4 Bring to the boil and boil rapidly until setting point is reached. Skim to remove the surface scum, then pour the jelly into warmed pots and cover in the usual way.

REDCURRANT JELLY: Prepare as above, but replace the blackcurrants with *1.4 kg (3 lb) redcurrants* and simmer them with only *600 ml (1 pint) water* until really soft.

Four Fruit Jelly

450 g (1 lb) redcurrants, washed
450 g (1 lb) raspberries, washed and hulled
450 g (1 lb) tart cherries, washed
450 g (1 lb) strawberries, washed and hulled

60 ml (4 tbsp) lemon juice or 5 ml (1 level tsp) citric or tartaric acid
600 ml (1 pint) water
sugar

1. Pick over the fruits, but do not remove the stalks from the redcurrants. Place all the fruit in a preserving pan with the lemon juice and water and simmer gently until the fruit is soft and pulped.
2. Strain through a clean cloth or jelly bag. Do not press the fruit but leave it to drip for several hours.
3. Measure the juice and weigh out 450 g (1 lb) sugar for every 600 ml (1 pint) of juice. Put the juice in the pan, add the sugar and stir over gentle heat until dissolved. Bring to the boil and boil rapidly until setting point is reached. Skim, pour into warmed pots and cover in the usual way.

As for other types of jam the fruit for marmalade must be well softened before the sugar is added. Since the peel on citrus fruit is tough, this may take over 2 hours by conventional methods, but you can use a pressure cooker to shorten the cooking time. Put the prepared fruit in the pressure cooker with a quarter of the water stated in the recipe, bring to medium (10-lb) pressure and cook for 10 minutes. Reduce pressure slowly, add the same amount of water again and stir in the sugar. Bring to the boil in the open pan and continue as usual.

Seville Orange Marmalade

1.4 kg (3 lb) Seville oranges, washed
juice of 2 lemons

3.4 litres (6 pints) water
2.7 kg (6 lb) sugar

Makes 4.5 kg (10 lb)

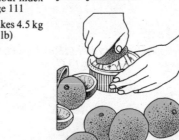

1 Halve the oranges and squeeze out the juice. Collect the pips and pulp in a piece of muslin and tie into a bag.

2 Slice the peel thinly with a sharp knife or vegetable slicer. Put the fruit juices and water in a preserving pan and tie the bag to the handle.

3 Add the peel and simmer for about 2 hours, until the peel is soft and the liquid reduced by about half.

4 Remove the muslin bag, squeezing it well between two plates to extract all the juice (this improves pectin content).

5 Add the sugar and stir until it has dissolved. Bring to the boil and boil rapidly for 15 minutes.

6 Test setting point, then leave to cool for 15 minutes. Stir, pot and cover in the usual way.

Chutneys

SEVILLE ORANGE MARMALADE MADE WITH FROZEN ORANGES: Seville oranges can be bought in season and then frozen until needed. Clean them, then freeze them whole in thick polythene bags. To make the marmalade using *1.4 kg (3 lb) oranges,* simmer the frozen whole oranges in a tightly covered saucepan with the *water* until really soft. Remove the fruit from the pan, let it cool a little and then cut it up roughly. Tie up the pips in muslin and add to the liquid in the pan with the *lemon juice.* Bring to the boil and boil for 5 minutes. Remove the muslin bag and squeeze the juice out of it back into the liquid. Now weigh the empty preserving pan. Put the cut-up fruit into it with the liquid from the saucepan. Calculate the weight of the mixture and boil until it weighs 2 kg (4½ lb). Add the *sugar* and finish as left.

Three Fruit Marmalade

Colour index page 111

Makes about 4.5 kg (10 lb)

4 lemons, 2 sweet oranges and 2 grapefruit, total weight 1.4 kg (3 lb)   *3.4 litres (6 pints) water*
2.7 kg (6 lb) sugar

1. Wash the lemons and oranges, halve them and squeeze out the juice and pips. Slice the peel thinly.
2. Wash the grapefruit, pare off the rind thickly with a knife or vegetable peeler and slice it thinly. Remove any thick white pith and membrane from the fruit and chop the flesh roughly.
3. Put the fruit juice and flesh, sliced peel and water in a preserving pan. Tie up the pith, membrane and pips in a piece of muslin and add to the pan. Simmer gently for about 1–1½ hours or until the peel is really soft and the liquid is reduced by about half. Remove the muslin bag and squeeze any juice back into the saucepan.
4. Add the sugar, stirring until it has dissolved. Bring to the boil and boil rapidly until setting point is reached, stirring frequently to prevent sticking. Leave the marmalade to cool for about 15 minutes, then pour the marmalade into warmed pots and cover in the usual way.

Lime Marmalade

Colour index page 111

Makes about 2.3 kg (5 lb)

700 g (1½ lb) limes, washed   *1.7 litres (3 pints) water*
1.4 kg (3 lb) sugar

1. Cut the stem end off the limes. Place the whole limes in a saucepan with the water and cover with a tightly fitting lid. Simmer for 1½–2 hours until the fruit is really soft.
2. Remove the limes from the pan and slice them very thinly, using a knife and fork. Discard the pips.
3. Weigh the empty preserving pan. Put the sliced fruit and juice and the cooking liquid in the pan. Calculate the weight of the mixture and, if necessary, boil it until it weighs 1.1 kg (2½ lb).
4. Add the sugar, stirring until it has dissolved. Bring to the boil and boil rapidly until setting point is reached, stirring frequently to prevent sticking. Leave the marmalade to cool for 15 minutes, pour it into warmed pots and cover in the usual way.

The distinctive texture and flavour of a chutney is achieved by long, slow cooking and by leaving it to mature for at least 2–3 months. Store chutneys, tightly covered, in a cool place to prevent fermentation.

Green Tomato Chutney

Colour index page 111

Makes about 1.4 kg (3 lb)

1.4 kg (3 lb) green tomatoes
450 g (1 lb) apples, peeled and cored
225 g (8 oz) onions, skinned
225 g (8 oz) sultanas
225 g (8 oz) demerara sugar

10 ml (2 level tsp) salt
400 ml (¾ pint) malt vinegar
4 small pieces dried root ginger
2.5 ml (½ level tsp) cayenne pepper
5 ml (1 level tsp) dry mustard

1 Scald the tomatoes and remove the skin (page 296). Slice them thinly with a sharp knife.

2 Mince the apples and onions finely and put them in a preserving pan with the sliced tomatoes.

3 Add the remaining ingredients and bring the mixture slowly to the boil. Reduce the heat.

4 Simmer until tender and thick. Remove the ginger, pot and cover with a vinegar-proof lid.

Dower House Chutney

Colour index page 111

Makes 2.3 kg (5 lb)

700 g (1½ lb) plums
900 g (2 lb) tomatoes, skinned and sliced
900 ml (1½ pints) malt vinegar
4 cloves garlic, skinned
350 g (12 oz) onions, skinned

1 kg (2¼ lb) apples, peeled and cored
225 g (8 oz) dried fruit
22.5 ml (1½ tbsp) pickling spice
450 g (1 lb) demerara sugar
20 ml (4 level tsp) salt

1. Wash the plums, halve them and remove the stones. Put the plums in a preserving pan with the tomatoes and vinegar and simmer gently until soft.
2. Mince the next four ingredients and stir into the cooked mixture. Tie the pickling spice in muslin and add to the mixture with the sugar and salt.
3. Simmer for about 2 hours until tender and reduced to a thick consistency. Remove the pickling spice, pot and cover with a vinegar-proof lid.

Pickles and other preserves

Vegetables for pickling are steeped in brine to remove excess water and then preserved in a spiced vinegar; fruit is generally preserved in a sweetened vinegar syrup. Mincemeat is a mixture of dried fruit and spices.

Colour index page 111

Spiced Orange Rings

8 thin-skinned sweet oranges
900 ml (1½ pints) water
700 g (1½ lb) sugar
300 ml (½ pint) distilled white vinegar
15 ml (1 tbsp) cloves
1½ sticks cinnamon
6 blades mace

1 Wipe the oranges, cut into 0.5-cm (¼-in) slices and discard the pips. Place the slices in a saucepan, cover with water and bring to the boil. Cover and simmer for 40 minutes until the peel is soft. Drain well.

Colour index page 111

Makes 2.7 kg (6 lb)

Pickled Onions

225 g (8 oz) salt
2.4 litres (4 pints) water
1.8 kg (4 lb) small onions

For the spiced vinegar:
1 litre (1¾ pints) vinegar
30 ml (2 tbsp) blade mace

15 ml (1 tbsp) whole allspice berries
15 ml (1 tbsp) cloves
18-cm (7-in) stick cinnamon
6 peppercorns

1. Mix the salt and water to make a brine, pour enough over the unskinned onions to cover them and leave for 12 hours. Peel them, cover with fresh brine and leave for 1–1½ days.
2. Put all the ingredients for the spiced vinegar in a saucepan, bring to the boil and pour into a bowl. Cover and leave to cool for 2 hours, then strain.
3. Remove the onions from the brine, rinse them in cold water and drain. Pack them into jars, pour the cold spiced vinegar over them and cover with a vinegar-proof lid. Leave for 3 months before use.

2 Heat the sugar and vinegar gently until sugar is dissolved and add the spices. Bring to the boil and boil for 3–4 minutes.

3 Put the orange slices in a pan and cover with vinegar syrup. Simmer, covered, for 30–40 minutes. Remove from heat.

Soaking the onions: Pour the brine over the onions; leave for 12 hours.

Packing onions into jars: Use a slotted spoon to transfer onions to jars.

4 Leave for 24 hours then lift the slices out of the syrup and pack them into jars. Cover with the vinegar syrup.

5 Keep topping up with syrup for 3–4 days; then cover with a vinegar-proof lid. Leave for at least 6 weeks before serving.

Colour index page 111

Makes 3.2 kg (7 lb)

Piccalilli

2.7 kg (6 lb) skinned and trimmed vegetables, eg. marrow, cucumber, beans, small onions, cauliflower
450 g (1 lb) salt
4.5 litres (8 pints) water
15 ml (1 level tbsp) dry mustard
250 g (9 oz) sugar

7.5 ml (1½ level tsp) ground ginger
1.8 litres (3 pints) distilled white vinegar
60 ml (4 level tbsp) plain flour
30 ml (2 level tbsp) turmeric

1. Dice the marrow and cucumber, slice the beans, halve the onions and break the cauliflower into small florets. Dissolve the salt in the water, add the vegetables, cover and leave for 24 hours. Remove the vegetables, rinse them and drain well.
2. Mix the mustard, sugar and ginger with 1.5 litres (2½ pints) vinegar in a preserving pan. Add the vegetables and simmer for 20 minutes. Blend the flour and turmeric with the remaining 300 ml (½ pint) vinegar and stir into the cooked vegetables.
3. Bring to the boil and cook for 1–2 minutes. Pot and cover with a vinegar-proof lid.

Colour index page 111

Makes about 2.3 kg (5 lb)

Spicy Mincemeat

225 g (8 oz) cooking apples, peeled and cored
450 g (1 lb) currants
450 g (1 lb) sultanas
450 g (1 lb) seedless raisins
100 g (4 oz) chopped mixed peel
175 g (6 oz) shredded suet
grated rind and juice of 1 lemon
2.5 ml (½ level tsp) salt
450 g (1 lb) demerara sugar

2.5 ml (½ level tsp) ground cinnamon
2.5 ml (½ level tsp) ground cloves
2.5 ml (½ level tsp) ground nutmeg
2.5 ml (½ level tsp) ground mace
2.5 ml (½ level tsp) ground allspice
200 ml (7 fl oz) brandy

1. Chop the apples finely and place them in a large bowl with all the remaining ingredients. Mix all the ingredients thoroughly together, cover and leave to stand for 2 days. Stir the mixture occasionally.
2. Stir well and pack into jars to within about 2.5 cm (1 in) from the top. Cover as for jam, and allow the mincemeat to mature for at least 2 weeks before using. Store in a cool place and use within a year of preparation.

DRINKS

For parties and summer picnics, complement the flavour of the food with home-made fruit drinks and punches or mix a big jugful of one of the more conventional cocktails. Choose generous-sized glasses to serve fruit drinks and smaller cocktail glasses for alcoholic drinks. Use a heatproof bowl and punch cups for hot drinks.

Lemon Drink

Colour index page 112

Makes 3.7 litres (6½ pints)

350 g (12 oz) sugar
15 ml (1 tbsp) finely grated lemon rind
350 ml (12 fl oz) hot water
350 ml (12 fl oz) lemon juice

To serve:
ice cubes
soda water or water

1 Put sugar and lemon rind into a 1.1-litre (2-pint) capacity screw-topped jar; add the water.

2 Screw the top on tightly. Shake until the sugar is dissolved and add the lemon juice. Chill well.

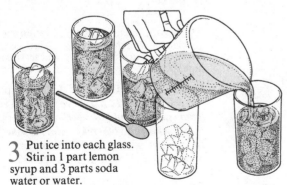

3 Put ice into each glass. Stir in 1 part lemon syrup and 3 parts soda water or water.

Pineapple Crush

Colour index page 112

Makes 1.7 litres (3 pints)

538-ml (19-fl oz) can unsweetened pineapple juice
juice of 1 orange
juice of 1 lemon

sugar
1 litre (1¾ pints) ginger ale, chilled
ice cubes

1. Combine the fruit juices in a large punch bowl, and sweeten to taste. Chill well.
2. Add the ginger ale and ice cubes and stir well.

Citrus Punch

Colour index page 112

Makes 3.7 litres (6½ pints)

1 small orange
3 175-g (6-oz) cans frozen lemon juice concentrate
750 ml (1¼ pints) unsweetened orange juice
750 ml (1¼ pints) bourbon or Scotch whisky

900 ml (1½ pints) soda water, chilled
ice cubes

1. Thinly slice the orange and flute the edges of the slices with a small sharp knife.
2. Mix all the ingredients in a large punch bowl and add the orange slices.

Mulled Wine

Colour index page 112

Makes 900 ml (1½ pints)

300 ml (½ pint) water
100 g (4 oz) sugar
4 cloves
5-cm (2-in) cinnamon stick

2 lemons, thinly sliced
1 bottle Burgundy or claret
1 orange, thinly sliced

1. Put the water, sugar and spices in a large saucepan; bring to the boil. Remove from the heat and stir in the lemons. Leave to stand for 10 minutes.
2. Add the wine and heat through without boiling. Strain into a heated punch bowl, add the orange slices and serve hot.

Glögg

Colour index page 112

Makes 2.2 litres (4 pints)

10 ml (2 tsp) grated orange rind
5 ml (1 level tsp) cloves
4 cardamom seeds, crushed
3 sticks cinnamon
2 bottles Burgundy

225 g (8 oz) dried apricots
175 g (6 oz) seedless raisins
1 bottle vodka or gin
175 g (6 oz) sugar
150 g (5 oz) blanched almonds

1. Tie the orange rind and spices in a small piece of muslin. Put one bottle of wine, the spice bag, apricots and raisins in a large saucepan; cover and simmer gently for 30 minutes.
2. Remove from the heat, discard the spice bag and stir in the remaining wine, the spirits and the sugar. Cover and leave to stand overnight.
3. Heat the punch without boiling, stirring occasionally. Ignite it and leave to burn for a few seconds, then cover to extinguish flames. Stir in almonds, pour into a heated bowl and serve hot.

Hot Cider Cup with Baked Apples

*3 large dessert apples,
wiped and cored
3.7 litres (6½ pints) dry
cider*

4 litres
(7 pints)

*nutmeg
175-g (6-oz) can frozen
lemon juice concentrate
175-g (6-oz) can frozen
orange juice concentrate
175 g (6 oz) soft light
brown sugar*

To serve:
*granulated sugar
cinnamon sticks*

1 Cut the apples in half
crossways and place
them, cut side down, in an
ovenproof dish. Bake at
180°C (350°F) mark 4 for
10 minutes or until tender
when tested with a fork.

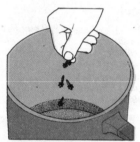

2 Meanwhile, pour 600 ml
(1 pint) cider into a
very large pan. Add the
spices; cover and simmer
for 10 minutes.

3 Add the remaining
cider, undiluted fruit
juice concentrates and
brown sugar. Heat
through without boiling,
stirring occasionally.

4 Pour the mixture care-
fully into a large
heated punch bowl.

5 Add the apples, skin
side up, and sprinkle
them with a little sugar.

6 Serve at once, ladling
the punch into heat-
proof punch cups. Garnish
each punch cup with a
short cinnamon stick.

Cocktails

Cocktails should always be served really cold, so use
plenty of ice or chill the ingredients thoroughly beforehand. Cocktails that are served with crushed or cracked
ice in them should ideally be made in a shaker, but you

spirits For example, gin and vodka are virtually
interchangeable and a Manhattan cocktail or Tom
Collins can be mixed using any spirit. If you want to
make a cocktail weaker or stronger, increase or decrease
the amount of ice you use.

Daiquiris

Colour index
page 112

Makes
1.1 litres
(2 pints)

*400 ml (¾ pint) white rum
150 ml (¼ pint) fresh lime
or lemon juice
30 ml (2 level tbsp) sugar
or sugar syrup
600 ml (1 pint) crushed ice*

1 Measure the rum into a
bowl with the lime juice
and sugar or sugar syrup.
Stir well, then cover and
chill thoroughly.

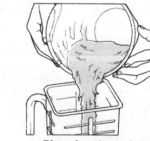

2 Place the mixture in a
blender with the
crushed ice and blend at
high speed for 30 seconds.

3 Pour the rum mixture
into cocktail glasses
and serve with two short
straws in each.

BLENDED WHISKY SOURS: Prepare as above,
but use *350 ml (12 fl oz) rye whisky, 150 ml (¼ pint)
lemon juice, 15 ml (1 level tbsp) sugar* or sugar syrup,
½ egg white and *600 ml (1 pint) crushed ice*. Garnish
each glass with a *maraschino cherry* and *half an
orange slice*. Colour index page 112

Margarita

Colour index
page 112

1 cocktail

*lemon or lime rind
salt
crushed ice
2 parts tequila*

*1 part curaçao
1 part lemon or lime
juice*

1. Rub the rim of a cocktail glass with the lemon or
lime rind and dip the rim in salt.
2. Put the ice in a cocktail shaker with the remaining
ingredients and shake well until a frost forms. Pour
into the prepared cocktail glass.

Party Bloody Mary

Colour index page 112

Makes 1.1 litres (2 pints)

1 litre (1¾ pints) tomato juice
225 ml (8 fl oz) vodka
10 ml (2 tsp) Worcestershire sauce
2.5 ml (½ tsp) Tabasco sauce, optional
2.5 ml (½ level tsp) salt, optional
freshly ground black pepper, optional
ice cubes
2 lemons or limes, quartered

1 Measure the tomato juice and vodka into a jug, add the seasonings and stir until well blended.

2 Put some ice into tumblers and divide the cocktail between them.

3 Squeeze a lemon or lime wedge into each tumbler and stir well.

INDIVIDUAL BLOODY MARY: Mix *1 part vodka* and *2 parts tomato juice* with a dash of *Worcestershire sauce* and a squeeze of *lime juice*. Pour over *ice cubes* in a tumbler and garnish with a *lime wedge*. Colour index page 112; 1 cocktail

Old Fashioned

Colour index page 112

1 cocktail

1 sugar lump
1–2 dashes Angostura bitters
cracked ice
1 measure whisky

For the garnish:
maraschino cherry
orange slice or lemon twist

1. Put the sugar lump in a glass, add the bitters and mix around in the glass to dissolve the sugar.
2. Fill the glass with cracked ice, pour the whisky over it and garnish with a maraschino cherry and orange slice or lemon twist.

Manhattan

Colour index page 112

1 cocktail

4–5 ice cubes
1 part rye whisky
1 part sweet vermouth
1–2 dashes Angostura bitters

2–3 dashes curaçao

For the garnish:
maraschino cherry

1. Mix all the ingredients together in a large jug.
2. Strain into a chilled cocktail glass and garnish with the maraschino cherry.

DRY MANHATTAN: Prepare as above, but substitute *dry vermouth* for sweet vermouth.

MEDIUM MANHATTAN: Prepare as above, but use half each of *dry vermouth* and *sweet vermouth*.

Virginia Mint Julep

Colour index page 112

1 cocktail

3 mint sprigs
5 ml (1 level tsp) sugar or sugar syrup
crushed ice

1 measure bourbon

For the garnish:
1 mint sprig

1. Put three sprigs of mint and the sugar into a cold tumbler or tankard and crush them together with the back of a spoon.
2. Fill the glass with crushed ice and pour in the bourbon, stirring well. Garnish with a mint sprig and, if you wish, serve with a long straw.

Martini

Colour index page 112

1 cocktail

2 parts dry vermouth
1 part gin
cracked ice

For the garnish:
stuffed olives or lemon rind curls

1. Put the vermouth and gin into a cocktail shaker with some cracked ice; shake until a frost forms.
2. Strain into a chilled cocktail glass and garnish with a stuffed olive or lemon rind curl.

DRY MARTINI: Prepare as above, but use equal parts of gin and vermouth.

VERY DRY MARTINI: Prepare as above, but use 2 parts gin and 1 part vermouth.

Tom Collins

Colour index page 112

1 cocktail

1 part gin
1 part lemon juice
5 ml (1 level tsp) sugar or sugar syrup
cracked ice
ice cubes
soda water

For the garnish:
maraschino cherry
orange slice or lemon twist

1. Put the gin, lemon juice and sugar or sugar syrup in a cocktail shaker with some cracked ice and shake well until a frost forms.
2. Put some ice into a tumbler and strain the mixture over. Top with soda water and stir well. Garnish with a cherry and an orange slice or lemon twist.

GIN RICKEY: Prepare as above, but use *2 parts gin* to *1 part lemon* and omit the sugar or syrup. Garnish with a *lemon twist*.

Stinger

Colour index page 112

1 cocktail

2 parts brandy
1 part crème de menthe

cracked ice

1. Put the brandy and the crème de menthe in a cocktail shaker with some cracked ice and shake well until a frost forms.
2. Strain the mixture into a chilled cocktail glass.

Brandy Alexander

Colour index page 112

1 cocktail

1 part crème de cacao
3 parts brandy

1 part cream
4–5 ice cubes

1. Put the crème de cacao, brandy and cream in a cocktail shaker with the ice cubes and shake well until a frost forms.
2. Strain the mixture into a cocktail glass.

Wines

When you are serving good food, you owe it the compliment of a good wine. Precisely which wine you choose is largely a matter of personal taste and the amount you want to spend, but there are a few guide-lines that it is wise to follow, as some wines are better suited than others to certain types of food. The chart opposite and on page 476 will provide a guide to the better known wines of Europe.

White wine is always better with fish but meat will take red, white or rosé. Pork, veal and chicken are good with a dry or medium-dry white wine, but also go well with a light red or rosé. Meats with a more pronounced flavour, such as beef, lamb or game, do justice to the fuller clarets and Burgundies. The very sweet, heavy, white wines, such as Sauternes, are best served with desserts, especially cakes and pastries.

SERVING WINE

When you are serving a dish that has been cooked in wine or is accompanied by a wine-based sauce, serve a wine of the same type and if you are serving a dish that has a particular national character, try to serve a wine that comes from the same country – for instance, an Italian pasta dish is excellent accompanied by Chianti Classico or Valpolicella.

The temperature at which wine is served is very important for its full enjoyment. White wine is generally at its best lightly chilled – putting it in the refrigerator for 30 minutes before serving will usually give the correct temperature. It should never be iced or served with ice in it. On the other hand, red wine is much better served at, or just below, room temperature. Leave the bottle to stand in a room with a temperature of about 18°C (65°F) for several hours before serving. Red wine is also best if it is uncorked about an hour before serving, to allow the air to get to it. A young wine may even benefit from being opened 2–3 hours before serving. Be careful not to warm wine too quickly or let it become over-heated as this will spoil the flavour. If you do not have the time to allow the wine to come to room temperature gradually, do not stand it on a radiator or hold it under a hot tap, as this could ruin it. Instead, warm an empty decanter in hot water, then carefully decant the wine into it.

If you are serving a fine old wine that has formed a large amount of sediment in the bottle, it will be necessary to decant it to prevent the wine becoming cloudy as the bottle is moved around during serving. Carefully pour the wine from the sediment into a decanter in one steady movement. Decanting also helps to 'air' the wine in the same way as uncorking it well in advance. If you are serving a cheap brand name wine, a carafe is a perfectly acceptable way of disguising its origins without giving it pretensions.

Although custom and fashion suggest using a different type of glass for different types of wine, this is an unnecessary trimming. A glass that allows you to enjoy not only the flavour, but also the aroma and colour of the wine, is suitable for any type of wine from sherry through to port. The choice between the rounded goblet or the taller 'tulip' shape is a matter of personal preference. A wine glass should be large enough to hold a generous helping without being more than half full, so as not to lose the bouquet of the wine the moment it is poured. For the same reason the bowl of the wine glass should be round, cupping slightly towards the top. Finally, the glass should be clear to enable you to see the true colour of the wine and it should have a stem, so that the warmth of your hand does not have to come into contact with the bowl.

COOKING WITH WINE

Wine can be used to add extra flavour to casseroles, soups, sauces and gravies, or may be mixed with other ingredients to make a marinade to tenderise and flavour a joint or a steak.

Using wine in this way need not be as expensive as it may sound. You do not have to use the finest wines, as a modest brand name wine or leftovers will give just as good a flavour to most dishes. Never throw away any wine left in a bottle; simply decant it into a smaller bottle, cork it tightly and keep it for cooking. You can also freeze leftover wine and use it for cooking, although it will no longer be suitable for drinking.

If you do not have any wine opened, dry or medium sherry or dry vermouth can often be used instead. Sherry is ideal for flavouring consommé or chicken soup. You can also pour it over veal or chicken and ignite it to give a rich flavour to the meat and a smooth texture to any sauce or gravy made with the juices from the meat. The lighter flavour of dry vermouth makes it a good substitute in any dish where you would otherwise be using white wine.

Wines are also used in many traditional sweet dishes, such as sherry in trifle, white wine or sherry in syllabub and Marsala in zabaglione. A little white wine or vermouth can be added to cream to give it extra flavour before being poured over a plain sweet. Hard fruits such as pears are excellent poached in red or white wine, while those with a stronger flavour, such as strawberries, are good with port or Marsala.

Any of the shapes illustrated are suitable as general purpose wine glasses. Remember that the glass should be no more than half or two-thirds full so the bouquet of the wine is not lost.

FRANCE	
Alsace	*White:* Fine, dry wines with a distinctive but delicate bouquet. *Examples:* The wines are generally named after the grape type: Gewürz-traminer, Riesling, Sylvaner.
Beaujolais	*Red:* Light-bodied, fruity wines with a distinctive bouquet. *Examples:* Beaujolais, Beaujolais-Villages, Fleurie, Moulin-à-Vent.
Bordeaux	*Red (claret):* Dry, dark, medium-bodied wines which age well. *Examples:* Bordeaux, Médoc (Margaux, Pauillac, Saint-Estèphe, Saint Julien), Saint-Emilion, Pomerol, Côtes de Blaye, Côtes de Bourg, Château Haut-Brion. *White:* Good dry and medium-dry wines and superlative sweet, full-bodied dessert wines. *Examples:* Entre-Deux-Mers (medium dry); Graves (dry); Bordeaux, Barsac, Sauternes (sweet).
Burgundy	*Red:* Full, smooth, fruity wines with a powerful bouquet and full body. *Examples:* Bourgogne, Mâcon, Beaune, Nuits-Saint-Georges, Gevrey Chambertin. *White:* Also smooth fruity wines, with less body than white Bordeaux. *Examples:* Bourgogne, Chablis, Meursault, Mâcon, Pouilly-Fuissé.
Champagne	*White (occasionally pink):* An unsurpassable sparkling wine that may be dry (Brut), medium-dry (Sec) or sweet (Demi-Sec). *Examples:* Sold under the brand names of the various houses, such as Moët et Chandon, Veuve Clicquot.
Côtes du Rhône	*Red:* Big, round, full-bodied wines with great depth of flavour. *Examples:* Côtes-du-Rhône, Côtes-du-Rhône-Villages, Hermitage, Châteauneuf-du-Pape. *Rosé:* Dry and full-flavoured wines. *Examples:* Tavel, Lirac.
Loire	*Red:* Light, dry and fresh wines. *Examples:* Touraine, Bourgeuil, Chinon. *Rosé:* Fragrant, medium-dry wines of excellent quality. *Examples:* Cabernet d'Anjou, Anjou. *White:* Light, dry or very dry wines; some are sparkling. *Examples:* Muscadet, Saumur, Sancerre, Pouilly-Fumé (dry); Vouvray (medium-dry); Coteaux-du-Layon (sweet).

GERMANY	
Moselle	*White:* Fragrant, crisp and delicate wines, best drunk young. Mainly from the Riesling grape. *Examples:* Bernkasteler, Piesporter.
Rhineland	*Red:* Some good, fruity wines, but rarely exported. *White (hock):* Full-flavoured, fine wines; some are sweet, few are thoroughly dry. Styles vary greatly according to the location of the vineyard and the grape; the name of the grape usually appears on the label. *Examples:* Riesling, Sylvaner, Scheurebe, Traminer, Müller-Thurgau.
Franconia	Dryer than most German wines, *Examples:* Steinwein, Mainviereck, Maindreieck, Steigerwald.
Nahe	Flowery, fresh, fruity, well-balanced wines with a clean flavour. *Examples:* Bad Kreuznach, Schloss Böckelheim.
Rheingau	Elegant, delicate, deep-flavoured wines, slow to mature. *Examples:* Kloster Eberbach, Schloss Vollrads, Schloss Johannisberg.
Rheinhessen	Slightly earthy, soft, sweetish wines. *Examples:* Liebfraumilch, Niersteiner, Oppenheimer.
Rheinpfalz	Varying widely, but generally fuller wines, some are sweet. *Examples:* Bad Dürkheim

ITALY	
Piedmont	*Red:* Dry, full-flavoured wines, often with a strong bouquet. *Examples:* Barolo, Barbaresco, Barbera, Nebbiolo. *White:* Dry, light, sparkling wines. *Examples:* Asti Spumante.
Tuscany	*Red:* Fruity, robust wines, coarse when drunk young (as they often are), but can be fine when aged. *Examples:* Chianti, Chianti Classico. *White:* Strong, dry wines, pleasant but rather earthy. *Examples:* Chianti.
Umbria	*White:* Soft, light wines, varying from medium-dry to rather sweet. *Examples:* Orvieto.
Veneto	*Red:* Lighter wines, with a soft, fresh flavour and bouquet. *Examples:* Valpolicella, Bardolino. *White:* Dry, fruity, fragrant wines. *Examples:* Soave, Terlano.

Wines

SPAIN	
Rioja	*Red (tinto)*: Smooth, rich wines with a full, dry flavour; some are [...] 'Reserva' Riojas are superb. [...] [rosado]: Excellent, subtle, fresh wines. *White (blanco)*: Dry wines better than the sweet, varying from delicate to full-bodied. *Examples*: Most Riojas are blends, the labels bearing the brand names of companies such as C.V.N.E. (North Spain Wine Company), Marqués de Riscal, Marqués de Murrieta, Federico Paternina, Bodegas Bilbainas, Bodegas Riojanas, Bodegas Franco-Españolas.
Catalonia	*Red*: Pleasant dry or slightly sweet wines. *Examples*: Tinto Abocado, Gran Coronas Reserva. *White*: Dry and sweet wines. *Example*: Viña Sol. *White, sparkling (blanco espumoso)*: Fine, fresh wines made by the champagne method. They may be dry, very dry or medium. *Examples*: Codorniu, Freixenet, Marqués de Monistrol. *Rosé, sparkling (rosado espumoso)*: Agreeable fruity wines, made by the champagne method, these are usually on the dry side. *Examples*: Torres, Codorníu, Freixenet, San Sadurní de Noya.
Navarre	*Red and white*: Strong, heavy wines, mainly dry. *Examples*: Senorio de Sarría, Las Campañas.
Valdepeñas	Good, light, red and white wines, generally drunk young.

FORTIFIED WINES	
Port	Made in Portugal from grapes grown in the upper valley of the Douro river. Port is partially fermented wine fortified with brandy; most is sweet. Port is usually served as a dessert wine, though white port may be chilled and served as an aperitif.
Vintage port	This is made from unblended wine, bottled after 2 years and matured in the bottle for 10–20 years.

FORTIFIED WINES *(continued)*	
Wood ports	These are wines from different years, blended and matured in the [...] tawny port, which may be a ruby that has matured to a fine, old port, or a blend of ruby port with an older wine; and white port which is made from white grapes.
Sherry	Sherry derives its name from Jerez de la Frontera, the southern Spanish town at the centre of the production of sherry. California, South Africa, Australia and Cyprus also produce their own type of 'sherry'. All are blends of wine, fortified with brandy and matured in casks. There are five main types:
Fino	A dry, pale-coloured wine, usually chilled and served as an aperitif.
Manzanilla	A delicate fino with a distinctive flavour. Served as an aperitif.
Amontillado	A matured fino with a deep fragrance, a darker gold colour and less dryness than fino. Generally served as an aperitif, but also drunk at other times.
Oloroso	A tawny-gold sherry with a rich bouquet. A genuine oloroso is dry, but many are sweetened for export as after-dinner sherry.
Brown sherries	Sweet, dark sherries, often called 'milk' or 'cream' indicating the richness of the texture of the wine. Usually drunk as dessert wines.
Madeira	Fortified dessert wine from the Portuguese island of Madeira. There are four main types corresponding to the grapes from which they are made:
Sercial	This is the driest and lightest Madeira; a pleasant aperitif.
Verdelho	A medium-dry wine, darker in colour and softer than Sercial; served before and after meals.
Bual	A velvety, medium-sweet, deep golden wine, ideal with dessert.
Malmsey	A rich, dark, sweet wine, drunk after dinner but also at other times.
Marsala	The famous wine of Sicily is made from a blend of local wines, brandy and unfermented grape juice. There are dry as well as sweet Marsalas, though these are rarely exported.

USEFUL
INFORMATION

Entertaining

Impromptu entertaining can be fun, but it can also be nerve-racking. Things will be easier all round, for host, hostess and guests, if parties are planned ahead: 2 weeks is enough time for your own preparations but 3-4 weeks notice is more likely to find the right people free on the right day. For a larger party you will want at least 4 weeks, to be sure of fitting everything in.

INVITATIONS

Invitations for an informal dinner party are normally given by telephone. This is also perfectly acceptable for larger, casual parties but it can take a lot of time and effort to telephone everybody involved, so most people opt for written invitations. Don't forget that your invitations should state not only the time and place, but also what type of party it will be, such as 'Buffet Supper', 'Lunch', 'Cheese and Wine', 'Snacks' or whatever is appropriate. An invitation to sherry or cocktails automatically assumes that only small cocktail snacks will be served.

Although a written invitation to a formal party such as a wedding or coming-of-age should normally receive a written reply, a note at the bottom that says 'R.S.V.P.' and gives your telephone number is often appreciated. Keep a list of the people you have invited and check them off as they reply, so that you can add up the numbers at the last moment.

DINNER PARTIES

When the hostess is cooking and serving without help, a simple, three-course meal is quite acceptable, even for comparatively formal dinner parties at home; cheese and fresh fruit may be offered as extras after the dessert. Keep the menu simple, selecting recipes that need the minimum of last minute preparation. It worries guests if the hostess has to spend long periods out of the room, attending to details in the kitchen.

As far as possible, choose dishes that will not spoil if kept waiting for late guests, or if the conversation over the main course is so absorbing that dessert is 10 minutes later than you expected. Think carefully how many hot dishes you can accommodate in your oven, along with the plates and dishes that have to be preheated for serving hot food. This usually means that at least one course and probably two will have to be cold. If you really want a hot starter as well as a hot main course, choose one that can be cooked on top of the stove, to relieve the pressure on oven space.

Plan also for balance within the meal;

make sure that the same major ingredient does not feature in more than one course. Try to produce a menu that gives variety of textures and flavours; follow a spicy dish with a mild one, serve a creamy dish accompanied by a crisp salad. And if you are in any doubt about the universal acceptability of any dish (shellfish, for instance, are difficult – some people are allergic to them) have a simple alternative on hand so that there need be no embarrassment. Pay attention, too, to the colours of the foods, look for contrasting colours and choose vegetables and garnishes with an eye to brightening up the presentation of the central dish.

Having planned your menu in good time, spread the rest of the preparation over several days. Make a list of the foods you need, check the store cupboard and shop for groceries and wines well ahead. If you want a special cut of meat, tell the butcher in advance; order any fresh vegetables and fruit to avoid disappointment on the day. Check the table linen and silver and attend to any special cleaning and polishing a day or two ahead of the occasion.

On the day itself, pick and arrange flowers and get the food preparation under control as early as possible. You may well think about the menu and decide 'I can easily do all that in 2 hours'; but if you leave it all until 6 o'clock before you start you will end up after your 2 hours, red-faced and steaming, totally unable to enjoy the occasion. Much better to work out an approximate timetable that lets you do all possible preparation in the morning, or the evening before if you are out working during the day, leaving only the final cooking for the evening. A checklist next to the cooker will ensure that nothing gets forgotten.

LARGE PARTIES

A buffet meal or drinks party will be your choice if you want to entertain a larger number of people. For these, the preparations are more complicated. Not only do you have to plan the food and drink, but you will need more than the normal household equipment for serving, and you will have to think carefully about how you are going to arrange the serving tables, bar and seating.

Glasses and china: Most off-licences will lend you glasses free of charge if you buy your wines and spirits from them. If yours does not, you can usually hire glasses, or it may be worth buying a cheap set of party glasses.

China is not quite so easy. For that you will need to find a hire company; the Yellow Pages section of the telephone directory is usually a good source. The same company will also be able to supply cutlery, ash-trays and so on. Don't forget serving dishes and trays.

Food and wines: Order wines and spirits well ahead, preferably on a sale or return basis. There is nothing worse than running out of wine, but it can work out very expensive if you over-order without making arrangements for returning unopened bottles. It is sensible not to offer too great a variety of drinks. For instance, a simple choice of red or white wine makes serving much easier and cuts down the cost in the end as the number of leftovers can be carefully controlled.

Plan to serve a high proportion of cold foods that can be prepared at least a day ahead, with a simple hot dish such as a soup that can be cooked ahead and reheated at the last moment. For menu ideas and guidance on setting a buffet table, see page 481.

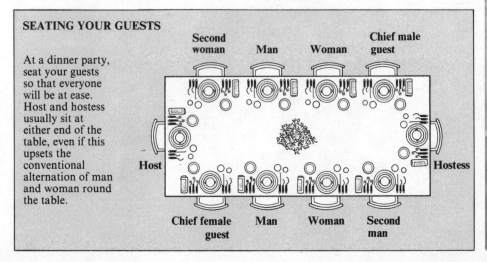

SEATING YOUR GUESTS

At a dinner party, seat your guests so that everyone will be at ease. Host and hostess usually sit at either end of the table, even if this upsets the conventional alternation of man and woman round the table.

Second woman · Man · Woman · Chief male guest

Host

Hostess

Chief female guest · Man · Woman · Second man

Brunch

Conveniently timed for late morning, yet early enough to allow for an afternoon of activity, brunch unites the good qualities of both lunch and breakfast. It is an ideal way of introducing weekend guests to local friends, or merely of anticipating a quiet Sunday. A selection of fresh fruit or a fruit drink may be served before the main dish. Alcoholic drinks are optional.

Birthday Brunch
12 servings

Buck's Fizz (orange juice with
Champagne)
Quiche Lorraine *page 156* (*make two*)
Creamed Finnan Haddie *page 180*
(*double quantity*)
Mixed Green Salad Bowl *page 318*
(*double quantity*)
Kolacky *page 443* (*make two*)
Coffee, served with crème de cacao,
brandy or whipped cream
Tea

Weekend Brunch
4 servings

Orange Juice
Baked Eggs *page 143*
Fried Sausages
Fried Apple Wedges *page 301*
Quick Muffins, toasted *page 424*
Coffee   Tea

Bacon Brunch
8 servings

Party Bloody Mary *page 473*
Chilled Apple Juice
Beignets *page 425*
Fried Eggs *page 143*
Fried Bacon
Coffee   Tea

Family Brunch
8 servings

Gingered Melon Wedges *page 310*
(*double quantity*)
Chicken Vol-au-Vents *page 269*
(*double quantity*)
Nut Bread and Butter *page 428*
Coffee   Tea

American-style Brunch
8 servings

Pineapple Juice
Waffles with Maple Syrup *page 427*
(*double quantity*)
Fried Sausages
Coffee   Tea

Quick and Easy Brunch
4 servings

Vegetable Cocktail Juice
Welsh Rarebit *page 154*
Waldorf Salad *page 322*
Coffee   Tea

Lunch

A lunch need be neither large nor elaborate to be considered a party. A light soup or fruit first course could be followed by a cold salad with hot bread and a rich dessert, or a hot casserole or hearty soup plus bread and a light dessert. If you prefer to miss the first course, serve a hot main dish with salad and a dessert.

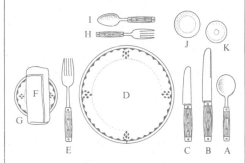

A. *Soup spoon*; B. *Main course knife*;
C. *Bread and butter knife*; D. *Liner plate for soup bowl*; E. *Main course fork*; F. *Napkin*;
G. *Side plate*; H. *Dessert fork*; I. *Dessert spoon*; J. *Water glass*; K. *Wine glass*

Lunch à la Marseillaise
6 servings

Bouillabaisse *page 137*
French Bread *page 436*
Spinach Salad with Lemon and
Mustard Dressing *page 318*
Cream Puff Ring *page 367*
Dry White Wine   Coffee

Winter Lunch
6 servings

Marinated Artichoke Hearts with
Mushrooms *page 319*
Simmered Chicken with Pasta *page 268*
French Beans with Thyme *page 280*
Crusty Rolls
Perfection Salad *page 323*
Oranges à la Turque *page 312*
Red Wine   Coffee

Business Lunch
4 servings

Crème Vichyssoise *page 130*
Roast Rack of Lamb with Apricot
Glaze *page 227*
Herby Baked Tomatoes *page 297*
Caesar Salad *page 318*
Strawberries Romanoff *page 305*
Red Wine   Coffee

Seafood Salad Lunch
4 servings

Crab Louis *page 325*
Plaited Herb Bread *page 437*
Cinnamon Apricots in Cream *page 302*
Brandy Snaps *page 407*

White Wine Coffee

Tea

Entertaining at tea-time is a delightful habit that gives a feeling of leisure in a life of rushing about. Tea should not be a heavy meal, but you have to provide variety, so make sure that everything comes, or can be divided into, small portions. Cut tiny sandwiches, with thinly sliced bread, ringing the changes between white and wholemeal breads. If you are serving a large cake, it may be either a creamy gâteau or a plainer cake. Tiny cakes or pastries, some home-made biscuits, cookies and sweets will add a touch of luxury.

In winter, a hot fireside tea is welcome. For this, toasted sandwiches or toasted muffins and crumpets, with butter and home-made jam are ideal.

As well as the conventional tea with milk, be prepared to offer tea with lemon for those who prefer it, and in the summer consider iced tea as a refreshing afternoon drink.

Fireside Tea
12 servings

Quick Muffins, toasted with butter
page 424
Strawberry Jam *page 467*
Honey
Apricot Coffeecake *page 443*
Scotch Pancakes *page 426*
Tea, with milk or lemon

Luxury Snack Tea
12 servings

Sponge Fingers with Whipped Cream
page 389
Deep-fried Walnuts *page 114*
Assorted Candied Fruits: orange slices,
apricots, figs, dates, pineapple
Indian and China Tea, with milk or
lemon

Village Party
20 servings

Pâté Pinwheels *page 459*
Tongue Salad Sandwiches *page 459*
Lemon Teabread *page 428*
Neapolitan Cookies *page 411*
Shell Cookies *page 409*
Chocolate-dipped Fruit *page 420*
Tea, with milk or lemon

Birthday Tea
12 servings

Ribbon Sandwiches *page 459*
Cream Cheese on Raisin Bread squares
page 443
Marzipan Fruits *page 419*
Tiny Meringues with Whipped Cream
Sachertorte *page 394*
Tea, with milk or lemon

Entertaining

Dinner

A dinner party is the perfect way to entertain people you would like to know better. The meal provides the centre of the party and a careful choice of guests, combining old friends with new acquaintances, should keep the conversation flowing easily. If you plan the menu and meal preparation well, you should have plenty of time to relax and talk to all your guests.

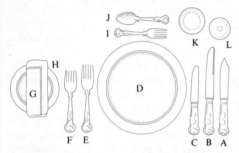

A. *Fish knife*; B. *Dinner knife*; C. *Bread and butter knife*; D. *Liner plate for first course*; E. *Dinner fork*; F. *Fish fork*; G. *Napkin*; H. *Side plate*; I. *Dessert fork*; J. *Dessert spoon*; K. *Water glass*; L. *Wine glass*

Friday Special Dinner
4 servings

Chicken and Rice Soup *page 130*
Marinated Halibut Steaks *page 182*
Creamed Parsnips *page 291*
Buttery Cucumber Rings *page 286*
Runner Beans
Lemon Meringue Pie *page 351*
Hock   Coffee

Mid-summer Party Dinner
6 servings

Chilled Cucumber Soup *page 129*
Sole Stuffed with Prawns *page 180*
Château Potatoes *page 293*
Stir-fried Broccoli *page 282*
Marinated Watermelon *page 310*
Dry White Wine   Coffee

Greek Dinner
8 servings

Spanakopitas *page 121*
Chicken Avgolemono *page 259*
(*double quantity*)
Greek Salad *page 320*
Baklava *page 371*
Retsina   Coffee

Chafing Dish Dinner
6 servings

Fried Oysters *page 161*
Turkey in Cider with Toast Flowers
page 260
Zesty Tangerine Salad *page 315*
(*use 9 tangerines*)
Walnut Tarts *page 357*
Cider

Anniversary Dinner
6 servings

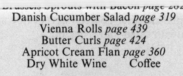

Brussels Sprouts with Bacon *page 282*
Danish Cucumber Salad *page 319*
Vienna Rolls *page 439*
Butter Curls *page 424*
Apricot Cream Flan *page 360*
Dry White Wine   Coffee

Traditional English Dinner
6 servings

Cream of Mushroom Soup *page 131*
Roast Rib of Beef with Yorkshire
Pudding *page 191*
Potatoes au Gratin *page 294*
Simmered Carrots and Celery *page 298*
Sherry Trifle *page 372*
Cheese Board
Claret   Coffee

Italian-style Dinner
4 servings

Tortellini in Cream Sauce *page 335*
Veal Escalopes with Lemon *page 236*
Risotto alla Milanese *page 339*
Pepper and Tomato Sauté *page 299*
Braised Fennel *page 287*
Italian Bread Sticks
Strawberry-orange Ice *page 381*
Chianti   Coffee

Parisian-style Dinner
4 servings

Artichokes with Béarnaise Sauce
page 277
Coq au Vin *page 257*
Potatoes Anna *page 294*
Sorrel Salad
French Bread
Camembert with fresh Pears
Burgundy   Coffee

Steak Dinner
6 servings

Dressed Crab *page 166*
Fillet Steak with Mustard-caper Sauce
page 195
Baked Potatoes *page 293* (*6 potatoes*)
French Beans with Courgettes and
Bacon *page 299*
Sesame Seed Bread *page 438*
Pears in White Wine *page 313*
Burgundy   Coffee

Retirement Dinner
8 servings

Eggs en Gelée *page 141*
(*double quantity*)
Individual Beef Wellingtons *page 192*
Peas
Cauliflower Polonaise *page 284*
Tomatoes Vinaigrette *page 319*
(*double quantity*)
Watermelon Ice *page 381*
Claret   Coffee

Chicken Dinner
6 servings

Party Chicken and Prawns *page 255*
Simmered Carrots and Celery *page 298*
California Salad *page 318*
Chocolate Cream Pie *page 353*
Dry White Wine   Coffee

Family Celebration Dinner
12 servings

Fresh Grapefruit
Roast Stuffed Turkey *page 249*
Spiced Carrots *page 284*
(*double quantity*)
Onions in Cream Sauce *page 291*
(*double quantity*)
Brussels Sprouts with Buttered Crumbs
page 282 (*double quantity*)
Cranberry and Apple Relish *page 305*
Chipolata Sausages
Strawberry Shortcake *page 369*
Apple Pie *page 346*
Whipped Cream
Red and White Burgundy   Coffee

Mexican-style Dinner
6 servings

Guacamole *page 124*
Soured Cream Chicken Enchiladas
page 270
Mixed Fruit Salad
Pecan Pie *page 356*
Beer   Coffee

Coffee Morning

Whether a purely social occasion or a fund-raising event for charity, a coffee morning provides the perfect opportunity for a chat and a snack. Most people will not want a lot to eat, but will be tempted by attractive pastries or cookies. Experiment with some interesting recipes.

Fund Raiser
24 servings

Danish Almond Cookies *page 409*
Boston Brownies *page 404*
Chocolate Cookies *page 406*
Chelsea Buns *page 444* (*double quantity*)
Apricot Butterfly Rolls *page 445*
Cherry Teabread *page 430* (*make two*)
Coffee, with choice of hot milk or cream

Neighbourhood Coffee Morning
12 servings

Danish Pastries *pages 450–451*
Luscious Apricot Squares *page 404*
Quick Ring Doughnuts *page 425*
(*half quantity*)
Vienna Cookies *page 410*
Raspberry Thumbprints *page 410*
Coffee, with choice of
hot milk or cream

Buffet Party

If you are entertaining a larger number of people but still want to provide a full meal, a buffet party will be your choice. Try to choose food that can be eaten easily without a table; a full set of cutlery should be available, but guests will find it much easier if they are able to eat with fork alone. Select a variety of savoury and sweet foods, some hot as well as cold dishes, and concentrate on setting the buffet table attractively, so that it will be the centre of attraction.

Summer Buffet Party
16 servings

Prawn Soup *page 132* (*triple quantity*)
Dinner Rolls *page 439* (*double quantity*)
Chicken Galantine *page 250* (*make 2*)
Roast Sirloin of Beef, sliced
Horseradish Cream *page 185*
Mixed Salad Vegetables; pepper strips, celery sticks, tomato wedges, cucumber wedges, sweetcorn kernels
Mayonnaise *page 462*
Meringue Basket with Fresh Fruit and Whipped Cream *page 364*
French Apple Flan *page 348*
Red or White Wine

Turkey Buffet
20 servings

Blue Cheese Dip *page 124*
Basket of Vegetables for Dipping
Hot Mushroom Turnovers *page 118*
Boned and Stuffed Turkey *page 251*
Caesar Salad *page 318*
(*4 × recipe quantity*)
Coleslaw Bowl *page 319*
(*4 × recipe quantity*)
Hot Potato Salad *page 320*
(*4 × recipe quantity*)
Party Marinated Watermelon *page 310*
Raspberry Ribbon Flan *page 354*
(*make 2*)
White Wine

Champagne Buffet
12 servings

Tiny Pâté-stuffed Tomatoes *page 126*
(*double quantity*)
Smoked Salmon Squares *page 115*
Blue Cheese and Aspic Canapés
page 116
Pineapple Glazed Baked Ham *page 220*
Salmon Mousse *page 184*
Baked Chicken *page 252*
(*double quantity*)
Assorted Salads: green pepper strips, tomato wedges, lettuce, spinach, cucumber; French Dressing
Chocolate and Cinnamon Torte
page 373
Minted Sherbet Ring *page 380*
(*make two*)
Champagne
Cheese Board
Coffee

Hot Fork Dinner
8 servings

Lemon Fruit Salad *page 322*
(*double quantity*)
Manicotti *page 334* (*double quantity*)
Baked Creamed Spinach *page 295*
(*double quantity*)
Canteloup Water Ice *page 310*
Valpolicella

Hot and Cold Buffet
12 servings

Bagna Cauda *page 125*
Cheese Spreads *page 124*
with assorted savoury biscuits
Rolled and Glazed Turkey Roast
page 250
Spiced Nectarine Slices *page 311*
Ratatouille *page 298* (*double quantity*)
Coleslaw Bowl *page 319*
(*double quantity*)
Chocolate and Walnut Layer Cake
page 387
Orange Praline Mousse *page 312*
Citrus Punch *page 471*

Cocktail Party

This is definitely an occasion for finger food only. Whether you have half a dozen friends seated in comfort or a large group of people jostling shoulder to shoulder, the food must be easy to handle without cutlery. Dips with vegetables or potato crisps for dunking and canapés are ideal; and one hot appetiser is always welcome.

Saturday Evening Drinks
6 servings

Fresh Vegetables with Peppery Mayonnaise Dip *page 124*
Scallops and Bacon *page 163*
Egg and Roe Rounds *page 115*
Salted Nuts and Pretzels
Cocktails

Sunday Cocktail Party
20–25 servings

Cheese Twists *page 114*
Fresh Vegetables with Chilli-tomato Dip *page 125*
Pissaladière *page 117*
Chicken Liver Pâté on Toast *page 122*
Pepper and Herb Cream Cheese
page 123
Crackers and Crispbreads
Tuna and Dill Rounds *page 115*
Steak Bites *page 119*
Cocktails

OPENING A CHAMPAGNE BOTTLE

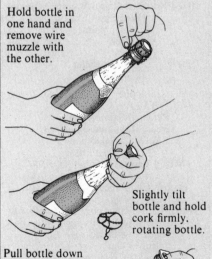

Hold bottle in one hand and remove wire muzzle with the other.

Slightly tilt bottle and hold cork firmly, rotating bottle.

Pull bottle down gently and slowly to reduce internal pressure Cork will come out with a soft 'pop'. Wipe rim before serving.

SETTING UP A BUFFET

Arrange the table so that guests can move easily around it, progressing naturally from plates and cutlery to the main dishes and the side dishes. If you wish to include the desserts on the same table, put them where they can be reached after other dishes are cleared away.

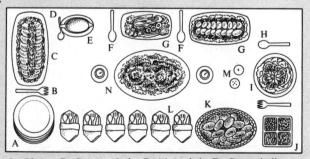

A. *Plates*; B. *Serving fork*; C. *Main dish*; D. *Sauce ladle*;
E. *Sauce boat*; F. *Serving spoon*; G. *Vegetable dish*;
H. *Salad servers*; I. *Salad bowl*; J. *Pickles and relishes*;
K. *Roll basket*; L. *Napkins and cutlery*; M. *Salt and pepper*;
N. *Centrepiece and candles*

Entertaining

Wedding Reception

A wedding reception is a grand occasion, when all the family will be nervous. It is essential to keep the menu simple, to be sure that nothing can go wrong. For a really large party, choose finger food only, a good variety of savoury and sweet tit-bits.will keep everybody happy and chatting over the Champagne. For a smaller number, it is reasonable to attempt a more substantial buffet meal, but avoid anything that needs last minute attention.

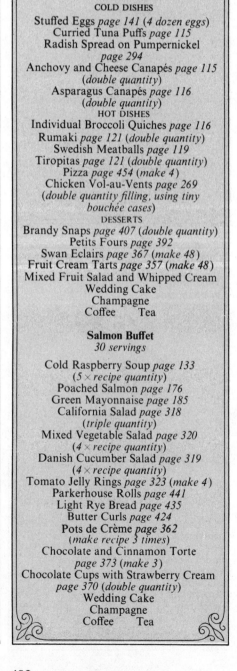

Finger Buffet
100 servings

COLD DISHES

Stuffed Eggs *page 141 (4 dozen eggs)*
Curried Tuna Puffs *page 115*
Radish Spread on Pumpernickel *page 294*
Anchovy and Cheese Canapés *page 115 (double quantity)*
Asparagus Canapés *page 116 (double quantity)*

HOT DISHES

Individual Broccoli Quiches *page 116*
Rumaki *page 121 (double quantity)*
Swedish Meatballs *page 119*
Tiropitas *page 121 (double quantity)*
Pizza *page 454 (make 4)*
Chicken Vol-au-Vents *page 269 (double quantity filling, using tiny bouchée cases)*

DESSERTS

Brandy Snaps *page 407 (double quantity)*
Petits Fours *page 392*
Swan Eclairs *page 367 (make 48)*
Fruit Cream Tarts *page 357 (make 48)*
Mixed Fruit Salad and Whipped Cream
Wedding Cake
Champagne
Coffee   Tea

Salmon Buffet
30 servings

Cold Raspberry Soup *page 133 (5 × recipe quantity)*
Poached Salmon *page 176*
Green Mayonnaise *page 185*
California Salad *page 318 (triple quantity)*
Mixed Vegetable Salad *page 320 (4 × recipe quantity)*
Danish Cucumber Salad *page 319 (4 × recipe quantity)*
Tomato Jelly Rings *page 323 (make 4)*
Parkerhouse Rolls *page 441*
Light Rye Bread *page 435*
Butter Curls *page 424*
Pots de Crème *page 362 (make recipe 3 times)*
Chocolate and Cinnamon Torte *page 373 (make 3)*
Chocolate Cups with Strawberry Cream *page 370 (double quantity)*
Wedding Cake
Champagne
Coffee   Tea

NAPKIN FOLDING

Add a decorative touch to your dinner table by folding napkins into one of the shapes below. Use starched linen or large,

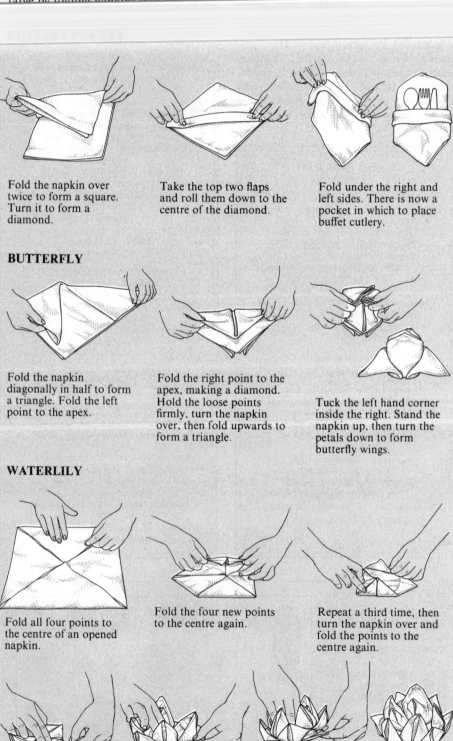

CUTLERY POCKET

Fold the napkin over twice to form a square. Turn it to form a diamond.

Take the top two flaps and roll them down to the centre of the diamond.

Fold under the right and left sides. There is now a pocket in which to place buffet cutlery.

BUTTERFLY

Fold the napkin diagonally in half to form a triangle. Fold the left point to the apex.

Fold the right point to the apex, making a diamond. Hold the loose points firmly, turn the napkin over, then fold upwards to form a triangle.

Tuck the left hand corner inside the right. Stand the napkin up, then turn the petals down to form butterfly wings.

WATERLILY

Fold all four points to the centre of an opened napkin.

Fold the four new points to the centre again.

Repeat a third time, then turn the napkin over and fold the points to the centre again.

Hold the centre firmly with your fingers, unfold a petal from underneath each corner.

Pull out four more petals between the first four; then pull out four more under the first petals.

The water lily now has 12 points.

Eating outdoors

Cooking outdoors on a barbecue is great fun for casual entertaining. Choose foods with robust flavours and use brightly coloured picnic plates and cups. Provide plenty of paper napkins for greasy fingers. At some parties the host does the cooking; at others, guests cook their own portions.

BARBECUE TOOLS

Brush

Skewers

Barbecue tongs   Oven mitts   Foil

SAFETY TIPS
Never use a charcoal grill indoors, or anywhere where there may not be adequate ventilation, such as in a garage, porch, tent or caravan; the carbon monoxide fumes given off are lethal. Position the barbecue away from the house and dry grass or bushes. Never leave the fire unattended.

BARBECUING TIPS
Several types of charcoal are available. The cheaper charcoal chips are easiest to light and give a good heat quickly, but they also burn away quite quickly; choose these if you are cooking only two or three steaks or chops. Briquettes of compressed charcoal are more difficult to light, and more expensive, but they give a longer lasting fire for cooking larger quantities.

Use enough charcoal to give a good, even layer in the fire box throughout cooking; you cannot add extra charcoal to the fire without lowering the cooking temperature. To get the fire started quickly, heap the charcoal into a pyramid. Use a proprietary charcoal lighter to start it, choosing from the liquid, solid or jelly types available; NEVER use petrol, paraffin, methylated spirits or any other highly volatile fuel. Light the fire at least 30 minutes before you want to start cooking, to give the coals time to get really hot. You should not cook while the charcoal is flaring; wait until it is reduced to embers, glowing red at night or lightly covered with grey ash in daylight.

When the coals are burning strongly, spread them out in an even layer in the bed of the fire box. Just before you are ready to cook, put the grid in position to heat up. To raise the temperature during cooking, you can either place the grid closer to the coals, or rake the coals together into a heap; to lower the temperature, move the grid further away or spread the coals out a little.

Fatty meat dripping on to the charcoal may cause flaring. Minimise this by tilting the cooking grid, so that fat runs down the wires and off at the edge of the fire. In the case of a real flare-up, remove the grid altogether and spray the fire with water from a plastic spray bottle.

Fisherman's Barbecue
6 servings

Grilled Sesame Trout *page 174*
Potatoes Baked in Charcoal
Grilled Courgette Halves
Mixed Bean Salad *page 321*
Cheese Scones *page 423*
Iced Melon
Iced Coffee
Sparkling White Wine

Chicken and Sweetcorn Barbecue
4 servings

Yogurt and Cream Cheese Dip *page 125*
Potato Crisps
Breadsticks
Vegetable Chunks
Savoury Chicken *page 261*
Corn-on-the-cob with Chive Butter
page 296
Sliced Tomatoes and French Beans
with French Dressing
Chocolate Feather Sponge Cake
page 389
Lemon Drink *page 471*
Iced Lager

Cheap and Cheerful Barbecue
4 servings

Barbecued Spareribs *page 216*
Braised Mixed Vegetables *page 298*
(*cooked in foil over the fire*)
Broad Beans with Soured Cream
page 279
Wholemeal Rolls
Poached Pears with Melba Sauce
Soft Drinks   Beer

Steak Grill
4 servings

Stuffed Eggs *page 141*
Devilled Porterhouse Steak *page 197*
Stir-fried Cabbage and Courgettes
page 299
Turkish Bean Salad *page 321*
Cherry and Kirsch Flan *page 355*
Red Wine
Pineapple Crush *page 471*

Picnics
Whether you are planning a light lunch on the beach, or a gala picnic for an annual sporting occasion, proper food preparation and packing are important. In hot weather, food left standing around will quickly rise to unsafe temperatures, leading to possible food poisoning. To ensure that picnic foods are safe as well as delicious, follow our packing suggestions.

Choose foods that keep well and can be eaten easily without a table. Cold roast chicken portions, marinated vegetable salads and fancy breads and pastries are favourites. Keep cooked foods in the refrigerator until the last minute before you leave the house. Carry hot and iced foods in vacuum containers and put a plastic box of ice cubes, or frozen ice-packs, in your insulated picnic bag or box. Divide food into convenient portions, so that you need only take out into the sun what is going to be eaten immediately; bring food out of the cool box only as needed.

Family Picnic
8 servings

Hot Peppery Walnuts *page 114*
Chilled Meat Loaf *page 207*
Cocktail Onions *page 126*
Rice Salad *page 325*
Olives
Cheese Crackers
Pineapple Upside-down Cake *page 384*
Soft Drinks   Red Wine

Point-to-Point Lunch
4 servings

Cream of Green Pea Soup *page 130*
Pâté de Campagne *page 122*
Herbed Mushrooms *page 126*
Salade Niçoise *page 324*
Onion Crackers *page 431*
Brie with Seedless Grapes
Rosé Wine

Beach Party
6 servings

Gazpacho *page 129*
Chicken or Turkey Salad *page 269*
Alfalfa Sprouts
Pitta Bread *page 447*
Cucumber and Carrot Sticks
Walnut Bars *page 404*
Apple Juice

Silverstone Picnic
6 servings

Tuna Dip *page 125*
Italian Cheese and Ham Pie *page 157*
Caponata *page 300*
Bananas or Nectarines
Madeira Cake *page 386*
Beer   Soft Drinks

Herbs and spices

Pick or buy fresh herbs as close as possible to the time you intend to use them as they wilt quickly. Dried herbs and spices will usually keep for up to 6 months but are best bought in small quantities; store them in tightly sealed containers in a cool, dry place. Smell them from time to time: if the aroma has gone, the

flavour will have gone too and they should be thrown away.

Fresh herbs have a milder flavour than dried, and quantities should be adjusted accordingly when following a recipe. As a rough guide, 15 ml (1 level tbsp) dried herbs are equivalent to 45 ml (3 level tbsp) chopped fresh herbs.

NAME	CHARACTERISTICS	USES
Allspice	Whole dark berries, larger than peppercorns, or ground, with flavour like a blend of cloves, cinnamon, nutmeg.	Whole in meat and fish dishes. Ground in pickles and relishes, cakes, fruit pies and milk puddings.
Aniseed	Whole seeds or ground, with strong flavour and aroma.	Use sparingly in salad dressings and some vegetable dishes, with fruit and in cakes, biscuits and pastry.
Basil	Fresh or dried, broken or ground leaves with pungent flavour and sweet aroma.	Use in raw or cooked tomato dishes and sauces; also in salads, in lamb dishes and with asparagus, green beans and broccoli.
Bay Leaves	Whole, fresh or dried leaves or ground, with strong flavour (especially if whole leaves are torn or crushed); ingredient in bouquet garni.	In meat and poultry dishes, particularly soups, pot roasts and stews; in fish and vegetable dishes; in pickles and in stuffings for poultry and meat.
Caraway Seed	Whole seeds with warm, sweet, slightly sharp taste.	In breads; in cheese spreads and dips, sauerkraut, sweet pickles; as garnish for breads, cheese, coleslaw.
Cardamom	Whole pods with seeds, ground seeds and pod, or seeds only, whole and ground; sweet, highly aromatic flavour.	In pickles and curries, beef and pork dishes; in bread, buns, biscuits and cakes and with fruit.
Celery Seed	Small whole seeds or ground, with slightly bitter, fresh-celery flavour; combined with salt to make celery salt.	In meat, cheese, egg and fish dishes; in barbecue sauces, pickles, soups and salad dressings.
Chervil	Fresh or dried leaves similar to parsley but with subtler, faintly sweet flavour reminiscent of tarragon.	In egg, cheese and chicken dishes, with vegetables, in soups, salads, meat sauces and stews.
Chilli Powder	Blend of spices with chilli pepper as basic ingredient.	In meat dishes, especially Spanish or Mexican style and curries; in pickles, barbecue sauces, cocktail dips and salad dressings, snack foods and seafood dishes.

NAME	CHARACTERISTICS	USES
Chives	Member of the onion family. Long, spiky, green leaves, fresh or dried and chopped.	Use wherever delicate onion flavour is wanted: in egg, cheese, fish and poultry dishes; with vegetables and as garnish for salads, soups and cooked vegetables.
Cinnamon	Reddish-brown sticks of rolled bark, or ground, with sweet, pungent aroma.	Sticks in preserving and mulled wines. Ground in cakes, milk puddings and in fruit pies, particularly apple.
Cloves	Whole nail-shaped bud or ground, with pungent, warm, sweet aroma.	Whole to stud roast ham and pork; in fruit punches and mulled wines; pickling fruit and apple pies. Ground in mincemeat and Christmas puddings, milk puddings and biscuits.
Coriander	Whole seeds or ground, with slightly orangey flavour and aroma.	Whole in pickling spice. Ground in pea soup, with roast pork, in casseroles, curries and apple pies.
Cumin	Whole seeds or ground, with strong, slightly bitter flavour.	In Spanish- and Mexican-style meat and rice dishes; in cheese and fish dishes. One of the chief ingredients in curry powder.
Curry Powder	A blend of many spices giving a distinctive flavour; degree of 'heat' depends on blend.	In meat, poultry, seafood, egg and cheese dishes and in soups, sauces and salad dressings.
Dill	Fresh or dried dill weed has distinctive yet mild, caraway-like flavour. Seeds are sharper, slightly bitter.	Dill weed as garnish for salads, in fish and seafood dishes and in casseroles. Dill seeds in pickles, cheese dishes, salad dressings, cocktail dips, with vegetables and potato salads.
Fennel	Whole seeds or ground, with sweet aniseed-like flavour.	With boiled fish or oily fish (to counteract richness); in sauces, dressings, apple dishes.

NAME	CHARACTERISTICS	USES
Ginger	Roots whole, fresh or dried, or dried and ground. Stem or green ginger fresh, or crystallised, or preserved in syrup. Pungent and hot.	Whole root in curries, pickles, sauces. Ground root in curries, preserves, cakes, biscuits, on melon. Stem in Chinese cooking and confectionery.
Mace	Dried, net-like casing around nutmeg, available whole or ground. Flavour and aroma similar to nutmeg but milder.	Whole in pickles and preserves. Ground in sauces, cheese dishes, meat and fish dishes, stewed fruits, hot punches, mulled wines.
Marjoram	Fresh, dried or ground leaves; similar to oregano, with spicy, slightly bitter flavour.	In meat particularly pork, poultry, fish, cheese, egg, vegetable and Italian-style dishes.
Mint	Fresh or dried leaves or flakes, with strong, sweet aroma and cool aftertaste.	Mint sauce or mint jelly to serve with lamb; flavouring for boiled new potatoes and peas; garnish for drinks.
Mustard Seed	Tiny, yellow or brown seeds, whole or powdered. Yellow seeds are odourless; brown seeds have sharp, irritating odour and both have pungent taste when moist.	In a condiment for meat, in pickles and relishes, salad dressings, cheese dishes, curries, cocktail dips, sandwich spreads.
Nutmeg	Large, whole seed, or ground with warm, sweet, aromatic flavour.	In cream soups, hot drinks, vegetable dishes, cakes, cheese dishes, custards and milk puddings.
Oregano	Dried leaves or ground. Flavour and aroma similar to marjoram but stronger.	In Italian-, Greek- and Mexican-style cooking, in meats, salads, dressings, buttered vegetables, egg dishes.
Paprika	There are two varieties: one is sweet and mild, the other has a slight bite. Buy in small amounts – it does not keep.	In meat, poultry, cheese dishes, salad dressings, snack foods, cocktail dips; as garnish for soups, eggs and salads.
Parsley	Fresh leaves and stems (stems contain the most flavour), or dried flakes; mild in flavour.	To flavour and garnish almost any savoury dish, raw or cooked.
Pepper	Black pepper is available as whole peppercorns and cracked or ground. White pepper (the core of the pepperberry) comes whole or ground and is milder.	In most main dishes and main-dish sauces and gravies, salads, salad dressings, snacks, appetisers and pickles.

NAME	CHARACTERISTICS	USES
Pepper, Red	Whole or crushed pods, or ground; varies from mild to intense, cayenne is hottest of all.	Whole in pickles, Mexican dishes. Ground in soups, meat, cheese and shellfish dishes. Use sparingly.
Poppy Seed	Tiny, whole, blue-grey seeds with sweet, mild, nutty flavour and aroma.	In salads and dressings; on vegetables, eggs and pastries, cakes and biscuits. As garnish for cheese dishes and snack foods.
Rosemary	Fresh or dried needle-shaped leaves with pungent tea-like aroma and bitter-sweet flavour.	In meat dishes, particularly lamb; in stuffings and marinades; with vegetables; in salads; as garnish for salads and breads.
Saffron	Dried stamens of a crocus, available as strands or ground. Deep orange in colour, with strong aroma and pleasant, slightly bitter taste.	In poultry, fish and shellfish dishes; in rice and cakes.
Sage	Fresh or dried leaves, rubbed or ground, with pungent, slightly bitter aroma.	In meat dishes, particularly pork and poultry; in sausages and stuffings and with cheese.
Savory	Leaves or ground, with pine-like, almost peppery aroma.	In egg dishes and with beans of all kinds; in tomato sauce and with veal and pork pies.
Sesame	Whole, small, white, flattish seeds with slightly nut-like aroma and flavour. Flavour is heightened by toasting before use.	In green salads, mashed potatoes, on fish or chicken; sprinkle on scones, breads, biscuits before cooking.
Tarragon	Fresh or dried leaves, or rubbed, with a sweet, aromatic flavour and piquant, aniseed-like tang.	In sauces, poultry, seafood, cheese and egg dishes; with vegetables; in salad dressings.
Thyme	Fresh or dried leaves or ground; pungent and aromatic in flavour.	In meat and poultry dishes; in soups, stuffings and salad dressings; on carrots, onions and mushrooms.
Turmeric	Ground root of plant related to ginger, brilliant yellow in colour, with fragrant, peppery aroma and slightly bitter flavour.	An essential ingredient of curry powder and often used in prepared mustard, also in pickles and relishes, salad dressings; used for colouring cakes and rice.

Storage guide

CUPBOARD STORAGE

Your kitchen storage cupboards should be as cool and dry as
possible. The ideal temperature is about 10°C (50°F) so, if you
have any choice in the matter, use cupboards on a cold north or
east-facing wall for food storage. Keep any cupboards over
radiators, or positioned where they catch the afternoon sun for
long periods, for storing china, glassware or saucepans. Cover
the shelves with a surface that can be wiped clean easily, such as
plastic laminate or spongeable shelf paper, and wipe up any
spills as soon as they happen.

STORAGE TIME CHART

Food	Storage Time	Special Notes
Bottled goods		
Gravy browning	1 year	
Sauces	6 months	
Salad oil	18 months	
Pickles and chutneys	1 year	Discard if fermented.
Lemon curd, bought home-made	2–3 months 1 month	
Jams and mincemeat	1 year	If mould occurs, scrape off mouldy part and use up remainder quickly.
Mayonnaise, salad cream (bought)	1 year	If home-made, store in refrigerator.
Honey	6 months	
Vinegar	2 years	
Cake decorations and flavourings		
Flavouring essence	1 year	
Block chocolate or chocolate chips	1 month	
Colourings	1 year	
Silver balls, vermicelli and other decorations	1 month	
Cans		
Fish, meat, fruit and juices	1 year	
Ham, up to 900 g (2 lb)	2 years	Store larger hams in refrigerator and use within 6 months.
Soups (including condensed)	1 year	
Vegetables, canned (including tomato juice and paste)	1 year	
Evaporated milk	6–8 months	
Condensed milk	4–6 months	
Cocoa, drinking chocolate	1 year	
Cereals		
Plain, self raising flour	6 months	Keep in original packet until opened, then transfer to storage jar with lid.
Wheatmeal flour	2–3 months	
Wholemeal flour	1 month	

Food	Storage Time	Special Notes
Cornflour, custard powder	1 year	
Dried vegetables – pearl barley, lentils, peas, beans	1 year	
Oatmeal	1 month	
Rice, sago, tapioca	1 year	
Breakfast cereals	1 month	Reseal opened packets carefully.
Dried fruit		
Currants, sultanas, raisins	2–3 months	Dried fruit will ferment if allowed to get damp.
Prunes, figs, apricots	2–3 months	
Candied peel, glacé cherries	2–3 months	
Herbs, spices and seasonings Allspice, bay leaves, cloves, celery seeds, cinnamon, dried herbs, ginger, mace, mixed spice, curry powder	6 months	Keep in air-tight container in dark cupboard.
Curry paste, mustard, pepper	1 year	
Salt	6 months	Keeps longer if perfectly dry.
Nuts		
Whole almonds, walnuts	1 month	
Ground almonds, shredded coconut	1 month	
Raising agents Baking powder, bicarbonate of soda, cream of tartar	2–3 months	
Dried yeast	6 months	
Sugars and syrups		
Granulated, caster, cubes	1 year	Keep in original packet until opened then transfer to storage jar with lid.
Icing, brown	1 month	
Golden syrup, treacle	1 year	
Miscellaneous		
Coffee (beans)	1 month	Unopened, vacuum-packed will keep for 1 year.
(ground)	1 week	Loose beans and open-pack ground coffee – keep in air-tight container.
Packet soups	1 year	
Dried milk, whole	1 month	Will keep a few weeks after opening if packet is resealed carefully, but inclined to go rancid.
skimmed	2–3 months	
Jellies and gelatine	1 year	
Tea	1 year	Store in original packet until opened, then transfer to air-tight container.

REFRIGERATOR STORAGE

Cover all food before you put it in the refrigerator and, if it has been cooked, allow it to go cold first. Store raw meat, bacon and fish in the coldest part, just under the frozen food compartment; cooked meat dishes should go on the middle shelves, salads and vegetables in the crisper at the bottom. Open the door as infrequently as possible to avoid excessive frosting.

The star rating given by refrigerator and frozen food manufacturers is a useful guide to how long you can keep frozen food in the frozen food compartment of a refrigerator.

Maximum temperature of frozen food compartment		Maximum storage time for:	
		Frozen foods	Ice cream
*	−6°C (21°F)	1 week	1 day
**	−12°C (10°F)	1 month	2 weeks
***	−18°C (0°F)	3 months	3 months

✱*** *indicates the storage temperature of a three star compartment, plus the ability to reduce the temperature to −24°C (−12°F) in order to freeze in fresh food.*

Food	Storage Time	How to Store
DAIRY PRODUCTS		
Fresh milk	3–4 days	In bottle or covered container.
Fresh cream	3–4 days / 2 days	In original container, sealed. Once opened, store in original container, covered.
Milk sweets, custards, etc.	2 days	In covered dishes.
Cultured milk	7 days	In original container.
Fats	2–4 weeks	In original wrapper, in door compartments.
Cheese	1–2 weeks	In original pack, polythene, or foil.
Cream cheese	5–7 days	In covered container, polythene or foil.
EGGS		
Fresh in shell	2 weeks	Small end down. Covered with water if whole.
Yolks	2–3 days	
Whites	3–4 days	In covered container.
Hard-boiled in shell	Up to 1 week	Uncovered.
FISH		
Raw	1–2 days	Covered loosely in polythene or foil.
Cooked	2 days	Covered loosely in polythene or foil. Or place in covered container.
Frozen	Depends on Star Rating	In original pack in frozen food compartment.

Food	Storage Time	How to Store
FRUIT AND VEGETABLES		
Soft fruits	1–3 days	Pick over but do not wash; refrigerate in a covered container.
Hard and stone fruits	3–7 days	Lightly wrapped or in the crisper.
Bananas		Never refrigerate.
Salad vegetables	4–6 days	Clean and drain, store in crisper or lightly wrapped in polythene or in a plastic container.
Greens	3–7 days	Prepare ready for use. Wrap lightly or place in the crisper.
Frozen	Depends on Star Rating	In original pack in frozen food compartment.
MEAT		
Joints	3–5 days	Rinse off any blood and wipe dry. Cover lightly with polythene or foil and refrigerate straight away.
Steaks	2–4 days	
Chops	2–4 days	Wrap tightly in foil or cling film.
Stewing meat	2–4 days	
Smoked ham	1 week	
Offal and mince	1–2 days	
Sliced bacon rashers	7–10 days	
Cooked meats		Wrap in foil or polythene or leave in the covered dish they were cooked in or any other covered container.
Joints	3–5 days	
Casseroles	2–3 days	
POULTRY		
Whole fresh	2–3 days	Draw, wash, dry and wrap loosely in polythene or aluminium foil.
Cooked poultry	2–3 days	Cool; remove stuffing, wrap or cover with polythene or foil and refrigerate straight away.
Frozen poultry	Depends on Star Rating; 2–3 days in main cabinet	In original pack in the frozen food compartment.
MISCELLANEOUS		
Yeast, fresh	Up to 1 month	Wrap tightly in foil.
Packet frozen foods	Depends on Star Rating	In original pack in frozen food compartment.
Leftover canned foods	2 days	Store in covered container.

Storage guide

FREEZER STORAGE

For freezer storage, always use heavy-duty polythene bags, cling film or foil as these are vapour-proof and will prevent the food drying out during storage. Correctly wrapped, the foods will remain in good condition for the times suggested below. Foods in thinner quality wrappings will remain in satisfactory condition for a much shorter time, then will begin to show deterioration in texture and flavour (though they will, of course, still be safe to eat).

HOME FROZEN FOODS

Food	Storage Time	Preparation
Biscuits	6 months	Pack in rigid containers, with waxed paper between layers.
Bread Crusty loaves, rolls Sandwiches	4 weeks 1 week 1–2 months	Wrap in polythene bags. Avoid salad fillings, hard-boiled egg; pack in polythene bags.
Cakes, scones, teabreads, plain Iced	6 months 2 months	Wrap in polythene bags, with waxed paper between layers. Pack small cakes and scones together in polythene bags. Decorate after thawing. Freeze iced cakes unwrapped until set, then wrap in polythene and protect with boxes; remove wrappings before thawing.
Cheese Soft, cream Hard	 6 months 1 month	Wrap in polythene. Hard cheese becomes crumbly, but can be used for cooking.
Cream, fresh	3 months	Freeze only double or whipping cream; best half-whipped.
Desserts Mousses, creams etc.	 2–3 months	Make and freeze in foil or freezerproof serving dishes.
Eggs	6 months	Separate for freezing. Pack in waxed cartons. To every 6 yolks, add 5 ml (1 level tsp) salt or 10 ml (2 level tsp) sugar.
Fats Butter and margarine, salted Butter, unsalted Fresh suet	 3 months 6 months 6 months	Overwrap blocks in foil or polythene. Pack in polythene bags.
Fish, raw Oily fish White fish Smoked fish Caviar Shellfish	 2 months 3 months 2–3 months Do not freeze 1 month	Freeze within 12 hours of catch. Freeze large, whole fish unwrapped until firm; dip in cold water to form thin ice. Return to freezer; repeat until ice is 0.5 cm ($\frac{1}{4}$ in) thick. Wrap in polythene. Wrap small fish and portions in polythene before freezing.
Fish, cooked Pies, fish cakes, croquettes etc.	1–2 months	Pack in foil dishes, or open freeze then wrap in polythene.

Food	Storage Time	Preparation
Fruit Currants, berries Hard fruit	 1 year 1 year	Pack in syrup in boxes.
Bananas Seville oranges, for marmalade	Do not freeze 6 months	Pack whole oranges in polythene bags.
Herbs, fresh	6 months	Freeze in bunches in rigid container; crumble while frozen. Or, chop first and store in small cartons.
Ice cream	3 months	Pack in rigid containers.
Meat, raw Beef Lamb Veal Pork Freshly minced meat Offal, sausages Cured and smoked meat (see page 218)	 8 months 6 months 6 months 6 months 3 months 3 months 1–4 months	Pack in meal-size quantities in polythene bags. Place polythene sheets between individual chops or steaks. Bacon freezes best in vacuum packs.
Meat, cooked Casseroles, stews, curries etc. Roast Loaves, pâtés	 2 months 2–4 weeks 1 month	Cook as usual. Pack in rigid cartons or foil dishes; or freeze in foil-lined cookware, then remove the foil package and overwrap with polythene. Remove from tin when cold; wrap in polythene.
Milk	1 month	Use homogenised milk. Do not freeze in bottle. Pack in rigid containers, leaving headspace.
Pancakes, unfilled Filled	2 months 1–2 months	Stack flat, wrap in polythene. Pack in foil dishes.
Pastry, raw Shortcrust Flaky, puff	 3 months 3–4 months	Most useful if rolled and shaped as required before freezing.
Pastry, cooked Unfilled pastry cases Meat pies Fruit pies Danish pastries, croissants	 6 months 3–4 months 6 months 4 weeks	Very fragile. Use foil or freezerproof ovenware; overwrap with polythene. Open freeze small pastries, then pack in rigid cartons with waxed paper between layers.
Poultry and game, raw Chicken Duck, goose Turkey Giblets Game birds	 1 year 4–5 months 6 months 2–3 months 6–8 months	Pluck, draw and truss as usual; do not stuff. Wrap tightly in a polythene bag. Freeze giblets separately. Hang game before freezing.
Poultry, cooked		As cooked meats.
Sauces, soups, stocks	2–3 months	Freeze in small portions in rigid containers.
Sponge puddings	3 months	Cook and freeze in foil basins or use freezerproof basins and overwrap with polythene.
Vegetables	1 year	See opposite.

FREEZING RAW VEGETABLES

Vegetables should be blanched before freezing to preserve the colour, flavour and texture. If not blanched, they show a deterioration in eating quality much more quickly; deterioration is noticeable in Brussels sprouts after only 3 days, in broad beans after 3 weeks, in runner beans after 1 month, in peas after 6 months.

Prepare the vegetables as you would for normal cooking then plunge them into boiling water, using not less than 3.5 litres (6 pints) water to each 450 g (1 lb) vegetables and make sure the water returns to the boil in 1 minute after the vegetables are added. Blanch for the times suggested in the chart below, starting to time when the water returns to the boil. Don't attempt to blanch more than 450 g (1 lb) at a time.

After blanching, remove the vegetables from the boiling water and plunge them quickly into ice-cold water to prevent over-cooking and to cool them quickly. Drain them and dry as much as possible on clean cloths or kitchen paper towel. Pack small vegetables in meal-size portions; free-flow packaging is difficult.

PREPARATION FOR FREEZING

Vegetable	Blanching Time	Preparation
Artichokes, globe	7–10 min.	Add lemon juice to blanching water. Drain upside down. Pack in rigid boxes.
Asparagus	Thin: 2 min. Thick: 4 min.	Grade before blanching. When cool, tie in small bundles. Pack in rigid boxes, bundles separated by waxed paper.
Aubergines	4 min.	Peel and cut in thick slices before blanching. Pack in boxes, with waxed paper between layers.
Beans, broad French runner	3 min. 2–3 min. 2 min.	Pack in polythene bags.
Beetroots	Small: 5–10 min. Large: Cook until tender.	Freeze tiny beetroots whole, larger ones sliced or diced; pack in cartons.
Broccoli	4 min.	Pack in boxes in one or two layers, tips to stalks.
Brussels sprouts	Small: 3 min. Large: 4 min.	Pack in polythene bags.
Cabbages	1½ min.	Shred finely before blanching. Pack in small quantities in polythene bags.
Carrots	3–5 min.	Slice or dice. Pack in polythene bags.
Cauliflowers	3 min.	Break into 5-cm (2-in) sprigs before blanching. Add lemon juice to blanching water. Pack in polythene bags.
Celery	3 min.	Cut into 2.5-cm (1-in) lengths before blanching. Pack in polythene bags. Use for cooked dishes only.
Chicory	Do not freeze.	

Vegetable	Blanching Time	Preparation
Courgettes	1 min.	Slice thickly. Blanch or sauté in butter. Pack in polythene bags or cartons.
Cucumbers	Do not freeze.	
Fennel	3 min.	Slice before blanching. Pack in polythene bags.
Jerusalem artichokes		Freeze only as soup or purée.
Leeks	4 min.	Slice thickly and sauté in butter or oil; pack in cartons. Use for casseroles or soups.
Lettuces	Do not freeze.	
Marrows	3 min.	Peel and slice thickly before blanching. Pack in rigid containers; leaving headspace.
Mushrooms	1 min.	Sauté in butter. Leave small mushrooms whole; slice large ones for use in casseroles and soups.
Okra	Do not freeze.	
Onions	Chopped: 2 min. Whole: 4 min.	Skin and chop before blanching; pack in small quantities. Blanch small onions whole.
Parsnips	2 min.	Peel and cut into strips before blanching. Pack in polythene bags.
Peas, green mange tout	1–2 min. 2–3 min.	Pack in polythene bags. Pack in rigid containers.
Peppers	3 min.	Slice or chop before blanching for use in casseroles; pack in small quantities in polythene bags. Or, blanch as halves.
Potatoes, old		Freeze fully cooked as purée, in cartons, or as croquettes or duchesse potatoes; open freeze then pack in boxes. Or, freeze as partially cooked chips, after first frying. Pack in polythene bags.
new	Cook fully.	
Radishes	Do not freeze.	
Spinach	2 min.	After blanching and cooling, press to remove excess moisture. Pack in rigid containers or polythene bags; leave headspace.
Swedes	Do not freeze.	
Sweetcorn	Small: 4 min. Medium: 6 min. Large: 8 min.	Pack individually in foil. Overwrap with polythene bags.
Tomatoes		Best as purée. Skin, core, simmer for 5 min., then purée in blender or press through a sieve. Pack in small cartons.
Turnips	2½ min.	Dice before blanching. Pack in rigid containers. Or, cook fully and freeze as purée.

Nutrition and calorie counting

When planning a family diet, it helps to know something of what is needed in the way of nutrients to keep healthy, and which foodstuffs contain them.

PROTEINS
Proteins are required for growth, the formation of new tissue and the repair and maintenance of the old tissue. They also supply heat and energy.
Sources: Meat, fish, poultry, milk, cheese, eggs, pulses, bread, cereals, nuts.

FATS AND OILS
These form a fundamental part of all cell structure, provide a concentrated form of energy and act as carriers for vitamins A, D, E and K.
Sources: Butter, margarine, lard, dripping, vegetable fats and oils, fish oils, meats (especially pork and bacon), cream, cream cheese, eggs.

CARBOHYDRATES
These provide heat and energy for muscular contraction.
Sources: Sugars and starches. With the exception of meat, fish, poultry and cheese, most foods contain a certain amount of carbohydrate. Foods that are high in carbohydrate content but low in other nutrients include white flour, polished rice, puffed or flaked cereals, sugar, jams, biscuits, cakes and pastries.

MINERALS
Minerals are necessary for the formation of body structure and for normal body functions. They are widely distributed in foods.
Sources: Calcium is found in milk, cheese, eggs, green and root vegetables, enriched white flour and bread. Phosphorus is found in fish, cheese, milk, eggs, meat, green vegetables, cereals. Iron is found in liver, kidney, heart, wholegrain cereals, meat, fish, pulses, green vegetables and potatoes. Sodium is found in salt.

VITAMINS
Vitamins are substances required in small amounts in our food to promote the normal health of the body. They can normally be found in plenty in a good diet of mixed natural foods.
Vitamin A keeps the mucous membranes healthy, also the skin, glands and bones, and is necessary for normal growth and development and for properly functioning eyesight.
Sources: Liver, butter, margarine, eggs, milk, cheese; carrots, spinach and other green vegetables, tomatoes, watercress, dried apricots and prunes; cod liver oil and halibut liver oil.
Vitamin B (that is, the vitamin B complex, including vitamin B_1, B_2, etc.) is necessary for the good condition of the nervous system, for normal appetite and digestion and for other processes.
Sources: Yeast and yeast extracts, wholegrain cereals, wheat-grain preparations; liver and other offal, lean meat, pork (including ham and bacon), fish, egg yolk, milk, cheese; vegetables, fruit, nuts. By law all flour must contain certain quantities of Vitamin B_1, and niacin.
Vitamin C increases resistance to infection and maintains a healthy condition of the skin; it improves the circulation and condition of the gums and other body tissues.
Sources: Rose-hip berries (as syrup), blackcurrants, kiwi fruit, citrus fruits and juices, fresh vegetables, provided correct cooking methods are used.
Vitamin D ensures the proper utilisation of calcium and phosphorus, directly influencing the structure of bones and teeth.
Sources: Fish liver oils, oily fish, egg yolk, butter, vitamin enriched margarine. This vitamin can also be manufactured in the body by the action of sunlight and ultraviolet light on the skin surface.

WATER
This is an essential constituent of all cells, and is present in all foods.

DAILY DIET
Everybody's daily diet should contain a selection of the above nutrients. This is easily achieved if, every day, the diet includes at least one helping of milk, cheese or eggs; one helping of meat, poultry or fish; one helping of bread or other cereals; a little butter or margarine; at least two helpings of fruit and vegetables.

The basic requirement of our daily diet is that it should provide us with sufficient energy to breathe, and for the body to develop and function correctly. On top of that we need a certain amount of extra energy for work or whatever other activities the day may bring. Any surplus energy intake will be converted into fat, and will ultimately reduce the efficiency of the body in all its functions.

Many people are lucky and, either naturally or by habit, are able to balance their intake of food against the particular energy requirements of their own bodies and their ways of life; these people maintain a steady body weight without needing to give it any special thought. Most of us, however, find that unless controlled, our habitual intake will be in excess of what is really necessary once adulthood is achieved and the body is fully grown, and that excess turns into fat, showing as a gradual increase in body weight over the years.

Anyone suffering from serious obesity should consult a doctor before adopting a weight-reducing diet. But for those simply wishing to shed a small amount of excess fat and then maintain a steady body weight, control of energy intake by counting calories is the easiest method.

The precise calorie requirements of any individual are dictated by the speed of his particular metabolism. But it has been found that people of the same sex and age, leading broadly similar ways of life, need roughly the same calories to keep them healthy and maintain a steady body weight. Use this chart as a guide.

DAILY CALORIE REQUIREMENTS		
Age range	kJ per day	kcal per day
Men		
18–35 years		
Sedentary	11297	2700
Moderately active	12552	3000
Very active	15062	3600
35–65 years		
Sedentary	10878	2600
Moderately active	12134	2900
Very active	15062	3600
65–75 years		
Sedentary	9832	2350
75 and over		
Sedentary	8786	2100
Women		
18–55 years		
Most occupations	9205	2200
Very active	10460	2500
55–75 years		
Sedentary	8577	2050
75 and over		
Sedentary	7950	1900
Pregnant, 3–9 months	10042	2400
Breast feeding	11297	2700
Schoolboys		
9–12 years	10460	2500
12–15 years	11715	2800
15–18 years	12552	3000
Schoolgirls		
9–12 years	9623	2300
12–15 years	9623	2300
15–18 years	9623	2300
Boys and girls		
0–1 year	3347	800
1–2 years	5021	1200
2–3 years	5858	1400
3–5 years	6694	1600
5–7 years	7531	1800
7–9 years	8786	2100

CALORIE COUNTING

A calorie is the heat unit commonly used to measure the energy value of foods. In nutritional studies the unit usually used is the kilocalorie (kcal), which is the amount of heat required to raise 1000 grams of water 1°C; a kilocalorie is colloquially referred to as a calorie. Another unit sometimes used is the kilojoule (kJ): 1 kcal = 4.19 kJ. The charts on pages 490, 491 and 492 show both units.

To reduce your intake of calories, eliminate foods that are high in carbohydrates and low in other nutrients, such as sugar, honey, jam, chocolates and sweets, and white flour products such as cakes, pastries and biscuits. Cut down on fats, too, by grilling meat instead of frying, using less butter on your bread and drinking skimmed milk. Keep your diet varied so you don't get bored.

CALORIE CONTENT OF FOODS

Food	kJ per 100 g	kcal per oz
CEREALS AND CEREAL PRODUCTS		
All-Bran	1295	88
Arrowroot	1488	101
Barley, pearl, dry	1504	102
Biscuits		
chocolate	2077	142
plain	1801	122
rich, sweet	2073	141
Bran	827	51
Bread, brown	990	66
malt	902	54
rye	1054	62
starch reduced	978	66
white	1057	72
wholemeal	1007	68
fried	2064	140
Buckwheat	1407	83
Cornflakes	1525	103
Cornflour, custard powder	1475	100
Crispbread	1329	90
Flour, white, plain, or self raising	1454	99
Flour, wholemeal	1351	79
Flour, rye	1428	83
Macaroni, raw	1525	103
Macaroni, wholemeal, raw	1525	103
Muesli	1475	100
Oatmeal, raw	1672	113
Rice, raw	1504	102
boiled	518	35
brown, boiled	518	35

Food	kJ per 100 g	kcal per oz
Sago, raw	1488	101
Semolina, raw	1554	109
Shredded Wheat	1375	93
Spaghetti, raw	1525	103
wholemeal, raw	1525	103
Sugar Smacks	1542	105
Tapioca	1504	102
Weetabix	1475	100
Wheatgerm	1475	100
EGGS		
Eggs, fresh (Quick measure 1 size 2 egg = 90 kcal (376 kJ) 1 size 4 egg = 80 kcal (334 kJ))	660	45
Egg white (Quick measure 1 egg white = 15 kcal (62 kJ))	158	11
Egg yolk (Quick measure 1 egg yolk = 65 kcal (271 kJ))	1454	99
FATS		
Butter	3114	211
Lard or compound white fat	3736	253
Margarine	3214	218
Vegetable oil	3757	255
FISH		
Anchovy (Quick measure 1 fillet = 7 kcal (29 kJ))	438	30
Fish fingers, raw	794	54
Herring, raw	794	54
Kipper, raw	919	62
Mackerel, on bone, raw	438	30
Pilchards, canned in tomato sauce	635	43
Prawns, shelled	438	30
Salmon, canned	555	38
Sardines, canned in oil	1191	81
Trout, on bone, raw	438	30
Tuna, canned in oil	1107	75
Whitebait, fried	2244	152
White fish, raw filleted: cod, haddock, hake, halibut, plaice, sole, coley, whiting	296–367	20–25

Food	kJ per 100 g	kcal per oz
FRUIT		
Apples, eating or cooking	192	13
Apricots, dried	760	52
Apricots, fresh	117	8
Bananas	326	22
Blackberries	117	8
Blackcurrants	117	8
Canned fruit, in syrup, average	367	25
Cherries	192	13
stewed without sugar	146	10
Cranberries	62	4
Currants, dried	1015	69
Dates, dried	1036	70
Figs, dried	890	60
Gooseberries	117	8
Grapefruit	91	6
Grapes, black or white	221	15
Lemons	29	2
Melon, yellow. weighed with skin	940	4
honeydew, weighed with skin	171	12
Oranges	146	10
Orange juice, canned, unconcentrated	192	13
Peaches	158	11
Pears	171	12
Pineapple	192	13
Plums	133	9
Prunes, dried	672	46
Raisins, dried	1036	70
Raspberries	104	7
Rhubarb	29	2
Strawberries	104	7
Sultanas, dried	1045	71
MEAT AND POULTRY		
Bacon, raw	1989	135
well grilled	890	60
Beef, corned	936	64
lean mince or stewing	890	60
silverside, boiled	1120	83
steak for grilling	735	50
topside or sirloin roasted	1178	80
Chicken, on bone, raw	601	30
boneless, raw	769	41
roast meat	760	52
Duck, roast meat	1312	89

Nutrition and calorie counting

Food	kJ per 100 g	kcal per oz
Frankfurters, cooked	1329	90
Ham, lean, boiled	890	60
Heart, ox, raw	438	30
Kidney, raw	438	30
Lamb, flesh only,		
average, raw	1387	94
leg, roast meat	1178	80
shoulder, roast		
meat	1400	95
Liver, raw	581	39
Luncheon meat	1358	92
Pork chop, on bone,		
grilled	589	40
fillet	1036	70
leg, roast meat	1329	90
Rabbit, on bone, raw	543	37
Sausage, pork	1542	105
Tongue	1295	88
Turkey, roast meat	819	56
Veal, pie meat, raw	518	35
roast meat	973	66
MILK AND MILK PRODUCTS		
Buttermilk	159	10
Cheese, Cheddar	1722	117
cottage	480	31
curd	589	40
Edam	1149	88
Cream, double:		
30 ml (2 tbsp)	434	104
single: 30 ml (2 tbsp)	167	40
soured: 30 ml (2 tbsp)	217	52
Milk, dried skimmed	1375	93
Milk, liquid		
whole: 30 ml (2 tbsp)	75	18
skimmed: 30 ml (2 tbsp)	37	9
Yogurt, fat free	171	12
fruit	326	22
natural	238	16
NUTS		
Almonds	2424	164
Coconut, desiccated	2541	172
Peanuts, roasted	2449	166
Walnuts	2227	151
PRESERVES AND COOKING INGREDIENTS		
Beef extract	338	23
Capers	75	5
Chocolate, milk or plain	2441	165

Food	kJ per 100 g	kcal per oz
Chutney, average	635	43
Curry powder	986	67
Gelatine	1036	70
Honey	1208	82
Jam and marmalade	1095	74
Malt, dried	1545	92
Mustard, made	trace	trace
Peanut butter	2508	170
Sugar	1651	112
Syrup, golden	1237	84
Toffees	1713	120
Tomato ketchup	413	28
paste	158	11
Treacle, black	1078	73
VEGETABLES		
Artichokes, globe, boiled	58	4
Artichokes, Jerusalem, boiled	75	5
Aubergine, raw	58	4
Avocado	367	25
Beans, baked in tomato sauce	384	26
broad, boiled	171	12
green, boiled	29	2
haricot, dried	1078	73
boiled	367	25
butter, boiled	388	26
soya, dried	495	29
beansprouts, raw	100	6
Beetroot, boiled	171	12
Broccoli, boiled	58	4
Brussels sprouts, boiled	67	5
Cabbage, boiled	29	2
raw	117	8
Carrots, boiled	75	5
raw	104	7
Cauliflower, raw	58	4
Celery, raw	29	2
Chicory, raw	45	3
Courgettes, raw	45	3
Cucumber, raw	45	3
Gherkins, pickled	45	3
Leeks, raw	113	9
Lentils, dried	1237	84
Lettuce, raw	45	3
Marrow, boiled	29	2
Mushrooms, raw	29	2

Food	kJ per 100 g	kcal per oz
Mustard and		
raw		
Onions, raw	104	7
Parsley, raw	204	14
Parsnips, boiled	267	18
Peas, fresh or frozen, raw	267	18
boiled	204	14
canned, processed	297	27
Peppers, green and red, raw	91	6
Potatoes, raw	326	22
boiled	338	23
fried chips	986	67
roast	518	35
Pumpkin, raw	58	4
Radishes, raw	58	4
Seakale, raw	29	2
Spinach, boiled	91	6
Spring greens, boiled	45	3
Swedes, boiled	75	5
Sweetcorn, fresh, frozen or canned, boiled	397	27
Tomatoes, raw or canned	58	4
Turnips, boiled	45	3
Watercress, raw	58	4
DRINKS: ALCOHOLIC		
Beer and stout	132	10
Brandy	919	65
Cider, dry	132	10
Gin	919	65
Liqueurs	1107	75
Rum	919	65
Sherry, dry	481	33
sweet	568	38
Vermouth, dry	585	35
Vodka	919	65
Whisky	919	65
Wine	271	18
DRINKS: NON-ALCOHOLIC		
Cordial, undiluted	438	30
Grapefruit juice	250	17
Lemon juice	171	12
Orange juice	238	16
Pineapple juice	204	14
Tomato juice	75	5
Tonic water	146	10

Glossary of food and cooking terms

à la: In the manner of.

al dente: Italian term used to describe pasta, cooked until it offers just slight resistance to the bite.

Amandine: Garnished with almonds.

Antipasto: Italian term for a mixed hors d'oeuvre.

Aperitif: A drink taken before a meal, to stimulate the appetite.

Appetiser: Food taken before the main meal, to stimulate the appetite.

Aspic: Savoury jelly used for setting and garnishing savoury dishes.

au gratin: Coated with a sauce, sprinkled with breadcrumbs and/or grated cheese and browned in the oven or under the grill; the food is usually served in the dish in which it was cooked.

Bain marie: A shallow, open vessel, half-filled with water which is kept at a temperature just below boiling point; used to keep sauces, soups etc. hot without further cooking, also used to prevent over-heating of custards and other egg dishes during cooking.

Bake: To cook in the oven by dry heat.

Barbecue: 1. To cook outdoors on a rack or spit, usually over a charcoal fire.
2. To coat with a highly seasoned sauce, as for outdoor cooking.

Bard: To cover the breast of a poultry or game bird with pieces of bacon fat to prevent it drying out during cooking.

Baste: To moisten meat, poultry or game during roasting or grilling by brushing or spooning over it the juices and melted fat from the tin.

Basting steak

Batter: A mixture of flour, liquid and sometimes other ingredients, of a thin, creamy consistency.

Beat: To agitate an ingredient or mixture vigorously with a fork, spoon, whisk or electric mixer.

Beurre manié: A liaison of equal quantities of butter and flour kneaded together to a paste. Used to thicken soups or stews after cooking is complete. Whisk a little of the paste into the hot liquid and bring back to the boil, adding a little more until the required thickness is reached.

Bind: To add a liquid, egg or melted fat to a dry mixture to hold it together.

Bisque: A thick, rich, puréed soup, usually of shellfish.

Blanch: To treat food with boiling water in order to whiten it, preserve its natural colour, loosen the skin or remove a flavour which is too strong. Vegetables are blanched before freezing to destroy harmful bacteria. Two common methods are:
1. To plunge the food into boiling water; use this method for skinning tomatoes, preparing vegetables for freezing.
2. To place food in cold water and bring slowly to the boil; use this method for reducing the saltiness of bacon and for whitening veal or sweetbreads.

Blanquette: A white, creamy stew.

Blend: 1. To mix together thoroughly two or more ingredients.
2. To prepare food in an electric blender.

Boil: To cook in liquid at a temperature of 100°C (212°F).

Bombe: A dessert of frozen mixtures arranged and frozen in a mould.

Bouchée: Small puff pastry patty, cut about 4 cm (1½ in) round, with a savoury filling; traditionally a mouthful only.

Bouquet garni: A small bunch of herbs tied together, often in muslin, and used to give flavour to stocks and stews; it is removed before the dish is served. Traditional ingredients include parsley, thyme, a bay leaf and a few peppercorns.

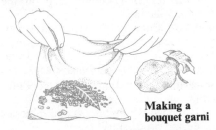

Making a bouquet garni

Braise: To cook in a small amount of simmering liquid in a tightly covered pan. The food may be browned first in a little hot fat.

Brine: A salt and water solution in which food is immersed, usually as a preliminary to pickling.

Brochette: French term for skewer.

Brûlée: Sprinkled with sugar and grilled until crusted with caramel.

Canapé: An appetiser consisting of a firm base of bread, toast, pastry etc. with a savoury and decorative topping. Each canapé should be one mouthful only.

Caramel: Sugar heated to a rich brown coloured syrup.

Carve: To cut meat or poultry in slices or pieces for serving.

Casserole: 1. An ovenproof dish with a lid, used for cooking stews and braises in the oven; the food is usually served straight from the dish.
2. Food prepared in a casserole.

Chantilly: Served with whipped cream, generally slightly sweetened and often flavoured with vanilla.

Charlotte: A custard; the classic dish is charlotte russe, which is a cream set with biscuits. For apple charlotte, a mould is lined with bread and filled with apple purée.

Chasseur: Hunter-style, cooked with mushrooms, shallots and white wine.

Chaudfroid: A jellied sauce with a béchamel base, used for masking cold fish, poultry and game.

Chill: To cool food, without freezing, in the refrigerator.

Chine: To sever the chine (back) bone from the rib bones on a loin or neck joint. The bone is usually left in place, attached by membrane, to hold the joint in shape during cooking; it is removed when cooking is complete.

Chop: To cut food into small pieces with a knife, blender or food processor.

Chowder: A thick American-style soup, a cross between a soup and a stew, often based on fish.

Clarify: To clear or purify. The term is used for the process of clearing or freeing fat or liquid from impurities so that it may be used for frying delicate dishes or making cakes such as a Genoese sponge.
To clarify butter or margarine: Heat the fat gently until it melts, then continue to heat slowly, without browning, until all bubbling ceases (this shows the water has been driven off). Remove from the heat and let it stand for a few minutes for the salt and sediment to settle; then pour off the fat. If there is much sediment, strain the fat through muslin.
To clarify dripping: Melt the fat and strain it through muslin into a large basin to remove any large particles. Now pour over it two or three times its own bulk of boiling water, stir well and allow to cool; the clean fat will rise to the top. When it is solid lift it off with a spoon, dry the underside with kitchen paper towel and scrape off any sediment that remains.

Coat: 1. To cover food that is to be fried with flour, egg and breadcrumbs or batter.
2. To cover cooked food with a thin layer of sauce, mayonnaise, etc.

Coating fish with egg and breadcrumbs

Glossary of food and cooking terms

Coating consistency: The consistency required in a sauce for coating. Test by stirring the sauce and holding the spoon upside down; when the consistency is correct the sauce will coat the back of the spoon.

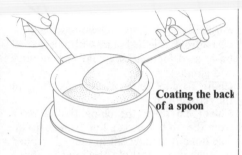

Coating the back of a spoon

Cocotte: Small earthenware, ovenproof dish in single portion size.
Compote: Fruit stewed in a sugar syrup and served either hot or cold.
Concassé: Roughly chopped.
Condiment: A seasoning or relish to add to food at the table.
Conserve: Whole-fruit jam.
Court bouillon: A seasoned liquid for poaching fish.
Cream: 1. The fat portion of milk; single cream has 18% fat content, whipping cream 38% fat content, double cream 48% fat content.
2. To beat together fat and sugar until they resemble whipped cream.
Croquette: A mixture of chopped or minced cooked food, shaped into a roll or cone, coated with egg and breadcrumbs and deep fried.
Croûte: 1. A round or finger of toasted or fried bread on which game and savouries may be served.
2. A pastry crust.
Croûton: A small cube of fried or toasted bread, used to garnish soups and salads.
Curd: 1. The solid part of soured milk or junket.
2. A creamy preserve made from fruit, usually lemons or oranges, with sugar, eggs and butter.
Curdle: To cause milk or a sauce to separate into curds and whey in the presence of acid or excessive heat.
Cure: To preserve fish, meat or poultry by salting, drying or smoking.
Cut in: To distribute solid fat in flour using a pastry blender or knife.
Dariole: A small, narrow mould with sloping sides, used for setting individual creams and jellies and for baking or steaming puddings and madeleines.
Daube: A braised dish of meat or poultry.
Devilled: Seasoned with a sharp, hot sauce and grilled or fried.

Dot: To scatter bits, as of butter or margarine, over the surface of food.

Dotting pastry with butter

Dough: A thick mixture of uncooked flour and liquid, often combined with other ingredients; the mixture can be handled as a solid mass.
Draw: To remove entrails from poultry, game or fish.
Dredge: To sprinkle food thickly and evenly with flour, sugar etc.
Dress: 1. To pluck, draw and truss poultry or game.
2. To coat a salad with dressing.
Dressing: Light sauce, usually for salad.
Dripping: The fat obtained from roasted meat during cooking, or from pieces of new fat that have been rendered down.
Dropping consistency: The consistency of some cake and pudding mixtures before cooking; if a spoonful of mixture is lifted from the basin, it should drop off the spoon in 5 seconds.
Dust: To sprinkle lightly with flour, sugar, spices or seasonings.
Enchilada: A tortilla, stuffed, rolled and served with a highly seasoned sauce.
Enriched: 1. Containing added goodness and fat, such as cream and eggs.
2. Resupplied with vitamins and minerals lost during processing.
Entrée: A hot or cold savoury dish served complete with sauce and garnish. In a formal menu the entrée follows the appetiser and fish courses, coming before the main course.
Escalope: A slice of meat, usually veal, cut from the top of the leg.
Farce, forcemeat: Stuffing used for meat, fish or vegetables. A farce is based on meat, bacon etc, while a forcemeat is made from breadcrumbs, suet, onion and herbs.
Farina: Fine starch flour made from wheat, potatoes or nuts.
Fillet: A prime cut of meat, fish or poultry, boneless, or with all bones removed.
Fines herbes: A mixture of chopped herbs, traditionally including parsley, tarragon, chives and chervil.
Flake: 1. To separate cooked fish into individual flakes.
2. To make close, horizontal cuts with a knife into the edge of a pie, before cooking, giving a flaked effect.

Flambé: Used to describe a dish flavoured with flamed alcohol. The alcohol, usually brandy or sherry, is ignited and allowed to burn without stirring, distributing over all the pan during cooking.

Making flambé pancake

Flute: To make decorative indentations, especially in pastry.
Fold in: To combine a light, whisked or creamed mixture with other ingredients so that it retains its lightness. Usually done with a metal spoon or rubber spatula.
Fondue: A dish cooked on the table, usually over a spirit heater. A Swiss fondue is of melted cheeses and wine, served with chunks of bread for dipping; a fondue bourguignonne is cubes of meat, deep fried in hot oil and served with cold dips and relishes.

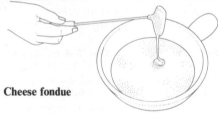

Cheese fondue

Fool: A cold dessert of puréed fruit, whipped cream and sometimes custard.
Freeze: To preserve food by deep refrigeration and storage at a temperature of 0°C (32°F) or below.
Freeze-dried: Commercially processed food, frozen so rapidly that most of the water content is removed.
Fricassee: A white stew of chicken, rabbit or veal, finished with cream and egg yolks.
Fritter: A portion of batter-coated food, deep fried until crisp.
Froth: To dredge the surface of roast game or meat with flour, and cook briskly to a rich brown colour in a hot oven.
Fry: To cook in hot fat or oil.
Shallow frying: Only a small quantity of fat is used, in a shallow pan. The food must be turned halfway through to cook both sides.
Deep frying: Sufficient fat is used to cover the food completely. The pan used must be deep enough to be only half full of fat before the food is added.
Galantine: A cold dish of boneless white meat, usually stuffed, rolled and pressed, glazed with chaudfroid sauce.

Garnish: An edible decoration added to a savoury dish to improve the appearance.

Glaze: To brush or coat with a liquid that will give the finished dish a glossy surface, improving appearance and flavour, eg. milk or beaten egg on pastry, sugar and water on sweet buns, concentrated meat stock on savoury dishes.

Grate: To rub food on a grater to produce fine shreds.

Grating a carrot

Grease: To coat the surface of a dish or tin with fat to prevent sticking.

Greasing a cake tin

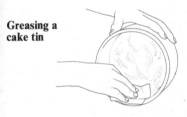

Grill: 1. To cook by direct, radiant heat. 2. The appliance or part of a cooker used for this type of cooking.

Grind: To reduce hard foods, such as nuts or coffee beans, to fine particles in a food mill, grinder or blender.

Grissini: Italian bread sticks.

Gumbo: A substantial soup or stew thickened with okra.

Hang: To suspend meat or game in a cool, dry place for a controlled period before butchery, to tenderise the meat and develop the flavour.

Hard sauce: Creamed butter and sugar, flavoured with brandy or rum and chilled until firm; served with hot puddings.

Hoisin sauce: A mixture of soya beans and vegetable extracts used in Chinese cookery.

Hors d'oeuvre: Appetiser.

Hull: To remove the calyx from soft fruits such as strawberries, raspberries and loganberries.

Icing: A decorative sugar mixture used to coat cakes and pastries.

Infuse: To extract flavour from spices and herbs by covering with boiling liquid and leaving to stand without further heating; the liquid is usually strained and the herbs or spices discarded.

Jardinière: Garnished with a variety of cooked spring vegetables.

Julienne: Garnished with fine strips of cooked or raw vegetables.

Kebab: Cubes of meat, marinated and cooked on a skewer.

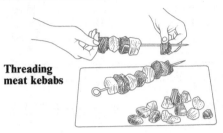

Threading meat kebabs

Ketchup: A sauce based on one major ingredient such as tomatoes or mushrooms, preserved with vinegar and spices.

Knead: To work a dough by hand or machine until smooth.

Lard: 1. The fat of pork, rendered and sold in solid form.
2. To insert small strips of fat bacon into the flesh of game, meat or poultry before cooking, to prevent it drying when roasted.

Liaison: A thickening agent, such as flour, cornflour, arrowroot, rice flour or egg yolk; used for sauces and soups.

Lukewarm: Just above blood heat, at about 38°C (100°F).

Marinade: A seasoned liquid, usually a blend of oil, wine or vinegar and seasonings, used for soaking meats in order to tenderise and add flavour.

Marinate: To soak in a marinade.

Mask: 1. To cover or coat a cooked dish with savoury jelly, glaze or sauce.
2. To coat the inside of a mould with a thin layer of jelly.

Meringue: Egg white whisked until stiff, mixed with sugar and baked until crisp.

Meunière: Cooked in butter, seasoned with salt, pepper and lemon juice and garnished with chopped parsley, usually of fish.

Mince: To cut into tiny pieces with a knife or mincing machine.

Mirepoix: A mixture of carrot, onion and celery, sometimes also bacon or ham, cut into large pieces, lightly fried and used as a bed on which to braise meat.

Mixed herbs: Usually a blend of dried herbs including parsley, tarragon, chives, thyme and chervil.

Mocca: A blend of chocolate and coffee.

Monosodium glutamate: A white crystalline salt that enhances the natural flavour of foods without adding any flavour of its own.

Navarin: A stew of mutton or lamb, usually with turnips.

Noisette: A neatly trimmed round of veal, lamb or beef, about 1 cm (½ in) thick.

Panada: A thick, binding sauce based on a roux, and used to bind croquettes and similar mixtures.

Papillote, en: Wrapped in greased paper or foil, in which the food is cooked and sent to the table; usually fish or meat.

Parboil: To boil for part of the normal cooking time, before finishing by some other method.

Parfait: A light, cream-enriched, iced dessert, often with a fruit purée.

Pasteurise: To sterilise by heating to 60–82°C (140–180°F); usually dairy products.

Pasty: Small, savoury, pastry pie made without a dish, on a baking sheet.

Pâte: Pastry.

Pâté: A minced or finely chopped savoury mixture, or purée, usually of meats and often with a liver base, cooked in a terrine or tin and sealed with bacon or fat, or sometimes wrapped in pastry.

Patty: A small individual pie.

Paupiette: A slice of meat rolled round forcemeat, or a rolled fillet of fish such as sole or plaice.

Pectin: Substance found in fruit and vegetables, necessary for setting jams and jellies.

Petits fours: Very small fancy cakes or almond biscuits served at the end of a formal meal.

Pilaf: Seasoned rice dish, usually with meat or poultry added.

Pipe: To force a soft mixture through a nozzle to give a decorative effect; used for icings, whipped cream, creamed potato, meringues etc.

Pith: The white cellular lining between the rind and flesh of a citrus fruit.

Poach: To cook in an open pan in simmering liquid.

Pot roast: To braise, usually used of whole joints or birds.

Praline: Flavoured with burnt almonds.

Prosciutto: A raw, smoked, Italian ham.

Purée: 1. To press food through a fine sieve or food mill, or blend in a blender or food processor, to a smooth, thick mixture.
2. The mixture thus made.

A traditional food mill

Quenelles: A light mixture of minced fish, poultry or meat, shaped into balls or ovals and poached.

Quiche: An open custard tart with a savoury filling.

Raspings: Crumbs made from stale bread, dried in the oven and then crushed until very fine.

Glossary of food and cooking terms

Réchauffé: Reheated; applied to hot dishes made up from leftover cooked foods.
Reduce: To reduce the volume of a liquid by rapid boiling in an open pan.

Refresh: To rinse freshly cooked food, usually vegetables, in cold water. This takes the heat from the food, preventing cooking continuing, and helps to retain a good colour and texture.
Relish: A sharp, spicy sauce.
Rice paper: Edible paper made from the pith of a Chinese tree.
Roulade: 1. Meat roll, or rolled meat.
2. Soufflé-type mixture served in a roll.
Roux: A mixture of fat and flour, cooked together to form the basis of a sauce and for thickening sauces and stews.
Rub in: To incorporate fat into flour using the fingertips; used mainly for shortcrust pastry and plain cakes.
Salmi: A ragout or stew, usually of game.
Sauté: To cook in an open pan in hot, shallow fat, tossing the food to prevent it sticking.
Scald: 1. To pour boiling water over food to clean it.
2. To heat a liquid, usually milk, to just below boiling point.
Scallop: 1. A mollusc (page 163).
2. To bake in a scallop shell or similar container; the food is usually coated with a creamy sauce, topped with breadcrumbs and surrounded with piped, creamed potato. It is served in the same dish.
3. To decorate the edge of a pie (page 343).
Score: To make shallow parallel or crisscross cuts in the surface of food to improve appearance and help it to cook more quickly; also to make similar marks without cutting, eg. with burnt sugar on an omelette (page 146).

Scoring steak

Sear: To brown the surface of meat quickly in hot fat before grilling or roasting. This seals the surface of the meat and helps to retain the juices.
Seasoning: Salt, pepper, spices, herbs etc. added to give depth of flavour.
Shred: To slice a food into very fine pieces; a knife or coarse grater is usually used.
Sieve: To rub or press a moist food, such as cooked vegetables or fruit, through a sieve.
Sift: To shake a dry ingredient through a sieve or flour sifter, to remove lumps.

Simmer: To cook in liquid at a temperature just below boiling point, approximately 96°C (205°F). The liquid should be brought to the boil first, then the temperature adjusted until the surface of the liquid just shivers.
Skewer: Pointed metal or wooden stick used to hold meat, poultry or fish in shape during cooking.
Skim: To remove scum or fat from the surface of a food.

**Skimming fat
from meat juices**

Souse: To pickle in brine or vinegar.
Spit: A rotating metal rod on which meat or poultry is impaled for cooking.
Steam: To cook in the steam from rapidly boiling water; a special steaming pan may be used, or an ordinary saucepan with a second container inside. The food should not come into contact with the water.
Sterilise: To destroy harmful microorganisms, usually by heating.
Stew: To cook slowly, and for a long period, in plenty of simmering liquid. The cooking liquid may be thickened and is served with the finished dish.
Stir: To mix with a circular action, usually with a spoon, fork or spatula.
Stir-fry: To cook quickly in a little hot fat, stirring constantly.
Stock: The liquid produced when meat, bones, poultry, fish or vegetables are simmered in water for a long period to extract the flavour. Herbs and spices are usually added for extra flavour.
Strain: To separate liquid from solids, using a sieve, colander, cloth etc.
Stuffing: A savoury mixture used to fill poultry, meat, fish, vegetables.
Sweat: To cook food gently in melted fat in a covered pan until the juices run.
Syrup: A concentrated solution of sugar in water. Golden syrup is a by-product of sugar refining.
Taco: A fried tortilla with a filling rolled or folded inside.
Tepid: Approximately at blood heat. Tepid water is obtained by adding two parts cold water to one part boiling water.
Terrine: 1. China or earthenware dish used for pâtés and potted meats.
2. The food cooked in a terrine.
Timbale: 1. A thimble-shaped mould for the preparation of savoury mixtures.
2. Food shaped in such a mould.

Toast points: Toast slices cut in half or quarters diagonally.
Torte: Rich, decorative, cake-type dessert of German origin.
Tortilla: Thin, Mexican, flat bread, made with cornmeal or flour.
Toss: 1. To mix foods lightly with a lifting motion, using two spoons or forks.
2. To turn quickly by throwing.
Tostada: Tortilla, fried until crisp and served flat, topped with beans or savoury meat mixture.
Tournedos: A steak of fillet of beef, cut into a small round and weighing about 150 g (5 oz).
Truffle: 1. A rare fungus, black, white or occasionally red, used mainly for garnishing. It grows underground.
2. A rich chocolate confection shaped to resemble a truffle.
Truss: To tie or skewer a poultry or game bird into a compact shape.
Turnover: A sweet or savoury pastry made flat on a baking sheet, by folding a square or round of pastry into a triangle or semicircle over the filling.
Vanilla sugar: Flavoured sugar made by storing a vanilla pod in the sugar jar.
Vol-au-vent: A round puff pastry case, filled with diced meat, poultry, game or fish in a well-flavoured sauce.

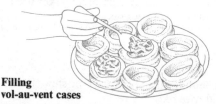

**Filling
vol-au-vent cases**

Whey: That part of milk which remains liquid when the rest forms curds.
Whip: To beat rapidly, to introduce air into a mixture; usually of cream.
Whisk: 1. To beat rapidly to introduce air into a light mixture.
2. The hooped metal implement that is used for whisking.
Wok: A Chinese cooking pan similar to a frying pan, but with a rounded base. This is the correct pan for stir-frying.

Wok and utensils

Zest: The coloured part of orange or lemon rind, containing the oil that gives the characteristic flavour.

INDEX

C

T

Acknowledgments

Illustrators
David Baird
Russell Barnett
Nigel Chamberlain
Helen Cowcher
Tony Graham
Vana Haggerty
Hayward and Martin Ltd
Gary Marsh
Coral Mula
Andrew Popkiewicz
Isobelle Pover
Jim Robins

Photographers
Barry Bullough
Paul Kemp
David Levin
Roger Phillips
Paul Williams
Tessa Traeger

Stylist
Fran Fisher

Home Economists
Jane Atkinson
Elaine Bastable
Carol Bowen
Zoë Camrass
Moya Clarke
Alex Dufort
Caroline Ellwood
Hilary Foster
Sylvia Ireland
Dinah Morrison
Janice Murray
Mary Pope
Jane Suthering
Home Economists on Request

Artwork Services
Frederick Ford and
 Mike Pilley of Radius
John Downton

Studio Services
Focus Ltd
Gilchrist Studios Ltd
Negs Photographic
 Services Ltd
W. Photoprint Ltd

Typesetting
Contact Graphics
C.E. Dawkins Ltd
TJB Photosetting Ltd

Reproduction
Arnoldo Mondadori
Company Ltd

Photographic Props
Dorling Kindersley *would
especially like to thank
all the following organizations
which have kindly loaned
props and equipment for the
photographs:*

The Conran Shop
77 Fulham Road
London SW3

Craftsmen Potters Association
of Great Britain
William Blake House
Marshall Street
London W1

Creda Cookers
Blythe Bridge
Stoke-on-Trent
Staffs

Elizabeth David
46 Bourne Street
London SW1

Dickins & Jones
(Harrods) Ltd
224 Regent Street
London W1

Framford Kitchens
Sunderland Road
Sandy
Beds

Frida Marketing Services
107 Long Acre
London WC2

The Glasshouse
65 Long Acre
London WC2

Grahame & Greene
7 Elgin Crescent
London W11

Peter Jones
Sloane Square
London SW1

Leisure Sinks
Meadow Lane
Long Eaton
Notts

Liberty & Co Ltd
Regent Street
London W1

David Mellor
4 Sloane Square
London SW1

The Reject Shop
245 Brompton Road
London SW3

Sunbeam Electric Ltd
14 Old Quebec Street
London W1

Worcester Royal Porcelain
Severn Street
Worcester
Worcs

Dorling Kindersley *would
like to thank the following staff
of Ebury Press for their
cooperation and help in the
production of this book:*
Barbara Argles, Renny Harrop,
Patricia MacKinnon, Janet
Marsh, Susanna Tee

*and the following individuals
and organisations:*
David Ashby, Rex Bamber,
Anne Billson, Sue Burt, Joan
Carr, John Cousins, Fast Flow
Ltd, Lesley Gilbert, David
Harris, Marlon John, Rory Kee,
Letterstream Ltd, Penny
Markham, Rob Matheson,
Lesley Prescott, Anne Savage,
Sue Thurley, Elaine Weedon